1-15 ✓
22-27 (through n.4) ✓
28-37 (through n.1) &
40-45 (through n.4). ✓
64-69 (through n.3)

135-39 (through n.3)
176-83 (through n.2) ✓
200-06 (through n.4) & 219 (n.8)
220-27 (through n.2)

260-85 (through n.5)
286-90 (through n.1) & ✓
292-97 (through n.5)

306-15 (through n.3)
322-32 (through n.5) ✓
add'l reading online

✓ 246-54 (through n.4).
256-62
271-73 (through n.3)

334-41 & 344-45 (n.5-6)
346-48 (through n.2)
✓ 350-60 & 362 (n.4)
362-69 (through n.2)
382-83

394-401, 406-11,
✓   416-19 (skim)
    video

471-74, 477 (n.6),
✓   484-88
492-95 & 499-500 (n.5)

✓ 564-66 (facts only)
604-25

644-50
Torrent (skim Two)
Cece agent & code
    transfer
        (Two)

M000117255

CASES AND MATERIALS ON
WATER LAW

Eighth Edition

■ ■ ■

By
Douglas L. Grant
E.L. Cord Foundation Professor of Law
University of Nevada, Las Vegas
William S. Boyd School of Law

Gregory S. Weber
Professor of Law
University of the Pacific
McGeorge School of Law

AMERICAN CASEBOOK SERIES®

WEST®
A Thomson Reuters business

Mat #40889049

American Casebook Series is a trademark registered in the U.S. Patent and Trademark Office.

© West, a Thomson business 2000, 2005
© 2010 Thomson Reuters
    610 Opperman Drive
    St. Paul, MN 55123
    1–800–313–9378
Printed in the United States of America

ISBN: 978–0–314–90799–8

Preface

The lineage of this casebook goes back to Frank G. Trelease, Harold S. Blumenthal & Joseph R. Geraud, Cases and Materials on Natural Resources Law (1965), followed by Frank G. Trelease, Cases and Materials on Water Law (2d ed. 1974). George A. Gould joined Frank Trelease as a coauthor of the Fourth Edition. Douglas L. Grant joined George Gould beginning with the Fifth Edition, and Gregory S. Weber joined the two of them for the Seventh Edition. With the retirement of George Gould in 2008, Douglas Grant and Gregory Weber prepared the Eighth Edition.

Users of prior editions will find the Eighth Edition familiar. Like preceding editions, it is a traditional casebook built around cases and supplemented by notes and statutory materials. It examines water law largely through the perspective of private water rights. Public rights, water quality protection, and other environmental regulation are covered extensively, but primarily in the context of how they affect long-established systems of private water rights—the appropriation doctrine and the riparian doctrine for streams, and various doctrines for groundwater. This approach illuminates the tension between affording stability of water rights and accommodating change, tension that lies at the heart of modern water law and policy. Interstate allocation, federal-state relations, and water distribution organizations are also extensively examined.

New principal cases and statutory materials have been added to reflect recent developments in the law. New notes have been added, and existing notes have been updated and rewritten for brevity. Despite the additions, the Eighth Edition is only eleven pages longer than the Seventh Edition, the increased length coming primarily from new materials in the chapters on federal water law and public rights and environmental protection.

Case and statutory citations, as well as footnotes, of courts and commentators have been omitted without so specifying. Numbered footnotes are from the original materials and retain the original numbering; lettered footnotes within the cases are those of the authors. Occasionally, paragraph structure has been altered from the original materials and headings and other organizational features have been omitted.

The authors thank Crystal D'Souza, Louinda V. Lacey, and Jessica Warne, Pacific McGeorge students, for their assistance in research, proofreading, cite checking, and similar editorial tasks. Without their skill and diligence, preparation of the book would have been much more difficult.

DOUGLAS L. GRANT

GREGORY S. WEBER

January 2010

Summary of Contents

Table of Contents

Table of Cases

The principal cases are in bold type. References are to pages.

CASES AND MATERIALS ON
WATER LAW

Eighth Edition

Chapter 1

INTRODUCTION TO WATER LAW

FRANK J. TRELEASE, FEDERAL–STATE RELATIONS
IN WATER LAW
Nat'l Water Comm'n, Legal Study No. 5, at 2-8 (1971).

[People use] water in many ways. * * * A boy swims in a neighbor's pond. A trout fisherman casts his fly into the riffles of a mountain stream. A vacationer tows his girl on water skis behind a power boat. The owner of a summer home merely sits and enjoys the view of a lake or brook. The tugs and barges of a navigation company ply a great river. A city discharges the wastes of its people and industries into the river.

* * * A power company's dam builds up the pressure that enables it to turn turbines and generators. A farmer diverts the water from a stream to irrigate his fields and orchards. A manufacturer withdraws it from an underground source to use as a raw material or to wash and treat other materials. A city pumps large quantities through its mains for use in homes and commercial establishments. Any of these users may store water for future use, or a government agency may build a great multipurpose reservoir project to supply them all.

* * *

All of the water uses described in the opening paragraphs are desired by and have utility and value to the users. Not all will be protected by law and given the property status of a "water right." The boy's desire to swim is outweighed by the neighboring landowner's right to full possession of his land. The trout fisherman and motorboater similarly may have no private rights if the stream or lake is on private land but they may have "public rights" and be entitled to protection if the water is open to the public under the governing law. The tugboat also operates under a public right of navigation, but if the captain finds his highway blocked by a dam constructed by the sovereign government he will have no recourse. The owner of the summer home, who receives not only pleasure but also increased land value from the lake or brook, may have a protected interest in the water in some states but not in others. The city which saves money by discharging raw sewage into a stream, spoiling it for others or imposing costs of treatment on them, has no property right to continue its use.

The hydroelectric power company needs legal protection for its substantial investment in dam and power plant. In most jurisdictions it has a perpetual water right, in others a right for a term of years sufficiently long to allow it to amortize its sunk costs. The farmer provides the best illustration of the way in which the law may be varied to reflect the desirability of an activity. In a western state where irrigation reclaimed the desert and is much favored, he has a water right as permanent as the title to his land. In an eastern state where irrigation is still somewhat new and strange, he may have no right at all if his land does not border on the stream, and if it does, his use is theoretically subject to displacement by some other more reasonable use of the water. Under some modern eastern water statutes he has a right that lasts for a term of years, or one that may be cancelled "in the public interest." The manufacturer withdrawing ground water receives different protection in different states, but in one way or another he is assured of a supply. The city supplying the domestic needs of its people has the firmest of water rights, preferred over all others, though it may have to pay damages if it injures other existing rights. Its customers may not have property rights in a strict sense, but they are protected by municipal or public utility law that guarantees them service at reasonable rates. The government has seen to it that its dam has a water right, but the consumers of the water stored behind it may have almost any sort of right ranging from a temporary use until the water is needed for another purpose, through a contract right that may be subject to an infinite number of agreed-upon terms, to a property right in the works.

GEORGE A. GOULD, WATER RIGHTS SYSTEMS
Water Rights of the Eastern United States 8-10 (Kenneth R. Wright ed. 1998).

The function of water law. What is the function of water law? What is society trying to accomplish through water law? Very simply, water law is concerned with resource allocation; water law determines who can use water and for what purposes. Resource allocation is not an end in itself. The end is, or should be, the advancement of social values and needs. Thus, in considering various water law systems from a public policy perspective, one should ask whether a system serves society.

Some persons may object that focusing on resource allocation places too much emphasis on commercial uses of water and minimizes the value of non-commercial uses, such as environmental preservation. This objection is without merit if resource allocation is broadly defined. Focusing on resource allocation does not mean that water cannot or should not be used to provide environmental or other non-commercial values. To be sure, traditional legal rules for allocating water and other resources favored commercial uses, and changes in the law have been required to reflect noncommercial values. Indeed, change in the law to reflect new social values has been the essence of the environmental movement over the last 30 years. Nevertheless, such laws, like traditional legal rules, allocate resources. Whether it involves competition between private parties over water or whether it involves efforts to provide water for public or environmental uses, water law is concerned with difficult choices that must be made about the allocation of a scarce resource.

Water resources. The law must necessarily reflect the nature of the legal problem to be resolved. Usually, the more complex the problem, the more complex must be the legal system. The allocation of water resources—the legal problem of water law—is quite complex. To begin with, rivers and streams are "flow" resources and it is flow, not quantity, that must be allocated. That is, at any point in time, the problem confronting the law is the division of the available flow among the competing demands. Adding to the complexity of the problem, both flow and demands for the flow are variable. By analogy one might envision a water tap discharging a stream of water and a number of persons trying to capture part of the stream with straws. The stream varies as the control valve is turned. Similarly, the number of persons trying to insert straws into the stream varies. The problem is not to allocate glasses or gallons of water; the problem is to determine which persons can have their straws in the stream at any time.

The East and the West have developed very different legal systems to solve this problem. This reflects very different water resources and demands for water. In the East, water resources are relatively abundant. The climate is humid, irrigation is not necessary for successful farming, and demand for water has historically been low. In addition, the flow of eastern streams is much less variable than the flow of western streams.[3] As a consequence, conflict is atypical; it is generally the result of extraordinary uses or exceptional shortages (drought). Applying the analogy to the water tap, the stream from the

---

3. On an eastern stream, flows may vary by a factor of two between the driest and wettest months and a factor of 24 between the driest and wettest years; on western streams these factors may be 40 and 85, respectively. See, New Challenge, New Direction, The Water Policy Report of the Western Governors' Association 7-9 (undated) and National Water Commission, Water Policies for the Future 5 (1973).

tap exceeds demand except when attempts are made to place an unusually large straw in the stream or when the valve is turned exceptionally low.

In the West, water resources are scarce and highly variable, both seasonally and from year-to-year. The climate is arid, irrigation is necessary for successful farming, and demand is high, particularly during the irrigation season. Conflict is frequent and predictable; it results from ordinary uses (principally irrigation) and periodic shortage (low, late summer flows). Using the water tap analogy, even in a normal year, the stream from the tap fluctuates widely and is insufficient during part of the year to fill all the straws inserted into the stream.

The role of government. Government plays a variety of roles with regard to water law; it enforces, it creates, and it regulates water rights; it also develops water supplies and uses water. Initially, water rights were created through private acts, and the role of government was simply to enforce such rights. More recently, [state] government has become the creator of water rights through permit systems. * * *

A third role, closely related to government's role as creator, is its role as a regulator of water rights. Government regulation is a widespread feature of modern society and is typically predicated on failure of market forces adequately to address certain problems. Historically, the western system of permits and administrative regulation was directed toward making the operation of the private water rights system more effective and efficient. Recently, however, most western states have become increasingly active in regulating toward other ends. Similarly, [a number of eastern states now regulate water use] motivated by the desire to increase the efficacy of private water rights and the desire to advance other social goals.

Government uses water and develops water supplies for use by its constituents. Municipal governments are particularly active in developing water supplies for their citizens. In the West, the federal government has been a major water developer, primarily in the form of reclamation projects which supply water for irrigation.

The relationship of the federal government and the states also deserves brief mention. Water rights are primarily a subject of state law. Although the federal government has extensive authority to deal with water pursuant to a number of constitutional powers, the federal government has never attempted to create a general system of water rights. Federal law is the source of limited rights held by the federal government and Indian tribes in the western United States. The federal government also regulates some activities related to water use pursuant to its power over interstate commerce and navigable waters. In addition, it has constructed a number of water projects.

Notes

1. **Governmental powers.** Some water uses are not made as an exercise of property rights but rather as an exercise of governmental powers. The United States, for instance, has no "water rights" for Hoover Dam on the Colorado River, but the Constitution and federal statutes authorize the U.S. Bureau of Reclamation to construct and operate it.

In an exercise of governmental power that crosses straightforwardly into the realm of property rights, many western states have authorized or directed state agencies or officials to acquire water rights to maintain instream flows. The purpose is to protect flow-based environmental values such as scenic beauty, recreational use, and fish and wildlife habitat.

Mostly, however, environmental values in water sources are not protected by assigning property-style water rights. Rather, these values are protected—to the extent they are protected—mainly through the exercise of state and federal regulatory powers. For example, a state permit system might require denial of a permit for any new water right that will have unacceptable environmental consequences. Other measures such as state or federal endangered species legislation might limit not only the creation of new private water rights but also the future exercise of long-standing private water rights in order to protect fish or wildlife habitat.

2. **Public rights.** Public rights empower members of the public to use certain waters in place for certain purposes. For example, the public has rights to use navigable waters for navigation, fishing, and recreation. The exercise of these public rights might be protected and enhanced by minimum streamflow water rights and environmental regulations.

3. **Water distribution organizations.** Much water is abstracted or stored by organizations that distribute it to their ultimate consumers. Institutional law relating to business organizations, cooperatives, public utilities, municipal corporations, and myriad forms of public districts may become "water law," especially insofar as it governs the rights of consumers between themselves, against the distributor, or against the holders of other water rights.

4. **A property-rights viewpoint.** As preceding materials suggest, water law includes much more than property rights in water. Property rights, however, are the basis of most water uses and are central to water allocation issues. For that reason, other water laws and water uses are conveniently studied by examining their impact upon property rights in water. The next three chapters of this book provide detailed exploration of property rights in water. The remaining chapters consider other elements of water law and their effect upon property rights.

OVERVIEW OF PROPERTY RIGHTS IN WATER

Surface Streams. Rights to abstract and use the water of streams in the United States are based on two quite different doctrines, the law of riparian rights and the law of prior appropriation. Each type of right is a property interest created by or obtained under state law, but they have very different characteristics.

The modern form of the riparian doctrine gives each owner of land bordering on a stream the right to make a reasonable use of the water and imposes liability on an upper riparian owner who unreasonably interferes with that use. The right exists whether or not the water is actually used, and a use may be initiated at any time. The use usually must be made on the riparian land and within the watershed of the stream. A nonriparian who uses water is liable to any riparian injured thereby, and conversely a riparian who initiates a use that interferes with a prior nonriparian use is subject to no liability. Some states do not give effect to attempts of riparian proprietors to grant their water rights to nonriparians.

Under the modern form of the appropriation doctrine, a water right may be described as a state administrative grant that allows the use of a specific quantity of water for a specific beneficial purpose, if water is available in the source free from the claims of others with earlier appropriations. The right is initiated by an application for a permit. The place of use is not restricted to riparian land or even to the watershed. The right may be sold and its purpose of use or place of use changed, and it may cease to exist if it is not used.

Riparian law, developed in the green countrysides of England and eastern America, seems to be based on the unspoken premise that if rights to the use of water are restricted to persons who have access to it through the ownership of the banks and if those persons will restrict their demands on the water to reasonable uses, there will be enough for all. Appropriation law, developed in the arid West, is usually regarded as a system for water-short areas. Where there is not enough for everyone, the rule of priority insures that those who obtain rights will not have their water taken by others who start later. The theory is that as demands arise, water rights to supply them will be given out until the water is exhausted, after which those with new demands must purchase rights. Because western streams fluctuate greatly, appropriation law places much emphasis on distribution of scarce water to the persons entitled to it. This is an ongoing process, while riparian law is more sporadic. While in some western states riparian law has been used to distribute shares of scarce water among riparian irrigators regardless of when they initiated their uses, much of the thrust of riparian law is to adjust uses so that all riparians can be accommodated. The late Professor Jacob Beuscher once said that eastern riparian law is not so much a system of water allocation as a fire-fighting device used to settle the few disputes that arise between users of the generally abundant supplies.

In general, the appropriation doctrine is western water law, and the riparian doctrine is eastern water law. Specifically, nine western states have pure appropriation law, the "Colorado Doctrine," and have had it from their beginnings. These are Alaska, Arizona, Colorado, Idaho, Montana, Nevada, New Mexico, Utah, and Wyoming. Nine other western states began with the "California Doctrine," which recognizes both riparian rights and appropriations, but all of them are now substantially appropriation states. In six of them—Kansas, North Dakota, Oregon, South Dakota, Texas, and Washington—riparian rights are the historical basis of some uses, but all new uses must be appropriative. Only in California, Nebraska, and Oklahoma is it possible to initiate new uses by exercising riparian rights; and in each of them, the new exercise of riparian rights is subject to limitations that did not exist historically.

It would be misleading to say that the water law of the other 32 states is common law riparianism. At least 14 of them control the initiation of substantially all new uses by administrative permits—Connecticut, Delaware, Florida, Georgia, Iowa, Kentucky, Maryland, Massachusetts, Minnesota, Mississippi, New Jersey, North Carolina, Virginia, and Wisconsin. Some permit states allow only riparian uses, but others apparently allow nonriparian uses as well. The remaining mainland states may have the doctrine of riparian rights as their common law, but it has been heavily overlaid with statutes that control dams on navigable streams (hydroelectric dams or all dams), statutes that authorize nonriparian use of water stored in dams, statutes that authorize and control the abstraction of water by cities, districts, state agencies, or other large users, and more recently, with statutes that control private uses for the protection of minimum flows and environmental values. In most "riparian states," these statutes rather than the common law are the important features of modern water law. Louisiana has riparian rights, though they stem from the Civil Code rather than the common law. Hawaii has a unique blend of ancient customary rights, appurtenant rights, and riparian rights overlaid with a permit system.

Groundwater. Groundwater that can be withdrawn in usable quantities is found in aquifers, which are porous earth formations such as gravel, sandstone, or fractured limestone that hold a substantial amount of water and permit it to move through the formation. Some narrowly confined aquifers have been treated as "underground streams," and the law of surface streams applies to them. Most groundwater, however, is so physically different from water in streams that historically it was treated differently. The first common law rule was absolute ownership, under which a landowner is regarded as owner of the water underneath the land and is allowed to take whatever quantity can be captured. The next common law rule to emerge was reasonable use, which requires that the landowner's use of groundwater must be reasonable and connected with use of the overlying land. A third common law rule is a rule of correlative rights similar to riparian doctrines of reasonable sharing. A fourth common law rule is prior appropriation. Many states now have superimposed substantial statutory regulation on the exercise of rights under these various common law doctrines.

Classification of states as to groundwater doctrine is significantly a matter of interpretation, and commentators disagree about particular states. Classification is especially problematic for a number of eastern states if one seeks to assess whether permit statutes or other regulatory measures have substantially superseded the common law rules. See generally Joseph W. Dellapenna, 3 Waters and Water Rights chs. 20-22 (Robert E. Beck, ed., 2003). Western states are somewhat easier to classify. Arizona applies the reasonable use doctrine but has replaced it in designated groundwater management areas with a statutory scheme designed over time to reduce existing pumping to the safe yield of aquifers. California adheres to the correlative rights doctrine. Hawaii used correlative rights for decades, but recent case law and legislation create uncertainty about how much of that doctrine survives. Nebraska has a combined reasonable use and correlative rights doctrine. Oklahoma once applied the reasonable use doctrine but has substantially altered it by statute. Texas adheres to the absolute ownership doctrine. The remaining western states use the appropriation doctrine. These include Alaska, Colorado, Idaho, Kansas, Montana, Nevada, New Mexico, North Dakota, Oregon, South Dakota, Utah, Washington, and Wyoming. In addition, groundwater districts that exercise many controls on withdrawals exist in California, Colorado, Nebraska, New Mexico, and Texas.

Note

Water measurement. The unit commonly used to measure the rate at which a stream flows is "cubic feet per second," abbreviated to second feet or c.f.s. To determine the flow in cubic feet per second, one multiplies the area of the cross-section of the stream in square feet by the velocity of the water in feet per second. The average velocity of the flow must be computed because near the sides and bottom of the river and at the surface the water will be slowed by friction and will flow at a lesser rate than at the center of the stream.

Cubic feet per second is also the official statutory unit for measuring water rights in most western states. For example, a water right might entitle its owner to divert water from a stream at the rate of five c.f.s. The "miner's inch is a unit that formerly was widely used in western states to measure small water diversions. It has been largely superseded by the cubic foot per second, but many older rights remain quantified in miner's inches. One miner's inch is the water flow through a one-inch square orifice under a certain pressure. The head of water above the orifice varied according to the custom of the locality, and since the greater the head, the higher the pressure and the greater the discharge, the flow described by "one miner's inch" can be translated into cubic feet per second only if the exact conditions of the measurement are known. In an effort to standardize measurement, many states have adopted legislative definitions. In Colorado, one second foot is equal to 38.4 miner's inches; in Arizona, California, Montana, Nevada, and Oregon, it takes 40 inches to make a cubic foot per second; and in Idaho, Nebraska, New Mexico, North Dakota, South Dakota, and Utah, it takes 50 inches.

The unit used to measure the rate of flow for pumped water, especially from underground sources, is "gallons per minute," abbreviated g.p.m. It takes 448.8 g.p.m. to equal one c.f.s.

When the total volume rather than the rate of flow is measured, the common unit is the "acre-foot." This is the amount of water that will cover one acre to a depth of one foot. It is 43,560 cubic feet, or 325,851 gallons. The right to store water in a reservoir is usually measured in acre-feet; if gallons were used, the capacity of large reservoirs would run into astronomical figures. The total volume delivered annually from a reservoir to land is given as "acre-feet per acre." A typical suburban family of five consumes approximately one acre-foot of water per year. Municipal uses, however, are often calculated in millions of gallons per day.

The relationship of flow rate to total volume is that one second-foot running for 24 hours will deliver 1.98 acre-feet. The total volume of flow of a stream can be expressed in "acre-feet per year."

CHARLES J. MEYERS, A HISTORICAL AND FUNCTIONAL ANALYSIS OF THE APPROPRIATION SYSTEM

Nat'l Water Comm'n, Legal Study No. 5, at 3-6 (1971).

Western courts developed a body of law that can be summarized as follows:

> A property right in the use of water is created by diversion of the water from a stream (or lake) and its application to a beneficial use. Water can be used at any location, without regard to the position of place of use in relation to the stream. In the event of a shortage of supply, water will be supplied up to a limit of the right in order of temporal priority: the last man to divert and make use of the stream is the first to have his supply cut off.

The function of this system of law was to ration a scarce resource and to promote economic development. The rationing principle adopted—first come, first served—is a familiar, if unsophisticated, means of allocating the use of a scarce resource. It is often used by parents to settle disputes among children over the use of toys; it is used by sponsors of such public events as football games and operas to allocate tickets; and it is used in some popular restaurants to allocate tables. Queuing, in short, is a familiar response of a simple social organism to the problem of shortage.

The rule of first-come, first-served is also found in the common law. * * * In the case of lost goods, many cases resolved the conflict between two claimants (neither the owner) by awarding the right to the first to take possession. The first possessor of wild animals (e.g., fish and foxes) was similarly protected. And as between trespasser on land owned by another, prior peaceful possession was protected against subsequent intrusion. * * *

This favor bestowed upon the appropriation system in the West cannot be explained solely by the necessity of adopting an elementary rule in a frontier society. The system has endured too long—as society, government and law became increasingly complex—for that explanation to do. It seems, rather, that the reason for the endurance of the appropriation system is found in the economic goals that the system serves. The system promotes investment by giving security of use. Prior appropriation said in effect: Come West, take up land and water, and they shall be yours. Thus the national (as well as regional) goals of settlement and development of the West were served (and continue to be served) by the appropriation system.

Note

The appropriation system and wise resource allocation. Frank J. Trelease, Federal-State Relations in Water Law, Nat'l Water Comm'n, Legal Study No. 5, at 5-6 (1971):

"Water uses may add substantially to the value of land, and most require a substantial investment in facilities for withdrawing and using it. The use of water is usually the basis of an enterprise which has a value as a going concern. The purpose behind much of water law is to insure that water users will receive a future water supply that will enable them to continue their uses, plan for the future and realize their expectations. While the law * * * may ascribe different degrees of security to different interests in or uses of a resource, it generally follows a strong policy of encouraging enterprise and development with a system of property rights that will give some assurance that the activity will not be subjected to premature termination without compensation.

"Another essential of water law is that it should follow and implement a wise policy of resource allocation, one that will insure the use of the resource to produce the maximum benefits for man and for society as a whole. This is generally accomplished by allocating the use of water to individuals who put it to use, so that private initiative is employed to increase the general as well as individual welfare. By giving security to water rights and protection to water uses, investments in water resources development and in enterprises dependent upon water use are encouraged. By permitting the grant and transfer of water rights, the use of water can be changed to higher and more beneficial uses through the economic process of purchase by persons and entities who can pay the price because of the greater value or productivity of the water in the new use. By regulations restricting water uses to those which are reasonable and beneficial, harmful uses and other undesirable effects are minimized. By other regulations restricting water uses that interfere with public uses and are contrary to the public interests, the public good is promoted and protected."

George A. Gould, Conversion of Agricultural Water Rights to Industrial Use, 27B Rocky Mtn. Min. L. Inst. 1791, 1791-92, 1801 (1982):

"There are two general solutions available to an industry needing new water supplies: it can develop new sources of water or it can transfer water from an existing use. While transfers have occurred for years, the more typical response in the past was to develop new sources. * * * The cheaply developed water was taken first. The water which remains consists largely of snowmelt run-off and flood water which require the construction of expensive storage facilities if a dependable supply is to be available. * * * [W]ater reallocation should begin to occur before all water is allocated; reallocation is less costly privately and socially. * * *"

CHARLES F. WILKINSON, WESTERN WATER LAW IN TRANSITION

56 U. Colo. L. Rev. 317, 321-22, 329, 344 (1985).[a]

[Western water law] has been dominated by themes of appropriation under state law; stable priority for historic uses; concern for private rights over public rights; preference for consumptive, usually commercial, uses; and the provision of subsidized water for irrigators. It goes virtually without saying that this range of nineteenth and early twentieth century priorities is not as broad as the spectrum of considerations that must be accommodated in current water policy.

First, we have become increasingly aware of budgetary restraints on governments. Subsidies of all stripes are increasingly being called into question. Second, the press of the continuing migration to the West has created unprecedented strains on water supplies, thus intensifying the scrutiny of wasteful practices. Third, post-World War II innovations in high-lift pumping equipment have allowed us to begin to tap the potential of the great reservoirs of ground water. But, as shortages have developed, we have learned that many ground water aquifers are not renewable resources in the sense that surface waters are; the annual recharge of some aquifers is so small that they amount

---

a. Copyright 1985. Reprinted with the permission of the University of Colorado Law Review.

to stock resources that can be mined out, much like oil or coal deposits. Further, we have learned that ground water is usually hydrologically related to surface water, so that the traditional system of managing surface water and ground water separately fails to reflect the hydrologic reality; conjunctive management of underground and surface resources is required when the two connect up. Fourth, we have become determined to abate water pollution, an issue given little or no attention in prior appropriation law.

Fifth, we have revolutionized our concept of what western water is. It is no longer simply a commodity to be removed from a watercourse for use on farmland or in a factory. There is life and beauty in water. It is a valid use of water simply to allow it to remain in a stream or lake. In a sense, after first rejecting the riparian rule so resoundingly, we reached a deeply held consensus that there is undeniable merit in some aspects of riparianism: sufficient water absolutely must be available to meet a broad range of public environmental, recreational, ecological, and aesthetic needs.

Finally, we have come to recognize that this body of water law and policy bred of the westward expansion must begin to account for the rights of Indians, to whom legally binding promises were made in order to open aboriginal land and resources for those who settled the West. * * *

The primary method for dealing with the critical issue of creating new water supplies will be to conserve water from existing supplies. For generations, water conservation has been defined chiefly as the construction of new water projects. But most of those proposals will have difficulty satisfying the scrutiny of this newly cost-conscious field. In addition, nearly all of the prime dam sites in the West have already been utilized. Even more fundamentally, water storage projects are conservation projects only in the sense that they capture water that would otherwise flow out to sea. True water conservation is a much broader concept requiring users to employ waste-saving practices designed to ensure that all, or a great percentage of, water is actually applied to the intended use and not to leaks, spill, or evaporation. A major source of new water is the conservation of water in existing uses. * * *

The ultimate problem, of course, is that the old doctrine forces us to proceed today according to the values of a century and a quarter ago. The promising young shoots in this time of transition all are nurtured by our determination to decide by contemporary standards, not those of a distant time.

Notes

1. **Last in time, last in right?** David E. Lindgren, The Colorado River: Are New Approaches Possible Now That the Reality of Overallocation Is Here?, 38 Rocky Mtn. Min. L. Inst. 25-1, 25-3 (1992):

"[T]he West has sustained a remarkable transformation. Industry and commerce replaced agriculture as the dominant economic force, and the region's population burgeoned as Americans abandoned the 'rust-belt' of the Northeast and Mid-West, and the environmental movement's growth during the last two decades changed the public's perception of the place environmental protection should occupy in matters of natural resources allocation and development.

"The pressures resulting from these societal changes have placed western water law—largely rooted in the appropriation doctrine of 'first in time, first in right'—in the throes of dynamic, fundamental change. Simply put, the urban and environmental interests who are 'last in time' are not willing to accept the proposition that, as supplies become fully allocated, western water law always places their interests 'last in right.'"

2. **Climate change.** Levi D. Brekke et al., U.S. Geological Survey, Circular 1331, Climate Change and Water Resources Management: A Federal Perspective 5-6 (2009):

"Reconstructions of the Earth's climate over the past 2,000 years have shown that while temperature has varied on multiple time scales, there appears to have been a significant increase during the most recent 100 years. * * *

"The changes to Earth's climate are caused by changes in the global energy budget, including surface and atmospheric energy exchanges, internal variability, and external forcing outside the climate system. The dominant drivers of change over the past 2,000 years are changes in the concentrations of greenhouse gases (GHGs), aerosols, volcanic activity, and solar radiation. * * * According to the IPCC [Intergovernmental Panel on Climate Change, a body created by the United Nations Environment Programme and the World Meteorological Organization], no driver other than GHGs provides a scientifically sound explanation of most of the warming observed both globally and nationally over the past few decades. * * *

"Temperature increases are expected to change the mix of precipitation toward more rain and less snow. Such precipitation shifts would affect the origin and timing of runoff, leading to less runoff from spring snowmelt and more runoff from winter rainfall, particularly in high-latitude or mountainous areas. * * * Increasing temperature may also increase potential evapotranspiration from vegetation and land surfaces and may thereby decrease the amount of water that then reaches streams, lakes, and reservoirs. Changing water temperatures and ocean circulation may change the intensity and frequency of coastal storms under future climate conditions, but there is still much uncertainty as to what those changes may be.

"Precipitation changes are expected to differ across the country, with some areas receiving more and others receiving less * * * There may also be changes in seasonal patterns and extremes of precipitation. Depending on location, these possible changes have led to concerns that droughts and floods, defined relative to past experiences, will occur more frequently and (or) be more severe under future climate conditions."

Two other possible effects of temperature increases are earlier melting of mountain snow pack and longer growing seasons. The former could diminish late-summer stream flows, and the latter could increase the use of irrigation water. Douglas Kenney et al., The Impact of Earlier Spring Snowmelt on Water Rights and Administration: A Preliminary Overview of Issues and Circumstances in the Western States, Final Project Report (review draft), Western Water Assessment, Univ. of Colo. & NOAA, Sept. 3, 2008 at 3, 11-12.

3. **Water use and public policy.** Nat'l Water Comm'n, Water Policies for the Future 2-3 (1973):

"[T]here are few water 'requirements,' except for relatively small amounts for drinking, cleaning, fire fighting in municipalities, and similar other essential social and environmental purposes. But there are 'demands' for water and water-related services that are affected by a whole host of other factors and policy decisions, some in fields far removed from what is generally considered to be water policy. For example, the invention of the kitchen garbage disposal unit greatly increased the load on municipal sewage treatment plants, and the decision to support the price of cotton led to vast increases in irrigated acreage on the High Plains of Texas. * * * How much water will be used, where, and for what purposes will depend on the policies that are adopted."

Wayne B. Solley et al., U.S. Dep't of the Interior, Circular 1200, Estimated Use of Water in the United States in 1995, at 2 (1998):

"Traditionally, water management in the United States has focused on manipulating the country's supplies of freshwater to meet the needs of users. A number of large dams were built during the early 20th century to increase the supply of freshwater for any given time. This era of building large dams to meet water demand in the United States has passed. As we approach the 21st century, the finite water supply and established infrastructure require that demand be managed effectively within the available sustainable supply. * * * "

Report of the Western Water Policy Review Advisory Comm'n, Water in the West: Challenge for the Next Century 3-51 to -52 (1998):

"The emphasis on the protection of fish and migratory waterfowl is one of the most dramatic changes in federal water policy since 1973 and is leading to a more holistic focus on the restoration and maintenance of healthy aquatic ecosystems. The 1973 [report of the National Water] Commission emphasized the incorporation of fish protection measures and flow release schedules into new projects, rather than the restoration of existing degraded systems. However, the events of the past 20 years have rendered this focus outdated—a key issue today is the potential re-operation of existing projects to help restore aquatic ecosystems * * *.

"The construction of dams and the diversion of water from river systems or basins have contributed to the decline of historic natural fish populations in many river basins throughout the West. Dams and water diversion patterns have also increased predation, reduced wildlife habitat, and increased pollution. * * *

"The immediate dilemmas facing modern water managers concern the preservation of existing native fish species and wildlife habitats, as well as the restoration of degraded habitats to increase their productivity. But there is also a growing recognition that the development of ecological baselines and the maintenance and restoration of health aquatic ecosystems are the best ways to avoid the bitter fish-versus-diversion conflicts that now pervade the West. There are three primary reasons for this. First, the ESA [Endangered Species Act] makes protection of listed fish and wildlife an absolute priority. The ESA directs the Fish and Wildlife Service * * * or the National Marine Fisheries Service * * * to list species, subspecies, or distinct populations of fish and wildlife as threatened or endangered; the difference reflects the degree of extirpation risk. Once a species is listed federal agencies or permittees may not take any action likely to jeopardize the continued existence of the species, including habitat destruction or modification. Second, the ESA applies to existing activities as well as to future ones. Third, there is increasing recognition that there are few 'natural' aquatic environments to preserve. More and more, the emphasis is on the restoration of degraded systems."

For more on sustainable water use from an ecosystem perspective, with examples of very different legislative approaches from around the world, see Stephan C. McCaffrey & Gregory S. Weber, Guidebook for Policy and Legislative Development on Conservation and Sustainable Use of Freshwater Resources (U.N. Environment Programme 2005).

4. **Continuity versus change.** The ideas and sentiments expressed in the last two principal excerpts (by Meyers and Wilkinson) and the accompanying Notes frame much of the current policy debate about water law. An interesting perspective on the debate comes from famed business management consultant and societal observer the late Peter Drucker. He saw "as central to society and civilization the tension between the need for continuity and the need for innovation and change." James W. Michaels, Jane Austen Novels and Management Manuals, Forbes, Mar. 10, 1997, at 14.

Chapter 2

PRIOR APPROPRIATION

SECTION 1. ORIGIN

IRWIN v. PHILLIPS
Supreme Court of California, 1855.
5 Cal. 140.

HEYDENFELDT, J., delivered the opinion of the Court. MURRAY, C.J., concurred.

The several assignments of error will not be separately considered, because the whole merits of the case depend really on a single question, and upon that question the case must be decided. The proposition to be settled is whether the owner of a canal in the mineral region of this State, constructed for the purpose of supplying water to miners, has the right to divert the water of a stream from its natural channel, as against the claims of those who, subsequent to the diversion, take up lands along the banks of the stream, for the purpose of mining. It must be premised that it is admitted on all sides that the mining claims in controversy, and the lands through which the stream runs and through which the canal passes, are a part of the public domain * * *, to which there is no claim of private proprietorship; and that the miners have the right to dig for gold on the public lands was settled by this Court in the case of Hicks et al. v. Bell et al., 3 Cal. 219.

It is insisted by the appellants that in this case the common law doctrine must be invoked, which prescribes that a water course must be allowed to flow in its natural channel. But upon an examination of the authorities which support that doctrine, it will be found to rest upon the fact of the individual rights of landed proprietors upon the stream, the principle being both at the civil and common law that the owner of lands on the banks of a water course owns to the middle of the stream, and has the right in virtue of his proprietorship to the use of the water in its pure and natural condition. In this case the lands are the property either of the State or of the United States, and it is

16

not necessary to decide to which they belong for the purposes of this case. It is certain that at the common law the diversion of water courses could only be complained of by riparian owners, who were deprived of the use, or those claiming directly under them. Can the appellants assert their present claim as tenants at will? To solve this question it must be kept in mind that their tenancy is of their own creation, their tenements of their own selection, and subsequent, in point of time, to the diversion of the stream. They had the right to mine where they pleased throughout an extensive region, and they selected the bank of a stream from which the water had been already turned, for the purpose of supplying the mines at another point.

Courts are bound to take notice of the political and social condition of the country which they judicially rule. In this State the larger part of the territory consists of mineral lands, nearly the whole of which are the property of the public. No right or intent of disposition of these lands has been shown either by the United States or the State governments, and with the exception of certain State regulations, very limited in their character, a system has been permitted to grow up by the voluntary action and assent of the population, whose free and unrestrained occupation of the mineral region has been tacitly assented to by the one government, and heartily encouraged by the expressed legislative policy of the other. If there are, as must be admitted, many things connected with this system, which are crude and undigested, and subject to fluctuation and dispute, there are still some which a universal sense of necessity and propriety have so firmly fixed as that they have come to be looked upon as having the force and effect of *res judicata*. Among these the most important are the rights of miners to be protected in the possession of their selected localities, and the rights of those who, by prior appropriation, have taken the waters from their natural beds, and by costly artificial works have conducted them for miles over mountains and ravines, to supply the necessities of gold diggers, and without which the most important interests of the mineral region would remain without development. So fully recognized have become these rights, that without any specific legislation conferring or confirming them, they are alluded to and spoken of in various acts of the Legislature in the same manner as if they were rights which had been vested by the most distinct expression of the will of the law makers; as for instance, in the Revenue Act "canals and water races" are declared to be property subject to taxation, and this when there was none other in the State than such as were devoted to the use of mining. * * * This simply goes to prove what is the purpose of the argument, that however much the policy of the State, as indicated by her legislation, has conferred the privilege to work the mines, it has equally conferred the right to divert the streams from their natural channels, and as these two rights stand upon an equal footing, when they conflict, they must be decided by the fact of priority, upon the maxim of equity, *qui prior est in tempore, potior est in jure.* The miner who selects a piece of ground to work, must take it as he finds it, subject to prior rights, which have an equal equity, on account of an equal recognition from the sovereign power. If it is upon a stream, the waters of which have not been taken from their bed, they cannot be taken to his prejudice; but if they have been already diverted, and for as high and legitimate a purpose as the one he seeks to accomplish, he has no right to complain, no right to interfere with the prior occupation of his neighbor, and must abide the disadvantages of his own selection.

It follows from this opinion that the judgment of the Court below was substantially correct, upon the merits of the case presented by the evidence, and it is therefore affirmed.

Notes

1. **Mining law origin.** "In January of 1848, two Americans, John A. Sutter and James T. Marshall, while building a sawmill on the American River in the mountain regions of California discovered gold in the mill race. * * * Within a period of two or three years the population of California increased from two or three thousand people to two or three hundred thousand people. * * *

"A vast and intricate field of mining law was to develop from these few simple rules as adopted in the early California mining districts. For a quarter of a century and more, mining law was the most significant field of law in the West. But the mining districts are of current significance not only because of the law of mining but also because of the law of water which owes its origin to them. A good many of the mines in California were placer mines. Water is essential to the operation of a placer mine. But a great many of these placer mines were situated a considerable distance from the stream and frequently entirely beyond the drainage of the stream. Just as there were not enough mines for all the people, there was not enough water for all the mines. Now the Anglo-American doctrine of riparian water rights was established on the premise that water belonged to the owner of the land adjacent to the stream and that while each land owner had a right to use the water still he was obligated to return it to the stream undiminished in quality and quantity for his neighboring riparian owner immediately below him on the stream. Such a law was of course worked out to meet the economic needs of a group of eastern factory owners and mill operators. It was a law made in a damp moist country, and simply did not fit the needs of the western miners. Hence, they were again thrown upon their own resources to work out a system wherein the greatest amount of good could be obtained from the limited amount of water.

"The miners met this problem just as they met the problem of adjusting the right to use a limited number of mines among a multitude of people. They applied the doctrine of prior appropriation to the water just as they did to the mining claims, and they limited the amount of water each person could use to the amount that he originally appropriated from the stream to operate his mine. The size of the ditch was used to determine the quantity of water originally taken. They also decreed that a failure to use the water for a given time worked an abandonment of the right to take the water just as a failure to work the mine worked an abandonment of the mine.

"It was soon discovered by those who went to farm that the water law as worked out by the miners was much more appropriate to their needs in such an arid country than the riparian rights which their ancestors had worked out in the humid East. Hence, the law of water, as originally worked out in the mining districts of California, was soon to become the water law of the entire arid west." John D. McGowen, The Development of Political Institutions on the Public Domain, 11 Wyo. L.J. 1, 8-14 (1956).

Compare the reasons for adopting prior appropriation, given by the California Supreme Court in *Irwin*, with the reasons advanced by the Colorado Supreme Court in Coffin v. Left Hand Ditch Co., infra p. 97.

2. **Mexican origin.** Decisions in Arizona and New Mexico trace statutes adopting the appropriation doctrine in those states to Spanish or Mexican law. See Maricopa County Mun. Water Cons. Dist. No. 1 v. Sw. Cotton Co., 4 P.2d 369 (Ariz. 1931); United States v. Rio Grande Dam & Irr. Co., 51 P. 674 (N.M. 1898). In contrast, Lux v. Haggin, 10 P. 674 (Cal. 1886), held that the Spanish and Mexican law applicable to territory ceded from Mexico was superseded by statutes adopting the common law. A confusing note was added by Motl v. Boyd, 286 S.W. 458 (Tex. 1926), in which dictum equated the Mexican law with riparian rights. However, some excellent scholarly research led the Texas courts to repudiate this dictum in State v. Valmont Plantations, 346 S.W.2d 853 (Tex. Civ. App. 1961), aff'd, 355 S.W.2d 502 (Tex. 1962). After an exhaustive study of historical and legal materials, it was concluded that a Spanish or Mexican grant of land riparian to the Rio Grande did not carry with it an appurtenant irrigation right, and that the Spanish and Mexican irrigation system was not a system of riparian law, but required a specific grant of the water.

3. **Mormon roots.** Seeds of prior appropriation have also been found in the Mormon settlement of Utah in 1847, six months before the discovery of gold in California. However, initial Mormon practice appears to have reflected a communitarian philosophy:

"During the earliest years, * * * the Mormon church approved the custom of diverting water by group effort and applying it to beneficial use, and supervised these operations. Early legislation made grants of water privileges, authorized the making of grants, and vested in the county courts control over appropriations of water. A statute passed in 1880 recognized accrued rights to water acquired by appropriation or adverse use, but did not contain a specific authorization to appropriate water. The principle of priority in time appears to have been recognized by custom before there was any general law on the subject." 1 Wells A. Hutchins, Water Rights Laws in the Nineteen Western States 163 (1971).

4. **Early common law.** Sir William Blackstone, apparently misinterpreting early cases basing the particular litigated water rights on prescription from ancient custom, stated: "If a stream be unoccupied, I may erect a mill thereon, and detain the water; yet not so as to injure my neighbor's prior mill, or his meadow: for he hath by the first occupancy acquired a property in the current." 2 William Blackstone, Commentaries *403. From this, Samuel Wiel, who considered riparian principles more progressive than appropriation principles, argued that prior appropriation was the common law of England before importation from France, via the United States, of "modern" riparian principles in the early nineteenth century. Samuel C. Wiel, Waters: American Law and French Authority, 33 Harv. L. Rev. 133 (1919). Subsequent scholarship exposed the fallacies of Blackstone and Wiel and asserted that early English law was riparian in nature. Arthur Maass & Hiller B. Zobel, Anglo-American Water Law: Who Appropriated the Riparian Doctrine?, 10 Pub. Pol'y 109 (1960). Carol M. Rose argues that pre-nineteenth century English law was neither riparian nor appropriative but preserved the status quo by protecting "ancient uses." Rose asserts that early nineteenth century English law, influenced by Blackstone, vacillated between ancient use principles and prior appropriation before rejecting both in favor of riparian reasonable use principles in mid-century. Carol Rose, Energy and Efficiency in The Realignment of Common-law Water Rights, 19 J. Legal Stud. 261 (1990).

5. **Other countries.** Frank J. Trelease, New Water Legislation: Drafting for Development, Efficient Allocation and Environmental Protection, 12 Land & Water L. Rev. 385, 414-16 (1977):

"I think one of those notions is that when a person has taken, used, become accustomed to, and made a livelihood from water, it becomes 'his water,' and that one who takes it from him has 'stolen his water.' I used to think that prior appropriation was an American invention, but now I am convinced it was simply the verbal identification of a very widespread human trait.

"Teclaff, in his survey of 57 countries, tells us that seniority in use is the most common of all bases for distributing water among users.[2] In its most explicit form, prior appropriation exists not only in 19 American states, but also in the four western provinces of Canada, in Taiwan (China), Iran, Rhodesia, Zambia and the Philippines. There are strong elements of it in several South American countries. The 1963 British Water Resources Act creates a 'protected right' indistinguishable from an appropriation, though enforced in an unusual roundabout manner.

"Protection based on temporal priority is to some degree implicit in many other laws. Before state controls came into being, customary water

---

2. Abstraction and Use of Water: A Comparison of Legal Regimes—U.N./ST/ECA/154 (1972).

rights, held from time immemorial or for prescriptive periods, were everywhere protected. When state authority to use water was instituted, the notion that a state should not make successive grants of the same water to different people appeared in most such laws. Permits, licenses or concessions, whatever they may be called, are not to be issued to the detriment of existing uses in most of the Spanish American countries, in several of the eastern United States, in Tanzania, and in Italy. Practically every new water code has given some sort of group preference to uses in existence when the code was adopted.

"Some evidence indicates a subliminal recognition of priority even where the law is specifically to the contrary. * * * Even under modern statutes that subject the allocation and distribution of water to administrative discretion, the administrators in Great Britain, Kenya and Mexico have eased their burden by issuing permits that authorize the withdrawal of water only when there is a surplus over the needs of existing users."

6. **California doctrine.** Despite the application of the appropriation doctrine in Irwin v. Phillips, in subsequent cases, culminating in Lux v. Haggin, 10 P. 674 (Cal. 1886), the California Supreme Court held that a federal patent to riparian land carried with it riparian rights. Thus, California recognized both appropriative and riparian rights in a system which came to be known as the "California doctrine." At one time at least nine other states—those on the west coast and the great plains—applied the California doctrine, but all except California, Nebraska, and Oklahoma now apply the appropriation doctrine exclusively.

Under the California doctrine, riparian rights on a particular tract of lands are subordinate to all appropriative rights (rights for the use of water on nonriparian lands) which are created before a federal patent for the particular tract is issued. They are superior to all appropriative rights created after the riparian lands are patented. Lux v. Haggin and the California doctrine are explored more fully in Chapter 3, Section 5.

7. **Federalism.** Private water rights are almost exclusively a matter of state law. An extensive legal and scholarly debate has raged over the theoretical basis for state jurisdiction over water rights in the West. Central to the debate is the relationship between ownership of western lands by the United States and legal control of water resources associated with those lands. Although frequently conducted with "sound and fury," it is a debate which has "signif[ied] [almost] nothing" where private water rights are concerned.[a] Notwithstanding what it might have done, the federal government left the creation and regulation of private water rights to the states. The debate has only had practical significance when the federal government has asserted rights on its own behalf or in connection with a federal program, project, or activity. Consequently, the debate is

---

a. "[I]t is a tale told by an idiot, full of sound and fury, signifying nothing." William Shakespeare, Macbeth, act 5, sc. 5, line 26 (G. Blakemore Evans ed., Houghton Mifflin Co. 1974).

left to Chapter 8, Section 2, in which federal powers and federal-state conflicts are developed in depth.

SECTION 2. ATTRIBUTES

A. Diversion

IN RE ADJUDICATION OF THE MISSOURI RIVER DRAINAGE AREA

Supreme Court of Montana, 2002.
311 Mont. 327, 55 P.3d 396.

JUSTICE W. WILLIAM LEAPHART delivered the Opinion of the Court.

The Montana Department of Fish Wildlife and Parks (DFWP) appeals a ruling by the Chief Water Judge on five pre-1973 water rights claims in the Missouri River basin. The five claims are based on diversions of water for purposes of fish, wildlife or recreation. The Water Court ruling refers to In the Matter of Dearborn Drainage Area (1988) * * * 766 P.2d 228 *(Bean Lake)* in remarking on the potential invalidity of the claims. * * * To provide guidance to the Water Court, we must resolve the *Bean Lake* confusion and address not only the question of whether fish, wildlife and recreation uses are recognized as beneficial uses for appropriation purposes, but also whether a diversion is required for appropriation purposes. * * *

The common law elements of a valid appropriation are intent, notice, diversion and application to beneficial use. However, in Montana, as in many western states, the flexibility of the prior appropriation doctrine has allowed acquisition of the right to use a specific amount of water through application of the water to a beneficial use. * * * Judicial opinions and scholarly commentators have repeatedly stated the rule that application to a beneficial use is the touchstone of the appropriation doctrine. See, e.g., * * * Thomas v. Guiraud (1883), 6 Colo. 530, 533 ("[t]he true test of appropriation of water is the successful application thereof to the beneficial use designed, and the method of diverting or carrying the same, or making such application, is immaterial").

Bean Lake involved a claim for inlake water rights for fish, wildlife and recreation purposes in a natural pothole lake. * * * To the extent *Bean Lake* suggests that fish, wildlife and recreation are not beneficial uses, it simply misstates Montana precedent and is hereby overruled. We next address whether *Bean Lake* correctly held that non-diversionary water rights for fish, wildlife and recreation purposes were not recognized in Montana under the doctrine of prior appropriation. * * *

After the *Bean Lake* Court concluded that prior to 1973, Montana did not allow appropriation of water for fish, wildlife and recreation purposes, the Court essentially skipped the traditional appropriation analysis. Rather than evaluating whether DFWP had intended to appropriate water and whether DFWP provided notice of its intent, the Court simply stated that because Montana did not recognize water rights for fish, wildlife and recreation purposes, DFWP could not have intended to appropriate water for those purposes, and thus adverse water users could not have had notice of any such intent. It is unclear from the opinion itself, whether the Court denied the appropriation for Bean Lake because there was no diversion or because it found there was no notice of intent to appropriate. To resolve the confusion engendered by *Bean Lake,* we now determine whether a valid appropriation of water may be established without a diversion where no diversion is physically necessary for the intended use.

While most traditional uses necessitated a diversion of water for application to beneficial use, the appropriation doctrine's history of flexibility and practicality support a holding that a diversion is not required where the application to beneficial use does not physically require a diversion. Common sense rebels against a rigid diversion requirement that would refuse to recognize an acknowledged beneficial use simply because application to the use does not require removal from and depletion of the water source. In accordance with the doctrine's flexibility, we find that a diversion is not a requisite element of an appropriation when it is not a physical necessity for application to a beneficial use.

More than one commentator has warned against the strict adherence to traditional elements, such as diversion, when the element no longer serves its original purpose. These scholars also note that beneficial use is the only essential element of a valid appropriation. See, e.g., Tarlock, Appropriation For Instream Flow Maintenance: A Progress Report on "New" Public Western Water Rights, 1978 Utah L. Rev. 211, 221 ("Most western water experts agree that the actual diversion requirement serves no function that cannot be served by other water law doctrines and statutory procedures. Thus the real issue is whether these uses are beneficial"); * * *

Under prior appropriation, a diversion traditionally served dual purposes providing notice of a user's intent to appropriate water, and defining the extent of the use. In Wheat v. Cameron * * * 210 P. 761, this Court explained that intent to appropriate is to be determined from the specific facts and circumstances pertaining. * * * In accordance with the historical flexibility of the doctrine of prior appropriation, the *Wheat* Court held that although intent could be *presumed* from actual diversion, intent could be proven through other facts and surrounding circumstances. Similarly, in *Bean Lake,* the Court noted that diversion could provide notice or proof of an intent to appropriate. *Bean Lake* * * * 766 P.2d at 233. These decisions do not require a diversion for proof of intent. To the contrary, the opinions suggest that although a diversion may provide proof, intent is the essential element and may be proven through means other than a diversion. In other words, a diversion, although sufficient to prove intent, is not necessary.

Decisions from this Court have not consistently required diversions for water appropriations. Indeed, despite the fact that most traditional beneficial uses of water, such as mining and irrigation, could not occur without a diversion, Montana has specifically recognized appropriations of water without diversions where no diversion was required for the intended beneficial use. See, e.g., Donich v. Johnson (1926), * * * 250 P. 963 (appropriation recognized for instream reservoir); Axtell v. M.S. Consulting, 1998 * * * 955 P.2d 1362 (domestic use recognized without a diversion). Those cases that do suggest that a diversion is an essential element of an appropriation involve uses that, of practical necessity, require a diversion for the application to beneficial use. See, e.g., * * * Sherlock v. Greaves (1938), 106 Mont. 206, 216, 76 P.2d 87, 89 (diversion by pipes and flumes from ditch for irrigation and domestic use). * * *

Ample case law depicting the evolution of the prior appropriation doctrine, and emerging from throughout the west, supports a conclusion that the doctrine should not rigidly demand a diversion where unnecessary to achieve the intended beneficial use. See, e.g., Empire Water & Power Co. v. Cascade Town Co. (8th Cir.1913), 205 F. 123, 129 ("[i]f nature accomplishes a result which is recognized and utilized, a change of process by man would seem unnecessary"); In re Water Rights in Silvies River (1925) * * * 237 P. 322, 336 ("[w]hen no 'ditch, canal, or other structure' is necessary to divert the water from its natural channel, the law does not vainly require such works, prior to an appropriation") * * *.

Only two short months after our *Bean Lake* decision, the Nevada Supreme Court decided a nearly identical controversy. In State v. Morros, the Nevada Court considered whether "Nevada law absolutely requires a physical diversion of water to obtain a water right" in a controversy involving an inlake appropriation claim for recreation purposes. State v. Morros (1988), * * * 766 P.2d 263, 265. After noting that the common law had evolved to allow appropriations for stock watering without a diversion when there was no practical need for a physical diversion, the Nevada Court validated an inlake appropriation for recreation purposes. *Morros,* 766 P.2d at 267. In protecting the inlake water right, the court held that just as the common law "conformed to the practical demands of stockwatering," so should it reflect the fact that "[d]iversions are not needed for and are incompatible with many recreational uses." *Morros,* 766 P.2d at 267. We find the Nevada Court's reasoning persuasive.

Any perception that Montana law required a diversion as a *sine qua non* to an appropriation arises from the fact that most traditional uses, such as agriculture and mining, had a practical need for a physical diversion. That necessity combined with the practice of using diversions as evidence of a user's intent to appropriate has undeniably led to confusion in our precedent, which likewise recognizes instream uses of water where no diversion is necessary for the beneficial use. See, e.g., Axtell v. M.S. Consulting, 1998 * * * 955 P.2d 1362; Donich v. Johnson (1926), * * * 250 P. 963; Montana Coalition, * * * 682 P.2d at 166; and *Greely,* * * * 712 P.2d at 763. Given Montana's long history of beneficially using water * * *, we resolve the confusion in favor of the *Axtell, Donich, Montana Coalition* and *Greely* line of authority and hold that the doctrine of prior appropriation does not require a physical diversion of water where no diversion is necessary to put the water to a beneficial use. Thus, instream/inlake appropriations of water for beneficial uses may be valid when the purpose (e.g., stock-watering, fish, wildlife and recreation) does not require a diversion.

Because beneficial use rather than diversion is the touchstone of the prior appropriation doctrine; because Montana has long recognized as beneficial the use of water for fish, wildlife and recreation; and because Montana has validated non-diversionary appropriations, we now hold that Montana law prior to 1973 did not absolutely require a diversion for a valid appropriation of water. * * *

Notes

1. **Elements of appropriation.** The "common law" elements—intent, notice, diversion, and beneficial use—listed in the principal case are typical of the physical acts used by many pioneer courts to define an appropriation. However, legislation regulating appropriations began to be adopted fairly early, and today the appropriation and use of water is subject to extensive statutory regulation. A central feature of such regulation in most states is an administrative permit system. Under this system, a government issued permit is required in order to make an appropriation. The common law elements remain relevant, but the practical importance of some of them has been greatly diminished by the permit system.

The descriptive parameters of an appropriative right, as distinct from the elements necessary to its creation, typically include the source of supply (e.g., a named stream or river), the point of diversion, the place of use, the purpose of use (e.g., irrigation, domestic use, municipal use), the quantity of water which can be taken, specified by rate of flow (e.g., cubic feet per second) or volume (e.g., acre-feet) or both, and the priority date.

Modern appropriative rights are often subjected to additional terms or limitations imposed to protect the "public interest" or the environment. (See, Chapter 2, Section 3C). The point of diversion and the place and purpose of use of a right can generally be changed, subject to certain limitations and pursuant to specified procedures. (See Chapter 2, Section 5).

2. **Defining "diversion."** A dam alone, which caused overflow of a meadow without the aid of ditches, was held sufficient in Thomas v. Guiraud, 6 Colo. 530 (1883). The construction and maintenance of fish ladders, fish passage facilities, a barrier dam, and a fish trap were recognized as a diversion in *In re* Dearborn Drainage Area, 766 P.2d 228, 232 (Mont. 1988). A so-called "nature dam" designed solely to return a stream to its "historic" channel to preserve the recreational and environmental benefits of flowing water was held to be a diversion in City of Thornton v. City of Fort Collins, 830 P.2d 915 (Colo. 1992). Colorado statutes authorize a "recreational in-channel diversion," defined as "the minimum stream flow as it is diverted, captured, or controlled, and placed to beneficial use between specific points defined by physical control structures * * * for a reasonable recreation experience in and on the water." Colo. Rev. Stat. §§ 37-92-103(7), (10.3).

3. **Early importance of a diversion.** The necessity of an actual diversion was of some importance in the early days of the West when pioneers took advantage of natural conditions. Nevada, New Mexico, and Utah held that reaping the benefits of natural overflow and percolation irrigation was not an appropriation of the water. Walsh v. Wallace, 67 P. 914 (Nev. 1902); State *ex rel.* Reynolds v. Miranda, 493 P.2d 409 (N.M. 1972); Hardy v. Beaver County Irr. Co., 234 P. 524 (Utah 1924). Oregon held that a water right was acquired by natural overflow in *In re* Silvies River, 237 P. 322 (Or. 1925), although the court suggested that as time passed the necessities of economy might require the appropriator to install a controlled system of diversion. Colorado codified this rule in its "meadow right" statute. See Broad Run Inv. Co. v. Duel & Snyder Improvement Co., 108 P. 755 (Colo. 1910). In contrast, lack of diversion prevented an appropriation of water seeping from a reservoir, although benefits from subirrigation resulted. Lamont v. Riverside Irr. Dist., 498 P.2d 1150 (Colo. 1972).

Where horses, cattle and sheep do their own diverting, stockwater appropriations have been upheld. See, e.g., Hunter v. United States, 388 F.2d 148 (9th Cir. 1967). In Utah, the animals may drink but the owner obtains no protectable right. Adams v. Portage Irr. Reservoir & Power Co., 72 P.2d 648 (Utah 1937).

4. **Constitutional claims that a diversion is required.** Several "diversion" cases have involved statutes which expressly provided for "instream" appropriations. Opponents of the appropriations argued that the statutes were unconstitutional because they authorized appropriations having no physical diversions. The opponents cited state constitutional provisions protecting the right to appropriate water, and argued that these provisions made a diversion a constitutional requirement. The con-

stitutional challenges were rejected and the statutes were all upheld. E.g., Colo. River Water Cons. Dist. v. Colo. Water Cons. Bd., 594 P.2d 570 (Colo. 1979); Neb. Game & Parks Comm'n v. The 25 Corp., 463 N.W.2d 591 (Neb. 1990).

5. **Instream appropriation in California.** Two California Courts of Appeal ruled that without a diversion no appropriation of instream flows could be made for fisheries. Cal. Trout, Inc. v. State Water Res. Control Bd., 153 Cal. Rptr. 672 (Cal. Ct. App. 1979); Fullerton v. State Water Res. Control Bd., 153 Cal. Rptr. 518 (Ct. Cal. App. 1979). However, a statute enacted in 1991 allows existing water rights to be changed to environmental uses "whether or not the proposed use involves a diversion of water." Cal. Water Code § 1707.

6. **Intent and notice.** The requirements of intent and notice are seldom an issue today because water rights in most states are initiated by filing an application for a permit accompanied by substantial engineering work. Perhaps clear proof that the application was filed only with intent to establish a paper claim could lead to its rejection. Compare Power v. Switzer, 55 P. 32 (Mont. 1898), where the turning of Uncle George's Creek out of its banks for no apparent purpose was held not to constitute an appropriation. Intent and notice can also be issues where pre-permit law rights are being adjudicated for the first time, as in the principal case.

In Colorado, which has no permit law, intent and notice are still important. An overt act sufficient to manifest intent and provide notice to interested persons of the proposed demand upon the water supply is sufficient to initiate a water right. This often takes the form of a survey of the land. However, in City of Aspen v. Colorado River Water Conservation District, 696 P.2d 758 (Colo. 1985), the court held that acts "on the land" were not required, reversing its earlier position. In *In re* Applications for Water Rights of the Upper Gunnison River Water Conservancy District, 838 P.2d 840 (Colo. 1992), the court held that acts of negotiating and executing a contract relating to reservoir operations were sufficient to manifest intent and provide notice. Some of the uncertainty regarding intent and notice has been removed by present Colorado appropriation procedures, discussed infra p. 126, Note 6, authorizing a prospective appropriator to file an application for a "conditional decree" with a "water court." An application for a conditional decree, accompanied by some other "substantial step" toward appropriation, satisfies intent and notice requirements. *In re* Vought, 76 P.3d 906 (Colo. 2003).

B. Beneficial Use

IDAHO DEPARTMENT OF PARKS v. IDAHO DEPARTMENT OF WATER ADMINISTRATION
Supreme Court of Idaho, 1974.
96 Idaho 440, 530 P.2d 924.

SHEPARD, CHIEF JUSTICE. * * * In 1971 the Idaho Legislature enacted I. C. § 67-4307. In essence the statute directs the Department of Parks of the State of Idaho to appropriate in trust for the people of Idaho certain unappropriated natural waters of the Malad Canyon in Gooding County, Idaho. Additionally, it declares (1) that the preservation of the waters for scenic beauty and recreation uses is a beneficial use of water; (2) that the public use of those waters is of greater priority than any other use save domestic consumption, and (3) that the unappropriated state land located between the highwater marks on either bank of these waters is to be used and preserved in its present condition as a recreational site for the people of Idaho. * * *

Pursuant to the statute the Idaho Department of Parks filed an application for a permit to appropriate the waters specified by the statute. The waters in question arise in part at least from springs in the canyon and are natural waters. There appears no argument but that there is unappropriated water available for appropriation. That application was protested by the Idaho Water Users Association, Twin Falls Canal Company, and North Side Canal Company under the provisions of I.C. § 42-203. Those parties are cross-appellants herein and are hereafter designated "Water Users." * * *

The Water Users * * * assert error in the trial court's determination that the preservation of aesthetic values and recreational opportunities for the citizens of this state is a beneficial use in the sense that they will support an appropriative water right under the Idaho Constitution. The foundation of the Water Users' argument is that the five uses specified in article 15, section 3 of the Constitution, i. e., domestic, agriculture, mining, manufacturing and power are exclusive and thus are the only uses that are cognizable beneficial uses under our Constitution. We reject that argument.

We find no support for the position of the Water Users in the discussions reported in II Idaho Constitutional Convention, Proceedings and Debate 1889 (1912), as pertaining to article 15, section 3. It appears that insofar as particular uses were mentioned in the debates, discussion was confined to the establishment of preferences for certain uses over others under certain circumstances. Such establishment of preferences appears to be a common feature of water law in the west. * * * While it is well established in western water law that an appropriation of water must be made for a "beneficial use," nevertheless in

Idaho at least the generic term "beneficial use" has never been judicially or statutorily defined. Our research does not disclose any case in which any court has attempted to define the term "beneficial use."
* * *

Consideration of the statute in question herein indicates clearly that the legislature has declared that "[t]he preservation of water in the area described for its scenic beauty and recreational purposes necessary and desirable for all citizens of the state * * * is hereby declared to be a beneficial use of such water." We note that numerous other western states have recognized through legislation that utilization of water for scenic or recreational purposes is a beneficial use. * * * Such legislation in other states carries no binding effect on this court but, in the absence of persuasive case law to the contrary, it would appear to indicate that the use of water for providing recreational and aesthetic pleasure represents an emerging recognition in this and other states of social values and benefits from the use of water. * * * The statute in question herein recognizes aesthetic and recreational values and benefits which will accrue to the people of the state in respect to the waters of Malad Canyon. We find no basis upon which to disturb that declaration of the legislature that in this instance those values and benefits constitute "beneficial uses." The decision of the district court upon this issue is affirmed. * * *

BAKES, JUSTICE (concurring specially). * * * Article 15 of the Idaho Constitution does not concern itself with abstract notions such as the relationship between the citizenry and their government, but instead concerns itself with the very practical question of water rights. I think we should look to very practical considerations in attempting to construe it. Prior to the time that the Constitution was adopted there were a number of common uses of water which were neither domestic, mining, agricultural nor manufacturing. A community would store water in a tank for use in fighting fires. The operator of a livery stable or a stockyard would water the stock kept there. Logging operations used water both to transport logs and for storage in mill ponds. Communities would use water wagons to settle dust on their dirt streets. The railroad used water for its steam engines and other uses related to the operation of the railroad. All of these uses were undoubtedly considered beneficial, but none of them were domestic, mining, agricultural or manufacturing. I do not believe that by adopting Article 15, § 3, of the Idaho Constitution that it was intended that uses such as these could no longer be considered beneficial uses. On the contrary, the universal expectation must have been that such uses could continue and could be the subject of an appropriation. Many of those uses still continue today, and the changing needs of our society are generating new uses for water which are neither domestic, agricultural, mining nor manufacturing. As an example, many privately owned public swimming pools or health facilities have applied for and received licenses to drill their own wells to supply their water needs. Natural hot water springs have been extensively developed into health resorts, e.g., Lava Hot Springs, upon the assumption that they have obtained a valid right to the use of the water in their facilities. Such uses, could not be considered as domestic, mining, agricultural or manufacturing as used in Article 15, § 3, without unduly broadening the definitions of the terms, yet such uses are no doubt beneficial from a societal point of view in that they contribute to the general welfare of the citizenry; and unless a valid water right could be obtained for such a use, not only would society suffer by the loss of such uses, but a great deal of capital which has been invested in reliance upon the validity of a right to such a use for water would be in jeopardy. I therefore conclude that uses other than those enumerated in Article 15, § 3, can be beneficial uses. * * *

With the exception of those uses elevated to beneficial status by Article 15, § 3, of the Constitution, the concept of what is or is not a beneficial use must necessarily change with changing conditions. For example, if we were now presented with a question of whether or not using water to operate a public swimming pool, a fountain, or to flood a tract to provide ice for a skating rink were beneficial uses, a good argument could be presented that such uses, although not domestic, mining, agricultural or manufacturing uses, were nevertheless beneficial. But we cannot say that such uses will always be beneficial because conditions might so change that these uses would be an unjustifiable use of water needed for other purposes. The notion of beneficiality of use must include a requirement of reasonableness. With the exception of the uses implicitly declared to be beneficial by Article 15, § 3, there is always a possibility that other uses beneficial in one era will not be in another and vice versa. * * *

MCFADDEN, JUSTICE (dissenting). * * * It is beyond dispute that scenic beauty and recreation are both of vital importance to modern day life in Idaho. But this does not ipso facto mean the state has the right to promote these beneficial ends by withdrawing waters from appropriation, given the guarantee contained in the Idaho Constitution. I note, however, that the effect of a proposed appropriation upon scenic beauty and recreation can and should be considered in determining whether the use contemplated is "beneficial" within the meaning of the Constitution. * * * In other words, where the benefits of a proposed use are outweighed by the attendant detriment to scenic beauty and recreation, the use is not a "beneficial use," and the application for a permit to appropriate public waters for that use should be denied. As always, the question of beneficial use must be determined on a case by case basis, since the benefits of a particular proposed appropriation may outweigh the detriment to recreation and scenic beauty. * * *

Notes

1. **A core principle.** Beneficial use is a core principle of the appropriation doctrine; many doctrinal rules are refinements or corollaries of the concept. The importance of beneficial use finds expression in judicial opinions and in statutes in many appropriation states. See, e.g., *In re Missouri River*, supra p. 22, referring to beneficial use as the "touchstone" of appropriation and citing approvingly a statement by the Colorado Supreme Court that application to beneficial use is the "true test" of appropriation); Ariz. Rev. Stat. § 45-141 (stating that "[b]eneficial use shall be the basis, measure and limit to the use of water").

2. **Instream appropriations.** Other states have also enacted statutes which authorize and regulate instream appropriations. See, e.g., Colo. Rev. Stat. § 37-92-102(3); Wyo. Stat. Ann. §§ 41-3-1001 to -1014.

Under the Colorado statute, recreational instream appropriations are limited to the "'minimum stream flow' necessary 'for a reasonable recreation experience in and on the water.' If an in-channel recreational appropriator seeks more than the minimum stream flow for a reasonable recreation experience in and on the water, then by definition, that would-be appropriator's intended use is not a beneficial use." Colo. Water Cons. Bd. v. Upper Gunnison Water Cons'y Dist., 109 P.3d 585, 598 (Colo. 2005).

Instream appropriations have also been recognized in states without express programs. See State v. Morros, 766 P.2d 263 (Nev. 1988); DeKay v. U.S. Fish & Wildlife Serv., 524 N.W.2d 855 (S.D. 1994). In *Morros*, the court confirmed an instream appropriation for recreation and fisheries by the United States Bureau of Land Management. The court found statutory authorization for an "in situ" appropriation in a statute recognizing recreation as a beneficial use. In *DeKay,* the court approved an appropriation by the United States Fish and Wildlife Service of the natural flow of six springs to maintain wetlands in a wildlife refuge, citing a statute which acknowledged "assigned beneficial uses of irrigation and wildlife propagation and stock watering."

3. **Private instream appropriations.** Many states restrict instream appropriations to designated public agencies. See, e.g., Colo. Rev. Stat. §37-92-102(3); Neb. Rev. Stat. § 46-2,108. Should private parties be able to make instream appropriations? Consider the following views:

"[I]nstream uses differ from water rights applied to the more traditional beneficial uses in that the public is the real beneficiary of the dedication. * * * Because the benefits of instream uses inevitably redound to the public generally rather than the claimant, only public rather than private bodies should be permitted to claim water for instream uses." A. Dan Tarlock, The Recognition of Instream Flow Rights: "New" Public Western Water Rights, 25 Rocky Mtn. Min. L. Inst. 24-1, 24-3 (1979).

"[T]he benefits [of privately held instream rights] for streamflows could be significant. * * * Parties who have invested significant sums in private rights are likely to be vigilant in seeing that their rights are protected. As these parties pressure watermasters to enforce private instream rights, state instream rights might be better enforced as well. * * * Private parties also can provide an important source of additional funds to supplement state efforts to maintain adequate instream flows for fish. Private parties operating in the free market can use their funds to acquire senior rights on important streams and tributaries, without harming the rights of other users." Jack Sterne, Instream Rights and Invisible Hands: Prospects for Private Instream Rights in the Northwest, 27 Envtl. L. 203, 232-33 (1997).

4. **Transfers to instream use.** Cal. Water Code § 1707(a) allows "[a]ny person entitled to the use of water, whether based upon an appropriative, riparian, or other right, [to] petition the board pursuant to this chapter * * * for a change for purposes of preserving or enhancing wetlands habitat, fish and wildlife resources, or recreation in, or on, the water." Consider also Or. Rev. Stat. § 537.348, authorizing private parties to convert existing appropriations to instream rights.

Does it make sense to restrict new instream appropriations but allow transfers of existing rights to instream uses? Frank Trelease suggested that one should "think land" when considering water policy issues. Frank J. Trelease, The Model Water Code, the Wise Administrator, and the Goddam Bureaucrat, 14 Nat. Resources J. 207 (1974). In previous centuries, the United States gave large amounts of public land to private parties—primarily homesteaders, miners, and railroad companies. Much like appropriation's "beneficial use" requirement, private parties were required to invest substantial resources in the development of such land before receiving title. Federal law, however, did not give public land to private parties for public parks, wildlife refuges, and similar reserves, although homesteaders, miners, and railroad companies were not prohibited from dedicating land to such purposes once title had been received from the federal government. Did it make sense to give land to those who would develop it economically but not to those who would preserve it or was this just another example of a bias in favor of consumption over preservation?

5. **Relinquishment of instream rights.** In Aspen Wilderness Workshop v. Colorado Water Conservation Board, 901 P.2d 1251 (Colo. 1995), the court held that the Colorado Water Conservation Board could not unilaterally decrease an instream appropriation. The court noted that, unlike other appropriators, the board acts on behalf of the people of the state in making instream appropriations and, thus, has "a unique statutory fiduciary duty to protect the public in the administration of its water rights decreed to preserve the natural environment." Shortly thereafter, the Colorado legislature amended the instream appropriation statutes to give the board such authority. Colo. Rev. Stat. § 37-92-102(4)(a). However, a board decision to decrease an instream appropria-

tion must be preceded by public notice and hearings. The decision is also subject to judicial review to determine that "the decreed appropriation as decreased will preserve the natural environment to a reasonable degree." Id. § 37-92-102(4)(b).

WASHINGTON DEPARTMENT OF ECOLOGY v. GRIMES
Supreme Court of Washington, 1993.
121 Wash.2d 459, 852 P.2d 1044.

SMITH, JUSTICE. * * * Appellants Clarence E. and Peggy V. Grimes (Grimeses) appeal from a decree adjudicating water rights pursuant to RCW 90.03.200 entered by the Pend Oreille County Superior Court. Respondents [include] the State of Washington Department of Ecology (Ecology). We affirm the Superior Court. * * *

The Grimeses submitted five claims for water rights, only the first of which is at issue in this appeal. This claim was for the use of waters for domestic supply, irrigation and recreational purposes. The Grimeses requested an instantaneous flow rate of 3 cubic feet per second (c.f.s.) for irrigation purposes, and a storage right of 1,520 acre feet of water in the Marshall Lake reservoir. The referee recommended that this claim be confirmed, but limited it to an instantaneous flow of 1.5 c.f.s. during irrigation season, and a storage right of 183 acre feet plus 737 acre feet for evaporative loss, for a total storage right of 920 acre feet. * * *

On January 5, 1990, after hearing testimony on the Grimeses' exceptions, the Superior Court entered its "Decree Adjudicating Water Rights Pursuant to RCW 90.03.200." The decree approved the "Report of Referee." * * * The appellants challenge the consideration of evidence by the referee and the trial court, as well as application of the law relating to appropriative water rights. * * *

The Doctrine of Prior Appropriation

* * *

"Beneficial use" is a term of art in water law, and encompasses two principal elements of a water right. First, it refers to the purposes, or type of activities, for which water may be used. Use of water for the purposes of irrigated agriculture is a beneficial use. The Grimeses' use of water to irrigate alfalfa fields is not at issue in this case.

Second, beneficial use determines the measure of a water right. The owner of a water right is entitled to the amount of water necessary for the purpose to which it has been put, provided that purpose constitutes a beneficial use. To determine the amount of water necessary for a beneficial use, courts have developed the principle of "reasonable use." Reasonable use of water is determined by analysis of the factors of water duty and waste. * * *

Water Duty

"[Water duty is] that measure of water, which, by careful management and use, without wastage, is reasonably required to be applied to any given tract of land for such period of time as may be adequate to produce therefrom a maximum amount of such crops as ordinarily are grown thereon. It is not a hard and fast unit of measurement, but is variable according to conditions."[40]

The referee based his determination of the volume of water necessary for irrigation in the Marshall Lake basin on a Washington State University Research Bulletin entitled "Irrigation Requirements for Washington—Estimates and Methodology" (Irrigation Report), and on the expert testimony of Jim Lyerla, the District Supervisor for seven Eastern Washington counties, including Pend Oreille County, in the Water Resources Program of the Department of Ecology. * * * The Irrigation Report provides information for water requirements for specific crops, given in inches per acre per irrigation season, in 40 locations around the state, including Newport, Washington, 5 miles south of Marshall Lake.

Based on the testimony of Mr. Lyerla and the Irrigation Report, the referee determined that an irrigated alfalfa crop grown in the Marshall Lake area requires 21 inches or 1.75 acre feet of water per acre during the irrigation season. The referee then applied an efficiency factor and increased this water duty to 2.5 acre feet per acre per year. The referee found this water duty to be "approximately commensurate with the duty utilized by the Department of Ecology in its quantity allocations in this geographic area under the water right permit system."

Because water rights are characterized in both total yearly allowance and instantaneous flow, the referee also established the maximum rate of diversion at 0.0166 c.f.s. per acre under irrigation. The referee first calculated a standard flow of 1 c.f.s. of water per 60 acres as a reasonable instantaneous flow for alfalfa irrigation in the Marshall Lake basin. In considering the Grimeses' claim, he determined that the Grimeses were entitled to sufficient flow to irrigate 73 acres, or a minimum of 1.21 c.f.s. He then calculated in an efficiency factor to increase this flow by 25 percent and awarded the Grimeses an instantaneous flow of 1.5 c.f.s. * * *

Waste

From an early date, courts announced the rule that no appropriation of water was valid where the water simply went to waste. Those courts held that the appropriator who diverted more than was needed

---

40. In re Steffens, 756 P.2d 1002, 1005-06 (Colo.1988) (quoting Farmers Highline Canal & Reservoir Co. v. Golden, 129 Colo. 575, 272 P.2d 629 (1954)); see In re Ahtanum Creek, 139 Wash. 84, 96, 245 P. 758 (1926).

for the appropriator's actual requirements and allowed the excess to go to waste acquired no right to the excess. A particular use must not only be of benefit to the appropriator, but it must also be a reasonable and economical use of the water in view of other present and future demands upon the source of supply. The difference between absolute waste and economical use has been said to be one of degree only.

Appellant Clarence E. Grimes acknowledged in his testimony that his existing irrigation system required a water flow of up to 3 cubic feet per second in order to deliver 1 cubic foot per second to the field, and that this system was highly inefficient, causing one-half to two-thirds loss of water. * * * While an appropriator's use of water must be reasonably efficient, absolute efficiency is not required. * * * Relying on a standard efficiency factor for irrigation sprinkler systems found in the irrigation report, [the referee] confirmed in the Grimeses a water right with one-fourth conveyance loss for a total of 1.5 cubic feet per second. * * *

The Reasonable Efficiency Test

In limiting the Grimeses' vested water right, the referee balanced several factors, including the water duty for the geographical area and crop under irrigation, the claimants' actual diversion, and sound irrigation practices. In his report, the referee described his method of calculating the Grimeses' water right as a "reasonable efficiency" test. * * *

Decisions of courts throughout the western states provide a basis for defining "reasonable efficiency" with respect to irrigation practices. While customary irrigation practices common to the locality are a factor for consideration, they do not justify waste of water. As this court stated in a case predating the Water Code of 1917:

> * * * [C]ustom can fix the manner of use of water for irrigation only when it is founded on necessity * * * [and] an irrigator is entitled to use only so much as he can put to a beneficial use, for the public policy of the people of the United States will not tolerate waste of water in the arid regions.[66]

Local custom and the relative efficiency of irrigation systems in common use are important elements, but must be considered in connection with other statutorily mandated factors, such as the costs and benefits of improvements to irrigation systems, including the use of public and private funds to facilitate improvements. * * * The referee alluded to a test incorporating factors that consider impacts to the water source and its flora and fauna. While consideration of these impacts is consonant with the State's obligations under RCW 90.03.005

---

66. Shafford v. White Bluffs Land & Irrig. Co., 63 Wash. 10, 13–16, 114 P. 883 (1911).

and 90.54.010(1)(a) and (2), these factors cannot operate to impair existing water rights.

There is some confusion in the record as to the legal standard used by the referee in determining beneficial use. * * * There is no discussion in the original report of any "reasonable efficiency" test. However, the referee rendered a supplemental report in response to exceptions taken by the Grimeses. * * * [I]n a footnote the referee set forth a detailed "test of reasonable efficiency" which he purportedly used in determining beneficial use. That "test" is stated as follows:

> (1) [C]ustomary delivery and application practices in the area, (2) technology and "practices" improvements feasible and available to reduce water consumptions and financial needs associated with implementation thereof, and (3) impacts of improvements of existing facilities and practices, if initiated, upon (a) the water source from which the diversion takes place, (b) the existing flora and fauna within the area of diversion, conveyance and actual uses, (c) other water rights from said water source, and (d) other water users on other water sources.

There is nothing in the record to support the referee's statement that he employed the reasonable efficiency test. Nowhere in the record does he discuss application of the elements of the so-called "test." If he had in fact applied the "test," it would be necessary for this court to reverse and remand. That test is without statutory authorization in an adjudication proceeding which relates exclusively to confirmation of water rights established or created under "other provisions of state law or under federal laws."

Adjudication proceedings cannot be used "to lessen, enlarge, or modify the existing rights of any riparian owner, or any existing right acquired by appropriation, or otherwise." The suggested test would be contrary to the vested rights of water users. * * * Included in the vested rights is the right to diversion, delivery and application "according to the usual methods of artificial irrigation employed in the vicinity where such land is situated."[75] The Legislature sets a standard clearly contradictory to the suggested test in RCW 90.03.040, which relates to eminent domain over water rights. The test is contrary also to long established principles of Western water law.

While we reject use of the specific test suggested by the referee, we affirm because (1) there is no indication in the record that he in fact applied the factors stated in the "test," and (2) he applied the actual beneficial use made by Grimes, taking into account the actual needs and use and the methods of delivery and application in the vicinity. * * *

---

75. RCW 90.03.040.

The Takings Argument

Appellants Grimes argue that diminishment of their prior appropriation in any way is a "taking" of their property right for which they must be compensated or have the decision of the trial court set aside. A vested water right is a type of private property that is subject to the Fifth Amendment prohibition on takings without just compensation. Nevertheless, the concept of "beneficial use," as developed in the common law and as described earlier in this opinion, operates as a permissible limitation on water rights. * * *

Notes

1. **Duty of water.** Contrary to the suggestion in the principal case, in many states "duty" is quite specific. See, e.g., Idaho Code § 42-202 (1 c.f.s. for 50 acres); S.D. Codified Laws § 46-5-6 (limiting appropriations for irrigation to 1 c.f.s. for 70 acres and 3 acre-feet per acre per year); Wyo. Stat. Ann. § 41-4-317 (1 c.f.s. for 70 acres); see also Cal. Water Code § 1004 (2 1/2 acre-feet per acre per year for the irrigation of uncultivated areas). Nevada and New Mexico have repealed their former fixed limit, replacing them with flexible standards. Nev. Rev. Stat. 533.070; N.M. Stat. Ann. § 72-5-18. In Kansas, which straddles the boundary between arid and humid zones, administrators allow 2 acre-feet per year in the western section, 11/2 in the central part, and 1 near the eastern boundary.

2. **Reservoirs.** Reservoirs require special rules. Since the purpose of constructing reservoirs is to balance out the lean and the fat years, the courts have been liberal in allowing "carryover storage." E. Side Canal & Irr. Co. v. United States, 76 F. Supp. 836 (Ct. Cl. 1948). In Idaho, storage rights for irrigation are limited to 5 acre feet per year. Idaho Code § 42-202. By administrative practice in California, storage in a reservoir in any year is usually limited to the maximum amount stored during the five-year period prior to the issuance of a license.

In most states the quantity which can be stored during a particular water year is governed by the capacity of the reservoir—what it will hold as a result of a single filling, not what it can be made to hold by successive fillings and emptyings. Windsor Reservoir & Canal Co. v. Lake Supply Ditch Co., 98 P. 729 (Colo. 1908). The one-filling rule is usually applied so that if at the beginning of a particular "water year" a reservoir is partly full with carryover storage, only the balance needed to fill it can be taken during that year. See N. Sterling Irr. Dist. v. Simpson, 202 P.3d 1207 (Colo. 2009) (upholding state engineer's use of November 1 to October 31 as the "water year" for the one-filling rule).

The one-filling rule reflects irrigation practices. Water is usually stored in irrigation reservoirs during the winter or spring, when demand is low or flows are high, and is later released to irrigate crops during late summer, when flows are low and demand is high. Thus, irrigation reservoirs typically fill only once a year. If such reservoirs were allowed to fill and empty several times during the same year under their original priority, the burden on the river would be substantially increased, to the detriment of parties holding junior rights. The one-filling rule prevents this, and, under such circumstances, the rule works well. However, the rule can require unnecessary construction of excess storage capacity if the demand for water from the reservoir is constant throughout the year, as for a city or industry, since it prevents the use of a small regulating facility that can be filled, partially drained and refilled to take full advantage of predictable river fluctuations. See Wheatland Irr. Dist. v. Pioneer Canal Co., 464 P.2d 533 (Wyo. 1970).

In City of Denver v. Northern Colorado Water Conservancy District, 276 P.2d 992 (Colo. 1954), the one-filling rule, added to the pioneer rule that the capacity of the ditch is the top measure of a water right, was used to block an imaginative feat of modern engineering. Denver filed a map and statement showing a diversion from the Blue River of 1600 cubic feet of water per second through a tunnel under the continental divide. This quantity of water was available only during short periods of spring run-off. Later, Denver proposed to save a major portion of construction costs by accumulating water in Dillon Reservoir at the rate of 1600 second feet when that quantity was available and carrying it away through a tunnel with a capacity of 788 second feet; i.e., Denver intended to use Dillon Reservoir for temporary storage until the accumulated water could be drained away by the smaller tunnel. Denver already had a late priority for storage for the full capacity of Dillon Reservoir. "One cannot add water to a full cup, and may not have a second decree for water from the same source to be held at the same time in the same reservoir to which a decree has already been ordered to its full capacity. Further, the rule is elementary that the first essential of an appropriation is the actual diversion of the water with intent to apply to a beneficial use. * * * Water can be actually diverted only by taking it from the stream. The amount so diverted is necessarily limited to the capacity of the ditch or tunnel through which diversion is made. * * * Where water is stored in a channel reservoir, a ditch headed in such reservoir has no right by virtue of direct use decree to deplete such storage." Id. at 998-99.

Three dissenting judges pointed out that with its junior priority the reservoir, as a practical matter, would never be full when the proposed diversion of 1600 second feet was being made. "Thus the illustration of the 'full cup' fails to hold water. * * * Unquestionably the city of Denver would have the right to appropriate the 1600 cubic feet per second of water by the construction of a tunnel of that capacity. This objective could be obtained with no grounds for opposition by the expenditure of an additional $10,000,000 of the peoples' money. If the same result can be obtained by the substitution of a mechanical operational equivalent to the larger tunnel I am at a loss to understand why the increased burden on the taxpayers should be required. * * * In all normal operations the Dillon Dam would serve two functions: (1) as a headworks for diverting Denver's direct appropriation through the tunnel; and (2) for catching an occasional flood in the late summer. * * * There is no reason why the Dillon Dam cannot fulfill in succession both the diverting and the storage functions." Id. at 1021-22.

The Colorado Supreme Court revisited Dillon Reservoir in 1998 in City of Grand Junction v. City of Denver, 960 P.2d 675 (Colo. 1998). In 1987, Denver sought a refill right for Dillon Reservoir to replace water lost through seepage, evaporation, and releases required by flood control obligations. Grand Junction, which has a junior priority to water from the Blue River, objected, citing a provision of the Blue River Decree which states that "as against junior appropriators * * * only one filling [of Dillon Reservoir] shall be allowed each year." Id. at 680.

Despite this provision, the Colorado Supreme Court affirmed a lower court decree awarding Denver refill rights with a 1987 priority. The court held that the Blue River Decree only prohibited Denver from filling Dillon Reservoir more than once under the priority awarded it in that decree. Thus, the court said, Denver's request for a new right with a 1987 priority was entirely consistent with the decree. In a footnote, the court said: "This provision [the one-fill provision in the Blue River Decree] is consistent with other 'one fill' limitations found in our case law. * * * '[T]he statute which provides for these decrees forbids the allowance of more than one filling on one priority in any one year.'" Id. at 683 n.6. The court also noted that the new refill right with a 1987 priority could not be exercised to the detriment of the 1946 priority right awarded Grand Junction in the Blue River Decree.

If a city can later obtain a right to refill a reservoir, why can it not obtain a refill right at the time it makes its original reservoir appropriation in those cases where it is efficient to successively fill, drain, and refill a reservoir several times during the same year? Would other parties who subsequently obtain junior rights be unfairly harmed by such a practice? Did the court overrule its earlier opinion *sub silentio*?

3. **Vested rights.** In *Grimes* the court stated that an appropriator has "vested rights * * * to diversion, delivery and application 'according to the usual methods of artificial irrigation employed in the vicinity where such land is situated.'" If the "usual methods" become more efficient over time, do an appropriator's rights "vest" in accordance with the "usual methods" on the date the right was initiated? On the date water was applied to beneficial use? On the date of adjudication? The court also noted that beneficial use "operates as a permissible limitation on water rights." As a result of the litigation in the principal case, the Grimeses were adjudicated rights to 1.5 c.f.s. If future improvements reduce the amount of water required for irrigation "according to the usual methods," can this figure be reduced? Justice Bakes, concurring in *Idaho Department of Parks*, supra p. 28, suggests that a use which is beneficial in one era may not be beneficial in another. Compare N.M. Stat. Ann. § 72-5-18 ("Improved irrigation methods or changes in agricultural practices resulting in conservation of water shall not diminish beneficial use or otherwise affect an owner's water rights or quantity of appurtenant acreage.") Can

the Grimeses' right be extinguished if their use—irrigation of alfalfa—ceases to be a beneficial use? Consider the following case.

IMPERIAL IRRIGATION DISTRICT v. STATE WATER RESOURCES CONTROL BOARD

California Court of Appeal, 1990.
225 Cal. App. 3d 548, 275 Cal. Rptr. 250.

FROELICH, ASSOCIATE JUSTICE. * * * In 1980 a private citizen requested the Department of Water Resources to investigate alleged misuse of water by IID [Imperial Irrigation District] which had resulted in a rise in the level of the Salton Sea, flooding the citizen's farmland. After an investigation, an initial conclusion of water waste, and unproductive communications with IID, the Department of Water Resources referred the matter to the Board for investigation and action. * * * On June 21, 1984, the Board issued its Decision Regarding Misuse of Water by Imperial Irrigation District, designated Decision 1600 (hereafter sometimes referred to as "Board Decision") which consisted of a 71-page review of the history of the proceedings, the evidence taken by the Board, the Board's findings and conclusions, and an order requiring certain action be taken by IID. * * *

[The trial] court undertook to review by writ of mandate the substance of Decision 1600. Using the independent judgment test (as directed by this court, ibid.), the court determined that the Board's findings were supported by the evidence, that its decision was "a reasonable and balanced directive for achieving compliance with Article X, Section 2," and that the writ should be denied. This appeal followed. * * *

As IID concedes in its brief, the essential facts of this case are not in dispute. The experts on any particular issue were never in complete agreement, but their differences were of degree, not kind. For instance, estimates of water lost through "canal spill" ranged from 53,000 to 135,000 acre feet per annum; and water lost through excessive "tailwater" ranged from 312,000 to 559,000 acre feet per annum. There was no dispute, however, that very large quantities of water in each case were being lost. The dispute is whether such loss (and this is but one example of such decisions made by the Board) was or was not reasonable. * * *

IID's water rights * * * are the result of federal statute, U.S. Supreme Court decision, and a seven-party agreement allocating water among Southern California users. Water rights within the state of California traditionally were derived from riparian rights or entitlement based upon prior appropriation. (See historical discussion in United States v. State Water Resources Control Bd. (1986) * * * 227 Cal.Rptr. 161.) It is conceivable that IID's water rights, based as they are upon a unique blend of statutory and contractual origins, could be characterized as somehow more stable or securely vested than water rights from traditional sources. IID does not, however, make this claim. It simply contends that a right to use water, no matter how derived, once vested, becomes a property right which cannot be undermined without due compensation.

Illustrative of IID's broad contention is the following quote from United States v. State Water Resources Control Bd., supra, * * * 227 Cal.Rptr. 161: "It is * * * axiomatic that once rights to use water are acquired, they become vested property rights. As such, they cannot be infringed by others or taken by governmental action without due process and just compensation." The essence of IID's contention, therefore, is that the Board was without power to deprive IID of its discretionary power of determination of water use without providing compensation (which the Board admittedly has no power to provide).

As a preliminary matter we should note exactly what the Board did require of IID. * * * IID was required within a period of eight months to submit a plan for reservoir construction and to affirm its intent to construct one reservoir per year. Once a general plan of water conservation was achieved, IID was required to submit progress reports every six months "until the objectives have been achieved." The Board reserved jurisdiction to monitor IID progress and to "take such other action" as might be required to assure compliance with an approved plan. There can be no doubt that the Board's intrusion into IID's previously untrammeled administration of the use of water in its district was substantial. As often stated in water law cases, "what is meant by a water right is the right to use the water. * * *" (Id. at * * * 227 Cal.Rptr. 161.) While the Board's decision in no way interfered with IID's contractual and statutory entitlement to Colorado River water, it most certainly presaged an interference with IID's utilization of that water once it traversed the All-American Canal.

Our conclusion that the Board Decision substantially impacted the practical use and administration by IID of its water does not, however, result in our acceptance of IID's contention of unconstitutional interference with "vested" rights. Historic concepts of water "rights" in California were dramatically altered by the adoption in 1928 of the above referenced constitutional amendment. Our Supreme Court, in Gin S. Chow v. City of Santa Barbara (1933) * * * 22 P.2d 5, acknowledged that the new provision altered previously vested rights. "As already observed the amendment purports only to regulate the use and enjoyment of a property right for the public benefit, for which reason the vested right theory cannot stand in the way of the operation of the amendment as a police measure. * * * It has been long established that all property is held subject to the reasonable exercise of the police power and that constitutional provisions declaring that property shall not be taken without due process of law have no application in such cases."

The concept of the dimension of rights remaining to the water user after the constitutional amendment was fully developed in Joslin v. Marin Mun. Water Dist. (1967) * * * 429 P.2d 889. In that case a lower user attempted to enjoin upstream diversion by a municipal water company upon the contention that the downstream prior use for deposit of sand and gravel was a vested, protectible use. The Supreme Court held that simply because a use is beneficial it does not become "reasonable" under the constitution. Denying the plaintiff's assertion of compensability for its loss of water, the court focused on the nature of water rights after 1928. "While plaintiffs correctly argue that a property right cannot be taken or damaged without just compensation, they ignore the necessity of first establishing the legal existence of a compensable property interest. Such an interest consists in their right to the reasonable use of the flow of water. * * * [While a] vested right as now defined may not be destroyed or infringed upon without due process of law or without just compensation * * * [there is] no provision of law which authorizes an unreasonable use or endows such use with the quality of a legally protectible interest merely because it may be fortuitously beneficial to the lands involved." (* * * see also * * * National Audubon Society v. Superior Court (1983) * * * 658 P.2d 709 ["After the effective date of the 1928 amendment, no one can acquire a vested right to the unreasonable use of water."])

Put simply, IID does not have the vested rights which it alleges. It has only vested rights to the "reasonable" use of water. It has no right to waste or misuse water. The interference by the Board with IID's misuse * * * does not constitute a transgression on a vested right. * * *

All things must end, even in the field of water law. It is time to recognize that this law is in flux and that its evolution has passed beyond traditional concepts of vested and immutable rights. In his review of our Supreme Court's recent water rights decision in In re Water of Hallett Creek Stream System (1988) * * * 749 P.2d 324, Professor Freyfogle explains that California is engaged in an evolving process of governmental redefinition of water rights. He concludes that "California has regained for the public much of the power to prescribe water use practices, to limit waste, and to sanction water transfers." He asserts that the concept that "water use entitlements are clearly and permanently defined," and are "neutral [and] rule-driven," is a pretense to be discarded. It is a fundamental truth, he writes, that "everything is in the process of changing or becoming" in water law.[5]

---

5. Freyfogle, Context and Accommodation in Modern Property Law, 41 Stanford Law Review (1989) 1529, 1546-1547.

In affirming this specific instance of far-reaching change, imposed upon traditional uses by what some claim to be revolutionary exercise of adjudicatory power, we but recognize this evolutionary process, and urge reception and recognition of same upon those whose work in the practical administration of water distribution makes such change understandably difficult to accept.

Notes

1. **Contrary views?** In Enterprise Irrigation District v. Willis, 284 N.W. 326 (Neb. 1939), the court in dicta suggested that retroactive application of a "duty" statute to reduce the quantity of water that can be diverted would unconstitutionally interfere with vested rights. McDonald v. Montana, 722 P.2d 598 (Mont. 1986), involved Mont. Code Ann. § 85-2-234 which required that decrees adjudicating water rights state "the amount of water included in the right." Prior to 1973, water rights in Montana were limited only by flow rate. The court first held that pre-1973 rights could be limited by volume as well as flow rate but then seemingly subverted this holding by stating that the amount required for beneficial use, not the volume limit, will control in "rare" cases where the volume specified cannot meet the requirements of beneficial use. Are these cases inconsistent with *Imperial*? In considering the question, note that the Board did not interfere with IID's contractual or statutory entitlements to water, but rather with the way the water was used.

2. **Relationship to beneficial use.** To what extent is the court's decision dependent on article X, section 2 of the California Constitution—prohibiting "waste or unreasonable use or unreasonable method of use of water"? What is the relationship between "reasonable use" and "beneficial use"? In an omitted part of the opinion, IID argued that even the excess water introduced into the district was used for beneficial purposes such as power generation and prevention of excess salinization of the Salton Sea. The court responded:

"IID is also in error in contending that all 'beneficial' uses are 'reasonable.' * * * The fact that a diversion of water may be for a purpose 'beneficial' in some respects (as for desalinization of lakes or generation of electric power) does not make such use 'reasonable' when compared with demands, or even future demands, for more important uses." 275 Cal. Rptr. at 265-66.

Assume that a California farmer is using no more water than is necessary to grow crops. Could the Board find that the farmer's use was "unreasonable" because there was a more important or valuable use for the water? See Brian E. Gray, "In Search of Bigfoot" The Common Law Origins of Article X, Section 2 of the California Constitution, 17 Hastings Const. L.Q. 225 (1988); Clifford W. Schulz & Gregory S. Weber, Changing Judicial Attitudes Towards Property Rights in California Water Resources: From Vested Rights to Utilitarian Reallocation, 19 Pac. L.J. 1031, 1086-93 (1988).

3. **Defining waste.** Nat'l Water Comm'n, Water Policies for the Future 304-05 (1973): "Substantial savings can be made through improved efficiency in the use of water for irrigation. * * * For example, a statement submitted to the Commission by the Utah-Idaho Sugar Company * * * indicates that Company achieved substantial reduction in water use when it switched in the early 1960's from gravity-flow irrigation to sprinkler irrigation on its Osgoode Project in Southeastern Idaho. The U-I Osgoode Project consists of approximately 6,000 acres of irrigated land and is not a federal reclamation project. Prior to the change to sprinkler irrigation, the Commission was told, the project had been 'water hungry.' After the change, which included squaring up fields and other modernizations, an additional 1,000 acres of land could be put under irrigation and the usage of water per acre for irrigation crops was cut in half."

A rancher in a high altitude, northern Idaho valley grows one crop of "wild hay" per year to supply winter feed for his cattle, drawing over 2 acre feet per acre in the short irrigating season, using "wild flood" irrigation methods. An equipment salesman tells him that with pumps and sprinklers he could grow the same or a slightly better crop with one-half the water. He does not buy the equipment. Is he wasting water? On the plains downstream from the rancher, the U-I Company could grow sugar beets of higher cash value than the hay grown by the rancher. Because of his early priority, however, the rancher gets the water. Is this waste?

If the irrigator's ditch is long or dug through porous soil, a considerable amount of water—sometimes called "carriage water"—may be lost by evaporation and seepage between the point where it is diverted and the place of use. In *Grimes*, supra p. 33, the referee added twenty-five percent for transportation losses. Is that a waste of water? The duty statutes cited supra p. 37, Note 1, appear to make no allowance for carriage water. If a duty statute accurately reflects the minimum quantity of water required for irrigation, an irrigator whose ditch is long and porous will not be able to irrigate all of his land unless he can afford to line his ditch. Is that a waste of land? If he can use carriage water instead of concrete to get the full amount needed on his land, is it a waste of concrete to line the ditch?

4. **Defining waste—third party and environmental benefits.** Water Policies for the Future, supra Note 3, at 305: "It must not be assumed, however, that all irrigation water in excess of consumptive use is lost to the system. In many cases * * * the water is returned to the stream as stream flow or serves to recharge ground water. Some excess water is needed in almost all irrigated areas to leach salts from the soil."

As the preceding quote suggests, one person's "waste" is sometimes another's supply. Environmental amenities are also often produced by inefficient uses of water. For example, a leaky earthen canal may increase stream flows or may create new wetlands; lining the canal may reclaim water previously lost to seepage, but may also decrease the instream flows or dry up the wetlands. See, e.g., United States v. Alpine Land & Reservoir Co., 510 F.3d 1035 (9th Cir. 2007) (upholding Nevada State

Engineer's determination that unlined ditch lead to beneficial 'lateral root irrigation' of vegetation consumed by grazing cattle); Protect the Historic Amador Waterways v. Amador Water Agency, 11 Cal. Rptr. 3d 104 (Cal. Ct. App. 2004) (environmental impact report was deficient because it did not adequately assess the affect that replacing an earthen canal with a pipeline would have on late summer stream flows created by canal leakage). Should the benefits of inefficient practices—either to other water users or to the environment—be considered in defining waste?

5. **Financial or physical feasibility.** In Colorado v. New Mexico, 459 U.S. 176 (1982), infra p. 484, Colorado sought a declaration that some water in the small Vermejo River was available for appropriation in that state, even though essentially all of the water in the stream was diverted and consumed downstream in New Mexico. The Special Master appointed had suggested that greater conservation in New Mexico would free water up for Colorado's intended use. O'Connor, J., concurring in a judgment, noted longstanding rules that, "the extent of the duty to conserve that may be placed upon the user is limited to measures that are 'financially and physically feasible,' Wyoming v. Colorado, 259 U.S. 419, 484 * * * (1922), and 'within practicable limits.' Ibid."

6. **Eliminating waste through regulation.** Is the elimination of "waste" by government regulation a good policy? Consider the following:

"With careful planning, none of the problems associated with reducing wasteful water rights is insurmountable. Legislatures can formulate measures, if required, to make resource tradeoff decisions and to distribute the cost of modernization through all sectors of the economy. There are indeed prices to be paid, but they must not be allowed to overshadow the need for proper water management. As growth continues in the arid West, the quality of life in the region will depend on maintaining a reliable water supply and natural streamflows. Without a commitment to efficient water use, not only will segments of the agricultural industry be threatened by increased problems of erosion and salinity, but all sectors of the economy could be undermined by the resulting water constraints. Consequently, the time has come for state governments to implement the move to water conservation." Steven J. Shupe, Waste in Western Water Law: A Blueprint for Change, 61 Or. L. Rev. 483, 521 (1982).

"Many writers seem to view the statutory and judicial prohibition of 'waste' with approval and argue that water should be put to 'beneficial' use. It is somewhat difficult to understand this position. The logic of the situation is the same as in the case of statutory preferences or the loss of water rights through non-use. It is not clear why a person should not be free to use his own property as he sees fit, providing losses are not imposed upon others. If water rights are salable, and if protection is provided to third parties, it is difficult to see how the problem of waste would become important. To deny rationality in the use of one's own water right is to question the basis of private decisions in the use of all resources. The problem here is to define water rights in such a way that they do become real property and susceptible to market allocation by the forces of supply and demand.

"The California case of *Chow v. Santa Barbara*[12] can be used to illustrate judicial judgments on waste of water. Chow, as a riparian water user, had used for many years the flood waters of a stream for leaching purposes on his riparian lands. In 1933 the California Supreme Court declared this use of water to be unreasonable and also wasteful. * * * As a result the city of Santa Barbara was allowed to appropriate the 'waste' waters formerly used by Chow *without* any compensation.

"There is probably little doubt that the economic worth of the water to the city exceeded the value of the water for leaching purposes. What is important here is that (1) the court took the responsibility of saying that the well-established practice of leaching was wasteful and unreasonable, and that (2) Chow was deprived of his use of water without compensation. If Chow's property right had been clearly defined, the city of Santa Barbara could have purchased that right in the ordinary manner of transfer of property. This case invites reflection upon the application of riparian law and upon the efficacy of judicial decision-making." Jerome W. Milliman, Water Law and Private Decisionmaking: A Critique, 2 J.L. & Econ. 41, 50-51 (1959).[b]

7. **Regulation versus the market.** Is there a role for both government regulation and the market in reducing water waste? Government regulation is usually justified by claims of market failure, and markets in water rights have been a failure. One source of market failure is alluded to in the Milliman article quoted in the preceding note—the lack of clearly defined property rights in water. Indeed, deficiencies in the definition of water rights under existing doctrines is the focus of Milliman's article. This problem and other legal, institutional, and practical impediments to the development of water markets are considered elsewhere in the book, particularly in Chapter 2, Section 5.

Although a variety of efforts are underway to eliminate impediments to transfers and facilitate the development of water markets, progress has been slow and success limited. Until such reforms are in place, government action to eliminate the most egregious instances of waste might be appropriate even in states firmly committed to water markets. In addition, even if most reform efforts are ultimately successful, residual transaction costs may prevent a number of economically positive transactions, particularly where inefficiencies are small individually but large collectively, i.e., where a large number of appropriators engage in inefficient practices. In such cases, government imposition of conservation measures may be appropriate, particularly if care is taken to observe the limitations regarding financial and physical feasibility of such measures suggested by Justice O'Connor supra p. 45, Note 5.

---

12. Chow v. City of Santa Barbara, 217 Cal. 673, 22 P.2d 5 (1933).

Government regulation can also encourage market solutions. The principal case provides an example. In 1989, IID entered into a contract with the Metropolitan Water District of Southern California (MWD) in which MWD agreed to finance conservation in the district in exchange for long-term rights to the water salvaged by the projects. Most observers agree that Decision 1600 of the California Water Resources Control Board—the subject of the principal case—was a significant factor in the consummation of the contract.

8. **Efforts to eliminate waste.** Only Arizona has made a concerted regulatory effort to eliminate waste. Although Arizona's efforts are aimed at curtailing serious groundwater overdraft problems, the Arizona conservation regulations also affect the use of surface waters. The Arizona conservation regulations are discussed infra p. 378, Note 1. Efforts to curtail waste are reviewed and critiqued in Janet C. Neuman, Beneficial Use, Waste and Forfeiture: The Inefficient Search for Efficiency in Western Water Use, 28 Envtl. L. 919 (1998).

CITY OF THORNTON v. BIJOU IRRIGATION CO.
Supreme Court of Colorado, 1996.
926 P.2d 1.

[The City of Thornton applied for new conditional water rights and for changes in use of existing water rights as part of a long-term project to meet the needs of projected population increases. The trial court awarded Thornton conditional water rights, rejecting objections raised by a several parties. (A "conditional water right" is decreed in Colorado when a party has taken an adequate "first step" toward appropriation but has not "perfected" the appropriation by applying water to beneficial use. A decree of a conditional water right is functionally similar to issuance of a permit to appropriate water in states utilizing a permit system. See infra p. 126, Note 6, discussing the Colorado appropriation system.)]

LOHR, JUSTICE. * * * [A]n applicant must establish an intent to appropriate water for application to beneficial use. Pursuant to the anti-speculation doctrine, an applicant's intent to appropriate cannot be based upon the subsequent speculative sale or transfer of the appropriative rights. In the present case, the trial court held that Thornton formed the necessary nonspeculative intent. Objectors NCWCD [Northern Colorado Water Conservancy District] and [City of] Fort Collins appeal this finding and argue that Thornton's plan violates the anti-speculation doctrine. Resolution of the issues raised by NCWCD and Fort Collins requires an examination of the anti-speculation doctrine as it applies to municipalities. Our specific analysis will be informed by a general overview of the anti-speculation doctrine as it has developed in Colorado water law.

Our seminal case in this area is Colorado River Water Conservation District v. Vidler Tunnel Water Co., * * * 594 P.2d 566 (1979). In that case, Vidler Tunnel Water Company (Vidler), a private corporation, sought a conditional storage decree for a reservoir as part of a planned transmountain diversion project. The corporation planned to sell the water to municipalities on the eastern slope for general municipal use but had not obtained firm contractual commitments binding those municipalities to purchase or receive the water. We held that Vidler's plan, which essentially depended on an unsubstantiated assumption that general population growth would produce a need for more water in the future and that municipalities would seek to satisfy this need from Vidler's supply, did not establish the necessary intent to apply the appropriated water to beneficial use. In the absence of firm contractual commitments for the use of water not intended by Vidler for its own use or of agency relationships between Vidler and the intended users, we held Vidler's application unduly speculative. * * *

Although *Vidler* has most often been cited as defining the anti-speculation doctrine, we did not articulate a new legal requirement in that case, but rather merely applied longstanding principles of Colorado water law. Thus, we must examine *Vidler's* predecessors to determine the scope of the application of the anti-speculation doctrine to municipal applicants.

The question of a municipality's ability to appropriate water to meet future needs first received significant attention from this court in City & County of Denver v. Sheriff, * * * 96 P.2d 836 (1939). In *Sheriff* * * * [w]e emphasized the necessity of preserving the flexibility of municipalities to exercise their managerial judgment in resolving their water supply problems, and made the following statement regarding the unique circumstances of municipal water providers:

> The concern of the city is to assure an adequate supply to the public which it serves. In establishing a beneficial use of water under such circumstances the factors are not as simple and are more numerous than the application of water to 160 acres of land used for agricultural purposes. A specified tract of land does not increase in size, but populations do, and in short periods of time. With that flexibility in mind, it is not speculation but the highest prudence on the part of the city to obtain appropriations of water that will satisfy the needs resulting from a normal increase in population within a reasonable period of time.

The *Sheriff* decision clearly counsels against a strict application of the anti-speculation doctrine to municipalities seeking to provide for the future needs of their constituents.

* * * [I]n City & County of Denver v. Northern Colorado Water Conservancy District, * * * 276 P.2d 992 (1954) (*Blue River*) * * *

[s]everal objectors challenged Denver's application on the ground that the city's water supply was adequate without the claimed Blue River water, and that to base a decree solely on projected future needs would be improperly speculative. We noted the divergent estimates of the future growth and needs of the city but ultimately reached the following conclusion:

> We cannot hold that a city more than others is entitled to decree for water beyond its own needs. However, * * * when appropriations are sought by a growing city, regard should be given to its reasonably anticipated requirements.

Thus, under *Blue River*, a city may appropriate water for its future needs without violating the prohibition on speculation so long as the amount of the appropriation is in line with the city's "reasonably anticipated requirements."

* * * [I]nterpreting *Vidler* in conjunction with *Sheriff* and *Blue River*, we do not read the requirements of firm contractual commitments or agency relationships applied to private parties in *Vidler* to apply with equal force to municipalities. This limited exception to the *Vidler* requirements is supported by actions taken by the General Assembly. In 1979, immediately following the *Vidler* decision, the legislature amended the definition of "appropriation" * * * to codify the prohibition on speculation articulated in *Vidler*. Following the amendment, subsection 103(3)(a) now states:

> (3)(a) * * * [N]o appropriation of water, either absolute or conditional, shall be held to occur when the proposed appropriation is based upon the speculative sale or transfer of the appropriative rights to persons not parties to the proposed appropriation, as evidenced by either of the following:

> (I) The purported appropriator of record does not have either a legally vested interest or a reasonable expectation of procuring such interest in the lands or facilities to be served by such appropriation, unless such appropriator is a governmental agency or an agent in fact for the persons proposed to be benefited by such appropriation.

> (II) The purported appropriator of record does not have a specific plan and intent to divert, store, or otherwise capture, possess, and control a specific quantity of water for specific beneficial uses.

By enacting the above provision, the General Assembly endorsed the *Vidler* holding with respect to private parties but also recognized the need for governmental agencies, which include municipalities and other agencies responsible for supplying water to individual users, to exercise some planning flexibility with respect to future water needs. This exception, however, does not completely immunize municipal applicants from speculation challenges. Rather, as part of the statute codifying *Vidler*, the exception must be read as consistent with the

[handwritten margin note: municipalities can speculate to a more reasonable degree than private parties]

scope of the exception recognized for municipalities in those decisions underlying *Vidler*, such as *Sheriff* and *Blue River*. Thus, under section 37-92-103(3)(a), a municipality may be decreed conditional water rights based solely on its projected future needs, and without firm contractual commitments or agency relationships, but a municipality's entitlement to such a decree is subject to the water court's determination that the amount conditionally appropriated is consistent with the municipality's reasonably anticipated requirements based on substantiated projections of future growth.

* * * We have reviewed numerous challenges to decrees based on the anti-speculation doctrine subsequent to *Vidler* and the enactment of section 37-92-103(3)(a). However, almost all of those cases concerned applications by private parties rather than by municipalities. Our sole post-*Vidler* case addressing speculation in the municipal application context is City & County of Denver v. Colorado River Water Conservation District (CRWCD), 696 P.2d 730 (Colo.1985).

* * * Our holding in Denver v. CRWCD must be viewed as limited to the unique facts of that case. Denver sought the claimed water to sell it for profit to parties outside its own boundaries. The city was acting in the capacity of a water supplier on the open market rather than as a governmental entity seeking to ensure future water supplies for its citizens. Accordingly, the municipal planning exception was simply inapplicable, and Denver was required to comply with the full range of requirements applicable to private parties under *Vidler*. Thus understood, Denver v. CRWCD does not eliminate a municipality's ability to plan for the future, and municipal appropriations for reasonably anticipated future requirements, including requirements for projected growth areas not presently within the municipal boundaries, are valid if the municipality substantiates such need. * * *

In the present case, the trial court evaluated the evidence pursuant to the proper legal standard. Furthermore, the trial court's factual findings that the decreed water is consistent with Thornton's reasonably anticipated water requirements and that the water will eventually be used to satisfy needs within Thornton's boundaries or service areas have an adequate basis in the record. Therefore, we accept these findings and uphold the court's determination that Thornton established a nonspeculative intent to appropriate the claimed water.

Notes

1. **Beneficial use, speculation, and municipal water supply.** A bias against speculation is inherent in the concept of beneficial use, and the views of the principal case on speculation are shared, to some degree, by all appropriation states. Relaxation of anti-speculative policies on behalf of municipalities—sometimes referred to as the "growing communities doctrine"—is also widely accepted. The policy is reflected in judicial

decisions, statutory provisions, and administrative regulations which give cities special consideration with regard to the completion ("perfection" or "vesting") of new appropriations or which excuse nonuse of water rights by cities. (Completion of new appropriations is examined in Chapter 2, Section 2C; loss of rights because of non-use—abandonment and forfeiture—is examined in Chapter 2, Section 4).

2. **Limits to relaxation.** In Pagosa Area Water & Sanitation District v. Trout Unlimited, 170 P.3d. 307 (Colo. 2007), the Colorado Supreme Court concluded that the trial court had failed to make sufficient findings to allow it to uphold a decree granting a conditional water right to a water district for 100 years. The reviewing court found unresolved disputes over the appropriate length of the planning period (40, 50 or 100 years) and the projections of future growth. Citing the principal case, the court urged the lower court to scrutinize closely claims for planning periods that exceed fifty years. It put the burden on the district to demonstrate that its needs were non-speculative. And it stated that conditional rights should not be based on conjectural population estimates that become self-serving vehicles for growth.

3. **Private suppliers.** Central Delta Water Agency v. State Water Resources Control Board, 20 Cal. Rptr. 3d 898 (Cal. Ct. App. 2004), presented a situation very similar to *Vidler* (discussed in the principal case), with similar results. A private entity, known as Delta Wetlands Properties, proposed a rather novel project to convert two "islands" in the Sacramento/San Joaquin Delta Estuary into storage reservoirs. Delta Wetlands planned to sell the stored water, but had no specific buyers for the water, relying instead on a general demand for water in California. Despite the lack of specificity regarding where and how the stored water would be used, the California Water Resources Control Board issued appropriation permits which identified potential places of use and purposes of use only generally. However, the permits provided that actual buyers had to be identified and that the Chief of the Division of Water Rights had to determine that water would be placed to beneficial use before water could be stored. The Court of Appeal set aside the permits, holding that "a statement of alternative, potential beneficial uses" did not satisfy constitutional and statutory requirements relating to beneficial and reasonable use of water and that the board could not satisfy its obligations by requiring that particular uses be identified and evaluated later. The court also held that the board's beneficial use obligations could not be delegated.

In Department of Ecology v. Theodoratus, 957 P.2d 1241 (Wash. 1998), the Washington Supreme Court refused to extend the growing communities doctrine to a private subdivision developer. The court affirmed a decision by the Department of Ecology (DOE) which held that the quantity of water awarded in a final certificate of appropriation must be based on water actually applied to beneficial use and not on the capacity of the supply system. In rejecting the capacity of the system as the measure of quantification, the court and DOE reversed a long-standing

Washington practice. The court noted that DOE could allow additional time to the developer to actually put water to use before seeking a final certificate, but reminded DOE that beneficial use must occur within a "reasonable time." The opinion also suggests that a certificated right previously quantified on the basis of system capacity may be vulnerable to partial forfeiture for nonuse where subdivision lots remain long vacant.

4. **Anti-speculation, transfers and severance.** In High Plains A & M, LLC v. Southeastern Colorado Water Conservancy District, 120 P.3d 710, 714 (Colo. 2005), again citing the principal case, the Colorado Supreme Court used the anti-speculation doctrine to reject applications to change water rights, previously used in one county for irrigation, to "any one of over fifty proposed uses in any of twenty-eight Colorado counties." (Transfer of appropriative water rights is examined in Chapter 2, Section 5.) *High Plains* "unreservedly embraces the public-as-supervisor model" of water reallocation, instead of "treating [previously] consumed water as private." Lawrence J. MacDonnell, Public Water-Private Water: Anti-Speculation, Water Reallocation, and High Plains A&M, LLC v. Southeastern Colorado Water Conservancy District, 10 U. Denv. Water L. Rev. 1, 3 (2006).

In Adaven Management, Inc. v. Mountain Falls Acquisition Corp., 191 P.3d 1189 (Nev. 2008), the Nevada Supreme Court clarified that the anti-speculation doctrine does not limit an entity's ability to acquire water rights from a private owner separately from the land to which the right is appurtenant. (Appurtenance of appropriative water rights is examined in Chapter 2, Section 2F.)

5. **Pueblo rights.** Some municipalities in the Southwest claim "pueblo rights," rights for municipal purpose that are superior to those of agricultural appropriators and that permit a city to expand its uses and take without compensation water put to use long before the city's exercise of the right. Such rights are generally said to be a remnant of the Southwest's Spanish heritage, stemming from Spanish or Mexican grants to agricultural villages which have since grown up into American cities. A document which established the village of Pitic in Sonora, Mexico, is claimed to have granted the inhabitants unrestricted rights to water and provided that pueblos established thereafter were to have like privileges.

Only in California are pueblo rights recognized. Pueblo rights in California are based on a discussion, albeit dicta, of Mexican law in Lux v. Haggin, 10 P. 674 (Cal. 1886). Subsequently, the California Supreme Court held that San Diego and Los Angeles have paramount rights to the San Diego River and Los Angeles River, respectively, for as much of the waters of the rivers as the expanding needs of the cities require. City of San Diego v. Cuyamaca Water Co., 287 P. 475 (Cal. 1930). Although modern research indicates that the plan of Pitic did not give pueblos the expansive rights claimed in Lux v. Haggin and other decisions, the California Supreme Court reaffirmed these rights in City of Los Angeles v. City of San Fernando, 537 P.2d 1250 (Cal. 1975), in part because of Los

Angeles' long reliance on them. Despite their long recognition in California, only San Diego and Los Angeles have been adjudicated pueblo rights.

In Cartwright v. Public Service Co., 343 P.2d 654 (N.M. 1959), the New Mexico Supreme Court adopted the pueblo rights doctrine in a suit involving the town of Las Vegas. However, in State *ex rel.* Martinez v. City of Las Vegas, 89 P.3d 47 (N.M. 2004), the New Mexico Supreme Court overruled *Cartwright*. While the court concluded that the historical evidence was not sufficiently clear to justify overruling *Cartwright*, the court held that the doctrine was incompatible with the New Mexico system of prior appropriation, particularly the principle of beneficial use. Although it rejected arguments that *Cartwright* established a "rule of property" which should be adhered to even if wrong or that it should be overruled only prospectively, the court remanded to determine an appropriate equitable remedy to balance Las Vegas' reliance on *Cartwright* with the reliance of others on the system of prior appropriation.

Texas, the only other state to consider the doctrine, rejected it, finding no basis for it in the law of New Spain. *In re* Contests of City of Laredo, 675 S.W.2d 257 (Tex. Ct. App. 1984).

6. **"Can and will doctrine."** Colo. Rev. Stat. § 37-92-305(9)(b), provides that a conditional right cannot be recognized unless it is "established that waters can and will be diverted." This statute focuses on the applicant's ability to complete the intended appropriation. "The factors a court considers under the 'can and will' requirement in diligence proceedings include, but are not limited to: 1) economic feasibility; 2) status of requisite permit applications and other required governmental approvals; 3) expenditures made to develop the appropriation; 4) ongoing conduct of engineering and environmental studies; 5) design and construction of facilities; and 6) nature and extent of land holdings and contracts demonstrating the water demand and beneficial uses which the conditional right is to serve when perfected." Pagosa Area Water & Sanitation Dist. v. Trout Unlimited, 170 P.3d. 307, 316 (Colo. 2007). While there is overlap between the can and will and the anti-speculation doctrines, they are not identical. City of Aurora v. ACJ P'ship, 209 P.3d 1076 (Colo. 2009). Apparently, the latter ensures that an identified beneficial use will result by the end of the relevant time; the former looks at a project's feasibility over that time.

In FWS Land & Cattle Co. v. Division of Wildlife, 795 P.2d 837 (Colo. 1990), the court held that a conditional decree to enlarge existing reservoirs was properly denied because the applicant lacked the legal ability to acquire lands which enlargement would inundate. Similarly in West Elk Ranch, L.L.C. v. United States, 65 P.3d 479 (Colo. 2002), it held that a conditional right to appropriate water from a spring in a national forest was appropriately denied because the United States Forest Service had refused to grant the applicant the special use permit needed for access. In Gibbs v. Wolf Land Co., 856 P.2d 798 (Colo. 1993), in contrast, the court held that lack of legal access to a stream does not violate the doctrine if the applicant can invoke a statutory right of private condemnation. Accord Lemmon v. Hardy, 519 P.2d 1168 (Idaho 1974). In *In re* Vought, 76 P.3d 906 (Colo. 2003), the court explained that the applicants in *FWS* and *West Elk* could not invoke the right of condemnation because both involved government lands which could not be condemned.

In City of Black Hawk v. City of Central, 97 P.3d 951 (Colo. 2004), however, the court indicated that the doctrine does not always require legal access or the ability to obtain access through condemnation. The court affirmed a lower court decision granting a conditional right to the City of Black Hawk to enlarge a reservoir owned by Central City despite a resolution by the city council of Central City denying Black Hawk access to the reservoir. The court distinguished *FWS* and *West Elk*, observing that, unlike those cases, the resolution did not constitute a final denial of access because it did not bind future Central City city councils. The court found it unnecessary to decide if Black Hawk could condemn access to the reservoir, saying that lack of current access is not typically dispositive of whether the can and will statute is satisfied and that the statute should not be rigidly applied in cases not involving speculation. Compare Natural Energy Res. Co. v. Upper Gunnison River Water Cons'y Dist., 142 P.3d 1265 (Colo. 2006) (distinguishing *Black Hawk* where applicant's proposed reservoir use was "inimical" to current use and it was unreasonable to expect applicant to ever get permission for its proposal).

The right of non-governmental parties to condemn property to facilitate the appropriation of water is examined in Chapter 2, Section 2H.

7. **Economic functions of speculation.** Although "speculation" and "speculator" often carry pejorative connotations, economists assert that speculation serves important economic functions. See, e.g., Stephen F. Williams, The Requirement of Beneficial Use as a Cause of Waste in Water Resource Development, 23 Nat. Resources J. 7 (1983). Williams argues that the requirement of beneficial use creates economic waste by encouraging uneconomic investments and premature development of resources. He suggests that unappropriated water should be allocated by state auction and that the purchasers should be allowed to hold their rights for speculative profit without beneficial use.

8. **Appropriation for the benefit of others.** Could the Izaak Walton League appropriate water for a reservoir to be stocked with fish and opened for public fishing? In Lake Shore Duck Club v. Lake View Duck Club, 166 P. 309, 310-11 (Utah 1917), the Utah Supreme Court said, "no": "for the purpose of effecting a valid appropriation of water under the statutes of this state * * * the beneficial use contemplated in making the appropriation must be one that inures to the exclusive benefit of the appropriator and subject to his complete dominion and control."

No other state seems to have similarly limited appropriations. In Scherck v. Nichols, 95 P.2d 74 (Wyo. 1939), the Wyoming court (in a different context) stated: "[I]t is not contrary to the policy of this state that a man may apply for the diversion of water for the ultimate use of it by another." Is the Utah rule consistent with the instream appropriations confirmed in the cases discussed supra p. 31, Note 2? With the appropriation of water by a district or distributing company for use by its consumers?

Nevada and Utah have statutes that attempt to prevent the United States Bureau of Land Management from appropriating water to be used by its grazing lessees to water livestock. See infra pp. 721-22, Note 5.

C. Priority

CITY OF DENVER v. NORTHERN COLORADO WATER CONSERVANCY DISTRICT
Supreme Court of Colorado, 1954.
130 Colo. 375, 276 P.2d 992.

[Proceedings for the adjudication of water rights to the Blue River. The Blue, Williams Fork and Fraser rivers are tributaries of the Colorado River, having their headwaters on the western slope of the continental divide. Denver is on the eastern slope. As early as 1914, Denver had made a reconnaissance of the western slope as a possible source of future water. In 1921 it employed a consulting engineer, who began surveys for diversions from the Fraser and Williams Fork. In 1922 he made preliminary surveys in the basin of the Blue, and filed with the State Engineer a map and statement for a transmountain diversion of 1200 c.f.s. through a tunnel headed on a tributary of the Blue. In 1926 another survey showed that a lower tunnel from the Blue itself could capture the water of several more tributaries through collection ditches, and in 1927 another filing was made for a 1600 c.f.s. tunnel at the new site. Several years of geological investigations disclosed unfavorable conditions along the line of the second proposed tunnel and plans were drawn for a third tunnel at about the same site but with a different direction. In 1941 further engineering work showed that a dam and reservoir at Dillon on the Blue River would eliminate the need for collection ditches, and a new filing was made showing the reservoir and a new location for the tunnel, 20 feet lower in elevation and 3500 feet farther down stream. Later, the plan of operation was revised to call for storage of water in the reservoir at the rate of 1600 c.f.s., and releases at a slower rate through a smaller tunnel with a capacity of 788 c.f.s. Work was begun on this tunnel in 1946.

In the meantime, Denver had proceeded to construct diversion works and tunnels for the waters of the Fraser and Williams Fork rivers, and reservoirs and works on the eastern slope to hold and distribute the western slope waters. In other proceedings, it was decreed rights to appropriate waters of the Fraser and Williams Fork.

In this proceeding, Denver claimed 1200 c.f.s. with a priority of 1921 and 400 c.f.s. with a priority of 1927. The Conservancy District resisted this claim and filed a claim for its large storage reservoir farther down on the Blue, with a priority of 1937. The district court allowed this claim, and decreed to Denver a right to 788 c.f.s. with a priority of 1946. Denver appeals.]

STONE, CHIEF JUSTICE. * * * [S]erious questions are raised by Denver's challenge to the priority date awarded the Blue River project in the decree. The basic law is not disputed, to wit: * * * (2) that as to the rights here involved a municipal corporation has no different status from that of an individual or any other party to the proceeding; (3) that although an appropriation is not complete until actual diversion and use, still the right may relate back to the time when the first open step was taken giving notice of intent to secure it; * * * (4) that right to relate back is conditional that construction thereafter was prosecuted with reasonable diligence, and conditional further that there was then "a fixed and definite purpose to take it up and carry it through," State of Wyoming v. Colorado, 259 U.S. 419 * * * and (5), that the questions of reasonable diligence and of fixed and definite purpose are questions of fact to be determined by the trial court from the evidence. * * *

There is no evidence that any work even of survey, on the Blue River project was begun on July 4, 1921, or at any time prior to the summer of 1922. The claim for the 1921 date is based solely on the fact that survey was started on that date on Denver's Williams Fork and Fraser River projects and the contention that those two projects and the Blue River project constitute in fact a single irrigation project, and consequently that in the determination of the date when the first step was taken, and also in the determination of reasonable diligence since such date, the three projects should be considered as a single project.

In determining the date "when the first step was taken," a survey made on the Fraser River or on the Williams Fork would of itself be no evidence of intent to appropriate water from the Blue River. Certainly such a survey in a far distant basin supplying water to another stream would constitute no notice to another appropriator of such intent. The filing of a plat of method of diversion from the Fraser or Williams Fork would be no evidence of intent to appropriate water from the Blue or notice of such intent. Therefore, there is nothing to support the contention that the priority should be dated as of July 4, 1921. At most, the priority for the Blue River project could date back only to the time when the first step was taken in construction of a project on the Blue River.

In determining reasonable diligence, also, we find no ground for holding, as urged by Denver, that the Blue River project, the Williams Fork project and Fraser River project are each units of a single project so that the construction work on those projects and the expenses incurred thereon can be considered as part of the construction of the Blue River project. Denver's claim for its Blue River project was made by survey, plat and filing entirely separate from those of its Fraser and Williams Fork projects. It seeks priority to water from an entirely separate stream, not even confluent with the Fraser River or Williams Fork except to the extent that each is ultimately a tributary of the Colorado River. It seeks water to be diverted from an entirely separate drainage basin. It was surveyed and planned after those projects. It directly affects other claimants who are protestants here but not directly affected by those projects. It is to be carried through an entirely separate conduit,—the Fraser River being diverted through the Moffat Tunnel and the Williams Fork through the Jones Pass Tunnel, and the Blue, as now planned, to be carried in the Montezuma Tunnel to be bored through the Continental Divide many miles to the south of the others. Its water rights are here sought to be adjudicated as entirely separate from the rights of those projects. It has even less relation to the Fraser River and Williams Fork projects than to Denver's South Platte water system with which it will share the same river channel and reservoirs. In fact, the only relation between the Blue River project and these other projects is that their several waters may ultimately rest in common filtration and concentration plants, and that by means of exchange they may be used cooperatively for supplying prior rights or filling storage reservoirs such as would be probable in the case of any other independent water right. The priority of appropriation which gives the better right under our Constitution is priority on a stream rather than on a project, and any diligence in construction to permit dating back of priority on the Blue River must be diligence relating to and promoting the Blue River appropriation. No such relation here appears. Therefore, diligence in the prosecution of the Fraser and Williams Fork projects cannot be imputed to the Blue River project. However, the fact that the City of Denver was engaged in the construction of these or other enterprises may properly be considered together with all other evidence as to existing facilities and ability of the city in determination of the issue of reasonable diligence. * * *

During the entire period from 1927 to 1946, substantially all the work done and all the money spent by Denver in connection with its Blue River project was for investigation and exploratory work or work in connection with Eastern Slope reservoirs which were not dependent on any one plan for diversion or even on Blue River water. This and similar evidence before the trial court presented substantial support to the contention of protestants that Denver had no fixed and definite plan and no definite point of diversion prior to * * * 1946, and supported the decree of the trial court consistent therewith.

As to the second question, that of diligence:

In summary, the evidence showed that the * * * plan of 1923 has been abandoned without any construction whatever; that following the filing of the * * * plan in 1927, no evidence of actual excavation work in connection with its proposed tunnel appeared until 1942, some fifteen years later, when a cut was made and a small exploratory tunnel was driven about 400 feet at a place then intended to be the west portal to ascertain the condition of the ground. The proposed location of the portal has since been changed and a part of the excavation has caved in. No other work was performed on the ground until July 1946 when work at the east portal of the tunnel was started. Denver's Chief Engineer testified that "That was the first actual construction work." * * *

It appears that throughout the period from 1936 to 1941 efforts were made by the City to induce the United States Bureau of Reclamation to build the project, but without success. There was no evidence of any effort by Denver to finance the project itself prior to the year 1946, but only of efforts to induce the United States to do so.

To support its contention that this work was sufficient to satisfy the requirements of reasonable diligence, Denver cites Tausig v. Moffat Tunnel Co., * * * 106 P.2d 363, wherein it was held that surveys, preparation of maps, acquiring of rights of way and options and obtaining a contract for the carriage of water through the Moffat Tunnel, drilling of test holes, clearing of timber along proposed ditch lines and other similar work was sufficient to satisfy the requirement of reasonable diligence in construction of a ditch leading to the Moffat Tunnel. However, there the party seeking diversion of the water was a private company of apparently limited resources. The dating back was apparently for a period of less than five years, and the decision of this court affirmed the finding of the trial court, holding that there was due diligence; while here, we are asked to hold such that expenditures on the part of a great city, without shown limitation upon its financial capacity, spread out over a period of nearly twenty years would require us to reverse the decision of the trial court and say that such expenditures were evidence of reasonable diligence as a matter of law.

Kinney, in his great work on irrigation, says: "Probably the best definition of the word diligence was given by Lewis, C.J., in rendering the opinion in an early Nevada case, Ophir Silver Min. Co. v. Carpenter, 4 Nev. 534. It is there defined as 'the steady application to business of any kind, constant effort to accomplish any undertaking.' 'It is the doing of an act or series of acts with all possible expedition, with no delay except such as may be incident to the work itself.'" Kinney on Irrigation and Water Rights, Vol. 2, § 735. * * *

It is undisputed that during a period of about twenty years, Denver had not even begun the actual construction of its project and had made no effort whatever as appears from the record towards financing it, but only a laudable but fruitless attempt after nine years of inaction to induce the United States Reclamation Service to finance it for the joint use of Denver and the South Platte Water Users Association. Meanwhile others have worked diligently and long to put a part of this water to actual use. The record before us does not show such conclusive evidence of "steady application" to the business of constructing the project or of such "constant effort to accomplish" it as to require us to hold that the trial court erred in refusal to date back Denver's appropriation, to the loss of such prior users. On the contrary, in order to sustain Denver's claim, we should have to establish as a law of Colorado that a great city or a great corporation, by the filing of a plat of a water diversion plan and the fitful continuance of surveys and exploratory operations, could paralyze all development in a river basin for a period of nineteen years without excavating a single shovel full of dirt in actual construction and without taking any step towards bond issue or other financing plan of its own for carrying out its purpose; that for nineteen years no farmer could build a ditch to develop his farm and no other city or industry could construct a project for use of water in that area without facing loss of their water when and if the city or corporation which filed the plat should actually construct its project. This we cannot do. * * *

MOORE, JUSTICE (dissenting). * * * *To what extent can a claimant of water change his plan of development without that change amounting to a relinquishment of his claim?*

As will be seen from the quotation in De Haas v. Benesch, supra, there are some changes which can be made in the plan of a water development which will not constitute a relinquishment of the project. One criterion for determination of this problem was used by the United States Supreme Court in the case of State of Wyoming v. Colorado, 259 U.S. 419 * * * where the changes planned had to do with the determination of "whether" the would-be appropriator would proceed at all with the diversion project. Such changes are to be distinguished from those which go rather to selection of the most economical or effective means to be employed for the accomplishment of a diversion and use of water, concerning which there already is a fixed and definite intention to take. Once the decision has been made to proceed with the project, continuing investigations and changes are simply evidence of diligence and endeavor to accomplish the greatest good at a minimum of cost to the public, not abandonment of the project. * * * Changes undertaken with the apparent intent to improve or make more efficient or less costly the whole work to be undertaken, should be regarded as the natural diligence of a prudent man rather than the want of constancy in the prosecution of the undertaking. * * *

May a claimant of water offer evidence to show that the water claimed is part of an interrelated system involving other water rights, and, if so, is work on various parts of such interrelated system to be considered in determining the diligence with which each of the component water rights in the system is being developed?

This question must be answered in the affirmative. With respect to the development of a water right to irrigate a single piece of land through a single ditch to which water is diverted through one headgate, it would be obvious that diligence could be shown by reference to work on any, or all, of the three component parts: diversion dam, carrying ditch, or distribution laterals.

As the works become more complex, including, several sources of supply, wider spread uses, and a variety of purposes, a project may cross county lines, irrigation district or irrigation division lines, and different jurisdictional lines for adjudicating the water rights involved. It does not appear that there is any point at which a water system becomes so large that its parts no longer relate to each other in such a way that work on one part may not constitute diligence with respect to completion of the whole including its other parts. It may well be that a single entity may have holdings so extensive that many of them are unrelated to others. In such a case, work on one holding would not constitute work on an unrelated holding.

It appears, therefore, that the test of the extent to which work on one part of a water system may properly relate to another for the purpose of determining due diligence, is whether the parts of the work relate to a single integrated purpose intimately enough that progress on one part has a direct bearing upon another part. What we are really considering is whether or not the work done is within the limits of what is reasonably to be considered as customary to an enterprise unified under single management and in which impairment of any part tends to directly impair the remaining parts, or in which construction of one part directly contributes to the whole which is comprised of other parts.

Much of the evidence which was admitted, and that which was erroneously excluded, established the fact that the city of Denver has one interrelated water system which should have been considered as a whole in so far as the question of reasonable diligence of the city in going forward with the Blue River diversion is concerned. Even without the full delineation of fact which might have been presented had the trial court not restricted evidence to the Blue River unit alone, the only evidence in the record concerning Denver's efforts shows a continuing good faith endeavor to accomplish the appropriation for which she now seeks a conditional decree. * * * The majority opinion comments that: "There was no evidence of any effort by Denver to finance the project itself prior to the year 1946, but only of efforts to induce the United States to do so." Unmentioned is the fact, which every citizen then living well knows, that in 1929 the whole nation trembled and lay prostrate in depression; that the public treasuries were empty; that for years thereafter any attempt to finance such a large under-taking upon the local level would have been sheer folly; and that the only hope for resources sufficient to warrant a start at construction was to seek the financial backing of the United States. In those years all business, both public and private, looked only to Washington for rescue from total collapse.

At about the time when another approach to the financial problem might reasonably have been expected to succeed, World War II broke out and thereafter for several years the productive energies of all the people were concentrated on the war effort. Men and materials were not to be had for any development of this kind, which could possibly wait. Just as soon as the conflict ended and war demands relaxed, construction of the tunnel began, and, despite inadequate financing and disappointments, the city has gone forward with the work.

For the foregoing reasons I am of the opinion that the City and County of Denver is entitled to a conditional decree for 1600 cubic feet per second, with a priority date as of October 19, 1927.

Notes

1. **Subsequent developments.** In 1990, the Colorado legislature adopted the views of the dissent. Colo. Rev. Stat. § 37-92-301(4)(b):

"The measure of reasonable diligence is the steady application of ef-fort to complete the appropriation in a reasonably expedient and efficient manner under all the facts and circumstances. When a project or inte-grated system is comprised of several features, work on one feature of the project or system shall be considered in finding that reasonable diligence has been shown in the development of the water rights for all features of the entire project or system." Accord Nev. Rev. Stat. 533.395(5).

2. **Priority date in permit states.** In states where a permit is re-quired for an appropriation (all appropriation states except Colorado), the priority of the appropriation dates from the filing of the permit applica-tion. See, e.g., Ariz. Rev. Stat. § 45-162B; Utah Code Ann. § 73-3-18. As in the principal case, this priority is retained only if the permittee completes the appropriation by applying water to beneficial use with reasonable diligence. See, e.g., Ariz. Rev. Stat. § 537.160; Utah. Code Ann. § 73-3-12. As discussed supra p. 50, Note 1, diligence requirements are relaxed for some public entities.

3. **Policies behind "relation back" and "diligence."** The priority rule is an application of the principle of "first possession" which finds broad expression in the common law. Like rights to the fox made famous in Pierson v. Post, 3 Cai. R. 175 (N.Y. Sup. Ct. 1805), rights to water are perfected only when water is physically captured (applied to beneficial use). Unlike the fox hunter, an appropriator obtains protected, albeit in-choate, rights to water by taking a "first step" toward appropriation—by

beginning the "chase" so to speak—a proposition expressly rejected by the court in Pierson v. Post. This deviation from *Pierson* is explained by the effort necessary to apply water to beneficial use. Application of water to beneficial use, particularly for large projects, requires large investments of capital and labor and may take a substantial time to complete. A party might be reluctant to make such investments if priority to an essential water supply could be lost to a competitor who is able to initiate and complete a project in a shorter time. To assuage such concerns, the appropriation doctrine holds that the priority "relates back" to the "first act" of appropriation. See Dallas Creek Water Co. v. Huey, 933 P.2d 27, 35 (Colo. 1997). To prevent hoarding and speculation, however, "relation back" is tempered by the "reasonable diligence" requirement. Id.

4. **Codification of "due diligence."** In several permit states, the requirement has been crystallized by statutes setting forth a specific time within which the work must be commenced (two years, Ariz. Rev. Stat. § 45-160; six months, Neb. Rev. Stat. § 46-238); the physical works must be completed (five years, N.M. Stat. Ann. § 72-5-6, Wyo. Stat. Ann. § 41-4-506); and the water applied to beneficial use (five years, Idaho Code § 42-204). These are often coupled with intermediate standards for diligence, such as that one-fifth of the work must be completed within one-half the time allowed. S.D. Codified Laws 46-5-25. In some states, progress reports must be filed with water officials. Nev. Rev. Stat. 533.390. Colorado requires the holder of a conditional decree—the functional equivalent of a permit—to obtain a finding of diligence from the water court every sixth year. Colo. Rev. Stat. §37-92-301(4).

For "good cause," very similar to "due diligence," state water officials may extend these periods. See Tulkisarmute Native Cmty. Council v. Heinze, 898 P.2d 935 (Alaska 1995). In some states, extensions may be granted almost routinely. For an extreme case, see Green River Development Co. v. FMC Corp., 660 P.2d 339 (Wyo. 1983), which involved permits that had been extended for more than sixty years without any significant development efforts. See also Carbon Canal Co. v. Sanpete Water Users Ass'n, 353 P.2d 916 (Utah 1960), where the court upheld extensions totaling thirty-six years, and 425 P.2d 405 (Utah 1967), where it finally lost its patience and terminated the permit.

5. **Excusing lack of progress.** In determining reasonable diligence, what is the relevance of financial troubles? See Maricopa County Mun. Water Cons. Dist. No. 1 v. Sw. Cotton Co., 4 P.2d 369 (Ariz. 1931) (pecuniary inability does not dispense with the need to complete an appropriation with diligence). Of economic uncertainty? See Pub. Serv. Co. v. Blue River Irr. Co., 753 P.2d 737 (Colo. 1988) (economic feasibility of the proposed development is a relevant factor in a diligence proceeding [but see the next paragraph of this Note]). Of litigation? See Metro. Suburban Water Users Ass'n v. Colo. River Water Cons. Dist., 365 P.2d 273 (Colo. 1961) (applicant satisfies diligence during pendency of adjudication proceedings by seeking to have claim allowed and opposing claims of others); Associated Enters., Inc. v. Toltec Watershed Improvement Dist. , 578 P.2d

1359 (Wyo. 1978) (extension of time for completion of appropriation is justified where litigation delayed construction and completion of reservoir). Of efforts to sell water? See Pub. Serv. Co. v. Blue River Irr. Co., 829 P.2d 1276 (Colo. 1992) (efforts to sell water are not evidence of reasonable diligence). Of age, psychological stress, and ill health? See *In re* Application No. 5189-3 to Extend Time, 467 N.W.2d 907 (S.D. 1991) (cumulative impact of such factors might have excused failure to complete construction but did not excuse failure to file for an extension of the permit); *Maricopa County Mun. Water Cons. Dist. No. 1,* supra (ill health does not dispense with the need to complete an appropriation with diligence).

Colo. Rev. Stat. § 37-92-301(4)(c) states: "current economic conditions beyond the control of the applicant which adversely affect the feasibility of perfecting a conditional water right * * * [shall not] be considered sufficient to deny a diligence application, so long as other facts and circumstances which show diligence are present." In Municipal Subdistrict, Northern Colorado Water Conservancy District v. Chevron Shale Oil Co., 986 P.2d 918 (Colo. 1999), the court upheld, pursuant to this section, a 1995 extension of conditional appropriations dating back to the 1950s although no actual construction activities had ever taken place and the applicant's studies indicated that the appropriations might not be completed until 2085. See also Mun. Subdistrict, N. Colo. Water Cons'y Dist. v. OXY USA, Inc., 990 P.2d 701 (Colo. 1999). In both cases, the rights are to be used in the development of shale oil projects; oil shale can yield petroleum, but production is not currently economically feasible.

Is the statute consistent with Colorado's policy of maximum beneficial use of water? What would cause the Colorado legislature to adopt such a statute? (The legislative history indicates that the statute, enacted in 1990, was adopted at least in part for the benefit of the oil shale industry.) Is it good policy to tie up water for an industry which may not become economically viable for almost 100 years?

6. **Commencement of diligence.** Although the date of permit application fixes the priority, diligence requirements do not commence until the permit is issued. In Wyoming, this led to "shelf filings" in which the State Engineer held applications for many years without taking action on them, thereby preserving applicants' priority dates without requiring any efforts toward development. Some states remedy this problem by requiring water officials to act on applications within fixed time limits. See, e.g., Mont. Code Ann. § 85-2-310.

7. **Protection of pre-application activities.** Since an application for a permit must be accompanied by detailed maps, plans, and other information, much planning, surveying, and engineering work must be completed before the application can be filed. A small project, inconsistent with a larger and more complex one, could be initiated and the application filed after much preliminary work was done on the larger project but before a filing could be made for it. To protect such pre-application efforts, New Mexico allows the filing of a notice of intention; this fixes the date of priority if a formal application for a permit is made within a reasonable

time. N.M. Stat. Ann. § 72-5-1. In Washington, a preliminary permit can be issued for up to five years (with extensions) to allow an applicant to develop and provide information to remedy deficiencies in the original application. Wash. Rev. Code § 90.03.290.

8. **Notice and opportunity to be heard.** If a permittee does not comply with diligence requirements established in a permit and does not apply for an extension, does due process require notice and an opportunity to be heard before the permit is canceled? See *In re* Application No. 5189-3 to Extend Time, 467 N.W.2d 907 (S.D. 1991) (suggesting that such requirements must be met before cancellation). In Colorado, a person holding a conditional right (one which has not been perfected by application to beneficial use) is required by statute to file an application for a finding of reasonable diligence every six years. Colo. Rev. Stat. § 37-92-301(4)(a)(I). In several cases, the Colorado Supreme Court held that failure to file before the deadline automatically terminates the right. See, e.g., Town of De Beque v. Enewold, 606 P.2d 48 (Colo. 1980). A second statute, Colo. Rev. Stat. §37-92-305(7) directs the water courts to give notice before cancellation or expiration of a conditional right. In *In re* Double RL Co., 54 P.3d 908 (Colo. 2002), the court held that the second statute prevents automatic termination if notice is not given. However, the court also held that such failure only extends the time for filing a diligence application; it does not relieve the applicant from proving that reasonable diligence occurred during the six-year diligence period.

9. **Priority in Colorado.** The priority date in Colorado continues to depend, in part, on the "first step" toward appropriation; disputes regarding the sufficiency of putative "first steps" occur frequently. See *In re* Vought, 76 P.3d 906 (Colo. 2003). To further complicate the matter, the date of the "first step" does not always determine the priority of an appropriation. Under Colorado's "postponement doctrine," rights filed with the water court in a particular year are junior to all rights filed in previous years, regardless of the dates the "first steps" were taken. See Colo. Rev. Stat. § 37-92-306; Bd. of County Comm'rs v. United States, 891 P.2d 952 (Colo. 1995). See infra p. 126, Note 6, for a discussion of Colorado appropriation procedures.

STATE EX REL. CARY v. COCHRAN
Supreme Court of Nebraska, 1940.
138 Neb. 163, 292 N.W. 239.

CARTER, JUSTICE. This is an action of mandamus brought by a number of irrigators under the Kearney canal, on behalf of themselves and others similarly situated, and by the Central Power Company, which, with the exception of one small user of water, is the owner of the oldest water appropriation on the Platte River and its tributaries. The respondents are the governor, the state engineer, and the chief of the bureau of irrigation and his subordinates. The petition prays for the issuance of a writ of mandamus compelling the proper administration and enforcement of the irrigation laws of the state for the purpose of protecting the irrigation and power rights of the relators from alleged unlawful diversions of water above relators' canal by junior appropriators. The trial court denied the writ and dismissed the petition of the relators. Relators thereupon perfected an appeal to this court.

It is not disputed that the waters of the Platte River and its tributaries are subject to appropriation for irrigation and power purposes upon the principle that priority of time bestows priority of right, and that pursuant to such principle the Central Power Company, through its predecessors in interest, was adjudicated and given a priority upon the Platte River, as of September 10, 1882, of 140 cubic feet per second of flow of water for power purposes, and a further appropriation, as of February 12, 1920, of 485 cubic feet per second for the same purposes. It is also admitted by the pleadings that 22 second-feet of water have been adjudicated to certain lands in Buffalo county for irrigation purposes with a priority dating of September 10, 1882, and which, for the purposes of this suit, will be treated as the property of certain of the relators claiming to be the owners thereof in this litigation. The foregoing appropriations of water, bearing the priority dating of September 10, 1882, are prior in time to all appropriations on the Platte River and its tributaries in Nebraska, except [one] * * *.

The respondents, as officers, agents and employees of the bureau of irrigation, are charged by law with the duty of the administration and enforcement of the irrigation laws of the state and the distribution of the waters of the Platte River and its tributaries within the state in accordance with adjudicated priorities. It is the contention of relators that respondents, in administering and enforcing the irrigation laws of the state and in the distribution of water for irrigation, have continuously permitted and allowed junior appropriators, situated above the headgate of the Central Power Company, to take and use water for irrigation, storage, and other purposes, without regard to priority and to the prejudice and damage of the relators. * * *

Losses from evaporation and transpiration are heavy, due to the wide and shallow character of the river. Changes of temperature and varying types of wind add to the uncertainty of the losses resulting from these changing conditions. Losses from percolation vary along the various sectors of the river. * * * Experts with experience on the river estimate that the loss in delivering water from North Platte to the headgate of the Kearney canal with a wet river bed amounts to three times the amount of delivery, and with a dry river bed that it is almost impossible to get water through without a flood or a large sustained flow. In other words, it requires approximately 700 second-feet of water at North Platte to deliver 162 second-feet at the headgate of the Kearney canal when the river bed is wet. The underlying sand and gravel beds thicken as the river moves east. With the bed of the river on the surface of these sand and gravel deposits, it requires a huge amount of water to recharge the river channel and surrounding water table after the river bed once becomes dry. Until the water table is built up to the surface of the river bed, the river channel will not support a continuous flow. * * *

Appropriations of water are made throughout the length of the river. The priority dates of these appropriations have no relation whatever to their location on the stream. Hence, very early appropriations may be found at the upper and lower ends of the stream, while very late appropriations are likewise found at both ends. In times of water shortage, the later appropriators are the first to be deprived of water. The closing of canals in accordance with the inverse order of their priority dates necessarily requires certain canals to close their headgates all along the stream at the same time. Water moves down the stream at approximately 25 miles per day with the result that it requires approximately ten days to deliver water from the state line to the Kearney headgate under normal conditions. The resulting lag therefore becomes an important factor to be considered. * * *

The real question to be decided, however, is the determination of the duty imposed upon the officers of the state in administering the waters of the stream when the available supply of water at the headgate of the Kearney canal is reduced to an amount less than the 162 second-feet to which the relators are entitled. The rights of relators to the use of this water as against all appropriators subsequent to September 10, 1882, cannot be questioned. It is the duty of the administrative officers of the state to recognize this right and to give force to relators' priority. This requires that junior appropriators be restrained from taking water from the stream so long as such water can be delivered in usable quantities at the headgate of the Kearney canal. If it appear that all the available water in the stream would be lost before its arrival at the headgate of the Kearney canal, it would, of course, be an unjustified waste of water to attempt delivery. Whether a definite quantity of water passing a given point on the stream would, if not diverted or interrupted in its course, reach the headgate of the Kearney canal in a usable quantity creates a very complicated question of fact. It therefore is the duty of the administrative officers of the state to determine from all available means, including the factors hereinbefore discussed, whether or not a usable quantity of water can be delivered at the headgate of the Kearney canal. * * *

After determination that a given quantity of water passing a certain point on the river would not, even if uninterrupted, reach the headgate of the Kearney canal in usable quantities, the administrative officers of the state may lawfully permit junior appropriators to divert it for irrigation purposes. This results ofttimes in having junior appropriators receiving a head of water at a time when an appropria-

tor farther downstream is getting none, though he is prior in time.
* * *

Amici curiae urges that the doctrine of reasonable use is in force
in this state and that it should be applied to the case at bar. * * * [W]e
cannot agree that the doctrine of reasonable use can be applied in a
case where delivery of a usable quantity of water can be made, although the losses suffered in so doing are great. To permit the officers
of the state the right to say whether prospective losses would or would
not justify the delivery of usable quantities of water would clothe such
officers with a discretion incompatible with the vested interests of the
relators, and destroy the very purpose of the doctrine of appropriation
existent in this state. When upstream appropriators applied for and
received adjudicated priorities, they did so with the knowledge that
there was an earlier appropriator at the lower end of the stream
whose rights had to be recognized. When the relators applied for and
received their adjudications, they are likewise presumed to have
known that other appropriators would obtain inferior rights above
them that would have to be recognized. Each is required to respect the
vested rights of the others, even though some hardships may be
thereby imposed. We therefore hold that the doctrine of reasonable
use does not extend so far as to authorize the administrator of the waters of the stream to refrain from delivering a usable quantity of water
to a senior appropriator because it might appear to him that excessive
losses would result. The duty of the administrator, in administering
the waters of the stream by virtue of the police power of the state, is to
enforce existing priorities, not to determine, change or amend them.
* * *

The administration of the waters of the stream must be in accordance with the law announced in this opinion. The administrator tes-
tifies to his willingness to so administer the stream and, in fact,
contends that he has so administered it. We doubt not that he will endeavor to so administer it in the future. * * * After a consideration of
the pleadings, the evidence, and all the circumstances, surrounding
the case, we think the trial court was justified in the exercise of such
discretion in denying the writ prayed for. * * *

Notes

1. **Wisdom of the decision.** The rule of this case has been criticized
as an example of waste built into the appropriation doctrine. See Clyde O.
Fischer, Jr., Western Experience and Eastern Appropriation Proposals, in
The Law of Water Allocation in the Eastern United States 75 (Haber &
Bergen eds., 1958). But see Frank J. Trelease, The Model Water Code, the
Wise Administrator and the Goddam Bureaucrat, 14 Nat. Resources J.
207 (1974):

"The 'waste' caused by the downstream senior on the dwindling stream should concern the easterner not at all. His streams gain water throughout their length, they do not lose it to desert soils. That such waste exists, even in the west, is doubtful. * * * A waste of 538 c.f.s.? The richer lands are at Kearney, and perhaps more can be produced there, at least the North Platte irrigators have never seen fit to buy out the Kearney irrigators. A better explanation is that the 538 c.f.s. feed the alluvial aquifer underlying a vast sea of corn and alfalfa that stretches along the valley, irrigated by thousands of wells. At any rate, the fault is not that of prior appropriation law but of historical accident.[91]"

The rule of the principal case may also provide another benefit not mentioned by Trelease—the preservation of instream flows. Note that the senior right of the Kearney Canal preserves a flow of at least 162 c.f.s. in the Platte River for some 250 miles when such flows are physically available. The existence of downstream senior rights has a similar effect on a number of western streams.

2. **A contrary view?** Would the principal case be followed in California (assuming that the water not reaching the Kearney Canal is wasted)? See *Imperial Irrigation Dist.*, supra p. 40.

3. **Effect of priority.** Frank J. Trelease, Climate Change and Water Law, in Climate, Climatic Change and Water Supply (National Research Council & National Academy of Sciences eds., 1977):

"The rule of priority operates even in a normal year, not only in time of shortage. On an unregulated stream (one without storage dams) from which many irrigators draw water, all may open their ditches in the spring as the mountain snowpacks melt and the stream is high. As the flow decreases during the dry summer, the diversion works are shut off in inverse order of priority. The last ditch is first closed; the first need never be. The entire burden of the lessened flow falls on the junior appropriator. He loses all his water; the senior, none. Some have called this a harsh rule, but it should be remembered that the low flow is insufficient for all, and that equal shares for everybody would be sufficient for none. The rule of priority does guarantee a firm supply to all for whom the source is sufficient, and the senior irrigators can build a stable agriculture unmatched in humid climes. The junior appropriator is not unlike the farmer in a semihumid area who must take his chances on rain. If he can only count on spring flood water, he will grow one crop of wild hay and will not plant a late maturing crop like sugar beets. The senior may grow an orchard or a vineyard, the junior will plant corn, since he may gamble on the loss of an annual crop but not of a permanent investment.

---

91. Nebraska was settled from east to west as the homesteaders encroached on Indian territory, so the early priorities are in the downstream east. In Colorado, however, the lands at the foot of the Rockies were settled first so the senior rights are there, and the downstream lands were settled later as the junior appropriators pushed eastward against the Cheyennes of the Smoky Hills.

"Since the low flow will accommodate so few users, storage is desirable to detain the spring flood for release in the late summer. The rule of priority also determines who will pay for the dam—it is the junior appropriator who will get the benefit from it. In return for his investment, he will often have a better right than many seniors, since his stored water will carry him late into the year when the base flow becomes insufficient for all but a few. For this reason, seniors will often join in a dam project in order to receive supplemental water to firm up their late season supply. * * *

"Applying the rule of priority to the physical results of drought or climatic change may have some unexpected effects. It is not correct to think that drought will simply fall upon the most junior appropriators and wipe them out. In the long run, of course, the juniors will be those squeezed out, but many holders of senior and intermediate priorities may be affected. It will depend in part on the nature of the change, whether it takes the form of an extraordinarily 'subnormal' water year, an 'unexpectedly long' series of low water years, or a 'permanent' change in climate that reduces the long-term yield to some new norm. In most subnormal years, the high water begins to drop at an earlier date than usual, and as the flow subsides each junior appropriator will 'go out of priority' and must close his intake some indeterminate number of days earlier than he would have if the year had been within the 'normal' range. On an unregulated stream, the odds will be changed on all the bets. The original marginal junior rights become untenable and forfeit, the moderately secure rights are now risky, and the relatively certain are smaller in number. If the subnormality consists of unusually low base flows, the seniors who depend on late summer flows may get hurt the worst. If the drought flattens out the peaks and there is less high water than expected, then junior storage projects bear the brunt. Where large-scale storage has been built to equate the supply, the planners had in mind some combination of bad years to be hurdled. If that 'design drought' were never exceeded, every right would be as good as any other; but if the dams are finally run dry, a substantial block of shares—all of those that depend on the junior project—will fail together.

"Variations in the pattern of multiyear drought will also change the incidence of hardship. The North Platte River, to take an example, is a fully regulated stream on which the annual and perennial fluctuations have been ironed out by two large projects with different priorities. The earliest, Pathfinder Dam, has low storage in proportion to the land it serves, while the more recent project, Seminoe Dam, has large storage but a late priority. A short-term drought with several years of very low flows would dry up Pathfinder but might be well within the carryover capacity of Seminoe, while a long sequence of mediocre years would hardly affect Pathfinder but would ruin the Seminoe project."

4. **Importance of priority.** Priority is the principle most associated with the appropriation doctrine; for example, it is frequently called "the doctrine of *prior* appropriation." But how important is it? Compare:

"The priority of a water right is * * * the most important stick in the water rights bundle. * * * The security and reliability of water rights turn on the enforceability of priorities when natural supply is not adequate to fill all decreed rights and administration of decreed rights is necessary to ensure the property value of water rights." Empire Lodge Homeowners' Ass'n v. Moyer, 39 P.3d 1139, 1148-49 (Colo. 2001).

"This article * * * argues that priority is an efficient rule of water allocation, but it is often more rhetoric than rule. * * *

"The fact that priority enforcement is more bluff than substance does not undermine the need for consistent and fair allocation rules, but it does call into question the sole reliance on enforcement of priorities to allocate water in temporary and chronic shortages. The principal assumption of this article is that experience will demonstrate that priorities are seldom enforced in practice. In many situations, the strict enforcement of prior appropriation would raise substantial fairness and efficiency concerns. * * * Thus, it is not surprising that states have taken extraordinary steps to ensure that the rule is never applied in practice and that federal, state and local water distribution agencies find alternative ways to ameliorate the rule when droughts occur.

"I do not argue that priority should be abandoned. There are no superior alternatives. Rather, I make a positive and normative argument. The positive one is simply that priority enforcement is generally the exception rather than the norm, and thus there is a need to examine more systematically what happens when scarcity occurs and how large and small systems cope. The normative argument is that the focus of water allocation should be on the actual expectations that lie behind a use, rather than the simple enforcement of the entitlement to understand that alternative ways of satisfying those expectations exist. The core idea of prior appropriation is the protection of investment-backed expectations from the risks of variable water years and perhaps now global climate change, and this idea remains a valid objective. The issue is whether the enforcement of priorities contributes to this objective." A. Dan Tarlock, Prior Appropriation: Rule, Principle, or Rhetoric?, 76 N.D. L. Rev. 881, 883-84 (2000).

5. **Ignoring priority—"futile calls."** In Colorado a senior appropriator's complaint that upstream juniors are taking his water and should be regulated is known as "calling the river." When shutting down the junior does not improve the senior's water supply, a "futile call" has occurred. Statutes deal with the matter both substantively and procedurally: "No reduction of any lawful diversion because of the operation of the priority system shall be permitted unless such reduction would increase the amount of water available to and required by water rights having senior priorities." Colo. Rev. Stat. § 37-92-102(2)(d).

"Each division engineer shall order the total or partial discontinuance of any diversion in his division to the extent the water being diverted is not necessary for application to a beneficial use; and he shall also order the total or partial discontinuance of any diversion in his division to the extent the water being diverted is required by persons entitled to use water under water rights having senior priorities, but no such discontinuance shall be ordered unless the diversion is causing or will cause material injury to such water rights having senior priorities. In making his decision as to the discontinuance of a diversion to satisfy senior priorities the division engineer shall be governed by the following: The materiality of injury depends on all factors which will determine in each case the amount of water such discontinuance will make available to such senior priorities at the time and place of their need. Such factors include the current and prospective volumes of water in and tributary to the stream from which the diversion is being made; distance and type of stream bed between the diversion points; the various velocities of this water, both surface and underground; the probable duration of the available flow; and the predictable return flow to the affected stream. * * * In the event a discontinuance has been ordered pursuant to the foregoing, and nevertheless such does not cause water to become available to such senior priorities at the time and place of their need, then such discontinuance order shall be rescinded." Colo. Rev. Stat. § 37-92-502(2).

6. **Contrasting treatment to other "futile calls."** Seepage and return flows sometimes recharge downstream segments of a stream even though diversions have completely depleted the flow upstream. Baker Ditch Co. v. District Court, Gallatin County, 824 P.2d 260 (Mont. 1992), involved such a situation. To protect instream flows, the water commissioner applied priority rules literally and refused to allow a downstream appropriator to divert water because there was no water available for upstream senior rights. Held, the downstream appropriator could divert water because it would cause no detriment to prior appropriators.

In contrast, in Fort v. Washington Department of Ecology, 135 P.3d 515 (Wash. Ct. App. 2006), the court insisted upon strict compliance with a 1921 decree establishing 18 prioritized classes of water rights on a stream. Plaintiff held rights to classes 1, 8 and 9. He was the last diverter on the creek. Thus he claimed that, if water was otherwise going to be wasted by the time it reached his point of diversion, he should be permitted to take water for his class 8 and 9 rights even though there was an order barring diversions for anything less senior than class 5. Held, the decree was to be enforced class by class, not individual by individual. Moreover, the court refused to adopt the "futile call" doctrine, finding it a matter for legislative, not judicial, attention.

7. **Priority and tributary flows.** Diversions from tributaries may be regulated in favor of senior appropriators from the main stream below the junction, Strickler v. City of Colorado Springs, 26 P. 313 (Colo. 1891), but not infrequently practical considerations lead to separate administration of intermittent tributaries. For example, in Nebraska v. Wyoming, 325 U.S. 589 (1945), infra p. 477, the Court adopted the Special Master's recommendation to protect out-of-priority diversions on tributaries of the North Platte River. "There is some out-of-priority diversion as we have

noted. But * * * practical difficulties of applying restrictions which would reduce the amount of water used by the hundreds of small irrigators would seem to outweigh any slight benefit which senior appropriators [on the main stream] might obtain." Id. at 624.

8. **Seasonal priorities.** Seasonal priorities exist in some states. They entitle the appropriator to take water only during certain periods, so that other persons with later rights may have a better claim to water during other times. Some courts have frozen the pioneer pattern of use, restricting the use of the lands to the original crop irrigated, or incorporating the original appropriator's personal habits into the water right. Thorne v. McKinley Bros., 56 P.2d 204 (Cal. 1936) (never at night); Santa Paula Waterworks v. Peralta, 45 P. 168 (Cal. 1896) (24 hours per week beginning Saturday noon); Oliver v. Skinner, 226 P.2d 507 (Or. 1951) (an appropriation for irrigating hay lands, never used after July 1st, cannot be used for crops requiring water later in the year).

More modern courts hold that unless the claim, permit or decree upon which the right is founded contains time limits, the appropriator can take the water any time it can be put to the beneficial use for which it was appropriated. See Harkey v. Smith, 247 P. 550, 553 (N.M. 1926).

9. **Reservoir storage.** Usually there is no division of the year into an irrigation season and a storage season, so as to give later direct users a seasonal preference over earlier reservoirs or vice versa. People *ex rel.* Park Reservoir Co. v. Hinderlider, 57 P.2d 894 (Colo. 1936). But see Neb. Rev. Stat. § 46-241 (forbidding the impounding of water when it is required for direct irrigation).

In El Dorado Irrigation District v. State Water Resources Control Board, 48 Cal. Rptr. 3d 468 (Ct. App. 2006), the California Water Board conditioned the reassignment of water rights dating from 1927 on the assignees' acceptance of a condition ("term No. 91") prohibiting diversion of water while junior permittees were releasing stored water upstream of assignees to meet water quality objectives downstream of assignees in the California Delta. The El Dorado Irrigation District challenged the condition because water users with rights junior to the District's were not subject to the same condition. The appellate court summarized:

"we agree with the trial court that the Board abused its discretion in imposing term No. 91 on El Dorado's permit, when it has not included that term in the permits and license of appropriators in the Delta watershed whose rights are junior to those of El Dorado. The Board's action contravened the rule of priority, which is one of the most fundamental principles of California water law, because appropriators junior to El Dorado can divert water when El Dorado cannot. Although the rule of priority is not absolute, the Board is obligated to protect water right priorities unless doing so will result in the unreasonable use of water, harm to values protected by the public trust doctrine, or the violation of some other equally important principle or interest." Id. at 473.

10. **Priority in a "regulatory drought."** In a physical drought, the rule of priority means that junior appropriators receive nothing while senior appropriators remain untouched. Should the result be the same in a "regulatory drought"—a shortage caused by laws which reduce the water available for diversion and use—or should the shortfall be allocated by different principles? See United States v. State Water Res. Control Bd., infra pp. 592-93, Note 1; Harrison C. Dunning, State Equitable Apportionment of Western Water Resources, 66 Neb. L. Rev. 76 (1987).

PHILLIPS v. GARDNER
Court of Appeals of Oregon, 1970.
2 Or. App. 423, 469 P.2d 42.

SCHWAB, CHIEF JUDGE. The defendant watermaster, who is charged with the duty of distributing water in Yamhill County in accordance with the rights of each user, threatened to cut off plaintiffs' domestic water supply and to empty plaintiffs' impoundment for that purpose to give water to a downstream user who holds the water right for irrigation prior in time to plaintiffs' domestic right. Plaintiffs brought suit to enjoin the defendant watermaster from so doing, claiming a statutory priority for domestic use under ORS 540.140. The trial judge granted the injunction and the defendant watermaster appeals, contending that ORS 540.140 has no application to the facts of this case. The plaintiffs' water certificate has a priority date of June 7, 1947; the downstream property owner's water certificate has a priority date of August 26, 1919.

During the months of August and September 1967, there was not sufficient water to serve both appropriators. The watermaster threatened to cut off plaintiffs' water supply and this gave rise to the suit in question. This controversy relates to surface water only, not to ground water available through wells.

ORS 540.140 was enacted in 1893. It reads:

> "When the waters of any natural stream are not sufficient for the service of all those desiring the use of the same, those using the water for domestic purposes shall, subject to such limitations as may be prescribed by law, have the preference over those claiming such water for any other purpose, and those using the water for agricultural purposes shall have the preference over those using the same for manufacturing purposes."

The statute has never been cited or discussed in any of the numerous opinions of the Oregon Supreme Court dealing with the application of Oregon water laws.

Oregon first adopted a comprehensive water code in 1909. Since then this code has been subject to major amendments. * * *

The 1909 Act established a system for the filing of applications for the appropriation of water with the state engineer in § 47 (ORS 537.130(1)), and provided in § 46 (ORS 537.140), that applications contain, among other information, the nature and amount of proposed use. Section 46 discloses that the legislature had in mind that there were varying uses of water for among the uses to which it there refers are those for agriculture, power, municipal water supply and mining. Section 54 (ORS 537.250(3)) provides "The right acquired by an appropriation shall date from the filing of the application in the office of the State Engineer."

The Act, § 73, provides "All laws and parts of laws so far as in conflict or inconsistent with the provisions of this act are hereby repealed."

The plaintiffs argue that despite the provisions of the 1909 Water Act the holder of a certificate for domestic water use has a preference by virtue of ORS 540.140 over a prior recorded water right for other purposes.

* * * Although the 1909 Act did not directly state that thereafter priorities should be based on priority in time and not on nature of use, the whole thrust of the Act clearly indicates such a purpose. The insufficiency of water in parts of Oregon is what gave rise to Oregon's comprehensive water code commencing with the 1909 Act. Priorities are meaningful only in times of shortage. If we were to apply ORS 540.140 as plaintiffs would have us do, in times of shortage—the only time when there is any reason for priorities—water would be allocated based upon the nature of the various uses involved, not on the basis of the effective date of appropriation. The result would be that the priorities established by the 1909 Act and subsequent additions to it would be effective only as to appropriators within similar categories of use. It is hard for us to conceive that the 1909 and subsequent legislatures could have intended such a result without one word in the statutes to indicate their desire to adopt such a complicated scheme. It may be that ORS 540.140 still has viability as to rights which were perfected prior to 1909 or as to rights bearing the same effective date. Since neither situation is involved in the case at bar, we need not consider those possibilities here.

Appealing as plaintiffs' humanistic arguments may be, if viewed from a single point of view, it is our opinion that the statutory interpretation they seek is in conflict with what we perceive as clear legislative intent—the substitution of priority based on time of appropriation for the pre-1909 statutory preference (ORS 540.140) based on the nature of the use.

Reversed and remanded for the entry of a decree in accordance with this opinion.

Notes

1. **Alternatives for the junior appropriator.** Does this decision mean that Gardner goes thirsty? See Chapter 2, Section 5.

2. **The meanings of "preference."** "Preference" can refer to one of several quite different things: (1) In times of shortage, the water is devoted to the preferred use instead of to a non-preferred purpose although the latter is prior in time—sometimes called a "true preference." (2) Where new applicants compete for permits to appropriate water insufficient for all proposed uses, the preferred user gets the water right, regardless of the relative priority of filing the applications. (3) Where a change is needed in the use of appropriated water, the preferred user may condemn and pay for a prior right for a non-preferred use. The principal case involves a putative preference of the first type. Preferences of the second type are discussed infra p. 158, Note 5, of the third, p. 215, Note 3.

3. **Subordination of priority.** Cal. Water Code § 106 provides that "the use of water for domestic purposes is the highest use of water and that the next highest use is for irrigation." In implementing this statute, the California authorities not only have chosen applications for preferred uses over presently competing applications, but have subordinated current non-preferred uses to future preferred uses, for example, by inserting into a permit for a hydroelectric power project the condition, "The right to store and use water for power purposes under this permit shall not interfere with future appropriation of said water for agricultural or municipal purposes." This procedure was upheld in East Bay Municipal Utility District v. Department of Public Works, 35 P.2d 1027 (Cal. 1934). Compare El Dorado Irr. Dist. v. State Water Res. Control Bd. , 48 Cal. Rptr. 3d 468 (Cal. Ct. App. 2006) (absent a finding that enforcing a senior water user's priority would impair public trust values or unreasonably use water, the state's interest in water quality in an important estuary did not justify subordinating the priority).

In Benz v. Water Resources Commission, 764 P.2d 594 (Or. Ct. App. 1988), a farmer used groundwater with a high boron content for irrigation. The accumulation of boron in the soil harmed the farmer's crops, and he sought a permit to appropriate winter flows to be used to leach boron from the soil. The Commission found that boron leaching was a beneficial use of water. However, it also found:

"[B]ecause boron leaching will require the application of large quantities of water, boron leaching is of less benefit overall than other potential future uses, junior in priority to the subject application, for which water should be conserved. Accordingly, [the Commission] allowed the appropriation for boron leaching on the condition that it be 'subordinate and inferior to both the storage and direct use of water for other consumptive beneficial uses of water.'"

The court affirmed the subordination of the appropriation, citing Oregon statutes requiring the Commission to consider various factors, including "the highest use of the water" and "the maximum economic development of the waters involved," in determining if a proposed use of water will be in the public interest.

Subordination can also be consensual. See, e.g., Board of County Commissioners v. Crystal Creek Homeowners' Ass'n, 14 P.3d 325 (Colo. 2000), in which the United States Bureau of Reclamation subordinated certain rights in the Gunnison River to junior rights for in-basin uses, but not to junior rights for out-of-basin uses. Why would an appropriator voluntarily subordinate the priority of a water right?

Is subordination proper for proposed projects requiring large capital expenditure? Will an applicant proceed with the project in such a case?

4. **"True preferences"?** S.D. Codified Laws § 46-1-5: "It is the established policy of this state: (1) That the use of water for domestic purposes is the highest use of water and takes precedence over all appropriative rights, if it is exercised in a manner consistent with public interest as provided in § 46-1-2."

[handwritten margin note: Domestic use overrides first in time rule]

Utah Code Ann. § 73-3-21: "Appropriators shall have priority among themselves according to the dates of their respective appropriations, so that each appropriator shall be entitled to receive his whole supply before any subsequent appropriator shall have any right; provided, in times of scarcity, while priority of appropriation shall give the better right as between those using water for the same purpose, the use for domestic purposes, without unnecessary waste, shall have preference over use for all other purposes, and use for agricultural purposes shall have preference over use for any other purpose except domestic use."

Are these "true preferences"? Or are they preferences of the third type, requiring compensation if a senior appropriator is required to relinquish water for a preferred junior use? See also *In re* 2007 Administration of Appropriations of the Waters of the Niobrara River, 768 N.W.2d 420 (Neb. 2009) (higher preference juniors in Nebraska may continue to divert but must compensate lower preference seniors.)

CACHE LA POUDRE WATER USERS ASS'N v. GLACIER VIEW MEADOWS

Supreme Court of Colorado, 1976.
191 Colo. 53, 550 P.2d 288.

GROVES, JUSTICE. The applicant Glacier View Meadows, a limited partnership, is a developer of residential lots in the mountains northwest of Fort Collins, Colorado. It filed with the water court two applications for approval of a plan of augmentation. The plans would provide future owners of presently unimproved lots with domestic water from wells to be drilled in the future. * * * The court granted approval of the plan for augmentation in the first two applications. We affirm with some modifications. * * *

The objector, Cache LaPoudre Water Users Association, is a non-profit protective association, whose members own substantial reservoir and direct flow decrees on the Cache LaPoudre River. * * *

The applicant owns 75 "preferred shares" of the Mountain and Plains Irrigation Company, which entitle applicant to both reservoir and direct flow water. Applicant acquired these 75 shares from Ideal Cement Company, Dreher Pickle Company and City of Fort Collins, which historically had made year-around use of their water. Under the plan some of applicant's reservoir rights will be used to replace consumptively used water from proposed wells. The water from the wells will be exclusively devoted to in-house, residential domestic use. Under the two applications which are the subject of the court's decree, there will be a maximum of 1892 single-family residential units. In some cases, one well will furnish water for more than one unit.

The reservoirs containing replacement water and the points of discharge of water therefrom into the stream, as well as all of the residential units and the points of return flow therefrom into the stream, lie above the points of diversion of any water of the objectors.

Of the 1892 units, at ultimate development 105 units are expected to use an evapotranspiration system of sewage disposal. The consumptive use for these 105 units will be 100% of the water diverted from wells. This 100% will be replaced entirely by reservoir water plus enough to account for evaporative losses during transportation in the stream.

The remaining 1787 units, when ultimately developed, will have septic-soil absorption sewage systems. From these latter diversions there will be a consumptive use of not more than 10% and at least 90% will constitute return flow to the stream. Replacement water for the 10%, plus an amount sufficient to embrace transportation losses, will be replenished by the aforementioned releases from the reservoirs.

* * * The entire consumptive use of well water (including those units having 100% consumptive use) will not exceed 89 acre feet per year. 55 of applicant's 75 shares will be devoted to replacement of this consumptively used water. 55 shares represent an amount of 94.71 acre feet per year. After deducting 5% for transportation losses, 89.97 feet remain for replacement. * * *

As mentioned earlier, the applicant acquired the 75 shares from Ideal Cement Company, Dreher Pickle Company and the City of Fort Collins. Historically, only 25% of the water used by these three returned to the stream. The plan allocates the water from 20 of the 75 shares of stock for use in the stream in lieu of the 25% return flow which no longer exists.

It is contemplated by the plan that, so long as its provisions are followed, there will be no injury to the holders of prior rights. However, if there is a call by a right superior to the association's priority rights, that call must be met. The water court concluded that the only thing that will upset the plan will be an extended period of drought. If such a drought causes insufficient water to be available for replacement, the well water users will be obliged to acquire additional water by lease or otherwise, or else to reduce their consumptive use, to the end that water consumptively used under the plan will not exceed that available for replacement. * * *

The principal argument of the objectors is that, except during flood stages, the Cache LaPoudre River is over-appropriated. With this we agree. The argument continues that, unless there is 100% replacement of the water taken from the wells, senior water rights will be injured and there will be a violation of the Water Right Determination and Administration Act of 1969 (section 37-92-101 et seq., C.R.S.1973, hereinafter called the "Act"), and the rules and regulations of the State Engineer's office. * * *

First, we look to the Act, and here quote some of the legislative declaration underlying it and the definition of "plan for augmentation":

"(1) * * *

"'Plan for augmentation' means a detailed program to increase the supply of water available for beneficial use in a division or portion thereof by the development of new or alternate means or points of diversion, by a pooling of water resources, by water exchange projects, by providing substitute supplies of water, by the development of new sources of water, or by any other appropriate means." Section 37-92-103(9), C.R.S.1973.

We find that the plan of augmentation has been formulated and approved consonant with, and in furtherance of, the purpose and intent of our recent statutes; and that the plan is valid.

We hold here * * * that under the plans for augmentation involved water is available for appropriation when the diversion thereof does not injure holders of vested rights.

Objectors cite Southeastern Colorado Water Conservancy District v. Shelton Farms * * * 529 P.2d 1321 (1974), in which this court ruled that one, who cuts down water-consuming vegetation (phreatophytes) along the Arkansas River, does not have a right to a decree for an equivalent amount of water to that consumed by the vegetation, free of the call of the river. In the opinion it was stated, "Appellees would substitute the priority doctrine with a lack of injury doctrine." The judgment was reversed and the cause remanded to the trial court with directions to vacate the decree. The indication * * * that *Shelton Farms* stands for the proposition that lack of injury does not cause water to be available for appropriation must be analyzed. *Shelton Farms* involved a factual situation * * * distinguishable from this. * * *

There, the senior rights had adjusted to the loss of the water caused by the growth of phreatophytes; and, once returned to the river, the water would still belong to the senior users in satisfaction of their decrees. In the instant case, the water to be used in replacement never was that of the senior users. Here, there is not displacement *"from the time and place of* their need." Under the findings here, the stream will be the same, irrespective of the well diversions.

Under the circumstances of this case, there is no significant difference between the prior appropriation doctrine, and the lack of injury doctrine. Here, where senior users can show no injury by the diversion of water, they cannot preclude the beneficial use of water by another. Fellhauer v. People * * * 447 P.2d 986 (1968), was cited as authority in *Shelton Farms.* It is likewise authority here. As was there said, "As administration of water approaches its second century the curtain is opening upon the new drama of *maximum utilization* and how constitutionally that doctrine can be integrated into the law of *vested rights.*"

We rule that * * * water is available for appropriation if the taking thereof does not cause injury. Therefore, the argument of the objectors, to the effect that water withdrawn from the wells must be replaced 100%, falls. *must prove injury*

Notes

1. **Priority and substitution.** "Plan of augmentation" is a predominantly Coloradan term, but the rule that a senior appropriator can be compelled to accept a substitute source of water or other modifications which allow a junior to use water without harming the senior is widely accepted. See, e.g., State *ex rel.* Office of State Eng'r v. Lewis, 150 P.3d 375 (N.M. Ct. App. 2006) (upholding complex augmentation plan for Pecos River). See generally Harrison C. Dunning, The "Physical Solution" in Western Water Law, 57 U. Colo. L. Rev. 445 (1986). More broadly, the rule is a corollary of the principle that the rights of the junior appropriator begin at the limits of the rights of the senior.

2. **Protection of junior instream flows.** In Colorado Water Conservation Board v. City of Central, 125 P.3d 424 (Colo. 2005), the Colorado Supreme Court required a plan of augmentation to protect downstream junior rights for instream appropriations. "We hold the noninjury requirement applicable to changes of water rights also applies to augmentation plans affecting instream flow rights. We likewise hold that an adjudicated instream flow right entitles its holder to maintain the stream conditions existing at the time of its appropriation and to resist proposed developments through changes of water rights or augmentation plans * * * that in any way materially injure instream flow rights."

3. **Other examples of substitution.** Senior appropriators may claim all the summer flow in the downstream reaches of a stream, while a reservoir site lies above them and undeveloped lands above the site. Junior appropriators may build the reservoir, appropriate the senior's natural flow for the upstream land and substitute the stored water on the downstream land. Reno v. Richards, 178 P. 81 (Idaho 1918). Where senior appropriators claim all the natural flow within a valley, a junior may import water from a different watershed, use the natural flow, and deliver the imported water to the senior. Bd. of Dirs. of Wilder Irr. Dist. v. Jorgenson, 136 P.2d 461 (Idaho 1943).

4. **Limits of senior rights.** The defining elements of an appropriative right serve not only to "measure" the right but also to limit it, much like a boundary description both measures and limits the rights of a landowner. Consequently, a senior appropriator has no right, as against a junior appropriator, to waste water, to increase the amount or extend the time of his diversion so as to put it to double use by irrigation of other lands, or to lend, rent or sell to others the excess water. Enlarged Southside Irr. Ditch Co. v. John's Flood Ditch Co., 183 P.2d 552 (Colo. 1947). In Colorado, this rule is described as the junior appropriator's vested right to the continuation of stream conditions as they existed at the time of his appropriation. See Farmers Highline Canal & Reservoir Co. v. City of Golden, infra p. 200.

This rule is an over-simplification that is subject to many exceptions, since the second user of water is not protected against its loss in every case of change in the first use. See Metro. Denver Sewage Disposal Dist. No. 1 v. Farmers Reservoir & Irr. Co., 499 P.2d 1190 (Colo. 1972). For thirty years Denver had deposited the effluent from its municipal sewage treatment plant into the South Platte River above the headgate of the irrigation company. When the plant became inadequate the sewage was transported to a large new metropolitan plant whose outfall was downstream from the plaintiff's point of diversion. Held, downstream appropriators have no vested right of control over the works of the upstream appropriator, and a change in the point of return to the stream is not subject to the no-harm rule. See also Chapter 2, Section 6.

5. **Senior appropriators not protected from every injury.** A senior appropriator is not protected against every detrimental change caused by junior appropriators. In Colorado's "dirty water case," A-B Cattle Co. v. United States, 589 P.2d 57 (Colo. 1978), irrigators from the Bessemer Ditch complained that the muddy water of the Arkansas River, which had sealed the ditch with silt, had been replaced by the Bureau of Reclamation with clear, clean reservoir water. This leaked out of the ditch so that less water arrived for their use. Held, in effect: plaintiffs had a water right, not a silt right, and no claim to compensation.

In City of Thornton v. Bijou Irrigation Co., 926 P.2d 1 (Colo. 1996), infra p. 588, Thornton proposed to divert water from the Poudre River above a plant owned by Eastman Kodak Company and replace it with a substitute supply below Kodak's plant. Although the proposal substantially reduced flows between the diversion and replacement points, sufficient flows remained for Kodak's water rights. Kodak opposed the proposal because it reduced the quantity of water in the river available to dilute wastewater discharged by Kodak. Kodak asserted that the flow reduction would require it to construct a new treatment facility costing nine to twelve million dollars to meet water quality standards for its discharged wastewater. The court ruled against Kodak, holding that the loss of diluting flows is not an injury against which a senior appropriator is protected. See Chapter 7, Section 2B.

6. **Interconnected surface water and groundwater.** Glacier View Meadows plans to use wells for its water supply. Why then is it concerned with the rights of appropriators from the Cache LaPoudre River? The groundwater and the river are interconnected and are being treated as a single source of supply. In Colorado, such groundwater is labeled "tributary groundwater." Like surface tributaries, the groundwater in *Glacier View* feeds the river. Pumping the groundwater will reduce flows in the river *in much the same way* as diversions from surface tributaries would. Because the river is over-appropriated, new diversions from tributary waters, whether surface or underground, are permissible only if the diverted water is replaced, as the developer proposed to do by releasing reservoir water.

Management of interconnected groundwater and surface water is addressed in Chapter 4, Section 2C.

7. **Dedication to protect juniors.** The Rio Grande River in New Mexico is fully appropriated. Groundwater in the Rio Grande basin is hydrologically connected to the river. To protect senior rights to river flows, the New Mexico State Engineer requires applicants for groundwater permits in the basin to acquire and "dedicate" (retire) sufficient surface water rights to offset the effects of pumping on the river, a practice upheld in City of Albuquerque v. Reynolds, 379 P.2d 73 (N.M. 1963). In theory, an alternative for a prospective groundwater user might be to acquire a surface right and transfer its point of diversion to a well.

The State Engineer, however, has addressed the purchase-and-retirement technique in guidelines issued for processing water right applications in several administrative areas. E.g., N.M. State Engineer, Roswell Basin Guidelines for Review of Water Right Applications (2005); N.M. State Engineer, Middle Rio Grande Administrative Area Guidelines for Review of Water Right Applications (2000). The guidelines vary for the different areas, but none allow deferred purchase and retirement. For example, the guidelines for the Middle Rio Grande Administrative Area, which includes the City of Albuquerque, close the aquifers hydrologically connected to the Rio Grande to new appropriations, except for domestic wells. The closure prevents use of the purchase-and-retirement technique for new applications. The guidelines allow that technique for applications pending when the guidelines became operative but without deferred identification and quantification of the surface water rights to be purchased and retired. The recipient of a new ground water permit conditioned upon purchase and retirement cannot start pumping until after purchasing the surface rights needed to offset future stream depletion and obtaining a transfer permit to change the purchased rights from consumptive use to offset use. The new permittee can lease the purchased surface rights for other purposes until they are needed for offset.

8. **Rotation.** Where there is water enough for each of several small appropriations, each appropriator in turn may take the total share of all for a short time, to give each an "irrigating head" of a manageable quantity of water and to cut down on seepage and evaporation. Such "rotation" does not violate priority rules; it is simply a variation in its administration. Similar practices apply among community ditch users, or owners of shares in mutual ditch companies or irrigation districts. Most of the western states have statutes permitting and regulating rotation by agreement. E.g., Wyo. Stat. Ann. § 41-3-612. Sometimes courts have imposed rotation upon appropriators by decree, where more efficient utilization of small flows will result. McCoy v. Huntley, 119 P. 481 (Or. 1911).

D. Waters Subject To Appropriation

WATER: THE YEARBOOK OF AGRICULTURE
United States Department of Agriculture, 1955.
pp. 42, 43.

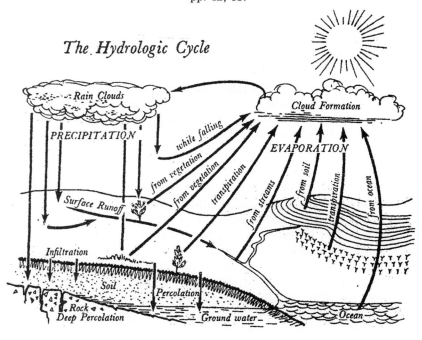

The Hydrologic Cycle

The unending circulation of the earth's moisture and water is called the water cycle. It is a gigantic system operating in and on the land and oceans of the earth and in the atmosphere that surrounds the earth. The cycle has no beginning or ending, but because our discussion must start someplace, we can think of it as beginning with the waters of the oceans, which cover about three-fourths of the earth's surface.

Water from the surface of the oceans is evaporated into the atmosphere. That moisture in turn is lifted and is eventually condensed and falls back to the earth's surface as precipitation. The part of the precipitation that falls as rain, hail, dew, snow, or sleet on the land is of particular concern to man and agriculture. Some of the precipitation, after wetting the foliage and ground, runs off over the surface to the streams. It is the water that sometimes causes erosion and is the main contributor to floods. Of the precipitation that soaks into the ground, some is available for growing plants and for evaporation. Some reaches the deeper zones and slowly percolates through springs and seeps to maintain the streams during dry periods. The streams in turn eventually lead back to the oceans, where the water originated. It is because of this never-ending circulation that the process has become known as the water cycle, or hydrologic cycle.

About 80,000 cubic miles of water are evaporated each year from the oceans. About 15,000 cubic miles are evaporated from the lakes and land surfaces of the continents. Total evaporation is equaled by total precipitation, of which about 24,000 cubic miles fall on the land surfaces. * * *

Rain that reaches the soil surface is wholly or partly absorbed by the soil in the process of infiltration. How much of it enters the soil depends upon the rate of rainfall and the receptiveness or infiltration rate of the soil. When the rainfall rate exceeds the infiltration rate, the excess rain becomes surface flow, which runs off quickly to streams. Surface flow is undesirable because it may erode the soil and also because it often produces damagingly rapid and high flows in streams during storms.

Note

Although scientists regard the hydrologic cycle as a unity, the law has usually applied different rules to different segments of the cycle. Historically, the legal problems of the past arose principally between persons competing for water at the same point in the cycle. Disputes between competitors for ground water or between users or drainers of diffused surface waters were not seen to require rules identical to those developed to settle conflicts over the use of stream flows, and scientific knowledge of the nature of water occurrence and the interrelationship of different classes of water was lacking. Thus each type of case was handled separately, and different bodies of law grew up concerned with different types of water occurrence. It is therefore important to determine the legal classification of an occurrence of water in order to discover the rules which the courts will apply to it.

Disputes between persons using water at different points in the hydrologic cycle have become more frequent, particularly where the use of groundwater has increased significantly. The problems associated with physically connected groundwater and surface water are examined in detail in Chapter 4, Section 2C.

STATE v. HIBER
Supreme Court of Wyoming, 1935.
48 Wyo. 172, 44 P.2d 1005.

[Adamson received a permit from the state to construct a reservoir on a "natural stream" known as Adamson Draw. The draw, described by several witnesses as a "swale," drained about 300 acres, mostly on the lands of Hiber, above Adamson's lands. The dam was partially constructed when Hiber built on his land, without a permit, a dam across the draw 200 feet long and 13 feet high. The state brought this action to abate Hiber's dam as an illegal structure and to enjoin him from interfering with the natural flow of the draw. The lower court found for the defendant. Other facts are stated in the opinion.]

BLUME, JUSTICE. * * * Under section 1, article 8 of the Constitution of the State, "the waters of all natural streams, springs, lakes or other collections of still water, within the boundaries of the state are hereby declared to be the property of the state." * * * The controlling question, accordingly, is as to whether or not the assertion that the draw is a natural stream is correct. Counsel for the state contend that in an arid region the term "natural stream" should be construed liberally. So much we may, for the purposes of this case, concede. But it is further contended that "the proper test of distinction, according to the rule laid down * * * as to what constitutes a natural stream or water course is whether or not the water is in such shape as to make it susceptible to application for beneficial use." The test proposed does not seem to be justified by any authorities * * *

If, then, the water in question here was surface water, or what comes to the same thing, if it was not the water of a natural stream, the court was right in finding for the defendant, as to his right to impound it. As to whether it is the one or the other in a specific case is not always easy to determine, and is generally, or often, a question of fact. * * * "Surface water," it has been said, is that which is diffused over the surface of the ground, derived from falling rains and melting snows, and continues to be such, and may be impounded by the owner of the land, until it reaches some well-defined channel in which it is accustomed to, and does, flow with other waters; or until it reaches some permanent lake or pond, and it then ceases to be surface water and becomes the water of the water course, or a lake or a pond, as the case may be. * * * This, accordingly, brings us directly to the point as to whether or not the waters in controversy reached such definite channel—in other words, whether Adamson Draw was a natural stream or water course. * * *

It is said by Kinney, supra, § 303, that "according to the great weight of authority, the essential characteristics of a water course are: A channel, consisting of a well-defined bed and banks, and a current of water." Some exceptions have been made, the definition has not been applied in all cases, and it may be difficult to give one that is universally applicable. Too much stress ought not, perhaps, be placed upon any one of the elements mentioned, and all should be given due consideration. However, the definition given has been approved in recent cases. * * * In Hutchinson v. Watson Slough Ditch Co., * * * 101 P. 1059, 1060, * * * which involved appropriation of water, the court held that: "a water course is a stream of water flowing in a definite channel, having a bed and sides or banks, and discharging itself into some other stream or body of water. The flow of water need not be constant, but must be more than mere surface drainage occasioned by extraordinary causes; there must be substantial indications of the existence of a stream, which is ordinarily a moving body of water." In Simmons v. Winters, * * * 27 P. 7, 9, * * * also involving appropriation of water, the Oregon court, after citing and quoting from a number of decisions, finally stated: "* * * a water-course is a stream of water usually flowing in a particular direction, with well-defined banks and channels, but that the water need not flow continuously,—the channel may sometimes be dry; that the term 'water-course' does not include water descending from the hills, down the hollows and ravines, without any definite channel, only in times of rain and melting snow; but that where water, owing to the hilly or mountainous configuration of the country, accumulates in large quantities from rain and melting snow, and at regular seasons descends through long deep gullies or ravines upon the lands below, and in its onward flow carves out a distinct and well-defined channel, which even to the casual glance bears the unmistakable impress of the frequent action of running water, and through which it has flowed from time immemorial, such a stream is to be considered a water-course, and to be governed by the same rules."

Courts of other western states have taken the same view; * * * Kinney, supra, § 302, says that: "A water course does not include surface water conveyed from higher to lower levels for limited periods, during the melting of snow, or during or soon after a heavy fall of rain, through hollows or ravines, which at all other portions of the year are entirely dry. These occasional bursts of water, which in times of freshets, or of melting ice or snow, descend from the hills and inundate the country, have none of the characteristics of a water course." The water, as already indicated, need not run through the entire year. On that subject Kinney, supra, says in section 307 that: "Those who are acquainted with the streams and water courses of the arid Rocky Mountain region of this country, draining as they do steep, mountain areas with their swift currents, running over gravelly and rocky bottoms, know that often in a dry summer month many of them are entirely dry, at least upon the surface. All of them, nevertheless, have well defined beds, channels, banks and currents of water, at least the greater portion of the year." Again, it is said that a water course does not include the water flowing in the hollows or ravines in land, which is mere surface water from rain or melting snow (i.e., snow lying and melting on the land) and is discharged through them from a higher to a lower level, but which at other times are destitute of water; that such hollows or ravines are not, in legal contemplation, water courses. * * * Kinney, supra, § 312. And it has been stated that "it is almost the unanimous doctrine that swales are not, in their strict legal sense, water courses." Kinney, supra, § 314. Farnham, supra, § 457, maintains that the source of water which flows in a channel claimed to be a water course is a more satisfactory test than is the presence or absence of a channel. But even he holds that there must be more than surface water, unless it comes from a large area of country, and is so continuous in its flow that it takes upon itself the character of a water course. So it is said in 27 R.C.L. 1064 that a "water course is the condition created by a stream of water having a well defined and substantial existence, and that if this substantial existence is present the fact that the stream is not strong enough to create for itself bed and banks is not sufficient to defeat its character as a water course." Hinkle v. Avery, * * * 55 N.W. 77, 78 * * * and Miller & Lux v. Madera Canal, etc., Co., * * * 99 P. 502 * * * are cited. In the Iowa case the water in question came from a spring, running continuously, at times in a well-defined channel with banks, at times spreading out several rods, later again coming together again in a narrow, well-defined, and single channel, with the current visible along the entire course. Here the substantial existence of the stream could not be questioned, and the case presents a feature altogether absent in the case at bar. In the California case it was held that where a stream flows in a continuous current, the fact that the water thereof, on account of the level character of the lands, spreads over a large area, without apparent banks, does not affect its character as a water course; the overflow caused by ordinary rainfall is but a part thereof. * * * So while too strict adherence to the definition that, to constitute a water course, there must be a stream flowing in a bed with banks, has at times given trouble, that definition is, ordinarily, correct and sufficient. * * *

Testing the facts in this case by these rules of law, we think we must hold that there was ample testimony to sustain the finding and judgment of the trial court, and that the state has failed, at least by a preponderance of the evidence, to show that Adamson Draw is a natural stream. According to most, if not all, of the evidence, it is dry nearly all the time; the main exception being in the spring. It is covered with grass; it has no banks; it is easily crossed by a vehicle almost everywhere; its main course is confined to the lands of the defendant. Its commencement is but a short distance beyond the north boundary thereof, and it has not been shown that it extends southward to a great length; at least, so far as the evidence shows it has no natural outlet. The run of the water therein is confined to a short period in the spring time when the snows melt; or heavy rains at other times may cause it to run for a short period of time. It is even doubtful, by reason of the porous soil, that any water would in any event reach [Adamson's] reservoir. Judging from the testimony, no one would instantaneously perceive that it is a water course. It is, of course, marked on the ground, as all draws are, but that it has been worn out by the water, in view of its grassy condition and the absence of banks, is not very likely, * * * The watershed is small; at least half of it, if not more, is confined to the lands of the defendant, and it would seem that the case may be said to resolve itself into the question as to whether or not the defendant has the right to impound water coming from melting snows and heavy rains, which fall onto his lands and on a small adjoining area, and which drain into a depression on defendant's lands. We think he has that right under the circumstances disclosed herein, or, at least, the trial court had the right to so find. * * *

The judgment of the trial court should, accordingly, be affirmed, and it is so ordered.

Notes

1. **Approaches to defining a watercourse.** Compare the descriptive definition in the principal case to the functional treatment in Hoefs v. Short, 273 S.W. 785 (Tex. 1925). Barilla Creek runs for one or two days after rains fall on its 350 square-mile watershed, from one to twenty-two times a year. The court said: "When it is said that a stream in order to be a natural watercourse to which water rights attach must have bed, banks, a current of water, and a permanent source of water supply, we have only described in detail such physiographic and meteorological characteristics as make the use of the stream for irrigation practicable. When it is once shown that the waters of a stream are so confined and persistent in their course, and flow with such frequency and volume that it is both practicable and valuable to irrigate therefrom, it is a stream to which such water rights attach. With reference to the phrase 'definite and permanent source of supply of water,' frequently used by the courts as describing a necessary requisite of an irrigable stream, all that is meant is that there

must be sufficient water carried by the stream at such intervals as may make it practicable to irrigate from or use the stream."

Did the court in the principal case partly rely on a functional test? (See its statement expressing doubt that any of water captured by the defendant would reach the reservoir of the downstream competitor.)

2. **Other exceptional cases.** In addition to the unusual natural features discussed in the principal case, consider the Fresno slough, which flows sometimes northward and sometimes southward, held part of a watercourse in Turner v. James Canal Co., 99 P. 520 (Cal. 1909). Consider also Medano Creek, which disappears into sand dunes only to reappear as Big and Little Spring Creeks. See Medano Ditch Co. v. Adams, 68 P. 431 (Colo. 1902). And what about groundwater which flows from an artesian well, via a ditch, into a lake formed by a dam on a creek: does the groundwater become surface water? See Edwards Aquifer Auth. v. Day, 274 S.W.3d 742 (Tex. Ct. App. 2008).

3. **Extent of "diffused surface waters."** In Oklahoma Water Resources Board v. Central Oklahoma Master Conservancy District, 464 P.2d 748 (Okla. 1968), a city owned the entire watershed of a small creek and, claiming "the right to capture water falling on its property for private use," dammed the stream. Held, an illegal appropriation of the stream: "Diffused surface waters lose their original character when they reach some well-defined channel in which they are accustomed to, and do, flow with other waters, or when they reach some permanent lake or pond. They then become 'a constituent part' of the stream, lake or pond, as the case may be. Diffused surface water may be appropriated by the owner of land over which it flows and become his property *when captured by him before it enters a definite stream.* Thereafter it is no longer subject to appropriation by the landowner." Id. at 754.

4. **Constitutional and statutory provisions.** The constitutions or statutes of several western states define water that is subject to appropriation in watercourse terms. E.g., Colo. Const. art. XVI, § 5 ("natural stream"); N.M. Const. art. XVI, § 2 ("perennial or torrential"). Several statutes define waters to exclude diffused surface water. See Ariz. Rev. Stat. § 45-141A; N.D. Cent. Code § 61-01-01. In contrast, the laws of some states refer to "all sources of water supply" or "all waters." E.g., Nev. Rev. Stat. 533.025; Utah Code Ann. § 73-1-1.

5. **Effect of soil conservation practices.** Harold E. Thomas, Hydrology v. Water Allocation in the Eastern United States, in The Law of Water Allocation in the Eastern United States 165, 173 (Haber & Bergen eds., 1958): "Of all the various 'diffused surface waters,' those that would be most likely to affect streamflow are the waters gathered on or flowing over the surface after precipitation. Such waters contribute materially to storm runoff, and especially to floods. Land owners within any drainage basin, therefore, by holding these 'diffused' waters on their land could reduce the streamflow materially; and if all overland flow could be prevented, the water in watercourses would consist largely of the discharge

from ground water reservoirs. Thus if the landowners have absolute ownership of both the ground water and diffused surface water on their lands, a surface water appropriator cannot be assured of a secure water right. * * * [I]t is reported that soil-conservation practices have reduced the flow of many streams in west Texas. At a water conference last September at Texas A & M College it was conceded that, with continuing reduction of base flow and reduction of storm runoff from minor storms, some surface-water appropriators would eventually have rights to nothing but the run-off during major floods."

Cal. Water Code § 1252.1: "An appropriation of water of any stream or other source of water under this part does not confer authority upon the appropriator to prevent or interfere with soil conservation practices above the point of diversion in the watershed in which such stream or other source originates, which practices do not themselves constitute an appropriation for which a permit is required by this part."

6. **Springs and lakes.** Springs which form a watercourse are usually held to be a part of the watercourse, and their use is governed by the law, riparian or appropriative, applicable to watercourses. In Arizona, "springs on the surface" are appropriable by statute, even though they do not flow beyond the boundary of the land on which they arise. Parker v. McIntyre, 56 P.2d 1337 (Ariz. 1936). Although the Oregon statutes appear to require a permit for diversions from all springs, case law holds that a permit is required only when the spring, if undiverted, flows beyond the boundaries on the land on which the spring arises. Norden v. State, 973 P.2d 910 (Or. Ct. App. 1999). California follows a similar rule as to springs arising on private lands, but springs which arise on public lands are appropriable even though their waters do not reach living streams. See Wells A. Hutchins, The California Law of Water Rights 407-13 (1956). If a dispute arises long after the diversion and development of spring waters, it may be difficult to determine whether the spring would flow beyond the property boundaries in its natural condition. See *Norden,* supra.

Several state constitutions and statutes mention lakes and ponds as sources of appropriable water. Generally, they are considered part of the watercourse which feeds them or originates from them. A lake may be appropriable though it lacks both a visible source of supply and an outlet. Proctor v. Sim, 236 P. 114 (Wash. 1925).

7. **Glacial ice.** In the 1980s glacial ice became a valuable novelty item for use in drinks because it makes more noise when melting than normal ice. In 1987, the Alaska Attorney General ruled that the Alaska appropriation statutes apply to glacial ice and icebergs. Thomas A. Meacham, 21 Water L. Newsl. No. 3, at 4 (Rocky Mtn. Min. L. Found., Westminster, Colo.) (1988).

R.J.A., INC. v. WATER USERS ASS'N OF DISTRICT NO. 6
Supreme Court of Colorado, 1984.
690 P.2d 823.

LOHR, JUSTICE. R.J.A., Inc. (applicant) appeals from a judgment * * * denying its application for a developed water right. The applicant based its claim on a project that will reduce water loss from a marshy mountain meadow by removing the underlying peat moss, thereby eliminating a saturated, seepy condition. This will decrease evaporation from the soil and surface and reduce evapotranspiration from grassy vegetation. We affirm the judgment.

R.J.A., Inc. operates a summer resort business on property located south of Estes Park, Colorado, in a mountain valley approximately 9000 feet above sea level. The property is situated at the headwaters of Tahosa Creek, which flows into St. Vrain Creek, a tributary of the South Platte River. This land originally included a 27-acre peat moss marsh which was approximately 3000 years old and, thus, was in existence long before any water rights were established on the South Platte River system. Historically, water entered this marsh from several surface streams and springs, and the area was much wetter than the surrounding lands. According to the applicant, loss of water to the atmosphere was higher from this peat moss marsh than from a well-drained mountain meadow of equivalent size. This is because the soil was saturated at or near surface level, resulting in relatively high rates of evaporation from the soil and standing water on the surface and evapotranspiration from the grassy vegetation growing throughout the marsh. While substantial amounts of water were lost to the atmosphere in this manner, the remaining water eventually moved through or around the marsh to become the headwaters of Tahosa Creek.

In the early 1970s, the applicant undertook a project to remove the extensive deposits of peat moss underlying the marsh, drain the land, and convert the marsh to a well-drained meadow more suitable for use in the applicant's resort business. At the time of the water court hearing in 1982, R.J.A., Inc. had completed about three quarters of the planned work.

In 1979, R.J.A., Inc. filed an application for a developed water right * * *, seeking a decree for 22.5 acre feet absolute and 20.8 acre feet conditional to be used for augmentation and other specified beneficial uses. * * * The applicant claimed that the drainage of the marsh and elimination of the saturated, seepy condition would reduce the rates of evaporation and evapotranspiration, and thereby would decrease consumptive use of water by 43.3 acre feet per year. Because this would represent a net gain to the stream, the applicant asserted that its water right should not be subject to administration under the priority system. * * *

The applicant contends that a developed water right for tributary water, free from the priority system, may be recognized where a claimant increases the natural flow of a stream by reducing consumptive uses that existed before the first appropriations were made on the stream. In support of this position, the applicant relies upon a line of cases in which we have recognized rights to developed water based upon addition of water to an existing supply. We hold that reduction of consumptive use of tributary water cannot provide the basis for a water right that is independent of the system of priorities on the stream.

As the trial court found, the water involved in the application before us is tributary to Tahosa Creek. The Water Right Determination and Administration Act of 1969, * * * (the 1969 Act), provides a comprehensive scheme for adjudication of rights to tributary water and for administration of the distribution of such water. That act provides for adjudication and administration under a system of priorities, implementing the constitutionally based right of prior appropriation in waters of natural streams. * * * Nowhere in the entire scheme of the 1969 Act is there a suggestion that rights to tributary water independent of the priority system can be obtained.

The applicant urges, however, that we have previously recognized that developed water rights, independent of the priority system, may be established as to tributary water in appropriate circumstances. We have stated on several occasions that one who increases the flow of a natural stream by adding water that otherwise would not reach the stream is entitled to the use of the water to the extent of the increase. * * *

Review of our cases relating to developed water brings us to the same conclusion that we reached in *Shelton Farms* that under prior case law "[no] person has been granted a water right free from the call of the river for water which has always been tributary to a stream." * * * 529 P.2d at 1325. Thus, the developed water cases provide no support for the applicant's position.

In *Shelton Farms* we considered an application with many similarities to the one now before us. There, we reversed judgments of the water court awarding water rights free from the call of senior decreed water rights on the Arkansas River. The trial court had decreed these rights based upon the reduction of evaporation and evapotranspiration effected by clearing phreatophytes from the land and filling in a marshy area. We concluded that, since the water in question had always been tributary to the stream and was not water new to the river system, the developed water cases were inapposite. We rejected the argument that demonstration of lack of injury to vested rights could serve as a basis for recognition of a water right outside the priority system and concluded:

[Present section 37-92-306, 15 C.R.S. (1973) prescribing the ranking of water rights by priorities] cannot be ignored * * *. There is nothing in the plain language of the statute to except appellees' plans [for award of water rights independent of the priority system] from the priority date system. Thus, we hold that all water decrees of any kind are bound to the call of the river, subject to any specific exceptions found within the law. To hold any other way would be to weaken the priority system, and create a superclass of water rights never before in existence.[7] * * * 529 P.2d at 1326.

In *Shelton Farms* we recognized the importance of maximizing beneficial use of Colorado's water. * * * We noted, however, that * * * the General Assembly had not authorized the creation of a water right outside the priority system through elimination of a prior consumptive use, as sought by the applicant here.

The applicant argues that *Shelton Farms* is not controlling because the phreatophytes in that case grew after the early water rights had been established on the river. Therefore, the plants were aptly characterized as "water thieves," and we visualized the generation of a new industry of "planting and harvesting trees to create water rights superior to the oldest decrees on the Arkansas * * *." * * * 529 P.2d at 1327. In the present case, however, the peat bog existed long before initiation of the earliest water right on the South Platte system. The water lost from the river system by evaporation and evapotranspiration from the seepy bog was never available for utilization by holders of senior rights. While this difference is real, we do not consider it controlling.

A separate strand of analysis supported our decision in *Shelton Farms*. We expressed concern over adoption of a rule of law that would encourage widespread destruction of plant life, with attendant likelihood of irreparable erosion and the creation of a barren wasteland. We said, "the waters of Colorado belong to the people, but so does the land. There must be a balancing effect, and the elements of water and land must be used in harmony to the maximum feasible use of both." * * * 529 P.2d at 1327. * * *

The water rights sought here are based upon alterations of long existing physical characteristics of the land. Alteration of natural con-

7. We distinguished between "developed" and "salvaged" water. The former is new water not previously part of the river system, i.e., it is imported or nontributary water. The latter is tributary water made available for beneficial use through elimination of waste. Only developed water can be made the basis of a right independent of the priority system. *Shelton Farms,* * * * 529 P.2d at 1324-25 * * *. One example of a developed water right described in *Shelton Farms* clearly involves tributary water—the capture, storage and utilization of flood waters. * * * 529 P.2d at 1324. There are valid reasons consistent with the priority system for entering a decree in favor of the person capturing such waters. Despite our dicta in *Shelton Farms,* such a decree does not involve a right to developed water independent of the priority system.

ditions and vegetation in order to save water carries with it the potential for adverse effects on soil and bank stabilization, soil productivity, wildlife habitat, fisheries production, water quality, watershed protection and the hydrologic cycle. * * * Whether to recognize such rights, and thus to encourage innovative ways of reducing historical consumptive uses by modifying conditions found in nature, is a question fraught with important public policy considerations. * * * [T]he question is especially suited for resolution through the legislative process.

In the 1969 Act, the General Assembly has used priority of appropriation as the sole criterion for ranking rights to tributary water. As we recognized in *Shelton Farms,* the general legislative policy of maximizing beneficial and integrated use of surface and subsurface water must be implemented with a sensitivity to the effect on other resources. The General Assembly has addressed the accommodation of the policy of maximum utilization of water and the policy of preservation of natural resources, but only in a limited way. It has expressed its concern that maximum utilization of water be balanced by preservation of the natural environment "to a reasonable degree" by authorizing appropriations on behalf of the people of the state of Colorado for that latter purpose. §§ 37-92-102(3) and 103(4), 15 C.R.S. (1973), the relevant portions of which were adopted in 1973 * * *.

Then, in 1975, shortly after the *Shelton Farms* case was decided, the General Assembly revised the definition of "plan for augmentation" to affirm that neither the salvage of tributary waters by eradicating phreatophytes nor the increase of runoff by making land surfaces impermeable provides an increased supply of water that may be utilized to support a plan for augmentation. § 37-92-103(9), 15 C.R.S. (1983 Supp.). These partial approaches to the problem reflect a cautious step-by-step legislative approach in addressing the issues. It is noteworthy, however, that in neither of these statutes has the legislature deviated from the basic priority system for tributary water when engrafting refinements upon the system.

The phreatophytes in *Shelton Farms* may have presented a factually more compelling case for rejection of recognition of a developed water right through their eradication than is present here. The larger consideration of achieving maximum feasible use of both land and water, however, is also present here, with the result that we find what we said in *Shelton Farms* equally applicable in this case:

> "No one on any river would be adverse to a schematic and integrated system of developing this kind of water supply with control and balancing considerations. But to create such a scheme is the work of the legislature, through creation of appropriate district authorities with right of condemnation on a selective basis, not for the courts. Until such time as the legislature responds, action such as appellees' should not be given court sanction. * * * 529 P.2d at 1327."

We affirm the judgment of the water court.

Notes

1. **Phreatophyte eradication.** Phreatophytes (Greek for "well-plants") literally pump water through their structure and transpire it from their foliage.

"Along many of the river valleys of the West, saltcedars and other generally worthless vegetation (willows, cottonwoods, mesquite, greasewood, and certain reeds and weeds) have crowded onto river bottom land to such an extent that they now cover nearly 16 million acres and discharge into the atmosphere an estimated 20 to 25 million acre-feet of water annually. These plants, having their roots in the ground water, have first call on available water supplies, leaving for man only that which they cannot use. Losses are particularly acute in the water shortage states of Arizona and New Mexico, where the warmer climate leads to greater consumption of water, particularly by the saltcedars. Elimination of the consumptive waste from these plants provides an excellent opportunity for increasing the usefulness of available water supplies." Senate Select Comm. on Nat'l Water Res., Report of the Committee Pursuant to S. Res. 48, S. Rep. No. 29, at 108-09 (1961).

Phreatophyte removal is controversial:

"A case in point is Arizona, where Federal agencies are studying or proposing the removal of phreatophytes—deep rooted vegetation—from the banks of many rivers in the state. The main purpose of the removal is to conserve water in that arid state. * * *

"Bitterly opposing the phreatophyte removal projects, some of which are already under way, are conservationists and wildlife proponents who say that the riverbank vegetation is the only major wildlife habitat in the arid state. Remove it, they say, and the adverse effects on wildlife will be devastating and sometimes irreversible. Some also mention indications, somewhat less supported by scientific evidence, that the effects on fisheries may be equally detrimental." Richard H. Gilluly, Wildlife Versus Irrigation, 99 Sci. News 184 (1971). Compare People v. Shirokow, 605 P.2d 859 (Cal. 1980), where the California Water Resources Control Board conditioned a permit on the eradication of phreatophytes.

2. **Water outside the priority system.** The court's statement in footnote 7 of the principal case that imported water is independent of the priority system should not be misunderstood. The court only means that imported water is outside the priority system in the basin to which it is imported. Such water is subject to the priority system in the basin in which it originates; i.e., water can be diverted from the basin of origin only when the diversion is in priority. Indeed, as public jurisdiction has been extended to other parts of the hydrologic cycle, it is difficult to find water that is not subject to appropriation or some other form of public administration (other than diffused surface water). For example, in Ripley v. Park Center Land & Water Co., 90 P. 75 (Colo. 1907), water

trapped in abandoned mine shafts was labeled "developed water" and was held to be free of the priority system, but more recently in *In re* General Determination of the Rights to Use of Surface and Ground Waters of Payette River Drainage Basin, 687 P.2d 1348 (Idaho 1984), it was held that the water emanating from a mine shaft was not "developed water" but was public ground water subject to appropriation.

3. **Stored water.** In footnote 7 of the principal case the court also notes that it was previously in error in categorizing stored water as developed water—water independent of the priority system. The court's confusion is understandable because stored water has some of the attributes of developed water. An appropriation is required to store water, and, like any appropriation, a storage appropriation is subject to the rule of priority. Thus, water in a stream or river can be captured for storage only when the right to store is in priority—i.e., only when more senior rights do not require the water. However, once lawfully stored, water is no longer subject to the claims of more senior appropriators; it can be held and used by the storing party without regard to "calls" by more senior appropriators. Thus, a right to *store* water is subject to the priority system, but the right to *use stored* water is independent of the system.

4. **Augmentation or return flows?** When computing the effect of an appropriation, return flows are generally offset against the amount diverted. See *Glacier View Meadows*, supra p. 76. The return flows are not considered "augmentation," but are simply a factor in determining the net depletion of an appropriation. The net depletion of an appropriation is sometimes called the "burden on the river."

Colo. Rev. Stat. § 37-92-103(9), cited in the principal case, provides that increased runoff resulting from making land surfaces impermeable cannot be used to support a plan of augmentation. Land development often replaces the natural terrain with impermeable surfaces, primarily paved roads and building roofs, thereby increasing surface runoff. If a land developer proposes an appropriation for a subdivision water supply, can increased surface runoff resulting from urbanization be used in determining the burden on the river of the proposed appropriation? Or is the use of such water to offset the effects of diversion prohibited under the above statute? I.e., should the increased runoff be classified as "augmentation" or as an incident of use analogous to return flows?

In State Engineer v. Castle Meadows, Inc., 856 P.2d 496 (Colo. 1993), the court found it unnecessary to determine the correct classification. It concluded that the legislature intended to remove the incentive for persons to increase water supplies by replacing natural land conditions with impermeable surfaces. Consequently, the court held that the use of such water to offset the effect of diversions would impermissibly contravene the legislative policy embodied in the statute, whether characterized as augmentation or as an incident of use.

5. **Injury to existing appropriators and water available for appropriation.** Collier v. Arizona Department of Water Resources, 722

P.2d 363 (Ariz. App. 1986), involved a spring which surfaced for the first time in 1979. Prior to surfacing, the water of the spring had been "percolating groundwater" and had contributed to the flow of Kirkland Creek. The Colliers built a dam to intercept the spring flow before it reached Kirkland Creek and applied for an appropriation. The application was protested by appropriators from Kirkland Creek who claimed that their appropriations included the spring water because of its hydrologic connection to the creek. The Colliers countered that the spring constituted a new source of unappropriated water. They noted that before surfacing it had been percolating groundwater which is not appropriable in Arizona and that after surfacing they had intercepted it before it had ever reached the creek. Thus, they reasoned that the water had never been part of the "appropriated" water of Kirkland Creek. The court agreed with the Colliers. Nevertheless, citing a statute barring any new appropriation which interferes with an existing one, it rejected the application.

6. **Artificially induced precipitation.** Although there have been some successes, the ability to increase water supplies through weather modification (cloud seeding) is controversial and largely unproven. See American Meteorological Society, Planned and Inadvertent Weather Modification (A Policy Statement) (1992).

Most of the litigation has involved unsuccessful attempts to collect damages for the harms allegedly caused by artificial precipitation; most of the legislation is concerned with regulatory and institutional controls of the activity. See, e.g., Ray J. Davis, Law and Urban-Induced Weather Change, 25 U. Tol. L. Rev. 379 (1994).

From the "water law" standpoint, the best article is still John M. Pierce, Legal Aspects of Weather Modification—Snowpack Augmentation in Wyoming, 2 Land & Water L. Rev. 273 (1967), speculating on the rights of the "rain maker" to capture, store, use and sell the water he adds to the natural stream flow. Consider Cal. Water Code § 401: "It is hereby declared that atmospheric water within the state which is caused to fall by weather resources management activities shall, for the purpose of water rights determinations, be considered as if it occurred as natural precipitation."

7. **Protection of instream uses.** Instream uses—uses associated with water in a stream, such as recreation, aesthetics, maintenance of fish and wildlife habitat and general environmental preservation—did not fare well historically under the appropriation doctrine because of its emphasis on consumptive use of water. Although limited acts to protect instream uses can be found earlier, the issue did not receive widespread attention until the 1970s. Since then, most western states have adopted legislation which provides for instream uses. In most cases, such legislation effectively withdraws water from appropriation.

The instream appropriation is the most widely used technique to protect instream uses. The use of this technique required the elimination of a diversion as an element of an appropriation and the recognition that the protection of instream values is a beneficial use of water. See *In re* Adjudication of the Mo. River Drainage Area, supra p. 22; Idaho Dep't of Parks v. Idaho Dep't of Water Admin., supra p. 28.

Other techniques include withdrawal of specified streams from appropriation (see Or. Rev. Stat. § 538.200); protection from diversion of state required minimum flows (see Wash. Rev. Code §§ 90.22.010-.060, 90.54.005-.920); reservation of water for instream flows by public agencies (see Mont. Code Ann. § 85-2-316); wild and scenic rivers designations to preserve the free-flowing nature of specified rivers (see federal Wild and Scenic Rivers Act, 16 U.S.C. §§ 1271-1287); regulation of the appropriation process to deny or condition new appropriations (see Chapter 2, Section 3C); application of the public trust doctrine (see Chapter 7, Section 1B); limitations on diversions under section 404 of the Clean Water Act (see Chapter 7, Section 2C) and the Endangered Species Act (see Chapter 7, Section 2D); imposition of flow requirements as water quality standards under sections 303 and 401 of the Clean Water Act (see City of Thornton v. Bijou Irr. Co. and accompanying Notes, infra p. 588; PUD No. 1 of Jefferson County v. Wash. Dep't of Ecology and accompanying Notes, infra p. 658); and flow requirements dictated by federal land agencies in permits issued for water development (see infra p. 604, Note 8).

E. Geographic Restrictions On Use

COFFIN v. LEFT HAND DITCH CO.
Supreme Court of Colorado, 1882.
6 Colo. 443.

HELM, J. Appellee, who was plaintiff below, claimed to be the owner of certain water by virtue of an appropriation thereof from the south fork of the St. Vrain creek. It appears that such water, after its diversion, is carried by means of a ditch to the James Creek, and thence along the bed of the same to Left Hand Creek, where it is again diverted by lateral ditches and used to irrigate lands adjacent to the last named stream. Appellants are the owners of lands lying on the margin and in the neighborhood of the St. Vrain below the mouth of said south fork thereof, and naturally irrigated therefrom.

In 1879 there was not a sufficient quantity of water in the St. Vrain to supply the ditch of appellee and also irrigate the said lands of appellant. A portion of appellee's dam was torn out, and its diversion of water thereby seriously interfered with by appellants. The action is brought for damages arising from the trespass, and for injunctive relief to prevent repetitions thereof in the future. The answer of appellants, who were defendants below, is separated into six divisions. * * * But it nowhere appears by sufficient averment that such appropriations of defendants making the same were actually made prior to the diversion of water through appellee's ditch. * * *

It is contended by counsel for appellants that the common law principles of riparian proprietorship prevailed in Colorado until 1876, and that the doctrine of priority of right to water by priority of appropriation thereof was first recognized and adopted in the constitution. But we think the latter doctrine has existed from the date of the earliest appropriations of water within the boundaries of the state. The climate is dry, and the soil, when moistened only by the usual rainfall, is arid and unproductive; except in a few favored sections, artificial irrigation for agriculture is an absolute necessity. Water in the various streams thus acquires a value unknown in moister climates. Instead of being a mere incident to the soil, it rises, when appropriated, to the dignity of a distinct usufructuary estate, or right of property. It has always been the policy of the national, as well as the territorial and state governments, to encourage the diversion and use of water in this country for agriculture; and vast expenditures of time and money have been made in reclaiming and fertilizing by irrigation portions of our unproductive territory. Houses have been built, and permanent improvements made; the soil has been cultivated, and thousands of acres have been rendered immensely valuable, with the understanding that appropriations of water would be protected. Deny the doctrine of priority or superiority of right by priority of appropriation, and a great part of the value of all this property is at once destroyed.

The right to water in this country, by priority of appropriation thereof, we think it is, and has always been, the duty of the national and state governments to protect. The right itself, and the obligation to protect it, existed prior to legislation on the subject of irrigation. It is entitled to protection as well after patent to a third party of the land over which the natural stream flows, as when such land is a part of the public domain; and it is immaterial whether or not it be mentioned in the patent and expressly excluded from the grant.

The act of congress protecting in patents such right in water appropriated, when recognized by local customs and laws, "was rather a voluntary recognition of a pre-existing right of possession, constituting a valid claim to its continued use, than the establishment of a new one." Broder v. Notoma W. & M. Co., 11 Otto, 274.

We conclude, then, that the common law doctrine giving the riparian owner a right to the flow of water in its natural channel upon and over his lands, even though he makes no beneficial use thereof, is inapplicable to Colorado. Imperative necessity, unknown to the countries which gave it birth, compels the recognition of another doctrine in conflict therewith. And we hold that, in the absence of express statutes to the contrary, the first appropriator of water from a natural stream for a beneficial purpose has, with the qualifications contained in the constitution, a prior right thereto, to the extent of such appropriation. * * *

It is urged, however, that even if the doctrine of priority or superiority of right by priority of appropriation be conceded, appellee in this case is not benefitted thereby. Appellants claim that they have a better right to the water because their lands lie along the margin and in the neighborhood of the St. Vrain. They assert that, as against them, appellee's diversion of said water to irrigate lands adjacent to Left Hand Creek, though prior in time, is unlawful.

In the absence of legislation to the contrary, we think that the right to water acquired by priority of appropriation thereof is not in any way dependent upon the *locus* of its application to the beneficial use designed. And the disastrous consequences of our adoption of the rule contended for, forbid our giving such a construction to the statutes as will concede the same, if they will properly bear a more reasonable and equitable one.

The doctrine of priority of right by priority of appropriation for agriculture is evoked, as we have seen, by the imperative necessity for artificial irrigation of the soil. And it would be an ungenerous and inequitable rule that would deprive one of its benefit simply because he has, by large expenditure of time and money, carried the water from one stream over an intervening watershed and cultivated land in the valley of another. It might be utterly impossible, owing to the topography of the country, to get water upon his farm from the adjacent stream; or if possible, it might be impracticable on account of the distance from the point where the diversion must take place and the attendant expense; or the quantity of water in such stream might be entirely insufficient to supply his wants. It sometimes happens that the most fertile soil is found along the margin or in the neighborhood of the small rivulet, and sandy and barren land beside the larger stream. To apply the rule contended for would prevent the useful and profitable cultivation of the productive soil, and sanction the waste of water upon the more sterile lands. It would have enabled a party to locate upon a stream in 1875, and destroy the value of thousands of acres, and the improvements thereon, in adjoining valleys, possessed and cultivated for the preceding decade. Under the principle contended for, a party owning land ten miles from the stream, but in the valley thereof, might deprive a prior appropriator of the water diverted there from whose lands are within a thousand yards, but just beyond an intervening divide. * * *

The judgment of the court below will be affirmed.

Notes

1. **Geographic restrictions.** Prior appropriation began with a rejection of the riparian watershed limitation, see Irwin v. Phillips, supra p. 16. Yet, in some states, a strong sectionalism has developed along the lines of basin divides, and local politics have produced inroads on the

freedom to transfer water from water-rich areas to water-short areas. Consider the following provisions of the California Water Code, relating to state "appropriations" of water and their assignment or release to actual appropriators and to authorization of the federal Central Valley Project and the California Water Plan:

"Section 10505. No priority under this part shall be released nor assignment made of any application that will, in the judgment of the commission, deprive the county in which the water covered by the application originates of any such water necessary for the development of the county.

"Section 11460. In the construction and operation by the department of any project under the provisions of this part a watershed or area wherein water originates, or an area immediately adjacent thereto which can conveniently be supplied with water therefrom, shall not be deprived by the department directly or indirectly of the prior right to all of the water reasonably required to adequately supply the beneficial needs of the watershed, area, or any of the inhabitants or property owners therein.

"Section 11463. In the construction and operation by the department of any project under the provisions of this part, no exchange of the water of any watershed or area for the water of any other watershed or area may be made by the department unless the water requirements of the watershed or area in which the exchange is made are first and at all times met and satisfied to the extent that the requirements would have been met were the exchange not made, and no right to the use of water shall be gained or lost by reason of any such exchange."

These statutes apply primarily to water rights held by the federal Central Valley Project and the State Water Project. In 1984, the legislature provided additional "area of origin" protection to designated river systems located in the northern and central part of the state. See Cal. Water Code §§ 1215-1222; see also §§ 12200-12228. For the most part, these statutes have lain dormant. As competition for California's water increases, more cases like El Dorado Irrigation District v. State Water Resources Control Board, 48 Cal. Rptr. 3d 468 (Cal. Ct. App. 2006), can be expected. There, the court concluded that the statutes did not give the irrigation district a priority to appropriate water, from the area of origin, that had been stored by the state or federal water projects. At most, it gave the district a priority to contract and pay for such project water.

2. **Compensatory storage.** Consider the limitation placed on the powers of Colorado water conservancy districts:

"Any works or facilities planned and designed for the exportation of water from the natural basin of the Colorado river and its tributaries in Colorado, by any district created under this article, * * * shall be designed, constructed and operated in such a manner that the present appropriations of water and, in addition thereto, prospective uses of water for irrigation and other beneficial consumptive use purposes, including consumptive uses for domestic, mining and industrial purposes, within the natural basin of the Colorado river in the state of Colorado, from which water is exported, will not be impaired nor increased in cost at the expense of the water users within the natural basin. The facilities and other means for the accomplishment of said purpose shall be incorporated in and made a part of any project plans for the exportation of water from said natural basin in Colorado." Colo. Rev. Stat. § 37-45-118(1)(b)(II).

This statute translates into a requirement for "compensatory storage;" a reservoir which the exporting district must construct on the western slope of the continental divide to replace with stored water the direct flow taken to the eastern slope, even though the water is not needed for present western slope uses. The City of Denver, although a major exporter of Colorado River water, is not bound by this law. Metro. Suburban Water Users Ass'n v. Colo. River Water Cons. Dist., 365 P.2d 273 (Colo. 1961). The Colorado constitutional guarantee that the right to appropriate water "shall never be denied" was held not to proscribe this limitation on the powers of an instrumentality of the state in Central Colorado Water Conservancy District v. Colorado River Water Conservation District, 526 P.2d 302 (Colo. 1974).

3. **Nebraska interbasin diversions.** In Nebraska, an 1895 statute required the return of unused irrigation water to the river of origin or the Missouri River. Neb. Rev. Stat. § 46-265. In 1936 this was held to prevent interbasin surface water diversions, since it would be impracticable to transport irrigation return flow back across the divide to the river of origin. The decision was perhaps influenced by the drought conditions of the 1930s and a fear that a large irrigation project planned for use of the Platte River in the Blue and Republican river basins might dry up the Platte River valley. Osterman v. Cent. Neb. Pub. Power & Irr. Dist., 268 N.W. 334 (Neb. 1936). *Osterman* was overruled in Little Blue Natural Resources District v. Lower Platte North Natural Resources District, 294 N.W.2d 598 (Neb. 1980). The Court noted that all of Nebraska is ultimately drained by the Missouri River, and ruled that cross-divide diversions are governed by the general statute permitting appropriations wherever there is unappropriated water and the appropriation would not be otherwise detrimental to the public welfare.

4. **Other restrictions on interbasin diversions.** See, e.g., Kan. Stat. Ann. § 82a-1502 (restricting exports to water which is surplus to the needs of the exporting area unless the benefits to the state of exporting water outweigh the benefits of not exporting it); Mont. Code Ann. § 85-2-301 (restricting exports to the Department of Natural Resources and Conservation, thereby forcing users to "lease" the water from the Department); Tex. Water Code Ann. § 11.085 (requiring that the benefits to the receiving basin outweigh the detriments to the exporting basin).

5. **Land use restrictions.** In Delta Wetlands Properties v. County of San Joaquin, 16 Cal. Rptr. 3d 672 (Ct. App. 2004), the court rejected a facial challenge to a county land use ordinance requiring a conditional use permit for reservoirs. The plaintiff, Delta Wetlands, held appropriation permits issued by the California Water Resources Control Board for the storage of water in reservoirs to be created by flooding several "islands" in

the Sacramento-San Joaquin Delta. The county adopted the ordinance after the board issued the permits because of concerns about various impacts of the project, particularly the loss of farmland resulting from the inundation of the islands.

Delta Wetlands argued that the state had impliedly preempted local regulation of matters considered by the board in issuing an appropriation permit. The court disagreed, holding that the board's exclusive jurisdiction over the appropriation of water and its authority to attach conditions to a permit in the public interest did not preempt county land use authority over reservoir siting. Because Delta Wetlands had not applied for a use permit from the county, the court refused to speculate as to specific county regulations that would be preempted by the appropriation permit.

In City of Colorado Springs v. Board of County Commissioners, 895 P.2d 1105 (Colo. Ct. App. 1994), a county successfully used its authority to regulate land use to block proposed transbasin diversions by two cities. The court found that the county was justified in denying use permits needed for construction of the projects because the cities failed to satisfy county regulations regarding wetlands protection and nuisance abatement. The county's authority was upheld against statutory and constitutional challenges.

6. **Purpose of geographic restrictions.** What is the purpose of such restrictions? To protect prior appropriators? To protect the future of slower growing regions? Are there any economic justifications for geographic restrictions? See Lawrence J. MacDonnell & Charles W. Howe, Area-of-Origin Protection in Transbasin Water Diversions: An Evaluation of Alternative Approaches, 57 U. Colo. L. Rev. 527 (1986). MacDonnell and Howe suggest that in a market setting like the West such statutes can be a means of assuring "economically efficient transbasin diversions" by making exporters accountable for costs which they impose on an area of origin. They conclude that requiring compensation to an area of origin is the most direct way of assuring economic efficiency. See also Nev. Rev. Stat. § 533.438 (authorizing a tax on groundwater that is appropriated for use outside the county of origin and requiring that all money raised by the tax be deposited in a trust fund to be used by the county "for purposes of economic development, health care and education").

7. **Interstate diversions.** In the absence of a statute, an appropriation may be made by diverting water with a ditch that taps the stream in one state and carries the water across a state line to a place of use in another state. The courts of the state where the diversion is made will protect the appropriation. Willey v. Decker, 73 P. 210 (Wyo. 1903). Most of the western states, however, enacted statutes designed to see that the benefits of water use remained within the state of origin. Limitations on exports of water took a number of forms: absolute embargoes, requirements of specific legislative approval, requirements for a discretionary permit, and (alone or in conjunction with permission for export) a requirement that the receiving state grant reciprocal privileges. Some statutes applied to all sources, others only to streams or to groundwater. In

1982 this pattern was considerably altered when Sporhase v. Nebraska *ex rel.* Douglas, 458 U.S. 941 (1982), invalidated a Nebraska statute that prevented the owner of a farm lying partly in Nebraska and partly in Colorado from piping water from a well on the Nebraska side across the state line to irrigate the Colorado field. The Court ruled that groundwater is an "article of commerce" subject to the potential, though unexercised, regulatory power of Congress, and held that Nebraska could not build into a water right restrictions that unreasonably burden interstate commerce. The Court discussed factors that might permit some preference for in-state uses. Several states have amended their laws to give as much protection to local needs as is permissible under *Sporhase.* The case and those laws are considered in Chapter 8, Section 1.

F. Appurtenance

SALT RIVER VALLEY WATER USERS' ASS'N v. KOVACOVICH

Arizona Court of Appeals, 1966.
3 Ariz. App. 28, 411 P.2d 201.

EDWIN THURSTON, SUPERIOR COURT JUDGE. These actions, consolidated for purpose of appeal, were brought by appellant in the Yavapai County Superior Court seeking a permanent injunction against appellees to enjoin the use of waters of the Verde River upon certain land situate in Yavapai County, and asking for determination with respect to whether or not valid and existing water rights were legally existing appurtenant to such land. * * * The statement of facts agreed to by the parties is as follows:

1. That the defendants and their predecessors in interest have made valid appropriations of water from the Verde River for irrigation purposes upon a portion of the lands owned by them;

2. That prior to 1933 in the Kovacovich action and prior to 1950 in the Ward action, certain additional lands owned by the respective defendants were not used for farming purposes nor was irrigation water applied thereon;

3. That neither the defendants nor their predecessors in interest ever made application under the Arizona Water Code to appropriate water for these additional lands;

4. That during and after 1933 in the Kovacovich action and during 1950 in the Ward action, the defendants, respectively, undertook in addition the cultivation of approximately thirty-five (35) acres and forty (40) acres of land adjacent to the land upon which the parties already had a valid water appropriation by irrigating said lands with water from the Verde River; and

5. That because of water-saving practices, no more water was thus used by the defendants to irrigate all of their lands here involved than was formerly used upon only their lands with a valid water appropriation.

The lower Court denied injunctive relief in each action and confirmed the right of appellees to beneficially use, as presently used, that quantity of water used by the appellee Kovacovich during or prior to 1933 and by the appellee Ward during or prior to 1950. * * *

In essence this case involves the narrow issue of whether or not an owner of land having a valid appurtenant water right may through water-saving practices apply the water thus saved to immediately adjacent lands owned by that person, without need to apply for the right to use such additional waters under the State Water Code. The further issue is that since the application of such waters would not result in less quantity of water flowing to the use of the appellants herein as owners of lower and subordinate water rights than would have previously occurred, have appellants been damaged whereby they are entitled to injunctive relief?

It was argued that decision of this issue in favor of appellants would result in penalizing persons who, through their industry, effort and expenses, engage in water-saving practices. The water-saving practices here referred to include improvement of ditches and concrete lining of ditches. This Court is of the opinion that the water-saving practices entered into by appellees not only result in conservation of water but also other benefits to appellees such as weed and vegetation growth control along such irrigation ditches and reduction of time and cost of maintenance of such ditches. Certainly any effort by users of water in Arizona tending toward conservation and more economical use of water is to be highly commended. However, commendable practices do not in themself create legal rights.

Historically, the development of water rights in Arizona created confusion by attempts to apply some of the strict concepts of common law riparian rights to the peculiar circumstances of not only the use of water but the need for its economical use prevalent in Arizona. The confusion concomitant with early attempts to apply the law with respect to use of water in Arizona progressed through several stages, including that where the right to use water appeared to be vested in the owner of land whereby same could be traded, leased or sold in much the same manner as other property. In an effort to achieve some degree of order out of the chaos then existing, our Courts through a series of decisions developed and applied what we today refer to as the "Doctrine of Beneficial Use." This doctrine is clearly enunciated in Gillespie Land & Irrigation Co. v. Buckeye Irr. Co. et al., 75 Ariz. 377, 384, 257 P.2d 393, 397, 398 (1953).

"* * * a water right is attached to the land on which it is beneficially used and becomes appurtenant thereto, and that the right is not in any individual or owner of the land. It is in no sense a floating right, nor can the right, once having attached to a particular piece of land, be made to do duty to any other land, with certain exceptions, e.g., where the land is washed away."

This doctrine was further implemented by enactment of a series of statutes, today referred to as the State Water Code, wherein matters pertaining to application of waters to new lands or changes in use of waters previously appropriated was placed under the jurisdiction of the Arizona State Land Department. In addition these statutes prescribe certain standards to be followed by the State Land Department with respect to applications for acquisition of change in the use of water. Title 45, Chapter 1, Articles 1-6, Arizona Revised Statutes.

This Court is of the opinion that the Doctrine of Beneficial Use precludes the application of waters gained by water conservation practices to lands other than those to which the water was originally appurtenant. * * * Under the doctrine of beneficial use, the appellees are not entitled under all circumstances to appropriate a given number of acre feet of water per year. Beneficial use is the measure and limit to the use of water. * * * The appellees may only appropriate the amount of water from the Verde River as may be beneficially used in any given year upon the land to which the water is appurtenant * * *. They may not take a quantity of water in excess of their appropriation even though they could beneficially use the same upon water right land. If in a given year, this should constitute an appropriation and use of all the water available at that particular point on the Verde River, subordinate owners of water rights have no cause to complain. However, in those years when water in excess of that which appellees may beneficially use upon the appurtenant land to which their water right attaches, all water which may flow to lower and subordinate owners of water rights is no longer of concern to appellees. Any practice, whether through water-saving procedures or otherwise, whereby appellees may in fact reduce the quantity of water actually taken inures to the benefit of other water users and neither creates a right to use the waters saved as a marketable commodity nor the right to apply same to adjacent property having no appurtenant water rights. * * *

The judgment of the lower Court is reversed with instructions to the lower Court to issue an injunction on behalf of appellant as against appellees as prayed for in appellant's complaints.

Notes

1. **Nature of the water right.** What is the nature of the "water right" in *Kovacovich?* A right to divert a quantity of water or a right to irrigate a specific piece of land?

2. **Purpose of appurtenance.** Charles J. Meyers, A Historical and Functional Analysis of the Appropriation System, in Nat'l Water Comm'n, Legal Study No. 1, at 17-18 (1971): "[T]his restriction was an understandable but misguided effort to get at what was regarded as the evil of speculation. Despite adoption of the permit system, it was believed that many pre-permit rights were inflated. In an effort to make more unappropriated water available at zero cost to new settlers—and in this sense, encourage development—statutes were enacted * * * making water rights appurtenant to land and nontransferable (subject to certain exceptions). The theory of these statutes * * * is that by attaching water rights indissolubly to land, the owner of the inflated right (who is unable to use all the water on his own land) will be unable to sell the excess for use on other land."

3. **Appurtenance and water rights transfers.** The foregoing note suggests that appurtenancy makes water rights nontransferable, "subject to certain exceptions." The exceptions have largely swallowed the rule. In most states, water rights may be transferred to new places or purposes of use pursuant to statutory procedures. Transfer procedures and substantive limits on transfers to protect other appropriators are examined in Section 5 of this Chapter. Unlike *Kovacovich*, in most transfers the original use is partially or completely discontinued.

4. **Appurtenance, transfers and third party ownership.** Where the owner of the land to which a water right is appurtenant does not also hold the water right, only the water right's holder can petition for a change in use. This can occur when a water district holds the water rights. See, e.g., Fort Vannoy Irr. Dist. v. Water Res. Comm'n, 162 P.3d 1066 (Or. Ct. App. 2007). The relationship between water districts and the water users they serve is addressed in Chapter 5.

5. **Trend away from *Kovacovich*.** Colorado and Utah permit an appropriator to enlarge the lands under irrigation if the expanded use will not injure other appropriators; i.e., if the appropriator's conservation measures have salvaged water that would otherwise be lost to the system and have not merely captured return flows relied on by other appropriators. In both states the statutory transfer procedures are used for this purpose. See Danielson v. Kerbs Ag., Inc., 646 P.2d 363 (Colo. 1982); E. Bench Irr. Co. v. Deseret Irr. Co., 271 P.2d 449 (Utah 1954). Several states have codified this approach to promote conservation. See Cal. Water Code §§ 1010, 1011; Mont. Code Ann. § 85-2-419; Tex. Water Code Ann. § 11.002 (4), (9). Such statutes do not appear to have been widely used, principally, it seems, because of high transaction costs and significant uncertainties associated with demonstrating lack of injury.

6. **Appurtenance and conveyancing.** In most states, a water right is "appurtenant" in a conveyancing sense; i.e., water rights pass in a conveyance of land unless expressly reserved. See, e.g., Utah Code Ann. § 73-1-11; Axtell v. M.S. Consulting, 955 P.2d 1362 (Mont. 1998).

In Joyce Livestock Co. v. United States, 156 P.3d 502 (Idaho 2007), the Idaho Supreme Court found that stock watering rights on federal public lands were appurtenant to the plaintiffs' predecessors' nearby patented property. Thus, these water rights were conveyed to plaintiffs even though the deeds conveying the patented property were silent.

In Dermody v. City of Reno, 931 P.2d 1354 (Nev. 1997), the court extended the rule to condemnation, holding that Reno acquired appurtenant water rights when it condemned land for airport expansion although the decree made no mention of the rights. In Wayt v. Buerkel, 875 P.2d 499 (Or. Ct. App. 1994), the court applied the rule to contract rights to water, holding that such rights were acquired by a purchaser of land at a foreclosure sale. However, in Colorado the question depends on the intent of the grantor, Bessemer Irrigating Ditch Co. v. Woolley, 76 P. 1053 (Colo. 1904), and in New Mexico the rule applies only to irrigation rights. Walker v. United States, 162 P.3d 882 (N.M. 2007). In Little v. Greene & Weed Investment, 839 P.2d 791 (Utah 1992), the court ruled that a right does not become appurtenant for conveyancing purposes until the state engineer issues a certificate of appropriation. If the land is divided, the amount appurtenant to each tract is the amount which was beneficially used on the tract prior to division, Stephens v. Burton, 546 P.2d 240 (Utah 1976), or is a proportionate share of the entire right. Crow v. Carlson, 690 P.2d 916 (Idaho 1984). Cf. Utah Code Ann. § 73-3-31 (watering right must be jointly acquired by public agency and the beneficial user before livestock can be watered on public lands.)

In Spears v. Warr, 44 P.3d 742 (Utah 2002), land developers orally represented to several buyers that irrigation water rights were included in the purchase price of lots, but deeds conveying the lots made no mention of water rights. Subsequently, the developers refused to convey the promised water rights, and the buyers sued for specific performance. The court ruled for the buyers, holding that enforcement of the oral agreements was not blocked by the merger doctrine, the parol evidence rule, or the statute of frauds. The Utah appurtenance statute noted above was not mentioned, apparently because the rights were being transferred from other lands and were not appurtenant when the lots sold.

G. Protection of Means of Diversion

STATE EX REL. CROWLEY v. DISTRICT COURT

Supreme Court of Montana, 1939.
108 Mont. 89, 88 P.2d 23.

JOHNSON, CHIEF JUSTICE. * * * The suit in question is for damages for alleged interference with plaintiff's use of irrigation water from the Madison River in 1935, 1936 and 1937. There are nine causes of action, which are grouped as to years. The first three relate to 1935, the next three to 1936, and the last three to 1937. Thus there are three causes of action with reference to each of the three years. * * *

The second group, comprising causes 2, 5 and 8, is based upon the allegations that the defendants [Montana Power Company et al] impounded by their dams the entire natural flow of the river so that the water level at plaintiff's point of diversion was so low that he could not divert water into his ditches by his diversion dam, although the latter was suitable and efficient for the purpose and was a reasonably adequate means of diversion, and reasonably constructed and maintained to divert water from the river to plaintiff's land in spite of the fluctuations in flow incidental to the reasonable and lawful use of water by all persons lawfully entitled to use the same. * * * The demurrers to these causes of action numbered 2, 5 and 8 were sustained. * * *

The allegations of the causes are those usual to actions of this kind. Defendants' contentions are that plaintiff has no cause of action merely because their acts so reduced the flow that he could not divert his appropriated water by his reasonably efficient diversion system; that he should have alleged that not enough was left to permit his diversion without leaving any water in the stream. In other words, they contend that plaintiff has no cause of action if there are 200 inches of water at his point of diversion, even though he cannot get the water into his ditches without a pump; that an appropriator's vested interest is only in the use of the quantum of water appropriated by him without reference to his means or manner of diversion, however reasonably efficient; that not reasonable efficiency but absolute efficiency is required. To this theory we cannot assent without doing violence to the entire principle of water rights by appropriation. If it is to be followed, there are few, if any, irrigation water rights in the state of Montana, however long established, which could not in effect be destroyed entirely by subsequent appropriations. One hundred per cent efficiency can be furnished by no system of diversion, and certainly by none financially available to the average water user. The law does not defeat its own end by requiring the impossible. The marginal character of many farming enterprises, and especially of the smaller ones, is well known, and if defendants' argument is followed, vested interests will be seriously affected and rights limited by the necessity of installing diversion systems by which the last drop may be taken from the stream.

There is no question that waste of our water resources must be minimized in the general interest, but it is equally manifest that there is a vanishing point at which the possible waste of water would be more than overcome by the waste incidental to the abandonment of reasonably efficient diversion systems and the establishment of diversion systems whose expense is neither warranted nor permitted by the benefit to be derived from the water.

It is well established that subsequent appropriators take with notice of the conditions existing at the time of their appropriations. In *prior appropriation are held to both Amount & Means*

(means doesn't include force, but how the water is diverted)

making their appropriation of storage or other water and their expenditures in connection therewith, defendants and their predecessors were chargeable with knowledge of the existing conditions, with reference not only to the amount of prior appropriations, but also to the existing diversion systems of prior appropriators. They cannot now argue that they are limited by the amount but not the means of prior appropriations, however reasonably efficient under the circumstances, or that so long as they leave the exact amount of plaintiff's appropriation in the river at his point of diversion, they have no further duty and that it is his worry and not theirs how or whether he can divert it upon his land. His right is to divert and use the water, not merely to have it left in the streambed; that is the essential difference between riparian and appropriation rights. * * *

court supports P, says D is required to fully uphold P's appropriation rights (i.e. including P's diversion rights)

Defendants contend that the case of Schodde v. Twin Falls Land & Water Co., 224 U.S. 107, * * *, sustains their contention that a prior appropriator has no vested interest in his means of diversion. It cannot be so construed. In that case plaintiff had appropriated 1250 inches of water from Snake River in Idaho, for use on his ranch of 429 acres, and diverted it by means of large waterwheels operated by the stream flow. The defendant thereafter constructed a dam nine miles below to supply water to about 5,000 settlers for the irrigation of approximately 300,000 acres of land. The dam backed the water up beyond plaintiff's waterwheels so that the current was no longer available to operate them. Plaintiff sued for damages in the federal court of Idaho, and defendant's demurrer was sustained. On appeal the Ninth Circuit Court of Appeals affirmed the trial court's action on the ground that there was no attempted appropriation of water to run the wheels, and that there could be none under the laws of Idaho without an actual diversion for the purpose, and upon the further ground that the statute expressly authorizing the use of rams and other machines to lift appropriated water from streams gave a mere license, and not an appurtenance to the water right appropriated. In other words, the right to the flow of the river constituted neither an appropriation of the flow nor an appurtenance to the irrigation water actually appropriated. It also held that where the method of diversion was obviously unreasonable and inefficient it could not be used where it interfered with the reasonable use of water by others. Obviously, of course, under the circumstances of that case, it was unreasonable to prevent the irrigation of 300,000 acres by an unusual and inefficient method of diverting water for 429 acres. The complaint there was not that the defendant had taken water out of the stream so as to interfere with the waterwheels; as a matter of fact, the defendant had confined more water there. What it had deprived plaintiff of was not the water, but the force of the water, which was no part of his appropriation. This can be made clear by an analogy. If, instead of building waterwheels to utilize the force of the stream, he had constructed wind-mills to employ the force of the wind, it would have been entirely clear that his complaint was not of water right interference, but of something entirely different. If the conditions were such that he could have recovered for an obstruction to the flow of the wind to his windmills, it would still have been something entirely apart from and not appurtenant to his water right. This is clear from the opinion of the Circuit Court of Appeals in 161 F. at page 45, as follows: "It is contended on the part of the plaintiff that the current of the river is necessarily appurtenant to the water location and that the means of utilizing that current is attached as an appurtenance to the appropriation. We have not been referred to any case—and we know of none—where either of these propositions has been upheld. The claim that the right to the current of the river is appurtenant to the water location is contrary to well-established principles of the common law governing such a relation. The water location was an appropriation and diversion of a certain quantity of the flowing water of the stream. The current of the river is part of the stream. There can be no right to the current of a stream as appurtenant to a diversion of the flowing waters of the stream. The two rights in such case would be equal and of the same character and quality, and one such right cannot be appurtenant to the other." The court then went on to show that there had been no diversion or appropriation of water for power purposes, so that plaintiff's asserted right against defendant's interference was not a water right, and concluded by quoting the decision of this court in Fitz-patrick v. Montgomery, 20 Mont. 181, 50 P. 416, 63 Am.St.Rep. 622, to the effect that the tendency and spirit of legislation in the northwest had been to prevent a monopoly of water.

On certiorari the United States Supreme Court, speaking through Mr. Chief Justice White, said: "The trial court recognized fully the right of the plaintiff to the volume of water actually appropriated for a beneficial purpose. It nevertheless dismissed the complaint on the ground that there was no right under the Constitution and laws of the state of Idaho to appropriate the current of the river so as to render it impossible for others to apply the otherwise unappropriated waters of the river to beneficial uses. The court did not find it necessary to deny that power might be one of the beneficial purposes for which appropriations of water might be made, but in substance held that to uphold as an appropriation the use of the current of the river to the extent required to work the defendant's wheels would amount to saying that a limited taking of water from the river by appropriation for a limited beneficial use justified the appropriation of all the water in the river as incident to the limited benefit resulting from the use of the water actually appropriated. The court said: '* * * there is no statute, nor so far as known, any judicial rulings, protecting him in the establishment and in the use of his water wheels, as he claims to, and must, use them for the diversion of water to his land.' * * * 'It is unquestioned that what he has actually diverted and used upon his land, he has appropriated; but can it be said that all the water he uses or needs to operate his wheels is an appropriation? As before suggested, there is neither statutory nor judicial authority that such a use is an appropriation. Such use also lacks one of the essential attributes of an appropriation,—it is not reasonable.'" * * *

The rule in this connection is well stated as follows in Long on Irrigation, 2nd ed., 202, 203, sec. 116: "The irrigator may employ any means best suited to the existing physical conditions, and all the circumstances of the case, though undoubtedly he will be required to employ reasonably economical means, so as to prevent unnecessary waste. * * * As already stated, the means of diversion employed must not be unnecessarily wasteful (Doherty v. Pratt, 34 Nev. 343, 124 P. 574), but when ditches and flumes are the usual and ordinary means of diverting water, parties who have made their appropriations by such means cannot be compelled to substitute iron pipes, though they will be required to prevent unnecessary waste by keeping their ditches and flumes in good repair (Barrows v. Fox, 9 Cal. 63, 32 P. 811)." * * *

Plaintiff alleges that he has diverted the water by means of a wing dam of brush, rocks and dirt, and proceeds to allege that the means of diversion was at the time in question "suitable and efficient for the diversion of water," and "a reasonably adequate means of diversion and reasonably constructed and maintained" for the purpose, notwithstanding the fluctuations incidental to the reasonable and lawful use of water by all those entitled, including defendants. These are statements of ultimate facts, and causes numbered 2, 5 and 8 sufficiently state causes of action. It follows that the demurrers should have been overruled. * * * *Court is protecting reasonable means of diversion*

Notes

1. **Illustration of unreasonable means of diversion.** In *Schodde,* distinguished in the principal case, both the trial court and the Supreme Court used the following illustration: "Suppose from a stream of 1000 inches a party diverts and uses 100, and in some way uses the other 900 to divert his 100, could it be said that he had made such a reasonable use of the 900 as to constitute an appropriation of it? Or, suppose that when the entire 1000 inches are running, they so fill the channel that by a ditch he can draw off to his land his 100 inches, can he then object to those above him appropriating and using the other 900 inches, because it will so lower the stream that his ditch becomes useless? This would be such an unreasonable use of the 900 inches as will not be tolerated under the law of appropriation." 224 U.S. 107, 119 (1912) (quoting the unpublished opinion of the trial court).

2. **Is "reasonableness" static or dynamic?** On remand, what standards will be used to determine if Crowley's means of diversion are "reasonably adequate": the standards when Crowley began to appropriate or the standards when the dispute with the defendant arose?

In Warner Valley Stock Co. v. Lynch, 336 P.2d 884 (Or. 1959), the court refused to protect the use of natural overflow to divert water from a lake for irrigation, although the rights at issue had been previously adjudicated. However, the earlier adjudication had found that the diversions were wasteful and were "privileges," not rights, to be enjoyed only until rendered impractical by fuller use of the stream. In distinguishing cases in which appropriators' means of diversion were protected, including the principal case, the court said simply, "in each of these cases the interest * * * which the court protected was a vested right." If Crowley has a "vested right" to his means of diversion, as *Warner* suggests, can he be required to adopt more efficient methods if economic changes, advances in irrigation technology, or changes in customary irrigation practices make his "wing dam" obsolete? See *Imperial Irrigation Dist.*, supra p. 40.

3. **Codification.** N.D. Cent. Code § 61-04-06.3: "Priority of appropriation does not include the right to prevent changes in condition of water occurrence, such as the increase or decrease of streamflow, or the lowering of a water table, artesian pressure, or water level, by later appropriators, if the prior appropriator can reasonably acquire his water under the changed conditions."

4. **An economic perspective.** R. H. Coase, The Problem of Social Cost, 3 J.L. & Econ. 1 (1960):

"This paper is concerned with those actions of business firms which have harmful effects on others. The standard example is that of a factory the smoke from which has harmful effects on those occupying neighboring properties. The economic analysis of such a situation has usually proceeded in terms of a divergence between the private and social product of the factory * * *. The conclusions to which this kind of analysis seems to have led most economists is that it would be desirable to make the owner of the factory liable for the damage caused to those injured by the smoke, or alternatively, to place a tax on the factory owner varying with the amount of smoke produced an equivalent in money terms to the damage it would cause, or finally, to exclude the factory from residential districts (and presumably from other areas in which the emission of smoke would have harmful effects on others). It is my contention that the suggested courses of action are inappropriate, in that they lead to results which are not necessarily, or even usually, desirable.

"The traditional approach has tended to obscure the nature of the choice that has to be made. The question is commonly thought of as one in which A inflicts harm on B and what has to be decided is: how should we restrain A? But this is wrong. We are dealing with a problem of a reciprocal nature. To avoid the harm to B would inflict harm on A. The real question that has to be decided is: should A be allowed to harm B or should B be allowed to harm A? The problem is to avoid the more serious harm. I instanced in my previous article the case of a confectioner the noise and vibrations from whose machinery disturbed a doctor in his work. To avoid harming the doctor would inflict harm on the confectioner. The problem posed by this case was essentially whether it was worth while, as a result of restricting the methods of production which could be used by the confectioner, to secure more doctoring at the cost of a reduced supply of confectionery products. * * *

"The court's decision established that the doctor had the right to prevent the confectioner from using his machinery. But, of course, it would have been possible to modify the arrangements envisaged in the legal ruling by means of a bargain between the parties. The doctor would have been willing to waive his right and allow the machinery to continue in operation if the confectioner would have paid him a sum of money which was greater than the loss of income which he would suffer from having to move to a more costly or less convenient location or from having to curtail his activities at this location or, as was suggested as a possibility, from having to build a separate wall which would deaden the noise and vibration. The confectioner would have been willing to do this if the amount he would have to pay the doctor was less than the fall in income he would suffer if he had to change his mode of operation at this location, abandon his operation or move his confectionery business to some other location. The solution of the problem depends essentially on whether the continued use of the machinery adds more to the confectioner's income than it subtracts from the doctor's. But now consider the situation if the confectioner had won the case. The confectioner would then have had the right to continue operating his noise and vibration-generating machinery without having to pay anything to the doctor. The boot would have been on the other foot: the doctor would have had to pay the confectioner to induce him to stop using the machinery. If the doctor's income would have fallen more through continuance of the use of this machinery than it added to the income of the confectioner, there would clearly be room for a bargain whereby the doctor paid the confectioner to stop using the machinery. That is to say, the circumstances in which it would not pay the confectioner to continue to use the machinery and to compensate the doctor for the losses that this would bring (if the doctor had the right to prevent the confectioner's using his machinery) would be those in which it would be in the interest of the doctor to make a payment to the confectioner which would induce him to discontinue the use of the machinery (if the confectioner had the right to operate the machinery). * * * With costless market transactions, the decision of the courts concerning liability for damage would be without effect on the allocation of resources. * * *

"Judges have to decide on legal liability but this should not confuse economists about the nature of the economic problem involved. * * * The doctor's work would not have been disturbed if the confectioner had not worked his machinery; but the machinery would have disturbed no one if the doctor had not set up his consulting room in that particular place.

* * * If we are to discuss the problem in terms of causation, both parties caused the damage. If we are to attain an optimum allocation of resources, it is therefore desirable that both parties should take the harmful effect (the nuisance) into account in deciding on their course of action. It is one of the beauties of a smoothly operating pricing system that, as has already been explained, the fall in the value of production due to the harmful effect would be a cost for both parties. * * *

"Of course, if market transactions were costless, all that matters (questions of equity apart) is that the rights of the various parties should be well-defined and the results of legal actions easy to forecast. But as we have seen, the situation is quite different when market transactions are so costly as to make it difficult to change the arrangement of rights established by the law. In such cases, the courts directly influence economic activity. It would therefore seem desirable that the courts should understand the economic consequences of their decisions and should, insofar as this is possible without creating too much uncertainty about the legal position itself, take these consequences into account when making their decisions. Even when it is possible to change the legal delimitation of rights through market transactions, it is obviously desirable to reduce the need for such transactions and thus reduce the employment of resources in carrying them out. * * *

"The problem which we face in dealing with actions which have harmful effects is not simply one of restraining those responsible for them. What has to be decided is whether the gain from preventing the harm is greater than the loss which would be suffered elsewhere as a result of stopping the action which produces the harm. In a world in which there are costs of rearranging the rights established by the legal system, the courts, in cases relating to nuisance, are, in effect, making a decision on the economic problem and determining how resources are to be employed. It was argued that the courts are conscious of this and that they often make, although not always in a very explicit fashion, a comparison between what would be gained and what lost by preventing actions which have harmful effects. But the delimitation of rights is also the result of statutory enactments. Here we also find evidence of an appreciation of the reciprocal nature of the problem. While statutory enactments add to the list of nuisances, action is also taken to legalize what would otherwise be nuisances under the common law. The kind of situation which economists are prone to consider as requiring corrective Government action is, in fact, often the result of Government action. Such action is not necessarily unwise. But there is a real danger that extensive Government intervention in the economic system may lead to the protection of those responsible for harmful effects being carried too far. * * *

"It would clearly be desirable if the only actions performed were those in which what was gained was worth more than what was lost. But in choosing between social arrangements within the context of which individual decisions are made, we have to bear in mind that a change in the existing system which will lead to an improvement in some decisions may well lead to a worsening of others. Furthermore we have to take into account the costs involved in operating the various social arrangements (whether it be the working of a market or of a Government department), as well as the costs involved in moving to a new system. In devising and choosing between social arrangements we should have regard for the total effect. This, above all, is the change in approach which I am advocating."

5. **Equity.** Note that Professor Coase puts "problems of equity" aside in concluding that it makes no difference in resource allocation whether or not, to translate into our terms, the priority of the first right includes the right to maintain an inefficient means of diversion. If in *Crowley* the loss to Crowley's crops is less than the benefit the power company obtains when the extra water required by the inefficient wing dam is held back, the water will be stored in the company's reservoir, whether the company has to pay Crowley or not. If the benefit to the company is less than the crop loss, the water will be released, either because if the company is liable it will be cheaper to release it than to pay damages, or if not liable the company will make a profit by accepting Crowley's offer to buy the water at a price somewhere between the company's benefit and his loss. Whether an improved dam will be built is similarly independent of the rule of liability. If the water is stored in the reservoir and if the cost of building an improved diversion dam is less than the crop loss, the dam will be built. If Crowley has no claim against the company, he will build it to eliminate his crop loss. If the company is liable, it will build it or pay Crowley to build it rather than continuing to pay the greater damages. If the water is released from the reservoir because it has less value to the company than to Crowley, the new dam will not be built. The "inefficient" wing dam then remains as the most efficient method of utilizing the resource.

What "problems of equity" remain? Assuming maximum efficiency in resource allocation is obtainable under either rule, *ought* the cost of constructing the improved dam be placed on the power company or on the irrigator? Should it make any difference if all the water users are irrigators?

If the prior appropriator's means of diversion is protected, does the relief given by the court make any difference? Crowley asked for damages. If he had sought and obtained an injunction, would the Coasian analysis of the situation change? Suppose there are a number of persons situated similarly to Crowley, all of whose diversion works need to be improved to get the desirable combination of irrigation and power. If each is given the right to an injunction, is the Coasian optimum more or less likely to be reached?

For a specific application of Coase to water rights, see C. Carter Ruml, Note, The Coase Theorem and Western U.S. Appropriative Water Rights, 45 Nat. Resources J. 169 (2005).

H. Access

HALLAUER v. SPECTRUM PROPERTIES, INC.
Supreme Court of Washington, 2001.
143 Wash. 2d 126, 18 P.3d 540.

MADSEN, J. Wilbur G. and Josephine Hallauer, who hold a certificated water right to water from a spring on neighboring land, seek to condemn a way across that land for transporting water to their property for domestic use, and to ponds for fish propagation. The Court of Appeals held that because the Hallauers' property is not landlocked and alternative sources of water are available, the Hallauers failed to prove a reasonable necessity for condemnation. We reverse the Court of Appeals and hold that the Hallauers are entitled to proceed with their condemnation action.

The Hallauers and respondents Ernesto C. and Madeliene B. Del Rosario own adjacent property on the shore of Lake Osoyoos in Okanogan County. Donald Thorndike was the Del Rosarios' predecessor in interest. In the mid-1970's, part of a bluff on Thorndike's property collapsed, revealing a natural spring. In the early 1980's the Hallauers built a home on their property with a heat pump and cooling system that used water from a well. The first winter, the heat pump froze because the water from the well was too cold for its proper operation. Mr. Hallauer learned that the water from the spring on Mr. Thorndike's property would be satisfactory for operation of the heat pump as well as for supplying water to ponds intended for fish propagation.

Mr. Thorndike and Mr. Hallauer agreed that Mr. Hallauer would apply to the Department of Ecology for a water right entitling him to withdraw water from the spring on the Thorndike property, and when the water right was granted Mr. Hallauer would pay Mr. Thorndike $500. * * *

Mr. Hallauer developed the spring and installed a pipeline to transport water from the spring to his property for the heat pump and fish ponds. The property on which the ponds are located was developed into the Champerty Shores development, a private community. In 1984, fish were added to the ponds. In October 1984, the Department of Ecology issued a certificate of water right.

* * * In October 1989, Mr. Del Rosario entered into a real estate contract for the purchase of [Thorndike's] property, took possession, and began managing an apple orchard on it. During roadwork on the property, the Hallauers' pipeline was discovered, and the Del Rosarios demanded that the pipeline be removed.

Litigation ensued. * * * The trial court held that the Hallauers had failed to show a reasonable necessity for a private condemnation.

On appeal, the Court of Appeals affirmed. This court granted discretionary review.

Although several other grounds for relief have been argued during litigation between the parties, the only matter before this court is whether the Hallauers are entitled to condemn an easement across the Del Rosarios' property for a pipeline to transport water from the spring to their property for use in the heat pump and cooling system and as a water supply for propagation of fish. The authority to condemn a right of way to transport water has long existed in this state, both by constitutional and statutory provisions. The chief question posed by this case is whether the showing of necessity to condemn a right of way to transport water is identical to the showing required to condemn a private way of necessity. The Court of Appeals held that "necessity" means the same in both contexts, relying on RCW 8.24.010. We disagree because RCW 8.24.010 does not apply in the context here.

As we explain below, RCW 90.03.040 provides the statutory authority for condemnation in this case. Among other things, the statute directs that "property or rights shall be acquired [through condemnation] in the manner provided by law for the taking of private property for public use by private corporations." RCW 90.03.040. Therefore, chapter 8.20 RCW (eminent domain by corporations), rather than chapter 8.24 RCW, provides the procedures for condemnation. * * *

In order to determine whether the Hallauers are entitled to an order of public use and necessity, we examine both public use and necessity * * *. Also, the public interest condition and the necessity condition "are generally subsumed under the definition of 'necessity'." City of Seattle v. Mall, Inc., 104 Wash.2d 621, 623, 707 P.2d 1348 (1985). The interrelatedness of the conditions is particularly apparent where water rights or rights of way to transport water are concerned. This is because of the adoption of the prior appropriation doctrine in this state for acquisition of new water rights; condemnation of rights of way to transport water is an integral component of application of water to beneficial use.

Accordingly, we begin by discussing the public use condition as a predicate to discussion of the necessity condition. Our analysis begins with article I, section 16 of the Washington State Constitution, which provides:

> Private property shall not be taken for private use, except for private ways of necessity, and for drains, flumes, or ditches on or across the lands of others for agricultural, domestic, or sanitary purposes. No private property shall be taken or damaged for public or private use without just compensation having been first made * * *.

As an initial matter, this constitutional provision does not require that condemnation for rights of way to transport water is subject to the same criteria as condemnation for private ways of necessity. The first sentence of article I, section 16 carves out two forms that a condemnation for "private" use may take. The constitution states the exceptions to the rule that private property may not be taken for private uses as: "except *for* private ways of necessity, *and for* drains, flumes, or ditches on or across the lands of others for agricultural, domestic, or sanitary purposes." Const. art. I, § 16 (emphasis added). * * *

[RCW 90.03.040] was enacted as part of the 1917 water code under which the prior appropriation doctrine became the sole method for acquisition of new water rights. It provides in part that "[t]he beneficial use of water is hereby declared to be a public use, and any person may exercise the right of eminent domain to acquire any property or rights now or hereafter existing when found necessary for the storage of water for, or the application of water to, any beneficial use." RCW 90.03.040.

This statute was needed in order to implement the prior appropriation doctrine. * * * [P]rior appropriation rights, by definition, do not require that the owner's land abut a stream or other water body. Where appropriative rights are concerned, there "need be no relationship between the source of the water and the locus of use." A. Dan Tarlock, Law of Water Rights and Resources § 5.24, at 5-41 (2000). Accordingly, there must be some means of delivering the appropriated water to the owner's land. The authority to condemn property for rights of way to transport water is thus an essential part of the prior appropriation scheme: "Access to water open to appropriation can generally be acquired by eminent domain. To prevent de facto riparianism, western states passed statutes permitting a water rights claimant to condemn the necessary rights of way to bring the water from the stream to the place of his use." Id. at 5-42.

The constitutionality of these statutes was originally at issue because the power of eminent domain was limited to public uses. Id. at 5-43. However, by the time RCW 90.03.040 was enacted the validity of such statutes was settled. In *Clark v. Nash,* 198 U.S. 361 * * * (1905), the Court upheld a Utah statute granting the right to condemn land for the purpose of conveying water in ditches across that land for irrigation of the condemnor's land alone. The Court observed that

> [w]here the use is asserted to be public, and the right of the individual to condemn land for the purpose of exercising such use is founded upon or is the result of some peculiar condition of the soil or climate, or other peculiarity of the State, where the right of condemnation is asserted under a state statute, we are always, where it can fairly be done, strongly inclined to hold with the state courts, when they uphold a state statute providing for such condemnation. The validity of

such statutes may sometimes depend upon many different facts, the existence of which would make a public use, even by an individual, where, in the absence of such facts, the use clearly be private.

Clark, 198 U.S. at 367-68 * * *. It is now settled that "[e]minent domain may be used to transport water so long as the use is beneficial; beneficial uses are presumed public uses." Tarlock, supra, § 5.24, at 5-42. * * *

In Galbraith v. Superior Court, 59 Wash. 621, 629, 110 P. 429 (1910), the court discussed this principle in the context of beneficial use of water. The court noted that article I, section 16, provides for eminent domain for certain private purposes, including ditches for agricultural purposes. * * * The court explained that the reclamation through irrigation of one small field by an individual promotes the development and adds to the taxable wealth of the state as well as reclamation by irrigation of large areas. Id. at 632, 110 P. 429.

> The benefit to the public which supports the exercise of the power of eminent domain for purposes of this character, is not public service, but is the development of the resources of the state, and the increase of its wealth generally, by which its citizens incidentally reap a benefit. Whether such development and increased wealth comes from the effort of a single individual, or the united efforts of many, in our opinion does not change the principal upon which this right of eminent domain rests.

Id. at 631, 110 P. 429 * * *. The same principle was discussed by the United States Supreme Court in *Clark,* quoted above. * * *

* * * "The Legislature can declare in the first instance that the purpose is a public one, and it remains the duty of the court to disregard such assertion if the court finds it to be unfounded." Id. A legislative declaration will be accorded great weight. Port of Seattle v. Isernio, 72 Wash.2d 932, 936, 435 P.2d 991 (1967) * * *.

We conclude that the Legislature's declaration that beneficial uses are public uses, coinciding with its choice of prior appropriation as the sole basis for acquisition of new water rights in this state in 1917, is entitled to deference. Our conclusion accords with the laws of other western states that provide that condemnation of any property or rights necessary to apply water to beneficial use is a condemnation for a public use.

— Public Use

Our discussion of the public use question sets the stage for discussion of the necessity question. RCW 90.03.040 provides that the right of eminent domain may be exercised by any person "to acquire any property ... *when found necessary for* ... the application of water to[ ] any beneficial use." (Emphasis added.) "The word 'necessary,' when used in or in connection with eminent domain statutes, means reasonable necessity, under the circumstances of the particular case." City of Tacoma v. Welcker, * * * 399 P.2d 330 (1965) * * *.

However, rather than determining whether the Hallauers established that a right of way across the Del Rosarios' land was necessary in order to put water from the spring to beneficial use, as RCW 90.03.040 directs, the Court of Appeals applied RCW 8.24.010. That court read RCW 8.24.010 as providing that an easement for transporting water may be condemned only where the land on which the water is to be used is landlocked. * * *

This analysis overlooks the fact that RCW 90.03.040 does more than declare that beneficial use of water is a public use. The statute also provides that any person can condemn a right of way to transport water where necessary to apply the water to beneficial use. * * * Thus, in marked contrast to RCW 8.24.010, RCW 90.03.040 does not require necessity based upon the landlocked nature of the condemnor's property, but expressly states the relevant necessity as "*necessary for* the storage of water for, or *the application of water to, any beneficial use.*" (Emphasis added.) * * * Because RCW 90.03.040 provides for condemnation of rights of way to transport water for application to beneficial use, the Del Rosarios and the Court of Appeals have mistakenly relied on cases involving private ways of necessity where necessity largely turned on the landlocked nature of the land of the party seeking condemnation. * * *

The necessity for the right of way is obvious. The water right that the Hallauers hold allows withdrawal of water from the spring on the Del Rosarios land. The only way in which the water can be conveyed to the Hallauers' property is over or through the Del Rosarios' land. Accordingly, the Court of Appeals' holding that necessity has not been established must be reversed. * * *

Notes

1. **Ditch rights.** A "ditch right" is a separate property interest from a water right. The acquisition of a water right does not automatically result in the acquisition of a right to transport the water across the lands of others. Often the two are linked, and, carrying out the intention of the parties, a conveyance of a ditch may carry with it the water right as an appurtenance, Williams v. Harter, 53 P. 405 (Cal. 1898), or the ditch may be regarded as an appurtenance of the water right and pass with a deed to the latter, Jacob v. Lorenz, 33 P. 119 (Cal. 1893). Often they are sufficiently separate that one can be sold independently of the other, or that abandonment of the water right does not bring the existence of the ditch right-of-way to an end. Ada County Farmers' Irr. Co. v. Farmers' Canal Co., 51 P. 990 (Idaho 1898).

2. **Acquisition of rights of way.** Rights of way for ditches can be acquired by purchase, or obtained by prescription where their existence

and use have been adverse to the servient estate for the relevant limitations period. Where oral permission has been given by the owner of the servient estate so that the use is not adverse, the water user may still have a permanent ditch right in the form of an "executed parol license" or a "license by estoppel." See Gustin v. Harting, 121 P. 522 (Wyo. 1912). The owner of an easement for a ditch has a secondary easement to enter and to inspect, repair, maintain or otherwise use the easement. O'Connor v. Brodie, 454 P.2d 920 (Mont. 1969).

3. **Rights of way on federal lands.** Rights of way for canals and ditches over the federal public domain were first authorized in 1866 and are now governed by section 501 of the Federal Land Policy and Management Act of 1976 (the "BLM Organic Act"). 43 U.S.C. § 1761. Rather elaborate procedures are required. Rights of way are limited to a reasonable term, are subject to an annual rental, and are highly regulated.

4. **Entry on another's land.** In Oregon, a person may enter another's land to locate a diversion point and survey ditch lines and reservoir sites. Or. Rev. Stat. § 537.320; see also Utah Code Ann. § 73-3-19.

5. **Modification of ditch rights of way.** As western cities expand over former farmlands, irrigation ditches following the contour of the country present problems to subdivision developers. Historically, the location of an easement cannot be changed by either the servient or the dominant owner without the other's consent. Stamatis v. Johnson, 224 P.2d 201 (Ariz. 1950), initially followed this rule, but on rehearing, the landowner was allowed to install a covered tile pipe on the original ditch right of way. 231 P.2d 956 (Ariz. 1951). In Roaring Fork Club, L.P. v. St. Jude's Co., 36 P.3d 1229 (Colo. 2001), the Colorado Supreme Court explicitly rejected the historic rule, adopting instead Restatement (Third) of Property (Servitudes) § 4.8. That rule allows the owner of the servient estate to move an easement provided that the owner of the dominant estate is not damaged. The court held, however, that the burdened owner cannot utilize self-help, but must seek court approval. In City of Boulder v. Farmer's Reservoir & Irrigation Co., 214 P.3d 563 (Colo. Ct. App. 2009), the court applied the rule to refuse to allow the city to reroute a public hiking trail through a culverted ditch.

Idaho Code § 42-1207 provides that the owner of the servient land "shall have the right" to move an irrigation ditch if it can be done without injury to the owner of the ditch, but a later clause requiring the "written permission of the owner" of the ditch seems to deprive the "right" of much utility. In Boz-Lew Builders v. Smith, 571 P.2d 389 (Mont. 1977), a developer filled in a ditch that had been used since 1866, and built an apartment over it. The developer was ordered to find a way to get the ditch water around or through his property and to pay damages.

SECTION 3. REGULATION

A. The Permit System

WYOMING HEREFORD RANCH v. HAMMOND PACKING CO.

Supreme Court of Wyoming, 1925.
33 Wyo. 14, 236 P. 764.

KIMBALL, J. This action involves rights to the use of the waters of Crow creek, a stream rising west of the city of Cheyenne, and flowing in a general easterly direction through that city and through lands owned by the Hammond Packing Company and the Wyoming Hereford Ranch. The plaintiff, the Wyoming Hereford Ranch, and the defendant the Hammond Packing Company are appropriators of the waters of said creek for the purpose of irrigation. * * *

In addition to its rights under [a] decree of 1888, the plaintiff claimed an appropriation through the Bolln ditch for the irrigation of about 200 acres. The decree of the district court upheld this claim and established the right as prior and superior to the rights of the defendant under its permits of 1909 and 1911 * * *. It is conceded that whatever right the plaintiff has to divert and use water through the Bolln ditch was acquired since the adoption of the Constitution and the enactment of the state water law of 1890. * * *

At the first session of the state Legislature, there was enacted a law approved December 22, 1890, "providing for the supervision and use of the waters of the state." * * *. Section 34 of that act provided, among other things, that any one thereafter intending to appropriate any of the public waters of the state should * * * make an application to the president of the board of control for a permit to make such appropriation. It requires that the application for a permit shall, among other things, state the source from which the appropriation is to be made, the amount of the appropriation, the location and character of the proposed works, and the time at which the application of water to beneficial purposes shall be made, which time is limited to the time required for the completion of the work when prosecuted with due diligence. If it is intended that the water should be used for irrigation, the application should describe the lands to be irrigated. * * * On receipt of the application, it is filed and recorded in the office of the state engineer, and if on investigation it is found that there is unappropriated water in the source of supply named in the application, and if the appropriation is not otherwise detrimental to the public welfare, the engineer shall approve the application. The application indorsed with such approval is then returned to the applicant, "who shall, on receipt thereof, be authorized to proceed with such work, and to take such measures as may be necessary to perfect such appropriation." It is further provided that—

> "If there is no unappropriated water in the source of supply, or if, in the judgment of the state engineer, such appropriation is detrimental to public interests, the state engineer shall refuse such appropriation, and the party making such application shall not prosecute such work, so long as such refusal shall continue in force."

There is provision for appeal from the action of the state engineer to the board of control and from the board to the courts. * * *

It is conceded as to the Bolln ditch that the plaintiff has never conformed to the provisions of this law, and we are required to decide whether, under the Constitution and the legislation of 1890, a lawful appropriation of waters can be made without a permit, and without an application therefor. The question is one of considerable importance and of some difficulty. Its solution requires a careful consideration of the foregoing provisions of the Constitution and statutes.

Directing our attention first to statute law of 1890, there would seem to be little need for construction or interpretation. * * * If an applicant for a permit has no right to divert waters until the application is approved, it surely was not intended that a person who has never made such application could legally divert and use the waters of the state. * * * It is argued, however, that section 3 of article 8 of the state Constitution, supra, requires a different construction, and that though a permit is necessary in order that the appropriator may have priority as of the date of filing the permit, an "appropriation" can still be made as under previous laws by diversion and use without a permit, with the only difference that such an appropriation will have priority only from the time of the application of the water to the beneficial use. The effect of the contention is that the statutes requiring a permit, if construed as preventing a diversion and use of the waters of the state without a permit, are unconstitutional.

The declaration of section 3, article 8, of the Constitution, that "priority of appropriation for beneficial uses shall give the better right," must be construed in connection with section 1 of the same article, declaring that the waters of all natural streams, etc., are the property of the state; section 2 providing that the board of control shall, under such regulations as may be prescribed by law, have the supervision of such waters and of their appropriation, distribution, and diversion, and the last sentence of section 3, that no appropriation shall be denied except when such denial is demanded by the public interest. * * *

In determining the meaning of a written law, it is proper to consider the evils sought to be remedied. The laws of the territory had permitted the diversion of water without any state supervision of the works and without any adequate notice and record of the amount, purpose, and date of the appropriation. Defective and badly located diversion works often made the use of water wasteful. No right became definite until it was adjudicated in court, and adjudications were often long delayed and then made on inaccurate testimony and without any disinterested measurements of the ditches or of the lands irrigated. Until such an adjudication, no subsequent appropriation could be made with safety, for no one could tell the amount of unappropriated water in the stream. The evils attendant on such a system, and the importance of providing a different system that would give the state the unquestioned right of control, had become well recognized at the time the Constitution was framed. * * * To correct these defects in the old system, it was provided by the Constitution not only that the waters of the state are the property of the state but also that those waters, and their appropriation, distribution, and diversion, shall be under the supervision of a state board of control. This supervision, it was hoped, would cure many of the evils of the old system, and we think that hope has been justified by the later events. The constitutional declaration that priority of appropriation for beneficial uses shall give the better right was not intended to prevent the Legislature from prescribing reasonable conditions that must be complied with before a lawful appropriation could be made. Their power in this respect is both recognized and limited by the further provision of the Constitution, carried into the statutes, that "no appropriation shall be denied except when such denial is demanded by the public interests." In interpreting this language, we must give consideration to the contemporaneous recognition not only of the importance of state supervision of the diversion of waters, but also of the fact that such supervision could not be effective, nor intelligently exercised, without accurate and complete information of proposed appropriations. The Legislature has decided that the public interests demand that such information shall be given to the state board by an application for a permit, and that until such an application is approved, no appropriation can be lawfully made. We believe these requirements are reasonable in so far at least as they are questioned in this case. * * *

A different decision would leave prevalent many of the acknowledged evils of the territorial system intended to be superseded by the system of state control contemplated by the Constitution and carried into effect by the law of 1890. The plaintiff is willing in this case to concede that its right under the Bolln ditch would take priority only from the date of the application of the water to the land. Another claimant of a similar right might not be willing to make that concession. If a right may be lawfully acquired by diversion and use since 1890 without compliance with the state laws, it might be impossible to

[handwritten note at bottom] so appropriation by diversion is not superior to a permit right

find a sufficient reason for holding that the right would not have priority as of the date of commencement of the work. If that condition should prevail, there would seem to be no advantage to be gained by proceeding under a permit, and we would be thrown back to the confusion incident to the haphazard methods of the old system. * * *

It follows that the part of the decree which gives the plaintiff a priority for use of water through the Bolln ditch cannot be upheld.

Notes

1. **Early procedures.** In the early history of appropriation law, the word "appropriation" was used in its crudest sense—as a taking of possession—and a legal right flowed from the physical acts of constructing a ditch, diverting the water and applying it to use. Nevertheless, a need was felt by the appropriators for improving their legal position, and following the common procedure of staking a mining claim, the custom arose of posting a notice of claim upon the bank of the stream near the point of diversion. The courts recognized such a notice as evidence of the possessory right to the water. Thompson v. Lee, 8 Cal. 275 (1857). Later these procedures were codified in a number of states by statutes which required the posting of a more elaborate notice and its recordation in the county where posted. These systems were optional. A failure to comply did not affect the validity of the rights acquired by diversion and application to beneficial use, though it did affect the date of priority. If an appropriator did not post and file a notice, his priority dated from the time of completion of the appropriation, but if he did, his priority related back to the start of work. Once the application to beneficial use was made, an unfiled appropriation was a complete and vested right, and took precedence over any subsequently initiated appropriations.

The defects in this system are obvious. "Claims are filed in the different counties, and as Montana rivers are long, the water-right records of a single stream are often found in several counties. Musselshell River forms a part of the boundary between Fergus and Meagher, Yellowstone, Dawson, and Custer counties. Ditches on one side of the stream are recorded in one county, and ditches on the other side of the river in another county. It would require a journey of several hundred miles and an examination of five sets of county records to ascertain the extent of the claims to this stream." Elwood Mead, Irrigation Institutions 301 (1903).

2. **Adoption of the permit system.** The permit system of initiating appropriations is now found in all of the states recognizing the appropriation doctrine except Colorado. It is the exclusive method in each state.

3. **Exceptions.** Some statutes contain express exceptions to the requirement of a permit for certain classes of small appropriations or appropriations from some sources. See Cal. Water Code §§ 1228-1229.1; S.D. Codified Laws § 46-5-8; Tex. Water Code Ann. §§ 11.142, 11.143.

4. **Procedures.** The procedures for obtaining a permit are not identical in all states. A person seeking a water right must carefully check

and follow the practice of the particular state. Typical steps include: (1) application to the designated agency or official, accompanied by required supporting documents such as maps and engineering plans, (2) publication of notice of the application and, in some states, notice to designated officials or agencies, such as the Department of Fish and Game, (3) acceptance of protests from interested parties, (4) internal agency processing, including an environmental assessment if required, (5) hearing, if protests have been filed or if the agency has made a preliminary decision to deny or condition the application, (6) issuance or denial of a permit, (7) construction of necessary facilities and application of water to beneficial use, and (8) issuance of a "certificate of appropriation" or other document confirming that the appropriation has been completed.

5. **Stored water.** Several states have a dual permit system for stored irrigation waters. The person intending to impound the waters must apply for a "primary permit" to construct the reservoir; the person intending to use the water on particular land can or must apply for a "secondary permit." E.g., Ariz. Rev. Stat. § 45-151.

6. **Colorado procedures.** Since the Colorado Constitution declares, "[t]he right to divert the unappropriated waters of any natural stream to beneficial uses shall never be denied" (art. XVI, § 6), it has generally been assumed that a permit system is unavailable in that state. Colorado was the first state to create the office of State Engineer, but the engineer's duties are confined to regulating the works of appropriators and distributing water according to decrees entered by courts in proceedings to adjudicate all rights to a stream or segment of a stream.

The Water Right Determination and Adjudication Act of 1969 carves the state into seven water divisions, each covering a major river basin. Colo. Rev. Stat. § 37-92-201. One district judge in the division is designated a "water judge." He is assisted by a "water clerk" who is in charge of all records of water matters and by such "water referees" as may be necessary. §§ 37-92-203, 37-92-204. Since amended in several procedural details, the act in effect makes each water court an administrative agency with complete records of and supervision over newly initiated and incomplete water rights ("conditional rights"). In effect, the act also creates a perpetual suit of adjudication in each water division.

"Any person who desires a determination of a water right or a conditional water right and the amount and priority thereof, including a determination that a conditional water right has become a water right by reason of the completion of the appropriation, * * * [or] finding of reasonable diligence * * * shall file with the water clerk a verified application setting forth facts supporting the ruling sought * * *." § 37-92-302(1)(a). The application must contain a detailed description of the right sought. Elaborate provisions for notice, protests of applications and investigations and rulings by the referee are set out. Twice a year the water judge holds hearings on protests to referees' rulings and orders referred to him by the referee, and enters a judgment and decree embodying his rulings on all cases before him. §§ 37-92-303, 37-92-304. A finding of reasonable diligence is required every sixth year for rights which have not become absolute, i.e., by finally using water beneficially. § 37-92-301(4).

An application for a conditional right functions like an application for a permit in other appropriation states; likewise the conditional right, if granted, functions like a permit. A conditional right holder must complete the appropriation with reasonable diligence to retain its priority, and, as noted above, in the interim, must obtain periodic findings of diligence. When the water has finally been put to beneficial use, an absolute right is sought from the water court; if granted, the absolute right functions like a certificate of appropriation. While theoretically an appropriation can be made without following this process, it can never receive an enforceable priority. Although the relative priorities of all water rights or conditional water rights applied for during a calendar year are determined, all of them must be decreed to be junior to all water rights granted in previous years. § 37-92-306.

B. Availability of Water

LOWER COLORADO RIVER AUTHORITY v. TEXAS DEPARTMENT OF WATER RESOURCES
Supreme Court of Texas, 1984.
689 S.W.2d 873.

KILGARLIN, JUSTICE. We reverse the judgments of the courts below because those courts have misconstrued and misapplied Tex. Water Code Ann. § 11.134. We hold that the term "unappropriated water" means the amount of water remaining after taking into account all existing uncancelled permits and filings valued at their recorded levels.

The Water District applied for a permit to impound over 500,000 acre-feet of water from the Colorado River at the Stacy Dam site southeast of Ballinger, Texas. * * *

The right to impound water had to be obtained by the Water District, through a Department permit. Tex. Water Code Ann. § 11.121. To acquire a permit, the Water District had to satisfy the statutory grounds of Tex. Water Code Ann. § 11.134(b)(2) & (3):

Action on Application * * *

(b) The commission shall grant the application only if: * * *

(2) unappropriated water is available in the source of supply; and

(3) the proposed appropriation: * * *

    (B) does not impair existing water rights or vested riparian rights; and

    (C) is not detrimental to the public welfare.

The Colorado River waters are presently charged with four types of outstanding water rights. There are vested riparian rights, certified filings, permits to appropriate water, and certificates of adjudication. The Colorado is an inconstant stream. There is insufficient water to satisfy the existing rights during drought, but the water supply is capable of supplying additional users during times of abundant rain.

The Department developed a sophisticated computerized model of the seasonally varying inflow to the Colorado at various points along the river. One goal of the computer model was to allow the staff to obtain a reasonably accurate scientific estimate whether there was "unappropriated water" at points along the river, at least during some seasons or months.

The computer model assumed that all existing recorded water rights in the Colorado River basin would be exercised in the maximum amounts authorized, or to the extent of water available from the inflows. The staff study concluded that "very little water would be available for appropriation at the proposed reservoir site. * * * The estimated firm yield of the reservoir for these quantities of appropriable water is 3,120 acre-feet per year * * *." * * *

The Water District rebutted the staff conclusion by expert studies and testimony. The studies used the hydrologic data from the staff report but discounted the recorded filings in a number of ways. As to certified filings, the experts presented historical use data to demonstrate that the maximum amount claimed under the filings had never in fact been used, and that some claims necessarily had not been "perfected." As to riparian rights, many of the riparian claims were invalid because they were based on Spanish and Mexican land grants that did not include riparian rights. Finally, experts testified that demographic projections and historical use data indicated that the full amounts authorized under uncancelled permits would not be used. By subtracting the estimated amounts that would not be used from the recorded filings, the Water District's expert witnesses concluded there was sufficient water available for the proposed Stacy Reservoir. Similarly, they concluded that downstream rights would not be impaired if occasional flow-throughs were allowed.

The Commission made finding 15 that there was "unappropriated water" within the meaning of section 11.134(b)(2).

　　　* * *

The undisputed evidence in this record is that existing uncancelled permits and filings, valued at their recorded levels, leave an insufficient supply of "unappropriated water for Stacy Dam." Sections 11.134(b)(2) & (3) are unambiguous in their statements that the Commission shall grant applications for new water rights only if there is available unappropriated water and the new appropriation does not impair existing water rights or vested riparian rights. Additionally, granting additional permits cannot be detrimental to public welfare. Basically, our decision is that the article prohibits "double permitting" or the stacking of appropriated waters on appropriated waters. * * *

Section 11.134(b)(2) finds its source in section 19 of the 1913 Act and its reenactment in section 24 of the 1917 Act. Representative D.W. Glasscock, a principal author of the 1913 Act, stated that the purpose of the 1913 Act was to prevent overappropriation of rivers and thus to insure the stability necessary to attract development capital. An initial purpose of the permit system has been to insure as much as possible that the water granted in a permit would be available when the project was completed. Section 11.146(e), by providing that water granted under *any* permit is not again subject to a new permit to appropriate until the permit has been canceled in whole or in part, is consistent with the overall legislative purpose.

* * * The court of appeals rationalized that the statement in Motl v. Boyd, 116 Tex. 82, 286 S.W. 458 (1926), that the Board of Water Engineers would merely consult their records to determine the amount of existing appropriations, was not contrary to its holding in this case. "Records," to the court of appeals, included the required annual reports which showed how much water the permittee actually used. The court of appeals reasoned that in consulting its records, to determine whether there existed "unappropriated water," the Board would consider how much of the recorded appropriation was going unused. That rationalization is directly contrary to the legislature's purpose. According to the 1953 Act, even if the records under the existing permit indicated the appropriator had not used any water at all for the last 10 years, it was still necessary to cancel the unused permit before the water covered by it would again be subject to a new appropriation. * * *

The majority of the court of appeals reasoned, through a series of rhetorical questions, that the term, "unappropriated water," included unused waters that were subject to existing permits. The court reasoned that any other construction would mean the Commission and its predecessor agencies had shirked their statutory duty by allowing Texas rivers to become overappropriated. There can be no doubt that the prevention of overappropriation was a principal goal of the legislative scheme. * * * The fact that some rivers are overappropriated does not mean the state's water agencies have failed in their duty. Because of changing circumstances, the vagaries of nature or the possibility of erroneous assumptions about the inflow amounts to the rivers, overappropriation may exist. These circumstances may make any river overappropriated, particularly during a drought period, and thus there can be no substitute for enforcement. The Texas statutes protect senior water rights from actual impairment. No matter how many permits the Commission issues, the action is purely administrative, and it cannot divest or impair prior rights.

Conclusion

Under the law, the Department may not grant permits when its own records show that the supply must come from an existing downstream permittee's water that the Department speculates he will not actually need. Section 11.025 places a limit on the amount of water that can be used beneficially or the amount the senior holders can claim, even though the face amount of their permits may be more. Among other things, that limitation serves to distribute the water appropriately when there is a drought. It does not mean the Department may intentionally overappropriate. A contrary decision would return water rights to the state of chaos that the act is designed to avoid. For example, upstream junior permit holders whose grants depended upon an overappropriation of the stream would suffer the most from deprivation of water in times of drought. The water source they had come to rely upon would be denied them. * * *

We reverse the judgments of the courts below and set aside the permit granted by the Texas Department of Water Resources to the Colorado River Municipal Water District. * * *

RAY, JUSTICE, concurring.

I agree with the court's conclusion that "unappropriated water" must not include water already granted under an existing, uncancelled permit. I do not agree with the court's disposition of setting aside the Commission's order. I would remand the case to the Commission for further proceedings in accordance with the opinion.

* * * The Commission's error was applying the wrong definition of "unappropriated water." This court had not previously expressly addressed the question. Had the water district presented its application under the proper standard, it could have simultaneously sought partial or total cancellations of unused water rights under existing certified filings and permits. Although the district can now file a new application using the proper definition, that action would not be a complete remedy. Both the priority of an appropriation and the claimant's right to use the water date from the filing of the *application* with the Department. Tex. Water Code Ann. § 11.141 (Supp. 1984). Since the misconception of the law caused the Commission to commit error, I believe it is appropriate to preserve the district's priority by remanding to the Commission for proper proceedings under the correct legal standard.

Opinion on Motion for Rehearing

KILGARLIN, JUSTICE.

* * * Because an examination of authorities on the issue demonstrates that a remand is more appropriate than a reversal and rendition, we reverse the judgments of the courts below and remand the cause to the Texas Department of Water Resources pursuant to our power under the Administrative Procedure and Texas Register Act, Tex.Rev.Civ.Stat.Ann. art. 6252-13a, § 19(e)(4) (Vernon Supp.1984). * * *

Notes

1. **Other states.** Statutes in a number of western states express criteria similar to those in Tex. Water Code Ann. § 11.134(b). See, e.g., Neb. Rev. Stat. § 46-235; Wyo. Stat. Ann. § 41-4-503.

2. **Determining if unappropriated water exists.** In Central Platte Natural Resources District v. Wyoming, 513 N.W.2d 847 (Neb. 1994), the director of the Department of Water Resources used the "historic flows" method to find unappropriated water available for a proposed instream appropriation. This method, which used actual flow records from gauging stations along the river, was similar to the method which the court rejected in the principal case. An opponent of the proposed appropriations, the State of Wyoming, challenged the finding, arguing that the director should have used a method which assumed that all existing rights would be fully exercised, similar to the method adopted by the court in the principal case. In concluding that the "historic flows" method was permissible the Nebraska court said:

"The beneficial use requirement limits the amount of water which the holder can actually appropriate. For example, if a landowner had an appropriation right to use 10 cfs for irrigation purposes, and if the landowner needed only 5 cfs in a given month, then the landowner would not be entitled to capture and sell the other 5 cfs. An appropriation right extends only as far as the beneficial use requirement will allow.

"It thus appears that an appropriation right can be measured in two ways. First, the right can be measured with reference to the appropriation limit. This is a fixed and theoretical limit—the most water that a particular holder is authorized to use. Second, the right can be measured with reference to the beneficial use limit. This is a fluctuating and practical limit—the amount of water that a particular holder is entitled to use at any given time.

"We find that the phrase 'subject to an existing appropriation right' refers to the appropriation right measured by the beneficial use limit. That is, when the director considers an instream flow application, the director must find that there is enough water that is not subject to another appropriator's beneficial use. The question then becomes how the director is to measure the water that is not subject to another appropriator's beneficial use.

"We find that the historic flow method is a permissible way of measuring the beneficial use limit. As explained above, the beneficial use limit fluctuates with the appropriators' needs. The appropriators' needs fluctuate with external factors. The most important external factor is the weather; in a dry year, the holders' need to divert water for irrigation increases dramatically. The historic flow method lends perspective to the fluctuations because the data is collected over a span of years. * * * In short, the amount of water that is actually in the river is a rough approximation of the amount of water not needed for beneficial use elsewhere. Accord Temescal Water Co. v. Dep't of Pub. Works, 44 Cal.2d 90, 280 P.2d 1 (1955) (stating that the amount of unappropriated water will depend on the stream's flow, the rainfall, and the nonuse of existing rights)." Id. at 855; accord *In re* Application for Water Rights of the Bd. of County Comm'rs, 891 P.2d 952 (Colo. 1995).

3. **Purpose of the rule.** Stream flow and water demand variability makes it likely that there will occasionally be unused flows even on the most heavily appropriated stream. Is it thus good policy to reject an appropriation because there is no unappropriated water? Consider the following from *In re* Hitchcock & Red Willow Irrigation District, 410 N.W.2d 101, 108 (Neb. 1987):

"'The Commission is charged with securing the maximum beneficial use and control of the state's water resources. Because streamflows vary greatly from year to year, disallowing further permits once the reliable flow had been appropriated would result in nonuse of the excess water available in years of greater than average water supply. It is the Commission's position that the maximum beneficial use of waters of the state is achieved by issuing a permit to anyone who is willing to attempt appropriation and use of whatever unappropriated water may become available, except where a basin program identifies a need to set aside some amount of unappropriated water for particular future uses.'" Benz v. Water Res. Comm'n, 764 P.2d 594, 599 (Or. 1988) (quoting with approval a decision of the Oregon Water Resources Commission * * *).

"While it is true that some unappropriated water is present during times of high flow at the proposed diversion point, to be available in a practical sense the supply of water must be fairly continuous and dependable. The director concluded that based on historical flow records, the appellants would not be able to withdraw any water in a number of years, sometimes consecutive. * * * Although appellants do not quarrel with that factual finding, it is their argument that the director is not entitled, as a matter of law to base his refusal to allow the application on the unlikelihood of success of the irrigation project.

"As early as 1910 in Young & Norton et al. v. Hinderlider, * * * 110 P. 1045 (1910), the New Mexico court held that it was proper to refuse an appropriation of water for a project which appeared doomed to failure." [*Hinderlider* is set out infra p. 135.]

4. **Frequency of unappropriated flows.** The principal case deals with the demand side of the equation. The supply side must also be considered, including the great fluctuations in the western stream flows. On

remand, which flows should the Texas Department of Water Resources use to calculate whether unappropriated water is available: a drought year? an "average" year? a high-flow year? How frequently must water be available before the agency can find unappropriated water?

"A showing of reasonable availability does not require a demonstration that water will always be available to the full extent applied for in the decree. The applicant need only prove * * * a substantial probability that the appropriation can and will be completed, based upon necessarily imperfect predictions of future conditions. This approach to obtaining a conditional water right decree promotes the development and maximum utilization of Colorado's scarce water resources." Aspen Wilderness Workshop, Inc. v. Hines Highlands L.P., 929 P.2d 718, 724 (Colo. 1996).

In *Hitchcock & Red Willow*, supra p. 132, Note 3, the Nebraska Supreme Court stated that the supply must be "fairly continuous and dependable." In *Central Platte Natural Resources District*, supra p. 131, Note 2 at 859, it said:

"A determination regarding water availability cannot and should not be divorced from the applicant's purpose. There are two ways in which the applicant's purpose affects the 'fairly continuous and dependable' standard.

"First, the nature of a fairly continuous and dependable flow may change depending upon the nature of the application. An application to divert water is not the same as an application for instream flows; an irrigation project is not the same as a habitat project. If an irrigation project fails because insufficient water was available, then there is a loss on the investment and a loss to any junior downstream appropriators who could have used the diverted water. In contrast, if a habitat project fails, then there is minimal, if any, loss of investment, and there is no loss to junior downstream appropriators, because the water was never removed from the stream.

"Second, in the context of instream flow applications, the threshold of a fairly dependable and continuous flow may change depending on the specific goals of the application. A wildlife project is not the same as a recreation project.

"In the context of an instream flow application to maintain existing wildlife habitats, we hold that 'fairly continuous and dependable' means the flow regime which the species can bear. Put another way, there is sufficient water available under § 46-2,115(1) when there is enough water to maintain the wildlife habitat sought by an applicant."

5. **Unadjudicated rights.** Unadjudicated claims to water exist in many states. An important example involves Indian and federal reserved rights. In several states there are also significant numbers of unadjudicated appropriative claims which pre-date the adoption of mandatory permit systems. (Adjudication of water rights is discussed in the next section. Indian and federal reserved rights are examined in Chapter 8, Section 3.) The validity and the quantity of unadjudicated claims is often in

question. How should such claims affect decisions on whether water is available for new appropriations? In Montana, which had statutory criteria similar to those in the principal case, the state Supreme Court held that no permits for new appropriations could be issued until Indian reserved rights claims have been adjudicated. *In re* Application for Beneficial Water Use Permit No. 66459-76L, 923 P.2d 1073 (Mont. 1995).

The Montana legislature quickly amended the appropriation statute to reverse the decision, which threatened to completely stop permits for new appropriations in Montana. A showing that "unappropriated waters" are available is no longer required. Instead an applicant is required to show that water for the proposed appropriation is "physically available" and "can reasonably be considered legally available." Mont. Code. Ann. § 85-2-311(1)(a). To further clarify, the preceding statute states that "[a] permit may be issued * * * prior to the adjudication of existing water rights in a source of supply." A companion statute specifies, however, that all permits issued prior to a final determination of existing water rights are only provisional and are subject to being reduced, modified, or revoked if necessary to protect adjudicated senior rights. § 85-2-313.

Shortly after the legislature adopted the amendment, the Montana Department of Natural Resources and Conservation announced its intent to issue new appropriation permits on the Flathead Reservation although the reserved rights associated with the reservation had not been adjudicated. In Confederated Salish & Kootenai Tribes v. Clinch, 992 P.2d 244 (Mont. 1999), the Montana Supreme Court enjoined the Department from issuing permits on the Flathead Reservation until the tribes' reserved rights are adjudicated, despite the legislative directive that permits can be issued prior to adjudication. The court noted that the term "legally available" in the amended statute is not defined and concluded that it should adopt a construction which would not render the section unconstitutional. The court reasoned that the issuance of permits on the reservation for the use of water which may belong to the tribes would violate Article IX, Section 3(1) of the Montana Constitution, which protects existing water rights whether adjudicated or unadjudicated. Thus, the court concluded that water is "legally available" only if it has not been reserved for the reservation, which, the court held, cannot be determined until the tribes' reserved rights are adjudicated and quantified.

After adjudication and quantification, the tribes' reserved rights may remain unexercised for years. How should such rights be accounted for in determining if water is "legally available" for appropriation? In adopting the amendments to the appropriation statutes referred to above, the legislature observed: "Because water is a resource that is subject to use and reuse, such as through return flows, and because at most times all water rights on a source will not be exercised to their full extent simultaneously, it is recognized that an adjudication is not a water availability study. Consequently, the legislature has provided an administrative forum for the factual investigation into whether water is available for new uses and changes both before and after the completion of an adjudication in the source of supply." Mont. Code Ann. § 85-2-101 (5). This observation seemingly indicates that the Department of Natural Resources and Conservation should investigate actual uses of water and apply its administrative expertise in determining whether water is available for appropriation. Nevertheless, *Confederated Tribes* implies that water required to satisfy Indian reserved rights is not "legally available" even if the Indians are not actually using the water and it appears the Indians may not use it for the foreseeable future. In other words, in the court's view, the Department cannot make the prescribed investigation, but must treat Indian water rights as fully exercised even if that is not actually the case. It is unclear whether this treatment is confined to Indian water rights. See infra pp. 700-01, Note 6, for other aspects of *Confederated Tribes*.

6. **Closing streams to further appropriations.** Are there valid administrative reasons for prohibiting additional appropriations when a stream is substantially overappropriated? Is it desirable to expend administrative effort to process applications if there is little likelihood that water will ever be put to use? Should records be cluttered up with appropriations which will seldom, if ever, be exercised? Are enforcement problems exacerbated by creating additional rights to an already inadequate supply? Consider Cal. Water Code §§ 1205-1207. These statutes authorize the Water Resources Control Board to declare streams fully appropriated and close them to further appropriation. The Board has declared some streams fully appropriated year-round and others only during specified months. The effect of the latter declaration is to require new appropriators to construct storage reservoirs.

In Postema v. Pollution Control Hearings Bd., 11 P.3d 726 (Wash. 2000), the court upheld the authority of the Washington Department of Ecology to close steams to further appropriation, despite the lack of explicit statutory authority. The court cited several provisions giving the Department authority to promulgate rules for the administration of water rights and protection of the environment. The court said: "Stream closures by rule embody Ecology's determination that water is not available for further appropriations." Id. at 742.

C. Public Interest

YOUNG & NORTON v. HINDERLIDER
Supreme Court of the Territory of New Mexico, 1910.
15 N.M. 666, 110 P. 1045.

On the 1st day of October, 1907, M.C. Hinderlider filed with the territorial engineer an application for a permit to appropriate 200 second feet of the flow of the La Plata river in San Juan county, N.M., and for the construction of a storage reservoir with a storage capacity of 12,406 acre feet for the purpose of reclaiming and irrigating about 14,000 acres of land in said county. On December 20, 1907, Messrs. Young & Norton for themselves and others filed with the territorial engineer an application for a permit to appropriate the waters of the same stream in the same county and territory, for the purpose of reclaiming and irrigating about 5,000 acres of land, being a part of the same land covered by the Hinderlider project. This last application included the construction of a storage reservoir with a storage capacity of 10,149 acre feet for the purpose of storing the flood waters of the said river and applying the same to the reclamation of the said 5,000 acres of land. After the publication of the notice required by law and on the 19th day of March, 1908, the said Young, Norton, and others filed with the territorial engineer a protest against the approval of the said Hinderlider application. That after a hearing before the territorial engineer and on July 20, 1908, he rendered an opinion sustaining said protest rejecting the Hinderlider application and approving the application of the protestants. * * *

[The Territorial Engineer found that Hinderlider's filing covered much public land as well as the private land owned by protestants, that his project would cost $40 per acre; that Young and Norton and others they represent are settled on about 5,500 acres of land, their project is for the irrigation of the settled land, and would cost about $20 per acre; that there was water available for about 5,000 to 6,000 acres, that either applicant could and would complete his appropriation, but that Young and Norton's project was more within the water supply. Hinderlider appealed to the Board of Water Commissioners, which ruled that the power of the Engineer to reject an application as contrary to the public interest is limited to cases in which the project would be a menace to the public health and safety, and ordered Hinderlider's application approved. The District Court affirmed, and Young and Norton appealed.]

ABBOTT, J. We think the decision of the district court was justified and probably required by the statement of facts on which it was heard; but we find that statement very incomplete and unsatisfactory as the basis of a decision in such a cause. If it were a matter of private interest alone, a question simply between two rival applicants for the right to use the waters in question, we should content ourselves with affirming the decision of the district court. But the question is much broader than that, and includes the public interest as well, by the terms of the statute under which the territorial engineer, the water commissioners, and the courts have jurisdiction of the subject-matter.

The view apparently adopted by the water commissioners in their decision that the power of the territorial engineer to reject an application, "if in his opinion the approval thereof would be contrary to the public interest" (section 28), is limited to cases in which the project would be a menace to the public health or safety is we think, not broad enough. There is no such limitation expressed in terms of the statute, and we think not by implication. The declaration in the first section of

[handwritten top margin: the amount of water must be sufficient to meet the need of the project]

[handwritten right margin: Stat.]

the statute that the waters therein described are "public waters," and the fact that the entire statute is designed to secure the greatest possible benefit from them for the public, should be borne in mind. It is, for instance, obviously for the public interest that investors should be protected against making worthless investments in New Mexico, and especially that they should not be led to make them through official approval of unsound enterprises. If there is available unappropriated water of the La Plata river for only 5,000 or 6,000 acres of land, it would be contrary to the public interest that a project for irrigating 14,000 acres with that water should receive an official approval which would, perhaps, enable the promoters of it to market their scheme, to sell stock reasonably sure to become worthless, and land which could not be irrigated, at the price of irrigated land. Such a proceeding would in the end result only in warning capital away from the territory. The failure of any irrigation project carries with it not only disastrous consequences to its owners and to the farmers who are depending on it, but besides tends to destroy faith in irrigation enterprises generally.

It may be said that the territorial engineer could have approved the Hinderlider project for the number of acres which could be irrigated from it. He makes it clear, however, from his report, that the cost of the works for that project would be much greater than for works fit to irrigate the land which could really be irrigated from the available water there. While that element is not conclusive on the question of public interest, we think it should be taken into account. It may be that, of the 5,000 or 6,000 acres there which it is claimed can be irrigated at an expense of $10 or $12 per acre under the Young-Norton project, a thousand acres could be irrigated at $5 per acre because of its being at a lower level or nearer the water than the other land. But that would not justify refusing the owners of the other 4,000 or 5,000 acres the privilege of irrigating their lands, under a plan which would increase the cost of irrigation to the owners of the thousand acres. And the same may be said of the Hinderlider project as compared with the Young-Norton project. The mere fact that irrigation under the former project would cost more per acre than under the latter is not conclusive that the former project should be rejected. But the attempt to cover too much land may have gone so far that the cost of irrigation under that project would be so excessive that the owners of land under the project could not pay the water rates and farm their lands at a profit. The statute provides that the charges for irrigation shall be "reasonable;" but what is reasonable in any case must depend largely on the cost of constructing and operating the irrigation works.

* * * The territorial engineer finds that the Young-Norton project is "better within the available water supply." But that furnished no reason why he should not have approved the earlier project for the

amount of land there is water for. He does not find that the cost of water under the Hinderlider project would be prohibitory or excessive, but only that it would be considerably greater per acre than under the Young-Norton project. The price which the owners of land can afford to pay for irrigation must depend in part on the use to which it can be put.

For ordinary farm crops $40 per acre for water might be prohibitory, while for fruit or garden truck in certain localities it might not be excessive. But neither the territorial engineer nor the water commissioners have touched on that point in their reports. The territorial engineer apparently bases his approval of the latter project as against the former on the fact that Young and Norton and their associates are actual settlers on the land, while Hinderlider is not a resident of the territory. We do not say this circumstance should have no weight in determining the question of the public interest, but we think it should not outweigh the other considerations to which we have referred.

On the other hand, the water commissioners find that there is available unappropriated flood water of the La Plata river, but do not find whether there is enough for 14,000 or any other number of acres, nor whether the cost of the Hinderlider project would be such as necessarily to make the irrigation charges under it prohibitory or excessive. * * *

The cause is therefore remanded to the district court to obtain facts through the water commissioners and territorial engineer, or by agreement of counsel, or otherwise, essential to a satisfactory decision of the cause. * * *

Notes

1. **Extent of public interest review.** Among appropriation states, only Colorado and Oklahoma do not require some form of public interest review of new appropriations. The statute in *Hinderlider* typifies older statutes which provide little guidance to administrators. At the other extreme is an Alaska statute which lists eight specific criteria: (1) the benefit to the applicant resulting from the proposed appropriation; (2) the effect of the economic activity resulting from the proposed appropriation; (3) the effect on fish and game resources and on public recreational opportunities; (4) the effect on public health; (5) the effect of loss of alternate uses of water that might be made within a reasonable time if not precluded or hindered by the proposed appropriation; (6) harm to other persons resulting from the proposed appropriation; (7) the intent and ability of the applicant to complete the appropriation; and (8) the effect upon access to navigable or public waters. Alaska Stat. § 46.15.080(b). Between these two extremes are states like California which do not define public interest comprehensively, but do provide substantial guidance. See Cal. Water Code §§ 1243, 1243.5, 1254, 1256-1259.

2. **Purpose of public interest review.** Douglas L. Grant, Public Interest Review of Water Right Allocation and Transfer in the West: Recognition of Public Values, 19 Ariz. St. L.J. 681, 702 (1987):

"In modern society, administrative agencies regulate diverse economic activities. Such regulation typically is predicated on a failure of market forces to deal adequately with particular structural problems. The problems vary with the economic activity regulated. With water resources use, the key problem is externalities. An externality exists when a person's water use affects others, negatively or positively, but the user does not consider those effects in deciding whether to engage in the use. In other words, some of the costs or benefits of the water use activity are external to the user's calculations in deciding whether to make the use. The difficulty with externalities is that they tend to cause resource misallocation. For example, suppose a farmer's diversion of water to irrigate sugar beets reduces opportunities for water-based recreation some distance downstream. The loss of downstream recreation is a cost of the farmer's water use. Suppose further that the law does not require the farmer to take that cost into account in deciding whether to irrigate. From a societal viewpoint, the result may be the use of too much water to produce sugar beets and too little water for downstream recreation use."

For a follow-up survey, and an argument that legislatures need to revisit their public interest statutes, see Douglas L. Grant, Two Models of Public Interest Review of Water Allocation in the West, 9 U. Denv. Water L. Rev. 485 (2006).

3. **Benefit-cost analysis.** In 1973 the State of Washington added an express benefit-cost formula to its statutes: "Allocation of waters among potential uses and users shall be based generally on the securing of the maximum net benefits for the people of the state. Maximum net benefits shall constitute total benefits less costs including opportunities lost." Wash. Rev. Code § 90.54.020(2).

4. **Opportunity costs.** "Opportunity costs" is the economists' term for benefits foregone when one alternative development is chosen rather than another. How concrete should the foregone alternative be if the loss of its benefits is to be considered "opportunity costs"? Consider Tanner v. Bacon, 136 P.2d 957, 964-65 (Utah 1943) (Wolfe, Chief Justice, concurring):

"I assume that the State Engineer could not reject an application on the ground that if approved it would 'prove detrimental to the public welfare' because in his mind he conceived some ultimate or remote public project which would need the water. A farsighted person with imagination and bold conceptions may visualize projects which in the future may be most beneficial to the state. * * * I do not conceive that ideal conceptions for future and better public use of water in the State Engineer's head can be the basis for refusing to approve an application."

5. **Effect of investment in physical works.** Why should a water administrator be concerned with possible future use of water at all? After

all, water in a stream or river is a "flow" resource, not a "stock" resource. Current use does not diminish future availability. Because no future benefits are foregone when a present use is made of water, is it not correct to say that a potential future use cannot be an opportunity cost of a present use? Indeed, should not the law encourage any present use of water so long as present benefits exceed present costs—a present use precludes no future benefits while the benefits lost when a present use is foregone can never be recovered? Except for contemporaneous competing projects or uses, are "opportunity costs" even relevant to flowing water? Consider Edgar S. Bagley, Some Economic Considerations in Water Use Policy, 5 Kan. L. Rev. 499, 510 (1957):

"[W]ater projects often involve large * * * investments in permanent or semi-permanent works. Decisions to undertake such works have a * * * physical inflexibility and irrevocability which underlines the importance of careful, long-range planning, regardless of the system of water rights in effect and whether * * * development is public or private."

6. **Beneficial use and public interest.** To what extent might the requirement of "beneficial use" substitute for a public interest standard? Is an appropriation which is not in the "public interest" a beneficial use of water? Colorado does not provide for "public interest" review of applications for appropriation of water. In *In re* Application for Water Rights of the Board of County Commissioners, 891 P.2d 952 (Colo. 1995), the Colorado Supreme Court refused to hold that a proposed appropriation was not a "beneficial use" of water because of its adverse effects on the environment, on recreation, and on similar values.

"Conceptually, a public interest theory is in conflict with the doctrine of prior appropriation because a water court cannot, in the absence of statutory authority, deny a legitimate appropriation based on pubic policy." Id. at 972, 973.

Compare the Justice McFadden's dissent in *Idaho*, supra p. 28.

SHOKAL v. DUNN
Supreme Court of Idaho, 1985.
109 Idaho 330, 707 P.2d 441.

[Dunn, the director of the Idaho Department of Water Resources, issued a permit to Trout Co. for an appropriation from Billingsley Creek for fish propagation and hydropower generation. Shokal and others who had protested the issuance of the permit appealed the decision to the district court. Judge Schroeder reversed and remanded Dunn's decision, finding the Department of Water Resources consideration of two issues inadequate: (1) The financial ability of the applicant to complete the project, and (2) the local public interest with respect to the project. On remand, Dunn again approved the permit, after substantial changes were made in the project to comply with water quality standards set by Dunn. An appeal was again taken to the district court, this time before Judge Smith. Judge Smith again reversed and remanded. Judge Smith's decision was appealed to the Idaho Supreme Court.]

BISTLINE, JUSTICE. * * * While we affirm the decision of the district court to remand for a new hearing, we differ on the matters necessary for consideration at the new hearing. We hold that Water Resources used the proper standard for and has adequately dealt with the financing question. In addition, although we in general affirm the district court's order as it related to public interest matters, we modify in part the district court's guidelines. * * *

Since Water Resources's decisions on financing are reinstated, the only matters for the agency to consider on remand are those which relate generally to the local public interest. I.C. § 42-203A(5)(e). We turn first to the interpretation of this provision * * *.

Under I.C. § 42-203A(5)(e), if an applicant's appropriation of water "will conflict with the local public interest, where the local public interest is defined as the affairs of the people in the area directly affected by the proposed use," then the Director "may reject such application and refuse issuance of permit therefor, or may partially approve and grant a permit for a smaller quantity of water than applied for, or may grant a permit upon conditions." * * *

The authority and duty of the Director to protect the public interest spring naturally from the statute; the more difficult task for us is to define "the local public interest." Public interest provisions appear frequently in the statutes of the prior appropriation states of the West, but are explicated rarely. I.C. § 42-203A provides little guidance. Fortunately, however, the legislature did provide guidance in a related statute, I.C. § 42-1501. We also derive assistance from our sister states and from the academic community.

In I.C. § 42-1501, the legislature declared it "in the public interest" that:

> the streams of this state and their environments be protected against loss of water supply to preserve the minimum stream flows required for the protection of fish and wildlife habitat, aquatic life, recreation, aesthetic beauty, transportation and navigation values, and water quality.

Not only is the term "public interest" common to both §§ 42-1501 and 42-203A, and the two sections common to the same title 42 (Irrigation and Drainage—Water Rights and Reclamation), but also the legislature approved the term "public interest" in both sections on the same day, March 29, 1978. Clearly, the legislature in § 42-203A must have intended the public interest on the local scale to include the public interest elements listed in § 42-1501: "fish and wildlife habitat, aquatic life, recreation, aesthetic beauty, transportation and navigation values, and water quality." * * *

In so intending, the legislature was in good company. Unlike other state public interest statutes, the Alaska statute enumerates the elements of the public interest. The public interest elements of I.C. § 42-1501 are almost precisely duplicated within the Alaska statute. * * *

The Alaska statute contains other elements which common sense argues ought to be considered part of the local public interest. These include the proposed appropriation's benefit to the applicant, its economic effect, its effect "of loss of alternative uses of water that might be made within a reasonable time if not precluded or hindered by the proposed appropriation," its harm to others, its "effect upon access to navigable or public waters," and "the intent and ability of the applicant to complete the appropriation." Alaska Stat. § 46.15.080(b).

Several other public interest elements, though obvious, deserve specific mention. These are: assuring minimum stream flows, as specifically provided in I.C. § 42-1501, discouraging waste, and encouraging conservation. * * *

The above-mentioned elements of the public interest are not intended to be a comprehensive list. As observed long ago by the New Mexico Supreme Court, the "public interest" should be read broadly in order to "secure the greatest possible benefit from [the public waters] for the public." Young & Norton v. Hinderlider, 15 N.M. 666, 110 P. 1045, 1050 (N.M.1910) * * *. By using the general term 'the local public interest,' the legislature intended to include any locally important factor impacted by proposed appropriations.

Of course, not every appropriation will impact every one of the above elements. Nor will the elements have equal weight in every situation. The relevant elements and their relative weights will vary with local needs, circumstances, and interests. For example, in an area heavily dependent on recreation and tourism or specifically devoted to preservation in its natural state, Water Resources may give great consideration to the aesthetic and environmental ramifications of granting a permit which calls for substantial modification of the landscape or the stream.

Judge Smith provided some specific guidelines, also needful of comment, to which our attention is now drawn.

1. *Finality of Design*

In order to be able to assess a project's impact on the public interest, the project's design must be definite enough to reflect its impacts and implications. Judge Smith held that because the applicant has the burden of proof to show a project is worthy of issuance of a permit, "the design of the proposed facility should be final, detailed and not schematic." He elaborated on the finality issue by stating:

The department should not have to issue a permit on conditions that the Department review the final plans. The final plans should be presented to the Department with the application for a permit. Thus, all interested parties could review the plans, cross-examine in regard thereto and offer suggestions that might be helpful in reducing any adverse impact. The issuance of the permit, therefore, would also constitute approval of the plan.

Any application for a permit that is not substantially complete in its engineering so that it cannot be properly evaluated for a here-and-now financial commitment or for impact on the public, can be readily denied by the Director. * * *

In our perception, Judge Smith's language requires an applicant to present "blueprint quality" plans at the outset of seeking a permit, much in the same vein as his "here and now" standard of financing required ready cash. We are not persuaded that blueprint quality plans of a facility are always necessary when applying for a permit to appropriate water. Rather, the design plan for a proposed facility depends on the nature of the facility, the complexity of the proposal, and the extent of the proposed appropriation's impact on the local area. In this particular case, the Department will determine at the hearing on the amended application whether blue print quality plans and drawings are a prerequisite to giving approval. In all cases the plans should be sufficient to generally apprise the public of the efficacy of the proposed use in the planned facility, and of its potential impact.

2. *Dewatering*

The dewatering of Billingsley Creek raises significant public interest and public trust concerns. In his discussion of the issue Judge Smith simply declared that "the rights of an appropriator prevail over riparian rights." Such a statement on its face fails to account for the state's policy of providing for minimum stream flows, and for the public's legitimate interests in the stream environment, wildlife, aesthetics, recreation, and alternative uses. However, after reviewing the record, we agree with Judge Smith that Water Resources has dealt properly with the dewatering issue. Therefore we affirm Judge Smith's holding that there is no "legal basis for reversing the Department decision on the grounds that a portion of Billingsley Creek would be dewatered from 125 CFS to a 25 CFS minimum for an approximate 700 ft. stretch of the creek."

3. *Health Hazard*

Judge Smith opined that the law will not allow Billingsley Creek to become a nuisance or a health hazard, adding also that "a permit cannot issue which would allow construction of a project contrary to the authority of the Board of Health in policing water for pollution." Hence, Judge Smith concluded that the Director had authority to consider whether the design of any particular facility will meet all environmental requirements.

We believe this to be a correct assessment of the law, but add a word of caution regarding the differing functions of Water Resources and the Department of Health and Welfare. Water Resources must oversee the water resources of the state, insuring that those who have permits and licenses to appropriate water use the water in accordance with the conditions of the permits and licenses and the limits of the law. It is not the primary job of Water Resources to protect the health and welfare of Idaho's citizens and visitors—that role is vested in the Department of Health and Welfare, including compliance with the water quality regulations and monitoring effluent discharge in our state's waterways. Nevertheless, although these agencies may have separate functions, Water Resources is precluded from issuing a permit for a water appropriation project which, when completed, would violate the water quality standards of the Department of Health and Welfare. It makes no sense whatsoever for Water Resources to blindly grant permit requests without regard to water quality regulations. Hence, Water Resources should condition the issuance of a permit on a showing by the applicant that a proposed facility will meet the mandatory water quality standards. Under this rule, Water Resources has the authority to withhold a permit application until it receives a proposed design which appears to be in compliance with the water quality standards. Once the conditional permit is granted, Water Resources has continuing jurisdiction over compliance with the conditions of the permit, including suspension or revocation of the permit for proven violations of the permit's conditions regarding water quality.

The Department of Health and Welfare continues to have the primary responsibility for policing water quality control in this state, and can exercise in personam jurisdiction over those who violate the state's water pollution laws. While it often may be both more feasible and more reasonable for Health and Welfare to take remedial steps against one violating the pollution laws, either by forcing compliance or shutting down a facility, than to resist an application for a permit in the first instance, Health and Welfare certainly has the right to be heard in proceedings before Water Resources. And, as appointed guardian of the quality of Idaho water, its views are entitled to consideration.

In sum, we agree with the district court, Judge Smith, that Water Resources cannot issue a permit which would allow construction of a project violative of the laws regulating water quality. However, later compliance with those laws after construction of a facility generally will be a proper concern of the Department of Health and Welfare.

The above elements of the public interest, together with other elements and factors which Water Resources deems relevant, will be considered at the hearing on the amended application. * * *

Notes

1. **Ad hoc approach.** The Nevada appropriation statutes contain a simple directive to the State Engineer to reject any application for appropriation which "threatens to prove detrimental to the public interest." In Pyramid Lake Paiute Tribe of Indians v. Washoe County, 918 P.2d 697 (Nev. 1996), a trial court remanded an approved application to the State Engineer with a directive to provide an administrative definition of the quoted phrase. On remand, the State Engineer did not provide a definition, but instead identified thirteen "guidelines" contained in the Nevada water statutes and again approved the application. The approval was again challenged on the grounds, inter alia, that the guidelines did not adequately define the "public interest." The challengers argued that Nevada should follow the lead of the principal case and define the public interest using criteria from the Alaska statute. They further asserted that the approval of the application was invalid under the Alaska definition because the State Engineer had not considered certain criteria identified in the Alaska statute. The Nevada Supreme Court rejected the argument saying, "we can find no indication that Nevada's legislature intended that the State Engineer determine public policy in Nevada by incorporating another state's statutes * * *." Although the dissent called the guidelines "rambling," "unresponsive," and "a useless summary of readily accessible statutory water law", the court affirmed the State Engineer's decision, finding that the "thirteen guidelines adequately defined the public interest *in this case*." (Emphasis added).

2. **Statutory directives regarding environmental and recreational considerations.** Cal. Water Code § 1257 directs water officials to consider the "relative benefit to be derived from * * * all beneficial uses of the water concerned including, but not limited to, use for * * * preservation and enhancement of fish and wildlife, [and] recreational * * * uses" in acting on applications to appropriate water. Section 1260(j) requires an application for a permit to appropriate water to set forth all data and information reasonably available to the applicant or that can be obtained from the Department of Fish and Game concerning the extent, if any, to which fish and wildlife would be affected by the appropriation, and a statement of any measures proposed to be taken for the protection of fish and wildlife in connection with the appropriation.

The Alaska Water Use Act requires that in the issuance of a permit one criterion for determining the public interest shall be "the effect on fish and game resources and on public recreational opportunities." Alaska Stat. § 46.15.080.

The Oregon Water Resources Board shall consider "Conserving the highest use of the water for all purposes, including * * * public recreation, protection of commercial and game fishing and wildlife, * * * navigation, scenic attraction or any other beneficial use to which the water may be applied for which it may have a special value to the public." Or. Rev. Stat. § 537.170(8)(a).

The Utah State Engineer is directed to reject an application for an appropriation if he has reason to believe that it will "unreasonably affect the public recreation or the natural stream environment." Utah Code Ann. § 73-3-8.

The Washington Water Resources Act of 1971 contains a "general declaration of fundamentals for utilization and management of water of the state," which includes:

"(3) The quality of the natural environment shall be protected and, where possible, enhanced as follows:

"(a) Perennial rivers and streams of the state shall be retained with base flows necessary to provide for preservation of wildlife, fish, scenic, aesthetic and other environmental values, and navigational values. Lakes and ponds shall be retained substantially in their natural condition. Withdrawals of water which would conflict therewith shall be authorized only in those situations where it is clear that overriding considerations of the public interest will be served." Wash. Rev. Code § 90.54.020.

3. **Endangered Species Acts.** The Nebraska Nongame and Endangered Species Conservation Act directs all state agencies "to insure that actions authorized * * * by them do not jeopardize the continued existence of * * * endangered species * * *." Neb. Rev. Stat. § 37-435(3) (recodified at § 37-807(3)). In Upper Big Blue Natural Resources District v. City of Fremont, 499 N.W.2d 548 (Neb. 1993), the Nebraska Department of Water Resources rejected several applications to appropriate water because it determined that the proposed projects would jeopardize endangered species. The Nebraska Supreme Court upheld the action.

In a later case, Central Platte Natural Resources District v. City of Fremont, 549 N.W.2d 112 (Neb. 1996), also involving permit applications which were denied because of jeopardy to endangered species, the court said:

"[T]he only way to satisfy the public interest, as declared in § 37-435(3), is by denying permits to appropriate waters when doing so would jeopardize the continued existence of an endangered or threatened species. Consequently, the director's evidentially supported finding that the district's proposed project would jeopardize the continued existence of the endangered whooping crane demanded that the district's applications be denied."

Endangered Species Acts are examined in Chapter 7, Section 2D.

4. **Valuation of environmental gains and losses.** Economists have long struggled with the problem caused by the lack of a market for many values affected by water projects. Over the years, much work has been done on "recreational values." Questions addressed include: How can such opportunities be fitted into the benefit-cost calculus? Can dollar val-

ues be assigned to the intangibles of pleasure? By valuing the facility as an asset, like a painting by an old master? By totaling gross expenditures by sportsmen? By capitalizing "derived values" from admittance fees and user charges for comparable private recreational opportunities? For an early look at these issues, see Frank J. Trelease, Policies for Water Law: Property Rights, Economic Forces and Public Regulation, 5 Nat. Resources J. 1, 18-23 (1965), and materials cited.

5. **Permit conditions.** In addition to the power to deny outright an application for a permit, the agency may grant it conditionally. See Kirk v. State Bd. of Irr., 134 N.W. 167 (Neb. 1912).

Such discretion is not unlimited, however. Bank of America National Trust & Savings Association v. State Water Resources Control Board, 116 Cal. Rptr. 770 (Ct. App. 1974), involved applications for two off-stream reservoirs to be used as water supplies for a large residential development. In approving the applications the Board imposed stream by-pass requirements to protect fish, which had been agreed to by the Bank and the California Department of Fish and Game. In addition, the Board required the applicant to open the reservoirs to public recreational use. The applicant appealed the latter requirement, designated as "condition 11" by the Board. In reversing the Board the court said:

"It becomes clear that the Board's reason for condition 11 was that the approved diversion would reduce the flow of the river which, in turn, would have an uncertain effect on the 'fishery.' Further, the diversion would result in "diminished recreational value" of the Cosumnes because of its lower level downstream. These two factors—the undetermined effect on fish and lessened recreational prospects caused by lower water level—prompted the Board to require as a 'trade-off' public access to the Rancho Murieta recreational reservoirs.

"While Fish & Game's determination that the [by-pass] formula fixed in the agreement is adequate to support fish life is not binding on the Board, Fish & Game's judgment in this matter is entitled to great weight. Charged with a statutory obligation, Fish & Game is the guardian and custodian of the public's deep and continuing interest in the fish and game resources of this state. It has the collective experience and expertise to make the essential determinations in the technical areas of water flows and fish maintenance. The agreed formula was negotiated and approved by Fish & Game and we cannot presume that its conclusions were not carefully reached. Of greater significance is the fact that nowhere in the record does there appear before the Board any evidence that adoption of the formula would adversely affect, diminish, or impair the fishery. We accordingly conclude that the first basis for imposition of the condition, preservation of the fish life in the Cosumnes downstream from the diversion, has been otherwise adequately assured.

"The remainder of our inquiry relates to whether substantial evidence in the record establishes a 'diminished recreational value' of the Cosumnes warranting a 'trade-off' or exchange for condition 11. Our review of the record discloses no such evidence. There are clear inferences from the record that the water level of the Cosumnes below the diversion during certain times of the year will be lower because of it, but there is no testimony as to its degree or, more importantly, as to its effect in terms of recreational use of the river, present or prospective. No testimony written or oral was presented which in any substantial manner pointed to the specifics of impairment of recreational activities.

"We note that one of the exhibits, a report prepared by the U.S. Department of the Interior, on the Feasibility of Water Supply Development, Cosumnes River Diversion of the Central Valley Project, described general recreational activities around *reservoirs* as 'boating, swimming, waterskiing, and fishing,' and that shoreline activity includes 'camping, picnicking, sightseeing, hiking and related activities.' We envision that the boating and waterskiing activities in a stream like the Cosumnes because of its size and configuration would be very limited with or without the diversion, but the remaining recreational uses will be unimpaired insofar as disclosed by the Board record. No evidence, written or oral, was presented which indicated that the lower water level would change or affect the recreational utilization of the Cosumnes downstream from the diversion.

"We have heretofore underscored the primacy of the 'public interest' in the considerations before the Board and have emphasized the broad discretion vested in it. Nonetheless, we apply a measure of substantiality in reviewing the evidence supporting the Board's action. * * *

"The record, in our view, is barren of evidence which is of 'ponderable legal significance' in support of the conclusion that the diversion would result in a reduction in the recreational value of the Cosumnes. While fully accepting the rule giving primacy to the public interest, we may not leave to speculation the nature of its impairment. Condition 11 constitutes an onerous burden. The Board, in our view, has the jurisdiction and the right to impose a condition requiring public access but only for precise and specific reasons founded on tangible record evidence.

"To summarize, we conclude that the record lacks substantial evidence supporting condition 11 and it must fail."

6. **Permit conditions v. instream appropriations**. "Some states (such as California) authorize retention of water in the source for purposes of fishery protection and recreation on a case-by-case basis when considering new applications to appropriate. This process is less desirable than that of the Model Water Code for two reasons. First, the Code's reservation device provides advance notice of a contemplated appropriation, while the case-by-case procedure does not allow a determination until a project has been fully planned and a specific applicant is before the appropriate administrative agency. Second, the extent of the reservation on a case-by-case basis will necessarily be determined by weighing the utility of the specific project against the value of the instream use instead of basing such reservation on general public policy. It is difficult for

noneconomic uses based on such policy to be broadly considered." Ronald B. Robie, Modernizing State Water Rights Laws: Some Suggestions for New Directions, 1974 Utah L. Rev. 760, 770 (1974).

The California Department of Fish and Game has complained that the use of permit conditions provides little permanent protection to instream values. The department has noted that bypass flows required of one appropriator often become a target for subsequent appropriation downstream, forcing it to make its case for instream protection again and again, with the possibility that it may be successful in nine cases only to lose on the tenth. See Anne J. Schneider, Legal Aspects of Instream Water Uses in California, at 44-45 (Governor's Comm'n to Review Cal. Water Rights Law, Staff Paper No. 6, 1978).

7. **Weighing public interest factors.** Most permit statutes provide little guidance concerning how to weigh various factors in deciding if a proposed appropriation is in the public interest. Is this a deficiency? See Frank J. Trelease, A Water Code for Alaska 17 (1962):

"Making decisions such as these will be very difficult. No law can make them, they must be made by people. No economic formula can solve these problems by push button techniques. Although * * * the proposed Code incorporate[s] the benefit-cost idea, * * * the balancing of benefits against cost must be performed by the exercise of judgment. Mathematical equivalents could be used if desired, to insure that some factors are not vastly overweighed. Indeed, the Code could be amended to delete the formula, yet surely the administrators would consider these same factors in determining the public interest. It is believed that the real strength of the Code lies in its procedures, which will enable all viewpoints to be brought together and all factors considered, so that choices will be made, not by action of an appropriator or polluter, and not to further the policy of a single-purpose agency, but on an informed basis by officials responsible to the State for 'maximum use consistent with the public interest', for the 'maximum benefit of (all) its people.'"

8. **Institutional competence and public interest decisions.** Consideration of the public interest in the regulation of water use raises difficult questions regarding the competence of various government institutions to address particular issues. For example, should a particular issue be addressed administratively or legislatively? Should it be addressed at the state or at a local level? If it is to be addressed administratively, what should be the make up of the body and what should be the scope of its authority? Should its authority be confined to technical issues or should it include broad discretion to choose between conflicting public values? Should it include authority to address matters which are typically addressed by other governmental institutions? Such questions arise in the context of statutory interpretation and in the development of sound public policy; i.e., *does* a water agency have the authority to address particular issues and *should* it have such authority? The latter question is relevant to addressing the former question, particularly when a statute simply directs the agency to promote the "public interest."

In re Application of Water Permit No. 4580A-3, South Dakota Water Management Board, discussed in Grant, supra p. 139, Note 2, at 698, illustrates the problem. There, the South Dakota Water Management Board considered the effect on adjacent public recreation areas of odors from a hog farm in determining whether a proposed appropriation for the farm was in the public interest. It concluded that the economic benefits of the facility outweighed the harm to recreation resulting from the occasional presence of unpleasant odors. It approved the appropriation. (Accord Chisholm v. Idaho Dept. of Water Res., 125 P.3d 515 (Idaho 2005) (dairy odors)).

Did the South Dakota Legislature intend the Water Management Board to consider land-use conflicts in determining the public interest with regard to water matters? Would it have been appropriate for the Board to deny the appropriation if local land use officials had considered the matter and approved the hog farm? Should such a decision be made at the state or local level? See Pyramid Lake Paiute Tribe of Indians v. Washoe County, supra p. 145, Note 1, in which the court concluded that the state engineer appropriately refused to consider alternatives to a proposed county water supply project because the legislature had assigned the responsibility for water supply planning and development to the county, and Serpa v. County of Washoe, 901 P.2d 690 (Nev. 1995), holding that approval of the water supply plans for a proposed subdivision by the state engineer did not preempt the authority of the county to disapprove the subdivision because of its effect on regional water resources. See also City of Colo. Springs v. Bd. of County Comm'rs, discussed supra p. 101, Note 5, in which a county blocked a transbasin appropriation through the exercise of its land use authority.

In 2003 the Idaho legislature amended the definition of "local public interest." The relevant section now reads: "'Local public interest' is defined as the interest that the people in the area directly affected by a proposed water use have in the effect of such use on the public water resource," Idaho Code § 42-202B (3). A statement of purpose accompanying the legislation which amended the definition states that the "local public interest" should not be construed to require the consideration of secondary effects of an activity simply because the activity happens to use water. The statement gives an example: "[T]he effect of a new manufacturing plant on water quality, resident fish and wildlife and the availability of water for other beneficial uses is appropriately considered under the local public interest criteria. On the other hand the effect of the manufacturing plant on air quality is not within the local public interest criteria because it is not an effect of the diversion of water but rather a secondary effect of the proposed plant. While the impact of the manufacturing plant is important this effect should be evaluated by [the Department of Environmental Quality under other legislation]." Statement of Purpose/Fiscal Impact of H.O. 284, 57th Leg., 1st Reg. Sess. (Idaho 2003). The statement indicates that the change was prompted by protests based on a broad range of social, economic, and environmental policy issues having nothing to do with impacts on water resources.

In *In re* Application of Sleeper, discussed infra p. 219, Note 9, a trial judge decided that the protection of cultural values outweighed the economic development which would result from a particular water use. Is a judge "competent" to make such a decision? Is the New Mexico State Engineer, whose decision was challenged in *Sleeper*, "competent" to make such a decision? If not, what body should address such questions?

9. **Police power regulation of water rights.** A California case provides a reminder that administrative permits are not the only basis for the regulation of water rights. In People v. Murrison, 124 Cal. Rptr. 2d 68 (Cal. Ct. App. 2002), Murrison claimed a water right based on an appropriation made before the state adopted a permit requirement in 1914. To exercise this right, he constructed a diversion dam in a stream without notifying the California Department of Fish and Game as required by a California statute. When challenged by state authorities, Murrison argued that his water right was not subject to statutory regulation because it was not based on a state permit. The court rejected the argument: "A water right, whether it predates or postdates 1914 is not exempt from reasonable regulation. Just as a real property owner does not have an unfettered right to develop property in any manner he or she sees fit, * * * an owner of a water right may be similarly restricted." Id. at 76.

UNITED PLAINSMEN ASS'N v. NORTH DAKOTA STATE WATER CONSERVATION COMMISSION
Supreme Court of North Dakota, 1976.
247 N.W.2d 457.

PEDERSON, JUSTICE. This is an appeal by the United Plainsmen Association, a North Dakota non-profit corporation, from a decision of the district court of Burleigh County dismissing the complaint for failure to state a claim upon which relief could be granted.

The complaint sought an injunction against the North Dakota State Water Conservation Commission and Vernon Fahy, State Engineer. Should this court find that the trial court erred, then United Plainsmen asks for a temporary restraining order against the Commission and the State Engineer pending trial on the merits. We hold that the district court did err in dismissing the complaint, we deny a temporary restraining order, and remand the case for further proceedings. * * *   √ why they rejected TRO

The injunction sought by United Plainsmen would have prevented the State Engineer from issuing future water permits for coal-related power and energy production facilities until there is a comprehensive short- and long-term plan for the conservation and development of the State's natural resources, which, United Plainsmen contends, is required by § 61-01-26, NDCC, and the common law Public Trust Doctrine existing in this State. Section 61-01-26 reads as follows:

> "In view of legislative findings and determination of the ever-increasing demand and anticipated future need for water in North Dakota for every beneficial purpose and use, it is hereby declared to be the water resources policy of the state that: * * *

> "4. Accruing benefits from these resources can best be achieved for the people of the state through the development, execution and periodic updating of comprehensive, coordinated and well-balanced short- and long-term plans and programs for the conservation and development of such resources by the departments and agencies of the state having responsibilities therefor;

> "5. Adequate implementation of such plans and programs shall be provided by the state through cost-sharing and cooperative participation with the appropriate federal and state departments and agencies and political subdivisions within the limitation of budgetary requirements and administrative capabilities; * * *

> "The provisions of this chapter shall not be construed to in any manner limit, impair or abrogate the rights, powers, duties or functions of any department or agency of the state having jurisdiction or responsibilities in the field of water and related land resources conservation, development or utilization."

United Plainsmen argues that the language of subsection 4 of that statute imposes mandatory planning responsibility upon the State Engineer, which constitutes a condition precedent to the issuance of temporary or permanent water permits in this State. We do not agree. In the light of the qualifying proviso at the end of § 61-01-26, we must conclude that subsection 4 thereof is "hortatory and precatory, but not mandatory." * * *

Although it is not mandatory, § 61-01-26, entitled "Declaration of state water resources policy," is a significant advisory policy statement. The last sentence therein clearly indicates that it is not to be construed to limit, impair or abrogate the rights, powers, duties or functions of any department or agency of the State. This statute provides but little support for United Plainsmen's contention that the State Engineer must complete short- and long-term planning as a condition precedent to the issuance of water permits.

* * *

The foregoing, however, does not relieve the Commission and State Engineer of mandatory planning responsibilities with respect to the issuance of water permits, and we note that counsel for the Commission emphasized in his argument that the State Engineer and the Commission do have plans and do not reject the concept of prior planning. We agree with United Plainsmen that the discretionary authority of state officials to allocate vital state resources is not without limit but is circumscribed by what has been called the Public Trust Doctrine.

This doctrine was first clearly defined in Illinois Central Railroad v. Illinois, 146 U.S. 387 * * * (1892), a case in which the United States Supreme Court was called upon to decide the competency of the State of Illinois to convey, by legislative grant, a portion of Chicago's harbor on Lake Michigan to the Illinois Central Railroad.

"That the State holds the title to the lands under the navigable waters of Lake Michigan, within its limits, in the same manner that the State holds title to soils under tide water, by the common law, we have already shown, and that title necessarily carries with it control over the waters above them whenever the lands are subjected to use. * * * It is a title held in trust for the people of the State that they may enjoy the navigation of the waters, carry on commerce over them, and have liberty of fishing therein freed from the obstruction or interference of private parties." 146 U.S. at 452, 13 S.Ct. at 118.

"The State can no more abdicate its trust over property in which the whole people are interested, like navigable waters and soils under them, so as to leave them entirely under the use and control of private parties, except in the instance of parcels mentioned for the improvement of the navigation and use of the waters, or when parcels can be disposed of without impairment of the public interest in what remains, than it can abdicate its police powers in the administration of government and the preservation of the peace." 146 U.S. at 453, 13 S.Ct. at 118. * * *

The Commission, the State Engineer, and the lower court, while acknowledging the existence of this doctrine in North Dakota, interpret it in a narrow sense, limiting its applicability to conveyances of real property. We do not understand the doctrine to be so restricted. The State holds the navigable waters, as well as the lands beneath them, in trust for the public. * * *

[Under North Dakota law,] those who seek use of public waters can petition the State Engineer for water permits. In the performance of this duty of resource allocation consistent with the public interest, the Public Trust Doctrine requires, at a minimum, a determination of the potential effect of the allocation of water on the present water supply and future water needs of this State. This necessarily involves planning responsibility. The development and implementation of some short- and long-term planning capability is essential to effective allocation of resources "without detriment to the public interest in the lands and waters remaining."

We believe that § 61-01-01, NDCC, expresses the Public Trust Doctrine. * * * Confined to traditional concepts, the Doctrine confirms the State's role as trustee of the public waters. It permits alienation

and allocation of such precious state resources only after an analysis
of present supply and future need.

The Legislature has indicated its desire to see such planning take
place, although not in mandatory language. Until the Legislature
speaks more forcefully, we think the Public Trust Doctrine requires,
as a minimum, evidence of some planning by appropriate state agencies and officers in the allocation of public water resources, and that
the Environmental Law Enforcement Act (Chapter 32-40, NDCC) requires more than a plenary dismissal of the action.

United Plainsmen has requested a temporary restraining order,
enjoining the further issuance of water permits pending trial on the
merits in the lower court. A temporary injunction or restraining order
may be granted if it appears by the complaint that the plaintiffs are
entitled to the relief requested, and that such relief consists of restraining acts which would, if continued, produce injury to the plaintiffs during the litigation. * * * We are not convinced that a temporary
restraining order is necessary or advisable in this instance.

During oral argument counsel for appellees stated that, of the total number of water permits considered each year, a very small percentage is in the industrial category relating to energy conversion. Of
that small percentage of industrial water-use applications considered,
only a few are actually granted and some that are granted will never
be used because of other causes which prevent the intended development.

We express no opinion about the ultimate outcome of the trial on
the merits, should that point be reached in this case. We acknowledge,
however, that there is merit in the argument that the extent of planning is somewhat related to the sums appropriated therefor by the
Legislature. It may be that the planning being done by the Commission, according to the oral argument made in this Court, is sufficient.

We hold that the dismissal was premature and improvident under
the circumstances. The amended complaint charges a failure to devise
any water conservation plan, as well as a failure to consider injury to
the public. For the purpose of the motion to dismiss, the trial court
and this Court must consider all allegations of the complaint to be
true. We hold, accordingly, that the complaint does state a claim upon
which relief could be granted, if proved, and, therefore, must be reinstated.

Reversed and remanded for further proceedings.

Notes

1. **Extent of planning.** Most western states have statutes which
provide for water planning of some sort. However, a 1988 survey indicated that in about half the states the process was essentially moribund;

i.e., plans were never completed or had become outdated and there were no ongoing planning efforts. David H. Getches, Water Planning: Untapped Opportunity for the Western States, 9 J. Energy L. & Pol'y 1, 44-45 (1988). With a few exceptions, e.g., Texas and California, the situation does not appear to have changed appreciably.

2. **Modern water planning.** Modern planning statutes establish a dynamic and comprehensive process. E.g., Kan. Stat. Ann.:

"§ 82a-901a. Legislative declaration."

"The people of the state can best achieve the proper utilization and control of the water resources of the state through comprehensive planning which coordinates and provides guidance for the management, conservation and development of the state's water resources."

"§ 82a-903. Same; formulation of state water plan; cooperation of state water agencies; advice of general public."

"In accordance with the policies and long-range goals and objectives established by the legislature, the office shall formulate on a continuing basis a comprehensive state water plan for the management, conservation and development of the water resources of the state. Such state water plan shall include sections corresponding with water planning areas as determined by the office. The Kansas water office and the Kansas water authority shall seek advice from the general public and from committees consisting of individuals with knowledge of and interest in water issues in the water planning areas. The plan shall set forth the recommendations of the office for the management, conservation and development of the water resources of the state, including the general location, character, and extent of such existing and proposed projects, programs, and facilities as are necessary or desirable in the judgment of the office to accomplish such policies, goals and objectives. The plan shall specify standards for operation and management of such projects, programs, and facilities as are necessary or desirable. The plan shall be formulated and used for the general purpose of accomplishing the coordinated management, conservation and development of the water resources of the state. The division of water resources of the Kansas board of agriculture, state geological survey, the division of environment of the department of health and environment, department of wildlife and parks, state conservation commission and all other interested state agencies shall cooperate with the office in formulation of such plan."

"§ 82a-907. State water resource planning act; considerations in formulation of state water plan."

"In formulating the state water plan the office shall consider:

(a) The management, conservation and development of the water resources of the state for the benefit of the state as a whole;

(b) the benefits to be derived from development of reservoir sites for the combined purposes of flood control, water supply storage and recreation;

(c) the safeguards to public health, aquatic and animal life established by K.S.A. 65-161 to 65-171t, inclusive, and amendments thereto, and the Kansas water quality management plan approved and adopted as provided by chapter 351 of the 1979 Session Laws;

(d) the water development policies, whenever possible, consistent with the beneficial development of other natural resources;

(e) the public health and general welfare of the people of the state;

(f) all appropriation and other rights to the use of water that exist pursuant to the Kansas water appropriation act and the state water plan storage act;

(g) the interrelationship of groundwater and surface water supplies and the effects of evapotranspiration on water supply;

(h) the alternative plans, programs and projects in the interest of effective water resource management, conservation and development;

(i) the means and methods for the protection of aquatic and other wildlife;

(j) the use of waters to augment the flow of surface streams for the support of aquatic and other wildlife and to improve the water quality of the stream and to protect the public health;

(k) the inclusion of conservation storage in reservoir development and planning for the regulation of streamflow for the purpose of quality control, such inclusion not to serve as a substitute for methods of controlling wastes at their sources;

(l) the maintenance, preservation and protection of the sovereignty of the state over all the waters within the state;

(m) plans, projects and recommendations of public corporations, the federal government and state agencies prepared pursuant to statutory authority;

(n) plans, recommendations and projects of private associations or organizations as they relate to the water resources of the state;

(o) the need of the state to control storage in federal reservoirs by purchase or agreement; and

(p) such other matters as the office deems proper or desirable."

3. **Modern water planning—California.** The California Water Plan, prepared by the Department of Water Resources in 1957 and approved by the legislature in 1959, was an example of an older, more static, type of plan—a list of 376 dams and related facilities on rivers and streams throughout the state. In effect, the plan was a blueprint for water development projects in the state.

Water planning in California, however, has evolved substantially. Beginning in 1966, the Department of Water Resources updated the plan. This process was codified in 1991 with a legislative directive to the Department to update the plan every five years. See Cal. Water Code §§ 10004-10005. Unlike the 1957 plan, the updates do not focus on water facilities. Instead, the updates collect and analyze extensive regional and statewide data and information on water use, on water management activities and proposals, and on contemporary and future issues and problems confronting water management efforts in California in an effort to assess present and future water supplies and demands and to evaluate progress and options in meeting future water needs. Although the updates make various recommendations, they are not binding policy documents; they are essentially descriptive and analytic. Indeed, the Water Code specifies that the "Plan" does not itself authorize the construction of any facilities. Cal. Water Code § 10005. It is simply "the master plan" for the state's water resource conservation, management and development.

Three aspects of the planning legislation merit attention. First, the Department must release, at least a year prior to each update, a "preliminary draft of the assumptions and other estimates upon which the study will be based." § 10004.6(c). The legislation details nine major topics that must be included in the report: 1) basin hydrology, 2) groundwater supplies, 3) current and projected land use patterns, 4) environmental water needs, 5) current and projected population, 6) current and projected interior and exterior residential, commercial, industrial, agricultural and park water use, 7) evapotranspiration rates for major crop types, 8) current and projected adoption of urban and agricultural conservation practices, and 9) current and projected supplies provided by water recycling and reuse. This preliminary report is designed to give interested parties a "heads up" about the key assumptions upon which the Department will be basing its ultimate recommendations. Among other matters, this allows controversy over underlying data to be dealt with in advance of controversy over water conservation, management or development options.

Second, the Department must convene an advisory committee. § 10004(b)(2). The statute specifies that members must include representatives of "agricultural and urban water suppliers, local government, business, production agriculture, and environmental interests * * *." Advisory committees, an ever increasing fixture of natural resources planning, allow the Department to receive stakeholder input to improve the planning process, as well as to build support for any eventual recommendations.

Finally, the legislation mandates that the plan contain a region by region analysis of "regional and local water projects * * * to improve water supplies to meet municipal, agricultural and environmental water needs and minimize the need to import water from other hydrologic regions." § 10013. The clear import of the section is that water-importing regions, particularly in Southern California, should thoroughly develop their own supplies and reuse capabilities before seeking additional interregional water imports.

The most recent update can be found at the Department's web site.[c]

4. **Effect of the water plan.** When one California water district applied for a permit to construct one of the listed dams in the 1957 Califor-

---

c. http://www.waterplan.water.ca.gov/b160/indexb160.html.

nia Water Plan and another sought approval of an inconsistent project that would displace the listed dam but better use existing facilities, the latter was preferred by the State Water Rights Board and its choice was upheld in Johnson Rancho County Water District v. State Water Rights Board, 45 Cal. Rptr. 589 (Cal. Ct. App. 1965). The court noted that the plan itself included a recommendation that more detailed studies of component features were necessary to determine their need, their engineering feasibility and their financial feasibility, and that further investigation might indicate alternative projects. The court also noted that the legislature had not made the plan binding but had merely directed the Board (now the Water Resources Control Board) to "give consideration to any general or coordinated plan * * * including the California Water Plan * * * and any modification thereto * * *."

Should a water plan be binding in water allocation decisions to the extent that it addresses particular issues? Should water officials at least be required to consider a water plan and justify inconsistent allocation decisions? If not, is a plan anything more than an "academic exercise"?

5. **Preference statutes.** Preference statutes are a more static form of planning:

N.D. Cent. Code § 61-04-06.1: "Preference in granting permits. When there are competing applications for water from the same source, and the source is insufficient to supply all applicants, the state engineer shall adhere to the following order of priority: (1) Domestic use. (2) Municipal use. (3) Livestock use. (4) Irrigation use. (5) Industrial use. (6) Fish, wildlife, and other outdoor recreational uses."

6. **Absolute preferences.** Cal. Fish and Game Code §§ 5937 and 5946 create another kind of preference. Section 5937 provides: "The owner of any dam shall allow sufficient water at all times to pass through a fishway, or in the absence of a fishway, allow sufficient water to pass over, around or thorough the dam, to keep in good condition any fish that may be planted or exist below the dam." Section 5946 states that all permits and licenses issued in a particular region of the state must be conditioned on full compliance with section 5937. Nevertheless, various water rights were issued to Los Angeles without the required conditions. In California Trout, Inc. v. State Water Resources Control Board, 255 Cal. Rptr. 184 (Cal. Ct. App. 1989), the court ordered water officials to amend Los Angeles' water rights:

"The legislative mandate of section 5946 was either overlooked or misconstrued in the actions of the Water Board granting the licenses here in issue. We agree with the Water Board that the mandate of section 5946 is a specific legislative rule concerning the public trust. Since the Water Board has no authority to disregard that rule, a judicial remedy exists to require it to carry out its ministerial functions with respect to that rule. The Legislature, not the Water Board, is the superior voice in the articulation of public policy concerning the reasonableness of water allocation. The unfortunate fact that the Water Board did not hear the Legislature's voice in 1974 does not warrant, by the passage of time, its turning a deaf ear now."

Is this absolute preference for fishery protection good public policy? What if the evidence showed only a small number of "trash" fish would be preserved by the flows but that alternate uses of the water were very valuable?

7. **Ecosystem management.** Ecosystem management is a type of planning that is receiving increasing interest. The concept is still relatively new and there is not complete agreement about its meaning. Nevertheless, the following description by one of its strongest advocates captures the essence of the ecosystem management:

"The concept of ecosystem management, though still often misunderstood, has now been defined with sufficient precision to constitute a viable natural resource management policy. Drawing heavily upon ecological and biological sciences, particularly the field of conservation biology, ecosystem management views the land and resource base in its entirety, as a holistic or integrated entity. Management focuses on entire ecosystems, not just individual resources such as timber and forage. Recognizing that natural systems often cross jurisdictional boundaries, ecosystem management emphasizes the need for inter-jurisdictional coordination to ensure ecological integrity and sustainable resource systems. The policy is designed to maintain and restore natural processes, including biodiversity levels and natural disturbance regimes. And because ecological systems evolve over time, often unpredictably, ecosystem management is intended to accommodate such instability and change. Human intervention, including commodity production and extraction activities, may be used to accomplish these goals, although this will vary depending upon the managing agency's organic mandate and basic philosophy." Robert B. Keiter, Beyond the Boundary Line: Constructing a Law of Ecosystem Management, 65 U. Colo. L. Rev. 293, 295 (1994).[d]

Ecosystem management is both narrower and broader than traditional water planning. It is narrower because it focuses primarily on environmental protection, particularly the preservation of biological diversity. It is broader because it emphasizes management of all resources within ecosystems rather than on management of water resources alone. While its proponents can identify a number of efforts at ecosystem management, the concept is not yet widely reflected in the law. If adopted, it would have a substantial impact on water management. Water is a major component of most ecosystems; indeed, the watershed is often identified as the logical geographic unit for ecosystem management.

8. **Public Trust Doctrine.** *Illinois Central Railroad* and other cases dealing with the public trust doctrine are found in Chapter 7, Section 1B.

---

d. Copyright 1994. Reprinted with the permission of the University of Colorado Law Review.

D. Adjudication and Enforcement

FARM INVESTMENT CO. v. CARPENTER
Supreme Court of Wyoming, 1900.
9 Wyo. 110, 61 P. 258.

POTTER, C.J. This suit was instituted in the district court of Johnson County for the purpose of securing a decree quieting the title of plaintiff to the right to use water from French creek for the irrigation of certain lands, as against each and all of the defendants, who, it is alleged, are asserting prior and superior rights to the plaintiff. An appropriation by plaintiff's grantor in the year 1879, and the continued use and application of the water so appropriated, are set out, and in consequence thereof a right superior to the defendants is alleged to reside in the plaintiff. The answer of but one of the defendants is in the record. Admitting the original appropriation alleged in the petition, and the ownership of plaintiff to the water right acquired thereby, if any, the answer, as a separate defense, after disclosing the claim of the answering defendant to the use of certain of the waters of the stream for irrigation purposes by reason of an appropriation in 1883, sets up an adjudication by the state board of control of the rights of the various claimants to the use of the water of said stream on or about October, 1893, in accordance with the provisions of chapter 8 of the Laws of 1890-91; the same being an act entitled "An act providing for the supervision and use of the waters of the state." * * * It is also alleged that by the order of the said board in that proceeding the defendant was awarded a certain priority for a definite quantity of water, for which a certificate was issued to him, and that "no amount of water whatever was awarded or decreed to the plaintiff or to any other person for use upon the lands described in said plaintiff's petition." Wherefore it is averred that the plaintiff has abandoned its rights, and is now estopped from asserting the same. * * *

[Counsel for plaintiff contended that the statutory provisions for the adjudication were unconstitutional on various grounds. The district court certified the constitutional questions directly to the supreme court for answer.]

The expressions of the constitution relating to irrigation and water rights are as follows: "Water being essential to industrial prosperity, of limited amount, and easy of diversion from its natural channels, its control must be in the state, which, in providing for its use, shall equally guard all the various interests involved." Article 1, § 31. "The waters of all natural streams, springs, lakes, or other collections of still water, within the boundaries of the state, are hereby declared to be the property of the state." Article 8, § 1. "There shall be constituted a board of control to be composed of the state engineer, and superintendents of the water divisions; which shall, under such regulations as may be prescribed by law, have the supervision of the waters of the state and of their appropriation, distribution and diversion, and of the various officers connected therewith. Its decisions to be subject to review by the courts of the state." Id. § 2. * * *

Pursuant to the constitutional requirements, the first state legislature, by an act entitled "An act providing for the supervision and use of the waters of the state," approved December 22, 1890, created the state board of control, divided the state into four water divisions, and provided for the appointment of a superintendent for each division. * * * By the act in question, also, a system of procedure to be inaugurated and conducted by the board is established, wherein and whereby the board is directed and empowered to ascertain, adjudicate, and determine the priorities of rights of the various claimants from the same stream, and the former legislation authorizing such adjudication by a special proceeding in the district court is repealed. * * *

Counsel for the plaintiff contend that the act of December 22, 1890, is unconstitutional, in so far as it confers upon the board of control authority to determine the priorities of rights to the use of water. * * * The position maintained by counsel is that a determination of the priorities of rights to the use of water involves solely a judicial inquiry into rights to property as between private parties, and that the jurisdiction to undertake such an investigation and adjudicate therein can be constitutionally lodged only in some court which is by article 5 of the constitution vested with judicial power. The statute nowhere attempts to devest the courts of any jurisdiction granted to them by the constitution to redress grievances and afford relief at law or in equity under the ordinary and well-known rules of procedure. A purely statutory proceeding is created, * * * a proceeding which is to result, not in a judgment for damages to a party for injuries sustained, nor the issuance of any writ or process known to the law for the purpose of preventing the unlawful invasion of a party's rights or privileges; but the finality of the proceeding is a settlement or adjustment of the priorities of appropriation of the public waters of the state, and is followed by the issuance of a certificate to each appropriator, showing his relative standing among other claimants, and the amount of water to which he is found to be entitled. * * *

The other fundamental principles expressed in the constitution are that control of the public waters must be in the state, which, in providing for their use, shall equally guard all the various interests involved. Such control shall consist in a supervision of the waters, their appropriation, distribution, and diversion, by a board of control, to be composed of certain designated officers, with an officer of technical and practical knowledge and experience at its head; and priority of appropriation shall give the better right. Let us inquire into the nature and subject of the supervisory power of the board. * * * It has already been suggested that the supervision of the board affects individual appropriations, and concerns the distribution of water to individual claimants. Any effort to supervise and control the waters of the state, their appropriation and distribution, in the absence of an effective ascertainment of the several priorities of rights, must result in practical failure in times when official intervention is most required. * * * In the development of the irrigation problem under the rule of prior appropriation, perplexing questions are continually arising, of a technical and practical character. As between an investigation in the courts and by the board, it would seem that an administrative board, with experience and peculiar knowledge along this particular line, can in the first instance, solve the questions involved, with due regard to private and public interests, conduct the requisite investigation, and make the ascertainment of individual rights, with greater facility, at less expense to interested parties, and with a larger degree of satisfaction to all concerned. In the opinion of an able law writer upon this subject, the powers of the board of control in this respect constitute one of the most praiseworthy features of our legislation. He says: "In the state of Wyoming, at least, there will no longer be the ludicrous spectacle of learned judges solemnly decreeing the right to from two to ten times the amount of water flowing in a stream, or, in fact, amounts so great that the channel of the stream could not possibly carry them; thus practically leaving the questions at stake as unsettled as before." Kin. Irr. § 493. * * *

The determination required to be made by the board is, in our opinion, primarily administrative rather than judicial in character. The proceeding is one in which a claimant does not obtain redress for an injury, but secures evidence of title to a valuable right,—a right to use a peculiar public commodity. That evidence of title comes properly from an administrative board, which, for the state in its sovereign capacity, represents the public, and is charged with the duty of conserving public as well as private interests. The board, it is true, acts judicially; but the power exercised is quasi judicial only, and such as, under proper circumstances, may appropriately be conferred upon executive officers or boards. The jurisdiction bears some resemblance to that of the land department of the government concerning the disposal of the public lands. * * *

We are not persuaded that the act is void, as conferring judicial power upon the board in violation of the constitution. That the board was expected to exercise quasi judicial functions is apparent from that provision of section 2 of article 8 of the constitution requiring its decisions to be subject to review by the courts. * * *

Notes

1. **Limitations of private litigation.** Private litigation has its limitations in adjudicating water rights. In a suit between two appropriators, the trial court decreed that the plaintiff owned the first right to divert the waters of the source and that the defendant owned a right, subject only to the plaintiff's prior right. Other appropriators, claiming rights prior to both, sought to set aside the decree. Denied. "Although [the decrees are] general in form, and broad enough in language to include the whole world, they can have no such effect. They are binding on the parties to the action and their privies, but upon no one else. As to strangers claiming rights in the waters of the lake the decrees in no manner affect them. The decrees are not even evidence of adverse rights. Strangers may proceed as if the decrees had never been entered." State *ex rel.* McConihe v. Steiner, 109 P. 57, 60 (Wash. 1910).

The rights of third persons likewise have no effect upon a judgment as to the litigants' relative rights. "Neither do we think that the trial court was called upon * * * to inquire into and pass upon the question whether appropriators of water below the mouth of the proposed canal of appellee would be injured by the construction of the canal. The rights of such persons will not, of course, be injuriously affected by the decree in this cause * * *." Gutierres v. Albuquerque Land & Irr. Co., 188 U.S. 545, 556-57 (1903).

Private litigation can even fail to adjudicate the relative rights of all parties to it. In one case, the parties' predecessors had been co-defendants in a 1916 action. The trial court enjoined the current defendants from diverting more water than was allocated to their predecessors in 1916. Reversed. "Although the [earlier] case adjudicated the rights of the Poplar Irrigation Company with respect to numerous upstream water users * * * the decision does not purport to determine the rights of the various codefendants as among themselves. In short, the [earlier] decision suffers from the inherent inability of private lawsuits to provide just the sort of 'comprehensive allocation' of water rights attributed to it by the trial court. As our Supreme Court has noted, 'This method of resolving controversies involving the rights of the users of water on the river is necessarily piecemeal, unduly expensive and obviously unsatisfactory.' It is just these sorts of shortcomings that a statutory streamwide adjudication is designed to overcome." Pleasant Valley Canal Co. v. Borror, 72 Cal. Rptr. 2d 1, 17-18 (Cal. Ct. App. 1998).

See also State v. Haggerman Water Rights Owners, Inc., 947 P.2d 409 (Idaho 1997), holding that a decree in a private adjudication is not binding in a subsequent comprehensive statutory adjudication.

2. **Development of special procedures.** In 1881, Colorado enacted a special round robin adjudication procedure. All claimants within a water district were joined, any party could contest any claim, and the validity, quantity and priority of each water right was settled in relation to all of the others. Since a district covered only a part of a stream system, co-

ordination between districts was accomplished by allowing users in one district to join in the proceedings in another, or to contest within four years the priorities awarded in another. The decrees were brought up to date from time to time and new uses were added to the list in supplemental adjudications, but no priority could be awarded that was earlier than the latest right adjudicated under the prior decree. Rights not brought to completion were awarded a conditional decree which could ripen into an appropriation if the water was later applied to beneficial use in compliance with the requirements for reasonable diligence. The procedures were modified and recodified in 1943.

The Colorado procedure served as the inspiration for the procedures described in the principal case and in Note 4 below. The Colorado Water Rights Determination and Administration Act of 1969, Colo. Rev. Stat. §§ 37-92-101 to -602, consolidated all decreed water rights into new "tabulations" as described infra p. 167, Note 11.

Montana clung to the classic lawsuit, only slightly modified, until 1973. See Albert W. Stone, Montana Water Rights—A New Opportunity, 34 Mont. L. Rev. 57 (1973). Professor Stone's role changed from that of a lone voice for reform to that of a major prophet with the enactment of the Montana Water Use Act of 1973, Mont. Code Ann. §§ 85-2-101 to -123.

3. **Constitutional barriers to administrative adjudication.** The Wyoming court's views on administrative and constitutional law were quite advanced for the period. Texas adopted the Wyoming system in 1917, but it was struck down in Board of Water Engineers v. McKnight, 229 S.W. 301 (Tex. 1921), as unconstitutionally giving an administrative board judicial power over vested property rights. The constitutionality of subsequent legislation, the Texas Water Adjudication Act of 1967, Tex. Water Code Ann. §§ 11.301-11.341, was upheld in *In re* Adjudication of Water Rights in the Upper Guadalupe River, 642 S.W.2d 438 (Tex. 1982). The court ruled:

"A significant difference between the 1917 Irrigation Act and the procedure under the Water Rights Adjudication Act is that the agency does not make the final determination of rights. There is a two-step procedure. The Commission makes its determination which is followed by an automatic and mandatory judicial review. * * *

"By statute, the standard of review under the Adjudication Act is neither a substantial evidence review nor a de novo review. It is a review made independently of the Commission's adjudication, and a review exercised on those parts of the Commission's determination to which exceptions were timely leveled. In passing on the exceptions, the court may, as in the case now before us, hear additional evidence. Tex. Water Code Ann. § 11.321. The exceptions are the pleadings which the court acts upon with or without a jury trial. The burden of proof is upon the one who levels the exceptions. * * * We conclude that the act, unlike the statutes construed in *McKnight,* 111 Tex. 82, 229 S.W. 301, * * * provides a constitutional method for adjudication."

4. **Adjudication systems.** Most states have adopted one of several variations on the Wyoming theme, combining in some degree the efficiency of the administrative action with the sanctity of a court decree. These systems are described and tabulated in Albert W. Stone, Montana Water Rights—A New Opportunity, 34 Mont. L. Rev. 57, 70-71 (1973):

"The Wyoming system authorizes the Board of Control to select streams for adjudication, to publish notice of the investigation and hearing, and (after a hearing by the Division Superintendent) to make the determination of rights which is conclusive and binding upon all. An aggrieved person may appeal to the courts.

"The Oregon system starts out similarly to the Wyoming system, in that the State Engineer publishes and mails notice, conducts an investigation and hearing, and makes a determination of all rights. But then this administrative order of determination is filed in a circuit court, where interested parties may file exceptions, and from which emanates a final court decree of adjudication which is conclusive and binding upon all, subject to appeal to the Supreme Court of Oregon.

"The Bien Code system derives its name from Morris Bien of the U.S. Reclamation Service who drafted this system of stream adjudication in 1903. It provides for an administrator such as the State Engineer to prepare a hydrographic survey and transmit it to the state Attorney General, who then brings an action in court based upon the Engineer's findings and determinations. Some of the states which use the Bien Code provide for publication of notice and a conclusive decree."

5. **Problems with comprehensive adjudications.** Modern statutes have not solved all of the problems associated with adjudications:

"Many of the western states have entered into ambitious efforts for the comprehensive adjudication of water rights. Unfortunately, most of these states have encountered serious obstacles in their adjudication efforts. Water right claimants, courts, legislatures, and agencies involved in water right adjudications are deeply frustrated by the complexity and resultant length and cost of these adjudications.

"* * *

"Given the myriad issues and interests involved in water rights adjudications, it is no surprise that adjudication efforts face some very real problems. There are, however, some real solutions to these problems. The solutions may include enactment of laws to address substantive issues, or adoption of procedures to make adjudications more effective, whether by statute, formal judicial orders or agency rules, or informal judicial or agency practices. But, given the many issues and interests involved in water rights adjudications, complexity is a fact that no amount of substantive or procedural tinkering can make disappear. The real solution thus becomes the collective efforts of all participants to promote an effective adjudication." A. Lynne Krogh, Water Right Adjudications in the Western States: Procedures, Constitutionality, Problems & Solutions, 30 Land & Water L. Rev. 9, 10-11 (1995).

6. Constitutional limits on legislative efforts to streamline adjudications. In San Carlos Apache Tribe v. Superior Court, 972 P.2d 179 (Ariz. 1999), the Arizona Supreme Court struck down provisions adopted by the legislature in 1995 to expedite the Gila River and Little Colorado River adjudications. These provisions fell into three general categories: (1) substantive provisions which were intended to clarify ambiguities in the law, (2) evidentiary rules and presumptions which were intended to simplify factual findings and legal determinations, and (3) changes to the adjudication process.

The court invalidated all the substantive provisions. Some evidentiary provisions survived, but many were struck on grounds that they impermissibly interfered with judicial powers. Noting that all the parties agreed that procedural changes may be applied retroactively, the court upheld the procedural provisions.

State *ex rel.* Higginson v. United States, 912 P.2d 614 (Idaho 1995), involved constitutional challenges to 1994 amendments to the Snake River adjudication statutes. Like the Arizona litigation, the challenges centered on separation of powers issues. Interpreting the Idaho constitution, the court invalidated some provisions and upheld others. Cf. Idaho Stat. § 42-1507 (Snake River water rights agreement minimum stream flows).

Fremont-Madison Irrigation District & Mitigation Group v. Idaho Ground Water Appropriators, Inc., 926 P.2d 1301 (Idaho 1996), involved a second challenge to the 1994 amendments. This challenge involved so-called "amnesty statutes" which attempted to protect appropriators who had changed or enlarged their appropriations without complying with mandatory statutory procedures. In effect, the amnesty statutes allowed changes or enlargements which had been made unlawfully to be confirmed in the adjudication process. The amnesty statutes were found to be constitutional, largely because changes or enlargements could be confirmed only if they did not harm water rights existing at the time of change or enlargement.

7. Coordination of rights determined in different adjudications. As to coordination of the priorities of parties to different adjudications of confluent streams, see Campbell v. Wyoming Development Co., 100 P.2d 124 (Wyo. 1940), and Alamosa-La Jara Water Users Protection Ass'n v. Gould, 674 P.2d 914 (Colo. 1983).

8. Adjudications involving federal and Indian water rights. The United States and Indian tribes have extensive claims to water in the West. Adjudications involving such rights present unique jurisdictional, procedural, and substantive complications, stemming largely from the sovereign immunity of the United States and Indian tribes and from the basis of rights in federal law, not state law. Chapter 8, Section 3, explores this subject.

9. Adjudication of rights in private proceedings. In states which provide for administrative adjudication of water rights, administrative agencies do not typically have exclusive jurisdiction, and unadjudicated rights may be litigated in suits between private parties. Territory of Haw. v. Gay, 32 Hawaii 404 (1932); Crawford Co. v. Hathaway, 93 N.W. 781 (Neb. 1903). In Simmons v. Ramsbottom, 68 P.2d 153 (Wyo. 1937), the Board of Control had given plaintiff's rights a general date of "1884," and defendant's rights a date of "February 1884." Held, the court can determine the relative priorities without first resubmitting the case to the Board of Control.

Even though administrative agencies do not have exclusive or primary jurisdiction, their decisions are binding on collateral attack. "The Board of Control was given complete and exclusive jurisdiction to make general adjudication of the waters of this state as to priority and amount to which the several appropriators are entitled. The jurisdiction of the courts is (aside from appeals) confined to determining the rights of the parties in individual cases to the extent that the Board has not acted." Campbell v. Wyo. Dev. Co., 100 P.2d 124 (Wyo. 1940).

10. **Adjudication of new rights.** After a general adjudication, new rights are typically added to the list of adjudicated priorities by procedures for separately adjudicating rights acquired by permits. See, e.g., Wyo. Stat. Ann. § 41-4-511.

11. **Inaccurate records.** The water records in many states do not accurately reflect actual water use. In some states, many streams have never been adjudicated. In such states, rights which predate the adoption of a mandatory permit requirement are often not reflected in water rights records. Similarly, rights which are not created by appropriation—e.g., reserved rights and riparian rights—are usually not reflected in the records of unadjudicated streams. In other cases, the adjudications are old and there is substantial divergence between rights as adjudicated and rights as exercised; e.g., changes in points of diversion or place and purpose of use have been made without following prescribed procedures or rights have been abandoned or forfeited (see Chapter 2, Section 4) but are still carried on the records. In addition, most states do not require that changes in ownership of water rights be recorded with water agencies. For example, the ownership of a ranch and appurtenant water rights might be transferred from A to B, but there is no requirement to notify water officials that B now owns the water rights.

Colorado probably has the best procedures for maintaining accurate records. The Colorado Water Right Determination and Adjudication Act of 1969, Colo. Rev. Stat. §§ 37-92-101 to -602, described partially supra p. 126, Note 6, requires a continuous adjudication in each of the state's seven water divisions. This assures that incomplete appropriations (conditional rights) and newly completed appropriations are adjudicated and integrated into the water rights records annually. In addition, each division engineer is required to make periodic tabulations (quadrennially beginning in 1988) in order of seniority of all water rights within his division. These tabulations reflect judgments and decrees entered by the water court since the previous tabulation. Objections to tabulations are permitted, revisions deemed appropriate are made, and the tabulations are filed with the water court. The tabulations form the basis for the administration of water rights by the state engineer and divisions engineers. However, the tabulations are not adjudications and do not themselves alter water rights.

Each division engineer must prepare a decennial abandonment list, noting all rights which appear to have been partially or totally abandoned. After an opportunity for protests and revision, these lists are filed with the water court. Once again, the statutes provide an opportunity for protests and a hearing. Thereafter, the water judge enters a decree which is conclusive as to rights determined to have been abandoned.

Major adjudication efforts underway in several western states will improve water records when completed. Washington and Idaho established deadlines, under penalty of loss, for registration of claims not represented by permits, certificates, or licenses. See Idaho Code §§ 42-241 to -247; Wash. Rev. Code §§ 90.14.010 to -.121. Registration of a claim does not establish its validity in either state. Utah also provides for registration of pre-permit claims, but registration is not mandatory, and the primary effect of registration appears to be evidentiary. See Utah Code Ann. § 73-5-13. Nevada and Idaho require conveyances of water rights to be recorded with water officials. See Idaho Code § 42-248; Nev. Rev. Stat. 533.382 -.387. Failure to record a conveyance appears not to affect the validity of the water right in either state, but administrative notice of actions affecting water rights need only be given to the record owner. The Nevada statutes also provide that recording imparts notice of a transfer to subsequent purchasers of the water right. Nev. Rev. Stat. 533.383.

RETTKOWSKI v. DEPARTMENT OF ECOLOGY
Supreme Court of Washington, 1993.
122 Wash. 2d 219, 858 P.2d 232.

DURHAM, JUDGE. A group of ranchers who water their cattle at the aptly named Sinking Creek have complained to the Department of Ecology (Ecology) for over two decades about the detrimental effect on the creek's flow of groundwater pumping by irrigation farmers in the surrounding area. After numerous investigations, Ecology determined that there was a connection between the groundwater withdrawals and the diminished flow of the creek. Ecology also decided that the water rights of the various ranchers were superior to those possessed by the irrigation farmers. Accordingly, Ecology issued cease and desist orders which prohibited the irrigation farmers from making any further groundwater withdrawals. * * * [T]he dispute was brought to this court to decide if Ecology possesses the authority to issue these orders. We hold that it does not. We also hold that the trial court correctly exercised its jurisdiction in hearing this matter. * * *

The resolution of this case turns on a fundamental rule of administrative law—an agency may only do that which it is authorized to do by the Legislature. * * *

Under RCW 90.03 (hereinafter the Water Code), a "first in time, first in right" rule is followed for appropriations of both groundwater and surface water. RCW 90.03.010. Ecology claims that it was attempting to follow this rule when it issued the cease and desist orders to the Irrigators. While Ecology cannot point to any statute which specifically authorizes the procedures it followed in issuing these orders, it argues that it derives inherent authority to do so from the penumbra of a number of statutes. Primarily, Ecology rests upon its enabling statute as vesting it with the plenary authority to protect senior water rights from encroachment or diminution by junior appropriators. That statute proclaims that Ecology "shall regulate and control the diversion of water in accordance with the rights thereto." RCW 43.21A.064(3). Ecology additionally points out that it is authorized to issue regulatory orders "whenever it appears to [Ecology] that a person is violating or is about to violate any of the provisions of [the Water Code]." RCW 43.27A.190.

However, these broad enabling statutes are silent as to how Ecology is to determine water rights in a regulatory context. This silence is even more telling when compared to the elaborate general adjudication process for determining water rights entrusted to the superior courts by RCW 90.03. Nowhere in Ecology's enabling statutes was it vested with similar authority to conduct general adjudications or even regulatory adjudications of water rights. * * * The absence of a specific grant to Ecology to determine water rights, coupled with an explicit grant to another branch of government to do exactly that, makes Ecology's determination of such rights seemingly ultra vires.

Since Ecology has no explicit statutory authority to rely upon, it asks instead that we extend a number of previous cases to allow it the authority to make "tentative determinations" of the priorities of existing water rights in order to regulate. Ecology argues that it only "tentatively determined" that the Irrigators' rights were junior to those of the Ranchers, and that a final determination would occur if the PCHB [Pollution Control Hearing Board] hearings were allowed to proceed. [Appeals from Ecology decisions are generally heard by the PCHB]

There are two problems with this argument. First, the concept of "tentative determinations" in the cases cited by Ecology was developed in a different context. Each of those cases dealt with the authority of Ecology (or its predecessor agency) to grant permits to appropriate water. The inquiry in that situation is relatively straightforward: is there water available to apportion, is the proposed use beneficial and not detrimental to the public interest, and is there any conflict with existing water rights. RCW 90.03.290. In the permitting situation,

Ecology's determination is limited to tentatively determining whether there are existing water rights with which the proposed use will conflict. Ecology investigates an application for a permit to tentatively determine the existence of water rights and the availability of water. If a conflict exists, it is resolved by denying the permit, not by determining who has the better claim. Ecology does not have to pass upon the validity of such existing or claimed rights in order to determine a potential conflict.

Once the permit has been granted, the situation is significantly different. Permit holders have a vested property interest in their water rights to the extent that the water is beneficially used. Unlike the permitting process, in which Ecology only tentatively determines the existence of claimed water rights, a later decision that an existing permit conflicts with another claimed use and must be regulated necessarily involves a determination of the priorities of the conflicting uses. In order to properly prioritize competing claims, it is necessary to examine when the use was begun, whether the claim had been filed pursuant to the water registration act, RCW 90.14 and whether it had been lost or diminished over time. These determinations necessarily implicate important property rights. It is because of the complicated nature of such inquiries, and their far-reaching effect, that the Legislature has entrusted the superior courts with responsibility therefor. RCW 90.03.110.

The second problem with Ecology's argument that it was only "tentatively determining" water rights is that the PCHB has no jurisdiction to conduct adjudicative hearings regarding such rights. The statute creating the PCHB specifically forbids it to conduct hearings on "[p]roceedings by [Ecology] relating to general adjudications of water rights." RCW 43.21B.110(2)(c). Both Ecology and the PCHB argue that this case did not involve a general adjudication, but rather an appeal of an administrative order issued by Ecology, which would be within the jurisdiction of the PCHB. RCW 43.21B.110(1)(b), (c).

This bootstrap argument is unpersuasive. The administrative orders in question were based upon Ecology's determinations of the existence, quantities, and relative priorities of various legally held water rights. Ecology cannot sustain the argument that it conducted only a little, or a limited, or a tentative, adjudication, so that it is then permitted to have the PCHB conduct a more thorough adjudication. The PCHB cannot adjudicate priorities between water users. Nor can Ecology determine allegedly senior water rights outside of the context of a general adjudication. * * *

Were Ecology allowed to allocate water resources solely on the basis of its own determination of priorities, general adjudications might become unnecessary. Ecology could circumvent the general adjudication process by conducting minor, ad hoc investigations and subsequent piecemeal adjudications throughout the state. This result could prove detrimental to the general adjudication process statewide in light of Ecology's statutory role as the initiator of general adjudications in the superior court. RCW 90.03.110. There would be no reason to grant a petition to initiate a general adjudication if Ecology could conduct its own investigation and solve the conflict as it sees fit. * * *

[U]nder the Water Code, a claim which allegedly dates back to the turn of the century may be found, upon closer examination, to be flawed for a variety of reasons. Ecology's orders assumed that the Ranchers' claims were entirely valid without ever undertaking the formal statutory process necessary to make such a determination. * * *

To summarize, we hold that Ecology had no authority to issue these cease and desist orders without first utilizing a general adjudication pursuant to RCW 90.03 in order to determine the existence, amount, and priorities of the water rights claimed in the Sinking Creek basin. * * * Although the conclusion Ecology reached as to the relative priorities of the water rights in the Sinking Creek basin may ultimately prove to be correct, the only method of ascertaining this will be through a general adjudication.

Notes

1. **Effect of *Rettkowski*.** Can the Department of Ecology ever enforce water rights? Even on a fully adjudicated stream, does not the enforcement of rights implicitly require an "adjudication" that none of the rights have been abandoned or forfeited? Would not a determination by DOE about forfeiture be a forbidden adjudication?

The court in the principal case stated that DOE can make "tentative determinations" of water rights in connection with the issuance of permits. It extended this concept in Okanogan Wilderness League, Inc. v. Town of Twisp, 947 P.2d 732 (Wash. 1997), to include DOE determinations regarding beneficial use in ruling on applications for changes in water rights. Should "tentative determinations" include the matters discussed in the prior paragraph?

The respective jurisdictions of the state engineer, or its equivalent, and the courts remain matters for litigation in states other than Washington. See, e.g., Howell v. Ricci, 197 P.3d 1044 (Nev. 2008) (state engineer could not resolve water rights question that turned on land title issues); El Dorado Util. v. State ex rel. D'Antonio, 110 P.3d 76 (N.M. Ct. App. 2005) (engineer did not adjudicate plaintiff's water rights). In Colorado, jurisdictional issues occur between the water court and the general trial court. See, e.g., Archuleta v. Gomez, 140 P.3d 281 (Colo. Ct. App. 2006) (trial court could resolve trespass questions but not water rights questions).

2. **Comprehensive administration of rights.** In some western states the actual distribution of water and regulation of headgates and storage works is performed by a state official, sometimes known as a water commissioner, working under a central state water agency. The Colorado system is typical:

"Here is an entire state * * * divided into districts covering every stream, creek, or runlet from which water is taken. And up and down these streams, creeks and runlets patrol in every irrigating season a small army of commissioners and deputies who have absolutely complete control of all the water. Not a drop may be diverted not only without their consent but without their actually setting the gates and superintending the diversion. All the districts are combined into divisions along drainage lines, and in each division there is an engineer, a captain over the privates; to him come frequent reports, perhaps daily, perhaps telegraphic, of the flow in every creek, of the rainfall in the headwaters and the mountains, from which he calculates the amount of water which will flow into each district on each day, and upon which, knowing from his records who is entitled to water, in what order, and how much, he 'marshals' the water of all the tributaries in the area and orders its distribution, perhaps from day to day, so that those who are entitled to water shall receive it, whether they be ditch or reservoir owners. At the top is the state engineer who commands the whole array. It is a most complete police system, controlling every phase of the distribution; and more." Moses Lasky, From Prior Appropriation to Economic Distribution of Water by the State, 1 Rocky Mtn. L. Rev. 161, 262 (1929).

The water commissioner's acts are ministerial, comparable to those of a sheriff or police officer, so that regulation of a headgate requires no notice or hearing. Hamp v. State, 118 P. 653 (Wyo. 1911). Disregard of commissioner orders, or opening a closed headgate, is in most states a misdemeanor. Persons aggrieved by the commissioner's acts may appeal to a supervisor and eventually to the central state water agency and to the courts. However, the administrative law doctrine of "exhaustion of administrative remedies" does not apply. The failure to appeal from an adverse decision of the commissioner up through the administrative hierarchy does not bind the courts in a later proceeding between two appropriators. Ryan v. Tutty, 78 P. 661 (Wyo. 1904). Nor does the doctrine of "prior resort" apply in Wyoming. An appropriator aggrieved by another's unlawful diversion may sue for damages or for an injunction without first calling upon the water commissioner to regulate the ditches. Van Buskirk v. Red Buttes Land & Live Stock Co., 156 P. 1122 (Wyo. 1916). Not so in New Mexico. A downstream senior on a regulated stream "must make his needs known," and cannot sue for damage to crops because upstream juniors took all the water, when he did not serve a demand on either the water master or the State Engineer. Worley v. U.S. Borax & Chem. Corp., 428 P.2d 651 (N.M. 1967).

3. **Subordination of unadjudicated rights.** For many years Idaho law allowed both "statutory" water rights obtained in compliance with the

permit statute and "constitutional" water rights self-initiated by diverting water and putting it to beneficial use. Idaho Code § 42-607 directs watermasters distributing water in time of shortage to treat constitutional rights which have never been adjudicated as "subsequent to any adjudicated, decreed, permit, or licensed right" regardless of alleged priority dates. In Nettleton v. Higginson, 558 P.2d 1048 (Idaho 1977), a plaintiff claiming that his prior unadjudicated right had been subordinated to junior recorded rights challenged the constitutionality of the statute on three grounds: deprivation of property without due process, denial of equal protection, and taking of property without just compensation. The court found the statute constitutional in all respects.

4. **Procedural problems in suits against water officials.** Suits by an appropriator against water officials raise difficult procedural problems of party joinder and res judicata. In Mitchell Irrigation District v. Whiting, 136 P.2d 502 (Wyo. 1943), a senior appropriator sued for a mandatory injunction requiring the water commissioner to close the headgates of junior ditches above the plaintiff's point of diversion. Held, the junior appropriators must be joined in the suit. In Merrill v. Bishop, 237 P.2d 186 (Wyo. 1951), a senior sought to enjoin the water commissioner from closing his headgate for the benefit of downstream juniors. Held, the juniors need not be joined. How can these be distinguished? See also McLean v. Farmers' Highline Canal & Reservoir Co., 98 P. 16 (Colo. 1908). In A's suit against a water commissioner, judgment by default was entered enjoining defendant from closing A's headgate except in favor of prior appropriators named in a particular decree. In A's later action against B, an appropriator claiming under another decree, the first suit was not res judicata as to B, even though B had notice of the first action and had been requested to defend it. Lower Latham Ditch Co. v. Louden Irr. Canal Co., 60 P. 629 (Colo. 1900). In contrast, where the first action was between appropriators, it was said: "[T]he question cannot be relitigated between the same parties or their privies, and the defendants, water officials, are in privity with the Ft. Lyon Company. They have no interest of their own. They must obey the decree." On application for rehearing this was qualified: "It is urged that the water officials are not privies to the Ft. Lyon Company. Perhaps not technically, but what we mean is that they must turn out the water according to the judgment of the court, and so are bound thereby as if they had been parties thereto." Reorganized Catlin Consol. Canal Co. v. Hinderlider, 253 P. 389 (Colo. 1927).

5. **Reference of matters to water agencies.** In Laramie Rivers Co. v. LeVasseur, 202 P.2d 680 (Wyo. 1949), plaintiff sued in district court for a declaration as to the relative rights of the parties, appropriators from the same stream. Defendant had previously obtained a permit to construct a reservoir. After plaintiff had sued, defendant began proceedings before the Board of Control for the adjudication of its right. The Board decreed to defendant a right prior to plaintiff's. Plaintiff appealed to the district court, and the appeal was consolidated with plaintiff's suit.

The district court confirmed Board's decision and ruled against the plaintiff in plaintiff's suit. On appeal to the supreme court, plaintiff contended that since the district court had first acquired jurisdiction of the subject matter, the Board lacked jurisdiction. The court disagreed: "we can find no good reason why the court may not avail itself of the aid which may be furnished by having a previous adjudication of the right made by the Board of Control, just as it might refer a case to a referee, and that is in substance the situation in this case." Id. at 695.

The California supreme court has repeatedly noted the trial courts' power to use state administrative agencies' expertise. In one case, it said, "The facilities of the commission can, in this manner, be made available to the trial court and that court can thus secure independent and impartial expert advice not colored by personal interest. Incidentally, the procedure outlined in this section will secure representation of the state in such actions, thus insuring the protection of the rights of the public." Tulare Irr. Dist. v. Lindsay-Strathmore Irr. Dist., 45 P.2d 972 (Cal. 1935). See also Kans. Stat. Ann. § 82a-725.

What would prompt the reverse practice, i.e., administrative use of the courts to enforce the water laws? See a 1973 Wyoming law:

"(a) Upon the request of the state engineer, the attorney general shall bring suit in the name of the state of Wyoming, in the proper district court, to enjoin the unlawful appropriation, diversion or use of the waters of the state, or the waste or loss thereof. A showing of injury in such suits shall not be required as a condition to the issuance of any temporary restraining order, preliminary or permanent injunction. If an appeal is taken from the judgment or decree entered by the district court in such suit, it shall be the duty of the supreme court, at the request of one (1) of the parties, to advance the appeal to the head of its docket and give it precedence over all other civil causes in the hearing and determination thereof." Wyo. Stat. Ann. § 41-2-111.

6. **Jurisdictional problems caused by federalism.** The existence of federal and state courts sometimes complicates the administration and enforcement of water rights. United States v. Alpine Land & Reservoir Company, 174 F.3d 1007 (9th Cir. 1999), involved an appeal to a state court of a decision of the Nevada State Engineer authorizing the transfer of water rights which had previously been adjudicated by the United States District Court for Nevada. On the State Engineer's motion, the federal court enjoined the state court action, holding that it had exclusive jurisdiction to hear the appeal. The Ninth Circuit affirmed, under the principle that the court which first gains jurisdiction over a *"res"* exercises exclusive jurisdiction over actions involving that *res*.

State Engineer v. South Fork Band of Te-Moak Tribe, of Western Shoshone Indians, 339 F.3d 804 (9th Cir. 2003), involved irrigation water rights adjudicated by the Nevada District Court under the Nevada general adjudication statutes. The lands and associated rights were later transferred to the United States for use by the Te-Moak Tribe. The Tribe denied Nevada water officials access to its lands to regulate the rights and stopped paying associated fees. The water officials initiated state court contempt proceedings. The United States removed the case to federal district court. Eventually, under Colorado River Water Conservation District v. United States, infra p. 724, the federal court abstained in favor of the state court proceedings. On appeal, the Ninth Circuit ruled that the federal court should have dismissed, rather than abstained, for want of jurisdiction. Applying the principles relied on in *Alpine,* which it labeled the doctrine of "prior exclusive jurisdiction," the Ninth Circuit held that since the state court first obtained jurisdiction over the water rights when it adjudicated them, the federal court could not exercise jurisdiction.

Critical to both Ninth Circuit decisions was the reservation of continuing jurisdiction by the court adjudicating the rights. Consequently, the doctrine of prior exclusive jurisdiction should not apply to suits to administer rights which were adjudicated administratively, or to suits to administer rights which were adjudicated judicially if the adjudicating court did not reserve jurisdiction. Thus, assuming federal jurisdiction were otherwise proper, a federal court would have jurisdiction in a dispute involving administration of water rights adjudicated statutorily in Wyoming, where the process is administrative, but would not have jurisdiction in an identical situation in Nevada, where a judicial process in which the court retains continuing jurisdiction is used for statutory adjudications. Should the jurisdiction of federal courts depend on the method of statutory adjudication which a state has adopted?

Colorado River Water Conservation District v. United States, infra p. 724, involved concurrent suits in state and federal courts to adjudicate water rights of the federal government. The Supreme Court ruled that both courts had jurisdiction, but held that the federal court should abstain in favor of the state court proceedings even though the federal court proceedings had been commenced first. Is the decision in *Te-Moak* consistent with *Colorado River?* In reconciling *Colorado River,* the Ninth Circuit said: "[The issue in *Colorado River* was] a question of *adjudication.* In contrast, the question here is one of administration. *Colorado River* stands for the unremarkable proposition that, *before* a res has been seized, both federal and state courts enjoy concurrent jurisdiction and may commence proceedings to decide questions about the allocation of water rights. * * * *Colorado River* is thus entirely consistent with the doctrine of prior exclusive jurisdiction. The doctrine is only triggered after a court has acquired jurisdiction over the res." Id. at 813. Is this explanation convincing? Did not the federal court in *Colorado River* first acquire jurisdiction over the "res"? If not, why not?

SECTION 4. LOSS

A. Abandonment

EAST TWIN LAKES DITCHES AND WATER WORKS, INC.
v. BOARD OF COUNTY COMMISSIONERS
Supreme Court of Colorado, 2003.
76 P.3d 918.

RICE, JUSTICE. East Twin Lakes Ditches and Water Works, Inc., ("ETLD") appeals the water court's holding that the water right in the Derry Ditch No. 1, owned by the Lake County Board of County Commissioners ("Lake County"), was not abandoned. ETLD contends that (1) the water right was abandoned due to non-use for approximately thirty years; and (2) the decision by the predecessors of Lake County to not line the ditch was affirmative proof of that abandonment. * * *

The Derry Ditch No. 1 is a senior water right with an appropriation date of 1879 and an adjudication date of 1904 * * * for the irrigation of two hundred acres on what is commonly known as the "Hallenbeck Ranch" in Lake County. * * * In 1972, the Hallenbeck Ranch and all of its water rights were purchased by the Twin Lakes Recreation Land Investment Company ("TLR") * * *. TLR purchased the Hallenbeck Ranch and its water rights with the intent of reselling it for residential development. Despite apparently diligent sales efforts, however, the ranch and its water rights did not sell until 1998 when they were purchased by Lake County.

During the entire twenty-six years that TLR owned the property, the ranch and its water rights were managed by Walter Clotworthy. Throughout this period of time, Clotworthy was unable to get the Derry Ditch No. 1 to carry water more than one-half to one mile down its length. The first section of the ditch was evidently so porous that even the full decree of four cfs would travel only a short distance before it seeped into the bottom of the ditch and disappeared. Clotworthy testified that at various times during his tenure he did grading and shovel work on the ditch in an unsuccessful attempt to improve its carrying capacity. He also made numerous diversions of water into the ditch in a similarly unsuccessful effort to saturate and seal the bottom of the ditch. * * *

[In 1985, Mickelson, one of TLR's general partners,] raised the issue of lining the ditch to the limited partners at a partnership meeting. Because the amount of money that could be assessed the limited partners had already been exhausted, and because it was believed that a sale of the ranch was imminent, Mickelson was unable to secure the partnership funds necessary to line the ditch. As a result, the

Derry Ditch No. 1 remained functionally inoperable for approximately another ten years, up until and after the ranch and water rights were sold to Lake County in 1998. * * *

Lake County concedes that the approximately thirty-year period between 1972 and 2002 during which the Derry Ditch No. 1 water right was not applied to beneficial use gave rise to a presumption of abandonment. The county contends, however, that there was no intent to abandon, that the county and TLR engaged in numerous activities that were inconsistent with an intent to abandon, and that the water court correctly concluded that the presumption had been rebutted. We agree. Our examination of the record reveals sufficient evidence to support the trial court's finding of no abandonment.

The principles of law governing the issue of abandonment in Colorado are well established. "Abandonment of a water right" is defined as "the termination of a water right in whole or in part as a result of the intent of the owner thereof to discontinue permanently the use of all or part of the water available thereunder." § 37-92-103(2), 10 C.R.S. (2002). This court has consistently held that a finding of abandonment requires the concurrence of two elements: a sustained period of non-use and an intent to abandon. The objector must prove abandonment by a preponderance of the evidence.

Because intent is a subjective element that is difficult for a complainant to prove by direct evidence, Colorado law provides that failure to apply water to a beneficial use for a period of ten years creates a rebuttable presumption of abandonment. § 37-92-402(11), 10 C.R.S. (2002). The presumption of abandonment shifts the burden of going forward to the water rights owner, but is insufficient in and of itself to prove abandonment. Rather, the element of intent remains the touchstone of the abandonment analysis, and the owner of the water right can rebut the presumption of abandonment by introducing evidence sufficient to excuse the non-use or demonstrate an intent not to abandon. Acceptable justifications for an unreasonably long period of non-use are limited, however, and a successful rebuttal requires objective and credible evidence, not merely subjective statements of intent by the water rights owner.

A review of our precedent reveals a number of different factors that Colorado courts have considered as indicative of an intent not to abandon a water right. Significantly, although failure to put the water to beneficial use may give rise to the presumption of abandonment in the first instance, it is not the standard by which the second element, intent to abandon, has been measured. Instead, in determining whether or not an owner intended to abandon his water right, Colorado courts have looked at such factors as: (1) repair and maintenance of diversion structures, (2) attempts to put the water to beneficial use, (3) active diversion records and non-appearance of the water right on the State Engineer's abandonment list, (4) diligent efforts to sell the water right, (5) filing documents to protect, change, or preserve the right, (6) leasing the water right, and (7) economic or legal obstacles to exercising the water right. While none of these factors is necessarily conclusive, their cumulative weight, as assessed by the water court, may be enough to rebut a presumption of abandonment. On the other hand, if these factors are insufficient or nonexistent, only then is the failure to put the water to a beneficial use enough by itself to sustain a finding of abandonment.

Because resolution of an abandonment case is largely based upon the weighing of evidence and assessing the credibility of witnesses, this court has consistently held that the water court's resolution of an abandonment case will not be disturbed on appeal unless the evidence contained in the record is "wholly insufficient to support the decision." * * * It is therefore incumbent upon this court to search the record for any evidence in support of the decision, and if successful, to uphold the decision even if, had this court been the trier of fact, it might have held differently. With these principles in mind, we now turn to the task of determining whether there was sufficient evidence * * * to support the water court's decision that the Derry Ditch No. 1 was not abandoned * * * between 1972 and 2002.

Two of the TLR general partners (Mickelson and Sims), Clotworthy, and a former Lake County Commissioner all testified that despite the problems with the carrying capacity of the Derry Ditch No. 1, it was never the intent of Lake County or TLR to abandon the water right. To the contrary, each asserted that the water rights associated with the Hallenbeck Ranch were exceedingly important assets, and of those rights, the Derry Ditch No. 1 was the most important because it was the most senior. Mickelson and Sims also indicated that all of the Hallenbeck Ranch water rights were critical components of their sales efforts. These statements, although valid evidence to be weighed by the water court, are necessarily subjective and therefore fall well short of the quantum of proof necessary to rebut a presumption of abandonment.

There is, however, an abundance of other objective evidence in the record regarding actions taken by TLR and Lake County that were inconsistent with an intent to abandon the Derry Ditch No. 1. These include attempts to repair the ditch and divert water, the filing of legal documents with regard to the water right, the fact that the water right never appeared on the State Engineer's abandonment list, the lease of the water right, diligent efforts to sell the ranch and water rights, and financial obstacles to exercising the water right. We turn now to an examination of this evidence.

There was a substantial amount of evidence in the record regarding maintenance and repair of the Derry Ditch No. 1. TLR engaged

Clotworthy as an on-site ranch manager almost immediately upon TLR's acquisition of the Hallenbeck Ranch in 1972. * * * Clotworthy made a number of attempts during his tenure to maintain the Derry Ditch No. 1 and apply the water to beneficial use. He testified that during the time period from 1985 to 1990, and perhaps earlier, he used a tractor, grader, and shovel in attempts to get the ditch to carry water. * * *

There was also evidence introduced at trial regarding attempts—although unsuccessful—to put the water right to beneficial use in the years between 1972 and 2002. Clotworthy testified that he diverted water into the ditch a number of times over his years at the ranch, either in an attempt to saturate and seal the bottom of the ditch, or to check the success of his grading efforts. * * * The Derry Ditch No. 1 was never listed during this time on the State Engineer's abandonment list.

TLR and Lake County also took legal and investigative actions during their years of ownership that were consistent with the use and protection of their water rights. Sims testified that during his involvement with the partnership, TLR actively investigated several other water rights applications and filed one statement of opposition, to ensure that its water rights were protected. In 1995, TLR filed several applications with the water court to correct invalid points of diversions in its water decrees, including a filing for the Derry Ditch No. 1. In 1998, Lake County filed jointly with the City of Aurora to the water court requesting that the Derry Ditch No. 1 be used as an alternate point of diversion in a change case.

The next evidence presented at trial of an intent not to abandon was the lease of the Derry Ditch No. 1. In 1980, TLR leased the Hallenbeck Ranch and all its water rights to Box Creek Mining Company, a business entity initially owned by Clotworthy. * * * The venture ultimately failed, however, evidently due to partnership squabbles and the failure to obtain financing, and the lease was terminated in 1992. Regardless of the failure of the mining venture, the lease of the Derry Ditch No. 1 by TLR to Box Creek Mining Company, even for an undecreed use, demonstrates an intent to not abandon the water right. * * *

Although not specific to the Derry Ditch No. 1, intent not to abandon was next demonstrated by TLR's consistent efforts to sell the ranch and its water rights throughout the duration of its ownership. * * * TLR introduced a voluminous exhibit at trial detailing the partnership's sales efforts from 1975 through 1998, including documentation of marketing efforts, preliminary letters of interest, sales proposals, two signed option agreements, and two signed sales contracts (which ultimately failed). * * *

The final type of evidence this court has considered in rebutting a presumption of abandonment is the presence of legal or economic obstacles to exercising a water right. * * * Such conditions were arguably present here; testimony indicated that the partnership declined to line the ditch because the amount of money that could be assessed the limited partners had already been exhausted, and because it was believed that a sales contract was imminent.

ETLD argues, however, that the partnership's failure to act, followed by approximately another ten years of non-use is instead affirmative proof of abandonment. The trial court took the opposite view, finding that the request Mickelson made to the limited partners to line the ditch was "indicative of a desire to maintain the ditch and is contrary to an intent to abandon." We find no error in the trial court's conclusion. The task before the court was to determine the intent of the partnership, as an entity, with regard to the use or abandonment of the water right. Such intent would be better evidenced by the general partner's actions than by an investment decision made by limited partners who likely had no familiarity whatsoever with the Derry Ditch No. 1.

In summary, the record indicated that Lake County and TLR took a number of actions inconsistent with an intent to abandon. * * * None of these actions was by itself conclusive nor sufficient to rebut the presumption of abandonment. Indeed, over a period of thirty years, many of these activities were inconsistent, sporadic, and subject to contradictory interpretations. Nevertheless, taken as a whole, we find there was sufficient evidence in the record to support the water court's finding of no abandonment. The water court's findings of fact in an abandonment case are accorded considerable deference and we will not reverse absent a showing of abuse of discretion. There was no such abuse here. * * *

HOBBS, JUSTICE, dissenting: * * * Beneficial use is essential to the establishment of a water right and its perpetuation. Knapp v. Colorado River Water Conservation Dist., 131 Colo. 42, 52, 279 P.2d 420, 425 (1955). "Speculation on the market, or sale expectancy, is wholly foreign to the principle of keeping life in a proprietary right and is no excuse for failure to perform that which the law requires." Id. at 56, 279 P.2d at 427; see Southeastern Colo. Water Conservancy Dist. v. Twin Lakes Assocs., 770 P.2d 1231, 1238 (Colo. 1989).

Our cases repeatedly provide that "[c]ontinued and unexplained nonuse of a water right for an unreasonable period of time creates a rebuttable presumption of *intent* to abandon." City & County of Denver v. Snake River Water Dist., 788 P.2d 772, 776 (Colo. 1990) (emphasis added) * * *. Here, the nonuse is explained, but this explanation supports abandonment, and not the water court's conclusion that the presumption of abandonment was rebutted. The explanation for nonuse is that the ditch could not deliver the water to its place of use, and the owner did not wish to make the investment an actual water user would be required to make to maintain the priority of the water right. * * *

Affirmatively deciding not to make repairs necessary to utilize a water right is convincing evidence of intent to abandon it. Southeastern Colo. Water Conservancy Dist., 770 P.2d at 1241 (upholding finding of abandonment when ditches deteriorated and were not repaired); Masters Inv. Co. v. Irrigationists Ass'n, 702 P.2d 268, 270 (Colo. 1985) (upholding finding of abandonment where ditch had washed away and was not replaced). Evidence of non-repair is especially persuasive where the owner ignored advice that the repairs were required. *Haystack Ranch,* 997 P.2d at 553. Failure to maintain the entire length of the ditch is also evidence of intent to abandon. Southeastern Colo. Water Conservancy Dist., 770 P.2d at 1236-37.

We have considered economic difficulty a justifiable excuse for nonuse in very limited circumstances. We recognized that the Great Depression, material and labor shortages during World War II, and federal regulatory requirements can provide an excuse for nonuse. Hallenbeck v. Granby Ditch & Reservoir Co., 160 Colo. 555, 568, 420 P.2d 419, 426 (1966). However, run-of-the-mill economic difficulties are not recognized. "Nonuse resulting from present economic difficulties, coupled with an expectation of a more favorable economic climate for future use, will not constitute justifiable excuse." Southeastern Colo. Water Conservancy Dist., 770 P.2d at 1238.

Without doubt, the investment partnership tried repeatedly to sell the ranch and the water rights. However, in *Knapp,* we held that intent to sell a water right, including listing the right with a real estate agent, was not sufficient to overcome the presumption of abandonment raised by a long period of nonuse. 131 Colo. at 55-56, 279 P.2d at 427.

I would distinguish our decision in Danielson v. City of Thornton, 775 P.2d 11 (Colo. 1989), from this case. There, a developer acquired the water rights for use in a central water system for a subdivision it was creating. It sought to obtain a change of point of diversion for the wells to effectuate its use. Upon finding that a centralized water system would be impractical, it diligently and continuously attempted to sell the water rights to a party who would use the water under the water rights. The wells were in good condition and capable of operation throughout the efforts to sell them. Within eight years, the developer sold the water rights. The water court held that, under the circumstances, eight years was a reasonable time period to effectuate sale of the water rights. On appeal, we applied a legal standard that took into account the "totality of the evidence in evaluating whether a water right [had] been abandoned" and concluded that it had not. In contrast, in this case, the investment partnership never had a use for the water, never effectuated a use, and when put on actual notice of the need to maintain the water rights, affirmatively decided not to repair the structure so the right could be utilized under its decree.

As we recognized in *Danielson,* efforts to sell the water right, in light of other evidence in the case, may be sufficient to overcome the presumption of abandonment arising from a prolonged period of non-use. But, we also said that the presumption of abandonment is a strong one. The *Knapp* anti-speculation basis for the abandonment doctrine continues to be good law, in my view. * * *

I disagree with the Majority conclusion that there is competent evidence in the record to rebut the strong presumption of abandonment arising from the investment partnership's prolonged period of nonuse. The investment partnership's decision not to repair the ditch is factually no different from those cases in which water courts and we have declared abandonment based upon prolonged failure to repair. Here, the evidence of holding the right for speculation is manifest. Like *Knapp,* this case involved twenty-six years of nonuse and "[o]n the whole their conduct is much more indicative of being speculative than operative." 131 Colo. at 51, 279 P.2d at 425. Accordingly, I * * * respectfully dissent.

Notes

1. **Questions on intent.** Can the differences between Justices Rice and Hobbs be explained by concluding that Justice Rice focuses on intent to abandon the water right while Justice Hobbs focuses on intent to abandon the use of water authorized by the right? If so, which approach is most consistent with the principle of beneficial use? If the correct focus is on abandonment of the water right, why would anyone intentionally abandon a valuable right, particularly a "senior water right?" Justice Rice says that "subjective statements of intent" are not sufficient to rebut the presumption of abandonment. Why not, if intent truly is the "touchstone" of abandonment? Certainly, present statements of past intent may be highly suspect from an evidentiary standpoint, but what about past statements? For example, what if an owner has given regular notices to water officials of the intent to retain a right? In terms of proving intent, what is the difference between such notices and efforts to sell a water right? Is the difference between mere statements and the acts relied on by Justice Rice to rebut the presumption of abandonment more a matter of effort than intent?

2. **Contrary authority on rebuttal evidence?** In *In re* Adjudication of the Clark Fork River, the court reaffirmed several decisions holding that to rebut the presumption of abandonment a party "must establish 'some fact or condition excusing the long period of nonuse,' not mere expression of hope or desire reflecting a 'gleam-in-the eye philosophy' regarding future uses of the water." 908 P.2d 1353, 1355 (Mont.

1995) (quoting CF&I Steel Corp. v. Purgatoire River Water Cons'y Dist., 515 P.2d 456 (Colo. 1973)). Can efforts to sell a water right help rebut the presumption in Montana? If "must" means "must", is intent really an element of abandonment in Montana?

3. **Miscellaneous holdings.** Where an appropriator sold land with a water right, and later repurchased the land and irrigated it with water obtained by renting other water rights, he abandoned his prior right. Brockman v. Grand Canal Co., 76 P. 602 (Ariz. 1904). Turning water into another ditch, but not using it, was a mere pretense not preventing abandonment in Parsons v. Fort Morgan Reservoir & Irrigation Co., 136 P. 1024 (Colo. 1913), but the yearly turning of water into a broken ditch, whence it shortly returned to the stream, negated an intent to abandon in Featherman v. Hennessy, 113 P. 751 (Mont. 1911). In Colorado, "economic, financial or legal difficulties or natural calamities" confronting an appropriator may excuse nonuse, Hallenbeck v. Granby Ditch & Reservoir Co., 420 P.2d 419 (Colo. 1966), but not the present economic infeasibility of a particular use, CF&I Steel Corp. v. Purgatoire River Water Conservancy District., supra p. 182, Note 2. Montana follows Colorado on the latter point, *In re* Adjudication of the Clark Fork River, supra p. 182, Note 2, but 79 Ranch, Inc. v. Pitsch, 666 P.2d 215 (Mont. 1983), held that an appropriator's lacks of funds to irrigate does not rebut the presumption of abandonment.

In re Adjudication of the Clark Fork River Drainage Area, 833 P.2d 1120 (Mont. 1992), held that the presumption of intent to abandon was not rebutted by carrying unused rights as an asset on the books of a municipal corporation. Cf. Mont. Rev. Code § 85-2-227 (criteria for presumption of municipal nonabandonment). Okanogan Wilderness League, Inc. v. Town of Twisp, 947 P.2d 732 (Wash. 1997), held that a municipality's "continuous existence and need for a municipal water supply" was not sufficient to rebut the presumption. United States v. Alpine Land & Reservoir Co., 27 F. Supp. 2d 1230 (D. Nev. 1998), held that the payment of taxes and assessments associated with water rights of an irrigation project can be considered in determining intent to abandon. Including water rights in deeds conveying real property was held not to be sufficient to rebut a presumption of abandonment in Haystack Ranch, LLC v. Fazzio, 997 P.2d 548 (Colo. 2000). That case also held that removal of water rights from a division engineer's abandonment list does not preclude a finding of abandonment, although it may be considered in determining abandonment. Nevada, apparently alone among western states, holds that long non-use does not give rise to a rebuttable presumption of abandonment, but only evinces an intent to abandon. United States v. Orr Water Ditch Co., 256 F.3d 935 (9th Cir. 2001) (Nevada law).

4. **Excess water.** Where an appropriator is decreed water in excess of his needs, the failure to put such excess to use constituted an abandonment. New Mercer Ditch Co. v. Armstrong, 40 P. 989 (Colo. 1895).

5. **Abandonment as a strategy.** In City of Denver v. Middle Park Water Conservancy District, 925 P.2d 283 (Colo. 1996), Denver found it-

self in the seemingly absurd position of defending its asserted abandonment of certain rights which it had purchased against the claim of Middle Park that Denver had not abandoned the rights. Why would Denver purchase and then attempt to abandon water rights? Denver diverts water for municipal supply upstream from the diversion points for the purchased rights, all of which were senior to Denver's right. By purchasing and abandoning the rights, Denver increased diversions to its project because it no longer had to bypass water to satisfy those rights.

Why would Middle Park object to abandonment of the rights? Middle Park apparently has rights which are junior to Denver's right and which are downstream from the purchased rights. Prior to Denver's purchase, Middle Park received the return flows from the purchased rights. The elimination of the bypass water also eliminated the return flows to Middle Park. Middle Park argued that Denver had not abandoned the purchased rights but was exercising them by diverting them to its municipal supply project. Middle Park had apparently hoped to force Denver to seek a formal transfer of the purchased rights. In such a formal transfer, Denver might be required to bypass flows equal to the historic return flows of the purchased rights. See Section 5 of this Chapter. The court, however, held that Denver had successfully (!) abandoned the rights.

B. Forfeiture

RENCKEN v. YOUNG
Supreme Court of Oregon, 1985.
300 Or. 352, 711 P.2d 954.

CAMPBELL, JUSTICE. This is a review of a decision by the Court of Appeals which affirmed an order of the Director of the Water Resources Department canceling the bulk of a water right owned by Rudolph G. Rencken. The water right had granted Rencken the use of the water from the East Branch of Mud Creek to irrigate 10 acres in Umatilla County. Following an administrative hearing, the Director found that Rencken had not used the water for "five successive years" as required by ORS 540.610(1) and canceled the right for irrigation except for .1 acre. * * * We remand to the Director with instructions to re-evaluate the evidence in light of this opinion.

Two of the chief issues in this case involve the interpretation of ORS 540.610(1) which provides: "Beneficial use shall be the basis, the measure and the limit of all rights to the use of water in this state. Whenever the owner of a perfected and developed water right ceases or fails to use the water appropriated for a period of five successive years, the right to use shall cease, and the failure to use shall be conclusively presumed to be an abandonment of water right. Thereafter the water which was the subject of use under such water right shall revert to the public and become again the subject of appropriation in the manner provided by law, subject to existing priorities."

* * * In 1979, 1980, 1981 and 1982, [Rencken] did not use the water granted by the right except to irrigate a garden of approximately .1 acre. The factual controversy in this case concerns * * * 1983. * * * During the fall season of 1983, Rencken excavated a small pond or sump near the East Branch of Mud Creek to receive and hold water from the channel of the stream. He then purchased and installed an electric centrifugal pump to pump the water from the sump into the pipeline serving the sprinkler irrigation system. The pump was purchased in September 1983 and a permit which authorized the connection of the electricity to it was obtained * * * on October 4, 1983.

Witnesses on Rencken's behalf testified that after the pump was installed, the alfalfa growing on the 10 acres was irrigated in late October or November 1983, with water from the East Branch of Mud Creek. The assistant water master for the area observed the subject land being irrigated with water from the same source on November 21, 1983. Two neighboring orchard owners, who were the proponents of the cancellation and interested witnesses, testified that the irrigation of the subject 10 acres with water from the East Branch of Mud Creek did not commence until after the end of October 1983.

The [Director] found that water from the East Branch of Mud Creek was not used by Rencken in 1983 to irrigate the 10 acres until after the end of the irrigation season on October 31. The Director's ultimate findings of fact in part were: "With the exception of the continued use of water from the East Branch of Mud Creek for irrigation of a garden area of approximately 0.1 acre in area, water from the East Branch of Mud Creek was not diverted and used for irrigation under the provisions of the water right in question during the years of 1979, 1980, 1981, 1982 and 1983, being a period of five successive years of nonuse." The Director then ordered that the right to use the water * * * for irrigation purposes be canceled as to 9.9 acres.

The principal issues in this case are: (1) Does ORS 540.610(1) provide for the "abandonment" or the "forfeiture" of water rights after a failure to use; (2) Does the term "five successive years" in ORS 540.610(1) mean "five successive calendar years" or "five successive irrigation seasons," and (3) Did the Director properly allocate the burden of proof in evaluating the evidence?

The distinction between "abandonment" and "forfeiture" is important to the correct determination of this case. The Director, relying upon Withers et al. v. Reed, * * * 243 P.2d 283 (1952), held that ORS 540.610(1) is a forfeiture statute. However, if ORS 540.610(1) is an abandonment statute and an intent to abandon the water right is required, the Director might have reached a different result because

there is uncontradicted evidence in the record that before the end of
the fifth irrigation season, Rencken dug a sump and bought an electrical pump to use the water from the East Branch of Mud Creek.

ORS 540.610(1) was passed by the Oregon Legislature in 1913 as
Chapter 279. * * * Oregon cases decided after the enactment of this
statute have not always drawn a clear distinction between abandonment and forfeiture. * * *

In Withers et al. v. Reed, supra, the sole question was whether
[the predecessor to ORS 540.610(1)], applied to the State of Oregon's
ownership of lands. * * * During the period of 13 years when the state
owned the land, it was not irrigated, although water was available for
that purpose. * * * Justice Lusk, writing for this court, held that
OCLA § 116-437, now ORS 540.610(1), applied to the state ownership
of lands and affirmed the circuit court. The 4-3 opinion of the court
said at * * * 243 P.2d 283:

> Under the statute in question, failure of "the owner of a perfected
> and developed water right" to use the water appropriated for a period
> of five successive years works a *forfeiture* of the right, not for the
> benefit of any individual as in the case of an ordinary statute of limi-
> tations—which this is not—but for the benefit of the public, to the
> end that the "water right shall revert to the public and become again
> the subject of appropriation in the manner provided by law." * * *
> (Emphasis added.) * * *

Two law professors and one attorney general agree that ORS
540.610(1) is a forfeiture statute. Professor Chapin D. Clark in Survey
of Oregon's Water Laws * * * at page 153 refers to ORS 540.610(1):
"This is a statutory declaration that failure to use a water right for
five successive years shall cause the right to be forfeited. Intent to
abandon, actual or inferred, is not an element of forfeiture." * * *

1942-44 Opinions of Attorney General 48 comments on OCLA
§ 116-437 (now ORS 540.610(1)): "Although the statute employs the
word 'abandonment', it clearly contemplates an involuntary forfeiture
through non-user rather than a voluntary abandonment. An intent to
relinquish the right is, of course, an essential element of abandonment, but the forfeiture provided by section 116-437 results without
regard to the owner's intent."

2 Hutchins, Water Rights Law in the Nineteen Western States
(1974), contains the following statement concerning ORS 540.610(1)
on page 320: " * * * The controlling sentence in the Oregon statute
reads: 'Whenever the owner of a perfected and developed water right
ceases or fails to use the water appropriated for a period of five successive years, the right to use shall cease, and the failure to use shall
be *conclusively presumed* to be an abandonment of water right.' [Em-
phasis in original.] This goes beyond the Kansas Legislature's 'shall

be deemed abandoned' and makes it clear that if 'conclusively presumed' means anything at all, it completely rules out the element of intent. Its ingredients are those of forfeiture—nonuse and lapse of time. Although this may purport to be an abandonment statute, it is in effect a forfeiture statute."

Since * * * Withers et al. v. Reed, supra, this court has consistently indicated that ORS 540.610(1) is a forfeiture statute. * * * We reaffirm Withers et al. v. Reed, supra.

Next we are requested to determine if * * * "five successive years" in ORS 540.610(1) means "five successive calendar years" or "five successive irrigation seasons." * * * Rencken contends that ORS 540.610(1) refers to calendar years. Therefore, even if the Director found that Rencken did not use the water during the fifth irrigation season which ended on October 31, 1983, his undisputed use of the water in November 1983 was within the fifth calendar year * * *. Under Rencken's position, this proceeding should be dismissed.

Even if we should decide that ORS 540.610(1) refers to "calendar years" and not "irrigation seasons," it does not help Rencken. His water right from the East Branch of Mud Creek was limited for irrigation to a season from March to October. Rencken's use of the water in November was not "the water appropriated" under the circuit court decree and referred to in ORS 540.610(1). * * * We hold that Rencken's use of the water from the East Branch of Mud Creek during November 1983 was not "appropriated water" within the limits of his adjudicated right. We are dealing with a decree that specifically limits the use of the water for irrigation from March to October of each year * * *.

The Director's findings of fact * * * contain the following statement: "The initial burden is on the proponents of cancellation to show that a period of five successive years of nonuse of water under the terms of the water right in question has occurred. With the exception of that portion of the water right in question appurtenant to the 0.1 acre garden area, proponents did meet that burden in regard to the use of water for irrigation. [¶] The burden of proof then shifted to the [Rencken] to refute the showing made by proponents. [Rencken] did not meet that burden."

The Director is mistaken. The burden of proof does not shift. There is no affirmative defense in this proceeding. "The burden of presenting evidence to support a fact or position in a contested case rests on the proponent of the fact or position." ORS 183.450(2). The proponents of cancellation have the burden to prove by reliable, probative and substantial evidence, ORS 183.450(5), that Rencken had ceased or failed to use the water appropriated for a period of five successive years. * * *

The proceeding is remanded to the Director of Water Resources to re-evaluate the evidence in light of this opinion.

Notes

1. **Legislative clarification?** Or. Rev. Stat. § 540.610(1) now reads: "Whenever the owner of a perfected and developed water right ceases or fails to use all or part of the water appropriated for a period of five successive years, the failure to use shall establish a rebuttable presumption of forfeiture of all or part of the water right." Does this change make it clear that forfeiture, not abandonment, is intended? See Hannigan v. Hinton, 97 P.3d 1256 (Or. Ct. App. 2004) (assuming without discussion that the preceding provision is a forfeiture statute).

2. **Unauthorized uses.** United States v. Alpine Land & Reservoir Co., 340 F.3d 903 (9th Cir. 2003), held that the use of rights appurtenant to one part of a farm to irrigate other parts of the farm forfeits the rights. Similarly, Hannigan v. Hinton, supra p. 188, Note 1, held that the use of water at an unauthorized location does not prevent forfeiture. Hennings v. Water Resources Department, 622 P.2d 333 (Or. Ct. App. 1981), held that the use of water to wet ground for plowing does not avoid forfeiture when "irrigation" is the authorized use. In contrast, Russell-Smith v. Water Resources Department, 952 P.2d 104 (Or. Ct. App. 1998), and Salt Lake City v. Silver Fork Pipeline Corp., 5 P.3d 1206 (Utah 2000), held that unauthorized changes in the diversion point do not forfeit the water rights.

3. **Forfeiture statutes.** The statutes vary considerably in their language and in the period of nonuse that will result in forfeiture. One common feature is a list of circumstances which excuse nonuse. See, e.g., Idaho Stat. § 42-223; Or. Rev. Stat. § 540.610(2); Wash. Rev. Code § 90.14.140. As the Oregon experience demonstrates, neither the legislatures nor the courts have carefully distinguished abandonment and forfeiture. See, for example, Scott v. McTiernan, 974 P.2d 966 (Wyo. 1999), in which the court repeatedly refers to "abandonment" while stating that "intent" to abandon need not be shown under the statute involved. (The statute, Wyo. Stat. Ann. Ann. § 41-3-401, uses both "abandoned" and "forfeit.") Cf. Hawley v. Kan. Dep't of Agric., 132 P.3d 870 (Kan. 2006) (finding legislative intent to enact a forfeiture statute from its phrase, "shall be deemed abandoned and shall terminate").

4. **Effect of forfeiture statutes on abandonment.** Adoption of a forfeiture statute does not necessarily result in rejection of abandonment. See Crow v. Carlson, 690 P.2d 916 (Idaho 1984); New Mexico ex rel. Martinez v. McDermett, 901 P.2d 745 (N.M. Ct. App. 1995). In Washington, which recognizes both concepts, cities are exempt from forfeiture but not from abandonment. Okanogan Wilderness League, Inc. v. Town of Twisp, 947 P.2d 732 (Wash. 1997). See also United States v. Alpine Land & Reservoir Co., 510 F.3d 1035 (9th Cir. 2007) (analyzing claims of abandonment and forfeiture under Nevada law).

5. **Involuntary nonuse.** Ramsay v. Gottsche, 69 P.2d 535 (Wyo. 1937), held that a forfeiture requires a "voluntary act," and did not occur when the appropriator was prevented from using water for several years by floods that washed out his diversion works. In 1973 the Wyoming legislature amended the forfeiture statute to provide that forfeiture will occur if the appropriator fails "either intentionally or unintentionally" to use water. Wyo. Stat. Ann. § 41-3-401. In Scott v. McTiernan, supra p. 188, Note 3, the court held that the amendment had not overruled *Ramsay*. The court said that "intent to abandon" need not be shown in order for a right to be extinguished under the statute, but nonuse must still be "voluntary," i.e., not the result of circumstance beyond the owner's control.

6. **Standing.** In Horse Creek Conservation District v. Lincoln Land Co., 92 P.2d 572 (Wyo. 1939), the court required the complaining party to show that he would be benefited by a declaration of forfeiture. It held that a late-priority junior appropriator with a "flood water right," who would receive little water whether the questioned right were used or not, had no standing to initiate the proceedings. A 1985 amendment expressly gives standing to any person having a right which is "equal to or junior in date of priority to the right for which abandonment is sought." Wyo. Stat. Ann. § 41-3-401. Held: A complaining party must still show it will benefit from forfeiture. Joe Johnson Co. v. Wyo. State Bd. of Control, 857 P.2d 312 (Wyo. 1993).

7. **Jurisdiction.** In Louth v. Kaser, 364 P.2d 96 (Wyo. 1961), the Wyoming Supreme Court held that the statutory procedure for declaration of forfeiture was not exclusive, and that the question of abandonment and forfeiture could be decided in private litigation. In 1973, the Wyoming legislature gave the State Board of Control exclusive original jurisdiction over forfeiture proceedings. Wyo. Stat. Ann. § 41-3-401.

8. **Concentration of water.** Will forfeiture lie if an irrigator concentrates water on only a part of the land included in the appropriation?

N.M. Stat. Ann. § 72-5-28F: "The owner or holder of a valid water right or permit to appropriate waters for agricultural purposes appurtenant to designated or specified lands may apply the full amount of water covered by or included in said water right or permit to any part of the designated or specified tract without penalty or forfeiture."

Wyo. Stat. Ann. § 41-3-401(f): "An appropriation for irrigation use is not subject to partial abandonment for failure of the appropriator to irrigate part of the lands described in his permit or certificate of appropriation during the successive five (5) year period if:

(i) Facilities to divert the water and to apply it to beneficial use upon the lands which were not irrigated existed in usable form during the period of nonuse; and

(ii) There was not a sufficient supply of water available, because of regulation for prior water rights or because shortage of supply resulted in insufficient water to satisfy the appropriation in full, to irrigate the lands for which abandonment is sought provided that a diligent effort was made to use the supply which was available."

In Russell-Smith v. Water Resources Department, 952 P.2d 104 (Or. Ct. App. 1998), the court held that use of water through an unauthorized diversion point does not forfeit the right.

9. **Revival by resumed use.** If the holder of the right does not use the water for the statutory period, but uses it again before a forfeiture declaration, is the right revived? In Town of Eureka v. State Engineer, 826 P.2d 948 (Nev. 1992), the court held that substantial use of water "cures" the forfeiture so long as no forfeiture proceeding has commenced. It cited Carrington v. Crandall, 147 P.2d 1009 (Idaho 1944), and Sturgeon v. Brooks, 281 P.2d 675 (Wyo. 1955), but acknowledged that contrary holdings had been given in Bausch v. Myers, 541 P.2d 817 (Or. 1975), and in *In re* Cancellation of Stabio Ditch Water Right, 417 N.W.2d 391 (S.D. 1987). The *Eureka* rule is codified in Arizona. See Ariz. Rev. Stat. § 45-188D. Oregon and Utah both require forfeiture proceedings to be brought within 15 years after a resumption of use. Or. Rev. Stat. § 540.610(2)(f); Utah Code Ann. § 73-1-4(3)(c). The Idaho Supreme Court reaffirmed the "resumption of use doctrine" in 2003 in Sagewillow, Inc. v. Idaho Department of Water Resources, 70 P.3d 669 (Idaho 2003), but deprived the doctrine of most of its practical significance by holding that a forfeited right may be revived by resumed use only where there are no junior appropriators who have used water during the forfeiture period.

10. **Notice and Hearing.** In *In re* Cancellation of Stabio Ditch Water Right, supra p. 190, Note 9, the court acknowledged that the forfeiture statute appeared to be self-executing—i.e., nonuse for the statutory period extinguished the right without any judicial or administrative action. Nevertheless, the court concluded that due process required a hearing before forfeiture occurred and that a right existed until the hearing on forfeiture was finalized. However, the court seemingly deprived this holding of much of its significance by ruling that a right cannot be revived by resuming use of water after the statutory forfeiture period. Did the court confuse the due process requirements for forfeiture with the requirements of a judicial or administrative determination that forfeiture has occurred? See Texaco, Inc. v. Short, 454 U.S. 516 (1982), in which the Supreme Court held that an Indiana statute which terminates severed mineral rights without notice or a hearing is constitutional. The Court noted, however, that due process notice and hearing requirements are applicable to procedures to determine if termination has occurred.

In Kansas, which has a five year forfeiture statute, the state engineer must notify any water rights holder who has failed for three consecutive years to report water use. Hawley v. Kan. Dep't of Agric., 132 P.3d 870 (Kan. 2006). If two more years pass without water use, or a sufficient excuse, the state engineer holds a hearing. At the hearing, a verified copy of the engineer's report of nonuse is prima facie evidence of forfeiture. The burden shifts to the water rights holder to rebut. Frick Farm Prop. v. State, 190 P.3d 983 (Kan. Ct. App. 2008).

11. **Conservation and forfeiture.** Prior appropriation law is sometimes criticized as conducive to waste or at least giving no incentive to save water. Cf. *Kovacovich* and notes, supra p. 103. To promote efficient water use, California allows an appropriator to keep for its own benefit water saved either by conservation efforts or by using reclaimed or polluted water in lieu of appropriated water. It also provides that cessation or reduction in the use of appropriated water from these activities is equivalent to a reasonable beneficial use of the appropriated water and will not forfeit the water right. Cal. Water Code §§ 1010, 1011.

12. **Effect on water records.** If vigorously enforced, forfeiture and abandonment procedures can help reduce the divergence between water records and actual water use. In Colorado, each division engineer must prepare a list of unused rights every ten years; these lists serve as a basis for abandonment proceedings in the water court. See supra p. 167, Note 11. In Nebraska, the Department of Water Resources must examine ditches "as often as necessary" and initiate cancellation proceedings on its own motion. Neb. Rev. Stat. § 46-229.01; see also Mont. Rev. Code § 85-2-405; Wyo. Stat. Ann. § 41-3-402; Tex. Water Rights Comm'n v. Wright, 464 S.W.2d 642 (Tex. 1971).

13. **Forfeiture and water rights transfers.** Does approval of a change in point of diversion, in place of use, or in purpose of use by a state water rights agency preclude a subsequent claim that the transferred right was forfeited or abandoned prior to its transfer? In Kerivan v. Water Resources Commission, 72 P.3d 659 (Or. Ct. App. 2003), the court answered yes, but in Sagewillow, Inc. v. Idaho Department of Water Resources, 70 P.3d 669 (Idaho 2003), the court held that res judicata and collateral estoppel did not preclude such a challenge unless forfeiture or abandonment was actually raised in the transfer proceeding.

14. **Duration of water rights.** Appropriation statutes are silent on the duration of water rights. The Supreme Court of the United States once said that an appropriation is a "vested right to take and divert from the same source, and to use and consume the same quantity of water annually forever." Arizona v. California, 283 U.S. 423, 459 (1931). Is the tenure of the water right like that of land held in fee simple absolute? Does a forfeiture statute make it more like a fee simple determinable, or a fee simple subject to condition subsequent?

In 1985, Montana enacted leasing legislation which limits the duration of water rights received by private parties. The legislation provides that only the Montana Department of Natural Resources and Conservation may make appropriations if water in excess of 4000 acre-feet a year and 5.5 cubic feet per second is to be consumed or if water is to be transported outside designated river basins. Private parties wishing to use water in such circumstances must lease it from the Department. The leases cannot exceed fifty years. See Mont. Code Ann. §§ 85-2-141, -301.

The Montana legislature apparently believed that large water users should not receive perpetual rights; that requiring payments from such users would provide an incentive to conserve; and that leasing would provide greater protection from environmental damage caused by transporting water out of watersheds. In addition, the legislature felt that the state could exercise greater regulatory control over the interstate movement of water by acting as a "proprietor" of water under the leasing statute. See John E. Thorson, Margery H. Brown & Brenda Desmond, Forging Public Rights in Montana's Waters, 6 Pub. Land L. Rev. 1, 43-44 (1985).

Oklahoma has placed temporal limits on water appropriated for use outside of the state. Okla. Stat. § 105.12(F) allows the Oklahoma State Board to review such permits "at least every ten (10) years" to determine if there have been any material changes in the circumstances the Board considered when first issuing the permit. Where the Board finds such changes, it can impose new conditions upon the permit.

C. Prescription

A   6

ARCHULETA v. GOMEZ
Supreme Court of Colorado, 2009.
200 P.3d 333.

HOBBS, JUSTICE. Plaintiff/Appellant Ralph L. [Lupe] Archuleta appeals a judgment entered by the District Court for Water Division No. 2. The judgment denied and dismissed Archuleta's complaint for an injunction against Theodore Gomez seeking restoration of three ditch rights-of-way and delivery of water through the ditches.

* * *

[Archuleta and Gomez own neighboring parcels in the Upper Huerfano River drainage of the Arkansas River Basin. Both parcels were originally owned by Sabino Archuleta. Archuleta Ditch runs through Gomez's upper parcel. Manzanares Ditch No. 1 runs through the western part of Gomez's lower parcel, across Lupe Archuleta's parcel, and onto the eastern part of Gomez's lower parcel. Manzanares Ditch No. 2 ends on the western side of Gomez's lower parcel.]

* * *

In Colorado, a party seeking to establish ownership of another person's water right by adverse possession has the burden of establishing that such possession is actual, adverse, hostile, and under claim of right, as well as open, notorious, exclusive, and continuous for the prescribed statutory period. Bagwell v. V-Heart Ranch, Inc., 690 P.2d 1271, 1273 (Colo.1984). Such a claim can be made only as between rival claimants to the possession and use of water, for the statutory period, behind the headgate, that is, after the water's diversion from the stream pursuant to an adjudicated water right. Mountain Meadow Ditch and Irrigation Co. v. Park Ditch and Reservoir Co., * * * 277 P.2d 527, 528 (1954).

Section 38-41-101(2), C.R.S. (2008), of Colorado's adverse possession statutes provides that no adverse possession claim may be made against "any ... water, water right ... whatsoever dedicated to or owned by the state of Colorado." Accordingly, Colorado law does not recognize a claim of adverse possession against the stream or against appropriators on the stream. * * *

A party may not adversely possess water from a stream because a water right does not represent actual ownership of any part of the public's water in the stream, but only the right to claim and divert at the headgate of the diversion works the amount of water actually needed for beneficial use, up to the volume of the adjudicated priority. * * *

[O]ur cases establish that no person can revive or adversely possess an abandoned water right. Farmers Reservoir & Irrigation Co. v. Fulton Irrigating Ditch Co., * * * 120 P.2d 196, 199 (1941) ("After abandonment becomes an accomplished fact, the attempt to exercise the abandoned right differs in no respect from an attempt by one who never had a right to assert...."); * * * Thus, adverse possession cases should address whether the deeded owner abandoned the water right. See, e.g., Nesbitt v. Jones, * * * 344 P.2d 949, 953 (1959); * * * If the right has been abandoned, the water belonging to it for beneficial use reverts to the stream, and the right cannot be revived through adverse possession.

Instead, the adverse possession claimant must show that the adjudicated irrigation water right at issue was continuously put to beneficial use on lands irrigated by the claimant, rather than the deeded owner, during the statutory period. * * *

As demonstrated by our cases, adverse possession is very difficult to establish. * * * In Loshbaugh v. Benzel, * * * 291 P.2d 1064, 1070-71 (1956), we stated, "It is not reasonable to suppose that priority of right to water, where water is scarce, or likely to become so, will be lightly sacrificed or surrendered by its owner. Nor should the owner of such a right be held to have surrendered it or merged it except upon reasonably clear and satisfactory evidence." * * * The *Losbaugh* case is instructive for the litany of evidence produced about lands that were or were not irrigated at various times, consensual arrangements between those irrigating from the ditch, unwarranted assumptions about percentage shares in the ditch understood or misunderstood at the time of purchase by successors-in-interest, and the wash-out and non-replacement of diversion works. Based upon the evidence in that case, we held the adverse possession claimant had not presented sufficient evidence to support his adverse possession claim. * * *

The fundamental question in an adverse possession water case is whether, under all the surrounding circumstances, the practices of water use between the rival claimants are consistent or inconsistent with the claimed adverse use. V-Heart Ranch, 690 P.2d at 1275-76. The water court should evaluate "all relevant circumstances surrounding the use of water in evaluating adverse possession claims to water rights." Id. at 1276.

We recognized in *V-Heart Ranch* that formal and informal arrangements between water right holders in an irrigation ditch are often "dictated more by day-to-day circumstances than by legal rights of ownership." Id. at 1275. Typically, rotation agreements involving irrigation rights indicate cooperation and permission among water users. By rotating the entire flow of the adjudicated priority for the ditch onto certain fields at various times in round robin fashion, the irrigators optimize use of the ditch's gravity flow to the irrigated fields served by the ditch. Such arrangements do not typically compromise the title interests of the individual irrigators, and do not demonstrate adverse possession except in unusual circumstances. For this reason, examining the issue of rotational water use, we have said that "the adoption of mutually agreeable rotation systems by the owners of water rights cannot be deemed conclusive proof of either the creation or the abandonment of particular ownership rights." Id.; see also Strole v. Guymon, 37 P.3d 529, 533 (Colo. App. 2001) (concluding that the rotation system of a ditch could not be used to quantify the plaintiff's water rights and that the plaintiff's water rights "exist independently of any rotation agreement").

* * *

The water court awarded all of Archuleta's deeded interests in the adjudicated water rights to Gomez. However, the facts contained in the record of this case suggest that a portion of Archuleta's adjudicated water rights may have been abandoned to the stream, a portion may have been adversely possessed by Gomez, and a portion may still belong to Archuleta. A quantification of the use actually made by Gomez and by Archuleta is required in order to determine how much, if any, of the beneficial consumptive use belonging to Archuleta's deeded interests in the adjudicated irrigation water rights belongs to Gomez or Archuleta, or has been abandoned to the stream.

Neither Archuleta in his injunction claim against Gomez, nor Gomez in his adverse possession claim against Archuleta, has yet demonstrated the actual beneficial use of the water rights at issue on their parcels of land. This showing is essential to both Archuleta's injunction claim and Gomez's adverse possession claim. First, Archuleta must prove the water rights he seeks to compel Gomez to restore deliveries for have not been abandoned because, if Lupe Archuleta abandoned all or a part of Archuleta's deeded water rights to the stream, Archuleta will have suffered no injury, or a diminished injury, upon which the water court may base an injunction against Gomez. In addition, Gomez cannot possess water rights Lupe Archuleta abandoned because such water belongs to the stream for use through adjudicated water rights in order of priorities. * * *

Second, Gomez can successfully prove his adverse possession of all or a portion of the Archuleta rights only by demonstrating actual beneficial use of that water, to the exclusion of Archuleta, on lands Gomez owns. This water must be in an amount above that which Gomez had available to him, and used, in exercising his own decreed water rights during the statutory 18-year period. [See Colo. Rev. Stat. § 38-41-101 (prescriptive period for obtaining fee simple absolute).] Without evidence of actual beneficial use of the water rights, Gomez has not shown "actual" use of the water rights as required to sustain a claim for adverse possession.

The water court based its adverse possession judgment on the following evidence produced by Gomez at trial. Gomez showed that he filled in one of the ditches that had historically run to Archuleta's land, Manzanares Ditch No. 2; he intercepted water bound for Archuleta's land through Manzanares Ditch No. 1; and the Archuleta ditch has not extended into Archuleta's land since at least 1968. Gomez also participated in rotational agreements regarding water delivery from the three ditches that did not include Lupe Archuleta. In addition, Lupe Archuleta had not contributed to ditch maintenance or paid ditch assessments during the adverse possession period.

Based on this evidence, Gomez asserts that Lupe Archuleta had not exercised any of the three irrigation water rights for at least 18 consecutive years and he, Gomez, now owns all of Archuleta's interest in the water rights. However, there is no evidence in the record that Gomez did anything other than intercept water in the ditches belonging to Archuleta's deeded interests in the adjudicated irrigation water rights. Interception of the water is not sufficient to prove the use element of adverse possession in a water case. The adverse claimant's use must be adverse, hostile, exclusive, and the claimant must actually beneficially consume all, or a specified portion, of the deeded owner's historical beneficial consumptive use entitlement for the irrigation water right during the statutory period, in order to deprive the deeded owner permanently of deeded interests in the right. In effect, what the adverse claimant owns, if successful, is the deeded owner's interest in the water right's adjudicated priority. * * *

Gomez failed to make the required showing of his actual beneficial consumptive use of Archuleta's deeded irrigation water rights. Gomez might have made such a showing by proof of their predecessor-in-interest, Sabino Archuleta's, actual beneficial consumptive use of the three ditch rights on the parcels Sabino Archuleta deeded to Gomez and Lupe Archuleta, in comparison to the use each made after those lands passed to them. Gomez might have shown that his parcels were water short when he only utilized the water rights he was deeded, or that he broke out additional acreage into irrigation utilizing Archuleta's rights, thereby demonstrating his need for and actual beneficial use of Archuleta's rights.

The fact that Gomez admitted to considerable sub-flow from his use of water on the western portion of his lower parcel to Archuleta's parcel suggests that Gomez was not beneficially consuming all, or perhaps even any portion of the water he claims to have been adversely possessing from Lupe Archuleta. To the contrary, Lupe Archuleta may have been using and beneficially consuming, through sub-irrigation, his deeded water rights during the claimed adverse possession period.

In any adverse possession case, the "extent of actual occupancy must be determined by the court when ascertaining the extent of the adverse interest." Anderson v. Cold Spring Tungsten, Inc., * * * 458 P.2d 756, 759 (1969). In this adverse water use case, a showing of the actual beneficial consumptive use that Gomez made of Archuleta's water rights for irrigation during the 18-year statutory period requires quantification, in acre feet, of the amount of Archuleta's water that Gomez beneficially used. Moreover, to successfully claim that he adversely possessed Archuleta's water rights, Lupe Archuleta must not have abandoned them to the stream. The court has a role in ascertaining whether all or part of Archuleta's water rights belong to the stream, and not to either Archuleta or Gomez. * * *

Gomez might defeat the abandonment presumption by showing that, during the ten-year period of Lupe Archuleta's non-use giving rise to a presumption of abandonment, § 37-92-103(2), C.R.S. (2008), Gomez was actually consumptively using the Archuleta rights he now claims to own. * * *

Based on the record before us, we conclude that Gomez has not met his burden of proof for adverse possession because he offered no evidence that he made actual beneficial consumptive use of all or any portion of the Archuleta water rights. The record shows the water court found that Gomez adversely possessed Archuleta's water rights based on Gomez's claim that Lupe Archuleta was not using any of his water, had not lent it out to others on the ditches, including Gomez, and Gomez had intercepted Lupe Archuleta's water adversely and hostilely for the statutory period. This was error because evidence of intercepting the water by itself does not prove actual beneficial use.

* * * On remand, the water court should allow the parties the opportunity to present supplemental evidence with regard to the injunction and adverse possession claims in this case. * * *

Quantification is also necessary to prevent an unlawful enlargement of Archuleta's deeded irrigation water right interests. A water right decreed for irrigation purposes cannot lawfully be enlarged beyond the amount of historical beneficial consumptive use belonging to the perfected right. *In re* Water Rights of Cent. Colo. Water Conservancy Dist., 147 P.3d 9, 14 (Colo. 2006). Depending on the water court's findings based on the evidence, the sum total of whatever consumptive use must be apportioned in this case among Archuleta, Gomez, and any amount abandoned to the stream cannot exceed the historical beneficial consumptive use, in acre feet of water, attributable to the exercise of Sabino Archuleta's portion of the adjudicated irrigation water rights in the three ditches upon which Gomez and Archuleta's interests in this case depend.

Accordingly, we reverse the water court's judgment and remand this case for further proceedings consistent with this opinion.

JUSTICE MARTINEZ, dissenting.

I dissent because the majority, for the first time, articulates the requirement that for a successful adverse possession claim against water rights, the party asserting the claim must show he beneficially used a specific quantity of water expressed in acre feet. I believe this is an inappropriate case in which to announce this new legal principle. The argument that beneficial use of a specific quantity of water is an element of an adverse possession claim was not directly raised at trial, and is not necessary to resolution of the issues before this court. Accordingly, I dissent.

Notes

1. **Scope of prescriptable interests.** The principal case indicates the limited way in which prescriptive rights can arise in Colorado. Such rights may not be obtained: 1) against the state, i.e., from unappropriated or public water; 2) against other decreed water rights holders who are appropriating from a stream; or 3) against a decreed rights holder who has previously abandoned the rights, as those rights have reverted to the state. Prescriptive rights can only be obtained "below the headgate," i.e., in water that has already been diverted, as it moves in ditches or pipes or other conveyancing or use facilities. Even in this limited realm, prescriptive rights will not be presumed simply because of one person's use of another's decreed water; the prescriptive use must be established as "adverse." In the often informal setting of adjoining farmers or ranchers, distinguishing "adverse" use from "neighborly" permission, or neighborly "looking the other way," requires a detailed showing. Are there policy or doctrinal reasons for treating "ditch prescription" differently from prescriptive claims to water which has not been diverted?

2. **Legislative abolition.** In 1937, the Utah Supreme Court allowed the prescription of an adjudicated water right. Hammond v. Johnson, 66 P.2d 894 (Utah 1937). Two years later, the Utah legislature overruled the decision by adding two provisions: "No right to the use of water either ap-

propriated or unappropriated can be acquired by adverse use or adverse possession." Utah Code Ann. § 73-3-1. "The provisions of this section are applicable whether such unused or abandoned water is permitted to run to waste or is used by others without right." Utah Code Ann. § 73-1-4(2)(d). An almost exactly parallel development took place in Nevada. Nev. Rev. Stat. 533.060; Application of Filippini, 202 P.2d 535 (Nev. 1949). Alaska and Kansas have similar statutes. Alaska Stat. § 46.15.040(a); Kan. Stat. Ann. § 82a-705. See also Mont. Code Ann. § 85-2-301(3): "A right to appropriate water may not be acquired by any other method, including by adverse use, adverse possession, prescription or estoppel. The method prescribed by this chapter is exclusive."

3. **Prescription of unappropriated water rejected.** In People v. Shirokow, 605 P.2d 859, 866-67 (Cal. 1980), the court said:

"Even if arguendo we were to hold defendant was not required to comply with the statutory appropriation procedures, his claim of a prescriptive right would fail for two reasons.

"First, public rights cannot be lost by prescription. Defendant alleged and the trial court agreed that as against the state he had perfected a prescriptive right. Both were mistaken. What is being challenged is the state's governmental interest in regulating the use of public waters rather than any proprietary interest in the water claimed by defendant. The stipulated facts do not reveal that the state was using the water; indeed, defendant admits the state, if successful in obtaining the injunction, will not make use of the water. Thus it is undisputed that the state's interest here at stake is nonproprietary.

"More than a century ago, in Hoadley v. San Francisco (1875) 50 Cal. 265, 274-276, we articulated the rule that property held by the state in trust for the people cannot be lost through adverse possession. * * *

"The second reason defendant cannot prevail in his claim of a prescriptive right is that the stipulated facts do not provide the necessary elements. Defendant has not shown his diversion was hostile to the interests of any downstream user; we are told only that there was general community knowledge that the dam and reservoir existed and water was impounded. Since it is axiomatic that common law prescriptive rights are based on adverse use, such rights could not have been obtained by defendant by a taking of excess water which did not invade the interests of another. * * * Not only did defendant fail to identify any downstream users having actual knowledge of his diversion (see Pabst v. Finmand (1922) * * * 211 P. 11), no downstream users were parties to this action. Accordingly, the court lacked jurisdiction to adjudicate their rights vis-à-vis those of defendant."

4. **Prescription in California after *Shirokow.*** While *Shirokow,* supra p. 198, Note 2, seemingly held that a permit is the exclusive method by which a new appropriation may be obtained vis-à-vis the state, prescription may still be viable in disputes between private parties. In Pleasant Valley Canal Co. v. Borror, 72 Cal. Rptr. 2d 1 (Cal. Ct. App.

1998), an upstream defendant claimed prescriptive rights against a downstream plaintiff and all other water users on the river, based on excess diversions. The court entertained the claim and discussed the requirements for prescription. It ruled against the defendant, finding no evidence that defendant's use of water had impaired the plaintiff's rights. The court also rejected the defendant's claim against other users on the river, citing *Shirokow*.

5. **Right of an adverse possessor.** Suppose a squatter, claiming adversely to a landowner, obtains title to the land by adverse possession. Does he become the owner of a water right which is appurtenant to the land, and which he used during the period of adverse possession? See Cook v. Hudson, 103 P.2d 137 (Mont. 1940).

6. **New Mexico's experience.** In Turner v. Bassett, 81 P.3d 564 (N.M. Ct. Appl. 2003), a New Mexico appellate court reviewed over 60 years of cases that had left the status of prescriptive water rights in that state still uncertain. Concluding that prescription would cripple the permit system, it squarely rejected the claims before it. On appeal, however, the New Mexico Supreme Court reversed on other grounds. 111 P.3d 701 (N.M. 2005). The issue thus remains open.

7. **Out of priority use.** In Lewis v. State Board of Control, 699 P.2d 822 (Wyo. 1985), upstream juniors argued that downstream seniors, the "BQ appropriators," had abandoned their right by permitting the juniors to divert water out of priority. In rejecting this argument the court said:

"The evidence is clear that the BQ appropriators utilized all the water that was available to them. In times when less than 16.5 c.f.s. were available, they consistently diverted the full amount that was available, and contacted a water official for administrative regulation. It is the duty of the officers charged with regulating water to make distribution in accordance with established priorities. Quinn v. John Whitaker Ranch Co., 92 P.2d 568 (Wyo. 1939). The BQ appropriators had the right to rely on the water officials to do their jobs. If said officials were not effective in their regulation, that alone will not work to effect a water abandonment, considering the facts herein that (1) the BQ appropriators consistently called for regulation when the flow of water in Twin Creek fell below 16.5 c.f.s.; (2) such regulation was attempted; and (3) such regulation failed primarily due to the refusal of contestants to abide by the lawful orders of the water officials." Accord Coryell v. Robinson, 194 P.2d 342 (Colo. 1948). Compare Idaho Code § 42-607: "So long as a duly elected watermaster is charged with the administration of the waters within a water district, no water user within such district can adversely possess the right of any other water user."

8. **Legalizing nonconforming uses.** Should states legalize long-continued uses and practices that do not square with the paper titles to water rights? See Colo. Rev. Stat. § 37-92-401(1)(b)(VI): "If, in the preparation of the tabulations provided for in this section, the application of the preceding principles [for determining priorities] would cause in any particular case a substantial change in the priority of a particular water

ticular case a substantial change in the priority of a particular water right to the extent theretofore lawfully enjoyed for a period of not less than eighteen years, then the division engineer shall designate the priority for that water right in accordance with historic practice."

SECTION 5. TRANSFER

interest of junior appropriators ↴

FARMERS HIGHLINE CANAL & RESERVOIR CO. v. CITY OF GOLDEN

Supreme Court of Colorado, 1954.
129 Colo. 575, 272 P.2d 629.

CLARK, JUSTICE. To review a judgment and decree favorable to defendant in error, City of Golden, in an action to change the point of diversion of certain water rights heretofore adjudicated to the Swadley ditch out of Clear Creek upstream a distance of some five miles to the headgate of the Church ditch, plaintiffs in error present the cause in our Court by writ of error. We will herein refer to the parties as they were aligned in the trial court where the City of Golden was petitioner and plaintiffs in error appeared as respondents.

Petitioner claimed ownership of said water rights by recent purchase and conveyance by deed, and sought to have changed, not only the point of diversion, but likewise, the manner of use, said rights having previously been employed under the Swadley ditch in the irrigation of farm lands, and petitioner is now seeking to devote the same to municipal uses by way of increase to the domestic supply of water for the City of Golden as well as for the irrigation of lawns, gardens and similar purposes within the city. The trial court granted the petition, and by its decree authorized the change of 0.844 cubic feet of water per second of time under priority number thirteen, dated May 14, 1861, and 0.92 cubic feet of water per second of time under priority number twenty-one under date June 1, 1862, for a total of 1.764 cubic feet of water per second of time. * * *

With respect to the facts, the parties hereto are in complete disagreement, and the evidence, limited and inadequate, as to us it seems to be, is in serious conflict. With respect to many legal issues, counsel for the respective parties are quite in accord. It is recognized that water is a property right, subject to sale and conveyance, and that under proper conditions not only may the point of diversion be changed, but likewise the manner of use. It further is recognized that such change may be permitted, by proper court decree, only in such instances as it is specifically shown that the rights of other users from the same source are not injuriously affected by such change, and that the burden of proof thereof rests upon petitioner. * * * Here, there appears no disagreement as to the law but a wide divergence of theory in its applicability.

There is absolutely no question that a decreed water right is valuable property; that it may be used, its use changed, its point of diversion relocated; and that a municipal corporation is not precluded from purchasing water rights previously used for agricultural purposes and thereafter devoting them to municipal uses, provided that no adverse effect be suffered by other users from the same stream, particularly those holding junior priorities.

Equally well established, as we have repeatedly held, is the principle that junior appropriators have vested rights in the continuation of stream conditions as they existed at the time of their respective appropriations, and that subsequent to such appropriations they may successfully resist all proposed changes in points of diversion and use of water from that source which in any way materially injures or adversely affects their rights. * * *

[I]n Enlarged Southside Irrigation Ditch Co. v. John's Flood Ditch Co., * * * 183 P.2d 552, * * * Mr. Justice Stone declared the principle that the owner of a priority for irrigation has no right, as against a junior appropriator, to waste water, to increase the amount or extend the time of his diversion so as to put it to double use by irrigation of other lands; nor to lend, rent or sell to others the excess water. "The well-recognized right to change either the point of diversion of the water right or its place of use is always subject to the limitation that such change shall not injure the rights of subsequent appropriators." * * *

Under subhead (d) of its findings, the trial court stated that it was convinced that, under no tenable theory of the case would any injury be done if 1.2 cubic feet of water per second of time out of priorities thirteen and twenty-one were allowed to be transferred, as requested by Golden. Then, under subdivision (e), the trial court "determined to authorize the change of point of diversion of Golden's priorities numbered thirteen and twenty-one, but effectuate the relinquishment of its priority number forty-four." True, under subhead (d) of its findings, the trial court further stated that it was not persuaded that water rights of any users appearing as protestants would be injured by granting decree for the full amount of all three priorities, but it specifically found that no injury would result if the diversion point of 1.2 cubic feet of water per second of time were authorized to be changed, and then proceeded to change the whole of the two oldest priorities for 1.764 cubic feet of water per second of time. This inconsistency of itself would be sufficient to justify a remand of the cause to the trial court for correction, but there appears a far more urgent necessity for reversal. As we have hereinbefore stated, the evidence presented before the trial court is conflicting and from our standpoint not altogether satisfactory. The principal witness who testified in behalf of the petitioner was one Wheeler, an engineer; while the principal witness who testified for protestants was one Lowe, likewise an engineer. Their testimony primarily was based upon two conflicting statistical theories, Mr. Wheeler using the Lowry-Johnson method, and Mr. Lowe the Blaney-Criddle method. The testimony of Mr. Wheeler was considerably more favorable to petitioner than was that of respondents' engineer; nevertheless, Mr. Wheeler testified that in his opinion there might be permitted, without injury to the stream, a change of point of diversion for 1.2 cubic feet of water. An effort was made to have him enlarge upon that amount, but he would not so commit himself other than to say that if an amount were transferred in addition to 1.2 cubic feet of water per second of time the effect on the stream would be so infinitesimal that it could not be measured. Mr. Wheeler's testimony was the extreme of all testimony before the court, both as to acreage irrigated under these decrees from the Swadley ditch, and the amount thereof for which point of diversion might properly be changed without injury to junior appropriators.

Regardless of this, the trial court, with no evidence whatever to support him, presumed to enter a finding that no injurious effect would result if the entire amount of the two older priorities, aggregating 1.764 cubic feet of water per second of time, was transferred, and that if any injury did result therefrom, it would be a general injury and could not affect any of the respondents specifically. The fallacy of such presumption is readily apparent. When any injury is permitted under the assumption that it is general to the stream, it immediately becomes clear that such instances multiplied might become very serious. Where general injury would result to the stream by the transfer, the change could not be authorized without injury to junior appropriators because it is their rights, proportionate with senior rights, that consume the whole stream. * * *

Where it appears that the change sought to be made will result in depletion to the source of supply and result in injury to junior appropriators therefrom, the decree should contain such conditions as are proper to counteract the loss, and should be denied only in such instances as where it is impossible to impose reasonable conditions to effectuate this purpose. City of Colorado Springs v. Yust, 126 Colo. 289, 249 P.2d 151. * * * What condition and limitation should be imposed depends upon the facts and surrounding circumstances in each particular instance. In this case it would require a full accounting not only of the amount of water reasonably required for the irrigation of Swadley lands and the proper return flow to the creek therefrom, but also should be taken into account the actual consumptive use of the City of Golden and the probable return flow to Clear Creek from such uses. If the return flow from the City use be shown to be greater than the return flow from the irrigation of farm lands, naturally the period and extent of use might be increased by the petitioner and the conditions imposed would not have to be so severe as where it would appear that the return flow was equal. It is the purpose of the law, both statutory and by decision, to protect all appropriators and holders of water rights; to this end all elements of loss to the stream by virtue of the proposed change should be considered and accounted for; and thereupon such appropriate provisions of limitation inserted in the decree as the facts would seem to warrant. * * *

[The action] is remanded with direction to the trial court to vacate the decree heretofore entered and for further proceedings in conformity with the rules and principles herein set forth.

Notes

1. **Meaning of "transfer."** As applied to water rights, "transfer" refers primarily to changes in water use, not to mere changes in ownership. Transfers of ownership, which typically accompany a transfer of the land on which the right is used, are quite routine and present few legal difficulties. As discussed supra p. 106, Note 6, water rights are usually appurtenant to land and, as such, are automatically transferred when land is conveyed unless expressly excepted in the deed. It may not even be necessary to notify water officials of a transfer of ownership. Changes in use, in contrast, present many legal complications, as the principal case illustrates. Such changes include changes in the type of use, changes in the place of use, changes in the point of diversion, and changes from direct diversion and use to storage of water. In all cases, the transferring party aims to retain the transferred right's priority.

Most transfers involve irrigation rights, as 80 to 90 percent of the water in the West is used for irrigation.

2. **Importance of transfers.** Water right transfers have been recognized almost from the inception of the appropriation doctrine. See McDonald & Blackburn v. Bear River & Auburn Water & Mining Co., 13 Cal. 220 (1859); Maeris v. Bicknell, 7 Cal. 261 (1857). Until recently, however, transfers have been relatively rare; new users typically developed new supplies to meet their needs. The convergence of multiple factors has led to a marked recent interest in transfers. These include: new demands for water generated by Western industrialization and urbanization West; the declining availability of unappropriated water; and the high cost of developing new supplies. Concern about environmental damage caused by large water projects and parochial opposition to the export of water, manifested in "area of origin" legislation discussed supra p. 99, Note 1, are also factors. Increased interest in transfers is reflected in new labels, such as "water marketing" and "water banking," which refer to efforts to make water transfers more responsive to market forces. Even some environmental advocates and others who previously objected to the "commodification" of water implied by water marketing have begun to view water transfers more favorably.

3. **"No-injury rule."** The principal difficulty in treating a water right as salable property is that many water uses are peculiarly interdependent. Since the same water can be reused by several persons, all may have water rights that entitle them to receive the same molecules of water. If the sale and transfer of one person's water right makes those molecules unavailable to another who also has a right to them, the first user has sold the latter's water as well as his own.

"Return flow is a common phenomenon in Western irrigated regions and many water rights are predicated wholly or partly upon it. For example, on streams such as the Provo in Utah, downstream development occurred first, and return flow from junior upstream diversions not only satisfied the requirements of earlier downstream appropriators but actually benefited them by prolonging the seasonal supply. In contrast, on the South Platte in Colorado, upstream development occurred first and the increasing return flow made progressive downstream development possible and eventually added materially to the value of the junior downstream rights." Wells A. Hutchins, Selected Problems in the Law of Water Rights in the West 331 (1942).

A sale that results in the transfer out of the watershed of the total diversion made by a seller whose use produced return flow will reduce the quantity of water available to appropriators below the point of return. If they are senior to the transferred right, the rule of priority protects them; if they are juniors, they are nevertheless protected by the rule against transfers that cause them harm, frequently referred to as the "no-injury rule." This results in the rule of thumb that the transferor can take only the amount consumed by the original use. Can a water right for a completely nonconsumptive use, e.g., for power or mining, never be sold? Could an irrigator of land on one side of a stream sell his entire diversion to his neighbor who wishes to irrigate the land on the other side? Could an appropriator upstream from both new and old diversion points ever show an injury that would prevent or limit the change? See CF&I Steel Corp. v. Rooks, 495 P.2d 1134 (Colo. 1972).

The principal case discusses a reduction in the rate of diversion to offset the loss of return flows relied on by junior appropriators. In addition to reducing the diversion rate, Colorado courts have imposed volumetric limitations (i.e., acre-feet) on transferred rights even though the original right lacked such limitation. See Farmers Highline Canal & Reservoir Co. v. City of Golden, 975 P.2d 189 (Colo. 1999). Limitations on diversion dates (e.g., May through October), approximating historic diversion periods under the original right, are also common. See id.

A decrease in return flows is not the only possible injury from a transfer. Anything which alters quantity, timing, or quality of flows at any point on a stream may cause injury unless appropriate conditions are imposed. A change in dates of diversion can cause injury by extending the period of use or shifting diversions from a period of low demand to a period of high demand; moving the point of diversion and place of use downstream of a junior appropriator can deprive the junior of return flows that previously supplied its appropriation; reducing the quantity diverted to compensate for increased consumption, as in the principal case, may eliminate late season return flows relied on by downstream appropriators. As the frequency of transfers has increased, junior appropriators and water officials have gotten more sophisticated in identifying potential injuries and in requiring mitigation. When proposed transfers are contested, the dispute frequently centers on the nature and sufficiency of proposed conditions. Problems encountered in transfers and possible solutions are discussed in George A. Gould, infra p. 206, Note 5.

4. **Historic use.** The Colorado Supreme Court adopted "historic use" in City of Westminster v. Church, 445 P.2d 52, 56-57 (Colo. 1968):

"It was proper, therefore, for the district court to examine the state engineer's records * * * to determine the historical use of the Eggleston No. 2 and McKenzie Ditch water rights during the period 1938-59. The purpose and effect of this inquiry was * * * simply to ascertain the extent of actual historical usage by Jenkins and the Rodgers.

"Perhaps defendant's allegations of error * * * stems from the fact that the term 'historical use' is not very prevalent in the prior decisions of this court and the belief that we had not heretofore sanctioned any such yardstick. * * * Precedent for the trial court's limitation of the direct flow rights finds sanction in the apropos language of this court to be found in Enlarged Southside Irrigation Ditch Company v. John's Flood Ditch Company, 116 Colo. 580, 183 P.2d 552, as follows:

'The owner of a priority for irrigation has no right, as against a junior appropriator, * * * to lend, rent or sell to others the excess water after irrigation of the land for which it was appropriated, to the detriment of junior appropriators, and such limitation of right of use cannot be circumvented by shifting the use to other lands. The well-recognized right to change either the point of diversion of the water right or its place of use is always subject to the limitation that such change shall not injure the rights of subsequent appropriators.'"

See also Wyo. Stat. Ann. § 41-3-104(a):

"The change in use, or change in place of use, may be allowed, provided that the quantity of water transferred by the granting of the petition shall not exceed the amount of water historically diverted under the existing use, not exceed the historic rate of diversion under the existing use, nor increase the historic amount consumptively used under the existing use, nor decrease the historic amount of return flow, nor in any manner injure other existing lawful appropriators."

Dallas Creek Water Co. v. Huey, 933 P.2d 27, 34 n.3 (Colo. 1997), explained the relationship between a decreed right and historic use:

"An absolute decree entitles the subsequent operation of the right in the amount of its decreed quantity, so long as the water is applied beneficially. River conditions vary from year to year, as does the need of the appropriator for the water. Over an extended period of time, a pattern of historic diversions and use under the decreed right will mature and become the measure of that right for change purposes."

The New Mexico Supreme Court, in contrast, insists that the decree, not historic use, fixes the extent of the right to be transferred. W.S. Ranch Co. v. Kaiser Steel Corp., 439 P.2d 714 (N.M. 1968).

In Santa Fe Trail Ranches Property Owners Ass'n v. Simpson, 990 P.2d 46 (Colo. 1999), water rights acquired for manufacturing purpose were long leased and used for irrigation, but required judicial approval for the lease was never obtained. Subsequently, an attempt was made to transfer the rights to supply an urban subdivision. Held: the rights could not be transferred because no evidence existed regarding the historic use of the rights for manufacturing and the use for irrigation could not be utilized to establish historic use because the transfer to irrigation use had not been judicially approved and, thus, might represent an expansion of the manufacturing use.

City of Westminster v. Church, supra, held that a prior unsuccessful abandonment action does not bar an examination of historic use in a transfer proceeding. Conversely, People v. City of Thornton, 775 P.2d 11 (Colo. 1989), held that implied limitations on a water right based on historic use are not relevant in abandonment proceedings.

Transfer proceedings can also raise complex questions regarding claim and issue preclusion. Farmer's Highline Canal & Reservoir Co. v. City of Golden, 975 P.2d 189 (Colo. 1999), involved rights which had been transferred from agricultural use to municipal use in the 1960s. The 1960s transfer decrees contained flow limitations but not volumetric limitations. Junior appropriators later sued, seeking to add volumetric limitations to the original decrees to reflect historic consumptive use. The court concluded that doctrine of claim preclusion barred the addition of volumetric limitations because historic consumptive use had been calculated and relied on in the formation of the earlier transfer decrees, which, as noted, contained no volumetric limitations. However, the court also held that the earlier proceedings did not bar claims that the transferee, the City of Golden, had subsequently enlarged its use of the transferred rights by changing municipal use patterns and increasing lawn irrigation. On appeal after remand, 44 P.3d. 241 (Colo. 2002), the court found that the flow limitations in the 1960s decrees were based on calculations that Golden would not irrigate more than 225 acres of lawn or apply more that 900 acre-feet of transferred water to lawn irrigation and held that these figures limited Golden's use of transferred water.

5. **Factual difficulties associated with no-injury rule.** George A. Gould, Water Rights Transfers and Third-Party Effects, 23 Land & Water L. Rev. 1, 20-21 (1988):

"Determining third-party effect is a complex process, frequently requiring the assistance of various experts and the accumulation of extensive data. For example, the prevention of an increase in consumption is a major concern in most transfer proceedings. * * * Actual data concerning the quantity of water diverted is frequently not available. Return flows may sometimes enter streams as discrete, identifiable, sources, but even so, these flows are seldom measured. More often return flows seep back over a broad stretch of the stream or percolate into groundwater which is tributary to the stream, making direct measurement impossible. Consequently, it is usually necessary to estimate consumption indirectly.

"Techniques such as the Blaney-Criddle method use temperature, sunshine, climatological data, and consumptive coefficients for various crops to estimate consumption. This approach requires the collection of data about the area irrigated and the crops grown. It also requires the assistance of agronomists, agricultural engineers, and other experts. It leads to an inevitable battle of experts concerning factual information and technical issues. Furthermore, this method assumes that only water used in the growing process is 'consumed.' Because the purpose of the transfer process is to preserve stream flow conditions, however, consumption properly includes all water lost to the stream, not just that used in the growing process. Thus, irrigation water which seeps into deep aquifers not tributary to the stream or which collects on the surface and evaporates is also 'consumed' and should be included in the amount available for transfer. Disputes involving the extent of such losses further complicates the transfer process.

"Although the effect on consumption is typically the central focus of transfer proceedings, other matters must also be evaluated. Like consumption and return flows, information concerning stream conveyance losses, the timing of return flows, the effects of alterations in diversion patterns, water quality changes resulting from a change in use, and other factors which must be evaluated to determine the effects of a proposed transfer, is sketchy or nonexistent and subject to varying interpretations. Gathering this information, evaluating it, and presenting it entail the same delays, expenses, and uncertainties as information concerning consumption."

6. **Burden of proof.** Who has the burden of proof? The Colorado statute requires the applicant for a change to show the "absence of any injurious effect." Colo. Rev. Stat. § 37-92-304(3). While the applicant bears the initial and ultimate burden of showing absence of injury, once the applicant meets the initial burden, objectors must come forward with evidence of injury. Farmers Reservoir & Irr. Co. v. Consol. Mut. Water Co., 33 P.3d 799 (Colo. 2001). Utah allocates burdens similarly, requiring the applicant to show initially that it has "reason to believe" that the change will not impair other water rights. Searle v. Milburn Irr. Co., 133 P.3d 382 (Utah 2006). But see Mont. Code Ann. § 85-2-402(5) (sometimes requiring proof by "clear and convincing evidence").

Colorado allows a trial period: "Any decision of the water judge * * * dealing with a change of water right * * * shall include the condition that the approval of such change * * * shall be subject to reconsideration by the water judge on the question of injury to the vested rights of others for such period * * * as is necessary or desirable to preclude or remedy any such injury." § 37-92-304(6). In Farmers Reservoir & Irrigation Co., supra, the court explained that historic consumptive use is to be determined in granting a transfer and that the retained jurisdiction provided by the foregoing statute cannot be used to reopen this determination; rather, the court said, retained jurisdiction provides a period for testing the change plan to determine if it operates as predicted to protect against injury and to make adjustments if it does not.

7. **Economic impact of the no-injury rule.** The transaction costs and the uncertainty generated by the no-injury rule substantially impede the transfer of water rights and the development of water markets. Some economists suggest that the no-injury rule would be unnecessary if water rights were redefined in terms of consumptive use of water. See, e.g., Timothy D. Tregarthen, Water in Colorado, Fear and Loathing of the Marketplace, in Water Rights, Scare Resource Allocation, Bureaucracy and the Environment 125-30 (Terry Anderson ed., 1983). For an argument that redefinition is impractical and would only provide a marginal solution, see George A. Gould, supra p. 206, Note 5.

8. **Transfers involving water companies and irrigation districts.** A lot of western water is supplied by mutual water companies and public irrigation districts which have constructed large dams and canals or have contracted for delivery of large quantities of water from U.S. Bureau of Reclamation projects. A water user's ability to sell its share of the district supply may turn upon legal issues of water rights ownership or appurtenance, rather than on the desirability of the change and whether injury would befall anyone. In some states, a district may veto the change; i.e., it must approve any such transfer. The district's power to sell water outside its service area may depend upon similar considerations, as well as on its enabling legislation or articles of incorporation, and on whether the water is "surplus" or in use.

Barton H. Thompson, Jr., Institutional Perspectives on Water Policy and Markets, 81 Cal. L. Rev. 673 (1993), concludes that the reallocation of water among users within the service areas of mutual water companies and irrigation districts occurs with much greater ease and frequency than formal transfers of water rights and plays a much more important role in local water transfers than is typically recognized. The article attributes this to the standardized nature of water entitlements created by such institutions, the availability of the institutions as clearinghouses to match potential buyers and sellers, the existence of distribution systems to redirect water within the service areas, and the fact that intra-institution transfers typically do not require the approval of state water officials. See, e.g., Dep't of Ecology v. Acquavella, 935 P.2d 595 (Wash. 1997) (holding that the trial court had correctly specified that water rights held by an irrigation district were appurtenant to all irrigable lands within the district rather than the lands actually irrigated because an irrigation district water right can be transferred and applied to any land within the district without administrative approval).

The transfer of water by members of mutual water companies and irrigation districts is discussed in greater detail in Chapter 5.

The transferability of Bureau of Reclamation water varies from project to project and may depend on the legislation authorizing it, whether the project is paid out, and the parties' residency. Administrative and legislative steps have been taken to clarify and simplify the transfer of federal project water. These steps are discussed infra pp. 690-91, Note 7.

9. **Transfer of permits and applications.** In Green River Development Co. v. FMC Corp., 660 P.2d 339 (Wyo. 1983), the court held that an inchoate permit cannot be transferred, reasoning that only water which has been beneficially used is transferable. Accord Hansen v. Turney, 94 P.3d 1 (N.M. Ct. App. 2004). In United States v. Alpine Land & Reservoir Co., 965 F.2d 731 (9th Cir. 1992), a federal court held that the reference to "water already appropriated" in the Nevada statutes precludes transfers if water has not been put to beneficial use. This holding contradicted a long-standing practice of the Nevada state engineer and cast into doubt many such transfers previously approved. In response the Nevada Legislature enacted Nev. Rev. Stat. § 533.324, which states that "'water already appropriated' includes water for whose appropriation the state engineer has issued a permit but which has not been applied to the intended use." The act adopting the statute states that the section clarifies rather than changes law and that the legislature ratifies the transfers previously approved by the state engineer.

10. **Transfer procedures.** In most states, the agencies that regulate the appropriation and distribution of water can approve or disapprove transfers after proceedings at which all interested parties are represented. E.g., Cal. Water Code §§ 1700-1707; Idaho Code § 42-222; Utah Code Ann. § 73-3-3; Wyo. Stat. Ann. § 41-3-104.

In Colorado, the type of transfer determines the relevant decision maker. For permanent changes, the "change in point of diversion" procedure illustrated in the principal case has been abolished and an application for a change is handled by the Water Judge. Colo. Rev. Stat. §§ 37-92-101 to -602. For many temporary changes, however, the state engineer has approval authority. See, e.g., Col. Rev. Stat. §§ 37-80.5-104 to -106 (water banks); 37-83-104 (exchanges); 37-83-105 (loans).

11. **Miscellaneous.** The lack of facilities to transport water is often a barrier to water transfers. In 1986, California enacted legislation to alleviate this problem. Cal. Water Code §§ 1810-1814. These statutes attempt to make available to transferees the unused capacity of water transportation facilities owned or operated by public agencies.

In Desert Irrigation, Ltd. v. State, 944 P.2d 835 (Nev. 1997), the Nevada State Engineer canceled permits to transfer irrigation water rights to residential land development after numerous extensions. The land developer argued that the water represented by the canceled transfer permits should revert to the original rights. The court ruled otherwise, holding that canceled rights revert to the public and are available for further appropriation. Compare Andersen Family Assoc. v. Ricci, 179 P.3d 1201 (Nev. 2008) (permits to change pre-statutory vested rights may be cancelled, but not the vested rights themselves).

Paloma Investment L.P. v. Jenkins, 978 P.2d 110 (Ariz. Ct. App. 1998), will revive unpleasant memories of the first year of law school for many students and lawyers. Jenkins acquired a contract right to purchase a ranch and appurtenant water rights. Jenkins later assigned the contract, and, simultaneously, entered into an agreement with the assignee giving Jenkins twenty per cent of all proceeds from the sale or lease of the water rights. A subsequent ranch purchaser sued to quiet title, alleging that he was not bound by the agreement. The court ruled that the agreement did not create an equitable mortgage or lien, nor did it constitute a covenant running with the land. Instead, Jenkins had retained a "royalty interest" which bound the subsequent purchaser.

BONHAM v. MORGAN
Supreme Court of Utah, 1989.
788 P.2d 497.

PER CURIAM: Plaintiffs appeal from a summary judgment which denied them standing to pursue count one of their complaint against the state engineer. * * * Plaintiff Stanley B. Bonham, who is not a water user, protested against a permanent change application filed under Utah Code Ann. § 73-3-3 (1980) in the office of the defendant state engineer (state engineer) in June of 1984 by defendants Salt Lake County Water Conservancy District and Draper Irrigation Company (applicants). Applicants sought to change the point of diversion, place, and nature of use of certain water rights in Bell Canyon, Dry Creek, Rocky Mouth Creek, and Big Willow Creek. At a subsequent hearing, Bonham produced evidence of substantial flooding and damage to plaintiffs' properties and adjacent public lands during 1983 and 1984. Bonham informed the state engineer that the flooding was the result of applicants' construction of a screw gate, pipeline, and diversion works after they obtained preliminary approval of their change application. According to Bonham, the flooding had occurred and would recur on a yearly basis whenever the applicants closed their screw gate, allowing the waters to be diverted down the hillside onto plaintiffs' properties and nearby property contemplated for use as a public park. Bonham objected that the proposed structures and improvements contemplated after final approval would detrimentally impact the public welfare.

The state engineer conducted on-site inspections but eventually issued his memorandum decision in which he concluded that he was without authority to address Bonham's claims in ruling on the permanent change application, as Bonham was not a water user, that the state engineer's authority was limited to investigating impairments of vested water rights, and that there was no evidence before him to indicate that the implementation of the change application would impair those rights. The state engineer then granted the permanent change application.

Plaintiffs sued in the district court in compliance with Utah Code Ann. § 73-3-14 (1980), which provides in pertinent part:

> In any case where a decision of the state engineer is involved any person aggrieved by such decision may within sixty days after notice thereof bring a civil action in the district court for a plenary review thereof * * *

Plaintiffs alleged that the state engineer's disclaimer of any authority to consider, in connection with a permanent change application, any damages caused to plaintiffs as a result of his approval of the application, was contrary to the clear mandate of section 73-3-8, which requires an evaluation of the factors there set out, including any and all damage to public and private property and the impact the application will have on the public welfare. * * *

Before any discovery was conducted, the district court granted the state engineer's motion for summary judgment after concluding that the change application process under section 73-3-3 did not contemplate a consideration of all the factors listed in section 73-3-8; that the issues raised by plaintiffs were outside the limited criteria governing approval and rejection of change applications contained in section 73-3-3; and that plaintiffs were, therefore, not "aggrieved persons" within the meaning of section 73-3-14 and could not bring an action to review the decision of the state engineer under section 73-3-3. * * *

Plaintiffs appealed. This Court granted the request of the National Parks and Conservation Association (NPCA) to intervene as amicus curiae and granted a like request by [9 water districts and municipalities] (the water users).

* * * At oral argument, the parties conceded that the question of whether plaintiffs are aggrieved persons within the meaning of section 73-3-14 turns on whether the scope of the considerations appropriate for the state engineer under a section 73-3-3 proceeding for a permanent change application is the same as that listed in section 73-3-8. If it is, the state engineer concedes that plaintiffs are aggrieved persons; if it is not, plaintiffs concede that they are not aggrieved persons and that summary judgment was proper. The issues before us may therefore be reduced to the question of whether in permanent change applications (section 73-3-3) the state engineer has the same duties with respect to approval or rejection of applications as he has when considering appropriation applications (section 73-3-8). We hold that the state engineer's duties under the two statutes are the same and that

plaintiffs therefore are aggrieved persons entitled to a trial on the merits of count one of their complaint. * * *

Utah Code Ann. § 73-3-3 (1980), at the time the state engineer rendered his decision, read in pertinent part:

> Any person entitled to the use of water may change the place of diversion or use and may use the water for other purposes than those for which it was originally appropriated, * * * Changes for an indefinite length of time with an intention to relinquish the original point of diversion, place or purpose of use are defined as *permanent changes. Temporary changes* include and are limited to all changes for definitely fixed periods of not exceeding one year. * * * No permanent change shall be made except on the approval of an application therefor by the state engineer. * * * *The procedure in the state engineer's office and rights and duties of the applicants with respect to applications for permanent changes of point of diversion, place or purpose of use shall be the same as provided in this title for applications to appropriate water;* * * * No temporary change shall be made except upon an application filed in duplicate with the state engineer. * * * The state engineer shall make an investigation and *if such temporary change does not impair any vested rights of others he shall make an order authorizing the change.* (Emphasis added.)

[handwritten margin note: amendment 73-3-8]

Section 73-3-8 (1985), at the time the state engineer rendered his decision, read in pertinent part:

> (1) * * * *If the state engineer, because of information in his possession obtained either by his own investigation or otherwise, has reason to believe that an application to appropriate water will interfere with its more beneficial use for irrigation, domestic or culinary, stock watering, power or mining development or manufacturing, or will unreasonably affect public recreation or the natural stream environment, or will prove detrimental to the public welfare, it is his duty to withhold his approval or rejection of the application until he has investigated the matter. If an application does not meet the requirements of this section, it shall be rejected.* (Emphasis added.)

Although the two statutes before us have remained virtually unchanged in their substantive provisions for over fifty years, the issue whether the state engineer must consider all the factors listed in section 73-3-8 when passing on a permanent change application under section 73-3-3 is one of first impression in this Court. * * * The language critical to our determination was added to section 100-3-3 in 1937. The amendment removed provisions addressing notice requirements and added for the first time language defining permanent and temporary changes. After setting out procedures relating to applications for permanent changes, the 1937 amendment continued:

> The procedure in the state engineer's office and the rights and duties of the applicant with respect to application for permanent changes of

point of diversion, place, or purpose of use shall be the same as provided in this title for applications to appropriate water. (Emphasis added.)

The appropriations statute, section 100-3-8, to which the amendment made cross-reference, contained then, as section 73-3-8 does now, a specification on the duties of the state engineer when acting on appropriation applications. These were to be granted if, and only if, they did not interfere with more beneficial use, public recreation, the natural stream environment, or the public welfare, as more specifically set out in the statute. In contrast to the cross-reference between *permanent change* applications and appropriations, the 1937 amendments prescribed different and very summary procedures for *temporary changes*, under which the state engineer "shall make an investigation and *if such temporary change does not impair any vested rights of others, he shall make an order authorizing the change.*" See also § 73-3-3 (1980). From these contrasting references and procedures, we draw the rational inference that in temporary change applications the review criteria (now contained in section 73-3-8) did not apply, but in considerations of permanent change applications they did. * * *

Plaintiffs and the NPCA * * * rely on those general provisions to underscore their position that neither the right to appropriate water nor the right to permanently change its use or place of use is absolute. The conditioning of that right, they say, was acknowledged by our Supreme Court in United States v. Caldwell, * * * 231 P. 434, 439 (1924), when it stated:

> [A]ppellants' right to change the place of diversion is not an absolute or vested right, but is only a conditional or qualified one. No such change can be made if thereby the public, or any other appropriator, prior or subsequent, is adversely affected. * * *

Even were we convinced * * * by the state engineer's argument that the "procedure in the state engineer's office" in section 73-3-3 refers only to his ministerial duties, the lack of precision in the cross-reference is of little avail to the state engineer. The further mention in that section of the "rights and duties" of the applicants and the reference to section 73-3-8 are sufficient by themselves to show that the legislature meant to require more than similar procedures alone. The only reasonable meaning to read into section 73-3-3 is that the state engineer must investigate and reject the application for either appropriation or permanent change of use or place of use if approval would interfere with more beneficial use, public recreation, the natural stream environment, or the public welfare. It is unreasonable to assume that the legislature would require the state engineer to investigate matters of public concern in water appropriations and yet restrict him from undertaking those duties in permanent change applications.

Carried to its logical conclusion, such an interpretation would eviscerate the duties of the state engineer under section 73-3-8 and allow an applicant to accomplish in a two-step process what the statute proscribes in a one-step process. For all that an applicant would need to do to achieve a disapproved purpose under section 73-3-8 would be to appropriate for an approved purpose and then to file a change application under section 73-3-3. * * *

We hold that the state engineer is required to undertake the same investigation in permanent change applications that the statute mandates in applications for water appropriations and that plaintiffs are aggrieved persons who have standing to sue him pursuant to Utah Code Ann. § 73-3-14 (1980) for a review of his decision approving the subject change application. The summary judgment in favor of the state engineer is vacated, and plaintiffs' complaint against him reinstated for trial on the merits.

Notes

1. **Other decisions.** Accord Clark v. Briscoe Irr. Co., 200 S.W.2d 674 (Tex. Civ. App. 1947). Contra *In re* Application of Sleeper, 760 P.2d 787 (N.M. Ct. App. 1988); but see N.M. Stat. Ann. §§ 72-5-23, -5-24, -12-7, -12B-1.

2. **Expansion of public interest review.** Douglas L. Grant, Public Interest Review of Water Right Allocation and Transfer in the West: Recognition of Public Values, 19 Ariz. St. L.J. 681, 684-85 (1987):

"Public interest review of water right transfers * * * has grown rapidly in recent years. In 1971, Nevada was the only state with a permit statute requiring denial of proposed transfers that would be detrimental to the public interest. Now, eight states have such statutes. Two more states have statutes that require consideration of certain public effects of proposed transfers."

In Colorado there is no public interest review of appropriations or transfers. Nevertheless, in City of Thornton v. Bijou Irrigation Co. , 926 P.2d 1 (Colo. 1996), the water court conditioned a proposed transfer on "revegetation" of lands which would be removed from irrigation pursuant to a transfer of water from agricultural to urban use. The revegetation requirements reflected statutory requirements found in legislation adopted in 1992. Colo. Rev. Stat. § 37-92-305(4.5). However, the 1992 legislation did not apply to the Thornton applications because they predated its adoption. Thornton asserted that the revegetation requirements were invalid, arguing that the water court could only impose conditions to prevent injury to other appropriators. The Colorado Supreme Court disagreed. It held that the legislation merely codified existing powers of the water courts. Reviewing past decisions, the court found that, in addition to promoting maximum beneficial use and protecting water rights, water judges must consider the potential impact of water use on other resources.

3. **Transfer restrictions.** A 1909 Wyoming statute restricted water rights to the land, place or purpose for which they were acquired. The provision, codified at Wyo. Stat. Ann. § 41-3-101, is so riddled with exceptions as to be almost meaningless. See Frank J. Trelease, Transfer of Water Rights—Errata and Addenda—Sales for Recreational Purposes and to Districts, 2 Land & Water L. Rev. 321 (1967).

In three states, restrictions on transfers of water rights have been adopted by substantially identical statutes. These require a water right to remain appurtenant to the land on which it is used. If, however, it becomes impracticable to beneficially or economically use the water on the appurtenant land, the right may be severed and transferred to other land without loss of priority. Such changes need the approval of the state water authorities and cannot harm existing rights holders. Nev. Rev. Stat. 533.040, .325; Okla. Stat. tit. 82, § 105.22; S.D. Codified Laws §§ 46-5-34 to -36. In Nevada the statute applies to all water rights, in the other states, only to irrigation rights. This leaves other rights freely transferable upon compliance with approval procedures.

In North Dakota a transfer may be made only to a "superior" use, as defined in the preference statute, N.D. Cent. Code § 61-04-15.1. The Washington Family Farm Water Act, Wash. Rev. Code §§ 90.66.010-.910, adopted by initiative in 1977, substantially restricts the transfer of agricultural water rights. See Wash. Rev. Code § 90.66.065. The transfer restrictions were applied in City of West Richland v. Department of Ecology, 103 P.3d 818 (Wash. Ct. App. 2004).

4. **Temporary transfers.** Several states have statutes that authorize temporary transfers. E.g., N.M. Stat. Ann. §§ 72-6-1 to -7; Wash. Rev. Code § 90.03.390. California has a particularly wide array of such statutes. See Cal. Water Code §§ 1725-1732 (temporary changes); §§ 1735-1737 (long-term transfers); §§ 1435-1442 (temporary urgency changes); §§ 1020-1031 (water leases). Colorado legislation authorizes expedited approval of "interruptible water supply agreements," Colo. Rev. Stat. § 37-92-309, and several states authorize loans or leases of water for instream uses. E.g., Colo. Rev. Stat. § 37-83-105; Or. Rev. Stat. § 537.348. Like the Utah statute in the principal case, these statutes create greater flexibility by facilitating short-term changes in use to meet temporary or one-time needs. In general, these statutes simplify or expedite transfer processes; they also automatically revert the right to its prior use at the end of the transfer period.

5. **Criticism of prior appropriation.** M. Mason Gaffney, Economic Aspects of Water Resource Policy, 28 Am. J. Econ. & Soc. 131, 140 (1969):

"Under the 'first in time, first in right' doctrine, appropriators are senior and junior to one another along a scale from the first to the last. When water falls low, the juniors drop out first and lose everything before the next senior appropriator loses anything. In result, there is no pooling of risk whatever. The top senior has a 100 per cent firm supply; the last junior has a supply so uncertain it is unusable. Two basic economizing principles are denied. One is marginal productivity. The junior appropriator who loses all his water obviously loses marginal units of high productivity, while the senior retains marginal units of low productivity. The other is pooling of risk. The doctrine is conceived in terms of an assumed necessity for vertical integration: that is, there is no market for the raw material, water, but every user rather owns his own supply. His supply is a piece of the larger common supply, but his piece is defined in such a way as greatly to increase the aggregate variability of supply above that which nature imposes; to increase the uncertainty as well; and, finally, to distribute these risks unequally."

To what extent can transfers alleviate Gaffney's criticisms?

6. **Water banking.** The State of California turned to "water banking" to deal with drought in 1991. In February 1991, precipitation for the water year, which began on October 1, 1990, was only 25 per cent of normal statewide. In addition, four prior years of drought had substantially depleted reservoirs. In response, the governor directed the Department of Water Resources, which operates the State Water Project, to establish a water bank to purchase water from willing sellers for reallocation to urban areas, critical agricultural uses such as orchards and vineyards, environmental protection, and carryover storage.

Through the bank, more than 800,000 acre-feet of water were transferred to buyers from farmers, who either fallowed land or pumped groundwater to replace surface water sold to the bank. The Department subsequently developed a permanent water drought water bank.

The drought water bank was largely considered successful. However, four factors may make it difficult to duplicate elsewhere. First, the extreme severity of the 1991 drought created a climate of cooperation which suppressed legal and political barriers that might otherwise have impeded the bank. Second, the Department of Water Resources provided funds to capitalize the bank and took the financial risks inherent in the bank. Third, because of California legal idiosyncrasies, most of the transfers did not have to be approved by the Water Resources Control Board. Finally, California has unparalleled facilities to move large quantities of water around the state.

Colorado, Kansas, Idaho, and Texas have adopted water banking legislation, Colo. Rev. Stat. §§ 37-80.5-104.5, Kan. Stat. Ann. §§ 82a-762 to -769, Idaho Code §§ 42-1761 to -1765A; Tex. Water Code Ann. §§ 15.701 to .708, but water banking is not yet greatly used in these states. Arizona has also created a state water bank. Ariz. Rev. Stat. §§ 45-2401 to -2472. A primary purpose of this legislation is to allow Arizona to use its entire allocation of Colorado River Water by storing ("banking") water in depleted groundwater basins. However, the legislation does allow the transfer of some water to users in California and Nevada, and helps assure firm rights to Indian communities. The interstate functions of the bank operate under federal regulations adopted by the Secretary of Interior. See 43 C.F.R. pt. 414. Colorado River issues are examined more fully in

Chapter 6, Section 3. Indian rights are examined more fully in Chapter 8, Section 3A.

7. **Economic and social effects of water rights transfers.** In City of Thornton v. Farmers Reservoir & Irrigation Co., 575 P.2d 382 (Colo. 1978), the Colorado Supreme Court upheld the right of the "home rule" city to condemn water rights without resort to the appointment of a commission otherwise required by non-home rule cities. The condemnation functioned as a "forced" transfer. (For some general provisions on condemnation of water rights, see infra p. 219, Note 4.) Gray & Nobe, Water Resource Economics, Externalities and Institutions in the United States, 1975 Proc., Int'l Conf. on Global Water Systems, Valencia, Spain, reviewed the implications of the city's eminent domain action:

"[A] brief historical perspective is in order. Thornton had developed rapidly during the 1950s as a suburb of Denver, the major metropolitan center of the intermountain region of the nation. Since its incorporation in 1956, the City of Thornton has grown so that it now encompasses 17 square miles and has a population of 27,000 people. During its period of rapid growth, the City of Denver provided adequately for its municipal water requirements so no serious thought was given to whether or not it would continue to do so indefinitely. In recent years, however, proposed additional trans-mountain diversions for augmenting Denver's water supply have been opposed because of adverse environmental impacts. Faced with a potential future limit to its growth due to an upper limit on its source of Denver water, the City of Thornton set out to satisfy its needs from alternative sources. This decision led in turn to the condemnation proceedings filed against the irrigation water users in the vicinity.

"The fact that the City of Thornton has resorted to condemnation proceedings is a clear indication of the great difficulty and high cost of obtaining alternative, new water supplies in its region. Thus, it can be inferred that such an option also does not exist for the irrigators if they lose their existing water rights. What are the adverse implications of this situation? First of all, it must be recognized that farmers in the area would not necessarily be forced out of agriculture. They could revert to dryland farming and continue to grow most of the crops now being produced. But yields will decline drastically and so will net incomes per acre (in the order of magnitude of dropping from a long term average of $200/acre under irrigation to $40/acre under dryland farming). In the short run, yields will drop even lower because, under irrigation, plant nutrients are applied in excess of the levels plants can utilize under dryland conditions, and it will take several years to leach out the excess.

"In addition, indirect—but nonetheless significant—adverse effects of the transfer of water rights in these cases would result. These are as follows:

1. Since real estate taxes are unlikely to decline in response to lower income yields under dryland farming, there would be abandonment of some farm land (presumably to other uses).

2. There will certainly be a displacement or loss of sunk capital invested by farmers in their irrigation systems, land leveling, and in equipment utilized in irrigated farming in excess of that required in dryland farming.

3. There will be a broadbased reduction in secondary benefits that have been accruing from irrigated agriculture to others in the vicinity, including farm labor jobs, farm machinery and fertilizer sales, plus lower sales volume in the food processing sector.

4. The farms affected are primary grain producers; the Front Range area of Colorado is already grain deficient and subsequent reduction in production will particularly affect a large number of grain dependent industries, including breweries, beef cattle feedlots, feed mills, and elevators.

5. Finally, there will be loss of open space as some of the agricultural area is built up in residential and industrial uses which will adversely affect the quality of life of the area via increased pollution and congestion (and will trigger another round of increasing water demand)."

The social and economic effects of fallowing land was of some concern in the operation of the California Water Bank, discussed supra p. 216, Note 6. One county unsuccessfully filed a claim seeking reimbursement for increased welfare costs allegedly resulting from water sales.

8. **Policy concerns.** Should the law require consideration of the negative social and economic effects associated with water rights transfers? Resource shifts are common in our economy and are the source of much economic growth. One economist has argued that there is little the government can or should do about the indirect economic and social dislocations which result from water transfers beyond existing wealth redistribution programs such as unemployment compensation and welfare. B. Delworth Gardner, The Untried Market Approach to Water Allocation, in New Courses for the Colorado River 166-67 (Gary Weatherford & F. Lee Brown eds., 1986). Another writer has objected that the consideration of such factors dulls market incentives because it increases the risk that a transfer will not be approved and makes the expectation of revenues from a transfer less certain. Stephen F. Williams, A Market-Based Approach to Water Rights: Evaluating Colorado's Water System, in Tradition, Innovation and Conflict: Perspectives on Colorado Water Law 113 (Lawrence J. MacDonnell ed., 1986).

Other writers have argued that water is a social good in which the interest of the public is paramount; to treat it as a commodity and allocate it on the basis of economic efficiency alone is a mistake. See, e.g., Joseph L. Sax, Understanding Transfers: The California Water Torture, in California Water Transfers: Gainers and Losers in Two Northern Counties (Raymond H. Coppock & Marcia Krieth, eds. 1992) (arguing that those who suffer economic loss as the result of water transfers should be compensated and that a transfer tax is the most expedient means to accomplish this).

Arizona legislation attempts to mitigate the loss of tax base caused by the transfer of groundwater from rural areas. The legislation requires cities to pay a "transportation fee," ranging from $3 to $30 per acre-foot, to counties in which groundwater originates. Ariz. Rev. Stat. § 45-556.

9. **A celebrated case.** *In re* Application of Sleeper, Rio Arriba County, Cause No. RA 84-53 (C) (N.M. 1st Jud. Dist. April 16, 1985), involved a proposal to transfer water from irrigation to a recreational lake associated with a ski area. On appeal from a decision of the state engineer, the district court denied the transfer application, holding that it was not in the public interest. The court, noting that the development would produce mostly menial jobs for local residents, said:

"[I]t is simply assumed by the Applicants that greater economic benefits are more desirable than the preservation of a cultural identity. This is clearly not so. Northern New Mexicans possess a fierce pride over their history, traditions and culture. This region of northern New Mexico and its living culture are recognized at the state and federal levels as possessing significant cultural value, not measurable in dollars and cents. The deep-felt and tradition bound ties of northern New Mexico families to the land and water are central to maintenance of that culture. * * *

"I am persuaded that to transfer water rights, devoted for more than a century to agricultural purposes, in order to construct a playground for those who can pay is a poor trade, indeed."

Did the court strike the appropriate balance between economic benefits and social costs? Should judges be deciding such issues? Should water officials be deciding such issues? Which official, agency, or institution is most competent to undertake this balancing process?

The New Mexico Court of Appeals reversed; it found that transfer statutes then in effect precluded the state engineer from considering the public interest. *In re* Application of Sleeper, 760 P.2d 787 (N.M. 1988). The statutes now require the state engineer to deny transfers which are not in the public interest. N.M. Stat. Ann. §§ 72-5-23, 5-24, -12-7, -12B-1.

10. **Condemnation powers.** In each western state, cities and towns can condemn water rights if needed for municipal supplies. In a sense, municipalities thus have a preferred right. Most of the statutes conferring the power are found in the laws relating to municipal governments and not in the water codes. Statutes granting a preference for domestic use are also construed as conferring the power of eminent domain. See Town of Sterling v. Pawnee Ditch Extension Co., 94 P. 339 (Colo. 1908).

In Nebraska and Idaho the constitutions give an order of precedence between various uses when the waters of a stream are insufficient. Each expressly provides for condemnation and compensation as the means of acquiring the water of the non-preferred user. Neb. Const. art. XV, § 6; Idaho Const. art. XV, § 3. Wyoming's statutory list of preferences is implemented by a combination of eminent domain and an administrative procedure authorizing the changed use. Wyo. Stat. Ann. §§ 41-3-102, -103.

SECTION 6. REUSE

DEPARTMENT OF ECOLOGY v. UNITED STATES BUREAU OF RECLAMATION

Supreme Court of Washington, 1992.
118 Wash. 2d 761, 827 P.2d 275.

EN BANC. The Washington State Department of Ecology (Department) granted to J.M. Hanson a permit to appropriate water from a stream running across his property. Hanson's property is located within the boundaries of a federal irrigation project and the stream carries * * * water that the project diverted from the Columbia River pursuant to the federal government's own rights of appropriation. * * *

The Columbia River Basin Irrigation Project is a massive federal project providing irrigation water for lands along the Columbia River. * * * The federal government, through the United States Bureau of Reclamation, contracted with local irrigation districts to operate and maintain the facilities and to deliver the water to the basin's farmlands. * * * Certain farmlands (known as "farm units") receive a direct water supply from the irrigation districts. In return, the farm units pay a proportionate share of the cost of the facilities.

After these farm units use the water for irrigation, significant amounts of the water seep through the land and accumulate, either above or below ground, within the project's borders. The parties refer to this water as "waste, seepage or return flow water", abbreviated as "WSRF water." * * *

Although some of the WSRF water returns to the Columbia River without being used for further irrigation, the project does recapture and reuse a portion of the used water. The irrigation districts enter into "water service contracts" with area landowners granting the landowners the right to divert the previously used water for purposes of further irrigation. These landowners pay a portion of the project's construction and maintenance costs, but a smaller portion than that charged to the landowners who used the water initially. The landowners entering into water service contracts pay for their own costs of capturing and diverting the runoff water.

J.M. Hanson owns farmland within the boundaries of the federal project and he receives water from the project to irrigate portions of his land. In the early 1980's, Hanson became interested in obtaining more water to irrigate an additional 30 acres of his land. Particularly, he wanted to divert water from an unnamed stream flowing across his property.

A significant portion of the water in Hanson's stream is WSRF water from other project lands. * * * The stream carries the water across Hanson's land and then, within a mile of his proposed point of diversion, empties into the Columbia River. The land downstream from Hanson's is undeveloped and currently has no use for project waters. The project currently has no facilities in place along this stream with which it could recapture this WSRF water, and it currently has no intention of building such facilities in the future. * * *

Hanson * * * applied to the Department of Ecology in order to obtain his own independent rights of appropriation in the stream. The United States Bureau of Reclamation opposed Hanson's application. The Bureau argued that the WSRF water in Hanson's stream had already been appropriated to the federal government, thereby precluding any further reappropriation.

The Department investigated Hanson's application and the Bureau's objection. It determined that the statutory requirements for granting the permit were met * * *. Accordingly, the Department granted Hanson's permit application.

* * * At particular issue is whether the water in Hanson's stream is still subject to the federal government's prior right of appropriation. If the federal right still applies to this water, then the Department may not grant any conflicting appropriation rights in the water.

The holder of a water right owns no title to any molecules of water until that water is diverted. Once an appropriator diverts water and brings it under his control and possession, the appropriator owns it as personal property. * * *

The appropriator's rights in the particular molecules of diverted water do not necessarily end when the water has been used once for irrigation. See Ide v. United States, 263 U.S. 497, 506, * * * (1924). An appropriator has a right to recapture and reuse this WSRF water, even under certain circumstances, when the water has left the appropriator's land and entered a natural watercourse.

This much the parties agree on. Where the parties differ is with regard to when the appropriator's rights in particular molecules of water end.[6]

The irrigation districts cite to a line of cases holding that an appropriator's rights in particular water molecules extend at least as long as the water remains within the boundaries of the appropriator's

---

6. As the Department of Ecology stresses in its brief, we are not being asked to determine whether the federal government has abandoned its water rights. Abandonment of water rights has broader consequences than abandonment of water molecules. Abandoning water molecules, as opposed to abandoning water rights, does not affect the party's right to change its practices so as to recapture future supplies of diverted water. See Stevens v. Oakdale Irr. Dist., 13 Cal.2d 343, 350, 90 P.2d 58 (1939).

property. We refer to this theory as the "geographical" test. In Miller v. Wheeler, * * * 103 P. 641 (1909), the court stated that landowners who irrigate using appropriated water retain the right to WSRF water while it remains on their land. This rule is also the law in other jurisdictions. One of the clearest statements of this rule is from Nevada:

> *So long as [waste] water exists upon [the plaintiffs'] lands, it is their property,* and they may consent to others acquiring rights therein upon their property and in ditches thereupon for the purpose of conveying such waters to the lands of such other parties. These waters, while upon the lands of the plaintiffs Bidleman, were certainly not subject to appropriation by the defendants. * * *

(Citation omitted. Italics ours.) Bidleman v. Short, * * * 150 P. 834 (1915). Similar pronouncements are found in cases from other Western States. See Barker v. Sonner, * * * 294 P. 1053 (1931) (water is not even considered waste water until it has left the land of the original appropriator); * * * Jones v. Warmsprings Irr. Dist., * * * 91 P.2d 542 (1939) (an irrigation district's water becomes free, unappropriated water when it leaves lands within an irrigation district and returns to the stream from which its was diverted, absent any attempt by landowners in the district to control it).

Here, the water in Hanson's stream is still within the boundaries of the irrigation project. Therefore, under the irrigation districts' theory, the water would still be appropriated to the project.

The Department counters that an appropriator's rights do not depend on the water's geographical location. It instead cites a number of authorities for the proposition that the duration of an appropriator's rights in particular molecules of water depends on continued control and possession of the water. One of the cases cited by the Department describes the test as follows:

> When possession of the actual water, or corpus, has been relinquished, or lost by discharge without intent to recapture, property in it ceases. This is not the abandonment of a water right, but merely an abandonment of specific portions of water, i.e., the very particles which are discharged or have escaped from control.

(Italics omitted.) Stevens v. Oakdale Irr. Dist., 13 Cal.2d 343, 350, 90 P.2d 58 (1939). General statements of this standard seem to be fairly well accepted in the Western States. * * *

The Department of Ecology argues that under its theory the water molecules in Hanson's stream are no longer appropriated to the federal government. According to the Department, once the water reaches Hanson's proposed point of diversion, the irrigation project has discharged the water without intent to recapture, as the water is headed toward the project's outer boundary and the project has no current plans to recapture this water.

It appears that both the Department's "control and possession" test and the irrigation districts' geographical test are wellfounded in the water law of the Western States. We therefore strive to construe these lines of authority so as to give greatest possible effect to each. We conclude that an appropriator's rights in particular molecules of water do not end while the water remains within the boundaries of the appropriator's property, and that after water has left those boundaries, the termination of the appropriator's rights depends on the "control and possession" test. Accordingly, once an appropriator has discharged water from his or her own property, then the issue becomes whether the appropriator nevertheless retains an intent to recapture that water, whether downstream on another piece of property or otherwise. * * * Thus, the theories may be fully reconciled by applying the geographical test until the water has left the appropriator's lands and the "control and possession" test after that point.

[W]e conclude the Department abused its discretion in granting Hanson's permit application. We cannot uphold the Department's interpretation of the law when doing so would run counter to the most directly applicable principle of western water law. * * *

Notes

1. **Policy behind the decision.** What policy does the decision serve? Is not the court simply allowing the Bureau to play the role of "dog in the manger"—denying the water to others although the Bureau has no use for it? In another part of the opinion the court said:

"Additional support for our decision flows from the fact that the original appropriator here is a federal irrigation project that was formed for the very purpose of supplying farmers like Hanson with irrigation water. Supplying this water is an expensive undertaking, and each farmer using the water—even those using WSRF water—is required to pay a share of the costs of building and maintaining the project's facilities. Under the Department's theory, Hanson would be able to obtain the water without having to pay his fair share of the system's costs.

"Moreover, if Hanson is allowed to obtain water rights without paying his portion of the system's costs, others similarly situated would have to be similarly treated. Even those landowners who currently obtain WSRF water through water service contracts—and who therefore currently contribute toward the payment of the system's costs—could potentially do so as well, for the water service contracts are terminable by landowners at the end of each year. The irrigation districts fear these landowners too would seek to avoid the system's true costs. The Bureau of Reclamation has gone so far as to maintain that the potential loss of repayment from these sources 'seriously jeopardizes the successful completion of the project.' While we cannot independently determine if this last assertion overstates the impact on the project, the potential for disruption to the system certainly is present." 827 P.2d at 281.

Is this case an example of a "hard case" making "bad law"? Is there some narrower legal basis on which Hanson might be forced to pay for project water like other irrigators? Does the answer lie in some other method of charging for project benefits? For example, instead of entering into "water service contracts," could the irrigation district assess the lands of those who use or could use WSRF water, including Hanson, for the benefits which the availability of WSRF water provides? See infra p. 430, Note 4. Would the court have the authority to impose such a charge if the enabling legislation in Washington does not provide for it?

If the court had held that Hanson could appropriate the WSRF water, would that have prevented the Bureau from recapturing and reusing the water at a future time? See the next case.

2. **More on the right to recapture.** In Binning v. Miller, 102 P.2d 54 (Wyo. 1940), the right to recapture waste water still on the original land and to reuse it on that land was apparently regarded as existing indefinitely, without time limit. Jones v. Warmsprings Irrigation District, 91 P.2d 542 (Or. 1939), held that the intent to recapture must exist at the time the water is appropriated, and that the water is abandoned to downstream users if that intent is not exercised within a reasonable time. In United States v. Haga, 276 F. 41 (D. Idaho 1921), the principal requisite was that the first appropriator be able to identify the recaptured water as that added by his operations.

3. **"In lieu diversion."** Nebraska v. Wyoming, 325 U.S. 589 (1945), infra p. 477, involved the Bureau of Reclamation's Kendrick Project, under construction on the North Platte River in Wyoming. The project would be supplied almost entirely by water stored in Seminoe Dam and diverted at Alcova Dam to the project lands in Wyoming. Return flows from the project were estimated to be 96,000 acre feet, 46,000 during the irrigation season. The Bureau did not wish to use the water below the point where it returned to the river, but could use it to enlarge the project. It therefore proposed to divert an amount equivalent to this return flow through the canal at Alcova "in lieu of" recapturing the actual return flow.

The Court refused to permit the diversion. "But we think the proposal is basically not in accord with the principle underlying [Ide v. United States, 263 U.S. 497 (1924)]. That principle is that although the water rights belong to the landowners, the owner of the irrigation project has an interest in the appropriative rights to the extent of obtaining the fullest use of the water for the project. It may therefore, retain control over the water until abandonment. We think it goes too far to say that when the return flows are abandoned, they may nevertheless be exchanged for upstream diversions by the same amount. When the return flows are abandoned, they become subject to appropriation downstream. * * * They no longer remain subject to control for further use in the project. Any claim to them or their equivalent under the form of an 'in lieu of' diversion is lost." 325 U.S. at 636-37.

FUSS v. FRANKS

Supreme Court of Wyoming, 1980.
610 P.2d 17.

[Waste-water from the plaintiffs' lands collected in a drainage ditch built by the Goshen County Irrigation District (G.I.D.) in the borrow pit of a "ditch-rider" road, which ran along the lower end of the plaintiffs' lands. The water was carried by the drainage ditch to the borrow pit of a state highway where it flowed for some distance, eventually crossing the highway in an underground pipe constructed by G.I.D. After the water crossed the highway, one of the plaintiffs, Fuss, had for many years used it to irrigate a piece of land. Fuss held no appropriation to use the water on this piece of land. The defendant, Franks, received an appropriation permit to construct a dam in the highway borrow pit to intercept the water and use it as a supplemental supply for his lands.]

ROSE, JUSTICE. * * * We will address these following issues, which we find to be dispositive of all material questions raised by the appellants:

* * *

Point 1: Was the water from the highway borrow pit lawfully appropriated by Franks?

Whether or not Franks' appropriation was lawful is resolved by answering whether or not the State Engineer had authority to approve the Franks permit in July of 1979. In this case, there was testimony that the seepage water in contest here would, if uninterrupted, flow into a natural stream. This is a qualifying requirement for appropriation. Binning v. Miller, 55 Wyo. 451, 102 P.2d 54 (1940).

In *Binning* we said:

"* * * And so it is held in a number of cases that seepage water which, if not intercepted, would naturally reach the stream, is just as much a part of the stream as the waters of any tributaries and must be permitted to return thereto, if the owner cannot make beneficial use thereof. * * * That would seem to be the more reasonable rule in irrigating states * * *."

This concept was reaffirmed in Bower v. Big Horn Canal Association, 77 Wyo. 80, 307 P.2d 593 (1957).

The permit having been issued to Franks, this constituted prima facie evidence of his right to take the water. Hunziker v. Knowlton, 78 Wyo. 241, 322 P.2d 141 (1958). This being so, it fell to appellants to allege facts sufficient to show that they had a right to the water superior to that of Franks, the permittee.

Appellants say in their brief:

"* * * The appropriator who captures upon his land waters not fully used for irrigation, sometimes referred to as waste water, may recapture the water for beneficial *use upon his premises for which the water had been appropriated.* * * * "(Emphasis supplied.)

That is a correct statement of law. It cannot, however, inure to the favor of appellants under the facts of this case.

We commented upon *Binning,* supra, where the facts were uniquely similar to those to be found here, when, in *Bower,* supra, we said:

"* * * The real question in the case [*Binning*] was whether the prior appropriation of what was termed in the original application as 'waste and seepage water' was good as against the owner of the land *from which said water came.* The court held that the seepage water which formed a natural stream might be appropriated, subject to the right of the land owner to use the water for beneficial purposes *upon the land for which the water forming the seepage was originally appropriated.*" (Emphasis and bracketed matter supplied.)

This language means that the owner of land upon which seepage or waste water rises has the right to use and reuse—capture and recapture—such waste waters for use only "upon the land for which the water forming the seepage was originally appropriated." When the water leaves the land for which it was appropriated and would, if left to flow uninterrupted, reach a natural stream, it becomes eligible to other and separate appropriation for other and different uses. It leaves the landowner upon which the seepage rose, and from which it has escaped, without any superior right to such water by reason of its having been utilized upon the land to which it was first appropriated.

We recognized this concept in *Bower,* supra, when we said:

"* * * Additionally, it is equitable, in accordance with the constitutional provisions of this State, and in line with our previous holdings, that we here decree seepage water arising on Bower's land to be subject *to appropriation* by him (subject to prescribed procedures) for lands *other than those upon which the seepage arises.* * * * " (Emphasis supplied.)

The "prescribed procedures" referred to are the application requirements for a water permit under the statutes. The rationale for this rule finds its genesis in the doctrine long since established in this state to the effect that waters become appurtenant to the lands for which they are acquired and, unless the statutes are followed with respect to change of use, the waters cannot be detached and assigned to other land without the loss of priority.

The water which accumulates in the collection ditch separating the Franks land from Bremers, Fusses and Baumgartner in Section 5, and which thereafter runs into the highway right-of-way originates on the land of the last three mentioned owners and is adjudicated in the name of the individual landowners for use upon their particular land tracts. This fact statement is undisputed. Therefore, once the water escapes the aforementioned Bremers, Fusses and Baumgartner lands in Section 5 and finds its way to the collection ditch and thence to the highway right-of-way, it must be regarded as having escaped the land to which it is appropriated and, since it would, if undisturbed, have flowed to a natural stream, it, therefore, becomes eligible for other appropriation.

Franks' permit was valid because the Fusses, Bremers and Baumgartner had no superior right to the water after it left their properties to accumulate in the collection ditch and from there flow to the highway right-of-way borrow pit. * * *

Notes

1. **Rights of juniors.** Comstock v. Ramsey, 133 P. 1107 (Colo. 1913), is the leading case holding that return flow seeping from the lands of a senior appropriator cannot be intercepted and reused *on different lands* when the water is tributary to the stream and junior appropriators have relied on it to serve their ditches downstream from the point of reentry. The same rule relied on in Farmers Highline Canal & Irrigation Co. v. City of Golden, supra p. 200—that junior appropriators are entitled to have conditions on the stream maintained as they were when the junior appropriations were made—was relied on in *Comstock*.

Why are junior appropriators entitled to have stream conditions maintained when a senior appropriator transfers water (*Highline Canal*) or tries to recapture water for use on different lands (*Comstock*) but not when the senior recaptures it for use on the same land? I.e., can the rule of *Comstock* and *Highline Canal* be reconciled with the rule permitting a senior appropriator to recapture return flows for reuse on the land for which it was initially appropriated to the detriment of junior appropriators who have come to rely on them?

2. **Appropriating return flows at the inception of a water right.** In Water Supply & Storage Co. v. Curtis, 733 P.2d 680 (Colo. 1987), an applicant for a water right requested a ruling that "the water may be used and reused and put to a succession of uses until totally consumed." In effect, the applicant attempted to appropriate its own return flows for future unspecified uses at the same time that it made the initial appropriation, thereby avoiding the problems encountered by Fuss in the principal case. The court indicated that such a ruling might be proper in a suitable case but denied the request because the applicant had no concrete plans for reuse of return flows and, thus, lacked the requisite "intent to appropriate."

3. **Protecting seepage with the law of servitudes.** A Californian court compelled the continuance of the source of the water. What kind of a right did the servient owner have in Krieger v. Pacific Gas & Electric Co., 173 Cal. Rptr. 751 (Ct. App. 1981)? The Utica Ditch originally crossed public land that was later patented to Krieger's predecessor. By federal statute the patented land was subject to a right of way for the ditch. When PG&E acquired the water right it began to line the ditch with liquid concrete ("gunite"). Krieger sought an injunction. PG&E cross-complained against Krieger for siphoning water from the ditch with a hose. The court held that the original earthen ditch "fixed the extent of the servitude," and enjoined further guniting as an enlargement of the easement, not within the "secondary easement" to make repairs. The "riparian vegetation" subsisting on the leakage was a benefit enjoyed by the landowner, said the court, and its loss would be an increase in the burden of the easement. No waste was involved, in the court's mind, the seepage was said to be beneficial to the riparian vegetation. Although the injunction against the siphon was held appropriate, the final declaration of the rights of the parties was, "The water flowing in the ditch is the property of PG&E, and [Krieger] has no right to that water; however, water which percolates, leaks or seeps through the ditch to [Krieger's] property thereby becomes his property."

4. **Tort liability for drainage.** "Waste water" or "tail water," surface return flow from irrigation, is common in irrigated country. Common law or civil law rules of drainage of natural surface waters do not apply to waters artificially brought upon the land. The owner of the upper irrigated land must acquire from the owner of the lower land permission or an easement to drain the waste water across the land. Loosli v. Heseman, 162 P.2d 393 (Idaho 1945). The upper owner may, however, discharge into a watercourse on the lower land reasonable quantities of excess waters if they can be drained without injury to the lower lands. Provident Irr. Dist. v. Cecil, 271 P.2d 157 (Cal. Ct. App. 1954). It has been said that every irrigation project eventually becomes a drainage project. Ditches to collect and redistribute waste water to other users, and to drain what would otherwise become seeped and boggy lands, are commonly constructed as part of modern projects, or as additions to older projects, by drainage districts or by the irrigation district that distributes the water.

THAYER v. CITY OF RAWLINS

Supreme Court of Wyoming, 1979.
594 P.2d 951.

ROSE, JUSTICE. This appeal concerns the rights of the defendant water users to effluent water discharged by the City of Rawlins. By virtue of water rights dating from 1900, the City of Rawlins has imported all of its municipal water supplies from the North Platte River and from Sage Creek, a tributary of the North Platte River. After using the water for municipal purposes, the City has historically discharged the resulting effluent into a channel, known as Sugar Creek, which connects with the North Platte River. In the past, the point of this discharge was above the points at which the defendants diverted the effluent for irrigation, stock water and other purposes. Defendants diverted the effluent pursuant to certificates of appropriations giving them priorities to the Sugar Creek effluent dating from 1914. To be in compliance with state and federal water-quality laws, the City must now meet certain minimum-quality standards before discharging water into Sugar Creek. To meet these standards, the City of Rawlins proposes to establish an aerated lagoon system at a location which will cause the purified water to reach Sugar Creek at a point below the defendants' point of diversion. In an effort to determine the legal effect of this proposal, the City sought and was granted a judgment declaring that the defendants were not entitled to compensation for the loss of this water. We will affirm the district court's judgment. * * *

Defendants premise their claim to compensation on the belief that Sugar Creek below the City of Rawlins has, due to the passage of a long period of time, become a natural stream subject to appropriation, thus entitling the defendants to protections afforded to other holders of water rights in the state. * * *

More than fifty years ago, this court stated, in Wyoming Hereford Ranch v. Hammond Packing Co., 33 Wyo. 14, 236 P. 764, 772 (1925):

> "* * * Even in this state, where the conservation of water for irrigation is so important, we would not care to hold that in disposing of sewage the city could not adopt some means that would completely consume it. It might, we think, be diverted to waste places, or to any chosen place where it would not become a nuisance, without any consideration of the demands of water users who might be benefitted by its disposition in some other manner. * * *"

While we may not rely on the Wyoming Hereford Ranch decision for a disposition of the present case—due to significant factual distinctions—it is somewhat prophetic with respect to the clash, between concepts of western water law and the directives of environmental-protection statutes, now before us. We will not, however, attempt to decide all of the potential questions that are bound to arise as the demands for cleaner environment begin to impinge on the availability of sufficient supplies of water. * * * As a result, our discussion and disposition of this case will be narrowly drawn.

The fundamental question becomes: Do the defendants have a right to compensation for a loss occasioned by the City's change in the point of discharge of imported waters? It has been stated that generally junior appropriators have vested rights in a continuation of stream conditions existing at the time of their appropriations, thus entitling them to resist changes in points of diversion or use which materially affect their rights. However, an importer of water—at least insofar as these defendants are concerned—has the right to reuse, successively use and make disposition of imported waters. See, City and County of Denver Bd. of Water Commissioners v. Fulton Irrigating Ditch Co., Colo., 179 Colo. 47, 506 P.2d 144 (1972). Even though, at the time of the Fulton Irrigation Ditch decision, there was a statute authorizing the conclusion reached, the Colorado Supreme Court opined that the rule would be the same without the statute, subject to contrary contractual obligations.

The right of the City to use such imported waters finds its roots in the common law of property and the Puritan ethic: One who by his own effort adds to the supply of a stream, is entitled to the water even though a senior priority might be without water. A person should reap the benefit of his own efforts, and a priority relates only to the *natural* supply of the stream at the time of appropriation.

These concepts are not new to Wyoming water law, since they have been applied to protect the right of a senior appropriator to recapture waste and seepage water. See, Binning v. Miller, 55 Wyo. 451, 102 P.2d 54 (1940). The lower landowner using such water merely takes his chances as to future supplies, no matter how long he uses such water.

Defendants seem to want this court to declare that the City has abandoned its right to make a change in the point of discharge of these imported waters. We indicated in Binning v. Miller, supra, that if the senior appropriator had allowed the lower landowner to use waste water for 35 years, but then legitimately began to use it himself, the lower landowner would have no right to complain—"The water is always different from year to year." This question, in its broad sense, was raised but not answered in the Fulton Irrigation Ditch case, supra. * * * We hold that in the imported-water context—which gives the importer the unrestricted right to reuse, successively use and make disposition—the importer's right to do these things is not subject to abandonment insofar as these defendants are concerned. It must be remembered that any other holding would be inconsistent with the fact that the defendants depend entirely on the City's sufferance—it is always free to terminate the importation. Under such circumstances, we are reluctant to declare an abandonment. * * *

We turn, then, to the statutory provisions which purportedly vest the State Engineer or Board of Control with primary jurisdiction over the City's proposed actions. Defendants claim that the City's water-treatment proposal constitutes either a change or expansion in use—because the water will be used as a purifying agent, instead of only as a flushing agent—or a change in the place of use, because the sewage will be transported for treatment to a place outside the city limits. The City, on the other hand, contends that there will be no change in use since the use will still be for municipal purposes, and that the place of use will remain with the City of Rawlins. The only change, according to the City, is a change in the place of discharge.

The difficulty in attempting to classify the changes required by water-pollution-control laws has been noted. * * * We find no need, * * * to put a label on what the City of Rawlins proposes to do, in order to determine whether the City must file a petition under § 41-3-104.

The purpose of § 41-3-104 is to provide a procedure for those wishing to change a water right *and* to place limitations on the quantity of water that can be transferred. We must ask why the City's proposal should be subjected to these procedures. The manifest result of a § 41-3-104 proceeding is the entry of a Board of Control order limiting the amount of water transferred by a change in use or a change in the place of use. Insofar as these defendants are concerned, we have already held that the City has the *unrestricted* right to reuse, successively use and make disposition of these imported waters. If these rights are not subject to restriction, it would be anomalous to require the City to submit to a procedure that assumes that restrictions are permissible and, indeed, required. As a result, we hold that the State Engineer and Board of Control have no jurisdiction, by virtue of § 41-3-104 over the controversy between these parties. * * *

ROONEY, JUSTICE, dissenting, with whom RAPER, CHIEF JUSTICE joins.

I dissent. I agree with the contention of the defendants that this matter is prematurely in the courts, and that the board of control should first apply its expertise in passing on the issues. * * *

The majority opinion lays its cornerstone on the proposition that an importer of water has the unobstructed right to reuse, successively use and make disposition of imported waters. The importer, then, would have supervision over the appropriation, distribution and diversion of such water. Imported water is no less precious than any other kind of water. The mere fact that it is transported from one basin to another does not make it more subject to waste, more subject to the whims of any private citizen, less subject to the requirement of beneficial use, or less subject to the constitutional supervision of the board of control. If there is case law to the contrary, I would reverse it. If there is statutory law to the contrary, I would hold such to be unconstitutional. * * *

This case had its origin in a very worthy direction to the City of Rawlins to clean up its discarded water. To do so will cost money. It would be incongruous, in view of the value of water in Wyoming, to not also direct the city to preserve the water as it cleans it—preserve it for additional beneficial use. This may cost more money. Cleaning water is no more worthy than preserving it. The board of control should determine the relation of beneficial use to other aspects of the project. The board may authorize the project as now planned. It may direct pumping to the original place of discharge. It may direct a different method of cleaning. It may require payment of just compensation to the damaged appropriators. It may require change in reservoir construction to provide for a deeper but less extensive body of water so as to reduce evaporation. It may reach the same conclusion as did the district court. * * *

I would reverse and remand with directions that the plaintiff be ordered to submit the plans for the project to the state engineer for review and approval.

Notes

1. **Abandonment and intent to reuse.** In City of Thornton v. Bijou Irrigation Co., 926 P.2d 1 (Colo. 1996), supra p. 47, the Colorado Supreme Court joined Wyoming in holding that the rights to reuse, to successively use, and to dispose of imported water are not subject to abandonment. *Bijou* also held that the importer need not prove it had intended to reuse the water at the time of initial appropriation.

2. **Use of natural facilities to transport and store imported water.** The City of Los Angeles brings water from the Owens River Valley to the San Fernando Valley. There, it spreads part in gravel pits and on other grounds so that it sinks beneath the surface to join other water under the valley floor. It sells other parts of it to valley farmers, 27 1/2% of which also sinks beneath the surface. Both the induced recharge and the return flows join waters normally present in the valley and eventually become part of the surface flow of the Los Angeles River, from which the city takes its water downstream. The cities of Glendale and Burbank pump water from wells in the valley. Held, Los Angeles has a prior right to both the recharge and the return flow. City of L.A. v. City of Glendale, 142 P.2d 289 (Cal. 1943). The court stated:

"Plaintiff had a prior right to the use of the water brought to the San Fernando Valley. It did not abandon that right when it spread the water for the purpose of economical transportation and storage. It used a similar storage system at the source of this supply in the Owens River Valley. By availing itself of these natural reservoirs, it spared its citizens the cost of financing the construction of additional dams, if, indeed, appropriate sites were available at the lower end of the aqueduct. * * * It would be as harsh to compel plaintiff to build reservoirs when natural ones were available as to compel the construction of an artificial ditch beside a stream bed. In making water available for irrigation, plaintiff sought not only to increase cultivation of the land, but to convey some of the water into the underground reservoir of the valley. Thus, in selling water to the farmers, as in spreading water, plaintiff was interested in its economical transportation and storage.

"The use by others of this water as it flowed to the subterranean basin does not cut off plaintiff's rights. * * *"

3. **When is water "imported?"** City of Thornton v. Bijou Irrigation Co., supra p. 47, at 81:

"Through its use of the Larimer County Canal, Thornton transports water from the Poudre River to an area that the river otherwise would not have reached. However, the area to which the water is carried is not within an entirely different watershed or drainage area. The water was initially diverted from the Poudre River, a tributary of the South Platte River, and the aquifer fed by the return flows from irrigation with this water remains a part of the tributary system of these rivers. Thus, unlike water imported from across the Continental Divide, Thornton's irrigation water is not new to the system; Thornton essentially changed only the place of use of that water. * * * Therefore, we decline to extend the special treatment afforded imported and developed water to the 'transbasin' diversion within the same general water system * * *."

Would the Colorado Supreme Court treat the water in the principal case as imported water? Note that Sugar Creek is a tributary of the North Platte River, the source of the water "imported" by Rawlins.

4. **Artificially stored groundwater.** In Jensen v. Department of Ecology, 685 P.2d 1068 (Wash. 1984), the court held that imported irrigation water which percolates into an aquifer is "artificially stored groundwater." As such, the court held the water is not subject to appropriation by another as public groundwater. The court rejected the argument that the importer, the Bureau of Reclamation, had abandoned or forfeited the water, finding that the Bureau intended to recapture it from the inception of the irrigation project and had, in fact, used natural and artificial systems to control and channel it. The court also rejected the argument that the water had lost its identity as artificially stored groundwater by being commingled with natural groundwater. Neb. Rev. Stat. § 46-226.01 essentially codifies *Jensen* by authorizing a permit to recapture groundwater which is "incidentally" stored through an appropriative use. The statute was upheld in Central Nebraska Public Power & Irrigation District v. Abrahamson, 413 N.W.2d 290 (Neb. 1987).

5. **Appropriation of unrecaptured return flows from imported water.** May others appropriate return flows from foreign water which are not recaptured by the importer? In Dodge v. Ellensburg Water Co., 729 P.2d 631 (Wash. Ct. App. 1986), the court held that foreign water abandoned by the developer does not become public water and is not subject to appropriation. Rather, the water may be used without appropriation by the "first taker," that is, by the first person to get physical control of the water at any point in time. The court also held that prescriptive rights could not be acquired in foreign water. As to the court's first point, compare Arizona Public Service Co. v. Long, 773 P.2d 988 (Ariz. 1989).

6. **Sale of return flows from transferred rights.** Allowance of sales of new return flows is urged as a partial solution to the problem faced by a water rights purchaser who buys all of a former user's diversion yet acquires only his consumptive use when transferring the right to a new use. The discrepancy between what the former user sells and what the new user gets may be 50%. If the purchaser can sell return flows from the new use, part of this loss can be recouped. The National Water Commission has joined in the suggestion, Water Policies for the Future, supra p. 44, Note 3, at 269.

7. **Rights in sewage effluent.** Compare Pulaski Irrigating Ditch Co. v. City of Trinidad, 203 P. 681 (Colo. 1922), with the principal case. The water for the City of Trinidad was taken from the Las Animas River. After use, it was deposited as raw sewage into settling pits, from which it seeped back into the river. When the city built a treatment plant, it wanted to sell the purified water. Senior appropriators downstream protested.

"The use of water in cities by which it is contaminated is principally as a vehicle for carrying away noxious matter; and when that duty has been discharged and the city * * * has withdrawn the solid matter from the water, the water should be returned to the stream. * * *

"It is said, however, that the city might have disposed of the sewage by evaporating the water from it, from which it is argued that it had a right to destroy the water; hence it could not belong to the public.

"It would seem that, according to the established public policy of this state, this right to destroy the water by evaporation can exist only when there is no other practicable method of disposing of the sewage; that is to say, if all other methods were very expensive as compared with the cost of evaporation, public policy might, in the interest of the community producing sewage, permit its disposal by the evaporation of the water. That case, however, is not before us. We are dealing with water which the city is voluntarily purifying.

"To turn this water back into the river will not increase the river's flow above what it would have been had the water not been diverted, and it is not therefore developed water. Applying the principle heretofore laid down, it seems clear that the water here in question does not belong to the city, and that it has no right to sell it." Id. at 682-83.

Cal. Water Code § 1211: "Prior to making any change in the point of discharge, place of use, or purpose of use of treated wastewater, the owner of any wastewater treatment plant shall obtain the approval of board for that change. The board shall review the changes pursuant to the provisions [relating to changes in use]." If the source of treated waste water was imported water could the board refuse to permit a change in use because it would deprive downstream junior appropriators of water they have come to rely on?

In Arizona Public Service Co. v. Long, 773 P.2d 988 (Ariz. 1989), the plaintiff entered into contracts to purchase sewage effluent from several

Arizona cities. The effluent, which had previously been discharged into the Gila River after treatment, was transported by pipeline some fifty miles to cool a nuclear power plant. Downstream irrigators who relied on the sewage effluent sued, alleging that the cities must continue discharging the effluent into the river. Although the court rejected the cities' argument that they owned the effluent, it nevertheless concluded that effluent is neither surface water nor groundwater under Arizona statutes and is not subject to regulation. Consequently, the court held, cities may sell the effluent. The court refused to create a regulatory system for sewage effluent by judicial decision but invited the legislature to do so.

In City of San Marcos v. Texas Commission on Environmental Quality, 128 S.W.3d 264 (Tex. Ct. App. 2004), the court held that the City of San Marcos did not retain ownership of sewage effluent after discharging it into the San Marcos River and, thus, could not divert the water for reuse downstream without obtaining an appropriation permit. Was the City simply being stubborn when it refused to apply for an appropriation permit? Who do you suppose objected to the City's planned permitless recapture of the effluent? The objectors' victory was short-lived. Legislation passed while the case was pending authorizes reuse projects similar to the San Marcos project. Tex. Water Code Ann. §11.042(b).

8. **Rights to reservoir water.** Should an appropriator who stores water in a reservoir be able to reuse and dispose of the water without regard to the injury caused to other appropriators? Do not the reasons which the court gives in *Thayer* for allowing unrestricted uses of imported water apply equally to stored water? In City of Westminster v. Church, 445 P.2d 52 (Colo. 1968), the Colorado Supreme Court seemed to so hold, but in Southeastern Colorado Water Conservancy District v. Fort Lyon Canal Co., 720 P.2d 133 (Colo. 1986), the court clarified its earlier decision and held that changes in the use of stored water are limited by historical use to prevent injury to other appropriators.

Chapter 3

RIPARIAN RIGHTS

SECTION 1. BASIS OF RIGHT

ANAHEIM UNION WATER CO. v. FULLER

Supreme Court of California, 1907.
150 Cal. 327, 88 P. 978.

SHAW, J. This is an action to enjoin the defendants from diverting water from the Santa Ana river. Judgment in favor of the plaintiffs as prayed for was given in the court below. The defendants appeal from the judgment, and from an order denying their motion for a new trial.

The plaintiffs own lands through which the Santa Ana river flows. They have been accustomed for many years to irrigate this land with waters from the river, and for that purpose there is required, during the irrigating season, a continuous flow of 400 miners' inches of water. The defendants * * * own land on the river, situated above the land of the plaintiffs, and upon it they had built a dam in the river and were thereby diverting water from the stream, which, by means of a ditch, they were conducting to other lands owned by them and were there using it for irrigation. The plaintiffs claim, and the court found, that the land which the defendants were thus irrigating with water from the river was not riparian thereto. * * *

Some distance below the land of the plaintiffs a tributary, known as "Chino creek," enters the Santa Ana river. Chino creek also has a tributary, known as "Mill creek," which enters Chino creek 1 1/2 miles above the confluence of the latter with the Santa Ana river. The defendants take the water from the river, above the land of the plaintiffs, in a ditch which extends across the low bottom to the high land or bluff, and then extends along the bluff, at a grade less than that of the river, gradually getting further above and away from the river until it reaches and crosses the divide, or summit of the elevated land, between the watershed of the river and that of Mill creek. The court found that the land irrigated with water from this ditch lies beyond

236

this divide, and is wholly within the watershed of Mill creek, and that it does not abut upon the stream of the Santa Ana, and is not riparian thereto. Land which is not within the watershed of the river is not riparian thereto, and is not entitled as riparian land, to the use or benefit of the water from the river, although it may be part of an entire tract which does extend to the river. * * *

The defendants claim that * * * this rule does not apply to the land they seek to irrigate, because, while it is wholly within the Mill creek watershed, it is also within the general watershed of the Santa Ana river, considered as an entirety including the valley from its sources to its mouth. This fact does not affect the case, at least so far as the land of the plaintiffs is concerned. The principal reasons for the rule confining riparian rights to that part of lands bordering on the stream which are within the watershed are that, where the water is used on such land, it will, after such use, return to the stream, so far as it is not consumed, and that, as the rainfall on such land feeds the stream, the land is in consequence entitled, so to speak, to the use of its waters. Where two streams unite, we think the correct rule to be applied, in regard to the riparian rights therein, is that each is to be considered as a separate stream, with regard to lands abutting thereon above the junction, and that land lying within the watershed of one stream above that point is not to be considered as riparian to the other stream. The fact that the streams are of different size, or that both lie in one general watershed, or drainage basin, should not affect the rule, nor should it be changed by the additional fact that the two watersheds are separated merely by the summit or crown of a comparatively low table land, or "mesa," * * * and not by a sharp or well-defined ridge, range of hills, or mountains. The reasons for the rule are the same in either case. In some cases it may be difficult to distinguish the line of separation. This seems to have been a case of that sort. Nevertheless, we think there is evidence sufficient to support the finding of the court that there is a dividing line between the two watersheds, and that the land irrigated by defendants lies upon the slope which descends into Mill creek. * * *

The evidence also supports the finding that the land irrigated by the defendants does not abut upon, or extend to, the river. If the owner of a tract abutting on a stream conveys to another a part of the land not contiguous to the stream, he thereby cuts off the part so conveyed from all participation in the use of the stream and from riparian rights therein, unless the conveyance declares the contrary. Land thus conveyed and severed from the stream can never regain the riparian right, although it may thereafter be reconveyed to the person who owns the part abutting on the stream, so that the two tracts are again held in one ownership. * * * All the land belonging to the defendants, including the Smith tract, which was in part irrigated, was originally a part of the Jurupa rancho, which abutted upon the river. The original owner of that rancho subdivided it by arbitrary lines, corresponding to the government surveys, and sold and conveyed it in parcels according to that survey. Under the rule above stated the conveyance by him of a tract not contiguous to the stream would sever such tract from the riparian interest and deprive it of subsequent participation in the use of the water of the river, the right to which previously attached to the entire rancho. The tract which includes the irrigated land of the defendants is not at any point contiguous to the river. At the time the action was begun it was owned by the defendant Smith. He was not the owner of any adjoining land which lay contiguous to the river. After the action was begun he conveyed this land, to certain of the other defendants, some of whom owned adjoining lands extending from the Smith land to the river. This subsequent conveyance gave those defendants a continuous ownership of land extending from the river to and including the Smith land. This contiguous ownership, however, did not confer upon the Smith land the riparian rights of which it was deprived, when Smith, or his predecessors, obtained it by a conveyance which severed it from the portion of the Jurupa rancho abutting upon the river. * * *

It is further contended that the plaintiffs' land is in no wise damaged by the diversion complained of, and hence that the diversion cannot be enjoined. * * *

On this point the defendants cite several cases in which it is held that a lower riparian owner cannot enjoin a diversion by another riparian proprietor above, unless he can show that such diversion works damage to him, and that it is more than a just proportion of the water to which the upper owner is entitled. Such decisions are not applicable to this case. Riparian owners have correlative rights in the stream, and neither is a trespasser against the other until he diverts more than his share and injures and damages the other thereby. Here the defendants were not, with respect to the land irrigated, riparian owners, but were trespassers on plaintiffs' property rights from the beginning, and the continuance of the trespass for a sufficient time would divest the right of the plaintiffs with respect to the water diverted. * * *

The defendants urge that inasmuch as the plaintiffs need but 400 inches of water for their land, and there remained in the stream, after defendants' diversion, more than 2000 inches, which flows down to and beyond the plaintiffs' land, and which is more than they can possibly use thereon, that it therefore follows that no damage can ever ensue, even if the diversion is unlawful and should ripen into a prescriptive right by continuance; and hence that their diversion should not be enjoined. The theory of the law of riparian rights in this state is that the water of a stream belongs by a sort of common right to the several riparian owners along the stream; each being entitled to sever his share for use on his riparian land. The fact that a large quantity of water flows down the stream by and beyond the plaintiffs' land does not prove that it goes to waste, nor that the plaintiffs are entitled to take a part of it, as against other riparian owners or users below. Nor can it be said that plaintiffs, on account of the present abundance, could safely permit defendants to acquire, as against them, a right to a part of the water. The riparian right is not lost by disuse, and other riparian owners above may take or others below may be entitled to take, and may insist upon being allowed to take, all of the stream, excepting only sufficient for the plaintiffs' land. In either alternative, the taking of a part of the water by the defendants would not leave enough for the plaintiffs' use. There is nothing in this case to show how much water is required above and below by those having rights in the stream. In view of the well-known aridity of the climate, and the high state of cultivation in the vicinity, the court could almost take judicial notice that in years of ordinary rainfall there is no surplus of water in the stream over that used by the various owners under claim of right. But, however this may be, it is settled by the decisions above cited that a party, situated as the plaintiffs are, can enjoin an unlawful diversion, in order to protect and preserve his riparian right.

* * *

The judgment and order are affirmed.

Notes

1. **Source of title test.** The "source of title" test of the extent of riparian lands was summarized in Boehmer v. Big Rock Creek Irrigation District, 48 P. 908 (Cal. 1897), by saying that the riparian right extends only to the smallest tract held under one title in the chain of title leading to the present owner. Under this rule, the amount of riparian land can only diminish. Express or implied preservation of riparian rights when a riparian tract is subdivided is discussed in Thompson v. Enz, infra p. 242 and accompanying Note 1.

2. **Unity of title test.** A contrasting theory is "unity of title." In Jones v. Conn, 64 P. 855, 858 (Or. 1901), the court said, "It would seem, therefore, that any person owning land which abuts upon or through which a natural stream of water flows is a riparian proprietor, entitled to the rights of such, without regard to the extent of his land, or from whom or when he acquired his title. The fact that he may have procured the particular tract washed by the stream at one time, and subsequently purchased land adjoining it, will not make him any the less a riparian proprietor, nor should it alone be a valid objection to his using the water on the land last acquired. The only thing necessary to entitle him to the right of a riparian proprietor is to show that the body of land owned by him borders upon a stream."

This rule is adopted by the American Law Institute in Restatement (Second) of Torts, § 843, cmt. c (1979).

3. **Government subdivision test.** In Crawford Co. v. Hathaway, 93 N.W. 781 (Neb. 1903), the court suggested that since the government disposed of the public domain in 40 acre tracts, riparian rights should be limited to such subdivisions, but in computing damages for loss of riparian rights by condemnation, the court later decided that damage to entire sections (640 acres) should be considered. McGinley v. Platte Valley Pub. Power & Irr. Dist., 271 N.W. 864 (Neb. 1937).

4. **Extent of riparian lands in eastern states.** Questions of the extent of riparian lands have not often been litigated in eastern states. The watershed limitation clearly finds acceptance, see William H. Farnham, The Permissible Extent of Riparian Land, 7 Land & Water L. Rev. 31 (1972). Farnham argues for the adoption of a "reasonable limit" rule that can be supported by an analysis of some cases. Eastern courts have not adopted either the "smallest tract" rule of *Boehmer*, supra p. 239, Note 1, or the "government subdivision" rule of *Crawford*, supra p. 240, Note 3.

5. **Necessity of bed ownership.** It was once thought that land to be riparian had to either include a part of the bed of the watercourse or border on a public watercourse whose bed is privately owned. Restatement of Torts, § 843 (1939). The Restatement (Second) of Torts § 843 (1979), now states that ownership of the bed is immaterial.

Some powers and privileges relating to the stream and commonly denominated as riparian rights may require either ownership of the bed or public access to the water. These include dam building and, probably, commercial ice cutting. Cases prohibiting an adjacent land owner from performing various acts deal with trespasses on another's land and not directly with the rights of the contiguous owner to use the water if he can do so without trespass. For example, some early cases found a right to the natural overflow of a stream which annually goes out of its banks. E.g., Lux v. Haggin, 10 P. 674 (Cal. 1886). Many cases allow a riparian owner to go upstream on the land of another and with permission divert water to the riparian land. E.g., Rose v. Mesmer, 75 P. 905 (Cal. 1904).

As to the status of the bed itself as riparian land, see the omitted portions of the opinion in the principal case (bottom lands, apparently sometimes overflowed). A statute granting owners bordering on tidal waters the sole right to plant and gather oysters in front of their lands for 500 yards seaward gives rights which are protected from private infringement, though subject to superior rights of the public and the state. Crary v. State Highway Comm'n, 68 So. 2d 468 (Miss. 1953). There are no cases dealing directly with the status as riparian proprietors of persons who have rights to tidelands affected by river water, but who own no uplands. However, such a status may be inferred from Grant v. United States, 192 F.2d 482 (4th Cir. 1951), which held that a person holding a lease from the state for cultivation of oysters on lands beneath tidal waters may complain of stream pollution which destroys the beds.

6. **Nonriparian use.** The principal case holds that a downstream riparian may enjoin a nonriparian use, even one causing no harm. More typically, courts hold that a nonriparian use may be enjoined if it causes "actual perceptible damage to the present or potential enjoyment" of a downstream riparian. E.g., Stratton v. Mt. Hermon Boys' School, 103 N.E. 87 (Mass. 1913). In the language of "reasonable use," discussed in the next section, a non-riparian use which causes injury is "per se" unreasonable. Similarly, a downstream nonriparian use is per se unreasonable and not entitled to protection against the acts of an upstream riparian. See Kennebunk, Kennebunkport & Wells Water Dist. v. Me. Tpk. Auth., 71 A.2d 520 (Me. 1950).

Perhaps no feature of riparian law has received more adverse and critical comment than the concept that the waters are reserved for the benefit of the lands along the stream, and that rights to the use of water are special privileges of the owners of such lands. See William L. Zeigler, Water Use under Common Law Doctrines, in Water Resources and the Law 49, 70–72 (1958):

"Apart from the problem of uncertainty and instability of a riparian's right to use water, there is the problem of supplying water to non-riparian land. It is impossible for all people to be riparians. The increasing population and industrial expansion require the utilization of lands which are not adjacent to surface water supplies. In most [riparian] states, use of stream or lake water on non-riparian land is prohibited. This is considered as unreasonable or as unlawful per se. The water of a stream or lake is for the riparians only. * * * The prohibition on non-riparian uses precludes the distribution of water from areas of plenty to areas of drought or great demand, and the water, where available, may be wasted."

Compare John E. Cribbet, Illinois Water Rights Law 28 (1958): "This does not appear to be a major problem. Practically, water can be most efficiently used close to its source and land with riparian rights can always be purchased just as one purchases oil land, gravel pits, etc. This is largely a matter of economics rather than a serious legal problem."

Which would be the preferable rule for determining the extent of riparian land, "source of" or "unity of" title? Would it make a difference whether the land was located in California, where appropriators may make non-riparian uses, but newer riparian uses have priority, or in a state where riparian rights are the only source of water rights?

7. **Nonriparian use by a riparian proprietor.** Under the Restatement (Second) of Torts § 855 (1979), a nonriparian use by a riparian proprietor is not per se unreasonable. The comments to the section state, however, that the use on a nonriparian parcel is one factor to be considered in determining reasonableness. The comments state that this rule follows the policy that riparian law should place no artificial or absolute

restrictions on the use of water. In contrast, under the Restatement (Second), the use of water by a nonriparian which causes harm to a riparian is per se unreasonable unless: (1) the nonriparian's use is under a grant from another riparian, (2) the nonriparian is exercising a right created by governmental authority, or (3) the nonriparian is exercising a public right. See Restatement (Second) of Torts §§ 856, 857. See also Pyle v. Gilbert, 265 S.E.2d 584 (Ga. 1980), infra p. 287.

Is the distinction which the Restatement (Second) makes between a nonriparian use by a riparian proprietor and a nonriparian use by a nonriparian proprietor valid? How can there ever be a nonriparian use by a nonriparian proprietor? In order to get access to a stream would not a nonriparian proprietor need a grant from a riparian and would not the grant convey either riparian lands, making the nonriparian a riparian, or riparian rights?

8. **Extent of the watershed limit.** Where plaintiff's land is situated below the junction of two branches of a stream, he cannot complain of the transportation, by a defendant who has riparian lands above the forks, of water out of one branch for irrigation in the watershed of the other branch. Rancho Santa Margarita v. Vail, 81 P.2d 533 (Cal. 1938).

9. **Characterization of riparian rights.** Riparian rights have been described as part and parcel of the land itself, corporeal hereditaments, incorporeal hereditaments, easements, appurtenances and as tenancies in common in the stream. What are the characteristics of these species of property? Is it appropriate to approach a problem concerning riparian rights in this way? See John K. Bennett, Some Fundamentals of Legal Interests in Water Supplies, 22 S. Cal. L. Rev. 1 (1948).

In Stewart v. Bridges, 292 S.E.2d 702 (1982), one lakeshore proprietor sued another to enjoin use of the water for irrigation. Held: the trial court erroneously instructed the jury that: (1) the parties had a tenancy in common in the water of the lake and the defendant irrigator therefore had no superior right to use the water to the exclusion of the plaintiff, and (2) the plaintiff, as the owner of the part of the lake bed, was entitled to possession and control of the water vertically above his land, and hence to "lateral support" for that water.

THOMPSON v. ENZ
Supreme Court of Michigan, 1967.
379 Mich. 667, 154 N.W.2d 473.

KAVANAGH, JUSTICE. Plaintiffs filed a complaint in the Barry county circuit court against defendants claiming violation of their rights as riparian owners on Gun Lake and seeking a declaratory judgment to that effect. * * * Plaintiffs were granted the relief requested. * * *

This case concerns certain property rights in and around Gun Lake * * *. The parties agree that this lake has approximately 2,680 acres of surface area and approximately 30 miles of shore line. The defendant corporation is a contract purchaser of a riparian parcel of land having approximately 1,415 feet of frontage on said lake, and the individual defendants are the sole stockholders of the corporation. Plaintiffs are riparian owners of other property abutting Gun Lake. * * *

Defendants are * * * developing and subdividing their parcel of land into from 144 to 153 lots. Of these lots, approximately 16 will abut on the natural shore line of the lake. The remainder of the lots will front on canals. To give the back lot purchasers access to the lake the defendants' plan calls for excavating across riparian lots Nos 13 and 76. The defendants purport to grant to the purchasers of those lots fronting on the canals riparian rights to the lake and rights of access through the excavation to the lake. The back lots would have frontage on the canals of approximately 11,000 feet.

The following questions are raised on appeal:

1. May a right of access to Gun Lake be created by dredging an artificial canal from the lake through lots having frontage on Gun Lake to back lots having no frontage thereon, and may ownership of such lots carry with it riparian rights? * * * *No*

"Riparian land" is defined as a parcel of land which includes therein a part of or is bounded by a natural watercourse. * * * Artificial watercourses are waterways that owe their origin to acts of man, such as canals, drainage and irrigation ditches, aqueducts, flumes, and the like. * * *

Land abutting on an artificial watercourse has no riparian rights. * * * We, therefore, conclude that parcels of land to be subdivided from the main tract of land bordering on Gun Lake have no riparian rights as: (1) they neither include therein a part of nor are they bounded by Gun Lake, and (2) the canal itself would be an artificial watercourse giving rise to no riparian rights.

The remaining question for decision is whether or not riparian rights may be conveyed to a grantee or reserved by the grantor in a conveyance which divides a tract of land with riparian rights into more than one parcel, of which parcels only one would remain bounded by the watercourse.   *No*

In the case of Harvey Realty Co. v. Borough of Wallingford * * * Justice Hinman, writing for the Court, stated (150 A. p. 63):

> "It is clear that the grantees or contractees, from the plaintiff, of lots separated from and not bordering on Pine Lake can have, of their own right, no riparian privileges in its waters. *And any attempted transfer of the right made by a riparian to a nonriparian proprietor is invalid.*" (Citing cases.) (Emphasis supplied.) * * *

We hold that riparian rights are not alienable, severable, divisible or assignable apart from the land which includes therein or is bounded by a natural watercourse.

Judgment of the Court of Appeals reversed.

BRENNAN, JUSTICE. * * * Here, the developer wishes to subdivide his property and convey back lots by deeds which will expressly grant easements for rights of way, permitting access to the lake through the canal. There is no doubt that a riparian owner can grant an easement over his land to permit a nonriparian owner to have access to the water.

A great many inland lakes in Michigan have been developed in this fashion, where cottages or homes do not have actual lake frontage, but do enjoy, in common with other property owners, the use of a granted or reserved easement providing for access to the water for recreational purposes. If the easement proposed in this case were a road, rather than a canal, no serious issue would be raised concerning the defendants' right to convey back lots with such an easement included in the grant. * * *

Notes

1. **Preservation of riparian status when land is subdivided.** Where a portion of riparian lands, not contiguous to the stream, was conveyed with "the same rights to the use of water that appurtained to said land in the hands of the party of the first part," the non-riparian land retained riparian rights. Strong v. Baldwin, 97 P. 178 (Cal. 1908). Where a land company which owned a large tract of riparian land organized another corporation to which it transferred the water right, and then sold the land in small parcels, giving with each parcel a certificate of stock in the water corporation entitling the holder to a certain part of the water, the purchaser of each parcel became vested with a proportionate part of the riparian right originally held by the land company. Copeland v. Fairview Land & Water Co., 131 P. 119 (Cal. 1913). The partition of a riparian tract among tenants in common does not destroy the riparian character of the off-stream plots. Rancho Santa Margarita v. Vail, 81 P.2d 533 (Cal. 1938). Where a right-of-way for a road was granted across a riparian tract the part of the tract separated from the stream by the right-of-way retained its riparian status. Pleasant Valley Canal Co. v. Borror, 72 Cal. Rptr. 2d 1 (Cal. Ct. App. 1998). A conveyance of an upland portion of a riparian tract did not include a riparian right. Harvey Realty Co. v. Borough of Wallingford, 150 A. 60 (Conn. 1930).

As for the status and rights of landowners on man-made bodies of water, see infra p. 262, Note 1.

2. **Riparian rights to continued access to watercourse.** The riparian right includes reasonable access to the watercourse even though the bed may belong to the state. E.g., Romeo v. Sherry, 308 F. Supp. 2d

128 (E.D.N.Y. 2004) (New York law). This includes the right to build a wharf out to the navigable portion of the water. See infra p. 529, Note 2. The principal case held that riparian rights could not be extended to non-riparian parcels by dredging an access channel. Where, however, siltation or other natural changes in a watercourse affect a riparian's continued access to the watercourse, courts have concluded that riparian rights may be *preserved* by dredging. Town of Oyster Bay v. Commander Oil Corp., 759 N.E.2d 1233 (N.Y. 2001).

3. **Conveyance of easement.** As the dissenting opinion in the principal case noted, many courts will allow a riparian owner to grant an easement to nonriparians to allow access to the watercourse. Little v. Kin, 644 N.W.2d 375 (Mich. App. 2002).

4. **Riparian rights of cities.** Under the majority rule, a city fronting a river or lake does not have a riparian right to take water for public water supply. E.g., Town of Purcellville v. Potts, 19 S.E.2d 700 (Va. 1942); but see City of Canton v. Shock, 63 N.E. 600 (Ohio 1902).

The rights of cities, public utilities, and public agencies furnishing water in "riparian rights states" that follow the majority rule are examined in Chapter 3, Section 3C. In several cases cities have been treated, without discussion, as if they were riparian proprietors. See, e.g., Sayles v. Mitchell, 245 N.W. 390 (S.D. 1932).

5. **Riparian rights to diffused surface water.** Riparian rights relate to watercourses, including springs and lakes, but not to every source. See State v. Hiber, supra p. 84 and accompanying Notes, for what constitutes a watercourse. Diffused surface water resulting from precipitation may be captured and used, or dammed and redirected, by the owner of the land on which the waters are found, even though these activities diminish the flow of a stream with adverse effects on downstream riparians. Broadbent v. Ramsbotham, 156 Eng. Rep. 971 (Exch. 1856).

6. **Drainage of diffused surface water.** Many controversies over surface water arise because the landowners are trying to get rid of it, rather than to capture and use it. Two drainage rules have competed for acceptance by the courts, and a third has developed. Some courts follow the "common enemy" rule, under which the possessor of land may protect himself against surface water as best he can, building dikes to keep the water off his land or drains to cast it down onto lower lands. E.g., Johnson v. Whitten, 384 A.2d 698 (Me. 1978). Others apply the "civil law" rule, borrowed from European countries. This subjects each piece of land to a servitude for the natural flow of water across it. A landowner cannot prevent water from coming to his land, nor may he collect it so it flows from his land in unusual quantities, or change the direction of the natural drainage. E.g., Dekle v. Vann, 182 So. 2d 885 (Ala. 1966).

Each of these rules has obvious disadvantages and both have been modified in some states by statute or decision. Thus some courts applying the civil law rule have held that the natural flow may be changed if damage is slight, or if the landowner is protecting himself from extraordinary flood water. E.g., McManus v. Otis, 143 P.2d 380 (Cal. Ct. App. 1943). Some courts have imposed liability despite the common enemy rule where the upper owner has discharged unusually large flows on the lower. Clark v. City of Springfield, 241 S.W.2d 100 (Mo. Ct. App. 1951), but now see Heins Implement v. Highway. & Transp. Comm'n, 859 S.W.2d 681 (Mo. 1993) (adopting "reasonable use" rule). Others restrict the upper owner from collecting the diffuse waters and discharging them "as a body." Bulldog Battery Corp. v. Pica Inv., Inc., 736 N.E.2d 333 (Ind. App. 2000). These modifications have been merged into a rule of "reasonable use," which is gaining increasing acceptance. This rule allows a landowner to modify natural drainage patterns provided the alteration does not unreasonably injure adjacent landowners. E.g., Whorton v. Malone, 549 S.E.2d 57 (W. Va. 2001). The distinction between surface water and water in watercourses is equally important here, for these rules do not permit an obstruction of a watercourse or its diversion into a new channel.

Most drainage is performed today by drainage districts—public bodies established to build works to drain a large area of land. They are formed with the approval of a court or county board when the majority of the landowners in the area desire the improvement. They are financed by assessments on all improved lands, and these assessments can be levied and enforced even if a minority landowner does not want to participate. Such public districts are not limited by private drainage laws. If damage is done to others the district may nevertheless proceed, providing compensation if necessary and adding it to the costs of the project.

7. **Drainage of wetlands.** Drainage and filling of swamps and marshes to produce farmland and residential sites was once "reclamation," encouraged and subsidized by the United States Department of Agriculture. Now it is "destruction of wetlands" and of the wilderness and wildlife habitat that wetlands provide. Protection of the environmental and ecological features of wetlands is now a function of water quality control, and is regulated by discharge permits and "dredge and fill" permits under sections 402 and 404 of the Federal Clean Water Act. See Chapter 7, Section 2.

SECTION 2. REASONABLE USE

HARRIS v. BROOKS
Supreme Court of Arkansas, 1955.
225 Ark. 436, 283 S.W.2d 129.

WARD, JUSTICE. The issues presented by this appeal relate to the relative rights of riparian landowners to the use of a privately owned nonnavigable lake and the water therein.

Appellant, Theo Mashburn, lessee of riparian landowners conducts a commercial boating and fishing enterprise. In this business he rents cabins, sells fishing bait and equipment, and rents boats to members of the general public who desire to use the lake for fishing and other recreational purposes. He and his lessors filed a complaint in chancery court on July 10, 1954 to enjoin appellees from pumping water from the lake to irrigate a rice crop, alleging that, as of that date, appellees had reduced the water level of the lake to such an extent as to make the lake unsuitable "for fishing, recreation, or other lawful purposes." After a lengthy hearing, the chancellor denied injunctive relief, and this appeal is prosecuted to reverse the chancellor's decision.

Factual Background. Horseshoe Lake, located about 3 miles south of Augusta, is approximately 3 miles long and 300 feet wide, and, as the name implies, resembles a horseshoe in shape. Appellees, John Brooks and John Brooks, Jr., are lessees of Ector Johnson who owns a large tract of land adjacent to the lake, including three-fourths of the lake bed. For a number of years appellees have * * * raised rice on Johnson's land and have each year, including 1954, irrigated the rice with water pumped from the lake. They pumped no more water in 1954 than they did in 1951 and 1952, no rice being raised in 1953. Approximately 190 acres were cultivated in rice in 1954.

* * * In March 1954 Mashburn leased * * * a relatively small camp site on the bank of the lake and installed the business above mentioned at a cost of approximately $8,000, including boats, cabins, and fishing equipment. Mashburn began operating his business about the first of April, 1954, and fishing and boat rentals were satisfactory from that time until about July 1st or 4th when, he says, the fish quit biting and his income from that source and boat rentals was reduced to practically nothing.

Appellees began pumping water with an 8 inch intake on May 25, 1954 and continued pumping until this suit was filed on July 10, and then until about August 20th. They quit pumping at this time because it was discovered fish life was being endangered. The trial was had September 28, 1954, and the decree was rendered December 29, 1954.

The Testimony. * * * 1952, 1953 and 1954 were unusually dry and the water levels in similar lakes in the same general area were unusually low in August and September of 1954. During August 1954 Horseshoe Lake was below "normal," but it is not entirely clear from the testimony that this was true on July 10 when the suit was filed. It also appears that during the stated period the water had receded from the bank where Mashburn's boats were usually docked, making it impossible for him to rent them to the public. There is strong testimony, disputed by appellees, that the *normal* level of the lake is 189.67 feet above sea level and that the water was below this level on July 10. Unquestionably the water was below normal when this suit was tried the latter part of September, 1954.

[Appellees] attempted to show that; they had used the water for irrigation several years dating back to 1931 and Mashburn knew this when he rented the camp site; although they had been pumping regularly since May 25, 1954 the water did not begin to fall in the lake until July 1st or 4th; an agent of the Arkansas Game and Fish Commission examined the lake and the water about July 2nd and found no condition endangering fish life, and similar examinations after suit was filed showed the same condition and; they stopped pumping about August 20th when they first learned that fish life was being endangered.

Issues Clarified. In refusing to issue the injunction the chancellor made no finding of facts, and did not state the ground upon which his decision rested. * * * If it be conceded that the testimony does show and the chancellor should have found that the water in Horseshoe Lake was at or below the normal level when this suit was filed on July 10th, then appellants would have been entitled to an injunction provided this case was decided strictly under the uniform flow theory mentioned hereafter. However as explained later we are not bound by this theory in this state. It appears to us there might have been some confusion as to the ground upon which appellants based their contention for relief. Under the pleadings it appears that they may be asking for relief on two separate grounds: (a) The right to fish and (b) The right to conduct a commercial boating enterprise. It was incumbent upon appellants to show that one or both rights were unreasonably interfered with when the water level sank below "normal." It is difficult to tell whether the testimony establishes this fact in either instance. (a) The only testimony in the first instance is that fish quit biting somewhere about the 4th of July but there was no conclusive evidence that this was caused by the lake being below "normal" level. It is common knowledge that fish quit biting some time for no apparent good reason. There was no testimony that fish life was endangered before July 10th but on the other hand there was positive testimony to the contrary. (b) Likewise there was no conclusive testimony showing that it was impractical to dock or run boats on the lake prior to July 10th. Moreover it would be pure conjecture to say that the same water level, whether normal or otherwise, controlled both fishing and boating. * * *

In view of the above situation it is urged by appellees that the case should therefore be affirmed, but we have concluded that the best interest of the parties hereto and the public in general will be served by concluding this case in the light of the announcements hereafter made and the conclusions hereafter reached. * * *

Riparian Doctrine. This doctrine, long in force in this and many other states, is based on the old common law which gave to the owners of land bordering on streams the right to use the water therefrom for certain purposes, and this right was considered an incident to the ownership of land. Originally it apparently accorded the landowner the right to have the water maintained at its normal level, subject to use for strictly domestic purposes. Later it became evident that this strict limitation placed on the use of water was unreasonable and un-utilitarian. Consequently it was not long before the demand for a greater use of water caused a relaxation of the strict limitations placed on its use and this doctrine came to be divided into (a) the natural flow theory and (b) the reasonable use theory.

(a) *Natural Flow Theory.* Generally speaking again, under the natural flow theory, a riparian owner can take water for domestic purposes only, such as water for the family, live stock, and gardening, and he is entitled to have the water in the stream or lake upon which he borders kept at the normal level. There are some expressions in the opinions of this court indicating that we have recognized this theory, at least to a certain extent.

Reasonable Use Theory. This theory appears to be based on the necessity and desirability of deriving greater benefits from the use of our abundant supply of water. It recognizes that there is no sound reason for maintaining our lakes and streams at a normal level when the water can be beneficially used without causing unreasonable damage to other riparian owners. The progress of civilization, particularly in regard to manufacturing, irrigation, and recreation, has forced the realization that a strict adherence to the uninterrupted flow doctrine placed an unwarranted limitation on the use of water, and consequently the court developed what we now call the reasonable use theory. * * * In 56 Am.Jur., page 728, it is stated that "The rights of riparian proprietors on both navigable and unnavigable streams are to a great extent mutual, common, or correlative. The use of the stream or water by each proprietor is therefore limited to what is reasonable, having due regard for the rights of others above, below, or on the opposite shore. In general, the special rights of a riparian owner are such as are necessary for the use and enjoyment of his abutting property and the business lawfully conducted thereon, qualified only by the correlative rights of other riparian owners, and by certain rights of the public, and they are to be so exercised as not to injure others in the enjoyment of their rights." It has been stated that each riparian owner has an equal right to make a reasonable use of waters subject to the equal rights of other owners to make the reasonable use, United States v. Willow River Power Co., [324 U.S. 499]. The purpose of the law is to secure to each riparian owner equality in the use of water as near as may be by requiring each to exercise his right reasonably and with due regard to the rights of others similarly situated. Meng v. Coffey, [93 N.W. 713].

This court has to some extent recognized the reasonable use theory. Thomas v. La Cotts, [257 S.W.2d 936]; Harrell v. City of Conway, [271 S.W.2d 924], but we have also said in the City of Conway case that the uniform flow theory and the reasonable use theory are inconsistent and, further that we had not yet made a choice between them. It is not clear that we made a choice in that case. The nucleus of this opinion is, therefore, a definite acceptance of the reasonable use theory. We do not understand that the two theories will necessarily clash in every case, but where there is an inconsistency, and where vested rights may not prevent, it is our conclusion that the reasonable use theory should control.

In embracing the reasonable use theory we caution, however, that we are not necessarily adopting all the interpretations given it by the decisions of other states, and that our own interpretation will be developed in the future as occasions arise. Nor is it intended hereby that we will not in the future, under certain circumstances, possibly adhere to some phases of the uniform flow system. It is recognized that in some instances vested rights may have accrued to riparian landowners and we could not of course constitutionally negate those rights. * * *

The result of our examination of the decisions of this court and other authorities relative to the use by riparian proprietors of water in non-navigable lakes and streams justifies the enunciation of the following general rules and principles:

(a) The right to use water for strictly domestic purposes—such as for household use—is superior to many other uses of water—such as for fishing, recreation and irrigation.

(b) Other than the use mentioned above, all other lawful uses of water are equal. Some of the lawful uses of water recognized by this state are: fishing, swimming, recreation, and irrigation.

(c) When one lawful use of water is destroyed by another lawful use the latter must yield, or it may be enjoined.

(d) When one lawful use of water interferes with or detracts from another lawful use, then a question arises as to whether, under all the facts and circumstances of that particular case, the interfering use shall be declared unreasonable and as such enjoined, or whether a reasonable and equitable adjustment should be made, having due regard to the reasonable rights of each.

Application to This Case. Some of the questions, therefore, which must be considered are these:

(a) Had appellees on July 10, 1954, by the continued use of water from Horseshoe Lake, destroyed appellants' right to fish and conduct the boating enterprise? If so, the injunction should be granted.

(b) If it is found however that appellants' rights had only been impaired at the stated time, then it must be judged, under all the facts and circumstances as before mentioned, whether such impairment is unreasonable. If it is so found then the injunction should issue. If it is found that appellants' rights have not been unreasonably impaired, having due regard to all the facts and circumstances and the injury which may be caused appellees as weighed against the benefits accruing to appellants, then the injunction should be denied.

We do not minimize the difficulties attendant upon an application of the reasonable use rule to any given set of facts and circumstances and particularly those present in this instance. It is obvious that there are no definite guide posts provided and that necessarily much must be left to judgment and discretion. The breadth and boundaries of this area of discretion are well stated in Restatement of the Law, Torts, § 852c in these words: "The determination in a particular case of the unreasonableness of a particular use is not and should not be an unreasoned, intuitive conclusion on the part of the court or jury. It is rather an evaluating of the conflicting interests of each of the contestants before the court in accordance with the standards of society, and a weighing of those, one against the other. The law accords equal protection to the interests of all the riparian proprietors in the use of water, and seeks to promote the greatest beneficial use of the water, and seeks to promote the greatest beneficial use by each with a minimum of harm to others. But when one riparian proprietor's use of the water harmfully invades another's interest in its use, there is an incompatibility of interest between the two parties to a greater or lesser extent depending on the extent of the invasion, and there is immediately a question whether such a use is legally permissible. It is axiomatic in the law that individuals in society must put up with a reasonable amount of annoyance and inconvenience resulting from the otherwise lawful activities of their neighbors in the use of their land. Hence it is only when one riparian proprietor's use of the water is unreasonable that another who is harmed by it can complain, even though the harm is intentional. Substantial intentional harm to another cannot be justified as reasonable unless the legal merit or utility of the activity which produces it outweighs the legal seriousness or gravity of the harm."

In all our consideration of the reasonable use theory as we have attempted to explain it we have accepted the view that the benefits accruing to society in general from a maximum utilization of our water resources should not be denied merely because of the difficulties that may arise in its application. In the absence of legislative directives, it appears that this rule or theory is the best that the courts can devise.

Our Conclusion. After careful consideration, an application of the rules above announced to the complicated fact situation set forth in this record leads us to conclude that the Chancellor should have issued an order enjoining appellees from pumping water out of Horseshoe Lake when the water level reaches 189.67 feet above sea level for as long as the material facts and circumstances are substantially the same as they appear in this record. We make it clear that this conclusion is not based on the fact that 189.67 is the normal level and that appellees would have no right to reduce such level. Our conclusion is based on the fact that we think the evidence shows this level happens to be the level below which appellants would be unreasonably interfered with. * * *

We think the conclusion we have reached is not only logical but practical. Although appellees had quit using water from the lake when this case was tried yet they testified that they intended to use water therefrom in 1955. We might assume that they would want to also use water in subsequent years, so it would seem to be to the best interest of all parties concerned to have a definite level fixed at which pumping for irrigation must cease in order to avoid useless litigation.

* * *

Reversed with direction to the trial court to enter a decree in conformity with this opinion.

Notes

1. **Historical development.** Restatement (Second) of Torts, Chapter 41, Interference with the Use of Water ("Riparian Rights"), Introductory Note on the Nature of Riparian Rights and Legal Theories for Determination of the Rights:[a]

"*Riparian rights—history.* In the early English common law there was little litigation over the private use of water. * * * With the advent of the Industrial Revolution there came a marked increase in the use of water for powering machinery, and industrial wastes added a new dimension to pollution problems. In the resulting increase of litigation over water use the underlying principle was brought forth and clearly stated: each riparian proprietor has a right to use the stream as it passes his property, but no riparian proprietor has a right to use water to the injury of another. This developed into what has been called the natural flow theory, which required the stream to be left substantially unchanged except for minor effects of reasonable means of harnessing and using it as it passed.

"As American industry grew it became obvious that many economically and socially desirable uses of water could not fit this pattern of leaving the streams substantially unchanged. A large mill required not merely a small dam to create a head of water but a reservoir for storage of

a. Copyright 1979. Reprinted with the permission of the American Law Institute.

water. The consumption of water increased as steam power freed the mills from the river banks, irrigation expanded and railroads and other industries multiplied. The idea of preserving the natural stream gave way to the need to alter it materially in order to enable the water to be put to these beneficial uses. The use, not the stream, came to be the thing protected by law, and injury to a reasonable use became the tort. * * * Under the reasonable use theory the primary or fundamental right of each riparian proprietor on a watercourse or lake is to be free from unreasonable uses that cause harm to his own reasonable use of the water. Emphasis is placed on a full and beneficial use of the advantages of the stream or lake, and each riparian proprietor has a privilege to make a reasonable use of water for any purpose, provided that his use does not cause harm to the reasonable uses of others. Each riparian must make his use in a manner that will accommodate as many other uses as possible. * * * The major advantage of this theory is that it tends to promote the beneficial use of water resources.

"The reasonable use theory has won an almost complete victory in the American courts, although a considerable amount of natural flow language can still be found. Some cases do not require a clear distinction, since the natural flow theory allows many reasonable accommodations between users and the reasonable use theory sometimes results in holdings that the maintenance of a stream or lake in its natural condition is reasonable under particular circumstances. Even when the reasonable use rule is applied in its strictest form, the natural flow preference for 'natural wants' is preserved in the form of a preference for domestic uses. Some courts have applied the reasonable use theory in cases between riparians and the natural flow theory in cases between a riparian and a nonriparian. In some western states the streams were regarded merely as sources for irrigating the arid land and the courts applied the reasonable use theory to its ultimate extreme and permitted the streams to be dried up completely. In eastern states, however, where a stream is regarded as an amenity that may add value to land though it remains unused, courts that usually apply the reasonable use rule will sometimes use natural flow language to preserve a living stream, although what is preserved is the minimum flow required to protect its values, not the full natural flow."

2. **Civil law origins?** Samuel C. Wiel, Waters, American Law and French Authority, 33 Harv. L. Rev. 133 (1919), argued that riparianism stems from the civil law, was imported into the United States in the early nineteenth century, and then found its way to England. More recent research has pretty well rejected Weil's theory. See supra p. 20, Note 4.

3. **Determination of reasonableness.** Restatement (Second) of Torts § 850A. Reasonableness of the Use of Water:[b]

b. Copyright 1979. Reprinted with the permission of the American Law Institute.

"The determination of the reasonableness of a use of water depends upon a consideration of the interests of the riparian proprietor making the use, of any riparian proprietor harmed by it and of society as a whole. Factors that affect the determination include the following: (a) The purpose of the use, (b) the suitability of the use to the watercourse or lake, (c) the economic value of the use, (d) the social value of the use, (e) the extent and amount of the harm it causes, (f) the practicality of avoiding the harm by adjusting the use or method of use of one proprietor or the other, (g) the practicality of adjusting the quantity of water used by each proprietor, (h) the protection of existing values of water uses, land, investments and enterprises, and (i) the justice of requiring the user causing harm to bear the loss.

"Comment: *a. Determination of reasonable or unreasonable use.* The reasonableness or unreasonableness of a use of water by a riparian proprietor must be determined by a court or jury from a number of points of view and upon the consideration of a number of factors. A conflict arising out of a claim of harm to one riparian proprietor caused by the water use of another proprietor involves an examination of the use or interest alleged to be harmed, the use causing the harm, the effect that the latter has upon the former and the effects upon society, the economy and the environment of making the uses and of resolving the conflict.

"In a suit between two riparian users of water the reasonableness of both uses is in issue. The plaintiff, in order to show he has a right that has been violated, must establish that his use of the water is reasonable."

4. **Application of reasonableness principles in** *Harris v. Brooks.* The court in *Harris*, quoting the Restatement of Torts, states that a determination of unreasonableness should not be an "unreasoned, intuitive conclusion" but should involve "an evaluating of the conflicting interests of each of the contestants and a "weighing of those, one against the other." Did the *Harris* court engage in such a process? The quoted language also provides that substantial harm to another riparian may not be unreasonable if the utility of the activity outweighs the gravity of the harm. Did the court follow this directive?

5. **Domestic use preference.** The preference for domestic use, referred to in *Harris*, permits an upper riparian to take the full flow of the stream even though such use would deprive a lower riparian of any use of the water whatever. This preference for "natural uses," had its origin in a dictum from Evans v. Merriweather, infra p. 271. *Evans* also suggested a preference for irrigation in areas where it is necessary for the successful cultivation of crops. This suggestion, however, was rejected in Watkins Land Co. v. Clements, 86 S.W. 733 (Tex. 1905) and Meng v. Coffey, 93 N.W. 713 (Neb. 1903). In City of Canton v. Shock, 63 N.E. 600 (Ohio 1902), expressing the minority view that a city may be a riparian proprietor, it was held that the city's domestic use would be entitled to a preference over manufacturing uses. In Prather v. Hoberg, 150 P.2d 405 (Cal. 1944), the court held that the domestic use preference might extend to a hotel or resort, although it indicated that the preference might be lost if

the use was too extensive. In United States v. Fallbrook Public Utility Dist., 108 F. Supp. 72 (S.D. Cal. 1952), the use of water for domestic purposes by 50,000 soldiers in a military camp was held a proper and reasonable riparian use, under *Prather*. However, the court gave it no preference. Later, the court limited the use of water to the maximum amount allowable for agricultural use on the ranch which had been purchased for the camp. 109 F. Supp. 28 (S.D. Cal. 1952).

6. **Adjustment of conflicting uses.** *Harris* also suggests that an equitable adjustment of uses may resolve the conflict between two riparians in some cases. See also Restatement (Second) of Torts § 850A(f) above. Did the court use this principle?

Hazard Powder Co. v. Somersville Manufacturing Co., 61 A. 519 (Conn. 1905), involved a conflict between the operators of two mill dams. The upstream defendant stored the entire flow of the stream during the night and used the water during the day. The downstream plaintiff, who operated day and night, objected to this practice because it was deprived of water for night operations. The court held for the defendant, finding that the conflict was caused by the inadequacy of storage capacity in the plaintiff's mill pond and that it would be feasible for the plaintiff to increase the capacity of its pond. Rancho Santa Margarita v. Vail, 81 P.2d 533 (Cal. 1938), involved a stream which was inadequate to meet the needs of two riparian ranchers during the summer. The court said it that the trial court should work out a "physical solution" to accommodate both riparians if possible; it suggested the construction of reservoirs as a solution.

Who should bear the costs of physical solutions? See Chapter 2, Section 2G. See also Restatement (Second) of Torts § 850A, cmt. h.

7. *De minimus* **harm.** Many "relative reasonableness" cases which favor a defendant's new use over a plaintiff's existing use seem to be holding either that the plaintiff's harm is not substantial in economic terms or that it is the type of inconvenience that is the inevitable result of progress. For example, in Gehlen v. Knorr, 70 N.W. 757 (Iowa 1897), the plaintiff complained of defendant's new dam for an ice pond, yet it was filled in two days and neither removal of ice nor seepage and evaporation from the dam materially affected plaintiff's mill. *De minimus non curat lex* and *damnum absque injuria* are important principles in riparian law, although the courts have not always identified them as such or distinguished the two.

8. **Disruption of natural flows.** In theory, in a pure natural flow jurisdiction, any retention of water infringes on the rights of downstream riparians. Thus, in City of Waterbury v. Town of Washington, 800 A.2d 1102 (Conn. 2002), the court stated that the existence of an upstream dam put downstream riparians on notice that a prescriptive right was accruing in favor of the dam owner.

Given the harsh and inefficient consequences of the pure natural flow doctrine, many courts modified it to permit substantial interference with such flows. J. H. Beuscher, Appropriation Water Law Elements in Riparian Doctrine States, 10 Buff. L. Rev. 448, 453 (1961):

"Dams often disrupt the natural flow of the stream, especially in dry periods when water flowing down the stream is held behind the dam to maintain the head or power potential. Cases from mill dam and logging dam days willingly (and understandably) sustained as reasonable the complete retention of the full flow of the river for days at a time. Economic needs dictated these blows at "natural flow" ideals. Far from protecting a bare technical right to the natural flow of the watercourse,[25] courts permitted complete disruption of the flow for sustained periods of time. Nor have the legislatures failed to react to similar pressures. A Wisconsin statute, for example, requires the hydro-dam proprietor to let by, not the entire natural flow, but as little as 25% of it."

ORR v. MORTVEDT

Supreme Court of Iowa, 2007.
735 N.W.2d 610.

HECHT, Justice.

The defendants appeal from the district court's ruling * * * declaring: (1) they have the right to use and enjoy only that portion of a man-made lake covering an abandoned rock quarry within the legal description of their deed; (2) the plaintiffs may erect a fence, berm or other structure in the lake marking the borders of their properties; and (3) the plaintiffs may drain the water covering their respective properties and reopen the quarry. We affirm.

I. Background Facts.

The Twedt family owned a rock quarry and land surrounding it in Hamilton County. The mining of the quarry was discontinued, and the excavated area consisting of approximately thirty acres became a lake filled by ground water springs and normal rainwater run-off. The Twedt family subsequently sold the real estate in a series of transactions over a period of years. Each of the transactions resulted in the conveyance of a portion of the lake bed and land surrounding it.

In the first transaction, [the Svedes] purchased approximately twenty acres of the lake bed along with adjacent land situated east, south and west of the lake in 1994. In the second transaction in the series, [the Mortvedts] purchased a tract west and north of the lake, including the northern tip of the lake bed, in 1996. In 1998, [the Orrs] acquired a parcel situated primarily on the east side of the lake and including that part of the lake bed located between the parts previously purchased by the Sevdes and the Mortvedts. In the last convey-

---

25. In United States v. Gerlach Live Stock Co., 339 U.S. 725 (1950), Mr. Justice Jackson said that such riparianism pressed to the limits of its logic enables one to play dog-in-the-manger.

ance * * *, the Orrs soon * * * conveyed a portion of the property they had acquired, including a part of the lake bed, to [Cameron].

A boundary dispute arose between the Mortvedts and the Orrs. * * * Disharmony also resulted from the neighbors' inability to agree about their respective rights to use the lake. The Sevdes and the Orrs objected when the Mortvedts used, for fishing and boating, parts of the lake beyond the boundaries of the lake bed owned by the Mortvedts.

The Orrs, the Sevdes, and Cameron filed this action seeking: * * * (2) an adjudication of whether the owners of the lake bed have a legal right to access the entire lake or only that portion of the lake within the legal descriptions of their respective deeds; (3) a declaration that they have the right to drain the water covering their property and fence it; * * * and (5) compensatory damages for trespass and injunctive relief to prevent future trespasses by the Mortvedts.

* * *

After a bench trial, the district court filed a decision declaring in relevant part: * * * (3) the Mortvedts are prohibited, absent express written permission, from entering upon or using the water overlaying the properties owned by the Sevdes, the Orrs, and Cameron, who are legally entitled to construct a fence, berm or other structure to mark the boundaries of their properties; and (4) the Sevdes, the Orrs, and Cameron are entitled to drain the water covering, mine minerals from, and restore wetlands upon their properties.* * *

The Mortvedts appeal * * *.

B. Ownership of the Lake Bed; Use and Control of the Lake Water.

We next address the parties' competing legal claims as to their rights to access the surface waters of the lake for boating and fishing, to fence or otherwise establish physical boundaries on the surface of the lake demarcating their respective claims to ownership of parts of the lake bed, and to drain the water from the lake. As we have noted, the district court concluded the parties have a legal right to go upon and use only the water overlaying the lake bed they own; and consequently, without the consent of the other lake bed owners, the Mortvedts may not go upon or use the water overlaying the plaintiffs' property.

The public generally has a right of access to navigable watercourses. *See* State v. Sorensen, 436 N.W.2d 358, 361-63 (Iowa 1989) (concluding the public trust doctrine requires the State to protect the public's right to use navigable watercourses). Accordingly, if the lake at issue in this case is navigable, the plaintiffs have no right to exclude the Mortvedts from using and enjoying any part of it. The determination of whether a watercourse was navigable at common law depended on the presence or absence of the tidal ebb and flow of water. McManus v. Carmichael, 3 Iowa 1, 3-6 (1856). But the jurisprudence of this country has extended the definition of "navigable" to refer to watercourses "susceptible of use for purposes of commerce" or "possess[ing] a capacity for valuable floatage in the transportation to market of the products of the country through which it runs." Monroe v. State, [175 P.2d 759, 761] (1946) (internal quotation marks and citation omitted). * * * The landlocked body of water which is the subject of this case consists of only approximately thirty acres and has never served as a highway of commerce. It has been used primarily for recreational purposes and is clearly nonnavigable.

The navigable or nonnavigable status of a watercourse generally determines whether the bed of a watercourse is owned by the state or by private parties. "In Iowa, the legal title to the beds of all navigable lakes to the high-water mark is in the state in trust for the use and benefit of the public." State v. Nichols, [44 N.W.2d 49, 57] (1950); * * * But "[i]f a body of water is nonnavigable, it is privately owned by those who own the land beneath the water's surface and the lands abutting it, and may be regulated by them." [Mountain Props., Inc., v. Tyler Hill Realty Corp., 767 A.2d 1096, 1099-1100 (Pa. Super. 2001)]. The nonnavigable lake in this case is thus privately owned by the parties because each of their deeds includes part of the lake bed.

We have not previously been asked to decide the fighting issue presented by the parties now before the court: Whether the owner of part of the bed of a nonnavigable lake has the legal right to use and enjoy the entire lake, or only that part covering the lake bed described in his deed? The authorities on this issue are divided. The majority rule, often referred to as the "common law rule," dictates that one is entitled to exclusive use and enjoyment of that portion of the nonnavigable lake covering the lake bed one owns. * * * In jurisdictions following the common law rule, owners of the lake bed may fence off their lake bed to promote their exclusive use and enjoyment. The common law rule thus conforms to the familiar legal maxim *cujus est solum, ejus est usque ad coelum et ad inferos*—"[w]hoever owns the soil owns everything up to the sky and down to the depths." Nichols v. City of Evansdale, 687 N.W.2d 562, 566 (Iowa 2004) (citing *Black's Law Dictionary* 1712 (8th ed. 2004)).

A lesser number of jurisdictions have adopted what has been described as the "civil law rule."[1] This rule holds that owners of any part

---

1. One scholar has noted that the rule commonly referred to as the "civil law rule" was not derived from either the civil law tradition of post-Roman continental Europe or ancient Rome, but rather from decisions of Scottish courts in the nineteenth century, and that the "common law rule," which pre-dates the English common law, actually originated in Roman civil law. *See* Nicholas Harling, Non-navigable Lakes and the Right to Exclude: The Common Misunderstanding of the Common Law Rule, 1 Charleston L. Rev. 157, 176-77 (2007). While we have no quarrel with the author's

of a nonnavigable lake are entitled to reasonable use and enjoyment of the entire surface of the lake, not merely that part covering the bed they own.

* * *

In the absence of legislative direction on the issue, we must determine whether the common law rule or the civil law rule should prevail in Iowa. Advocates of the civil law rule claim it is to be preferred because it avoids "the difficulties presented by attempts to establish and obey definite property lines." [Beacham v. Lake Zurich Prop. Owners Ass'n, [526 N.E.2d 154, 157] (1988).] Where, as in the case now before the court, multiple parties claim an ownership interest in an unfenced lake, it may be difficult to discern precisely where the boundaries of one's property are located. The civil law rule avoids this problem by granting the owner of part of a nonnavigable lake bed access to the entire lake. The rule arguably "promotes rather than hinders the recreational use and enjoyment of lakes." *Id.* Perhaps more importantly, the civil law rule discourages the placement of fences or other barriers along boundary lines in the water that "frustrate the cooperative and mutually beneficial use" of water resources, *id.,* and arguably promotes the aesthetic enjoyment of those who use them.

Notwithstanding the notable positive features of the civil law rule, however, we reject it and join the majority of jurisdictions that have adopted the common law rule. The principal advantage of the rule we adopt today is its consistency with prevailing norms of real estate ownership in this state. The common law rule recognizes the legal significance of property boundaries and protects the interests of owners when neighbors are unwilling or unable to coexist cooperatively. Finally, we adopt the common law rule as the default rule, realizing that the several owners of nonnavigable lakes may bargain among themselves to adopt other mutually acceptable arrangements for the use and mutual enjoyment of water resources.

IV. Conclusion.

* * * The district court correctly concluded: (1) the plaintiffs have the legal right to exclude the Mortvedts from access to parts of the lake covering the lake bed owned by the plaintiffs; (2) the plaintiffs are legally entitled to drain and fence the water covering their respective properties and reopen the quarry; * * *.

AFFIRMED.

All justices concur except CADY, J., who dissents.

CADY, J. (dissenting).

---

historical analysis, we choose to refer to the two rules by the names ascribed to them by other American courts.

I respectfully dissent from the majority's adoption of the common law rule regarding littoral rights in nonnavigable waters in Iowa. The decision of the majority is based largely on its allegiance to "one of the oldest rules of property known to the law that the title of the owner of the soil extends, not only downward to the center of the earth, but upward *usque ad coelum*." Hannabalson v. Sessions, [90 N.W. 93, 95] (1902). The "logical extension" of this rule leads one to conclude "[a]n owner 'is entitled to exclusive dominion over his land, including the areas above and below its surface.'" Andrea B. Carroll, Examining a Comparative Law Myth: Two Hundred Years of Riparian Misconception, 80 Tul. L.Rev. 901, 907 (2006) (citation omitted) [hereinafter Carroll]. Indeed, the logical extension of the rule in this case leads the majority to conclude lake bed owners of nonnavigable lakes have absolute ownership in the waters above their lands. But such an extension is not justified because it is based on the anachronistic rule that our property rights "'extend from heaven to hell.'" *Id.* (citation omitted). The march of time, the evolution of society, and the inherent differences between land, water, and air clearly demonstrate they do not. The majority's adoption of what is called the "common law rule" only furthers this antiquated abstraction. *See id.* at 940 (suggesting the common law rule should be called "the Roman rule," "traditional rule" or "exclusive dominion" rule instead).

Moreover, the application of such a rule to Iowa today is unreasonable. As the majority recognizes, the rule presents difficulties in "attempt [ing] to establish and obey definite property lines," and leads to "impractical consequences," such as the "erection of booms, fences, or barriers." Beacham v. Lake Zurich Prop. Owners Ass'n., [526 N.E.2d 154, 157] (1988). The Scots recognized and solved this problem long ago. *See* Carroll, 80 Tul. L.Rev. at 927 ("[T]he rule of free access to the surface of nonnavigable lakes has its genesis nowhere but in the Scottish legal system, and that it was born out of the Scots' desire to simplify the problems of boundary demarcation and enforcement on those water bodies."). Their solution was embodied in what could be called the "free access" rule, or what the majority calls the "civil law rule." *See id.* at 940 (suggesting the civil law rule should be called the "Scottish rule," the "modern rule," or the "free access" rule). The reasonableness of the free access rule is readily apparent--even to the majority. The majority correctly recognizes it "promotes rather than hinders the recreational use and enjoyment of lakes." Beacham, 526 N.E.2d at 157. In addition, vis a vis the exclusive dominion rule, it has several recognized advantages:

> (1) the [exclusive dominion] rule is too difficult to follow with regard to lakes; (2) there can be no private ownership in the waters or in the fish of a nonnavigable lake and, thus, use of the surface should be open to all riparian landowners, (3) common use of the surface of

nonnavigable lakes is customary; [and] (4) economic policy requires the adoption of the [free access rule].

Carroll, 80 Tul. L.Rev. at 910 (footnotes omitted).

Nevertheless, the majority adopts the exclusive dominion rule. It reasons that the principle is the "majority" rule, that owners could modify the rule by private agreement, and that it comports with the property norms in this state. In my view, these arguments are unpersuasive. First, the traditional rule is definitely not, when put into context, the "majority" rule. *See* Nicholas Harling, Non-Navigable Lakes & the Right to Exclude: The Common Misunderstanding of the Common Law Rule, 1 Charleston L. Rev. 157, 170 & n. 88, 183 (recognizing most courts have adopted the common law rule, but that because "many other[ ] [courts] have been unduly influenced by the common law rule's historic mislabeling and a mistaken belief that their decision places the state's law squarely within the common law tradition ... no true majority rule exists in America"). Second, the parties in this case clearly demonstrate that a private agreement between them is nearly impossible so that when cases like this arise there really is no other choice.

Finally, if the exclusive dominion rule is consistent with our prevailing norms regarding real estate ownership, it is only because it is based on an antiquated concept that fails to consider the nature of the property in this case. * * *.

Perhaps most importantly, the free access rule is not detrimental to prevailing norms. *See* Eric T. Freyfogle, The Particulars of Owning, 25 Ecology L.Q. 574, 585 (1999) ("This trend of tailoring rights to the land poses little real threat to the core values of property. Once people see what is going on, once they realize that property rights now depend in part on the land itself, expectations can be adjusted and life can go on, with as much economic growth, personal privacy, and civic harmony as ever before.") * * *. In fact, I do not believe a free access rule would necessarily limit the existing property rights of lake bed owners, such as the Orrs in this case. The free access rule simply "permits a riparian landowner 'to use the surface of the entire lake for fishing, boating, and bathing as long as he does not unduly interfere with the rights of the other [riparian landowner] proprietors.'" Carroll, 80 Tul. L. Rev. at 909-10 (quoting James W. Cullis, Note, *Extent of Private Rights in Nonnavigable Lakes,* 5 U. Fla. L. Rev. 166, 176 (1952)).

Property law is not set in stone, but depends "entirely on the law of the nation" where the property is located. Johnson & Graham's Lessee v. M'Intosh, [21 U.S. 543, 572] (1823). It is perhaps noteworthy that Illinois and Minnesota, apparently Iowa's only two border states that have considered the issue, have adopted the free access rule. *See*

Beacham, 526 N.E.2d at 157; Johnson, 100 N.W.2d at 696-97. Moreover, in light of the benefits of the free access rule, it is not too much for our law to require lake bed owners to permit the reasonable use of surface water by other lake bed owners. This approach best reflects our modern values of free use and enjoyment of lakes and streams in Iowa and still protects the rights and ownership of lake bed owners by only permitting others to use the surface water in a reasonable manner, and not terminating any rights a lake bed owner has in the land.

I do not know how many Iowans share the shores of nonnavigable lakes around the state so as to be affected by the holding in this case, but I suspect there are many. In each instance, the inflexible rule adopted by the majority could leave unwanted consequences. For example, it will permit lake bed owners to build fences into the lake to mark boundary lines. It will also give rise to claims of trespass for operating boats in waters over land owned by another or for merely "casting a fishing line into water" over land owned by another. Carroll, 80 Tul. L.Rev. at 908. We, of course, know of the uncivilized conduct exhibited by the property owners in this case. This is not the Iowa our laws should create.

                    * * *

The policy behind the free access rule best reflects life in Iowa in the twenty-first century. Rigid property rights of the past centuries should give way to the simple and fair solution of boundary disputes offered by the better reasoned free access rule. Our laws pertaining to land, air, and water must begin to reflect that we coexist on Earth as one.

Notes

1. **Use of the surface above beds owned by another.** As the principal case indicates, courts take different approaches to both the "rules" and the nomenclature. However named, the approach followed by the majority in the principal case limits access of riparian owners to the specific waters overlying their portion of the privately owned lake bed. Some of the courts who apply the rule, however, will not presume that the non-riparian use is adverse to the riparians' interests. Rather, they will require clear and convincing evidence of an adverse use. E.g., Carnahan v. Moriah Prop. Owners Ass'n, 716 N.E.2d 437 (Ind. 1999).

Beginning with Beach v. Hayner, 173 N.W. 487 (Mich. 1919), the common use rule supported by the dissent in the principal case has taken hold in several states where water recreation is of special importance. E.g., Duval v. Thomas, 114 So. 2d 791 (Fla. 1959); Johnson v. Seifert, 100 N.W.2d 689 (Minn. 1960).

For some states, the applicable rule turns on whether the non-navigable lake is artificial or natural; for these states, the common use rule applies to natural lakes only. Compare Anderson v. Bell, 433 So. 2d

1202, 1204 (Fla. 1983) (artificial lake) and Duval v. Thomas, supra (natural lake); Thompson v. Enz, 154 N.W.2d 473 (Mich. 1967) (artificial extension of lake) and W. Mich. Dock & Market Corp. v. Lakeland Inv., 534 N.W.2d 212 (Mich. Ct. App. 1995) (natural lake); Wickouski v. Swift, 124 S.E.2d 892, 894 (Va. 1962) (lands submerged under artificial lake) and Improved Realty Corp. v. Sowers, 78 S.E.2d 588 (Va. 1953) (natural lake).

2. **Navigability.** "Navigability" has different meanings in different contexts. As in the principal case, it may determine ownership of submerged lands and the incidents of ownership. It may also be used to determine state regulatory authority, as in Muench v. Public Service Commission, infra p. 302. It is treated at greater length in Chapter 7, Section 1, and Chapter 8, Section 1.

3. **Common public users.** If you were persuaded by Justice Cady's dissent in the principal case, would you extend to each riparian "common user" the right to have his or her guests use the lake's surface as well? What if one of the riparian owners was a state agency who wished to open the lake to public recreation? The next case explores these issues.

BOTTON v. STATE
Supreme Court of Washington, 1966.
69 Wash.2d 751, 420 P.2d 352.

HILL, JUDGE. The State of Washington, through its Department of Game, acquired by purchase a waterfront lot on Phantom Lake (nonnavigable) which it has developed to be used as a public fishing access area. Its use or abuse, for that purpose, has resulted in the present action by other owners of waterfront property on the lake, asking that the state be enjoined from maintaining its public access area.

The trial court made very comprehensive findings of fact:

Since the defendant, through its Game Department, put in the public access area, the plaintiffs have suffered the following as a result of it:

1. The fair market value of plaintiffs' property has been decreased.

2. Thievery on the lake has greatly increased, particularly the stealing of boats, oars, outdoor furniture, tools and miscellaneous items of personal property of all kinds. In many of the cases it was definitely ascertained that the thieves gained access to the lake from the public access area.

3. Persons relieving themselves in the lake as well as on the property and front yards of various of the plaintiffs, to the considerable embarrassment and annoyance of the plaintiffs, their families and guests.

4. Beer cans, worm cans, sandwich bags, pop bottles, rafts, and other assorted trash has been deposited in the lake and on the plaintiffs' beaches in considerable quantity.

5. Repeated and frequent trespasses on the plaintiffs' front yards, docks, beaches and property. In addition to the trespasses by persons coming in by the access area, numerous other trespassers have crossed the plaintiffs' yards, docks, beaches and property from other adjoining residential areas, and which trespassers, when confronted by the plaintiffs, have justified their actions by saying to the effect that, "Well, now, it's a public lake, isn't it."

6. Numerous of the plaintiffs, their children and grandchildren, have severely and frequently been cut by broken beer bottles left on the beaches.

7. Fishermen using plaintiffs' docks, and fishing immediately adjacent to their beaches and front yards, would refuse to leave when requested and would stare and make remarks when plaintiffs, their wives and daughters would try to use their beaches for sun bathing, swimming or the entertainment of guests. The plaintiffs, as a result of this, cut down very considerably in their use of their front yards and beaches.

8. Although hunting and shooting on the lake are illegal, hunters come in and hunt and shoot on the lake. Persons also come in and shoot at ducks with air rifles.

9. Speed boating on the lake has greatly increased. In some cases it has increased to the extent that it has become a danger to the plaintiffs' children.

10. The public use of the lake has interfered with the plaintiffs' use of the lake for boating, swimming, fishing and recreational purposes.

11. The noise on the lake has substantially increased.

From these findings, the trial court drew the legal conclusions that the state's opening up of the lake to public use through its access area, without resorting to eminent domain, constituted a taking and damaging of private property without compensation to the owners thereof; and that the state's opening up of the lake to public use constituted an unreasonable interference with the rights of the plaintiffs.

Based on these conclusions, the trial court entered an injunction enjoining the state

from maintaining its public access area on Phantom Lake as a public access area and from admitting the public to Phantom Lake and across the access area until such time as it condemns the plaintiffs' property and property rights in the manner provided by law.

The state appeals, urging that as a riparian owner on a nonnavigable lake it can permit the public to enjoy the right to fish from boats

over every portion of the lake so long as this does not constitute an unreasonable interference with the rights of the other riparian owners.
This implies an obligation to police and control the use of the nonnavigable lake by the public to prevent such use becoming an unreasonable interference with the rights of the other riparian owners thereon.

The lake is small and shallow, covering 63.2 acres, and with
depths running from extremely shallow to a maximum of 47 feet near
the middle. The shore of the lake is partly surrounded with nice homes
(most of the homeowners reside on the lake the year-round) and partly
by as yet undeveloped properties. It lies between Lake Washington
and Lake Sammamish (within only a few hundred feet of the latter),
both of which are large, navigable lakes with many public access areas, parks, and beaches. There are no commercial establishments, resorts or public beaches on Phantom Lake. Nor were there any public
streets, roads, or street ends which would give the public an access to
the lake, until the state, acting through its Department of Game, acquired approximately a hundred feet of lake frontage, extending back
some 800 feet to a public thoroughfare, and developed it to provide an
access for fishermen and their boats.

There has been no serious attempt by the state to limit access to
the lake to fishermen; and the trial court found that this access area
had been open to any member of the public. We do not question the
right of the state, as a riparian owner, to ignore the county's zoning
regulations and to permit the public, as its licensees, access to the lake
over its property. There is, however, a limitation, and that is that it
cannot permit such use of its property as constitutes an unreasonable
interference with the rights of the other riparian owners.

We have stated the law applicable in the present case quite succinctly in Snively v. Jaber, * * * 296 P.2d 1015, 1019, * * * (1956):

> We hold that with respect to the boating, swimming, fishing,
> and other similar rights of riparian proprietors upon a nonnavigable
> lake, these rights or privileges are owned in common, and that any
> proprietor or his licensee may use the entire surface of a lake so long
> as he does not unreasonably interfere with the exercise of similar
> rights by the other owners. This rule does not have the effect of mak-
> ing the nonnavigable lake public, since a stranger has no right to en-
> ter upon the lake without the permission of an abutting owner. The
> rule we have announced affords equal protection to the interest of all
> riparian owners in the use of the water and seeks to promote the
> greatest beneficial use by each with a minimum of harm to other
> owners.

In that case, the defendant Jaber had a dance hall, picnic
grounds, and a swimming area on Angle Lake (nonnavigable) and
rented some 30 rowboats to the public. The conduct of the licensees in

rented rowboats was such that the trial court found it necessary to enjoin that operation for a 2-year period, and this we affirmed.

The depredations and conduct of Jaber's licensees, which warranted an injunction in that case, could be characterized as a Sunday-school picnic as compared with the indecencies and obscenities to which the other riparian owners on Phantom Lake have been subjected. Added to this is the physical danger to other riparian owners, their children and grandchildren from broken beer bottles left on the beaches and from the operation of speed boats dangerously close to bathers and swimmers near the shore. While the trial court's injunction was justified at the time of trial, it was too extensive in time and was not properly conditioned as to termination.

The dedicated people who make up the great fishing fraternity in this state should not be deprived of the opportunity and pleasure of fishing for perch, crappie, and the like (the water is too warm for trout) because of the conduct of a relatively few hooligans.

The state, as a riparian owner, does not have to acquire by condemnation the rights of the other riparian owners before it permits fishermen in reasonable numbers access to the waters of Phantom Lake; but it does have the obligation, and counsel for the state so concede, to so regulate the number and conduct of its licensees as to prevent any undue interference with the rights of other riparian owners.

The injunction should be continued only until the state, through its Department of Game, presents a plan for the controlled operation of its property that satisfies the trial court that the rights of other riparian owners will be adequately safeguarded. The state is entitled to all the rights of a riparian owner, but it should also accept the responsibility of a riparian owner for the conduct of its licensees.

We are in accord with the trial court's conclusion, from the facts in this case, that there has been an unreasonable interference by the state's licensees with the rights of other riparian owners and that an injunction was properly granted, but it should be modified and limited as indicated herein; and the cause is remanded for that purpose. * * *

FINLEY, JUDGE (concurring specially in the majority opinion). We are confronted in this appeal with a complex natural resources problem certain to become more and more acute in this age of a geometrically increasing demand by more and more people for outdoor recreational and leisure time activities. The problem is one of insuring that the greatest possible number of Washingtonians, and others, are able to utilize reasonably the natural resources of our state for recreational activity. * * *

If the problem is approached strictly in the sense of the legal concept of "riparian rights," its solution will be a restricted and limited one, and probably inadequate, in terms of its recognition of either the rights of the public or the rights of the individual lakefront owners. The same kind of danger or limitation is apparent in approaching the problem solely in terms of the legal concept of state ownership of the waters of nonnavigable lakes. Again, in the best tradition of the common law, some gloss upon the legal concept of "riparian rights" and upon the legal concept of state ownership of the waters of the lake seems indicated and necessary for a juristic accommodation of the conflicting interests and rights of members of the public and the private owners of water front on Phantom Lake. Without employing or adverting to the foregoing nomenclature, or characterization, it seems to me the reasoning of the majority opinion by Judge Hill resolves the problem in a common-sense, practicable way—again, in the best tradition of the common law—and that the results reached constitute an adequate and highly desirable solution of the problem involved. * * *

OTT, JUDGE (concurring in part and dissenting in part). Phantom Lake has been open for public fishing continuously since 1926. It is not a popular fishermen's lake because it is stocked only with spiny ray fish. On opening day in 1963, only 50 fishermen appeared, who caught a total of 9 fish. The evidence was undisputed that seldom were more than 6 boats on the lake at any one time. It is this limited use by the public that the riparian owners wish to exclude entirely.

The majority sustain the injunction until such time as the Department of Game "presents a plan for the controlled operation of its property that satisfies the trial court that the rights of other riparian owners will be adequately safeguarded." With this holding, I do not agree for the following reasons:

(1) One who builds his home on the shore of public waters of this state is aware that the public will use those waters for recreational purposes, and that such use may be abused by relatively few members of the public and by other riparian owners. The debits of such living must be measured against the credits of the scenic beauty and the many recreational pleasures enjoyed by those who are the owners of waterfront property.

(2) The majority do not suggest what type of "plan" will be acceptable to this court. Are 50 boats on opening day and less than 6 boats a day thereafter too many on this 63-acre lake? I do not believe that this use is excessive or that regulations limiting the number of boats on Phantom Lake have been shown to be necessary.

Should the "plan" of the game department require that the Sheriff of King County station a deputy on Phantom Lake from daylight until dark to keep under surveillance the operators of the 6 boats in order to arrest the offenders if the general misdemeanors complained of are committed? I doubt whether the sheriff could find, much less afford, sufficient officers to police so intensively the myriad lakes in King County.

Should the "plan" require that the game department be authorized to police all of the lakes of this state, including Phantom Lake, to prevent violation of the general misdemeanor laws? Such a plan must be submitted to the legislature, not to the courts. The legislature has vested in the game protectors of this state limited authority to enforce only the game laws. RCW 77.12.070. A game protector has no more authority to arrest a person for general misdemeanors than has a riparian owner.

The legislature, in the exercise of its discretion, has vested solely in the local authorities power to enforce the general misdemeanor laws. The record before us establishes that the riparian owners on Phantom Lake never sought the aid of such officers when they observed these laws being violated. Any "plan" which the game department might suggest would be advisory only to those authorities whose duty it is to enforce the general misdemeanor laws of this state.

Notes

1. **Limits on filling privately owned beds.** Bach v. Sarich, 445 P.2d 648 (Wash. 1968), involved riparian owners on Bitter Lake, a small 19-acre non-navigable lake in Seattle. The bed was privately owned, and a zoning ordinance allowed apartment use on the defendant's portion of the bed. Defendant began constructing an apartment building that would have extended 180 feet into the lake, built partly on lake fill and partly on piers. Plaintiffs, claiming a common right to use the surface, objected. The court said that the building was not a reasonable use of the lake surface by the defendant. Indeed, it was not a riparian use at all, as it was not "intimately associated with the water." See Ralph W. Johnson & G. Richard Morry, Filling and Building on Small Lakes—Time for Judicial and Legislative Controls, 45 Wash. L. Rev. 27 (1970).

2. **Protection of aesthetic values.** A "right to view" was recognized in City of Los Angeles v. Aitken, 52 P.2d 585 (Cal. 1935). The city, condemning littoral rights to lands surrounding a lake to be drained for municipal supply, objected to substantial damages being awarded persons who withdrew no water from the lake.

"Mono Lake is situated on the now famous Tioga Highway connecting Los Angeles with Lake Tahoe. From Mono a frequently traveled thoroughfare extends through a timbered country to the Yosemite Valley. The picturesque beauty, the highly colored rocks and precipitous walls and the rare surroundings of Mono Lake attract an increasing number of tourists to its popular resorts. John Muir, the late famous exploring scientist, half a century ago said of this locality: 'This beauty * * * is of a still higher order, enticing us lovingly on through gentian meadows and groves of rustling aspen to Lake Mono, where, spirit-like, our happy stream vanishes. * * * Mountains, red, gray, and black, rise close at hand on the right, whitened around their bases with banks of enduring snow; on the left swells the huge red mass of Mount Gibbs, while in front the eye wanders down the shadowy canon, and out on the warm plain of Mono, where the lake is seen gleaming like a burnished metallic disk, with clusters of lofty volcanic cones to the south of it.'

"But this limitation of riparian rights of owners of land to a necessary use for beneficial purposes does not mean that the water must be actually used in irrigating the land or consumed for domestic purposes. It does not authorize the appropriation of littoral rights to land bordering on the margin of a lake without the payment of just compensation therefor, when the very value of the land depends on the maintenance of the lake in its natural condition. Irrigation and household uses of water are not the only reasonable or beneficial purposes for which it may be employed, even though the presence of mineral salts or alkali in the water renders it unfit for human consumption or domestic use.

"For the reason that the existence of Mono Lake in its natural condition, with all of its attractive surroundings, is the vital thing that furnishes to the respondents' marginal land almost its entire value, and that the draining of the lake will nearly destroy the value of their properties and the incident littoral rights thereto, it seems clear that the lake is not being used by the respondents for an unreasonable or nonbeneficial purpose, but, upon the contrary, that their use of the lake in its natural condition is reasonably beneficial to their land, and the littoral rights thereof may therefore not be appropriated, even for a higher or more beneficial use for public welfare, without just compensation therefor."

Cases, like *Aitken*, finding a right to a view include: Lee County v. Kiesel, 705 So. 2d 1013, 1015-16 (Fla. Ct. App.1998) (loss of view of waterway from landowner's property caused by government bridge was compensable) and DBL, Inc. v. Carson, 585 S.E.2d 87, 91 (Ga. 2003) (landowners may sue marina because marina's docks obstructed landowners' view of water), cert. denied (2003).

In Center Townhouse Corp. v. City of Mishawka, 882 N.E.2d 762 (Ind. Ct. App. 2008), however, the Indiana court rejected such a right.

Other cases protecting riparians from the loss of land values resulting from drying up a stream or lowering lake levels include Collens v. New Canaan Water Co., 234 A.2d 825 (Conn. 1967) and Taylor v. Tampa Coal Co., 46 So. 2d 392 (Fla. 1950).

3. **Protection of public values.** As with prior appropriation law, riparian law, although concerned with private rights, can help enhance and produce public recreational opportunities. In Snively v. Jaber, cited in the principal case, and in *Botton* itself, the Washington court permits riparian proprietors operating a commercial resort and a public park to invite the public to share in their riparian rights to recreational uses of water. In a famous eastern case, however, McCord v. Big Brothers Movement, 185 A. 480 (N.J. Ch. 1936), the use of water for a swimming pool used by a large number of boys at a summer camp was enjoined. "Ripar-

ian rights can be claimed only by the owner thereof, and they include the use of the waters of a stream for ordinary and reasonable bathing privileges, which extend only to the owner, his family, and inmates and guests of his household. The transfer to a large number of invitees of the bathing use of transported waters exceeds the reasonable use to which the riparian owner is entitled."

The rules of riparian law that preserve living streams, restrict the extent of riparian land and restrict non-riparian uses offer a form of blunt-instrument protection of some environmental values. For a more finely tuned provision, see Cal. Water Code § 1707. That provision allows both riparian and appropriative rights holders to dedicate their rights to preserve or enhance "wetlands habitat, fish and wildlife resources, or recreation in, or on, the water." The transfers require approval of the State Water Resources Control Board. The Board may approve the petition if it neither will "increase the amount of water the petitioner is entitle to use" nor will "unreasonably affect any legal user of water." Cal. Water Code § 1707(b)(1) & (2). Petitioners may also indicate the extent to which such dedications are meant "to satisfy any applicable federal, state, or local regulatory requirements governing water quantity, water quality, instream flows, fish and wildlife, wetlands, recreation, and other instream beneficial uses." Through this latter provision, the Board serves as a clearinghouse, recording credits towards petitioners' externally imposed legal obligations.

4. **Regulation of water levels in lakes.** The water level in natural lakes, and often as well in man-made reservoirs, has important implications for residential, recreational and environmental values. Several states have imposed extensive controls on fluctuations and minimum levels. Reservoir levels may be fixed, e.g., Minn. Stat. § 103G.401. Natural lake levels are the subject of regulation in some states, e.g., Vermont. Vt. Stat. Ann. tit. 10 §§ 905, 1421-1426.

5. **Reasonableness and equality.** After retrial, on a second appeal of Thompson v. Enz, supra p. 242, the Michigan supreme court ruled that the developer's canals that would give boat access to the lake from 128 back lots would violate the riparian rights of other lakefront property owners. The evidence showed, however, that several other large tracts had been similarly subdivided and canalized. The trial court had said, "Defendants contend that plaintiffs and others are contributing their share to the congestion. * * * The answer to this is that the others were there before the breaking point was reached." The supreme court approved the trial judge's finding but held that the injunction could not issue, the plaintiffs being estopped because, with notice of the dredging, they had stood by while nearly all the defendants' canals had been excavated before seeking preventive relief. The dissenting judge stated, "These defendants do not propose to exercise any rights or inaugurate any uses which are in the slightest fashion more detrimental to the lake than the existing uses of other lake owners. * * * The trial court would brand these defendants' use as the 'straw that broke the camel's back,' and in

the name of preserving to these plaintiffs a quasi-monopoly to use a lake which belongs to the people of Michigan, our Court would approve the arbitrary, unlawful and unconstitutional confiscation of the defendants' property without payment of compensation therefor." Thompson v. Enz, 188 N.W.2d 579 (Mich. 1971).

Riparians supposedly have "equal" rights. Are the rights of Botton and the state to use Phantom Lake "equal"? But for estoppel, how equal would be the rights of plaintiff and defendants in Thompson v. Enz?

EVANS v. MERRIWEATHER
Supreme Court of Illinois, 1842.
3 Scam. (4 Ill.) 492.

LOCKWOOD, JUSTICE, delivered the opinion of the court: This was an action on the case, brought in the Greene Circuit Court, by Merriweather against Evans, for obstructing and diverting a water course. The plaintiff obtained a verdict, and judgment was rendered thereon. * * * After the cause was brought into this court, the parties agreed upon the following statement of facts, as having been proved on the trial, to wit: " * * * Smith and Baker, in 1834, bought of T. Carlin six acres of land, through which a branch ran, and erected a steam mill thereon. They depended upon a well and the branch for water in running their engine. About one or two years afterwards, John Evans bought of T. Carlin six acres of land, on the same branch, above and immediately adjoining the lot owned by Smith & Baker, and erected thereon a steam mill, depending upon a well and the branch for water in running his engine.

"Smith & Baker, after the erection of Evans' mill, in 1836 or 1837, sold the mill and appurtenances to Merriweather, for about $8,000. Evans' mill was supposed to be worth $12,000. Ordinarily there was an abundance of water for both mills; but in the fall of 1837, there being a drought, the branch failed, so far that it did not afford water sufficient to run the upper mill continually. Evans directed his hands not to stop, or divert the water, in the branch; but one of them employed about the mill did make a dam across the branch, just below Evans' mill, and thereby diverted all the water in the branch into Evans' well. * * * After the diversion of the water into Evans' well, as aforesaid, the branch went dry below, and Merriweather's mill could not and did not run, in consequence of it, more than one day in a week, and was then supplied with water from his well. Merriweather then brought this suit, in three or four weeks after the putting of the dam across the branch for the diversion of the water, and obtained a verdict for $150. * * * It is further agreed, that the branch afforded usually sufficient water for the supply of both mills, without materially affecting the size of the current, though the branch was not depended upon exclusively for that purpose. * * * "

Upon this state of facts, the question is presented, as to what extent riparian proprietors, upon a stream not navigable, can use the water of such stream? The branch mentioned in the agreed statement of facts, is a small natural stream of water, not furnishing, at all seasons of the year, a supply of water sufficient for both mills. There are no facts in the case showing that the water is wanted for any other than milling purposes, and for those purposes to be converted into steam, and thus entirely consumed. * * *

Each riparian proprietor is bound to make such a use of running water as to do as little injury to those below him as is consistent with a valuable benefit to himself. The use must be a reasonable one. Now the question fairly arises, is that a reasonable use of running water by the upper proprietor, by which the fluid itself is entirely consumed? * * * But where the water * * * is not sufficient for each proprietor living on the stream, to carry on his manufacturing purposes, how shall the water be divided? We have seen that, without a contract or grant, neither has a right to use all the water; all have a right to participate in its benefits. Where all have a right to participate in a common benefit, and none can have an exclusive enjoyment, no rule, from the very nature of the case, can be laid down, as to how much each may use without infringing upon the rights of others. In such cases, the question must be left to the judgment of the jury, whether the party complained of has used, under all the circumstances, more than his just proportion.

It appears, from the facts agreed on, that Evans obstructed the water by a dam, and diverted the whole into his well. This diversion, according to all the cases, both English and American, was clearly illegal. For this diversion, an action will lie. * * *

For these reasons I am of opinion that the judgment ought to be affirmed, with costs.

Notes

1. **Difficulties of sharing.** Sharing of shortages has an egalitarian appeal but creates difficulties. If competing uses cannot both exist in a reduced amount, an equal sharing of the supply might effectively destroy one or both. An irrigator of annual crops might reduce the acreage he waters so long as he will have water enough to mature the remainder of his crop, but if reducing his share means that he would be cut off completely in mid season, he may lose the entire crop. Cutting the supply of a fruit grower could result in loss of trees. The reduction of water power below a point may stop a mill completely. A reduced water supply may allow one enterprise to continue operation at reduced levels of production and profit, while it may put another out of business if profitability depends upon maintenance of a high level of production because of fixed costs. The irrigator who lowers a lake level may spoil for a summer some recrea-

tional features on which a resort depends and may induce ecological changes which have an even more lasting effect on fishing.

2. **Sharing v. over-development.** When do the virtues of sharing become the evils of "common pool exploitation?" What is a shortage? Suppose a drought of the same severity in 1830 had reduced the branch to the 1837 flow. Was there then a shortage? Suppose another drought in 1835, after the Smith & Baker mill was erected but before Evans' was in operation? How many more mills will (or should) riparian law allow to be built on the branch?

3. **Unreasonable sharing.** What happens if a shortage becomes so acute or demand so large that the shares are sufficient for no one? The riparian vineyardists of the Napa Valley ward off frost damage by pumping water from the Napa River and spraying their vines with a fine mist. In a cold snap all spray together, which threatens to dry up the river and create a water shortage for all the growers. The State Water Board sought to force construction of a storage reservoir on the river by obtaining a declaratory judgment that the simultaneous diversion of unstored water was an unreasonable use and method of use proscribed by the California Constitution. (See *Joslin,* infra p. 278, Note 1). Held, the Board's complaint states a cause of action and the court should determine whether, under the circumstances of the case, these simultaneous uses of unstored water were unreasonable. People *ex rel.* State Water Res. Control Bd. v. Forni, 126 Cal. Rptr. 851 (Cal. Ct. App. 1976).

4. **Allocation among riparian irrigators.** In the West, where shortage is common even in the absence of drought, the courts have sometimes allocated fixed proportions of water among riparian irrigators. For example, Hunter Land Co. v. Laugenour, 250 P. 41 (Wash. 1926), involved three riparians who owned 133, 70 and 2 acres respectively, in a basin containing 1040 irrigable riparian acres. They were decreed rights to 133/1040, 70/1040 and 2/1040 of the water of the stream. This method of allocation was approved in Wiggins v. Muscupiabe Land & Water Co., 45 P. 160, 163-64 (Cal. 1896): "The amount of irrigable land belonging to each party, rather than the amount of land already under cultivation, would be properly made a controlling element in adjusting their respective rights to the flow of the stream; otherwise a readjustment would be necessary whenever either party should cultivate a greater or less area." See also Harris v. Harrison, 29 P. 325 (Cal. 1892), in which the court approved an order which allowed to riparian irrigators to each use the full flow of the small stream for 3 1/2 days per week, and Southern California Inv. Co. v. Wilshire, 77 P. 767 (Cal. 1904), in which it was held error to divide the water solely on the basis of the proportion of the frontage of the owners' lands upon the stream. A decree apportioning shares among riparians is binding only so long as the conditions on which it is based remain unchanged. See City of L.A. v. Baldwin, 53 Cal. 469 (1879) (Rhodes J., concurring specially).

Compare Lone Tree Ditch Co. v. Cyclone Ditch Co., 128 N.W. 596, 598 (S.D. 1910): "the amount of water, in inches, to which a riparian owner may be entitled for irrigation as against other riparian owners, is absolutely impossible of estimation, as it must continually vary, not only from the varying volume of water flowing down the stream at different times of the year or during different years, but also from the amount of land that may have been settled upon; and the extent of the use of water for the so-called ordinary or natural purposes which in itself varies with the population of the riparian district and the number of domestic animals kept thereon." In Seneca Consol. Gold Mines Co. v. Great Western Power Co., 287 P. 93, 98 (Cal. 1930), the court held that a riparian right does not entitle one to "any specific concrete amount of water." It stated, "[t]he moment a right * * * is defined in a concrete inflexible amount, at that moment the right becomes one of priority and not riparian." *Seneca Consolidated* was applied in Pleasant Valley Canal Co. v. Borror, supra p. 244, Note 1, to hold that a prior suit had adjudicated only appropriative rights because the decree awarded specific quantities of water.

5. **Sharing of water power.** Warren v. Westbrook Manufacturing Co., 33 A. 665 (Me. 1895): "To make water power of economic value, the rights to its use and the division of its use, according to those rights, should be determined in advance. This prior determination is evidently essential to the peaceful and profitable use by the different parties having rights in a common power. To leave them in their uncertainty, to leave one to encroach upon the other, is to leave the whole subject matter to possible waste and destruction."

6. **Sharing in appropriation states.** Sharing of shortages by persons similarly situated is widely practiced in western irrigation districts, which take water wholesale and retail it to consumers. When water is insufficient to supply in full the district's appropriation, the shortage is shared *pro rata* by the irrigators. See infra pp. 448-50, Note 6.

FARRELL v. RICHARDS
New Jersey Court of Chancery, 1879.
30 N.J.Eq. 511.

THE CHANCELLOR. The bill is filed by the owners and lessee of the property in Atlantic county long known as the Pleasant Mills, but now, also, as the Nescochague Mills, against Augustus H. Richards, to restrain him from diverting, to the damage of the complainants, as owners and lessee of the mill property, a stream known as the Forge stream, by which one of the two ponds of the complainants, known as the Forge pond, is supplied with water. From that pond the other, called the Pleasant Mills pond, and on which their mills are, draws part of its supply; and the mills, which are driven by water-power, depend wholly on the ponds for their power. The two ponds are connected by a ditch or canal. This connection between the ponds, and the use of the water in both of them to drive the machinery of the mills, have existed for over fifty years, though there was an interval of about ten years from the time when the mills were burned to the time when they were rebuilt (which was in or about 1860) when the mill site was not used.

The defendant, by various conveyances to him from the year 1858, has become the owner of a large tract of land, of about two thousand five hundred acres, extending from the head of the Forge stream up and along that stream for about three miles and a half. This property, or a considerable part of it, is used by him for the production of cranberries. In 1876 (according to the evidence it was probably in the summer and fall), he dug a large ditch, extending from the upper part of that tract to the Forge pond. His object in digging the ditch was, to irrigate his land. He also, at the same time, for the purpose of diverting the water of the stream into the ditch, constructed, with stones, brickbats and pieces of fence-rails driven into the bottom of the stream by way of piling, a dam in the stream. He and his witnesses say that it extended only partially across the stream; but some of the complainants' witnesses testify that it is entirely across the main body of the stream.

In the summer of 1877, the complainants, William E. Farrell (he is the owner of two undivided thirds of the Pleasant Mills property) and Lucius H. Warren (lessee of the other third), were operating the mills as partners. They then, in the month of August, perceived a sudden and very considerable diminution of their water-power, which was found to be due to the decrease of the water in the Forge pond. The season being an unusually wet one, and they being unable to account for the diminution of the water, set on foot investigations which resulted in the discovery of the existence of the dam and ditch. The ditch was then found to be draining the water from the Forge stream in large quantities. In January, 1878, they filed their bill in this cause for relief, praying that the defendant may be restrained from interfering in any way with the natural and ancient flow of the water down the Forge stream, and from storing or retaining the water of the stream, and that the dam built by him, or so much of it as may be found to interfere with the natural, ancient flow of the water in the stream, may be decreed to be a nuisance. They show, by the bill, a case of irreparable injury. On the filing of the bill, an order to show cause why an injunction should not be issued was made, and under it numerous affidavits were taken on both sides, which have been read without objection.

* * * The proof is that, as soon as the ditch began to withdraw the water from the stream the effect was perceived at the mills, and in August, 1877, the effect was so great that the operations of the mills were seriously affected. These facts are conclusive as to the amount withdrawn, and the consequent injury to the complainants. The defendant has no right to so use the water as to diminish its quantity to the prejudice of the complainants. While every riparian owner has a

right to use the water flowing through his land for the proper irrigation of his land, his use for that purpose must be such as not essentially to interfere with the natural flow of the stream, or essentially and to the material injury of the proprietors below to diminish the quantity of water that goes to them. * * *

I do not deem it necessary to discuss the evidence. A careful consideration of it leads me to the conclusion that the defendant, by means of the dam and ditch, has withdrawn from the stream so much water as seriously to affect the complainants' water-power, and to do them irreparable injury. He still claims the right to divert the water, but insists that, in so doing, he does the complainants no injury, and causes no diminution whatever of the water in the pond. The evidence satisfies me that, by the withdrawal of the water, he not only causes diminution of the water in the pond, but diminishes it to such an extent as to cause very serious injury to the complainants. The complainants, when he began to divert the water, had enjoyed the unquestioned right of the water for over half a century. They are entitled to the protection of this court. * * *

The defendant should be restrained from diverting the water and maintaining the dam. There will be an injunction accordingly.

Notes

1. **Priority in the riparian doctrine.** Is *Farrell* merely a "natural flow" decision now supplanted by "reasonable use" cases? Or does it bear out Professor Beuscher's dictum, supra p. 255, Note 8, "There is actually much more protection given to the prior user of water as against a subsequent water claimant than one would have any reason to expect from a mere recitation of black-letter riparianisms?" Recall also the answer given by the Michigan Supreme Court in Thompson v. Enz, supra p. 270, Note 6, when the defendants pointed out that their proposed development, which the court had decided was "unreasonable," created no more congestion that several existing developments: "The answer to this is that the others were there before the breaking point was reached."

The reasonable use rule typically omits any reference to temporal priority. Some cases expressly say it is immaterial, e.g., McCarter v. Hudson County Water Co., 65 A. 489 (N.J. Ch. 1906). Nevertheless, it is occasionally stated as a factor: "It is also material, sometimes, to ascertain which party first erected his works and began to appropriate the water." Strobel v. Kerr Salt Co., 58 N.E. 142, 147 (N.Y. 1900).

2. **Mill dams and priority.** "Mill dam acts gave a private eminent domain power to entrepreneurs who chose to construct dams on streams flowing through riparian lands, a power to build the dam, flow the lands of an upstream riparian and be free of any obligation except to pay the value of the flowage right if the damaged landowner sued in time. More striking, * * * however, is the express guarantee of appropriative status

given to the riparian who first constructed a dam. No subsequent dam could be erected to the injury of any mill lawfully existing. * * * American courts have protected the earlier dam against upstream or downstream structures which threatened to impair the power potential. Similar protections are accorded hydroelectric dams erected in accordance with state-granted permits or franchises." J.H. Beuscher, supra p. 255, Note 8.

3. **Priority v. sharing.** Priority in time and sharing are not necessarily incompatible. Priority might limit the demand to the dependable supply; i.e., new uses might be prohibited once the dependable supply is exhausted. But, sharing, not priority, might allocate water among permitted uses when an atypical shortage makes the supply inadequate.

The leading cases requiring riparian irrigators to restrict withdrawals were all triggered by drought or unusually low flows. E.g., Half Moon Bay Land Co. v. Cowell, 160 P. 675 (Cal. 1916); Nesalhous v. Walker, 88 P. 1032 (Wash. 1907). When flows are above normal each riparian may take as much as he wants as long as he causes no harm. Half Moon Bay Land Co. v. Cowell, supra.

Dependable flow was used as the basis for making an equitable apportionment between states in Wyoming v. Colorado, 259 U.S. 419 (1922). See infra pp. 475-76, Note 4. Some indication that the courts will stop further development when the capacity of the stream has been reached is found in Mason v. Hoyle, 14 A. 786 (Conn. 1888): "These men of moderate capital, investing their means in mills upon our lesser streams should be protected against such a use of the streams by mills disproportioned to their capacities as would practically deprive them of water and ruin their privileges."

4. **Contrasting views of the first and second Restatements on priority.** The first Restatement says that a riparian whose use of water causes substantial harm to another riparian's use is liable for the harm caused "unless the utility of use outweighs the gravity of the harm." Restatement of Torts §§ 851, 852 (1939). Under this rule a new, more valuable use can apparently displace an otherwise reasonable established use. Indeed, the flexibility to replace old uses with new ones is sometimes considered to be one of the virtues of the riparian doctrine.

The Restatement (Second) states that one of the factors to be considered in determining if a riparian use is reasonable is the protection of "existing values" in water uses, land, investments and enterprises. Restatement (Second) of Torts § 850A. This translates to a rule of priority, although the comments to the section indicate that the rule is not as absolute as that found in prior appropriation law: "The effect given to priority by the law of riparian rights is very different from its effect under the western law of appropriation. That law not only protects uses of the normal flow from harm caused by new withdrawals, but also protects the elder uses in times of temporary shortage. The senior appropriator may withdraw the total quantity allowed by his appropriation even thought this might leave the junior appropriator none at all. In contrast, similarly situated riparians would normally be required to share the reduced supply without regard to priority of use." Restatement (Second) of Torts § 850A, cmt. k (1979)[c]. See also the Restatement (Second) of Torts § 850A, associate reporter's notes to comment k (1982), indicating that the priority factor may be "of little moment" if the other factors of § 850A (see supra p. 253, Note 3) are present.

The Restatement (Second) acknowledges that only a few cases have expressly mentioned priority, but states that it can be deduced from the results of cases which favor the prior user in almost every case in which a new use threatens a substantial investment of a the prior user. See supra comment k and associate reporter's notes. But see Joseph W. Dellapenna, Introduction to Riparian Rights, 1 Water and Water Rights § 703(d) (Robert E. Beck ed., 1991), asserting that outside dual-system states virtually all authority rejects priority as relevant except perhaps in otherwise evenly balanced cases.

5. **An uncompensated reallocation of water.** Joslin v. Marin Municipal Water Dist., 429 P.2d 889 (Cal. 1967), is a rare case in which an established riparian use was extinguished without compensation in favor of a new, more valuable use, albeit an appropriative (nonriparian) use. The water district constructed a water supply reservoir upstream from Joslin's gravel operation. The reservoir obstructed flows which had replenished Joslin's supply of sand and gravel prior to its construction. Despite Joslin's allegations of substantial damages, the court sustained the trial court's grant of summary judgment to the district. The court held that Joslin had no property interest in continued replenishment of sand and gravel by the stream. Relying on an amendment to the California constitution (Art. X, § 2), which prohibits all unreasonable uses of water, the court said: "Is it 'reasonable' then, that the riches of our streams, which we are charged with conserving in the great public interest, are to be dissipated in the amassing of mere sand and gravel which for aught that appears subserves *no* public policy? * * * We are satisfied that * * * the use of such water as an agent to expose or to carry and deposit sand, gravel and rock, is as a matter of law unreasonable within the meaning of the constitutional amendment."

Is "reasonableness" under the California constitution the same as "reasonableness" under common law riparian rights? The court said that the purpose of the constitutional amendment was to extend to disputes between an appropriator and a riparian "the rule of reasonableness of use as a measure of water rights which had theretofore been applied between [riparian] claimants."

6. **The remedy when a prior use is displaced.** The Handy Horsecollar Company manufactures harnesses, using the waters of the small stream on its property to tan leather. Horse harnesses are of very little utility today, demand is low, and the company is barely getting along. Ford Motors acquires the land upstream and builds a $40,000,000

---

c. Copyright 1979. Reprinted with the permission of the American Law Institute.

plant to manufacture emission control devices for its new compact cars. It takes all the water for drinking, sanitary and processing purposes in its plant, and pipes all its waste water to a metropolitan sewage treatment plant so that none of it returns to the stream. The Handy Company sues Ford for damages. What result? The Handy Company sues for an injunction. What result?

7. **The compensation principle.** "The Pareto criterion says that a change that makes at least one individual better off and leaves no individual worse off represents an increase in welfare. This criterion is usually interpreted to mean that welfare is increased by a change rendering it 'possible' to make at least one individual better off and leave no individual worse off by compensating the losers. Most of the discussion in the new welfare economics deals with this compensation principle." S. V. Ciriacy-Wantrup, Concepts Used as Economic Criteria for a System of Water Rights, in The Law of Water Allocation in the Eastern United States 531, 546 (Haber and Bergen eds., 1958).

The compensation principle has respectable support in the law. The leading riparian rights case is Strobel v. Kerr Salt Co., 58 N.E. 142, 145-47 (N.Y. 1900): "[The defendant's acts] would amount to a virtual confiscation of the property of small owners in the interest of a strong combination of capital. * * * We have never adopted that rule [of destroying one water use by another which would produce greater wealth] in this state and no public necessity exists therefor, even if it would ever warrant the courts in relaxing rules for the protection of property of small value in the interests of some business required to develop the resources of the state and in which much capital had embarked, giving employment to a great number of people." A leading case protecting a riparian right against uncompensated public impairment is United States v. Gerlach Live Stock Co., 339 U.S. 725 (1950). A California riparian's use of water was destroyed by the Friant Dam built by the United States. The United States Supreme Court held, "But the public welfare, which requires claimants to sacrifice their benefits to broader ones from a higher utilization, does not necessarily require that their loss be uncompensated any more than in other takings where private rights are surrendered in the public interest. * * * No reason appears why those who get the waters should be spared from making whole those from whom they are taken. Public interest requires appropriation: it does not require expropriation." The Court also emphasized the loss distribution factor and pointed out that the project beneficiaries could well afford to reimburse the riparian for his loss of irrigation.

8. **Water rights and water pollution.** Courts have applied the reasonable use rule (and the original 1939 Restatement rule) to both water supply and pollution cases. The utility-harm formula of § 852 of the original Restatement is exactly the same as the formula applied to determine a nuisance under § 826. The Restatement (Second) of Torts (1979) includes water pollution in the chapter on nuisances. It restricts its chapter on riparian rights to acts affecting the physical volume of the water, e.g.,

a diversion, withdrawal, obstruction, storage, or consumption that interferes with a beneficial use of water. Chapter 41, Scope Note.

SECTION 3. NONRIPARIAN USES: PRESCRIPTION, GRANT, AND MUNICIPAL SUPPLY

A. Prescription

PABST v. FINMAND
Supreme Court of California, 1922.
190 Cal. 124, 211 P. 11.

LENNON, J. This action was instituted by the plaintiffs, Charlie Lee Pabst and the Priors, against H.H. Finmand and N.H. Finmand and the Cambrons, to quiet title to the waters of Eagle creek, in the county of Modoc, state of California. Eagle creek, rising in the Warner Mountains, west of the lands of both plaintiffs and defendants, flows in a single channel until just before it reaches the land of the plaintiffs, Priors, and the defendant, N.H. Finmand. There it forks and the north branch flows across the northwest corner of N.H. Finmand's lands and across the Prior lands. The south branch flows across the south portion of N.H. Finmand's lands and thence onto and across the lands of plaintiff Pabst.

The lands of the other defendant, H.H. Finmand, are not riparian to the creek. They lie to the west of the lands of the plaintiffs Priors and to the northwest of the lands of the plaintiff Pabst and the defendant N.H. Finmand, and are irrigated by means of two ditches, the "Gee" and the "Grider" ditches, which run from the main channel of Eagle creek before it forks, northerly to the lands of H.H. Finmand.

The trial court found that the lands of the defendant N.H. Finmand were riparian to Eagle creek, and that the defendant N.H. Finmand was entitled, as an appropriator, to a first right to 300 inches of the water of Eagle creek, * * * and that said defendant also had a prescriptive right to said quantity of water. The court found that the defendant H.H. Finmand was entitled to a first right of 200 inches of water from Eagle creek through what is known as the "Gee" ditch, and a first right to 200 inches of water through what is known as the "Grider" ditch, both under a right by prior appropriation and by prescription. Judgment was accordingly rendered and entered in favor of the defendant N.H. Finmand for 300 miner's inches of water * * * and in favor of H.H. Finmand for 400 miner's inches of water * * * for the irrigation of his lands through the Gee and Grider ditches. It is from this judgment that plaintiffs appeal.

The N.H. Finmand lands being riparian, whereas the H.H. Finmand lands are nonriparian, the rights arising from the use of water on these different tracts are necessarily based upon different principles, and for this reason these different tracts of lands will be considered separately.

As to the rights of the N.H. Finmand lands, it is conceded by counsel for defendants that the right to the amount of water awarded to the defendants by the judgment of the trial court must rest upon a prescriptive right alone. This is so for the reason that, as admitted by defendants, the right by appropriation is not supported by the evidence, and, while the trial court found that N.H. Finmand was a riparian owner, no judgment was given such defendant based upon his right as a riparian owner, and no attempt was made to apportion the waters among the plaintiffs and defendants as riparian owners.

The judgment for a prescriptive right was given in favor of the N.H. Finmand lands against both the Prior lands and the Pabst lands. The N.H. Finmand lands claimed this right, and it was adjudged to those lands upon the theory that said lands had gained it by adverse use of the water which was taken from the south fork of the creek. As to the Prior lands no right could be gained by prescription. This is so because the water used on the N.H. Finmand lands was taken from the south fork of the stream, which runs below and does not border the Prior lands, whereas the water diverted for use on the Prior lands is taken from the north fork of the creek, which runs by a small portion of the northwest corner of the N.H. Finmand lands and on to the Prior lands. The Prior lands, therefore, are riparian only to the north fork of the stream. A right can be gained by prescription only by acts which operate as an invasion of the rights of the person against whom the right is sought and which afford a ground of action by such party against such claimant, * * * a lower use, since it interferes in no way with the flow above, constitutes no invasion of the upper riparian owner's right, and cannot, therefore, afford any basis for a prescriptive right. * * *

As to the Pabst lands, the N.H. Finmand lands are the upper riparian lands, and the Pabst lands are lower riparian lands. It is the contention of defendants that the continuous use of a certain amount of water each year for the statutory period of time gave to them a prescriptive right to that certain quantity of water so used by them, and this in spite of the fact that the use of the water by the lower riparian owner was never in any manner interrupted or interfered with by such use, and in the absence of any indication or bringing of knowledge home to the lower riparian owner that the upper riparian owner was claiming such right, not as a riparian owner, but adversely to him. This contention cannot be maintained. In the absence of a showing that the upper owner is using the water under a claim of prescriptive right, the lower owner has the right to presume that such owner is only taking that to which he is entitled as a riparian owner by virtue of his riparian right. * * * Such use was not hostile unless there was an actual clash between the rights of the respective owners. While there was sufficient water flowing down the stream to supply the wants of all parties, its use by one was not an invasion of the rights of the other. * * *

* * * The rights of riparian proprietors are correlative, and the "reasonable" amount to which any one riparian owner is entitled is to be measured by comparison with the needs of the other riparian proprietors. The fact that there was always sufficient water coming down the creek for the Pabst lands with the exception of the two years prior to the trial is undisputed by any evidence offered by the defendants. And, so long as defendants left sufficient water in the stream for the use of the lower riparian proprietors, it cannot be said that they were using an unreasonable amount, and, so long as they were not using an "unreasonable" amount, the plaintiffs had no cause to complain, nor was any right of theirs invaded. * * *

The adverse use must be such as to raise a presumption of a grant of an easement as the only hypothesis on which to account for the other party's failure to complain thereof. * * * In the absence of any facts showing an actual knowledge by plaintiffs of the adverse nature of defendants' claim or of any facts sufficient to create a presumption of a knowledge of that claim, it cannot be said that a failure of plaintiffs to assert their rights by bringing an action against the defendants was such a submission as could be accounted for only on the hypothesis of a grant. Indeed, defendants have not shown such an unreasonable use of the water on their lands as to put plaintiffs on notice of their claim. We do not mean to hold that a right may not be gained by an upper riparian proprietor by prescription, but to do so it must be clearly shown either that actual notice of the adverse claim of such owner has been brought home to the other party, or that the circumstances are such, as, for instance, the use of all of the water of the creek, that such party must be presumed to have known of the adverse claim. In the instant case there was nothing to indicate to the lower riparian owners that the owners of the N.H. Finmand lands were exercising, or attempting to exercise, any more than their riparian rights, and, in the absence of such indication to plaintiffs that the owners of the N.H. Finmand lands were asserting a right hostile to the rights of the plaintiffs, no prescriptive title was acquired. Even if the upper riparian owner is using all the water of the stream, still, if the lower riparian owner is not then using any and has no desire to do so, such use by the upper riparian owner would not be adverse, and, and if continued five years, would not gain him a prescriptive right. * * *

It is the contention of plaintiffs that there was no invasion of plaintiffs' riparian rights by the nonriparian owners of the H.H. Finmand lands by the diversion by such nonriparian owners of water which the riparian owners did not need, and therefore no prescriptive right to the use of the water could be acquired in the absence of a showing of actual damage to the lands of the riparian owners caused by a deprivation of the water. As to a nonriparian owner the riparian owner is under no duty to share the waters of the creek, and the slightest use by such nonriparian owner diminishes to some extent the flow of the stream. * * * The initial step in the diversion of the water by the nonriparian owner is therefore an invasion of the right of the lower riparian owner, and every subsequent diversion is a further invasion of that right. Against a person who seeks to divert water to nonriparian lands, the riparian owner is entitled to restrain any diversion, and he is not required to show any damage to his use. Although no damage to the present use of the riparian owner results from the diversion, yet damage to the future use may result, and an injunction will be granted to prevent the diversion from growing into a right by the lapse of the statutory period. * * * In the instant case the adverse use of the water on nonriparian lands was continued "openly and notoriously" for a period longer than five years, and, the slightest use by the owners of these lands being notice to all the lower riparian owners that a hostile right was being asserted, a prescriptive right was acquired by such adverse use on those lands. * * *

Judgment reversed.

Notes

1. **Noninjury, injunctive relief, and prescription.** A 1928 amendment to the California constitution, now found at Article X, Section 2, limits riparian rights to reasonable beneficial use and removes the right of a riparian owner to enjoin a nonriparian use which is not causing present injury. Logically, the amendment should have eliminated the acquisition of prescriptive rights through a nonriparian use which causes no present injury. However, the California courts initially exhibited confusion on the point. While acknowledging that a riparian owner could no longer enjoin a nonriparian use that was causing no present injury, some cases held that to protect future uses a riparian owner was entitled to declaratory relief to prevent the nonriparian use from ripening into a prescriptive right. See Peabody v. City of Vallejo, 40 P.2d 486 (Cal. 1935) and Tulare Irr. Dist. v. Lindsay-Strathmore Irr. Dist., 45 P.2d 972 (Cal. 1935). Finally, in 1949 the court held "[p]rescriptive rights are not acquired by the taking of surplus or excess water, since no injunction may issue against a taking and the appropriator may take the surplus without giving compensation." City of Pasadena v. City of Alhambra, 207 P.2d 17, 29 (Cal. 1949), infra p. 370.

2. **Harmless use rule.** If a nonriparian use causes no present harm but is enjoined to prevent the acquisition of a prescriptive right, a "dog in the manger" situation results in which desirable uses of water resources are inhibited. New York solved this problem with its "harmless use law," N.Y. Envtl. Conserv. Law § 15–0701:

"An alteration * * * in the natural flow, quantity, **quality** or condition of a natural watercourse or lake situated in this state * * * effected by the use either on or off riparian land, withdrawal, impoundment, or obstruction of the water in such watercourse or lake, or by the **addition** of water thereto, or by changes in the banks, bed, course or other **physical** characteristics of such watercourse or lake, is reasonable and lawful as against any person, * * * having an interest in such watercourse or lake, unless such alteration is causing harm to him or it, or would cause him or it immediate harm if and when begun. No action for nominal damages or for an injunction shall be maintainable because of such an alteration against any person or corporation, whether a riparian owner or not, on the ground that such alteration is an infringement of the plaintiff's private rights and privileges in the waters of, or with respect to, such watercourse or lake unless such alteration is causing plaintiff harm, or would cause him or it immediate harm if and when begun. * * *

"The cause of action essential to the initiation and creation of a prescriptive right or privilege against a private riparian owner to continue an alteration in the natural condition of such a watercourse or lake shall not be supplied by such an alteration until it shall have caused such riparian owner harm and then only if it is unreasonable."

If the rule allowing a riparian landowner to enjoin a harmless nonriparian use is so obviously bad policy, why did the California courts cling to it until forced to abandon it by the 1928 constitutional amendment? Was the rule merely an archaic vestige of the natural flow theory which the California courts felt compelled to follow out of misguided loyalty to stare decisis? Was the rule completely one-sided, favoring only riparian landowners? Or did it sometimes favor nonriparian appropriators? Who benefitted from the rule in *Pabst*, the riparian landowner or the nonriparian appropriator? See infra p. 329, Note 2.

3. **Prescription against upstream riparians.** Since in most cases a downstream use causes no harm to an upstream riparian, a long-continued downstream nonriparian use does not create a prescriptive right that can receive protection against a new upstream use that causes harm to it. Kennebunk, Kennebunkport & Wells Water Dist. v. Me. Tpk. Auth., 84 A.2d 433 (Me. 1951). In the West this rule has become epitomized as "prescription does not run upstream." But see Dontanello v. Gust, 150 P. 420 (Wash. 1915).

4. **Extent of prescriptive rights.** "[W]hen a party has, for the prescriptive period, diverted all the water from a watercourse, it has established a prescriptive easement to divert all the water, regardless of whether the diversion was later reduced, or the scope of the diversion

fluctuated. Second, if a party has, for that period, not diverted all, but only a portion, of the water from a watercourse, however, then it will have established an easement only for an amount that has become customary between the parties. Finally, if there is subsequently a significantly increased change in usage, that new use may be considered unreasonable, and a new prescriptive period would start to run as to that increased usage." City of Waterbury v. Town of Wash. , 800 A.2d 1102, 1154 (Conn. 2002).

Should the extent of a prescriptive right be fixed in terms of a specific quantity of water, or should it be measured by the proportion of the total flow of the stream that was diverted? In Mally v. Weidensteiner, 153 P. 342 (Wash. 1915), the court put both limitations on an adverse claimant who had diverted and used 1 1/2 c.f.s., but never more than one-third of the stream. However, in Akin v. Spencer, 69 P.2d 430 (Cal. Ct. App. 1937), an adverse user of six inches of water was held to be absolutely entitled to this quantity as against downstream riparians, and could not be compelled to prorate very low flows with the riparians.

5. **Right to compel continuation of use by another party.** Can principles of prescription or estoppel create a right to the continuation of a long-existing use by another? In Kray v. Muggli, 86 N.W. 882 (Minn. 1901), the court enjoined the removal of 40-year old mill dam:

"The dam in question, * * * must be taken to be a permanent obstruction; and, it having existed and been maintained as such for so great a length of time, the artificial conditions created thereby must be deemed to have become the natural conditions. * * * In the case at bar even nature herself became adapted to the new surroundings. A native growth of hard-wood timber sprang up along the shore of the lakes formed by the raise of the river, thus giving a natural effect and appearance to the conditions created by the dam. The government, * * * recognized the artificial as the natural state, and surveyed the public lands with reference to the lakes, meandering them precisely as other natural bodies of water are surveyed and meandered."

But see Kiwanis Club Foundation Inc. of Lincoln v. Yost, 139 N.W.2d 359 (Neb. 1966).

Some states may require the owners of dams to maintain them against their will. See Minn. Stat. § 103G.401; Wis. Stat. § 31.185. How can these be enforced perpetually? In New Jersey, a dam 20 years old or older, upon which other landowners have made permanent improvements, may be ordered maintained, but if the expense would be an undue burden on the owner the landowners around the reservoir may be ordered to pay part or all of it. N.J. Stat. Ann. § 58:4–10.

B. Grant

DUCKWORTH v. WATSONVILLE WATER & LIGHT CO.

Supreme Court of California, 1910.
158 Cal. 206, 110 P. 927.

[Plaintiff Duckworth owns lands riparian to Pinto Lake, formerly owned by McKinley, who deeded to defendant company all the water rights pertaining to the land. Defendant diverts water and sells it to persons who use it on nonriparian lands. Plaintiff is now irrigating his lands from the lake, and brings this action to quiet his title to the water. Held, defendant's right to take water from the lake in any quantity, for any purpose, is superior to the plaintiff's.]

SHAW, J. I concur. * * * Perhaps something more should be said regarding the effect of a conveyance, by the owner of riparian land, of his riparian right therein, to another for nonriparian use. The court below seems to have been of the opinion that the riparian right consisted of the ownership of a definite quantity of the water of the lake, a quantity equal only to the amount which could be beneficially used on the riparian land concerned, and that the conveyance merely transferred to the grantees that quantity from the lake, leaving the riparian grantor free to take thereafter an equal or greater quantity therefrom and use it on the identical land, provided only that he must leave enough to furnish to the grantees the definite quantity which, by this theory, was conveyed, or if the grantees were using less, then enough to provide for their actual use from time to time. This was not the legal effect of the conveyance. The riparian right exists solely because the land abuts upon the water. It is parcel of the land. It extends to all the water which may be reached from the land, and not to any specific particles or definite quantity or area of it. It is the right to make reasonable use and consumption of the water on the adjoining land and to a reasonable use of the water, in place, in connection with and for the benefit of the land. The water cannot be severed from the land and transferred to a third person so as to give him the title and right to remove it, as against other riparian owners. The grantor alone will be estopped by such a conveyance. The estoppel against him, with respect to the use and consumption of the water, or diversion from its natural position, must be as complete and extensive as was the right he conveyed. The McKinley deeds conveyed the entire right to use this water for irrigation on these lands to the defendant's predecessors, and it now belongs to the defendant, and not to Duckworth. A man may not eat his cake and have it. A man who sells a right to do a thing cannot thereafter exercise the right himself, except by permission of the buyer, and it is immaterial that the buyer may not be using or exercising it. If the water company had obtained similar deeds from the owners of all the lands abutting upon the lake and its tributaries, it would have obtained a complete estoppel against such landowners which would have prevented them from interfering with any use it saw fit to make of the water, and such estoppel would undoubtedly extend to all the water of the lake. If, having this right of estoppel, it chose to use only a part of the water, or none of it, this neglect to use it would not give any of the owners the right to take that which the company suffered to remain unused. A judgment which purported to give such owners the unqualified right to use the water on their respective tracts, as against the company, would operate to deprive the company of the property which it had bought and paid for and to return that property to the person who sold it and received payment of the price. The same principle must apply when the estoppel has been obtained as to one, only, of the riparian owners. He is absolutely estopped to use any part of the water on the land, except as specified in the deed by which he is bound. These propositions are fully established by the * * * authorities. * * *

Notes

1. **Other Cases.** Cases finding ineffective, against other riparians, a grant to a non-riparian, include Hendrix v. Roberts Marble Co., 165 S.E. 223 (Ga. 1932) and Roberts v. Martin, 77 S.E. 535 (W. Va. 1913).

2. **Statutory Proscription of Transfers.** In Stoesser v. Shore Drive Partnership, 494 N.W.2d 204, 208 (Wisc. 1993), the Wisconsin Supreme Court concluded that "riparian rights can be conveyed to non-riparian owners by easement." In response, the Wisconsin Legislature adopted Wisconsin Statutes § 30.133. That section bars transfers of riparian rights "by easement or by a similar conveyance . . . except for the right to cross the land in order to have access to the navigable water." The statute does not bar a transfer of rights that are accompanied by a transfer of the appurtenant real property interests. ABKA, L.P. v. Wis. Dept. of Natural Res., 648 N.W.2d 854 (Wis. 2002).

PYLE v. GILBERT
Supreme Court of Georgia, 1980.
245 Ga. 403, 265 S.E.2d 584.

HILL, JUSTICE. This is a water rights case involving a non-navigable watercourse. It presents a confrontation between the past and the present. Plaintiffs are the owners of a 140-year-old water-powered gristmill. They emphasize the natural flow theory. Defendants are upper riparians using water to irrigate their farms. They emphasize the reasonable use theory of water rights.

The plaintiffs, Willie and Arlene Gilbert, own property commonly known as Howard's Mill located on Kirkland's Creek, a non-navigable stream in Early County which goes into the Chattahoochee River. They acquired a partial interest in the property in 1974. The other interest was acquired at the same time by their daughter and son-in-law. In 1977, they purchased the other interest and now own the fee. Until August 31, 1978, the Gilberts owned and operated a water-powered gristmill on their property. They also rented boats for profit and permitted fishing and swimming in the 40-acre pond. * * *

On July 7, 1978, the Gilberts filed a complaint against Sanford Hill, who is an owner of property that is upper riparian in relation to the Gilbert's property, alleging that since 1975 he has been diverting and using water from Kirkland's Creek for irrigation * * *.

The testimony at a hearing on July 18, 1978, revealed to plaintiffs that other upper riparian owners also had irrigated with water from the creek. The plaintiffs subsequently added four defendants: George Edgar Pyle, Jimmy Doster, Philip Buckhalter and Vinson Evans.[2] Following discovery, the trial court made an extensive examination of our water law and granted the plaintiffs' motions for summary judgment as to liability against all defendants, holding that the defendants' use of the water for irrigation constituted a diversion, a trespass, a nuisance and an unreasonable use as a matter of law, and enjoining any future use. The issue of damages was reserved for trial. The defendants appeal. * * *

We do not find that the record supports the conclusion that the uses complained of were unreasonable as a matter of law. Whether the use of water for irrigation is reasonable or unreasonable presents a triable question. White v. East Lake Land Co., supra, * * *, 23 S.E. 393; Price v. High Shoals Mfg. Co., supra, * * * 64 S.E. 87. It was error to grant summary judgment to the plaintiffs.

In its detailed analysis of Georgia water law, the trial court had to apply Hendrix v. Roberts Marble Co., * * * 165 S.E. 223, 226 (1932), to the effect that "* * * riparian rights are appurtenant only to lands which actually touch on the watercourse, or through which it flows, and that a riparian owner or proprietor can not himself lawfully use or convey to another the right to use water flowing along or through his property * * *." Thus *Hendrix* held water could only be used on riparian lands. Yet four years later, in reversing the denial of an injunction against the use of water on non-riparian land, the court did not rely heavily on *Hendrix,* supra. Instead the court (Russell, C.J., writing the opinion in both cases) based its decision more on general riparian water law principles than on the non-riparian use. Robertson v. Arnold, * * * 186 S.E. 806 (1936). To the extent that Robertson v. Arnold

---

2. Vinson Evans owns non-riparian property which he admits having irrigated with the alleged permission of a riparian owner. The evidence does not show that he owns any riparian property. The second and fourth findings of fact by the trial court must be reversed to the extent that they imply he is an upper riparian landowner to the plaintiffs.

might reflect ambivalence as to the rule announced in *Hendrix,* that concern is well-founded.

A major study of Georgia water law concluded that "Another disadvantage of this doctrine is that it permits the use of stream water only in connection with riparian land." Institute of Law and Government, University of Georgia Law School, A Study of the Riparian and Prior Appropriation Doctrines of Water Law (1955), p. 104. Likewise, the American Law Institute now recommends allowing use of water by riparian owners on non-riparian land, Rest. Torts 2d § 855, as well as allowing non-riparian owners to acquire a right to use water from riparian owners. Id., § 856(2) * * *. The Restatement relies on two principles: that riparian rights are property rights and as such could normally be transferred, and that water law should be utilitarian and allow the best use of the water. Id., Comment b. Also, the Institute considers the acquisition of water rights by condemnation a "grant of riparian right." Id., Comment c.

Georgia recognizes the power to condemn riparian rights; in fact, this court relied on that principle in affirming an injunction in City of Elberton v. Hobbs, * * * 49 S.E. 779 (1905) (see also the second City of Elberton v. Hobbs, * * * 49 S.E. 780 (1905)). City of Elberton, in turn, was relied on by the court in Hendrix for the proposition that water could not be used on non-riparian lands. In our view, City of Elberton is not good authority for that rule; rather, it established that the right to use water on non-riparian lands can be acquired by condemnation. We agree with the American Law Institute that the right to use water on non-riparian land should be permitted and if that right can be acquired by condemnation, it can also be acquired by grant. Thus we find that the right to the reasonable use of water in a non-navigable watercourse on non-riparian land can be acquired by grant from a riparian owner. The contrary conclusion in Hendrix v. Roberts Marble Co., supra, will not be followed.

In summary, the grant of summary judgment, and the permanent injunction based thereon, against each of the defendants must be reversed. On remand, the issues must be tried in accordance with the foregoing decision, looking always to see if, insofar as injunctive relief is concerned, all the uses of the creek and pond can be accommodated.

Judgment reversed.

Note

Lease of water. In Smith v. Stanolind Oil & Gas Co., 172 P.2d 1002 (Okla. 1946), the riparian owner leased water to the company for drilling on nonriparian lands. A lower riparian sought an injunction. Held, the company's right to use water depended upon the extent of the rights of the riparian owner who granted it. Since a riparian owner's use on nonriparian lands would not be unreasonable per se, the nonriparian grantee could similarly use the water so long as the plaintiff's present uses for domestic and stock water were not substantially impaired.

STATE v. APFELBACHER

Supreme Court of Wisconsin, 1918.
167 Wis. 233, 167 N.W. 244.

Action by George Apfelbacher against the State of Wisconsin and others. Judgment for plaintiff, and defendants bring error. Affirmed.

[From the trial court's findings] it appears:

That the defendant Humphrey and his predecessors have for many years operated a gristmill at the outlet of Lake Nagawicka in Waukesha county. Lake Nagawicka * * * and its waters are held and maintained * * * by a dam owned and controlled by defendant Humphrey at this outlet. The stream forming the inlet and outlet to this lake is Bark river. One mile below Lake Nagawicka and on Bark river plaintiff and his predecessors had for many years also maintained a dam and operated a similar mill. The millpond at this point was about 25 acres in extent and held only sufficient water supply to run plaintiff's mill for a few hours. The mill and water power of defendant Humphrey was the elder of the two.

In 1906 the State of Wisconsin established a fish hatchery just below Nagawicka Lake with ponds numbered 1, 2, and 3 just below the lake and on the north side of the Bark river, and ponds numbered 4, 5, and 6 south thereof. Ponds 1, 2, and 3 were supplied with water from a spillway on Lake Nagawicka; ponds 4, 5, and 6 by a 12-inch pipe running from the waters of Lake Nagawicka through or under ponds 1, 2, and 3 and the Bark river. The waters from these six ponds, save such as is lost by seepage or evaporation, ultimately find their way into Bark river above the plaintiff's dam. * * *

That for upwards of 20 years prior to 1906, as the two water powers were being operated by their respective owners, and with the natural flow of the Bark river between them, the upper mill had been operated practically every day continuously, and the plaintiff was thereby enabled to also operate his mill continuously.

By a written contract made in 1906 between the defendant Humphrey and the State of Wisconsin it was agreed that the state might place and maintain in Lake Nagawicka, for the purpose of drawing water for use in the fish hatchery, the 12-inch pipe connected with the ponds numbered 4, 5, and 6, and might use for the hatchery so much of the waters of Lake Nagawicka as could be drawn through such pipe, and that, if at any time such use by the state and by defendant Humphrey in connection with his mill should lower the waters in the lake to a point 12 inches below a certain high-water mark, then the said Humphrey * * * would absolutely desist and refrain from using any water from said lake for the running of the mill property, or for any other purpose, until the waters of said lake should again reach a point within 12 inches below such high-water mark.

That the defendant state by reason of such agreement claimed to have the right to, and did, exercise practical control over the waters at said dam, and did at several times subsequent to 1906 shut off the outflow of the waters in Lake Nagawicka so that for periods of one or two weeks each the plaintiff was practically deprived of the use of the waters of Bark river and forced thereby to shut down his mill. * * * The operation of plaintiff's mill prior to the agreement between defendants in 1906 was of substantial value to him, but by the exercise by the state of such claim of right under the agreement there has been a substantial interference with, if not destruction of, the plaintiff's business. * * *

As conclusions of law the court found that the defendant state of Wisconsin has made an unreasonable use of the waters of Lake Nagawicka and Bark river, and that both defendant state and the defendant Humphrey should be restrained from exercising or attempting to exercise, the power attempted to be given under the agreement between them so far as it affected the detaining of the water from Bark river in such manner as theretofore done under such claim of right and except only when such detention is a reasonable one having relation to the correlative rights and duties existing between the plaintiff and the defendant Humphrey as riparian owners. From such judgment the defendants appeal.

ESCHWEILER, J. (after stating the facts as above). * * * In this state the owner of an upper dam has the right to withhold the waters of the stream at certain periods in order that there may be thereby created a sufficient storage of water to more properly and efficiently carry out the purpose to which he, as riparian owner, may put the waters of the stream. * * *.

But the right to detain for a time, * * * the waters of the stream flowing through or by his land is restricted always to that which is a reasonable detention or a reasonable use, and these terms are to be measured and determined by the extent and capacity of the stream, the uses to which it is and has been put, and the rights that other riparian owners on the same stream also have. There can be no absolute or fixed standard for the measure of such relative rights. The essential question to be determined by the court or jury trying the issues between the parties in each particular case is what is reasonable under the circumstances there presented. This was the view adopted by the trial court, and his finding, therefore, that the state's withholding at times the flow of water from Lake Nagawicka was not a reasonable or necessary use of the waters of Lake Nagawicka and the Bark river for the proper carrying on of the fish hatchery, is the controlling fact in this case. * * *

The right that defendant Humphrey has to hold back the waters of Lake Nagawicka * * * when below the high-water mark so that the supply of water may thereby be increased * * * cannot be severed from his entire rights as riparian owner so that this particular element of those rights that is, to withhold the natural flow of the Bark river, can be, in a measure, carved out therefrom and transferred to some one else, and by that person used in a manner that would be unreasonable if the use were by Humphrey himself. The conveyance by Humphrey to the state confers no greater right with reference to these flowing waters than Humphrey himself had. The condition of reasonable use attached to it before he conveyed it, and remained with it after such conveyance. The state stands in no better position with reference to its exercise than did or would the defendant Humphrey.

Note

Compare Farmers Highline Canal & Reservoir Co. v. City of Golden, supra p. 200.

C. Municipal Supply

ADAMS v. GREENWICH WATER CO.
Supreme Court of Errors of Connecticut, 1951.
138 Conn. 205, 83 A.2d 177.

INGLIS, JUDGE. The plaintiffs, who are riparian owners along the Mianus River in Greenwich, instituted this action to enjoin the defendant from diverting, and from attempting to take by condemnation, any of the waters of that stream. The defendant filed a cross complaint claiming a declaratory judgment determining whether it has the right to condemn the water rights although part of the benefits may accrue to inhabitants of Port Chester, New York. * * *

The defendant is a corporation specially chartered by the Connecticut General Assembly in 1880. * * * By virtue of its charter and amendments thereof, it has the franchise to furnish water for public and domestic use in the town of Greenwich, in a small portion of the town of Stamford adjacent to the Mianus River, in the town of Rye, New York, including Port Chester, and in Westchester County, New York, whenever that use in Westchester County will not curtail the supply adequate for the inhabitants of Connecticut. * * *

A period of extreme drought occurred in the summer of 1949. The defendant's water supply diminished rapidly. By August 1 its reservoirs were only about 60 per cent full. * * * Thereupon, on August 9, 1949, the defendant began pumping water, at the rate of about a million gallons daily, from the Mianus River at Farms Road into a pipe line which led into one of its reservoirs. When this came to the attention of the plaintiff Altschul, inquiries were made of the defendant on her behalf and a series of conferences and letters between the parties ensued. The defendant acknowledged that it had no legal right to divert the water as it was doing without purchasing or condemning the water rights but took the position that conditions required it to do so. * * * On January 1, 1950, the defendant had less than forty days' supply of water on hand, * * *. This necessitated the installation of an additional pump and the pumping of a greater quantity of water from the Mianus. Between August 9, 1949, and June 1, 1950, the approximate date of the trial of this case, the defendant diverted from the river an average of 1.56 million gallons daily. During that same period the average flow of the river was 16.2 million gallons daily. At no time did the defendant cut off the flow in the river completely, although during the driest period of the diversion the defendant was taking more than half of the flow. During most of the period the flow of the river was in such quantity that the diversion resulted in no inconvenience or detriment to the plaintiffs. Even during the driest periods the plaintiffs suffered no actual or substantial damage.

The original charter of the defendant granted it the right to take by eminent domain any land or water in the town of Greenwich for its corporate purpose. * * * In 1927, after its franchise had been extended in 1925 to include the furnishing of water to Rye * * * the General Assembly granted it authority, for the purpose of supplying water for public or private use, to take by eminent domain, purchase or otherwise all or any part of the waters of the Mianus River * * * and to take by eminent domain, purchase or otherwise such property as it might deem necessary for the construction of reservoirs, the protection of its watershed or any other corporate purpose. * * *

A water company in the situation of the defendant should plan for a supply of water to meet conditions as they will be at least ten and preferably fifteen or twenty years in the future. The safe yield of the defendant's present water supply system * * * based on experience during the dry year June 1, 1949—June 1, 1950, is only about four million gallons daily. In 1949 Greenwich consumed about five million gallons daily and Port Chester and Rye about four million. It is estimated that in 1960 there will be required for Greenwich 6.8 million gallons a day and for Port Chester and Rye 4.3 million, while in 1970 Greenwich will take 8.75 million gallons daily and Port Chester and Rye 4.65 million. Thus it appears that the safe yield of the defendant's own system * * * was not adequate in 1948-49 to take care of the needs of the defendant's Connecticut customers alone, and as time goes on this yield will become less able to do so. To meet this condition, the defendant plans to construct a reservoir by damming the Mianus River above Farms Road. This will give the defendant additional storage capacity of approximately 2,200 million gallons. From this reservoir certain quantities of water will be conducted through the present pipe line into Rockwood Lake. The defendant will be bound to allow enough water to flow down the river to meet the needs of the New York, New Haven and Hartford Railroad Company, and its plan is to release sufficient water down the stream to equalize the flow over the entire year. A portion of the proposed reservoir and a major portion of its watershed will be in New York state, and the land for that portion will be acquired by the Port Chester Water Works, Inc. The defendant has no permanent source of water storage available to it other than the Mianus River.

On the foregoing facts the trial court concluded that, because the damage suffered by the plaintiffs from the diversion of the water of the river was far outweighed by the utility of the defendant's conduct and the interests of the public therein, no injunction should issue against future diversion. It also decided * * * that the defendant may exercise its right of eminent domain in respect to lands and water rights on the Mianus River, "including those of the plaintiffs," in order to increase its water supply storage, although a portion of such additional supply may be delivered to and used by those inhabitants of the state of New York to whom the defendant may supply water under existing legislative grants. It followed from this that the prayer for an injunction against such condemnation was denied.

We will first consider the question whether the defendant has the power to condemn the water rights of the plaintiffs for the purpose of constructing its proposed reservoir. Clearly, the General Assembly, by the amendment of the defendant's charter in 1927, purported to grant it that right. The taking of water by a water company chartered to supply water to the public is a taking for a public use. * * * When the legislature endows a public utility company with the power to take by eminent domain such property as is necessary to fulfill its corporate purposes without restriction, the determination of what is necessary to be taken lies in the discretion of the company. The courts will interfere with the exercise of that discretion only in cases of bad faith or unreasonable conduct. * * * Upon the subordinate facts found, there can be no question that it is reasonably necessary for the defendant to acquire water rights for the construction of a reservoir in the Mianus River in order to continue to furnish an adequate supply of water to its customers in Connecticut, to say nothing of the users of its water in New York state. The court would not be warranted in concluding the contrary. * * *

We turn now to a consideration of the plaintiffs' prayer for an injunction restraining the defendant from further diverting the water of the Mianus by pumping. * * * [A] riparian owner is entitled to have the water of the stream upon which he borders continue to flow in its wonted manner. * * * Any infringement of that right entitles him to relief, at least by way of damages, even though the actual, provable damage is small. * * * It does not necessarily follow, however, that he is entitled to relief by way of injunction, for the granting of such relief lies in the sound discretion of the court. * * *

The trial court denied the injunction in this case because it concluded that to grant it would result in damage to the defendant disproportionate in amount to the damage refusal of the injunction would cause the plaintiffs and would be detrimental to the public interest. * * *

The limitations on the propriety of the denial of an injunction on the theory of comparative damage between the parties do not apply to the refusal of an injunction which, if issued, would seriously affect public interest. It is well within a court's discretion to deny an injunction against the infringement of riparian rights if to grant it would adversely affect the interest of the public. * * * The subordinate facts found amply supported the court's conclusion in the instant case that the issuance of the injunction prayed for would seriously and adversely affect the public interest at the time the case was tried. Except for one consideration, therefore, the denial of the plaintiffs' prayer for that injunction was correct.

That consideration is this: The plaintiffs do have property rights to the accustomed flow of the Mianus River. In the emergency of a drought the public interest may require the court to refuse to protect those rights by way of injunction. However, the riparian owners ought not to be deprived permanently of those rights without compensation. If the judgment of the trial court stands in its present form, there is nothing to prevent the defendant from continuing indefinitely to pump water from the river as the most economical way of getting its required supply. By doing this it might well be able to avoid the building of its proposed reservoir. The result would be that the plaintiffs would for many years continue to be deprived of their rights without any compensation except that which they might recover by a multiplicity of actions. It is obviously not doing equity to leave them in such a position. Under the circumstances of this case, equity demanded that the defendant be allowed a reasonable time within which to make adequate compensation to the plaintiffs for the permanent taking of their water rights if it intends to acquire them, and, if that compensation is not made within such reasonable time, the defendant should be enjoined from further diversion of the waters of the stream. * * * Although the granting or withholding of an injunction lies in the discretion of a trial court, when the only reasonable conclusion is that a plaintiff is, in equity, entitled to an injunction in a given form, it is competent for us to order such an injunction even though the trial court has refused it. * * * The trial court was in error in unconditionally denying the injunction against the diversion of the waters of the stream.

[T]he case is remanded with direction to hear the parties and determine what will be a reasonable time to be allowed to the defendant to acquire the water rights of the plaintiffs by condemnation or otherwise—that to be the sole issue of fact to be tried—and then to enter a judgment which shall (1) direct that unless compensation is made within that reasonable time the defendant shall be enjoined from further diversion of the waters of the stream as prayed, (2) deny the prayer for an injunction against condemning such water rights of the plaintiffs as will be taken for the construction of the proposed reservoir * * *.

Notes

1. **Aftermath.** What will the city acquire by condemning plaintiffs' water rights? We are told that in subsequent eminent domain proceedings no claims for compensation were pressed because the riparian owners felt they would collect only nominal damages. Robert L. Leonard, An Economic Evaluation of Connecticut Water Law: Water Rights, Public Water Supply and Pollution Control, Report No. 11, Institute of Water Resources, University of Connecticut 11 (1970).

2. **Inverse condemnation.** In most states "inverse condemnation" is available. Ferguson v. Village of Hamburg, 5 N.E.2d 801 (N.Y. 1936), was a suit for an injunction brought by downstream riparians claiming injury from a diminution caused by a reservoir built by defendant village. The lower court granted relief in the form of an injunction which would go into effect unless the village sued to acquire the riparian rights. The Court of Appeals reversed, with orders to the lower court to ascertain the damages and issue an injunction unless within a reasonable time the defendant tendered to the plaintiff the damages so fixed. A simpler form of inverse condemnation is the ordinary damage action brought against the city for injury to the plaintiff's riparian rights. See Pernell v. City of Henderson, 16 S.E.2d 449 (N.C. 1941).

3. **Application of riparian principles.** In New Jersey, basic riparian principles govern cities and water companies. City of Paterson v. E. Jersey Water Co., 70 A. 472 (N.J. Ch. 1908), aff'd 78 A. 1134 (N.J. 1910).

4. **Basis of municipal authority.** Cities and public water supply companies were originally given powers to procure their supplies by special acts or charters. More commonly today, the power is given in general statutes applicable to all municipalities or water companies.

5. **Special municipal rights in public waters.** On some public waters (see Chapter 7) cities have been held to partake of the public's superior rights; they thus can take water without compensating injured riparians. Watuppa Reservoir Co. v. City of Fall River, 18 N.E. 465 (Mass.

1888) (great ponds); Minneapolis Mill Co. v. Bd. of Water Comm'rs of St. Paul, 58 N.W. 33 (Minn. 1894) (navigable waters).

HUDSON RIVER FISHERMAN'S ASS'N v. WILLIAMS
New York Supreme Court, Appellate Division, 1988.
139 A.D.2d 234, 531 N.Y.S.2d 379.

YESAWICH, J. Respondent Spring Valley Water Company, Inc. (hereinafter Spring Valley) provides water for approximately 88% of the residents of petitioner Rockland County and various industrial users from four major sources: (1) 57 wells, (2) the Lake De Forest Reservoir and Filter Plant, (3) the Ramapo Valley Well Field, and (4) the Stony Point Reservoir and Filter Plant. In 1979, Spring Valley submitted a water supply application to respondent Department of Environmental Conservation (hereinafter DEC) for permission to construct an additional water source named the Ambrey Pond project on a 364-acre site near the Town of Stony Point, Rockland County, * * *; acquisition of land to construct the reservoir and filtration plant is contemplated by the first stage of this multistage undertaking. The project, capable of adding a dependable yield of approximately 7.5 million gallons per day (mgd) to the utility's water distribution capacity, was sought to meet three perceived needs: (1) a present water supply deficit in the Haverstraw-Stony Point area of the Spring Valley system that is currently being met * * * by pumping water from lower elevations in the system at a substantial cost; (2) an anticipated inability to meet peak demand throughout the system in the short-term future; and (3) a projected system-wide inability to meet average demand further into the future. A primary factor requiring a new supply is the growth of Rockland County's population, though other factors include the contamination of six wells, the antiquation of the Stony Point treatment facility, the unavailability of water from the Ramapo Valley Well Field during periods of drought * * *.

During the course of extensive hearings, the inevitability of the need for an additional water supply became obvious; there was, however, a great deal of disagreement as to when this need would become manifest. The inherent uncertainty in determining precisely when the project would be necessary prompted Spring Valley and the Department of Public Service, which had expressed interest in increasing the peaking capacity of Spring Valley's system, to suggest that a "trigger mechanism" tying the date of the project's implementation to the demand for water be utilized. So that preliminary steps could be taken without authorizing premature construction and yet avoid a redundant new hearing which might perilously delay development of the proposed water supply, respondent Commissioner of Environmental Conservation (hereinafter the Commissioner) approved the project but "triggered" issuance of construction permits upon Spring Valley's experiencing an average demand of 27.9 mgd for two consecutive years. * * * Although Spring Valley expects to reach its maximum peak demand capacity well before it approaches the limit of its average demand capacity, the "trigger mechanism" was linked to the average demand because it more accurately reflects the relatively smooth trend of increased demand than the erratic peak demand which is heavily influenced by such vagaries as the weather. The point at which Spring Valley's current peak demand capacity would be exhausted was approximated by divining an appropriate ratio between average and peak demands to determine at which average demand level the peak demand capacity would be exhausted; that average demand figure was then adjusted downwards to allow for the three to four years' construction time required for the project. A regrettable and apparently inescapable consequence of the Ambrey Pond project is the likely destruction of a major naturally reproducing trout population due to the diversion of most of the flow from Rockland County's best trout stream into the Ambrey Pond Reservoir. * * *

Petitioners argue initially that Spring Valley failed to demonstrate the "public necessity" which ECL 15-1503 (2) requires as a precondition to construction of a water supply project. Citing Matter of Country Knolls Water Works v. Reid, * * * 383 N.Y.S.2d 661, they assert that because Spring Valley concedes that it does not have a present need for which the proposed source will be developed in the "immediate future," the application should have been denied * * *. This argument is flawed in several respects. First, ECL 15-1503 (2) authorizes the granting of permits based on a number of factors including "future needs for sources of water supply." It is also important to note the posture of the Country Knolls case. There we held that the DEC could deny a permit because a present need was not sufficiently shown; we did not concomitantly hold that the DEC must wait for the need to become dire and then only issue permits belatedly. Second, aside from the present water supply deficit in the Haverstraw-Stony Point area, there is substantial evidence of an unavoidable, if not imminent, necessity for greater peak demand capacity. Third, the trigger mechanism itself insures that the construction permits will not be issued until the need for an expanded water supply is close at hand, at least to the extent that such a demand can be foretold. The time required to construct dams, a filtration plant and a diversion pipeline necessitates that some sort of predictive mechanism be used. Given the many variables affecting the demand for water, it is hardly surprising that there was great divergence in the trigger proposals advanced by the various parties or that the figures relied upon have changed over the course of the long application process. Nevertheless, this does not equate to a showing of irrationality for the Commissioner's decision to conditionally authorize the project

Petitioners maintain further that the Commissioner's choice of the crucial 27.9 mgd trigger which actuates the process for issuing the construction permits was irrational; specifically that there is no historical foundation for relying on average demand to forecast peak demand. Reliance on average demand is undeniably a logical indicator here because of its stability and, though not faultlessly predictive of peak demand, the ratio between the two has remained between 1.4 and 1.9, thus providing the Commissioner with a rational and not unreasonable means of judging when to authorize additional water supply construction.

* * * Viewed in the context of the problems facing Spring Valley and considering that the basic dispute is one of timing, the trigger mechanism was a particularly apt resolution, for it postpones costly construction if the water demand does not grow as expected while allowing Spring Valley to acquire property in the inevitable reservoir basin, and yet allows it adequate time to construct the project when the demand for water begins pressing the limits of the existing system. * * *

Notes

1. **Regulation of public water supply projects.** R.I. Gen. Laws § 46–15–2: "No municipal water department or agency, public water system, including special water districts or private water company, or the water resources board, engaged in the distribution of water for potable purposes shall have any power: (1) To acquire or take a water supply or an additional water supply from an existing approved source * * * until the municipal water department or agency, special water district, or private water company has first submitted the maps and plans therefor to the director of the department of health, the commissioner of environmental protection for the department of the environment, the state planning council and the board, as hereinafter provided, and until the director of the department of the environment, after receiving the recommendations of the director of the department of health and the commissioner for environmental protection and the division of statewide planning, shall have approved the recommendations or approved the recommendation with modifications as he or she may determine to be necessary; provided, however, this subsection shall not apply to any area presently served by any municipal water department or agency, or special water district."

2. **Priority applied to competing public water supply projects.** In 1939 Pennsylvania created a priority system among public water supply agencies, 32 Pa. Cons. Stat. §§ 631–641. Unused water rights of any such agency were declared null and void, § 632, and all other water rights had to be registered with and their validity determined by the Water and Power Review Board, §§ 633 and 634. Compliance with the Act was made the exclusive method of acquiring water rights, § 635. A permit to acquire (by purchase, eminent domain, payment of damages, etc.) designated wa-

ter rights (of riparians) must be applied for, § 636. If the rights are not acquired within one year or the water is not actually taken within four years, the permit may be revoked, but, "if the project required for the taking of water has been commenced in good faith or if the commencement thereof has been prevented by events beyond the control of the permittee, the board shall have the power, upon application of the permittee, to grant such extensions of said period as the board deems to be necessary to enable the permittee to complete the project required for the taking of water." § 638.

3. **Other rules governing competition between water supply agencies.** There has been little litigation on the relative rights of eastern cities that are competing for the same water, but in it the courts have given a rule for every taste. In Massachusetts priority was the basis of the decision. The legislature in 1926 authorized the town of Somerset "to take by eminent domain * * * or acquire by purchase or otherwise * * * the waters of the Segreganset River." Prior to 1961 the only use of the river was to recharge the town's well field by flooding it in dry years. In that year a survey was undertaken for a diversion of water from the stream to an off-stream reservoir, money was appropriated to purchase land for the project, and bonds for construction funds were authorized. Meanwhile, the Dighton Water District had been established by legislative act in 1950 and authorized to acquire water from any stream within its service area "not already appropriated and used for the purpose of public water supply." Learning of Somerset's plans in 1962, the District hastily recorded an "order of taking" which purported to appropriate all the water of the Segreganset not already appropriated and used for public water supply. Held, the District's authority should be construed to mean that it could not take water "appropriated *or* used" for public supply, and that "appropriated" meant "permitted by legislative authority to be taken." Town of Somerset v. Dighton Water Dist., 200 N.E.2d 237 (Mass. 1964).

In New York, an "administrative allocation" was made. The City of Syracuse long ago was given legislative authority to take from Skaneateles Lake, through a 30 inch pipe, water not needed for the Erie Canal. In the twentieth century it almost doubled its withdrawals under authority of an order of the Water Power and Control Commission that contained the following clause, "The Commission reserves the right from time to time to authorize the amount of water found reasonably necessary for the supply of other parts of the state and the inhabitants thereof to be taken from Skaneateles Lake and applicant shall have no claim for compensation to the water so diverted unless it shall render a service in connection therewith * * *." In 1935 the Commission ordered the city to share its supply with the village of Jordan, which had no water works of its own. On appeal, affirmed. "The city accepted the determination and acted upon it, necessarily assumed and agreed to any burdens it imposed and is not now in any position to question the propriety of the limitations, conditions, or restrictions fixed or the power of the Commission to impose them." The order was held reasonable and fully sustained by the evidence. City of Syracuse v. Gibbs, 28 N.E.2d 835 (N.Y. 1940).

An interstate case was decided on riparian sharing. The Hackensack River flows from New York into New Jersey. In New York it is used by defendant Village of Nyack and several neighboring villages. Once used, the water is not returned to the Hackensack but is released into the Hudson. In New Jersey the plaintiff Hackensack Water Company diverts most of the water to serve 800,000 people in several cities. The plaintiff has several dams, some built in New York under authority of the New York Water Resources Commission, some in New Jersey, approved by that state's Department of Commerce and Development, Division of Water Policy and Supply. When Nyack took steps to increase its supply, claiming the right to do so under the terms of the New York Commission's orders allowing the dams, the plaintiff claimed that as builder of the dams it was entitled to the undiminished flow of the regulated river, and brought this action to determine its right to compensation for the proposed "withdrawal without return." The case came up on a motion for a summary judgment. In the stated facts it appeared that the plaintiff company owned 90% of the riparian land in New Jersey, but the defendant Village's holdings, if any, were not mentioned, and the reason for treating both parties as riparian proprietors was not discussed. Nevertheless the court set out at some length the "respective rights of upstream and downstream riparian owners," and discussed riparian principles applicable to diversions without return to the stream, domestic consumption and reasonable use. "From the foregoing it is apparent that the right of the plaintiff to the undiminished flow of the Hackensack River cannot be established as a matter of law. On the other hand, it is by no means clear that as a matter of fact the defendant's use of water of the Hackensack River is reasonable." The court overruled the motion and set these issues of fact for trial. Hackensack Water Co. v. Vill. of Nyack, 289 F. Supp. 671 (S.D.N.Y. 1968).

4. **Federal regulation of public water supply projects.** The Ambrey Pond project in the principal case probably required a permit from the Army Corps of Engineers under section 404 of the Clean Water Act, regulating the discharge of "dredge and fill materials" in most waters. (See Chapter 7, Section 2C). Could the Corps refuse to issue the permit because of the effect which the project will have on the trout fishery even though New York authorities have apparently concluded that the need for public water supplies outweighs the damage to the fishery? See infra pp. 601-02, Note 3. Could the Administrator of the U.S. Environmental Protection Agency veto a permit for the project because of its effects on the fishery without considering local water supply needs? See James City County v. Environmental Protection Agency, infra p. 602, Note 4. How would the authority and responsibilities of the Corps and EPA be affected if the trout were a listed species under the federal Endangered Species Act. See Riverside Irrigation Dist. v. Andrews, infra p. 595, and Chapter 7, Section 2D.

SECTION 4. STATE REGULATION

MUENCH v. PUBLIC SERVICE COMMISSION
Supreme Court of Wisconsin, 1952.
261 Wis. 492, 53 N.W.2d 514.

On March 8, 1950, the Namekagon Hydro Company (hereinafter * * * "Company") filed an application with the Public Service Commission to construct, operate, and maintain a hydro-electric dam on the Namekagon River in Washburn county. The Conservation Commission entered its appearance and objected to construction of the dam on the ground that it was violative of public rights and in particular the right declared by sec. 31.06(3), Stats., to *"the enjoyment of natural scenic beauty."* The Conservation Commission was represented at the hearing by the attorney general acting on the express direction of the governor of the state. * * *

* * * [T]he commission issued its findings, conclusions, and certificate of permit to the Company. The effect of the Public Service Commission's findings was to determine that the statutory requirements entitling the Company to a permit to construct the dam existed, and that there were no public rights which required denial of the application.

After the permit was issued both the Conservation Commission and the petitioner Muench filed motions for rehearing before the Public Service Commission, which motions were denied by an order entered December 6, 1950. Muench, a private citizen who is also president of the state division of the Izaak Walton League, had appeared as a party at the original hearing before the Public Service Commission. * * *

CURRIE, JUSTICE. We are concerned in this case with the problem of the nature of public rights in the navigable streams of the state and the beds underlying the same, and the protection of such rights. * * *

After the Revolutionary War, the original thirteen states were impoverished and were confronted with the problem of paying the debts created by the war. States without western lands demanded that Virginia and other states claiming such lands to the west should cede the same to the Confederation to be sold to pay such debts. In 1783 the Virginia legislature authorized the ceding of the Northwest Territory to the Confederation, and the actual deed of conveyance was executed March 1, 1784. This cession was made upon two conditions: (1) The new states to be admitted as members of the Federal Union were to have the same rights to sovereignty as the original states; and (2) The navigable waters flowing into the Mississippi and the St. Lawrence rivers, and the carrying places between them were to be forever free public highways. These conditions were incorporated into the Northwest Ordinance of 1787, which set up the machinery for the government of the Northwest Territory.

Art. IX, sec. 1, of the Wisconsin Constitution, adopted by the Territorial Convention on February 17, 1848, * * * incorporated verbatim the wording of the Northwest Ordinance with respect to navigable waters, such section reading as follows:

> "The state shall have concurrent jurisdiction on all rivers and lakes bordering on this state so far as such rivers or lakes shall form a common boundary to the state and any other state or territory now or hereafter to be formed, and bounded by the same; and the river Mississippi and the navigable waters leading into the Mississippi and St. Lawrence, and the carrying places between the same, shall be common highways and forever free, as well to the inhabitants of the state as to the citizens of the United States, without any tax, impost or duty therefor." * * *

One of the early cases which established the "saw-log" test of navigability in the state is that of Olson v. Merrill, 1877, 42 Wis. 203, 212. * * *

* * * Wisconsin, in adopting the saw-log test of navigability, based the same on commercial considerations. * * * In Diana Shooting Club v. Husting, 1914, * * * 145 N.W. 816, 820, * * * the defendant Paul O. Husting * * * entered his hunting boat floating upon the waters of Rock river, and with the aid of a pole and paddle propelled it down the river to the place of the alleged trespass for the purpose of shooting wild ducks * * *. This case is significant in that the navigability was established not through any commercial use, such as floating of logs, but through the use of shallow draft boats for purposes of recreation. * * *

In 1911 Wisconsin enacted the first Water Power Act, * * * which was very similar in wording to our present sec. 30.01(2), Stats., which reads:

> "All rivers and streams which have been meandered and returned as navigable by the surveyors employed by the government of the United States, and all rivers, streams, sloughs, bayous and marsh outlets, whether meandered or nonmeandered *which are navigable in fact for any purpose whatsoever* are hereby declared navigable to the extent that no dam, bridge, or other obstruction shall be made in or over the same without the permission of the legislature."

Therefore, since 1911 it is no longer necessary in determining navigability of streams to establish a past history of floating of logs, or other uses of commercial transportation, because any stream is *"navigable in fact"* which is capable of floating any boat, skiff or canoe, of the shallowest draft used for recreational purposes. * * *

Our present Water Power Law dates from 1915, * * * and such act contained a provision * * * which required the Railroad Commission (predecessor to the Public Service Commission), in granting a permit to construct a dam upon a navigable stream, to find that "the proposed dam will not materially obstruct existing navigation *or violate other public rights*." This same provision is now contained in sec. 31.06(3), Stats.

The nature of these *"other public rights"* referred to in sec. 31.06(3) Stats., is elucidated in the opinion of this court in Nekoosa-Edwards Paper Co. v. Railroad Comm., 1930, * * * 228 N.W. 144, 147, 229 N.W. 631. * * *

> "Many of the meandered lakes and streams of this state, navigable in law, have ceased to be navigable for pecuniary gain. They are still navigable in law; that is, subject to the use of the public for all the incidents of navigable waters. As population increases, these waters are used by the people for *sailing, rowing, canoeing, bathing, fishing, hunting, skating and other public purposes.* While the public right may have originated in the older use or capacity of the waters for navigation, such public right having once accrued, it is not lost by the failure of pecuniary profitable navigation, but resort may be had thereto for any other public purpose. Our state has for many years been extensively engaged in the propagation of fish and the stocking of the waters of the state with fish fry in order that the public may more fully enjoy the sport and recreation of fishing. By reason of the state's enterprise in behalf of the public, the small streams of the state are fishing streams to which the public have a right to resort so long as they do not trespass on the private property along the banks."
> * * *

The 1929 legislature * * * amended sec. 31.06, Stats., so as to provide that *the enjoyment of scenic beauty is a public right* to be considered by the Public Service Commission in making findings as to whether a permit for a proposed dam shall be issued. Thus we have a further public right in navigable streams recognized by legislative enactment which is highly illustrative of the trend to extend and protect the rights of the public to the recreational enjoyment of the navigable waters of the state. * * *

The second question to be passed upon is whether the petitioner Muench is a person *"aggrieved"* and *"directly affected,"* under the provisions of sec. 227.16(1), Stats., by the decision of the Commission in this instance which is reviewable under sec. 227.15, Stats. The Company contends that Muench is not directly affected by the Commission's decision because he has no direct pecuniary interest which would be jeopardized by the issuance of a permit to erect the dam. The right of the citizens of the state to enjoy our navigable streams for recreational purposes, including the enjoyment of scenic beauty, is a legal right that is entitled to all the protection which is given financial rights. * * *

Such rights would be severely limited, curtailed, or endangered if we did not hold that any citizen who has appeared at a hearing of the Public Service Commission, * * * [on] an application to erect a dam in a navigable stream is *"aggrieved"* and *"directly affected"* by a decision of the Commission finding that public rights will not be violated by erection of a proposed dam so as to entitle him to petition for review under sec. 227.15, Stats. We conclude that petitioner Muench was therefore entitled to petition the circuit court for review.

Our holding in this respect is in keeping with the trend manifested in the development of the law of navigable waters in this state to extend the rights of the general public to the recreational use of the waters of this state, and to protect the public in the enjoyment of such rights. * * *

The state contends that the Namekagon river, on which the proposed dam is to be erected, is famous throughout the eastern half of the United States because of its scenic beauty, desirability for float trips and canoeing, and for a type of fishing water which the Federal Fishing and Wildlife Service has described as rapidly disappearing from the state of Wisconsin. The Public Service Commission will be required to make findings as to whether public rights for the recreational enjoyment of this stream in its present natural condition outweigh the benefits to the public which would result in the construction of the dam.

Judgment reversed [and the matter remanded to the Commission] for further proceedings in accordance with this opinion.

Notes

1. **Origins of state regulation.** Much of the movement for statutory regulation of water uses in the eastern states is directed at environmental protection. Wisconsin was a leader in this regard as its legislature and courts built on the "public rights" concept, and *Muench* (case and man) should not be forgotten.

2. **Basis of state regulation.** Much early water legislation authorized the construction of dams, operation of log booms and diversions to canals. These were mostly limited, like the statute in the principal case, to navigable waters over which the state had clear powers. "Navigability" was not a limiting factor in Wisconsin, which has so broad a definition of navigability that it applied to quite small streams. As one Wisconsin official said, "If a perch can swim in it—even on his side like a flounder—it's navigable, and we'll take charge." Some of the earliest statutes, however, were directed at the use of non-navigable water. The mill dam statutes of New England gave the privilege of erecting dams across non-navigable streams and allowed dam owners to flood the lands of upper riparians.

Today it is generally recognized that state powers over navigable waters are not the only source of water legislation and that the general police power is the basis for statutes affecting all types of waters.

3. **Regulation of particular uses**. Many eastern states have long had limited permit systems for certain uses, like Wisconsin's Water Power Law. Typical examples involve dam construction, e.g., Conn. Gen. Stat. §§ 22a–401 to 22a–410; W. Va. Code. §§ 22–14–1 to 22–14–18. Some apply only to navigable rivers while many deal only with safety licensing and inspection. The Arkansas Soil and Water Conservation Commission not only controls and regulates the building of dams, but also some relations between water users. A permit is required, but only surplus water may be impounded. "Surplus" is whatever remains in excess of a continuous discharge, fixed by the Commission in amount to protect lower riparian rights and fish and wildlife. The person constructing the dam under a permit has an exclusive right to the use of the water impounded. Ark. Code Ann. § 15–22–210.

VILLAGE OF TEQUESTA v. JUPITER INLET CORP.
Supreme Court of Florida, 1979.
371 So. 2d 663.

[The Jupiter Inlet Corporation owned property on which it planned to build a 120 unit condominium project, supplied with water from an underlying shallow aquifer. The property was less than a quarter of a mile from the well field that supplied the Village of Tequesta with water from seven wells which pumped more than one million gallons per day from a depth of 75 to 90 feet. This is the entire "safe yield" of the shallow aquifer, since greater withdrawals would induce the intrusion into the aquifer of salt water from the nearby Intracoastal Waterway, a canal connected to the Atlantic Ocean. The only other nearby source of fresh water is a deep artesian aquifer which can be tapped only by 1200 foot wells, at greatly increased drilling and pumping costs.

Florida's common law gave the overlying landowner a right to reasonable use of the ground water, modified by the correlative rights of adjacent landowners to use the same water. Reasonableness of a landowner's particular use was determined in much the same way as the reasonableness of a riparian use of water in a water course. As explained in the opinion, the Florida Water Resources Act of 1972 applies to both stream water and ground water, requires a permit for all substantial new withdrawals and provides for regularizing existing common law withdrawals by issuing permits for them. Tequesta applied for and received permits for its wells. When Jupiter applied for a permit to take water from the shallow aquifer, its application was denied. Jupiter now sues Tequesta in inverse condemnation, claiming that Tequesta had deprived Jupiter of the beneficial use of its property rights and thereby took the property without compensation. The legal problem is essentially identical to that which would exist if Jupiter's property were riparian to a small stream, upstream from a point where Tequesta took the entire flow for municipal supply.]

ADKINS, JUSTICE. * * * Florida operates under an administrative system of water management [under] the Florida Water Resources Act. * * * (1972). The law prior to the Florida Water Resources Act did not allow ownership in the corpus of the water, but only in the use of it. Even then, the use was bounded by the perimeters of reasonable and beneficial use. Legislation limiting the right to the use of the water is in itself no more objectionable than legislation forbidding the use of property for certain purposes by zoning regulations. Village of Euclid v. Ambler Realty Co., 272 U.S. 365, * * * (1928).

The Florida Water Resources Act, in recognizing the need for conservation and control of the waters in the state (Section 373.016 * * *) makes all waters in the state subject to regulation, unless otherwise specifically exempt. § 373.023(1) * * *. The Department of Environmental Regulation and the various water management districts are given the responsibility to accomplish the conservation, protection, management, and control of the waters of the state. § 373.016(3) * * *. In order to exercise such controls a permitting system is established which requires permits for consumptive use of water, exempting only "domestic consumption of water by individual users" from the requirements of a permit. § 373.219(1) * * *. Jupiter, in serving a 120-unit condominium, does not qualify as an individual user and thus must secure a permit in order to draw water from beneath its property. Without a permit Jupiter has no such property right to the use of water beneath its land for which, upon deprivation, it must be compensated through inverse condemnation.

The Water Resources Act of 1972 recognizes a right to use water under the common law as separate from the right to use water under a permit granted pursuant to the act. This is done by a provision concerning the termination of the common-law right and a transitional procedure. The holder of such a common-law water-use right was given two years to convert the common-law water right into a permit water right. § 373.226(3) * * *. In order to qualify for the initial permit under section 373.226(2) * * * the right must have been exercised prior to the implementation of the Florida Water Resources Act by a water management district with geographical jurisdiction in that area. Otherwise the right is abandoned and extinguished requiring a new application for a permit. Tequesta had acquired the permit and Jupiter was merely a proposed user. The Florida Water Resources Act makes no provision for the continuation of an *unexercised* common-law right to use water. Jupiter had perfected no legal interest to the use of the water beneath its land which would support an action in inverse condemnation.

Section 373.1961 * * * provides additional powers and duties for the governing boards of the water management district. Subsection (7) provides that the governing board:

> May acquire title to such interest as is necessary in real property, by purchase, gift, devise, lease, eminent domain, or otherwise, *for water production and transmission* consistent with this section. However, the district shall not use any of the eminent domain powers herein granted to acquire water and water rights already devoted to reasonable and beneficial use or any water production or transmission facilities owned by any county, municipality, or regional water supply authority. [Emphasis supplied].

Condemnation of "water rights" is not granted in the first sentence of this subsection. The authority granted is specifically limited to the acquisition of land for the purpose of constructing and operating well fields and other withdrawal facilities and for the right-of-way necessary for the transmission of water to consumers. The second sentence prohibits the use of eminent domain to acquire such "water rights" which were *already* being put to a reasonable and beneficial use. The statutory prohibition of the use of eminent domain in one situation cannot be used as authority for its use by implication in another, as the statute must be strictly construed. Canal Authority v. Miller, 243 So. 2d 193 (Fla.1970). All that Section 373.1961(7) * * * accomplishes is to further protect presently existing legal uses of water. No implication can be drawn that this section intends to include any "water right" other than the permit that may be granted by a water management district. After all, if a use of water is both preexisting and also reasonable and beneficial, after two years, it must be either under permit or it is conclusively presumed to be abandoned. There was no necessity for the Water Resources Act to provide for the condemnation of an unexercised right to use water, as the owner became subject to the permit provisions of the law. There was no "taking" of this right.

Jupiter's remedy is only through proper application for a permit under the Florida Water Resources Act.

Notes

1. **Comprehensive permit systems ("regulated riparianism").** At least seventeen states have adopted permit systems. Ala. Code §§ 9–10B–1 to –30; Ark. Code Ann. §§ 15–22–201 to –622; Conn. Gen. Stat. §§ 22a–365 to –380; Del. Code Ann. tit. 7, §§ 6001-6031; Fla. Stat. §§ 373.013 to -.71; Ga. Code Ann. §§ 12–5–20 to –31, 12–5–43 to –53; Iowa Code §§ 455B.261 to -.281; Ky. Rev. Stat. Ann. §§ 151.010 to -.600; Md. Nat. Res. Code Ann. §§ 8–101 to –204, 5–501 to –514; Mass. Gen. Laws ch. 21G, §§ 1-19; Minn. Stat. §§ 103G.255 to -.315; Miss. Code Ann. §§ 51–1–5 to –3–55; N.J. Stat. Ann. §§ 58:1A–1 to –17; N.Y. Envtl. Conserv. Law

§§ 15–1501 to –1529; N.C. Gen. Stat. §§ 143–215.11 to –215.22; Va. Code Ann. §§ 62.1–242 to –253; Wis. Stat. §§ 30.18, 30.28, 30.292, 30.294, 30.298. See also Haw. Rev. Stat. §§ 174C–1 to –101, and infra p. 332, Note 6. Professor Joseph W. Dellapenna used the term "regulated riparianism" to describe such systems and that term is increasingly accepted. See Joseph W. Dellapenna, Owning Surface Water In the Eastern United States, 6 Proc. E. Min. L. Found. 1–1, 1–33 to 1–34 (1985); American Society of Civil Engineers, The Regulated Riparian Model Water Code (Joseph W. Dellapenna, ed. 1997).

Although they vary greatly, the common theme of these statutes is government regulation of water use through an administrative permit system. While this theme is shared by western permit systems under the appropriation doctrine, these other systems differ substantially from their western counterparts. Notably, the role of priority in time is greatly reduced (typically, it receives no explicit mention), permits expire after a specified period or may be canceled administratively, and administrative officials are given greater discretion to allocate water in time of shortage and to reallocate water to new (presumably better) use as needs and values change. Descriptions and analyses of eastern permit systems are found in Joseph W. Dellapenna, Introduction to Riparian Rights, 1 Waters and Water Rights, ch. 9 (Robert E. Beck ed., 1991); Richard Ausness, Water Rights Legislation in the East: A Program for Reform, 24 Wm. & Mary L. Rev. 547 (1983); Peter N. Davis, Eastern Water Diversion Permit Statutes: Precedents for Missouri, 47 Mo. L. Rev. 429 (1982); George W. Sherk, Eastern Water Law: Trends in State Legislation, 9 Va. Envtl. L.J. 287 (1990).

2. **Reasons for eastern permit systems.** The eastern permit systems respond to perceived inadequacies in common law riparian rights. Critics charge that: riparian rights are vague, inherently unstable, and do not provide a sound basis for investment in water development; because the system is "litigation driven," determination and enforcement of rights are slow, expensive, and the outcomes are unpredictable; the doctrine poorly protects environmental and public values associated with water; the doctrine poorly allocates water during drought; and limiting the use to riparian lands is economically unsound. See, e.g., Joseph W. Dellapenna, Special Challenges to Water Markets in Riparian States, 21 Ga. St. U. L. Rev. 305 (2004).

3. **The Florida permit system.** The Florida permit system has been a substantial success in two respects: in the registration and quantification of preexisting uses and in the control of the initiation of new withdrawals. The applicant for a permit must demonstrate that the proposed use will be "reasonable-beneficial," that it will not interfere with any presently existing legal water use, and that it will be consistent with the public interest. Fla. Stat. § 373.223(1). The reasonable-beneficial standard limits water use to the quantity needed for economic and efficient utilization for a purpose and in a manner both reasonable and in the public interest. § 373.019(13). The new use must comport with the state's

water plan which may not only provide for development, protection and management of water resources but may also prohibit or restrict uses on designated streams that might impair public recreation or harm fish and wildlife. § 373.036(3). Further environmental protection is given by minimum flow requirements setting the limit at which further withdrawals would be significantly harmful to the area's water resources or ecology. § 373.042.

Priority. In practice, the success of the permit granting process seems largely attributable to putting as much priority into the system as possible. The requirement of non-interference with existing uses is heavily stressed. Some permits have been conditioned to coordinate withdrawals, rotating the pumping of different users, scheduling withdrawals to avoid depletion of minimum flows or fluctuation of lake levels, and when visual effects are offensive by allowing pumping only at night. Some actual priority is practiced—some permits forbid withdrawals when they would interfere with the supply of an existing permit holder, and some permittees have been required to build retaining ponds to store water for use during times of peak demand. See Harloff v. City of Sarasota, 575 So. 2d 1324 (Fl. Dist. Ct. App. 1991) (priority to existing user). Cf. § 373.223(1)(b) (protection of existing uses).

The permit statutes of other states either outright prohibit the water agency from issuing new permits that impair the rights of existing water users or require the relevant authority to consider the effect on existing uses when issuing new permits. See Conn. Gen. Stat. § 22A–373(b)(2); Ga. Code Ann. § 12–5–31(g); Ky. Rev. Stat. Ann. § 151.170(2); Mass. Gen. Laws ch. 21G, § 7(4). Nearly all of the eastern statutes provide for registration and quantification of pre-existing uses.

Nonriparian uses. The Florida statutes apparently authorize permits for nonriparian uses: "The governing board or department may authorize the holder of a use permit to transport and use ground or surface water beyond overlying land, across county boundaries, or outside the watershed from which it is taken * * *." Fla. Stat. § 373.223(2). Transfer of water between water management districts, although not expressly permitted, was approved in Osceola County v. St. Johns River Water Management District, 504 So. 2d 385 (Fla. 1987). See also Ark. Code. Ann. § 15–22–304(b), specifically authorizing the transfer of "excess surface water" to nonriparians, and Wis. Stat. § 30.18(6)(b), permitting the irrigation of contiguous nonriparian lands. Although most states do not specifically authorize nonriparian uses, none expressly limit permits to riparians. A few early statutes were administered as if the permits were merely regulatory measures affecting riparian rights. See Nekoosa-Edwards Paper Co. v. Pub. Serv. Comm'n, 99 N.W.2d 821 (Wis. 1959).

4. **Administrative discretion.** The Florida statute is taken almost verbatim from Frank Maloney, Richard Ausness & James Morris, A Model Water Code (1972). A severely critical review of the book raised strong objections to administrative distribution of water in times of

shortage. Frank J. Trelease, The Model Water Code, The Wise Administrator and the Goddam Bureaucrat, 14 Nat. Resources J. 207 (1974):

"Reduction, restriction, changes in permits, suspension of permits, apportionment, rotation, limitation, prohibition—these are what the water user may expect. The Code's solution to the legal uncertainties of riparian rights is the substitution of these administrative uncertainties.

"To what end? Protection of the public, the environment? No—that is all taken care of. To understand the choice between property rights and administrative distribution, it must be very clearly kept in mind that all we are talking about is water already allocated to private use, that the state and its administrators have issued permits for its use, that every use is reasonable-beneficial, that all the uses can be made in times of water plenty. It must be remembered that all minimum flow requirements are met, that all other environmental factors are protected, and that the state water plan is observed and even furthered. The 'public interest' stands neutral, and the only question is, which people get to use the water. The choice is between giving people, industries and cities water rights that entitle them to water under stated conditions, rights that they may use as they see fit and adjust among themselves as they may agree, or giving the regulatory official the power to determine in his discretion which water users get water in times of shortage, and to shift water between uses and users as time progresses."

Since that article was written the shortage plans of the decentralized water management districts have been revised and adopted and many of these terrible things have not occurred. Each district is required by Fla. Stat. § 373.246(1) to prepare a shortage plan. These extensive documents are essentially plans for periods of subnormal precipitation that require temporary cutbacks when the supply drops below the level usually sufficient for all. The shortage plans all follow a pattern, although all are not identical. The Water Shortage Plan of the St. Johns River Water Management District is typical (Fl. Admin. Code Ch. 40C–21). Uses are classified by source of water, type of use, and method of abstraction or diversion. Shortages are classified as moderate, severe, extreme and critical, or as emergencies. Target cutbacks are set at 15% through 30%, 45% and 60%. Voluntary reductions in use are primarily relied on in the early stages. As the shortage deepens strict provisions against waste and careless or profligate use are instituted, fountains are shut off, and irrigation of lawns, trees and golf courses is limited by day of the week, hour of use, and time of day. Car washing and street and sidewalk flushing are restricted. Overhead spray irrigation of agricultural crops is restricted by day, hour and length, flood irrigation to a few days a month, and frost protection to forecasts of severe freeze.

Essentially, these shortage plans set up mechanisms for sharing a temporary drought in a usually abundant supply. Sharing, of course, occurs among householders during droughts in cities of other states, and among irrigators in western irrigation districts when project supplies are below normal. Sharing among persons similarly situated is functional as long as the shares do not become too small for everyone. When not all uses are the same, however, less than a full supply may stop some processes. Perhaps for this reason the Florida shortage plans typically contain very specific rules for mines and processing plants.

Areas of bureaucratic rule over the fortunes of water users may remain. The system of classification allows uses and users to be ranked according to official notions of which are least essential and can be cut off first. Farmers, however, are the most vulnerable. Irrigated agriculture is the largest water user and receives the brunt of the cutbacks. In an extreme shortage or emergency, an overall allocation is made to each class of water. The total agricultural irrigation allocation is set, but it is not necessarily shared equally. "The share available to each user will be based on any prioritization among crops the District establishes based on economic loss and equity considerations and the acreage and quantity of withdrawals for which the user has been permitted." Fla. Admin. Code §§ 40C–21.641(2)(a)(6); 40C–21.651(2)(a)(6).

In other states administrators are given wide discretionary powers in times of shortage to determine who gets water and who does not, guided only by vague and general criteria such as "the best interests of the public" (Ky. Rev. Stat. Ann. § 151.200(1); giving priority to "(1) sustaining life; (2) maintaining health; and (3) increasing wealth" (Ark. Code Ann. § 15–22–217(c)); "to protect adequately such citizens or water resources" (Ga. Code Ann. § 12–5–31(l)); or allocating to each user "an equitable portion of available water" (Ark. Code Ann. § 15–22–217(a)).

5. **Inadequate control of over-development.** In the eastern states, a "shortage" seems to be conceived of as a one-sided phenomenon, a temporary subnormal supply of natural origin. There appears to be little recognition that demands upon normal supplies can exceed the available quantity and thus create a shortage. Although in the *Tequesta* case a new permit was refused because increased drafts on the supply would ruin the entire source for everyone, there are no statutes or cases which recognize that too many permits can produce a permanent shortage or that on a fluctuating source each new permit will cause the next "shortage" to cut deeper, and will bring the one after that sooner. There is no apparent recognition that as the permit-granting process continues the existing uses will be impaired by having their shares reduced during the next below-normal year. There are no statutory requirements that call for halting the issuance of permits when some limit of safe yield or dependable supply is reached. The Florida shortage plans mention no reduction in future use or restrictions on new permits, but seem to assume the resumption of business as usual with the return of the rains.

6. **Flexibility, reallocation, and time-limited permits.** Some method must be devised to accommodate new demands and uses and to reallocate water in use to different and more productive purposes if the limits of supply are reached. Water transfers—voluntary or involuntary—can facilitate such reallocations. The time-limited permits in regulated riparian states give administrators an option not found in western states,

where permits may last in perpetuity: regulated riparian administrators can simply deny the renewal of a permit and award the water to a higher use. Joseph W. Dellapenna, supra p. 309, Note 2, however, concludes that this does not readily occur:

"Theoretically, one purpose of the regulated riparian system is to enable the administering agencies to force these transfers through the non-renewal of permits. In practice, however, the agencies free up far less water through the renewal process than theory suggests because the agencies prefer to tighten conditions on existing uses rather than to deny renewals outright. Non-renewal of permits will likely remain an infrequent and cumbersome device unless states are willing to create a good deal of investment insecurity."

Frank J. Trelease, The Model Water Code, the Wise Administrator and the Goddam Bureaucrat, 14 Nat. Resources J. 207 (1974), summarizes other problems with time-limited permits.

"Under the Model Code [and most eastern codes], the mechanism to accomplish these shifts is the issuance of new permits to newly-favored users upon the expiration of old and now-to-be-discarded uses. I see several difficulties with this process. First, to the extent that the 'normal' permit lasts twenty years, flexibility is surrendered during its life. If the application for the new use does not coincide with permit expirations, the new user may have to wait a fairly long time before water becomes available. Second, the investment may have been only partly amortized during the 20-year (or shorter) period. Third, the holder will in most cases lose an asset more valuable than his investment, that is, the going concern value of his enterprise, the continuing opportunity to make a profit, which is presumably a contribution to the economy. Fourth, if it were my enterprise, I would suspect that some Bureaucrat might solve the first problem and aggravate the second and third by simply granting the permit and squeezing the water out of me and other less favored users under the shortage plans and emergency measures."

How transferable is a 20-year water right in its 17th year? Suppose an irrigation system of pumps and sprinklers, which initially cost $40,000, hopelessly breaks down in the 15th year. Will it be replaced?

A mid-western farmer with sandy soils can, under normal rainfall, grow small grain that brings him $50 per acre. With irrigation, he can grow vegetable crops that bring in $200 per acre. He obtains an irrigation permit, borrows $40,000 from the bank, and buys pumps, pipes and sprinklers. After ten years the mortgage is paid off. His permit is then canceled, or expires and is not renewed. Has he suffered a loss? Suppose a western appropriator whose permit runs "in perpetuity" sells his land with appurtenant water right at $500 per acre when dry land in the neighborhood is selling at $100 per acre. Has he made a "windfall profit?" Suppose he sells an acre's worth of water right at $400?

Suppose an Iowa farmer has a permit to irrigate, but the irrigation often reduces the stream to its minimum flow. A downstream cannery needs a water supply, and could pay the farmer more than he realizes through irrigation. Iowa Code § 455B.273 provides, "A permittee may sell, transfer, or assign a permit by conveying, leasing, or otherwise transferring the ownership of the land described in the permit * * *." Will the water move to its "highest and most productive use?"

7. **Other criticisms of eastern permit systems.** Others besides Frank Trelease (supra Notes 4 and 6) have criticized eastern permit systems Professor Richard Ausness, one of the draftsmen of the Model Water Code, has criticized such statutes: (1) because there is no coordination between water resource planning and administration of the permit system, (2) because permits are of short duration, have no certainty of renewal, and leave the allocation of water during shortages uncertain, thereby undermining the confidence of permit holds and discouraging capital investments, and (3) because there is no explicit mechanism for reallocation of water. Richard Ausness, supra p. 314, Note 1. Professor Robert Abrams identifies three evident drawbacks of a standard permit system: its rigidity, its tendency to overregulate, and its lack of articulated policy objectives. Robert H. Abrams, Replacing Riparianism in the Twenty-First Century, 36 Wayne L. Rev. 93 (1989). In addition, each state exempts many uses. Individually or collectively, these exemptions may be substantial. For example, in Georgia, virtually all "farm uses" are exempt. Ga. Code Ann. §§ 12-5-31(a)(3), 12-5-105(a). Dellapenna, supra p. 309, Note 2.

W. Baron A. Avery, Disenfranchising the Non-Riparian: Alabama's Water Resource Management Program, 39 Cumb. L. Rev. 437 (2009), makes a very different critique. Avery notes the widespread existence of long-standing, non-riparian, non-permitted water diversions in Alabama. "This non-riparian water use continues in spite of the common law rules militating against the practice and in spite of statutory and regulatory prohibitions. The rules are simply ignored." He concludes, however, that "the current regulatory regime in Alabama should be amended so that it does not discriminate against the non-riparian water users and thereby increase the opportunity for economic development in the state."

8. **Constitutional objections.** Constitutional objections to eastern permit systems are discussed infra p. 328, Note 1, and p. 330, Note 3.

9. **A revisionist view?** Not all commentators lament the litigation-driven core of common law riparianism. D. S. Pensley, The Legalities of Stream Interventions: Accretive Challenges to New York State's Riparian Doctrine Ahead?, 25 Pace Envtl. L. Rev. 105 (2008), finds that the large gaps in New York's regulated riparian regime leave many practical watershed management questions inadequately addressed. In a paean to traditional riparianism, he urges the common law to fill the gaps:

"This Article proposes a variety of additional grounds for riparian suit, such as enjoining the clearing of an obstructive point bar, forcing the redesign of a poorly located stormwater conduit, or seeking damages for the drying up of a beautiful river. Considering that the 'wall of environmental law enacted in the 1970s remains . . . tremendously valuable at slowing disaster, but [is] ultimately not enough without additional systemic changes,' small-time litigation within the ambit of the common law represents a populist, place-by-place, and potentially equitable tool to convert the rights of one landowner to riparian health into the duties of another to act or to forebear in effecting changes to a watercourse. As the evolution of New York's groundwater doctrine illustrates, courts' incremental approach justifiably infuses 'what the law is' with 'what the law ought to be' when faced with an increasing number of land use conflicts around related issues; the judiciary is educated, in the best of cases, by deepening scientific understanding of geologic and ecologic phenomena.

"* * *

"Whereas it is false to say that regulated riparianism has supplanted riparianism, it is true to say that alongside regulated riparianism, the common law doctrine is in the process of supplanting itself, creatively and accretively, and potentially enriching the statutory realm thereby. While instrumentalist and needs-based yet, the doctrine is well on its way to a full-fledged prescriptive and ecological destination, but one no longer allocative or distributive. Rooted firmly in precedent, today's riparianism is capable of weighing time, place, circumstance, and above all, a normative view of the 'things of nature.'"

SECTION 5. ABOLITION AND COMBINATION (INCLUDING THE "CALIFORNIA DOCTRINE")

COFFIN v. LEFT HAND DITCH CO.
Supreme Court of Colorado, 1882.
6 Colo. 443.

[See opinion, supra p. 101.]

Notes

1. **Cases rejecting the doctrine in other jurisdictions.** The cases in other states that have extinguished riparian rights to the use of water and adopted the "Colorado doctrine" include Van Dyke v. Midnight Sun Mining & Ditch Co. (Alaska) 177 F. 85 (9th Cir. 1910) and Drake v. Earhart, 23 P. 541 (Idaho 1890).

2. **Meaning of statutes adopting the common law.** In Boquillas Land & Cattle Co. v. Curtis, 213 U.S. 339 (1909), a riparian, seeking to protect his unused right against an upstream appropriation, argued that the Arizona statute adopting the common law of England conferred upon him property rights not subject to legislative change. Mr. Justice Holmes disposed of this contention with one of his famous aphorisms, that this statute "is far from meaning that patentees of a ranch on the San Pedro are to have the same rights as owners of an estate on the Thames."

3. **Riparian rights in appropriation jurisdictions.** The phrase "riparian rights" frequently describes rights to ownership of land, such as the bed of a stream or fast land created by accretion, rights to protect the bank from stream erosion, rights to fish in waters, and rights to access to waters. For the status of these rights in Colorado doctrine states, see Note, Riparian Rights in Appropriation States, 9 Wyo. L.J. 130 (1955). See also Chapter 7, Section 1.

LUX v. HAGGIN
Supreme Court of California, 1886.
69 Cal. 255, 10 P. 674.

[Henry Miller, the "Cattle King," head of the firm of Miller & Lux, owned land for 120 miles on both sides of the San Joaquin River and other streams of California's Central Valley. In the southern end of his domain vast areas of "grass lands" were naturally irrigated by annual spring floods of the Kern River, which split into numerous channels and sloughs. When the floods subsided, the water was spread over the land by dams thrown across the sloughs. Huge quantities of native hay were produced in this fashion. The lands had been purchased in 1872 from the State of California, which had acquired them from the federal government in 1850 under the terms of the Federal Swamp Land Act, granting overflowed lands to the states.

Haggin was the promoter of the Kern River Land & Canal Company, a large irrigation project. In 1875 he and the company acquired an appropriation of 74,000 inches of the Kern. His point of diversion was on federal public lands upstream from the land of Miller & Lux. Some of these facts, and more background, are found in Samuel Wiel, Fifty Years of Water Law, 50 Harv. L. Rev. 252, 256 (1937).

Miller & Lux sued Haggin to enjoin the proposed diversion on the ground that it would interfere with their riparian rights to the overflow. The trial court denied relief. By four votes to three, the California Supreme Court reversed. The majority opinion on rehearing, by McKinstry, J., dealt extensively with the development of water law in the West, and covered 200 pages in the California reports and 110 in the Pacific Reporter.]

A grant of public land of the United States carries with it the common-law rights to an innavigable stream thereon, unless the waters are expressly or impliedly reserved by the terms of the patent, or of the statute granting the land, or unless they are reserved by the congressional legislation authorizing the patent or other muniment of title.
* * *

[A] grant of a tract of land bounded by a river or creek not navigable, conveys the land to the thread of the stream; and from a very early day the courts of this state have considered the United States government as the owner of such running waters on the public lands of the United States, and of their beds. Recognizing the United States as the owner of the lands and waters, and as therefore authorized to permit the occupation or diversion of the waters as distinct from the lands, the state courts have treated the prior appropriator of water on the public lands of the United States as having a better right than a subsequent appropriator, on the theory that the appropriation was allowed or licensed by the United States. It has never been held that the right to appropriate waters on the public lands of the United States was derived directly from the state of California as the owner of innavigable streams and their beds; and, since the act of congress granting or recognizing a property in the waters actually diverted and usefully applied on the public lands of the United States, such rights have always been claimed to be deraigned by private persons under the act of congress, from the recognition accorded by the act, or from the acquiescence of the general government in previous appropriations made with its presumed sanction and approval. * * *

It has never been held by the supreme court of the United States, or by the supreme court of this state, that an appropriation of water on the public lands of the United States (made after the act of congress of July 26, 1866, or the amendatory act of 1870) gave to the appropriator the right to the water appropriated as against a grantee of riparian lands, under a grant made or issued prior to the act of 1866, except in a case where the water so subsequently appropriated was reserved by the terms of such grant.

Since, as before, September 28, 1850, the United States has been the owner of lands in California, with power to dispose of the same in such manner, and on such terms and conditions * * * as it deemed proper. But neither the legislation of congress with respect to the disposition of the public lands, nor its apparent acquiescence in the appropriation by individuals of waters thereon, *subsequent* to the act of September, 1850, granting the swamp lands to the state, can affect the title of the state to lands and waters granted by that act. * * *

In Broder v. Water Co., 101 U.S. 274, it appeared: In the year 1853 the defendant completed a canal, through which it had continuously conducted waters and distributed them for mining, agricultural, and other uses; that a portion of the land through which the canal ran was included in the land granted to the Pacific Railroad (under whom plaintiff claimed) by the act of July 2, 1864; that the plaintiff also claimed as a pre-emptor, the inception of his claim as such being a declaratory statement filed August 6, 1866. The court held that the plaintiff was not entitled to have the canal running through his land abated as a nuisance by reason of his pre-emption right, because previous to the initiation of proceedings to secure pre-emption, on the twenty-sixth of July, 1866 * * * congress had enacted a statute, the ninth section of which contained the declaration "that wherever, by priority of possession, rights to the use of water for mining, agricultural, manufacturing, or other purposes have vested and accrued, and the same are recognized and acknowledged by the local customs, laws, and the decisions of courts, the possessors and owners of such vested rights shall be maintained and protected in the same; and the right of way for the construction of ditches and canals, for the purposes aforesaid, is hereby acknowledged and confirmed." The court also held that the plaintiff was not entitled to relief under his deraignment of title from the railroad company, because the grant to the company of July 2, 1864, contained the following reservation:

> "Any lands granted by this act, or the act to which this is an amendment, shall not defeat or impair any pre-emption, homestead, swamp-land, or other *lawful claim,* nor include any government reservation or mineral lands, or the improvements of any *bona fide* settler on any lands returned or denominated as mineral lands, and the timber necessary to support his said improvements as a miner or agriculturist."

In the opinion of the court the section of the act of 1866 above quoted "was rather a voluntary recognition of a pre-existing right of possession, constituting a valid claim to its continued use, than the establishment of a new one," and that the claim of the defendant to the right of way was such a "lawful claim" as was unaffected by the grant to the railroad company made before the act of 1866 was passed. * * *

In the case at bar the grant of the lands to the state (containing no reservation of the waters of flowing streams, express or to be implied from its terms) was made nearly 30 years before the first appropriation of water by the defendant, which was *after* the act of congress of July, 1866, and the amendatory act of 1870. * * *

In Osgood v. Water Co., 56 Cal. 571, it was held that where a person acquired a right, by appropriation, to water upon the public lands of the United States, *before* the issuance of a patent to another for lands through which the stream ran, the patentee's rights were, "by express statutory enactment, subject to the rights of the appropriator." The court cited the amendatory act of congress above referred to, the seventeenth section of which reads:

> "That all patents granted, or pre-emptions or homesteads allowed, shall be subject to any vested and accrued water-rights, or rights to ditches and reservoirs used in connection with such water-rights, as may have been acquired under or recognized by the ninth section of the act of which this is amendatory." * * *

Both Broder v. Water Co. and Osgood v. Water Co. are (by strongest implication) authority for the statement that one who acquired a title to riparian lands from the United States prior to the act of July 26, 1866, could not (in the absence of reservation in his grant) be deprived of his common-law rights to the flow of the stream by one who appropriated its waters after the passage of that act.

Much stress is laid by counsel on the language used in Broder v. Water Co., supra, with reference to the clause in the act of 1866, that water-rights recognized or acknowledged by the local customs, etc., "shall be maintained and protected," "was rather a recognition of a pre-existing right of possession, constituting a valid claim to its continued use, than the establishment of a new one." But this language is to be interpreted in view of the context. The language cannot be construed as a recognition by the court of vested rights in appropriators of water, created by mere appropriation and independent of statute. The case proceeds on the assumption that neither the plaintiff nor the defendant had any rights except such as were granted or recognized by acts of congress. It holds that appropriators of water from streams on (or flowing to) the lands granted by the act of 1864 were "recognized" or admitted to have rights which were protected by that act, because the act by its terms reserved from the grant to the railroad company every "lawful claim;" that one who had been permitted to divert water from those lands had a claim which was not in itself unlawful; and that the reservation included "*every honest claim* evidenced by acts of possession." There is no statement in the opinion in Broder v. Water Co., that except for the reservation found in the act of 1864, and the provision in the act of 1866, the defendant would have any right to the water as against the grantees named in the act first named, or their successors in interest. The court holds that Broder acquired no right by virtue of his preemption, because his proceedings to secure it were begun after the act of 1866, which recognized the prior appropriation of the water as being a right in the appropriator, and that Broder acquired no right under the railroad grant, because the water previously appropriated was reserved in that grant. * * *

[Reversed.]

Notes

1. **California Doctrine.** This is the "California Doctrine" in its purest form, though the term is often applied to any system recognizing both riparian and appropriative rights. Since the early appropriations had been from streams "on the public domain," the California courts later seized upon this phrase and gave it new significance, requiring that the actual diversion of the water must take place on public land. Thus, the California rule came to be that where an appropriator diverted the water from the stream at a point where it touched private land, no rights were acquired that were superior to the later uses of upstream riparians who subsequently acquired their lands. San Joaquin & Kings River Canal & Irr. Co. v. Worswick, 203 P. 999 (Cal. 1922).

2. **Relationship between federal land patents and local law.**
Must a patentee of public domain land analyze federal land statutes to
determine whether the land acquired riparian rights? Or whether a state
may authorize an appropriation of water? Or whether, as between private
rights' holders, one type of right is superior to the other? See Connecticut
v. Massachusetts, 282 U.S. 660 (1931). Compare Sturr v. Beck, 133 U.S.
541 (1890), with Boquillas Land & Cattle Co. v. Curtis, 213 U.S. 339
(1909), as to the effect of local law on the incidents of ownership of land
acquired by patent. In neither case does the Court make a direct connection, but is it merely coincidence that in Dakota, where the Territory had
codified riparian law, the patentee had riparian rights, while in Arizona,
where neither the Territory nor the preceding Mexican State of Sonora
recognized such rights, the patentee acquired none?

In California Oregon Power Co. v. Beaver Portland Cement Co., 295
U.S. 142 (1935), the Supreme Court concluded that federal land laws left
to the states the "power * * * to legislate in respect of waters and water
rights as they deemed wise in the public interest * * * with the right in
each to determine for itself to what extent the rule of appropriation or the
common law rule in respect to riparian rights should obtain. For since
'Congress cannot enforce either rule upon any state,' State of Kansas v.
Colorado, 206 U.S. 46, 94, the full power of choice must remain with the
state." Compare also Borax, Consol. v. City of L.A., 296 U.S. 10 (1935),
and Or. *ex rel.* State Land Bd. v. Corvallis Sand & Gravel Co., 429 U.S.
363 (1977).

As to the extent to which the federal laws reserve to the national
government a residuum of "title to unappropriated water" within the public domain, see Chapter 8, Section 2B.

3. **Riparian rights in Texas.** Texas, by statute, established a cutoff date after which a person acquiring public land would not receive riparian rights. Tex. Water Code Ann. § 11.001. Moreover, Spanish and
Mexican grants of land along the lower Rio Grande have no riparian
rights. State v. Valmont Plantations, 346 S.W.2d 853 (Tex. Civ. App.
1961), aff'd 355 S.W.2d 502 (Tex. 1962). This ruling was modified in State
v. Hidalgo County Water Control & Improvement District No. 18, 443
S.W.2d 728 (Tex. Civ. App. 1969), the case from which *Valmont Plantations* was spun off. The court recognized several "equitable" water rights,
including some held by owners of riparian tracts in Spanish land grants
whose land had been irrigated under the claim to riparian rights rejected
in *Valmont.* The decision was motivated by the "unprecedented situation"
resulting from the fact that two large reservoirs had been constructed on
the Rio Grande by the federal government pursuant to a treaty with Mexico, which had made large quantities of water available for use in Texas
at no expense to irrigators. On "water-short Cibolo Creek," however, the
court refused to find an "equitable right" for use on a riparian Spanish
land grant tract. *In re* Water Rights of Cibolo Creek Watershed, 568
S.W.2d 155 (Tex. Civ. App. 1978).

In 1895 Nebraska passed a comprehensive water code, which the court held prevented the acquisition of any riparian rights in lands thereafter acquired. Crawford Co. v. Hathaway, 93 N.W. 781 (Neb. 1903). Nevertheless, in Brummund v. Vogel, 168 N.W.2d 24 (Neb. 1969), the owner of farm property which abutted a creek claimed the right to use water from this stream for domestic purposes superior to an appropriator's right to build a dam upstream. The landowner was held to have this riparian right despite the fact that he neither pleaded nor proved that he or his predecessors had owned the land before the cutoff date of April 4, 1895. In Koch v. Aupperle, 737 N.W.2d 869, 881 (Nev. 2007), however, the Nebraska Supreme Court rejected *Brummund*: "To the extent *Brummund* suggests that riparian rights can be asserted without proof of their existence, or that there may be a nonriparian common-law right to surface water, it is disapproved."

4. **Additional limitations on riparian rights.** Although riparians are generally regarded as having rights in navigable waters, the Supreme Court of Washington held that since that state's constitution declares that the state owns the bed and shores of all navigable waters up to the line of ordinary high water, an owner of the shore of a navigable lake cannot make a riparian claim to the waters of the lake for irrigation that is good against the state, or against one who appropriates water under state law. State *ex rel.* Ham v. Superior Court, 126 P. 945 (Wash. 1912).

A similar approach in Texas confined riparian rights to low-water flows, with the result that large quantities of the annual flow of variable streams were reserved for use by appropriators. In Motl v. Boyd, 286 S.W. 458 (Tex. 1926), the court said that riparian rights could attach only to waters below the line of highest ordinary flow, which it defined as the highest line of flow which the stream reaches and maintains for a sufficient length of time to become characteristic when its waters are in their ordinary normal and usual condition, uninfluenced by recent rainfall or surface runoff. Texas water officials, trying to introduce some certainty into the rule as a guide to determining the availability of water for appropriation, translated the court's definition of "highest ordinary flow" into "modal flow," that level of water most frequently occurring in daily measurements of the actual flow of the stream. Carter, Proceedings, Water Law Conferences, University of Texas School of Law, 194 (1954).

5. **Economic efficiency in the California Doctrine.** Until the 1928 constitutional amendment on reasonable use, discussed supra p. 283, Note 1, the California Supreme Court generally held that a riparian landowner could enjoin an upstream appropriation even though it caused no present injury. See Anaheim Union Water Co. v. Fuller, supra p. 236, and Pabst v. Finmand, supra p. 280. Nevertheless, there were cases prior to the amendment in which the California Supreme Court refused to enjoin an upstream appropriation. E.g., Chow v. City of Santa Barbara, 22 P.2d 5 (Cal. 1933). In Chowchilla Farms v. Martin, 25 P.2d 435, 450 (Cal. 1933), the court reconciled these two lines of cases by distinguishing ordinary and extraordinary floodwaters: "A consideration of the authorities

upon this subject leads to the conclusion that flood waters in a stream which can be put to a reasonably beneficial use by riparian owners on the stream are not subject to appropriation by an upstream claimant. On the other hand, if the flood waters are not being used by riparians and cannot be put to any beneficial use by them, then, under [Gin Chow], they are, to the extent that the riparian owners cannot put them to any beneficial use, subject to appropriation.

Mark T. Kanazawa, Efficiency in Western Water Law: The Development of the California Doctrine, 27 J. Legal Stud. 159 (1998), reconciles these cases differently. The author tentatively concludes that the court selectively applied these two lines to promote economic efficiency. He hypothesizes that injunctions without regard to injury make economic sense when the number of competing riparians is small because they pave the way for voluntary transfers from riparians to appropriators by giving well-defined property right to the riparians; i.e., the appropriator can pay the riparians to have the injunction lifted if the appropriator's use is sufficiently valuable. This is exactly what happened after the decision in Lux v. Haggin according to the author; the parties in that case negotiated an exchange in which Miller & Lux gave Haggin water and Haggin paid part of the costs of a dam to augment the supply. However, when the number of competing riparians is large, Kanazawa hypothesizes, voluntary transfers are much less likely because of the greater transaction costs associated with negotiating with more parties. In such cases, a court concerned with economic efficiency would not automatically enjoin diversions by appropriators; it would only enjoin them selectively depending on the damage caused to downstream riparians.

6. **Reassessment of *Lux v. Haggin*.** Lux v. Haggin is reassessed in Eric T. Freyfogle, Lux v. Haggin, The Common Law Burden of Modern Water Law, 57 U. Colo. L. Rev. 485 (1986). Professor Freyfogle suggests that the case was burdened by 19th century views of property rights and the common law which continue to dominate modern water law.

FRANCO-AMERICAN CHAROLAISE, LTD. v. OKLAHOMA WATER RESOURCES BOARD

Supreme Court of Oklahoma, 1990.

855 P.2d 568.

OPALA, JUSTICE. This appeal challenges the constitutionality of the 1963 amendments to Oklahoma's water law insofar as the amendments regulate riparian rights. * * * We hold that the Oklahoma riparian owner enjoys a vested common-law right to the reasonable use of the stream. This right is a valuable part of the property owner's "bundle of sticks" and may not be taken for public use without compensation. We further hold that, inasmuch as 60 O.S.1981 § 60, as amended in 1963, limits the riparian owner to domestic use and declares that all other water in the stream becomes public water subject to appropriation without any provision for compensating the riparian owner, the statute violates Art. 2 § 24, Okl. Const. * * *

Since 1897, both the common law and the statutes have operated in Oklahoma to confer riparian and appropriative rights. Though these rights have coexisted in the State for almost 100 years, they are theoretically irreconcilable. The common-law riparian right extends to the reasonable use of the stream or to its natural flow, depending on the jurisdiction; the appropriative right attaches to a fixed amount. The last riparian use asserted has as much priority as the first; the appropriator who takes first has the senior right. In 1963 the legislature attempted to reconcile the two doctrines. * * *

[T]he 1963 amendments provided a validation mechanism as a method for protecting pre-existing beneficial uses, including those of the riparian owner and pre-existing appropriators. All subsequent rights to the use of stream water, except for riparian domestic uses, are to be acquired by appropriation. The stream's natural flow is considered public water and subject to appropriation. The riparian owner may not assert his (or her) common-law right to the use of stream water other than for the domestic uses. * * *

The issue here is whether the legislature can validly abrogate the riparian owner's right to initiate non-domestic reasonable uses in stream water without affording compensation. Art. 2, § 24, Okl. Const. provides in part: "Private property shall not be taken or damaged for public use without just compensation." Private property protected by Art. 2, § 24 includes "easements, personal property, and *every valuable interest which can be enjoyed and recognized as property.*"[42] Further, In Oklahoma Water Resources Board v. Central Oklahoma Master Conservancy District[43] we held: "A 'vested right' is the power to *do certain actions* or possess certain things lawfully, and is substantially a property right. It may be created by common law, by statute or by contract. Once created, it becomes absolute, and is protected from legislative invasion * * * " Therefore, the common-law riparian right to use stream water, as long as that use is reasonable, has been long recognized in Oklahoma law as a private property right.

[T]he legislature may restrict the use of private property by exercise of its police power for the preservation of the public, health, morals, safety and general welfare without compensating the property owner. In Phillips Petroleum Co. v. Corporation Comm'n[46] this court defined the permissible exercise of police power: "[T]he police power is usually exerted merely to regulate the use and enjoyment of property

---

42. Graham v. City of Duncan, Okla., 354 P.2d 458, 461 (1960).

43. Okla., 464 P.2d 748, 755 (1969) (Emphasis added).

46. Okla., 312 P.2d 916 (1956) (quoting 29 C.J.S. §6); * * *.

by the owner, or, if he is deprived of his property outright, it is not taken for public use, but rather destroyed in order to promote the general welfare. * * * " Therefore, in C. C. Julian Oil & Royalties Co. v. Capshaw [292 P. 841 (1930)] we declared that the legislature could regulate a landowner's use and enjoyment of natural resources to prevent waste and infringement on the rights of others. Thus, a statutory regulation of the methods to be used in extracting hydrocarbons was a constitutional exercise of police power where none of the hydrocarbons was taken for public use. Then, in Frost v. Ponca City[48] we held that in the interest of health and safety, the city could exercise its police power to restrict the plaintiff's right to capture hydrocarbons underlying his property, but the city could not remove the hydrocarbons and sell them without compensating the plaintiff.

We, therefore, hold that the 1963 water law amendments are fraught with a constitutional infirmity in that they abolish the right of the riparian owner to assert his (or her) vested interest in the prospective reasonable use of the stream. The riparian owner stands on equal footing with the appropriator. His ownership of riparian land affords him *no right* to the stream water except for limited domestic use. * * *

The OWRB argues the 1963 amendments are a permissible exercise of the police power just as a zoning ordinance would be. That contention is inapposite when, as here, the use of stream water is *not just restricted but is taken for public use.*

Although the 1963 water law amendments provided a mechanism for a riparian owner to "perfect" all beneficial uses initiated prior to the legislation, that mechanism falls short of protecting the riparian owner's common-law appurtenant right. * * * The heart of the riparian right is the right to assert a use at *any time* as long as it does not harm another riparian who has a corresponding right. Further, yesterday's reasonable use by one riparian owner may become unreasonable tomorrow when a fellow riparian owner asserts a new or expanded use. After the 1963 amendments, the riparian owner who wants to expand a use or assert a new use may do so *only as an appropriator.* His use is not judged by its reasonableness but only by its priority in time.

Furthermore, the validation mechanism attempted to forever set in stone the maximum amount of stream water the landowner, *as a riparian owner*, can use. Any use asserted by the landowner, *as an appropriator*, is either denied because no water is available or is given a lower priority than all other uses, including those of appropriators who are non-riparian to the stream. * * * This result is antithetical to the very nature of the common-law riparian right, which places no stock in the fact of past use, present use, or even non-use. * * *

---

48. Okla., 541 P.2d 1312, 1324 (1975).

To assure that the state's resources are put to the most reasonable and beneficial use, we adopt the approach of the Supreme Court of Nebraska in Wasserburger v. Coffee.[54] *Wasserburger* holds that the rights of the riparian owner and the appropriator are to be determined by relative reasonableness. On remand, the trial court shall balance the riparian owners' uses against those of the City * * *.

LAVENDER, VICE CHIEF JUSTICE, concurring in part; dissenting in part:

I must respectfully dissent from that part of the majority opinion holding the 1963 legislative amendments to our State's stream water law unconstitutional under the guise the amendments effected a taking of property without just compensation in violation of Okla. Const. art. 2, § 24. In reaching this result the majority makes several errors.

Initially, it misperceives that future, unquantified use of stream water by a riparian is a vested property right that can only be limited or modified pursuant to judicially mandated common law factors that were generally used to decide piecemeal litigation between competing riparians in water use disputes. Secondly, it misinterprets the plain and unambiguous legislation at issue and it fails to recognize that even assuming a vested property right is at issue, such rights in natural resources like water, may be subject to reasonable limitations or even forfeiture for failure to put the resource to beneficial use. Thirdly, its analysis of the law as to what constitutes a taking of private property requiring just compensation is flawed. In my view the majority errs in such regard by failing to view the legislation as akin to zoning regulation, which although may limit a riparian's open-ended common law right to make use of the water to benefit his land and thereby effect the value of his land, does not deprive him of all economic use of his land or absolutely deprive him of water. The lack of water to a riparian, if it occurs, is caused by his own neglect or inaction by years of failure either to put the water to beneficial use or failure to gain an appropriation permit from the Oklahoma Water Resources Board (OWRB) for uses being made prior to passage of the 1963 amendments or uses made or sought to be made between passage of the amendments and the * * * appropriation at issue here. This mistake of the majority is particularly egregious because it wholly ignores the virtually admitted fact that neither riparians or appropriators own the water they are being allowed to use. All of the people in this State own the water and that ownership interest by the legislation before us is merely being channeled by the Legislature, for the benefit of those owners (i.e. the people), to those uses deemed wise.

The majority has failed to consider persuasive case law from the highest courts of other jurisdictions upholding analogous legislation

---

54. 180 Neb. 149, 141 N.W.2d 738, 743 (1966).

over similar attacks and pronouncements of the United States Supreme Court which lead me to conclude the legislation *on its face* is constitutional. * * * In place of the statutory scheme drafted by the Legislature after years of study and debate the majority acts as a super-legislature by rewriting the water law of this State in accord with its views of prudent public policy * * *. The foundation of this judicial "legislation," relying as it does on the so-called California Doctrine, is illusory at best because the majority ignores pronouncements from the California Supreme Court which has itself recognized the common law doctrine of unquantified future riparian use of stream water is not a vested right, even in the face of a California constitutional provision specifically interpreted to protect it, *when it may impair the promotion of reasonable and beneficial uses of state waters and, in effect, constitute waste of the resource.*[2] * * *

* * * In essence, the majority indicates it relies on the so-called California Doctrine for its position. It, however, nowhere discusses recent authority from California that sheds serious doubt on its analysis. In the case of In Re Waters of Long Valley Creek Stream System[40] the California Supreme Court was not so generous. There it held that the state, through its water board, *may subordinate any future unexercised riparian right below any appropriation awarded prior to user by the riparian when conducting stream wide adjudications because doing so will promote the state's interest in fostering the most reasonable and beneficial uses of scarce water resources.* * * * In my view our Legislature has accomplished nothing more than that approved by the California Supreme Court via the legislation at issue here and its limitations and modifications in regard to the common law reasonable use doctrine.

[E]ven if it be assumed the majority is correct that the riparian had a protectible property interest to some unquantified right to make use of the water at some unspecified time in the future, this common law right could be lost or forfeited by nonuse or, at least, limited to domestic use and appropriative uses granted by the OWRB as sought to be accomplished by the legislation under review. To rule otherwise simply places a common law doctrine as an impenetrable barrier to

---

2. In re Waters of Long Valley Creek Stream System, [599 P.2d 656, 661, f.n. 3 (1979)]. In said case the California Supreme Court said: [A]ppellant also asserts that these common law cases disclose his future right to an unquantified amount of water has become "vested." The assertion is without merit. * * * [R]iparian rights are limited by the concept of reasonable and beneficial use, and they may not be exercised in a manner that is inconsistent with the policy declaration of article X, section 2 of the [California] Constitution. Thus, to the extent that a future riparian right may impair the promotion of reasonable and beneficial uses of state waters, it is inapt to view it as vested. (Emphasis added).

40. [599 P.2d 656 (1979).]

efficient management of a natural resource never deemed to be owned by private landowners.

The majority further fails in its analysis in the area of just compensation law. It relies on the case of Frost v. Ponca City[57] which ruled although a city may exercise its police power to restrict a landowner's right to capture hydrocarbons underlying his property in the interest of health and safety, if a city (or a public entity) itself removes the hydrocarbons and sells them the private landowner must be compensated. The majority fails to see at least two significant distinguishing factors between the situation involved in Frost and that facing us today. One, Frost relied on the fact hydrocarbons, such as oil and gas underlying a landowner's property, were subject to the law of capture, i.e. the landowner had the exclusive right to drill for, produce, or otherwise gain possession of such substances and when reduced to actual possession, the landowner obtained an absolute ownership interest in the substance. After the ownership interest was established the landowner could sell the hydrocarbons. *Riparians were never deemed to have such exclusive rights in regard to stream water as shown above and the majority admits this.*

Secondly, in Frost the landowners were *totally restricted from removing the hydrocarbons themselves or reducing them to actual possession under the law of capture. Here Appellee riparians are not totally restricted from gaining the use of stream water in the future.* The only requirement is that they apply for an appropriation permit. Of course they also may use the water for domestic purposes without a permit and the legislation provided an opportunity to protect preexisting uses. No State or public law prohibits their use of stream water, but only inaction on their part. In view of these differences it is inapposite for the majority to rely on *Frost.*

Instead of placing unwarranted reliance on *Frost* to strike down the legislation under review I would uphold it by ruling it is akin to zoning regulations which have long been upheld by the courts. * * *

The United States Supreme Court has long recognized that land use regulations normally do not effect a taking of property as long as the regulations at issue substantially advance legitimate state interests and do not deny a landowner economically viable use of his land. No one argues here, including the majority, that the statutory scheme under review does not substantially advance legitimate state interests. The State interests advanced are numerous. Among them are direct promotion of the efficient management of our State's water resources by preventing waste. It provides a semblance of certainty in the area of water rights and distributes this valuable resource *which is owned by all the public* in response to demonstrated need. There-

FROST

---

57. 541 P.2d 1321 (Okla. 1975).

fore, the only real question in the taking context is whether the legislation has deprived riparians of the economically viable use of their land. * * *

Nowhere is there evidence in this record that the legislation itself has rendered the use of riparian land economically unviable. Riparians are not estopped from using their land for any purpose or gaining water rights in connection therewith as specified above. * * * In sum, I would hold the legislation on its face did not constitute a taking of private property for which compensation is required just as land use regulation does not constitute a taking of private property when the owner is not denied economically viable use of his land. * * *

Notes

1. **Abolition of riparian rights in other states.** Oregon was the first California Doctrine state to incorporate riparian rights into its appropriation system. The Water Code of 1909 made all waters within the state appropriable for beneficial use, provided no "vested rights" were taken away or impaired. The vested rights of riparian proprietors were defined to include only the actual application of water to a beneficial use prior to the passage of the Act. Or. Laws 1909, ch. 216, p. 319. The "Oregon plan" has been upheld as constitutional. Cal. Or. Power Co. v. Beaver Portland Cement Co., 73 F.2d 555 (9th Cir. 1934), aff'd on other grounds 295 U.S. 142 (1935). The statute made no provision for compensating the riparian owner for the loss of his unused rights. A similar Kansas statute was upheld by a three-judge federal court, in a decision affirmed without opinion by the United States Supreme Court. Baumann v. Smrha, 145 F. Supp. 617 (D. Kan. 1956), aff'd 352 U.S. 863 (1956).

In re Adjudication of Water Rights in the Upper Guadalupe River, 642 S.W.2d 438 (Tex. 1982), upheld that part of the Texas Water Adjudication Act that limited riparian claimants to the quantity of water actually beneficially used during one of the five years between 1963 and 1967. The court held that after notice and upon reasonable terms, the statute's termination of the riparians' continuous nonuse of water is not a taking of their property. The court cited the Oregon and Kansas cases, and drew additional support from Texaco, Inc. v. Short, 454 U.S. 516, 530 (1982). In that case, the Supreme Court said:

"We have concluded that the State may treat a mineral interest that has not been used for 20 years and for which no statement of claim has been filed as abandoned; it follows that, after abandonment, the former owner retains no interest for which he may claim compensation. *It is the owner's failure to make any use of the property*—and not the action of the State—that causes the lapse of the property right; there is no 'taking' that requires compensation. The requirement that an owner of a property interest that has not been used for 20 years must come forward and file a current statement of claim is not itself a 'taking.'"

Although Washington adopted a water code in 1917 which provided for appropriation through a permit system and stated that "any right [to water] * * * shall be hereafter acquired * * * in the manner provided and not otherwise," it was not until 1985 that courts established that the code terminated riparian rights which had not been exercised within a reasonable time after the code's adoption. *In re* Deadman Creek Drainage Basin, 694 P.2d 1071 (Wash. 1985). The court determined that 15 years was a reasonable time and held that all riparian rights not exercised by 1932 were relinquished.

Unused riparian rights have been effectively abolished and the post-statute water user must go the appropriation route in all of the other California Doctrine states, except California, Oklahoma, and Nebraska. The Oregon system was expressly adopted in South Dakota (except for domestic uses), S.D. Codified Laws § 46–1–9. Under the South Dakota statutes, S.D. Codified Laws §§ 46–1–9(2), 46–1–5(1), 46–1–6(7), a riparian owner has vested rights to use stream water for irrigation purposes only to the extent of previous beneficial use, but he has the further right to use water for domestic use (irrigation of gardens, trees, shrubbery or orchards and stock watering), and such use takes precedence over all appropriative rights. Belle Fourche Irr. Dist. v. Smiley, 204 N.W.2d 105 (S.D. 1973).

2. **Diminished importance of riparian rights in California.** California, which gave the doctrine its name, remains the quintessential California Doctrine or "dual-system" state. Nevertheless, a variety of factors has diminished the practical importance and theoretical primacy of riparian rights. Such factors include use of the "source of title" test for riparian lands, supra p. 239, Note 1, which produces a continuing contraction in riparian lands. Similarly, the exclusion of multi-season storage from a riparian's rights is a significant limitation because seasonal storage is often necessary where dependability is important. See Colo. Power Co. v. Pac. Gas & Elec. Co., 24 P.2d 495 (Cal. 1933).

Ironically, however, a rule that seemingly gave riparian rights the greatest primacy over appropriate rights has most undermined that primacy: the riparian proprietor's pre-1928 ability to enjoin an appropriative use even though that use caused no injury. See Anaheim Union Water Co. v. Fuller, supra p. 236. This rule made it easier for appropriators to acquire prescriptive rights against riparians because any appropriative use started the limitations statute running against downstream riparians. See Pabst v. Finmand, supra p. 280. More significantly, reaction to a particularly egregious application of the rule in Herminghaus v. Southern California Edison Co., 252 P. 607 (Cal. 1926), produced an amendment to the California constitution which has significantly altered the relationship between riparian and appropriative rights. The amendment, referred to in footnote 2 of Justice Lavender's dissent in the principal case, requires all uses to be "reasonable." Thus, in a conflict between riparian and appropriative uses, only "reasonable" riparian uses prevail.

Initially, it appeared that the amendment, now found at Article X, Section 2, was purely remedial; that is, it appeared that a riparian proprietor could not enjoin an upstream appropriation which interfered with the riparian's "unreasonable" use of water but could obtain damages. See, e.g., United States v. Gerlach Live Stock Co. , 339 U.S. 725 (1950). However, in Joslin v. Marin Municipal Water District, 429 P.2d 889 (Cal. 1967), the court held that the amendment substantively modified riparian rights to preclude even an award of damages for unreasonable riparian uses. In addition, although early cases interpreting the amendment, equated "unreasonable" uses with "waste," *Joslin* seems to hold that a riparian use may become "unreasonable" simply because socially or economically more valuable uses develop. See supra p. 278, Note 5. See also Clifford W. Schulz & Gregory S. Weber, Changing Judicial Attitudes Towards Property Rights in California Water Resources: From Vested Rights to Utilitarian Reallocations, 19 Pac. L.J. 1031 (1988); Eric T. Freyfogle, Context and Accommodation in Modern Property Law, 41 Stan. L. Rev. 1529 (1989).

The amendment has significantly impacted unexercised riparian rights. In Tulare Irrigation District v. Lindsay-Strathmore Irrigation District, 45 P.2d 972 (Cal. 1935), the court found that the amendment protects the "prospective reasonable beneficial use" of riparians and held unconstitutional a statutory provision which terminated riparian rights after ten years of nonuse. Nevertheless, in the *Long Valley* case, the California Supreme Court held that unexercised riparian rights can be "subordinated" to appropriations in a statutory streamwide adjudication of water rights conducted by the state water board. See the text accompanying footnote 40 of the dissenting opinion in the principal case. "Subordination" can include a loss of priority to appropriations existing at the time of adjudication and to any future appropriations which are authorized before riparian rights are exercised. For all practical purposes, "subordination" is equivalent to extinguishment of unexercised riparian rights, albeit subordination can result only from a statutory adjudication by the state water board, not from private litigation. In reaching its conclusion, the court in *Long Valley* relied heavily on the amendment's directive to foster reasonable uses of water, finding that unexercised riparian rights deter water development, foster costly piecemeal litigation, and impair state administration of water rights.

3. **Alteration of riparian rights by eastern permit systems.** In the eastern states which adopted permit systems, most exercises of riparian rights initiated in the future (in the areas where the statutes apply) require a permit, the issuance of which is to some degree discretionary. Permits are not specifically limited to riparians in most states. See, e.g., Del. Code Ann. tit. 7, §§ 6003, 6004; Fla. Stat. § 373.219.

It is not clear in all of these states just what effect the statutes have on existing uses under riparian law. In some states it is specifically stated that the uses must be confirmed by a permit. Fla. Stat. § 373.226; N.J. Stat. Ann. § 58:1A–6. All of the other statutes are subject to the interpretation that a permit is required for continuation of an existing use, and all permits are subject to denial on various grounds of administrative discretion. All are issued for short terms and many are subject to discretionary cancellation. In many cases the quantity of water a riparian may withdraw and the arrangement for distribution of water among permit holders in times of shortage may be changed from what would have been allowable under common law.

These extensive changes in riparian rights might raise constitutional questions. Much of discussion of such questions has occurred, but no courts have ruled. Few commentators have qualms. E.g., National Water Commission, Water Policies for the Future, supra p. 44, Note 3, at 282–283.

4. **Purchase of unused riparian rights.** One way to eliminate unused riparian rights is for an appropriator to buy them. In *Tulare,* supra p. 330, Note 2, speaking of the powers of condemnation enjoyed by public districts, the court said, "as to prospective uses, however, it is obvious that when, as here, the appropriator takes the water and devotes the same to a public use, prior to the time such prospective needs arise, a public use has intervened as to the quantity required for such future uses. The appropriator may not desire to appropriate the water and to construct large and expensive works with the possibility constantly in the offing that the riparians, who have been protected by a declaration of their rights in the water for future purposes will increase their reasonable and beneficial use of the water, so that ultimately, perhaps, none is left for appropriation. The appropriator may and probably would desire to condemn the riparians' right to use of the water in the stream for these prospective purposes. No good reason suggests itself why the appropriator should not be permitted to do this in the injunction suit by means of an inverse condemnation. The same compelling reasons that exist for permitting such a procedure when the entire riparian right is sought to be condemned likewise exists where the appropriator simply desires to condemn the right of the riparian to whatever additional water he may later need for prospective reasonable beneficial purposes. In both cases, the all important fact must exist that a public use has attached, but once that is present, this procedure seems to us sensible and well calculated to prevent multiplicity of suits and interminable delays." 45 P.2d at 990-91.

5. **Resolving riparian/appropriation conflicts by augmenting supply.** Some of California's riparian-appropriation controversies have been given the "California solution" under which water problems are solved by pouring water on them, i.e., by augmenting supply rather than regulating demand. The United States Bureau of Reclamation's Central Valley Project and the State Department of Water Resource's State Water Project annually release water from their reservoirs to supply 370,300 acre feet to Sacramento River riparians and 295,000 acre feet for use on land riparian to the Feather, Yuba and Bear Rivers, in addition to releases of appropriated water for delivery pursuant to contracts with districts serving non-riparian irrigated land. David B. Anderson, Riparian

Water Rights in California 6-8 (Staff Paper No. 4, Governor's Comm'n to Review California Water Rights Law (1977)).

6. **A reversal of the historic trend.** In a reversal of the usual historic pattern, the Hawaii Supreme Court in 1973 adopted common law riparian rights. McBryde Sugar Co. v. Robinson, 504 P.2d 1330 (Haw. 1973). Subsequently, several large irrigators sued, alleging that enforcement of the *McBryde* decision would terminate their existing transbasin diversions of water and would result in a taking of property contrary to the federal constitution. In Robinson v. Ariyoshi, 753 F.2d 1468 (9th Cir. 1985), the Ninth Circuit agreed. The Ninth Circuit assumed that the Hawaii Supreme Court was free to overrule the territorial cases and adopt a new water law. However, the court ruled that the new law could only be applied prospectively and could not "divest" rights that were "vested" before the *McBryde* decision. Finding that the plaintiffs' transbasin diversions were vested rights, the court held that these rights could not be divested except through the state's exercise of its powers of eminent domain. Subsequently, the United States Supreme Court vacated the judgment and remanded the case to the Ninth Circuit for reconsideration on ripeness grounds. 477 U.S. 902 (1986). Ultimately, the Ninth Circuit dismissed the case. Finding that the state, to that date, had not interfered with the plaintiffs' diversions, the court held that the "inchoate and speculative cloud" created by the *McBryde* decision was insufficient to make the controversy ripe. 887 F.2d 215 (9th Cir. 1989).

In 1987 Hawaii adopted a water code, Haw. Rev. Stat. 174C. The code requires all existing users to file a declaration of use, § 174C–27; except for personal domestic use, permits are required of all users in water management areas (designated water short regions), § 174C–48. Water use is not regulated outside water management areas, but riparian principles, including restrictions on transbasin diversions, apparently apply. Within water management areas, the code allows permits to be issued for transportation and use of water outside the watershed of origin "the common law of the State to the contrary notwithstanding." § 174C–49(c). The law of water rights in Hawaii and the affect of the water code are examined in Douglas W. MacDougal, Testing the Current: The Water Code and the Regulation of Hawaii's Water Resources, 10 U. Haw. L. Rev. 205 (1988).

7. **Water rights and constitutional "takings."** For a recent case exploring the application of takings principles to water rights, see Tulare Lake Basin Water Storage Dist. v. United States, 49 Fed. Cl. 313 (2001), infra p. 608 (contractual entitlements). For a general discussion of constitutional "takings" and water rights see Joseph L. Sax, The Constitution, Property Rights and the Future of Water Law, 61 U. Colo. L. Rev. 257 (1990); see also Jan G. Laitos, Regulation of Natural Resource Use and Development in Light of the "New" Takings Clause, 34 Rocky Mtn. Min. L. Inst. 1 (1988). On the question of whether courts "take" property in overruling earlier decisions and altering property rights see Williamson Chang, Unraveling Robinson v. Ariyoshi: Can Courts "Take" Property,

2 U. Haw. L. Rev. 57 (1979); Bradford H. Lamb, Robinson v. Ariyoshi: A Federal Intrusion Upon State Water Law, 17 Envtl. L. 325 (1987); Barton H. Thompson, Jr., Judicial Takings, 76 Va. L. Rev. 1449 (1990).

       8. **Critique of *Franco-American Charolaise.*** The principal case is reviewed and critiqued in Gary D. Allison, Franco-American Charolaise: The Never Ending Story, 30 Tulsa L.J. 1 (1994).

Chapter 4

GROUNDWATER

SECTION 1. DOCTRINES

JAMES W. CROSBY, III, A LAYMAN'S GUIDE TO GROUNDWATER HYDROLOGY

Charles E. Corker, Groundwater Law, Management and Administration, National Water Commission, Legal Study No. 6, Chapter II, 38-45, 65, 68-70 (1971).

A. What is Groundwater

[W]e adopt the definition of groundwater employed by Professor William C. Walton (1970, p. 29) in Groundwater Resource Evaluation:

> "Water that exists in the interstices of rocks is called subsurface water * * *; that part of subsurface water in interstices completely saturated with water is called groundwater."

* * * The subsurface water which Walton excludes from his definition of groundwater is * * * water above the zone of saturation, not generally capable of withdrawal through wells but available, in part, to plant life. * * *

To understand the groundwater environment, one needs only to consider the void spaces, or *porosity*, of an accumulation of sand or gravel; or to view the fractures and crevices in the granites or limestones that form the walls of a road cut; or to note the open spaces that occur between the successive lava flows exposed in the walls of a valley. Picture then, the environment that would exist if these unconsolidated or consolidated rock masses were partially submerged beneath water, perhaps by rising waters of a lake or reservoir. The air occupying the different types of openings would be displaced by water which, in the natural setting, would be called groundwater. The upper surface of the water-saturated zone, or the air-water interface, would be called the water table. Should impermeable materials be present at the normal position of the upper surface of the zone of saturation, no water table exists. Groundwater sometimes is confined under pressure between or under impermeable or semi-permeable rocks in much the

334

same manner that water is pressurized in a pipeline network. Water in wells penetrating through impermeable material into the underlying permeable materials may rise above the top of the aquifer or water-bearing formation. Such groundwater is said to be under artesian pressure. The pressure is from gravity, just as is the water pressure on a dam impounding water in a surface reservoir.

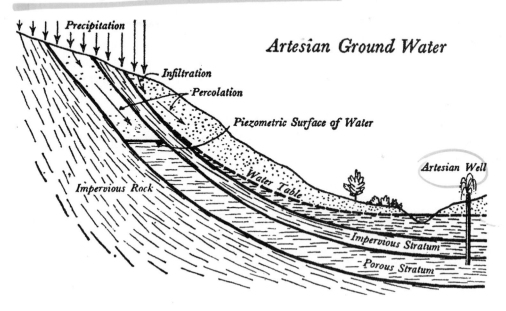

Artesian Ground Water

Depending upon the type of rock material saturated, the voids or empty spaces can be expected to range from about one percent to more than 30 percent. At saturation, in other words, such rocks can contain between one and 30 or more percent of their total volume as water. Much of this water might be contained in voids so small that, even given the opportunity, it could never drain out; it would be retained as though the rock were a blotter. Such water would not flow into wells, and hence it could not be extracted from the ground by any normal means.

The capacity of a rock to transmit water through its interconnected pore spaces is called its *permeability*. The capacity of a porous material to store water need have no bearing on its capacity to transmit water. Thus, a clay usually has high porosity but low permeability. On the other hand, an unconsolidated gravel may have both high porosity and high permeability. * * *

The relatively small size of rock openings and the tortuous nature of the tunnel-like interconnected pore spaces present tremendous frictional resistance to the movement of groundwater. This factor is dominant in establishing the permeability of a porous material. Frictional limitations to flow, coupled with the typically low gradients (or slopes), contribute to the very low flow velocities prevalent in the groundwater environment. Normal flow velocities range from five feet per day to five feet per year. However, velocities as high as 100 feet per day have been reported.

The saturated, permeable earth materials from which significant quantities of water can be produced are called *aquifers*. [W]e must distinguish still further between unconfined (water table) aquifers and confined (artesian) aquifers. The water level in wells penetrating water table aquifers will stand at the level of the water table where the pressure is that of the atmosphere. On the contrary, the water level in an artesian well will stand at the elevation of an imaginary pressure surface, some distance above the aquifer.

When water table wells are pumped, stored waters are removed by physically dewatering the pore spaces, first those in the immediate cone of depression. This is not true for confined conditions. When an artesian well flows or is pumped, a cone of depression is created in the pressure surface but no physical dewatering of aquifer pore volume occurs. The pores remain at full saturation as long as confinement exits, and throughout the confined portion of the aquifer. Waters released from storage are derived entirely from elastic rebound of the aquifer, from expansion of the aquifer skeleton and from expansion of the water. Each of these, in turn, is attributable to the relief of pressure. Because neither rock material nor water is notably compressible it is obvious that the quantities of stored waters made available by their expansion will be small. The amount of water released from storage for each foot of water level decline in the artesian case is much less than for the comparable water table case.

The astute layman will immediately wonder about the circumstance in which the pressure surface of an artesian aquifer drops below the bottom of the confining stratum. Will not physical dewatering of the aquifer then occur? Obviously, yes. When the confining pressure is dissipated, the system reverts to the water table condition and removal of waters from the interstices follows. * * *

[A] special class of hydrogeologic conditions are known as perched water bodies and have perched water tables. Perched waters form whenever the conditions of geologic structure and permeability restrict the free gravitational seepage of * * * waters, causing their build-up in local accumulations at elevations above the regional water table. An analogous condition would be presented by a porcelain saucer buried in a tank of sand through which waters are allowed to seep. Some of the downward moving water would be captured by the saucer and would form a suspended zone of saturation.

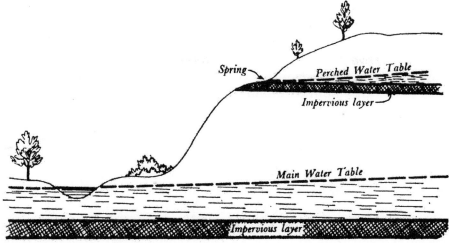

[A9465]

Underground rivers flowing through caverns are rare * * *. However, moving water which is groundwater in one location, surface water in another location, and again groundwater is a very common phenomenon which complicates water "ownership." Nearly all groundwater originates from surface sources and is subject to just such a succession of metamorphoses. Depending upon the fluid circulation pattern, the time sequence can be measured in minutes, days, years, or geologic periods.

Note

Importance of groundwater. Devin L. Galloway et al., U.S. Geological Survey Circular No. 1247, Evolving Issues and Practices in Managing Ground-Water Resources: Case Studies on the Role of Science 1 (2003):

"Ground water is among the Nation's most important natural resources. It is the source of drinking water to more than 140 million residents, or about half of the Nation's population. It is the primary source of drinking water for nearly all of the rural population, as well as for some of our largest metropolitan areas. Nearly 50 billion gallons of ground water are used each day in support of the Nation's agricultural economy. In several midwestern states, ground water provides more than ninety percent of the water used for irrigation. Ground water also plays a crucial role in sustaining stream flow, particularly during droughts and other low-flow periods. Moreover, in recent years, increased attention has been given to the integral role of ground water in maintaining the health of riparian, aquatic, and wetland ecosystems."

STATE v. MICHELS PIPELINE CONSTRUCTION, INC.
Supreme Court of Wisconsin, 1974.
63 Wis. 2d 278, 217 N.W.2d 339.

WILKIE, JUSTICE. * * * Michels Pipeline Construction, Inc., contracted with the Metropolitan Sewerage Commission of Milwaukee
county to install a 60-inch-diameter sewer in the Root River Parkway,
Greenfield, Wisconsin. * * * The complaint alleged that in September
of 1972 the defendants began pumping water from wells in the city of
Greenfield at a rate of 5,500 gallons per minute in order to dewater
the soil to a depth sufficient to permit tunneling for the sewer, approximately 40 feet beneath the ground surface. The complaint alleged
that numerous citizens were caused great hardship by the drying up of
wells, decreasing capacity and water quality in others, and by the
cracking of foundations, basement walls and driveways, due to subsidence of the soil. The State asked that the defendants be ordered to
conduct construction of the sewer so as not to create a nuisance and to
take action to eliminate or ameliorate the hardship and adverse effect
imposed upon state citizens.

The defendants demurred to the complaint on the ground that it
did not state facts sufficient to constitute a cause of action. * * * The
trial court granted the demurrer [because] Huber v. Merkel[14] established that there is no cause of action for interference with ground water. This is a correct statement of the holding of that case. In Huber v.
Merkel an owner of real estate attempted to have another landowner
in his vicinity enjoined from wasting and unreasonably using water
from artesian wells on the person's property. The defendant allowed
his wells to flow continuously, the excess simply spilling on the ground
and this adversely affected the artesian pressure of all the wells which
tapped the same aquifer. This court held that it was the almost universal consensus of judicial opinion that: "* * * If the waters simply
percolate through the ground, without definite channel, they belong to
the realty in which they are found, and the owner of the soil may divert, consume, or cut them off with impunity. * * *"

The basis for this rule of absolute ownership of percolating
ground water was a feeling that the ways of underground water were
too mysterious and unpredictable to allow the establishment of adequate and fair rules for regulation of competing rights to such water.
So the English courts adopted the position that everyone was permitted to take and use all of which they could get possession. * * *

[T]oday scientific knowledge in the field of hydrology has certainly
advanced to the point where a cause and effect relationship can be established between a tapping of underground water and the level of the

---

14. (1903), 117 Wis. 355, 94 N.W. 354.

water table in the area so that liability can be fairly adjudicated consonant with due process. Our scientific knowledge also establishes the interdependence of all water systems.

* * * The Huber v. Merkel case certainly gives no explanation of why a property right in ground water should be an exception to the general maxim—*sic utere tuo ut alienum non laedas.*

Also, although at the time of the decision of Huber v. Merkel the English rule did probably prevail, it was not a common-law rule of venerable, entrenched and ancient origin. The first decisions which enunciated the doctrine were decided in the early 1840's only a short time before Wisconsin achieved statehood. * * *

For the reasons discussed above, we overrule our decision in Huber v. Merkel and for that reason we find it necessary to adopt a rule of law more in harmony with present scientific and legal principles.

What rule should this court now adopt as to the use of percolating ground water? There are three distinct doctrines applied in various American jurisdictions regarding rights in percolating water:

(a) The English or common-law rule:

"* * * the person who owns the surface may dig therein, and apply all that is there found to his own purposes at his free will and pleasure; and if, in the exercise of such right, he intercepts or drains off the water collected from underground springs in his neighbor's well, this inconvenience to his neighbor falls within the description of damnum absque injuria, which cannot become the ground of an action. * * *"

There is one limitation that the actions may not be motivated by malice and waste of water can be actionable. Although framed in property language this doctrine is really a rule of capture. The landowner may sell and grant his right to withdraw the water to others.

(b) Reasonable Use:

As stated in Corpus Juris Secundum:

"In some states, the rule of the common law followed in early decisions has given way to the doctrine of reasonable use limiting the right of a landowner to percolating water in his land to such an amount of water as may be necessary for some useful or beneficial purpose in connection with the land from which it is taken, not restricting his right to use the water for any useful purpose on his own land, and not restricting his right to use it elsewhere in the absence of proof of injury to adjoining landowners. * * *"

(c) Correlative rights:

Again Corpus Juris Secundum defines this doctrine as:

"Under the rule of correlative rights, the rights of all landowners over a common basin, saturated strata, or underground reservoir are coequal or correlative, and one cannot extract more than his share of the water, even for use on his own land, where others' rights are injured thereby."

* * * This doctrine applies the basic rules of the reasonable use doctrine, but calls for apportionment of underground water where there is not a sufficient supply for all reasonable uses. We are not shown here that water conditions in Wisconsin are so critical as to necessitate the adoption of this doctrine. Also the administrative difficulties of a court trying to make such an apportionment would militate against its adoption.

The "reasonable use" doctrine has been widely adopted in the United States. However, a close reading of the language of the doctrine shows that it is not a very radical departure from the common-law rule. It still contains quite a broad privilege to use ground water. * * * This is because the term "reasonable" has a very special restricted meaning. [A] use of water that causes harm is nevertheless reasonable if it is made in connection with the overlying land. * * * The withdrawal of water for use elsewhere for beneficial purposes such as municipal supply or domestic supply is not "reasonable" in this special sense, but such removal may be made without liability if no harm results.

The "reasonable use" rule basically only affords protection from cities withdrawing large quantities of water for municipal utilities. The rule forces cities to pay those affected by such excessive use damages or the cost of new wells and pumping equipment and is very much in accord with policies of loss distribution and requiring the beneficiaries of harmful activities to pay the costs thereof. However, under the rule there is no apportionment of water as between adjoining landowners. If water is withdrawn for a beneficial use on the land from which it is taken there is no liability for any harm to adjoining property owners. In effect, the rule gives partial protection to small wells against cities or water companies, but not protection from a large factory or apartment building on the neighboring land.

We choose not to adopt any of the three rules here discussed, but rather to adopt the rule set forth in Tentative Draft No. 17 of the Restatement of the Law Second, Torts, as proposed on April 26, 1971, for adoption by the American Law Institute. * * * The proposed section of the Restatement Second reads as follows:

"Sec. 858A. NON-LIABILITY FOR USE OF GROUND WATER — EXCEPTIONS. "A possessor of land or his grantee who withdraws ground water from the land and uses it for a beneficial purpose is not subject to liability for interference with the use of water by another, unless (a) The withdrawal of water causes unreasonable harm through lowering the water table or reducing artesian pressure, * * *."

Thus the rule preserves the basic expression of a rule of nonliability—a privilege if you will—to use ground water beneath the land. The formulation of the exception to this basic rule recognizes that there is usually enough water for all users so that apportionment is not necessary but that the problem is who shall bear the costs of deepening prior wells, installing pumps, paying increased pumping costs, etc., necessitated by a lowering of the water table by a large user. The common law placed the burden of making improvements on each user. The "reasonable use" rule gives protection to existing wells if the water withdrawal is taken off the land for use elsewhere but not if the water is used for beneficial purposes on the overlying land. The proposed rule of the Restatement Second would place the matter of cost on the same rational basis as the rule applicable to surface streams, the reasonableness of placing the burden upon one party or the other.

The comment on the meaning of "unreasonable harm" as used in the Restatement rule explains that as in other situations, reasonableness will vary with the circumstances. Later users with superior economic resources should not be allowed to impose costs upon smaller water users that are beyond their economic capacity. The comment also address [sic] itself to the fear of the respondents that a change in the rule concerning use of percolating water will allow the first user to dictate the depth of wells and the water table to all later users. The comment explains that it is usually reasonable to give equal treatment to persons similarly situated and to place similar burdens on each.

In adopting the rule proposed in the Restatement of Torts, we necessarily overrule the order of the trial court sustaining the demurrer here, and we remand for further proceedings in the trial court.

Notes

1. **Absolute ownership doctrine.** The English doctrine of absolute ownership survives in some eastern states and Texas. The Maine Supreme Court refused to depart from it in Maddocks v. Giles, 728 A.2d 150 (Me. 1999). The court's reasons were that the absolute ownership doctrine was not shown to interfere with water use or result in unwise water policy; the state legislature, not the judiciary, "should be weighing the heavy policy considerations involved in this issue, not the least of which is the reliance of land owners on the present property laws"; and the legislature had recently chosen not to act on the recommendation of a study it commissioned that urged it to adopt reasonable use principles.

Texas has long supplemented the absolute ownership doctrine with legislation, repeatedly modified, providing for local groundwater conservation districts. For decades, the few districts that were created had limited powers and engaged in little groundwater management. In 1997, the

Texas Legislature enacted Senate Bill 1 to facilitate creating local districts in areas expected to experience groundwater problems, to require permits from districts for large wells, and to give districts authority to regulate water transfers outside their boundaries.

In Sipriano v. Great Spring Waters of Am., Inc., 1 S.W.3d 75, 78-80 (Tex. 1999), the Texas Supreme Court rejected a claim that it should replace the absolute ownership doctrine with the reasonable use doctrine:

"[In Senate Bill 1,] the Legislature expressly stated that '[g]roundwater conservation districts * * * are the state's preferred method of groundwater management.' * * * [B]y Senate Bill 1 the Legislature has chosen a process that permits the people most affected by groundwater regulation in particular areas to participate in democratic solutions to their groundwater issues. It would be improper for courts to intercede at this time by changing the common-law framework within which the Legislature has attempted to craft regulations to meet this state's groundwater-conservation needs. Given the Legislature's recent actions to improve Texas's groundwater management, we are reluctant to make so drastic a change as abandoning our rule of capture and moving into the arena of water-use regulation by judicial fiat. It is more prudent to wait and see if Senate Bill 1 will have its desired effect, and to save for another day the determination of whether further revising the common law is an appropriate prerequisite to preserve Texas's natural resources and protect property owners' interests."

In 2001, the Legislature enacted Senate Bill 2 to strengthen the regulatory powers of local groundwater conservation districts. For example, districts may regulate the spacing of wells and limit groundwater production based on tract size to minimize well interference, prevent land subsidence, protect water quality, and minimize as far as practicable the drawdown of a water table or reduction of artesian pressure. Tex. Water Code Ann. § 36.116. Senate Bill 2 addresses conflict between rights under the absolute ownership doctrine and conservation district regulation by stating that landowners' rights in groundwater "are hereby recognized * * * except as those rights may be limited or altered by rules promulgated by a district." § 36.002.

2. **Reasonable use doctrine.** *Michaels Pipeline* reported that the reasonable use doctrine has been widely adopted in the United States. This statement is more true of eastern states than western states.

Arizona has long adhered to the reasonable use doctrine, In re General Adjudication of All Rights to Use Water in Gila River System & Source, 857 P.2d 1236 (Ariz. 1993), but a 1980 groundwater management act supplanted it in large parts of the state designated as groundwater management areas. See infra p. 378, Note 1. Even where the doctrine still applies, there have been significant statutory modifications, e.g., to allow freer transportation of water and generally prohibit irrigation of new overlying acreage in Irrigation Non-Expansion Areas. Ariz. Rev. Stat. §§ 45-437, -453, -544.

Many cases adopting the reasonable use doctrine are titled "_____ v. City of _____." Why?

3. **Correlative rights doctrine.** The leading correlative rights state is California, where the doctrine traces back to Katz v. Walkinshaw, 74 P. 766, 772 (Cal. 1903):

"The controversies arising will naturally divide into classes. There will be disputes between persons or corporations claiming rights to take such waters from the same strata or source for use on distant lands. There is no statute on this subject, as there now is concerning appropriations of surface streams; but the case is not without precedent. * * * The principles which, before the adoption of the Civil Code, were applied to protect appropriations and possessory rights in visible streams, will, in general, be found applicable to such appropriations of percolating waters, either for public or private use, and will suffice for their protection as against other appropriators. Such rights are usufructuary only, and the first taker who with diligence puts the water in use will have the better right. * * * In controversies between an appropriator for use on distant land and those who own land overlying the water-bearing strata, there may be two classes of such landowners—those who have used the water on their land before the attempt to appropriate, and those who have not previously used it, but who claim the right afterwards to do so. Under the decision in this case the rights of the first class of landowners are paramount to that of one who takes the water to distant land, but the landowner's right extends only to the quantity of water that is necessary for use on his land, and the appropriator may take the surplus. As to those landowners who begin the use after the appropriation, and who, in order to obtain the water, must restrict or restrain the diversion to distant lands or places, it is perhaps best not to state a positive rule. * * * Disputes between overlying landowners, concerning water for use on the land, to which they have an equal right, in cases where the supply is insufficient for all, are to be settled by giving to each a fair and just proportion. And here again we leave for future settlement the question as to the priority of rights between such owners who begin the use of the waters at different times. The parties interested in the question are not before us."

The California Supreme Court soon supplied the two rankings missing from *Katz*. It held in Burr v. Maclay Rancho Water Co., 98 P. 260 (Cal. 1908), that an overlying landowner who has not yet used groundwater on the land can obtain a declaratory judgment to protect the paramount right to do so as against an appropriator who has previously put the water to use. In Hudson v. Dailey, 105 P. 748 (Cal. 1909), it said without mentioning priority of use that the rights of overlying landowners are equal and correlative. Among overlying owners, however, uncertainty remains about the specifics of what *Katz* called a "fair and just proportion" for each.

An overlying city's withdrawal for municipal supply is not a correlative right but rather an appropriation; the city does not become substituted as administrator of the rights of its inhabitants owning overlying land. City of San Bernadino v. City of Riverside, 198 P. 784 (Cal. 1921).

4. **Judicial mixing of the reasonable use and correlative rights doctrines and legislative modification.** In MacArtor v. Graylyn Crest III Swim Club, Inc., 187 A.2d 417 (Del. Ch. 1963), a large well that supplied the club's swimming pool lowered the water table below a neighboring householder's shallow well. Both parties apparently were overlying users. Applying what it called the "doctrine of reasonable use," the court said the club's abnormally large withdrawal compared to the householder's domestic use "was not unqualifiedly reasonable," and it required the club to share equally in the cost of deepening the householder's well.

Olson v. City of Wahoo, 248 N.W. 304 (Neb. 1933) stated in dicta that Nebraska combines the doctrine of reasonable use on overlying land and the correlative rights rule that "if the natural underground supply is insufficient for all owners, each is entitled to a reasonable proportion of the whole." Neb. Rev. Stat. § 46-702 now codifies this approach, subject to other statutes establishing water use preferences (e.g., domestic use over all other uses), § 46-613, authorizing groundwater use on nonoverlying land in specified circumstances, §§ 46-638(1), 46-691 to -691.03, and providing for natural resources districts with broad water and related land management powers over entire basins, §§ 2-3203, -3229. See Bamford v. Upper Republican Natural Res. Dist., 512 N.W.2d 642 (Neb. 1994) (upholding district regulations limiting the amount of groundwater that can be used per acre for irrigation).

5. **Restatement.** Proposed Restatement (Second) of Torts § 858A set forth in part in *Michels Pipeline* was revised by the American Law Institute and became Official Draft § 858.[a]

"§ 858. Liability for Use of Ground Water

"(1) A proprietor of land or his grantee who withdraws ground water from the land and uses it for a beneficial purpose is not subject to liability for interference with the use of water by another, unless

"(a) the withdrawal of ground water unreasonably causes harm to a proprietor of neighboring land through lowering the water table or reducing artesian pressure,

"(b) the withdrawal of ground water exceeds the proprietor's reasonable share of the annual supply or total store of ground water, or

"(c) the withdrawal of the ground water has a direct and substantial effect upon a watercourse or lake and unreasonably causes harm to a person entitled to the use of its water.

"(2) The determination of liability under clauses (a), (b) and (c) of Subsection (1) is governed by the principles stated in §§ 850 to 857."

---

a. Copyright 1979. Reprinted with the permission of the American Law Institute.

The official comment to section 858 elaborates as follows: A "grantee" is one to whom a proprietor has assigned the right to extract groundwater; the grantee need not acquire the overlying land. Clause (1)(a) protects owners of small wells using water on overlying land against harm from large municipal or industrial wells supplying water to nonoverlying lands (like the common law reasonable use doctrine). Clause (1)(a) also extends protection to owners of small wells against harm from unreasonably large wells supplying water for use on overlying lands (unlike the common law reasonable use doctrine).

Subsection 2, by referencing §§ 850-857, incorporates the reasonableness concept of riparian law for surface waters. Subsection 2 thus rejects what *Michels Pipeline* called the "very special restricted meaning" of reasonableness under the common law reasonable use doctrine for groundwater.

Section 858 was followed in Cline v. American Aggregates Corp., 474 N.E.2d 324 (Ohio 1984), and perhaps in Maerz v. United States Steel Corp., 323 N.W.2d 524 (Mich. Ct. App. 1982), but cf. Michigan Citizens for Water Cons. v. Nestle Waters N. Am. Inc., 709 N.W.2d 174 (Mich. Ct. App. 2005) (rejecting the "contention that *Maerz* made a wholesale adoption of the Restatement's rule"). Section 858 was rejected in favor of continued adherence to the absolute ownership doctrine in Maddocks v. Giles, supra Note 1, and Wiggins v. Braz. Coal & Clay Corp., 452 N.E.2d 958 (Ind. 1983).

6. **Underground streams.** The common law doctrines discussed in *Michels Pipeline*—absolute ownership, reasonable use, and correlative rights—apply only to percolating groundwater. In contrast, underground streams are governed by the common law doctrine that a state applies to surface streams, whether that be the riparian doctrine or the appropriation doctrine. Pima Farms Co. v. Proctor, 245 P. 369 (Ariz. 1926); Verdugo Canon Water Co. v. Verdugo, 93 P. 1021 (Cal. 1908).

Like a surface stream, an underground stream must have a bed and banks and a flow of water. This usually means only that the groundwater must be in a narrow confined aquifer, not that it must flow freely in a cavernous opening. At the same time, however, most states rebuttably presume that underground waters are percolating. Woodsum v. Twp. of Pemberton, 412 A.2d 1064 (N.J. Super. Ct. Law Div. 1980). One form of an underground stream is the subflow of a surface stream. This is water beneath the surface stream that supports it or feeds it and moves generally in a direction corresponding with the surface flow. Montecito Valley Water Co. v. City of Santa Barbara, 77 P. 1113 (Cal. 1904); City of L.A. v. Pomeroy, 57 P. 585 (Cal. 1899); N. Gualala Water Co. v. State Water Res. Control Bd., 43 Cal. Rptr.3d 821 (Cal. Ct. App. 2006).

The division of groundwater into underground streams and percolating waters has been criticized for ignoring physical reality. Charles E. Corker, Groundwater Law, Management and Administration, Nat'l Water Comm'n, Legal Study No. 6, at 147 (1971).

STATE ex rel. BLISS v. DORITY
Supreme Court of New Mexico, 1950.
55 N.M. 12, 225 P.2d 1007.

BRICE, CHIEF JUSTICE. The State of New Mexico, upon relation of its State Engineer John H. Bliss, brought separate suits against Bert Troy Dority, Loman Wiley and S. A. Lanning, Jr., the purpose of which was to enjoin the respective defendants from unlawfully using for irrigating lands, waters drawn from what is known as the Roswell Artesian Basin, and the valley fill above it, which plaintiff asserts under Ch. 131, N.M.L. 1931, 1941 Comp. § 77-1101 et seq., are subject to appropriation as provided therein. * * * The defendants admit that they have been using, and will continue to use, the water without a permit unless enjoined from so doing. They deny that their use of it is in violation of law. The principal contention is that the New Mexico statutes providing for the appropriation of sub-surface water is [sic] unconstitutional upon several grounds stated.

The statutes of New Mexico declaring that the artesian and shallow ground water from which defendants obtained the water to irrigate their land belongs to the public and providing for their appropriation for beneficial use, are as follows:

"The waters of underground streams, channels, artesian basins, reservoirs, or lakes, having reasonably ascertainable boundaries, are hereby declared to be public waters and to belong to the public and to be subject to appropriation for beneficial use."

* * *

"Any person, firm or corporation desiring to appropriate for irrigation or industrial uses any of the waters described in this act shall make application to the state engineer * * *."

"Existing water rights based upon application to beneficial use are hereby recognized. Nothing herein contained is intended to impair the same or to disturb the priorities thereof."

* * *

The principal question raised is whether the Act of 1931, which we have quoted, that declared the ownership of the waters in question to be in the public, violates the 14th Amendment to the Constitution of the United States and Sec. 18 of Art. 2 of the Constitution of New Mexico, in that it authorizes the state to deprive its citizens and others of their property without due process of law, and denies them the equal protection of the laws; and violates Sec. 20 of Art. 2 of the Constitution of New Mexico in that it authorizes the taking of private property for public use without just compensation.

The whole argument is based on the assumption that the water described in Sec. 1 of the Act of 1931 belongs to the owners of the overlying land. Each of the defendants claims that the underground water under his land is his property acquired through mesne conveyances from the United States, beginning with the patent from the Government and that such patent and mesne conveyances transferred to him the water underlying the land conveyed. In other words, that the common law, or at least the law of correlative rights in such waters, is the law of this state. * * * The substance of the contention of each of the appellants is that he has a vested interest in the title to the water under his lands, to the center of the earth, of which he cannot be deprived by any legislative act.

This question was settled by this court in Yeo v. Tweedy, [286 P. 970 (N.M. 1929)]. It was held in that case that the title to the water described in Sec. 1 of the 1931 Act belonged to the public and was subject to appropriation for beneficial uses. * * * It was stated in Yeo v. Tweedy that Sec. 1 of Ch. 182, N.M.L. 1927, almost identical with the 1931 Act, had always been the law in this jurisdiction. [Yeo v. Tweedy invalidated the nearly identical 1927 groundwater act because of a technical defect in the legislative process by which it was passed.]

There is another consideration which requires the affirmance of the trial court's decree. The decision of Yeo v. Tweedy, supra, has become a rule of property. In the nineteen years since that decision it may be assumed that many thousands of acres of the one hundred thousand irrigated with water from the Roswell Artesian basin and the valley fill have been sold to purchasers who relied on that decision as determining title to the right to use the water here involved, and the water rights to which would be injured or destroyed if Yeo v. Tweedy is overruled. Whether it stated the correct rule of law (and we are of the opinion that it did), it is now a rule of property that we will not disturb. * * *

Notes

1. **Legislation adopting the appropriation doctrine.** Twelve western states now have legislation adopting the appropriation doctrine for groundwater. They apply the doctrine to all groundwater, thus avoiding the false dichotomy in the common law between underground streams and percolating groundwater. Some of them have a separate groundwater code. Idaho Code §§ 42-226 to -239; Nev. Rev. Stat. § 534.010-.350; N.M. Stat. Ann. §§ 72-12-1 to -28; Or. Rev. Stat. §§ 537.505-.796; S.D. Codified Laws Ann. §§ 46-6-1 to -31; Wash. Rev. Code §§ 90.44.020-.450; Wyo. Stat. Ann. §§ 41-3-901 to -938. The others have a single code for surface water and groundwater. Alaska Stat. §§ 46.15.010-.270; Kan. Stat. Ann. §§ 82a-701 to -734; Mont. Code Ann. §§ 85-2-101 to -520; N.D. Cent. Code §§ 61-01-01, 61-04-01 to -04-32; Utah Code Ann. §§ 73-3-1 to -29.

The state codes typically require a permit to appropriate groundwater. The New Mexico code exempts from the permit requirement wells in basins not declared by the state engineer to have reasonably ascertainable boundaries. N.M. Stat. Ann. § 72-12-20. Nearly every state code exempts small domestic wells. The exemption apparently rests on the premise that it is not worth the time and trouble to require a permit for de minimis uses. That premise is challenged in Robert Jerome Glennon & Thomas Maddock, III, The Concept of Capture: The Hydrology and Law of Stream/Aquifer Interactions, 43 Rocky Mtn. Min. L. Inst. 22-1 (1997), where the authors report the existence of almost two and one-half million domestic wells in western states, many of which probably are in close proximity to rivers. They argue: "It is not sound policy to address the problem of large capacity groundwater wells interfering with surface flow and at the same time exempt small capacity wells which, cumulatively, may have an equally dramatic effect."

2. **Constitutionality of appropriation doctrine legislation.** Knight v. Grimes, 127 N.W.2d 708 (S.D. 1964), took a more direct approach than *Dority* to the constitutionality of superimposing a groundwater appropriation statute upon the rule of absolute ownership. South Dakota had recognized the absolute ownership doctrine by statute since territorial days, and the court acknowledged that the new appropriation statute invaded a pre-existing right or interest of landowners. Nonetheless, the court ruled the legislature was justified in finding that the public welfare requires maximum protection and utilization of the water supply, and that the police power permitted adoption of a statute imposing regulations that are not unreasonable or arbitrary. The new statute validated existing groundwater uses and abolished only unexercised absolute ownership rights. Accord, Baumann v. Smrha, 145 F. Supp. 617, 624-25 (D. Kan.), aff'd mem., 352 U.S. 863 (1956) (upholding a Kansas statute adopting the appropriation doctrine for groundwater that validated existing groundwater uses and adversely affected only unexercised rights). Compare statutory abolition of unexercised riparian rights in streams in *Franco-American*, supra p. 322.

3. **Colorado groundwater law.** Colorado is unique in recognizing four groundwater categories: tributary groundwater, designated groundwater, nontributary groundwater outside of a designated basin, and Denver Basin groundwater. Colo. Ground Water Comm'n v. N. Kiowa-Bijou Groundwater Mgmt. Dist., 77 P.3d 62 (Colo. 2003).

a. Tributary groundwater. Groundwater tributary to a surface stream is administered as part of the stream under the appropriation doctrine. Water Right Determination and Administration Act, Colo. Rev. Stat. §§ 37-92-101 to -602. Tributary groundwater was involved in Cache La Poudre Water Users Ass'n v. Glacier View Meadows, supra p. 76, where new wells were approved for operation under augmentation plans designed to avoid injury to senior surface appropriations. Tributary groundwater also was involved in Alamosa-La Jara Water Users Protection Ass'n v. Gould, infra p. 406.

b. Designated groundwater. This is groundwater located within the boundaries of a basin that has been designated by the Colorado Groundwater Commission. Generally designated basins are in the eastern plains of the state. In addition to being in such a basin, the groundwater (i) must not be available to and required to fill surface rights or (ii) must be in areas not adjacent to a natural stream wherein groundwater withdrawals have constituted the principal water usage for fifteen years prior to the first hearing on proposed designation of the basin. Colo. Rev. Stat. § 37-90-103(6)(a). Designated groundwater is administered under appropriation principles "modified to permit the full economic development of designated ground water resources." § 37-90-102(1). Designated groundwater was involved in Fundingsland v. Colorado Ground Water Commission, infra p. 356.

c. Nontributary groundwater outside of a designated basin. This is groundwater "located outside the boundaries of any designated basins * * *, the withdrawal of which will not, within one hundred years, deplete the flow of a natural stream * * * at an annual rate greater than one-tenth of one percent of the annual rate of withdrawal." Colo. Rev. Stat. § 37-90-103(10.5). It is administered under a version of the reasonable use doctrine that allows withdrawals by overlying owners based on an aquifer life of 100 years. § 137-90-137(4).

d. Denver Basin groundwater. The Denver Basin underlies the most populous area of the state, extending from the foothills west of Denver eastward for fifty miles or more to Limon, and from near Greeley on the north to Colorado Springs on the south. The basin contains four deep, mostly confined, aquifers that lie one under another. Some of the groundwater in the Denver Basin aquifers is within a designated groundwater basin; some is not. Either way, unless the groundwater is tributary to a surface stream, it is allocated based on overlying land ownership and an aquifer life of 100 years. §§ 37-90-137(4)(b)(I), (II), 37-90-111(5). To determine whether Denver Basin groundwater is tributary or nontributary, the one-hundred-year/one-tenth-of-one-percent depletion standard noted above is used, but the standard is applied in a relaxed way that fictionally expands the waters regarded as nontributary. Colo. Ground Water Comm'n v. N. Kiowa-Bijou Groundwater Mgmt. Dist., 77 P.3d 62, 73 (2003). Furthermore, even if the relaxed depletion standard is exceeded, the groundwater is not treated as tributary and administered under the appropriation doctrine if it is located outside of a designated basin. Rather, it is classified as "not nontributary" and administered on the basis of land ownership as if it were nontributary provided an augmentation plan is devised to avoid injury to surface water rights. Colo. Rev. Stat. § 37-90-103(10.7); N. Kiowa-Bijou Groundwater Mgmt. Dist., 77 P.3d at 73-74.

4. **Permits in nonappropriation states.** Appropriation doctrine states are not the only ones that require permits. Many other states now have water codes requiring permits. As in appropriation doctrine states, some of these codes apply only to groundwater while others apply to both surface water and groundwater. See A. Dan Tarlock, Law of Water Rights and Resources §§ 4:30 to -:31 (2008).

SECTION 2. PROBLEMS

PHYSICAL DIFFERENCES BETWEEN GROUNDWATER AND SURFACE WATER

Groundwater and surface water differ markedly in physical occurrence. Four differences particularly affect groundwater law and should be borne in mind as the materials in this section are studied.

First, groundwater is hidden from sight. The physical characteristics of an aquifer are not visible, and the effects of pumping cannot be observed easily. The science of hydrology has made great progress in understanding the principles that determine groundwater behavior. Typically, however, it is necessary to monitor existing wells and to drill and monitor additional wells over a broad geographical area for an extended period before these principles can be applied to a particular aquifer. Because this process is expensive and time consuming, adequate data are often unavailable. This is reflected in the lawyer's adage that in groundwater litigation, the person with the burden of proof loses. The advent of computers has enabled the construction of models in which the physical characteristics of a groundwater system are translated into mathematical language and the effects of groundwater withdrawals can be simulated. Groundwater modeling is discussed in Robert E. Schween & Steven P. Larson, Groundwater Modeling: Capabilities and Limitations, Use and Abuse, 32 Rocky Mtn. Min. L. Inst. 22-1 (1986). As one court observed, however, these models are "vulnerable to 'garbage in, garbage out,' that is, computer computations [are] only as good as the validity of the data supplied." Sorensen v. Lower Niobrara Natural Res. Dist., 376 N.W.2d 539, 543 (Neb. 1985). Consequently, the uncertainties in a particular situation can remain substantial due to inadequate physical data.

Second, surface streams are primarily a flow resource. Annual stream flow limits annual water use, except for carryover storage in reservoirs that is often modest relative to annual stream flow. In contrast, the water available for use in most aquifers consists of both annual recharge and water accumulated in significant quantity over many years. Annual recharge does not physically limit groundwater use when significant accumulated storage is available. The ratio of average annual recharge to accumulated storage varies from one aquifer to another, but overall average annual recharge in the contiguous forty-eight states totals perhaps one billion acre-feet while the groundwater storage that can be withdrawn with modern technology totals about forty-six billion acre-feet. Nat'l Water Comm'n, Water Policies for the Future 230 (1973). The presence in aquifers of large quantities of accumulated storage presents opportunities, creates problems, and raises policy issues not arising with surface streams.

Third, because groundwater is below the surface, wells must be drilled and often pumps must be installed if the water is to be used. The expense associated with groundwater use varies directly with the depth at which it is available. Although the legal issue of protecting a water user's means of diversion can arise with surface streams, see Chapter 2, Section G., this issue tends to be more prominent with groundwater.

Fourth, groundwater flows much more slowly than surface water. As noted in the excerpt from Crosby, supra p. 334, normal flow velocities for groundwater range from five feet per day to five feet per year. In contrast, the North Platte River was reported in State ex rel. Cary v. Cochran, 292 N.W. 239 (Neb. 1940), to be flowing at the rate of twenty-five miles per day. The physical effects of pumping groundwater may spread outward from a well more rapidly that the groundwater flow velocity itself. See, e.g., Dist. 10 Water Users Ass'n v. Barnett, 599 P.2d 894 (Colo. 1979) (recounting expert testimony that pumping groundwater tributary to a stream from a particular well would affect the stream flow in 40 years, while the groundwater if left undisturbed would take about 171 years to proceed from the location of the well to the stream). Nonetheless, it typically takes much longer for groundwater pumping to adversely affect other users from the supply than for a surface stream diversion to affect downstream users. Conversely, when an adverse impact is occurring, closure of the interfering well typically takes much longer to restore the supply to the other users than is true of closure of an interfering surface stream diversion. Time lag complicates groundwater management.

A. Managing Storage: Mining, Safe Yield, and Related Concepts

JAMES W. CROSBY, III, A LAYMAN'S GUIDE TO GROUNDWATER HYDROLOGY

Charles E. Corker, Groundwater Law, Management and Administration, National Water Commission, Legal Study No. 6, Chapter II, 56-67, 68, 72-74 (1971).

C. Where Does Groundwater Come From?

For all practical purposes, the origin of groundwater can be regarded as meteoric, meaning that it comes from the atmosphere. There is also water derived from sources within the earth which is not associated with the hydrologic cycle but which may accrue from geologic processes. This is called magmatic primary, or juvenile water.While the subject has not been without controversy, the consensus of professional opinion is that such water is not added in useful quantify and quality. The important sources of groundwater are:

1. Precipitation

This is indirectly the source of all fresh groundwater, except for the water just mentioned, and directly the source of much groundwater. Much of the precipitation falling on the earth's surface infiltrates the soil zone where it is utilized by plants and satisfies the capillary requirements (soil moisture deficiency) of the soil. Infiltrating precipitation in excess of these requirements tends to move downward through the zone of aeration under the influence of gravity until it reaches the water table. Some of the excess precipitation moves directly or indirectly by flow over the land surface to streams, from which it may, in part, move into a groundwater body.

2. Stream Flow

Surface streams are sometimes classified as gaining streams or losing streams (or, in the language of the technologist, effluent streams or influent streams, respectively). That is, they acquire water from or lose water to the groundwater body, depending on whether the stream is incised below or elevated above the water table. * * *

Ground Water to Stream

Stream to Ground Water

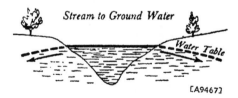

[A9467]

3. Return Flow to Groundwater

Most diversions of groundwater for use are not totally consumed and may return, in part, to some groundwater aquifer. Because irrigation is the major consumptive use of groundwater, it warrants special attention. Depending upon the physical setting and the quantity of groundwater pumped for irrigation, as much as half the diversion may return to groundwater source. Other types of diversions, including that of local surface waters, may also contribute return flow to the groundwater resource. Surface waters often are imported in tremendous quantities for irrigation and substantial percentages ultimately accrue to groundwater. The large available quantities of return flow of sewage in urban areas have prompted their ever increasing use, after treatment, in artificial groundwater recharge. In these operations soil mechanisms are called upon to further upgrade partially treated sewage. Any, or all, of these return flows can be important sources of recharge to a given groundwater basin. * * *

4. Artificial Recharge

Water may be imported to a drainage basin or existing basin waters may be allocated for the express purpose of storage underground. Or this storage may be an incidental and, ordinarily, welcomed circumstance, even when not undertaken for the specific purpose. Groundwater recharge may be induced or facilitated by spreading over areas of high infiltration capacity or by injection into deep wells under pressure. * * *

D. How is Groundwater Discharged?

Groundwater does not cease its movement after reaching an underground reservoir or aquifer. However, in rare instances groundwater may reach a closed basin from which no outflow other than evapotranspiration is possible. Such basins must be lower than all possible avenues of outflow or isolated by impermeable geologic barriers. Otherwise, groundwater is eventually discharged to the surface. The rate of movement varies widely, depending on the permeability of the underground material and the slope of the water table or hydraulic gradient. * * *

1. Natural Discharge

Outflow of groundwater by seepage to lakes, streams, and oceans has already been described. Outflow visibly concentrated in a single location is a spring. Groundwater near enough to the surface to be penetrated by roots of plants is consumed by natural processes of evaporation and transpiration and loss to the atmosphere. * * *

Springs, like surface streams, flow under the influence of gravity. A spring is formed at a point of natural groundwater discharge from an aquifer. Such discharges occur where the land surface intersects a perched or general water table, usually in a valley wall or a hillside slope. More rarely springs are formed where fractures or similar openings in the earth intersect and release confined, or artesian, waters. Hydraulic head, or potential, induced by gravity produces the outflow in all but a few rare spring types characterized by thermal driving mechanisms.

2. Artificial Discharge

Water is produced from underground aquifers by wells which are dug, drilled, or bored. * * *

3. Interconnecting Aquifers

Within any groundwater basin some natural communication between the individual aquifers can be expected under undisturbed conditions. Transfer of water between aquifers can be increased when wells are drilled which penetrate two or more water-bearing zones. Such transfers can be controlled by casing requirements for each well. Failure to provide such controls usually results in dewatering of the upper aquifers and the "drying up" of shallow water supplies. * * *

F. What is the Nature of Groundwater Storage

An unconfined aquifer may be viewed as an underground reservoir. As with a surface reservoir, one important characteristic of an aquifer is the quantity of withdrawable water which it contains. Still more pertinent is the amount of water that can be withdrawn from storage for each foot of water-level decline. Another characteristic is the capacity of the reservoir to contain water, regardless of whether at a given time it is full, partly full, or empty. In an unconfined groundwater reservoir capacity to store water is a function of the volume of the water-bearing materials, and the percentage of those materials which consist of voids or spaces capable of receiving water. * * *

The water remaining in storage at a given time is a resultant of the extent to which portions of the water-bearing material have been dewatered. It can be estimated from driller's and geophysical well logs, from depths to groundwater in various portions of the aquifer, and from comparative quantities of inflow and outflow. Available storage capacity of an aquifer can change with time and further complicate storage calculations. As water-bearing sediments are dewatered, they tend to undergo compaction, which reduces pore volume. Recharge may or may not restore some or all of the lost storage capacity lost by compaction.

Notes

1. **Aquifer equilibrium, capture, and storage depletion.** Under natural conditions, water in an aquifer moves slowly from areas of recharge to areas or points of discharge. Over millennia, the aquifer reaches a state of equilibrium in which the average natural recharge over a climatic cycle approximately equals the average natural discharge.

The introduction of wells disrupts the natural equilibrium, as explained by the following definition of the hydrologists' term "capture": "Water withdrawn artificially from an aquifer is derived from a decrease in storage in the aquifer, a reduction in the previous discharge from the aquifer, an increase in the recharge, or a combination of these changes. The decrease in discharge plus the increase in recharge is called capture." S.W. Lohman et al., U.S. Geological Survey, Water- Supply Paper No. 1988, Definitions of Selected Groundwater Terms—Revisions and Conceptual Refinements 3 (1972).

An analogy is used to clarify how pumping disrupts aquifer equilibrium in Robert Jerome Glennon & Thomas Maddock, III, The Concept of Capture: The Hydrology and Law of Stream/Aquifer Interactions, 43

Rocky Mtn. Min. L. Inst. 22-1, 22-11 to -12 (1997): Suppose you are a consumer whose income and expenditures are equal (groundwater recharge and discharge are in equilibrium). You decide to purchase a new Porsche (extract water by wells). You have three options to cover the payments: increase your income by moonlighting (increase recharge), decrease your expenditures by foregoing fancy restaurants (decrease discharge), or withdraw money from your savings (reduce storage).

The effects over time of continued groundwater pumping are explained in U.S. Geological Survey, Water-Supply Paper 2250, National Water Summary 1983—Hydrologic Events and Issues 36 (1984):

"When pumpage of ground water is initiated, the immediate response is a withdrawal of ground water from storage * * *. As water is withdrawn from storage, ground-water levels decline; this in turn causes a reduction in the natural discharge to streams, to the sea, or to evapotranspiration, and may sometimes also bring about increases in recharge. As natural discharge diminishes and as recharge increases, the amount of water that must be withdrawn from storage to supply the pumpage decreases. In effect, water that was formerly directed toward natural avenues of discharge is now diverted to the pumping centers, and increases in recharge may provide an additional source to sustain the pumpage. Ultimately, withdrawal from storage may cease, and a new equilibrium may be established in which the new rate of recharge balances the pumpage and the remaining natural discharge. On the other hand, if the pumping rate exceeds the reductions in natural discharge and the increases in recharge that can be effected in the system, withdrawal from storage will continue until falling water levels force a reduction in pumping rates. An equilibrium is then established in which the remaining natural discharge and this reduced pumping rate are balanced by the recharge. In many applications, of course, a part of the pumpage is returned to the aquifer or to streams after a cycle of use. To the extent that this occurs, the impact of the pumpage on water supply is reduced; however, it frequently is replaced by an impact on water quality."

The Porsche analogy can be extended to parallel the effects of continued pumping groundwater. Suppose initially you cover the payments on your new Porsche by dipping into savings (depleting storage). Later you forego fancy restaurants or take a second job, or both,(decrease discharge, increase recharge, or both) in order to bring your income and expenditures into balance (recharge/discharge equilibrium). You thereby cease depleting your savings account. On the other hand, if you do not sufficiently increase your income or decrease your expenditures (increase recharge or decrease discharge), your savings account will continue to shrink (water levels will continue to decline), and at some point economics may force you to get rid of the Porsche (quit pumping).

2. **Groundwater mining.** Capture is a key concept in groundwater management because withdrawals by wells in excess of capture necessarily reduce storage. The sustained withdrawal of groundwater in excess of capture is called mining.

A physical consequence of groundwater mining is aquifer water level decline, which in turn has the economic consequence of increasing the cost of withdrawing water as wells need to be deepened. Water level decline may cause other physical consequences depending on the circumstances. These include land surface subsidence; aquifer compaction that causes loss of transmissivity and storage capacity; intrusion into the aquifer of oceanic saltwater or poor quality water from a neighboring aquifer; and depletion of surface lakes, streams, wetlands, and adjacent aquifers.

After noting some of these potential consequences, the National Water Commission concluded: "Mining ground water is not inherently wrong. It is wrong, however, when the water is mined out without taking account of the future value of the water and the storage capacity of the reservoir." National Water Commission, Water Policies for the Future 239 (1973).

3. **Controlling groundwater mining.** Absent controls, overdepletion of storage is likely because of the typical "common pool" nature of groundwater. If a groundwater pool is shared by users, as it usually is, there is little incentive for individual users to conserve the water in storage for future use because water they do not pump now will be taken by someone else. This results in the parties undervaluing and overusing water presently.

As one means of controlling withdrawals, the National Water Commission suggested that pump taxes should be imposed at a rate equal to the predicted future value of the water discounted to present value. Id. at 240-41. But pump taxes are a far less common control than regulation. The principal cases and notes that follow illustrate various regulatory approaches taken by courts, legislatures, and administrative agencies. These materials reveal both different substantive policies on managing storage and different approaches to calculating whether withdrawals exceed the substantive policy.

FUNDINGSLAND v. COLORADO GROUND WATER COMMISSION
Supreme Court of Colorado, 1970.
171 Colo. 487, 468 P.2d 835.

PRINGLE, JUSTICE. * * * Mr. Fundingsland (hereinafter referred to as the plaintiff) filed an application with the Colorado Ground Water Commission (hereinafter referred to as the commission) for a permit to drill a well on certain property located in the Northern High Plains Designated Ground Water Basin in Kit Carson County. [T]he plaintiff's application was denied by the commission on the basis that there was over appropriation in the area where the well was to be drilled.
* * *

The plaintiff appealed the decision of the commission to the district court, and a trial de novo was held * * *. The trial judge entered a judgment denying the plaintiff's application, and the plaintiff brings writ of error to this Court from that judgment. [Plaintiff] alleges as grounds for reversal (1) that the denial of his application was not supported by the evidence and was arbitrary and capricious * * *. This Court finds no error, and we affirm the judgment of the district court.

* * * Under 148-18-6 the commission is empowered to deny an application if it finds that the proposed appropriation will unreasonably impair existing water rights from the same source, or will create unreasonable waste. The act further provides in 148-18-6(5):

> "In ascertaining whether a proposed use will create unreasonable waste or unreasonably affect the rights of other appropriators, the commission shall take into consideration the area, and geologic conditions, the average annual yield and recharge rate of the appropriate water supply, the priority and quantity of existing claims of all persons to use the water, the proposed method of use, and all other matters appropriate to such questions. With regard to whether a proposed use will impair uses under existing water rights, impairment shall include the unreasonable lowering of the water level, or the unreasonable deterioration of water quality, beyond reasonable economic limits of withdrawal or use."

[T]he trial court made detailed findings of fact concerning the proper tests to be used in determining whether the proposed use of water by the plaintiff would unreasonably impair existing water rights from the same source or create unreasonable waste. * * *

[T]he trial court determined that a so-called three mile test provided a reasonable basis for assessing the effect of a proposed use on other users in the district. The three mile test was developed for use in the Northern High Plains. It is partly based on policy and partly based on fact and theory. Using that test, a circle with a three mile radius is drawn around the proposed well site. A rate of pumping is determined which would result in a 40% depletion of the available ground water in that area over a period of 25 years. If that rate of pumping is being exceeded by the existing wells within the circle, then the application for a permit to drill a new well may be denied.

The three mile test takes into account all of the considerations specified in the statute. The factors involved in the three mile test were explained to the court by Mr. Erker, senior engineer in the ground water section of the State Engineer's office. He testified that the three mile circle represents the area over which a well, located at the center, would have an effect if permitted to pump intermittently for 25 years. Intermittent pumping, he explained, meant approximately 100 days per year. Other factors which are considered are the saturated thickness of the aquifer within the three mile circle, the number of wells located within the circle, and the yield of those wells. Multiplying the number of wells within the circle times the yield of those wells gives the total, present appropriation within the three mile circle.

Mr. Romero, an assistant water resource engineer for the State of Colorado Division of Water Resources, testified that * * * in determining the balance of water in the aquifer, he considered the fact that there was only intermittent pumping, the amount of recharge to the aquifer due to precipitation and ground water inflow from outlying areas, recharge due to excess irrigation, and possibly recharge from some other source such as leakage from ditches or rivers.

There does not seem to be any contention that the 40% depletion figure is unreasonable or irrational. The assumption in the three mile test is that a 40% depletion of the aquifer within that area would constitute lowering of the water balance beyond reasonable economic limits of withdrawal or use for irrigation.

Likewise, the selection of 25 years as the period during which the 40% depletion is to be allowed is not contested. Mr. Leslie, a farm and ranch loan representative for Northwestern Mutual Life Insurance Company, testified that 25 years was a reasonable, average period in which a loan for the construction of well facilities would have to be repaid.

The testimony and other evidence in the record before the district court support the reasonableness of the three mile test and establish that the three mile test takes into account the factors specified by the statute. If the three mile test was a proper method for the court to use in determining the effect of plaintiff's proposed use on the ground water supply in the district, then the decision of the district court must be upheld.

[I]t was admitted on both sides that the commission is dealing in a complex area about which little is known. Experts testifying for the commission stated that the three mile test is the best tool they presently have to work with, and that it will be refined as they continue to learn more about the area.

The plaintiff's application did not present the court with a close question of whether the granting of a new permit would work unreasonable injury to existing wells. According to the three mile test, seventeen wells in the three mile circle pumping intermittently with a 1,000 gallon capacity per minute would deplete the water resource 40% in 25 years. There were 28 registered wells within the three mile circle encompassing the plaintiff's proposed well site. These 28 wells had a registered yield of 29,700 gallons per minute while the maximum yield allowable under the three mile test would be 17,000 gallons per minute. * * *

Ground water existing in designated underground water basins is made subject to the doctrine of prior appropriation by 1965 Perm. Supp., C.R.S. 1963, 148-18-1. The statute further provides:

"* * * While the doctrine of prior appropriation is recognized, such doctrine should be modified to permit the full economic development of designated ground water resources. Prior appropriations of ground water should be protected and reasonable ground water pumping levels maintained, but not to include the maintenance of historical water levels. * * *"

Underground water basins require management that is different from the management of surface streams and underground waters tributary to such streams. In the case of the latter waters, seasonal regulation of diversion by junior appropriators can effectively protect the interests of more senior appropriators and no long range harm can come of over appropriations since the streams are subject to seasonal recharge. The underground water dealt with by 148-18-1 is not subject to the same ready replenishment enjoyed by surface streams and tributary ground water. It is possible for water to be withdrawn from the aquifer in a rate in excess of the annual recharge creating what is called a mining condition. Unless the rate of pumping is regulated, mining must ultimately result in lowering the water balance below a level from which water may be economically withdrawn. Due to the slow rate at which underground waters flow through and into the aquifer, it may be many years before a reasonable water level may be restored to a mined aquifer.

It is clear that the policies of protecting senior appropriators and maintaining reasonable ground water pumping levels set forth by the underground water act require management which takes into account the long range effects of intermittent pumping in the aquifer. In this case all of the experts testifying before the commission and the district court were in agreement that a mining condition exists in the Northern High Plains Designated Ground Water Basin. The commission has determined that proper use of the ground water resource requires that the mining be allowed to continue. However, the maximum allowable rate of depletion, at least when considering applications for permits to drill new wells, has been set at 40% depletion in 25 years. We have pointed out that the depletion rate in the area which would be affected by the plaintiff's proposed well is in excess of the rate allowed by the commission and approved by the district court.

If the plaintiff were permitted to proceed on his theory of "unappropriated water" and pump water from his proposed well until such time as it was no longer economically feasible to withdraw water from the aquifer, then no subsequent regulation of his pumping could protect senior appropriators, and all pumping from the basin within the area of influence of the plaintiff's well would have to cease until a reasonable pumping level was restored through the slow process of recharge. This is not the concept of appropriation contained in the statute, and not the one this Court will follow.

When, as in this case, water is being mined from the ground water basin, and a proposed appropriation would result in unreasonable harm to senior appropriators, then a determination that there is no water available for appropriation is justified. * * *

Notes

1. **Examples of controlled mining.** *Fundingsland* illustrates one approach to the controlled mining of groundwater. For the Northern High Plains Basin, the Ground Water Commission allowed 40% depletion of the available groundwater within a three-mile circle over twenty-five years. The Commission later increased the period for 40% depletion to 100 years. Rules and Regulations for the Management and Control of Designated Ground Water, 2 Colo. Code Regs. § 5.2.2.2.

Southwest Kansas Groundwater Management District No. 3 allows 40% depletion of the available groundwater within a township over twenty-five years. Kan. Admin. Regs. § 5-23-4a. Townships are squares six miles on each side, so the management area is a six-mile square rather than a circle with a three-mile radius.

Oklahoma's Groundwater Law, Okla. Stat. tit. 82, §§ 1020.1 to -.22, allows overlying landowners and their lessees to withdraw water for reasonable use up to but not exceeding a basin or subbasin's maximum annual yield, as determined by the state water resources board. The board must base the maximum annual yield of major basins or subbasins on a minimum life of twenty years. The law does not specify a minimum life for minor basins or subbasins. § 1020.5.

The first appellate case on controlled mining was Mathers v. Texaco, Inc., 421 P.2d 771 (N.M. 1966). Texaco was given a permit to appropriate 350 acre-feet per year from the Lea County underground water basin to use for water flooding an oil field. The fresh water in the basin is recharged only by a very limited surface precipitation that is just about equaled by natural discharge. The state engineer calculated the amount of water that could be withdrawn from a township of overlying land and still leave one-third of the water in storage at the end of forty years, at which point it would no longer be economically feasible to withdraw water for agricultural and most other purposes. Existing appropriators using water for agricultural purposes protested issuance of the permit. In upholding the permit in the face of a statute protecting existing water rights against impairment from new wells, the court said:

"The administration of a non-rechargeable basin, if the waters therein are to be applied to a beneficial use, requires giving to the stock or supply of water a time dimension, or, to state it otherwise, requires the fixing of a rate of withdrawal which will result in a determination of the economic life of the basin at a selected time.

"The very nature of the finite stock of water in a non-rechargeable basin compels a modification of the traditional concept of appropriable supply under the appropriation doctrine. * * *

"The rights of the protestants to appropriate water from this basin are subject to this time limitation, just as are the rights of all other appropriators. A lowering of the water level in the wells of protestants, together with the resulting increase in pumping costs and the lowering of pumping yields, does not constitute an impairment of the rights of protestants as a matter of law. These are inevitable results of the beneficial use by the public of these waters." Id. at 243-44, 246.

2. **Refinement of the *Fundingsland* test.** Thompson v. Colorado Ground Water Commission, 575 P.2d 372 (Colo. 1978), modified the *Fundingsland* three-mile circle when it would have extended across the Nebraska state line. The Commission considered only the portion of the circle located in Colorado and water development in Colorado, and determined that the area around plaintiff's proposed well was overappropriated. If the Commission had considered the entire circle and Nebraska development within it, the area would not have been overappropriated. The court upheld the Commission's state-line policy, saying: "Expert testimony supported the Commission's position that overappropriation of the aquifer at the state line, with the intent to stabilize or reverse the aquifer flow to the benefit of Colorado, would seriously injure vested Colorado rights far west of the state line and could ignite a destructive aquifer depletion race with Nebraska, an adjoining state. Evidence that a portion of Colorado's groundwater naturally flows into adjoining states, when considered in the context of the Commission's overall groundwater policy, does not establish a breach of statutory duty by the Commission in its determination."

Further refinement of *Fundingsland* was reported in Berens v. Colorado Ground Water Commission, 614 P.2d 352, 354-55 (Colo. 1980):

"[T]he standard three-mile formula did not, in practice, result in a 40% depletion rate in 25 years. [B]ecause a small shift in a proposed well site could eliminate from consideration those senior wells lying on the perimeter of a fully-appropriated circle, and cause the acceptance of the proposed well, the circle could, as a result, be overappropriated. * * * Commission studies suggest[] that a number of fully-appropriated townships were actually overappropriated by about 40%. * * * As a result, the Commission has recently modified its standard three-mile formula to take into account the percentage of overappropriation thought to be inherent in that formula. Based on the Commission studies suggesting that a 40% overappropriation resulted from the use of the Commission's standard formula, the Commission modified the formula to achieve a 40% reduction in its estimate of the amount of available ground water for each three-mile circle."

3. **Depletion deduction.** Internal Revenue Code § 611(a) allows a cost depletion deduction for mines, oil and gas wells, "and other natural deposits." United States v. Shurbet, 347 F.2d 103 (5th Cir. 1965), ruled that an irrigator taking groundwater from the Ogallala formation under the Southern High Plains of Texas was entitled to the depletion deduction. The court noted that under Texas law, an irrigator "owns the soil

and the percolating water which is part of the soil." Soon thereafter, the Internal Revenue Service announced it would also allow the depletion deduction for irrigators using water from the Ogallala formation in the Southern High Plains of New Mexico, where the appropriation doctrine rather than the absolute ownership doctrine applies. Rev. Rul. 65-296, 1965-2 C.B. 181. Later, the Internal Revenue Service announced its willingness to allow the depletion deduction for persons taking water from the Ogallala formation outside the Southern High Plains where it can be shown that the groundwater is being depleted and recharge is so low that, once extracted, the groundwater will be lost to the taxpayer and immediately succeeding generations. Rev. Rul. 82-214, 1982-2 C.B. 115; see also Priv. Ltr. Rul. 82-26-022 (Mar. 10, 1982).

4. **When available groundwater is depleted.** What happens to existing groundwater users when uneconomic pumping depths are reached? Irrigators might simply quit pumping and return to dry land farming or allow the land to revert to prairie. Another possibility is to supplement supplies by importing water. For example, much of the early growth of Los Angeles was based on groundwater drawn from overdrafted aquifers. This provided Los Angles with cheap water on which to develop the economic strength to begin importing water in 1913 from the Owens Valley 300 miles away.

Critics of groundwater mining argue that it frequently creates a crisis, leading to demands for a "rescue project" to supply supplemental water at subsidized prices. An example is the Central Arizona Project, which transports Colorado River water to Central Arizona. Although not originally conceived as a rescue project, when finally approved by Congress in 1968, its purpose was exactly that. As the project neared completion a quarter century later, it had to be restructured to accommodate the inability of various irrigation districts to pay for water at the originally scheduled, subsidized rates. Even lower rates were provided for agricultural users, though eventually this water will be shifted to municipal and industrial users at higher rates.

DOHERTY v. OREGON WATER RESOURCES DIRECTOR
Supreme Court of Oregon, 1989.
308 Or. 543, 783 P.2d 519.

FADELEY, JUSTICE. This is a judicial review of the state Water Resources Director's amended order, entered in 1986, declaring 274 square miles in Umatilla and Morrow counties a critical ground water area. Several agricultural irrigators challenge the order which can lead to controls on volume of water pumped from area wells. The Court of Appeals upheld the declaration of the Butter Creek Critical Ground Water Area with subareas, as well as the order that no new applications be accepted to appropriate ground water or to expand or change existing uses. * * *

* * * ORS 537.730 and ORS 537.735 authorized the director to establish a critical ground water area if the available supply is "being or about to be overdrawn," water levels "are declining or have declined excessively," or if wells "interfere substantially with one another." * * * The statute provides that, after hearing, the director "shall" by order declare an area to be a critical ground water area if "any" of the statutory factors exist and he further finds that public welfare, health, and safety require that corrective controls be adopted. * * *

The director entered * * * "findings of fact" * * * as follows:

"The record indicates that approximately 500 wells serve as the source of water needed for domestic and stock water use by residents within the subject area. Although the volume of water withdrawn * * * for domestic and stock water needs is not large in comparison to the amount withdrawn for irrigation and other permitted uses, maintaining adequate and safe supplies of ground water in the subject reservoir for continuing these necessary uses is of considerable significance to the health, safety and welfare of the residents of the area. * * *

"The sustained yield of a ground water basin is the amount of water that can be withdrawn from it annually without exceeding the long-term mean annual water supply to the reservoir. Withdrawals exceeding this supply must come from storage within the reservoir which results in long-term water level declines.

"Any draft in excess of the sustained yield of the basalt ground water reservoir in the proposed Butter Creek Critical Ground Water Area is overdraft."

The director found that testimony and evidence in the hearing record established both overdraft and excessive decline in water levels during the period for which records of well levels have been kept in the Butter Creek area. The director found that "existing developments have reached or exceeded the sustained yield capacity of the reservoir" in each subarea.

The "opinion" portion of the director's order related the facts found to the statutory policy stated in the Ground Water Act of 1955 as follows:

"ORS 537.525(1)[,(3),] and (9) provide the declared policy of the Oregon Legislature to be that the beneficial use of the available ground water resource be limited to the 'capacity of the available sources' and that 'whenever * * * overdrawing of the ground water supplies * * * exists or impends, controlled use of the ground water concerned be authorized or imposed * * *.' This declared policy requires that the ground water be managed to provide for development and use of the resource within the sustained yield capacity of the ground water reservoir. The sustained yield concept of ground water management is further supported by ORS 537.525(7) which provides, 'Reasonably stable ground water levels be determined and maintained.'"

* * *

Petitioners argue that public welfare is best served if they are permitted to pump as much as they can use on crops which may be sold at a profit after pumping and other costs are paid. * * *

Petitioners further argue that the statutes permit any amount of drawdown or any level of depletion of the underground water resource, if a current farmer can clear a profit on an irrigated crop. * * * Petitioners contend that the portion of ORS 537.525(8) which states "Depletion of ground water supplies below economic levels * * * be prevented or controlled within practicable limits" supports their claim that economic feasibility must be read into all other policy subsections of the ground water act as a limiting factor. The water should be looked at as a resource similar to gold in a mine and withdrawn totally so long as it is economically feasible to do so, they urge. Writers, whom they cite in support of this concept, advocate that the government establish a time period, such as 25 years, for using up all of the water.

This argument would say that the statutory words of "overdraft" and "excessive decline" in water levels cannot be interpreted to apply to the practice of progressively lowering water levels or permanent depletion of the resource in annual steps if the practice nonetheless provides profitable agriculture today. That is, if the farmer can afford the electricity to pump the water from greater depth and still raise a profitable crop, it cannot be overdraft or excessive decline. In that circumstance, they contend, there is no interference with public health, safety, and welfare, even though no irrigating agriculturalist has suggested that a profit can only be made by pumping the reservoir dry within the next 25 years or any other short-term period. A logical corollary of this mining-analogy argument is that the public health, welfare, and safety are simply not involved where the current generation profitably extracts all of the resource and leaves agricultural ghost towns.

The statutory scheme in the Ground Water Act of 1955 does not support this argument. Instead, the act is designed to prevent that result. The act established the critical area mechanism to assure a reasonably stable, adequate water supply which may be beneficially used only within the capacity of the available resource and is protected against overdrawing, declining water levels, and interference among wells.

We agree with the director and the Court of Appeals that ORS 537.525(8) does not mandate depletion to the lowest water level from which irrigation water may be profitably pumped today. A fair reading of subsection (8) casts it as a restriction on, rather than a justification for, depletion of ground water. The water-mining theory fails because it is inconsistent with the legislative act.

Petitioners assert that the director used an annual reservoir recharge rate as the guideline by which he interpreted the statutory term "overdrawn." They invite our inquiry on review to whether an annual overdraft standard is too stringent. The petitioners are equally dissatisfied with the 15-year study and, were the director to select a 50-year period, apparently would still assert error. They contend that the proper period for determining whether an overdraft in excess of reservoir recharge is occurring would be in the thousands of years. They assert that present day recharge comes from the Blue Mountains only intermittently, sometimes arriving at the reservoir thousands of years after the precipitation supplying the recharge fell there.

The argument is not supported by the record. Absent evidence needed to support the assertion that a cycle of millennial recharge exists, neither we nor the director should speculate upon that theory. In any event, the director determined overdraft by relying on cumulative overdraft over a 15-year period, not by an annual recharge standard. Moreover, the legislative direction under which he acted gives no hint that it is designed to accommodate pumping the reservoir dry on an expectation of refilling sometime within the next few thousand years. We need not reach any issue about whether "overdrawn" may be interpreted to mean overdraft for only one year. [T]he director did not rely upon annual overdraft but rather the "sustained yield * * * concept" in interpreting and applying ORS 537.525(7), which provides that "reasonably stable ground water levels be determined and maintained."

The director found that precipitation in the area in recent years was higher than long-term averages, but that cumulative decline in water levels continued. He also found that the sustained yield of the ground water basin should be defined in terms of "the long-term mean annual water supply to the reservoir." We agree with the director that a sustained yield concept is consistent with the words of ORS 537.525(7) and the policy of ORS 537.525. The claim of error fails because the director's approach is consistent with the statute.

Petitioners point out that the Butter Creek area is only a part of the Umatilla structural basin [encompassing more than 2,200 square miles] and that others, outside the Butter Creek area, are using up the same general underground reservoir but are not being subjected to the usage controls which the critical area designation threatens to visit upon them. They contend that no critical area may be formed unless all irrigators using the interconnected underground water source are similarly regulated. They argue that partial regulation would be ineffective and ineffective regulation does not promote public welfare. The Ground Water Act of 1955 appears to contemplate an area-by-area enforcement, especially because interference among wells is one ground for creating a critical area. Simultaneous enforcement throughout a basin is not required by statute. The record does not show that partial regulation would be ineffective and thereby does not show that partial regulation fails to promote public welfare, health, or safety. [The record indicated that there were "a number of separate, interconnected subpools within the aquifer."]

* * * The decision of the Court of Appeals is affirmed.

Notes

1. **Phased implementation of Oregon's sustained yield policy.** The Oregon Water Resources Commission issued rules to reduce pumping in the Butter Creek Critical Ground Water Area to the "sustainable annual yield," which the rules defined as "the volume of water that can be pumped on an annual basis while maintaining reasonably stable water levels." Instead of immediately implementing the policy, the rules provided for reduction of the existing overdraft to be phased in over five years. In Waterwatch of Oregon v. Oregon Water Resources Dep't, 852 P.2d 902 (Or. Ct. App. 1993), the petitioner argued that phased rather than immediate reduction of overdraft violated the statutory requirement that "[r]easonably stable ground water levels be determined and maintained." The court disagreed. After noting that another statutory provision states that the depletion of groundwater supplies below economic levels should be "prevented or controlled within practicable limits," the court concluded: "The problem with petitioner's argument is that it focuses on only one objective of the statute and disregards other statutory objectives. The challenged rules strike a balance between stabilization of water supplies and providing an interim during which agricultural practices can be accommodated to the regulatory stabilization mechanism."

2. **Safe yield.** Some states have statutes limiting groundwater withdrawals to safe yield. E.g., Kan. Stat. ann. § 82a-711; Kan. Admin. Regs. § 5-3-9, -11, -22-7; N.J. Stat. Ann. § 58:1A-15; Utah Code Ann. § 73-5-15.

Safe yield is neither an unambiguous standard nor a simple one to implement. Crosby, supra p. 334, at 75-77:

"Safe yield has been variously defined. Todd (1959) states, 'The safe yield of a groundwater basin is the amount of water which can be withdrawn from it annually without producing an undesired result.' * * * Meinzer (1923b, p. 55) had earlier defined safe yield as, 'the rate at which water can be withdrawn from an aquifer without depleting the supply to such an extent that withdrawal at this rate is harmful to the aquifer itself, or to the quality of the water, or is no longer economically feasible.'

"[The term] is inherently ambiguous because it may or may not invite subjective and/or economic judgments above the gravity of the risk from a water shortage. It has the additional disadvantage that decisions made in good faith may prove to be, in time, poorly considered. A regimen of totally 'safe' operation which avoided all risks would utilize much less than the optimum usable storage capacity."

Charles L. McGuinness, U.S. Geological Survey, Circular No. 117, Water Law, with Special Reference to Ground Water 11 (1951):

"Regulation of water use to prevent over-development of an aquifer, or a part of it, involves the determination of a safe or optimum rate of withdrawal and the holding of withdrawals to it. This is true whether the doctrine of prior appropriation or that of correlative rights is applied. Such a determination generally is much more difficult for a ground-water reservoir than for a surface stream or reservoir, for it inevitably involves the economic feasibility of a given means of withdrawal or a given pumping lift, not only in an aquifer as a whole but in different parts of it. * * * [I]n most aquifers the distribution of wells affects the perennial yield significantly. With a given distribution of wells, an enforced reduction in pumping by cutting off the later appropriators (or, under correlative rights, by reducing the pumpage of all in proportion to the estimated perennial yield of the aquifer and to the amount of land owned by each user) may not prevent local overdevelopment. Reducing the pumpage in one part of an aquifer may not result in an equivalent addition to the supply for other wells, either for a long time or, if the reduction simply results in an increase in the natural discharge from the aquifer, possibly not at all."

U.S. Geological Survey, Water Supply Paper No. 2250, National Water Summary 1983—Hydrologic Events and Issues 36 (1983):

"As it is often used, 'safe yield' seems to refer to the pumpage that can be sustained at equilibrium, without continued withdrawal from storage. However, sustained withdrawal from storage, or as it is often termed 'ground-water mining,' is no more 'unsafe' than the mining of any other mineral resource, provided it is recognized and planned. Neither should pumpage at equilibrium necessarily be considered 'safe,' unless the attendant impacts, such as reduced streamflow or degradation of water quality, are deemed acceptable. The expression 'safe yield' can, in fact only be defined in terms of specific impacts of pumpage. The consequences of pumpage must be assessed for each level of development, and 'safe yield' must be taken as the maximum pumpage for which the consequences are considered acceptable."

3. **Average annual recharge.** A variation of the safe-yield standard limits groundwater withdrawals to average annual recharge. Idaho Code § 42-237a(g) ("the reasonably anticipated average rate of future natural recharge"); S.D. Codified Laws § 46-6-3.1 ("the average estimated annual recharge").

Baker v. Ore-Ida Foods, Inc., 513 P.2d 627 (Idaho 1973), involved twenty irrigation wells that were causing the water level in an aquifer to drop by twenty feet a year. The average annual recharge was 5500 acre-feet. The court said Idaho's statute limiting annual withdrawals to average natural recharge prohibits mining, which the court defined as "perennially withdrawing ground water at rates beyond the recharge rate." The court affirmed a trial court decree that enjoined pumping by all but the four most senior wells, which together consumed the entire average annual recharge.

Suppose the senior wells thereafter continued to withdraw 5500 acre-feet annually. Would not storage still be mined to whatever extent there was natural discharge from the aquifer unless an offsetting increase in natural recharge were to be induced? See the concept of capture in Note 1, supra p.354.

The *Baker* court assigned further administration of the aquifer to the Department of Water Resources. The department then recalculated the parties' rights based on their actual historical use. Rather than assume that well owners had pumped at their full licensed rates for 24 hours a day 180 days per year, as the court apparently had done, the department examined power company records for each pump to determine the hours and days each year that the pump was operated. It found that the actual length of the pumping season was from 150-160 days per year, and it fixed the annual water right of each of the twenty wells in the basin at the highest five-year average withdrawal, expressed in acre-feet per year. This reduced the water rights by 28% to 38% and allowed more appropriators to pump. Then, based on the premise that in a dry year good farming practice might require the use of more than the annual water right, while in a wet year an irrigator might not need the total water right, the department allowed each water user to pump any amount of water necessary in a given year so long as the water user did not pump over five times the annual water right in any consecutive five-year period. The case was again appealed on a narrow point, Briggs v. Golden Valley Land & Cattle Co., 546 P.2d 382 (Idaho 1976), where the above findings were recited but not reviewed.

The Idaho Legislature later amended the average-natural-recharge statute. It retained average natural recharge as the basic limit on groundwater withdrawals but added language allowing withdrawals in excess of average natural recharge if (1) the department finds such withdrawals will be in the public interest, (2) a program exists or will exist to increase recharge or decrease withdrawals within a time period acceptable to the department to bring withdrawals into balance with recharge, and (3) senior groundwater appropriators will not be required to pump from below reasonable pumping levels.

Average annual recharge is a less definitive groundwater management tool than may first appear: "[A]verage recharge does not imply any particular average water level. When natural discharge is reduced as much as pumpage the level will stabilize. This may occur at many levels and the maximum may be near the original level or it may not be reached until the stored water is largely depleted. Moreover, lowering the level may bring increased recharge." Edgar S. Bagley, Water Rights Law and Public Policies Relating to Ground Water "Mining" in the Southwestern States, 4 J. Law & Econ. 144, 166 n.78 (1961).

As indicated in Note 1, supra p. 354, withdrawals by wells must come either from aquifer storage or from capture, i.e., induced greater recharge or induced lesser natural discharge. Given the physical unity of the hydrologic cycle, induced greater recharge might come from (that is, reduce) surface water supplies to the detriment of senior stream appropriators or environmental interests. Similarly, induced lesser natural discharge from an aquifer might translate into less flow in a surface stream, a loss of water supply for phreatophytes, or a loss of wetlands. The average-natural-recharge limit on withdrawals, standing alone, fails to address the policy question of the desirability of aquifer drawdown and surface water depletion.

A further complication is that the physical consequences of pumping, in the form of aquifer drawdown and stream depletion, will vary with local conditions: "There is no valid generic rule, such as pumping the natural recharge, that will lead to a desirable economic or stable (non-depleting) level of groundwater development. Subject to local permeability and storage conditions, such a rule can cause either greatly excessive and increasing drawdown or costly constraints on resource use regardless of the rate of natural recharge. * * * The effects of concern to water policy are primarily aquifer diffusivity, location [of wells in relation to each other and to any surface stream], and time of pumpage. The natural recharge rate is unrelated to any parameters controlling the primary water policy concerns." W.P. Balleau, Water Appropriation and Transfer in a General Hydrogeologic System, 28 Nat. Resources J. 269, 280 & n.26 (1988); see also Gregory S. Weber, Twenty Years of Local Groundwater Export Legislation in California: Lessons from a Patchwork Quilt, 34 Nat. Resources J. 657, 672-77 (1994) (discussing hydrologists' criticisms of the groundwater management concepts of mining, overdraft, safe yield, and average recharge).

4. **Reducing groundwater withdrawals.** If withdrawals by wells must be reduced to comply with governing policy on managing storage, how should that be done? In an appropriation doctrine state, must priorities be strictly enforced as in *Baker*? Compare Wyo. Stat. Ann. § 41-3-915):

"(a) * * * If the state engineer finds * * * that the underground water in the control area is insufficient for all of the appropriators, he may by order adopt one or more of the following corrective controls: * * *

(ii) He may determine the permissible total withdrawal of underground water in the control area for each day, month or year, and, insofar as may be reasonably done, he shall apportion such permissible total withdrawal among the appropriators holding valid rights to the underground water in the control area in accordance with the relative dates of priority of such rights.

(iii) If he finds that withdrawals by junior appropriators have a material and adverse effect upon the supply available for and needed by senior appropriators, he may order such junior appropriators to cease or reduce withdrawals forthwith.

(iv) If he finds that cessation or reduction of withdrawals by junior appropriators will not result in proportionate benefits to senior appropriators, he may require and specify a system of rotation of use of underground water in the control area.

"(b) * * *

"(c) Appropriators of underground water from a control area may agree to any method or scheme of control of withdrawals, apportionment, rotation or proration of the common supply of underground water. The state engineer shall encourage and promote such agreements and supply the parties with information and advice."

In Kansas, another appropriation doctrine state, pumping had to be reduced in the Walnut Creek Intensive Groundwater Use Control Area because it was about twice the safe yield. The chief engineer of the state water agency did not do this by strictly enforcing priorities. Instead, he divided appropriators into two groups, those with priorities of October 1, 1965 or earlier and those with later priorities. He ordered irrigators in the senior group to cut back by 22 or 33 percent, depending on their location, on the rationale that they needed to be more reasonable and efficient. He ordered irrigators in the junior group to cut back by 64 or 71 percent, depending on their location. Dissatisfied irrigators appealed the administrative action asserting inverse condemnation, but the matter was settled before judicial resolution of the takings issue. John C. Peck, Property Rights in Groundwater—Some Lessons from the Kansas Experience, 12 Kan. J.L. & Pub. Pol'y 493, 499-500, 503, 504-05 (2003) (reporting these facts and arguing that "if one accepts the proposition that the chief engineer has the power to control and reduce waste, the [administrative order] might stand.".

Under the correlative rights doctrine, a court may not impose pumping reductions in an overdrafted basin using equitable principles that ignore the superiority that the doctrine gives to water rights for overlying land compared to those for nonoverlying land. City of Barstow v. Mojave Water Agency, 5 P.3d 853 (Cal. 2000).

CITY OF PASADENA v. CITY OF ALHAMBRA
Supreme Court of California, 1949.
33 Cal. 2d 908, 207 P.2d 17.

[Numerous persons, municipalities, and water companies had pumped water for many years from a forty square mile aquifer known as the Raymond Basin. The City of Pasadena brought this action to determine the rights to groundwater in the basin and to enjoin an alleged overdraft. The trial court found that the safe annual yield of the Western Unit of the basin was 18,000 acre-feet per year, and that annual withdrawals totaled 24,000 acre-feet. This condition had existed since about 1913, and the water table had been steadily lowered toward the point of unreasonable depletion and possible destruction of the source. Most of the parties entered into a stipulation restricting total withdrawals to the annual yield, and the trial court entered a judgment substantially enforcing the stipulation against all parties, allocating to each about two-thirds of the amount previously pumped, and enjoining all pumping in excess of the rights decreed to each party. The California-Michigan Land and Water Company, not having joined in the stipulation, appealed.]

GIBSON, CHIEF JUSTICE. * * * Rights in water in an underground basin, so far as pertinent here, are classified as overlying, appropriative, and prescriptive. Generally speaking, an overlying right, analogous to that of a riparian owner in a surface stream, is the right of the owner of the land to take water from the ground underneath for use on his land within the basin or watershed; the right is based on ownership of the land and is appurtenant thereto. The right of an appropriator depends upon an actual taking of water. Where a taking is wrongful, it may ripen into a prescriptive right. * * *

In the present case some of the parties * * * have pumped water solely for use on their own land, and their rights at the outset were overlying. The principal takers of water, however, are public utility corporations and municipalities which have either exported water or have used it within the Western Unit for municipal purposes or for sale to the public, and their taking, when commenced, was entirely appropriative. * * *

[I]f no prescriptive rights had been acquired, the rights of the overlying owners would be paramount, and the rights of the appropriators would depend on priority of acquisition under the rule that the first appropriator in time is the first in right. The latest in time of the appropriations would then be the first to be curtailed in limiting total production of the area to the safe yield. If such were the case, the overdraft could be eliminated simply by enjoining a part of the latest appropriations, since the record shows that there is ample water to satisfy the needs of all the overlying users and most of the appropriators * * *.

The principal dispute between appellant and respondents, however, concerns whether any water rights in the Western Unit have become prescriptive and, if so, to what extent. Respondents assert that the rights of all the parties, including both overlying users and appropriators, have become mutually prescriptive against all the other parties and, accordingly, that all rights are of equal standing, with none prior or paramount. * * *

The record shows that there has been an actual adverse user of water in the Western Unit. There was an invasion, to some extent at least, of the rights of both overlying owners and appropriators commencing in the year 1913-1914, when the overdraft first occurred. Each taking of water in excess of the safe yield, whether by subsequent appropriators or by increased use by prior appropriators, was wrongful and was in injury to the then existing owners of water rights, because the overdraft, from its very beginning, operated progressively to reduce the total available supply. Although no owner was immediately prevented from taking the water he needed, the report demonstrates that a continuation of the overdraft would eventually result in such a depletion of the supply stored in the underground basin that it would become inadequate. The injury thus did not involve an immediate disability to obtain water, but, rather, it consisted of the continual lowering of the level and gradual reducing of the total amount of stored water, the accumulated effect of which, after a period of years, would be to render the supply insufficient to meet the needs of the rightful owners. * * *

The lowering of the water table resulting from the overdraft was plainly observable in the wells of the parties * * *. This evidence is clearly sufficient to justify charging appellant with notice that there was a deficiency rather than a surplus and that the appropriations causing the overdraft were invasions of the rights of overlying owners and prior appropriators. The elements of prescription being present in the record, the statute of limitations ran against the original lawful holders of water rights to whatever extent their rights were invaded. * * *

[A]t first glance it would seem to follow that the parties who wrongfully appropriated water for a period of five years would acquire prior prescriptive rights to the full amount so taken. The running of the statute, however, can effectively be interrupted by self help on the part of the lawful owner of the property right involved. * * * [A]lthough the pumping of each party to this action continued without interruption, it necessarily interfered with the future possibility of pumping by each of the other parties by lowering the water level. The original owners by their own acts * * * thus retained or acquired a right to continue to take some water in the future. The wrongdoers also acquired prescriptive rights to continue to take water, but their rights were limited to the extent that the original owners retained or acquired rights by their pumping.

[I]t seems probable that the solution adopted by the trial court will promote the best interests of the public, because a pro tanto reduction of the amount of water devoted to each present use would normally be less disruptive than total elimination of some of the uses.

We hold, therefore, that prescriptive rights were established by appropriations made in the Western Unit subsequent to the commencement of the overdraft, that such rights were acquired against both overlying owners and prior appropriators, that the overlying owners and prior appropriators also obtained or preserved, rights by reason of the water which they pumped, and that the trial court properly concluded that the production of water in the unit should be limited by a proportionate reduction in the amount which each party had taken throughout the statutory period. * * * [Affirmed.]

Notes

1. **Limitations on the mutual prescription doctrine.** The California Supreme Court later recognized that "[a] possible undesirable side effect of the so-called mutual prescription doctrine is that it may encourage a 'race to the pumphouse' after overdraft commences, each party endeavoring to increase the volume of continuous use on which his prescriptive right will be based." City of L.A. v. City of San Fernando, 537 P.2d 1250 (Cal. 1975).

In *San Fernando*, the court limited the mutual prescription doctrine in several ways. First, it interpreted a state statute to exempt cities from loss of their water rights by prescription. Cities can still acquire prescriptive rights against other pumpers but cannot have their own rights cut down by prescription. (A 1968 amendment to the statute extends the same status to public utilities.) Second, the court ruled that times of groundwater surplus break the running of the five-year prescriptive period. The prescriptive period must consist of five consecutive years of overdraft. Third, the court emphasized that the commencement of overdraft is only one requirement for the prescriptive period to commence running. Another requirement is that the persons against whom prescription is asserted must have notice of the overdraft. Mere notice that others are pumping is not sufficient because their pumping might be drawing from surplus. Fourth, the court suggested that unexercised overlying rights would not necessarily be subject to loss by prescription. 537 P.2d at 1318 n.100.

Further limitation came in Tehachapi-Cummings County Water District v. Armstrong, 122 Cal. Rptr. 918 (Cal. Ct. App. 1975), which held that mutual prescription does not apply if all the parties in a groundwater basin adjudication are overlying users. The correlative rights doctrine governs, and if the water supply is insufficient for all, each user gets a proportionate share of the supply based upon his reasonable need. The share "is predicated not on his past use over a specified period of time, nor on the time he commenced pumping, but solely on his current reasonable and beneficial need for water."

2. **Overdraft, surplus, and safe yield.** *Pasadena* predicated the running of the prescriptive period on the occurrence of basin overdraft. In the passage quoted below, *San Fernando* elaborated on overdraft and the related concepts of surplus and safe yield. The court's discussion is potentially relevant to any state with a policy of safe yield management, regardless of whether that policy exists under the correlative rights doctrine or another doctrine:

"A ground basin is in a state of surplus when the amount of water being extracted from it is less than the maximum that could be withdrawn without adverse effects on the basin's long term supply. * * * Overdraft commences whenever extractions increase, or the withdrawable maximum decreases, or both, to the point where the surplus ends. * * *

"The trial court defined 'surplus' and overdraft' in terms of 'safe yield.' The findings state that '[s]urplus is that condition which exists when the draft on the ground water supply is less than the safe yield,' and that over-draft exists when such draft 'exceeds the safe yield.' 'Safe yield' is defined as 'the maximum quantity of water which can be withdrawn annually from a ground water supply under a given set of conditions without causing an undesirable result.' The phrase 'undesirable result' is understood to refer to a gradual lowering of the ground water levels resulting eventually in deple-tion of the supply.

"Although the parties differ sharply over the correct meanings of 'sur-plus' and 'overdraft' under the present facts, they are in accord over the concept of 'safe yield' and the essential correctness of the method by which the referee and the expert witnesses computed the safe yield of the ULARA [Upper Los Angeles River Area] and its component basins for particular years. Basically, safe yield was deemed equivalent to an adjusted figure for net ground water recharge, consisting of (A) recharge from (1) native pre-cipitation and associated runoff, (2) return flow from delivered imported water, and (3) return flow from delivered ground water less (B) losses in-curred through natural ground water depletions consisting of (1) subsur-face outflow, (2) excessive evaporative losses in high ground water areas and through vegetation along streams, (3) ground water infiltration into sewers, and (4) rising water outflow, or water emerging from the ground and flowing past Gauging Station No. F57 down the river channel to the sea. The component figures for the particular safe yield year being deter-mined were adjusted to eliminate the effect of fluctuations extraneous to the long range calculation. The adjustment of chief importance here was the use of a 29-year base period, consisting of the water years 1928-1929 through 1956-1957, for the computation of all items dependent upon pre-cipitation. This 29-year period was selected as one for which (1) adequate hydrological data was available and (2) precipitation figures were represen-tative, in both average level and fluctuations, of the 85 years for which weather records were relatively complete.

"Plaintiff contends that the trial court's definition of overdraft as a condition in which draft exceeds safe yield, although consistent with the *Pasadena* decision, is insufficient for the facts of the present case. Accord-ing to plaintiff, overdraft commenced in the ULARA only when (1) total ex-tractions exceeded safe yield and (2) the available water storage capacity of the basin was sufficient to permit cycling of the safe yield throughout the 29-year base period of wet and dry years without causing a waste of water in the wet years. The referee's report as well as other evidence showed that when ground basin levels were relatively high, and storage space corre-spondingly diminished, waste occurred. Ground basin levels tended to vary in accordance with wide fluctuations in precipitation. Thus if a rising level of extractions were halted at the point of the safe yield based on the 29-year average, ensuing heightening of ground water levels during years of higher-than-average precipitation would cause waste. Since this waste would constitute a loss of basin water in addition to the safe yield extrac-tions, it would eventually create enough additional storage space to stop further similar waste, but the wasted water itself would be lost to any beneficial use. On the other hand, a withdrawal of water from the basin over and above its safe yield in the amount necessary to create the storage space sufficient to prevent the waste would result in a net addition to the beneficially used supply.

"We agree with plaintiff that if a ground basin's lack of storage space will cause a limitation of extractions to safe yield to result in a probable waste of water, the amount of water which if withdrawn would create the storage space necessary to avoid the waste and not adversely affect the basin's safe yield is a temporary surplus available for appropriation to beneficial use. Accordingly, overdraft occurs only if extractions from the basin exceed its safe yield plus any such temporary surplus."

3. **Local groundwater regulation in California.** The lack of administrative regulation of groundwater extraction at the state level in California has resulted in serious overdraft of a number of groundwater basins despite the common law safe-yield limit of *Pasadena* and *San Fernando*. In the absence of safe-yield enforcement by the state or by private litigation, some local governments decided to regulate groundwater withdrawals. The local regulation commonly prohibits groundwater withdrawals for export and use elsewhere. Ellen Hanak & Caitlin Dyckman, Counties Wresting Control: Local Responses to California's Statewide Water Market, 6 U. Den. Water L. Rev. 490 (2003); Gregory S. Weber, Twenty Years of Local Groundwater Export Legislation in California: Lessons from a Patchwork Quilt, 34 Nat. Resources J. 657 (1994). Baldwin v. County of Tehama, 36 Cal. Rptr. 2d 886 (Cal. Ct. App. 1994), held that state law did not preempt a county ordinance regulating the extraction of groundwater for use elsewhere.

4. **Unexercised overlying rights.** In re Waters of Long Valley Creek Stream System, supra p. 326, footnote 2, held an administrative adjudication of a stream system could subordinate unexercised riparian rights to existing riparian and appropriative water uses. In private groundwater litigation, could a court subordinate unexercised overlying rights to existing overlying and appropriative water uses? No, according to Wright v. Goleta Water District, 219 Cal. Rptr. 740 (Ct. App. 1985). The court viewed *Long Valley* as limited to statutory adjudications of streams by the State Water Resources Control Board. It ruled *Long Valley* could not be extended to groundwater because no similar statutory scheme exists for the comprehensive determination of all groundwater rights in a basin.

TOWN OF CHINO VALLEY v. CITY OF PRESCOTT
Supreme Court of Arizona, 1981.
131 Ariz. 78, 638 P.2d 1324.

STRUNKMEYER, CHIEF JUSTICE. * * * The Town of Chino Valley lies approximately fifteen miles north of the City of Prescott in Yavapai County, Arizona. Prescott owns 164 acres of land in the Chino Valley. In 1948, it drilled wells on some of its Chino Valley property and began transporting groundwater through a seventeen-mile pipeline to its municipal customers. In 1962, * * * the State Land Department established the Granite Creek Critical Groundwater Area. On September 20, 1970, the Town was incorporated. It was within the Granite Creek Critical Groundwater Area and it owned lands and was withdrawing groundwater from the same underground basin as Prescott. Prescott, itself, was not within the Granite Creek Critical Groundwater Area.

This action was filed on August 21, 1972, seeking to enjoin the pumping of groundwater by Prescott. * * * The lawsuit proceeded at a desultory pace until the order of dismissal on November 3, 1980. * * *

[I]n June of 1980, the Legislature enacted the Groundwater Management Act, herein called the Act or the 1980 Act.* It * * * abolished critical groundwater areas, substituting geographic units of groundwater management called Active Management Areas and Irrigation Non-Expansion Areas. Certain areas which had been declared critical groundwater areas under former laws were included in the Active Management Areas. By A.R.S. § 45-411(A)(3), the Prescott Active Management Area was established. It includes the Little Chino and Upper Agua Fria Sub-basins. Both the Town of Chino Valley and Prescott are within the Little Chino Sub-basin of the Prescott Active Management Area.

By A.R.S. § 45-541(A) of the 1980 Act, transportation of groundwater is allowed within a sub-basin of an Active Management Area. Pres-

---

* The 1980 Act provided for the establishment of Active Management Areas which are geographical areas where groundwater supplies are imperiled. Active Management Areas encompass a whole groundwater basin or basins. Groundwater basins are areas designated as enclosing a relatively hydrologically distinct body or related bodies of groundwater. Groundwater sub-basins are areas designated so to enclose a smaller hydrologically distinct body of groundwater found within a groundwater basin. The 1980 Act provides limitations on use of groundwater in Active Management Areas. In general the Act restricts new uses of water drawn from Active Management Areas. The Act sets up a system of determining grandfathered rights to use groundwater in Active Management Areas, defining certain usages of groundwater previously being made and allowing these usages to continue. The Act also establishes the rights of cities, towns, private water companies and irrigation districts in Active Management Areas to withdraw as much groundwater as is needed from within their service areas to serve their customers although restrictions are provided on extensions of service areas and the types of service that may be provided by these entities. The Act also specifies a few other new uses of groundwater that may be made in Active Management Areas. It allows limited new withdrawals for domestic purposes. It also sets up a system for obtaining permits to withdraw new amounts of water for certain specific purposes.

Provided withdrawal is permitted under any of the provisions of the Act, transportation of groundwater within the same sub-basin may be made without payment of damages. Transportation of groundwater between sub-basins or away from Active Management Areas is also authorized if the groundwater is allowed to be withdrawn under the Act's provisions, but damages must be paid for any injury caused. Rules for determining damage are set out. The transportation rules apply whether in or outside of Active Management Areas, although the restrictions on new uses of groundwater do not apply outside of Active Management Areas. * * *

cott, being within the Little Chino Sub-basin from which it was drawing water, moved for dismissal of the Town's complaint for injunctive relief. The Superior Court granted Prescott's motion, but ordered that the Town have twenty days in which to file an amended complaint specifying any damages. The Town's appeal from that portion of the trial court's order dismissing appellants' claim for injunctive relief is based upon the asserted unconstitutionality of the Act of 1980 since the Act, by permitting the transportation of groundwater, legitimatizes the prospective withdrawal of groundwater from the Little Chino Sub-basin by Prescott. Appellants' principal attack is that the Act takes property without due process of law and without just compensation. * * *

Appellants rely on the cases of Howard v. Perrin, 8 Ariz. 347, 76 P. 460 (1904), and Maricopa County Water Conservation District No. 1 v. Southwest Cotton Co., 39 Ariz. 65, 4 P.2d 369 (1931), for their basic proposition that they own the water percolating beneath their lands under the doctrine of reasonable use. * * * The question therefore is, what are a landowner's rights in the water percolating under his lands?

In our recent case of Town of Chino Valley v. State Land Dept., 119 Ariz. 243, 580 P.2d 704 (1978), we said: "Under the doctrine of reasonable use property owners have the right to capture and use the underground water beneath their land for a beneficial purpose on that land * * *." In the absolute sense, there can be no ownership in seeping and percolating waters until they are reduced to actual possession and control by the person claiming them because of their migratory character. Like wild animals free to roam as they please, they are the property of no one. * * *

We therefore hold that there is no right of ownership of groundwater in Arizona prior to its capture and withdrawal from the common supply and that the right of the owner of the overlying land is simply to the usufruct of the water.

This brings us to conclude that appellants' position that the 1980 Act violates the Fifth and Fourteenth Amendments to the Constitution of the United States and art. 2, § 17 of the Constitution of the State of Arizona as a taking of private property without due process of law and just compensation cannot be sustained.

The Legislature, in Ch. 2 of the 1980 Act, A.R.S. § 45-401, declared:

"A. The legislature finds that the people of Arizona are dependent in whole or in part upon groundwater basins for their water supply and that in many basins and sub-basins withdrawal of groundwater is greatly in excess of the safe annual yield and that this is threatening to destroy the economy of certain areas of this state and is threatening to do substantial injury to the general economy and welfare of this state and its citizens. The legislature further finds that it is in the best interest of the general economy and welfare of this state and its citizens that the legislature evoke its police power to prescribe which uses of groundwater are most beneficial and economically effective.

"B. It is therefore declared to be the public policy of this state that in the interest of protecting and stabilizing the general economy and welfare of this state and its citizens it is necessary to conserve, protect and allocate the use of groundwater resources of the state and to provide a framework for the comprehensive management and regulation of the withdrawal, transportation, use, conservation and conveyance of rights to use the groundwater in this state."

We do not doubt but that the overdraft of groundwater in this state is a serious problem which has no chance of correcting itself, and that it is necessary for comprehensive legislation to both limit groundwater use and allocate its use among competing interests. * * *

Legislation which denies or restricts rights to use property necessarily results in a diminution of that property's value. Yet the United States Supreme Court has on numerous occasions upheld under the state's police power regulations of land use which have virtually destroyed private interests. * * * In the present case, appellants may make such use of their property as they choose, except that their lands may not be irrigated if they were not legally irrigated in the last five years. The 1980 Act furthers legitimate state interests.

Legislatures of various states have from time to time abolished the prevailing uses of groundwater and substituted other plans for its use. State courts have uniformly rejected the idea that groundwater percolating through the soil may not be limited and regulated and must be acquired by eminent domain. * * *

The order of the court below is affirmed.

Notes

1. **The Arizona Groundwater Management Act.** The amazing story of the Groundwater Study Commission that prepared the first draft of the complicated groundwater act, the federal pressure on the state to enact a code, and the negotiations, concessions, and compromises of the cities, mining companies, and farmers whose "hired guns" hammered out the final bill in a lengthy "rump session" preceding the legislative session is told in Desmond D. Connall, Jr., A History of the Arizona Groundwater Management Act, 1982 Ariz. St. L.J. 313. The next two excerpts provide further details on the genesis and key substantive provisions of the act.

Frank J. Trelease, Conjunctive Use of Groundwater and Surface Water, 27B Rocky Mtn. Min. L. Inst. 1853, 1877-78 (1982):

"The 1980 Arizona Groundwater Management Act is the culmination of a long struggle to bring some order out of the chaos resulting from the disastrous judicial adherence to the so-called 'reasonable use rule' that allowed every landowner unrestricted pumping for use on his land, but severely limited the transportation of water to places where it was needed for municipal and industrial use. The rate of overdraft was checked by the [earlier] legislative restriction of new wells in critical areas, but cities, mining companies, and farmers hacked away at Arizona's very slowly recharging aquifers until overdraft of groundwater reached 2.2 million acre-feet per year. The Act is carefully designed to impose strict controls on previously unregulated groundwater withdrawals with the least possible disruption. All existing uses of groundwater are converted into 'grandfathered rights' and adjusted in quantity to meet new standards of conservation. The law's main design is to reduce overdraft, so it requires maximum use of surface water before groundwater is used. 'Surface water' will include a very large block of Colorado River water imported under the Central Arizona Project (CAP) * * *."

U.S. Advisory Comm'n on Intergovernmental Relations, Coordinating Water Resources in the Federal System: The Groundwater-Surface Water Connection 33-35 (1991):

"The importation and use of water, when CAP is operating at its full capacity of 1.2 million acre-feet per year, is expected to reduce reliance on groundwater supplies in central and southern Arizona enough to cut the overdraft by as much as two-thirds. * * * [N]o new agricultural lands may be brought into production using CAP water (except on Indian lands), and existing agricultural users of groundwater who receive water from the CAP must reduce pumping by equivalent amounts. In times of shortages, municipal and industrial uses of CAP water have an absolute priority over agricultural uses. * * *

"The remaining one-third or more of the statewide overdraft is to be solved by management and conservation methods. The Groundwater Management Act * * * designates four active management areas (AMAs) and two irrigation non-expansion areas (INAs) with boundaries approximately coterminous with those of major groundwater areas * * *. Eighty percent of Arizona's population and 70 percent of its water consumption are located within the four AMAs. [Later, the Act was amended to create a fifth AMA out of part of one of the original four, and a third INA was designated by administrative action.] The goal of the legislation is to establish a balance between water supply and demand within the AMAs by 2025 (except in the predominantly agricultural Pinal AMA, where a controlled mining operation will be pursued). Within each AMA, a director is responsible for the implementation of the act, with the recommendations of a five-member AMA advisory council. * * *

"The act established a formal decisionmaking structure that centralizes authority in the governor and the Department of Water Resources (DWR) and its director, and creates weaker authority in the local agencies. * * * The governor appoints the DWR director as well as the local AMA advisory council members. The DWR director appoints the AMA directors and is responsible for making a series of 10-year management plans for each AMA (with tighter water use restrictions during each period). The director is authorized to determine maximum water duties for irrigation and water conservation requirements for municipalities and industries within the AMAs, review the plans of local authorities for reducing groundwater withdrawals in critically overdrafted areas, file for civil and criminal penalties for violators of regulations promulgated under the act, set water withdrawal fees, and, ultimately, take land out of agricultural production if necessary.

"The 45-year period from 1980 to 2025 has been divided into five management periods to establish step-by-step control and eventual elimination of groundwater overdrafting. In the first period, from 1980 to 1990, the Department of Water Resources registered wells and defined groundwater rights through an application-and-permit program, with different classes of withdrawal rights but without many requirements or restrictions. The intention was to bring the implementation of the Code along relatively slowly at first, to try to heighten compliance with the first stages before the more restrictive provisions are applied. * * *

"[Apart from some de minimis uses that are not heavily regulated, the act recognizes and regulates three types of rights to withdraw groundwater within AMAs: grandfathered rights, service area rights, and withdrawal permit rights. Although nonirrigation grandfathered rights are recognized, the major grandfathered rights are for irrigation.] Lands that were not irrigated at some time between January 1, 1975, and January 1, 1980, do not qualify for a grandfathered irrigation right and may not be brought into irrigated agricultural production. The clear intention is to freeze the level of irrigated agricultural production that existed in 1980. Reductions in irrigated agricultural acreage and water consumption are reserved for later management periods.

"Grandfathered irrigation rights remain with the land and can be used by a new owner. The groundwater may be used only on the overlying land, however, and the rights remain with the land. If lands with grandfathered irrigation rights are sold for uses other than irrigated agriculture, the rights transfer at a predetermined rate of 3 acre-feet per year. * * *

"Municipalities, water companies, and irrigation districts apply for permits for service area rights to withdraw, transport, and distribute groundwater, provided they remain within per capita water conservation requirements set by the DWR director. Persons not eligible for grandfathered * * * rights or service area rights may apply for groundwater withdrawal permits for [certain] nonirrigation purposes.

"Within the irrigation non-expansion areas, no new land may be brought into irrigated agricultural production. * * * Water withdrawal and consumption for other types of uses [that are reasonable and beneficial, Ariz. Rev. Stat. Ann. § 45-453] may develop [largely] without restriction. * * *

"Groundwater management activities are financed on a 50-50 basis with appropriations from the state General Fund and funds raised from water withdrawal fees assessed against groundwater pumping. Groundwater users who are required to meter their wells and annually report their pumpage are also required to pay the 'pump tax.' The withdrawal fee is set by the DWR director within the guidelines of the law, with a cap of $5.00 per acre-foot. * * *

"The 1990-to-2000 management period calls for the implementation of a plan to augment water supplies. The director may propose any means of augmentation from artificial recharge to weather modification. The 2000-to-2010 management period includes the possibility, after 2006, of purchasing and retiring agricultural land to meet water conservation goals and ensure a balance between demand and supply."

The Arizona Legislature later supplemented the 1980 Act with measures designed to promote water conservation and water supply augmentation. A study done near the end of the second ten-year management period found, however, that the Act will not likely achieve the goal of safe yield by 2025 that it sets for the Prescott, Phoenix, and Tucson AMAs. This is because of numerous grandfathered rights that cannot be reduced significantly and because of restrictions on DWR's regulatory authority, e.g., DWR must issue groundwater permits for industrial and mineral extraction uses if the applicants meet certain criteria. Auditor General, Report No. 99-8, Performance Audit of the Arizona Department of Water Resources (1999). See also Robert J. Glennon, "Because That's Where the Water Is": Retiring Current Water Uses to Achieve the Safe-Yield Objective of the Arizona Groundwater Management Act, 33 Ariz. L. Rev. 89 (1991) (arguing that water conservation programs and water supply augmentation from CAP and other sources will be insufficient to achieve the safe-yield goal, and proposing a program for retiring current agricultural water rights to meet the goal).

2. **More on an overlying landowner's unexercised groundwater rights.** The Arizona court recently clarified its statement in *Chino Valley* that prior to the capture and withdrawal of groundwater, "the right of the owner of the overlying land is simply to the usufruct of the water." In Davis v. Agua Sierra Resources, L.L.C., 203 P.2d 506, 510 (Ariz. 2009), the court said its recognition that overlying landowners have a usufructary right to water under their lands "does not mean landowners have some vested real property right in the potential use of groundwater." It explained that "the landowner's right is perhaps better described as an unvested expectancy insofar as it concerns the potential future use of groundwater that has never been captured or applied." Because an overlying landowner lacks a real property interest in the potential use of such groundwater, the court invalidated a clause in a land deed purporting to reserve unused commercial groundwater rights in the grantor.

Sorensen v. Lower Niobrara Natural Resources District, 376 N.W.2d 539, 548 (Neb. 1985), concerned condemnation of both exercised and *unexercised* groundwater rights of an overlying owner under Nebraska's doctrine of "reasonable use and correlative rights," as the court called it. The court said "the right to use ground water is an attribute of owning fee simple title to land overlying a source of ground water and is inseparable from the land to which it applies," and therefore the right is a "proprietary appurtenance" protected by the takings clause of the state constitution from being taken without just compensation.

In an appropriation doctrine state, suppose unappropriated water in quantities usable by City *Y* underlies *X*'s irrigable land, and the city desires to drill a well on the land and build a pipeline across it. What would the city buy or condemn from *X*, and how would just compensation be measured? Suppose alternatively that (a) the city's withdrawals will not prevent *X* from obtaining a permit for a groundwater appropriation to irrigate the land, or (b) because of well-spacing requirements or safe-yield restrictions, the city's well will prevent *X* from obtaining an appropriation to irrigate the land.

DEVIN GALLOWAY ET AL., LAND SUBSIDENCE IN THE UNITED STATES
4 (U.S. Geological Survey Circular No. 1182, 1999).

We begin with five case histories in which overdraft of susceptible aquifer systems has resulted in regional, permanent subsidence and related ground failures. In alluvial aquifer systems, especially those that include semiconsolidated silt and clay layers (aquitards) of sufficient thickness, long-term ground-water-level declines can result in a vast one-time release of "water of compaction" from compacting aquitards, which manifests itself as land subsidence. Accompanying this release of water is a largely nonrecoverable reduction in the pore volume of the compacted aquitards, and thus an overall reduction in the total storage capacity of the aquifer system. This "water of compaction" cannot be reinstated by allowing water levels to recover to their predevelopment status. * * *

The five case studies demonstrate how agricultural and municipal-industrial ground-water use have combined to deplete critical ground-water resources and create costly regional-scale subsidence. We begin in the "Silicon Valley" in northern California, where early agricultural ground-water use contributed to subsidence that has increased flood risks in the greater San Jose area. Silicon Valley (properly the Santa Clara Valley) was the first place in the United States where subsidence due to ground-water pumpage was recognized; since the late 1960s, the ground-water resource there has been successfully managed to halt subsidence. In nearby San Joaquin Valley, the single largest human alteration of the Earth's surface topography resulted from excessive ground-water pumpage to sustain an exceptionally productive agriculture. In the Houston-Galveston area in Texas, early production of oil and gas, and a long history of ground-water pumpage, have created severe and costly coastal-flooding hazards and affected a critical environmental resource—the Galveston Bay estuary. In Las Vegas Valley ground-water depletion and subsidence have accompanied the conversion of a desert oasis into a thirsty and fast-growing metropolis. Finally, in south-central Arizona, importation of Colorado River water and conversion of water-intensive agriculture to lower-water-demand urban land uses has [sic] helped to partly arrest subsidence and forestall further fissuring of the Earth's surface.

Notes

1. **Negligence liability for subsidence damage.** Friendswood Development Co. v. Smith-Southwest Industries, Inc., 576 S.W.2d 21 (Tex. 1978):

"[I]n 1975 the Legislature undertook to retard further subsidence in Harris and Galveston Counties by creating a subsidence district with power to prevent future [location of wells too close together] and excessive pumping of the nature alleged to have occurred in this case. Previously, in 1949 the Legislature provided for the creation of districts for the purpose of 'conservation, preservation, protection, recharging, and prevention of waste of underground water * * *.'" In 1973, the Legislature added to such purposes the authority "to control subsidence caused by withdrawal of water * * *."

"[No] Texas case has dealt specifically with land subsidence resulting from * * * pumping of underground waters. In other jurisdictions adhering to the English ground water rule, liability for neighboring land subsidence has been denied. * * *

"We agree that some aspects of the English or common law rule as to underground waters are harsh and outmoded, and the rule has been severely criticized since its reaffirmation by this Court in 1955. Most of the critics, however, recognize that it has become an established rule of property law in this State, under which many citizens own land and water rights. The rule has been relied upon by thousands of farmers, industries, and municipalities in purchasing and developing vast tracts of land overlying aquifers of underground water. * * * The very wells which brought about this action were drilled after the English rule had been reaffirmed by this Court in 1955. * * *

"As heretofore mentioned, the Legislature has entered the field of regulation of ground water withdrawals and subsidence. * * * With a rule that recognizes ownership of underground water by each individual under his own land, but with no limitation on the manner and amount which another individual landowner might produce (absent willful waste and malicious malice), legislative action was essential in order to provide for conservation and protection of public interests. * * *

"This case, however, gives the Court its first opportunity to recognize, and to encourage compliance with, the policy set forth by the Legislature and its regulatory agencies in an effort to curb excessive underground water withdrawals and resulting land subsidence. It also affords us the opportunity to discard an objectionable aspect of the court-made English rule as it relates to subsidence by stating a rule for the future which is more in harmony with expressed legislative policy. We refer to the past immunity from negligence which heretofore has been afforded ground water producers solely because of their "absolute" ownership of the water.

"As far as we can determine, there is no other use of private real property which enjoys such an immunity from liability under the law of negligence. This ownership of underground water comes with ownership of the surface; it is part of the soil. Yet, the use of one's ground-level surface and other elements of the soil is without such insulation from tort liability. Our consideration of this case convinces us that there is no valid reason to continue this special immunity insofar as it relates to future subsidence proximately caused by negligence in the manner which wells are drilled or produced in the future. It appears that the ownership and rights of all landowners will be better protected against subsidence if each has the duty to produce water from his land in a manner that will not negligently damage or destroy the lands of others.

"Therefore, if the landowner's manner of withdrawing ground water from his land is negligent, willfully wasteful, or for the purpose of malicious injury, and such conduct is a proximate cause of the subsidence of the land of others, he will be liable for the consequences of his conduct. The addition of negligence as a ground of recovery shall apply only to future subsidence proximately caused by future withdrawals of ground water from wells which are either produced or drilled in a negligent manner after the date this opinion becomes final."

What does the negligence standard of *Friendswood* mean for pumpers who cause subsidence? Compare Olin L. Browder et al., Basic Property Law 187-88 (5th ed. 1989) (might approach strict liability), with David Todd, Common Resources, Private Rights and Liabilities: A Case Study on Texas Groundwater Law, 32 Nat. Resources J. 232, 253 (1992) (might require high levels of negligence or foreseeability).

2. **Other liability theories for land subsidence.** Indiana, which like Texas has the absolute ownership doctrine for groundwater rights, adds another legal theory to make a groundwater pumper liable for subsidence damage. In City of Valparaiso v. Defler, 694 N.E.2d 1177 (Ind. Ct. App. 1998), the court analogized to Indiana cases holding miners liable for subsidence caused by their removal of subjacent support from overlying land. The court expressly left open, however, whether to borrow the rule of strict liability from mineral cases or to use another standard of liability (presumably negligence) when subsidence is caused by the removal of groundwater rather than the removal of minerals.

Alabama, which has the reasonable use doctrine for disputes between competing water users, Martin v. City of Linden, 667 So. 2d 732 (Ala. 1995), applies nuisance law when the dewatering of a quarry causes subsidence damage to a neighboring house. Henderson v. Wade Sand & Gravel Co., 388 So. 2d 900 (Ala. 1980).

California uses the correlative rights doctrine for water use disputes, but a city whose groundwater pumping caused subsidence damage to neighboring buildings was held liable under the theory of inverse condemnation. Los Osos Valley Assocs. v. City of San Luis Obispo, 36 Cal. Rptr. 2d 758 (Ct. App. 1994). The court relied on Restatement (Second) of Torts § 818: "One who is privileged to withdraw subterranean water, oil, minerals or other substances from under the land of another is not for that reason privileged to cause a subsidence of the other's land by the withdrawal."

B. Protection of Means of Diversion

JAMES W. CROSBY, III, A LAYMAN'S GUIDE TO GROUNDWATER HYDROLOGY
Charles E. Corker, Groundwater Law, Management and Administration,
National Water Commission, Legal Study No. 6, Chapter II, 45-47, 95 (1971).

[1]. Wells and Well Hydraulics

* * * In hard rocks, wells are frequently open holes, whereas in unconsolidated materials support in the form of lengths of pipe or casing may be required. So that groundwater can enter the casing, a screen or section of perforated casing is generally emplaced opposite the productive aquifer.

Water in a properly-constructed well will rise to the level of the water table. If artesian, or pressure conditions exist, the water will rise to the level of the *pressure surface*. If the pressure surface is above ground surface, the well will flow freely unless capped. * * *

As pumping is commenced in a well, a quantity of water is discharged by the pump, lowering the water level in the well and nearby formation below the initial water surface in the formation. A gradient, therefore, is created between the nearby water table and the more distant water table. This gradient causes additional water to flow toward the well under the influence of gravity. The water table near the well takes the form of a hole or depression formed in the groundwater surface. Because it appears as an inverted cone around the pumping well, it is appropriately called the *cone of depression*. When the cones of depression of two or more wells overlap, interference results and decline of the water table is accelerated.

If the water-bearing formation has a high permeability, only a small gradient is required to produce a relatively large quantity of water. However, if the permeability is low, it may be found that the gradient required to produce a desired quantity of water exceeds the limit established by the depth at which the pump intake is set. The capacity of the well is exceeded and the pump soon starts sucking air. It is well to note that although the well is sucked dry in this situation, the pump can be turned off and after a period of recovery, the water in the well will return to nearly its original level. The groundwater has in no way been exhausted by the pumping. Rather, the well went dry temporarily and only because the formation was expected to release its stored water at a rate in excess of its physical capabilities.

[2]. Well Interference

* * * A groundwater reservoir requires serious consideration of well spacings to accommodate well interference effects. These phenomena become problems when the cones of depression (cones of pressure relief) of two or more nearby producing wells overlap. Where such overlaps occur the rate of water level decline is substantially increased. The total quantity of water in storage may be quite adequate, but its availability to pumps at particular locations may be inadequate without incurring excessive pumping lifts. These effects can vary greatly and depend in large part on the transmissivity of the aquifer.

[3]. What is a "Reasonable" Pump Lift?

The groundwater statutes of certain states prescribe protection of a prior appropriator to a "reasonable pump lift" or terms of similar import. Herein lies one of the single greatest obstacles to groundwater management in states recognizing appropriative doctrines.

What is a reasonable pump lift? Is it based upon economic or social criteria? What may be reasonable to an irrigator may be totally unacceptable to a farmer dependent upon groundwater for his domestic supply and yet these people must share the fruits of the same resource. All too frequently the development of deep, highly productive irrigation wells has had a detrimental effect upon shallower domestic wells, occasionally causing them to go completely dry. Proper management, however, might provide adequate protection for the shallow production or replacement by supplemental sources.

Notes

1. **Causes of interference with means of diversion: mining versus overlapping cones.** The term "mining" is occasionally used to refer to any removal of water from storage, including that associated with a cone of depression around a well even though, as Crosby notes, the water table may recover around the well nearly to its original level during nonpumping periods. More commonly, however, "mining" refers only to sustained overdraft that permanently depletes storage in a basin or subbasin. See, e.g., U.S. Geological Survey, Water-Supply Paper No. 2250, supra p. 355, Note 2; Baker v. Ore-Ida Foods, Inc., supra p. 367, Note 3.

Obviously, mining in the sense of sustained overdraft can render the means of diversion of existing wells inadequate. A state's decision to allow mining in that sense, even on a controlled basis, implies that existing diversion methods will not be protected against water level decline in a well due to mining. When the New Mexico court in Mathers v. Texaco, Inc., supra p. 360, Note 1, allowed two-thirds of the water in a basin receiving very limited recharge to be mined over forty years, it stated: "A lowering of the water level in the wells of protestants, together with the resulting increase in pumping costs and the lowering of pumping yields, does not constitute an impairment of the rights of protestants as a matter of law. These are inevitable results of the beneficial use by the public of these waters."

Mining in the sense of sustained overdraft is not the only cause of interference with the means of diversion of existing wells. As the Crosby excerpt points out, a new well's cone of depression (or pressure relief in a confined aquifer) might interfere with existing wells if the new well is too large and close to the existing ones given aquifer transmissivity. This happens even though, as Crosby puts it, "[t]he groundwater has in no way been exhausted by the pumping." Such interference with existing wells can often be avoided or at least minimized by well spacing requirements.

2. **Legal protection of a means of diversion.** If a well goes dry because of sustained overdraft contrary to state policy on mining, its owner can seek enforcement of that policy. But if an overlap of cones of depression is the cause, the well owner would need a different legal theory. The next case and some of the Notes following it explore possible theories.

CURRENT CREEK IRRIGATION CO. v. ANDREWS
Supreme Court of Utah, 1959.
9 Utah 2d 324, 344 P.2d 528.

WADE, JUSTICE. * * * The central problem is whether prior appropriators of water from an underground basin, who receive it by means of flowing wells and springs, have a vested right to continue receiving water by artesian pressure; and whether subsequent appropriators, whose withdrawals of water lower the water table and reduce the flow of prior wells, must restore the pressure or bear the expense of replacing the water of prior appropriators.

All of the wells and springs belonging to the parties are in a single broad alluvial fan, which slopes westward from the Wasatch Mountains, in north Juab Valley. * * * Fowkes are owners of 11 artesian wells and one spring which are located well up eastward on the alluvial fan and toward its northern part: the use is for domestic purposes and for irrigation of approximately 115 acres of land. * * *

Andrews are the owners of a spring and five flowing wells located roughly one-half mile southeast of the Fowkes wells and therefore higher on the fan, which are used to irrigate about 150 acres of land. They date to 1915 or before but are later in priority than the Fowkes wells. Andrews also own the right to use water from a number of seeps and springs which irrigate meadow land and which also have been so used since before 1903. They have further initiated a claim as of March 14, 1950, for a pump well which produces six second feet of water. This was by application to the State Engineer and use is permitted only during the irrigation season.

Current Creek Company's main water source is known as Mona Reservoir, which lies at the center of the valley near its north end. The water is transported about 12 miles to the south for irrigation. The company has also initiated a claim to appropriate 18 second feet of underground water * * *. Current Creek contracted with Andrews to permit the drilling of two wells on the latter's property. * * * The priority date of application for these wells is 1951, although they were not drilled until 1954. They flow by natural pressure about 2.74 second feet of water and are allowed to flow during the entire year for storage in the Mona Reservoir.

[W]hen the Andrews' pump well is started, the water level drops and the pressure ceases in Andrews' other wells, and in the wells owned by Fowkes; when the pump well is turned off the level pressure rises in the others. Opening and closing the Current Creek Company's wells has the same, although somewhat less, effect. The evidence indicates that the hydrostatic pressure in the Fowkes' and Andrews' flowing wells decreased from about 11 feet above ground in the beginning of 1953 to about 8.5 feet below ground in October, 1956. * * *

When the operation of the Current Creek wells resulted in stopping the flow in the Fowkes' and Andrews' flowing wells, which had never occurred before, Andrews closed the Current Creek wells on their land and insisted that they be kept closed or damages paid. * * * Current Creek's rejoinder is that it was not their wells, but Andrews' own pump well that depleted the Andrews' and Fowkes' flowing wells, and they also assert that Andrews and Fowkes have no absolute rights to artesian pressure, but must use reasonable means and pumping equipment to get their water.

The trial court found that the relative time priorities of the parties to the water in the basin were: (1) springs owned by Andrews and Fowkes, (2) the flowing wells of Andrews and Fowkes, (3) the Andrews' pump well, and (4) the Current Creek Company wells. * * * The court found that there is unappropriated water within the basin. * * *

The court further found that the pump wells of both Andrews and Current Creek interfered with the flow of the flowing wells of Andrews and Fowkes. As to Andrews, it refused to find that the interference in their flow well was caused by the Current Creek wells, as distinguished from the effect caused by their own pump well, and therefore refused to allow them any redress. The decree required Andrews and Current Creek Company to replace for Fowkes 1.775 second feet of water during the irrigation season and 27.11 gallons of water per minute during the nonirrigation season to be supplied by furnishing and installing pumps and sources of power, the cost to be shared equally between them. It further prohibited Andrews and Current Creek from using their pump wells and required them to desist from pumping water until and unless they replaced the water to Fowkes as just stated. * * *

Prior appropriators of this underground water who have beneficially used it through the natural flow of springs or artesian wells are entitled to have the subsequent appropriators restrained from drawing the water out of and lowering the static head pressure of this underground basin unless they replace the quantity and quality of the water by pumping or other means to the prior appropriators at the sole cost of the subsequent appropriators. The same rule should apply to all junior appropriators present and future. They can appropriate water to a beneficial use from the underground basin if it is available but they must replace the flow of the wells and springs at the prior appropriator's place of diversion solely at their own cost. * * *

There can be no doubt that the above is a correct statement of the rules governing this situation. Section 73-3-23, U.C.A. 1953, expressly grants the right of replacement to any junior appropriator whose appropriation diminishes the quantity or quality of previously appropriated underground water at the sole cost or expense of the junior appropriator. The wording of this statute is clear, unambiguous and positive. * * *

The facts of our present case do not indicate that less water will be beneficially used if we continue to follow the right to static head pressure theory. Before the static head pressure was lowered Fowkes received their water without pumping. Now Current Creek gets more water than Fowkes claims from a lower elevation without pumping. There is no reason to believe that the cost of replacement to Current Creek will be prohibitive but that the cost of pumping to Fowkes will be otherwise. So far as this case is concerned, we have the choice between protecting a junior or senior appropriator with nothing whatever to indicate that more water will be beneficially used one way or the other. * * *

CROCKETT, CHIEF JUSTICE (dissenting). * * * The difficulty with preserving to the prior user the absolute right to water and also to the pressure and means of diversion is that projecting its application to basins where there are a great number of users reveals that it does not work to serve the necessary purpose of maximum development and use of water. [W]hen the water table of an underground basin is maintained at a high enough level to sustain pressure in flowing wells in the higher areas, there will be water above and near the surface in the lower areas forming ponds, marshes and swamps. This results in wasteful losses from surface evaporation and from consumption by water-loving plants, tules, reeds and rushes, indigenous to such areas, which are of little or no value. There is often further wastage from drainage of the basin by streams or by leakage and seepage out of it.

* * * The administrative problems relating to the determination of costs of maintaining pressure for prior users, and allocation against later users, would be insuperable. In addition thereto the cost imposed

upon the initiator of a new well might be prohibitive, so that even where there was unused water in the basin it would not be put to use. * * *

In fairness I must concede that the language of Sec. 73-3-23, U.C.A. 1953: "In all cases replacement shall be at the sole cost and expense of the applicant" may reasonably be given the meaning espoused by the majority opinion. * * * However, the preceding language, which provides the foundation for "replacement," states that "the right of replacement is hereby *granted* to any junior appropriator whose appropriation may diminish the quantity or injuriously affect the quality of [prior] appropriated underground water." (Emphasis added.) Thus *granting* the junior appropriator the *right* of replacement does not necessarily make it mandatory that he maintain pressure and means of diversion under all circumstances. * * * My interpretation of [Utah precedents] is that the prior appropriator gets the right to use the water and to such means of diversion as is reasonably efficient and does not cause undue waste of water.

Notes

1. **A different policy—protection of a reasonable means of diversion.** In City of Colorado Springs v. Bender, 366 P.2d 552 (Colo. 1961), owners of a well used to irrigate approximately fifty acres sued to enjoin interference by the larger, junior wells of a municipality, a hotel, and a water company—all of whom transported the water for use at places remote from the aquifer. The court said:

"At his own point of diversion on a natural water course, each diverter must establish some reasonable means of effectuating his diversion. He is not entitled to command the whole or a substantial flow of the stream merely to facilitate his taking the fraction of the whole flow to which he is entitled. This principle applied to diversion of underflow or underground water means that priority of appropriation does not give a right to an inefficient means of diversion, such as a well which reaches to such a shallow depth into the available water supply that a shortage would occur to such senior even though diversion by others did not deplete the stream below where there would be an adequate supply for the senior's lawful demand. * * *

"In determining [the aquifer water level at which a junior appropriator must cease diverting water to meet the demands of a senior appropriator,] the conditions surrounding the diversion by the senior appropriator must be examined as to whether he has created a means of diversion from the aquifer which is reasonably adequate for the use to which he has historically put the water of his appropriation. * * *

"A determination of these questions is necessary. The court must determine what, if anything, the plaintiffs should be required to do to make more efficient the facilities at their point of diversion, due regard being given to the purposes for which the appropriation had been made, and the 'economic reach' of plaintiffs. The plaintiffs cannot reasonably 'command the whole' source of supply merely to facilitate the taking by them of the fraction of the entire flow to which their senior appropriation entitles them. On the other hand, plaintiffs cannot be required to improve their extraction facilities beyond their economic reach, upon a consideration of all the factors involved." Id. at 555-56.

2. **Retreat from *Current Creek*?** In Wayman v. Murray City Corp., 458 P.2d 861 (Utah 1969), five householders within the city had small artesian wells that diminished in flow when the city changed its diversion from seven old wells with rights aggregating 750 g.p.m. to a new large well from which it drew the 750 g.p.m. The artesian basin had a natural outflow of 34,000 acre feet per year, so it appeared that there was enough water for all users. A statute provided that no change in point of diversion could be made that would impair any vested right of another without just compensation. The district court directed the state engineer to include in his order approving the change in point of diversion a requirement that the city must at its sole cost replace the plaintiffs' water in an amount and quality equal to their former use. The Utah Supreme Court reversed. It distinguished *Current Creek* because there junior wells interfered with senior wells, while in *Murray City* some of the city's old wells had priorities senior to the householders' wells and those senior priorities transferred to the new city well. The court remanded the case and directed the district court to apply a 'rule of reasonableness," requiring it to analyze the total situation and balance individual rights in relationship to each other in a reasonable way that would best serve the overall objective of seeing all available water put to beneficial use. The court said that, to some degree, the rights of each individual should be subordinate to and correlated with reasonable conditions and limitations established by law for the general good. It thus concluded that all users must, where necessary, employ reasonable and efficient means in taking their own waters in relation to the others.

3. **Domestic wells.** The owners of domestic wells have gotten mixed results in seeking protection of their means of diversion against the owners of newer, higher-capacity wells providing water for nondomestic purposes:

Erickson v. Crookston Waterworks Power & Light Co., 117 N.W. 435 (Minn. 1908) (correlative rights doctrine): the domestic well owner was obligated "to suffer a reasonable inconvenience for the common good of others equally dependent upon the same gift of nature" and had to pay the full cost of deepening his well if the water company could not feasibly get the water it needed for nondomestic use from another source.

MacArtor v. Graylyn Crest III Swim Club, Inc., supra p. 344, Note 4 (reasonable use doctrine): the domestic well owner and a swim club, both apparently overlying users, were required to share equally in the cost of deepening the domestic well or providing replacement water from the swim club's well.

Prather v. Eisenmann, 261 N.W.2d 766 (Neb. 1978) (reasonable use/correlative rights doctrine modified by a statute giving preference to domestic wells over all other wells): the owners of artesian domestic wells were entitled to impose on the owners of an interfering irrigation well the full cost of restoring their water supply.

Bishop v. City of Casper, 420 P.2d 446 (Wyo. 1966) (appropriation doctrine supplemented by a statute protecting "adequate" domestic wells against unreasonable interference): the owner of a domestic well twenty-four feet deep was not protected against interference by the city's junior deep wells because the domestic well was not adequate).

Fraser v. Water Rights Comm'n, 294 N.W.2d 784 (S.D. 1980) (appropriation doctrine as supplemented by a statute "protecting water for reasonable domestic use, without the necessity of requiring maintenance of artesian head pressure"): although the statute precludes absolute protection of artesian pressure for domestic wells, it does not to give the state water agency unbridled power to approve irrigation wells without considering the maintenance of artesian head pressure for domestic wells; a balancing of interests is required.

Parker v. Wallentine, 650 P.2d 648 (Idaho 1982) (appropriation doctrine): the owner of a domestic well with a 1964 priority was absolutely protected in his historic means of diversion, but the owner of an interfering deep junior irrigation well had a right of replacement, as in *Current Creek*, though no statute specifically authorized that; a longstanding statute protecting appropriators only in reasonable pumping levels was held not to apply to domestic wells, and a 1978 amendment thereto clearly subjecting domestic wells to the reasonable pumping level rule was held not to apply to domestic wells predating its enactment.

Restatement (Second) of Torts § 858(1)(a), supra p. 344, Note 5, imposes liability if a well "unreasonably" harms another well by lowering the water table or artesian pressure. According to comment f, interference by a large well with the diversion method of a domestic well making small withdrawals "usually" will be unreasonable when the large well produces water "for more lucrative purposes."

Nev. Rev. Stat. § 534.110(5) states that when a permit is sought to pump one-half cubic foot per second or more for municipal, quasi-municipal, or industrial use, "the state engineer shall include as a condition of the permit that pumping water pursuant to the permit may be limited or prohibited to prevent any unreasonable adverse effects on an existing domestic well located within 2,500 feet of the well, unless the holder of the permit and the owner of the domestic well have agreed to alternative measures that mitigate those adverse effects."

4. **Who should pay?** Suppose A, B, C, and D sequentially drill wells in an aquifer, each one month after the last. B imposes added pumping costs on A, C on A and B, and D on A, B, and C. In time, as a result of capture, a new condition of equilibrium is reached in which pumping and natural discharge are in balance with recharge. All four parties can continue thereafter to pump from the new, lower level. Did B "cause harm" to A, C to B and A, etc.? Review Ronald H. Coase, The Problem of Social Cost,

supra pp. 112-15, Note 4. Which rule, "junior pays senior's added costs" or "each pays his own costs," will optimize social welfare, the amount and value of product from the water that just equals the costs of producing the water? Is there any other criterion which tells which rule is "best"?

Edgar S. Bagley, Water Rights Law and Public Policies Relating to Ground Water "Mining" in the Southwestern States, 4 J.L. & Econ. 144, 161 (1961):

"In some cases the value of the water to a junior appropriator would be great enough to warrant his compensating or supplying the senior appropriator. This might be true if there are not many senior appropriators and if the supply available to the junior appropriator is large. But if there are many hundreds or thousands of prior appropriators who must be compensated for falling water levels additional appropriations may be effectively blocked. Under these conditions unappropriated parts of the perennial yield might go to waste. Considerations of economic effects as well as equity dictate, however, recognition of the fact that falling water levels create burdens on water users. The mere fact that water may be wasted unless junior appropriators are allowed to take supplies without compensating senior appropriators as long as perennial yield is not exceeded or economic pumping limits not yet reached does not imply that allowing such appropriations will enlarge net economic benefits. The higher pumping costs to prior appropriators is a real cost—and there is a question whether cheap methods of obtaining the water with some waste are more economical than more expensive methods which utilize supplies more completely. On the other hand, there may also be a difficult, if not impossible, administrative task which entails expensive costs in measuring the amount of damage additional withdrawals will inflict on prior appropriators. The best policy from an economic standpoint will depend on the facts of the case and would not necessarily always be one way or the other."

5. **What is a "reasonable" means of diversion?** Most appropriation doctrine states have statutes that protect a senior appropriator only in the maintenance of a reasonable pumping lift or reasonable static water level. In general, these statutes give little specific guidance on what is a "reasonable" pumping life or static water level. An important theme—explicit in some of the statutes and likely implicit in the others—is tension between two economic considerations. One is concern about protecting senior appropriators against water level decline that drops below what the *Bender* court, supra Note 1, called their "economic reach." The other is Bagley's concern, supra note 4, that full economic development should not be blocked by burdening new appropriators with liability for the increased withdrawal costs of existing appropriators. Douglas L. Grant, Reasonable Groundwater Pumping Levels Under the Appropriation Doctrine: The Law and Underlying Economic Goals, 21 Nat. Resources J. 1 (1981). A companion article, Douglas L. Grant, Reasonable Groundwater Pumping Levels Under the Appropriation Doctrine: Underlying Social Goals, 23 Nat. Resources J. 53 (1983), discusses policy considerations other than economics and concludes as follows:

"The earlier article opened by quoting the following statement about the reasonable pumping level concept from a National Water Commission study: 'No definitive guidelines exist as to what the measure of reasonableness is or how it will be applied.' Although the reasonable pumping level statutes incompletely enumerate factors that should bear on the measure of reasonableness, the root cause of the uncertainty lies deeper. Additional factors can be ascertained from study of appropriation doctrine laws and traditions, albeit with varying degrees of clarity. Definitive guidelines in the sense of rules that will yield mechanical answers, however, are impossible or at least unwise. Unless one is willing to accept a simplistic, tunnel vision approach, the need is inevitable to weigh potentially competing concerns about economic efficiency, wealth and merit good distribution, and (perhaps) other social goals."

6. **The full statutory mosaic.** Whatever a statute protecting reasonable static water level or reasonable pumping lift might mean in isolation, it will not necessarily operate independent of other elements of the state's water or groundwater code. In *Fundingsland*, supra p. 356, the Colorado court construed a statute calling for "full economic development" of groundwater and protecting existing appropriators in the maintenance of "reasonable groundwater pumping levels" to allow depletion of 40% of the available groundwater supply over twenty-five years. But in *Baker*, supra p. 367, Note 3, the Idaho court read a similar statute calling for "full economic development" of groundwater and protecting existing appropriators in "the maintenance of reasonable groundwater pumping levels" to prohibit mining. The court ruled this statute did not supersede or modify another statute limiting withdrawals to average natural recharge. Similarly, in *Doherty*, supra p. 362, the Oregon court held that a statute calling for "[d]epletion of ground water supplies below economic levels [to] be prevented or controlled within practicable limits" did not implicitly authorize mining down to the economic reach of irrigators because that statute had to be read in the context of other statutes requiring sustained-yield management and reasonably stable groundwater levels.

C. Physically Connected Groundwater and Surface Water

NATIONAL WATER COMMISSION, WATER POLICIES FOR THE FUTURE
233 (1973).

Ground water is often naturally interrelated with surface water: ground water feeds springs and surface streams, and surface water charges ground water reservoirs. Nevertheless, there persists in the laws of many States myths (long ago abandoned by hydrologists) that ground water is separate from and unrelated to surface water. * * *

As a consequence of the faulty perception of hydrology that ground water is separate from and unrelated to surface water, different legal regimes were applied to surface water and ground water, and only recently and in only a few water-short Western States has an effort been made to coordinate the administration of the integrated surface water-ground water supply. As Colorado and New Mexico have discovered, when the coordination effort comes late—after an economy has been developed in reliance on two different legal systems for one interrelated supply—achieving coordinated administration is very difficult. The problem in those two States is that surface water users generally came first, followed by ground water users pumping from aquifers interdependent with the surface stream. Over time, depletion of the underground aquifer reduced surface flow so that senior surface users were deprived of water by junior pumpers. Untangling this confusion has been a persistent problem in parts of the West.

Notes

1. **The Texas struggle with the myth of separateness.** The hydrologically unrealistic separate legal treatment of groundwater and surface water has led to protracted difficulties in Texas regarding the Edwards Aquifer. The Edwards Aquifer is a confined aquifer in south central Texas underlying 3600 square miles. It discharges primarily through large springs at its eastern end, which in turn feed surface streams. The aquifer is the sole or primary source of water for many pumpers, including the City of San Antonio, and the spring-fed surface streams also supply many water users. Around 1989, environmental interests began to complain that unregulated pumping decreased water flow in the springs and threatened several endangered species.

In 1991, the Sierra Club sued the Secretary of the Interior and the U.S. Fish and Wildlife Service in federal district court under the Endangered Species Act (ESA) to require them to take measures to maintain the water level in the aquifer high enough to provide sufficient spring flows for critical species habitat. The court ordered the U.S. Fish and Wildlife Service to determine the minimum spring flows needed to protect the listed species and advise other federal agencies of its findings so they could perform their duties under the ESA should Texas fail to regulate aquifer withdrawals as needed to protect listed species. Sierra Club v. Lujan, 36 Env't Rep. Cas. (BNA) 1533 (W.D. Tex. 1993), appeal dismissed, Sierra Club v. Babbitt, 995 F.2d 571 (5th Cir. 1993).

Responding to the federal pressure, the Texas Legislature passed the Edwards Aquifer Act, available at http://www.edwardsaquifer.org. The act created the Edwards Aquifer Authority (EAA), capped annual withdrawals, and charged the EAA with developing a mandatory permit system for groundwater withdrawals and also a critical period management plan to reduce withdrawals when aquifer water levels and spring flows fall enough to harm or jeopardize the listed species.

Activity by the EAA was stalled first by a U.S. Justice Department ruling that the method of selecting EAA board members violated the federal Voting Rights Act and then by state trial court rulings against the constitutionality of the Edwards Aquifer Act that eventually were overturned on appeal. Barshop v. Medina County Underground Water Cons. Dist., 925 S.W.2d 618 (Tex. 1996).

In 1994, during a drought and with no functioning EAA board, the *Sierra Club* federal district court appointed a monitor to develop an emergency plan for staged reductions of pumping. Fall rains then eliminated the need to implement the plan. In 1996, the Sierra Club sued again, and the federal district court again appointed a monitor to develop an emergency plan to reduce pumping. The court later entered a preliminary injunction activating the plan, but the Fifth Circuit vacated it under the Burford abstention doctrine, which calls for abstention to allow a state's comprehensive regulatory scheme to operate without the risk of competing attempts by the federal courts to exercise control over the same entity. Sierra Club v. City of San Antonio, 112 F.3d 789 (5th Cir. 1997).

The Edwards Aquifer Act instructed the EAA to issue permits to existing pumpers for their maximum historical water use to the extent water is available for permitting. The EAA proceeded to issue permits for 572,000 acre-feet, though that exceeded the act's cap on withdrawals. In 2007, the legislature raised the cap to 572,000 acre-feet but imposed tighter critical period rules that will require the reduction of groundwater withdrawals at higher aquifer water levels and spring flows than before. The legislature left in place a requirement that the EAA must implement methods and practices that will produce minimum spring flows need to protect the listed species by 2012.

In Edwards Aquifer Authority v. Day, 274 S.W.3d 742 (Tex. Civ. App. 2008), petition for review filed Feb. 2, 2009, the owners of overlying land argued that EAA's order limiting their groundwater withdrawals to fourteen acre-feet per year unconstitutionally took their property without just compensation. The court ruled the landowners had a constitutionally protected vested property right in the groundwater beneath their land and remanded for further proceedings based on that ruling.

Further details of the Edwards Aquifer story are reported in Todd H. Votteler, The Little Fish that Roared: The Endangered Species Act, State Groundwater Law, and Private Property Rights Collide Over the Texas Edwards Aquifer, 28 Envtl. L. 845 (1998), and Todd H. Votteler, Raiders of the Lost Aquifer? Or, the Beginning of the End to Fifty Years of Conflict Over the Texas Edwards Aquifer, 15 Tul. Envtl. L.J. 257 (2002).

Apart from the Edwards Aquifer Act, 1997 Senate Bill 1 acknowledges the reality of frequent hydrologic connection between groundwater and surface water in Texas. It requires the Texas Commission on Environmental Quality when processing permits to appropriate surface waters to consider the effects, if any, on groundwater or groundwater recharge. Tex. Water Code Ann. § 11.151. It also requires groundwater conservation districts, in coordination with surface water management entities on a regional basis, to develop comprehensive management plans that address, inter alia, conjunctive surface water management issues. Id. § 36.1071.

2. **The Arizona struggle with the myth.** Arizona applies the appropriation doctrine to streams and their subflow but not to percolating groundwater, the latter being governed by the reasonable use doctrine or by a 1980 groundwater act, see supra p. 378, Note 1. As part of the ongoing Gila River adjudication, Arizona has been struggling with how to define subflow subject to the appropriation doctrine.

The Arizona Supreme Court long ago defined subflow as "waters which slowly find their way through the sand and gravel constituting the bed of the stream, or the lands under or immediately adjacent to the stream," and which cannot be extracted without tending "to diminish appreciably and directly the flow of the surface stream." Maricopa County Mun. Water Cons. Dist. No. 1 v. Sw. Cotton Co., 4 P.2d 369, 380 (Ariz. 1931). Much later, the Gila River adjudication trial court adopted a 50%/90-day test for determining whether wells in the younger alluvium of the valley should be treated as pumping subflow. The test created a presumption that a well takes subflow if 90 days of continuous pumping will deplete the stream by 50% or more of the total volume pumped. The Arizona Supreme Court rejected this test as impermissibly broadening its longstanding definition of subflow. The court said the longstanding definition had served as the backdrop for vast investments in the state and should not be altered. The court added a measure of hydrologic reality, however, by saying that "if the cone of depression of a well has expanded to the point that it intercepts a stream, it almost certainly will be pumping subflow." *In re* General Adjudication of All Rights to Use Water in Gila River System & Source, 857 P.2d 1236, 1245 (Ariz. 1993).

On remand, the trial court ruled that the Gila River subflow is limited to a narrow strip called the saturated floodplain Holocene alluvium. But taking a cue from the supreme court, the trial court also ruled that a well outside the subflow zone is pumping subflow if its cone of depression extends to the subflow and its continued pumping will measurably deplete the volume of subflow and stream flow. The Arizona Supreme Court upheld these rulings, declaring that its earlier cases defining subflow "should not serve as a straitjacket that restricts us from reaching in the direction of the facts and, so far as possible under those decisions, conforming to hydrological reality." *In re* General Adjudication of All Rights to Use Water in Gila River Sys. & Source, 9 P.3d 1069, 1076, 1079 (Ariz. 2000).

On remand, the trial court developed an 11-step approach to applying the cone-of-depression test. The Arizona Supreme Court denied an interlocutory appeal to challenge that. *In re* Gen. Adjudication of All Rights to Use Water in Gila River Sys. & Source, No. WC-05-001-IR (Ariz. Sup. Ct. May 23, 2007). An Arizona expert on groundwater modeling predicts the trial court's approach is likely to cause nearly all of the wells in Arizona to be treated as pumping appropriable groundwater. Jon R. Ford, "The Role of Injury Determinations in Adjudicating Conjunctively Managed Resources: Modeling in the Context of Developing a Case (Analysis of the Arizona Cone of Depression Test)," Ford – 6, *in* Colorado Bar Ass'n CLE, *Conjunctive Management of Ground and Surface Water Resources* (Sept. 10, 2006).

3. **The Restatement.** The Restatement of Torts imposes liability on a well owner whose "withdrawal of groundwater has a direct and substantial effect upon a watercourse or lake and unreasonably causes harm to a person entitled to the use of its water." See supra p. 344, Note 5.

4. **Coordinated administration when the appropriation doctrine governs both groundwater and surface water.** Most western states that apply the appropriation doctrine to both groundwater and surface water now have statutes or case law adopting, at least to some degree, the principle of coordinated administration of priorities. The next three principal cases illustrate issues that arise under that principle.

POSTEMA v. POLLUTION CONTROL HEARINGS BOARD

Supreme Court of Washington, 2000.
142 Wash.2d 68, 11 P.3d 726.

MADSEN, J. These two consolidated cases, one of which involves four consolidated cases, present numerous issues arising from the Department of Ecology's denial of applications for groundwater appropriation permits on the basis that the groundwater sources are in hydraulic continuity with surface water sources and further appropriations are foreclosed under the criteria of RCW 90.03.290 [one of the criteria prohibits issuance of a permit for an appropriation that will "impair existing rights"]. In the five individual cases before this court, the Pollution Control Hearings Board [PCHB] upheld Ecology's denial of the groundwater applications. * * *

Ecology's understanding of hydraulic continuity has altered over time, as has its use of methods to determine hydraulic continuity and the effect of groundwater withdrawals on surface waters. In 1996, the United States Geologic Services published a report by Morgan and Jones regarding three-dimensional computer modeling for the complex geologic and hydrogeologic basins of Puget Sound. The report concluded that the effects of pumping always reaches [sic] some of the surface water boundaries, and can do so over many square miles. Prior to issuance of this report, there was no such model. Ecology maintains that in a complex hydrologic system, use of a three-dimensional computer model is the best method for determining the effects groundwater withdrawals will have on surface water flow and senior surface water right holders. Ecology concluded that the Morgan and Jones model could be used in decisions on the Jorgensen appellants' applications because the climate, topography, and geology in the Green-Duwamish, Snohomish, and Cedar-Sammamish watersheds were similar.

The primary issues common to these appeals concern the impact of groundwater withdrawals on surface waters having minimum flow requirements set by rule which are unmet a substantial part of the year, and on surface waters closed to further appropriation. * * * Appellant Postema contends that there must be a significant measurable effect on surface waters before a groundwater application may be denied even though hydraulic continuity between the ground and surface waters is established. In general, the appellants in the Jorgensen cases argue that minimum flows are limited rights, and that Ecology's regulations require a direct and measurable effect of groundwater withdrawal on surface waters using standard stream measuring equipment, which has effective limits of about five percent of stream flow, before hydraulic continuity has any legal significance vis-a-vis minimum flow rights. If, using these methods, no effect is measurable, these appellants reason, Ecology has no authority to deny a groundwater application because of any affect on or relationship to surface waters. * * *

Once established, a minimum flow constitutes an appropriation with a priority date as of the effective date of the rule establishing the minimum flow. RCW 90.03.345. Thus, a minimum flow set by rule is an existing right which may not be impaired by subsequent groundwater withdrawals. * * *

The appellants' arguments that there must be measurable effects on stream flows raise the question of how impairment must be determined. There seems to be no dispute that Ecology has revised its view of the interconnection of groundwater and surface water in hydraulic continuity as new information has become available. There is also no dispute that Ecology has altered the methods by which it determines the impact of groundwater withdrawal on surface waters. Ecology points to PCHB decisions upholding use of qualitative analysis, such a hydrological studies and conceptual modeling, and quantitative modeling, such as analytical equations or numeric models.

Ecology may use new methods to determine impairment as they are developed. Also, as the King County Superior Court reasoned [in the Jorgensen cases], logically one cannot actually measure the impact of a well which does not yet exist. That court said that the statutes and regulations do not prohibit use of modeling, and modeling may be the only means of quantifying effect, impact or conflict. * * *

We reject the Jorgensen appellants' claim that a direct and measurable impact on surface water must be shown using standard stream measuring devices before an application for a groundwater permit may be denied. We also reject Postema's argument that a significant measurable effect on stream flows is required. * * * The statutes do not authorize a de minimis impairment of an existing right. RCW 90.03.290

plainly permits no impairment of an existing right. This does not mean, however, that there is no need to show any impact on the surface water resource, nor does it mean that measurement is irrelevant to the inquiry. As explained, though, Ecology is entitled to use more advanced techniques as they become available and scientifically acceptable. Applicants should then be provided the opportunity to challenge Ecology's factual determinations.

We also reject the Board's holding that hydraulic continuity, where minimum flows are unmet a substantial part of the year, equates to impairment of existing rights as a matter of law. As the King County Superior Court noted, existing rights may or may not be impaired where there is hydraulic continuity depending upon the nature of the appropriation, the source aquifer, and whether it is upstream or downstream from or higher or lower than the surface water flow or level, and all other pertinent facts.

Additionally, we reject the premise that the fact that a stream has unmet flows necessarily establishes impairment if there is an effect on the stream from groundwater withdrawals. The Board held that the number of days the minimum flow levels are not met may be considered in determining water availability, but declined to rule on whether it can be the sole consideration. * * * The conclusion is correct. While the number of days minimum flows are unmet is a relevant consideration, it may be, for example, that due to seasonal fluctuations and time of withdrawal, groundwater withdrawal affecting the stream level will not impair the minimum flow rights. However, where minimum flows would be impaired, then an application must be denied.

We hold that hydraulic continuity of an aquifer with a stream having unmet minimum flows is not, in and of itself, a basis for denial of a groundwater application * * *. However, where there is hydraulic continuity and withdrawal of groundwater would impair existing surface water rights, including minimum flow rights, then denial is required. Ecology may use new information and scientific methodology as it becomes available and scientifically acceptable for determining hydraulic continuity and effect of groundwater withdrawals on surface waters.

In each of the rulings in the cases consolidated in Jorgensen, the Board ruled that as a matter of law Ecology could not grant a groundwater application for consumptive use where the groundwater is in hydraulic continuity with surface water which has been closed by rule. The King County Superior Court disagreed, holding that as in the case of streams with minimum flow rights, hydraulic continuity is a factual question which does not satisfy any of the criteria in RCW 90.03.290 for denying a water application. The Jorgensen appellants argue, as they do with respect to minimum flow rights, that hydraulic continuity alone is an insufficient ground for denial. Insofar as they contend that standard stream measuring devices, with five percent limits, must establish a direct and measurable impact on the surface water flow or levels, we disagree for the reasons discussed above. * * *

Note

Other standards on the amount of impact and method of proving impact needed for coordinated administration. Colorado integrates priorities to surface streams and tributary groundwater. Colo. Rev. Stat. § 37-92-102(1)(a). Although Colorado does not require a permit to appropriate water, it requires a permit to construct a well. § 37-90-137(1) (wells outside designated groundwater basins). The statutory standard for the state engineer to issue a permit is whether the proposed well would "materially injure" existing water rights. § 37-90-137(2)(b). Similarly, the state engineer cannot shut down an existing well under the priority principle unless it causes or will cause "material injury" to a senior water right. § 37-92-502(2).

Idaho has a material injury standard for coordinated administrative enforcement of surface water and groundwater priorities, supplemented by policy of reasonable water use. A senior appropriator can obtain administrative enforcement only if he is suffering material injury and is diverting and using water efficiently without waste. Idaho Admin. Code Rules 37.03.11, Rule 40.03. See Am. Falls Reservoir Dist. No. 2 v. Idaho Dep't of Water Res., 154 P.3d 433 (Idaho 2007) (rejecting a claim that the administrative rules were unconstitutional on their face.

Utah has a substantial interference standard for priority enforcement. In Salt Lake City v. Silver Fork Pipeline Corp., 5 P.3d 1206 (Utah 2000), SFPC claimed an appropriation of approximately .5 c.f.s. of groundwater that it intercepted in a mine and transported for residential use. Previously Salt Lake City had appropriated nearly the entire flow of a creek to which the groundwater was tributary. The court considered the adequacy of Salt Lake City's proof of substantial interference with its appropriation:

"SFPC argues that the district court erred in finding substantial interference without requiring Salt Lake to proffer actual measurements of water flowing in the creek at the mouth of the canyon, illustrating that diversion of water at the mine significantly diminished the flow in the creek. We disagree * * *. Measurements of water flow are often not available to prove interference, and when they are, their value is limited to the extent that other environmental factors dictate flow, such as season and amount of precipitation. It is especially difficult to demonstrate by empirical evidence the extent to which interception of percolating water interferes with a surface body of water to which it is tributary. Hydrogeological characteristics in a particular area may extend to decades the time it takes for underground water to percolate through the soil before reaching the surface, only then making the effect of interception evident based on diminished water levels.

"Given the difficulty in obtaining reliable measurements of water flow that accurately reflect the effects of interception of underground source waters, we cannot agree that a finding of interference must be premised on this type of evidence. If nearly .5 c.f.s. of water intercepted in the mine would naturally flow into the creek but for the existence of the mine, it is reasonable to infer that Salt Lake has suffered, or will eventually suffer, a diminution in its water right of approximately 362 acre-feet of water each year. This evidence is sufficient to support the trial court's finding of substantial interference." Id. at 1215.

TEMPLETON v. PECOS VALLEY ARTESIAN CONSERVANCY DISTRICT
Supreme Court of New Mexico, 1958.
65 N.M. 59, 332 P.2d 465.

H. VEARLE PAYNE, DISTRICT JUDGE. * * * The appellees filed with the State Engineer their applications to drill wells in the Roswell Shallow Water Basin. Although these were on the usual forms for applications to appropriate underground waters, it was agreed by all of the parties that in effect these applications constituted applications for the changing of the point of diversion of waters from points in the Rio Felix to points in the Valley Fill of the Roswell Shallow Water Basin. The applications were denied by the State Engineer, and an appeal was perfected to the District Court of Chaves County. Upon hearing before the District Court, judgment was entered in favor of the applicants from which the Pecos Valley Artesian Conservancy District and S.E. Reynolds, State Engineer of the State of New Mexico, have appealed. * * *

* * * The water rights of the appellees were to irrigate certain land out of the Rio Felix. The amount of water in the Rio Felix has decreased in recent years for the reasons hereinafter mentioned, so that the water in the river is insufficient to irrigate the land of the appellees and they have applied for permits to drill wells to supplement this water to the extent necessary to produce the amount of water originally appropriated. * * *

The Rio Felix is a small water course which crosses Chaves County from the west toward the east, and empties into the Pecos River. There are two underground bodies of water in this area. The deepest one is known as the Roswell Artesian Basin, and the upper body of water is known as the Roswell Shallow Water Basin. These two bodies of water are separated by impervious red shale and gypsum, known as the Pecos Red Beds. Below the Pecos Red Beds is the body of artesian water and above the Pecos Red Beds is the Roswell Shallow Water Basin. Above the Pecos Red Beds and spreading over the basin is what is known as the Valley Fill which consists of topsoil, sand, gravel, shale, clay, and boulders which have been washed in and deposited through the centuries. The Shallow Water Basin is held in this Valley Fill and varies in thickness from nothing on the west to two hundred and fifteen feet or more on the east.

The Rio Felix channel passes across this Valley Fill and at places is as deep as twenty-five feet or more into the Valley Fill. The water flow of this river, except for flood waters, rises into the channel from the Valley Fill wherever the waters of the Shallow Basin are higher than the bed of the river.

The Rio Felix is a stream that heads in the foothills of the Sacramento Mountains and runs down to the Pecos River. It is not a continuous stream except in flood times. The waters that fall on the headwaters of the stream run for a distance and then they lose themselves in the ground. In other words, the headwaters of the Rio Felix sink and become a part of the Valley Fill except for the times when the stream is in flood stage. * * *

Until the year 1952, the flow of the Rio Felix supplied enough water for the irrigation of the lands involved, but about that time the water table began to lower materially, and thus decreased the amount of water which, except for floods, flowed into the Rio Felix, so that the appellees have been unable to secure sufficient waters from the river to properly irrigate their lands. This decrease in the water table was due to the pumping of water from irrigation wells which have been drilled into the Shallow Water Basin in later years, aggravated by several years of drouth. * * *

Witness Brown is an Engineer with many years of experience. He testified as follows:

"Q. Is there any difference in the water that is produced by the shallow wells, or wells in the shallow basin, from the Felix water? A. No, and I would like to explain that this way. In a natural state, the shallow ground water is discharged into the Felix, as described by prior witnesses, because the Felix is cut down below the ground water table. When the first shallow wells were drilled and pumped, the effect of withdrawal of water from the shallow wells was to intercept the ground water that was migrating toward the Felix, so that it reduced the discharge into the Felix, but as the wells were pumped, and the levels of the ground water was lowered, the water level in the wells got down to where they were below the bed of the Felix, and when water is withdrawn under that condition, instead of intercepting water which is going to the Felix, it actually diverts water from the Felix, just as certainly as if it was pumped out of the river, or as if a person had built a dam and taken it off through a canal. Likewise, these appellants, when their wells are put down and water is pumped from them, they will be withdrawing water from the Felix to some extent, the same as these shallow waters in the surrounding area are now doing."

* * *

The Court concluded that the water of appellees appropriated from the natural flow of the Rio Felix included the waters in the Valley Fill that would have naturally reached the river, except for the acts of subsequent appropriators. The Court further concluded that the restoration to the appellees of the quantity of water originally appropriated by means of wells sunk into the Valley Fill at the locations designated by the appellees, cannot and does not impair any other water right. * * *

[T]he appellants [contend] that the proposed change of point of diversion amounts to a new appropriation in an underground basin that is fully appropriated. This proposition is based on the assumption that there is no connection between the surface flow of the Rio Felix and the underground water basin. The findings of the lower court do not support this assumption. The lower court found that the headwaters of the Rio Felix sank into the ground and became a part of the Valley Fill and then rose again into the river and that the appropriations made by the appellees amounted to appropriations out of the Valley Fill.

In 93 C.J.S. Waters § 170, p. 909, is found the following: "An appropriation when made follows the water to its original source, whether through surface or subterranean streams or through percolations."

In the case of Richlands Irrigation Company v. Westview Irrigation Company, 96 Utah 403, 80 P.2d 458, 465, the Supreme Court of Utah had the following to say:

> "The entire watershed to its uttermost confines, covering thousands of square miles, out to the crest of the divides which separate it from the adjacent watersheds, is the generating source from which the water of a river comes or accumulates in its channel. Rains and snows falling on this entire vast area sink into the soil and find their way by surface or underground flow or percolation through the sloping strata down to the central channel. This entire sheet of water, or water table, constitutes the river and it never ceases to be such in its centripetal motion towards the channel. Any appropriator of water from the central channel is entitled to rely and depend upon all the sources which feed the main stream above his own diversion point, clear back to the farthest limits of the watershed."
>
> * * *

Applying the foregoing principles to this case would lead to the conclusion that the appellees were entitled to the waters of the Valley Fill that flowed into the Rio Felix at the time of their appropriation. It seems that there is nothing in the law that would prevent them from following this water through an application for a change of point of diversion, provided that it does not impair any other existing rights. In other words, their applications do not amount to a request for a new appropriation in the underground water basin, but merely a request to follow the source of their original appropriation. * * *

The appellants argue that this amounts to a change from a river or surface water right to an underground water right. If the river and the underground waters had two separate sources of supply and if there were no connection between them, this argument might be sound, but under the facts set forth above, the Valley Fill was the source of the flow of the river.

The next contention of the appellants, was that the change of point of diversion would impair existing rights. This was a question of fact which was determined by the lower court against the appellants * * *. The appellants objected that [this] finding of fact * * * is contrary to [another finding by the lower court that] "the shallow waters of the Roswell Basin were closed to further appropriation on August 1, 1937, by Order of the State Engineer, which recited that all of said waters were fully appropriated."

Apparently this [objection] is based on the assumption that the appellees are seeking a new appropriation. As pointed out above, they are not seeking a new appropriation but merely seeking a change in the point of diversion. Previously the water flowed from the Valley Fill into the Rio Felix and was then lifted on to the land by means of dams or pumping plants. The appellees now intend to lift the water directly out of the Valley Fill, due to the fact that the water table has been lowered. This does not mean that it is a new appropriation at all, but merely a change in the method of extracting the water from the Valley Fill. * * *

[Affirmed.]

Notes

1. **Reasons for a _Templeton_ well.** Why would a senior stream appropriator whose right is unfilled choose to install a supplemental well rather than seek priority enforcement against junior appropriators whose wells are depleting the stream? Perhaps the state lacks an effective process to enforce priorities administratively, so that closure of junior wells would require expensive and time-consuming litigation to determine which individual wells are reducing the stream flow, by how much, at what times, and where on the stream their impacts occur. Or perhaps even swift closure of junior wells would fail to restore the stream flow soon enough because of the distance the junior wells are from the stream and the slow movement of groundwater.

2. **Extension of _Templeton_.** Langenegger v. Carlsbad Irrigation District, 483 P.2d 297 (N.M. 1971), extended _Templeton_ further back in the hydrologic cycle. The Pecos River was supplied partly by base flows that passed through the Valley Fill shallow aquifer and partly by flood flows from precipitation within the river drainage. The Red Beds that supported the Valley Fill and confined the underlying artesian Roswell Underground Basin in this area leaked water upwards from the artesian basin into the overlying shallow aquifer. Thus, the base flows supplying

the river included some water from the artesian basin. The court held that a senior appropriator from the Pecos River could drill a supplemental well through the Valley Fill and the Red Beds and tap the artesian water. Moreover, the court allowed him to take water from the new artesian wells as needed to satisfy his full right, rather than take only that percentage of historically available stream flow coming from the artesian basin or even from base flows.

3. **More on *Templeton*.** Herrington v. State, 133 P.3d 258 (N.M. 2006), stressed that a *Templeton* well must tap the same groundwater that was the source of the original stream appropriation. The court also said the same-source requirement might be met even if the supplemental well is located below the stream diversion because once junior wells lower the water table, groundwater formerly discharged to the stream at or above the original point of diversion might instead discharge at a lower elevation.

The court also distinguished between installing a *Templeton* well and changing the point of diversion from a surface stream to groundwater pursuant to a statutory transfer. It said the same-source requirement for a *Templeton* well is stricter than what is required for a statutory transfer. The latter merely requires that the water at the old and new points of diversion be "hydrologically connected," which means the two diversion points only need to "draw from the same hydrologic unit." Id. at 269-70. The new diversion after statutory transfer need not draw the same groundwater that was the source of the original stream appropriation.

The New Mexico transfer statute, as is typical of western transfer statutes, does not allow a change in point of diversion that will impair any other water right. Is there also a no-impairment limitation on a *Templeton* well? Or is an existing junior well never legally "impaired" by a *Templeton* well even if the junior well goes dry provided the senior stream appropriator could have shut down the junior well under the priority principle instead of installing a *Templeton* well?

If a *Templeton* well and an affected existing junior well both continue to operate, the latter perhaps pumping from a greater depth, what will be the long-term consequences to the water system? See Note 1, supra p. 354.

2. **Voluntary versus mandated switch from a surface water to a groundwater diversion.** The issue in *Templeton* was whether a senior stream appropriator could switch voluntarily to a groundwater diversion. A key issue in the next case is whether a senior stream appropriator could be *required* to switch to a groundwater diversion rather than insist that junior wells be shut down to restore stream flow.

ALAMOSA-LA JARA WATER USERS PROTECTION ASS'N v. GOULD

Supreme Court of Colorado, 1983.
674 P.2d 914.

DUBOFSKY, J. This is an appeal from a judgment of the district court for Water Division 3 regarding rules promulgated by the Colorado State Engineer limiting the use of surface and underground water in the San Luis Valley. Curtailment of water use in the valley is required by the terms of an interstate stipulation under which Colorado must meet its Rio Grande Compact obligation to deliver scheduled amounts of Rio Grande water at the Colorado-New Mexico border on an annual basis. The dispute over the proposed rules concerns the distribution of that curtailment * * * between well owners and surface diverters. The water court * * * disapproved rules which phased out all wells in the San Luis Valley unless each well owner could demonstrate a lack of material injury to senior surface water users or provide a plan of augmentation to replace the water taken by a well. * * *

The upper 6000 feet of fill below the valley surface consists of unconsolidated clay, silt, sand, and gravel, and interbedded lava flows, containing an estimated two billion acre-feet of underground water. Some of the underground water is in an unconfined aquifer system at shallow depths. Beneath the unconfined aquifer are relatively impermeable beds of clay and basalt and beneath these confining layers are substantial quantities of water which comprise the confined aquifer. The confining clay layer generally does not exist around the valley's perimeter, and the confined aquifer system is recharged from surface flow to the underground water system at the edges of the valley. Because the recharge areas are higher in elevation than the floor of the valley, the confined aquifer is under artesian pressure, resulting in the free flow of water from some artesian wells and springs at natural breaks in the confining layer. In some places, where the confining layer is less thick and more transmissive, water from the confined aquifer will leak upward through the confining clay layers into the unconfined aquifer. The unconfined aquifer is directly connected with the surface streams in some places. To varying degrees, the surface streams, the unconfined aquifer, and the confined aquifer are hydraulically connected.

The first appropriations from streams in the valley began in the 1850s on the Conejos River. The first appropriation on the Rio Grande mainstem was in 1866, and the most extensive development for irrigation purposes on both rivers was between 1880 and 1890. By 1900, the natural flow of all surface streams in the valley was over-appropriated. High spring runoff and low summer flows in valley streams, coupled with years of severe drought, resulted in undependable water supplies for irrigation; thus, farmers turned to wells and reservoirs to supplement and regulate their water supply.

Well construction in the valley began as early as 1850. Between 1880 and 1891, about 2,000 artesian wells were drilled. Withdrawals from the confined aquifer by wells remained relatively constant until the early 1950s when a number of large capacity wells were constructed. In 1972, the state engineer ceased issuing permits for wells to be drilled into the confined aquifer after determining that both aquifers were tributary to the surface streams in the valley. * * *

In 1975, the state engineer promulgated the proposed rules * * *. [T]he underground water rules provide for phasing out of underground water diversions unless the underground water user submits proof to the division engineer that the user's well is operating under a decreed plan of augmentation or has a decree as an alternate point of diversion, or that the underground water appropriation can occur without impairing the right of a senior appropriator. * * *

At trial * * * all parties agreed that historical hydrologic patterns in the valley have changed dramatically, particularly since 1950, because of a combination of natural and man-made causes, resulting in an overall reduction in surface water supplies. The state and the Conejos District asserted that the primary cause of the reduction is increased well pumping, but there was also evidence that decreased snowpack runoff and more efficient irrigation are responsible causes. The theories were supported by studies, which contrasted stream system inflow and outflow, and computer modelling, which estimated overall stream depletions from well withdrawals. Farmers testified to the effect of loss of surface water on their ability to grow crops and the need for supplemental well water when surface supplies are undependable. Finally, evidence was presented that the natural consumptive use of water by evapotranspiration from native grasses and phreatophytes, such as cottonwood, greasewood and rabbitwood, accounts for a large portion of the annual loss of water in the valley. Expert testimony indicated, and the water court found, that when wells are pumped, lowering the water table below phreatophyte root zones, the result is a substantial salvage of water, perhaps as much as one million acre-feet a year, that would otherwise be lost through evapotranspiration. * * *

The water court disapproved the underground water rules, suggesting that section 37-92-502, C.R.S. requires that the state engineer must determine that each well causes material injury to a senior appropriator before that well may be curtailed and holding the rules to be inconsistent with the statutory and judicial policy of maximum utilization of water. The court held * * * that in some instances senior appropriators may be required to drill new wells to augment or replace their surface water diversions before curtailment of junior rights can be required. * * * The state and the Conejos District appeal the water court's disapproval of the underground water rules. * * *

In support of the underground water rules, the state engineer introduced voluminous exhibits which showed that well pumping decreases artesian pressure, resulting in increased recharge to the confined aquifer from the streams in the recharge areas and decreased flow into surface streams from springs fed from the confined aquifer, and ultimately, in streamflow depletion. The state engineer estimated that well diversions from both aquifers annually deplete the Rio Grande mainstem by 17,700 acre-feet and the Conejos River by 16,400 acre-feet. He concluded that junior well diversions were causing material injury to senior water rights throughout the valley.

The water court found that the underground water was tributary to the surface streams; that surface decrees were experiencing increasing curtailment; and that underground water withdrawals had accelerated in recent years, affecting surface flows. The court also found that the effect of underground water withdrawals had not been specifically quantified and had not been attributed to individual wells. None of the parties take issue with the water court's general factual findings. Instead the rules' proponents challenge the legal bases of the water court's disapproval of the underground water rules. * * *

In disapproving the underground water rules, the water court looked to language in section 37-92-502(2), C.R.S. which prohibits the curtailment of a diversion unless the diversion is causing material injury to senior water rights. The water court stressed the statutory reference to "each case" and "each diversion" and concluded that the materiality of injury must be determined individually for each well * * *. To the extent that the water court ruling disapproves the rules because they presume material injury to senior rights from all junior groundwater diversions in the valley, and to the extent that the ruling requires the division engineer to reprove in each individual well determination the existence of material injury which has already been proven on a valley-wide basis, the ruling is in error. * * * The purpose of the materiality of injury requirement is to prevent the futile curtailment of underground water diversions, not to erect a procedural roadblock to effective regulation of wells. * * *

[W]here, as here, streams are over-appropriated and underground water diversions from an aquifer have been found to significantly affect stream flow, it may be presumed that each underground water diversion materially injures senior appropriators. The state engineer, therefore, will not be required to repeat for every well curtailed the painstaking analysis which led to the aquifer-wide determination of material injury. * * *

The water court disapproved the well regulations because they did not contain a requirement that stream appropriators tap the enormous supply of water underlying the surface of the valley. Relying upon the reasonable-means-of-diversion requirement adopted in Colorado Springs v. Bender, 148 Colo. 458, 366 P.2d 552 (1961) and codified in section 37-92-102(2)(b), C.R.S.; the policy of "maximum utilization" of the State's water as recognized in Fellhauer v. People, 167 Colo. 320, 447 P.2d 986 (1968); and the requirement under section 37-92-102(1), C.R.S., of integration of administration of underground water tributary to a stream with the use of surface water, the water court held that, under certain circumstances, surface stream appropriators have a duty to withdraw underground water tributary to the stream in order to satisfy their surface appropriations. The court observed that this may take the form of requiring senior appropriators to drill new wells to augment or replace their surface water diversions before they can require curtailment of junior rights, and that *Bender* provides that the sole limitation on seniors' duty to effectuate reasonable means of diversion is that senior appropriators cannot be required to improve their extraction facilities beyond their economic reach.

The state engineer asserts that the proposed rules properly place the burden of remedying the injury caused to senior appropriators on junior water users and that the water court's ruling is a misapplication of law. The state engineer relies upon the principle, codified in section 37-92-102, C.R.S., that the priority system governs water allocation and that junior water rights from whatever source are not entitled to divert water that otherwise would be available for use by senior water rights. Under the prior appropriation doctrine, it is argued, the burden of integrating surface and groundwater rights falls upon junior water users, primarily through plans for augmentation under section 37-92-103(9), C.R.S. * * *

Here, several witnesses testified that the water in storage in the valley's aquifers provides the support for the water above it to move to the streams. The well owners and the communities argue that it is not unreasonable to require surface diverters to deepen their headgates if the water from the stream is beneath their feet. The argument continues that the surface owners have lost nothing except a gravity flow source of supply which is cheaper and easier to divert, and that the loss only occurs at times when the surface stream is inadequate to fill the surface diverters' priorities. A reasonable means of diversion in this case, it is argued, is one that eliminates the need for supporting the surface stream, thereby freeing the underground water for maximum beneficial use.

The Conejos District * * * argues that augmentation is one of the means provided to achieve maximum utilization under the 1969 [Water Right Determination and Administration] Act, and that because the proposed rules require junior wells to augment, the rules are consistent with the policy of maximum utilization. Evaluation of different means of achieving maximum utilization, however, is a matter of policy, and therefore a task to be performed by the state engineer after full consideration of the available alternatives. In proposing the instant rules, the state engineer * * * excluded consideration of the reasonableness of surface diversions, concluding that the prior appropriation doctrine prevented any means of maximizing utilization of the waters of the San

Luis Valley other than what could be accomplished by augmentation plans developed by junior well owners.

* * * The prior appropriation doctrine is not a legal barrier to the concurrent consideration by the state engineer of the various methods of implementing the state policy of maximum utilization set out in the 1969 Act. See Trelease, Conjunctive Use of Ground Water and Surface Water, 27 Rocky Mtn. Min. L. Inst. 1853 (1982); Harrison & Sandstrom, The Ground Water Surface Water Conflict and Recent Colorado Water Legislation, 43 U. Colo. L. Rev. 1 (1971). * * *

The water court held that, under certain circumstances, surface stream appropriators may be required to withdraw underground water tributary to the stream in order to satisfy their surface appropriations. We affirm this legal conclusion and return the proposed well rules to the state engineer for consideration of whether the reasonable-means-of-diversion doctrine provides, in this case, a method of achieving maximum utilization of water—a consideration which the state engineer erroneously believed was foreclosed. We note that the policy of maximum utilization does not require a single-minded endeavor to squeeze every drop of water from the valley's aquifers. Section 37-92-501(e) makes clear that the objective of "maximum use" administration is "optimum use." Optimum use can only be achieved with proper regard for all significant factors, including environmental and economic concerns. See section 37-92-102(3), C.R.S. (recognizing the need to correlate the activities of mankind with reasonable preservation of the natural environment); Harrison & Sandstrom, supra, at 14-15 (An increase of well diversions at the expense of maintenance of a surface flow would increase the efficiency of irrigation at the expense of other environmental and economic values.). See also Trelease, supra, at 1866-1872 (Determination of what constitutes a reasonable means of diversion may be more a question of the proper allocation of the costs of more efficient diversion than of the quantity of water ultimately diverted.). The water court observed that the state engineer's reconsideration might take the form of requiring senior appropriators to drill new wells before requiring curtailment of junior rights and listed a number of suggestions for increasing utilization. Similarly, the state engineer's reconsideration might result in assessment to junior appropriators of the cost of making those improvements to seniors' diversions which are necessitated by junior withdrawals. Selection among these and other possibilities, including retention of the scheme of the proposed rules, is a policy decision to be made by the state engineer, after consideration of all relevant factors.

[W]e affirm the water court's disapproval of the underground water rules. [W]e remand the rules for the state engineer's consideration of the policy of maximum utilization and the reasonable-means-of-diversion doctrine. * * *

Notes

1. **Subsequent events.** On remand, the state engineer avoided having to grapple with repromulgating the rules. A moratorium on new wells, strict administration of water rights, and the addition to the Rio Grande of shallow groundwater salvaged by a Bureau of Reclamation project combined to enable full compact compliance without the rules. See Simpson v. Cotton Creek Circles LLC, 181 P.3d 252, 255-57 (Colo. 2008).

Nonetheless, conjunctive management remained a big issue in the San Luis Valley. In 1998, the legislature expressed interest in greater development of the confined aquifer, which is tributary to the stream system because of its leakage into the unconfined aquifer. The legislature directed the state engineer to develop more data on the connection between the confined aquifer and surface water and then issue rules for new wells in the aquifer. It instructed him that the rules must "recognize that unappropriated water is not made available and injury is not prevented as a result of the reduction of water consumption by nonirrigated native vegetation." Act of May 26, 1998, 1998 Colo. Legis. Serv., ch. 231 (H.B. 98-1011) (West).

In 2004, the legislature directed the state engineer to regulate the confined and unconfined aquifers "to maintain a sustainable water supply in each aquifer system." Colo. Rev. Stat. § 37-92-501(4)(a)(I). It instructed him not to "recognize the reduction of water consumption by phreatophytes as a source of replacement water for new water uses or to replace existing depletions" and not to "require senior surface water right holders with reasonable means of surface diversions to rely on underground water to satisfy their appropriative water right." § 37-92-501(4)(b)(III), (IV). He later issued rules for new wells in the confined aquifer that the Colorado Supreme Court approved in *Cotton Creek Circles*, supra.

2. **Complexities of integrating priorities under the appropriation doctrine.** Integrated administration of groundwater and surface water rights under the appropriation doctrine can be complicated. One complication is described in David L. Harrison & Gustave Sandstrom, Jr., The Groundwater-Surface Water Conflict and Recent Colorado Water Legislation, 43 U. Colo. L. Rev. 1, 18 (1971):

"It is worthwhile to emphasize the time dimension of this problem. * * * When a user or water official discovers that a senior right is being damaged by a well far away in terms of [the time lag between pumping and impact on stream flow], it may be too late to cure the situation. The well pumping can be shut down immediately but it may be days before the effect of the shutdown is felt. For the irrigator the water must be delivered at a crucial time; a delay may mean crop destruction."

Another complication is noted in *In re* Arkansas River, 581 P.2d 293, 295-96 (Colo. 1978):

"When water in the aquifer is brought to the surface by a well and there is a consumptive use of that water * * *, generally the surface supply is depleted by the amount of such consumptive use. The evidence and findings in this case demonstrate, however, that the restriction of wells does not necessarily result in a comparable increase in the supply of surface water. There are countereffects which offset or modify the depletive use of well water. Some of these are: variations in the amount of river flow; more winter irrigation; reduction in evaporation and phreatophyte losses as a result of lowering of water tables; changes in ground water storage; extent of alluvium recharge occurring during wet cycles or as a result of widespread winter irrigation practices; and increased irrigation efficiencies. Other factors which may also be involved are increased ground water storage, stock ponds, municipal sewage lagoons, potholes, changes in side channel inflows, and cyclical fluctuations through wet and dry periods."

See also Douglas L. Grant, The Complexities of Managing Hydrologically Connected Surface and Groundwater Under the Appropriation Doctrine, 22 Land & Water L. Rev. 63, 64-65 (1987).

3. **Coordination when different legal doctrines govern surface water and groundwater.** In City of Lodi v. East Bay Municipal Utilities District, 60 P.2d 439 (Cal. 1936), the city had a right under the correlative rights doctrine to pump from an aquifer recharged by percolation from the Mokelumne River. As a nonoverlying user, the city's groundwater right was inferior to all overlying uses but was governed by the priority principle as against other nonoverlying uses. See supra p. 343, Note 3. The utility district had an appropriation from the river that was junior in time to the city's groundwater use. The trial court enjoined the utility district from making stream diversions that would lower the water table at the city's wells. The California Supreme Court reversed and remanded:

"One of the expert witness called by the plaintiff conceded that its wells could go down at least 25 feet below their present levels without danger or substantial injury to the plaintiff. Assuming a lowering of one foot a year by the District's operations, as found by the trial court, it is apparent that the plaintiff's water supply is in no immediate danger. [T]he cause should be sent back to the trial court to permit it to take evidence as to the levels to which plaintiff's wells may be lowered without substantial danger to the city's water supply. In fixing this danger level an adequate safety factor in favor of the city should be allowed. * * * The decree should then be reframed to provide that the duty rests upon the District to maintain the levels of the plaintiff's wells above the danger level so fixed by the trial court; that in the event the levels of the wells reach the danger points, the duty be cast upon the District to supply water to the city, or to raise the levels of the wells above the danger mark; * * * ." Id. at 451-52.

Suppose the plaintiff had been an overlying rather than a nonoverlying groundwater user. Should it have fared worse than the city did for lack of an appropriative right that could be compared in priority with the district's appropriation?

Nebraska allocates surface water primarily under the appropriation doctrine and groundwater under a reasonable use/correlative rights doctrine (see supra p. 344, Note 4). The state also bifurcates administration of the two water sources. The Department of Natural Resources (DNR) administers surface water, and local natural resources districts have the primary responsibility for administering groundwater. Over time, it became clear that this bifurcated structure was inadequate to deal with conflicts between surface water and groundwater users.

The Nebraska legislature addressed the problem in 2004. It required DNR to designate river basins or parts thereof that are fully appropriated or over appropriated and to identify within these areas where hydrologic connections exist between surface water and groundwater. For each designated area, DNR and the local natural resources district or districts involved must jointly develop and implement an integrated management plan (IMP). New uses of surface water and groundwater are stayed until an IMP is in place. An IMP must contain controls aimed at achieving a sustainable balance between water supply and demand. If DNR and the local district or districts cannot agree on an IMP, an Interrelated Water Review Board, consisting of the governor or governor's designee and four other persons appointed by the governor, will break the impasse. Nebraska Ground Water Management and Protection Act §§ 46-701 to -753.

In 2005, with the new statutory scheme in its infancy, the Nebraska Supreme Court adopted Restatement (Second) of Torts § 858 to resolve litigation between users of surface water and groundwater. Spear T Ranch, Inc. v. Knaub, 691 N.W.2d 116 (Neb. 2005). Section 858, quoted supra p. 344, imposes liability for a groundwater withdrawal that "has a direct and substantial effect upon a watercourse or lake and unreasonably causes harm to a person entitled to the use of its water."

4. **Hydrologic and policy considerations in coordinated management.** W.P. Balleau, Water Appropriation and Transfer in a General Hydrogeologic System, 28 Nat. Resources J. 269, 271-74, 278-80 (1988):

[Generally,] the reliable baseflow of streams was diverted early for irrigation. * * * Reclamation projects later stored the winter and peak flows and claimed much of the remaining yield from the river systems. Groundwater development followed in the 20th century and has reduced the baseflow of many streams. * * *

"The degree of effect on a stream due to groundwater development varies in each case. The effects on some streams are insignificant, while other stream reaches have changed from perennial to intermittent flow because the regional water table has declined below the stream bed. * * * With wells nearby the surface streams, the total system yield may be expanded in the short term. The system then rapidly adjusts to a new equilibrium with little net gain in the system yield. At greater distances from the surface water bodies, the spacing of the wells and the groundwater hydraulics may allow major expansion of the total supply for centuries. In all cases, the eventual reduction in surface water supply as a result of groundwater development creates an issue in water rights administration.

"The administration of groundwater in the priority system is not straightforward because the source of groundwater has two components:

groundwater storage and induced recharge of surface water. Development of aquifer storage interjects an additional source of water into the otherwise well-ordered surface water scheme. Groundwater storage is relatively large. Variation in supply is not a consideration until the decline in water level becomes an economic problem. Diversions from wells, however, are physically linked to surface depletions in the form of induced recharge from the surface streams. * * *

"The timing of effects on adjacent streams caused by groundwater withdrawal depends upon the aquifer diffusivity and the distance from the wells to the surface water body. The major factor in determining the rate of effects on surface supplies is the distance of withdrawals from the surface sources. For radial flow of groundwater, a 10-fold increase in distance from the surface water body causes a 100-fold delay in the response time, whereas a change in diffusivity is linearly proportional to the response time.

"Every groundwater development * * * begins with 100 percent of withdrawals being derived from storage. The timing of the change from storage depletion (mining) to induced recharge from surface water bodies is key to the water policy question. * * * The management category of mineable, nontributary or unrechargeable water is a reasonable one to apply to wellfield areas that would not progress beyond the earliest stages of [transition from storage depletion to induced recharge from surface supplies] within a reasonable planning horizon. * * *

"The rate at which dependence on groundwater storage converts to dependence on surface water depletion is highly variable and is peculiar to each case. * * * The distinct category of groundwater mining depends entirely upon the time frame. All groundwater developments initially mine water, and finally do not."

Balleau makes the important point that groundwater pumping may expand the total system yield significantly during the period that storage is being consumed, but over the long term a new equilibrium will be reached with little net gain in the system yield. He focuses on the induced recharge element of capture. (To review capture, see supra p. 354, Note 1.) Another possible element of capture is reduced natural discharge. In *Alamosa-La Jara,* for example, the trial court found that lowering the water table below phreatophyte root zones through pumping would capture perhaps one million acre-feet per year by reducing natural discharge (evapotranspiration) from the saturated zone. Would Balleau's point—that groundwater pumping will produce little net gain in system yield over the long term—be valid for an area like the San Luis Valley, where instead of increasing recharge the pumping would reduce natural discharge?

The answer is yes if the "total system yield" prior to lowering of the water table is understood to encompass not just discharge through wells but also the natural discharge, including the one million acre-feet of annual natural discharge to phreatophytes. If the junior wells in *Alamosa-La Jara* were to continue to operate, the annual system yield would increase during the period that storage is being depleted. But once storage depletion ceases because of capture (whether in the form of greater induced recharge or decreased natural discharge) and a new equilibrium is reached, the total annual system yield would return more or less to what it was. In the process, however, part of the total system yield would be reallocated: The one million acre-feet per year that phreatophytes formerly consumed would go instead to junior wells. Moreover, senior stream appropriators would have to take their shares of the total system yield from underground through wells rather than from surface sources that have dried up.

Balleau says the timing of the transition from storage depletion to capture is key to water policy. If the transition will occur within the planning horizon, then a further a key to deciding policy would be comparing (a) the benefits of permanently depleting some storage and (b) the costs of such depletion in the form of increased pumping expenses, phreatophyte and stream flow losses, and other possible adverse consequences such as land subsidence and loss of wetlands—all calculated over the planning horizon and discounted to present value. How long should a planning horizon be? What should the discount rate be? How should the policymaker compare expected costs and benefits in the absence of perfect economic and hydrologic data?

D. Conjunctive Management of Groundwater and Surface Water

INTRODUCTION

Conjunctive management, though universally praised, lacks precise meaning. Different people use the phrase differently depending on the ground water supply issue being addressed. Frank J. Trelease, Conjunctive Use of Groundwater and Surface Water, 27B Rocky Mtn. Min. L. Inst. 1853, 1853-54 (1982). In its narrowest sense, the phrase refers to administering rights in physically connected groundwater and surface water under the same legal doctrine and on an integrated basis. E.g., Musser v. Higginson, 871 P.2d 809 (Idaho 1994). In broader usage, the phrase encompasses a wide variety of measures to coordinate the use of available water supply sources and storage capacity, including underground storage capacity, in an effort to maximize the net benefits from them over time. This might include coordinated management of surface and underground water sources that are not even physically connected. And whether or not the sources are connected, it might involve the use of some creative management ideas and tools. The notes that follow illustrate different techniques of coordinating the use of available water supplies to maximize the benefits from them.

Notes

1. **Purchase and retirement of surface rights.** In City of Albuquerque v. Reynolds, 379 P.2d 73 (N.M. 1962), the city applied for permits to appropriate 6000 acre-feet per year from a groundwater basin physically connected with the fully appropriated Rio Grande River. Over the next seventy-five years, about half the water the city proposed to pump would come from basin storage and about half from depletion of surface flows. The state engineer found that the proposed wells would impair existing surface rights in violation of state statute. He ruled that the permits could issue, however, upon the condition that the city would have to purchase and retire enough surface water rights to offset the effects of its groundwater pumping on the river. The court upheld the state engineer's power to impose the condition because it would increase beneficial water use and because his statutory authority to deny permits to protect existing rights implied authority to issue permits conditioned upon purchase and retirement of existing rights.

Due to the time lag between pumping groundwater and impact on stream flow, as outlined by Balleau supra, p. 414, the purchase-and-retirement technique would enable total beneficial use of surface water and groundwater to increase for decades. Ultimately, of course, total beneficial water use would decrease due to stream depletion, and water would be reallocated from stream-supplied irrigation to groundwater-supplied municipal uses in the City of Albuquerque.

After *City of Albuquerque*, the state engineer issued more groundwater permits, usually for municipal and industrial use, conditioned upon future purchase and retirement of existing surface rights to offset the effects of pumping. He followed a practice of not identifying or quantifying the surface rights to be retired in the future. Instead, a permit would only specify a date by which surface rights must be retired. Later, as the date approached, the permittee would have to identify and quantity the surface rights to be purchased subject to approval by the state engineer.

In N.M. Op. Att'y Gen. No. 94-07 (Dec. 23, 1994), the attorney general ruled that deferred identification and quantification of the surface rights to be retired was illegal. He said here was no specific statutory authority for it, and it violated various statutes on new appropriations and water right transfers, e.g., it did not comply with a statute requiring scrutiny of whether a new appropriation would impair existing rights, would be contrary to the conservation of water within the state, or would be detrimental to the public welfare. The attorney general also concluded that the failure to provide notice of which surface rights would be retired and an opportunity to protest during the initial permit proceeding violated the procedural due process rights of people whose water rights might be impaired.

2. **Exchanges, by-pass pumping, and artificial recharge.** A discussion of conjunctive management tools under Colorado law is found in David L. Harrison & Gustave Sandstrom, Jr., The Groundwater-Surface Water Conflict and Recent Colorado Water Legislation, 43 U. Colo. L. Rev.

1, 37-48 (1971). Although this article is not recent, it still provides a useful explanation of different physical tools. These include water exchanges, in which water stored in a surface reservoir is released to replace stream flow that is diminished by groundwater by pumping (as in *Glacier View Meadows*, supra p. 76); "by-pass pumping," in which a fraction of the groundwater pumped is passed on to the stream to replace natural flow; and artificial recharge of groundwater, including storage of stream water during periods of high flows in aquifer-reservoirs for later withdrawal by wells during low flow seasons or drought years. For three case studies of conjunctive management in Colorado, see Lawrence J. MacDonnell, Colorado's Law of "Underground Water": A Look at the South Platte Basin and Beyond, 59 U. Colo. L. Rev. 579 (1988).

   3. **Economic management tools.** Nat'l Water Comm'n, Water Policies for the Future 234-36 (1973):

   "[A water] management agency might use economic tools in lieu of, or in addition to, regulatory ones. A water management agency having the power to impose pump charges would be able to introduce incentives to affect decisions of water users in the interest of the best use and conservation of the resource. Through taxing or pricing mechanisms a management agency may, in effect, efficiently ration ground and surface water.

   "An illustration is provided by the management scheme employed by the Orange County Water District in Southern California. The District can buy imported water from the Metropolitan Water District of Southern California. Ground water is also available, but sole reliance on it would cause an overdraft, as it has in the past. Each year the Orange County Water District determines how much of the water demand shall be supplied from ground water and how much from imported water. The determination of the amount of ground water withdrawal is based in part on the quantity in storage in the aquifer and the anticipated recharge, including artificial recharge.

   "Suppose in a given year that the District decides to meet demand with 60 percent ground water and 40 percent surface water; these percentages establish each user's 'fair share' of basin supply. Then the District establishes the cost differential between pumped water and imported water. Suppose imported water costs $14 per acre-foot more than pumped water. If a water user takes a total of 100 acre-feet of water during the year, pumping 60 percent and taking imported water for the other 40 percent, he pays no special charge, although he has, of course, paid a premium of $14 per acre-foot for the imported water. If the user takes the full 100 acre-feet in ground water, he must pay a Basin Equity Assessment of $14 per acre-foot on 40 of the 100 acre-feet that he pumped. If another user takes his 100 acre-feet all in imported water (paying the $14 per acre-foot premium on the total imported), the District will credit him with $14 per acre-foot for the 60 acre-feet he could have pumped from the aquifer. As a consequence, all water users in the District pay approximately the same price per acre-foot for water no matter what the source, and all water users pay part of the costs for importing water even though some may use no part of it. Even in the absence of a supply of imported water, a similar pricing system can be used to apportion withdrawals between indigenous surface supply and ground water supply."

4. **California's mix of tools.** U.S. Advisory Comm'n on Intergovernmental Relations, Coordinating Water Resources in the Federal System: The Groundwater-Surface Water Connection 36-37 (1991):

"California has not adopted a comprehensive statewide groundwater management law, but has pursued a policy of encouraging local water users to develop governance structures for water management (usually through the combined efforts of special water districts and water users' associations) with the support of state agencies such as the Department of Water Resources. * * *

"Artificial recharge projects in southern California, using groundwater basins to store surface waters for later use, date back at least to the 1920s. Flood waters were moved out of stream channels, diked and ponded in permeable areas, and allowed to sink into the underground strata. Temporary dams were constructed in more permeable stream channels to obstruct surface flows and increase recharge to groundwater basins, which could then serve both storage and transmission purposes. In the 1980s, over 2 million acre-feet of water per year were placed in underground storage by local water agencies.

"In some locations, extensive spreading grounds were constructed, some of which were designed to recharge the groundwater supply while providing surface recreational opportunities for local residents. The Orange County Water District was a leader in this multipurpose facility development. Groundwater pumping was taxed by local special water districts to provide the funds for artificial replenishment programs that primarily benefited pumpers and consumers. Later innovations included 'in-lieu replenishment' (whereby water users in basins with access to both surface and groundwater supplies are encouraged to take surface water in lieu of pumping groundwater when surface supplies are plentiful) and the use of reclaimed water for basin recharge and sea water barrier projects. * * *

"* * * Environmental concerns and budgetary constraints have largely eliminated the prospect of future water development projects. Local water agencies have focused increasingly on the use of pricing to regulate the demand side of the water supply equation, on reaping new supply availability from conservation, and on interlocal agreements and water rights transfer to move water from wasteful and lower valued uses to higher valued uses."

BOARD OF COUNTY COMMISSIONERS v. PARK COUNTY SPORTSMEN'S RANCH, L.L.P

Supreme Court of Colorado, 2002.
45 P.3d 693.

[Park County Sportsmen's Ranch (PCSR) owned 2,037 acres in a high mountain valley. It sought a conditional permit for a project to store water in aquifers underlying approximately 115 square miles of the mountain valley. PCSR planned to construct six surface reservoirs to artificially recharge the aquifers and twenty-six wells to extract water from them for transport to a distant municipality. The Park County Board of Commissioners and two landowners in the valley (Landowners) sued for a declaration that PCSR's use of aquifer storage space under their lands would constitute trespass and could not be done without their consent or condemnation of an easement. None of PCSR's surface reservoirs or wells would be located on the Landowners' land, and the Landowners did not allege that the use and enjoyment of their property would be compromised in any way. Instead, they asserted trespass based on the common law doctrine "cujus est solum ejus est usque ad coelum et ad inferos," which translates as "to whomsoever the soil belongs, he owns also to the sky and to the depths." The water court ruled that the movement of recharge water through aquifers underlying Landowners' lands would not constitute a trespass. The Colorado Supreme Court affirmed.]

JUSTICE HOBBS * * * . To support their theory, the Landowners invoke our decisions in Walpole v. State Board of Land Commissioners, 62 Colo. 554, 163 P. 848 (1917) and Wolfley v. Lebanon Mining Co., 4 Colo. 112 (1878). [*Walpole* and *Wolfley* held that a landowner owns minerals under the surface of the land.] The Landowners invoke *Walpole* and *Wolfley* for the assertion that their "fee ownership includes the space underneath the land" and therefore they have a right to withhold consent and require compensation for PCSR's project.

* * * The Ohio Supreme Court has rejected a very similar contention in Chance v. BP Chemicals, Inc., 77 Ohio St.3d 17, 670 N.E.2d 985 (1996). In that case, a property owner claimed that the migration of injected liquid into portions of a very deep aquifer underlying its property constituted a trespass. Determining that the injectate mixed with "waters of the state" in the aquifer, the Ohio Supreme Court rejected the property owner's claim of ownership and trespass based on the cujus doctrine. * * *

We find the Ohio Supreme Court's discussion of state waters and limitations upon absolute subsurface ownership rights to be of particular significance to the case before us, in light of Colorado's strong constitutional, statutory, and case law holding all water in Colorado to be a public resource and allowing holders of water rights decrees the right of passage for their appropriated water through and within the natural surface and subsurface water-bearing formations. * * *

[W]e determine that the General Assembly, in authorizing the use of aquifers for storage of artificially recharged waters pursuant to decreed conjunctive use projects, has further supplanted the Landowners' common-law property ownership theory. * * *

When parties have use rights to water they have captured, possessed, and controlled, they may place that water into an aquifer by artificial recharge and enjoy the benefit of that water as part of their decreed water use rights, if the aquifer can accommodate the recharged water without injury to decreed senior water rights. This authority resides in a number of statutory sections that implement the "Colorado Doctrine," which is that all water in the state is a public resource dedicated to the beneficial use of public and private agencies, as prescribed by law. Sections 37-92-305(9)(b) and (c) provide that the Water Court may issue a conditional decree for storage of water in underground aquifers if the applicant can and will lawfully capture, possess, and control water for beneficial use which it then artificially recharges into the aquifer. Section 37-87-101(1) provides that the right to store water of a natural stream is a right of appropriation in order of priority, and section 37-87-101(2) provides that underground aquifers can be used for storage of water that the applicant artificially recharges into the aquifer pursuant to a decreed right. * * *

We now turn to water use rights and property ownership rights under Colorado law. Colorado law differs fundamentally from the English common law it replaced. * * * Advancing the national agenda of settling the public domain required abandonment of the pre-existing common-law rules of property ownership in regard to water and water use rights. Reducing the public land and water to possession and ownership was a preoccupation of territorial and state law from the outset. A new law of custom and usage in regard to water use rights and land ownership rights, the "Colorado Doctrine," arose from "imperative necessity" in the western region. * * * When first announcing the Colorado Doctrine, we said that "rules respecting the tenure of private property must yield to the physical laws of nature, whenever such laws exert a controlling influence." Yunker v. Nichols, 1 Colo. 551, 553 (1872) (Hallett, C.J.). * * *

Accordingly, by reason of Colorado's constitution, statutes, and case precedent, neither surface water, nor ground water, nor the use rights thereto, nor the water-bearing capacity of natural formations belong to a landowner as a stick in the property rights bundle. Section 37-87-103, 10 C.R.S. (2001), for example, codifies this longstanding aspect of the Colorado Doctrine. It provides that water appropriated by means of a reservoir impoundment and then released for travel to its place of beneficial use shall enjoy the right of passage through the natural formation in the administration of water use rights. * * *

[T]he Landowners claim a common-law property right to require consent or just compensation for an easement to use the subsurface estate for artificial recharge and storage of water in aquifers extending through their properties, asserting that "fee ownership includes the space underneath the land" which the water occupies. The Landowners rely on *Walpole* and *Wolfley* for this proposition, but these are mineral cases which are clearly distinguishable from water cases * * *.

Allowing property owners to control who may store water in natural formations, or charging water right use holders for easements to occupy the natural water bearing surface or underground formations with their appropriated water, would revert to common-law ownership principles that are antithetical to Colorado water law and the public's interest in a secure, reliable, and flexible water supply made available through the exercise of decreed water use rights. It would disharmonize Colorado's historical balance between water use rights and land ownership rights. It would inflate and protract litigation by adding condemnation actions to procedures for obtaining water use decrees. It would counter the state's goals of optimum use, efficient water management, and priority administration. * * * [36]

Notes

1. **Other rationales for holding artificial recharge is not a trespass or taking.** South West Sand & Gravel, Inc. v. Central Arizona Water Conservation District, 212 P.3d 1 (Ariz. Ct. App. 2008), concerned a 1986 Arizona recharge statute that authorizes an importer of water to turn it into the channel of a natural stream where gravity will cause it to infiltrate into an aquifer. The court ruled that artificial recharge accomplished under this statute was neither a taking nor a trespass because the owner of a streambed and adjacent land has no right to exclude the recharge water from its land. The landowner never had any such right, said the court, because the 1986 statute merely codified a longstanding background principle of Arizona law that reserves natural river channels for the transport and storage of water by appropriators. The court interpreted the longstanding principle to extend to the transport and storage of imported water.

In Niles Sand & Gravel Co. v. Alameda County Water District, 112 Cal. Rptr. 846 (Ct. App. 1974), the county water district artificially recharged the Niles Groundwater Basin with water taken from Alameda Creek. The recharge raised the water table enough to flood the gravel company's deep pits, although the water table was still below its natural level prior to any pumping in the basin. To enable quarrying, the gravel company pumped the water out of its pits and dumped it back into Alameda Creek. The court enjoined the gravel company from continuing to do that because it was a waste of water. The court also rejected the company's claim of inverse condemnation because the correlative rights doctrine made the company's overlying land subject to a "public servitude" that allows recharge water to fill empty aquifer storage space. The correlative rights doctrine calls for a water table to be maintained at a certain level, see *City of Pasadena*, supra p. 370, and *City of San*

---

36. We are not presented here with a cause of action in tort for interference with surface uses due to recharge that raises the groundwater table or with any claim to interference with the use and enjoyment of the Landowners' surface or subsurface estates. Our opinion should not be read as altering the otherwise applicable law regarding injury caused by alteration of natural surface drainage patterns.

Fernando, supra p. 373, and apparently the servitude allows recharge to bring the water table back to that level.

In re Application U-2, 413 N.W.2d 290 (Neb. 1987), involved "incidental recharge" due to seepage into an aquifer from a public power and irrigation district's 600 miles of canals. The district filed an application claiming the storage under a Nebraska statute allowing an appropriator who incidentally recharges an aquifer to obtain a right to the water. Landowners overlying the area challenged the statute for taking their exclusive right to the empty storage space under their lands without just compensation. They offered no evidence of harm to their lands. The court said a raised water level does not deprive an overlying owner of property unless it prevents an act the owner desires to do or diminishes profit or enjoyment the owner would otherwise derive from the property—a no-harm, no-taking rule.

2. **Recharge statutes.** Most western states have legislation authorizing recharge projects. For example, Nebraska legislation addresses not only incidental recharge, as indicated in Note 1, but also the appropriation of water for intentional recharge and recovery, and it allows a recharger to levy a reasonable fee for withdrawals by others. Neb. Rev. Stat. §§ 46-233, -240 to -242, -295, -296, -299 to -2,106. The California Water Code declares that the storage of water underground is a beneficial use for which stream water can be appropriated if the stored water will thereafter be applied to some beneficial use. § 1242. The Water Code also authorizes various public entities, including water replenishment districts covering more than one county, to store water for future use. §§ 60000-60622. If the storage operation is performed by a water replenishment district, no person can acquire any property or right in the waters, § 60351; and the district may charge water rates to cover operating expenses, § 60245, may tax real property to the extent water rates fail to cover expenses, §§ 60250, 60252, and may levy replenishment assessments on pumpers, § 60325.

Arizona has extensive recharge legislation. One chapter of the state code creates an elaborate system of permits for activities involving underground water storage, savings, and replenishment. Ariz. Rev. Stat. §§ 45-801.01 to -898.01. Other chapters authorize—or in some cases, obligate—various districts to engage in and finance groundwater recharge activities, e.g., §§ 48-3771 to -3783 (multi-county water conservation districts), §§ 48-4401 to -4575 (groundwater replenishment districts). In addition, the Arizona Legislature established a water banking authority empowered to recharge depleted aquifers with Colorado River water transported through the Central Arizona Project. §§ 45-2401 to -2473.

An important motivation for creating the Arizona water banking authority was the state's expected inability to use its full Colorado River apportionment of 2.8 million acre-feet annually until 2035. Groundwater recharge by the water banking authority enables Arizona to store unused water from its annual apportionment, rather than having to stand by and let California take the unused part. The water banking authority is also authorized to enter into interstate banking agreements, under which water can be stored in Arizona aquifers on behalf of California and Nevada.

Such storage would enable those two states later to divert water from the Colorado River in excess of their annual apportionments and because water previously stored in Arizona aquifers on their behalf would go to replace water that Arizonans otherwise would be entitled to take from the Colorado River. Margaret Bushman La Bianca, Note, The Arizona Water Bank and the Law of the River, 40 Ariz. L. Rev. 659 (1998). Bureau of Reclamation rules establish a framework for the Secretary of the Interior to consider, participate in, and administer interstate storage and release agreements among the Lower Basin states. 43 C.F.R. pt. 414. In 2002, Arizona, Nevada, and the United States signed an agreement for the storage in Arizona of up to 200,000 acre-feet per year on behalf of Nevada, to a cumulative total of 1.2 million acre-feet. Storage and Interstate Release Agreement, http://www.usbr.gov/lc/region/g4000/SIRA/finagmt.pdf. See also Agreement for the Development of Intentionally Created Unused Apportionment, http://www.azwaterbank.gov/awba/documents/2002/icua_agreement_12-18-02.pdf.

3. **Allocation of aquifer storage space.** In Central & West Basin Water Replenishment District v. Southern California Water Co., 109 Cal. App. 4th 891, 135 Cal. Rptr. 2d 486 (Cal. Ct. App. 2003), 148 entities that collectively held all the rights to pump water from a groundwater basin extending over 277 square miles wanted to use subsurface space to store imported water. About 645,000 acre-feet of storage space was available. The pumper entities sought a decree allocating the unused storage space to them on a pro rata basis, e.g., an entity holding 5% of the rights to extract water would also have 5% of the available storage space. Their efforts were opposed by a water replenishment district created and operating under California legislation referenced in Note 2. The court ruled that extraction and storage rights are not linked, that the storage space is a public resource not owned by the pumper entities, and that the legislature authorized the water replenishment district, not the pumper entities, to store waters in the space for conjunctive use.

The Nevada recharge legislation creates a three-tiered permit system—a permit to operate a recharge and recovery project, a permit to appropriate the water that will be used for recharge, and a permit for the recovery wells. Nev. Rev. Stat. 534.0145, -.250 to -.340. A permit to operate a recharge and recovery project requires (1) the technical and financial capability to construct and operate the project and (2) an approved appropriation of water for recharge.

Chapter 5

WATER DISTRIBUTION ORGANIZATIONS

SECTION 1. PRIVATE CORPORATIONS

JACOBUCCI v. DISTRICT COURT
Supreme Court of Colorado, 1975.
189 Colo. 380, 541 P.2d 667.

ERICKSON, JUSTICE. On November 14, 1973, the City of Thornton instituted an action in eminent domain in the Jefferson County District Court against Farmers Reservoir and Irrigation Company, the City of Westminster, a shareholder in Farmers, the Treasurer of Jefferson County, the Treasurer of Boulder County, and other unknown persons claiming any interest in the proceeding. Farmers Reservoir and Irrigation Company (Farmers) is a mutual ditch company, organized pursuant to section 7–42–102 et seq., C.R.S. 1973, as a Colorado corporation.

* * * The petitioners, [ten] shareholders in Farmers, filed a cross-petition * * * to intervene as defendants in the condemnation proceedings. This motion was denied by the District Court on February 11, 1975, after the court concluded that the shareholders of Farmers were not indispensable parties to the proceeding. Thereafter, this court was petitioned, pursuant to its original jurisdiction under C.A.R. 21, to grant the petitioners relief. The petition requested an order permitting the shareholders to intervene and compelling their joinder as parties in the condemnation proceeding. We issued a rule to show cause why the relief requested should not be granted.

The issue we address in this original proceeding, which renders the other issues moot, is whether the individual shareholders of a mutual ditch company are indispensable parties in an action to condemn the shareholders' decreed water priorities. We hold that they are.

Farmers, a mutual ditch company, administers an extensive water distribution system divided into four divisions. The Standley Lake Division includes a storage reservoir known as Standley Lake located in Jefferson County. The decreed water rights of this reservoir are used to irrigate approximately 15,000 acres of land * * *. Property rights administered by the Standley Lake Division are the subject of the condemnation action which created the issues in this proceeding.

At the time of the institution of the condemnation proceeding, Farmers represented a total of 1,105 shareholders, 271 of whom owned shares allocated to the Standley Lake Division of Farmers. * * * The record title to the physical properties of the ditches, reservoir, lands, and rights-of-way stands in the name of Farmers.

In order to determine whether the shareholders of Farmers are indispensable parties to the condemnation proceedings, we must define the nature of their relationship to the mutual ditch company and to the rights and properties administered by the corporation. The history behind the growth and purposes of mutual ditch companies is necessary to an analysis of the issue which is before us.

* * * The construction and maintenance of canals and ditches required the outlay of large sums of money. The average farmer did not have sufficient means to construct, own, or operate an irrigation ditch to convey water to his land. The most economical solution was to convey the water over a great distance through a single large main and laterals and then distribute it to consumers by means of smaller laterals.

In response to the enormous task of supplying water to the parched farmlands, farmers banded together and formed mutual ditch companies for the express purpose of storing and conducting water for irrigation purposes. Farmers who may have previously owned ditches as tenants-in-common would transfer their ownership rights to mutual ditch companies and in return receive stock representing their water rights. This made possible the distribution of water over large areas of land, often remote from the source of supply, and increased the availability of irrigated farmland at reasonable costs. Not only was the management of the ditches and reservoirs made more efficient, but capital was made more available through the operation of these companies.

Mutual ditch companies in Colorado have been recognized as quasi-public carriers. Farmers is not organized for profit or hire and exists primarily for the benefit of its shareholders. Farmers is engaged in the business of storing and transporting water to shareholders who own the right to use the water.

Mutual ditch companies like Farmers were formed expressly for the purpose of furnishing water to shareholders, not for profit or hire.

Delivery of water to the consumers is conditioned upon the payment of an annual assessment levied by the company to meet operating expenses and, if they exist, debt installments. * * *

The relationship between the mutual ditch corporation and its shareholders arises out of contract, implied in a subscription for stock and construed by the provisions of a charter or articles of incorporation. * * * The corporation is not only obligated to furnish a proper proportion of water to each of its shareholders, but it is liable in damages for the failure to do so. The corporation must protect and preserve the interests of the shareholders by keeping the ditches, canals, reservoir, and other works in good repair, the expense of which is paid from the special assessment. Sections 7–42–104, 7–42–107, 7–42–108, C.R.S. 1973.

The shares of stock in a mutual ditch corporation represent the "consumer's interest in the reservoir, canal and water rights." Beaty v. Board of County Comm'rs. of Otero County, 101 Colo. 346, 73 P.2d 982 (1937). The benefit derived from the ownership of such stock is the right to the exclusive use of the water it represents, the water being divided pro-rata according to the number of shares of stock held by each shareholder. The shareholders have the right to change the place of the use of the water if other users are not injured thereby.

As a mutual ditch company, Farmers is merely the vehicle by which its owners operate and manage its affairs. The corporation, like other mutual ditch companies, was organized solely for the convenience of its members in the management of the irrigation and reservoir systems. The ownership of the shares of stock is merely incidental to the ownership of the water rights by the shareholders. We wish to emphasize that the shares of stock owned by Farmers' shareholders represent a definite and specific water right, as well as a corresponding interest in the ditch, canal, reservoir, and other works by which the water right is utilized.

The City of Thornton seeks to analogize the position of the shareholders in Farmers to that of the shareholders in any other corporation. On this basis, they argue that the shareholders in Farmers are not necessary parties to this litigation, because the corporation, under principles of corporation law, is bound to protect their interests. We have held that a mutual ditch corporation is responsible for maintaining actions in the corporate name to secure or protect the consumers' water rights or other property and to represent the shareholders in civil actions. Inasmuch as Farmers holds legal title to the physical properties sought to be condemned, Thornton argues that Farmers is the real party in interest, not the shareholders.

In the first place, as petitioners rightly point out, a mutual ditch corporation is not organized under the general corporation laws, but under a separate and independent statutory provision. We find that the unique character of these corporations mandates different treatment which is not fully in accord with the principles applicable to corporations in general. As noted above, the shares of stock held by the consumers in a mutual ditch corporation represent a specific property interest in a water right. * * * While the "naked title" may stand in the name of Farmers, the ditch, reservoir and water rights are actually owned by the farmers who are served thereby. The shareholders are the real parties in interest in the condemnation action, not the corporation.

In our view, shareholders are indispensable parties. * * * The condemnation action here in issue has the potential of seriously disrupting the shareholders' property interests. That the water rights owned by Farmers' shareholders are property rights is well established by Colorado law.

At least 271 shareholders, as of the date of the petition in condemnation, are faced with the prospect of having their farmlands denied a substantial source of water. The productivity and value of their lands, as well as the assurance of their livelihoods, is in many cases entirely dependent upon the continuing flow of water from Standley Reservoir. No court can ignore the magnitude of disruption which would result in a successful condemnation action by the City of Thornton. Moreover, each shareholder stands in a different position from the others and is likely to be affected differently by the condemnation action. Their ability to protect those individualized interests would surely be impaired if this action were allowed to proceed in their absence.

The evidence in the present case does not suggest that joinder would be infeasible. All shareholders of Farmers similarly situated to the petitioners herein are subject to service of process. * * * Therefore, * * * the District Court should join as parties to the condemnation action those shareholders in the Standley Lake Division of Farmers whose water rights would be affected by the condemnation action of Thornton as of the date of the initiation of the condemnation action and all parties in interest.

Accordingly, the rule to show cause is made absolute, and we remand to the District Court for further proceedings consonant with the views expressed in this opinion.

Notes

1. **Just compensation and indispensable parties.** The *Jacobucci* court said that the condemnation action would likely affect shareholders differently and that their ability to protect their individualized interests would be impaired if they were not parties. To understand why, consider who would be entitled to just compensation and how it would be meas-

ured. In City of Boulder v. Snyder, 396 F.2d 853 (10th Cir. 1968), a municipal paving project destroyed a small mutual company ditch that carried water to a shareholder. The shareholder sued the municipality for taking her water supply. The court treated her loss of water as a partial taking, for which just compensation was the difference in the value of her property before the taking (land with appurtenant water) and its value after the taking (land without water). Before-and-after valuation is a standard measure of just compensation for partial takings. 4A Julius L. Sackman, Nichols' the Law of Eminent Domain § 14.02[1].

2. **Mutual companies.** Private associations of irrigators that provide water at cost to their members are called variously mutual water companies, mutual ditch companies, or mutual irrigation companies. Most of them, like the one in *Jacobucci*, are organized as nonprofit corporations. *Jacobucci* reports that in Colorado such companies are incorporated under special legislation rather than under the state's general corporation laws. In some states, they are organized under the general corporation laws, but typically there are supplemental special provisions limiting formation of the companies and regulating shareholder relations.

The characteristics of mutual water companies vary. Sometimes much of the land irrigable by the corporation's works was already irrigated under existing individual water rights, and the mutual company was formed to construct a new, more efficient ditch as a substitute method of carrying water to the farmers. In this situation, the farmers might either have retained their old water rights or have conveyed them to the company in return for rights as stockholders to a share of the company's water rights.

Other mutual water companies were organized prior to settlement by the farmers. In fact, many mutual companies were created as subsidiaries of land promotion companies. A "land company" or "land and water company," a commercial venture financed with private capital (often from eastern states, England, and Europe) purchased or obtained control of a large area of land and constructed irrigation works, subdivided the land, and sold farms to settlers together with shares in a subsidiary "water company" or "ditch company."

Still other mutual water corporations were formed to replace commercial enterprises originally organized to profit from the sale of water. The failure of such ventures, and their abandonment by their managers, forced the consumers to take over the system on a cooperative basis, either by purchase in bankruptcy or by more informal methods.

A few "Carey Act corporations" still exist. To encourage the reclamation of arid western lands, Congress enacted the Carey Act, 28 Stat. 372 (1894), as amended, 43 U.S.C. § 641. The Act provided that 1,000,000 acres of arid lands of the public domain would be donated to each of the western "public land states," if those states would see to its reclamation and settlement. Most of these states contracted with private companies to build and operate the reclamation works necessary to bring the water to the lands. The state then sold the lands to settlers who bought their water rights from the construction company in the form of stock in a mutual water corporation formed to operate the works. Many of the projects were not carefully planned and were economically infeasible so that the settlers were in trouble from the start, and many Carey Act corporations have been reorganized into irrigation districts.

Another form of mutual water company is the "water users' association," a corporation formed under state law to contract with the Secretary of the Interior for repayment to the government of the reimbursable costs of a federal reclamation project. The association levied assessments against the landowners, secured by liens on both stock and land, thus collecting on behalf of the United States the costs of construction, operation, and maintenance of the project. Today the Bureau of Reclamation prefers to deal with irrigation districts, and many of these associations have changed their form, though they are still used to a considerable extent in Arizona and Utah.

Mutual water companies are discussed and contrasted with other forms of organization in U.S. Dep't of Agric., Circular No. 934, Irrigation-Enterprise Organizations (1953); Theodore W. Russell, Mutual Water Companies in California, 12 S. Cal. L. Rev. 155 (1939); Raphael J. Moses, Irrigation Corporations, 32 Rocky Mtn. L. Rev. 527 (1960).

3. **Mutual company stock.** Usually mutual water companies issue shares based on the number of acres a stockholder irrigates, e.g., one share of stock for each acre of land, and each irrigator is entitled to a pro rata share of the water available to the company based on the amount of his land (or stock) relative to the total held by all stockholders. Shares in some companies, however, entitle the holder to a specific quantity of water or to a specific fraction of the water available to the company regardless of the acreage irrigated. For example, if existing water users formed the company to construct a ditch to replace their individual works, shares might well have been issued according to the quantities of the individual water uses and with no provision for pro rata sharing during shortage.

4. **Assessments.** Mutual water companies generally have statutory authority to levy assessments against their stockholders to raise funds for operation and maintenance, and for other proper charges such as for making improvements or for paying off bonds or other indebtedness. By statute or by the corporate articles or bylaws, stockholder assessments might have to be levied on a pro rata basis.

Payment of an assessment is enforced in the first instance simply by denying water to the nonpaying stockholder. Beyond that, the company articles, bylaws, or stock certificates typically provide that an unpaid assessment shall be a lien upon the stock, which may be forfeited to the company for nonpayment or sold to other water users. By agreement between the company and its stock subscribers, assessments may be made a lien upon the water user's land or a personal obligation as well.

5. **Other private organizations.** Although the incorporated mutual company is the major form of private water distribution organization, other forms exist. Ditches shared by several people under more informal arrangements are called variously joint, common, and partnership ditches. The relationships between these persons, their interests in the water, and their responsibilities for maintenance costs generally are governed by the law of property, contract, or partnership. In some states, however, these matters are elaborately regulated by statute.

Another private organization is the commercial, or for-profit, company that contracts to distribute water to users for a fee. The company might sell water it owns to customers, Willis v. Neches Canal Co., 16 S.W.2d 266 (Tex. Comm'n App. 1929). Alternatively, it might provide the service of carrying water to persons who own the water right, Denver v. Brown, 138 P. 44 (Colo. 1914). The carrier-ditch concept reached its high point in Slosser v. Salt River Valley Canal Co., 65 P. 332 (Ariz. 1901), where the court analogized the delivery ditch to a public road. The facts of the case support the comparison: Slosser first drew his water from the Chivari Ditch; when that ditch was washed out by a flood, he switched to the Farmers' Ditch; and when the great Salt River Valley Canal was built above the small ditches, encircling and capable of serving all the land, he drew his water from it, paying an annual charge to the company that built it. Clearly, he was the owner of his own water right, and the canals just carried his water, much as a railroad might carry his goods.

Private commercial companies are rare today. Many of the early ones made contracts for permanent service at fixed rates, and rising costs forced most of them into bankruptcy and reorganization as mutual corporations or irrigation districts. A number still exist, however, in Colorado and Texas. For some of the Texas problems, see R. Richard Roberts, Problems Connected with the Distribution of Irrigation Water in Texas, Proceedings, Water Law Conferences 79 (Univ. of Tex. 1952, 1954).

6. **Acequias.** Acequias, or community ditches, are a unique feature of New Mexico and Colorado law. Acequias derived from a mixture of Indian customs and Moorish-Spanish institutions brought by the first colonists, though early Mormon settlers added some features of the mutual ditch company. They are found in the Upper Rio Grande watershed. Typically, land ownership in acequia communities is organized around gravity fed earthen irrigation ditches that give each landowner arable, irrigated land. The ditches and the water flowing through them are supervised by elected mayordomos (ditch bosses) and comisionados (commissioners). See, e.g., Wilson v. Denver, 961 P.2d 153 (N.M. 1998). Water users contribute labor. In times of shortage, water will be shared under a variety of arrangements.

Tension exists between the preservation of traditional acequia practices and their viability under contemporary water law. These tensions are explored in Gregory A. Hicks & Devon G. Peña, Community Acequias in Colorado's Rio Culebra Watershed: A Customary Commons in the Domain of Prior Appropriation, 74 U. Colo. L. Rev. 387 (2003). For discussions of the New Mexican acequia organization, see Christopher J. De-Lara, Note, Who Controls New Mexico's Acequias? Acequia Government and Wilson v. Denver, 40 Nat. Resources J. 727 (2000); Jose A. Rivera, Irrigation Communities of the Upper Rio Grande Bioregion: Sustainable Resource Use in the Global Context, 36 Nat. Resources J. 731, 736 (1996). Cf. Robert E. Clark, New Mexico Water Resources Law 47-52 (1964).

BADGER v. BROOKLYN CANAL CO.
Supreme Court of Utah, 1996.
922 P.2d 745.

STEWART, ASSOCIATE CHIEF JUSTICE. * * * The dispute at issue arises out of a decision by the Brooklyn Canal Company to change its method of agricultural irrigation from a "flood" method to a high-pressure sprinkler method. Brooklyn is a nonprofit mutual water corporation formed for the purpose of distributing water to its shareholders in Sevier County. Brooklyn has traditionally distributed its water by means of the Brooklyn Canal to individual shareholders who have employed ditches and furrows to water their crops. The canal draws most of Brooklyn's water right directly from the Sevier River, but a small portion has also been drawn from several artesian wells. In early 1992, it was proposed that the irrigation method be changed. At a shareholders' meeting held on February 18, 1992, the plan to switch to a pressurized sprinkler method was approved, with 72% of the shareholders present voting in favor of it.

Switching to a pressurized sprinkler system apparently necessitated transferring water to an underground pipe linked to a diversion point several miles upstream from the diversion point that supplies the Brooklyn Canal. The State Engineer must approve any adjustment in a point of diversion of a water right. Consequently, Brooklyn filed a change application for approval of the proposed upstream diversion point. In that change application, Brooklyn proposed to divert its entire water right of 31.27 cubic feet per second from the Sevier River at the new upstream diversion point. Brooklyn has conceded that this change would require abandonment of the artesian wells.

[Dissident Brooklyn shareholders filed protests with the State Engineer asserting impairment of their vested rights.] After receiving evidence submitted by Brooklyn and the various protestants, the State Engineer issued a memorandum decision approving the change in Brooklyn's diversion point. * * *

A number of the protestants then filed for de novo review before the district court * * *. Relying solely on the pleadings, Brooklyn moved for summary judgment, asserting that plaintiffs had no standing as shareholders to contest Brooklyn's corporate decisions.[5] [The trial court] granted Brooklyn's summary judgment motion, subsequently issuing a written order * * * stating * * * the shareholder plaintiffs did not have "standing" to protest Brooklyn's change application * * *. Plaintiffs now appeal the grant of summary judgment * * *.

With respect to their claims of vested rights, the shareholder plaintiffs assert that they possess "vested real property rights which are represented by their individual shares of water stock." They thus claim to hold an independent water right apart from their status as mere shareholders in a mutual water corporation. * * *

Our holding in East Jordan Irrigation Co. v. Morgan, 860 P.2d 310, 316 (Utah 1993), * * * directly addressed the issue of a shareholder's rights to act in derogation of a water corporation's policy. *East Jordan* held that a shareholder did not have the right to file a change application without corporate consent. We quoted with approval a California case which summarized the difficulties inherent in treating shareholder rights as independent water rights:

> "[I]t would seem to be too clear for argument that neither one nor any number of such stockholders would or could possess the legal right to take or receive the amount of water to which [they] may be entitled by another manner or means than those supplied by the corporation itself." To recognize such a right "would necessarily be to admit the possession of similar rights in each and every stockholder in each of said corporations to go and do likewise, and it is too plain for argument that such an admission would result in a state of inextricable discord and confusion among the owners of water rights of various sorts * * *."

Id. at 315 (citations omitted).

Given these prudential concerns, there is no reason for drawing a distinction, as the shareholder plaintiffs request us to do, between the right to file a change application and the right to contest one. Permitting either would lead to the same "state of inextricable discord and confusion" and would nullify the ability of mutual water or irrigation corporations to act as a cohesive unit for the benefit of their shareholders.

* * * [T]he legal relationship of a water company and its shareholders necessarily implicates both benefits and burdens. Where individual holders of water rights might meet insuperable obstacles in attempting to maintain their own diversion points and canal or pipe systems for distribution, the pooling of resources under a contractual

---

5. The parties to this litigation have generally characterized this issue as a question of whether plaintiffs have "standing" before the State engineer or the district court. More accurately, however, the question addresses the authority or jurisdiction of the office of the State Engineer to consider and resolve the claims presented to it.

corporate system permits many individuals to benefit from the resources available through unified action.

Unified action also necessarily entails a certain sacrifice of the autonomy an individual shareholder could retain by refusing to take on the burdens and obligations accompanying the benefits of participating in a corporate body. Where, for instance, the governance of a mutual water corporation dictates that a majority vote of the shareholders will control the obligations of all, individuals who do not agree with the majority will always suffer a certain detriment simply by virtue of their position in the minority. That is the nature of the legal relationship undertaken. Were we to adopt the reasoning proposed by plaintiffs, shareholders could evade their obligations, which would result in an unacceptable interference with the constitution and maintenance of mutual water corporations.

Perhaps even more critical, adoption of the shareholder plaintiffs' argument would impermissibly expand the authority of the State Engineer. Assuming Brooklyn has violated any enforceable obligations it owes to its shareholders with respect to manner, mode, or quantity of delivery, then those shareholders possess a cause of action in a court of competent jurisdiction. Apparently, the plaintiffs in this case have already filed such an action. See Badger v. Madsen, 896 P.2d 20, 21-22 (Utah Ct. App. 1995). Although the State Engineer would not necessarily be required to adjudicate the specific obligations of the corporation vis-à-vis its shareholders, the Engineer's treatment of the shareholders' rights in any context would necessarily interfere with the authority of the court that was required to adjudicate those obligations. For example, assume hypothetical plaintiffs take their case before a district court and that court determines that the corporation has not violated its obligations. If the State Engineer simultaneously or subsequently determines that plaintiffs have suffered an impairment of their rights, then the effect of the district court's ruling could be called into question. We cannot require the State Engineer's office to assume a role which thus undermines the jurisdiction of the courts.

These prudential policy concerns also accord with the intent and the language of the statute at issue. The context of the entire statute makes it clear that the State Engineer does not have the authority to adjudicate all the issues that may arise in the context of a change application. A change application is required for a change in place of diversion, place of use, or purpose of use, but no such change may be made "if it impairs any vested right without just compensation." Utah Code Ann. § 73-3-3(2). The Code further provides, "The state engineer shall follow the same procedures, and the rights and duties of the applicants with respect to applications for permanent changes of point of diversion, place, or purpose of use shall be the same, as provided in this title for applications to appropriate water." Id. § 73–3-3(5)(a).

With respect to change applications, the jurisdiction of the State Engineer's office is thus circumscribed by the criteria upon which the statute permits it to base its decisions. Those criteria are largely set forth in § 73-3-8(1), which states in relevant part: "It shall be the duty of the state engineer to approve an application if: * * * (b) the proposed use will not impair existing rights or interfere with the more beneficial use of the water * * *." In this respect, the shareholder plaintiffs essentially argue that they possess individual rights which are protected as "existing rights" by § 73-3-8(1).

Clearly, the shareholder plaintiffs' rights are necessarily intertwined with the rights of the corporation of which they are shareholders and to which they have contractually delegated the authority to act on their behalf. The right and ability of the majority of shareholders to manage their own rights in a collective manner is dependent upon the ability of the corporation to function as a unified organization. If we were to accept the interpretation proposed by the shareholder plaintiffs, minority shareholder "existing rights" would be elevated above the "existing rights" of majority shareholders. We do not believe that the legislature intended such an anomalous result. We therefore hold that in the context of mutual water or irrigation corporations, "existing rights," as that term is employed by § 73–3–8, refers to the right held by the corporation representing its shareholders as a body. Therefore, the statutory authority of the State Engineer does not extend to the resolution of disputes between shareholders and their corporations regarding the distribution of their shares. It follows that because the statutory authority of the State Engineer does not include jurisdiction over cases more properly presented in other forums, the district court correctly refused to address plaintiffs' shareholder rights on de novo review. * * *

Notes

1. **Ownership.** Whether the water distribution organization or the consumer "owns" the water right often presents perplexing problems of semantics. Doctrines of ownership in the consumer seem to have arisen from a need to protect the water user by giving the user a permanent right to water, instead of leaving the user to the mercy of the distributor.

Regardless of whether the private water distribution entity is a mutual company, a commercial company, or a community ditch, three distinct types of cases can be identified: (1) the water users might squabble among themselves, (2) a water user might be at odds with the distribution organization, and (3) the organization might dispute with other appropriators outside the organization over priorities and shares of the stream. In results, a surprisingly uniform pattern has arisen.

Between water users, one is protected against any attempt by another to increase the latter's share at the expense of the former. Between a water user and the distributor, the most frequent problem arises when the distributor tries to stop delivering water to the user. Western courts have been quick to find some sort of enforceable right in the user to continued service because the user's livelihood is at stake. In disputes involving the outside world, that is, other appropriators from the stream, the usual solution is to leave the defense of the water right to the diverter-distributor as the representative of all its consumers.

As noted earlier, irrigators supplied by a mutual company might have had individual pre-existing rights that they retained when the company was organized, which of course protects them from other users seeking to take more than their share from the ditch. When there were no individual pre-existing rights or none that survived formation of the mutual company, shareholder rights under corporation laws or corporate by-laws prevent one consumer from encroaching on the other. When the interests of consumers of water carried by one mutual company conflict with the interests of consumers under another ditch, the company is regarded as the representative of its consumers; and a decree defining the company's appropriation is binding not only on it but on the consumers of water under its ditch. Combs v. Farmers High Line Canal & Reservoir Co., 88 P. 396 (Colo. 1907). For external purposes, then, the distributing company is the "owner."

Commercial water companies seeking to make a profit might naturally come in conflict with their customers. Denver v. Brown, 138 P. 44 (Colo. 1914), held that farmers supplied water by a commercial company were appropriators permanently entitled to water supply, but because that seemed contrary to *Combs*, the court later described *Brown* as establishing that the company was only "in effect" the appropriator. People *ex rel.* City & County of Denver v. Dist. Court, 168 P. 260 (1917). Consumers have property rights that the court will protect against arbitrary action by the commercial company; but in external relations between the project and outside interests, the commercial company is the "owner."

In a carrier ditch or community acequia, the consumer owns the water right. Slosser v. Salt River Valley Canal Co., 65 P. 332 (Ariz. 1901); Snow v. Abalos, 140 P. 1044 (N.M. 1914). In *Slosser*, this rule protected a consumer against the distributor. In *Snow*, it protected a consumer against outside appropriators.

Other solutions to the problem of protecting the irrigator have been found without declaring the irrigator to be the owner of the appropriation. In some states, constitutional and statutory rights perform this function instead of property rights. Idaho avoided the "ownership" bog in Hard v. Boise City Irr. & Land Co., 76 P. 331 (Idaho 1904), by citing Idaho Constitution Art. 15, § 4, which makes a sale, rental, or distribution of water for agricultural purposes an exclusive dedication to such use that protects the irrigator from being deprived of the water as long as the irrigator pays for it and complies with terms prescribed by law. In Texas the distributor owns the appropriation, Willis v. Neches Canal Co., 16 S.W.2d 266, 269 (Tex. Comm'n App. 1929); but a statute recognizes a permanent customer right that can be exercised according to the terms of the delivery contract or, if there is no contract, at a reasonable and nondiscriminatory price. Tex. Water Code Ann. § 11.040.

In several states, ownership of the right to water stored in a reservoir is vested in the landowner by a device known as a "secondary permit." The organization receives a "primary permit" to construct the dam and store the water. The consumer applies for a "secondary permit" to apply the stored water to beneficial use upon the land, and the water right is eventually adjudicated to the consumer. Ariz. Rev. Stat. Ann. § 45–161; Nev. Rev. Stat. § 533.440; Or. Rev. Stat. § 537.400; Wash. Rev. Code Ann. § 90.03.370; Wyo. Stat. §§ 41–3–301, –302.

The role of ownership in the context of water distribution organizations is discussed in Barton H. Thompson, Jr., The Relevance of "Ownership" to Water Markets and Other Issues, in WATER ORGANIZATIONS IN A CHANGING WEST (Nat. Resources L. Center, U. Colo. School of Law, 14th Annual Summer Program, June 14-16, 1993).

2. **Relation of stock and land.** When a mutual company issues stock based on the acres a stockholder irrigates, the stock usually is made appurtenant to the land. The stock certificate for appurtenant stock will specifically describe the land. Appurtenant stock may be made inseverably appurtenant by a provision in the corporate articles or bylaws. Riverside Land Co. v. Jarvis, 163 P. 54 (Cal. 1917). Alternatively, appurtenant stock may be severable from the land, so that while it would pass with a conveyance of the land if not mentioned in the deed, it can be expressly retained by the grantor upon sale of the land.

3. **Stock transfers.** Mutual company stock that is not appurtenant or is appurtenant but severable can be sold separately from land. But the corporate articles or bylaws of some mutual companies impose restrictions. E.g., in *In re* Water Rights of Fort Lyon Canal Co., 762 P.2d 1375 (Colo. 1988) (en banc) a bylaw stated that the place where water is delivered to a stockholder could be changed only if, in the opinion of the company's board of directors, the change would not injure the company, its canal, or other stockholders. The court upheld the restriction but said a finding of injury by the board would be subject to judicial review of whether it acted arbitrarily or capriciously or abused its discretion.

Uniform Commercial Code (U.C.C.) article 8 governing investment securities generally does not apply of its own force to mutual water company shares. This is because the shares typically are neither traded on a securities exchange nor a medium of investment expressly made subject to article 8. See U.C.C. § 8-102(a)(15) (definition of "security"). The Utah legislature, however, has made the procedures of article 8 applicable to mutual water company shares.

4. **Statutes regulating water right transfers.** Mutual company stock transfers might be limited by state statutes regulating water right transfers. In *East Jordan*, discussed in the principal case, a city purchased mutual company shares not restricted as to transfer by the com-

pany's articles or bylaws. Then the city applied to the state engineer to change the point of diversion to a city-owned well, from which it wanted to take water for year-round municipal use. Utah Code Ann. § 73–3–3(2) allows a "person entitled to the use of water" to change the point of diversion, place of use, or purpose of use if the vested rights of others will not be impaired. The court ruled that the city was not a person entitled to the use of water within the meaning of the statute. Only the mutual company was eligible to file the transfer application. The court did say, however, that judicial relief would be available to the city should the mutual company unreasonably refuse to apply for a transfer.

5. **Other limits on transfer.** Are there any limits on transfer apart from those found in a corporation's articles and bylaws and in state water transfer statutes? In *Consolidated People's Ditch Co.*, a California decision quoted in the principal case, a purchaser of mutual company shares was enjoined from changing the point of diversion upstream from the company's ditch. The shares were nonappurtenant, and the court did not mention any statute or any corporate article or bylaw preventing the change. But to avoid what it called inextricable discord and confusion, the court ruled that a stockholder has a right to a proportionate share of the available water supplied *through company facilities*, not a right to receive that amount of water through some other means. In contrast, the Colorado court allowed a mutual company stockholder to transfer water to lands beyond the service area of the company's ditch and transport it through another ditch, so long as he continued to bear his proportionate share of the cost of maintaining the company's ditch. Wadsworth Ditch Co. v. Brown, 88 P. 1060 (Colo. 1907).

YUCAIPA WATER CO. NO. 1 v. PUBLIC UTILITIES COMMISSION
Supreme Court of California, 1960.
54 Cal.2d 823, 357 P.2d 295.

TRAYNOR, JUSTICE. In this proceeding Yucaipa Water Company No. 1 attacks an order of the Public Utilities Commission determining that it is a public utility water corporation subject to the jurisdiction of the commission and directing it to file a financial report and cease and desist from increasing its rates to the Yucaipa Domestic Water Company pending further commission action.

No. 1 is organized as a nonpublic utility mutual water company and has not heretofore been regulated by the commission. Domestic is a regulated public utility water corporation. It secures all of its water from No. 1 and owns approximately 5 percent of No. 1's stock. In 1959 a dispute arose between the two companies over a substantial increase in the rate No. 1 proposed to charge Domestic and extensions of service by Domestic into areas served by No. 1. * * * The parties stipulated that the commission should first determine whether or not No. 1 is a public utility subject to its jurisdiction, and its determination of that issue is the only question before us for review. The commission found that No. 1 is a public utility that has dedicated its property to public use and that it is not exempt from regulation under section 2705 of the Public Utilities Code. No. 1 attacks both of these findings.

No. 1 operates in an area of about 3,500 acres including Yucaipa township. It was organized in 1910 and initially supplied water primarily for irrigation purposes. At the present time, however, about 74 percent of its sales are to domestic users. It also provides service to the Yucaipa Domestic Water Company, poultry farms, trailer parks, scheduled water users, and special users at specified rates. Special users include hospitals, schools, churches, parks, and other large users. With the exception of one domestic user, it supplies water only to its shareholders and lessees of shares from its shareholders. Its shares are freely transferable and are not appurtenant to the land, and users may obtain water in addition to the per-share entitlement by paying special rates. In 1959 No. 1 had about 2,000 domestic users and supplied water to over 100 lessees of shares. It maintained a list of shareholders who were willing to lease shares and referred nonshareholder applicants for service to them. It billed lessees of shares directly, but held the shareholder liable for any unpaid bill. In each of the years 1956, 1957, and 1958 it added 80 to 100 new domestic users to its system, and to increase the number of permissible service connections, it split its stock to permit a connection for each half share instead of each share.

No. 1 contends that since it is organized as a nonpublic utility mutual water corporation that supplies water only to its shareholders, lessees of shares from its shareholders, and one other person, it has not held itself out as willing to supply water to the public or any portion thereof and that it has not therefore dedicated its property to public use. No. 1's organization as a mutual and its formal limitations on its services do not preclude a finding of dedication, however, if it has held itself out as willing to supply water to the public or any portion thereof. * * *

The evidence supports the commission's finding of dedication in this case. It is true that No. 1 did not expressly offer service to everyone in its service area on condition that prospective consumers purchase shares of stock from it. Had it done so, its holding itself out to serve the public would be patent, and the attaching of a condition that any member of the public could meet would not affect its offer. Dedication may also be shown by implication, however, and in the present case, it may clearly be inferred. Thus, No. 1 steadily increased the number of its service connections; it split its shares to double the permissible number of such connections; it supplied water to a substantial number of lessees of shares; and it expedited the leasing of shares to those who wished water service. There is no evidence that anyone in its service area who wished water service could not obtain it by purchasing or leasing half a share or more. Under these circumstances, the commission could reasonably infer that No. 1 supplied its shareholders and lessees of its shares not merely for the reason "peculiar and particular to them" that they were such, but primarily for the reason that they were members of the public in No. 1's service area who accepted its offer of service by becoming shareholders or lessees of shares.

No. 1 contends that even if it has dedicated its property to public use, it is exempted from public utility regulation by section 2705 of the Public Utilities Code. That section provides:

> "Any corporation or association which is organized for the purpose solely of delivering water to its stockholders or members at cost, and which delivers water to no one except its stockholders or members, or to the State or any agency or department thereof, or to any school district, or to any other mutual water company, at cost, is not a public utility, and is not subject to the jurisdiction, control or regulation of the commission. * * * "

The exemption created by section 2705 indicates a legislative determination that when a mutual water corporation is substantially customer-controlled and delivers water at cost, the usual judicial contract remedies available to those who deal with it are an adequate substitute for public utility regulation. * * *

In the present case, however, the evidence supports the commission's finding that No. 1 delivered water to others than stockholders; it delivered water to over 100 lessees of shares of stock and one other person. Even if it is assumed that the latter delivery was *de minimis*, the deliveries to lessees were not. Lessees of shares are not stockholders, and to interpret the word "stockholders" in section 2705 to mean "stockholders or lessees of stock" would not only require reading into the statute words that are not there but violate the basic principle of customer control on which the exemption is based. * * * No. 1 was not obligated to deliver water to lessees of shares, for it could have insisted, in accord with its declared corporate purpose, on delivering water only to shareholders. Instead, however, it actively expedited the leasing of shares to those who wished water service, and such activity coupled with its other activities set forth above clearly supported the commission's finding that it had dedicated its property to public use. * * *

The order is affirmed.

Notes

1. **Public utility status.** A companion case, Corona City Water Co. v. Public Utilities Commission, 357 P.2d 301 (Cal. 1960), considered whether the Temescal Water Company was subject to regulation as a

public utility. Temescal was organized as a mutual water company. Nineteen percent of its shares were owned by Corona, a public utility that received its entire water supply from Temescal as a shareholder of Temescal. Temescal dominated Corona through majority ownership of Corona's stock and interlocking boards of directors and officers. The water delivery operations of the two companies were closely integrated, with each sometimes using the other's facilities. Held: Temescal dedicated its property to public use because of its close collaboration with a public utility. Moreover, the exemption of section 2705 did not apply because Corona was a "captive" stockholder with no voice in the management of the mutual company and in no position to enforce its rights as a stockholder.

In the legislative session following these two cases, the California State Assembly amended section 2705 to permit a mutual company to keep its nonpublic status though it delivers water at cost to nonstockholders in certain situations, including delivery to a lessee of its stock or to land leased by a stockholder to a nonstockholder.

2. **Regulation of public utilities.** Public utility status subjects many of a company's financial and operational matters to public regulation. In many states, a water utility must procure a certificate of convenience and necessity, i.e. a license, to enter the business. E.g., Cal. Pub. Util. Code § 1001. A utility must render service to consumers within its service area, Olsen v. Union Canal & Irr. Co., 119 P.2d 569 (Ariz. 1941), within the limits of its water supply, Butte County Water Users' Ass'n v. R.R. Comm'n, 196 P. 265 (Cal. 1921). It cannot discriminate between its customers by giving preferred services or rates to some. Id; Live Oak Water Users' Ass'n v. R.R. Comm'n, 219 P. 65 (Cal. 1923). Its transactions with other companies and its acquisitions or dispositions of property are subject to scrutiny by the regulatory commission for conformity with the public interest. Corona City Water Co. v. Pub. Util. Comm'n, supra Note 1. It cannot discontinue its services, even by going out of business, without the permission of the commission. Van Hoosear v. R.R. Comm'n, 194 P. 1003 (Cal. 1920).

Most important, the rates a utility charges for services are regulated. Rates are fixed to cover operating expenses, including depreciation on company properties, and a fair return on the value of the properties devoted to public use. In most states, rates are fixed by a state public utility commission. In Colorado, though, county commissioners can establish reasonable maximum rates to be charged. Colo. Rev. Stat. Ann. § 37-85-103. In Texas, rate-setting power is given to the Texas Natural Resource Conservation Commission. Tex. Water Code Ann. §§ 11.002(1), 12.013(a).

3. **Municipal water supply.** A water company supplying a municipality is not necessarily a public utility unless declared so by statute. Junction Water Co. v. Riddle, 155 A. 887 (N.J. Ch. 1931). Most such companies are declared so by statute.

A water company's contract with a city may give the city power to require service and to this extent supersede the powers of the state public utility commission. Portsmouth, Berkley & Suffolk Water Co. v. Portsmouth, 70 S.E. 529 (Va. 1911). A city's charter may empower it to impose regulations in lieu of the public service commission. New York v. N.Y. Water Serv. Corp., 8 N.E.2d 294 (N.Y. 1937).

Residents of a city who consume water that is diverted, stored, and distributed by a public utility company do not own appropriations of water or water rights of any kind. Instead they have rights to service arising under public utility law.

SECTION 2. PUBLIC AGENCIES

SULLIVAN v. BLAKESLEY
Supreme Court of Wyoming, 1926.
35 Wyo. 73, 246 P. 918.

Plaintiff, E.J. Sullivan, brings this action, on behalf of himself and others similarly situated, against Lou Blakesley, county treasurer of Big Horn county, and the commissioners of the Greybull Valley irrigation district. The petition alleges the due organization of said irrigation district under the laws of this state; that an assessment against the lands in said district was made in 1925 to meet the expenses of the district for the current year; that plaintiff is the owner of lands affected by such assessment, and that the county treasurer of said county threatens to sell such land for the nonpayment of such assessment; that the commissioners of said irrigation district threaten to issue and sell the bonds of said district, said bonds to be paid by assessments levied against the property of plaintiff and others similarly situated; that the irrigation district law of this state is unconstitutional for various specified reasons, and plaintiff accordingly seeks an injunction against the collection of said tax and the issuance of the bonds aforesaid. [W]e are asked to answer whether or not the irrigation district law of this state is in conflict with * * * the Constitution of this state. * * *

The irrigation district law [was] passed by the Legislature of this state in 1920. * * * For the purposes of this case, it will be sufficient to state the following provisions of the law: A certain number of owners or holders of land in the district may sign and present to the district court a petition, stating therein the name of the proposed district, the necessity of the proposed work, the object and purpose thereof, a general description of the lands proposed to be included in the district, the names of the freeholders owning lands therein, and a prayer for the organization of the district. A preliminary engineering report of the feasibility of the project must accompany the petition. The court or the judge thereof must cause notice to be given of the presentation of the petition, fixing the date for the hearing thereon. Upon the hearing, the district court may approve and confirm the petition, define the boundaries of the district, and establish it as a corporation by the name proposed with powers to sue and be sued, adopt a corporate seal, have perpetual succession, exercise the power of the eminent domain and generally carry out the purposes of the organization. Commissioners are appointed by the court, who are required to organize, who constitute the corporate authority of the district, who are declared to be public officers, and for whom successors are provided by election. Other lands may subsequently be included in the district, and lands originally embraced therein may be excluded therefrom. Immediately after the organization of the district, the commissioners thereof are required to cause surveys, a map, plans, and specifications to be made of the proposed work, and determine, as near as may be, the cost of said work. They must assess against the lands embraced within the district the total amounts of benefits, such benefits to constitute the basis of all assessments; apportion and assess the cost of construction with certain exceptions which need not be noted here, against the several benefited tracts in the irrigation district, in proportion to the benefits which have been assessed against the same, and apportion the water right, expected to be acquired by the proposed work, to each tract of land assessed. A report of such action must be made to the court. Notice of the hearing thereon must be given to all parties interested. Upon such hearing, the court may confirm the report of the commissioners and the assessments made as aforesaid, which assessments may be made payable in installments, as fixed by the court. Additional assessments may be made subsequently, to be confirmed by the court upon due notice given to the interested parties. The assessments become a lien upon the various tracts assessed, and may be enforced in the same manner as a judgment, or may be assessed and collected as taxes. The commissioners may borrow money and issue the bonds of the district therefor and such bonds are declared to be a lien upon the assessments for the repayment of the principal and interest thereof. More specific provisions as to some of these matters will be set forth in the opinion.

BLUME, J. (after stating the facts as above). 1. An irrigation district, reclaiming as it does, desert lands in the state, and accordingly, conferring a benefit, not alone upon the private individuals within the district, but also upon the people of the state as a whole, is a public rather than a private, corporation. * * * Such districts have at times been designated as municipal corporations, and they might be such within the meaning of laws or constitutional provisions not now under consideration, but it is clear that they are not municipal corporations as generally understood. They are merely special state organizations for state purposes with limited powers, created to perform certain work which the policy of the state requires or permits to be done, and to which the state has given a certain degree of discretion in reclaiming desert lands. * * *

There is no special constitutional limitation that we know of limiting the mode or method of the establishment of such districts provided that it is done under a general law. It may be left to a board or commission, or the court. The Legislature has seen fit to cause such districts to be created upon petition of a certain number of people owning or holding lands therein, and upon a hearing, after due notice, upon such petition by the district court. The method of thus establishing the districts is, we think, constitutional.

* * * The exactions authorized to be made by such districts may, in a broad sense, be termed taxes, but they are distinguishable therefrom, for they are levied for local benefits to be spread on the property in the districts in proportion to the peculiar advantages accruing to each parcel therein from the improvement made. Whether in the form of special assessments or in the form of taxes, they are essentially assessments for local benefits, and not levied for general governmental purposes. * * *

2. We come, then, to the consideration as to whether or not the legislation in question is in violation of section 13, art. 15, of the Constitution, which provides that no tax shall be levied except in pursuance of law, and that each law imposing a tax shall state distinctly the object of the same, to which only it shall be applied. * * * The argument is far afield. * * * We might accordingly very well pass this subject without anything further; but inasmuch as we are also asked whether the irrigation district law is in violation of section 33, article 1, that "private property shall not be taken or damaged for public or private use without just compensation," and inasmuch as a complete answer perhaps involves the subject-matter referred to by counsel, we shall discuss it somewhat at length. * * * It has been held [by several courts] that bonds issued by an irrigation district constitute a general lien obligation of the district. The contrary has been held in [Colorado and Utah]. And the Supreme Court of Colorado [reasoned] that to consider such bonds as general lien obligations of the district would be violative of both state and federal Constitutions, presumably because of taking property without due process of law or taking property without just compensation. * * * The difference in opinion as to the character of such bonds may, to some extent at least, be accounted for by the difference in the laws of the several states, and, in order to arrive at the proper conclusion herein, it will be necessary to consider the laws of this state that bear upon the point in question. * * *

We do not think, as contended by counsel, that these provisions leave in doubt the character or extent of the lien of the various assessments. * * * The Legislature evidently intended to make the assessments a general lien against all of the assessed property in the district, within the limitation * * * hereafter mentioned, since it has provided for the levy in each year of an amount sufficient to meet the principal and interest that may fall due during that year, to be apportioned to all the lands to which benefits are assessed, just as payments of principal and interest are met on general municipal bonds. But there is a limitation. The assessments cannot be in excess of the benefits assessed against the several parcels of land in the district. The objection accordingly urged by the Colorado Supreme Court * * * does not, we think, hold good under the laws of this state even if it were true that the principle there stated would apply in the absence of such limiting provisions of the statute. Made as the assessments are, because and on the theory that they equal the amount of the benefits, they do not constitute a taking of property without due process of law or without just compensation, in the case of irrigation districts any more than under a like situation in the case of municipal improvements generally, and it is well settled that in the latter case there is no violation of constitutional provisions in that regard. It was held in Re Drainage District, 24 Wyo. 143, 161, 156 P. 610, that assessments made for the purpose of constructing drains are not in violation of section 33, article 1, of our Constitution. Assessments made in drainage districts are similar in kind to assessments in irrigation districts. They are all based upon the same underlying principle. It may, possibly, happen, as suggested that the benefits assessed to all or part of the lands within the irrigation district by reason of the construction of improvements, may become exhausted before the full amount of the cost of such improvement is paid. But it is not shown that such contingency will arise, and we are not called upon to anticipate it any more than we are called upon to anticipate that the total cost of making the improvements might happen to be greater than the total amount of the **benefits**. We answer, accordingly, that the irrigation district law of this state is not in conflict with either of the two constitutional provisions last herein discussed. * * *

Notes

1. **Formation of a district.** All seventeen contiguous western states have laws authorizing the formation of irrigation districts, though some are called water conservation, water improvement, or reclamation districts. Historically, they all stem from California's Wright Act, Cal. Stat. 1887, ch. 34. In most states, the petition for formation of a district is presented to the board of county commissioners, rather than to a court as in the principal case, and a citizen vote on formation is held. There are variations from state to state in eligibility to vote (electors, landowners, owners of agricultural lands) and in the majorities required. In some states, approval of the state irrigation officials is required for the project or the engineering aspects of it.

2. **Bonds and liens.** An irrigation district that wants to construct facilities such as a dam and a canal system usually will need to issue bonds to fund construction. As indicated in the principal case, the commissioners of a Wyoming irrigation district may issue bonds after formation of the district has been approved. More commonly, statutes require the submission of proposed bond issues to district electors at a special election. Also common are statutory proceedings initiated by the governing officers of the district, in which all questions relating to the organization of the district and the proceedings of the board with respect to the issue and sale of the bonds may be judicially approved and confirmed. These proceedings are in rem and are conclusive as to the validity of the bonds.

The principal case discusses the concept of a general lien against land in the district to provide security for the bondholders. A general lien has been described as follows: "The district thus may impose assessments on all assessable lands in the district until a bond * * * is retired. By this means, cumulative assessments may be made against district lands to meet deficiencies arising from nonpayment of assessments by some landowners." 3 Report of the President's Water Resources Policy Comm'n, Water Resources Law 173 (1950). In contrast, a specific lien makes each parcel of land subject only to its proportionate share of the debt; recurring assessments on a parcel to make up for delinquencies by other landowners are not allowed.

3. **Assessments and water charges.** The principal case also gives the rule that assessments levied by the district against land must be apportioned among the landowners in accordance with the actual benefits received by the property. Under this rule, it is illegal to treat all land as equal and levy an equal assessment against each acre. Wheatland Irr. Dist. v. Short, 339 P.2d 403 (Wyo. 1959). It is permissible, however, to divide land into classes according to size, topography, soil classification, etc., fix a value for each class, and apply the formula to all acres in the district. Kansas-Bostwick Irr. Dist. No. 2 v. Mizer, 270 P.2d 261 (Kan. 1954).

Not all states require assessments to be apportioned according to benefits received. Some allow assessment on an ad valorem basis, at a standard rate against property valued at market or cash value. See Reed v. Oroville-Wyandotte Irr. Dist., 304 P.2d 731 (Cal. Dist. Ct. App. 1956). Others allow assessment according to area, whereby an equal charge is levied against each irrigable acre.

Another source of revenue for districts is a direct charge for water delivered: "The statutes of various States authorize the obtaining of revenue through tolls or charges for use of water. These tolls or charges are fixed by the board of directors, either in addition to the levying of assessments or in lieu thereof. * * * Tolls are used by many California districts, usually in addition to assessments. They are used to a lesser extent in some of the other Western States." U.S. Dep't of Agric., Circular No. 934, Irrigation-Enterprise Organizations 39 (1953).

4. **Federal reclamation projects.** Many irrigation districts were organized primarily as fiscal agents for the United States Bureau of Reclamation. Reclamation projects are built with federal financing, obviating an irrigation district's issuance of bonds for construction funds. Certain construction costs of reclamation projects are "reimbursable," however, and must be repaid to the United States. The irrigation district will enter into a repayment contract with the Secretary of the Interior in which it agrees to collect assessments from water users supplied by the project to cover operation and maintenance costs and construction charges.

5. **Ownership.** Usually there is no controversy over whether an irrigation district or other public agency that distributes water "owns" the water rights as against the consumer. The relations and duties of districts to their consumers are fixed by the statutes under which they are created, and those statutes without exception clearly empower the districts to appropriate or purchase water rights.

California recognizes a special property right to protect the consumer, but it is not a water right. A California public agency that distributes water "owns" the water rights as against the consumer, but this ownership is construed to be a trusteeship for the beneficial owners, the water users. Lindsay-Strathmore Irr. Dist. v. Wutchumna Water Co., 296 P. 933 (Cal. Dist. Ct. App. 1931). The trust ownership generated controversy recently in the rural Imperial Valley. The Imperial Irrigation District in response to pressure from its water supplier, the U.S. Bureau of Reclamation, agreed to transfer 300,000 acre-feet per year from irrigation use within the district to municipal use outside the district under long-term leases. It is argued that the transfer violates the district's trust duties to district water users in Shannon Baker-Branstetter, The Last Stand of the Wild West: Twenty-first Century Water Wars in Southern California, 38 Envtl. L. Rep. News & Analysis 10726 (2008).

Oregon also uses the trust concept. Or. Rev. Stat. § 540.510(1) limits eligibility to apply for a change in nature of use, point of diversion, or place of use to "the holder of any water use." Fort Vannoy Irr. Dist. v. Water Resources Comm'n, 188 P.3d 277 (Or. 2008), ruled that the holder of a water use is the irrigation district, not a district member using water. The court said that because the district holds legal title to the water right in trust for its members, to allow a member to apply for transfer "would run afoul of the trust relationship by permitting a beneficiary to manage the trust property." Id. at 296.

Water users served by an irrigation district do not have rights appurtenant to their land independent of the district. Where individual landowners opt out of a district and vote to form their own district, they do not take with them a share of the original district's water right. Madera Irr. Dist. v. All Persons, 306 P.2d 886 (Cal. 1957), rev'd on other grounds, Ivanhoe Irr. Dist. v. McCracken, 357 U.S. 275 (1958).

The Washington statutes on water adjudications generally require personal service of process or publication of notice to all persons claiming the right to divert the water involved, who must then appear in the proceeding or be subject to loss of their rights. Wash. Rev. Code Ann. § 90.03.120 provides, however, that persons claiming the right to use water by virtue of a contract with a claimant of the right to divert the water shall not be necessary parties. The Yakima River adjudication covered 6062 square miles, 475,000 irrigated acres, and over 40,000 people. Most water users were served by irrigation districts, canal companies, ditch companies, and municipalities. In State, Department of Ecology v. Acquavella, 674 P.2d 160 (Wash. 1983), the court acknowledged that individual landowners receiving water from a distribution entity have a vested interest in the water right to the extent that the water is beneficially used on their lands. Nonetheless, the court held that due process did not require service on such individual water users because of the extremely large scale of the proceeding and an identity of interest between the distributor and its water users. The court suggested that its holding might not apply to a smaller adjudication and that even in the Yakima River adjudication, due process might at some point require "service of process, or some other remedy, to protect the interests of water users not adequately represented by their distributing entities."

6. **Water allocation among district members.** Statutes in some states direct or authorize districts to issue "equitable" rules for distributing water to their members. E.g., Idaho Code § 43-304; Or. Rev. Stat. § 545.221; Utah Code Ann. § 17B-2a-510. In Nelson v. Big Lost River Irrigation Dist., 219 P.3d 804 (Idaho 2009), the district delivered water stored in its reservoir to members by using the stream channel. Water was lost in-transit by seepage from the porous stream channel. The farther downstream a member's diversion was located, the greater the seepage loss. The district allocated the total seepage loss pro rata among all its members, rather than based on their individual diversion points. The court held the water distribution complied with the Idaho statute requiring equitable distribution rules. The court noted that a district cannot vary assessments to its members based on the cost of delivering water to them, and it said seepage loss is simply a cost of delivering water.

Statutes in many states are silent about water allocation during shortage, in which case it is generally assumed that all landowners are to be treated equally. Those statutes that address shortages do so with varying clarity. Mont. Code Ann. § 85–7–1911(2) requires proportionate reduction. Ariz. Rev. Stat. Ann. § 48-2991 requires districts to distribute water "upon certain or alternate days to different localities as the board deems for the best interests of all persons affected, and so that the available water is distributed in as nearly equal proportions as possible to all lands of the district subject to the laws of priorities." Utah Code Ann. § 17B-2a-515 provides that a district "may distribute water as [its] board considers best for all concerned, subject to distribution and apportionment requirements of a district contract with the United States and applicable federal law, rule, and regulation."

California has a unique statutory structure on allocation. The main distributors of irrigation water are "irrigation districts" and "California water districts." In many of these districts, annual arrangements must be made to accommodate variable water requirements of irrigators. The basic statute for both kinds of districts requires them to distribute water "ratably to each landowner based on the basis of the ratio which the last assessment against his land for district purposes bears to the whole sum assessed to the district for district purposes," except as otherwise provided by statute. Cal. Water Code §§ 22250, 35420. Other statutes authorize a district's board to require irrigators to file applications by a date the board sets in order to receive water during the ensuing irrigation season (either for all crops or only for annual crops and new plantings). The board can require a cash deposit that is subject to forfeiture for water an applicant does not use if the district has water available. In case of shortage, the board may "give preference to or serve only the land for which application was filed prior to the date set and the land for which no application was required." Id. §§ 22252.1, 35450-35453.

During an extreme drought in 1977, the California Legislature added more provisions:

"In districts where meters or other volumetric measuring instruments or facilities are not available or are inadequate to measure substantially all agricultural water deliveries, the district may establish annual water requirements in the district for growing each type of crop grown in the district, accept such applications for water based on proposed crops to be grown and acreage of each proposed crop, and determine the quantity of water apportioned under [the above statutes] expressed in terms of acreage of each type of proposed crop to be served. In such a district, the district may refuse to deliver water to, or assess penalties on, the landowner who uses such water on a greater acreage of such crops than such landowner's share of the estimated available water will bring to maturity based on the requirements established for growing such crops in the district.

"In establishing annual water requirements for growing particular types of crops, * * * the district * * * may designate the number of irrigation runs and the amount of water to be allocated to each run with respect to each crop, and may give the water user water credits measured by the designated irrigation runs with respect to each such crop as to which the water user has notified the district he intends to underirrigate.

"This section provides a means of measuring the allocation of water to land based on the type of crop grown and does not authorize a district to designate, the crops to be grown on such land." Id. §§ 22252.3, 35454.5.

Although sponsors of this legislation called it "a measurement statute," not an "allocation statute," its effect is to establish an allocation scheme according to crop and acreage. The practice seems to be to give preference to the needs of perennial plants (orchards, vineyards) over annual crops. Apparently if a district has accurate metering devices, this legislation does not apply.

Another kind of California public water agency, county water districts, may have even broader powers. These districts are authorized "to restrict the use of district water during any emergency caused by drought, or other threatened or existing water shortage, and to prohibit the wastage of district water during such periods, for any purpose other than household uses or such other restricted uses as may be determined to be necessary by the district and may prohibit the use of such water during such periods for specific uses which the district may from time to time find to be nonessential." Cal. Water Code § 31026.

7. **Transfers by districts or district members.** Many states have statutes authorizing water districts to sell or lease surplus water for use outside the district. E.g., Colo. Rev. Stat. Ann. § 37–42–135 (lease for up to twenty years); Mont. Code Ann. § 85–7–1911(3) (sell or dispose); Utah Code Ann. §§ 17B–2a–503 (sell or lease for up to five years). California has one of the more detailed statutory schemes. Local and regional public water agencies can sell, lease, exchange or otherwise transfer for outside use water that is surplus to the needs of their water users and water that their users voluntarily forego the use of during the transfer period. Cal. Water Code § 382. They cannot, however, transfer water for use within the boundaries of another public water agency that furnishes the same water service without the consent of the latter agency. Id. § 385. Nor can they make any transfer that will unreasonably affect instream beneficial uses or the overall economy of the area from which the water is transferred. Id. § 386.

Some states authorize district members to transfer their rights to receive water if the district consents. E.g., Ariz. Rev. Stat. Ann. § 45–172; Idaho Code § 42–108; Utah Code Ann. § 17B–2a–514 (limited to one year at a time; new place of use must be in the district). A district's water right typically is appurtenant to all the irrigable lands within its borders, so a transfer by one irrigator to another within the district is not deemed a change in place of use that triggers usual statutory limits on transfer such as the no-injury rule. E.g., Nev. Rev. Stat. Ann. § 539.230(3); State, Dep't of Ecology v. Acquavella, 935 P.2d 595 (Wash. 1997).

For further discussion of transfers by districts or district members, see Barton H. Thompson, Jr., Institutional Perspectives on Water Policy and Markets, 81 Cal. L. Rev. 671 (1993). The article also proposes reforms to facilitate transfers for use beyond district boundaries.

IN RE RENO PRESS BRICK CO.
Supreme Court of Nevada, 1937.
58 Nev. 164, 73 P.2d 503.

Taber, Justice. Respondent corporation is the owner of 33 acres of land included within the boundaries of appellant irrigation district. Acting under the provisions of section 44 of the Irrigation District Act, as amended, respondent, on April 30, 1936, applied in writing to appellant's board of directors for the exclusion from the district of said piece of land. After considering the application, the board of directors of the irrigation district, on July 9, 1936, rejected respondent's application in whole. Thereafter, respondent petitioned the district court to set aside said order of appellant's board of directors, and to direct that said land be excluded from the district. The matter was later tried, and, in December, 1936, the district court granted respondent's application, and adjudged that said land be excluded from the irrigation district. This appeal is taken from said judgment, and from an order of said district court denying a motion for a new trial.

The portion of said section 44 of the Irrigation District Act with which we are primarily concerned, reads as follows: "The board of directors of any district now or hereafter formed under the provisions of this act, either upon its own initiative or upon the application in writing of any holder of title or of evidence of title to land in the district, may, by a majority vote, exclude from the district any land or lands theretofore included in the district, and change the boundary lines of the district so as to exclude or leave out certain tracts or portions of tracts when the proposed system or systems of irrigation cannot practically include land or lands, or when such land or lands would not be benefited by the district or by any improvement it might make." Respondent's application for exclusion of its land was and is based upon the contention that said land would not be benefited by certain improvements contemplated by the district.

The tract of land sought to be excluded from the irrigation district adjoins the city of Reno on the north. No part of it is within the city limits, but its southern boundary line is identical along its whole length with a portion of the northern boundary line of the city of Reno. The land has been irrigated for the past twenty or twenty-one years. For the first five or six years, two crops of alfalfa were grown upon it annually. After that, it was allowed to go to pasture. With an ample supply of water, it will produce good pasturage crops. * * *

During the three or four years that Parker Brick Company owned this property, it was used for the manufacture of brick, and to that extent the statement heretofore made, that this land has been irrigated for some twenty or twenty-one years, must be qualified. The buildings and machinery which had been used by Parker Brick Company in the manufacture of brick on said premises were of small value at the time the property was purchased by respondent. The premises have not been used for brick making at any time since respondent has owned them. * * *

Without water the land in controversy would be valueless for agricultural purposes. With an adequate water right it would be worth from $125 to $150 per acre for agricultural purposes. With the exception of about three and one-half acres, the land is susceptible of irrigation by gravity. * * * It is estimated that this property would be worth about $400 an acre if subdivided for residential purposes. * * *

There is no substantial conflict in the testimony in this case. The question we have to determine is the interpretation to be put on the word "benefited" as applied to the undisputed facts disclosed by the testimony. Upon respondent rests the burden of proving by a fair preponderance of evidence that the Truckee river upstream storage project will not benefit its 33-acre tract of land.

Appellant contends that this court should follow the decisions of courts of other states in holding that the benefit to the land, as contemplated by said amended section 44 of the Irrigation District Act, may be indirect as well as direct. * * * Respondent takes the position that, in Nevada, land within an irrigation district should be excluded therefrom on application of the owner when such land will not be directly benefited by the district or by any improvement it might make. * * *

We find it unnecessary to decide whether, in Nevada, an indirect benefit to land, within the meaning of amended section 44 of the Irrigation District Act, may be sufficient to justify a refusal to exclude such land from an irrigation district, because the uncontradicted evidence satisfies us that respondent has not met the burden imposed upon it by the statute to show that its said land will not be directly benefited by the Truckee river upstream storage project. We shall proceed to set forth some of the reasons which have influenced us in reaching this conclusion.

The land is not now being used for the manufacture of clay products, and will probably not be so used for at least ten or twelve years, because the supply of superior clay where respondent company is now manufacturing its products will, it is estimated, last that long, and respondent has other clay deposits superior in quality to that in its said 33-acre tract. * * *

It will not be necessary for respondent to go to any considerable expense in irrigating this land, because a neighboring farmer has offered to allow respondent to carry water through his ditch for a very small consideration. * * *

If the land were not susceptible of any use for agriculture * * *; if irrigation would constitute a detriment to the clay content of the land; or if the land were now being used for the manufacture of clay products, or definite plans were now being made to use it for that purpose within a reasonably short time, we might well have decided to affirm the judgment of the district court.

It does not result from the refusal to allow respondent's 33-acre tract to be excluded from the district that respondent must irrigate the land. It need not exercise that right unless it so chooses, and, so far as the court can see, respondent may rent or otherwise dispose of it. * * *

The court is not to be understood as holding that respondent may not at some future time be entitled to have this land excluded from the district; but viewing the situation, as we must, as it existed at the time of the filing of respondent's application and at the time of the trial in the district court, it is the court's opinion that, under the law, respondent is not entitled at this time to have said tract excluded from appellant conservation district. We find nothing in the law which would prevent respondent's filing another application for exclusion of this land from the district at a time when conditions may be different from those shown by the evidence to exist in this case.

The judgment and order appealed from are reversed.

Notes

1. **Grounds for exclusion of land.** Apart from the grounds for exclusion in the Nevada statute, another common statutory ground for excluding land is that it is irrigated from another water source, unless district facilities are used to transport the water to the land or the district furnishes supplemental water to the land. However, if a district is formed to protect future as well as present underground water resources, or if one of its purposes is to replenish groundwaters, any overlying land may be considered benefited by the district. Atchison, Topeka & Santa Fe Ry. v. Kings County Water Dist., 302 P.2d 1 (Cal. 1956); Hobe v. Madera Irr. Dist., 274 P.2d 874 (Cal. Dist. Ct. App. 1954).

2. **Third-party beneficiaries.** An irrigator might wish to sue the United States Bureau of Reclamation for alleged violation of its contractual obligation to deliver water to an irrigation district that in turn supplies water to the irrigator. The irrigator can sue on the contract between the Bureau and the district only if the irrigator is an intended third-party beneficiary of it. Courts have found intended beneficiary status with some contracts, H.F. Allen Orchards v. United States, 749 1571 (Fed. Cir. 1984); Klamath Irr. Dist. v. United States, 67 Fed. Cl. 504 (2005), and not with others, Orff v. United States, 358 F.3d 1137 (9th Cir. 2004), aff'd on other grounds, 545 U.S. 596 (2005); Klamath Water Users Protective Ass'n v. Patterson, 204 F.3d 1206 (9th Cir. 1999)

PEOPLE EX REL. ROGERS v. LETFORD
Supreme Court of Colorado, 1938.
102 Colo. 284, 79 P.2d 274.

KNOUS, JUSTICE. This is an original proceeding in quo warranto upon information of the Attorney General to try the right of respondents to occupy the office and exercise the duties of directors of Northern Colorado Water Conservancy District * * *.

The Colorado act was passed by the Thirty-First General Assembly and became effective on May 13, 1937. It was intended to make possible the organization of what is designated as "Water Conservancy Districts." Section 1 of the act states the purpose of the Legislature in passing the law in the following words:

"It is hereby declared that to provide for the conservation of the water resources of the State of Colorado and for the greatest beneficial use of water within this state, the organization of water conservancy districts and the construction of works as herein defined by such districts are a public use and will:

"a. Be essentially for the public benefit and advantage of the people of the state of Colorado.

"b. Indirectly benefit all industries of the state.

"c. Indirectly benefit the State of Colorado in the increase of its taxable property valuation.

"d. Directly benefit municipalities by providing adequate supplies of water for domestic use.

"e. Directly benefit lands to be irrigated from works to be constructed.

"f. Directly benefit lands now under irrigation by stabilizing the flow of water in streams and by increasing flow and return flow of water to such streams.

"g. Promote the comfort, safety and welfare of the people of the State of Colorado, and it is therefore declared to be the policy of the State of Colorado: * * * 3. To cooperate with the United States under the Federal Reclamation laws now or hereinafter enacted and other agencies of the United States Government for the construction and financing of works in the State of Colorado as herein defined and for the operation and maintenance thereof."

The act is general in its nature, and upon compliance with its terms a water conservancy district can be formed at any place within the State of Colorado. * * *

Pursuant to this act * * *, the district court of Weld county, on September 20, 1937, entered its findings and decree organizing the Northern Colorado Water Conservancy District, which includes generally the lands in the agricultural areas in the vicinity of the St. Vrain, Big Thompson, Cache la Poudre rivers, and of the Platte river from Platteville to the eastern line of Colorado. The approximate present total valuation of these farm lands and improvements thereon within the district is alleged to be $40,000,000, in addition to which it is said there has been an economic development within the district of approximately $100,000,000, making a total assessed valuation of all property within the district, both real and personal, of approximately $140,000,000. This economic development has resulted from the building of the cities of Greeley, Eaton, Boulder, Fort Collins, Longmont, Loveland, Fort Morgan, Brush, Sterling and Julesburg, and numerous other towns and hamlets of various size. In this economic development is also embraced a number of sugar factories, extensive public carrier and utility developments, and other large and prosperous businesses, all of which is due principally to the agricultural development which has been made in the district by application of water for the irrigation of the lands therein. The projected further development of this section by the construction of what is commonly known as the "Colorado-Big Thompson Project" allegedly is the motivating cause for the formation of the Northern Colorado Water Conservancy District. The Colorado-Big Thompson Project contemplates the construction of a number of large reservoirs on the western slope of the Continental Divide on the Colorado river and its tributaries, and the diversion of the waters of that river through the Continental Divide by means of canals and tunnels to the Big Thompson river on the eastern slope of the Continental Divide, from whence, through a series of reservoirs, canals, and other facilities, the water ultimately is destined for delivery to the municipalities and lands in the district. As an integral part of the project, the construction of a reservoir on the Blue river on the western slope for the purpose of replacement of water diverted to the eastern slope and to compensate and stabilize the flow of the Colorado river is included. After a detailed survey made under its auspices, with funds provided by the United States, the Bureau of Reclamation has approved the feasibility of the project. * * *

Preliminary to the consideration of the various constitutional questions involved and as decisive of many of these points, it is necessary to determine the legal nature and character of the corporation intended to be created under the Water Conservancy Act. The act itself, in section 7, declares that: "The district shall be a political subdivision of the State of Colorado and a body corporate with all the powers of a public or municipal corporation." While a legislative declaration of this nature is not conclusive upon a court, it must be seriously regarded in the construction of an act. In this connection also must be considered the purpose of the law, not only as disclosed by its words, but also in the light of the physical conditions of the state, its needs, and the character and extent of the projected benefits. * * *

These circumstances demonstrate, and we conclude, as the language of the act states, that its objects are of sufficient public benefit and advantage to the people of Colorado as a whole to constitute a public purpose and that the water conservancy districts authorized thereby are state agencies and public corporations. * * *

Our Legislature did not confer the ordinary functions of local governments enjoyed by towns and cities on the Water Conservancy Districts contemplated, but did vest in them powers which have come to be associated with true municipal corporations, including the power of taxation to further its purpose. * * *

Section 15 of our Conservancy Act is as follows:

"Section 15. Classification of Taxes and Assessments—Powers.

"In addition to the other means of providing revenue for such districts as herein provided, the Board shall have power and authority to levy and collect taxes and special assessments for maintaining and operating such works and paying the obligations and indebtedness of the district by any one or more of the methods or combinations thereof, classified as follows:

"Class A. To levy and collect taxes upon all property within the district as hereinafter provided.

"Class B. To levy and collect assessments for special benefits accruing to property within municipalities for which use of water is allotted as hereinafter provided.

"Class C. To levy and collect assessments for special benefits accruing to lands within irrigation districts for which use of water is allotted as hereinafter provided.

"Class D. To levy and collect assessments for special benefits accruing to lands for which use of water is allotted as hereinafter provided."

Under class A the Legislature has authorized districts to levy and collect general taxes on all property, real and personal, within the district, and in classes B, C, and D to levy and collect assessments for special benefits.

The express authorization for power to levy taxes conferred by the Legislature upon the district here involved is found in article 10, § 7, of the Colorado Constitution, which reads as follows: *Municipal taxation.*—The general assembly shall not impose taxes for the purposes of any county, city, town or other municipal corporation, but may by law, vest in the corporate authorities thereof respectively, the power to assess and collect taxes for all purposes of such corporation."

In this grant of power lies the distinction between a water conservancy district under this act and the irrigation districts authorized by the Colorado Irrigation District Act of 1905, as amended. The public character of the water conservancy district is the occasion for this difference. * * *

The relator contends that the due process clauses of the Federal Constitution, the Fourteenth Amendment, and the Colorado Constitution, art. 2, § 25, are contravened by numerous provisions of the Water Conservancy Act. Under this head it is said the act is fatally defective because no appraisal of benefits or hearing thereon is provided either as to the general mill levy or special assessments.

Our determination that the general tax authorized is for a public purpose and is not a special assessment in effect disposes of the specially urged contention, based generally upon the objection last discussed as to lack of benefits, that the order of court creating the district and the act itself violate the due process clauses as to the owners of: (1) Real property within the limits of incorporated cities and towns lying within the district; (2) lands not susceptible of irrigation; (3) lands already having an adequate water supply; and (4) personal property. All of these owners are subject to the general ad valorem tax by reason of the situs of their property in the same manner as property owners in ordinary political subdivisions are liable for taxation to support the diversified activities of such subdivisions, which liability is not contingent upon direct benefits, and, as to such tax, as we have indicated, the due process clauses have no application. Under the terms of the act, personal property under no circumstances can be directly liable for the special assessments therein contemplated. The liability of landowners under classes 2 and 3 for special assessments can arise only by a contractual relation initiated by them, and those in class 1 can be affected solely when the town or city in which they reside assumes the special assessments by agreement, in which event the urban landowner, in common with his fellow residents, is subject only to a corporate tax imposed by the authorities of said city or town to pay the special assessment for the domestic water supply contracted for, and for which a general liability would exist if domestic water was secured. To this situation, * * * the due process clauses have no application.

We now refer to the power conferred by the Water Conservancy Act to levy special assessments. As a general proposition, special assessments are permitted by authorized governmental agencies upon the theory that the property against which they are levied derives some peculiar benefit by reason of the projected improvement different from that enjoyed by other property in the community in which the improvement is to be made. The so-called assessments for special benefits provided for in classes B, C, and D of section 15 of the act are unique in character and are not directly analogous to special assessments as they generally are known in ordinary local improvement districts. This difference lies in the fact that under the act the liability for these assessments can arise only by the voluntary act of the individuals and corporations affected, whereas in ordinary cases the special assessments are imposed upon the property owners involuntarily on the basis of the benefit fixed by some public board or authority. In effect, the individuals, cities, towns, irrigation districts, and mutual ditch companies who become liable for such special assessments through agreement with the water conservancy district themselves ascertain the amount of the benefit and the extent of their liability in applying for the water which they deem necessary for their purposes. These contracts are the basis for the lien created by the act against the property of the applicant for water. The terms of an act authorizing such assessments cannot be held violative of due process of law, as each individual landowner and designated corporation agrees to process before he or it becomes subject to any special assessment. * * *

The demurrer of relator is overruled and the writ discharged.

Notes

1. **Ad valorem taxation.** Other courts have sustained districts with ad valorem taxing powers against attacks on state constitutional grounds. Santa Barbara County Water Agency v. All Persons, 306 P.2d 875 (Cal. 1975), rev'd on other grounds, Ivanhoe Irr. Dist. v. McCracken, 357 U.S. 275 (1958); Nebraska Mid-State Reclamation Dist. v. Hall County, 41 N.W.2d 397 (Neb. 1950); *In re* Arch Hurley Cons'y Dist., 191 P.2d 338 (N.M. 1948); Patterick v. Carbon Water Cons'y Dist., 145 P.2d 503 (Utah 1944), overruled on another point by Timpanogos Planning & Water Mgmt. Agency v. Central Utah Water Cons'y Dist. , 690 P.2d 562 (Utah 1984).

The Colorado River Storage Project legislation, which deals with comprehensive development of the water resources of the Upper Colorado River Basin, requires that "prior to construction of irrigation distribution facilities, repayment contracts shall be made with an 'organization' * * * which has the capacity to levy assessments upon all taxable real property located within its boundaries to assist in making repayments." 43 U.S.C. § 620c.

2. **Varieties of water districts.** Many states have statutes authorizing multipurpose districts that control water not only for irrigation but also for purposes such as drainage, flood control, municipal water supply, production of hydroelectric power, control of ground water withdrawals, and ground water replenishment. When the production of hydroelectric power is a feature, a common financial device is the issuance of revenue bonds secured by a pledge of income from the sale of electric energy.

In a number of states, general statutes provide for many types of single purpose and multipurpose districts having water as their central object. These give the careful legal shopper a choice of organizations, powers, and financial arrangements. In some states, most notably Texas and California, the legislatures have created many districts by special acts tailored to meet particular situations. According to one study, "California has * * * 38 general acts establishing water districts of different kinds with different powers, and 100 special acts, each of which creates a single district for a specified area. California contains approximately 1,000 of all types of local water districts engaged in all types of functions." U.S. Advisory Comm'n on Intergovernmental Relations, Coordinating Water Resources in the Federal System: The Groundwater-Surface Water Connection 59 (1991).

3. **State projects.** States themselves—as distinguished from districts created under state law—have not been particularly active in building or operating water storage and delivery projects. See Western States Water Council, State/Federal Financing and Western Water Resource Development 16-86 (1984). California is the most notable exception, with its large State Water Project (SWP) that impounds surplus northern California water and distributes it to the San Francisco Bay area, the San Joaquin Valley, and Southern California. A key feature of the SWP, which is operated by the Department of Water Resources, is the impoundment of water in the Feather River watershed behind Oroville Dam in Butte County. From there it flows through natural channels to the Sacramento-San Joaquin Delta. The North Bay Aqueduct and South Bay Aqueduct divert water to the San Francisco Bay area for agricultural, municipal, and industrial use. Water is pumped from the Delta into the California Aqueduct, which runs south into the San Joaquin Valley and supplies agriculture and cities there. The remaining water in the California Aqueduct is pumped over the Tehachapi Mountains to flow into Southern California, with a west branch serving Los Angeles and other coastal cities and an east branch serving the Antelope Valley and San Bernardino, Riverside, Orange, and San Diego Counties.

As once conceived, the SWP was expected to deliver 4.2 million acre-feet annually to 31 contracting agencies through nearly 700 miles of canals, pipelines, and tunnels. As presently constructed, its delivery capacity is about 2.4 million acre-feet annually. Future deliveries are likely to be constrained by the need to leave more water in the Delta to solve water quality and endangered species problems. See infra pp. 592-93, Note 1.

Various types of financing have been used for the SWP. Funds derived from the sale of California Water Resources Development Bonds and a portion of the state's tideland oil and gas revenues are deposited in the California Water Fund as authorized by the Burns-Porter Act, Cal. Water Code §§ 12930-12944. Revenue bond financing was authorized by the Central Valley Project Act, id. §§ 11100-11925. Authority to issue revenue bonds was confirmed in Warne v. Harkness, 387 P.2d 377 (Cal. 1963). The fund also receives miscellaneous receipts derived from payments and appropriations authorized by a variety of legislative actions and special contracts and cost-sharing agreements.

The history of the SWP is told in Norris Hundley, Jr., The Great Thirst: Californians and Water, 1970s-1990s, at 272-98, 309-30, 369-73 (1992).

MILLIS v. BOARD OF COUNTY COMMISSIONERS
Supreme Court of Colorado, 1981.
626 P.2d 652.

LOHR, JUSTICE. The appellants are nonresidents of Colorado who own vacation property in the High Drive Water District (District) near Estes Park. On August 13, 1975, the Larimer County Board of County

Commissioners (Board) adopted a formal resolution approving the modified service plan submitted by the District to provide domestic water for district residents. The appellants filed suit against the Board and the District, seeking relief * * * on the basis that the Board's approval exceeded its jurisdiction and was an abuse of discretion. * * * We affirm that judgment.

* * * The District consists of approximately 120 to 130 residences or parcels eligible for service, only 9 of which are owned by persons who utilize their property year-around. The majority of the parcels are owned by persons who, like the appellants, live out of state. * * * [T]he District was organized in 1974. The petition for organization carried by a vote of 27 to 21. * * *

The District's board of directors proposed to issue general obligation bonds in the amount of $350,000 to finance the construction and installation of a water system. Pursuant to section 32–4–124, C.R.S. 1973, the question of issuing the bonds was submitted to the qualified voters of the District, and the measure passed.

As part of the procedure for formation of the District, a service plan projecting the sale of bonds totaling $350,000 and bearing interest at 7% per annum had been submitted to and approved by the Board. Subsequent to the organization of the District, bond market rates rose. It appeared that the bonds could not be sold at a 7% interest rate and, upon recommendation of the underwriter of the proposed bond issue, the District's board of directors proposed a modified service plan raising the authorized interest on the bonds to 9%. Pursuant to section 32–1–209(3), C.R.S. 1973, the District submitted the modified service plan to the Board for approval. A public hearing was held on that plan, after which the Board approved it.

The appellants then filed a complaint in the Larimer County district court, claiming principally that the modified service plan was economically unfeasible. * * * The appellants also challenged the Board's approval of the modified service plan as a taking of property without due process of law. They apparently claim that the ad valorem tax burden necessary to finance the proposed water system is confiscatory and will not benefit the appellants, for they use their property only in the summer months. We do not agree with this analysis.

A water district is organized not for the improvement of land or to benefit only landowners. Such a district is created to "promote the health, safety, prosperity, security and general welfare" of its inhabitants. Section 32–4–101, C.R.S. 1973. * * * The District's board of directors therefore has the power to levy general ad valorem taxes upon property within the District without according a benefit in proportion to the tax burden imposed. Section 32–4–114, C.R.S. 1973. The fact that the appellants' property may be taxed according to its value regardless of whether the appellants choose to participate in the proposed water system, therefore, does not have any constitutional significance. The United States Supreme Court has held that the Fourteenth Amendment does not "prohibit unwise taxes, merely because they are unwise, or unfair or burdensome taxes, merely because they are unfair or burdensome." International Harvester Co. v. Wisconsin Department of Taxation, 322 U.S. 435, 444, 64 S. Ct. 1060, 1065, 88 L. Ed. 1373, 1381 (1944). * * *

Although the due process guarantee may not impose a significant limitation on the District's power to levy ad valorem taxes in order to finance the proposed water system, section 32–1–205, C.R.S. 1973, does require that the service plan for the District reflect an ability to provide economical and sufficient service to the area and that the area included within the District have sufficient financial ability to discharge any proposed indebtedness on a reasonable basis. The Board was charged with assessing these criteria when it approved the modified service plan. It is to the validity of that approval which we now turn.

A water district may not provide domestic water to its inhabitants except pursuant to a service plan which has been approved by the Board and, with respect to an original service plan, by the district court. Sections 32–1–202 to 209, C.R.S. 1973. * * *

Section 32–1–205, C.R.S. 1973, sets forth the reasons for which a service plan or modification thereof may be disapproved. For purposes of this challenge subsections (d) and (e) are relevant. Respectively, these allow disapproval of the modified plan if:

"(d) The proposed special district is incapable of providing economical and sufficient service to the area within its proposed boundaries; or (e) The area to be included in the proposed district does not have, or will not have, the financial ability to discharge the proposed indebtedness on a reasonable basis."

The primary dispute over the modified plan concerned projections as to how many persons would "tap in" to the proposed water system. It was conceded that a decrease in the income from tap fees and water charges caused by a smaller number of persons utilizing the system would have to be made up by increases in the ad valorem tax burden on all District property, increases in tap fees and water charges to those who were on the system, or a combination of such increases. Witnesses for the District, nevertheless, testified that such a decrease would not render the plan economically unfeasible. Although there was testimony at the hearing that some District landowners would not tap in, there was no proof that a substantial number would not do so.

The district court may not substitute its judgment for that of the Board, nor may we. * * * Upon review of the record, we conclude that the district court's finding that competent evidence exists to support the Board's decision is correct. The judgment of the district court is affirmed.

Notes

1. **Domestic water districts.** Practically all states authorize the creation of various districts empowered to supply water for domestic and household purposes outside of incorporated areas. For the most part, these districts depend on fees and charges for water delivered to obtain revenue for operation and maintenance and for bond retirement, though some have general taxing powers.

The Colorado Legislature repealed the statutes discussed in *Millis*, along with separate statutes governing various other quasi-municipal corporations serving purposes unrelated to water, and it replaced them all with a single Special District Act. The new act governs entities ranging from ambulance districts to water districts. Colo. Rev. Stat. §§ 32–1–101 to –1702. The repealed *Millis* statutes all have counterparts in the new act, including a provision allowing the county commissioners to approve a service plan only if the district can provide "economical and sufficient service" and the area included in the district will have "the financial ability to discharge the proposed indebtedness on a reasonable basis." Id. § 32–1–203(2).

2. **Farmers Home Administration financing**. Districts that supply domestic water in rural areas may be eligible for grants and low interest loans from the Farmers Home Administration (FmHA). See 7 U.S.C. § 1926(a).

BALL v. JAMES
Supreme Court of the United States, 1981.
451 U.S. 355, 101 S. Ct. 1811, 68 L. Ed. 2d 150.

JUSTICE STEWART delivered the opinion of the Court.

This appeal concerns the constitutionality of the system for electing the directors of a large water reclamation district in Arizona, a system which, in essence, limits voting eligibility to landowners and apportions voting power according to the amount of land a voter owns. The case requires us to consider whether the peculiarly narrow function of this local governmental body and the special relationship of one class of citizens to that body releases it from the strict demands of the one-person, one-vote principle of the Equal Protection Clause of the Fourteenth Amendment.

The public entity at issue here is the Salt River Project Agricultural Improvement and Power District, which stores and delivers untreated water to the owners of land comprising 236,000 acres in central Arizona. The District, formed as a governmental entity in 1937, subsidizes its water operations by selling electricity, and has become the supplier of electric power for hundreds of thousands of people in an area including a large part of metropolitan Phoenix. Nevertheless, the history of the District began in the efforts of Arizona farmers in the 19th century to irrigate the arid lands of the Salt River Valley, and * * * the primary purposes of the District have always been the storage, delivery, and conservation of water. * * *

This lawsuit was brought by a class of registered voters who live within the geographic boundaries of the District, and who own either no land or less than an acre of land within the District. The complaint alleged that the District enjoys such governmental powers as the power to condemn land, to sell tax-exempt bonds, and to levy taxes on real property. It also alleged that because the District sells electricity to virtually half the population of Arizona, and because, through its water operations, it can exercise significant influence on flood control and environmental management within its boundaries, the District's policies and actions have a substantial effect on all people who live within the District, regardless of property ownership. * * *

Reynolds v. Sims, [377 U.S. 533, 84 S. Ct. 1362 (1964)], held that the Equal Protection Clause requires adherence to the principle of one-person, one-vote in elections of state legislators. * * * In Hadley v. Junior College District, 397 U.S. 50, 90 S. Ct. 791, 25 L. Ed. 2d 45, the Court extended *Reynolds* to the election of trustees of a community college district because those trustees "exercised general governmental powers" and "perform[ed] important governmental functions" that had significant effect on all citizens residing within the district. But in that case the Court stated: "It is of course possible that there might be some case in which a State elects certain functionaries whose duties are so far removed from normal governmental activities and so disproportionately affect different groups that a popular election in compliance with *Reynolds* * * * might not be required * * *."

The Court found such a case in [Salyer Land Co. v. Tulare Lake Basin Water Storage Dist., 410 U.S. 719, 93 S. Ct. 1224 (1973).] The Tulare Lake Basin Water Storage District involved there encompassed 193,000 acres, 85% of which were farmed by one or another of four corporations. Under California law, public water districts could acquire, store, conserve, and distribute water, and though the Tulare Lake Basin Water Storage District had never chosen to do so, could generate and sell any form of power it saw fit to support its water operations. The costs of the project were assessed against each landowner according to the water benefits the landowner received. At issue in the case was the constitutionality of the scheme for electing the directors of the district, under which only landowners could vote, and voting power was apportioned according to the assessed valuation of the voting landowner's property. The Court recognized that the Tulare Lake Basin Water Storage District did exercise "some typical governmental powers," including the power to hire and fire workers, contract for construction of projects, condemn private property, and issue general obligation bonds. Nevertheless, the Court concluded that the district had "relatively limited authority," because "its primary purpose, indeed the reason for its existence, is to provide for the acquisition, storage, and distribution of water for farming in the Tulare Lake Basin." The Court also noted that the financial burdens of the district could not but fall on the landowners, in proportion to the benefits they received from the district, and that the district's actions therefore disproportionately affected the voting landowners. The *Salyer* Court thus held that the strictures of *Reynolds* did not apply to the Tulare District * * *.

[T]he services currently provided by the Salt River District are more diverse and affect far more people than those of the Tulare Lake Basin Water Storage District. Whereas the Tulare District included an area entirely devoted to agriculture and populated by only 77 persons, the Salt River District includes almost half the population of the State, including large parts of Phoenix and other cities. Moreover, the Salt River District, unlike the Tulare District, has exercised its statutory power to generate and sell electric power, and has become one of the largest suppliers of such power in the State. Further, whereas all the water delivered by the Tulare District went for agriculture, roughly 40% of the water delivered by the Salt River District goes to urban areas or is used for nonagricultural purposes in farming areas. Finally whereas all operating costs of the Tulare District were born by the voting landowners through assessments apportioned according to land value, most of the capital and operating costs of the Salt River District have been met through the revenues generated by the selling of electric power. Nevertheless, a careful examination of the Salt River District reveals that * * * these distinctions do not amount to a constitutional difference.

First, the District simply does not exercise the sort of governmental powers that invoke the strict demands of *Reynolds*. The District cannot impose ad valorem property taxes or sales taxes. It cannot enact any laws governing the conduct of citizens, nor does it administer such normal functions of government as the maintenance of streets, the operation of schools, or sanitation, health, or welfare services.

Second, * * * even the District's water functions, which constitute the primary and originating purpose of the District, are relatively narrow. The District [does] not own, sell, or buy water, nor [does it] control the use of any water [it has] delivered. The District simply stores water behind its dams, conserves it from loss, and delivers it through project canals. It is true * * * that as much as 40% of the water delivered by the District goes for nonagricultural purposes. But the distinction between agricultural and urban land is of no special constitutional significance in this context. The constitutionally relevant fact is that all water delivered by the Salt River District, like the water delivered by the Tulare Lake Basin Water Storage District, is distributed according to land ownership, and the District does not and cannot control the use to which the landowners who are entitled to the water choose to put it. As repeatedly recognized by the Arizona courts, though the state legislature has allowed water districts to become nominal public entities in order to obtain inexpensive bond financing, the districts remain essentially business enterprises, created by and chiefly benefiting a specific group of landowners. As in *Salyer*, the nominal public character of such an entity cannot transform it into the type of governmental body for which the Fourteenth Amendment demands a one-person, one-vote system of election.

Finally, neither the existence nor size of the District's power business affects the legality of its property-based voting scheme. * * * [T]he provision of electricity is not a traditional element of governmental sovereignty, and so is not in itself the sort of general or important governmental function that would make the government provider subject to the doctrine of the *Reynolds* case. In any event, since the electric power functions were stipulated to be incidental to the water functions which are the District's primary purpose, they cannot change the character of that enterprise. * * *

The appellees claim * * * that the sheer size of the power operations and the great number of people they affect serve to transform the District into an entity of general governmental power. But no matter how great the number of nonvoting residents buying electricity from the District, the relationship between them and the District's power operations is essentially that between consumers and a business enterprise from which they buy. * * *

The functions of the Salt River District are therefore of the narrow, special sort which justifies a departure from the popular-election requirement of the *Reynolds* case. And as in *Salyer*, an aspect of that limited purpose is the disproportionate relationship the District's functions bear to the specific class of people whom the system makes eligible to vote. The voting landowners are the only residents of the District whose lands are subject to liens to secure District bonds. Only these landowners are subject to the acreage-based taxing power of the District * * *.

As in the *Salyer* case, we conclude that the voting scheme for the District is constitutional because it bears a reasonable relationship to its statutory objectives. Here, according to the stipulation of the parties, the subscriptions of land which made * * * the District possible might well have never occurred had not the subscribing landowners been assured a special voice in the conduct of the District's business. Therefore, as in *Salyer*, the State could rationally limit the vote to landowners. Moreover, Arizona could rationally make the weight of their vote dependent upon the number of acres they own, since that number reasonably reflects the relative risks they incurred as landowners and the distribution of the benefits and the burdens of the District's water operations. * * *

Notes

1. *Ball* and *Salyer* in the lower courts. Two California water district cases illustrate the confusion created by *Ball* and *Salyer*. Moores v. Edelbrock, 272 Cal. Rptr. 919 (Cal. Ct. App. 1990), upheld a statute allowing only landowners to vote to elect directors and apportioning votes according to the assessed valuation of the land. Bjornestad v. Hulse, 272 Cal. Rptr. 864 (Cal. Ct. App. 1990), struck down a law that limited voting to elect directors to landowners, with one vote per parcel, because it violated the equal protection guarantees of the state and federal constitutions. The cases are not necessarily inconsistent because they involved water districts organized under different statutes, possessing different powers, and having different voting schemes. Nevertheless, the two courts clearly took different views of the scope of the exception to the "one-person, one-vote" principle in *Ball* and *Salyer*.

While *Bjornestad* was on appeal to the California Supreme Court, the state legislature narrowed the water district's governmental powers, stripping it of all powers relating to sanitation services, recreational facilities, and fire protection facilities. The supreme court remanded the case to the intermediate court of appeal for reconsideration in light of this change. The latter court then found that although the primary purpose of the restructured district was to provide domestic water and sewer services to residents, voting still could not be limited to landowners because the district served nonlandowning as well as landowning residents, and thus still did not meet the *Ball* and *Salyer* requirement of being "a special limited-purpose district that disproportionately affects landowners as a group." 281 Cal. Rptr. 548 (Cal. Ct. App. 1991).

2. Voting by nonresident landowners. The *Bjornestad* remand involved another legislative change that allowed both residents and nonresident landowners to vote in future district elections. This presented the question of whether enfranchising nonresident landowners unconstitutionally diluted the votes of residents. The court found that although the district was not a special limited-purpose district disproportionately affecting landowners, the district lacked general purposes and powers. Therefore, the court tested the constitutionality of the voting scheme by applying the "rational basis" test rather than the more demanding "compelling interest" test. It concluded that the legislature had a rational basis to allow nonresident landowners to vote along with residents because the district lacked general governmental purposes and powers, the area served was primarily a second-home, vacation community in a mountain area with a relatively low number of permanent residents, and the district's financial burdens were borne largely by landowners.

The Colorado water district in *Millis*, supra p. 459, also served mountain vacation property. The district financed its facilities by general obligation bonds payable out of ad valorem taxes levied on property within its boundaries. The statute on voting in elections for formation of the district and for approval of its plans enfranchised only "taxpaying electors," a term defined to exclude nonresidents of Colorado. Thus, landowners in the district who did not reside there could vote if they resided elsewhere in Colorado but not if they resided in another state. In a challenge to this differential treatment of nonresident landowners, the United States Supreme Court affirmed without opinion a federal district court decision finding no violation of the Equal Protection Clause of the Fourteenth Amendment. Millis v. High Drive Water Dist., 439 U.S. 802 (1978).

3. **State constitutional provisions.** After *Salyer* but before *Ball*, the California Supreme Court struck down a statute making landowner-ship a qualification for election to the board of directors of the Imperial Irrigation District. The district supplies 500,000 acres and 100,000 residents with irrigation and domestic water, electric power, drainage, flood control, sewage disposal, and recreational facilities. The court distinguished *Salyer* by pointing out differences between the districts in the two cases. Some of the differences may be of questionable Fourteenth Amendment significance after *Ball*, but the court's ruling was based not only on equal protection under the Fourteenth Amendment but also on the equal protection provision of the California Constitution. Choudhry v. Free, 552 P.2d 438 (Cal. 1976).

Foster v. Sunnyside Irrigation District, 687 P.2d 841 (Wash. 1984), held that a statute enfranchising the owners of agricultural or horticultural lands but not other landowners in an irrigation district violated the state constitutional guarantee of "free and equal" elections. The court said the irrigation district lacked general governmental powers that would trigger the "one-person, one-vote" rule of *Reynolds v. Sims,* but it ruled that the state constitution goes further to safeguard the right to vote than does the Equal Protection Clause of the Fourteenth Amendment.

4. **Voting Rights Act.** The federal Voting Rights Act prohibits states and their political subdivisions from imposing any voting qualification that denies the right to vote on account of race or color. 42 U.S.C. § 1973. The effect of this act upon the Arizona district involved in *Ball* was addressed in Smith v. Salt River Project Agricultural Improvement & Power District, 109 F.3d 586 (9th Cir. 1997). The court ruled that the district, though a limited-purpose entity, is a political subdivision of the state for purposes of the Voting Rights Act. The court concluded, however, that the district's land ownership requirement for voting did not violate the act even though only 40% of African-American heads-of-households within the district own homes while 60% of white heads-of-households do. There was no violation because the district had no history of racial politics and the land ownership qualification for voting had been established and continued in force for reasons unrelated to race.

FULGHUM v. SELMA

Supreme Court of North Carolina, 1953.
238 N.C. 100, 76 S.E.2d 368.

[Selma Mill Village is a small unincorporated community just outside the town of Selma. In 1946, the town contracted to sell water to plaintiff Fulghum for distribution to the inhabitants of the village through Fulghum's pipes. The town delivered the water was at a meter just inside the town limits at the same rate charged to residents of the town. Fulghum charged somewhat higher rates to the inhabitants of the village.

The delivery contract had no fixed duration. In 1952 the town passed an ordinance amending its rates to charge five times more for water supplied for use outside the town limits than within the town. Fulghum sued to have the ordinance declared void and to enjoin the city from shutting off his water supply. The trial court dismissed the action.]

ERVIN, JUSTICE. There may be more than a modicum of truth in the assertion of the plaintiffs that the defendant enacted the ordinance and its amendment for the coercive purpose of inducing Fulghum to abandon his water service to the inhabitants of Selma Mill Village and transfer his pipe lines to the defendant at less than their value. Be this as it may, we must remember that hard cases are the quicksands of the law and confine ourselves to our appointed task of declaring the legal rights of the parties.

The crucial question raised by the appeal is this: Does the evidence of the plaintiffs suffice to show that Fulghum has the legal right to compel the Town of Selma to supply water to him at the rates charged consumers within its corporate limits for resale beyond its boundaries?

The plaintiffs insist initially that this question must be answered in the affirmative on the ground that the contract made by Fulghum with the Town of Selma in 1946 gives Fulghum this legal right. * * * Where the parties to a contract calling for a continuing performance fix no time for its duration and none can be implied from the nature of the contract or from the surrounding circumstances, the contract is terminable at will by either party on reasonable notice to the other. * * *

The plaintiffs maintain secondarily that their evidence is sufficient to establish a legal right in Fulghum to the relief sought irrespective of the matter of contract right. They argue in this connection that when the Town of Selma established its waterworks and undertook to distribute water for compensation, it became the legal duty of the Town of Selma to supply Fulghum water for any purpose at the same rates as those charged consumers residing within its corporate limits. * * *

A municipality which operates its own waterworks is under no duty in the first instance to furnish water to persons outside its limits. It has the discretionary power, however, to engage in this undertaking. G.S. § 160–255. When a municipality exercises this discretionary power, it does not assume the obligations of a public service corporation toward nonresident consumers. G.S. § 62–30(3). It retains the authority to specify the terms upon which nonresidents may obtain its water. In exerting this authority, it "may fix a different rate from that charged within the corporate limits". G.S. § 160–256.

The rates fixed by the ordinance and the amendment for water supplied by the Town of Selma for consumption outside its corporate limits are not discriminatory in a legal sense. They apply alike to all nonresidents who purchase town water. The Town of Selma was empowered by law to make these rates different from those charged within its corporate limits. Since a nonresident must pay the uniform rates fixed by the Town of Selma for other nonresidents in order to obtain town water, it is immaterial that he deems such rates to be exorbitant or unreasonable. * * *

When a municipality engages in supplying water to its inhabitants, it owes the duty of equal service in furnishing water only to consumers within its corporate limits. It is under no legal obligation to supply water to a resident for resale to others either within or without its municipal limits.

Fulghum does not seek to have the water in controversy furnished to him as a consumer residing within the boundaries of the Town of Selma. His sole purpose is to resell the water to persons living outside its corporate limits. This being true, he cannot complain of the refusal of the Town of Selma to furnish him the water in controversy at the same rate charged resident consumers of the same quantity of water.

[Affirmed.]

Notes

1. **Municipal supply to nonresidents.** Generally municipal corporations have express or implied authority to supply water to consumers outside the corporate limits. See Richards v. City of Portland, 255 P. 326 (Or. 1927); Corp. of Mt. Jackson v. Nelson, 145 S.E. 355 (Va. 1928). The authority, even if express, might be construed narrowly, however, as applying only to surplus water not needed by municipal residents. Crandall v. Safford, 56 P.2d 660 (Ariz. 1936).

Whether a municipality (or a municipally owned public service company) with authority to supply nonresidents can be compelled to do so is a different question. *Fulghum* illustrates the usual view that nonresidents have no enforceable right to service from the city. Accord, Fairway Manor Inc., v. Bd. of Comm'rs, 521 N.E.2d 818 (Ohio 1988); Five Mile Prairie v. City of Spokane, 755 P.2d 836 (Wash. Ct. App. 1988).

In some states, a city that serves nonresidents in a particular area becomes subject to public utility commission regulation and must serve other nonresidents in the same area. Milwaukee v. Pub. Serv. Comm'n, 66 N.W.2d 716 (Wis. 1954); Recent Cases, 101 U. Pa. L. Rev. 160 (1952). But see Dateline Builders v. City of Santa Rosa, 194 Cal. Rptr. 258 (Cal. Ct. App. 1983) (no statutory basis exists for public utility commission jurisdiction over municipal utilities); County Water Sys. v. Salt Lake City, 278 P.2d 285 (Utah 1954) (municipalities are exempt from public utility commission jurisdiction in supplying water both to their residents and to nonresidents). Even in states where extraterritorial service can subject a municipality to public utility regulation, incidental service to a small number of nonresidents does not give rise to a duty to render additional nonresident service that would jeopardize service within the municipality. Mongiello v. Highstown, 112 A.2d 241 (N.J. 1955).

2. **Terms of nonresident service.** *Fulghum* illustrates the traditional rule that because a municipality is under no duty to supply nonresidents, it is free to set its own rates and other terms in contracting for extraterritorial service. The rule does not apply in states where extraterritorial service triggers public utility commission jurisdiction to regulate rates. Furthermore, courts increasingly are departing from the traditional rule by requiring that nonresident rates be reasonable and nondiscriminatory, although this does not necessarily mean that nonresident rates must be the same as for residents. Barr v. First Taxing Dist. of Norwalk, 192 A.2d 872 (Conn. 1963); Texarkana v. Wiggins, 246 S.W.2d 622 (Tex. 1952); Platt v. Town of Torrey, 949 P.2d 325 (Utah 1997) (suggesting higher nonresident rates could be justified by increased costs to serve nonresidents, by greater resident contributions to water system costs through general fund tax payments, or by greater potential resident responsibility for tort liability or replacement of the system). Bennett Bear Creek Farm & Water Sanitation District v. City & County of Denver, 928 P.2d 1254 (Colo. 1996), regarded rate classifications as legislative in nature and thus judicially reviewable under the rational basis test. More specifically, it said rates must be rationally related to legitimate governmental utilities purposes such as making additional development pay its way and providing a reasonable rate of return on investment based on plant value. Where the service provider makes the appropriate showing, courts have upheld nonresident surcharges of 100%. Usher v. City of Pittsburg, 410 P.2d 419 (Kan. 1966).

High rates are not the only potential problem for nonresidents. Cities sometimes use a monopoly position to exact terms unrelated to water supply or distribution, such as requiring nonresidents desiring water to accept other city services or agree to annexation. See Wayne v. Vill. of Sebring, 36 F.3d 517 (6th Cir. 1994); Five Mile Prairie v. City of Spokane, supra Note 1; Carvalho v. Levesque, 191 A.2d 165 (R.I. 1963).

Chapter 6

INTERSTATE ALLOCATION

SECTION 1. EQUITABLE APPORTIONMENT

KANSAS v. COLORADO
Supreme Court of the United States, 1907.
206 U.S. 46, 27 S. Ct. 655, 51 L. Ed. 956.

On May 20, 1901, * * * upon leave obtained, the State of Kansas filed its bill in equity in this court against the State of Colorado. To this bill the defendant demurred. * * * In delivering the opinion of the court [185 U.S. 125, 22 S.Ct. 552, 46 L.Ed. 838 (1902)] the Chief Justice disclosed in the following words the general character of the controversy, and the conclusions arrived at (p. 145, S.Ct. p. 559, L.Ed. p. 846):

"The gravamen of the bill is that the State of Colorado, acting directly herself as well as through private persons thereto licensed, is depriving and threatening to deprive the State of Kansas and its inhabitants of all the water heretofore accustomed to flow in the Arkansas River through its channel on the surface, and through a subterranean course across the State of Kansas; that this is threatened not only by the impounding and the use of the water at the river's source, but as it flows after reaching the river. Injury, it is averred, is being, and would be, thereby inflicted on the State of Kansas as an individual owner, and on all the inhabitants of the State, and especially on the inhabitants of that part of the State lying in the Arkansas Valley. The injury is asserted to be threatened, and as being wrought, in respect of lands located on the banks of the river; lands lying on the line of a subterranean flow; and lands lying some distance from the river, either above or below ground, but dependent on the river for a supply of water. And it is insisted that Colorado, in doing this, is violating the fundamental principle that one must use his own so as not to destroy the legal rights of another.

"The State of Kansas appeals to the rule of the common law that owners of lands on the banks of a river are entitled to the continual

471

flow of the stream; and while she concedes that this rule has been modified in the Western states so that flowing water may be appropriated to mining purposes and for the reclamation of arid lands, and the doctrine of prior appropriation obtains, yet she says that that modification has not gone so far as to justify the destruction of the rights of other states and their inhabitants altogether; and that the acts of Congress of 1866 and subsequently, while recognizing the prior appropriation of water as in contravention of the common-law rule as to a continuous flow, have not attempted to recognize it as rightful to that extent. In other words, Kansas contends that Colorado cannot absolutely destroy her rights, and seeks some mode of accommodation as between them, while she further insists that she occupies, for reasons given, the position of a prior appropriator herself, if put to that contention as between her and Colorado. * * *"

The issue between these several parties having been perfected by replications, a commissioner was appointed to take evidence, and after that had been taken and abstracts prepared, counsel for the respective parties were heard in argument, and upon the pleadings and testimony the case was submitted. * * *

MR. JUSTICE BREWER delivered the opinion of the court: * * *

[T]he Supreme Court is granted jurisdiction of all controversies between the States which are justiciable in their nature. * * *

One cardinal rule, underlying all the relations of the states to each other, is that of equality of right. Each state stands on the same level with all the rest. It can impose its own legislation on no one of the others, and is bound to yield its own views to none. Yet, whenever * * * the action of one state reaches through the agency of natural laws, into the territory of another state, the question of the extent and the limitations of the rights of the two states becomes a matter of justiciable dispute between them, and this court is called upon to settle that dispute in such a way as will recognize the equal rights of both and at the same time establish justice between them. In other words, through these successive disputes and decisions this court is practically building up what may not improperly be called interstate common law. This very case presents a significant illustration. Before either Kansas or Colorado was settled the Arkansas River was a stream running through the territory which now composes these two States. Arid lands abound in Colorado. Reclamation is possible only by the application of water, and the extreme contention of Colorado is that it has a right to appropriate all the waters of this stream for the purposes of irrigating its soil and making more valuable its own territory. But the appropriation of the entire flow of the river would naturally tend to make the lands along the stream in Kansas less arable. It would be taking from the adjacent territory that which had been the customary natural means of preserving its arable character. On the other hand, the possible contention of Kansas, that the flowing water in the Arkansas must, in accordance with the extreme doctrine of the common law of England, be left to flow as it was wont to flow, no portion of it being appropriated in Colorado for the purposes of irrigation, would have the effect to perpetuate a desert condition in portions of Colorado beyond the power of reclamation. Surely here is a dispute of a justiciable nature which might and ought to be tried and determined. If the two States were absolutely independent nations it would be settled by treaty or by force. Neither of these ways being practicable, it must be settled by decision of this court. * * *

In deciding this case on demurrer we said:

"[T]he mere fact that a state had no pecuniary interest in the controversy would not defeat the original jurisdiction of this court, which might be invoked by the state as *parens patriae,* trustee, guardian, or representative of all or a considerable portion of its citizens; * * *.

"In the case before us, the State of Kansas files her bill as representing and on behalf of her citizens, as well as in vindication of her alleged rights as an individual owner, and seeks relief in respect of being deprived of the waters of the river accustomed to flow through and across the State, and the consequent destruction of the property of herself and of her citizens and injury to their health and comfort. The action complained of is state action, and not the action of state officers in abuse or excess of their powers."

[Kansas] is in no manner evading the provisions of the 11th Amendment to the Federal Constitution.[a] It is not acting directly and solely for the benefit of any individual citizen to protect his riparian rights. Beyond its property rights it has an interest as a state in this large tract of land bordering on the Arkansas River. Its prosperity affects the general welfare of the State. The controversy rises, therefore, above a mere question of local private right and involves a matter of state interest, and must be considered from that standpoint. * * *

[T]he diminution of the flow of water in the river by the irrigation of Colorado has worked some detriment to the southwestern part of Kansas, and yet, when we compare the amount of this detriment with the great benefit which has obviously resulted to the counties in Colorado, it would seem that equality of right and equity between the two States forbids any interference with the present withdrawal of water in Colorado for purposes of irrigation.

Summing up our conclusions, we are of that opinion that * * * the appropriation of the waters of the Arkansas by Colorado, for purposes

---

a. The Eleventh Amendment provides: "The judicial power of the United States shall not be construed to extend to any suit in law or equity, commenced or prosecuted against one of the United States by Citizens of another State * * *."

of irrigation, has diminished the flow of water into the State of Kansas; that the result of that appropriation has been the reclamation of large areas in Colorado, transforming thousands of acres into fertile fields, and rendering possible their occupation and cultivation when otherwise they would have continued barren and unoccupied; that while the influence of such diminution has been of perceptible injury to portions of the Arkansas Valley in Kansas, particularly those portions closest to the Colorado line, yet, to the great body of the valley it has worked little, if any, detriment, and regarding the interests of both States, and the right of each to receive benefit through irrigation and in any other manner from the waters of this stream, we are not satisfied that Kansas has made out a case entitling it to a decree. At the same time it is obvious that if the depletion of the waters of the river by Colorado continues to increase there will come a time when Kansas may justly say that there is no longer an equitable division of benefits, and may rightfully call for relief against the action of Colorado, its corporations and citizens, in appropriating the waters of the Arkansas for irrigation purposes.

The decree which, therefore, will be entered, * * * will also dismiss the bill of the State of Kansas as against all the defendants, without prejudice to the right of the plaintiff to institute new proceedings whenever it shall appear that, through a material increase in the depletion of the waters of the Arkansas by Colorado, its corporations or citizens, the substantial interests of Kansas are being injured to the extent of destroying the equitable apportionment of benefits between the two States resulting from the flow of the river. * * *

Notes

1. **Supreme Court jurisdiction.** The Supreme Court's jurisdiction of controversies between states is original and exclusive. Const. art. III, § 2, cl. 2; 28 U.S.C. § 1251(a). In the principal case, the Court appointed a commissioner to hear testimony and prepare abstracts of it. Later the Court settled on the practice of appointing a special master to take evidence and submit a report containing findings of fact, conclusions of law, and a recommended disposition of the case.

2. **Private interstate water suits.** Litigation over interstate waters has not been limited to suits between states in the Supreme Court. Individual water users from different states have litigated allocation disputes in other courts.

Private suits raise issues of judicial jurisdiction. A court lacks power to issue an in rem decree affecting a water right outside its territorial jurisdiction. But the court can obtain personal jurisdiction over the right holder if that person appears voluntarily, is served while present in the forum state, or is served elsewhere under a long-arm statute. The court can then issue an in personam decree that regulates the person's water use. Vineyard Land & Stock Co. v. Twin Falls Salmon River Land & Water Co., 245 F. 9 (9th Cir. 1917). The decree can be enforced by contempt proceedings. Brooks v. United States, 119 F.2d 636 (9th Cir. 1941).

Private suits also raise issues of choice of law. The doctrine of equitable apportionment plays no role if the Supreme Court has not yet decreed an apportionment between the states. *Vineyard Land & Stock Co.,* supra. If the private litigants come from states that both have the appropriation doctrine, courts have determined and enforced priorities across the state boundary. E.g., Bean v. Morris, 221 U.S. 485 (1911); Albion-Idaho Land Co. v. Naf Irr. Co., 97 F.2d 439 (10th Cir. 1938); United States v. Walker River Irr. Dist., 11 F. Supp. 158 (D. Nev. 1935); Willey v. Decker, 73 P. 210 (Wyo. 1903). If the litigants come from states with different water law doctrines, neither existing water cases nor general choice-of-law principles provide much guidance on what law should govern. See Douglas L. Grant, Private Interstate Suits, in 3 Waters and Water Rights §§ 44.05(b)-.05(b)(2) (Robert E. Beck & Amy K. Kelley eds., 3d ed. 2009) (suggesting approaches to the choice-of-law issue).

3. **Further Arkansas River litigation.** The Arkansas River controversy between Kansas and Colorado returned to the Court in Colorado v. Kansas, 320 U.S. 383 (1943). Colorado sought to enjoin private suits brought by Kansas citizens in lower courts asserting claims that Colorado alleged were inconsistent with the principal case. Kansas responded that Colorado users had increased their diversions, and it again asked the Court to apportion the Arkansas River. The Court enjoined the lower court suits but still denied Kansas an equitable apportionment decree for failure to show that its substantial interests were being injured.

The Court also stated: "The reason for judicial caution in adjudicating the relative rights of states in such cases is that, while we have jurisdiction of such disputes, they involve the interests of quasi-sovereigns, present complicated and delicate questions, and, due to the possibility of future change of conditions, necessitate expert administration rather than judicial imposition of a hard and fast rule. Such controversies may appropriately be composed by negotiation and agreement, pursuant to the compact clause of the Federal constitution. We say of this case, as the court has said of interstate differences of like nature, that such mutual accommodation and agreement should, if possible, be the medium of settlement, instead of invocation of our adjudicatory power." Id. at 392. Kansas and Colorado responded by negotiating an apportionment in the Arkansas River Compact. 63 Stat. 145 (1949).

4. **The Laramie River apportionment.** The Court's first apportionment of an interstate river came in Wyoming v. Colorado, 259 U.S. 419 (1922). The Laramie River begins in northern Colorado and flows north into Wyoming, where it eventually empties into the North Platte River. Wyoming sued to prevent a large new diversion from the Laramie River in Colorado. Both states applied the appropriation doctrine internally, and a key issue was the whether Court should base the equitable apportionment on priority of appropriation. The Court said:

"We conclude that Colorado's objections to the doctrine of appropriation as a basis of decision are not well taken, and that it furnishes the only basis which is consonant with the principles of right and equity applicable to such a controversy as this is. The cardinal rule of the doctrine is that priority of appropriation gives superiority of right. Each of these States applies and enforces this rule in her own territory, and it is the one to which intending appropriators naturally would turn for guidance. The principle on which it proceeds is not less applicable to interstate streams and controversies than to others. Both States pronounce the rule just and reasonable as applied to the natural conditions in that region, and to prevent any departure from it the people of both incorporated it into their Constitutions. It originated in the customs and usages of the people before either State came into existence, and the courts of both hold that their constitutional provisions are to be taken as recognizing the prior usage rather than as creating a new rule. These considerations persuade us that its application to such a controversy as is here presented cannot be other than eminently just and equitable to all concerned."

The Court did not directly enforce priorities, however. It found that the Laramie River had an average dependable flow of 312,250 acre-feet per year and that existing water rights totaled 296,750 acre-feet (272,500 in Wyoming and 24,250 in Colorado). This left only 15,500 acre-feet of the average dependable flow available for the new Colorado diversion, and the Court's decree was in form an injunction against diversion of more than this amount. 259 U.S. 496 (1922). In practical operation, the decree guaranteed Colorado 39,750 acre-feet (24,250 + 15,500) and awarded Wyoming the remaining flow each year. Consequently, Wyoming's share would vary depending on how much the flow in a given year exceeded or fell below the average dependable flow. The Court later described the fixed award to Colorado as a "mass allocation." Nebraska v. Wyoming, 325 U.S. 589 (1945).

During the irrigation season immediately after entry of the Laramie decree, the river flow was far below average. Wyoming appropriators with priorities as early as 1883 received no water while the new Colorado project got its 15,500 acre-feet despite having only a 1909 priority. Wyoming's top water official remarked: "Why this situation? Simply because the Court of last resort in its wisdom granted to Colorado rights [to] a certain volume of water for use each year, regardless of the seasonal flow of the river. * * * What was heralded as a victory for Wyoming was indeed an empty one." Frank C. Emerson, Discussion, 90 Transactions Am. Soc'y Civ. Eng'rs 1052, 1052-53 (1927).

5. **Effect of an apportionment decree on individual rights.** During a year of very low flow in the Laramie River, could a Wyoming appropriator with an 1883 priority circumvent the Court's decree by bringing a private suit to enjoin diversion upstream by a 1909 priority Colorado appropriator? In later litigation between the two states, the Court said that although individual water users were not parties to the suit that

resulted in the apportionment decree, they were represented by their respective states and were bound by the decree. 286 U.S. 494 (1932).

6. **The Delaware River apportionment.** The Court's second apportionment of an interstate river came in New Jersey v. New York, 283 U.S. 336 (1931). The Delaware River rises in New York and forms all or part of the boundaries between New York and Pennsylvania, Pennsylvania and New Jersey, and New Jersey and Delaware—all riparian doctrine states. New Jersey sued to prevent New York from diverting water from the Delaware River or its tributaries for use in a different watershed. It sought strict application of the riparian doctrine to prevent water use outside the Delaware River watershed.

The Court refused to base its apportionment on the riparian doctrine, saying: "The different traditions and practices in different parts of the country may lead to varying results but the effort always is to secure an equitable apportionment without quibbling over formulas. * * * The removal of water to a different watershed obviously must be allowed at times unless States are to be deprived of the most beneficial use on formal grounds." 283 U.S. at 343.

In making its apportionment, the Court considered the adverse effects of New York's proposed diversion on navigation, recreation, water power, agricultural use, municipal and industrial use, the oyster industry, and shad fisheries in the downstream states. The Court limited the daily quantity of water that New York could divert, required it to release water from storage when the river flow fell below a certain rate, and required it to construct an efficient sewage treatment plant to address downstream water quality concerns.

NEBRASKA v. WYOMING
Supreme Court of the United States, 1945.
325 U.S. 589, 65 S.Ct. 1332, 89 L.Ed. 1815.

MR. JUSTICE DOUGLAS delivered the opinion of the Court.

Nebraska brought this suit in 1934 against Wyoming, invoking our original jurisdiction * * *. Colorado was impleaded as a defendant. The United States was granted leave to intervene. * * *

The controversy pertains to the use for irrigation purposes of the water of the North Platte River, a non-navigable stream. * * * The North Platte River rises in Northern Colorado in the mountainous region known as North Park. It proceeds in a northerly direction on the east side of the Continental Divide, enters Wyoming west of Cheyenne, and continues in a northerly direction to the vicinity of Casper. There it turns east across the Great Plains and proceeds easterly and southerly into and across Nebraska. About 40 miles west of the Nebraska line it is joined by the Laramie River. At North Platte, Nebraska, it is joined by the South Platte, forming the Platte River. It empties into the Missouri River at Plattsmouth, near the western border of Iowa. * * *

[The earliest water development from the river occurred near the Nebraska-Wyoming line. Some of the early canals were diverting water in Wyoming and serving Wyoming land. Several others, known as the State Line canals, were diverting water in Nebraska at the Tri-State Dam, located about a mile east of the state line, and serving Nebraska land. The French Canal was diverting in Wyoming but supplying land in both states.

In 1904 the United States Bureau of Reclamation started the North Platte Project with construction of Pathfinder Reservoir located just above Casper, Wyoming. Later it built Guernsey, a small auxiliary reservoir below Casper. Water from these reservoirs was being released into the river and diverted in eastern Wyoming at Whalen Dam into the Interstate Canal and the Fort Laramie Canal. These canals extend far into Nebraska. They were irrigating some land in Wyoming and a very large acreage in Nebraska.

Above Pathfinder, Wyoming ranchers were irrigating about 168,000 acres of hay lands, mostly from tributaries, and Colorado ranchers were irrigating about 131,000 acres of hay lands. Most of these water rights were junior to the State Line Canals, and about half of them were junior to Pathfinder.

In 1931 the Bureau of Reclamation started the Kendrick Project, consisting of Seminoe Reservoir above Pathfinder and the Casper Canal to deliver to Wyoming land. A few years later, it added Alcova Reservoir, just below Pathfinder.

Unfortunately, the decade from 1931 through 1940 was the driest on record. In every year but one, the annual river flow was below the mean for the period from 1904 through 1930.]

The commencement of this dry cycle plus the initiation of the Kendrick project precipitated the present controversy. Nebraska rests her case essentially on evidence of shortage and of misappropriation of water by the upper States since 1930 and of threats of more serious shortage and diversions in the future. * * *

* * * Colorado moves to dismiss the proceeding. She asserts that the pleadings and evidence both indicate that she has not injured nor presently threatens to injure any downstream water user. * * * The argument is that the case is not of such serious magnitude and the damage is not so fully and clearly proved as to warrant the intervention of this Court under our established practice. * * *

We fully recognize those principles. But they do not stand in the way of an entry of a decree in this case. The evidence supports the finding of the Special Master that the dependable natural flow of the river during the irrigation season has long been overappropriated. A genuine controversy exists. The States have not been able to settle their differences by compact. * * *

What we have then is a situation where three States assert against a river, whose dependable natural flow during the irrigation season has long been over appropriated, claims based not only on present uses but on projected additional uses as well. * * *

The equitable apportionment which Nebraska seeks is based on the principle of priority of appropriation applied interstate. Colorado and Wyoming have the rule of priority of appropriation as distinguished from the rule of riparian rights. * * * The rights asserted by Nebraska in this suit are based wholly on appropriations which have been obtained and recognized under Nebraska law. The appropriation system is dominant in the regions of Nebraska which are involved in the present litigation. Hence we, like the Special Master, treat the case as one involving appropriation rights not only in Colorado and Wyoming but in Nebraska as well. * * *

* * * The Special Master recommended a decree based on that principle. That was indeed the principle adopted by the Court in State of Wyoming v. Colorado, where an apportionment of the waters of an interstate stream was made between two States, each of which had the rule of appropriation. * * * Since Colorado, Wyoming, and Nebraska are appropriation States, that principle would seem to be equally applicable here.

That does not mean that there must be a literal application of the priority rule. We stated in State of Colorado v. Kansas, supra, that in determining whether one State is "using, or threatening to use, more than its equitable share of the benefits of a stream, all of the factors which create equities in favor of one state or the other must be weighed as of the date when the controversy is mooted." 320 U.S. page 394, 64 S.Ct. 181, 88 L.Ed. 116. That case did not involve a controversy between two appropriation States. But if an allocation between appropriation States is to be just and equitable, strict adherence to the priority rule may not be possible. For example, the economy of a region may have been established on the basis of junior appropriations. So far as possible those established uses should be protected though strict application of the priority rule might jeopardize them. Apportionment calls for the exercise of an informed judgment on a consideration of many factors. Priority of appropriation is the guiding principle. But physical and climatic conditions, the consumptive use of water in the several sections of the river, the character and rate of return flows, the extent of established uses, the availability of storage water, the practical effect of wasteful uses on downstream areas, the damage to upstream areas as compared to the benefits to downstream areas if a limitation is imposed on the former—these are all relevant factors.

They are merely an illustrative not an exhaustive catalogue. They indicate the nature of the problem of apportionment and the delicate adjustment of interests which must be made.

Colorado. Practical considerations of this order underlie Nebraska's concession that the priority rule should not be strictly applied to appropriations in Colorado, though some are junior to the priorities of appropriators in Wyoming and Nebraska. As the Special Master points out the flowage time of water from North Park to Bridgeport, Nebraska is between two and three weeks. If a canal in North Park were closed to relieve the shortage of a senior appropriator in Nebraska, it would be highly speculative whether the water would reach the Nebraska appropriator in time or whether the closing of the Colorado canal would work more hardship there than it would bestow benefits in Nebraska. Moreover, there is loss of water in transit from the upper to the downstream sections, increasing with the distance. The lower appropriator thus receives less than the upper appropriator loses. And there is evidence that a river-wide priority system would disturb and disrupt long established uses. * * *

We are satisfied that a reduction in present Colorado uses is not warranted. The fact that the same amount of water might produce more in lower sections of the river is immaterial. State of Wyoming v. Colorado, supra, page 468, 42 S.Ct. page 558, 66 L.Ed. 999. The established economy in Colorado's section of the river basin based on existing use of the water should be protected. Cf. State of Colorado v. Kansas, supra, 320 U.S. page 394, 64 S.Ct. page 181, 88 L.Ed. page 116. Appropriators in Colorado junior to Pathfinder have made out-of-priority diversions of substantial amounts. Strict application of the priority rule might well result in placing a limitation on Colorado's present use for the benefit of Pathfinder. But as we have said, priority of appropriation, while the guiding principle for an apportionment, is not a hard and fast rule. Colorado's countervailing equities indicate it should not be strictly adhered to in this situation. * * *

Colorado State Line to Pathfinder and Guernsey. The Special Master recommends that Wyoming be enjoined from diverting water from the main river above Guernsey and from its tributaries above Pathfinder for the irrigation of more than 168,000 acres. [M]ost of the land under irrigation in the section above Pathfinder is irrigated from tributaries. The rights are small but very numerous. The total acreage under irrigation is 153,000 acres, allowing for a margin of error. Below Pathfinder and above Guernsey the Special Master dealt only with diversions from the main river. He concluded that the run-off of the tributaries becomes so far exhausted before any shortage of water occurs in the main river that any regulation of the tributary diversions would be of no material benefit. The tributary inflow is greater than the depletion of the river. There is some out-of-priority diversion as we have noted. But possibilities for future developments are largely non-existent. The Special Master concluded that if Wyoming were limited to the irrigation of 15,000 acres (which is the extent of present irrigation with a margin of error) natural conditions would militate against this section getting more than its equitable share of the water.

We think that is a practical and fair adjustment. So far as the tributaries above Pathfinder are concerned, practical difficulties of applying restrictions which would reduce the amount of water used by the hundreds of small irrigators would seem to outweigh any slight benefit which senior appropriators might obtain. This does not seem to be denied. * * *

Pathfinder, Guernsey, Seminoe and Alcova Reservoirs and the Casper Canal. [For this section of the river, the Court accepted the Special Master's recommendation to apply the rule of priority.]

Whalen to Tri-State Dam. This is the pivotal section of the river around which the central problems of this case turn. Apart from the Kendrick project, the demand for water is as great in this short section of the river as in the entire preceding 415 miles from North Park to Whalen. The lands irrigated from the river in this section total 326,000 acres as compared with 339,200 acres in the upper valley—main river and tributaries. The consumptive use on this 326,000 acres far exceeds that of the upper sections combined. * * *

As respects priority, the canals * * * fall into thirteen groups, seven in Wyoming and six in Nebraska. The earliest in priority are some canals in Wyoming, then some in Nebraska, then others in Wyoming and so on. * * *

[The Special Master] proposes that the natural flow water in this section between May 1 and September 30 each year be apportioned [daily] on the basis of 25 per cent to Wyoming and 75 per cent to Nebraska. He recommends that Nebraska be given the right to designate from time to time the portion of its share which shall be delivered to the Interstate, Ft. Laramie, French and Mitchell Canals for use on Nebraska lands served by them and that Wyoming be enjoined from diversions contrary to this apportionment.

None of the parties agrees to this apportionment. * * *

Wyoming argues for a mass allocation, e.g. 705,000 acre feet to be allocated to Nebraska for diversion in this section during the irrigation season for Nebraska lands. The Special Master rejected that method. He concluded that it was based on an assumption of dependability of flow which would be bound to result in injustice to one or other of the States * * *. We [conclude] that the inadequacy of the supply is too clear to permit adoption of Wyoming's formula. * * *

The United States and Nebraska advance as their preferred alternative a strict priority apportionment in which the rights of each appropriator would be fixed. * * * The Special Master [recommended against] an interstate priority schedule for this section [on the grounds] (1) that it would deprive each State of full freedom of intrastate administration of her share of the water and (2) that it would burden the decree with administrative detail beyond what is necessary to an equitable apportionment. Our judgment is that these * * * considerations without more are sufficient justification for rejection of the strict priority allocation * * *. An equitable apportionment may be had without fashioning a decree of that detail. And greater administrative flexibility may be achieved within the respective States by choice of another alternative.

* * * We conclude that the early Wyoming uses, the return flows, and the greater storage water rights which Nebraska appropriators have in this section as compared with those of Wyoming appropriators tip the scales in favor of the flat percentage system recommended by the Special Master. It should be noted, moreover, that that method of apportionment, though not strictly adhering to the principle of priority, gives it great weight and does not cause as great a distortion as might appear to be the case. * * *

Notes

1. **Modification versus enforcement of a decree.** In a later opinion modifying the North Platte decree, the Court distinguished between modification and enforcement of a decree:

"In an enforcement action, the plaintiff need not show injury. When the alleged conduct is admitted, the only question is whether that conduct violates a right established by the decree. To be sure, the right need not be stated explicitly in the decree. * * * [W]hen the decree is silent or unclear, it is appropriate to consider the underlying opinion, the Master's Report, and the record in the prior proceedings to determine whether the Court previously resolved the issue. The parties' course of conduct under the decree also may be relevant. But the underlying issue primarily remains one of interpretation. In a modification proceeding, by contrast, there is by definition no pre-existing right to interpret or enforce. At least where the case concerns the impact of new development, the inquiry may well entail the same sort of balancing of equities that occurs in an initial proceeding to establish an equitable apportionment. * * * [W]hen the plaintiff essentially seeks a reweighing of equities and an injunction declaring new rights and responsibilities, we think the plaintiff still must make a showing of substantial injury to be entitled to relief. That is so not only because a new injunction would work a new infringement on sovereign prerogatives, but also because the interests of certainty and stability counsel strongly against reopening an apportionment of interstate water rights absent considerable justification." 507 U.S. at 592-93 (1993).

In a follow-up opinion, the Court said adverse effects on wildlife or wildlife habitat, if proved, would be a relevant factor in balancing the equities. 515 U.S. 1 (1995).

2. **Barriers to Supreme Court apportionment.** The Court has equitably apportioned only the Laramie, Delaware, and North Platte Rivers. It has declined to apportion several other rivers under a principle stated as follows in New York v. New Jersey, 256 U.S. 296 (1921): "Before this court can be moved to exercise its extraordinary power under the Constitution to control the conduct of one state at the suit of another, the threatened invasion of rights must be of serious magnitude and it must be established by clear and convincing evidence." See Colorado v. Kansas, supra p. 475, Note 3; Washington v. Oregon, 297 U.S. 517 (1936); Connecticut v. Massachusetts, 282 U.S. 660 (1931).

Another barrier to Supreme Court apportionment is that the United States might have sufficient interest in a river to require its presence in an equitable apportionment suit, but sovereign immunity prevents it from being joined without its consent. In Arizona v. California, 298 U.S. 558 (1936), Arizona petitioned for leave to sue the other states in the Colorado River basin for apportionment of the unappropriated water in the river. The Court dismissed the petition on the ground that the United States was an indispensable party because of its paramount power over the unappropriated waters for the purpose of controlling navigation. Similarly, the Court dismissed Texas v. New Mexico, 352 U.S. 991 (1957) (a suit for breach of an interstate water compact), after six years of litigation because of the absence of the United States as an indispensable party. There, the interest of the United States arose from its role as trustee for Indian tribes.

Although the United States cannot be compelled to appear in a water apportionment suit between states, it may appear voluntarily. For example, the United States intervened in Arizona v. California, 344 U.S. 919 (1953).

Federal interests in a river do not always raise a sovereign immunity bar to equitable apportionment. The principal case, Nebraska v. Wyoming, involved the nonnavigable North Platte River. Wyoming moved to dismiss on the ground that the Secretary of the Interior was an indispensable but absent party. The Court responded: "The bill alleges, and we know as [a] matter of law, that the Secretary and his agents, acting by authority of the Reclamation Act and supplementary legislation, must obtain permits and priorities for the use of water from the State of Wyoming in the same manner as a private appropriator or an irrigation district formed under the state law. His rights can rise no higher than those of Wyoming, and an adjudication of the defendant's rights will necessarily bind him. Wyoming will stand in judgment for him as for any other appropriator in that state. He is not a necessary party." Nebraska v. Wyoming, 295 U.S. 40 (1935).

COLORADO v. NEW MEXICO
Supreme Court of the United States, 1982.
459 U.S. 176, 103 S. Ct. 539, 74 L. Ed.2d 348.

JUSTICE Marshall delivered the opinion of the Court. * * *

The Vermejo River is a small, nonnavigable river that originates in the snow-belt of the Rocky Mountains in southern Colorado and flows southeasterly into New Mexico for a distance of roughly 55 miles before it joins the Canadian River. The major portion of the river is located in New Mexico. The Colorado portion consists of three main tributaries that combine to form the Vermejo River proper approximately one mile below the Colorado-New Mexico border. At present there are no uses of the water of the Vermejo River in Colorado, and no use or diversion has ever been made in Colorado. In New Mexico, by contrast, farmers and industrial users have diverted water from the Vermejo for many years. In 1941 a New Mexico state court issued a decree apportioning the water of the Vermejo River among the various New Mexico users.

In 1975, a Colorado corporation, Colorado Fuel and Iron Steel Corporation ("C.F. & I."), obtained in Colorado state court a conditional right to divert 75 cubic feet per second from the headwaters of the Vermejo River. C.F. & I. proposed a transmountain diversion of the water to a tributary of the Purgatoire River in Colorado to be used for industrial development and other purposes. * * *

The Special Master found that most of the water of the Vermejo River is consumed by the New Mexico users and that very little, if any, reaches the confluence with the Canadian River. He thus recognized that strict application of the rule of priority would not permit Colorado any diversion since the entire available supply is needed to satisfy the demands of appropriators in New Mexico with senior rights. Nevertheless, applying the principle of equitable apportionment established in our prior cases, he recommended permitting Colorado a transmountain diversion of 4,000 acre-feet of water per year from the headwaters of the Vermejo River. * * *

Explaining his conclusion, the Special Master noted that any injury to New Mexico would be restricted to the [Vermejo] Conservancy District, the user in New Mexico furthest downstream, since there was sufficient water in the Vermejo River for the three other principal New Mexico water users, Vermejo Park, Kaiser Steel, and Phelps Dodge. He further found that the "Vermejo Conservancy District has never been an economically feasible operation." * * *

Equitable apportionment is the doctrine of federal common law that governs disputes between states concerning their rights to use the water of an interstate stream. It is a flexible doctrine which calls for "the exercise of an informed judgment on a consideration of many factors" to secure a "just and equitable" allocation. Nebraska v. Wyoming, 325 U.S. 589, 618, 65 S.Ct. 1332, 1350–1351, 89 L.Ed. 1815 (1945). * * *

In reaching his recommendation the Special Master did not focus exclusively on the rule of priority, but considered other factors such as the efficiency of current uses in New Mexico and the balance of benefits to Colorado and harm to New Mexico. New Mexico contends that it is improper to consider these other factors. It maintains that this Court has strictly applied the rule of priority when apportioning water between states adhering to the prior appropriation doctrine, and has departed from that rule only to protect an existing economy built upon junior appropriations. Since there is no existing economy in Colorado dependent upon the use of water from the Vermejo River, New Mexico contends that the rule of priority is controlling. We disagree with this inflexible interpretation of the doctrine of equitable apportionment.

Our prior cases clearly establish that equitable apportionment will protect only those rights to water that are "reasonably acquired and applied." Wyoming v. Colorado, 259 U.S. 419, 484, 42 S.Ct. 552, 564, 66 L.Ed. 999 (1922). Especially in those Western states where water is scarce, "[t]here must be no waste * * * of the 'treasure' of a river * * *. Only diligence and good faith will keep the privilege alive." Washington v. Oregon, 297 U.S. 517, 527, 56 S.Ct. 540, 544–545, 80 L.Ed. 837 (1936). Thus, wasteful or inefficient uses will not be protected. Similarly, concededly senior water rights will be deemed forfeited or substantially diminished where the rights have not been exercised or asserted with reasonable diligence.

We have invoked equitable apportionment not only to require the reasonably efficient use of water, but also to impose on states an affirmative duty to take reasonable steps to conserve and augment the water supply of an interstate stream. In Wyoming v. Colorado, Wyoming brought suit to prevent a *proposed* diversion by Colorado from the Laramie River. This Court calculated the dependable supply available to both states, subtracted the senior Wyoming uses, and permitted Colorado to divert an amount not exceeding the balance. In calculating the dependable supply we placed on each state the duty to employ "financially and physically feasible" measures "adapted to *conserving and equalizing* the natural flow." 259 U.S. at 484, 42 S.Ct., at 564 (emphasis added). * * *

We conclude that it is entirely appropriate to consider the extent to which reasonable conservation measures by New Mexico might offset the proposed Colorado diversion and thereby minimize any injury to New Mexico users. Similarly, it is appropriate to consider whether Colorado has undertaken reasonable steps to minimize the amount of diversion that will be required.

In addition, we have held that in an equitable apportionment of interstate waters it is proper to weigh the harms and benefits to competing states. In Kansas v. Colorado, supra, where we first announced the doctrine of equitable apportionment, we found that users in Kansas were injured by Colorado's upstream diversions from the Arkansas River. 206 U.S. at 113-114, 117, 27 S.Ct., at 674, 675-676. Yet we declined to grant any relief to Kansas on the ground that the great benefit to Colorado outweighed the detriment to Kansas. Similarly, in Nebraska v. Wyoming, we held that water rights in Wyoming and Nebraska, which under state law were senior, had to yield to the "countervailing equities" of an established economy in Colorado even though it was based on junior appropriations. 325 U.S. at 622, 65 S.Ct., at 1352. We noted that the rule of priority should not be strictly applied where it "would work more hardship" on the junior user "than it would bestow benefits" on the senior user. Id., at 619, 65 S.Ct., at 1351. The same principle is applicable in balancing the benefits of a diversion for *proposed* uses against the possible harms to existing ones.

We recognize that the equities supporting the protection of existing economies will usually be compelling. The harm that may result from disrupting established uses is typically certain and immediate, whereas the potential benefits from a proposed diversion may be speculative and remote. Under some circumstances, however, the countervailing equities supporting a diversion for future use in one state may justify the detriment to existing users in another state. This may be the case, for example, where the state seeking a diversion demonstrates by clear and convincing evidence that the benefits of the diversion substantially outweigh the harm that might result.[13] In the determination of whether the state proposing the diversion has car-

---

13. Our cases establish that a state seeking to prevent or enjoin a diversion by another state bears the burden of proving that the diversion will cause it "real or substantial injury or damage." Connecticut v. Massachusetts, supra, 282 U.S., at 672, 51 S.Ct., at 290. This rule applies even if the state seeking to prevent or enjoin a diversion is the nominal defendant in a lawsuit. * * *

New Mexico must therefore bear the initial burden of showing that a diversion by Colorado will cause substantial injury to the interests of New Mexico. In this case New Mexico has met its burden since *any* diversion by Colorado, unless offset by New Mexico at its own expense, will necessarily reduce the amount of water available to New Mexico users.

The burden has therefore shifted to Colorado to establish that a diversion should nevertheless be permitted under the principle of equitable apportionment. Thus, with respect to whether reasonable conservation measures by New Mexico will offset the loss of water due to Colorado's diversion, or whether the benefit to Colorado from the diversion will substantially outweigh the possible harm to New Mexico, Colorado will bear the burden of proof. It must show, in effect, that without such a diversion New Mexico would be using "more than its equitable share of the benefits of a stream." Id., at 394, 64 S.Ct., at 181. Moreover, Colorado must establish not only that its claim is of a "serious magnitude," but also that its position is supported by "clear and convincing evidence." Connecticut v. Massachusetts, 282 U.S., at 669, 51 S.Ct., at 289.

ried this burden, an important consideration is whether the existing users could offset the diversion by reasonable conservation measures to prevent waste. This approach comports with our emphasis on flexibility in equitable apportionment and also accords sufficient protection to existing uses. * * *

We conclude, therefore, that in the determination of an equitable apportionment of the water of the Vermejo River the rule of priority is not the sole criterion. While the equities supporting the protection of established, senior uses are substantial, it is also appropriate to consider additional factors relevant to a just apportionment, such as the conservation measures available to both states and the balance of harm and benefit that might result from the diversion sought by Colorado.

Applying the doctrine of equitable apportionment, the Special Master recommended that Colorado be permitted to divert 4,000 acre-feet of water per year from the headwaters of the Vermejo River. Because all of the water of the Vermejo River is currently consumed by New Mexico appropriators, the recommended diversion would necessarily reduce the amount of water available to New Mexico.

In explaining the basis for his recommendation, the Special Master stated that the diversion would not "materially affect" existing New Mexico appropriations. This conclusion appears to reflect certain assumptions about the ability of New Mexico users to implement water conservation measures. The Special Master also concluded that any injury to New Mexico would be "more than offset" by the benefits to Colorado. Both the availability of conservation measures and a weighing of the harm and benefits that would result from the diversion are factors relevant to the determination of a just and equitable apportionment. However, the Special Master did not clearly state the factual findings supporting his reliance on these factors. * * * We remand for specific factual findings relevant to determining a just and equitable apportionment of the water of the Vermejo River between Colorado and New Mexico.

It is so ordered.

JUSTICE O'Connor, with whom JUSTICE POWELL, joins, concurring in the judgment.

The doctrine of prior appropriation includes the requirement that the appropriator's use of water be beneficial and reasonable. What is reasonable, of course, does not admit of ready definition, being dependent upon the particular facts and circumstances of each case. In this case, the Special Master has cast an accusatory finger at the Vermejo Conservancy District, concluding that "[t]he system of canals used to transport the water to the fields is inefficient."

Undoubtedly, there is evidence in the record indicating that large losses of water occur through seepage and evaporation in transporting waters of the Vermejo through open ditches for irrigation and stock watering. It is a leap, however, from observing that large losses occur to concluding, as Colorado would have the Court do, that the practices of the Conservancy District are wasteful or unreasonable. As the Court observes, the extent of the duty to conserve that may be placed upon the user is limited to measures that are "financially and physically feasible," Wyoming v. Colorado, 259 U.S. 419, 484, 42 S.Ct. 552, 564, 66 L.Ed. 999 (1922), and "within practicable limits." Ibid. Nevertheless, in concluding that the Conservancy District's distribution system is "inefficient," the Special Master made no factual finding that improved economy in that system is within the practicable means available to the District.

Colorado would have the Court assess the Conservancy District's "waste" and "inefficiency" by a new yardstick—i.e., not by comparing the economic gains to the District with the costs of achieving greater efficiency, but by comparing the "inefficiency" of New Mexico's uses with the relative benefits to Colorado of a new use. The Special Master has succumbed to this suggestion. His recommendation that Colorado be permitted a diversion embodies the judgment that, because Colorado can, in some *unidentified* sense, make "better" use of the waters of the Vermejo, New Mexico may be forced to change her present uses.

Today the Court has also gone dangerously far toward accepting that suggestion. The Court holds that it is appropriate in equitable apportionment litigation to weigh the harms and benefits to the competing States. It does so notwithstanding its recognition that the potential benefits from a *proposed* diversion are likely to be speculative and remote, and therefore difficult to balance against any threatened harms, and its concession that the equities supporting protection of an existing economy will usually be compelling.

COLORADO v. NEW MEXICO
Supreme Court of the United States, 1984.
467 U.S. 310, 104 S. Ct. 2433, 81 L. Ed.2d 247.

JUSTICE O'CONNOR delivered the opinion of the Court.

* * * Last Term, because our initial inquiry turned on the factors relevant to determining a just apportionment, the Court explained in detail the law of equitable apportionment. This Term, because our inquiry turns on the evidentiary material Colorado has offered in support of its complaint, we find it necessary to explain the standard by which we judge proof in actions for equitable apportionment. * * *

Last Term, the Court made clear that Colorado's proof would be judged by a clear-and-convincing-evidence standard. * * * Requiring

Colorado to present clear and convincing evidence in support of its proposed diversion is necessary to appropriately balance the unique interests involved in water rights disputes between sovereigns. The standard reflects this Court's long-held view that a proposed diverter should bear most, though not all, of the risks of erroneous decision * * *. In addition, the clear-and-convincing-evidence standard accommodates society's competing interests in increasing the stability of property rights and in putting resources to their most efficient uses * * *. In short, Colorado's diversion should and will be allowed only if actual inefficiencies in present uses or future benefits from other uses are highly probable. * * * Upon our independent review of the record, we find that Colorado has failed to meet its burden.

To establish whether Colorado's proposed diversion could be offset by eliminating New Mexico's nonuse or inefficiency, we asked the Master to make specific findings concerning existing uses, supplies of water, and reasonable conservation measures available to the two States. After assessing the evidence both States offered about existing uses and available supplies, the Master concluded that "current levels of use primarily reflect failure on the part of existing users to fully develop and put to work available water." Moreover, with respect to reasonable conservation measures available, the Master indicated his belief that more careful water administration in New Mexico would alleviate shortages from unregulated stockponds, fishponds, and water detention structures, prevent waste from blockage and clogging in canals, and ensure that users fully devote themselves to development of available resources. He further concluded that "the heart of New Mexico's water problem is the Vermejo Conservancy District," which he considered a failed "reclamation project [that had] never lived up to its expectations or even proved to be a successful project, * * * and [that] quite possibly should never have been built." Though the District was quite arguably in the "middle range in reclamation project efficiencies," the Master was of the opinion "that [the District's] inefficient water use should not be charged to Colorado." Furthermore, though Colorado had not submitted evidence or testimony of any conservation measures that C.F. & I. would take, the Master concluded that "it is not for the Master or for New Mexico to say that reasonable attempts to conserve water will not be implemented by Colorado."

We share the Master's concern that New Mexico may be overstating the amount of harm its users would suffer from a diversion. * * * Nevertheless, * * * we cannot agree that Colorado has met its burden of identifying, by clear and convincing evidence, conservation efforts that would preserve any of the Vermejo River water supply. * * * [I]t did not actually point to specific measures New Mexico could take to conserve water. * * *

Colorado's attack on current water use in the Vermejo Conservancy District is inadequate for much the same reason. Our cases require only conservation measures that are "financially and physically feasible" and "within practicable limits." See, e.g., Colorado v. New Mexico, supra, 459 U.S., at 192, 103 S.Ct., at 550; Wyoming v. Colorado, 259 U.S. 419, 484, 42 S.Ct. 552, 564, 66 L.Ed. 999 (1922). New Mexico submitted substantial evidence that the District is in the middle of reclamation project efficiencies and that the District has taken considerable independent steps—including, the construction, at its own expense and on its own initiative, of a closed stockwater delivery system—to improve the efficiency of its future water use. * * * Colorado has not identified any "financially and physically feasible" means by which the District can further eliminate or reduce inefficiency and, contrary to the Master's suggestion, we believe that the burden is on Colorado to do so. A State can carry its burden of proof in an equitable apportionment action only with specific evidence about how existing uses might be improved, or with clear evidence that a project is far less efficient than most other projects. Mere assertions about the relative efficiencies of competing projects will not do.

Finally, there is no evidence in the record that "Colorado has undertaken reasonable steps to minimize the amount of the diversion that will be required." Colorado v. New Mexico, supra, 459 U.S., at 186, 103 S.Ct., at 547. Nine years have passed since C.F. & I. first proposed diverting water from the Vermejo River. Yet Colorado has presented no evidence concerning C.F. & I.'s inability to relieve its needs through substitute sources. Furthermore, there is no evidence that C.F. & I. has settled on a definite or even tentative construction design or plan, or that it has prepared an economic analysis of its proposed diversion. * * *

[W]e do not believe Colorado has produced sufficient facts to show, by clear and convincing evidence, that reasonable conservation efforts will mitigate sufficiently the injury that New Mexico successfully established last Term that it would suffer were a diversion allowed. No State can use its lax administration to establish its claim to water. But once a State successfully proves that a diversion will cause it injury, the burden shifts to the diverter to show reasonable conservation measures exist. Colorado has not carried this burden.

We also asked the Master to help us balance the benefits and harms that might result from the proposed diversion. The Master found that Colorado's proposed interim use is agricultural in nature and that more permanent applications might include use in coal mines, timbering, power generation, domestic needs, and other industrial operations. The Master admitted that "[t]his area of fact finding [was] one of the most difficult [both] because of the necessarily speculative nature of [the] benefits * * *" and because of Colorado's "natural reluctance to spend large amounts of time and money developing plans, operations, and cost schemes * * *." Nevertheless, because the diverted water would, at a minimum, alleviate existing water shortages in Colorado, the Master concluded that the evidence showed considerable benefits would accrue from the diversion. * * *

Again, we find ourselves without adequate evidence to approve Colorado's proposed diversion. Colorado has not committed itself to any long-term use for which future benefits can be studied and predicted. Nor has Colorado specified how long the interim agricultural use might or might not last. All Colorado has established is that a steel corporation wants to take water for some unidentified use in the future.

By contrast, New Mexico has attempted to identify the harms that would result from the proposed diversion. New Mexico commissioned some independent economists to study the economic effects, direct and indirect, that the diversion would have on persons in New Mexico. * * * No doubt, this economic analysis involved prediction and forecast. But the analysis is surely no more speculative than the generalizations Colorado has offered as "evidence." New Mexico, at the very least, has taken concrete steps toward addressing the query this Court posed last Term. Colorado has made no similar effort.

Colorado objects that speculation about the benefits of future uses is inevitable and that water will not be put to its best use if the expenditures necessary to development and operation must be made without assurance of future supplies. We agree, of course, that asking for absolute precision in forecasts about the benefits and harms of a diversion would be unrealistic. But we have not asked for such precision. We have only required that a State proposing a diversion conceive and implement some type of long-range planning and analysis of the diversion it proposes. Long-range planning and analysis will, we believe, reduce the uncertainties with which equitable apportionment judgments are made. If New Mexico can develop evidence to prove that its existing economy is efficiently using water, we see no reason why Colorado cannot take similar steps to prove that its future economy could do better. * * *

As a final consideration, the Master pointed out that approximately three-fourths of the water in the Vermejo River system is produced in Colorado. He concluded, therefore, that "the equities are with Colorado, which requests only a portion of the water which it produces." Last Term, the Court rejected the notion that the mere fact that the Vermejo River originates in Colorado automatically entitles Colorado to a share of the river's waters. Both Colorado and New Mexico recognize the doctrine of prior appropriation, and appropriative, as opposed to riparian, rights depend on actual use, not land ownership. It follows, therefore, that the equitable apportionment of appropriated rights should turn on the benefits, harms, and efficiencies of competing uses, and that the source of the Vermejo River's waters should be essentially irrelevant to the adjudication of these sovereigns' competing claims. To the extent the Master continued to think the contrary, he was in error. * * *

Note

Foundation of the doctrine of equitable apportionment. In Idaho *ex rel.* Evans v. Oregon, 462 U.S. 1017 (1983), the Court extended the doctrine of equitable apportionment from allocating interstate rivers to allocating interstate runs of anadromous fish (chinook salmon and steelhead trout). In justifying the extension, the Court added a new thought about the foundation of equitable apportionment:

"The doctrine of equitable apportionment is neither dependent on nor bound by existing legal rights to the resource being apportioned. The fact that no State has a pre-existing legal right of ownership in the fish does not prevent an equitable apportionment. Conversely, although existing legal entitlements are important factors in formulating an equitable decree, such legal rights must give way in some circumstances to broader equitable considerations. * * *

"At the root of the doctrine is the same principle that animates many of the Court's Commerce Clause cases: a State may not preserve solely for its own inhabitants natural resources located within its borders. Consistent with this principle, States have an affirmative duty under the doctrine of equitable apportionment to take reasonable steps to conserve and even to augment the natural resources within their borders for the benefit of other States. Even though Idaho has no legal right to the anadromous fish hatched in its waters, it has an equitable right to a fair distribution of this important resource." Id. at 1025.

SECTION 2. INTERSTATE COMPACTS

HINDERLIDER v. LA PLATA RIVER & CHERRY CREEK DITCH CO.
Supreme Court of the United States, 1938.
304 U.S. 92, 58 S. Ct. 803, 82 L. Ed. 1202.

MR. Justice BRANDEIS delivered the opinion of the Court.

The La Plata River & Cherry Creek Ditch Company, a Colorado corporation, owns a ditch by which it diverts from that river in Colorado water for irrigation. On July 5, 1928, it brought in the district court for La Plata county a suit which charged that since June 24, 1928, the defendants, Hinderlider, State Engineer of Colorado, and his subordinates, have so administered the water of the river as to deprive the plaintiff of water which it claims the right to divert. A mandatory injunction was sought.

The defendants admit that in administering the water of the stream during the period named they shut the headgate of the Ditch Company so as to deprive it of water for purposes of irrigation; but assert that they did so pursuant to the requirements of the La Plata River Compact entered into by the States of Colorado and New Mexico with the consent of the Congress of the United States [in 1925]. The Compact provides that each State shall receive a definite share of water under the varying conditions which obtain during the year, and, among other things: * * *

"3. Whenever the flow of the river is so low that in the judgment of the State engineers of the States the greatest beneficial use of its waters may be secured by distributing all of its water successively to the lands in each State in alternating periods, in lieu of delivery of water as provided in the second paragraph of this article, the use of the waters may be so rotated between the two States in such manner, for such periods, and to continue for such time as the State Engineers may jointly determine."

* * * During the ten days commencing June 24, 1928, all the water of the river (except small amounts diverted in Colorado for domestic and stock requirements) was thus allowed to pass to New Mexico; and during the succeeding ten-day period all the water in the stream was similarly allowed to be diverted in Colorado. The defendant water officials contend that in so rotating the water of the stream they administered it as required by the Compact and wisely. * * *

The relative rights of all claimants to divert in Colorado water from the La Plata River were adjudicated in a proceeding under the Colorado statutes. By decree therein of January 12, 1898 (and later amended), the Ditch Company was declared entitled to divert 39¼ cubic feet of water per second, subject to five senior priorities aggregating 19 second feet. On June 24, 1928, there was in the stream, at the recognized Colorado gauging station, 57 second feet of water. The Ditch Company claimed that by reason of the 1898 decree it was entitled to all the water in the stream except that required to satisfy the Colorado priorities. If it had been permitted to draw all that water, none would have been available to the New Mexico water claimants, who, under similar laws, had made appropriations. Some of them were earlier in date than the Ditch Company's.

[Colorado courts rejected the compact defense and ordered the defendants to permit the plaintiff to divert water whenever there was water in the stream not subject to prior Colorado appropriations. The United States Supreme Court reversed on the following rationale:]

First. As the La Plata River flows from Colorado into New Mexico and in each State the water is used beneficially, it must be equitably apportioned between the two. The decision below in effect ignores that rule. It holds immaterial the fact that the acts complained of were being done in compliance with the Compact, and does so on the ground that the Compact authorizing diversion and rotation violated rights awarded by the January 12, 1898 decree in the Colorado water proceeding * * *.

It may be assumed that the right adjudicated by the decree of January 12, 1898 to the Ditch Company is a property right, indefeasible so far as concerns the State of Colorado, its citizens, and any other person claiming water rights there. But the Colorado decree could not confer upon the Ditch Company rights in excess of Colorado's share of the water of the stream; and its share was only an equitable portion thereof. * * *

Second. The declared purpose of the Compact was, as the preamble recites, equitable apportionment. * * * The extent of the existing equitable right of Colorado and of New Mexico in the La Plata River could obviously have been determined by a suit in this Court * * *. But resort to the judicial remedy is never essential to the adjustment of interstate controversies, unless the States are unable to agree upon the terms of a compact, or Congress refuses its consent. The difficulties incident to litigation have led States to resort, with frequency, to adjustment of their controversies by compact. * * *

Third. Whether the apportionment of the water of an interstate stream be made by compact between the upper and lower States with the consent of Congress or by a decree of this Court, the apportionment is binding upon the citizens of each State and all water claimants, even where the State had granted the water rights before it entered into the compact. * * *

Fourth. As the States had power to bind by compact their respective appropriators by division of the flow of the stream, they had power to reach that end either by providing for a continuous equal division of the water from time to time in the stream, or by providing for alternate periods of flow to the one State and to the other of all the water in the stream. To secure "the greatest beneficial use of" the water in the stream, the Compact provided that the water may be "rotated between the two States, in such manner for such periods, and to continue for such time as the State Engineers may jointly determine." That such alternate rotating flow was then a more efficient use of the stream than if the flow had been steadily divided equally between the Colorado and the New Mexico appropriators was conclusively established by the evidence. That is, the rotating supply which the Compact authorized, and the two State Engineers agreed upon, was clearly more beneficial to the Ditch Company than to have given to it and other Colorado appropriators steadily one-half of the water in the river. The delegation to the State Engineers of the authority to determine when the waters should be so rotated was a matter of detail clearly within the constitutional power. There is no claim that the authority conferred was abused.

Fifth. As Colorado possessed the right only to an equitable share of the water in the stream, the decree of January 12, 1898, in the Colorado water proceeding did not award to the Ditch Company any right greater than the equitable share. Hence the apportionment made by the Compact can not have taken from the Ditch Company any vested right, unless there was in the proceedings leading up to the Compact or in its application, some vitiating infirmity. No such infirmity or illegality has been shown. * * *

Notes

1. **Formation and significance of water apportionment compacts.** Article I, Section 10, Clause 3 of the United States Constitution provides: "No State shall, without the Consent of Congress, * * * enter into any Agreement or Compact with another State * * *." The interstate compact has become far more popular among states than equitable apportionment litigation for allocating interstate waters. See Douglas L. Grant, Water Apportionment Compacts Between States § 46.01, in 3 Waters and Water Rights (Robert E. Beck & Amy K. Kelley, eds., 3d ed. 2009) (table listing each water allocation compact, the signatory states, and the Statutes at Large citation to it).

The most detailed study of interstate water compacts is Jerome C. Muys, Interstate Water Compacts: The Interstate Compact and Federal-Interstate Compact (National Water Comm'n, Legal Study No. 14, 1971). All the water allocation compacts, as well as various other compacts pertaining to water resources, are reprinted in George William Sherk, Dividing the Waters: The Resolution of Interstate Water Conflicts in the United States (2000).

It has been suggested that "[m]ost compacts represent compromises reached by the water resource establishments of the signatory states against a background of urgent need (or at least desire) for federal benefits that are contingent upon agreement being reached." Charles J. Meyers, The Colorado River, 19 Stan. L. Rev. 1, 48 (1966). The federal benefits typically were the funding and building of water development projects using interstate waters, projects that by common understanding were not likely to be funded by Congress absent agreement by the affected states regarding allocation of the interstate waters.

Recently, Congress sought expressly to induce agreement between Nevada and Utah on allocating interstate groundwater. The Southern Nevada Water Authority (SNWA) proposed to pump groundwater from basins in east central Nevada and export it to the Las Vegas area through a 285-mile pipeline. One of the basins extends into Utah and at least one more likely has significant hydrologic connection to the interstate basin. The pipeline will require rights-of-way across federal lands. In the Lincoln County Conservation, Recreation, and Development Act of 2004, Pub.

L. No. 108-424, § 301, 118 Stat. 2403, 2413-14, Congress gave SNWA the needed rights-of-way but prohibited the transbasin diversion of groundwater it pumps from the interstate groundwater flow system until the two states reach an agreement dividing the water.

2. **The Supreme Court's role in compact disputes.** In Oklahoma v. New Mexico, 501 U.S. 221 (1991), which concerned the Canadian River Compact, the Special Master recommended to the Court that it should not allow states to invoke its original jurisdiction in compact disputes without certifying they had negotiated in good faith to try to resolve their differences. The Court declined to make that a jurisdictional prerequisite.

Texas v. New Mexico, 462 U.S. 554 (1983), concerned a provision in the Pecos River Compact stating New Mexico "shall not deplete by man's activities the flow * * * at the New Mexico-Texas state line below an amount which will give to Texas a quantity of water equivalent to that available to Texas under the 1947 condition." The compact included a detailed inflow-outflow formula to implement this provision for varying annual amounts of precipitation and inflow to the river. The compact also created a commission empowered to adopt any alternative "more feasible method" for quantifying New Mexico's delivery obligation and to determine the occurrence of any shortfalls in the flow promised to Texas. The commission has one voting representative from each of the two states and a nonvoting federal member. Soon after the compact became operative, the detailed inflow-outflow formula proved unworkable because it was based on badly flawed data and assumptions. The two state commissioners were unable to agree on the cumulative shortfalls under the flawed inflow-outflow formula or on an improved method of calculating them.

The Special Master recommended to the Supreme Court that it should break the 1-to-1 deadlock by rewriting the compact to add a tie-breaking mechanism, such as giving the federal commissioner a vote. The Court rejected the idea because "congressional consent transforms an interstate compact * * * into a law of the United States, [so] no court may order relief inconsistent with its expressed terms." Id. at 564.

The Court still had to decide what role, if any it could play in resolving the deadlock. New Mexico argued the compact commission was the exclusive forum for resolving disputes between the states, and the Court's only role was to review actions by the commission under the deferential model of judicial review of administrative action. This meant the Court would have to dismiss the case because with the commissioners deadlocked, there was no commission action to review. The Court responded: "[T]he mere existence of a compact does not foreclose the possibility that we will be required to resolve a dispute between the compacting States. * * * It is difficult to conceive that Texas would trade away its right to seek an equitable apportionment of the river in return for a promise that New Mexico could, for all practical purposes, avoid at will. In the absence of an explicit provision or other clear indication that a bargain to that effect was made, we shall not construe a compact to preclude a state from seeking judicial relief when the compact does not provide an equivalent method of vindicating the state's rights." The Court added that "[u]nder the Compact as it now stands the solution for impasse is judicial resolution of such disputes as are amenable to judicial resolution, and further negotiation for those disputes that are not." Id. at 565.

To aid judicial resolution, the Court asked the Special Master to recommend how the flawed inflow-outflow formula should be modified. The Court later approved his recommendation. 467 U.S. 1238 (1984).

3. **Defenses to breach of compact and the burden of proof.** Under the modified inflow-outflow methodology for the Pecos River Compact that the Court approved, New Mexico's shortfall in delivering water to Texas from 1950 through 1983 totaled 340,100 acre-feet. New Mexico sought to avoid liability for breach by arguing the shortfall resulted from good-faith misunderstanding of its compact obligation. The Court rejected that defense because "[a] Compact is, after all, a contract," and under contract law, good-faith differences about the scope of a contractual undertaking do not relieve either party from performance. 482 U.S. 124, 128-29 (1987).

In Kansas v. Colorado, 514 U.S. 673 (1995), Colorado sought to defend a suit for breach of the Arkansas River Compact by arguing that Kansas was barred by laches. The Court responded:

"This Court has yet to decide whether the doctrine of laches applies in a case involving the enforcement of an interstate compact. Cf. Illinois v. Kentucky, 500 U.S. 380, 388 (1991) (in the context of an interstate boundary dispute, 'the laches defense is generally inapplicable against a State'); Block v. North Dakota, 461 U.S. 273, 294 (1983) (O'Connor, J., dissenting) ('The common law has long accepted the principle "nullum tempus occurrit regi"—neither laches nor statutes of limitations will bar the sovereign'); Colorado v. Kansas, 320 U.S. at 394 (in the context of a suit seeking an equitable apportionment of river flows, facts demonstrating a delay in filing a complaint 'might well preclude the award of the relief requested. But in any event, they gravely add to the burden the plaintiff would otherwise bear'). We need not, however, foreclose the applicability of laches in such cases, because we conclude that Colorado has failed to prove an element necessary to the recognition of that defense [namely, lack of diligence by Kansas in asserting its claim]." Id. at 687-88.

Colorado also argued Kansas should have to prove breach by clear and convincing evidence instead of a preponderance of the evidence. The Court avoided deciding the issue by accepting the Special Master's finding that Kansas had proved breach under either standard.

4. **Remedies for breach of compact.** After finding in Texas v. New Mexico that New Mexico had shorted Texas on water compact deliveries by 340,100 acre-feet between 1950 and 1983, the Special Master recommended that the Court order New Mexico to make up the deficit by delivering an additional 34,010 acre-feet annually for ten years. Although the Master thought money damages might be better for the parties, he noted that the compact called for the delivery of water, and he concluded relief

498 INTERSTATE ALLOCATION Ch. 6

inconsistent with the compact could not be ordered. The Court disagreed, ruling that the lack of a specific compact provision authorizing money damages did not preclude that remedy. 482 U.S. 124 (1987).

The Special Master also recommended that the Court appoint a river master to calculate New Mexico's future annual water delivery obligations under the compact formula. Although the Court said it generally is reluctant to appoint continuing agents to administer its decrees, it agreed that such an agent was needed. This was because the compact formula was not mechanical but rather would require the exercise of judgment, and the Court wished to forestall repeated litigation arising from "the natural propensity of the two states to disagree if an allocation formula leaves room to do so." Id. at 134. The Court added, however, that its decree did not displace the authority of the compact commission to agree upon a more feasible method for quantifying New Mexico's water delivery obligation.

The two states settled the liability issue for $14 million. Texas v. New Mexico, 494 U.S. 111 (1990). To enable future compliance with its compact water delivery obligation, New Mexico undertook a $70 million program to purchase irrigated land in the state and retire the water rights. In view of *Hinderlider*, supra p. 492, was it legally necessary for the state to spend public funds on a purchase program? The reasons for adopting the program and the ensuing difficulties with it are described in G. Emlen Hall, High and Dry: The Texas-New Mexico Struggle for the Pecos River ch. 7 (2002) (other chapters relate the fascinating story of the compact litigation and its key players).

The Court continued to develop the law on damages for breach of compact in Kansas v. Colorado, 533 U.S. 1 (2001). The Arkansas River Compact states that "the Arkansas River * * * shall not be materially depleted in usable quantity or availability for use to the water users in Colorado and Kansas [by] future development." The compact became operative in 1949. Colorado breached it by allowing new wells that pumped groundwater tributary to the Arkansas River and materially depleted the stream flow available for use in Kansas.

The Court approved the Special Master's recommendation to award money damages to Kansas running from 1950 when stream depletion began. Damages were based on Kansas's losses, not Colorado's profits. The award included direct damages from reduced crop yields and increased water supply costs plus secondary damages for decreased economic activity such as fertilizer and machinery sales. For more detail on the direct and indirect damages, see David B. Willis et al., Secondary Damages in Interstate Water Compact Litigation, 48 Nat. Resources J. 679 (2008). Although the damages compensated for economic losses suffered by Kansas citizens, the award was payable to the state to use as it wished and thus would not necessarily end up on the pockets of those suffering the losses.

The damage award also included prejudgment interest from when the suit was filed in 1985 though Colorado's liability was unliquidated until the entry of judgment years later. Three Justices opposed any prejudgment interest because they thought federal common law barred it for unliquidated claims at the time the states formed the compact, and therefore Colorado had no reason to anticipate such liability. Four Justices thought that by the time of compact formation, federal common law allowed prejudgment interest on unliquidated claims if fairness demanded it. They thought fairness required prejudgment interest dating from 1969 when Colorado knew or should have known its postcompact wells were depleting the stream flow. The remaining two Justices thought prejudgment interest should run only from when Kansas filed suit in 1985. To enable entry of a judgment, the four Justices who favored 1969 joined the two favoring 1985 to produce a majority for the latter date. See also Kansas v. Colorado, 543 U.S. 86 (2004) (clarifying that prejudgment interest accrued only on damages that arose after suit was filed in 1985, and did not start accruing in 1985 on damages from earlier years).

5. **Federal-interstate compacts.** A variation of the interstate compact is the federal-interstate compact, in which the United States joins as a signatory party along with the states. Two federal-interstate water compacts have long been operative. The first is the Delaware River Basin Compact—among Delaware, New Jersey, New York, Pennsylvania, and the United States. The second, which is closely patterned after the first, is the Susquehanna River Basin compact—among Maryland, New York, Pennsylvania, and the United States. Jerome C. Muys, supra Note 1, gives a full history of the negotiations for both compacts.

The Delaware River Basin Compact established the Delaware River Basin Commission comprised of the governor of each state (or a delegate) and a federal member. The commission's main charge was to produce a comprehensive plan for development and use of the basin's waters and then to adopt annually a six-year water resources program based on the plan. The commission licenses each project to be undertaken and can itself construct and operate projects. It has "power from time to time as need appears, in accordance with the doctrine of equitable apportionment, to allocate the waters of the basin to and among the states signatory to this compact and to and among their respective political subdivisions, and to impose conditions, obligations and release requirements related thereto." § 3.3. The commission can also regulate withdrawals of surface and ground waters in areas of shortage and cases of emergency. §§ 10.4, 10.5. It exercised these powers during an extended drought that reached the emergency stage in 1965, curtailing New York City's withdrawals and Philadelphia's water intakes.

The major legal concern with the Delaware compact was the relationship of the Commission's comprehensive plan to federal programs. Conflicts with the federal power over navigation were seen as difficult, and were avoided by leaving that subject outside the scope of the Commission's activities. The compact provides that no expenditures or construction shall occur for any project, including federal projects, if the project is not included in the comprehensive plan. The federal government has only one vote on the five-member Commission, so as the compact is written, state members on the Commission could veto a federal project. This was unacceptable to the federal government, so in the congressional consent legislation a reservation recites that while nothing in the compact shall impair the constitutional authority of the United States or any of its rights or authority under existing or future legislation, the exercise of those federal powers shall not substantially conflict with a Commission plan concurred in by the federal member. Also, the President may suspend any provision of the plan in the national interest. See Jerome C. Muys, supra Note 1, at 206a-225.

In addition to the Delaware and Susquehanna compacts, the United States became a signatory party to two abortive compacts—the Apalachicola-Chattahoochee-Flint River Basin Compact, Pub. L. No. 105-104 111 Stat. 2219 (among Alabama, Florida, and Georgia) and the Alabama-Coosa-Tallapoosa River Basin Compact, Pub. L. No. 105-105, 111 Stat. 2233 (1997) (between Alabama and Georgia). These similarly structured compacts did not actually allocate water between states but rather created a commission charged with developing an allocation formula for equitably apportioning basin waters while protecting water quality, ecology and biodiversity. Each state had one vote on the compact commission, and unanimity of the states was required for all decisions. A federal commissioner had no vote but could veto an allocation formula the states developed upon giving reasons based on federal law. The compacts provided for their automatic termination should the states fail to develop an allocation formula by December 31, 1998, unless the states agreed to extend the deadline. After numerous extensions, both compacts ended for lack of agreement on either an allocation formula or any further deadline extension.

SECTION 3. CONGRESSIONAL APPORTIONMENT

ARIZONA v. CALIFORNIA
Supreme Court of the United States, 1963.
373 U.S. 546, 83 S. Ct. 1468, 10 L. Ed.2d 572.

MR. Justice BLACK delivered the opinion of the Court.

In 1952 the State of Arizona invoked the original jurisdiction of this Court by filing a complaint against the State of California and seven of its public agencies. Later, Nevada, New Mexico, Utah, and the United States were added as parties either voluntarily or on motion. The basic controversy in the case is over how much water each State has a legal right to use out of the waters of the Colorado River and its tributaries. * * * As we see this case, the question of each State's share of the waters of the Colorado and its tributaries turns on the meaning and the scope of the Boulder Canyon Project Act passed by Congress in 1928. That meaning and scope can be better understood when the Act is set against its background—the gravity of the Southwest's water problems; the inability of local groups or individual States to deal with these enormous problems; the continued failure of the States to agree on how to conserve and divide the waters; and the ultimate action by Congress at the request of the States creating a great system of dams and public works nationally built, controlled, and operated for the purpose of conserving and distributing the water.

The Colorado River itself rises in the mountains of Colorado and flows generally in a southwesterly direction for about 1,300 miles through Colorado, Utah, and Arizona and along the Arizona-Nevada and Arizona-California boundaries, after which it passes into Mexico and empties into the Mexican waters of the Gulf of California. On its way to the sea it receives tributary waters from Wyoming, Colorado, Utah, Nevada, New Mexico, and Arizona. The river and its tributaries flow in a natural basin almost surrounded by large mountain ranges. * * * Much of this large basin is so arid that it is, as it always has been, largely dependent upon managed use of the waters of the Colorado River System to make it productive and inhabitable. * * * In the second half of the nineteenth century a group of people interested in California's Imperial Valley conceived plans to divert water from the mainstream of the Colorado to give life and growth to the parched and barren soil of that valley. As the most feasible route was through Mexico, a Mexican corporation was formed and a canal dug partly in Mexico and partly in the United States. Difficulties which arose because the canal was subject to the sovereignty of both countries generated hopes in this country that some day there would be a canal wholly within the United States, an all-American canal.

During the latter part of the nineteenth and the first part of the twentieth centuries, people in the Southwest continued to seek new ways to satisfy their water needs, which by that time were increasing rapidly as new settlers moved into this fast-developing region. But none of the more or less primitive diversions made from the mainstream of the Colorado conserved enough water to meet the growing needs of the basin. The natural flow of the Colorado was too erratic, the river at many places in canyons too deep, and the engineering and economic hurdles too great for small farmers, larger groups, or even States to build storage dams, construct canals, and install the expensive works necessary for a dependable year-round water supply. Nor were droughts the basin's only problem; spring floods due to melting snows and seasonal storms were a recurring menace, especially disastrous in California's Imperial Valley where, even after the Mexican canal provided a more dependable water supply, the threat of flood remained at least as serious as before. Another troublesome problem was the erosion of land and the deposit of silt which fouled waters, choked irrigation works, and damaged good farmland and crops.

    * * *

The prospect that the United States would undertake to build as a national project the necessary works to control floods and store river waters for irrigation was apparently a welcome one for the basin States. But it brought to life strong fears in the northern basin States that additional waters made available by the storage and canal projects might be gobbled up in perpetuity by faster growing lower basin areas, particularly California, before the upper States could appropriate what they believed to be their fair share. * * * Nor were such fears limited to the northernmost States. Nevada, Utah, and especially Arizona were all apprehensive that California's rapid declaration of appropriative claims would deprive them of their just share of basin water available after construction of the proposed United States project. It seemed for a time that these fears would keep the States from agreeing on any kind of division of the river waters. Hoping to prevent "conflicts" and "expensive litigation" which would hold up or prevent the tremendous benefits expected from extensive federal development of the river, the basin States requested and Congress passed an Act on August 19, 1921, giving the States consent to negotiate and enter into a compact for the "equitable division and apportionment * * * of the water supply of the Colorado River."

Pursuant to this congressional authority, the seven States appointed Commissioners who, after negotiating for the better part of a year, reached an agreement at Santa Fe, New Mexico, on November 24, 1922. The agreement, known as the Colorado River Compact, failed to fulfill the hope of Congress that the States would themselves agree on each State's share of the water. The most the Commissioners were able to accomplish in the Compact was to adopt a compromise suggestion of Secretary of Commerce Herbert Hoover, specially designated as United States representative. This compromise divides the entire basin into two parts, the Upper Basin and the Lower Basin, separated at a point on the river in northern Arizona known as Lee Ferry. Article III(a) of the Compact apportions to each basin in perpetuity 7,500,000 acre-feet of water a year from the Colorado River System, defined in Article II(a) as "the Colorado River and its tributaries within the United States of America." In addition, Article III(b) gives the Lower Basin "the right to increase its beneficial consumptive use of such waters by one million acre-feet per annum." Article III(c) provides that future Mexican water rights recognized by the United States shall be supplied first out of surplus over and above the aggregate of the quantities specified in (a) and (b), and if this surplus is not enough the deficiency shall be borne equally by the two basins. Article III(d) requires the Upper Basin not to deplete the Lee Ferry flow below an aggregate of 75,000,000 acre-feet for any 10 consecutive years. Article III(f) and (g) provide a way for further apportionment by a compact of "Colorado River System" waters at any time after October 1, 1963. While these allocations quieted rivalries between the Upper and Lower Basins, major differences between the States in the Lower Basin continued. Failure of the Compact to determine each State's share of the water left Nevada and Arizona with their fears that the law of prior appropriation would be not a protection but a menace because California could use that law to get for herself the lion's share of the waters allotted to the Lower Basin. Moreover, Arizona, because of her particularly strong interest in the Gila, intensely resented the Compact's inclusion of the Colorado River tributaries in its allocation scheme and was bitterly hostile to having Arizona tributaries, again particularly the Gila, forced to contribute to the Mexican burden. Largely for these reasons, Arizona alone, of all the States in both basins, refused to ratify the Compact.

Seeking means which would permit ratification by all seven basin States, the Governors of those States met at Denver in 1925 and again in 1927. As a result of these meetings the Governors of the upper States suggested, as a fair apportionment of water among the Lower Basin States, that out of the average annual delivery of water at Lee Ferry required by the Compact—7,500,000 acre-feet—Nevada be given 300,000 acre-feet, Arizona 3,000,000, and California 4,200,000, and that unapportioned waters, subject to reapportionment after 1963, be shared equally by Arizona and California. * * * This proposal foundered because California held out for 4,600,000 acre-feet instead of 4,200,000 and because Arizona held out for complete exemption of its tributaries from any part of the Mexican burden.

Between 1922 and 1927 Congressman Philip Swing and Senator Hiram Johnson, both of California, made three attempts to have Swing-Johnson bills enacted, authorizing construction of a dam in the canyon section of the Colorado River and an all-American canal. * * *

Finally, the fourth Swing-Johnson bill passed both Houses and became the Boulder Canyon Project Act of December 21, 1928, 45 Stat. 1057. The Act authorized the Secretary of the Interior to construct, operate and maintain a dam and other works in order to control floods, improve navigation, regulate the river's flow, store and distribute waters for reclamation and other beneficial uses, and generate electrical power. The projects authorized by the Act were the same as those provided for in the prior defeated measures, but in other significant respects the Act was strikingly different. The earlier bills had offered no method whatever of apportioning the waters among the States of the Lower Basin. The Act as finally passed did provide such a method, and, as we view it, the method chosen was a complete statutory apportionment intended to put an end to the long-standing dispute over Colorado River waters. To protect the Upper Basin against California should Arizona still refuse to ratify the Compact, § 4(a) of the Act as finally passed provided that, if fewer than seven States ratified within six months, the Act should not take effect unless six States including California ratified and unless California, by its legislature, agreed "irrevocably and unconditionally * * * as an express covenant" to a limit on its annual consumption of Colorado River water of "four million four hundred thousand acre-feet of the waters apportioned to the lower basin States by paragraph (a) of Article III of the Colorado River compact, plus not more than one-half of any excess or surplus waters unapportioned by said compact." Congress in the same section showed its continuing desire to have California, Arizona, and Nevada settle their own differences by authorizing them to make an agreement apportioning to Nevada 300,000 acre-feet, and to Arizona 2,800,000 acre-feet plus half of any surplus waters unapportioned by the Compact. The permitted agreement also was to allow Arizona exclusive use of the Gila River, wholly free from any Mexican obligation, a position Arizona had taken from the beginning. Sections 5 and 8(b) of the Project Act made provisions for the sale of the stored waters. The Secretary of the Interior was authorized by § 5 "under such general regulations as he may prescribe, to contract for the storage of water in said reservoir and for the delivery thereof at such points on the river and on said canal as may be agreed upon, for irrigation and domestic uses * * *." Section 5 required these contracts to be "for permanent service" and further provided, "No person shall have or be entitled to have the use for any purpose of the water stored as aforesaid except by contract made as herein stated." Section 8(b) provided that the Secretary's contracts would be subject to any compact dividing the benefits of the water between Arizona, California, and Nevada, or any two of them, approved by Congress on or before January 1, 1929, but that any such compact approved after that date should be "subject to all contracts, if any, made by the Secretary of the Interior under section 5 hereof prior to the date of such approval and consent by Congress."

The Project Act became effective on June 25, 1929, by Presidential Proclamation, after six States, including California, had ratified the Colorado River Compact and the California legislature had accepted the limitation of 4,400,000 acre-feet as required by the Act. Neither the three States nor any two of them ever entered into any apportionment compact as authorized by §§ 4(a) and 8(b). After the construction of Boulder Dam the Secretary of the Interior, purporting to act under the authority of the Project Act, made contracts with various water users in California for 5,362,000 acre-feet, with Nevada for 300,000 acre-feet, and with Arizona for 2,800,000 acre-feet of water from that stored at Lake Mead.

The Special Master appointed by this Court found that the Colorado River Compact, the law of prior appropriation, and the doctrine of equitable apportionment—by which doctrine this Court in the absence of statute resolves interstate claims according to the equities—do not control the issues in this case. The Master concluded that, since the Lower Basin States had failed to make a compact to allocate the waters among themselves as authorized by §§ 4(a) and 8(b), the Secretary's contracts with the States had within the statutory scheme of §§ 4(a), 5, and 8(b) effected an apportionment of the waters of the mainstream which, according to the Master, were the only waters to be apportioned under the Act. The Master further held that, in the event of a shortage of water making it impossible for the Secretary to supply all the water due California, Arizona, and Nevada under their contracts, the burden of the shortage must be borne by each State in proportion to her share of the first 7,500,000 acre-feet allocated to the Lower Basin, that is, $4.4/7.5$ by California, $2.8/7.5$ by Arizona, and $.3/7.5$ by Nevada, without regard to the law of prior appropriation.

Arizona, Nevada, and the United States support with few exceptions the analysis, conclusions, and recommendations of the Special Master's report. * * * California is in basic disagreement with almost all of the Master's Report. * * *

ALLOCATION OF WATER AMONG THE STATES AND DISTRIBUTION TO USERS

We have concluded, for reasons to be stated, that Congress in passing the Project Act intended to and did create its own comprehensive scheme for the apportionment among California, Arizona, and Nevada of the Lower Basin's share of the mainstream waters of the Colorado River, leaving each State its tributaries. Congress decided that a fair division of the first 7,500,000 acre-feet of such mainstream waters would give 4,400,000 acre-feet to California, 2,800,000 to Arizona, and 300,000 to Nevada; Arizona and California would each get one-half of any surplus. Prior approval was therefore given in the Act for a tri-state compact to incorporate these terms. The States, subject to subsequent congressional approval, were also permitted to agree on a compact with different terms. Division of the water did not, however, depend on the States' agreeing to a compact, for Congress gave the Secretary of the Interior adequate authority to accomplish the division. Congress did this by giving the Secretary power to make contracts for the delivery of water and by providing that no person could have water without a contract.

A. *Relevancy of Judicial Apportionment and Colorado River Compact.*—We agree with the Master that apportionment of the Lower Basin waters of the Colorado River is not controlled by the doctrine of equitable apportionment or by the Colorado River Compact. It is true that the Court has used the doctrine of equitable apportionment to decide river controversies between States. But in those cases Congress had not made any statutory apportionment. In this case, we have decided that Congress has provided its own method for allocating among the Lower Basin States the mainstream water to which they are entitled under the Compact. Where Congress has so exercised its constitutional power over waters courts have no power to substitute their own notions of an "equitable apportionment" for the apportionment chosen by Congress. Nor does the Colorado River Compact control this case. Nothing in that Compact purports to divide water among the Lower Basin States nor in any way to affect or control any future apportionment among those States or any distribution of water within a State. * * *

B. *Mainstream Apportionment.*—The congressional scheme of apportionment cannot be understood without knowing what water Congress wanted apportioned. Under California's view, which we reject, the first 7,500,000 acre-feet of Lower Basin water, of which California has agreed to use only 4,400,000, is made up of both mainstream and tributary water, not just mainstream water. Under the view of Arizona, Nevada, and the United States, with which we agree, the tributaries are not included in the waters to be divided but remain for the exclusive use of each State. Assuming 7,500,000 acre-feet or more in the mainstream and 2,000,000 in the tributaries, California would get 1,000,000 acre-feet more if the tributaries are included and Arizona 1,000,000 less. * * *

C. *The Project Act's Apportionment and Distribution Scheme.*— The legislative history, the language of the Act, and the scheme established by the Act, for the storage and delivery of water convince us also that Congress intended to provide its own method for a complete apportionment of the mainstream water among Arizona, California, and Nevada. * * *

In the first section of the Act, the Secretary was authorized to "construct, operate, and maintain a dam and incidental works * * * adequate to create a storage reservoir of a capacity of not less than twenty million acre-feet of water" for the stated purpose of "controlling the floods, improving navigation and regulating the flow of the Colorado River, providing for storage and for the delivery of the stored waters thereof for reclamation of public lands and other beneficial uses * * *," and generating electrical power. The whole point of the Act was to replace the erratic, undependable, often destructive natural flow of the Colorado with the regular, dependable release of waters conserved and stored by the project. Having undertaken this beneficial project, Congress, in several provisions of the Act, made it clear that no one should use mainstream waters save in strict compliance with the scheme set up by the Act. Section 5 authorized the Secretary "under such general regulations as he may prescribe, to contract for the storage of water in said reservoir and for the delivery thereof at such points on the river * * * as may be agreed upon, for irrigation and domestic uses * * *." To emphasize that water could be obtained from the Secretary alone, § 5 further declared, "No person shall have or be entitled to have the use for any purpose of the water stored as aforesaid except by contract made as herein stated." The supremacy given the Secretary's contracts was made clear in § 8(b) of the Act, which provided that, while the Lower Basin States were free to negotiate a compact dividing the waters, such a compact if made and approved after January 1, 1929, was to be "subject to all contracts, if any, made by the Secretary of the Interior under section 5" before Congress approved the compact.

These several provisions, even without legislative history, are persuasive that Congress intended the Secretary of the Interior, through his § 5 contracts, both to carry out the allocation of the waters of the main Colorado River among the Lower Basin States and to decide which users within each State would get water. The general authority to make contracts normally includes the power to choose with whom and upon what terms the contracts will be made. When Congress in an Act grants authority to contract, that authority is no less than the general authority, unless Congress has placed some limit on it. * * *

APPORTIONMENT AND CONTRACTS IN TIME OF SHORTAGE

We have agreed with the Master that the Secretary's contracts with Arizona for 2,800,000 acre-feet of water and with Nevada for 300,000, together with the limitation of California to 4,400,000 acre-feet, effect a valid apportionment of the first 7,500,000 acre-feet of mainstream water in the Lower Basin. There remains the question of what shall be done in time of shortage. The Master, while declining to make any findings as to what future supply might be expected, nevertheless decided that the Project Act and the Secretary's contracts require the Secretary in case of shortage to divide the burden among the three States in this proportion: California $4.4/7.5$; Arizona $2.8/7.5$; Nevada $.3/7.5$. While pro rata sharing of water shortages seems equitable on its face, more considered judgment may demonstrate quite the contrary. Certainly we should not bind the Secretary to this formula. We have held that the Secretary is vested with considerable control over the apportionment of Colorado River waters. And neither the Project Act nor the water contracts require the use of any particular formula for apportioning shortages. While the Secretary must follow the standards set out in the Act, he nevertheless is free to choose among the recognized methods of apportionment or to devise reasonable methods of his own. This choice, as we see it, is primarily his, not the Master's or even ours. And the Secretary may or may not conclude that a pro rata division is the best solution.

It must be remembered that the Secretary's decision may have an effect not only on irrigation uses but also on other important functions for which Congress brought this great project into being—flood control, improvement of navigation, regulation of flow, and generation and distribution of electric power. Requiring the Secretary to prorate shortages would strip him of the very power of choice which we think Congress, for reasons satisfactory to it, vested in him and which we should not impair or take away from him. * * *

None of this is to say that in case of shortage, the Secretary cannot adopt a method of proration or that he may not lay stress upon priority for use, local laws and customs, or any other factors that might be helpful in reaching an informed judgment in harmony with the Act, the best interests of the Basin States, and the welfare of the Nation. It will be time enough for the courts to intervene when and if the Secretary, in making apportionments or contracts, deviates from the standards Congress has set for him to follow, including his obligation to respect "present perfected rights" as of the date the Act was passed. * * *

MR. JUSTICE HARLAN, whom MR. JUSTICE DOUGLAS and MR. JUSTICE STEWART join, dissenting in part.

I dissent from so much of the Court's opinion as holds that the Secretary of the Interior has been given authority by Congress to apportion, among and within the States of California, Arizona, and Nevada, the waters of the mainstream of the Colorado River below Lee Ferry. * * *

The Court professes to find this extraordinary delegation of power principally in § 5 of the Project Act, the provision authorizing the Secretary to enter into contracts for the storage and delivery of water. But § 5 * * * had no design resembling that which the Court now extracts from it. Rather it was intended principally as a revenue measure, and the clause *requiring* a contract as a condition of delivery was inserted at the insistence not of the Lower but of the Upper Basin States in an effort to insure that nothing would disturb that basin's rights under the Colorado River Compact. There was no thought that § 5 would give authority to apportion water among the Lower Basin States. * * *

It is manifest that § 4(a), on which the Court so heavily relies, neither apportions the waters of the river nor vests power in any official to make such an apportionment. * * *

MR. JUSTICE DOUGLAS, dissenting. * * * The Court relies heavily on the terms and history of a proposed tri-state compact, authorized by § 4(a) but never adopted by the States concerned, viz., Arizona, California and Nevada. The proposed tri-state compact provided for a division of tributary waters identical to that made by the Court, insofar as the Gila is awarded to Arizona. The Court in reality enforces its interpretation of the proposed tri-state compact and imposes its terms upon California. * * *

Notes

1. **Commentary.** The principal case is thoroughly analyzed in Frank J. Trelease, Arizona v. California: Allocation of Water Resources to People, States and Nation, 1963 Sup. Ct. Rev. 158, 166–83.

2. **Congressional revision of the Lower Basin apportionment.** The Court's decision left California vulnerable to reduction of its annual supply below 4.4 m.a.f. in a year of shortage. California was protected against the risk of getting less than 4.4 m.a.f., however, so long as Arizona was using much less than its full 2.8 m.a.f. annually. Moreover, Arizona was incapable of greatly increasing its use of Colorado River water unless Congress funded construction of the Central Arizona Project to bring the water to the Phoenix and Tucson areas. Not surprisingly, California opposed federal funding for that project. Arizona had little chance of obtaining such funding over opposition by California's congressional delegation. To gain California's support for the project, Arizona had to agree to congressional revision of the Court's decision regarding allocation among the Lower Basin states in times of shortage. The Colorado River Basin Project Act of 1968, § 301, 43 U.S.C. § 1521, authorized construction of the Central Arizona Project but guaranteed California 4.4 m.a.f. annually in times of shortage.

3. **Continuing Colorado River controversy.** Competition for the waters of the Colorado River has resulted in a complex body of state, federal, and international law known collectively as the "law of the river." One report lists forty-six "major components" of the law of the river. Dale Pontius, Colorado River Basin Study: Final Report, Report to Western Water Policy Review Advisory Comm'n, app. B (1997). The list of course includes the Colorado River Compact, 70 Cong. Rec. 324 (1928), the Boulder Canyon Project Act, 43 U.S.C. §§ 617-617t, and the Arizona v. California decree. Some other items on the list are the Treaty with Mexico Respecting Waters of the Colorado and Tijuana River, Feb. 3, 1944, 59 Stat. 1219, T.S. No. 994, the Upper Colorado River Basin Compact, 63 Stat. 31 (1949), the Colorado River Storage Project Act, 43 U.S.C. §§ 620-620o, the Colorado River Basin Project Act, 43 U.S.C. §§ 1501-1556 (referred to in Note 2); and the Colorado River Basin Salinity Control Act, 43 U.S.C. §§ 1571-1599.

Despite this extensive body of law, controversy over the river persists. In part, this is because of ambiguities and inconsistencies in the documents making up the law of the river. It is also because fundamental errors in the assumptions on which the law of the river is based have produced unanticipated problems. Most notable is an error in the assumption about the flow of the Colorado River on which the Colorado River Compact was based. The compact negotiators assumed an average annual virgin flow at Lee Ferry, Arizona, of at least 16.4 m.a.f. More recent studies suggest that the quarter century immediately preceding negotiation of the compact was unusually wet and that the long-term average annual flow is only about 15 m.a.f. Tree ring studies that reveal climate and precipitation on an annual basis spanning centuries indicate there have been cycles when the annual flow was much less than that.

For years, the errors, ambiguities, and inconsistencies in the law of the river produced much speculation but few actual disputes because water supply generally exceeded water demand. Recently, however, controversy intensified for various reasons. First, the compact allocates 7.5 m.a.f. per year for consumptive use in each basin and allows the Lower Basin to consume an additional 1 m.a.f. in years of surplus flow. But great disparity has developed between Upper and Lower Basin water demands. In recent years, Upper Basin consumptive use has been about 4.2 m.a.f. while Lower Basin consumptive use has sometimes surpassed its basic 7.5 m.a.f. allotment.

Second, although California is allocated 4.4 m.a.f. of the first 7.5 m.a.f. available for consumptive use in the Lower Basin, its use long exceeded that, reaching a high point of about 5.3 m.a.f. in 2002. Oversupply to California was possible because for decades the other two Lower Basin states underused their shares of the first 7.5 m.a.f. However, completion of the Central Arizona Project and an exploding population in the metropolitan Las Vegas area have all but eliminated the underuse.

Third, Colorado River Indian tribes hold unexercised rights to large quantities of river water, and they want to realize an economic return from this water through leasing or sale. Finally, environmental forces are calling for steps to remedy environmental problems on the Colorado River, including instream flows to protect a number of endangered species under federal law. See David E. Lindgren, supra p. 13, Note 1.

4. **The Secretary of Interior as Lower Basin watermaster.** The Secretary of Interior continues to be is a key player in allocating Lower Basin waters. Dale Pontius, supra Note 3: "The Boulder Canyon Project Act of 1928, as interpreted by the Supreme Court in Arizona v. California, vested extraordinary authority with the Secretary to serve as 'water master' for the Lower Basin. * * * The Secretary has the authority to define what is 'reasonable beneficial use,' to contract for the disposition of hydropower, to develop an annual operating plan for the reservoirs, and to establish surplus and shortage criteria, among other things."

In 2001, the Secretary issued interim guidelines for determining whether a surplus exists for the Lower Basin. In 2007, the Secretary issued interim guidelines on (1) Lower Basin shortages, (2) coordinated operation of the two major Colorado River reservoirs, Lake Powell and Lake Mead, (3) modification and extension of the 2001 interim surplus guidelines, and (4) the creation and delivery of "intentionally created surplus" to be generated by conservation, supply augmentation, and similar measures. U.S. Dep't of the Interior, Record of Decision—Colorado River Interim Guidelines for Lower Basin Shortages and the Coordinated Operations for Lake Powell and Lake Mean (Dec. 13, 2007), available at http://www.usbr.gov/lc/region/programs/strategies/RecordofDecision.pdf. The 2007 interim guidelines are effective until 2026. They largely reflect a proposal from the seven Colorado River Basin states submitted upon the Secretary's invitation. The guidelines are analyzed in Douglas L. Grant, Collaborative Solutions to Colorado River Shortages: The Basin States' Proposal and Beyond, 8 Nevada L.J. 964 (2008).

5. **The Truckee-Carson-Pyramid Lake congressional apportionment.** Whether Congress intended the Boulder Canyon Project Act to apportion Lower Basin waters was hotly contested in Arizona v. California. An indubitable exercise by Congress of its power to apportion interstate waters came in the 1990 Truckee-Carson-Pyramid Lake Water Rights Settlement Act, which is Title II of the Fallon Paiute Shoshone Indian Tribes Water Rights Settlement Act, Pub. L. No. 101-618, 104 Stat. 3289.

The Settlement Act provides for apportionment between California and Nevada of the Truckee River, the Carson River, and Lake Tahoe. More broadly, it seeks to resolve more than a century of interstate and intrastate controversies and litigation about these waters. The various conflicts involve claims and needs of Indian tribes, a federal wildlife refuge, a large federal reclamation project, and municipalities in the Reno-Sparks area. Further complicating the picture is the presence in Pyramid Lake, fed by the Truckee River, of two species of fish listed under the Endangered Species Act, the cui-ui and Lahontan cutthroat trout.

Between 1969 and 1971, California and Nevada ratified a compact apportioning the Truckee and Carson Rivers and Lake Tahoe. The states immediately began to abide by its provisions. However, Congress refused multiple times to consent to the compact because of opposition from the United States Departments of Justice and Interior. Those agencies objected primarily because they thought the compact did not adequately protect Indian and federal claims. Although the two states eventually gave up on obtaining congressional consent, they continued voluntarily to abide by the compact.

The 1990 Settlement Act apportions the Tahoe Basin based on the failed interstate compact and the Truckee and Carson Rivers based largely on federal court water adjudication decrees. The act also addresses objections that federal officials had to the failed compact and seeks to resolve longstanding disputes and problems. It provides for payments to the Pyramid Lake Paiute Tribe that will create a fisheries fund and an economic development fund. It requires measures to protect wetlands, wildlife, and the endangered fish species. Because solutions to many of the problems necessarily involve the operation of reservoirs and other facilities, the Settlement Act contemplates adoption of an operating agreement for these facilities by the United States, the two states, and certain other parties. The operating agreement needed to resolve some complex issues, so its adoption was not assured. The Settlement Act states that its interstate water apportionment is not effective until the operating agreement is adopted (and several other conditions precedent are met). The operating agreement that the parties reached appears at 43 C.F.R. pt. 419.

In the spirit of the Arizona v. California majority opinion, which recounted the enormous and intractable Colorado River problems to explain why Congress decided to apportion that river, the Senate committee report on the Settlement Act traced the long history of conflict and unsuccessful efforts to resolve problems in the Truckee-Carson-Pyramid Lake area. The report characterized the problems as involving "special and unique circumstances" warranting the exercise by Congress of its apportionment power. S. Rep. No. 101-555 (1990). This characterization seems designed to pacify those members of Congress who generally oppose interstate water apportionment by that body. To further justify the exercise of congressional power, the report described the Act as making a "voluntary" apportionment—indicating that Congress would not be forcing anything upon either state against its will.

5. **Congressional apportionment of the Missouri River?** The Missouri River straddles the 98th meridian—the line between East and West, between humid and arid zones. In the upstream western part of the basin, the primary water uses have been diversions from the river for farms, municipalities, and energy development. In the downstream eastern part of the basin, the primary water use is instream flow to transport freight by barge and tugboat. In the Flood Control Act of 1944, 33 U.S.C. §§ 701-709b, Congress authorized the Pick-Sloan Plan, which actually is an amalgam of competing plans—the Pick Plan for Army Corps of Engineers dams to provide flood control, hydroelectric power, and navigation to downstream cities and states, and the Sloan Plan for Bureau of Reclamation dams upstream to supply water for irrigation, municipal and other uses. The Pick Plan is practically complete. Significant parts of the Sloan Plan remain unbuilt, and some parts of it may never be built. The Flood Control Act and its history are analyzed in John P. Guhin, The Law of the Missouri, 30 S.D. L. Rev. 346 (1985).

The O'Mahoney-Milliken Amendment to the Flood Control Act, 33 U.S.C. § 701-1(b), provides that "use for navigation * * * of waters arising in States lying wholly or partly west of the ninety-eighth meridian shall be only such use as does not conflict with any beneficial consumptive use, present or future, in [those] States * * * of such waters for domestic, municipal, stock water, irrigation, mining, or industrial purposes." South Dakota claimed this provision apportions water for upstream consumptive uses, including irrigation projects still to be built, over navigation uses in downstream states. During the 1980s, the Supreme Court twice denied South Dakota leave to file a complaint asserting this theory against downstream states. South Dakota v. Nebraska, 485 U.S. 902 (1988); South Dakota v. Nebraska, 475 U.S. 1093 (1986). The Court did not explain the denials, but a commentator suggested the probable reason was that the Court viewed the basic controversy as really being between South Dakota and the United States over the operation of federal dams on the Missouri River rather than between South Dakota and other basin states. Vincent L. McKusick, Discretionary Gatekeeping: The Supreme Court's Management of its Original Jurisdiction Docket Since 1961, 45 Me. L. Rev. 185, 199, 207 (1993).

Later, South Dakota shifted strategy and sued the Corps of Engineers to enjoin it from releasing water from a reservoir in that state to maintain downstream navigation. South Dakota asserted that the release would interfere with fish spawning, and it argued the Flood Control Act obligates the Corps to maximize all river interests, including recreational fishing. The Eighth Circuit denied a preliminary injunction. It said that while the Flood Control Act makes flood control and navigation the Corps's primary concerns, the act also recognizes secondary uses such as irrigation, recreation, fish, and wildlife and gives the Corps discretion about how to balance the competing interests. South Dakota v. Ubbelohde, 330 F.3d 1014, 1027 (8th Cir. 2003).

In a further round of litigation, various parties filed suits in different federal district courts challenging the Corps's management of dams on the Missouri River under its 2004 Master Manual. These suits were consolidated in a single federal district court and ultimately reached the Eighth Circuit. The Eighth Circuit said that although the Flood Control Act makes navigation a primary concern, it does not specify what level of river flow or length of navigation season is required to give navigation primacy over secondary uses. The court reaffirmed that the Corps has discretion about how to balance primary and secondary water uses, and it ruled the Corps did not abuse its discretion by including rules in the 2004 Master Manual that would preclude downstream navigation during extreme drought years. *In re* Operation of the Missouri River System Litigation, 421 F.3d 618 (8th Cir. 2005).

6. **Implicit apportionment by federal water project legislation?** The Colorado River Compact allocated 7.5 million acre-feet per year to the Upper Basin states but did not make any allocation among those states. At the close of World War II, the Bureau of Reclamation announced a plan to develop the Upper Basin that listed a number of possible projects in each state. However, the Secretary of the Interior announced he would not push for congressional authorization of the projects until the Upper Basin states reached agreement on their respective shares of the water allocated to that basin. H.R. Doc. No. 80-419. The Bureau had no wish to construct a project within a state and later find that the state did not have a legal claim to sufficient water for it. It has been clear since the 1963 opinion in Arizona v. California, however, that Congress has power to apportion water between states and that such an apportionment places the water beyond the power of the Court to reassign. Could it now be inferred that Congress intends an implicit allocation of water among states whenever it provides for construction of federal projects on interstate rivers? In other words, could it be said that Congress

surely would not want to waste money constructing a project that lacks an adequate water supply, and therefore Congress must have intended an apportionment by the legislation authorizing the project (or if that alone is not enough, by the authorizing legislation plus the appropriation of construction funds)?

7. **Federal regulatory legislation affecting water use between states.** The Water Resources Development Act of 1986 does not directly apportion water between states, but its provisions affect water use as between states. It prohibits all federal agencies from studying any river basin plan or future federal project that would transfer water from the Columbia River basin to another region unless the study is approved by the governors of all affected states. 33 U.S.C. § 2265. It also bars anyone from exporting water from any portion of the Great Lakes within the United States for use outside the Great Lakes basin, unless the study is approved by all the governors of the Great Lakes states; and it bars federal agencies from studying the feasibility of such export unless all the Great Lakes governors approve or the study is done pursuant to the Boundary Waters Treaty of 1909 with Canada. 42 U.S.C. § 1962d-20(d), (e).

Modern federal environmental statutes are not aimed at apportioning interstate rivers between states, but they may provide a downstream state with new tools to block or modify proposed water development upstream in another state that would reduce flows in the downstream state. This potential is illustrated by Roanoke River Basin Association v. Hudson, 940 F.2d 58, (4th Cir. 1991). The Roanoke River flows from Virginia into North Carolina. A Virginia city wanted to divert up to 60 million gallons of water daily from the river system for municipal use. The city needed a permit from the Army Corps of Engineers under Rivers and Harbors Act § 10, 33 U.S.C. § 403, and Clean Water Act § 404, 33 U.S.C. § 1344. When the Corps issued a permit, North Carolina sued and argued it was issued in violation of the two sections cited above and the National Environmental Policy Act. North Carolina expressed concern that the city's water diversion would damage downstream water quality and striped bass. Although the Fourth Circuit upheld issuance of the permit, North Carolina's efforts did result in the addition to the permit of a mitigation requirement designed to maintain adequate downstream flow during bass spawning season.

See also Riverside Irrigation District v. Andrews, infra p. 595, involving the federal Endangered Species Act and Clean Water Act § 404. The habitat needs of an endangered species along an interstate river in Nebraska prevented an upstream Colorado appropriator from qualifying for a nationwide dredge and fill permit under § 404.

Chapter 7

PUBLIC RIGHTS AND ENVIRON-MENTAL PROTECTION

SECTION 1. PUBLIC RIGHTS

A. Navigation

STATE EX REL. MEEK v. HAYS
Supreme Court of Kansas, 1990.
246 Kan. 99, 785 P.2d 1356.

LOCKETT, JUSTICE. Jasper R. Hays constructed a fence across Shoal Creek, in part to prevent canoeists and others from using that portion of the stream which flows through his land located in southeast Cherokee County. Christopher Y. Meek, the Cherokee County Attorney, filed a petition for declaratory judgment seeking to confirm the public's right to use Shoal Creek for recreational purposes. On June 11, 1988, the district court ordered Hays to remove the fence pending a hearing on the State's petition. On September 22, the district court denied the State's petition and dissolved its temporary restraining order. * * *

The State appeals, claiming that (1) Shoal Creek is a navigable stream; (2) the public has acquired the right to use Shoal Creek by prescriptive easement; and (3) the public has the right to use Shoal Creek under the public trust doctrine. * * *

Navigability. If Shoal Creek is a navigable stream, the Hays' ownership extends only to the banks. If the stream is nonnavigable, the Hays own the bed of the stream by the same title that they own the adjoining land. If the stream is nonnavigable, the Hays, who own the land adjoining both sides of the stream, may put a fence across the stream to prevent trespassers upon their property.

In England, streams were considered navigable only in so far as they partook of the sea, and to the extent that their waters were affected by the ebb and flow of the tide, and only so far was the title of the riparian owner limited to the bank; above such point, even though the stream was large enough to be used, and in fact was used, for purposes of navigation, the riparian owner owned the soil ad medium filum aquae—to the middle thread of the stream. * * * [T]he better and more generally accepted rule in this country is to apply the term "navigable" to all the streams which are in fact navigable; and in such case to limit the title of the riparian owner to the bank of the stream. This is true in Kansas and most states where the lands have been surveyed and patented under the federal law.

To determine navigability, the first question is whether title to the riverbed passed to the State upon admittance into the Union. The critical case on this point is United States v. Holt Bank, 270 U.S. 49 (1926), which established that ownership of the beds of navigable streams and lakes is a federal question to be resolved according to principles of federal law and under federal definitions. *Holt Bank* also established the specific criteria to be used in determining whether particular bodies of water are deemed navigable for purposes of vesting the state with title to the beds. Under this test, bodies of water are navigable and title to the beds under the water are vested in the state if: (1) the bodies of water were used, or were susceptible of being used, as a matter of fact, as highways for commerce; (2) such use for commerce was possible under the natural conditions of the body of water; (3) commerce was or could have been conducted in the customary modes of trade or travel on water; and (4) all of these conditions were satisfied at the time of statehood. 270 U.S. at 55-56 * * *.

The last navigability case to come before this court was Webb v. Neosho County Comm'rs * * * 257 P. 966 (1927). * * * The *Webb* court found the Neosho River was not navigable. * * * As Professor Wadley notes, [the definition applied in *Webb*] "appears to track the [Holt Bank] federal title test in all relevant areas except for the requirement that the criteria be satisfied as of the time of statehood." Wadley, Recreational Use of Nonnavigable Waterways, 56 J.K.B.A. 27, 31 (Nov./Dec. 1987).

In its analysis, the *Webb* court first stated that navigability "is a question of fact to be determined from the evidence." * * * Did title to the Shoal Creek stream bed pass to the State upon entry into the Union or is there sufficient evidence to declare Shoal Creek navigable? The trial court made these findings of fact: "(10) Shoal Creek cannot be floated without getting out of the canoe or boat at various locations. (11) John Link, Jr., owner of Ozark Quality Products, Inc., travels Shoal Creek several times a year collecting plants used in his business. * * * (12) There is no evidence that Shoal Creek has ever been used for valuable floatage in transportation to market of the products of the country through which it runs. (13) During times of drouth, portions of Shoal Creek are impassable by even a canoe or small boat. * * * (14) Shoal Creek has been used for recreational purposes for more than fifteen years. (15) A canoe rental business exists, known as Holly Haven, which rents canoes to be used on Shoal Creek. The point of entry is near Joplin, Missouri, with the point of exit at Schermerhorn Park, Galena, Kansas, where the business picks up the canoes and their occupants for the return trip to Holly Haven." Based on these findings, the district court held that Shoal Creek did not meet the *Webb* standard for navigability.

The State does not challenge the trial court's findings; rather, it argues that findings (11) and (15) indicate that the stream is susceptible of being used for commerce, thus meeting the *Webb* standard for navigability. The Kansas Wildlife Federation adds: "Because Shoal Creek is in the same natural condition as it was at the time of statehood, any commercial use of the river today conclusively demonstrates that the river was 'susceptible of use' at the time Kansas was admitted to the Union."

Based on the trial court's finding of facts, Shoal Creek is less "navigable" than the Neosho River. Under both the federal (*Holt Bank*) and current state (*Webb*) tests for navigability, title to the Shoal Creek stream bed did not pass to the State upon entry into the Union.

Though federal and state laws set the criteria to determine the issue of navigability for purposes of determining state title, individual states are relatively free to regulate the consumptive and nonconsumptive use of water within their borders. State regulatory concerns may depart from state ownership of the beds of navigable bodies of water as the primary criterion by which public need or access to water is secured.

Based on the public's increasing desire to use water for nonconsumptive recreational purposes, the State urges us to adopt a "modern" view of navigability which would not affect landowners' title to the riverbeds. Other states have taken such action.

In Day v. Armstrong, 362 P.2d 137, 145-46 (Wyo. 1961), the court determined that, under the Wyoming Constitution, title to the water is in the State. Neither the Wyoming Constitution nor the act of Congress admitting the state into the Union limited the kind or type of use the State may make of its waters. Therefore, the legislature had the power to allow persons to float on the streams. In addition, the court determined that the public, while floating on the state's waters, may hunt, fish, or do anything which is not otherwise made unlawful.

In People v. Mack, * * * 97 Cal. Rptr. 448 (1971), the California court recognized that under the prior California law, a stream is navigable if it is susceptible to the useful commercial purpose of carrying the products of the country (citing Wright v. Seymour, * * * 10 Pac. 323 (1886)) or when declared navigable by the legislature. A navigable stream may be used by the public for boating, swimming, fishing, hunting, and all recreational purposes. * * * It then determined that a stream that can be boated or sailed for pleasure is also navigable.

In Southern Idaho F. & G. Ass'n v. Picabo Livestock, Inc., * * * 528 P.2d 1295 (1974), the Idaho court found that, while the federal test of navigability determines the title to stream beds, as the present action did not involve title to the bed of a navigable stream, the federal test of navigability does not preclude a less restrictive state test of navigability. It upheld the legislature's enactment that any stream which, in its natural state, will float logs or any other commercial or floatable commodity, or is capable of being navigated by oar or motor propelled small craft, for pleasure or commercial purposes, is navigable. The Idaho court concluded that, where a stream is navigable, the public's right to use the stream for fishing extended to boating, swimming, hunting, and all recreational purposes.

* * *

The Hays claim the adoption of a "modern" test for navigability by this court would be a radical change in current state law, citing People v. Emmert, 597 P.2d 1025 (1979), where the Colorado Supreme Court held that the defendants did not have any right under the state constitution to float on nonnavigable streams within boundaries of privately owned property without the consent of the property owner. In that case, Emmert and two others were convicted of criminal trespass after they rafted down a nonnavigable stream without first obtaining the riparian landowner's permission. They challenged the convictions, claiming a right to use the stream under the following state constitutional provision:

> "The water of every natural stream, not heretofore appropriated, within the state of Colorado, is hereby declared to be the property of the public, and the same is dedicated to the use of the people of the state, subject to appropriation as hereinafter provided." Colo. Const. art. XVI, § 5.

In affirming the convictions, the Colorado Supreme Court held that this provision, which appeared under a section entitled "Irrigation," did not open state waters for public recreational use. The court found support for this interpretation in state statutes which: (1) codified the common—law rule of cujus est solum, ejus est usque ad coelum—he who owns the surface of the ground has the exclusive right to everything which is above it; (2) authorized the State Wildlife Commission to contract for public hunting and fishing on private land; and (3) made unauthorized entry upon private land a crime.

The Colorado court in *Emmert* concisely summarized the Hays' position: "'If a change in long established judicial precedent is desirable, it is a legislative and not a judicial function to make any needed change.'" * * * 597 P.2d 1025. * * *

Prescriptive Easement. The State also claims that the public has acquired the right to use Shoal Creek by prescriptive easement. Though we have never determined whether an individual can acquire a prescriptive easement to use the nonnavigable waterways of this state, in State, ex rel., Akers, * * * 140 P. 637, we found that title to the waters or bed of a navigable stream cannot be acquired through private use or occupancy, whether adverse or by permission, however long continued, or by prescription. * * *

We agree that the doctrine of prescriptive easement for public highways extends to streams and rivers of this state. * * * For the public to obtain a prescriptive easement for recreational travel, both the *Shanks* test [adverse use for the prescriptive period] and *Kratina* requirement for official public action are required. Neither occasional use of the creek by a large number of canoeists nor frequent use by a small number of canoeists gives rise to a prescriptive right in the public to use nonnavigable streams. A public prescriptive right arises during the prescribed period when public use becomes so burdensome that government must regulate traffic, keep the peace, invoke sanitary measures, and insure that the natural condition of the stream is maintained. Because public officials have taken no such action, there is no public prescriptive easement on Shoal Creek.

The Public Trust Doctrine. The State finally contends that the public is entitled to use Shoal Creek under the public trust doctrine. The essence of the public trust doctrine was articulated by Professor Sax: "When a state holds a resource which is available for the free use of the general public, a court will look with considerable skepticism on any government conduct which is calculated either to reallocate that resource to more restricted uses or to subject public uses to the self-interest of private parties." Sax, The Public Trust Doctrine in Natural Resource Law: Effective Judicial Intervention, 68 Mich.L.Rev. 473, 490 (1970). * * *

At least one state, Montana, has applied the public trust doctrine under facts similar to those presented by this case. The Montana Supreme Court determined that, under the public trust doctrine and the 1972 Montana Constitution, "any surface waters that are capable of recreational use may be so used by the public without regard to streambed ownership or navigability." Montana Coalition for Stream Access v. Curran * * * 682 P.2d 163 (1984). The constitutional provision to which the Montana court referred * * * provides: "All surface, underground, flood and atmospheric waters within the boundaries of the state are the property of the state for the use of its people and subject to appropriation for beneficial uses as provided by law."

The State analogizes the Montana constitutional provision with K.S.A. 82a-702, which provides:

"Dedication of use of water. All water within the state of Kansas is hereby dedicated to the use of the people of the state, subject to the control and regulation of the state in the manner herein prescribed."

While the broad language in 82a-702 is similar to that which appears in the Montana Constitution and others, * * * our legislature did not intend to incorporate the State's position when it passed that statute. * * * [T]hese statutes were intended to address problems related to the consumptive use of water, and not nonconsumptive, recreational use. Statutory provisions concerned with consumptive appropriation cannot be applied to subvert a riparian landowner's right to exclusive surface use of waters bounded by his land.

* * *

Owners of the bed of a nonnavigable stream have the exclusive right of control of everything above the stream bed, subject only to constitutional and statutory limitations, restrictions, and regulations. Where the legislature refuses to create a public trust for recreational purposes in nonnavigable streams, courts should not alter the legislature's statement of public policy by judicial legislation. If the nonnavigable waters of this state are to be appropriated for recreational use, the legislative process is the proper method to achieve this goal.

The public has no right to the use of nonnavigable water overlying private lands for recreational purposes without the consent of the landowner.

Notes

1. **Decoupling public use and navigability.** The principal case discusses the Colorado Supreme Court's decision in People v. Emmert. That court upheld a trespass conviction where public users of a nonnavigable waterway leave their boats and step ashore. The rights of public users in Colorado to simply float over nonnavigable waterways remains an open question. See Lori Potter, Steve Marlin & Kathy Kanda, Legal Underpinnings of the Right to Float Through Private Property in Colorado: A Reply to John Hill, 5 U. Denv. L. Rev. 457 (2002).

A Wyoming case, Day v. Armstrong, also discussed in the principal case, decouples the issue of public use from the question of navigability and adopts the reasoning rejected in *Emmert*. After holding that the waters involved are nonnavigable and after noting that the Wyoming Constitution declares that the state is the owner of all streams, rivers and lakes, the court said:

"The title to waters within this State being in the State, in concomitance, it follows that there must be an easement in behalf of the State for a right of way through their natural channels for such waters upon and over lands submerged by them or across the bed and channels of streams or other collections of waters. * * * The waters not being in trespass upon or over the lands where they naturally appear, they are available for such uses by the public of which they are capable. When waters are able to float craft, they may be so used."

In Parks v. Cooper, 676 N.W.2d 823 (S.D. 2004), the South Dakota Supreme Court concluded that, under the South Dakota public trust doctrine, the public had rights to use nonnavigable surface waters overlying private lands, but only the state legislature could determine the scope of those uses.

In several other cases, it is debatable whether the court is decoupling public use from navigability or merely adopting a new test of navigability. See Mont. Coalition for Stream Access v. Curran, 682 P.2d 163 (Mont. 1984); Elder v. Delcour, 269 S.W.2d 17 (Mo. 1954). Cf. Madison v. Graham, 126 F. Supp. 2d 1320 (D. Mont. 2001).

2. **Great Ponds.** The Massachusetts Bay Colony Ordinance of 1641–1647 provides, "And for great ponds lying in common * * * it shall be free for any men to fish or foul there, and may pass and repass on foot through any man's property for that end, so they trespass not upon any man's corn or meadow." This concept, still applicable to most fresh water lakes in Maine, Massachusetts and New Hampshire, now includes access for most water recreation.

3. **Legislative declarations.** Some states have made certain waters public by statute. Minnesota has declared eleven categories of water to be "public waters." Minn. Stat. Ann. § 103G.005(15)(a). Additionally, the determination of the public or private status of a watercourse does not depend exclusively on bed ownership or watercourse navigability. Minn. Stat. Ann. § 103G.005(15)(b). Indiana has claimed control of all lakes "used by the public with the acquiescence of a riparian owner" for fishing, boating, swimming and the storage of water to maintain water levels. Ind. Code Ann. §§ 14–26–2–3, 14–26–2–5. California gives the public rights to fish in *all* reservoirs. Cal. Fish & Game Code § 5943(a).

"Takings" arguments which might be raised by legislative expansion of public rights in waters are assessed in Chris A. Shafer, Public Rights in Michigan's Streams: Toward A Modern Definition of Navigability, 45 Wayne L. Rev. 9 (1999).

4. **Use of privately owned beds of public waterways.** Where the bed is privately owned but the public has a right to use a waterway, what right does the public have to use the bed? Compare Day v. Armstrong with Montana Coalition for Stream Access v. Curran, both cited in the principal case. *Day* held that the public can float the stream, touch or scrape the bed when incidental to floating, and even disembark and walk on the bed to get watercraft around shoals, rapids, and obstacles; it may

not, however, wade or walk the stream except when incident to floating. *Curran* held that the public could use the bed and banks up to the ordinary high water mark ("OHWM") and could even go above that mark to get around obstacles. *Curran* expressly, and *Day* implicitly, held that the public may not cross privately owned lands to access streams.

In Conaster v. Johnson, 194 P.3d 897 (Utah 2008), the Utah Supreme Court concluded that the public may touch privately owned beds when incident to any lawful water-related recreational activities, including hunting, fishing, swimming and wading. The public must, however, act reasonably in touching the water's bed. And it may not unnecessarily injury the landowner. Compare Galt v. State Department of Fish, Wildlife, & Parks, 731 P.2d 912 (Mont. 1987), in which the court held that statutes giving the public the right to build duck blinds and boat moorages, to camp, and to engage in big game hunting on private lands below the OHWM confiscated property unconstitutionally. The court also held unconstitutional a statute requiring landowners to bear the cost of constructing portage routes around artificial barriers.

With so much at stake, disputes over the location of the OHMW often arise. See, e.g., *In re* Sanders Beach, 147 P.3d 75 (Idaho 2006) (OHWM determined "as of statehood;" lack of vegetation only one factor to consider in setting the mark).

5. **State ownership of beds of navigable waters.** State ownership of the beds of navigable waters is rooted in constitutional theory. Upon independence, the original colonies, as successors to the English Crown, became the owners of the beds of navigable bodies of water. The Constitution requires that new states be admitted to the Union on an "equal footing." Under the "equal footing doctrine," the United States held the title to territorial lands under navigable waters in trust for future states; such lands passed automatically to new states upon admission, Utah v. United States, 403 U.S. 9 (1971), except where title to such lands was conveyed to someone prior to admission or where there was a clear congressional intent to withhold title from the state. See United States v. Cherokee Nation, 480 U.S. 700 (1987). The equal footing doctrine passes title to navigable intrastate water courses, as well as water courses which are part of a navigable interstate or international highway. United States v. Utah, 283 U.S. 64 (1931). But see James R. Rasband, The Disregarded Common Parentage of the Equal Footing and Public Trust Doctrines, 32 Land & Water L. Rev. 1 (1997). Professor Rasband argues that state ownership of submerged lands is better explained as a principle of federal common law. He notes that the principle was essentially codified by the Submerged Lands Act of 1953, which confirms state ownership of all land under navigable waters not expressly reserved or granted by the United States prior to statehood. See 43 U.S.C. §§ 1301(a), 1311(b)(1), 1313(a).

6. **Title and state tests of navigability.** Since, as the principal case indicates, navigability for title is a federal test, what is the effect in title disputes of more liberal state tests? What if the lands involved were previously the subject of litigation in which the state test was applied?

Does it matter if the rival claimant to the submerged lands is the federal government or is a private party whose title originated in a federal patent? Would the same problems exist if the state has adopted a more stringent test of navigability for title? See Borax, Consol. v. City of L.A., 296 U.S. 10 (1935); Or. *ex rel.* State Land Bd. v. Corvallis Sand & Gravel Co., 429 U.S. 363 (1977).

For an analysis of navigability for title and public use, see Richard M. Frank, Forever Free: Navigability, Inland Waterways, and the Expanding Public Interest, 16 U.C. Davis L. Rev. 579 (1983).

7. **Float planes.** In Alaska v. United States, 754 F.2d 851 (9th Cir. 1985), Alaska claimed title to a lake bed used as by floatplanes. It argued that floatplane use was a customary mode of trade and travel on water at the time of statehood in 1959. Noting that the central theme of navigability is the movement of people or goods from point to point on the water, the court disagreed: "The floatplanes go to and from the lake; they do not travel on the water." Id. at 854.

8. **Title to nonnavigable tidal waters.** In Phillips Petroleum Co. v. Mississippi, 484 U.S. 469 (1988), the Supreme Court affirmed "longstanding precedents" that upon admission to the Union a state received ownership of all lands under waters subject to the ebb and flow of the tide even if those waters are not navigable in fact.

9. **Bed ownership and private rights.** Bed ownership can be important for reasons other public rights. If the bed is exposed, valuable surface uses may arise. More commonly, bed ownership is important for purposes of determining title to minerals lying under the bed. An extensive discussion of title problems in inland bodies of water is found in Kemp Wilson, Ownership of Mineral Interests Underlying Inland Bodies of Water and the Effects of Accretion and Erosion, 30 Rocky Mtn. Min. L. Inst. 14–1 (1984).

Somewhat similar questions arise when waterways form the boundaries between parcels of land. The common law rule for nonnavigable bodies puts the boundary at the thread of the stream. If the location of a body shifts or recedes slowly ("accretion," "reliction," or "erosion") the boundary shifts with it. The boundary does not shift, however, if the body of water changes location rapidly ("avulsion"). However, there is no uniform treatment of what qualifies as a rapid or slow shift. Kemp Wilson, supra, discusses these matters and related complications.

10. **Title problems.** In most states, there has been no systematic effort to determine the ownership of submerged lands. Consequently, title to submerged lands is often unresolved unless a particular watercourse has been the subject of litigation regarding its navigability. The potential "equal footing" claim of the state to the bed tends to cloud the title of upland riparian owners, even where the watercourse is almost certainly nonnavigable. In 1987, Arizona adopted legislation to reduce such clouds in response to aggressive assertion of equal footing claims by state officials. The legislation relinquished outright the state's equal footing claims

to waters where navigability was doubtful—all waters except the Colorado River and three other rivers. Where navigability was somewhat more viable—the named rivers other than the Colorado—the legislation provided that the state's claims would be relinquished to the upland owners upon receipt of a nominal fee. In Arizona Center for Law in the Public Interest v. Hassell, 837 P.2d 158 (Ariz. Ct. App. 1992), the court found that the legislation violated both the public trust doctrine and a constitutional prohibition against gifts of state property.

Hassell suggested that an administrative process which provided for a systematic investigation and evaluation of each of the state's claims would be acceptable. In response, the legislature in 1992 created the Arizona Navigable Stream Adjudication Commission to collect evidence, make an initial determination of navigability, and make recommendations to the legislature. The legislature disclaims title to the beds if it concurs with the commission's recommendation that a particular watercourse is nonnavigable. Conversely, it directs the State Land Department to claim title and bring a quiet title action if it concurs with a recommendation of navigability. In Defenders of Wildlife v. Hull, 18 P.3d 722 (Ariz. Ct. App. 2001), the Arizona Court of Appeal found that these disclaimers also violated both the public trust doctrine and the gift clause. In Arizona Laws 2001, Ch. 166, the Arizona legislature enacted new disclaimer provisions to address the court's concerns.

11. **"Navigability" in other contexts.** Navigability can be significant in contexts besides public rights and title to beds. Navigability has historically provided a basis for state and federal regulatory activities involving water. See Muench v. Pub. Serv. Comm'n and accompanying Notes, supra p. 302, and Kaiser Aetna v. United States and accompanying Notes, infra p. 640. A related context is the "navigation servitude" under which the federal and state governments can sometimes "take" private property without compensation. See United States v. Rands and Kaiser Aetna v. United States and accompanying Notes, infra pp. 635-44. The public trust doctrine, discussed briefly in the principal case and explored more fully in the next subsection, had its origins in navigable bodies of water and is still tied to navigable waters in many jurisdictions. Admiralty jurisdiction involves another application of navigability. See Propeller Genesee Chief v. Fitzhugh, 53 U.S. (12 How.) 443 (1851). "Navigability" can vary depending on the context even within a single jurisdiction; thus, a body may be navigable in one context but not another.

BRANNON v. BOLDT
Florida District Court of Appeal, 2007.
958 So. 2d 367.

EN BANC, ALTENBERND, Judge. This court has elected to review en banc a very narrow, but significant issue:

> What rights do the residents in a neighborhood receive, as dominant estate holders under an implied easement created by a denotation on

a plat map of an "easement for ingress and egress" to a body of water, when the servient estate is part of a residential lot on which there exists an occupied family dwelling?

The issue in this case arises directly from a dispute over the interpretation of this court's opinion in *Cartish v. Soper*, 157 So.2d 150 (Fla. 2d DCA 1963). In *Cartish*, this court considered whether the dominant estate holders of a similar easement received riparian rights that could allow them to rebuild a dock at the water's edge of the servient estate. * * *

[T]he lot owners in the neighborhood involved in this case are not primarily seeking to build a dock. Instead, they are seeking the right to sit and stand on the lands within the easement to fish, watch fireworks, watch the sunset, and generally enjoy the view of Boca Ciega Bay. The servient estate * * * [is] owned and occupied by the Brannons, subject to the "easement for ingress and egress" given to the other lot owners by virtue of a notation on the relevant plat map. The Brannons perceive their neighbors to be trespassers on their property when they remain within the easement for periods longer than reasonably necessary to gain access to the water. The neighbors perceive that they have the right to stay within the easement for as long as they wish in order to enjoy their "riparian" rights.

If "good fences make good neighbors," * * * bad easements can make for bad neighborhoods.[1] * * * Realizing that there are many neighborhoods in Florida affected by similar plat maps and that confusion in this area of the law can create great friction and hostility within a neighborhood, we have concluded that this matter is one of "exceptional importance" warranting the collective judgment of all active members of this court. * * *

I. THE BASIC LAYOUT OF BAY PARK GARDENS

This case involves a neighborhood that is west of Park Street on 37th Avenue North in St. Petersburg, Florida. Thirty-seventh Avenue essentially dead ends at Boca Ciega Bay. This neighborhood was platted as "Bay Park Gardens" in 1953. It was designed to include twenty-two lots along 37th Avenue North and four tracts of land near the water's edge. The four tracts were designated A, B, C, and D * * *. The original developer was Chestley E. Davis. In 1958, he sold tracts A and B to William and Virginia Norris, who built a personal residence on the two lots. Thus, for all practical purposes, these two tracts have been a single lot since the late 1950s. As explained later, the Brannons now own the home built by the Norrises.

---

1. Robert Frost, "Mending Wall," *Seven Centuries of Verse: English and American*, 588 (Charles Scribners Sons, 3d ed., 1967).

An examination of the original plat map reveals much about Mr. Davis's vision as a developer. None of the lots along 37th Avenue North had direct access to the water. The two most valuable tracts, C and D, each had approximately 100 feet of waterfront with the tracts extending down to the mean high-water mark. Without an easement, there would have been limited ability to have a driveway into tracts C and D, and no ability to reach tracts A and B. Thus the development was platted with a twenty-two-foot-wide easement running north and south at the eastern edge of tracts C and D, primarily to give automobile access to those lots. At the north end of this easement, Mr. Davis designated an easement running east and west. Mr. Davis placed the entire twenty-two-foot east/west easement on tracts A and B, the land he developed for himself * * *. The entire grant of easement states: "22' easement for ingress & egress and utilities."

If Mr. Davis had only been concerned about motor vehicle traffic, the east/west easement could have ended at the eastern property line of tract B. However, he extended the * * * easement to the mean high-water mark. By reference to the plat map in the deeds of all of the lots, the purchasers of those lots were given an easement by implication providing them with ingress and egress to the water at the mean high-water mark. Thus, the purchasers of the lots knew that although they would not own waterfront property, they were purchasing the right to reach the water in a convenient manner.

The vision of developers and the reality of development have often parted ways in Florida. * * * The Norrises built their home on tracts A and B, positioned so the easement runs down the driveway, adjacent to the garage and very close to their living room and kitchen before it enters the backyard. Thus * * * anyone who owns the home on tracts A and B will always have a sense that neighbors are invading their personal space when the neighbors use the easement.

The owners of tracts C and D, as well as Mr. Davis, also built a seawall on this property in 1957 or 1958. Like so many other seawalls, this wall kept the sea out, but it also tended to erode the beach available to the public below the mean high-water mark. * * * [T]here is [now] little, if any, public beach below the mean high-water mark at the edge of the easement where any normal person would choose to fish or enjoy a sunset. Thus, the easement now runs to a location of little or no value to someone who holds only public riparian rights.

* * *

The Brannons purchased tracts A and B in December 2000. By that time, tracts C and D were * * * owned by Mr. and Mrs. Henter. The Brannons installed two gates across the easement. * * * [The] second gate is locked, rendering a portion of the easement inaccessible to the owners of the other lots in the neighborhood. As a result of these gates, a dispute over the easement erupted again and the entire neighborhood became interested in their rights to the easement.

* * *

IV. RIPARIAN RIGHTS NECESSARY TO AN IMPLIED EASEMENT
* * *

Riparian rights are rights to use the water.[3] *Broward v. Mabry*, * * * 50 So. 826, 829 (1909). There are two categories of riparian rights. *Id.* at 830. The public has the right to use navigable waters for navigation, commerce, fishing, and bathing and "other easements allowed by law." *Id.* Owners of riparian land share these rights with the public. *Id.* The public's right to use navigable waters or the shore derives from the public trust doctrine. See *Hayes v. Bowman*, 91 So.2d 795, 799 (Fla. 1957). The doctrine embodies the common law rule that the sovereign held title to all the land below the high-water mark in trust for the use of the people. *Id.*

> The specific nature of the trust in favor of all the subjects * * * was that those subjects should have the free use of such waters and shores. The waters * * * were of common right, public for every subject to navigate upon and fish in without interruption; * * * the shore was also of common right public. The use of each was in the subjects for the inherent privileges of passage and navigation and fishing, as public rights * * *.

State v. Black River Phosphate Co., [13 So. 640, 643 (1893)] * * *.

Private riparian rights to navigable waters are given to those whose land extends to the high-water mark. As explained in *Broward*:

> Those who own land extending to ordinary high-water mark of navigable waters are riparian holders who, by implication of law, and in addition to the rights of navigation, commerce, fishing, boating, etc., common to the public, have in general certain special rights in the use of waters opposite their holdings; among them being the right of access from the water to the riparian land and perhaps other easements allowed by law. * * *.

50 So. at 830. Florida has recognized greater private riparian rights than merely the right of access to and from the water. In Florida and in most other states, riparian owners take title to land added to their property by accretion and reliction. *See Bd. of Trustees of the Internal Improvement Trust Fund v. Sand Key Assocs., Ltd.*, 512 So.2d 934, 936 (Fla.1987). Most notably and apparently unique to Florida, riparian

---

3. "In common usage 'riparian' is generally used to define property having water frontage. In fact, the term 'riparian' refers specifically to land abutting non-tidal or navigable river waters whereas 'littoral' refers to the land abutting navigable ocean, sea, or lake waters." *Kester v. Tewksbury*, 701 So.2d 443, 444 n. 2 (Fla. 4th DCA 1997). Although the use of "riparian" in this case is technically incorrect, it is consistent with the accepted usage in Florida cases. * * *.

owners have the right to an unobstructed view over the waters. *See Thiesen v. Gulf, Fla. & Ala. Ry. Co.*, [78 So. 491, 507 (1917)]; * * *.

In this case, of course, there is no dispute that all of the parties have public riparian rights in the waters of Boca Ciega Bay. Thus, they are all free to boat and swim in the waters of the bay. If and when accretion were to add a sandy beach below the mean high-water mark in front of the seawall on the Brannons' property, all members of the public could use that beach if they entered from the water, and the residents of this neighborhood would clearly be free to use the easement to gain access to the public beach to fish, watch fireworks, enjoy sunsets, and engage in typical beach activities.

But the current reality is that little or no land exists below the mean high-water mark at the location of the easement. * * * [I]t appears that the only way to fish or view a sunset from this location would require the use of land above the mean high-water mark and within the easement. This land is owned by the Brannons subject to the easement rights of the lot owners.

Under * * * *Cartish* * * * the lot owners have the legal right by virtue of the easement to apply for a permit to place a dock on the edge of the Brannons' property * * *.

However, the primary right that the lot owners wish to possess is the right to view the water from the land within the easement. If the easement by implication gives them all of the riparian rights of the Brannons, including the right to a view, then there is a good argument that they can view the water, sunsets, and fireworks from this portion of the Brannons' backyard.

We conclude that in the absence of a more elaborate written easement, the purpose of this implied easement is merely to give the lot owners access, i.e., ingress and egress, to the water and to the public riparian rights possessed by all people below the high-water mark. * * * To achieve that purpose they receive the right to cross the Brannons' property in a reasonable amount of time, but they do not receive the right to fish from or remain on the Brannons' property for extended periods. The right to view the water, albeit a private riparian right, is not a right necessary to or consistent with the purpose of this implied easement.

By way of analogy, we note that this property also borders on a public park. If the easement had been given as an ingress and egress easement to the public park, no one would argue that the lot owners received the right to linger in the easement. They would merely receive the right to cross the easement to reach and enjoy the public park. We conclude that the right of ingress and egress to the location where public riparian rights commence, i.e., the mean high-water mark, is essentially no greater than the right of ingress and egress to an adjacent parcel of land.

In sum, the lot owners have the legal right to build a dock at the water's edge of this easement if otherwise permitted by law. They have the right to cross the property without undue delay to reach any area below the mean high-water mark where public riparian rights exist. They may cross the property to launch any small boat, canoe, or floatation device that can be reasonably launched from the existing seawall. They do not have the right to remain within the easement for extended periods to view the water, fireworks, or the sunset.

Affirmed in part, reversed in part, and remanded.

Notes

1. **Public access to navigable waters.** The principal case involved the scope of private easement holders' rights to access navigable waters. A recurring problem where riparians own the shores of navigable waters involves public access to the waters. A Wisconsin statute provides that the county board may condemn a right of way for any public highway to any navigable stream or lake. In Branch v. Oconto County, 109 N.W.2d 105 (Wis. 1961), Branch had purchased a 100-foot strip completely around a 390-acre lake which was two to four feet deep and while not suitable for fishing or swimming was excellent for duck hunting. The county condemned a road to the lake. Held, Branch was not entitled to the diminution of the value of his property due to loss of exclusive use.

In State v. Bollenbach, 63 N.W.2d 278 (Minn. 1954), the court held that a similar statute, permitting condemnation of access to "public waters * * * upon which the public has a right to hunt and fish" had no application to private non-navigable waters. The lake involved was considerably bigger than the lake in *Oconto County,* but the Minnesota court limited public waters to those navigable by the federal test.

2. **Right to wharf out.** For the right of the riparian to "wharf out" into navigable waters, see Sheldon J. Plager, Interference with the Public Right of Navigation and the Riparian Owners' Claim of Privilege, 33 Mo. L. Rev. 608 (1968). For other access issues, see supra pp. 244-45, Note 2.

3. **Special rights of riparians to use navigable waters.** In State v. Bleck, 338 N.W.2d 492 (Wis. 1983), the Wisconsin Supreme Court considered a state statute that required a permit to place a ski jump in a navigable lake. The court upheld the state agency's decision to grant such permits only to riparian owners. It stated, "The fact that sec. 30.12 allows only riparians to apply for permits is simply an acknowledgement by the legislature of certain common law riparian rights that are incidents of their ownership of property abutting the water."

B. Public Trust Doctrine

ILLINOIS CENTRAL RAILROAD v. ILLINOIS
Supreme Court of the United States, 1892.
146 U.S. 387, 13 S. Ct. 110, 36 L. Ed. 1018.

MR. JUSTICE FIELD delivered the opinion of the court.

This suit was commenced on the 1st of March, 1883, in a circuit court of Illinois * * * by the attorney general of the state * * * against the Illinois Central Railroad Company, a corporation created under its laws * * *.

The object of the suit is to obtain a judicial determination of the title of certain lands on the east or lake front of the city of Chicago * * * which have been reclaimed from the waters of the lake, and are occupied by the tracks, depots, warehouses, piers, and other structures used by the railroad company in its business, and also of the title claimed by the company to the submerged lands, constituting the bed of the lake, lying east of its tracks * * *.

We proceed to consider the claim of the railroad company to the ownership of submerged lands in the harbor, and the right to construct such wharves, piers, docks, and other works therein as it may deem proper for its interest and business. The claim is founded upon [a statute enacted April 16, 1869, by the Illinois Legislature that purported to grant the land in question.]

* * * On the 15th of April, 1873, the legislature of Illinois repealed the act. The questions presented relate to the validity of the section cited, of the act, and the effect of the repeal upon its operation. * * *

The act, * * * placed under the control of the railroad company nearly the whole of the submerged lands of the harbor, subject only to the limitations that it should not authorize obstructions to the harbor, or impair the public right of navigation, or exclude the legislature from regulating the rates of wharfage or dockage to be charged. * * * A corporation created for one purpose, the construction and operation of a railroad between designated points, is by the act converted into a corporation to manage and practically control the harbor of Chicago, not simply for its own purpose as a railroad corporation, but for its own profit generally. * * *

The question, therefore, to be considered, is whether the legislature was competent to thus deprive the state of its ownership of the submerged lands in the harbor of Chicago, and of the consequent control of its waters; or, in other words, whether the railroad corporation can hold the lands and control the waters by the grant, against any future exercise of power over them by the state.

That the state holds the title to the lands under the navigable waters of Lake Michigan, within its limits, in the same manner that the state holds title to soils under tide water, by the common law, we have already shown; and that title necessarily carries with it control over the waters above them, whenever the lands are subjected to use. But it is a title different in character from that which the state holds in lands intended for sale. It is different from the title which the United States hold in the public lands which are open to pre-emption and sale. It is a title held in trust for the people of the state, that they may enjoy the navigation of the waters, carry on commerce over them, and have liberty of fishing therein, freed from the obstruction or interference of private parties. The interest of the people in the navigation of the waters and in commerce over them may be improved in many instances by the erection of wharves, docks, and piers therein, for which purpose the state may grant parcels of the submerged lands; and, so long as their disposition is made for such purpose, no valid objections can be made to the grants. It is grants of parcels of lands under navigable waters that may afford foundation for wharves, piers, docks, and other structures in aid of commerce, and grants of parcels which, being occupied, do not substantially impair the public interest in the lands and waters remaining, that are chiefly considered and sustained in the adjudged cases as a valid exercise of legislative power consistently with the trust to the public upon which such lands are held by the state. But that is a very different doctrine from the one which would sanction the abdication of the general control of the state over lands under the navigable waters of an entire harbor or bay, or of a sea or lake. Such abdication is not consistent with the exercise of that trust which requires the government of the state to preserve such waters for the use of the public. The trust devolving upon the state for the public, and which can only be discharged by the management and control of property in which the public has an interest, cannot be relinquished by a transfer of the property. The control of the state for the purposes of the trust can never be lost, except as to such parcels as are used in promoting the interests of the public therein, or can be disposed of without any substantial impairment of the public interest in the lands and waters remaining. It is only by observing the distinction between a grant of such parcels for the improvement of the public interest, or which when occupied do not substantially impair the public interest in the lands and waters remaining, and a grant of the whole property in which the public is interested, that the language of the adjudged cases can be reconciled. General language sometimes found in opinions of the courts, expressive of absolute ownership and control by the state of lands under navigable waters, irrespective of any trust as to their use and disposition, must be read and construed with reference to the special facts of the particular cases. A grant of all the lands under the navigable waters of a state has never been adjudged to be within the legislative power; and any attempted grant of the kind would be held, if not absolutely void on its face, as subject to revocation. The state can no more abdicate its trust over property in which the whole people are interested, like navigable waters and soils under them, so as to leave them entirely under the use and control of private parties * * * than it can abdicate its police powers in the administration of government and the preservation of the peace. In the administration of government the use of such powers may for a limited period be delegated to a municipality or other body, but there always remains with the state the right to revoke those powers and exercise them in a more direct manner, and one more conformable to its wishes. So with trusts connected with public property, or property of a special character, like lands under navigable waters; they cannot be placed entirely beyond the direction and control of the state.

The harbor of Chicago is of immense value to the people of the state of Illinois, in the facilities it affords to its vast and constantly increasing commerce; and the idea that its legislature can deprive the state of control over its bed and waters, and place the same in the hands of a private corporation, created for a different purpose,—one limited to transportation of passengers and freight between distant points and the city,—is a proposition that cannot be defended.

The area of the submerged lands proposed to be ceded by the act in question to the railroad company embraces something more than 1,000 acres, being, as stated by counsel, more than three times the area of the outer harbor, and not only including all of that harbor, but embracing adjoining submerged lands, which will, in all probability, be hereafter included in the harbor. It is as large as that embraced by all the merchandise docks along the Thames at London; is much larger than that included in the famous docks and basins at Liverpool; is twice that of the port of Marseilles, and nearly, if not quite, equal to the pier area along the water front of the city of New York. And the arrivals and clearings of vessels at the port exceed in number those of New York, and are equal to those of New York and Boston combined. * * * It is hardly conceivable that the legislature can divest the state of the control and management of this harbor, and vest it absolutely in a private corporation. Surely an act of the legislature transferring the title to its submerged lands and the power claimed by the railroad company to a foreign state or nation would be repudiated, without hesitation, as a gross perversion of the trust over the property under which it is held. So would a similar transfer to a corporation of another state. It would not be listened to that the control and management of the harbor of that great city—a subject of concern to the whole people of the state—should thus be placed elsewhere than in the state itself. All the objections which can be urged to such attempted transfer may be urged to a transfer to a private corporation like the railroad company in this case.

Any grant of the kind is necessarily revocable, and the exercise of the trust by which the property was held by the state can be resumed at any time. Undoubtedly there may be expenses incurred in improvements made under such a grant, which the state ought to pay; but, be that as it may, the power to resume the trust whenever the state judges best is, we think, incontrovertible. The position advanced by the railroad company in support of its claim to the ownership of the submerged lands, and the right to the erection of wharves, piers, and docks at its pleasure, or for its business in the harbor of Chicago, would place every harbor in the country at the mercy of a majority of the legislature of the state in which the harbor is situated.

We cannot, it is true, cite any authority where a grant of this kind has been held invalid, for we believe that no instance exists where the harbor of a great city and its commerce have been allowed to pass into the control of any private corporation. But the decisions are numerous which declare that such property is held by the state, by virtue of its sovereignty, in trust for the public. The ownership of the navigable waters of the harbor, and of the lands under them, is a subject of public concern to the whole people of the state. The trust with which they are held, therefore, is governmental, and cannot be alienated, except in those instances mentioned, of parcels used in the improvement of the interest thus held, or when parcels can be disposed of without detriment to the public interest in the lands and waters remaining.

* * *

In Newton v. Commissioners, 100 U. S. 548, it appeared that by an act passed by the legislature of Ohio in 1846 it was provided that upon the fulfillment of certain conditions by the proprietors or citizens of the town of Canfield the county seat should be permanently established in that town. Those conditions having been complied with, the county seat was established therein accordingly. In 1874 the legislature passed an act for the removal of the county seat to another town. Certain citizens of Canfield thereupon filed their bill setting forth the act of 1846, and claiming that the proceedings constituted an executed contract, and prayed for an injunction against the contemplated removal. But the court refused the injunction, holding that there could be no contract and no irrepealable law upon governmental subjects, observing that legislative acts concerning public interests are necessarily public laws; that every succeeding legislature possesses the same jurisdiction and power as its predecessor; that the latter have the same power of repeal and modification which the former had of enactment,—neither more nor less; that all occupy in this respect a footing of perfect equality; that this is necessarily so, in the nature of things; that it is vital to the public welfare that each one should be able at all times to do whatever the varying circumstances and present exigencies attending the subject may require; and that a different result would be fraught with evil.

As counsel observe, if this is true doctrine as to the location of a county seat, it is apparent that it must apply with greater force to the control of the soils and beds of navigable waters in the great public harbors held by the people in trust for their common use and of common right, as an incident to their sovereignty. The legislature could not give away nor sell the discretion of its successors in respect to matters, the government of which, from the very nature of things, must vary with varying circumstances. * * * We hold, therefore, that any attempted cession of the ownership and control of the state in and over the submerged lands in Lake Michigan, by the act of April 16, 1869, was inoperative to affect, modify, or in any respect to control the sovereignty and dominion of the state over the lands, or its ownership thereof, and that any such attempted operation of the act was annulled by the repealing act of April 15, 1873, which to that extent was valid and effective. There can be no irrepealable contract in a conveyance of property by a grantor in disregard of a public trust, under which he was bound to hold and manage it.

Notes

1. **Federal law or state law.** Did the Supreme Court apply state or federal law in *Illinois Central?* The opinion sounds like a constitutional decision. Yet in Appleby v. City of New York, 271 U.S. 364, 395 (1926), the Court stated that the "conclusion reached [in *Illinois Central*] was necessarily a statement of Illinois law." In 1988, in Phillips Petroleum Co. v. Mississippi, 484 U.S. 469 (1988), the Court seemingly reaffirmed this conclusion, saying that the states have the authority "to recognize private rights in [public trust] lands as they see fit."

What principles of Illinois law did the legislative grant contravene? A principle found in the Illinois Constitution? In the common law? Could the common law invalidate an act of the Illinois Legislature?

2. **More on the jurisprudential basis of the doctrine.** The jurisprudential basis of the public trust doctrine remains elusive. Its historical origins are clearly in English law and courts and commentators usually assume that it is a common law doctrine, often without much examination. This assumption is problematic, particularly when the doctrine is construed as a constraint on the power of state legislatures to dispose of trust resources. One writer has argued that the public trust doctrine is rooted in the commerce clause of the federal constitution and that the states are prohibited from entirely abrogating the doctrine. See Charles F. Wilkinson, The Headwaters of the Public Trust: Some Thoughts on the Source and Scope of the Traditional Doctrine, 19 Envtl. L. 425 (1989). However, Professor Wilkinson states that he does not wish to make "too much" of this point because he concludes that the states have such broad

discretion in determining the content of the trust that the constitutional limitation will seldom be called into play.

Another writer has found support for the doctrine in the due process and equal protection clauses of the Constitution. Richard A. Epstein, The Public Trust Doctrine, 7 Cato J. 411 (1987). Emphasizing "property" principles, Professor Epstein draws parallels to the "takings" doctrine which protect private property from legislative actions. He argues that both doctrines provide protection against those who seek to manipulate political process to redistribute property to themselves.

Others have suggested that the doctrine is rooted in sovereignty. According to this view, state ownership of submerged lands is a fundamental attribute of "sovereignty" which cannot be abrogated except pursuant to trust purposes. See Michael C. Blumm, Harrison C. Dunning, & Scott W. Reed, Renouncing the Public Trust Doctrine: An Assessment of the Validity of Idaho House Bill 794, 24 Ecology L.Q. 461 (1997).

The authors of the last cited article also argue that the public trust doctrine is a federal requirement, based on the equal footing doctrine. Like Professor Wilkinson, they acknowledge that the states have great discretion in the management of trust resources but are not free to entirely abrogate the doctrine. James R. Rasband, supra p. 522, Note 5, stresses the common parentage of the public trust and the equal footing doctrines but draws very different conclusions. Professor Rasband notes that conveyances of the beds of navigable waters receive disparate treatment under the two doctrines. The equal footing cases treat pre-statehood conveyances by Congress of such beds as a question of congressional intent, not congressional power, while the public trust cases treat post-statehood conveyance by state legislatures of the same lands as a question of power, not intent. He argues that consistency requires that both types of cases be treated similarly; that is, that both be treated as questions of intent or as questions of power. He concludes that it would be preferable to treat both as questions of intent because that permits judges to do that which they do best—determine legislative intent—and preserves for the legislative branch the "quintessential legislative task" of determining how public resources should be used.

More recently, Professor Douglas Grant has argued that the reserved powers doctrine best explains the decision. In Underpinnings of the Public Trust Doctrine: Lessons from Illinois Central Railroad, 33 Ariz. St. L.J. 849 (2001), Professor Grant develops his thesis that "*Illinois Central*, at its core, concerned the Contract Clause of the Federal Constitution and the reserved powers doctrine that the Court used to reduce the ambit of that clause. When *Illinois Central* is read in light of this widely neglected point, the public trust doctrine applied by the Court is seen to fit within the broader reserved powers doctrine. A search for the underpinnings of the public trust doctrine thus becomes a search for the underpinnings of the reserved powers doctrine." Id. at 852. Rejecting the federal law basis advanced by others, he argues that "the reserved powers doctrine is grounded in widely found state constitutional provisions on 'legislative power.'" Id.

According to Prof. Grant, a critical passage to understanding *Illinois Central* comes in the last three paragraphs set out in the case excerpt:

"By establishing the public character of state-owned navigable waters and their beds, [Justice Field] implicitly distinguished the submerged land in the Chicago harbor from state-owned nonpublic land, such as a farm acquired by escheat from an intestate decedent. The legislature could freely convey state-owned nonpublic land to a private grantee, but that was not true of state-owned navigable waters and their beds. The public character of navigable waters and their beds enabled Field to invoke the well-established reserved powers doctrine of the Contract Clause cases. In full context, the reference at the end of the above quotation to a public trust does not rely on the concept of trust ownership alone to explain why the legislature was incompetent to grant the submerged land to the railroad company. Rather, that reference is a link in the chain of reasoning that brings the case within the broader reserved powers doctrine." Id. at 868-69.

He continues:

"*Illinois Central* has been unjustly criticized for relying on cases that were inapposite and for not making its reasoning explicit. Although Justice Field rightly acknowledged a lack of direct authority, the case represents a reasoned extension of the reserved powers doctrine applied in *Newton.* Field's discussion of cases concerning state ownership of navigable waters and their beds in trust was not intended by itself to justify the conclusion that the legislature was incompetent to grant the submerged land to the railroad company. Rather, that discussion was intended to lay the foundation for extending the established reserved powers doctrine from the public welfare concern involved in *Newton* (public access to the seat of government) to the public welfare concern involved in *Illinois Central* (public access to navigable waters)." Id. at 872.

He concludes that the reserved powers' "theoretical bases indicate that the * * * doctrine is not confined to Contract Clause cases and has continuing vitality to support the public trust doctrine notwithstanding the modern decline in importance of the Contract Clause." Id. at 852.

3. *Illinois Central* **re-examined.** In The Origins of the American Public Trust Doctrine: What Really Happened in Illinois Central, 71 U. Chi. L. Rev. 799 (2004), Professors Joseph S. Kearney and Thomas W. Merrill exhaustively reexamined the Chicago waterfront land grants, development proposals, title issues, and lobbying campaigns that were the context for the Illinois Legislature's 1869 and 1873 enactments. Professors Kearney and Merrill rejected what they describe as "the standard *Illinois Central* narrative"—"monopoly privilege subverting the public interest." Id. at 806. They concluded that, at least up to 1869, the railroad acted legitimately and purely defensively to protect the substantial in-

vestments it had made in the face of efforts by rival Chicago interests to obtain their own title to the waterfront in question.

Along the way, they sought to debunk what they concluded are two myths: 1) the 1869 legislation gave the railroad monopoly control over the entire waterfront, and 2) the waterfront grants promoted no public interest. As to the monopoly charge, the 1869 legislation, they countered, gave the railroad no control over either the entrance to the Chicago River or the extensive harbor facilities located on that River. The authors believe that, instead of considering the legislation as an exclusive license to an entire harbor, it is better analogized to a license to build a private road that would parallel an existing public right of way. The second "myth"— that there was no public interest in the legislative license—the authors ascribed to Professor Sax's comments in The Public Trust Doctrine in Natural Resource Law: Effective Judicial Intervention, 68 Mich. L. Rev. 471 (1970). See infra p. 547, Note 1. Contrary to Sax's assertions, they found no suggestion in any of the legislative debates or newspaper accounts they examined that either public funding or public willingness existed to build the needed new, outer harbor on the areas encompassed by the legislative grant.

The authors did find some evidence of improper efforts to influence some legislators. These efforts notwithstanding, the authors concluded that the state legislators who overwhelmingly voted in favor of the grant to the railroad could do so with a clean conscience, reasonably believing that they were voting in the public's interest. As Professors Kearney and Merrill see it, the legislative battle was between Chicago and Illinois over who would benefit financially from the grant of private development rights to the waterfront. Chicago opposed the legislation because it would have precluded city leaders' desires to award lucrative development contracts to their cronies in a deal that would have provided no tax revenues to anyone other than Chicagoans. In contrast, the Illinois Central proposal included a 7% tax upon the railroad's gross receipts, payable into the state's coffers. For a legislator from outside of Chicago, the railroad's proposal easily beat the City's.

4. **Loss of government control.** In *Illinois Central*, the Court is primarily concerned with the loss of government control over the harbor and not with the loss by the state of legal title to the submerged beds. Was it necessary to invalidate the grant to preserve the state's regulatory power over the harbor? See Richard J. Lazarus, Changing Conceptions of Property and Sovereignty in Natural Resources: Questioning the Public Trust Doctrine, 71 Iowa L. Rev. 631 (1986), suggesting that *Illinois Central* can be explained by the limited view which courts took of the police power at the time the case was decided. But see Eric Pearson, Illinois Central and the Public Trust Doctrine in State Law, 15 Va. Envtl. L.J. 713 (1996), arguing that at the time of *Illinois Central* it was well established under Illinois law that a grantee of state property is not immunized from police power regulation.

5. **Standards for valid grants of submerged lands.** The Court indicates in the principal opinion that grants of submerged lands which promote or which do not substantially impair trust values are valid. Subsequent cases have dealt with these exceptions in various ways. According to one scholar, who made an extensive study of trust cases, the decisions gravitate around three types of standards: (1) a requirement that the grant satisfy trust purposes, which in some cases may mean little more than that it satisfy some public purpose; (2) a requirement that the grant occur only after consideration of its impact on trust resources and then only if the impact is minimal or necessary; and (3) a requirement that there be specific legislative authorization for the grant. Richard J. Lazarus, supra p. 537, Note 4.

A North Dakota statute provides that the owners of lands bordering navigable waters take title to the low watermark. N.D. Cent. Code § 47–1–15. In State *ex rel.* Spryncznatyk v. Mills, 523 N.W.2d 537 (N.D. 1994), North Dakota asserted that it owned title to lands between the low and highwater marks of navigable water under the equal footing and public trust doctrines, notwithstanding the statute. Conversely, the landowner asserted absolute ownership of such lands under the statute. Held: neither party has absolute title; they have coexistent, overlapping interests in the area.

6. **Compensation for improvements.** James R. Rasband, Equitable Compensation for Public Trust Takings, 69 U. Colo. L. Rev. 331 (1998), explores, and ultimately finds relatively non-controversial, Justice Field's statement that when taking back trust lands a state "ought to pay" for a grantee's improvements.

7. **Application to federal property.** To what extent is the federal government subject to state public trust limitations? In some states, such as California, a grant of trust lands is not invalid but the property is impressed with a "public trust easement" which restricts the uses which the grantee may make of the property. See People v. Cal. Fish Co., 138 P. 79 (Cal. 1913). In United States v. 11.037 Acres of Land, 685 F. Supp. 214 (N.D. Cal. 1988), the United States filed an action to condemn trust lands conveyed by the state to the City of Oakland. The California Lands Commission asserted that condemnation by the United States would not, and could not, extinguish the public trust easement, arguing that the public trust is an attribute of state sovereignty. Citing the Supremacy Clause of the U.S. Constitution, the court said that the state was powerless to frustrate or limit the federal power of eminent domain and held that the public trust easement was extinguished by the condemnation action. But see United States v. 1.58 Acres of Land, 523 F. Supp. 120 (D. Mass. 1981). Cf. Norton v. Town of Long Island, 883 A.2d 889 (Maine 2005) (federal government did not take state public trust interest when it condemned state land; subsequent grantee thus took the land subject to the trust).

8. **Reallocations from one trust use to another.** In Zack's Inc. v. City of Sausalito, 81 Cal. Rptr. 3d 797 (Cal. Ct. App. 2008), the city had been delegated, by statute, the state's trust authority over a strip of tide-

lands. In the course of its discussion, the court discussed the city's authority to change the balance among trust protected uses. "The purposes of the public trust would almost certainly be frustrated over time if a tidelands trustee could not accommodate changing public needs through the reallocation of resources to new public uses. While there are circumstances in which government may irrevocably commit the use of land to a particular public purpose * * * or must do so * * * no such circumstances are here presented. Ordinarily, a public trustee's decision that trust land shall be used for a specific purpose * * *, stands only until the trustee decides to reallocate the land to some other public purpose or to dispose of it if that is congenial to the interests protected by the trust. As we have said, the questions regarding such a reallocation are whether the other use would be more restricted than the present use or elevate the interests of private parties over the public interest." It is this kind of flexibility in resource allocation that excites many public trust supporters, and frustrates many public trust opponents.

9. **Continued importance of littoral rights along the Great Lakes.** As to the continued importance of the public trust along the shores of the Great Lakes, see Glass v. Goeckel, 703 N.W.2d 58 (Mich. 2005), and State *ex. rel.* Merrill v. Ohio Dep't of Natural Res., 2009 WL 2591758 (Ohio App. 2009). In *Glass,* the Michigan Supreme Court held that the public trust doctrine gave the public the right to walk along the shores of Lake Huron below the OHWM. In contrast, in *Merrill,* the Ohio Appellate Court concluded that littoral owners take to the water's edge— including the land between the ordinary high and low marks.

NATIONAL AUDUBON SOCIETY v. SUPERIOR COURT
Supreme Court of California, 1983.
33 Cal. 3d 419, 189 Cal. Rptr. 346, 658 P.2d 709.

BROUSSARD, JUSTICE. Mono Lake, the second largest lake in California, sits at the base of the Sierra Nevada escarpment near the eastern entrance to Yosemite National Park. The lake is saline; it contains no fish but supports a large population of brine shrimp which feed vast numbers of nesting and migratory birds. Islands in the lake protect a large breeding colony of California gulls, and the lake itself serves as a haven on the migration route for thousands of Northern Phalarope, Wilson's Phalarope, and Eared Grebe. Towers and spires of tufa on the north and south shores are matters of geological interest and a tourist attraction.

Although Mono Lake receives some water from rain and snow on the lake surface, historically most of its supply came from snowmelt in the Sierra Nevada. Five freshwater streams—Mill, Lee Vining, Walker, Parker and Rush Creeks—arise near the crest of the range and carry the annual runoff to the west shore of the lake. In 1940, however, the Division of Water Resources, the predecessor to the present California Water Resources Board, granted the Department of

Water and Power of the City of Los Angeles (hereafter DWP) a permit to appropriate virtually the entire flow of four of the five streams flowing into the lake. DWP promptly constructed facilities to divert about half the flow of these streams into DWP's Owens Valley aqueduct. In 1970 DWP completed a second diversion tunnel, and since that time has taken virtually the entire flow of these streams.

As a result of these diversions, the level of the lake has dropped; the surface area has diminished by one-third; one of the two principal islands in the lake has become a peninsula, exposing the gull rookery there to coyotes and other predators and causing the gulls to abandon the former island. The ultimate effect of continued diversions is a matter of intense dispute, but there seems little doubt that both the scenic beauty and the ecological values of Mono Lake are imperiled.

Plaintiffs filed suit in superior court to enjoin the DWP diversions on the theory that the shores, bed and waters of Mono Lake are protected by a public trust. Plaintiffs' suit was transferred to the federal district court, which requested that the state courts determine the relationship between the public trust doctrine and the water rights system, and decide whether plaintiffs must exhaust administrative remedies before the Water Board prior to filing suit. The superior court then entered summary judgments against plaintiffs on both matters, ruling that the public trust doctrine offered no independent basis for challenging the DWP diversions * * *.

This case brings together for the first time two systems of legal thought: the appropriative water rights system which since the days of the gold rush has dominated California water law, and the public trust doctrine which, after evolving as a shield for the protection of tidelands, now extends its protective scope to navigable lakes. Ever since we first recognized that the public trust protects environmental and recreational values (Marks v. Whitney (1971) * * * 491 P.2d 374), the two systems of legal thought have been on a collision course. They meet in a unique and dramatic setting which highlights the clash of values. Mono Lake is a scenic and ecological treasure of national significance, imperiled by continued diversions of water; yet, the need of Los Angeles for water is apparent, its reliance on rights granted by the board evident, the cost of curtailing diversions substantial. * * *

1. Background and history of the Mono Lake litigation. DWP supplies water to the City of Los Angeles. * * * After purchasing the riparian rights incident to Lee Vining, Walker, Parker and Rush Creeks, as well as the riparian rights pertaining to Mono Lake,[4] the

---

4. Between 1920 and 1934, the city purchased lands riparian to creeks feeding Mono Lake and riparian rights incident to such lands. In 1934, the city brought an eminent domain proceeding for condemnation of the rights of Mono Lake landowners. (City of Los Angeles v. Aitken (1935) 10 Cal. App .2d 460, 52 P.2d 585.)

city applied to the Water Board in 1940 for permits to appropriate the waters of the four tributaries. At hearings before the board, various interested individuals protested that the city's proposed appropriations would lower the surface level of Mono Lake and thereby impair its commercial, recreational and scenic uses.

The board's primary authority to reject that application lay in a 1921 amendment to the Water Commission Act of 1913, which authorized the board to reject an application "when in its judgment the proposed appropriation would not best conserve the public interest." ([Codified now at] Wat. Code, § 1255.) The 1921 enactment, however, also "declared to be the established policy of this state that the use of water for domestic purposes is the highest use of water" (id., now codified as Wat. Code, § 1254), and directed the Water Board to be guided by this declaration of policy. Since DWP sought water for domestic use, the board concluded that it had to grant the application notwithstanding the harm to public trust uses of Mono Lake.[6]

The board's decision states that "[i]t is indeed unfortunate that the City's proposed development will result in decreasing the aesthetic advantages of Mono Basin but *there is apparently nothing that this office can do to prevent it.* The use to which the City proposes to put the water under its Applications * * * is defined by the Water Commission Act as the highest to which water may be applied and to make available unappropriated water for this use the City has, by the condemnation proceedings described above, acquired the littoral and riparian rights on Mono Lake and its tributaries south of Mill Creek. This office therefore has *no alternative but to dismiss all protests based upon the possible lowering of the water level in Mono Lake and the effect that the diversion of water from these streams may have upon the aesthetic and recreational value of the Basin.*" * * *

2. The Public Trust Doctrine in California. * * *

(a) The purpose of the public trust. The objective of the public trust has evolved in tandem with the changing public perception of the

---

6. DWP calls our attention to a 1940 decision of the Water Board involving Rock Creek, a tributary of the Owens River, in which the board stated that "the Water Commission Act requires it to protect streams in recreational areas by guarding against depletion below some minimum amount consonant with the general recreational conditions and the character of the stream." (Div.Wat.Resources Dec. 3850 (Apr. 11, 1940), at p. 24.) The decision concluded that the board had insufficient information to decide what conditions, if any, to place upon DWP's application to divert water from Rock Creek for hydroelectric generation.

We do not know why the board was seemingly more willing to limit diversions to protect recreational values for Rock Creek than for the creeks flowing into Mono Lake. (Neither do we know the eventual outcome of the Rock Creek application.) The language of the board's opinions suggests that the crucial distinction was that the application for the Mono Lake streams was for domestic use, the highest use under the Water Code, while the Rock Creek application was for power generation.

values and uses of waterways. As we observed in Marks v. Whitney, supra * * * 491 P.2d 374, "[p]ublic trust easements [were] traditionally defined in terms of navigation, commerce and fisheries. They have been held to include the right to fish, hunt, bathe, swim, to use for boating and general recreation purposes the navigable waters of the state, and to use the bottom of the navigable waters for anchoring, standing, or other purposes." We went on, however, to hold that the traditional triad of uses—navigation, commerce and fishing—did not limit the public interest in the trust res. In language of special importance to the present setting, we stated that "[t]he public uses to which tidelands are subject are sufficiently flexible to encompass changing public needs. In administering the trust the state is not burdened with an outmoded classification favoring one mode of utilization over another. There is a growing public recognition that one of the most important public uses of the tidelands—a use encompassed within the tidelands trust—is the preservation of those lands in their natural state, so that they may serve as ecological units for scientific study, as open space, and as environments which provide food and habitat for birds and marine life, and which favorably affect the scenery and climate of the area."

Mono Lake is a navigable waterway. It supports a small local industry which harvests brine shrimp for sale as fish food, which endeavor probably qualifies the lake as a "fishery" under the traditional public trust cases. The principal values plaintiffs seek to protect * * * are recreational and ecological—the scenic views of the lake and its shore, the purity of the air, and the use of the lake * * * by birds. Under Marks v. Whitney * * * 491 P.2d 374 * * * protection of these values is among the purposes of the public trust.

(b) The scope of the public trust. Early English decisions generally assumed the public trust was limited to tidal waters and the lands exposed and covered by the daily tides; many American decisions, including the leading California cases, also concern tidelands. * * * It is, however, well settled in the United States generally and in California that the public trust is not limited by the reach of the tides, but encompasses all navigable lakes and streams. * * *

Mono Lake is, as we have said, a navigable waterway. The beds, shores and waters of the lake are without question protected by the public trust. The streams diverted by DWP, however, are not themselves navigable. Accordingly, we must address in this case a question not discussed in any recent public trust case—whether the public trust limits conduct affecting nonnavigable tributaries to navigable waterways. * * *

We conclude that the public trust doctrine, as recognized and developed in California decisions, protects navigable waters from harm caused by diversion of nonnavigable tributaries.[19]

(c) Duties and powers of the state as trustee. In the following review of the authority and obligations of the state as administrator of the public trust, the dominant theme is the state's sovereign power and duty to exercise continued supervision over the trust. One consequence, of importance to this and many other cases, is that parties acquiring rights in trust property generally hold those rights subject to the trust, and can assert no vested right to use those rights in a manner harmful to the trust.

* * *

In summary, the foregoing cases amply demonstrate the continuing power of the state as administrator of the public trust, a power which extends to the revocation of previously granted rights or to the enforcement of the trust against lands long thought free of the trust * * *. Except for those rare instances in which a grantee may acquire a right to use former trust property free of trust restrictions, the grantee holds subject to the trust, and while he may assert a vested right to the servient estate * * * and to any improvements he erects, he can claim no vested right to bar recognition of the trust or state action to carry out its purposes.

Since the public trust doctrine does not prevent the state from choosing between trust uses * * * the Attorney General of California, seeking to maximize state power under the trust, argues for a broad concept of trust uses. In his view, "trust uses" encompass all public uses, so that in practical effect the doctrine would impose no restrictions on the state's ability to allocate trust property. We know of no authority which supports this view of the public trust, except perhaps the dissenting opinion in Illinois Central R. Co. v. Illinois * * *. Most decisions and commentators assume that "trust uses" relate to uses and activities in the vicinity of the lake, stream, or tidal reach at issue. The tideland cases make this point clear; after City of Berkeley v. Superior Court, supra, * * * 606 P.2d 362, no one could contend that the state could grant tidelands free of the trust merely because the grant served some public purpose, such as increasing tax revenues, or because the grantee might put the property to a commercial use.

Thus, the public trust is more than an affirmation of state power to use public property for public purposes. It is an affirmation of the duty of the state to protect the people's common heritage of streams, lakes, marshlands and tidelands, surrendering that right of protection

---

19. In view of the conclusion stated in the text, we need not consider the question whether the public trust extends for some purposes—such as protection of fishing, environmental values, and recreation interests—to nonnavigable streams. * * *

only in rare cases when the abandonment of that right is consistent with the purposes of the trust.

3. The California Water Rights System. "It is laid down by our law writers, that the right of property in water is usufructuary, and consists not so much of the fluid itself as the advantage of its use." (Eddy v. Simpson (1853) 3 Cal. 249, 252.) Hence, the cases do not speak of the ownership of water, but only of the right to its use. * * * Accordingly, Water Code section 102 provides that "[a]ll water within the State is the property of the people of the State, but the right to the use of water may be acquired by appropriation in the manner provided by law." * * *

"[In 1913 the state enacted] the Water Commission Act, which created a Water Commission and provided a procedure for the appropriation of water for useful and beneficial purposes. The main purpose of the act was 'to provide an orderly method for the appropriation of [unappropriated] waters.' * * * By amendment in 1923, the statutory procedure became the exclusive means of acquiring appropriative rights. (§ 1225, Stats. 1923, ch. 87.) The provisions of the Water Commission Act, as amended from time to time, have been codified in Water Code, divisions 1 and 2. (Stats. 1943, ch. 368.)" [People v. Shirokow, 605 P.2d 859.]

According to the courts, the function of the Water Board was restricted to determining if unappropriated water was available; if it was, and no competing appropriator submitted a claim, the grant of an appropriation was a ministerial act. (Tulare Water Co. v. State Water Com. (1921) 187 Cal. 533, 202 P. 874.)

In 1926, however, a decision of this court led to a constitutional amendment which radically altered water law in California and led to an expansion of the powers of the board. In Herminghaus v. South California Edison Co. (1926) * * * 252 P. 607, we held not only that riparian rights took priority over appropriations authorized by the Water Board, a point which had always been clear, but that as between the riparian and the appropriator, the former's use of water was not limited by the doctrine of reasonable use. That decision led to a constitutional amendment which abolished the right of a riparian to devote water to unreasonable uses, and established the doctrine of reasonable use as an overriding feature of California water law. * * *

This amendment does more than merely overturn *Herminghaus*— it establishes state water policy. All uses of water, including public trust uses, must now conform to the standard of reasonable use. * * *

The 1928 amendment itself did not expand the authority of the Water Board. The board remained, under controlling judicial decisions, a ministerial body with the limited task of determining priorities between claimants seeking to appropriate unclaimed water. More recent statutory and judicial developments, however, have greatly enhanced the power of the Water Board to oversee the reasonable use of water and, in the process, made clear its authority to weigh and protect public trust values. * * *

[T]he function of the Water Board has steadily evolved from the narrow role of deciding priorities between competing appropriators to the charge of comprehensive planning and allocation of waters. This change necessarily affects the board's responsibility with respect to the public trust. The board of limited powers of 1913 had neither the power nor duty to consider interests protected by the public trust; the present board, in undertaking planning and allocation of water resources, is required by statute to take those interests into account.

   4. *The relationship between the Public Trust Doctrine and the California Water Rights System.* [T]he public trust doctrine and the appropriative water rights system administered by the Water Board developed independently of each other. * * *

In our opinion, both the public trust doctrine and the water rights system embody important precepts which make the law more responsive to the diverse needs and interests involved in the planning and allocation of water resources. To embrace one system of thought and reject the other would lead to an unbalanced structure, one which would either decry as a breach of trust appropriations essential to the economic development of this state, or deny any duty to protect or even consider the values promoted by the public trust. Therefore * * * we reach the following conclusions:

   a. The state as sovereign retains continuing supervisory control over its navigable waters and the lands beneath those waters. This principle, * * * applies to rights in flowing waters as well as to rights in tidelands and lakeshores; it prevents any party from acquiring a vested right to appropriate water in a manner harmful to the interests protected by the public trust.

   b. As a matter of current and historical necessity, the Legislature, acting directly or through an authorized agency such as the Water Board, has the power to grant usufructuary licenses that will permit an appropriator to take water from flowing streams and use that water in a distant part of the state, even though this taking does not promote, and may unavoidably harm, the trust uses at the source stream. The population and economy of this state depend upon the appropriation of vast quantities of water for uses unrelated to in-stream trust values. California's Constitution * * *, its statutes * * *, decisions * * *, and commentators * * * all emphasize the need to make efficient use of California's limited water resources: all recognize, at least implicitly, that efficient use requires diverting water from in-stream uses. Now that the economy and population centers of this state have developed in reliance upon appropriated water, it would be disingenuous to hold that such appropriations are and have always been improper to the extent that they harm public trust uses, and can be justified only upon theories of reliance or estoppel.

c. The state has an affirmative duty to take the public trust into account in the planning and allocation of water resources, and to protect public trust uses whenever feasible.[27] Just as the history of this state shows that appropriation may be necessary for efficient use of water despite unavoidable harm to public trust values, it demonstrates that an appropriative water rights system administered without consideration of the public trust may cause unnecessary and unjustified harm to trust interests. As a matter of practical necessity the state may have to approve appropriations despite foreseeable harm to public trust uses. In so doing, however, the state must bear in mind its duty as trustee to consider the effect of the taking on the public trust (see United Plainsmen v. N.D. State Water Con. Commission (N.D.1976) 247 N.W.2d 457, 462–463), and to preserve, so far as consistent with the public interest, the uses protected by the trust.

Once the state has approved an appropriation, the public trust imposes a duty of continuing supervision over the taking and use of the appropriated water. In exercising its sovereign power to allocate water resources in the public interest, the state is not confined by past allocation decisions which may be incorrect in light of current knowledge or inconsistent with current needs.

The state accordingly has the power to reconsider allocation decisions even though those decisions were made after due consideration of their effect on the public trust.[28] The case for reconsidering a particular decision, however, is even stronger when that decision failed to weigh and consider public trust uses. In the case before us, the salient fact is that no responsible body has ever determined the impact of di-

---

27. Amendments to the Water Code enacted in 1955 and subsequent years codify in part the duty of the Water Board to consider public trust uses of stream water. (See, ante, p. 363 of 189 Cal. Rptr., p. 726 of 658 P.2d). The requirements of the California Environmental Quality Act (Pub. ResourcesRes. Code, § 21000 et seq.) impose a similar obligation. (See Robie, op. cit. supra, 2 Ecology L.Q. 695.)

These enactments do not render the judicially fashioned public trust doctrine superfluous. Aside from the possibility that statutory protections can be repealed, the noncodified public trust doctrine remains important both to confirm the state's sovereign supervision and to require consideration of public trust uses in cases filed directly in the courts without prior proceedings before the board.

28. The state Attorney General asserts that the Water Board could also reconsider the DWP water rights under the doctrine of unreasonable use under article X, section 2. DWP maintains, however, that its use of the water for domestic consumption is prima facie reasonable. * * * In view of our reliance on the public trust doctrine as a basis for reconsideration of DWP's usufructuary rights, we need not resolve that controversy.

verting the entire flow of the Mono Lake tributaries into the Los Angeles Aqueduct. This is not a case in which the Legislature, the Water Board, or any judicial body has determined that the needs of Los Angeles outweigh the needs of the Mono Basin, that the benefit gained is worth the price. Neither has any responsible body determined whether some lesser taking would better balance the diverse interests. Instead, DWP acquired rights to the entire flow in 1940 from a water board which believed it lacked both the power and the duty to protect the Mono Lake environment, and continues to exercise those rights in apparent disregard for the resulting damage to the scenery, ecology, and human uses of Mono Lake.

It is clear that some responsible body ought to reconsider the allocation of the waters of the Mono Basin. No vested rights bar such reconsideration. We recognize the substantial concerns voiced by Los Angeles—the city's need for water, its reliance upon the 1940 board decision, the cost both in terms of money and environmental impact of obtaining water elsewhere. Such concerns must enter into any allocation decision. We hold only that they do not preclude a reconsideration and reallocation which also takes into account the impact of water diversion on the Mono Lake environment. * * *

This opinion is but one step in the eventual resolution of the Mono Lake controversy. We do not dictate any particular allocation of water. Our objective is to resolve a legal conundrum in which two competing systems of thought—the public trust doctrine and the appropriative water rights system—existed independently of each other, espousing principles which seemingly suggested opposite results. We hope by integrating these two doctrines to clear away the legal barriers which have so far prevented either the Water Board or the courts from taking a new and objective look at the water resources of the Mono Basin. The human and environmental uses of Mono Lake—uses protected by the public trust doctrine—deserve to be taken into account. Such uses should not be destroyed because the state mistakenly thought itself powerless to protect them.

Let a peremptory writ of mandate issue commanding the Superior Court of Alpine County to vacate its judgment in this action and to enter a new judgment consistent with the views stated in this opinion.

Notes

1. **Development of the modern public trust doctrine.** Until 1970, the public trust doctrine was largely confined to issues involving ownership of submerged lands. In that year, an article by Professor Joseph Sax infused the doctrine with new vigor. Joseph L. Sax, The Public Trust Doctrine in Natural Resource Law: Effective Judicial Intervention, 68 Mich. L. Rev. 471 (1970). Professor Sax saw the public trust doctrine largely as a procedural device used by the courts to "mend perceived im-

perfections in the legislative and administrative process." He argued that sometimes legislatures and agencies ignore broad based public interests because a well-organized minority is able to gain political advantage over a diffuse, disorganized majority. Thus, Sax asserted, the courts use the public trust doctrine as an instrument for democratizing decision-making. Frequently, he said, courts accomplish this by moving a decision from one constituency to another. For example, a court may find that an agency cannot divert trust property to a use which lessens public use without specific legislative authority, thereby moving the decision from the agency, with a narrow constituency, to the legislature, with a broad constituency. Professor Sax later gave the doctrine greater substantive content, stating that it protects public expectations against destabilizing changes. Joseph L. Sax, Liberating the Public Trust Doctrine, 14 U.C. Davis L. Rev. 185, 188 (1980).

Since the publication of the 1970 article, courts have remarkably expanded both the resources subjected to the trust and the interests protected by it. Although many states still require some connection to navigable waters, the doctrine is no longer confined to waters which are navigable for title purposes. It has been extended to bodies navigable only under more liberal state tests, to nonnavigable waters, and to resources which have no direct connection to water. E.g., Wade v. Kramer, 459 N.E.2d 1025 (Ill. 1984) (wildlife); Save Ourselves, Inc. v. La. Envtl. Control Comm'n, 452 So. 2d 1152 (La. 1984) (noting state constitution's extension of doctrine to all natural resources); Gould v. Greylock Reservation Comm'n, 215 N.E.2d 114 (Mass. 1966) (state parks). As *National Audubon* illustrates, the interests protected have been extended to include recreation, esthetics, and environmental preservation.

2. **Scholarly support for the modern public trust doctrine.** Four decades after Sax's seminal article, the doctrine still commands substantial scholarly attention. The weight of scholarly comment favors the expansion of the public trust doctrine as a means of furthering environmental protection.

3. **Criticisms of the public trust doctrine.** Not everyone views the public trust doctrine positively:

"Most simply put, the historic function of the public trust doctrine has been to provide a public property basis for resisting the exercise of private property rights in natural resources deemed contrary to the public interest. * * * By continuing to resist a legal system that is otherwise being abandoned, the public trust doctrine obscures analysis and renders more difficult the important process of reworking natural resources law. Of even broader concern, the doctrine threatens to fuel a developing clash in liberal ideology between furthering individual rights of security and dignity, bound up in notions of private property protection, and supporting environmental protection and resource preservation goals, inevitably dependent on intrusive governmental programs designed to achieve longer-term collectivist goals."

Lazarus, supra p. 537, Note 4.

4. **Outcome of the principal case.** In 1994, the California Water Resources Control Board modified Los Angeles's licenses in the Mono Basin to protect public trust resources and to establish fishery protection flows in tributaries feeding Mono Lake. California Water Resources Control Bd., Water Rights Decision 1631 (1994). The order implements the decisions of *National Audubon* and California Trout, Inc. v. State Water Resources Control Board, discussed supra p. 158, Note 6.

The order limits diversions from the Mono Basin to restore Mono Lake to an average elevation of 6392 feet over 20 years. The elevation of Mono Lake was approximately 6417 feet in 1941 when Los Angeles commenced its diversions. The historic low was 6372 feet, and the elevation was 6375 feet in 1994. (The Lake's current level can be found at http://www.monolake.org/today/water.) During the transition period, diversions by Los Angeles are expected to average 12,300 acre-feet per year. After the transition period, diversions are expected to average 30,900 acre-feet per year. By comparison, Los Angeles's diversions averaged 83,000 acre-feet per year from 1974 to 1989. Thus, the order reduces diversions during the transition period to about 15% of the pre-1989 average; after the transition period it reduces diversions to about 37% of the pre-1989 average. The Water Board estimated that it will cost about $27.8 million annually to replace lost water during the transition period and $17.9 million annually thereafter.

The order, however, is not based solely on the public trust doctrine, and the doctrine's significance in the outcome is unclear. The 6392-foot restoration elevation was selected as much to meet ambient air quality standards under the Clean Air Act (triggered by blowing sand from the relicted lake bed) as to protect public trust resources. In addition, mandatory fishery protection flows required in the tributaries by provisions of the Fish and Game Code and *California Trout* will reduce diversion by an average of 35,200 acre-feet per year. These flows would have restored the lake to an elevation of 6388 to 6390 feet, although the restoration period would have been considerably longer had additional public trust requirements not been imposed. During the transition period, public trust requirements reduce Los Angeles's diversions by an additional 32,300 acre-feet per year. However, after the transition period, public trust requirements only reduce the diversions by 8,500 acre-feet per year.

For a more complete review of the aftermath, see Craig Anthony (Tony) Arnold, Leigh A. Jewel, Litigation's Bounded Effectiveness and the Real Public Trust Doctrine: The Aftermath of the Mono Lake Case, 14 Hastings W.-N.W. J. Envtl. L. & Pol'y 1177 (2008). See also Richard Roos-Collins, Lessons from the Mono Lake Cases for Effective Management of Public Trust Resources, 15 Southeastern Envtl. L.J. 171 (2006).

5. **Development of the public trust doctrine in California.** Gregory S. Weber, Articulating the Public Trust: Text, Near-Text, and Context, 27 Ariz. St. L.J. 1155 (1995), is an in-depth study of the applica-

tion of the public trust doctrine to water rights in California in the first dozen years after *National Audubon*. Professor Weber observes that the handful of California appellate decisions which have considered the doctrine have added almost nothing of substance to *National Audubon* and have not produced a single reallocation of water to trust uses. In contrast, he notes that the California Water Resources Control Board has developed a sizeable body of pronouncements regarding the trust's meaning and its relationship to the system of water rights and has ordered several reallocations of water to trust uses. He concludes that the Water Board has articulated a vision of accommodation which gives it the fullest possible power to allocate surface water, places practical limits on the ability of other parties to invoke these powers, and acknowledges the necessity of permitting continued diversions of water.

6. **Legislative renunciation of the doctrine.** The Idaho Supreme Court has expressed an expansive view of the public trust in relation to water rights on several occasions, albeit always in dicta. See, e.g., Idaho Cons. League, Inc. v. State, 911 P.2d 748 (Idaho 1995). In reaction, the Idaho legislature adopted Idaho Code § 58–1203. That statute states that the doctrine is "solely a limitation on the power of the state to alienate or encumber the title to the beds of navigable waters." More pointedly, it states that the doctrine shall not apply to "[t]he appropriation or use of water, or the granting, transfer, administration, or adjudication of water or water rights * * * or any other procedure or law applicable to water rights in the state of Idaho." See Michael C. Blumm, et al, supra p. 534, Note 2, questioning the authority of the Idaho legislature to abrogate the public trust doctrine. Compare supra p. 523, Note 10, addressing the Arizona legislature's repeated efforts to disclaim title to ownership of trust-bound submerged lands.

7. **Impact on water rights in other western states.** Although a number of western courts have recognized the public trust doctrine in disputes involving rights to submerged lands and public use of waters, the doctrine has very limited application to water rights outside California. Only the North Dakota, Idaho and Hawaii supreme courts have explicitly declared that the doctrine applies to water rights. The North Dakota Supreme Court actually preceded the California Supreme Court in applying the doctrine to water rights, United Plainsmen Ass'n v. North Dakota State Water Conservation Commission, supra p. 151. However, that case involved new appropriations, not reallocations of water already appropriated; the doctrine was only used to impose water planning; and the result could have been reached on other grounds. The Idaho Supreme Court's expansive embrace of the doctrine and the subsequent legislative renunciation are discussed in the preceding note.

The Hawaii Supreme Court, however, has given a broad reading to the trust's application. In *In re* Water Use Permit Application, 9 P.3d 409 (Haw. 2000), commonly cited as the *"Waiahole Ditch"* case, the court concluded that the trust's application in Hawaii was even broader than under *National Audubon Society*. For example, the court applied the doctrine to both surface and subsurface water. In reaching its decision, the court was aided by both aboriginal Hawaiian law as well as a state constitutional provision. See Denise E. Antolini, Water Rights and Responsibilities in the Twenty-First Century: A Foreword to the Proceedings of the 2001 Symposium on Managing Hawaii's Public Trust Doctrine, 24 U. Haw. L. Rev. 1 (2001).

8. **Assertion of public trust issues in general adjudications.** Statutes in Idaho and Arizona precluding the adjudication of public trust issues in general stream adjudications met very different fates. In Idaho Conservation League, Inc. v. State, 911 P.2d 748 (Idaho 1995), the Idaho Supreme Court denied the petition of environmental groups to intervene in the Snake River Basin Adjudication (SRBA) to assert public trust issues. The Supreme Court held that the SRBA court is a separate division of the district courts which exercises unique jurisdiction given it by the legislature to adjudicate "proprietary" water rights. Noting that all water rights are impressed with the public trust doctrine, the court found that the doctrine is not an element of a water right for purposes of determining competing proprietary claims. Conversely, legislation in Arizona which expressly precludes the consideration of public trust issues in stream-wide adjudications was struck down by the Arizona Supreme Court. San Carlos Apache Tribe v. Superior Court, 972 P.2d 179 (Ariz. 1999 (Gila River Adjudication.) It held that the legislature lacked the power to make the doctrine inapplicable in judicial proceedings.

9. **Applicability to federal water rights.** The United States holds California water rights, most notably the Bureau of Reclamation's rights for the Central Valley Project. Are these rights subject to readjustment under *National Audubon*? See supra p. 538, Note 8, and California v. United States, infra p. 666. Are federal water rights which were not created by state law, such as federal reserved water rights (see Chapter 8, Section 3) subject to state public trust restrictions?

SECTION 2. ENVIRONMENTAL PROTECTION

INTRODUCTORY NOTE

Environmental law covers many facets of human relations to nature—land, air, water, plants and animals. Environmental law is much broader than water law, but the two touch at many points. Earlier materials in this book examine laws that enhance or preserve recreation, scenic enjoyment, fish and wildlife habitat, and other environmental values. However, those provisions are part of the *water law* of particular jurisdictions; i.e., they are a component of the law regulating the rights-based allocation of water. This section examines the impact of general environmental statutes on the law of water allocation. Most of the laws considered here are federal statutes, but many states have adopted comparable ones. Furthermore, federal law often relies heavily on state administration and enforcement.

A. Environmental Assessment

NATIONAL ENVIRONMENTAL POLICY ACT OF 1969
Public Law 91–190, 42 U.S.C. §§ 4331–4335.

PURPOSE

Sec. 2. [42 U.S.C. § 4321] The purposes of this Act are: To declare a national policy which will encourage productive and enjoyable harmony between man and his environment; to promote efforts which will prevent or eliminate damage to the environment and biosphere and stimulate the health and welfare of man; to enrich the understanding of the ecological systems and natural resources important to the Nation; and to establish a Council on Environmental Quality.

Title I

Declaration of National Environmental Policy

Sec. 101. [42 U.S.C. § 4331] (a) The Congress, recognizing the profound impact of man's activity on the interrelations of all components of the natural environment, particularly the profound influences of population growth, high-density urbanization, industrial expansion, resource exploitation, and new and expanding technological advances and recognizing further the critical importance of restoring and maintaining environmental quality to the overall welfare and development of man, declares that it is the continuing policy of the Federal Government, in cooperation with State and local governments, and other concerned public and private organizations, to use all practicable means and measures, including financial and technical assistance, in a manner calculated to foster and promote the general welfare, to create and maintain conditions under which man and nature can exist in productive harmony, and fulfill the social, economic, and other requirements of present and future generations of Americans.

(b) In order to carry out the policy set forth in this Act, it is the continuing responsibility of the Federal Government to use all practicable means, consistent with other essential considerations of national policy, to improve and coordinate Federal plans, functions, programs, and resources to the end that the Nation may—

(1) fulfill the responsibilities of each generation as trustee of the environment for succeeding generations;

(2) assure for all Americans safe, healthful, productive, and aesthetically and culturally pleasing surroundings;

(3) attain the widest range of beneficial uses of the environment without degradation, risk to health or safety, or other undesirable and unintended consequences;

(4) preserve important historic, cultural, and natural aspects of our national heritage, and maintain, wherever possible, an environment which supports diversity and variety of individual choice;

(5) achieve a balance between population and resource use which will permit high standards of living and a wide sharing of life's amenities; and

(6) enhance the quality of renewable resources and approach the maximum attainable recycling of depletable resources.

(c) The Congress recognizes that each person should enjoy a healthful environment and that each person has a responsibility to contribute to the preservation and enhancement of the environment.

Sec. 102. [42 U.S.C. § 4332] The Congress authorizes and directs that, to the fullest extent possible: (1) the policies, regulations, and public laws of the United States shall be interpreted and administered in accordance with the policies set forth in this Act, and (2) all agencies of the Federal Government shall—

(A) utilize a systematic, interdisciplinary approach which will insure the integrated use of the natural and social sciences and the environmental design arts in planning and in decisionmaking which may have an impact on man's environment;

(B) identify and develop methods and procedures, in consultation with the Council on Environmental Quality established by title II of this Act, which will insure that presently unquantified environmental amenities and values may be given appropriate consideration in decisionmaking along with economic and technical considerations;

(C) include in every recommendation or report on proposals for legislation and other major Federal actions significantly affecting the quality of the human environment, a detailed statement by the responsible official on—

(i) the environmental impact of the proposed action,
(ii) any adverse environmental effects which cannot be avoided should the proposal be implemented,
(iii) alternatives to the proposed action,
(iv) the relationship between local short-term uses of man's environment and the maintenance and enhancement of long-term productivity, and

(v) any irreversible and irretrievable commitments of resources which would be involved in the proposed action should it be implemented.

Prior to making any detailed statement, the responsible Federal official shall consult with and obtain the comments of any Federal agency which has jurisdiction by law or special expertise with respect to any environmental impact involved. Copies of such statement and the comments and views of the appropriate Federal, State, and local agencies, which are authorized to develop and enforce environmental standards, shall be made available to the President, the Council on Environmental Quality and to the public as provided by section 552 of title 5, United States Code, and shall accompany the proposal through the existing agency review processes;

(D) study, develop, and describe appropriate alternatives to recommended courses of action in any proposal which involves unresolved conflicts concerning alternative uses of available resources;

(E) recognize the worldwide and long-range character of environmental problems and, where consistent with the foreign policy of the United States, lend appropriate support to initiatives, resolutions, and programs designed to maximize international cooperation in anticipating and preventing a decline in the quality of mankind's world environment;

(F) make available to States, counties, municipalities, institutions, and individuals, advice and information useful in restoring, maintaining, and enhancing the quality of the environment;

(G) initiate and utilize ecological information in the planning and development of resource-oriented projects; and

(H) assist the Council on Environmental Quality established by title II of this Act. * * *

Sec. 104. [42 U.S.C. § 4334] Nothing in Section 102 or 103 shall in any way affect the specific statutory obligations of any Federal agency (1) to comply with criteria or standards of environmental quality, (2) to coordinate or consult with any other Federal or State agency, or (3) to act, or refrain from acting contingent upon the recommendations or certification of any other Federal or State agency.

Sec. 105. [42 U.S.C. § 4335] The policies and goals set forth in this Act are supplementary to those set forth in existing authorizations of Federal agencies.

CALVERT CLIFFS' COORDINATING COMMITTEES, INC. v. UNITED STATES ATOMIC ENERGY COMMISSION

United States Court of Appeals, District of Columbia Circuit, 1971.
449 F.2d 1109.

[The AEC adopted rules for incorporating NEPA requirements into its procedures for licensing atomic power plants that limited the scope and time of considering environmental impacts, relied on the parties and intervenors to raise environmental issues and supply information, and relied on determinations and standards supplied by other agencies. In disapproving these, Circuit Judge J. Skelly Wright issued a directive to all federal agencies:]

In these cases, we must for the first time interpret the broadest and perhaps most important of the recent statutes: the National Environmental Policy Act of 1969 (NEPA). We must assess claims that one of the agencies charged with its administration has failed to live up to the congressional mandate. Our duty, in short, is to see that important legislative purposes, heralded in the halls of Congress, are not lost or misdirected in the vast hallways of the federal bureaucracy.

NEPA * * * is cast in terms of a general mandate and broad delegation of authority to new and old administrative agencies. It takes the major step of requiring all federal agencies to consider values of environmental preservation in their spheres of activity, and it prescribes certain procedural measures to ensure that those values are in fact fully respected. * * * Section 101 sets forth the Act's basic substantive policy: that the federal government 'use all practicable means and measures' to protect environmental values. Congress did not establish environmental protection as an exclusive goal; rather, it desired a reordering of priorities, so that environmental costs and benefits will assume their proper place along with other considerations. In Section 101(b), imposing an explicit duty on federal officials, the Act provides that "it is the continuing responsibility of the Federal Government to use all practicable means, consistent with other essential considerations of national policy," to avoid environmental degradation, preserve "historic, cultural, and natural" resources, and promote "the widest range of beneficial uses of the environment without * * * undesirable and unintended consequences."

Thus the general substantive policy of the Act is a flexible one. It leaves room for a responsible exercise of discretion and may not require particular substantive results in particular problematic instances. However, the Act also contains very important "procedural" provisions—provisions which are designed to see that all federal agencies do in fact exercise the substantive discretion given them. These provisions are not highly flexible. Indeed, they establish a strict standard of compliance.

556 PUBLIC RIGHTS • ENVIRONMENTAL PROTECTION Ch. 7

NEPA, first of all, makes environmental protection a part of the mandate of every federal agency and department. * * * Perhaps the greatest importance of NEPA is to require the Atomic Energy Commission and other agencies to *consider* environmental issues just as they consider other matters within their mandates. * * *

The sort of consideration of environmental values which NEPA compels is clarified in Section 102(2)(A) and (B). In general, all agencies must use a "systematic, interdisciplinary approach" to environmental planning and evaluation "in decisionmaking which may have an impact on man's environment." In order to include all possible environmental factors in the decisional equation, agencies must "identify and develop methods and procedures * * * which will insure that presently unquantified environmental amenities and values may be given appropriate consideration in decisionmaking along with economic and technical considerations." "Environmental amenities" will often be in conflict with "economic and technical considerations." To "consider" the former "along with" the latter must involve a balancing process. In some instances environmental costs may outweigh economic and technical benefits and in other instances they may not. But NEPA mandates a rather finely tuned and "systematic" balancing analysis in each instance.

To ensure that the balancing analysis is carried out and given full effect, Section 102(2)(C) requires that responsible officials of all agencies prepare a "detailed statement" covering the impact of particular actions on the environment, the environmental costs which might be avoided, and alternative measures which might alter the cost-benefit equation. The apparent purpose of the "detailed statement" is to aid in the agencies' own decision making process and to advise other interested agencies and the public of the environmental consequences of planned federal action. Beyond the "detailed statement," Section 102(2)(D) requires all agencies specifically to "study, develop, and describe appropriate alternatives to recommended courses of action in any proposal which involves unresolved conflicts concerning alternative uses of available resources." This requirement, like the "detailed statement" requirement, seeks to ensure that each agency decision maker has before him and takes into proper account all possible approaches to a particular project (including total abandonment of the project) which would alter the environmental impact and the cost-benefit balance. Only in that fashion is it likely that the most intelligent, optimally beneficial decision will ultimately be made. Moreover, by compelling a formal "detailed statement" and a description of alternatives, NEPA provides evidence that the mandated decision making process has in fact taken place and, most importantly, allows those removed from the initial process to evaluate and balance the factors on their own. * * *

Unlike the substantive duties of Section 101(b), which requires agencies to "use all practicable means consistent with other essential considerations," the procedural duties of Section 102 must be fulfilled to the "fullest extent possible." * * * Thus the Section 102 duties are not inherently flexible. They must be complied with to the fullest extent, unless there is a clear conflict of *statutory* authority. Considerations of administrative difficulty, delay or economic cost will not suffice to strip the section of its fundamental importance.

We conclude, then, that Section 102 of NEPA mandates a particular sort of careful and informed decisionmaking process and creates judicially enforceable duties. The reviewing courts probably cannot reverse a substantive decision on its merits, under Section 101, unless it be shown that the actual balance of costs and benefits that was struck was arbitrary or clearly gave insufficient weight to environmental values. But if the decision was reached procedurally without individualized consideration and balancing of environmental factors— conducted fully and in good faith—it is the responsibility of the courts to reverse. * * * Compliance to the "*fullest*" possible extent would seem to demand that environmental issues be considered at every important stage in the decision making process concerning a particular action—at every stage where an overall balancing of environmental and nonenvironmental factors is appropriate and where alterations might be made in the proposed action to minimize environmental costs. * * *

NEPA establishes environmental protection as an integral part of the Atomic Energy Commission's basic mandate. The primary responsibility for fulfilling that mandate lies with the Commission. Its responsibility is not simply to sit back, like an umpire, and resolve adversary contentions at the hearing stage. Rather, it must itself take the initiative of considering environmental values at every distinctive and comprehensive stage of the process beyond the staff's evaluation and recommendation. * * *

NEPA mandates a case-by-case balancing judgment on the part of federal agencies. In each individual case, the particular economic and technical benefits of planned action must be assessed and then weighed against the environmental costs; alternatives must be considered which would affect the balance of values. The magnitude of possible benefits and possible costs may lie anywhere on a broad spectrum. Much will depend on the particular magnitudes involved in particular cases. In some cases, the benefits will be great enough to justify a certain quantum of environmental costs; in other cases, they will not be so great and the proposed action may have to be abandoned or significantly altered so as to bring the benefits and costs into a proper balance. The point of the individualized balancing analysis is to ensure that, with possible alterations, the optimally beneficial action is finally taken.

Notes

1. **Applicability of NEPA.** NEPA applies only to federal agencies. It can be triggered by a federal project, but it will more often be triggered by a private project or activity for which a federal permit or license is required, as in the principal case. Because water rights are primarily a subject of state law, acquisition of a water right alone will not usually activate NEPA, although acts required to use the water right may trigger the statute. For example, construction of a diversion structure by the owner of a water right may require a section 404 dredge and fill permit from the Army Corps of Engineers (See subsection C), thereby triggering NEPA. Similarly, water development in western states often occurs on federal lands. Diversion works and transportation facilities on federal lands require rights-of-way or special use permits from federal agencies, compelling the issuing agency to observe NEPA.

2. **State environmental policy acts.** A number of states have adopted environmental policy acts, patterned generally after NEPA, which express a similar policy and which contain directives to state agencies similar to NEPA. See, e.g., The California Environmental Policy Act, Cal. Pub. Res. Code §§ 21000-21177; Washington Environmental Policy Act, Wash. Rev. Code, ch. 43.21C. In states which require a permit or license to create water rights, the issuance of the permit or license can activate the state environmental assessment process. See Stempel v. Dep't of Water Res., 508 P.2d 166 (Wash. 1973).

NEPA AT 19: A PRIMER ON AN "OLD" LAW WITH SOLUTIONS TO NEW PROBLEMS
Dina Bear, 19 Envtl. L. Rep. 10060, 10061-10065 (1989).

The Environmental Impact Assessment Process Under NEPA

Background. As one means of implementing the goals of the Act's national environmental policy, Congress included the well-known §102(2)(C), directing all federal agencies to include, in proposals for legislation and other major federal actions significantly affecting the quality of the human environment, a "detailed statement" by the responsible official. * * *

Title II of NEPA created the Council on Environmental Quality (CEQ) in the Executive Office of the President, composed of three Members appointed by the President with the advice and consent of the Senate. CEQ has a number of responsibilities, including preparation of an annual report on environmental quality, developing and recommending to the President national environmental policies, and documenting and defining environmental trends.

CEQ Guidance and Regulations. * * * [T]he environmental impact assessment process, or "NEPA process," as it frequently is referred to in the federal establishment, acquired some unfortunate "barnacles" during the mid-1970s. The most frequent complaints were the length of EISs and the delays that the NEPA process was perceived to cause in the decisionmaking process. Observers believed that the lack of uniformity throughout the government and uncertainty about what was required accounted to a large degree for these problems. Consequently, in 1977 President Carter issued Executive Order 11991, directing CEQ to issue binding regulations to federal agencies in an effort to make the process more uniform and efficient. The regulations were to cover all procedural provisions of NEPA, and to include procedures for referral to CEQ of conflicts between agencies concerning the environmental impacts of proposed major federal actions. * * *

Regulatory Structure. The CEQ regulations implementing the procedural provisions of NEPA apply to all federal agencies of the government, excluding Congress and any of its institutions, the judiciary, and the President, including the performance of staff functions for the President. The CEQ regulations are generic in nature, and do not address the applicability of the various procedural requirements to specific agency actions. Instead, each federal department and agency is required to prepare its own NEPA procedures that address that agency's compliance in relation to its particular mission. CEQ reviews and approves all agency procedures and amendments to those procedures.

The agency procedures are required to establish specific criteria for and identification of three classes of actions: those that require preparation of an environmental impact statement; those that require preparation of an environmental assessment; and those that are categorically excluded from further NEPA review. Additionally, agencies are required to address NEPA compliance for actions initiated outside of the federal government that require federal approval, the introduction of supplemental EISs into the administrative record, the integration of NEPA analysis into the agency decisionmaking process, and to name a contact office for further information or documents prepared under NEPA.

Categorical Exclusions. "Categorical exclusions" refer to acts falling within a pre-designated category of actions that do not individually or cumulatively have a significant effect on the human environment. Thus, no documentation of environmental analysis is required. Agencies may list either very specific actions, or a broader class of actions with criteria and examples for guidance. However, federal officials must be alert to extraordinary circumstances in which a normally excluded action may have a significant environmental effect. A categorical exclusion is not an exemption from compliance with NEPA, but merely an administrative tool to avoid paperwork for those actions without significant environmental effects.

Environmental Assessments. An environmental assessment (EA) is supposed to be a concise public document that may be prepared to achieve any of the following purposes: to provide sufficient evidence and analysis for determining whether to prepare an EIS; to aid an agency's compliance with NEPA when no EIS is necessary; and to facilitate preparation of an EIS if one is necessary. An EA should include a brief discussion of the need for the proposal, of alternatives as required by NEPA § 102(2)(E), and of the environmental impacts of the proposed action and alternatives. It should list agencies and persons consulted. An EA is followed by one of two conclusions: either a Finding of No Significant Impact (FONSI) or a decision to prepare an EIS. A FONSI briefly presents the reasons why an action, not otherwise categorically excluded, will not have a significant effect on the human environment. It may include a summary of the EA, or simply be attached to the EA. Neither EAs nor FONSIs are filed in a central location (unlike EISs, which are filed with the Office of Federal Activities in the Environmental Protection Agency). However, they are public documents, and the agency responsible for their preparation must involve the public in an appropriate manner. * * *

Environmental Impact Statements. The primary purpose of an EIS is to serve as an action-forcing device to ensure that the policies and goals defined in NEPA are infused into the ongoing programs and actions of the federal government. It must provide full and fair discussion of significant environmental impacts and shall inform decisionmakers and the public of the reasonable alternatives that would avoid or minimize adverse impacts or enhance the quality of the human environment. In preparing EISs, agencies should focus on significant environmental issues and alternatives and reduce paperwork and the accumulation of extraneous background data. Texts should be concise, clear, and to the point, and should be supported by evidence that the agency has made the necessary environmental analyses. An EIS is more than a disclosure document; it should be used by federal officials to plan actions and make decisions.

The threshold requirement for preparation of an EIS is, of course, the statutory threshold of a "major federal action significantly affecting the quality of the human environment." As interpreted by the CEQ regulations and case law, "major federal actions" include a wide range of actions, certainly much more than the construction projects most commonly associated with NEPA compliance. For example, "actions" include adoption of rules, regulations, and interpretations of policy under the Administrative Procedure Act (APA), legislative proposals, treaties and international conventions or agreements, and adoption of programs. Actions include circumstances where the responsible official fails to act and that failure to act is reviewable by courts or administrative tribunals under the APA or other applicable law as agency action. The only items specifically excluded as "actions" under NEPA are judicial or administrative enforcement actions (both civil and criminal) and funding assistance solely in the form of general revenue sharing funds distributed under the State and Local Financial Assistance Act of 1971, with no federal agency control over the subsequent use of such funds.

The question of what is "significant," thus making EIS preparation necessary, has often been a difficult one. In fact, disagreement about whether a proposed action has "significant effects" has been the most frequent reason for NEPA litigation over the past 19 years. CEQ's regulations do not define which particular federal actions are "significant" for purposes of NEPA; rather, they provide a discussion of the factors that should be considered by each agency when drafting their own NEPA procedures and when considering proposed actions. The regulations emphasize the need to consider "significantly" in terms of both context and intensity. "Context" means that the significance of the proposed action must be analyzed in relation to the societal and environmental framework in which the action would occur. Factors to be considered in evaluating "intensity" include the degree to which the proposed action affects public health and safety, unique characteristics of the geographic area involved, the degree of controversy about the environmental impacts, the degree to which the possible effects on the human environment are highly uncertain or involve unique or unknown risks, the precedential value of the action, the presence of cumulative effects, the possible effects on historic, scientific, or cultural resources, the degree to which the action may adversely affect an endangered or threatened species or its habitat, and whether the proposed action would be a violation of a federal, state, or local law. One frequently overlooked point is that the NEPA standard of significance applies to both beneficial and adverse impacts.

Few federal courts have attempted to formulate a definition of the phrase "significantly affecting" that goes beyond the factual circumstances of a particular case. Instead, a review of the cases shows that almost all have been decided by the court determining whether the evidence in a given case pointed to the presence of potentially significant environmental effects and then deciding whether the agency's decision not to prepare an EIS was reasonable under the circumstances. Generally, however, the courts have rejected specific size or monetary factors as a guide to determining the significance of an action. Courts are also increasingly concerned with adequate consideration of cumulative and indirect effects. Although social and economic impacts alone do not trigger the requirement to prepare an EIS under NEPA, the courts have required the inclusion of such impacts once the threshold requirement for preparation of an EIS has been reached.

Two types of EISs that have received less attention than the typical project-specific EIS are the programmatic EIS and the legislative EIS. Programmatic EISs must be prepared prior to an agency's decision regarding a major program, plan, or policy with significant environmental impacts. It may be broad in scope, followed by site-specific EISs or EAs prepared at subsequent stages. The process of preparing a broad statement and subsequent, more narrowly focused NEPA documents is referred to as tiering. Legislative EISs meet the statutory requirement for a "detailed statement on proposals for legislation which would significantly affect the quality of the human environment." Although there are some modifications, the procedures for preparation of legislative EISs are similar to EISs prepared for proposals for executive branch action.

Once the decision is made to prepare an EIS of any type, the proponent federal agency publishes a Notice of Intent (NOI) in the Federal Register. The NOI should describe the proposed action and possible alternatives, the agency's intent to prepare an EIS, the agency's proposed scoping process, and any planned scoping meetings and the name and address of a contact person in the agency.

The agency must then engage in the "scoping process," a process to determine the scope of issues to be addressed in the EIS and for identifying the significant issues related to a proposed action. Scoping may or may not include meetings, but the process should involve interested parties at all levels of government, and all interested private citizens and organizations. Scoping is also the appropriate point to allocate responsibilities among lead and cooperating agencies,[49] identify other environmental requirements that are applicable to the proposal, set any time and page limits, and, in general, structure the process in such a way that all identifiable participants are informed and involved at appropriate points. A well designed scoping process can have an extremely positive ripple effect throughout the rest of the NEPA process.

The next step is preparation of a draft EIS. The EIS may be prepared either by the lead agency, with assistance from any cooperating agencies, or by a contractor. However, if a contractor prepares the EIS, the contractor should be chosen by the agency and must execute a disclosure statement prepared by the lead agency, specifying that the contractor has no financial or other interest in the outcome of the project. The agency may accept information from any party, including

---

49. "Lead agency" and "cooperating agency" designations are used when there is more than one federal agency either proposing an action or involved in the same action or group of actions. Federal, state, or local agencies, including at least one federal agency, may act as joint lead agencies. For criteria and responsibilities of lead and cooperating agencies, see 40 C.F.R. §§ 1501.5 and 1501.6. For resolution of disputes over which agency should be lead agency, see 40 C.F.R. § 1501.5(c).

the applicant, but it always has the duty to independently evaluate such information.

The content requirements of an EIS, from cover sheet to appendices, are set out in the CEQ regulations. The "heart" of the EIS is the alternatives analysis, which inevitably leads to the question of which alternatives must be analyzed. The answer to that, like the answer to the question of what is "significant," is addressed on a case-by-case basis, with the key judicial standard being that of reasonableness.

If the proposed action is the subject of a request for a federal permit or regulatory approval for a proposed action, the federal agency must consider both public and private purpose and need. Courts have stressed the need to consider the objectives of the permit applicant, but they have also emphasized the requirement for the agency to exercise independent judgment as to the appropriate articulation of objective purpose and need. Thus, NEPA requires the agency to consider both public and private purpose and need in formulating the alternatives to be examined in an EIS.

Once the draft EIS is prepared, it must be circulated for at least 45 days for public comment and review. Federal agencies with jurisdiction by law or special expertise with respect to any of the relevant environmental impacts are expected to comment, although this may take the form of a "no comment" letter. At the conclusion of the comment period, the agency must evaluate the comment letters and respond to the substantive comments in the final EIS. The final EIS is sent to all parties who commented on the draft EIS. No decision may be made concerning the proposed action until at least 30 days after the Notice of Availability of the final EIS or 90 days after the publication of the Notice of Availability of the draft EIS, whichever is later.

At the time of decision, the decisionmaker must sign a Record of Decision (ROD). The ROD states what the decision is, identifies which alternatives were considered by the agency in making the decision, specifies which alternatives were considered to be environmentally preferable, and discusses factors that were balanced by the decisionmaker. Further, the ROD states whether all practical methods to avoid or minimize environmental harm are being adopted, and if not, why not. The ROD also includes a description of any applicable enforcement and monitoring programs.

Notes

1. **Guidelines.** Largely unchanged since their adoption in 1978, the CEQ guidelines are found at 40 C.F.R. §§ 1500.1–1508.28.

2. **EPA responsibilities.** The EPA has NEPA implementation responsibilities. Clean Air Act § 309, 42 U.S.C. § 7609, directs the EPA Administrator to review and comment in writing on the environmental

impact of various activities taken by federal agencies including Environmental Impact Statements. The Administrator must publish a determination and refer to CEQ any activity determined to be "unsatisfactory from the standpoint of public health or welfare or environmental quality." EPA is also the repository for all EISs. Under this authority, EPA has developed a system for reviewing and rating actions and underlying EISs.

NATIONAL WILDLIFE FEDERATION v. HARVEY
United States District Court, Eastern District of Arkansas, 2006.
440 F. Supp. 2d 940.

WILSON, District Judge.

* * *

I. Introduction

Completion of the Grand Prairie Project ("GPP") and the protection of the Ivory-billed Woodpecker ("IBW") are at the heart of this case. The question is whether the two interests conflict; i.e., will completion of the Grand Prairie Project diminish the Ivory-billed Woodpecker's chance for survival?

Some doubt the existence of the IBW. Often things in the natural world, as well as in other worlds, cannot be proved to a certainty. And it may well be that doubts in this instance are justified * * *. Here, however, the parties have stipulated that the IBW exists, so for purposes of this case, it does. * * *

A. The Grand Prairie Project

The GPP is designed to prevent the depletion of the Alluvial and Sparta aquifers by pumping water from the White River and delivering it to some of the Grand Prairie farmland, by constructing a pumping station, and employing a system of canals, pipelines, and streams. * * * The potential depletion and destruction of the aquifers is of great concern to economic and agricultural interests-it is also an important environmental concern.

* * * Importantly, the GPP's impact area will include the White River National Wildlife Refuge-home of the largest remaining bottomland ecosystem on any tributary of the Mississippi River. The area is * * * the last known North American refuge of the IBW.

B. The Ivory-billed Woodpecker

The IBW is the largest woodpecker in the United States and the second largest in the world. Before 2004, it was believed to be extinct. It was last seen in northeastern Louisiana in the 1940's. In April 2005, scientists confirmed that it was seen in the Cache River National Wildlife Refuge, and heard in the White River National Wildlife Refuge, several miles to the South.

The bird's moniker is "Lord God Bird," because, according to lore, it is so majestic that, when it was seen, people exclaimed, "Lord God!" It is also known as the "Grail" bird, because, in the last 60 years, searching for it was akin to searching for the Holy Grail.

The IBW thrived in the once untouched forests that covered the southeastern United States-in the delta of the Mississippi and Ohio Rivers. It is a reclusive bird that prefers large expanses of bottomland swamp forest and extensive wilderness. * * *

II. Background

In 1996, Congress authorized the Grand Prairie Region and Bayou Meto flood control project. [The initial environmental review was upheld, after challenge, by the District Court and 8th Circuit.] * * *

On April 28, 2005, the FWS announced the rediscovery of the IBW. After this, the Corps suspended construction. Beginning in May 2005, the Corps evaluated the effects of the GPP on the IBW and issued a Biological Assessment on May 24, 2005. In its assessment, the Corps concluded that the GPP is not likely to adversely affect this Woodpecker.

Before entering a formal concurrence, the FWS issued a letter telling the Corps that it had to meet specific requirements. * * * Water flow monitoring was required because, even with the minimum flow cutoff, the project's operation will alter water levels in the area-making some forested wetlands slightly drier-and affecting the "flood plain resources." * * *

Plaintiffs filed a complaint, alleging that the FWS violated the ESA, the [Administrative Procedure Act, "APA"], and that the Corps violated NEPA. * * *

According to Plaintiffs, the Corps and the FWS arbitrarily concluded that the GPP would not adversely affect the IBW. They allege that jeopardy is likely because: (1) the Corps will destroy 135 acres of forest without ruling out the possibility that it may include the bird's nesting, roosting, and foraging trees; (2) the GPP will draw down one hundred fifty eight (158) billion gallons of water each year from the White River, and this will significantly reduce the water levels in the wetland forests; (3) some tree species will die when water levels fall, and the forest will gradually decline; (4) the FWS never revealed which trees would be most threatened by the change in water level; (5) the Corps is rushing to construct a massive pumping station located fourteen miles away from the IBW sighting; (6) the canals and pipelines will fragment the bottomland forest, which may adversely affect IBW habitat; and (7) the noise and human activity involved in construction and pumping activity will adversely affect the IBW. Plaintiffs point out that there is very little known about the IBW, and more study is necessary before beginning such a large, irreversible commitment of federal resources.

* * *

IV. Discussion[a]

A. NEPA

1. Requirements of NEPA

While NEPA does not require results, it does prescribe a necessary process. [Robertson v. Methow Valley Citizens Council, 490 U.S. 332, 335 (1989)]. The process required by NEPA is preparation of an EIS or a supplemental EIS. As long as adverse environmental effects are adequately identified and evaluated by the EIS, the agency complies with NEPA, even if it decides that other values outweigh environmental risks. [Strycker's Bay Neighborhood Council, Inc., 444 U.S. at 227-228].

Some statutes impose substantive environmental obligations on federal agencies. [*Robertson*, 490 U.S. at 351, n. 14 (the Supreme Court holds that the Endangered Species Act creates substantive rights)]. But NEPA prohibits uninformed, not unwise, agency action. [*Id.* at 351]. The EIS must describe the environmental consequences of agency action-nothing more. [42 U.S.C. § 4332(2)(C)].

Adequate agency consideration is shown by an EIS's form, content, and preparation. * * *. It must include a detailed statement on the following: (1) the environmental impact of the proposed action; (2) adverse effects that cannot be avoided; (3) alternative, less intrusive action; (4) the relationship between local short term gain and universal long term benefit; and (5) irreversible commitment of resources to the proposed action. [42 U.S.C. § 4332(2)(C)] * * *

Often an initial EIS is sufficient, but sometimes an EIS must be supplemented. [Marsh v. Oregon Natural Resources Council, 490 U.S. 360, 370-374 (1989)]. The Council on Environmental Quality implements NEPA regulations, which require agency supplementation when there are "*significant* new circumstances or information relevant to environmental concerns." [40 C.F.R. § 1502.9(c)(1)(ii) (2003) (emphasis added)]. * * *

In *Marsh,* the Supreme Court considered NEPA when new information emerged, and held that an agency must take a "hard look" at new information to determine if supplementation is necessary. [*Marsh*, 490 U.S. at 385]. The Court explained that an agency must apply a rule of reason and prepare a supplemental EIS: (1) when a

---

a. For readability, the court's footnotes have been eliminated and the citations moved to the text.

major federal project is pending; (2) the new information significantly affects environmental quality; or (3) the environment is affected to an extent not already considered. [*Id.* at 374]. Courts should carefully review the record to determine that the agency made a reasoned decision based on its evaluation of the significance of the new information. [*Id.* at 360, 378]. * * *.

Applying these directions, the Corps and the FWS are required to: (1) take a "hard look" at the rediscovery of the IBW; (2) consider its significance to the environment; (3) decide on reasonable grounds if completion and operation of the project will have a substantial effect on the IBW; and (4) determine if the IBW is a species that is so unique compared to other area wildlife, that effects on its recovery and survival were not considered when the project was first conceived.

2. Standards of Review under the APA

The APA sets forth the standard of review for NEPA requirements. * * * Under the APA, an agency administrative decision may be set aside only if it is "arbitrary, capricious, and an abuse of discretion, or otherwise not in accordance with law," [5 U.S.C. § 706(2)(A)]; "in excess of statutory authority;" [*Id.* at § 706(2)(C)]; or "without observance of procedure required by law." [*Id.* at § 706(2)(D)]. A decision is arbitrary or capricious if the agency relied on factors forbidden by Congress, did not consider an important aspect of the problem, and offered an explanation that is implausible or contrary to the evidence. * * * Unless it is shown that the Corps and FWS blocked out informed opinion and overextended their reach, their judgment should be accepted.

On the other hand, despite this highly deferential standard of review, courts shouldn't rubber-stamp administrative decisions that are inconsistent with statutory purpose or frustrate congressional policy. * * * Even if the agency uses flawed data, its decision will be set aside only if "there is a significant chance that, but for the errors, the agency might have reached a different result." [*Central South Dakota Co-op. Grazing District v. Secretary of United States Department of Agriculture*, 266 F.3d 889, 899 (8th Cir. 2001).]

3. Injunctive Relief under NEPA

There is no statutory authority for injunctive relief under NEPA; therefore, any request for a preliminary injunction is governed by Fed.R.Civ.P. 65 and traditional equitable doctrine. Plaintiffs must show: (1) the threat of irreparable harm; (2) the balance between this harm and the injury that granting the injunction will inflict on other parties; (3) the probability of success on the merits; and (4) the public interest. [*Dataphase Systems, Inc. v. C.L. Systems, Inc.*, 640 F.2d 109 (1981)]. * * *

4. Analysis

The impact of the GPP on the White River, its wetlands, and bottomland forest was addressed by the earlier decision. The Court found that the "stop-pump" provision described in the original EIS adequately addressed potential environmental damage to the area.

Once the IBW was discovered, the Corps evaluated the possible impact to particular areas of the forest considered most suitable to the IBW. An interagency team of the FWS, the Arkansas Game and Fish Commission ("ACFC"), and the Corps participated in field surveys and examined forest areas that would be disturbed by the canals, pipelines, and the pump station.

During their surveys, the interagency team identified the species and age of trees closest to construction sites and did not find trees typically used by the IBW for nesting, roosting, and foraging. The Corps designed the right-of-way of some pipelines to minimize detrimental effects to mature forest and moved the location of the pump station to avoid destruction of old-growth trees. After the survey, the Corps concluded that there would be no significant effect because: (1) there were no sightings of the IBW in the project zone; (2) the bottomland hardwoods and wetlands were not seriously threatened by the water withdrawal; and (3) the project would only involve destruction of 135 acres of trees in an area consisting of 263,662 acres of forest and wetlands. For the most part, the FWS agreed with the Corps' conclusions but suggested some additional preventative measures.

The FWS conceded that the "stop-pump" provision may not completely offset water reduction and its effects to "flood plain resources." To address those concerns, the FWS insisted on long-term water-flow monitoring. * * *

Applying NEPA directives under the APA standard of review-the Corps and the FWS did not act arbitrarily or capriciously. * * *

The Corps based its opinions on scientific observations of IBW habitat recorded by Hoyt in 1905, Tanner in the 1930s and 1940s, and Dennis in 1948. It then examined the effect of the GPP on trees preferred for nesting, roosting, and foraging. By studying the specific habitat of the IBW, the Corps and the FWS took a "hard look" at the rediscovery of the IBW; considered what is known about its habitat; reasonably evaluated the sites of the pumping station, and the largest pipeline; took steps to ensure that the water flow would be controlled to benefit the bottomland forest; and committed to pre-construction surveys to prevent habitat destruction.

In view of the highly deferential APA standard of review, Defendants conformed to NEPA directives. The FWS's conclusion that environmental effects on the IBW would not be significant enough to warrant a supplemental EIS complies with NEPA.

Under standards for injunctive relief outlined above, Plaintiffs did not show a likelihood of success on the merits. The request for preliminary injunctive relief under NEPA is DENIED. [The Court's ESA discussion is set out infra, p. 604.]

Notes

1. **Reiteration of NEPA's procedural emphasis.** NEPA is often described as "stop, think and disclose statute." The Supreme Court has repeatedly upheld that NEPA only imposes procedural duties. E.g., Strycker's Bay Neighborhood Council v. Karlen, 444 U.S. 223 (1980); Robertson v. Methow Valley Citizens Council, 490 U.S. 332 (1989). In the latter case, the Court said:

"The sweeping policy goals announced in § 101 of NEPA are thus realized through a set of 'action forcing' procedures that require that agencies take a 'hard look' at environmental consequences, and that provide for broad dissemination of relevant environmental information. Although these procedures are almost certain to affect the agency's substantive decision, it is now well settled that NEPA itself does not mandate particular results, but simply prescribes the necessary process. If the adverse environmental effects of the proposed action are adequately identified and evaluated, the agency is not constrained by NEPA from deciding that other values outweigh the environmental costs. * * * Other statutes may impose substantive environmental obligations on federal agencies, but NEPA merely prohibits uninformed—rather than unwise-agency action." (internal quotation marks omitted).

2. **Mandate to consider the environment.** Although NEPA may not require federal agencies to actually protect the environment, it is substantive in at least one regard; it requires agencies to consider environmental consequences in their decisionmaking. State environmental policy acts have a similar effect. See, e.g., Stempel v. Dep't of Water Res., supra p. 558, Note 4, holding that the Washington Department of Water Resources was required by the state environmental policy act to consider environmental effects in issuing a water right permit, although prior to the adoption of the act the Department had no such authority under a water law statute directing it to consider the "public welfare."

However, NEPA does not expand a federal agency's regulatory powers. Thus, in Natural Resources Defense Council v. Environmental Protection Agency, 859 F.2d 156 (D.C. Cir. 1988), the court held that while the EPA's authority to regulate the discharge of pollutants under the Clean Water Act allows it to impose "NEPA-inspired" conditions on discharges, NEPA does not expand EPA's authority to regulate discharges into a mandate to regulate plants and facilities producing the discharges.

3. **Utility of nonsubstantive environmental policy acts.** If an environmental policy act does not provide substantive protection to the environment, what is the utility in requiring the identification and exposition of environmental effects? Identification of environmental effects

may cause the agency to change a project or decision, to pursue alternatives, or to abandon it altogether. Pressure from other governmental agencies who review the EIS or public reaction to the disclosures of the EIS may result in modification or abandonment of the proposed action. The environmental consequences revealed in the EIS may also trigger the application of substantive environmental statutes, such as the Endangered Species Act, discussed in subsection D. Finally, the NEPA process itself is fertile ground for administrative and judicial challenges which can be used to delay agency decisions or force their reconsideration.

4. **Effectiveness of NEPA.** Kathleen A. McGinty, *transmittal letter* to Council on Environmental Quality, The National Environmental Policy Act, A Study of Its Effectiveness After Twenty-five Years, at iii (1997):

"Overall, what we found is that NEPA is a success—it has made agencies take a hard look at the potential environmental consequences of their actions, and it has brought the public into the agency decision-making process like no other statute. * * * Despite these successes, however, NEPA's implementation at times has fallen short of its goals. For example, this NEPA Effectiveness Study finds that agencies may sometime confuse the purpose of NEPA. Some act as if the detailed statement called for in the statute is an end it itself, rather than a tool to enhance and improve decision-making. * * * The Study finds that agencies sometimes engage in consultation only after a decision has—for all practical purposes—been made. * * * Other matters of concern to participants in the Study were the length of NEPA processes, the extensive detail of NEPA analyses, and the sometime confusing overlay of other laws and regulations."

5. **Substantive state environmental policy acts.** Many of the state environmental policy acts are more substantive than NEPA. Where feasible, several state acts require that an agency minimize or mitigate environmental effects or that it adopt less destructive alternatives. E.g., Cal. Pub. Res. Code § 21081; Minn. Stat. § 116D.04, subd. 6. The Minnesota statute states that "economic considerations alone" shall not justify agency action where a less destructive alternative exists. Although the Washington Supreme Court said that the state's environmental policy act (SEPA) did not mandate any particular substantive result in Stempel v. Department of Water Resources., supra p. 558, Note 2, a later decision by the Washington Court of Appeals said that if there are no important benefits to offset severe environmental consequences the courts would be warranted in holding that government action violates the substantive policies of SEPA. Ullock v. City of Bremerton, 565 P.2d 1179 (Wash. Ct. App. 1977).

6. **Wild and Scenic Rivers Act.** Balancing costs and benefits project by project, even with careful consideration of environmental factors, may keep a river in constant jeopardy and subject to small incursions that may add up to ruin. Congress opted for absolutes in the Wild and Scenic Rivers Act of 1968, 16 U.S.C. § 1271, which declared a policy that certain selected rivers, and their immediate environments, which possess

outstandingly remarkable scenic, recreational, geologic, fish and wildlife, historic, cultural or similar values, should be preserved in free-flowing condition and their environment protected for the benefit and enjoyment of present and future generations. Congress declared that the established national policy of dam and other construction on rivers needed to be complemented by a policy that will preserve other selected rivers or sections thereof. Section 3 of the Act identified three types of eligible streams: (1) wild rivers, free of impoundments and generally inaccessible except by trail, "vestiges of primitive America," (2) scenic rivers, free of impoundments with shoreline or watersheds largely primitive and undeveloped, but accessible in places by roads, and (3) recreational rivers, already accessible by road or railroad, that have some developments and impoundments upon them. 16 U.S.C. § 1273. The Act designated eight rivers as the National Wild and Scenic River System, and named more for further study. Others may be studied by the Secretary of the Interior (or the Secretary of Agriculture if they flow through national forest) and, if the Secretaries so recommend, may be included in the system by Congress. States may nominate still others, which will be recommended to the Congress if approved by the Secretary of the Interior. By 1995 over 150 rivers were included and many more were under study.

The principal effect of designation as a component of the National Wild and Scenic River System is the institution of a land use planning and management system for the banks and environs of the river. In addition, the Act prohibits the Federal Energy Regulatory Commission from licensing the construction of any dam, powerhouse, or transmission line on or directly affecting the rivers in the system or designated for study, and no other federal department may assist by loan, grant, license or otherwise in the construction of any water resources project that would have a direct and adverse effect on the values for which the river was established, except with the express permission of the Secretary of the Interior or Secretary of Agriculture, whichever is in charge of administering the particular river. The Act provides interim protection for rivers under study by the Secretaries.

B. Water Quality Regulation

INTRODUCTORY NOTE

Relation to Water Law. Water quality control presents only a peripheral aspect of water law. Traditionally, water law is concerned primarily with the allocation of water, i.e., with quantity, not quality. A person who gets rid of a noxious or offensive substance by discharging it into water does receive a benefit, and the discharge may make the water as unavailable to another as if it had been consumed. Conversely, a person who reduces the flow of a stream that dilutes a downstream influx of foreign matter may increase the concentration of the substance to intolerable limits. (See, e.g., Colorado Wild, Inc. v.

U.S. Forest Serv., 122 F. Supp. 2d 1190 (D. Colo. 2000) (ski resort's diversions for artificial snowmaking would increase concentration of toxic metals).) Nevertheless, historically, there has been little interplay between water law and pollution control law. The discharger was seldom treated as a water user, and while the diverter might be restrained, it would be by water law, not pollution law.

Sometimes a riparian proprietor was said to have the right to freedom from harmful water pollution, Sandusky Portland Cement Co. v. Dixon Pure Ice Co., 221 F. 200 (7th Cir. 1915); sometimes an upper riparian's use of a stream for waste disposal was said to be an unreasonable exercise of his riparian rights; and sometimes a polluter defended fouling the stream as an exercise of his riparian rights, Hazeltine v. Case, 1 N.W. 66 (Wis. 1879). In many cases, however, these property theories had no application. In some the polluter was not a riparian, in some the plaintiff had no status as a riparian although he suffered serious harm. E.g., Kennebunk, Kennebunkport & Wells Water Dist. v. Me. Tpk. Auth., 71 A.2d 520 (1950).

In the western states similar problems are raised by attempts to apply appropriation law to pollution problems. An appropriator may complain of pollution of his water supply, Game & Fish Commission v. Farmer's Irrigation Co., 426 P.2d 562 (Colo. 1967), but can a riparian who is not an appropriator complain of water pollution in an appropriation state? See Conley v. Amalgamated Sugar Co., 263 P.2d 705 (Idaho 1953). Does an appropriator obtain a prior right to water quality that cannot be impaired by later upstream users of the stream? See Dripps v. Allison's Mines Co., 187 P. 448 (Cal. 1919). Does an appropriator whose use deteriorates the quality of water returned to the stream obtain a prior right to continue this "use" although it prevents beneficial use by subsequent downstream appropriators? Compare State v. Cal. Packing Corp., 141 P.2d 386 (Utah 1943), with Suffolk Gold Mining & Milling Co. v. San Miguel Consol. Mining & Milling Co., 48 P. 828 (Colo. 1897).

Riparian and appropriation law did not produce very satisfactory results in pollution cases. The emphasis on property doctrines tended to obscure the real factors of decision. Better results were obtained when the courts applied nuisance theories, as in American Cyanamid Co. v. Sparto, 267 F.2d 425 (5th Cir. 1959). In western states which gave no recognition to riparian rights, nuisance was often used in water pollution cases. E.g., N. Point Consol. Irr. Co. v. Utah & Salt Lake Canal Co., 52 P. 168 (Utah 1898). The American Law Institute has taken the firm position that "[t]he pollution of water by a riparian proprietor that creates a nuisance by causing harm to another proprietor's interest in land or water is not the exercise of a riparian right." Restatement (Second) of Torts, § 849(2) (1979).

Pollution of surface and groundwaters was a fertile field for litigation, and there were many suits for redress of wrongs and injunctions against permanent damage. These cases built up a substantial body of doctrine. Nuisance law has its intricacies—e.g., balancing utility against harm, public nuisance, and coming to the nuisance. None of this litigation had much effect upon the overall quality of water, and all these questions lie outside the field of water law as such.

THE CLEAN WATER ACT

Prior to 1948 pollution control was almost entirely a state effort. The first Water Pollution Control Act, 62 Stat. 1155 (1948), offered state agencies a program of investigations, research and funds for operations and treatment works. It set up a complex enforcement system of notices, conferences, hearings and legal proceedings to abate pollution of interstate waters, but it was completely ineffective. In 1961, the Act was extended to all navigable waters, and in 1965 more amendments required the states to establish water quality standards for interstate streams. To simplify enforcement, federal proceedings could be brought against persons who violated the standards even though no harm or threat to health was shown. Where numbers of polluters were involved, however, problems of proof were difficult, and practical and economic difficulties were excuses for non-compliance and variances.

The sleeping beauty of federal water pollution control turned out to be section 13 of the Rivers and Harbors Act of 1899, 33 U.S.C. § 407. This law made it unlawful to discharge or deposit any refuse of any kind, other liquids flowing from streets and sewers, into navigable waters without a permit from the Secretary of the Army. For years this provision was applied only to discharges that threatened to impede navigation. Dusted off in 1970, rechristened the "Refuse Act," applied to all industrial discharges, administered by the Corps of Engineers under guidelines issued by the EPA, the Act became the first effective federal regulation of water pollution. It became the model for the comprehensive Federal Water Pollution Control Act Amendments of 1972. The "amendments" rewrote the old Act completely and replaced the Refuse Act. They have since been renamed the Clean Water Act, codified at 33 U.S.C. §§ 1251 et seq.

The 1972 amendments departed sharply from prior federal efforts in policy and approach. First, Congress made a philosophical shift regarding pollution. Prior to 1972, pollution was unacceptable only if it threatened the health or welfare of people or violated water quality standards, based on federally required, state-promulgated "receiving water standards." In contrast, the 1972 amendments indicate that it is no longer acceptable to use waterways to dispose of waste. This policy is embodied in section 101(a)(1), 33 U.S.C. § 1251(a)(1), which states that "it is the national goal that the discharge of pollutants be eliminated." The amendments recognized that some pollution would continue, at least for the short term, not because it was acceptable but because it was technologically impossible to eliminate all pollution. Second, the 1972 amendments "federalize" water pollution control efforts; federal law and federal agencies have the dominant role, although the states remain important participants. Third, the principal focus of the amendments is on the pollutants, not on the harm done or the water itself. "Effluent limitations," based on technologically achievable treatment, are imposed on all "point source" discharges into surface waters. A system of permits transforms the general effluent limitations into specific treatment and clean-up requirements for each discharger.

Point Source Pollution. The Clean Water Act makes its most vigorous and successful attack on "point source pollution." The act defines a "point source" as "any discernible, confined, and discrete conveyance, including but not limited to any pipe, ditch, channel, tunnel, conduit, well, discrete fissure, container, rolling stock, concentrated animal feeding operation, or vessel or other floating craft from which pollutants are or may be discharged." 33 U.S.C. § 1362(14). With limited exceptions, it is illegal to discharge pollutants from a point source unless a permit issued pursuant to the National Pollution Elimination Discharge System (NPDES) has been obtained. See 33 U.S.C. §§ 1311 and 1342. The NPDES permit sets maximum discharge levels for various pollutants based on uniform national effluent limitations that reflect various levels of technological capabilities. Id. The permit also establishes monitoring and reporting requirements and delineates the permittee's obligations. 33 U.S.C. § 1342(a)(2).

While the act provides for the consideration of economic factors in some situations, technology provides the basic determinant in setting the limitations. The act sets various general standards (e.g., "best available technology economically achievable," "best conventional pollutant control technology," called "BAT" and "BCT" respectively) for existing sources of various types of pollutants (e.g., "toxic pollutants," "conventional pollutants,") and establishes deadlines for achieving the standards. See 33 U.S.C. § 1311. The standards and deadlines have been modified several times since adoption of the 1972 amendments. Toxic pollutants and new sources of pollution are required to meet separate standards. 33 U.S.C §§ 1316, 1317. The general standards have limited intrinsic meaning and must be translated into specific limitations which are established for various industries or for classes or categories within a particular industry. Effluent limitations may be expressed in various ways, including maximum allowable concentrations (e.g., pounds per day), maximum rates of discharge (e.g., parts per million), or maximum discharges per unit of production (e.g., pounds per ton of steel produced).

Nonpoint Source Pollution. Much water pollution originates from nonpoint sources, such as farm lands, city streets, construction sites, road building, logging operations, cleared lands, junkyards, and dumps. In general, nonpoint source pollution is generated by land use activities, is discharged into waters by natural processes, such as run-off and precipitation, rather than being deliberately discharged, and is not susceptible to "end-of-pipe" treatment. Congress recognized that the number and variety of nonpoint sources of pollution, the site-specific nature of such pollution, the lack of known control technologies, and the perception that many of the problems could only be addressed through land use control, a traditional state function, made nonpoint source pollution unsuited to the NPDES.

In the 1972 amendments, Congress chose to address nonpoint source pollution through the section 208 planning process. 33 U.S.C. § 1288. Section 208 requires the governor of each state to designate a local planning agency to develop a "continuing areawide waste treatment management process" for areas that have substantial water quality control problems. Id. § 1288(a)-(b). A section 208 plan must identify nonpoint source pollution. Id. § 1288(b)(2)(F). The plan must also identify methods to control nonpoint source pollution, primarily through "best management practices" or land use controls. Id. Section 319, 33 U.S.C. § 1329, added in 1987, directed states to submit to EPA a report describing nonpoint source problems and to develop and submit a management plan for controlling nonpoint source pollution.

Water Quality Standards. Although effluent limitations are the primary control device, the Clean Water Act retains water quality standards in a secondary role. The act requires states to establish and periodically review water quality standards, pursuant to regulations developed by EPA. 33 U.S.C. § 1313. Water quality standards consist of "designated uses" for each body of water and "water quality criteria" sufficient to protect such uses. 33 U.S.C. §§ 1313(c)(2)(A), 40 C.F.R. § 130.2(d). Waste transport and waste assimilation are not permissible designated uses, 40 C.F.R. § 131.10; an antidegradation policy is required, 40 C.F.R. § 131.12(a); where actual quality allows a water to be fishable and swimmable, that quality must be maintained "except to accommodate economic or social development in the locality," id. § 131.12(a)(2); water quality of "outstanding natural resources" must be maintained and protected, id. § 131.12(a)(3).

States must identify and prioritize waters for which the technology based effluent limitations are not stringent enough to implement applicable water quality standards, known as "water quality limited segments." 33 U.S.C. § 1313(d)(1)(A), 40 C.F.R. §§ 130.2 (j), 131.3(h). States must establish the "total maximum daily load" (TMDL) for various pollutants in each water quality limited segment. 33 U.S.C. § 1313(d)(1)(C), 40 C.F.R. § 130.7(c)(1). A TMDL is the maximum amount of a pollutant that a water can receive without violating water quality standards. 33 U.S.C. § 1313(d)(1)(C), 40 C.F.R. § 130.2(e)-(i). TMDLs are allocated to contributing point and nonpoint sources of pollution, 40 C.F.R. § 130.2(g)-(h), and can result in the application of more stringent effluent limitations through the NPDES process. See 33 U.S.C. § 1313(e)(3)(A), 40 C.F.R. §130.7. Unlike the NPDES process, which focuses on individual discharges, the TMDL process focuses on the cumulative effect on a water body of all pollution. More stringent effluent limitations can also be imposed to meet the act's goal of making all water fishable and swimmable. 33 U.S.C. § 1312.

Federal and State Roles. The Environmental Protection Agency has initial responsibility for administering the NPDES program. 33 U.S.C. § 1342(a). A state may assume administration if it has an approved program meeting specified criteria, and most have done so. Id. § (b). EPA retains the authority to review each permit and veto those it determines are not incompliance with the act. Id. § (d). EPA may withdraw approval of a state program if it determines the program is not being administered in accordance with the act. Id. § (c)(3). EPA also establishes NPDES effluent limitations. 33 U.S.C. § 1314(b). The states initially set water quality standards, but EPA must review and approve the standards and can set them if a state fails to do so or if it sets unsatisfactory standards. 33 U.S.C. §1313(a)-(c). EPA identifies pollutants that are suitable for the TMDL approach, 33 U.S.C. § 1314(a)(2), and must review and approve state identified water quality limited segments and established TMDLs. 33 U.S.C. § 1313(d)(2). Although the states have primary responsibility for nonpoint source pollution, EPA must approve section 208 plans and section 319 assessment reports and management plans. 33 U.S.C. §§ 1288(b)(3), 1329(d); see also section 303(e), 33 U.S.C. § 1313(e).

For a historical overview of federal legislative efforts to control water pollution, with a contemporary focus on the TMDL program, see Kenneth M. Murchison, Learning From More Than Five-And-A-Half Decades of Federal Water Pollution Control Legislation: Twenty Lessons for the Future, 32 B.C. Envtl. Aff. L. Rev. 527 (2005).

FRIENDS OF THE EVERGLADES v. SOUTH FLORIDA WATER MANAGEMENT DISTRICT
United States Court of Appeals, Eleventh Circuit, 2009.
570 F.3d 1210.

CARNES, Circuit Judge:

This appeal turns on whether the transfer of a pollutant from one navigable body of water to another is a "discharge of a pollutant" within the meaning of the Clean Water Act, 33 U.S.C. § 1362(12). If it is, a National Pollution Discharge Elimination System permit is required. 33 U.S.C. §§ 1311(a), 1342(a). The Act defines "discharge of a pollutant," but the meaning of that definition is itself disputed. During the course of this litigation, the Environmental Protection Agency adopted a regulation addressing this specific matter. The issue we face * * * is whether we owe that EPA regulation deference under Chevron, U.S.A., Inc. v. Natural Res. Defense Council, Inc., [467 U.S. 837 (1984)].

I.

The unique geography of South Florida is once again before us. * * * Lake Okeechobee is part of that geography. Historically, the lake had an ill-defined southern shoreline because during rainy seasons it overflowed, spilling a wide, shallow sheet of water overland to the Florida Bay. * * *

In the 1930s the Herbert Hoover Dike was built along the southern shore of Lake Okeechobee. It was intended to control flooding but failed during the hurricanes of 1947 and 1948. Congress then authorized the Central and Southern Florida Flood Project * * *. Under * * * that project, nearly all water flow in South Florida is controlled by a complex system of gates, dikes, canals, and pump stations.

The area south of Lake Okeechobee's shoreline was designated the Everglades Agricultural Area. The Corps dug canals there to collect rainwater and runoff from the sugar cane fields and the surrounding industrial and residential areas. Not surprisingly, those canals contain a loathsome concoction of chemical contaminants including nitrogen, phosphorous, and un-ionized ammonia. The water in the canals is full of suspended and dissolved solids and has a low oxygen content.

Those polluted canals connect to Lake Okeechobee, which is now virtually surrounded by the Hoover Dike. The S-2, S-3, and S-4 pump stations are built into the dike and pump water from the lower levels in the canals outside the dike into the higher lake water. * * *. This process moves the water containing Agricultural Area contaminants uphill into Lake Okeechobee, a distance of some sixty feet. The pumps do not add anything to the canal water; they simply move it through pipes. * * *. The South Florida Water Management District operates the pumping stations.

* * *

III.

* * * [W]e turn now to whether the S-2, S-3, and S-4 pumps require NPDES permits. The Clean Water Act bans the "discharge of any pollutant" without a permit. 33 U.S.C. §§ 1311, 1342(a)(1). "Dis-

charge" is defined as "any addition of any pollutant to navigable waters from any point source." 33 U.S.C. § 1362(12).

It is undisputed that the agricultural and industrial runoff in the canals contains "pollutants," that Lake Okeechobee and the canals are "navigable waters," and that these three pump stations are "point sources" even though they add nothing to the water as they move it along. *See* S. Fla. Water Mgmt. Dist. v. Miccosukee Tribe, [541 U.S. 95, 102, 105 (2004)]. The question is whether moving an existing pollutant from one navigable water body to another is an "addition * * * to navigable waters" of that pollutant. The district court decided that it is, but that decision came before the EPA adopted its regulation. * * *

A.

The Water District's central argument is based on the "unitary waters" theory. That theory is derived from the dictionary definition of the word "addition," which is not defined in the Act. * * * The dictionary definition of "addition" is "to join, annex, or unite" so as to increase the overall number or amount of something. *Webster's Third New International Dictionary* 24 (1993).

The unitary waters theory holds that it is not an "addition * * * to navigable waters" to move existing pollutants from one navigable water to another. An addition occurs, under this theory, only when pollutants first enter navigable waters from a point source, not when they are moved between navigable waters. The metaphor the Supreme Court has adopted to explain the unitary waters theory is: "If one takes a ladle of soup from a pot, lifts it above the pot, and pours it back into the pot, one has not 'added' soup or anything else to the pot." *Miccosukee*, [541 U.S. at 110] (alteration and quotation marks omitted). Under that metaphor the navigable waters of the United States are not a multitude of different pots, but one pot. Ladling pollution from one navigable water to another does not add anything to the pot. So no NPDES permit is required to do that.

* * *

In sum, all of the existing precedent and the statements in our own vacated decision are against the unitary waters theory. * * * If nothing had changed, we might make it unanimous. But there has been a change. An important one. Under its regulatory authority, the EPA has recently issued a regulation adopting a final rule specifically addressing this very question. Because that regulation was not available at the time of the earlier decisions, they are not precedent against it. We are the first court to address the "addition * * * to navigable waters" issue in light of the regulation—to decide whether the regulation is due *Chevron* deference.

B.

The EPA's new regulation, which became final on June 13, 2008, explains that it was adopted to:

> clarify that water transfers are not subject to regulation under the National Pollution Discharge Elimination System (NPDES) permitting program. This rule defines water transfers as an activity that conveys or connects waters of the United States without subjecting the transferred water to intervening industrial, municipal, or commercial use.

NPDES Water Transfers Rule, 73 Fed.Reg. 33,697-708 (June 13, 2008) (codified at 40 C.F.R. § 122.3(i)). Everyone agrees that the EPA's regulation is entitled to *Chevron* deference if it is a reasonable construction of an ambiguous statute. * * *

In other words, there must be two or more reasonable ways to interpret the statute, and the regulation must adopt one of those ways. * * *

C.

Both sides pitch several decisions to us. The Water District * * * throws us National Wildlife Federation v. Consumers Power Co., 862 F.2d 580 (6th Cir. 1988), and National Wildlife Federation v. Gorsuch, 693 F.2d 156 (D.C. Cir. 1982). In those cases the courts concluded that the "discharge of a pollutant" language in the Clean Water Act was ambiguous and deferred to the EPA's view that dams did not add pollutants, which meant that no NPDES permits were necessary. 862 F.2d at 584-85; 693 F.2d at 183. The issues those cases addressed, however, were different from the one before us.

In *Gorsuch* the National Wildlife Federation sued the EPA for failing to require NPDES permits for dams. 693 F.2d at 161. The man-made dams and their reservoirs caused changes in the water's temperature, nutrient loads, and oxygen content, and the affected water was then released through the dams into the rivers below. Id. The EPA gave two reasons why no permit was required: (1) the changes caused by the dams were not pollutants; and (2) even if they were, releasing water through a dam did not add those pollutants to the water because the water would have reached the downstream river anyway, and its passage through the dam did not change it. Id. at 165. The D.C. Circuit concluded that neither the language of the statute nor its legislative history conclusively supported either side's position about what "discharge of a pollutant" meant under the circumstances of that case, so the court deferred to the EPA's position. * * *

In doing so, the *Gorsuch* court accepted the EPA's position that colder water and changes in oxygen and dissolved nutrient content were not pollutants at all. Id. at 174. That rendered irrelevant whether the changed water was being "added" to navigable water by its movement through a dam. In any event, the water was moving from a river above a dam to the same river below it. * * *

The other decision the Water District pitches us is *Consumers Power*. In that case a power plant sucked water containing some unlucky fish out of Lake Michigan, pumped the water uphill, and then directed it and the fish back downhill through turbines that generated electricity. 862 F.2d at 581. In the process the turbines pureed some of the fish and spewed the fish puree back into Lake Michigan. Id. at 581-82. The plant was a "dam" for permitting purposes because part of the generating process involved impounding water. Id. at 589-90. Deferring to the EPA's position, the Sixth Circuit concluded that "any entrained fish released with the ... facility's turbine generating water originate in Lake Michigan and do not enter the Lake from the outside world." Id. at 585. Fish, living or dead, are biological material under the Clean Water Act, and the fish in *Consumers Power* had always existed in the same lake to which the power plant returned them. *See id.* * * *

Gorsuch and *Consumers Power* involved water that wound up where it would have gone anyway. That is not the case here. Water from the agricultural canals would not flow upstream into Lake Okeechobee if the S-2, S-3, and S-4 pumps did not move it there. Here, unlike in *Gorsuch* and *Consumers Power*, pollutants are being moved between meaningfully distinct water bodies. * * *

The Friends of the Everglades, arguing against ambiguity, pitch us other decisions. * * * Because they all came out before the EPA's new regulation went into effect, none of those decisions addressed * * * whether the EPA's interpretation of the statutory language is reasonable, even if we might prefer another one. * * *

IV.

In the first step of *Chevron* analysis we apply the traditional tools of statutory construction to ascertain whether Congress had a specific intent on the precise question before us. *See Chevron*, [467 U.S. at 843 n. 9]. * * * If Congress did, then the statute is not ambiguous and *Chevron* has no role to play. The traditional tools of statutory construction include "examination of the text of the statute, its structure, and its stated purpose." Miami-Dade County v. EPA, 529 F.3d 1049, 1063 (11th Cir. 2008) * * *.

A.

The Clean Water Act outlaws "the discharge of any pollutant" subject to several exceptions, one of which is where an NPDES permit is obtained. 33 U.S.C. §§ 1311, 1342(a)(1). "Discharge" includes "any addition of any pollutant to navigable waters from any point source." 33 U.S.C. § 1362(12). "Navigable waters," in turn, is defined as "the waters of the United States." 33 U.S.C. § 1362(7). * * *

The question is whether "addition ... to navigable waters"—meaning addition to "the waters of the United States"—refers to waters in the individual sense or as one unitary whole. * * * Because the statutory language could be used either way, we turn next to its immediate context.

B.

* * * The Water District argues that the context of 33 U.S.C. § 1362(12) demonstrates that Congress intentionally selected each word in the definition of "discharge" to deliver a specific meaning. It asserts that the Friends of the Everglades' reading of the statute would require us to add words to the law, which is impermissible.

"Discharge" is defined in the Act as "[a]ny addition of any pollutant to navigable waters from any point source." 33 U.S.C. § 1362(12). According to the Water District, the conspicuous absence of "any" before "navigable waters" in § 1362(12) supports the unitary waters theory because it implies that Congress was not talking about *any* navigable water, but about *all* navigable waters as a whole. The Friends of the Everglades' reading effectively asks us to add a fourth "any" to the statute so that it would read: "Any addition of any pollutant to *any* navigable waters from any point source."

* * *

[The] context does not, however, establish that the meaning of the statutory language is clear. Although Congress did use the term "any navigable waters" in the Clean Water Act to protect individual water bodies, it also used the unmodified "navigable waters" to mean the same thing. * * *

The result so far is that we are not persuaded that the meaning of the statutory provision at issue, read either in isolation or in conjunction with similar provisions, is plain one way or the other. The statutory context indicates that sometimes the term "navigable waters" was used in one sense and sometimes in the other sense.

C.

The "broader context of the statute as a whole" does not resolve the ambiguity. *Robinson*, [519 U.S. at 341]; *see also Koons Buick*, [543 U.S. at 60] (explaining that a seemingly ambiguous provision may be clarified by the broad context of the statute if "only one of the permissible meanings produces a substantive effect that is compatible with the rest of the law"). The general purpose of the Clean Water Act is broad and ambitious:

> The objective of this chapter is to restore and maintain the chemical, physical, and biological integrity of the Nation's waters. In order to achieve this objective it is hereby declared that, consistent with the provisions of this chapter—(1) it is the national goal that

the discharge of pollutants into the navigable waters be eliminated by 1985 * * *.

33 U.S.C. § 1251(a). The NPDES permitting program is the center-piece of the Clean Water Act. * * * In light of the sweeping goals of the Act, the Senate Conference Report states that the "conferees fully intend that the term 'navigable waters' be given the broadest possible constitutional interpretation * * *"[9] S. Rep. No. 92-1236 (1972) (Conf. Rep.), *reprinted in* 1972 U.S.C.C.A.N. 3776, 3822. The Friends of the Everglades argue that * * * the Clean Water Act's ambitious anti-pollution goals make it absurd to read the Act as implicitly creating a sizeable exception to the NPDES permitting program for pollutants that come from other navigable waters.

* * * If an "addition * * * to navigable waters" occurs only at a pollutant's first entry into navigable waters, and not when it is transferred to a different water body, then the NPDES program—the centerpiece of the Clean Water Act—would require no permit to pump the most loathsome navigable water in the country into the most pristine one.

These horrible hypotheticals are frightening enough that we might agree with the Friends of the Everglades that the unitary waters theory does not comport with the broad, general goals of the Clean Water Act. * * * But we "interpret and apply statutes, not congressional purposes." In re Hedrick, 524 F.3d 1175, 1188 (11th Cir. 2008); * * * And there are other provisions of the Clean Water Act that do not comport with its broad purpose of restoring and maintaining the chemical, physical and biological integrity of the Nation's waters. (Which may help explain why the Act's express goal of completely eliminating all discharge of pollutants into the navigable waters by 1985 was not met.)

No one disputes that the NPDES program is restricted to point sources. Non-point source pollution, chiefly runoff, is widely recognized as a serious water quality problem, but the NPDES program does not even address it. *See generally* Rapanos, [547 U.S. at 777] (Kennedy, J., concurring) (observing that agricultural runoff from farms along the Mississippi River creates an annual hypoxic "dead zone" in the Gulf of Mexico that is nearly the size of New Jersey) * * *. Not only are ordinary non-point sources outside the NPDES program, but Congress even created a special exception to the definition of "point source" to exclude agricultural storm water discharges and re-

---

9. That statement appears intended to extend the application of the Clean Water Act to cover as much water as the Commerce Clause would allow. *See generally Rapanos v. United States,* 547 U.S. 715 * * * (2006). The question before us is not the constitutional reach of the Act but the meaning of specific statutory language where the Act does apply.

turn flows from irrigation, despite their known, substantially harmful impact on water quality. 33 U.S.C. § 1362(14).

The point is that it may seem inconsistent with the lofty goals of the Clean Water Act to leave out of the permitting process the transfer of pollutants from one navigable body of water to another, but it is no more so than to leave out all non-point sources, allowing agricultural run-offs to create a huge "dead zone" in the Gulf of Mexico. Yet we know the Act does that. What this illustrates is that even when the preamble to legislation speaks single-mindedly and espouses lofty goals, the legislative process serves as a melting pot of competing interests and a face-off of battling factions. What emerges from the conflict to become the enactment is often less pure than the preamble promises. The provisions of legislation reflect compromises cobbled together by competing political forces, and compromise is the enemy of single-mindedness. * * *

As the Supreme Court once said, "[a]fter seizing every thing from which aid can be derived we are left with an ambiguous statute." United States v. Bass, [404 U.S. 336 (1971)]. There are two reasonable ways to read the § 1361(12) language "any addition of any pollutant to navigable waters from any point source." One is that it means "any addition * * * to [any] navigable waters;" the other is that it means "any addition * * * to navigable waters [as a whole]." As we have held before, "the existence of two reasonable, competing interpretations is the very definition of ambiguity." United States v. Acosta, 363 F.3d 1141, 1155 (11th Cir. 2004) (quotation marks omitted).

D.

Having concluded that the statutory language is ambiguous, our final issue is whether the EPA's regulation, which accepts the unitary waters theory that transferring pollutants between navigable waters is not an "addition * * * to navigable waters," is a permissible construction of that language. *Chevron* [467 U.S. at 843]. * * * Because the EPA's construction is one of the two readings we have found is reasonable, we cannot say that it is "arbitrary, capricious, or manifestly contrary to the statute." [Id. at 844].

Sometimes it is helpful to strip a legal question of the contentious policy interests attached to it and think about it in the abstract using a hypothetical. Consider the issue this way: Two buckets sit side by side, one with four marbles in it and the other with none. There is a rule prohibiting "any addition of any marbles to buckets by any person." A person comes along, picks up two marbles from the first bucket, and drops them into the second bucket. Has the marble-mover "add[ed] any marbles to buckets"? On one hand, as the Friends of the Everglades might argue, there are now two marbles in a bucket where there were none before, so an addition of marbles has occurred. On the other hand, as the Water District might argue and as the EPA would decide, there were four marbles in buckets before, and there are still four marbles in buckets, so no addition of marbles has occurred. Whatever position we might take if we had to pick one side or the other we cannot say that either side is unreasonable.

Like the marbles rule, the Clean Water Act's language about "any addition of any pollutant to navigable waters from any point source," 33 U.S.C. § 1362(12), is ambiguous. The EPA's regulation adopting the unitary waters theory is a reasonable, and therefore permissible, construction of the language. Unless and until the EPA rescinds or Congress overrides the regulation, we must give effect to it.

In the defendants' appeal, we REVERSE the district court's judgment that the operation of the S-2, S-3, and S-4 pumps without NPDES permits violates the Clean Water Act. * * *

Notes

1. **Jurisdictional scope of the Clean Water Act.** The Clean Water Act regulates the "discharge of a pollutant" into "navigable waters." In South Florida Water Management District v. Miccosukee Tribe, 541 U.S. 95 (2004), cited in the principal case, and involving many of the same parties and issues, the Supreme Court addressed both elements.

It first rejected the District's interpretation of "discharge":

"In its opening brief on the merits, the District argued that the NPDES program applies to a point source 'only when a pollutant originates from the point source,' and not when pollutants originating elsewhere merely pass through the point source. * * *

"This initial argument is untenable, and even the District appears to have abandoned it in its reply brief. A point source is, by definition, a 'discernible, confined, and discrete conveyance.' § 1362(14) (emphasis added). That definition makes plain that a point source need not be the original source of the pollutant; it need only convey the pollutant to 'navigable waters'; which are, in turn, defined as 'the waters of the United States.' § 1362(7). Tellingly, the examples of 'point sources' listed by the Act include pipes, ditches, tunnels, and conduits, objects that do not themselves generate pollutants but merely transport them. § 1362(14). * * * We therefore reject the District's proposed reading of the definition of 'discharge of a pollutant' contained in § 1362(12). That definition includes within its reach point sources that do not themselves generate pollutants."

As the *Miccosukee* Court itself noted, the implications of this holding upon water conveyers in general, and voluntary water transfers in particular, was potentially sweeping. The EPA regulation upheld in the principal case was designed to avoid these implications.

The *Miccosukee* Court then reviewed the Clean Water Act's various references to the waters protected as "the Nation's water," "the navigable waters" and "the waters of the United States." These are essentially all water courses in the United States, not merely the classically "navigable waters of the United States" discussed infra pp. 632-34, Notes 2-3. In *Miccosukee*, because of the parties' failure to raise the issue below, the Court declined to rule on the "unitary" theory of "waters of the United States." This theory had been rejected by all of the appellate courts that had considered it until the court in the principal case. And, as discussed in the principal case, that court upheld the theory because it concluded it was required to defer to the EPA's regulation under the landmark administrative law case, *Chevron v. United States.*

2. **Failure of nonpoint source controls.** The NPDES program has made significant progress in reducing point source pollution. In contrast, much less progress has been made in controlling nonpoint source pollution. George A. Gould, Agriculture, Nonpoint Source Pollution and Federal Law, 23 U.C. Davis L. Rev. 461, 463-64 (1990):

"Nonpoint sources cause the predominant amount of pollution in sixty-five percent of streams and rivers in the United States not meeting water quality standards. In all but seventeen states, nonpoint sources exceed any other category of pollution in water quality impaired rivers and streams and account for more than ninety percent of the problem in five states. Nonpoint sources cause the predominant pollution in seventy-six percent of lake acres not meeting water quality standards. In all but eight states, nonpoint sources exceed any other category of pollution in water quality impaired lakes and cause one hundred percent of the problem in six states. Nonpoint sources account for forty-five percent of impaired estuarine waters and cause the predominant effects in nine of sixteen states reporting impaired estuarine waters."

The lack of success in controlling nonpoint source pollution stems partly from the complexity of the problem. Nonpoint source pollution cannot be controlled simply by attaching end-of-pipe treatment devices to production facilities, as can be done with point source pollution. See, e.g., Or. Natural Desert Ass'n v. U.S. Forest Serv., 550 F.3d. 778 (9th Cir. 2008) (grazing cattle are not "point sources"). Control of nonpoint source pollution requires fundamental changes in the activities and practices that generate the pollution. Such changes are not easy to induce. However, the failure to control nonpoint source pollution also stems from the lack of effective regulation. The act does not directly regulate nonpoint source pollution. Rather, it leaves it to the states to develop controls. See, e.g., Am. Wildlands v. Browner, 260 F.3d 1192 (10th Cir. 2001) (EPA has no direct authority over nonpoint sources). The states have relied primarily on voluntary strategies, and neither sections 208 nor 319 provide effective provisions to induce or require the states to implement mandatory controls.

3. **Implementation of the TMDL process.** The TMDL process has become the centerpiece of efforts to resolve the remaining water pollution problems. Initially, EPA made only limited efforts to discharge its responsibilities regarding the TMDL provisions, in large part because imple-

mentation of the point source provisions of the 1972 amendments consumed most of its energy. In addition, postponing vigorous implementation of the TMDL provisions was not wholly inconsistent with the CWA. The act requires that TMDLs be developed only for those waters for which application of uniform effluent limitations will not achieve water quality standards. Thus, it made some sense to delay implementation of the TMDL provisions until effluent limitations had been developed and the effect of their application on water quality through the NPDES process was clearer.

Completed implementation of the NPDES program freed EPA to focus on the TMDL provisions in the early 1990s. The persistence of serious water pollution problems, particularly those resulting from nonpoint sources, indicated that additional pollution control efforts were needed. EPA did not fully embrace the TMDL process, however, until prodded by several lawsuits. See, e.g., Idaho Sportsmen's Coalition v. Browner, 951 F. Supp. 962 (W.D. Wash. 1996). Between 1996 and 2000, EPA provided new policy guidance to the states and EPA regions, took steps to force state compliance with TMDL provisions, appointed a federal advisory committee to develop consensus among the states, environmental groups and affected dischargers about the future form of the TMDL process, and developed new regulations to clarify and strengthen TMDL regulatory requirements. See 64 Fed. Reg. 46,012 (1999). Not surprisingly, environmentalists have continued to challenge the pace of TMDL implementation. See, e.g., Thomas v. Jackson, 581 F.3d 658 (8th Cir. 2009); Pronsolino v. Nastri, 291 F.3d 1123 (9th Cir. 2002).

EPA's recent focus on the TMDL process is supported, indeed demanded, by many environmental advocates. Because of its emphasis on the effects of all sources of pollution on receiving waters, they argue that the TMDL process is more "holistic" than the effluent limitation approach of the NPDES program. They, like EPA, are hopeful that the TMDL process will provide a successful attack on nonpoint source pollution. Although EPA has consistently taken the position that the TMDL provisions apply to nonpoint sources, agricultural groups and others whose activities are major sources of point source pollution, and some federal agencies with close ties to such groups, argue that the TMDL provisions do not apply to nonpoint source pollution. On the other hand, many state officials and industry representatives favor the TMDL approach because of its emphasis on local control.

The history of the TMDL provisions and the difficulties confronting their successful application are discussed in a series of articles by Oliver A. Houck, culminating in TMDLs IV: The Final Frontier, 29 Envtl. L. Rep. 10469 (1999). Professor Houck observes that the emphasis on state-dominated, water quality-based regulation, represented by the TMDL process, is a throwback to the pre-1972 approach to water pollution control. He notes that the TMDL process is beguilingly simple to describe and frustratingly difficult to implement. It is, he says, expensive, site-specific, and heavily reliant on science, monitoring, and the will and ability of states and local governments. While he notes many significant problems which make the success of the TMDL approach far from certain, he concludes that TMDLs hold the best prospect for coming to grips with the last major sources of water pollution.

4. **Agricultural drains.** Natural Resources Defense Council v. Train, 396 F. Supp. 1393 (D.D.C. 1975), held that EPA had exceeded its authority in exempting agricultural return flows from the NPDES program. Congress responded by amending the definition of point source to exclude "return flows from irrigated agriculture." 33 U.S.C. § 1362(14). Congress also prohibited EPA from requiring a permit for discharges "composed entirely of return flows from irrigated agriculture." 33 U.S.C. § 1342(l)(1).

5. **Stricter State Provisions.** Where authorized by state law, state water quality programs may impose permit terms that are stricter than federal requirements. See, e.g., City of Burbank v. State Water Res. Control Bd., 108 P.3d 862 (Cal. 2005) (when imposing stricter-than-federal standards, state agency may take economic factors into account). See generally, David Cory, Linda Sheehan, Terry Young, Waste Discharge Requirements: Beyond the Point Source, 57 Hastings L.J. 1281 (2006) (California law).

6. **Control of injection wells.** The Safe Drinking Water Act of 1974, 42 U.S.C. §§ 300h to 300h–7, includes requirements for state programs to control underground injections in order to protect public water systems from contamination, pursuant to regulations issued by EPA. Id. at § 300h. The act emphasizes protection of aquifer recharge zones and on control waste injection wells that might damage drinking water supplies. See David H. Getches, Controlling Groundwater Use and Quality: A Fragmented System, 17 Nat. Resources Law. 623, 631 (1985).

7. **Other approaches.** Section 304(e) of the CWA, 33 U.S.C. § 1314(e), gives EPA authority to require best management practices for toxic and hazardous pollutants. These include methods for control of plant site runoff, spillage or leaks, sludge or waste disposal, and drainage from raw material storage when these might contribute significant amounts of pollutants to waters.

In the struggle to protect people against harm from toxic substances, the emphasis has shifted away from protection of waters to management and control of the substances themselves. The Toxic Substances Control Act, 15 U.S.C. §§ 2601 et seq., regulates the testing, manufacture and distribution of chemicals that present a risk of injury to health and the environment. The Resources Conservation and Recovery Act, 42 U.S.C. §§ 6921 et seq., regulates the current and future handling, storage, treatment, transportation and disposal of hazardous wastes. The Comprehensive Environmental Response, Compensation, and Liability Act, 42 U.S.C. §§ 9601 et seq., establishes four measures directed toward cleanup of existing uncontrolled dump sites. It requires owners of hazardous sites to notify EPA of their existence and nature; it gives EPA authority to clean up the dump if the owner cannot be found or does not act; it establishes the "superfund" for cleanup, replenished by a tax on petrochemical plants and crude oil importers; and it creates liability for cleanup and restitution costs.

The Safe Drinking Water Act, 42 U.S.C. § 300f–j, attacks in still another direction, by preventing the use of contaminated supplies. Most water destined for domestic use is treated to some degree before being delivered to consumers. The act empowers EPA to set maximum levels for contaminants in delivered water and to establish standards for monitoring, delegating enforcement to states with approved programs.

CITY OF THORNTON v. BIJOU IRRIGATION CO.
Supreme Court of Colorado, 1996.
926 P.2d 1.

[The City of Thornton applied for a water exchange as part of a large water development project. See supra page 47 for other aspects of this case]

LOHR, JUSTICE. * * * We turn now to issues relating to the potential water quality impacts of the Northern Project. The first of these issues on appeal concerns the water court's resolution of certain water quality issues raised by objector Eastman Kodak Company * * *. Kodak operates a manufacturing plant on the Poudre River near Windsor, Colorado. As part of its industrial processes, Kodak uses between 1.1 and 1.3 million gallons of water per day. * * * Following the use of this water at the plant, it is collected and treated at Kodak's on-site industrial wastewater treatment plant. After treatment, Kodak discharges the water into the Poudre River.

Kodak's discharge of treated wastewater is conducted under a wastewater discharge permit issued by the Colorado Department of Health Water Quality Control Division (Water Quality Division or Division). Pursuant to this permit, Kodak's discharge must meet or remain below certain effluent limits for various chemicals, including ammonia. These effluent limits are based in part on an average low-flow value in the river in the vicinity of Kodak's discharge point,[80] and Kodak has consistently met these current limitations through operation of its existing treatment facility.

Thornton's proposed Poudre River exchange will have a negative, if indirect, impact on Kodak's waste treatment operations. The ex-

---

80. * * * The effluent limits are calculated to ensure that water quality standards developed by the Water Quality Commission will be met in each relevant area of the stream. One controlling variable in calculating effluent limits is the volume of water in the stream just upstream of the discharge point. * * * [A] reduction in average low-flow conditions in a stream may result in stricter effluent limits in a discharge permit.

change proposed by Thornton contemplates the diversion of water from the Poudre River above the location of Kodak's plant and return of the substitute supply into the Poudre below the plant. The water being exchanged upon is not water necessary to satisfy Kodak's appropriative rights—i.e., the amount of water remaining in the river after the exchange diversion will be sufficient to allow Kodak to divert the full amount of its appropriative right. * * * The effect of the exchange about which Kodak complains, however, is the substantial depletion of Poudre River flows at Kodak's plant. Kodak presented evidence that this depletion in flow will affect the average low-flow rates on which Kodak's effluent limits are based and result in stricter unionized ammonia limits on Kodak's discharged water. Kodak alleges that such more stringent standards would require the construction of an entirely new treatment facility at a cost of between nine and twelve million dollars. * * *

In its Memorandum of Decision, the trial court interpreted Kodak's request for protective terms and conditions as a request for a minimum instream flow right for waste dilution purposes, and held that it was forbidden to decree such a right except as specifically authorized by statute. * * * Kodak appeals the trial court's decision to approve the Poudre River exchange without specifically addressing the impact of the exchange on Kodak's water treatment operations.

1. Relation Between Appropriation Doctrine and Quality Issues

From the earliest cases, Colorado courts have given at least some recognition to water quality concerns, holding, for example, that a water right does not include the right to discharge pollutants that detrimentally affect downstream users. However, beyond recognition of this general prohibition on unreasonable discharges, the system of water quality regulation in Colorado reflects a continued conflict with and subordination to the prior appropriation system. Rather than consolidating the power to regulate water quantity and water quality in the same body, Colorado divides responsibilities for these matters between two very distinct entities. The prior appropriation system, embodied in the adjudication of appropriative rights to water, is presided over by the judiciary in general and the water court in particular. * * * Although the water court must consider the effects on other water users when a water right owner seeks a change of water right, water court protection of such other users has traditionally been limited to ensuring that they do not suffer a decrease in the quantity of water available through exercise of their rights. The court is explicitly required to consider water quality issues only in the case of an exchange whereby water is being actively substituted into the stream for the use of other appropriators. * * *

In the Colorado Water Quality Control Act * * * the legislature delegated authority over water quality regulation to the Water Quality Control Commission and the Water Quality Division. These agencies were created to develop and enforce water quality standards across the state. Although these agencies exercise considerable authority over water users, the legislature made clear its intention that this authority cannot be exercised in a manner that significantly compromises the appropriative rights of present or future water users. The Water Quality Control Act states in pertinent part:

> * * * Nothing in this article shall be construed, enforced, or applied so as to cause or result in material injury to water rights.

§ 25-8-104(1), 11A C.R.S. (1989). Water quality regulation that affects water rights without causing material injury or impairment is not necessarily prohibited. However, section 25-8-104(1) serves notice that despite the importance of water quality regulation, the legislature's primary emphasis in enacting this scheme is to maximize beneficial use and to minimize barriers to further beneficial appropriation. The result of this policy decision is essentially to focus water quality regulation on uses culminating in unreasonable discharges, as such discharges are not part of any appropriative right under common law.

For better or worse, this dual system limits the ability of both the water court and the water quality control agencies to address certain water quality issues. The plight of appropriators in Kodak's situation, who allege quality impacts as a result of appropriative depletion rather than substandard discharge or supply water, is a prime example of the limitations of the present system to provide remedies for all types of injuries. The statutory scheme governing water exchange proposals places a clear limitation on the "discharge" aspect of all exchanges—i.e., the provision of the substituted supply of water.* * * These statutory provisions are intended to protect the quality of the substitute supply for those senior appropriators who receive this water. To ensure compliance with this requirement in the present case, the trial court included these conditions in the decree to be administered by the state engineer. Neither the statute nor the decree, however, provides relief to an appropriator in Kodak's situation. Under the decreed operation of the Poudre River exchange, Thornton will return the substitute supply water to the river below the location of Kodak's plant. Kodak is physically unable to receive any of this substitute supply. Thus, the discharge-oriented water quality provisions relating to exchanges fail to protect appropriators in Kodak's position.

2. Relation Between Quality and Cognizable Injury

Kodak argues, however, that under the "no-injury" statute, § 37–92–305(3), 15 C.R.S. (1990), the trial court can and must take into account quality impacts not related to substitute supply and impose any terms and conditions necessary to ensure that operation of the exchange will not "injuriously affect" Kodak's water rights. * * * Whether section 37-92-305(3) applies to all water exchange projects is not clear from the statutory language. However, we need not decide that issue in the present case. Even assuming that "no-injury" review of Thornton's exchange was required, we agree with the trial court that the legislative water quality scheme is not designed to protect against quality impacts unrelated to discharges or substitute water and specifically prohibits the water court from imposing the protective measures necessary to remedy depletive impacts of upstream appropriations on an appropriator in Kodak's situation.

Kodak does not allege that operation of the Poudre River exchange will reduce the quantity of water available in the river to a volume less than the amount of its appropriative right. Kodak also cannot contend that the substitute supply provided by Thornton in the Poudre River exchange will affect the quality of the water diverted to its plant. [The sole negative impact of the Poudre River exchange on Kodak's treatment operations results from a diminution in the flow of excess river water—i.e., water that would otherwise flow by Kodak's plant but that is in excess of the amount that can be diverted under Kodak's water right.] Because the volume of water in a stream just upstream of the discharge point is a controlling variable in the formula to set effluent limits, Kodak contends that diminution in flow caused by operation of the exchange will necessarily result in more stringent effluent limits for Kodak. However, to avoid this impact on Kodak's treatment operations, the trial court would have had to impose conditions that required maintenance of sufficient volume in the stream to preserve the average low-flow values that determine Kodak's effluent limits. Despite Kodak's arguments to the contrary, such protection would necessarily require the imposition of conditions creating a private instream flow right for Kodak for the purpose of waste dilution or assimilation.

3. Relation Between Quality and Minimum Stream Flow

The legislature expressed a clear intent to prohibit private parties from adjudicating instream flow rights. Pursuant to section 37-92-102(3), 15 C.R.S. (1990), the General Assembly vested exclusive authority in a state entity, the Colorado Water Conservation Board (CWCB), to appropriate minimum stream flows and limited the purpose for these appropriations to "preserv[ation of] the environment to a reasonable degree." * * * The meaning of this exclusive delegation of authority is clear—the judiciary is without authority to decree an instream flow right to any private entity.

* * *

Even in the absence of a specific legislative prohibition, the type of right sought by Kodak is inconsistent with Colorado law and policy concerning appropriations. Kodak currently diverts the full amount of its appropriative right, which it exercises pursuant to its water allotment contract with NCWCD, and the company does not argue that Thornton's exchange will affect its future ability to divert its maximum appropriated amount. Instead, Kodak claims an additional amount of water, above that amount which it can lawfully divert, to ensure the less expensive exercise of its right. Because this additional water exceeds the amount to which Kodak is entitled under its water right, Kodak cannot claim such water as part of its original appropriation. * * * Without an appropriative right or otherwise established beneficial use, Kodak is not entitled to protection of its incidental use of this water against lawful appropriations by other users. * * * We decline Kodak's invitation to avoid the effect of the specific prohibition on private instream flow rights by creating such a right in the guise of a condition imposed on the lawful appropriations of others. Under the current system, with its emphasis on maximum beneficial use, Kodak's reliance on unappropriated water in excess of its appropriative right is subject to the risk that a lawful appropriator will appropriate that excess water.

4. Conclusion

* * * [W]e affirm the trial court's decision not to include conditions in the final decree designed to protect Kodak's waste treatment operations.

Notes

1. **Different views.** The Sacramento-San Joaquin Delta in California is the setting for one of the most complex and long-running conflicts between water quality and water rights laws. The Delta is an important environmental resource, it is a source of water for several adjacent communities, and it serves as a transit facility for two large water projects, the federal Central Valley Project (CVP) administered by the Bureau of Reclamation and the California Water Project. Both projects store water in reservoirs in northern California. When needed, the water is released into rivers which flow into the Delta and is pumped from the Delta for transportation to central and southern California via large canals. The Delta has serious water quality problems, primarily consisting of salt water intrusion from San Francisco Bay. This intrusion can be controlled only by regulating water flows into, and pumping from, the Delta.

In 1978, the California Water Resources Control Board, which administers water quality and water rights laws in California, set water quality standards for the Delta in Decision 1485. To enforce the standards, D 1485 modified the water rights of the two projects referred to above. Challenges to D 1485 were addressed in United States v. State Water Resources Control Board., 227 Cal. Rptr. 161 (Ct. App. 1986). After concluding that the Water Board had erred in setting the standards the court turned to enforcement:

"California, of course, has already combined both water resource functions within the exclusive jurisdiction of the Board. The stated purpose of this merger was to ensure that 'consideration of water pollution and water quality' would become an integral part of the appropriative rights process. * * *

"The U.S. Bureau and federal contractors argue strongly that the Board had no authority to modify or interfere with the appropriative rights held by the U.S. Bureau for operation of the CVP. They contend that once an appropriation permit is issued, it is final and nonmodifiable. We disagree and will conclude that the Board's actions are supported on two independent grounds.

"*Reserved Jurisdiction.* In the present proceedings the Board explicitly grounded its authority to impose water quality standards on the CVP on its reserved jurisdiction. * * *

"*Unreasonable Use.* Independent of its reserved powers, we think the Board was authorized to modify the permit terms under its power to prevent waste or unreasonable use or methods of diversion of water. * * * That independent basis of authority vests jurisdiction in the Board to compel compliance with the water quality standards insofar as the projects' diversions and exports adversely affect water quality.

"*Enforcement of Water Quality Standards for Nonconsumptive, Instream Uses.* In addition to protecting consumptive uses of the Delta, the Board formulated revised standards of water quality to protect fish and wildlife, a function expressly authorized by state and federal law. * * * In the proceedings below the Bureau argued the Board had no authority to modify an appropriation permit once issued, and that the new standards for the protection of fish and wildlife will result in impairment of its vested appropriative rights. * * *

"The issue is now clearly controlled by National Audubon Society v. Superior Court, supra, 33 Cal.3d 419, 189 Cal. Rptr. 346, 658 P.2d 709, decided after the proceedings below. * * * This landmark decision directly refutes the Bureau's contentions and firmly establishes that the state, acting through the Board, has continuing jurisdiction over appropriation permits and is free to reexamine a previous allocation decision."

Cf. *In re* State Water Res. Control Bd. Cases, 39 Cal. Rptr. 3d 189 (Cal. Ct. App. 2006), cert. denied, 127 S. Ct. 318 (overturning water rights decision attempting to implement 1995 Bay-Delta water quality control plan); *In re* Bay-Delta Programmatic Envtl. Impact Report Coordinated Proceedings, 184 P.3d 709 (Cal. 2008) (upholding environmental review documents for Board's Bay-Delta program).

See also Shokal v. Dunn, supra p. 140, holding that a permit cannot be issued for a new appropriation if it would result in a violation of water quality laws. Gregory J. Hobbs, Jr. & Bennett W. Raley, Water Quality Versus Water Quantity: A Delicate Balance, 34 Rocky Mtn. Min. L. Inst. 24–1 (1988), argues that the regulation of diversions to achieve water quality standards is contrary to the congressional policy which prohibits the use of dilution to avoid point and nonpoint source controls. Cf. Colo. Wild, Inc. v. U.S. Forest Serv. , 122 F. Supp. 2d 1190 (D. Col. 2000) (Clean Water Act permit not required for ski resort's diversions for artificial snowmaking even though diversions would increase concentration of toxic metals).

2. **Implementation of Water Quality Plans.** As for the water quality and water rights issues in the Sacramento-San Joaquin Delta addressed in the preceding note, the California State Water Resources Control Board's Decision 1485 was replaced in 1995 by Decision 1641. That Decision promulgated new water quality standards for the Delta and the San Francisco Bay. Implementation of the decision on the Sacramento River threatened to spark major litigation between the state and federal projects and senior upstream water rights holders over the latter's responsibility, if any, to help meet the Decision 1641 water quality objectives. In effect, the senior rights holders argued that all of the harm caused in the Delta was attributable to the junior projects; the latter, in turn, argued that all upstream diverters bore some responsibility for meeting water quality objectives. Formal water rights hearings and inevitable litigation challenging the results of those hearings was averted, at least in the short term, by the 2002 adoption of a so-called "Short Term Settlement Agreement" among the major upstream rights holders, the junior diverters, and the users in the export areas in the Central Valley and Southern California.

3. **Federalism.** Federalism plays a role in the conflict between water quality and water allocation. Water allocation is primarily a matter of state law; water quality law is dominated by the federal government. Conflicts between the two bodies of law inevitably raise questions about the appropriate roles of the state and federal governments. In particular, western states have long feared that water quality laws will be used by federal agencies to usurp state control of water allocation, particularly to provide instream flows. This fear was given added credence by a remark by Justice O'Connor in PUD No. 1 of Jefferson County v. Washington Department of Ecology, infra p. 658:

"Petitioners also assert more generally that the Clean Water Act is only concerned with water 'quality,' and does not allow the regulation of water 'quantity.' This is an artificial distinction. * * * [T]here is recognition in the Clean Water Act itself that reduced stream flow, i.e., diminishment of water quantity can constitute water pollution. First, the Act's definition of pollution as 'the man-made or man induced alteration of the chemical, physical, biological, and radiological integrity of water' encompasses the effects of reduced water quantity. 33 U.S.C. § 1362(19). This broad conception of pollution—one which evinces Congress' concern with the physical and biological integrity of water—refutes petitioners' assertion that the Act draws a sharp distinction between the regulation of water 'quantity' and water 'quality.' Moreover, § 304 of the Act expressly recognizes that water 'pollution' may result from 'changes in the movement, flow, or circulation of any navigable waters * * *, including changes caused by the construction of dams.' 33 U.S.C. § 1314(f)."

Two Clean Water Act provisions address the relationship between the act and state water laws, sections 101(g) and 510(2), 33 U.S.C. §§ 1251(g) and 1370(2). Section 101(g) provides that "it is the policy of Congress that the authority of each State to allocate quantities of water within its jurisdiction shall not be superseded, abrogated, or otherwise impaired by this chapter." Section 510(2) states that nothing in the act shall "be construed as impairing or in any manner affecting any right or jurisdiction of the States with respect to waters * * * of such States." As *Jefferson County* and *Riverside* (the next principal case) show, these provisions may give the states less protection than initially seems apparent.

4. **Use of state water quality standards to avoid federal pre-emption.** Section 401 of the Clean Water Act, 33 U.S.C. § 1341, provides that no federal license or permit can be issued for an activity which may result in a discharge into navigable waters unless the applicant has obtained a state certification that the discharge will comply with state water quality standards. See PUD No. 1 of Jefferson County v. Wash. Dep't of Ecology, infra p. 658 and accompanying Notes, regarding the use of this provision to prevent preemption of state environmental laws by federal agencies.

C. Wetlands Regulation (Clean Water Act Section 404)

RIVERSIDE IRRIGATION DISTRICT v. ANDREWS
United States Court of Appeals, Tenth Circuit, 1985.
758 F.2d 508.

MCKAY, CIRCUIT JUDGE. The issue in this case is whether the Corps of Engineers exceeded its authority when it denied plaintiffs a nationwide permit for deposit of dredge material for construction of Wildcat Dam and Reservoir. The Corps based its decision on the potential downstream impact on an endangered species due to the resulting increased consumptive use of water.

Plaintiffs seek to build a dam and reservoir on Wildcat Creek, a tributary of the South Platte River. Because construction of the dam involves depositing dredge and fill material in a navigable waterway,[1] the plaintiffs are required to obtain a permit from the Corps of Engineers under Section 404 of the Clean Water Act, 33 U.S.C. § 1344. The regulations under the Clean Water Act create categories of nationwide permits that provide automatic authority to place fill material if cer-

---

1. We assume, for purposes of this appeal, that Wildcat Creek is a navigable waterway as defined in the Clean Water Act. While plaintiffs claim to have reserved the right to argue this point in later proceedings, they have not argued the point before this court.

tain conditions are met. 33 C.F.R. § 330.4. If the conditions are not met, the party must seek an individual permit through a public notice and hearing process. The Corps determined that the proposed deposit did not meet the required conditions because the increased use of water that the resulting reservoir would facilitate would deplete the stream flow and endanger a critical habitat of the whooping crane, an endangered species. The Corps therefore informed the plaintiffs that they would be required to obtain an individual permit before the project could proceed.

Plaintiffs filed this suit seeking declaratory and injunctive relief and review of the agency action, claiming that the project is entitled to proceed under a nationwide permit and that the Corps exceeded its authority when it considered the effect of depletions caused by consumptive use of the water to be stored in the reservoir. * * * [T]he district court held that the engineer had acted within his authority and that he was required, under the Clean Water Act and the Endangered Species Act, to deny the nationwide permit. Plaintiffs appeal.

A nationwide permit is one covering a category of activities occurring throughout the country that involve discharges of dredge or fill material that will cause only minimal adverse effects on the environment when performed separately and that will have only minimal cumulative effects. See 33 U.S.C. § 1344(e)(1). Such a permit is automatic in that if one qualifies, no application is needed before beginning the discharge activity. * * * The Corps has the authority and duty, however, to ensure that parties seeking to proceed under a nationwide permit meet the requirements for such action. One condition of a nationwide permit is that the discharge not destroy a threatened or endangered species as identified under the Endangered Species Act, or destroy or adversely modify the critical habitat of such species. 33 C.F.R. § 330.4(b)(2). The regulations thus are consistent with the Corps' obligation, under the Endangered Species Act, to ensure that "any action authorized, funded, or carried out by such agency * * * is not likely to jeopardize the continued existence of any endangered species or threatened species or result in the destruction or adverse modification of habitat of such species which is determined by the Secretary * * * to be critical." 16 U.S.C. § 1536(a)(2).

No one claims that the fill itself will endanger or destroy the habitat of an endangered species or adversely affect the aquatic environment. However, the fill that the Corps is authorizing is required to build the earthen dam. The dam will result in the impoundment of water in a reservoir, facilitating the use of the water in Wildcat Creek. The increased consumptive use will allegedly deplete the stream flow, and it is this depletion that the Corps found would adversely affect the habitat of the whooping crane.

the problem

The Endangered Species Act does not, by its terms, enlarge the jurisdiction of the Corps of Engineers under the Clean Water Act. * * * However, it imposes on agencies a mandatory obligation to consider the environmental impacts of the projects that they authorize or fund. * * * The question in this case is how broadly the Corps is authorized to look under the Clean Water Act in determining the environmental impact of the discharge that it is authorizing.

* * *

Plaintiffs argue that, even if the Corps can consider effects of changes in water quantity, it can do so only when the change is a direct effect of the discharge. In the present case, the depletion of water is an indirect effect of the discharge, in that it results from the increased consumptive use of water facilitated by the discharge. However, the Corps is required, under both the Clean Water Act and the Endangered Species Act, to consider the environmental impact of the discharge that it is authorizing. To require it to ignore the indirect effects that result from its actions would be to require it to wear blinders that Congress has not chosen to impose. The fact that the reduction in water does not result "from direct federal action does not lessen the appellee's duty under § 7 [of the Endangered Species Act]." National Wildlife Federation v. Coleman, 529 F.2d 359, 374 (5th Cir. 1976). The relevant consideration is the total impact of the discharge on the crane. Id. at 373. In *National Wildlife Federation*, the Fifth Circuit held that the federal agency was required to consider both the direct and the indirect impacts of proposed highway construction, including the residential and commercial development that would develop around the highway interchanges. Similarly, in this case, the Corps was required to consider all effects, direct and indirect, of the discharge for which authorization was sought.

* * *

There is no authority for the proposition that, once it is required to consider the environmental impact of the discharge that it is authorizing, the Corps is limited to consideration of the direct effects of the discharge. The reduction of water flows resulting from the increased consumptive use is an effect, albeit indirect, of the discharge to be authorized by the Corps. The discharge thus may "destroy or adversely modify" the critical habitat of an endangered species, and the Corps correctly found that the proposed project did not meet the requirements for a nationwide permit.

Plaintiffs claim that the Corps cannot deny them a nationwide permit because the denial impairs the state's right to allocate water within its jurisdiction, in violation of section 101(g) of the Act (the

"Wallop Amendment").[3] Even if denial of a nationwide permit is considered an impairment of the state's authority to allocate water, a question that we do not decide, the Corps acted within its authority. As discussed above, the statute and regulations expressly require the Corps to consider changes in water quantity in granting nationwide permits. Section 101(g), which is only a general policy statement, "cannot nullify a clear and specific grant of jurisdiction, even if the particular grant seems inconsistent with the broadly stated purpose." Connecticut Light and Power Co. v. Federal Power Commission, [324 U.S. 515, 527(1945)]. Thus, the Corps did not exceed its authority in denying a nationwide permit based on its determination that the depletion in water flow resulting from increased consumptive use of water would adversely affect the critical habitat of the whooping crane.

The Wallop Amendment does, however, indicate "that Congress did not want to interfere any more than necessary with state water management." National Wildlife Federation v. Gorsuch, 693 F.2d 156, 178 (D.C. Cir. 1982). A fair reading of the statute as a whole makes clear that, where both the state's interest in allocating water and the federal government's interest in protecting the environment are implicated, Congress intended an accommodation. Such accommodations are best reached in the individual permit process.

→ *compromise btwn state water right + federal law*

* * *

Affirmed.

Notes

1. **Importance of wetlands.** Wetlands used to be called "swamps," and filling and draining them used to be encouraged as "land reclamation." Modern science, however, recognizes that wetlands perform important ecological and economic functions:

"The swamps, bogs, sloughs, marshes, bottomlands, wet meadows, prairies, ponds, seeps, potholes, dune grasses and seabeds of the American landscape are the primary pollution control systems of the nation's waters, and the primary determinants of their water quality. They remove heavy metals at efficiencies ranging from twenty to one hundred percent. They remove up to ninety-five percent of phosphorous, nutrients and conventional pollutants, the equivalent of multi-million dollar treatment systems. A recent report concludes that a loss of fifty percent of America's remaining wetlands would result in increased sewage treatment plant expenditures of up to $75 billion for the removal of a single pollutant, nitrogen, alone. These same wetlands purify and recharge

---

3. The Wallop Amendment provides that: It is the policy of Congress that the authority of each State to allocate water within its jurisdiction shall not be superseded, abrogated or otherwise impaired by this Act. It is the further policy of Congress that nothing in this Act shall be construed to supersede or abrogate rights to quantities of water which have been established by any State. 33 U.S.C. § 1251(g) (1982).

groundwater, providing municipal drinking water supplies for towns and cities across the country. The loss of these wetland functions is, moreover, a phenomenon felt by states and federal off-shore waters hundreds of miles downstream. Nutrient loadings to the Mississippi River from the farm states of the American midwest have created a summer "dead zone" of anaerobic water across 6800 square miles of the Louisiana coast. Similar pollution from a half-dozen states seriously threatens the life and the economy of the Chesapeake Bay. * * *

"[W]etlands perform related functions of equal importance and of a similar, transboundary nature. Their biomass is the building block for the world's fisheries. More than seventy percent of America's commercial seafood harvest, with an estimated annual value of $3.6 billion and total economic output of $31 billion, originates in the shallow seagrasses and the salt, intermediate and brackish marshes of coastal estuaries. Up to 100 million migratory waterfowl breed in the prairie potholes, lakeshores and wet tundra of North America and winter along the coastal marshes of California, Louisiana and the Chesapeake Bay. The hydrology and nutrients of these systems are, in turn, regulated and protected by freshwater systems upstream, as is the abundance of their wildlife. Clearcutting along salmon spawning streams in Idaho degrades the commercial fisheries of Washington and Oregon. Prairie pothole drainage in North Dakota has threatened to eliminate Canvasback, Redhead and other wintering waterfowl of Virginia, Maryland and Delaware. More than seventeen million Americans own fishing licenses and generate an estimated fifteen billion dollars annually in related revenue; in 1980 another 5.3 million Americans hunted migratory birds, spending $638 million in the process. Fifty-five million Americans spent almost $10 billion in 1980 simply to watch and photograph wetland-dependent species of birds. This commerce, use and enjoyment begins, and will end, with wetlands. * * * In the natural world—and in an ever increasingly unnatural one—they are aptly seen as biological factories, producing interstate goods.

"Perhaps the most dramatic of these goods is flood control. * * * Wetlands along the coast perform a more direct flood-proofing function, buffering storm surges and protecting interior properties. A mile of vegetated wetlands can reduce storm wave heights by one foot. There are fifty miles of marshes between New Orleans and the sea.

"These values are in jeopardy. The coastal wetlands of Louisiana are disappearing at the rate of forty square miles each year. Waterfowl breeding grounds that once spread from Minnesota to Montana have been reduced to a thin wedge in North Dakota. It seems no coincidence that of the 595 plant and animal species listed in the United States as threatened or endangered, nearly sixty percent rely on wetlands during some part of their life cycle. * * *

"These losses are mirrored in every state. Of an estimated 215 million acres of wetlands found in America at the time of European discovery, fewer than half remain. They continue to disappear at a rate approaching 300,000 acres per year." Oliver A. Houck & Michael Rolland,

Federalism in Wetlands Regulation: A Consideration of Delegation of Clean Water Act Section 404 and Related Programs to the States, 54 Md. L. Rev. 1242, 1244-51 (1995).

2. **Section 404.** Section 404 provides that the Army Corps of Engineers "may issue permits * * * for the discharge of dredged or fill material into the navigable waters at specified disposal sites." "Navigable waters" is not limited to traditionally navigable waters but includes most of the waters of the United States. Cf. infra pp. 633-34, Note 3. Still, in Solid Waste Agency v. United States Army Corps of Engineers, 531 U.S. 159 (2001), the Court concluded that an abandoned sand and gravel pit was not a "navigable water" of the United States, at least under Section 404. The Court found no evidence of Congressional intent to extend the statute to include hydrologically isolated, seasonal wetlands found wholly within a state. Subsequently, a fractured court in Rapanos v. United States, 547 U.S. 715 (2006), infra p. 626, further addressed the need for hydraulic continuity between a regulated "wetland" and "navigable waters."

As for the other part of the statutory definition—"discharge of dredged or fill material"—the phrase is carried over from earlier law but its meaning is considerably broader. The Corps of Engineers regulations define "dredged material" as "material that is excavated or dredged from waters of the United States." 33 C.F.R. § 323.2(c). "Discharge of dredged material" is "any addition of dredged materials into, including any redeposit of dredged materials other than incidental fallback within, the waters of the United States." 33 C.F.R. § 323.2(d)(1). "Fill material" is "any material used for the primary purpose of replacing an aquatic area with dry land or of changing the bottom elevation of a waterbody." 33 C.F.R. § 323.2(e). "Discharge of fill material" is defined as "the addition of fill material into the waters of the United States * * * [including], placement of fill that is necessary to the construction of any structure in a water of the United States; the building of any structure or impoundment requiring rock, sand, dirt, or other material for its construction; site-development fills for recreational, industrial, commercial, residential, and other uses; causeways or road fills; dams and dikes; artificial islands; property protection and/or reclamation devices such as riprap, groins, seawalls, breakwaters, and revetments; beach nourishment; levees; fill for structures such as sewage treatment facilities, intake and outfall pipes associated with power plants and subaqueous utility lines; and artificial reefs. The term does not include plowing, cultivating, seeding and harvesting for the production of food, fiber, and forest products." 33 C.F.R. § 323.2(f).

The permit system is administered by the Corps of Engineers under both EPA guidelines and Corps regulations. Permits are issued by the Secretary of the Army, acting through the Chief of Engineers, and are subject to veto by the EPA Administrator. The states may assume administration of the section 404 permit process if they have an approved program. To date, only two states, Michigan and New Jersey, have such programs. See 43 C.F.R. §§ 233.70, -.71.

The rather unusual administrative arrangement established in section 404 is the result of a political compromise. The Corp, which historically has had responsibility for regulating development in navigable waters was perceived by environmental interests as too insensitive to environmental values; conversely, EPA was perceived by development interests as too environmentally-oriented.

The Corps of Engineers' general regulations require a "public interest review" in which, "the decision whether to issue a permit will be based on an evaluation of the probable impacts, including cumulative impacts, of the proposed activity and its intended use on the public interest. * * * The benefits which reasonably may be expected to accrue from the proposal must be balanced against its reasonably foreseeable detriments. The decision whether to authorize a proposal, and if so the conditions under which it will be allowed to occur, are therefore determined by the outcome of the general balancing process. That decision should reflect the national concern for both protection and utilization of important resources. All factors which may be relevant to the proposal must be considered including the cumulative effects thereof. Among those are conservation, economics, aesthetics, general environmental concerns, wetlands, cultural values, fish and wildlife values, flood hazards, floodplain values, land use, navigation, shore erosion and accretion, recreation, water supply and conservation, water quality, energy needs, safety, food and fiber production, mineral needs, considerations or property ownership, and, in general, the needs and welfare of the people." 33 C.F.R. § 320.4(a)(1).

The EPA guidelines allow a permit to issue only if (a) there is no practicable alternative that will have less adverse impact on the aquatic ecosystem (if an activity is not "water dependent" there is a presumption that practical alternatives exist); (b) the discharge will not violate state water quality standards or certain federal toxic pollutant prohibitions, will not jeopardize an endangered or threatened species or destroy critical habitat, and will not violate certain requirements under federal marine sanctuary legislation; (c) the discharge will not significantly degrade the waters of the United States; and (d) appropriate and practicable steps have been taken to minimize adverse impacts on the ecosystem. 40 C.F.R. § 230.10.

Although the EPA Administrator's actions are exempt from NEPA, section 404 permits issued by the Corps may be major federal actions significantly affecting the quality of the environment. The public interest review is thus not limited to direct effects of the placement of the material or structure in the stream nor to effects on water quality alone. See, e.g., Wyoming Outdoor Council v. United States Army Corps of Engineers, 351 F. Supp. 2d 1232 (D. Wyo. 2005) (striking down, under both NEPA and §404, a general permit issued to coalbed methane gas production in Wyoming). NEPA processes may trigger consideration of the Endangered Species Act (16 U.S.C. §§ 1531–1534), the Fish and Wildlife Coordination Act (16 U.S.C. § 662), the Wild and Scenic Rivers Act (16 U.S.C. §§ 1271–

1276), the Antiquities Act (16 U.S.C. § 433), and the Coastal Zone Management Act (16 U.S.C. §§ 1451–1464).

3. **Federalism and protection of minimum stream flows under section 404.** What if the dam on Wildcat Creek would have no effect on water quality and would involve none of these federal acts, but would adversely affect trout habitat and recreational features of the creek and the South Platte River? Assume that the Colorado Water Conservation Board has not appropriated a minimum stream flow in the creek or the river under Colo. Rev. Stat. § 37–92–102(3), and the Riverside District has a conditional decree for the appropriation and storage of the water for irrigation, municipal and industrial purposes under Colorado water law, although water is expected to be available only during fall and winter flows. May the wetlands permit be conditioned to preserve the fish and the fishing if the minimum flow release would make it impossible to store enough water to make the project feasible? What is the effect of section 101(g), discussed in *Riverside*? What does it add to section 510, which declares that courts should not construe the CWA "as impairing or in any manner affecting any right or jurisdiction of the state with respect to the waters (including boundary waters) of such states?"

Perhaps the ultimate solution might be for the state to take over administration of the section 404 permit program by incorporating it into their state water rights granting and regulating activities and procedures, as allowed by sections 404(g)–(t), upon a showing that the laws of the state provide adequate authority to carry out the program. The EPA Administrator would retain authority to veto a permit.

4. **Standards for EPA vetoes.** In James City County v. Environmental Protection Agency, 12 F.3d 1330 (4th Cir. 1993), the EPA vetoed a section 404 permit for a dam and reservoir to be used to supply water to various entities in Virginia's Lower Peninsula. It based the veto solely on the effect which the project would have on fish, wildlife, and natural habitat. It gave no consideration to the county's need for water. There was no indication that any endangered species were involved or that any of the other acts cited supra p. 600, Note 2, were implicated.

In upholding the EPA veto, the court said:

"[The EPA's] authority to veto to protect the environment is practically unadorned. It is simply directed to veto when it finds that the discharge 'will have an unacceptable adverse effect on municipal water supplies, shellfish beds and fishery areas (including spawning and breeding areas) wildlife, or recreational areas.' * * *. This broad grant of power to the EPA focuses only on the agency's assigned function of assuring pure water and is consistent with the mission assigned to it throughout the Clean Water Act.

"We think it significant that the only mention of responsibility for the quantities of water available to communities is contained in section 101(g) entitled 'Authority of States over water' * * *. In our view, the EPA's only function relating to the quantities of available water is limited to assuring purity in whatever quantities the state and local agencies provide. For these reasons, we think its veto based solely on environmental harms was proper." Id. at 1336.

As of 2008, EPA had exercised its section 404 veto only 12 times.

5. **Judicial review of decisions to issue 404 permits.** In Preserve Endangered Areas of Cobb's History, Inc. v. United States Army Corp of Engineers, 87 F.3d 1242 (11th Cir. 1996), the court held that a citizens group could not challenge a decision by the Corp to issue a section 404 permit nor a decision by EPA not to veto its issuance. The court found that the CWA does not "clearly and [un]ambiguously waive sovereign immunity in regard to the Army Corps of Engineers." Id. at 1249. Section 505(a)(2), 33 U.S.C. § 1365(a)(2), authorizes suits against the EPA Administrator for alleged failures to perform any act or duty "which is not discretionary." However, the court held that the decision not to veto a section 404 permit is discretionary.

In Alliance to Save the Mattaponi v. United States Army Corps of Engineers, 515 F. Supp. 2d 1 (D.D.C. 2007), the court agreed that that the Clean Water Act did not permit a citizen's suit against either the Army Corps, for issuing a permit, or the EPA, for failing to veto a permit. But it concluded that the EPA could be sued under the Administrative Procedures Act (APA) for failure to veto a permit. Cf. Nat'l Wildlife Fed'n v. Hanson, 859 F.2d 313 (4th Cir. 1988) (on a theory rejected by *Mattaponi*, upholding a Clean Water Act citizen's suit against the Army Corps).

For a novel third-party beneficiary theory to support a citizen's challenge to a 404 permit, see Justin Massey, Applying the Third Party Beneficiary Theory of Contracts to Enforce Clean Water Act § 404 Permits: A California Case Study, 18 J. Envtl. L. & Litig. 129 (2003).

6. **Exemption for agricultural activities.** The CWA exempts from the permit requirements activities undertaken "for the purpose of construction or maintenance of farm or stock ponds or irrigation ditches or the maintenance of drainage ditches." (§ 404(f)(1)(C).) The regulations clarify the scope of the exemption by adding, "[d]ischarges associated with siphons, pumps, headgates, wingwalls, weirs, diversion structures and such other facilities as are pertinent and functionally related to irrigation are included in this exemption." 33 C.F.R. § 323.4(a)(3). Note that intake structures for municipal and industrial uses are not exempted.

Suppose that the Wildcat Creek Dam was a diversion structure and that irrigation was the sole beneficial use to be made of the water. Is there a "Catch 22" in section 404(f)(2)? "Any discharge of dredged or fill material into the navigable waters incidental to any activity having as its purpose bringing an area of the navigable waters into a use to which it was not previously subject, where the flow or circulation of navigable waters may be impaired or the reach of such waters be reduced, shall be required to have a permit under this section." The regulations give two examples: "[A] permit will be required for the conversion of a cypress swamp to some other use or the conversion of a wetland from silvicultural to agricultural use when there is a discharge of dredged or filled material into waters of the United States in conjunction with construction of dikes, drainage ditches or other works or structures used to effect such conversion." 33 C.F.R § 323.4(c).

7. **Federal regulation of water rights under section 404.** Many water diversions require a section 404 permit. Does section 404 provide federal authority to regulate water rights to implement water quality standards? See Environmental Protection Agency, Question & Answers on Antidegradation 11: "Where a planned diversion would lead to a violation of water quality standards, a 404 permit associated with the diversion should be suitably conditioned if possible and/or additional nonpoint and/or point source controls should be imposed to compensate." Is this policy consistent with section 101(g)?

8. **Federal regulation of water rights pursuant to use of federal lands.** Rights of way for diversion works and transmission facilities on federal lands are governed by the Federal Land Policy and Management Act (43 U.S.C. §§ 1751ff). Two cases have upheld the Forest Service's authority to impose bypass flows as a condition of granting a right-of-way permit for a water facility. County of Okanogan v. Nat'l Marine Fisheries Serv., 347 F.3d 1081 (9th Cir. 2003) (prior permits specifically preserved full USFS discretion to impose new conditions); Trout Unlimited v. U.S. Dep't of Agric., 320 F. Supp. 2d 1090 (D. Colo. 2004) (finding no abuse of discretion in failing to require bypass flows from reservoir).

Bypass flows were the subject of a controversial Forest Service task force. See Janet C. Neuman & Michael C. Blumm, Water for National Forests: The Bypass Flow Report and the Great Divide in Western Water Law, 18 Stan. Envtl. L.J. 3 (1999). Cf. United States v. New Mexico, infra p. 714.

D. Endangered Species

NATIONAL WILDLIFE FEDERATION v. HARVEY

[The facts in this case are set out supra p. 564].

B. The Endangered Species Act

1. Substantive and Procedural requirements of the Act

The Supreme Court characterized the Endangered Species Act ("ESA") as "the most comprehensive legislation for the preservation of endangered species ever enacted by any nation." [*Tennessee Valley Authority v. Hill* 437 U.S. 153, 180 (1978) (In one of the most celebrated environmental decisions, the Supreme Court approved an injunction against the operation of a dam constructed by the Tennessee Valley Authority which would have destroyed the habitat of a small fish known as the snail darter)]. * * * The plain intent of Congress by enacting the ESA was to halt and reverse extinction of endangered species "whatever the costs." [*T.V.A. v. Hill*, 437 U.S. at 157]. * * * Unlike NEPA, the ESA imposes substantial, continuing, and affirmative obligations on federal agencies. * * *.

The Act empowers the Secretary of Commerce to recommend: (1) when a species should be listed as endangered; and (2) what habitat should be listed as a critical. [*See* 16 U.S.C. § 1533(a)(2)(A).] * * * After a species is identified as endangered, the Interior Secretary is to develop plans for its survival. [*See* 16 U.S.C. § 1533(f)].

The [Ivory Billed Woodpecker, "IBW"] was one of the first species listed as endangered under the ESA. * * * Very little is known about its numbers, preferences and habitat; therefore, no critical habitat has been identified and designated.

The mavens of the law and regulations pertaining to the Endangered Species Act refer to the heart of the Act as "Section 7." [16 U.S.C. § 1536 (Although there is no "Section Seven" in this statute)]. It sets out requirements for all federal agencies to ensure that any action they authorize, fund, or carry out is not likely to jeopardize a listed species or adversely modify its critical habitat. [16 U.S.C. § 1536(a)(2)].

The word "jeopardize" is defined in the federal regulations. An agency will "jeopardize an endangered species if it reasonably would be expected, directly or *indirectly*, to reduce appreciably the likelihood of both the survival and *recovery* of a listed species ... by reducing the reproduction, numbers, or distribution." [50 C.F.R. § 402.02 (emphasis added)]. * * *

The ESA requires a procedural consultation when an agency proposes an action that *may* affect an endangered species. [*See* 16 U.S.C. § 1536; 50 C.F.R. § 402.14(a) (emphasis added)]. As part of this process, an agency must use the best scientific and commercial data available, and consult with the [Fish & Wildlife Service, "FWS"], if it has reason to believe that an endangered species may be present in the area of a proposed action. [16 U.S.C. § 1536(a)(3) and 16 U.S.C. § 1536(c)(1)]. * * *

An incremental approach * * * determine[s] the project's impact on a listed species-(1) the presence of a species is established; (2) potential effects on the species are identified; (3) adverse effects are singled out; and (3) whether a species will be jeopardized by the adverse affects is evaluated. [50 C.F.R. § 402.14]. The regulations provide several different avenues for making such determinations: Biological Assessment, Informal Consultation, and Formal Consultation.

A Biological Assessment is a study prepared under the direction of the FWS, that evaluates the potential effects of the project on an endangered species. [*Id.*] Such an assessment is to be performed when a major construction project is about to take place. The assessment must be completed before the project begins. 50 C.F.R. § 402.12.

An important first step in a Biological Assessment is determining whether a listed species may be present in the project area. * * * Before beginning construction, an agency must submit either a written request to the Director of the FWS asking for a list of endangered species present in the action area, or written notification that an endangered species is in the area. [50 C.F.R. § 402.12.] * * *

If the species may be there, the agency must prepare an evaluation of the project's "potential effects" on the species and decide whether a species is likely to be adversely affected. [50 C.F.R. § 402.12(a)]. If the Biological Assessment concludes that the proposed action "is not likely to adversely affect" a listed species, and the FWS concurs in writing, the project may go forward. Otherwise, the agency must request Formal Consultation. [50 C.F.R. § 402.12(k)].

An Informal Consultation is a process that includes all discussions and correspondence between the FWS and the action agency that take place before a Formal Consultation is necessary. Like the Biological Assessment process, if, during informal consultation, the agency finds no adverse effect, and the FWS concurs, consultation is terminated. If it appears that an endangered species is likely to be affected by the project, then Formal Consultation is required.

Formal Consultation requires an in-depth analysis of a project's possible impact. * * * During Formal Consultation, the FWS * * * must produce a Biological Opinion that should contain precise, in-depth information. [50 C.F.R. § 402.14(g)].

* * * In this case the Corps and the FWS concluded that Formal Consultation was not essential. Plaintiffs assert that a Formal Consultation is crucial for the IBW's protection and survival.

* * *

4. Analysis

This case is as distinct as the IBW. After disappearing from sight for 60 years, the IBW suddenly reappeared within the GPP area, compelling the Corps and the FWS to balance the interest of ensuring the survival of the IBW and preventing depletion of the Alluvial aquifer. The decisions made by the Corps and the FWS are at the center of this case.

When the IBW was discovered, the Corps immediately suspended activity on the GPP and began to engage in the procedural process required by the ESA and its regulations. The Corps started work on a Biological Assessment and engaged in Informal Consultation with the FWS. The FWS accepted this approach, and by-passed Formal Consultation.

The Biological Assessment submitted by the Corps included a partial survey of the action area to determine the IBW's possible presence. * * *

In its June 2005 concurrence letter, the FWS admitted that "[t]he surveys were not specifically designed to collect visual records of IBW, or locate cavity trees or bark scaling," and recognized that less than eight percent of the action area had been searched for IBW presence. * * *

The FWS and the Corps did not conduct on-site surveys in the "action area" to make this initial determination. Instead, the FWS designated the entire GPP area as "potential" habitat, and without conducting any additional surveys, the FWS and the Corps concluded that construction, laying pipeline, and diverting water in this "potential" habitat would have no adverse impact. They put the cart before the horse. Without conducting on-site surveys that adequately identify IBW habitat in the action area, the FWS and the Corps cannot rationally explain a "no adverse impact" decision.

* * *

[T]he FWS and the Corps acted within the scope of their legal authority by opting for a Biological Assessment combined with an Informal Consultation. However, within that context, they failed to properly follow recommended procedures.

The plan agreed to by the Corps and FWS provides, at best, hit or miss protection for the IBW, because it calls for surveys to be done while the construction activity continues. This violates the purpose of the ESA which forbids the commitment of federal funds *before* determining if the species is present and threatened. Without appropriate habitat data within the "action area," any conclusion that the IBW will not be adversely affected by the GPP is without a rational basis and is, therefore, arbitrary and capricious.

* * *

For the reasons set out above, the conclusion of no adverse effect by the Corps and FWS lacks rational foundation. Therefore, Plaintiffs have shown a likelihood of success by showing that the Corps and FWS acted arbitrarily and in violation of APA and the ESA. Next, I am required to balance equities, consider the competing public interest, and the threat of irreparable harm.

When an endangered species is allegedly jeopardized, the balance of hardships and public interest tip in favor of the protected species. [*Hill*, 437 U.S. at 174 (Congress intended endangered species to be afforded the highest of priorities).] Here, there is evidence that the IBW may be jeopardized. The FWS has already partially halted construction, until the Corps conducts additional surveys. Issuing a preliminary injunction to ensure that the FWS-required surveys are rational

254 P.2d 606

and based on the best scientific information, will not unreasonably burden completion of the GPP. The public interest in preserving the Alluvial aquifer will be better served by determining whether the GPP will jeopardize the IBW, before further commitment of time and money are made to a project that may be doomed by unanticipated discoveries.

* * * The Motion for Preliminary Injunction under the Endangered Species Act is GRANTED.

Notes

1. **Administrative responsibilities.** ESA administration is assigned to the Secretary of Commerce (marine species and anadromous fish) and the Secretary of Interior (all other species). See 16 U.S.C. § 1532(15). The Secretary of Interior has delegated most authority to the Fish and Wildlife Service; the Secretary of Commerce has delegated most authority to the National Marine Fisheries Service (NOAA Fisheries).

2. **ESA section 7.** Section 7 applies not just to activities undertaken by federal agencies themselves, but also to actions "authorized" by federal agencies, such as permits and licenses issued to private parties. For the exercise of water rights, section 7 is frequently triggered by the requirement to obtain a section 404 permit from the Army Corps of Engineers. See, e.g., *Riverside* , supra p. 595. Section 7 can also be triggered when private parties seek permits to use federal lands to divert, store, or transport water (see supra p. 604, Note 8) or when private parties seek electrical hydropower licenses from the Federal Energy Regulatory Commission (see Chapter 8, Section 2A). Section 7 may also be triggered when the EPA is asked to approve a state's water quality control plans. Joint regulations of the Fish and Wildlife Service and the National Marine Fisheries Service implementing section 7 are found at 50 C.F.R. pt. 402.

Until the consultation process described in the principal case is completed, the ESA prohibits "any irreversible or irretrievable commitment of resources with respect to the agency action which has the effect of foreclosing the formulation or implementation of any reasonable and prudent alternative measures." Section 7(d), 16 U.S.C. § 1536(d).

A biological opinion may be accompanied by an "incidental take statement" (ITS) if the biological agency determines that takings will not violate the act. The statement must specify reasonable and prudent measures to minimize the impact on listed species and terms and conditions implementing such measures. Section 7(b)(4), 16 U.S.C. § 1536(b)(4); 50 C.F.R. § 402.14(i).

Following the issuance of a biological opinion, the agency proposing the action must determine how to proceed in light of its section 7 obligations and the biological opinion. 50 C.F.R. § 402.15(a). Although it technically can ignore a "jeopardy biological opinion," practically, it cannot because the opinion makes it almost impossible to defend against claims that it has violated section 7. Similarly, it can ignore conditions in an ITS, but if it does so, it and its employees lose the protection of section 7(o)(2), 16 U.S.C. § 1536(o)(2), which provides that a taking in compliance with an ITS is not a "prohibited taking."

Despite the mandatory language of section 7, few projects are actually stopped by the ESA. See Oliver A. Houck, The Endangered Species Act and Its Implementation By the U.S. Departments of Interior and Commerce, 64 U. Colo. L. Rev. 277 (1993). Professor Houck attributes this to a combination of the availability of non-jeopardizing alternatives and the extremely discretionary attitude toward jeopardy reflected in the regulations and practices of the biological agencies.

Section 7 applies only to "discretionary" acts by federal agencies. 50 C.F.R. § 402.03; Nat'l Ass'n of Homebuilders v. Defenders of Wildlife, 551 U.S. 644 (2007). Cf. Cal. Sportsfishing Protective Alliance v. Fed. Energy Regulatory Comm'n, 472 F.3d 593 (9th Cir. 2006) (continued operation of a dam during the last few years of a 30 year license is not a "final agency action" triggering consultation); W. Watersheds Project v. Matejko, 468 F.3d 1099 (9th Cir. 2006) (BLM's failure to exercise discretion was not discretionary act triggering consultation requirement). Section 7(e), 16 U.S.C. § 1536(e), creates a panel of cabinet-level federal officials (known irreverently as the "God Squad") with authority to grant exemptions to section 7.

3. **Taking a species.** The principal case involved ESA § 7. Section 9 makes illegal the taking, possessing, selling, importing, exporting or transporting of a protected species. The statute defines "take" broadly to mean "to harass, harm, pursue, hunt, capture, shoot, wound, kill, trap, capture or collect or to attempt to engage in any such conduct." 16 U.S.C. § 1532(19). The Secretary of the Interior, however, may permit a taking "if such taking is incidental to, and not the purpose of, the carrying out of an otherwise lawful activity." 16 U.S.C. §1539(a)(1)B). "Incidental take permits" formally give such permission. To get such a permit, the applicant must develop a conservation plan. 16 U.S.C. §1539(a)(2)(A).

4. **Habitat modification.** Regulations promulgated by the Secretary of Interior provide that "harm" in the definition of "take" under section 9 "may include significant habitat modification or degradation where it actually kills or injures wildlife by significantly impairing essential behavior patterns, including breeding, feeding, or sheltering." 50 C.F.R. § 17.3(c)(3). In Babbitt v. Sweet Home Chapter of Communities for a Greater Oregon, 515 U.S. 687 (1995), the Supreme Court upheld the definition. Most exercises of most water rights modify habitat. Thus, the definition greatly increases the ESA's potential impact on water law. An example of the potential impact is the dispute over the Edwards Aquifer in Texas, discussed supra pp. 395-97, Note 1. As indicated in that note, the ESA has forced the Texas legislature to substantially modify the "rule of capture," which allowed unregulated pumping, by the enactment of legislation to manage the aquifer and limit pumping.

The impact of *Babbitt* may have been blunted by the 9th Circuit's decision in Arizona Cattle Growers' Association v. United States Fish & Wildlife Service, 273 F.3d 1229 (9th Cir. 2001). In that case, the Fish and Wildlife Service (FWS) issued a Biological Opinion (BiOp) governing 288 livestock grazing entitlements on over 1.6 million acres of public land. The FWS issued ten Incidental Take Statements (ITS) for various listed or candidate species which it believed were present within the allotments. These statements placed substantial conditions on some grazing operations, including a complete ban on cattle grazing on certain floodplains and riparian corridors. The Ninth Circuit found that the FWS had acted arbitrarily and capriciously when it issued ITS for two species. For those species, the court found that FWS had no specific evidence that grazing would cause direct harm to the listed species. See Ruth Langridge, The Right to Habitat Protection, 29 Pub. Land & Resources L. Rev. 41 (2008). But see City of Tacoma v. Fed. Energy Regulatory Comm'n, 460 F.3d 53 (D.C. Cir. 2006) (under *Arizona Cattle Growers'*, "the BiOps and the ITS must be upheld as long as the agencies 'considered the relevant factors and made a rational connection between the facts found and the choices made'").

Many scholars have reviewed the constitutionality of the ESA in light of recent Commerce Clause jurisprudence. According to one writer, the articles break down into four groups. "One viewpoint holds that the habitat modification provisions of the ESA are unconstitutional because such regulations are land use regulations that should be governed by local governments. A second concludes that habitat modification is constitutional only if it regulates a commercial activity or if the protected species has a clear connection to commerce. A third determines that the ESA is constitutional based on the treaty Power, and a fourth finds that the ESA is constitutional based on the Commerce Clause." Omar N. White, Comment, The Endangered Species Act's Precarious Perch: A Constitutional Analysis Under the Commerce Clause and the Treaty Power, 27 Ecology L.Q. 214 (2000). See also Chapter 8, Section 1.

5. **"Take" and Tort Law.** In Priority, Probability, and Proximate Cause: Lessons from Tort Law about Imposing ESA responsibility for Wildlife Harm on Water Users and Other Joint Habitat Modifiers, 33 Envtl. L. 595 (2003), Professor James Rasband argues that "the current approach of federal wildlife agencies and courts to causation of wildlife harm, particularly in cases involving water users, fails to properly account for background risks, multiple habitat modifiers, and, in prior appropriation settings, for priority." He proposes using classic tort causation principles to better address these issues. In addition, he suggests that, consistent with other tort law trends, the courts should abandon joint and several liability for ESA violations in favor of more equitable apportionment. Such an apportionment, he concludes could better adapt principles of priority and proportionality.

6. **Impact of the ESA on western water activities.** In California, no law has a greater contemporary impact on water exports, via the state

and federal projects, from the state's two major rivers and the estuary into which they flow. In particular, orders issued in 2007 and 2008 by federal judge Oliver Wanger to protect the endangered delta smelt and various salmon runs, greatly curtailed the amounts and timing of export pumping from the Delta of the Sacramento and San Joaquin Rivers. Those exports support substantial agricultural activities in the San Joaquin Valley and extensive municipal uses in Southern California. See Pac. Coast Fed'n of Fishermen's Ass'ns v. Gutierrez, 606 F. Supp. 2d 1122 (E.D. Cal. 2008); Natural Res. Def. Council v. Kempthorne, 506 F. Supp. 2d 322 (E.D. Cal. 2007). Sitting in his Fresno, CA, courtroom, Judge Wanger has become somewhat of a water czar for the Delta, controlling much of how and when pumping can occur.

Beyond California, the ESA's impact is also potentially huge. Michael R. Moore et al., Water Allocation in the American West: Endangered Fish Versus Irrigated Agriculture, 36 Nat. Resources J. 319 (1996), examines the potential impact of the ESA on irrigated agriculture in the western United States. The article notes the strong correlation between areas of extensive surface water irrigation and concentration of ESA-listed fish species and concludes that there is a high potential for disruption of irrigated agriculture because of the ESA. The article also notes that the involvement of the United States Bureau of Reclamation in western agriculture increases the potential impact of the ESA because of the Bureau's responsibilities under section 7 of the act. See Stockton E. Water Dist. v. United States and accompanying Notes, infra p. 680. See also J. David Aiken, Balancing Endangered Species Protection and Irrigation Water Rights: The Platte River Cooperative Agreement, 3 Great Plains Nat. Resources J. 119 (1999), reviewing the impact of the ESA on water rights and water development activities in the Platte River basin and discussing the agreement entered into between the governors of Colorado, Wyoming, and Nebraska and the Secretary of Interior to develop a cooperative approach to the problem.

The impact of the ESA could be particularly great in river basins with a heavy federal presence, such as the Colorado and Columbia River Basins. See, e.g., Nat'l Wildlife Fed'n v. Nat'l Marine Fisheries Serv., 524 F.3d 917 (9th Cir. 2008) (Columbia River salmon ESA issues). Species of native fish are endangered in both of these basins, in significant part because of federal water development and regulatory activities. Consequently, section 7 is particularly significant, both in its own right and as a means of implementing "recovery plans" required for listed species by section 4(f) of the ESA, 16 U.S.C. § 1533(e).

Efforts to implement the ESA in the Colorado and Columbia River Basins are examined and critiqued in Mary Christina Wood, Reclaiming the Natural Rivers: The Endangered Species Act as Applied to Endangered River Ecosystems, 40 Ariz. L. Rev. 197 (1998). Professor Wood suggests that these river basins are in a class of their own in terms of ESA implementation because of the extent and complexity of their ecosystems, the heavy federal presence in the basins, and the frontal challenge which recovery of endangered species presents to status quo operations. She finds the results in both basins disappointing and concludes that political resistance to change has seriously infected implementation of the ESA despite the strong mandate of section 7. See also Michael C. Blumm, Erica J. Thorson, Joshua D. Smith, Practiced at the Art of Deception: The Failure of Columbia Basin Salmon Recovery under the Endangered Species Act, 36 Envtl. L. 709 (2006).

7. **Fish runs as "species"?** The ESA defines "species" to include "any subspecies * * * and any distinct population segment (DPS) of any species * * * which interbreeds when mature." 16 U.S.C. §1532(16). In applying this definition, two issues have arisen regarding protected fish populations. First, how should the ESA treat hatchery-raised populations of otherwise endangered native fish? Second, how should it treat fish, e.g., salmon, that are endangered in only a portion of their range, but are otherwise in no danger of going entirely extinct?

As to the first issue, the National Marine Fisheries Service (NMFS) developed a "Hatchery Listing Policy" (HLP). The policy professes a focus on the preservation of naturally sustaining populations. Among other matters, the policy required the agency to identify all populations of fish—natural and hatchery raised—but, in its decisions to list a species as endangered or threatened, to include hatchery fish only to the extent that those fish contribute to the viability of the natural populations. In other words, the agency considers case-by-case basis the negative and positive impact of hatchery programs on naturally spawning fish. Water diverters argued that the agency should fully county hatchery fish when deciding whether to list; environmentalists argued the agency should, basically, ignore hatchery fish in listing decisions. The HLP was upheld against both challenges in Trout Unlimited v. Lohn, 559 F.3d 946 (9th Cir. 2009).

As to the second issue, NMFS uses use two different methods to determine when to list, as DPS, fish that are endangered in only a portion of their range. It originally developed "Evolutionarily Significant Units" (ESU). An ESU is: 1) substantially reproductively isolated from other conspecific populations; and 2) represent an important component in the species' evolutionary legacy. It later joined with the Fish and Wildlife Service to develop a "Joint DPS Policy." Under this policy, the agencies consider: 1) the discreteness of the population segment when compared to the overall population; 2) the significance of the population segment to the overall population; and 3) the degree to which the population segment would, if considered by itself, meet ESA listing requirements. See *Trout Unlimited*, supra, (upholding downlisting, from endangered to threatened, of Upper Columbia steelhead ESU). See also Ctr. for Biological Diversity v. U.S. Fish & Wildlife Serv., 274 Fed. Appx. 542 (9th Cir. 2008) (upholding determination that DPS of Coastal Cutthroat Trout was not threatened in Lower Columbia River, but reversing decision not to list DPS for agency's failure to consider whether estuary and marine areas were significant portion of DPS.)

8. **The ESA and Indian water rights.** The regulations use a "first-in-time, first-in-right" approach in implementing section 7. The effects of a proposed action are not considered in isolation but include the effects of existing activities, federal actions for which section 7 consultation has been completed, and contemporaneous state and private activities. If the jeopardy threshold is not reached, the proposed action can proceed as proposed, except perhaps for steps to minimize the effect on listed species which may be required by an incidental take statement. See 50 C.F.R. §§ 402.14(i)(1) & (5). Conversely, if the jeopardy threshold is breached, the proposed action cannot proceed unless "reasonable and prudent alternatives" which prevent jeopardy are adopted. See supra p. 608, Note 2. (In determining jeopardy, the effects of future state or private activities which are "reasonably certain to occur" must also be considered. See 50 C.F.R. §§ 402.02 (definition of "cumulative effects" and 402.14(g)(3). While this is a deviation from the first-in-time rule, it does not affect the rule as applied to competing federal actions.)

Thus, the "conservation burden" falls almost solely on actions which are proposed after the jeopardy threshold is reached, while earlier activities and actions, including other federal projects, which contribute to the problem and may have been responsible for the listing of species in the first place, bear none of the burden. In effect, each action "appropriates" part of a pool of "permissible" adverse effects, until the pool is exhausted; thereafter, no new federal action can proceed unless mitigation measures are adopted which reduce the effects below the jeopardy threshold.

This approach when applied in an aquatic environment is somewhat congruent with the doctrine of prior appropriation. Assume for example that a minimum stream flow of 25 c.f.s. is required to avoid jeopardy to listed species. A proposed federal project which would reduce the flow below that level would result in jeopardy opinion and could not proceed, unless mitigative measures could be developed. The flow necessary to prevent jeopardy is like a senior appropriation, and the effect on the proposed action resembles the denial of an appropriation application because no unappropriated water is available.

Whatever its merits in general, some writers have argued that this approach is unfair when applied to Indian Tribes. See, e.g., Brian A Schmidt, Reconciling Section 7 of the Endangered Species Act with Native American Reserved Water Rights, 18 Stan. Envtl. L. J. 109 (1999). Under the reserved rights doctrine (Chapter 8, Section 3A), Indian tribes often have undeveloped water rights with a very early priority. Large-scale development of such rights is almost certain to involve federal agencies and federal funding, thereby triggering section 7. If the exercise of non-Indian rights, which are legally junior, has pushed a listed species to or past the threshold of jeopardy, these writers argue that the priority approach adopted by the section 7 regulations could prevent development of the Indian rights.

Comments on proposed regulations preceding adoption of the present regulations implementing section 7, 51 Fed. Reg. 19926, 19933 (1986), state: "In order to determine the effects of the action when a water project is the subject of consultation in a State which follows the prior appropriation doctrine, the project's operation plan should indicate the priority of the project's water rights under State law and account for the future effects of senior conditional water rights." Does this suggest that the effects of junior rights, whether conditional or perfected, can be ignored? In other words, when an Indian water project is the subject of consultation in jurisdictions applying the appropriation doctrine, does the quote indicate that the project should account only for the effects of rights senior to the Indian rights?

Section 9 of the ESA provides the basis for another argument for ignoring the effects of junior water rights when considering Indian water projects. Schmidt, supra, argues that priority should be used in determining which rights to regulate to maintain critical stream flows in order to prevent a "taking" of a listed species under section 9, i.e., he argues that rights should be regulated (shut off) in order of priority to maintain instream flows sufficient to prevent a "taking." Thus, Schmidt reasons, the effect of junior non-Indian water rights should be ignored in making section 7 jeopardy determinations associated with the development of Indian rights because the effects resulting from the Indian project can be eliminated by regulating the non-Indian rights under section 9. (But see Harrison C. Dunning, State Equitable Apportionment of Western Water Resources, 66 Neb. L. Rev. 76 (1987), suggesting that "equitable apportionment" should be used to allocate regulatory burdens of this sort.)

9. **Application of section 7 to federal reservoir operations.** Southwest Center for Biological Diversity v. United States Bureau of Reclamation, 143 F.3d 515 (9th Cir. 1998), involved an attempt to limit the storage of water in Lake Mead, a major Colorado River reservoir. In 1996, the Bureau of Reclamation issued a biological assessment which found that rising water levels in Lake Mead due to normal storage activities were inundating a stand of native willows which had grown in the Lake Mead delta during a dry period. This 1,148 acre stand, the largest contiguous stand in the Southwest, was an important nesting area for the Southwestern Willow Flycatcher, an endangered species.

In response to the Bureau's biological assessment, the Fish and Wildlife Service (FWS), issued a draft biological opinion which determined that the Bureau's activities on the Lower Colorado would jeopardize the Flycatcher. Initially, the FWS proposed a reasonable and prudent alternative (RPA) which required the Bureau to protect the delta habitat by lowering the water level in Lake Mead or, alternatively, to defer the use of conservation space in Roosevelt Lake, Arizona, to maintain Flycatcher habitat there. The Bureau informed the FWS that under the "law of the river" it lacked discretion to reduce the level of Lake Mead except for purposes of river regulation, water supply, and power generation. The Secretary of Interior, acting through the FWS, then adopted a final RPA which did not require the Bureau to protect the delta or defer the use of conservation space in Roosevelt Lake, but did require other measures to protect the Flycatcher, including a program to procure alternative habitat. The RPA was accompanied by an incidental take statement which permitted an "unquantifiable" take of Flycatchers at Lake Mead.

Southwest sued, seeking to force the Bureau to protect the delta habitat by lowering the water level in Lake Mead, an action which allegedly would have required the release of 3.5 to 5 million acre-feet of water. A second claim against the Secretary of Interior under the Administrative Procedure Act (APA) asserted that the adoption of the final RPA was arbitrary, capricious, and contrary to the ESA. The district court dismissed Southwest's claim for injunctive relief, holding that Southwest had not given sixty days notice of the alleged violation of the ESA before filing suit as required by section 1540 of the ESA, 16 U.S.C. § 1540(g)(2)(A)(i), and granted summary judgment for the Secretary on the APA claim.

The Ninth Circuit affirmed the decision of the district court on all points. It found that in determining whether the Secretary's adoption of the final RPA was arbitrary, capricious, or an abuse of discretion the district court only needed to determine whether the final RPA will avoid jeopardy to the Flycatcher. Reviewing the evidence, the Ninth Circuit held that the district court had not erred in finding that the final RPA will avoid jeopardy. Consequently, no review of the Bureau's claimed lack of discretion was required.

The opinion does not address the applicability of section 7 of the ESA to ongoing operations of a project to pursuant to longstanding policies and procedures. The Bureau of Reclamation apparently never questioned its applicability and the question became moot once the court concluded that the final RPA satisfied the ESA. Note, however, that section 7 refers to "any action" by a federal agency and the regulations state that "action" means "all activities or programs of any kind." 50 C.F.R. § 402.02. See also Pac. Rivers Council v. Thomas, 30 F.3d 1050 (9th Cir. 1994), holding that an ongoing policy or decision is an "agency action" each time it is applied. Cf. Grand Canyon Trust v. U.S. Bureau of Reclamation, 623 F. Supp. 2d 1015 (D. Ariz. 2009) (upholding ESA challenges to experimental operations of Glen Canyon Dam).

10. **Transboundary application of the ESA.** The ESA was the basis for another challenge to the Bureau of Reclamation's Colorado River operations, but one that presented an international twist. The Colorado River Delta, which begins just across the U.S.-Mexican border south of Yuma, Arizona, was once one of the richest wetlands in North America. See generally Charles Berman, Red Delta: Fighting for Life at the End of the Colorado River (2002). Ecosystem decline in the delta began with the filling of Lake Mead and continued through the filling of Lake Powell. Several species listed by the United States as endangered make their homes in the Delta and in adjoining areas in the United States. In Defenders of Wildlife v. Norton, 257 F. Supp. 2d 53 (D.D.C. 2003), plaintiffs claimed that the impacts of the Bureau of Reclamation's management of the lower Colorado River on the Mexican habitat of the listed species violated the ESA. In particular, they alleged that the Bureau had a duty to

consult with the designated biological agencies regarding the transboundary impacts of its water management operations.

In contrast to the United States Supreme Court's decision in Lujan v. Defenders of Wildlife, 504 U.S. 555 (1992), the district court found that the plaintiffs had standing to raise their claim. Nevertheless, the court granted summary judgment to the United States. The court agreed with the defendants that "even if Reclamation's actions have extraterritorial effects on the protected species in the delta, the consultation requirements of Section 7(a)(2) have no application to non-discretionary acts." Here, the court concluded, there was no discretion for the Bureau to adjust the time or amount of its water deliveries. Rather, the court concluded, the Bureau's hands were effectively tied by the "Law of the River." (For an overview of the law governing water use in the Colorado River basin, see Ch. 6, Section 3.) The court concluded that "it seems unlikely that any case will more clearly make any agency's actions nondiscretionary than this one: a Supreme Court injunction, an international treaty, federal statutes, and contracts between the government and water users that account for every acre foot of lower Colorado River." In combination, the applicable law gave the Bureau no flexibility to alter water deliveries to make more water available for species in Mexico. Absent such discretion, the court concluded that no ESA consultation obligation existed. Cf. Consejo de Desarollo Economico de Mexicali, A.C. v. United States, 482 F.3d 1157 (D. Nev. 2007) (Mexican and American non-profit organizations lacked standing under ESA to object to lining of canal to prevent seepage of water to Mexico.)

The international legal and political challenges presented by ecosystem restoration in the Colorado River Delta have been the subject of numerous recent articles. See, e.g., David H. Getches, Water Management in the United States and the Fate of the Colorado River Delta in Mexico, 11 U.S. Mex. L.J. 107 (2003). For a more general discussion of the problems presented by international rivers, see A. Dan Tarlock, Safeguarding International River Ecosystems in Times of Scarcity, 3 U. Denv. L. Rev. 231 (2000).

11. **State Endangered Species Acts.** Several states have endangered species acts which closely parallel the federal act and which can affect water rights activities. See, e.g., Dep't of Fish & Game v. Anderson-Cottonwood Irr. Dist., 11 Cal. Rptr. 2d 222 (Cal. Ct. App. 1992) (district liable for take of endangered fish under the California Endangered Species Act); and Central Platte Natural Res. Dist. v. City of Fremont, 549 N.W.2d 112 (Neb. 1996) (state water agency could not issue a permit to appropriate water which would jeopardize a species listed under the state act). Cf. Envtl. Prot. & Info. Ctr. v. Cal. Dep't of Forestry & Fire Prot., 187 P.3d 888 (Cal. 2008) (exploring the relationship between the state ESA and the public trust doctrine as both apply to wildlife). See also Dale D. Goble et al., Local and National Protection of Endangered Species: An Assessment, 2 Envtl. Sci. & Pol'y 43 (1999) (concluding that state endangered species legislation is far less comprehensive than federal law).

TULARE LAKE BASIN WATER STORAGE DISTRICT v. UNITED STATES

United States Court of Claims, 2001.
49 Fed. Cl. 313.

WIESE, Judge. * * *

This case concerns the delta smelt and the winter-run chinook salmon—two species of fish determined by the United States Fish and Wildlife Service ("USFWS") and the National Marine Fisheries Service ("NMFS") to be in jeopardy of extinction. The efforts by those agencies to protect the fish—specifically by restricting water out-flows in California's primary water distribution system—bring together * * * the Endangered Species Act and California's century-old regime of private water rights. The intersection of those concerns, and the proper balance between them, lie at the heart of this litigation.

The development of California's water system has a long and detailed history well chronicled in case law. * * * That system, in brief, involves the transport of water from the water-rich areas in northern California to the more arid parts of the state. Various water projects or aqueduct systems have been built to facilitate that goal; two—the Central Valley Project ("CVP") and the State Water Project ("SWP")—are the focus of the present litigation.

Although CVP is a federal project managed by the Bureau of Reclamation ("BOR") and SWP is a state project managed by the Department of Water Resources ("DWR"), the two projects share a coordinated pumping system that requires, as a practical matter, that the systems be operated in concert. * * *

Both BOR and DWR are granted water permits by the State Water Resources Control Board ("SWRCB" or "the Board")—a state agency with the ultimate authority for controlling, appropriating, using and distributing state waters. * * * BOR and DWR in turn contract with county water districts, conferring on them the right to withdraw or use prescribed quantities of water. Of the present plaintiffs, two—Tulare Lake Basin Water Storage District and Kern County Water Agency—have contracts directly with the [SWP], and three—Hansen Ranches, Lost Hills Water District, and Wheeler Ridge-Maricopa Water Supply District—have subsidiary contracts with Tulare and Kern County. Under its contract with DWR, Kern County's allotment of entitlement water was set at 1,153,400 acre-feet per year during the period in question (1992-1994), while Tulare's allocation was 118,500 acre-feet. * * *

Against this backdrop of water transportation and entitlements, Congress passed the Endangered Species Act in 1973 * * * ("ESA"). That act was designed to "halt and reverse the trend toward species extinction, whatever the cost." * * *.

In fulfillment of the duties assigned to it under the ESA, the [NMFS] initiated discussions with the [BOR] and [DWR] to determine the impact of the [CVP] and the [SWP] on the winter-run chinook salmon. As a result of those discussions, the NMFS issued a biological opinion on February 14, 1992, concluding that the proposed operation of SWP and CVP was likely to jeopardize the continued existence of the salmon population. Included in the agency's findings was a reasonable and prudent alternative ("RPA")[2] designed to protect the fish by restricting the time and manner of pumping water out of the Delta. As a result, water that would otherwise have been available for distribution by the water projects was made unavailable. * * *

The RPAs were thus implemented in each of the years in question, giving rise to the present claims. According to plaintiffs, the restrictions imposed by the RPAs deprived Tulare Lake Basin WSD of at least 9,770 acre-feet of water in 1992; at least 26,000 acre-feet of water in 1993, and at least 23,050 acre-feet of water in 1994. Kern County Water Agency, by contrast, is alleged to have lost a minimum of 319,420 acre-feet over that same period.

DISCUSSION The Fifth Amendment to the United States Constitution concludes * * * "nor shall private property be taken for public use, without just compensation." The purpose of that clause * * * is "to bar Government from forcing some people alone to bear public burdens which, in all fairness and justice, should be borne by the public as a whole." At issue, then, is not whether the federal government has the authority to protect the winter-run chinook salmon and delta smelt under the Endangered Species Act, but whether it may impose the costs of their protection solely on plaintiffs.

    * * *

II. Turning then to the merits of plaintiffs' claim, we begin by determining the nature of the taking alleged. Courts have traditionally divided their analysis of Fifth Amendment takings into two categories: physical takings and regulatory takings. A physical taking occurs when the government's action amounts to a physical occupation or invasion of the property, including the functional equivalent of a "practical ouster of [the owner's] possession." * * * When an owner has suffered a physical invasion of his property, courts have noted that "no matter how minute the intrusion, and no matter how weighty the public purpose behind it, we have required compensation." Lucas v. South Carolina Coastal Council [505 U.S. 1003, 1015, (1992)].

---

2. Where the activities of a federal agency are seen to jeopardize the continued existence of listed species or cause the destruction or adverse modification of critical habitats, the Endangered Species Act directs the Secretary to suggest "reasonable and prudent alternatives" to avoid such harms. 16 U.S.C. § 1536(b)(3)(A)(1994).

A regulatory taking, in contrast, arises when the government's regulation restricts the use to which an owner may put his property. In assessing whether a regulatory taking has occurred, courts generally employ the balancing test set forth in *Penn Central*, weighing the character of the government action, the economic impact of that action and the reasonableness of the property owner's investment-backed expectations. Penn Central Transp. Co. v. New York [438 U.S. 104, 124-125 (1978)]. Regulations that are found to be too restrictive, however—i.e., those that deprive property of its entire economically beneficial or productive use—are commonly identified as categorical takings and, like physical takings, require no such balancing. *Lucas*, [505 U.S. at 1015-1016].

Plaintiffs urge us to consider this action as a case involving a physical taking of property. Under that theory, plaintiffs possessed contract rights entitling them to the use of a specified quantity of water. By preventing them from using that water, plaintiffs argue, the government deprived them of the entire value of their contract right.

Defendant sees the case differently. In defendant's view, the court must examine the government's conduct under the three-part test that *Penn Central* prescribes for the evaluation of regulatory action that interferes with an owner's use of his property. Under that rubric * * * the claim must fail because plaintiffs' reasonable contract expectations were necessarily limited by regulatory concern over fish and wildlife; and because the economic loss asserted here—a fraction of the master contract's overall value—was de minimis.

Of the two positions, plaintiffs', we believe, is the correct one. Case law reveals that the distinction between a physical invasion and a governmental activity that merely impairs the use of that property turns on whether the intrusion is "so immediate and direct as to subtract from the owner's full enjoyment of the property and to limit his exploitation of it." United States v. Causby [328 U.S. 256, 265 (1946) (frequent overflights "took" property)]. * * *.

* * * In the context of water rights, a mere restriction on use—the hallmark of a regulatory action—completely eviscerates the right itself since plaintiffs' sole entitlement is to the use of the water. * * * Unlike other species of property where use restrictions may limit some, but not all of the incidents of ownership, the denial of a right to the use of water accomplishes a complete extinction of all value. Thus, by limiting plaintiffs' ability to use an amount of water to which they would otherwise be entitled, the government has essentially substituted itself as the beneficiary of the contract rights with regard to that water and totally displaced the contract holder. That complete occupation of property—an exclusive possession of plaintiffs' water-use rights for preservation of the fish—mirrors the invasion present in *Causby*. To the extent, then, that the federal government, by preventing plaintiffs

from using the water to which they would otherwise have been entitled, have rendered the usufructuary right to that water valueless, they have thus effected a physical taking. * * *

III. Having concluded that a deprivation of water amounts to a physical taking, we turn now to the question of whether plaintiffs in fact owned the property for which they seek to be compensated. * * * Defendant argues that both the terms of plaintiffs' contracts and the background principles of state law impose limits on plaintiffs' titles that render their loss of water non-compensable. * * *

i. Contract Language as a Limitation on Title Under the terms of the water supply contracts, neither the state nor its agents may be held liable for "any damage, direct or indirect, arising from shortages in the amount of water to be made available for delivery to the Agency under this contract caused by drought, operation of area of origin statutes, or any other cause beyond its control." Para. 18(f). Defendant reads that language to mean that plaintiffs are entitled to receive water only to the extent that water is available to DWR. * * *

* * * Paragraph 18(f) [however, only] insulates DWR from liability for circumstances beyond its control; not the federal government. The inclusion of Paragraph 18(f) in the contract does not render plaintiffs' interest in the water contingent; it merely provides DWR with a defense against a breach of contract action in certain specified circumstances. With that exception, plaintiffs' contract rights are otherwise fully formed against DWR, and certainly against a third party seeking to infringe on those rights. * * *.

ii. The Public Trust Doctrine, the Doctrine of Reasonable Use and Nuisance Law In addition to its contract-based argument, defendant offers a number of common law justifications for limiting the scope of plaintiffs' property right: specifically, that plaintiffs can have no vested right in a use or method of diverting water that is unreasonable or violates the public trust. The difficulty with defendant's argument, however, is that the water allocation scheme in effect for the period 1992-1994, as set forth in D-1485, specifically allowed for the allocations of water defendant now seeks to deem unreasonable. * * *

Whether a particular use or method of diversion is unreasonable or violative of the public trust is a question committed concurrently to the [SWRCB] and to the California courts. See National Audubon Soc'y v. Superior Court of Alpine County [33 Cal.3d 419, 451-452 (1983)]. Thus, while we accept the proposition that plaintiffs have no right to use or divert water in an unreasonable manner, nor in a way that violates the public trust, the issue now before us is whether such a determination has in fact been made.

Plaintiffs argue that the [SWRCB's] decision D-1485—a comprehensive water rights scheme balancing the needs of and allocating water rights among competing users—defines the full scope of their contract rights. In plaintiffs' view, D-1485 represents the state's determination of various water rights, thereby reflecting the amount of water, under state law, they reasonably can expect and to which they are reasonably entitled. * * *

In defendant's view, D-1485 fails to encapsulate the Board's approach to the endangerment of the delta smelt and salmon, both because it was promulgated before the fish were found to be in jeopardy, and because the [B]oard enacted D-95-1—a 1995 decision whose provisions adopt measures found in the RPAs—to protect the fish. Additionally, defendant argues that D-1485 should be read as an evolving document, one informed by later developments in water needs and altered by subsequent state actions. * * *

We cannot accept defendant's position. As an initial matter, the responsibility for water allocation is vested in the [SWRCB]. * * * Once an allocation has been made—as was done in D-1485—that determination defines the scope of plaintiffs' property rights, pronouncements of other agencies notwithstanding. While we accept the principle that California water policy may be ever-evolving, rights based on contracts with the state are not correspondingly self-adjusting. Rather, the promissory assurances they recite remain fixed until formally changed. * * *

Defendant argues against this position, urging us to anticipate how the Board or the California courts would apply the doctrine of reasonable use if the issue were before them. * * * The issue, defendant contends, is not what limitations the state in fact imposed on plaintiffs' titles, but what limitations the state could have imposed under state background principles. * * *

That the use now being challenged was not always unlawful is evident from the fact that it was specifically authorized by the state in D-1485. Were we now to deem that use a nuisance, we would not be making explicit that which had always been implied under background principles of property law, but would instead be replacing the state's judgment with our own. That we cannot do.

* * * The public trust and reasonable use doctrines each require a complex balancing of interests—an exercise of discretion for which this court is not suited and with which it is not charged.

To the extent that water allocation in California is a policy judgment—one specifically committed to the SWRCB and the California courts—a finding of unreasonableness by this court would be tantamount to our making California law rather than merely applying it. * * *

[W]e conclude that plaintiffs' right to divert water in the manner specified by their contracts and in conformance with D-1485 continued until a determination to the contrary was made either by the SWRCB or by the California courts. As no such determination was made during * * * 1992-1994, and subsequent amendments to policy cannot, for contract purposes, be made retroactive, plaintiffs were * * * entitled to the water use provided for * * * in their contracts.

CONCLUSION * * * It is the Board that must provide the necessary weighing of interests to determine the appropriate balance under California law between the cost and benefit of species preservation. The federal government is certainly free to preserve the fish; it must simply pay for the water it takes to do so. * * *

Notes

1. **Physical v. regulatory takings.** The impacts of environmental restrictions upon water diverters and users have led to repeated claims of compensable "takings" under the 5th Amendment. That Amendment states that private property shall not be "taken" for public use without just compensation. The Supreme Court has recognized two types of takings: physical and regulatory. See generally, Zachary C. Kleinsasser, Public and Private Property Rights: Regulatory and Physical Takings and the Public Trust Doctrine, 32 B.C. Envtl. Aff. L. Rev. 421 (2005).

As the principal case indicates, a physical taking occurs when the government's action amounts to a physical occupation or invasion of the property. Neither the size of the intrusion nor the significance of the public purpose behind it matters. See Lucas v. S.C. Coastal Council, 505 U.S. 1003 (1992). In the context of water rights, courts have found a physical taking where the government has physically diverted water for its own consumptive use or decreased the amount of water accessible by the owner of the water rights. See Casitas Municipal Water District v. United States, 543 F.3d 1267 (Fed. Cir. 2008) (finding physical taking after reviewing Dugan v. Rank 372 U.S. 609 (1963), United States v. Gerlach Live Stock Co., 339 U.S. 725 (1950), and Int'l Paper Co. v. United States, 282 U.S. 399 (1931).)

In contrast, a regulatory taking occurs when the government's regulation severely restricts the use to which an owner may put his property. The Supreme Court has declined to develop a precise formula for determining whether a regulatory taking has occurred, beyond the deprivation of "all economically viable use of the land." See, e.g., City of Monterey v. Del Monte Dunes at Monterey, Ltd., 526 U.S. 687 (1999). Where some economically viable uses remain, courts generally apply Penn Central Transportation Co. v. New York, 438 U.S. 104, 124-25 (1978). Under *Penn Central,* courts weigh the character of the government action, the economic impact of that action and the reasonableness of the property owner's investment-backed expectations. Compare *City of Monterey,* supra, (finding submission of regulatory taking issue to jury appropriate when the City had repeatedly rejected the developer's application to develop a parcel of land and each time imposed more rigorous demands) with Tahoe-Sierra Pres. Council, Inc. v. Tahoe Reg'l Planning Agency, 535 U.S. 302 (2002) (finding that a 32-month moratorium on development did not constitute a temporary taking.)

In the principal case, the decision to label the impact of the water delivery cutbacks a "physical taking" made plaintiffs' case substantially easier. As indicated above, under this doctrine, any physical intrusion, no matter how slight, is a "taking." Was the court's use of the physical takings case law here appropriate? While the specific amount of water that was not delivered to the contract holders was not available to them for their use that year, they did not suffer a complete cessation of deliveries. Is the cutback that they suffered any different from, say, land zoning requirements that require a set-aside of a portion of land for open space? These restrictions have long been upheld against regulatory takings claims. See, e.g., Gorieb v. Fox, 274 U.S. 603 (1927) (setbacks). Cf. Hadachek v. Sebastian, 239 U.S. 394 (1915) (no taking even though property lost 87.5% of overall value). But even if this argument were sufficient to address the facts in the principal case, how would it apply to the irrigators in the Klamath Basin? In 2001, under the mandate of the ESA, the Bureau of Reclamation stopped all deliveries of irrigation water to project contractors. Shortly after their victory in the principal case, the attorneys for the successful plaintiffs filed a similar suit on behalf of Klamath Basin irrigators. See Klamath Irr. Dist. v. United States, 67 Fed. Cl. 504 (2005) (finding *Tulare* "wrong on some counts, incomplete on others, and distinguishable, at all events.")

Takings scholarship is rich and diverse. See, e.g., articles cited supra p. 332, Note 7.); Hannah Jacobs Wiseman, Notice and Expectation under Bounded Uncertainty: Defining Evolving Property Rights Boundaries Through Public Trust and Takings, 21 Tul. Envtl. L.J. 233 (2008).

2. Background principles of California Water Law. A regulation that reflects the application of "background principles" of state property law will not trigger a taking. Lucas v. S.C. Coastal Council, 505 U.S. 1003, 1030 (1992). In the principal case, the court notes that under both the California reasonable use and public trust doctrines, no water user can acquire a right to use water unreasonably or in violation of the public trust. And the court also notes that both the California Water Resources Control Board and the courts have concurrent jurisdiction to enforce those two doctrines. Yet the court refused to second guess the state board's approval of the diversions in question. Was this appropriate? Did the California State Water Resources Control Board, in its Decision 1485, actually authorize deliveries of water that would themselves violate the ESA? How would a California state court have ruled on the validity of such deliveries, had a suit been brought in state court under either the reasonable use or public trust doctrines? Even if a California state court might have second guessed the state board, did the federal court in the principal case take the correct approach so that it did not have to guess what a California state court might have done? Or is such guessing part of the court's job when presented with such state law questions? See

Klamath Irr. Dist. v. United States, 67 Fed. Cl. 504, 538 (2005) (criticizing *Tulare* for failure to more thoroughly consider, inter alia, background principles of state law); Michael C. Blumm, Lucas Ritchie, Lucas's Unlikely Legacy: The Rise of Background Principles as Categorical Takings Defenses, 29 Harv. Envtl. L. Rev. 321 (2005).

3. **Impact of decision.** The court in the principal case was the first court to find a compensable taking for an ESA impact on a water right, albeit a contractual right to purchase water as opposed to a common law or statutory right to divert. As the first such case, it received a lot of attention from regulators, environmentalists, and water rights holders alike. Is it a landmark decision, or is it distinguishable on its unique facts? For an article setting out the latter argument, see Melinda Harm Benson, The Tulare Case: Water Rights, The Endangered Species Act, and the Fifth Amendment, 32 Envtl. L. 551 (2002). Benson argues that the case involved a unique concatenation of relationships. As noted in the principal case, the California State Water Project has a unique Coordinated Operating Agreement with the federal Bureau of Reclamation; this set of federal-state relationships is not likely to be duplicated elsewhere. Moreover, *Tulare Lake* was not a suit by a project's contractor against the project's operators itself. As the principal case notes, there are usually provisions within the water delivery agreements that only obligate the project operator to deliver such water as is available to them in a given year. Indeed, until 2009, suits by federal contractors against federal project operators for ESA-induced water delivery curtailments had been barred by such contractual provisions. See, e.g., O'Neill v. United States, and Rio Grande Silvery Minnow v. Keys, both discussed infra p. 687, Note 3. In 2009, however, a federal court distinguished *O'Neill*. Stockton E. Water Dist. v. United States and accompanying Notes, infra p. 680. See also infra, p. 625, Note 5.

Initial judicial treatment of *Tulare* has been largely critical. Indeed, in Klamath Irrigation District v. United States, 67 Fed. Cl. 504, 538 (2005) and Casitas Municipal Water District v. United States, 76 Fed. Cl. 100 (2007), reversed, 543 F.3d 1276 (Fed. Cir. 2008), the Court of Claims itself concluded that *Tulare* had been wrongly decided.

The *Casitas* claim involved compensation for the value of water required to be diverted to a fish ladder. The Court of Claims denied the claim. On appeal, however, the Court of Appeals for the Federal Circuit reversed. It found that the required diversion was a physical taking. In a footnote, it distinguished the post-*Tulare* opinions:

"We do not opine on whether *Tulare* was rightly decided, but note that the *Tulare* decision has been criticized. First, *Tulare* has been criticized for failing to engage in a thorough analysis of whether the plaintiff had a vested property right in the water in question. *See Klamath Irr. Dist. v. United States,* 67 Fed. Cl. 504, 538 (2005) (criticizing *Tulare* for failing to adequately consider whether the contracts were limited in the event of water shortage by prior contracts, prior appropriations, or other state law principles); *Allegretti & Co. v. County of Imperial,* 42

Cal.Rptr.3d 122, 131-32 * * * (4th Dist. 2006) (same) * * *. In the instant case, the government has conceded that Casitas has a valid property right in the water at issue. Second, *Tulare* has been criticized for focusing on the results of the government action rather than on the character of the government action. *See Allegretti,* 138 Cal.App.4th at 1275, 42 Cal.Rptr.3d 122 (criticizing *Tulare* for its conclusion "that the government's imposition on pumping restrictions is no different than an actual physical diversion of water" because "the government's passive restriction, which required the water users to leave water in the stream, did not constitute a physical invasion or appropriation"). In the instant case, the government's admissions made clear that it did not merely require water to be left in stream, but instead actively caused the physical diversion of water away from the Robles-Casitas Canal and towards the fish ladder."

4. **Denouement.** In the article cited in the preceding note, Benson concluded that the "decision will be of lasting significance only if the federal government fails, for political reasons, to appeal the decision." Benson, supra p. 624, Note 3, at p. 551. If you were the federal attorney in charge of the case, would you have recommended that the United States appeal? On the one hand, any damages owed to the plaintiffs will come out of the Treasury. On the other hand, would you be concerned that a decision upholding the matter by the Federal Circuit or the United States Supreme Court would make for even stronger precedent than the Court of Claims decision? Or would there be other factors influencing your decision? In late 2004, the United States decided not to appeal and agreed to pay plaintiffs $16.7 million dollars as compensation for the "taking."

5. **Breach of contract defenses.** In Stockton East Water District v. United States, 583 F.3d 1344 (Fed. Cir. 2009), the Federal Circuit considered another claim for compensation resulting from reduced water deliveries. The different approach taken by the parties and the court in that case is set out infra, p. 680. Interestingly, *Stockton East* does not even mention *Tulare* and cites but does not discuss *Casitas.*

Chapter 8

FEDERAL WATER LAW

SECTION 1. CONSTITUTIONAL POWERS

RAPANOS v. UNITED STATES
Supreme Court of the United States, 2006.
547 U.S. 715, 126 S.Ct. 2208, 165 L. Ed.2d 159.

Justice SCALIA announced the judgment of the Court and delivered an opinion, in which the Chief Justice, Justice Thomas and Justice Alito join.

[The Clean Water Act (CWA or Act) makes it unlawful to discharge dredged or fill material into "navigable waters," §§ 301, 502(12), 33 U.S.C. §§ 1311, 1362(12), without a permit from the Army Corps of Engineers issued under § 404, 33 U.S.C. § 1344. The Act defines the jurisdictional trigger "navigable waters" as "the waters of the United States." § 502(7), 33 U.S.C. § 1362(7).]

For a century prior to the CWA, we had interpreted the phrase "navigable waters of the United States" in the Act's predecessor statutes to refer to interstate waters that are "navigable in fact" or readily susceptible of being rendered so. After passage of the CWA, the Corps initially adopted this traditional judicial definition for the Act's term "navigable waters." After a District Court enjoined these regulations as too narrow, the Corps adopted a far broader definition. The Corps' new regulations deliberately sought to extend the definition of "the waters of the United States" to the outer limits of Congress's commerce power.

The Corps' current regulations interpret "the waters of the United States" to include, in addition to traditional interstate navigable waters, 33 CFR § 328.3(a)(1) (2004), "[a]ll interstate waters including interstate wetlands," § 328.3(a)(2); "[a]ll other waters such as intrastate lakes, rivers, streams (including intermittent streams), mudflats, sandflats, wetlands, sloughs, prairie potholes, wet meadows, playa lakes, or natural ponds, the use, degradation or destruction of which could affect interstate or foreign commerce," § 328.3(a)(3); "[t]ributaries of [such] waters," § 328.3(a)(5); and "[w]etlands adjacent to [such] waters [and tributaries] (other than waters that are themselves wetlands)," § 328.3(a)(7). The regulation defines "adjacent" wetlands as those "bordering, contiguous [to], or neighboring" waters of the United States. § 328.3(c). It specifically provides that "[w]etlands separated from other waters of the United States by man-made dikes or barriers, natural river berms, beach dunes and the like are 'adjacent wetlands.'" Ibid.

We first addressed the proper interpretation of 33 U.S.C. § 1362(7)'s phrase "the waters of the United States" in United States v. Riverside Bayview Homes, Inc., 474 U.S. 121, 106 S.Ct. 455, 88 L.Ed.2d 419 (1985). [W]e upheld the Corps' interpretation of "the waters of the United States" to include wetlands that "actually abut[ted] on" traditional navigable waters. Id., at 135, 106 S.Ct. 455. [Then, in Northern Cook County v. Army Corps of Engineers, 531 US. 159, 121 S.Ct. 675, 148 L.Ed.2d 576 (2001) (SWANCC)], we held that "nonnavigable, isolated, intrastate waters"—which, unlike the wetlands at issue in *Riverside Bayview*, did not "actually abu[t] on a navigable waterway,"—were not included as "waters of the United States." * * *

In these consolidated cases, we consider whether four Michigan wetlands, which lie near ditches or man-made drains that eventually empty into traditional navigable waters, constitute "waters of the United States" within the meaning of the Act. [The Corps determined that they do, and the lower courts agreed.]

We have twice stated that the meaning of "navigable waters" in the Act is broader than the traditional understanding of that term, *SWANCC,* 531 U.S., at 167, 121 S.Ct. 675; *Riverside Bayview,* 474 U.S., at 133, 106 S.Ct. 455. We have also emphasized, however, that the qualifier "navigable" is not devoid of significance, *SWANCC, supra,* at 172, 121 S.Ct. 675.

We need not decide the precise extent to which the qualifiers "navigable" and "of the United States" restrict the coverage of the Act. Whatever the scope of these qualifiers, the CWA authorizes federal jurisdiction only over "waters." 33 U.S.C. § 1362(7). The only natural definition of the term "waters" [indicates] that "the waters of the United States" in § 1362(7) cannot bear the expansive meaning that the Corps would give it.

The Corps' expansive approach might be arguable if the CWA defined "navigable waters" as "water of the United States." But "the waters of the United States" is something else. The use of the definite article ("the") and the plural number ("waters") shows plainly that § 1362(7) does not refer to water in general. In this form, "the waters" refers more narrowly to water "[a]s found in streams and bodies forming geographical features such as oceans, rivers, [and] lakes," or "the flowing or moving masses, as of waves or floods, making up such streams or bodies." Webster's New International Dictionary 2882 (2d ed. 1954) (hereinafter Webster's Second). On this definition, "the waters of the United States" include only relatively permanent, standing or flowing bodies of water. The definition refers to water as found in "streams," "oceans," "rivers," "lakes," and "bodies" of water "forming geographical features." Ibid. All of these terms connote continuously present, fixed bodies of water, as opposed to ordinarily dry channels through which water occasionally or intermittently flows. Even the least substantial of the definition's terms, namely, "streams," connotes a continuous flow of water in a permanent channel—especially when used in company with other terms such as "rivers," "lakes," and "oceans." None of these terms encompasses transitory puddles or ephemeral flows of water. * * *

Even if the phrase "the waters of the United States" were ambiguous as applied to intermittent flows, our own canons of construction would establish that the Corps' interpretation of the statute is impermissible. As we noted in *SWANCC*, the Government's expansive interpretation would "result in a significant impingement of the States' traditional and primary power over land and water use." 531 U.S., at 174, 121 S.Ct. 675. Regulation of land use, as through the issuance of the development permits sought by petitioners in both of these cases, is a quintessential state and local power. The extensive federal jurisdiction urged by the Government would authorize the Corps to function as a *de facto* regulator of immense stretches of intrastate land—an authority the agency has shown its willingness to exercise with the scope of discretion that would befit a local zoning board. We ordinarily expect a "clear and manifest" statement from Congress to authorize an unprecedented intrusion into traditional state authority. The phrase "the waters of the United States" hardly qualifies.

Likewise, just as we noted in *SWANCC*, the Corps' interpretation stretches the outer limits of Congress's commerce power and raises difficult questions about the ultimate scope of that power. See 531 U.S., at 173, 121 S.Ct. 675. (In developing the current regulations, the Corps consciously sought to extend its authority to the farthest reaches of the commerce power. See 42 Fed.Reg. 37127 (1977).) Even if the term "the waters of the United States" were ambiguous as applied to channels that sometimes host ephemeral flows of water (which it is not), we would expect a clearer statement from Congress to authorize an agency theory of jurisdiction that presses the envelope of constitutional validity.

In sum, on its only plausible interpretation, the phrase "the waters of the United States" includes only those relatively permanent, standing or continuously flowing bodies of water "forming geographic features" that are described in ordinary parlance as "streams[,] * * * oceans, rivers, [and] lakes." See Webster's Second 2882. The phrase does not include channels through which water flows intermittently or ephemerally, or channels that periodically provide drainage for rainfall. * * *

[In *Riverside Bayview,* w]e acknowledged, however, that there was an inherent ambiguity in drawing the boundaries of any "waters". Because of this inherent ambiguity, we deferred to the agency's inclusion of wetlands "actually abut[ting]" traditional navigable waters * * *. The difficulty of delineating the boundary between water and land was central to our reasoning in the case: "In view of the breadth of federal regulatory authority contemplated by the Act itself and *the inherent difficulties of defining precise bounds to regulable waters,* the Corps' ecological judgment about the relationship between waters and their adjacent wetlands provides an adequate basis for a legal judgment that adjacent wetlands may be defined as waters under the Act." Id., at 134, 106 S.Ct. 455 (emphasis added).

When we characterized the holding of *Riverside Bayview* in *SWANCC,* we referred to the close connection between waters and the wetlands that they gradually blend into: "It was the *significant nexus* between the wetlands and 'navigable waters' that informed our reading of the CWA in *Riverside Bayview Homes.*" 531 U.S., at 167, 121 S.Ct. 675 (emphasis added). In particular, *SWANCC* rejected the notion that the ecological considerations upon which the Corps relied in *Riverside Bayview*—and upon which the dissent repeatedly relies today—provided an *independent* basis for including entities like "wetlands" (or "ephemeral streams") within the phrase "the waters of the United States." *SWANCC* found such ecological considerations irrelevant to the question whether physically isolated waters come within the Corps' jurisdiction. It thus confirmed that *Riverside Bayview* rested upon the inherent ambiguity in defining where water ends and abutting ("adjacent") wetlands begin, permitting the Corps' reliance on ecological considerations *only to resolve that ambiguity* in favor of treating all abutting wetlands as waters. Isolated ponds were not "waters of the United States" in their own right, see 531 U.S., at 167, 171, 121 S.Ct. 675, and presented no boundary-drawing problem that would have justified the invocation of ecological factors to treat them as such.

Therefore, *only* those wetlands with a continuous surface connection to bodies that are "waters of the United States" in their own right, so that there is no clear demarcation between "waters" and wetlands, are "adjacent to" such waters and covered by the Act. Wetlands with only an intermittent, physically remote hydrologic connection to "waters of the United States" do not implicate the boundary-drawing problem of *Riverside Bayview,* and thus lack the necessary connection to covered waters that we described as a "significant nexus" in *SWANCC*. 531 U.S., at 167, 121 S.Ct. 675. Thus, establishing that wetlands such as [the ones in these consolidated cases] are covered by the Act requires two findings: first, that the adjacent channel contains a "wate[r] of the United States," (*i.e.*, a relatively permanent body of water connected to traditional interstate navigable waters); and second, that the wetland has a continuous surface connection with that water, making it difficult to determine where the "water" ends and the "wetland" begins. * * *

Because the Sixth Circuit applied the wrong standard to determine if these wetlands are covered "waters of the United States," and because of the paucity of the record in both of these cases, the lower courts should determine, in the first instance, whether the ditches or drains near each wetland are "waters" in the ordinary sense of containing a relatively permanent flow; and (if they are) whether the wetlands in question are "adjacent" to these "waters" in the sense of possessing a continuous surface connection that creates the boundary-drawing problem we addressed in *Riverside Bayview*.

Justice KENNEDY, concurring in the judgment.

The Court in *Riverside Bayview* did note, it is true, the difficulty of defining where "water ends and land begins," *id.*, at 132, 106 S.Ct. 455, and the Court cited that problem as one reason for deferring to the Corps' view that adjacent wetlands could constitute waters. Given, however, the further recognition in *Riverside Bayview* that an overinclusive definition is permissible even when it reaches wetlands holding moisture disconnected from adjacent water bodies, *id.*, at 135, and n. 9, 106 S.Ct. 455, *Riverside Bayview's* observations about the difficulty of defining the water's edge cannot be taken to establish that when a clear boundary is evident, wetlands beyond the boundary fall outside the Corps' jurisdiction. * * *

Consistent with *SWANCC* and *Riverside Bayview* and with the need to give the term "navigable" some meaning, the Corps' jurisdiction over wetlands depends upon the existence of a significant nexus between the wetlands in question and navigable waters in the traditional sense. The required nexus must be assessed in terms of the statute's goals and purposes. Congress enacted the law to "restore and maintain the chemical, physical, and biological integrity of the Nation's waters," 33 U.S.C. § 1251(a), and it pursued that objective by restricting dumping and filling in "navigable waters," §§ 1311(a), 1362(12). With respect to wetlands, the rationale for Clean Water Act regulation is, as the Corps has recognized, that wetlands can perform critical functions related to the integrity of other waters—functions such as pollutant trapping, flood control, and runoff storage. 33 CFR § 320.4(b)(2). Accordingly, wetlands possess the requisite nexus, and thus come within the statutory phrase "navigable waters," if the wetlands, either alone or in combination with similarly situated lands in the region, significantly affect the chemical, physical, and biological integrity of other covered waters more readily understood as "navigable." * * *

Justice STEVENS, with whom Justice Souter, Justice Ginsburg, and Justice Breyer join, dissenting.

* * * Rejecting more than 30 years of practice by the Army Corps, the plurality disregards the nature of the congressional delegation to the agency and the technical and complex character of the issues at stake. * * * The Corps' * * * decision to treat these wetlands as encompassed within the term "waters of the United States" is a quintessential example of the Executive's reasonable interpretation of a statutory provision.

Contrary to the plurality's revisionist reading today, *Riverside Bayview* nowhere implied that our approval of "adjacent" wetlands was contingent upon an understanding that "adjacent" means having a "continuous surface connection" between the wetland and its neighboring creek. * * * [Furthermore, Congress] acquiesce[d] in the Corps' regulations in 1977. Both Chambers conducted extensive debates about the Corps' regulatory jurisdiction over wetlands [and] rejected efforts to limit this jurisdiction * * *.

While I generally agree with [parts] of Justice Kennedy's opinion, I do not share his view that we should replace regulatory standards that have been in place for over 30 years with a judicially crafted rule distilled from the term "significant nexus" as used in *SWANCC*. * * *

[W]hile both the plurality and Justice Kennedy agree that there must be a remand for further proceedings, their respective opinions define different tests to be applied on remand. Given that all four Justices who have joined this opinion would uphold the Corps' jurisdiction in both of these cases—and in all other cases in which either the plurality's or Justice Kennedy's test is satisfied—on remand each of the judgments should be reinstated if *either* of those tests is met.

Notes

1. **The meaning of *Rapanos*.** A guidance memorandum on *Rapanos* issued by the Corps of Engineers on December 2, 2008, states: "When there is no majority in a Supreme Court case, controlling legal principles may be derived from those principles espoused by five or more justices [citing Marks v. United States, 430 U.S. 188, 193-94 (1977)]. Thus, regulatory jurisdiction under the CWA exists if either the plurality's or Justice Kennedy's standard is satisfied." http://www.epa.gov/owow/wetlands/pdf/ CWA _ Jurisdiction_Following_Rapanos120208.pdf.

U.S. v. Cundiff, 555 F.3d 200, 208 (6th Cir. 2009) found that CWA regulatory "jurisdiction is proper here under each of the [three] primary

Rapanos opinions and therefore we do not have to decide here, once and for all, which test controls in all future cases." The court added:

"In its short life, *Rapanos* has indeed satisfied any "bafflement" requirement. The first court to decide what opinion was controlling decided to ignore all of them and instead opted for earlier circuit precedent which it felt was clearer and more readily applied. United States v. Chevron Pipe Line Co., 437 F. Supp. 2d 605, 613 (N.D. Tex. 2006). The Courts of Appeals have not fared much better. The Ninth Circuit has stated that Justice Kennedy's test applies in most instances, Northern California River Watch v. City of Healdsburg, 496 F.3d 993, 1000 (9th Cir. 2007), while the Eleventh Circuit has held that the Act's coverage may be established *only* under his test. United States v. Robison, 505 F.3d 1208, 1219-22 (11th Cir. 2007). By contrast, the First and the Seventh Circuits, though differing somewhat in their analyses, have followed Justice Stevens' advice and held that the Act confers jurisdiction whenever *either* Justice Kennedy's or the plurality's test is met. United States v. Johnson, 467 F.3d 56, 60-66; United States v. Berke Excavating, Inc., 464 F.3d 723, 725 (7th Cir. 2006)."

2. **The Commerce Clause and the traditional concept of navigable waters.** The traditional concept of navigable waters of the United States goes back to three nineteenth century cases on the power of Congress under Article I, Section 8 of the Constitution "To regulate Commerce * * * among the several States." Gibbons v. Ogden, 22 U.S. (9 Wheat.) 1 (1824), and Gilman v. City of Philadelphia, 70 U.S. (3 Wall.) 713 (1865) established that Congress's power to regulate interstate commerce extends to navigable waters of the United States. The third case, The Daniel Ball, 77 U.S. (10 Wall.) 557, 563 (1870), defined such waters. Departing from the English common law definition of navigability, which generally was limited to the sea and waters affected by the ebb and flow of the tides, the Court stated in *Daniel Ball*:

> Those rivers must be regarded as public navigable rivers in law which are navigable in fact. And they are navigable in fact when they are used, or are susceptible of being used, in their ordinary condition, as highways for commerce, over which trade and travel are or may be conducted in the customary modes of trade and travel on water. And they constitute navigable waters of the United States within the meaning of the acts of Congress, in contradistinction from the navigable waters of the States, when they form in their ordinary condition by themselves, or by uniting with other waters, a continued highway over which commerce is or may be carried on with other States or foreign countries in the customary modes in which such commerce is conducted by water.

Much later, in United States v. Appalachian Electric Power Co., 311 U.S. 377 (1940), the Court elaborated on the *Daniel Ball* test. The Court said a river is navigable in fact if it either (a) presently is used or susceptible of being used as a highway for commerce, (b) in the past was so used or susceptible of being used even though it no longer is, or (c) in the future could be so used. The Court added that a river's susceptibility for use as a highway for commerce in its "ordinary condition" should be judged by whether it could be so used if reasonable improvements were made to it. The phrase "ordinary condition" thus refers to the volume of water, gradients, and regularity of flow, not to whether artificial aids are required before commercial navigation can be undertaken.

Consistent with the English common law on navigability, lower federal courts have treated the traditional Commerce Clause concept of navigable waters of the United States as including not only waters meeting the *Daniel Ball* test but also waters affected by the ebb and flow of the tide even though they are not used or usable as highways for interstate commerce. E.g., United States v. Sasser, 967 F.2d 993 (4th Cir. 1992); United States v. Stoeco Homes, Inc., 498 F.2d 597 (3d Cir. 1974).

Finally, in Kaiser Aetna v. United States, 444 U.S. 164, 173 (1979), the Court noted that Congress's Commerce Clause regulatory power has expanded since the traditional concept of navigable waters of the United States made its appearance in the nineteenth century:

> "Reference to the navigability of a waterway adds little if anything to the breadth of Congress' regulatory power over interstate commerce. [A] wide spectrum of economic activities 'affect' interstate commerce and thus are susceptible of congressional regulation under the Commerce Clause irrespective of whether navigation, or, indeed, water, is involved. The cases that discuss Congress' paramount authority to regulate waters used in interstate commerce are consequently best understood when viewed in terms of [affect-interstate-commerce] analysis than by reference to whether the stream in fact is capable of supporting navigation or may be characterized as 'navigable water of the United States.'"

3. **Current significance of the traditional concept.** The evolution of Commerce Clause jurisprudence does not mean the traditional concept of navigable waters has become obsolete under older legislation. One example is section 10 of the Rivers and Harbors Appropriation Act of 1899 (RHA). This statute requires a Corps of Engineers permit to excavate, fill, or otherwise alter the channel of "any navigable water of the United States" or to build any structures in such water. Corps of Engineers regulations implementing RHA § 10 define "navigable water of the United States" in accordance with the traditional concept, i.e., water that is navigable in fact for interstate commerce or is affected by the ebb and flow of the tide. See 33 C.F.R. §§ 322.2, 329.4.

A second example is section 23(b) of the Federal Power Act (FPA), 16 U.S.C. § 817. This requires a license from the Federal Energy Regulatory Commission (FERC), the successor of the Federal Power Commission, for nonfederal hydroelectric projects that either (1) are located on "navigable waters of the United States," (2) are located on other waters "over which Congress has jurisdiction under its authority to regulate commerce with foreign nations and among the several states * * * if * * * the interests of interstate or foreign commerce would be affected," (3) occupy federal public lands or reservations, or (4) use surplus water from a federal dam. The first two grounds for licensing jurisdiction are based on the Commerce Clause. (The last two are based on the Property Clause, infra Note 4.)

The FPA defines the first jurisdictional ground—navigable waters of the United States—by using the navigability-in-fact component of the traditional concept of navigable waters of the United States. FPA § 3(8), 16 U.S.C. § 796(8). The second jurisdictional ground—interstate or foreign commerce would be affected—means a project on a nonnavigable river requires a license if it will affect interstate commerce by generating electric power for interstate transmission, even though it will have no impact on downstream navigability. Fed. Power Comm'n v. Union Elec. Co., 381 U.S. 90 (1965).

The second jurisdictional ground has not swallowed up the first one. If a proposed hydroelectric project will be located on a navigable waterway, that alone supports regulatory jurisdiction. There is no need for FERC to inquire whether the project will affect interstate commerce. Thus, in City of Centralia v. FERC, 661 F.2d 787 (9th Cir. 1981), a small municipal hydroelectric plant was not shown to impact interstate commerce enough to require a license under the first basis for jurisdiction; but later the same plant was held to need a license under the "navigable waters" jurisdictional basis, 851 F.2d 278 (9th Cir. 1988).

4. **Other constitutional powers.** Besides the Commerce Clause, several other constitutional grants of power to Congress justify federal water regulation and water development. The Property Clause, Article IV, Section 3, states: "The Congress shall have power to dispose of and make all needful Rules and Regulations respecting the Territory or other Property belonging to the United States." The Property Clause enables the production and sale of hydroelectric power at federal dams. Ashwander v. TVA, 297 U.S. 288, 330 (1936). Also, federal ownership of the public domain sustained the Reclamation Act of 1902.

Article I, Sections 8 and 9 empower Congress to declare war and to levy taxes and appropriate money to provide for the common defense of the United States. In the 1916 National Defense Act, Congress authorized the President to investigate means of producing nitrates and other products for war munitions, and to designate sites on rivers and public lands suitable for generating power for the production of nitrates and other useful products. The Wilson Dam on the Tennessee River was constructed under this authority and later was incorporated into the system of the Tennessee Valley Authority. Its hydroelectric energy was sold in peacetime for distribution in the Tennessee Valley. In *Ashwander*, the Court ruled the dam and power plant were "adapted to the purposes of national defense" and their maintenance in operating condition to assure abundant electric energy in case of war made them national defense assets.

The General Welfare Clause, Article I, Section 8, empowers Congress to levy taxes and to appropriate funds to provide for the general welfare of the United States. In United States v. Gerlach Live Stock Co., 339 U.S. 725 (1950), the Court said that one of the largest federal water development projects—the Central Valley Project in California—could be sustained under this power.

Treaties made under Article II, Section 2 become under Article VI "the supreme Law of Land." Treaties of the United States with Canada and Mexico impose limitations on state action affecting boundary waters and other waters that flow across the boundary or into boundary waters. Treaty obligations of the United States give the Nation an additional basis for authorizing works of improvements on international waterways. Arizona v. California, 283 U.S. 423 (1931).

UNITED STATES v. RANDS
Supreme Court of the United States, 1967.
389 U.S. 121, 88 S. Ct. 265, 19 L. Ed.2d 329.

MR. JUSTICE WHITE delivered the opinion of the Court.

In this case the Court is asked to decide whether the compensation which the United States is constitutionally required to pay when it condemns riparian land includes the land's value as a port site. Respondents owned land along the Columbia River in the State of Oregon. They leased the land to the State with an option to purchase, it apparently being contemplated that the State would use the land as an industrial park, part of which would function as a port. The option was never exercised, for the land was taken by the United States in connection with the John Day Lock and Dam Project, authorized by Congress as part of a comprehensive plan for the development of the Columbia River. Pursuant to statute the United States then conveyed the land to the State of Oregon at a price considerably less than the option price at which respondents had hoped to sell. In the condemnation action, the trial judge determined that the compensable value of the land taken was limited to its value for sand, gravel, and agricultural purposes and that its special value as a port site could not be considered. The ultimate award was about one-fifth the claimed value of the land if used as a port. The Court of Appeals for the Ninth Circuit reversed, apparently holding that the Government had taken from respondents a compensable right of access to navigable waters and concluding that "port site value should be compensable under the Fifth Amendment." 367 F.2d 186, 191 (1966). We granted certiorari because of a seeming conflict between the decision below and United States v. Twin City Power Co., 350 U.S. 222, 76 S.Ct. 259, 100 L.Ed. 240 (1956). We reverse the judgment of the Court of Appeals because the principles underlying *Twin City* govern this case and the Court of Appeals erred in failing to follow them.

The Commerce Clause confers a unique position upon the Government in connection with navigable waters. "The power to regulate commerce comprehends the control for that purpose, and to the extent necessary, of all the navigable waters of the United States * * *. For this purpose they are the public property of the nation, and subject to all the requisite legislation by Congress." Gilman v. City of Philadelphia, 3 Wall. 713, 724–725, 18 L.Ed. 96 (1866). This power to regulate navigation confers upon the United States a "dominant servitude," which extends to the entire stream and the stream bed below ordinary high-water mark. The proper exercise of this power is not an invasion of any private property rights in the stream or the lands underlying it, for the damage sustained does not result from taking property from riparian owners within the meaning of the Fifth Amendment but from the lawful exercise of a power to which the interests of riparian owners have always been subject. Thus, without being constitutionally obligated to pay compensation, the United States may change the course of a navigable stream or otherwise impair or destroy a riparian owner's access to navigable waters, even though the market value of the riparian owner's land is substantially diminished.

The navigational servitude of the United States does not extend beyond the high-water mark. Consequently, when fast lands are taken by the Government, just compensation must be paid. But "just as the navigational privilege permits the Government to reduce the value of riparian lands by denying the riparian owner access to the stream without compensation for his loss, * * * it also permits the Government to disregard the value arising from this same fact of riparian location in compensating the owner when fast lands are appropriated." United States v. Virginia Elec. & Power Co., 365 U.S. 624, 629, 81 S.Ct. 784, 788, 5 L.Ed.2d 838 (1961). Specifically, the Court has held that the Government is not required to give compensation for "water power" when it takes the riparian lands of a private power company using the stream to generate power. United States v. Chandler-Dunbar Water Power Co., 229 U.S. 53, 73-74, 33 S.Ct. 667, 676, 57 L.Ed. 1063 (1913). Nor must it compensate the company for the value of its uplands as a power plant site. Id., at 76, 33 S.Ct. at 677. Such value does not "inhere in these parcels as upland," but depends on use of the water to which the company has no right as against the United States: "The government had dominion over the water power of the rapids and falls, and cannot be required to pay any hypothetical additional value to a riparian owner who had no right to appropriate the current to his own commercial use." Ibid.

All this was made unmistakably clear in United States v. Twin City Power Co., 350 U.S. 222, 76 S.Ct. 259, 100 L.Ed. 240 (1956). The United States condemned a promising site for a hydroelectric power plant and was held to be under no obligation to pay for any special value which the fast lands had for power generating purposes. The value of the land attributable to its location on the stream was "due to the flow of the stream; and if the United States were required to pay the judgments below, it would be compensating the landowner for the increment of value added to the fast lands if the flow of the stream were taken into account." 350 U.S., at 226, 76 S.Ct., at 261.

We are asked to distinguish between the value of land as a power site and its value as a port site. In the power cases, the stream is used as a source of power to generate electricity. In this case, for the property to have value as a port, vessels must be able to arrive and depart by water, meanwhile using the waterside facilities of the port. In both cases, special value arises from access to, and use of, navigable waters. With regard to the constitutional duty to compensate a riparian owner, no distinction can be drawn. * * * We are dealing with the constitutional power of Congress completely to regulate navigable streams to the total exclusion of private power companies or port owners. As was true in *Twin City,* if the owner of the fast lands can demand port site value as part of his compensation, "he gets the value of a right that the Government in the exercise of its dominant servitude can grant or withhold as it chooses. * * * To require the United States to pay for this * * * value would be to create private claims in the public domain." 350 U.S., at 228, 76 S.Ct., at 263. * * *

Notes

1. **History and rationale of the federal navigation servitude.** Eva H. Morreale, Federal Power in Western Waters: The Navigation Power and the Rule of No Compensation, 3 Nat. Resources J. 1 (1963), recounts the development of the federal navigation servitude from its origin in an ancient English public right of passage and fishing in navigable waters: The ancient public right existed on navigable waterways whether or not they were otherwise private property. Obstruction or destruction of the public right of passage was a public nuisance abatable by the Crown, and no compensation was owed to the tortfeasor. (The Crown not only had power to abate such nuisances but also had a duty not to do anything itself to derogate the public right, a duty that evolved into the modern public trust doctrine covered supra pp. 530-51.) The ancient public right survived the American Revolution, with the new states succeeding to the power of the Crown to preserve public navigation. Then the adoption of the Constitution gave Congress the superior power to protect and to improve navigation in aid of interstate commerce. While the superior power of Congress over navigation does not explain why private property interests must yield without compensation, "[t]he historical notion of the paramount right of the community to navigate and fish its navigable waterways free from any interference does explain it." Id. at 30.

The Supreme Court has relied on this history to justify the navigation servitude: "The owner's use of property riparian to a navigable stream long has been limited by the right of the public to use the stream in the interest of navigation. * * * There thus has been ample notice over

the years that such property is subject to a dominant public interest."
United States v. Kan. City Life Ins. Co., 339 U.S. 799 (1950). Professor
Morreale (now Hanks) found the notice rationale insufficient to justify
many modern judicial applications of the servitude: "[A] good deal of the
difficulty lies in the manner in which the navigation servitude has been
permitted to grow from a rule securing free and unhindered passage on
navigable waterways to its present scope." 3 Nat. Resources J. at 76. She
noted that originally the Supreme Court applied the federal navigation
servitude only when Congress acted to protect or improve navigation in
aid of interstate commerce. But over time, she reported, "[c]ongressional
activity in the name of navigation has expanded—as has the concept of
navigable streams. The cases have not taken account of either development and its respective effects on notice." Id. at 31.

2. **The navigation servitude and nonnavigable streams.** In
United States v. Grand River Dam Authority, 363 U.S. 229 (1960), a state
agency owned a power site on a nonnavigable tributary of the navigable
Arkansas River. The United States condemned the site for construction of
a federal dam as part of a comprehensive river basin plan to develop electric power and to improve navigation and flood control on the Arkansas
River. The Court applied the navigation servitude to deny the agency's
claim of $10 million for loss of water power rights: "When the United
States appropriates the flow either of a navigable or a nonnavigable
stream pursuant to its superior power under the Commerce Clause, it is
exercising established prerogatives and is beholden to no one." Id. at 233.

3. **Congressional waiver of the navigation servitude.** Congress
reversed *Rands* in section 111 of the Rivers and Harbors and Flood Control Act of 1970, 33 U.S.C. § 595a:

"In all cases where real property shall be taken by the United States
for the public use in connection with any improvement of rivers, harbors,
canals, or waterways of the United States, and in all condemnation proceedings by the United States to acquire lands or easements for such improvements, the compensation to be paid for real property taken by the
United States above the normal high water mark of navigable waters of
the United States shall be the fair market value of such real property
based upon all uses to which such real property may reasonably be put,
including its highest and best use, any of which uses may be dependent
upon access to or utilization of such navigable waters. In cases of partial
takings of real property, no depreciation in the value of any remaining
real property shall be recognized and no compensation shall be paid for
any damages to such remaining real property which result from loss of or
reduction of access from such remaining real property to such navigable
waters because of the taking of real property or the purposes for which
such real property is taken."

Rands was so directly based on *Twin City* that a shot aimed at the
former should also hit the latter. What of *Chandler-Dunbar*, which *Rands*
mentioned and was the basis of *Twin City*? There, the federal government condemned uplands and instream hydropower generating facilities

of a power company, and the company unsuccessfully claimed compensation for the water power capacity of the rapids and falls of the river. If the same facts arose today, could the company's claim be phrased as one to recover for the value of its uplands as a power plant site?

Does section 111 apply when government regulation of navigable water deprives fast land of essentially all value, but the government does not actually acquire title to any of the land? In United States v. 30.54 Acres of Land, 90 F.3d 790 (3rd Cir. 1996), the owners of a 102-acre parcel on the Monongahela River used it to load coal on barges. This use depended upon a coal tipple that was grounded on their land but extended over the river to load the barges. Subsequently, the Corps of Engineers prohibited coal loading on the water in the area of the tipple because it endangered navigation. The landowners claimed just compensation because the prohibition deprived their parcel of all economically reasonable use. But the court ruled: "Section 111 applies only to 'real property taken by the United States above the high water mark.' Here the United States did not acquire above the high-water mark real property * * *; rather, it prohibited use of the tipple—a structure jutting one hundred feet into a navigable waterway. * * * Congress intended to modify the rule of United States v. Rands only to the extent of paying full compensation based on riparian location in cases of actual acquisition of above the high-water mark real property." Id. at 796 (alternative holding).

4. **State navigation servitude.** California has a state navigation servitude arising from the state's ownership of navigable waterways in trust for the public benefit. In Colberg, Inc. v. State ex rel. Department of Public Works, 432 P.2d 3 (Cal. 1967), the court invoked the servitude to deny just compensation to shipyard owners when the state built two freeway bridges over a channel that blocked access to the shipyards by large ships. Although the bridges impaired navigation, they facilitated commercial traffic on the freeway. The court said the servitude applies when the state acts relative to navigable waterways in any manner that improves commercial traffic and intercourse, whether or not navigation is improved.

5. **Whether or not navigation is improved?** Would the federal navigation servitude apply if Congress acting under its Commerce Clause power had authorized the two freeway bridges over the channel in Colberg? In United States v. Gerlach Live Stock Co., 339 U.S. 725 (1950), Congress authorized the Central Valley Project, the Nation's largest reclamation project, under the Commerce Clause and included navigation improvement as one project purpose. As part of the project, Friant Dam on the San Joaquin River stores water for delivery to irrigators. The plaintiffs owned grasslands that were naturally irrigated by spring high water before the dam was built. The dam ended the natural overflow irrigation. The plaintiffs sought just compensation for deprivation of riparian rights, arguing Friant Dam itself had no navigation benefits. The Court noted that the navigation benefits of the whole project were "economically insignificant" compared to the irrigation benefits. But because Congress

provided the Reclamation Act governed the project and that Act required compensation, the Court said: "[W]e need not ponder whether by virtue of a highly fictional navigational purpose, the Government could destroy the flow of a navigable stream and carry away its waters for sale to private interests without compensation to those deprived of them. We have never held that or anything like it, and we need not here pass on any question of constitutional power * * *." 339 U.S. at 737.

Justice Douglas concurred in the result but read the Court's navigation servitude precedents more broadly than the majority did: "[W]e have repeatedly held that there are no private property rights in the waters of a navigable river. * * * [T]he existence of property rights in the waters of a navigable stream are not dependent upon whether the United States is changing the flow of the river in aid of navigation or for some other purpose." Id. at 756.

KAISER AETNA v. UNITED STATES
Supreme Court of the United States, 1979.
444 U.S. 164, 100 S. Ct. 383, 62 L. Ed.2d 332.

MR. JUSTICE REHNQUIST delivered the opinion of the Court.

[Kuapa Pond on the island of Oahu, Hawaii, was originally a shallow 523-acre lagoon separated by a barrier beach from Maunalua Bay and the Pacific Ocean. The early Hawaiians installed sluice gates across two openings from the pond to the bay, and used the pond to raise fish. Water from the bay and ocean entered the pond through the gates during high tide, and during low tide the flow reversed toward the ocean. Kuapa Pond and similar fishponds were always considered private property by the people and government of Hawaii. In 1961 Kaiser Aetna acquired the site for development of Hawaii Kai, a marina-style subdivision. Kaiser Aetna then deepened the pond and cut a channel connecting it to the bay and the ocean. A community of 22,000 persons was developed. The marina was used by the residents of waterfront lots, many residents of back lots, and some nonresident boat owners—all of whom paid fees for maintenance, privacy, and security.

Section 10 of the Rivers and Harbors Appropriation Act of 1899 (RHA), 33 U.S.C.A. § 403, requires a permit to excavate, fill, or otherwise alter the channel of "any navigable water of the United States" or to build any structures in such water. Kaiser Aetna did its initial dredging and channel cutting with the acquiescence of the U.S. Army Corps of Engineers that no permit was needed. In 1972, however, the Corps asserted that the pond had become navigable water of the United States, and therefore a RHA § 10 permit would be needed for future excavation, filling, or construction in the marina. The Corps also asserted that the pond was subject to a federal navigation servitude that obligated Kaiser Aetna to allow public access to the pond. Kaiser Aetna initially disputed both assertions, but when the case got to the Supreme Court, the only matter that Kaiser Aetna still contested was whether the navigation servitude applied to the pond.]

The question before us is whether the Court of Appeals erred in holding that petitioners' improvements to Kuapa Pond caused its original character to be so altered that it became subject to an overriding federal navigational servitude * * *.

* * * When petitioners dredged and improved Kuapa Pond, the Government [contends], the pond—although it may once have qualified as fast land—became navigable water of the United States. The public thereby acquired a right to use Kuapa Pond as a continuous highway for navigation, and the Corps of Engineers may consequently obtain an injunction to prevent petitioners from attempting to reserve the waterway to themselves.

The position advanced by the Government, and adopted by the Court of Appeals below, presumes that the concept of "navigable waters of the United States" has a fixed meaning that remains unchanged in whatever context it is being applied. While we do not fully agree with the reasoning of the District Court, we do agree with its conclusion that all of this Court's cases dealing with the authority of Congress to regulate navigation and the so-called "navigational servitude" cannot simply be lumped into one basket. * * *

Although the Government is clearly correct in maintaining that the now dredged Kuapa Pond falls within the definition of "navigable waters" as this Court has used that term in delimiting the boundaries of Congress' regulatory authority under the Commerce Clause, this Court has never held that the navigational servitude creates a blanket exception to the Takings Clause whenever Congress exercises its Commerce Clause authority to promote navigation. Thus, while Kuapa Pond may be subject to regulation by the Corps of Engineers, acting under the authority delegated it by Congress in the Rivers and Harbors Appropriation Act, it does not follow that the pond is also subject to a public right of access. * * *

In light of its expansive authority under the Commerce Clause, there is no question but that Congress could assure the public a free right of access to the Hawaii Kai Marina if it so chose. Whether a statute or regulation that went so far amounted to a "taking," however, is an entirely separate question. * * *

The navigational servitude is an expression of the notion that the determination whether a taking has occurred must take into consideration the important public interest in the flow of interstate waters that in their natural condition are in fact capable of supporting public navigation. * * *

Here, the Government's attempt to create a public right of access to the improved pond goes so far beyond ordinary regulation or improvement for navigation as to amount to a taking * * *. More than one factor contributes to this result.[9] It is clear that prior to its improvement, Kuapa Pond was incapable of being used as a continuous highway for the purpose of navigation in interstate commerce. Its maximum depth at high tide was a mere two feet, it was separated from the adjacent bay and ocean by a natural barrier beach, and its principal commercial value was limited to fishing.[10] It consequently is not the sort of "great navigable stream" that this Court has previously recognized as being "[incapable] of private ownership." See, e.g., United States v. Chandler-Dunbar Co., 229 U.S., at 69, 33 S.Ct., at 674. And, as previously noted, Kuapa Pond has always been considered to be private property under Hawaiian law. Thus, the interest of petitioners in the now dredged marina is strikingly similar to that of owners of fast land adjacent to navigable water.

[W]hat petitioners now have is a body of water that was private property under Hawaiian law, linked to navigable water by a channel dredged by them with the consent of the Government. While the consent of individual officials representing the United States cannot "estop" the United States, it can lead to the fruition of expectancies embodied in the concept of "property"—expectancies that, if sufficiently important, the Government must condemn and pay for before it takes over the management of the landowner's property. In this case, we hold that the "right to exclude," so universally held to be a fundamental element of the property right, falls within this category of interests that the Government cannot take without compensation. This is not a case in which the Government is exercising its regulatory power in a manner that will cause an insubstantial devaluation of petitioners' private property; rather, the imposition of the navigational servitude in this context will result in an actual physical invasion of the privately owned marina. * * * Thus, if the Government wishes to make what was formerly Kuapa Pond into a public aquatic park after petitioners have proceeded as far as they have here, it may not, without invoking its eminent domain power and paying just compensation, require them to allow free access to the dredged pond while petitioners' agreement with their customers call for an annual $72 regular fee.

Accordingly the judgment of the Court of Appeals is reversed.

---

9. We do not decide, however, whether in some circumstances one of these factors by itself may be dispositive.

10. * * * Although Kuapa Pond clearly was not navigable in fact in its natural state, the dissent argue that the pond nevertheless was "navigable water of the United States" prior to its development because it was subject to the ebb and flow of the tide. This Court has never held, however, that whenever a body of water satisfies this mechanical test, the Government may invoke the "navigational servitude" to avoid payment of just compensation irrespective of the private interests at stake.

Mr. Justice Blackmun, with whom Mr. Justice Brennan and Mr. Justice Marshall join, dissenting.

* * * I believe the Court errs by implicitly rejecting the old and long-established "ebb and flow" test of navigability as a source for the navigational servitude the Government claims. * * * I take it the Court must concede that, at least for regulatory purposes, the pond in its current condition is "navigable water" because it is now "navigable in fact." I would add that the pond was "navigable water" prior to development of the present marina because it was subject to the ebb and flow of the tide. * * *

Notes

1. **Navigability for purposes of the navigation servitude.** *Kaiser Aetna* shows that the test of navigability for purposes of the navigation servitude is not coextensive with the traditional Commerce Clause concept of navigability for regulatory purposes because it does not include the ebb-and-flow test. Beyond that, *Kaiser Aetna* generates difficult questions about the test of navigability for navigation servitude purposes.

Was the majority's rejection of the ebb-and-flow test based on unique factors in *Kaiser Aetna*, or was it a broader rejection that will apply in other fact situations? Earlier in the litigation, the federal district court said: "[I]f it were not for the unique legal status of Hawaiian fishponds such as Kuapa Pond as strictly private property, free and clear of any claim by the Crown either to the beds thereof or the waters thereon under Hawaiian law prior to annexation, and their protection then and thereafter as such by statute and Constitution, application of the ebb and flow test would have established a public right of access to Kuapa Pond." United States v. Kaiser Aetna, 408 F. Supp. 42, 50 (D. Haw. 1976). Was the Supreme Court referring to this statement when it said, without elaborating, "we do not fully agree with the reasoning of the District Court"?

If navigability for servitude purposes excludes at least some waters that ebb and flow with the tide, might it also exclude at least some waters that meet the navigable-in-fact branch of the classical Commerce Clause test? Justice Blackmun, dissenting in *Kaiser Aetna*, thought the majority would have to concede that Kuapa Pond had become navigable in fact under the traditional test. If he was correct, the majority opinion stands for the proposition that not all waters navigable-in-fact in the classical Commerce Clause sense are navigable for purposes of the navigation servitude. But if that is so, which traditional navigable-in-fact waters are subject to the servitude and which are not? Does the servitude apply to all waters that *prior to improvement* were capable of being used as continuous highways for navigation in interstate commerce? How much confusion is added by footnote 9 of the majority opinion?

2. **Private riverbed interests not deriving value from the use of or access to navigable water.** In United States v. Cherokee Nation,

480 U.S. 700 (1987), an Indian tribe owned portions of the bed of the Arkansas River. The tribe's submerged lands contained sand and gravel deposits that were damaged by federal navigation improvements to the river. The Tenth Circuit ruled that because the tribe's ownership interest, i.e., the sand and gravel deposits, was unrelated to any navigational use of the river, the no-compensation rule of the navigation servitude should not apply automatically, and instead a balancing of public and private interests should be used to determine whether just compensation must be paid. The Supreme Court reversed: "We think the Court of Appeals erred in formulating a balancing test to evaluate this assertion of the navigational servitude. No such 'balancing' is required where, as here, the interference with in-stream interests results from an exercise of the Government's power to regulate navigation * * *."

SPORHASE v. NEBRASKA EX REL. DOUGLAS
Supreme Court of the United States, 1982.
458 U.S. 941, 102 S. Ct. 3456, 73 L. Ed.2d 1254.

JUSTICE STEVENS delivered the opinion of the Court.

Appellants challenge the constitutionality of a Nebraska statutory restriction on the withdrawal of ground water from any well within Nebraska intended for use in an adjoining State. * * *

Appellants jointly own contiguous tracts of land in Chase County, Nebraska, and Phillips County, Colorado. A well physically located on the Nebraska tract pumps ground water for irrigation of both the Nebraska tract and the Colorado tract. Previous owners of the land registered the well with the State of Nebraska in 1971, but neither they nor the present owners applied for the permit required by § 46–613.01 of the Nebraska Revised Statutes. That section provides:

> "Any person, firm, city, village, municipal corporation or any other entity intending to withdraw ground water from any well or pit located in the State of Nebraska and transport it for use in an adjoining state shall apply to the Department of Water Resources for a permit to do so. If the Director of Water Resources finds that the withdrawal of the ground water requested is reasonable, is not contrary to the conservation and use of ground water, and is not otherwise detrimental to the public welfare, he shall grant the permit if the state in which the water is to be used grants reciprocal rights to withdraw and transport ground water from that state for use in the State of Nebraska."

Appellee brought this action to enjoin appellants from transferring the water across the border without a permit. The trial court rejected the defense that the statute imposed an undue burden on interstate commerce and granted the injunction. The Nebraska Supreme Court affirmed. It held that, under Nebraska law, ground water is not "a marketable item freely transferable for value among private parties, and therefore [is] not an article of commerce." * * *

I

In holding that ground water is not an article of commerce, the Nebraska Supreme Court and appellee cite as controlling precedent Hudson County Water Co. v. McCarter, 209 U.S. 349, 28 S.Ct. 529, 52 L.Ed. 828 (1908). [*Hudson County* held that a New Jersey statute prohibiting the transfer of water outside the state was not subject to the Commerce Clause under Geer v. Connecticut, 161 U.S. 519, 16 S.Ct. 600, 40 L.Ed. 793 (1896).]

* * * *Geer*, which sustained a Connecticut ban on the interstate transportation of game birds captured in that State, was premised on the theory that the State owned its wild animals and therefore was free to qualify any ownership interest it might recognize in the persons who capture them. One such restriction is a prohibition against interstate transfer of the captured animals. * * * In expressly overruling *Geer* three years ago, this Court traced the demise of the public ownership theory and definitively recast it as "'but a fiction expressive in legal shorthand of the importance to its people that a State have power to preserve and regulate the exploitation of an important resource.'" Hughes v. Oklahoma, 441 U.S. 322, 334, 99 S.Ct. 1727, 1735, 60 L.Ed.2d 250 (1979) (quoting Toomer v. Witsell, 334 U.S. 385, 402, 68 S.Ct. 1156, 1165, 92 L.Ed. 1460 (1948)). * * *

Appellee insists, however, that Nebraska water is distinguishable from other natural resources. [W]ater, unlike other natural resources, is essential for human survival. Appellee, and the *amici curiae* that are vitally interested in conserving and preserving scarce water resources in the arid Western States, have convincingly demonstrated the desirability of state and local management of ground water. But the States' interests clearly have an interstate dimension. Although water is indeed essential for human survival, studies indicate that over 80% of our water supplies is used for agricultural purposes. The agricultural markets supplied by irrigated farms are worldwide. They provide the archetypical example of commerce among the several States for which the Framers of our Constitution intended to authorize federal regulation. The multistate character of the Ogallala aquifer—underlying appellants' tracts of land in Colorado and Nebraska, as well as parts of Texas, New Mexico, Oklahoma, and Kansas— confirms the view that there is a significant federal interest in conservation as well as in fair allocation of this diminishing resource.

The Western States' interests, and their asserted superior competence, in conserving and preserving scarce water resources are not irrelevant in the Commerce Clause inquiry. Nor is appellee's claim to public ownership without significance. Like Congress' deference to state water law, these factors inform the determination whether the burdens on commerce imposed by state ground water regulation are reasonable or unreasonable. But appellee's claim that Nebraska ground water is not an article of commerce goes too far: it would not only exempt Nebraska ground water regulation from burden-on-commerce analysis, it also would curtail the affirmative power of Congress to implement its own policies concerning such regulation. * * * Ground water overdraft is a national problem and Congress has the power to deal with it on that scale.

II

Our conclusion that water is an article of commerce raises, but does not answer, the question whether the Nebraska statute is unconstitutional. For the existence of unexercised federal regulatory power does not foreclose state regulation of its water resources, of the uses of water within the State, or indeed, of interstate commerce in water. Determining the validity of state statutes affecting interstate commerce requires a more careful inquiry:

"Where the statute regulates evenhandedly to effectuate a legitimate local public interest, and its effects on interstate commerce are only incidental, it will be upheld unless the burden imposed on such commerce is clearly excessive in relation to the putative local benefits. If a legitimate local purpose is found, then the question becomes one of degree. And the extent of the burden that will be tolerated will of course depend on the nature of the local interest involved, and on whether it could be promoted as well with a lesser impact on interstate activities." Pike v. Bruce Church, Inc., 397 U.S. 137, 142, 90 S.Ct. 844, 847, 25 L.Ed.2d 174 (1970) (citation omitted).

The only purpose that appellee advances for § 46-613.01 is to conserve and preserve diminishing sources of ground water. The purpose is unquestionably legitimate and highly important, and the other aspects of Nebraska's ground water regulation demonstrate that it is genuine. Appellants' land in Nebraska is located within the boundaries of the Upper Republican Ground Water Control Area * * *. Pursuant to § 46-666(1), the Upper Republican Natural Resources District has promulgated special rules and regulations governing ground water withdrawal and use. The rules and regulations define as "critical" those townships in the control area in which the annual decline of the ground water table exceeds a fixed percentage; appellants' Nebraska tract is located within a critical township. The rules and regulations require the installation of flow meters on every well within the control area, specify the amount of water per acre that may be used for irrigation, and set the spacing that is required between wells. They also strictly limit the intrastate transfer of ground water: transfers are only permitted between lands controlled by the same ground water user, and all transfers must be approved by the district board of directors.

The State's interest in conservation and preservation of ground water is advanced by the first three conditions in § 46-613.01 for the withdrawal of water for an interstate transfer. Those requirements are "that the withdrawal of the ground water requested is reasonable, is not contrary to the conservation and use of ground water, and is not otherwise detrimental to the public welfare." Although Commerce Clause concerns are implicated by the fact that § 46-613.01 applies to interstate transfers but not to intrastate transfers, there are legitimate reasons for the special treatment accorded requests to transport ground water across state lines. Obviously, a State that imposes severe withdrawal and use restrictions on its own citizens is not discriminating against interstate commerce when it seeks to prevent the uncontrolled transfer of water out of the State. An exemption for interstate transfers would be inconsistent with the ideal of evenhandedness in regulation. At least in the area in which appellants' Nebraska tract is located, the first three standards of § 46-613.01 may well be no more strict in application than the limitations upon intrastate transfers imposed by the Upper Republican Natural Resources District.

Moreover, in the absence of a contrary view expressed by Congress, we are reluctant to condemn as unreasonable measures taken by a State to conserve and preserve for its own citizens this vital resource in times of severe shortage. Our reluctance stems from the "confluence of [several] realities." Hicklin v. Orbeck, 437 U.S. 518, 534, 98 S.Ct. 2482, 2491, 57 L.Ed.2d 397 (1978). First, a State's power to regulate the use of water in times and places of shortage for the purpose of protecting the health of its citizens—and not simply the health of its economy—is at the core of its police power. For Commerce Clause purposes, we have long recognized a difference between economic protectionism, on the one hand, and health and safety regulation, on the other. Second, the legal expectation that under certain circumstances each State may restrict water within its borders has been fostered over the years not only by our equitable apportionment decrees, but also by the negotiation and enforcement of interstate compacts. Our law therefore has recognized the relevance of state boundaries in the allocation of scarce water resources. Third, although appellee's claim to public ownership of Nebraska ground water cannot justify a total denial of federal regulatory power, it may support a limited preference for its own citizens in the utilization of the resource. In this regard, it is relevant that appellee's claim is logically more substantial than claims to public ownership of other natural resources. Finally, given appellee's conservation efforts, the continuing availability of ground water in Nebraska is not simply happenstance; the natural resource has some indicia of a good publicly produced and owned in which a State may favor its own citizens in times of shortage. A facial examination of the first three conditions set forth in § 46-613.01 does not, therefore, indicate that they impermissibly burden interstate commerce. Appellants, indeed, seem to concede their reasonableness.

Appellants, however, do challenge the requirement that "the state in which the water is to be used grants reciprocal rights to withdraw and transport ground water from that state for use in the State of Nebraska"—the reciprocity provision that troubled the Chief Justice of the Nebraska Supreme Court. Because Colorado forbids the exportation of its ground water, the reciprocity provision operates as an explicit barrier to commerce between the two States. The State therefore bears the initial burden of demonstrating a close fit between the reciprocity requirement and its asserted local purpose.

The reciprocity requirement fails to clear this initial hurdle. For there is no evidence that this restriction is narrowly tailored to the conservation and preservation rationale. Even though the supply of water in a particular well may be abundant, or perhaps even excessive, and even though the most beneficial use of that water might be in another State, such water may not be shipped into a neighboring State that does not permit its water to be used in Nebraska. If it could be shown that the State as a whole suffers a water shortage, that the intrastate transportation of water from areas of abundance to areas of shortage is feasible regardless of distance, and that the importation of water from adjoining States would roughly compensate for any exportation to those States, then the conservation and preservation purpose might be credibly advanced for the reciprocity provision. A demonstrably arid state conceivably might be able to marshal evidence to establish a close means-end relationship between even a total ban on the exportation of water and a purpose to conserve and preserve water. Appellee, however, does not claim that such evidence exists. We therefore are not persuaded that the reciprocity requirement—when superimposed on the first three restrictions in the statute— significantly advances the State's legitimate conservation and preservation interest; it surely is not narrowly tailored to serve that purpose. The reciprocity requirement does not survive the "strictest scrutiny" reserved for facially discriminatory legislation. * * *

The reciprocity requirement of Neb. Rev. Stat. § 46–613.01 violates the Commerce Clause. We leave to the state courts the question whether the invalid portion is severable. The judgment of the Nebraska Supreme Court is reversed and the case is remanded for proceedings not inconsistent with this opinion. It is so ordered.

Notes

1. **The *El Paso* cases.** The City of El Paso, Texas, sits below New Mexico's southern border. The city applied to the New Mexico State Engineer for permits to appropriate 296,000 acre-feet of water annually from wells in New Mexico to serve its growing population and stimulate eco-

nomic growth. The State Engineer denied all the applications under a New Mexico statute banning the interstate export of groundwater. New Mexico defended the facially discriminatory statute by arguing it was needed to avoid a projected statewide water shortage by the year 2020. New Mexico relied on the *Sporhase* statement that a demonstrably arid state might be able to show a close fit between conserving and preserving water and a total ban on export. New Mexico's projected shortage was based on estimated water needs not just for public health and safety but also for economic activities. In City of El Paso v. Reynolds (*El Paso I*), 563 F. Supp. 379 (D.N.M. 1983), the court struck down the statute. It said that under *Sporhase,* a state's discrimination in favor of its citizens is limited to water essential to human survival. "Outside of fulfilling human survival needs, water is an economic resource." Id. at 389.

The New Mexico Legislature then enacted new legislation requiring a permit to appropriate underground water for export and use outside the state. The legislation authorizes the State Engineer to issue a permit only if the proposed use would not impair existing water rights, would not be contrary to water conservation within the state, and would not be otherwise detrimental to the public welfare of New Mexico citizens. In applying these criteria, the legislation directs the State Engineer to consider six factors. The first four relate to water conditions within New Mexico— water supply, water demand, whether shortages exist, and the feasibility of transporting water from the proposed point of diversion to alleviate shortages within the state. The remaining two factors relate to water supply and demand conditions in the state of proposed export. In City of El Paso v. Reynolds (*El Paso II*), 597 F. Supp. 694 (D.N.M. 1984), El Paso argued that this legislation on its face violated the Commerce Clause. The court held, however, that requiring an exporter to meet the statutory conservation and public welfare criteria is not facially discriminatory because similar requirements apply to new appropriations for local use. And it said that comparing water supply and demand conditions in New Mexico with water supply and demand conditions in the importing state was a necessary step in applying the balancing test prescribed by *Sporhase.* "Simple economic protectionism" is still forbidden, said the court, but some burdens on commerce may be valid if outweighed by "non-economic local benefits."

The new legislation applies both to new appropriations for export and to transfers of existing appropriations from in-state to out-of-state use. El Paso sought permits to export water from four existing New Mexico wells to Texas. At the time of *El Paso II*, New Mexico allowed intrastate transfers if existing water rights would not be impaired; it did not subject intrastate transfers to the conservation and public welfare requirements applicable to interstate transfers. The *El Paso II* court held, therefore, that the portion of the new legislation dealing with transfers of existing appropriations was facially unconstitutional for imposing an extra burden on interstate transfers. The state legislature responded to *El*

Paso II by adopting conservation and public welfare requirements for intrastate transfers, N.M. Stat. Ann. § 72-5-23.

After *El Paso I* and *II*, the New Mexico State Engineer invoked a completely different state statute to deny all the City of El Paso's applications. N.M. Stat. Ann. § 72-1-9 provides that a municipality cannot hold unused water rights in excess of its projected needs for the next forty years. The State Engineer found that El Paso's present water supply would meet its needs until 2020, which was forty years from the date of El Paso's applications. El Paso again sought review in federal court, asserting that the forty-year requirement unduly burdens interstate commerce. The parties ended the litigation, however, by a settlement in which El Paso withdrew its applications.

2. **Congressional consent to state burdens on interstate commerce.** In Intake Water Co. v. Yellowstone River Compact Commission, 769 F.2d 568 (9th Cir. 1985), the water company planned a transbasin diversion of water from the Yellowstone River for use in Montana and North Dakota. The Yellowstone River Compact provides: "No waters shall be diverted from the Yellowstone River Basin without unanimous consent of all the signatory states." The compact was ratified by the three signatory states, and Congress enacted legislation consenting to it in accordance with the Compact Clause of the Constitution. The water company challenged the restriction as state action placing an unreasonable burden on interstate commerce. The court held that congressional consent to the compact converted it into federal law and thus immunized it against attack under the negative Commerce Clause, which limits the power of the states but not of Congress.

SECTION 2. FEDERAL LEGISLATIVE PROGRAMS (AND PREEMPTION OF STATE LAW)

A. Licensing and Permitting of Nonfederal Projects

FIRST IOWA HYDRO-ELECTRIC COOPERATIVE v. FEDERAL POWER COMMISSION
Supreme Court of the United States, 1946.
328 U.S. 152, 66 S. Ct. 906, 90 L. Ed. 1143.

MR. JUSTICE BURTON delivered the opinion of the Court.

This case illustrates the integration of federal and state jurisdictions in licensing water power projects under the Federal Power Act. The petitioner is the First Iowa Hydro-Electric Cooperative, a cooperative association organized under the laws of Iowa with power to generate, distribute and sell electric energy. On January 29, 1940, pursuant to § 23(b) of the Federal Power Act, it filed with the Federal Power Commission a declaration of intention to construct and operate a dam, reservoir and hydro-electric power plant on the Cedar River, near Moscow, Iowa.

On April 2, 1941, it also filed with the Commission an application for a license, under the Federal Power Act, to construct an enlarged project essentially like the one it now wishes to build. [The application] calls for an 8,300 foot earthen dam on the Cedar River near Moscow, an 11,000 acre reservoir at that point and an eight mile diversion canal to a power plant to be built near Muscatine on the Mississippi.
* * *

The Cedar River rises in Minnesota and flows 270 miles southeasterly through Iowa to Moscow which is 10 miles west of the Mississippi. From there it flows southwesterly 29 miles to Columbus Junction where it joins the Iowa River and returns southeasterly 28 miles to the Mississippi. The proposed diversion will take all but about 25 c.f.s. of water from the Cedar River at Moscow. This will correspondingly reduce the flow in the Iowa River while the diverted water will enter the Mississippi at Muscatine, about 20 miles above its present point of entry at the mouth of the Iowa River. * * *

On November 4, 1941, the Commission granted the State of Iowa's petition to intervene and, since then, the State has opposed actively the granting of the federal license.

On January 29, 1944, after extended hearings, the Commission rendered an opinion including the following statements:

> "As first presented, the plans of the applicant for developing the water resources of the Cedar River were neither desirable nor adequate, but many important changes in design have been made. * * * The present plans call for a practical and reasonably adequate development to utilize the head and water available, create a large storage reservoir, and make available for recreational purposes a considerable area now unsuitable for such use, all at a cost which does not appear to be unreasonable. * * *

The Commission also expressly found that—

> "The applicant has not presented satisfactory evidence, pursuant to § 9(b) of the Federal Power Act, of compliance with the requirements of applicable laws of the state of Iowa requiring a permit from the State Executive Council to effect the purposes of a license under the Federal Power Act, and the pending application, as supplemented, should be dismissed without prejudice."

The laws of Iowa which that State contends are applicable and require a permit from its Executive Council to effect the purposes of the federal license are all in Iowa Code Ann. §§ 7767-7796.1, constituting Chapter 363, entitled "Mill Dams and Races." Section 7767 of that chapter is alleged to require the issuance of a permit by the Executive

Council of the State and is the one on which the Commission's order must depend. * * *

To require the petitioner to secure the actual grant to it of a State permit under § 7767 as a condition precedent to securing a federal license for the same project under the Federal Power Act would vest in the Executive Council of Iowa a veto power over the federal project. Such a veto power easily could destroy the effectiveness of the federal act. It would subordinate to the control of the State the "comprehensive" planning which the Act provides shall depend upon the judgment of the Federal Power Commission or other representatives of the Federal Government.

For example, § 7776 of the State Code requires that "the method of construction, operation, maintenance, and equipment of any and all dams in such waters shall be subject to the approval of the executive council." This would subject to State control the very requirements of the project that Congress has placed in the discretion of the Federal Power Commission. A still greater difficulty is illustrated by § 7771. This states the requirements for a State permit as follows:

> "7771 When permit granted. If it shall appear to the council that the construction, operation, or maintenance of the dam will not materially obstruct existing navigation, or materially affect other public rights, will not endanger life or public health, and *any water taken from the stream in connection with the project is returned thereto at the nearest practicable place* without being materially diminished in quantity or polluted or rendered deleterious to fish life, it shall grant the permit, upon such terms and conditions as it may prescribe." (Italics supplied.)

This strikes at the heart of the present project. The feature of the project which especially commended it to the Federal Power Commission was its diversion of substantially all of the waters of the Cedar River near Moscow, to the Mississippi River near Muscatine. * * * It is this diversion that makes possible the increase in the head of water for power development from a maximum of 35 feet to an average of 101 feet, the increase in the capacity of the plant from 15,000 kw. to 50,000 kw. and its output from 47,000,000 kwh. to 200,000,000 kwh. per year. It is this diversion that led the Federal Power Commission, on January 29, 1944, to make its favorable appraisal of the enlarged project in contrast to its unfavorable appraisal * * * of the smaller project. It is this feature that * * * gives the project its greatest economic justification.

If a state permit is not required, there is no justification for requiring the petitioner, as a condition of securing its federal permit, to present evidence of the petitioner's compliance with the requirements of the State Code for a state permit. Compliance with State requirements that are in conflict with federal requirements may well block

the federal license. For example, compliance with the State requirement that the water of the Cedar River all be returned to it at the
nearest practicable place would reduce the project to the small one
which is classified by the Federal Power Commission as "neither desirable nor adequate." Similarly, compliance with the engineering requirements of the State Executive Council, if additional to or different
from the federal requirements, may well result in duplications of expenditures that would handicap the financial success of the project.
* * * On the other hand, there is ample opportunity for the Federal
Power Commission, under the authority expressly given to it by Congress, to require by regulation the presentation of evidence satisfactory to it of the petitioner's compliance with any of the requirements
for a State permit on the state waters of Iowa that the Commission
considers appropriate to effect the purposes of a federal license on the
navigable waters of the United States. This evidence can be required
of the petitioner upon the remanding of this application to the Commission.

In the Federal Power Act there is a separation of those subjects
which remain under the jurisdiction of the states from those subjects
which the Constitution delegates to the United States and over which
Congress vests the Federal Power Commission with authority to act.
To the extent of this separation, the Act establishes a dual system of
control. The duality of control consists merely of the division of the
common enterprise between two cooperating agencies of Government,
each with final authority in its own jurisdiction. The duality does not
require two agencies to share in the final decision of the same issue.
Where the Federal Government supersedes the state government
there is no suggestion that the two agencies both shall have final
authority. * * * A dual final authority, with a duplicate system of state
permits and federal licenses required for each project, would be unworkable. "Compliance with the requirements" of such a duplicated
system of licensing would be nearly as bad. Conformity to both standards would be impossible in some cases and probably difficult in most
of them. * * *

The Act leaves to the states their traditional jurisdiction subject
to the admittedly superior right of the Federal Government, through
Congress, to regulate interstate and foreign commerce, administer the
public lands and reservations of the United States and, in certain
cases, exercise authority under the treaties of the United States. * * *

Sections 27 and 9 are especially significant in this regard. Section
27 expressly "saves" certain state laws relating to property rights as to
the use of water, so that these are not superseded by the terms of the
Federal Power Act. It provides:

    "Sec. 27. That nothing herein contained shall be construed as af-
fecting or intending to affect or in any way to interfere with the laws

of the respective States relating to the control, appropriation, use, or distribution of water used in irrigation or for municipal or other uses, or any vested right acquired therein." 16 U.S.C.A. §821.

The effect of § 27, in protecting state laws from supersedure, is limited to laws as to the control, appropriation, use or distribution of water in irrigation or for municipal or other uses of the same nature. It therefore has primary, if not exclusive reference to such proprietary rights. The phrase "any vested right acquired therein" further emphasizes the application of the section to property rights. * * *

Section 9(b) does not resemble § 27. It must be read with § 9(a) and (c). The entire section is devoted to securing adequate information for the Commission as to pending applications for licenses. Where § 9(a) calls for engineering and financial information, § 9(b) calls for legal information. * * * It does not itself require compliance with any state laws. Its reference to state laws is by way of suggestion to the Federal Power Commission of subjects as to which the Commission may wish some proof submitted to it of the applicant's progress. The evidence required is described merely as that which shall be "satisfactory" to the Commission. * * *

* * * Section 9(b) says that the Commission may wish to have "satisfactory evidence" of the progress made by the applicant toward meeting local requirements but it does not say that the Commission is to assume responsibility for the legal sufficiency of the steps taken. In so far as [local] laws have not been superseded by the Federal Power Act, they remain as applicable and effective as they were before its passage. The State of Iowa, however, has sought to sustain the applicability and validity of Chapter 363 of the Code of Iowa in this connection, on the ground that the Federal Power Act, by the implications of § 9(b), has recognized this chapter of Iowa law as part of a system of dual control of power project permits, cumbersome and complicated though it be. * * *

The inappropriateness of such an interpretation is apparent in the light of the circumstances which culminated in the passage of the Federal Water Power Act in 1920. * * * It was the outgrowth of a widely supported effort of the conservationists to secure enactment of a complete scheme of national regulation which would promote the comprehensive development of the water resources of the Nation, in so far as it was within the reach of the federal power to do so * * *.

The detailed provisions of the Act providing for the federal plan of regulation leave no room or need for conflicting state controls. * * * It is the Federal Power Commission rather than the Iowa Executive Council that under our constitutional Government must pass upon these issues on behalf of the people of Iowa as well as on behalf of all others.

We accordingly reverse the judgment of the court below with directions to remand the case to the Federal Power Commission for further proceedings in conformity with this opinion.

Notes

1. **Federal Power Act licensing criteria.** Key licensing criteria under the Federal Power Act (FPA) are set forth in sections 4(e) and 10(a), 16 U.S.C. §§ 797(e), 803(a). Section 4(e) authorizes the Commission to issue a license if it determines the project is "desirable and justified in the public interest for the purpose of improving or developing a waterway or waterways for the use or benefit of interstate or foreign commerce." A 1986 amendment broadens the section 4(e) inquiry: "[T]he Commission, in addition to the power and development purposes for which licenses are issued, shall give equal consideration to the purposes of energy conservation, the protection, mitigation of damage to, and enhancement of, fish and wildlife (including related spawning grounds and habitat), the protection of recreational opportunities, and the preservation of other aspects of environmental quality."

Section 10(a) requires that "the project * * * shall be such as in the judgment of the Commission will be best adapted to a comprehensive plan for improving or developing a waterway or waterways for the use or benefit of interstate or foreign commerce, for the improvement and utilization of water-power development, for the adequate protection, mitigation, and enhancement of fish and wildlife (including related spawning grounds and habitat), and for other beneficial public uses, including irrigation, flood control, water supply, and recreational and other purposes referred to in section 4(e) * * *." A 1986 amendment added the references to fish and wildlife, irrigation, flood control, water supply, and recreation.

The word "Commission" in sections 4(e) and 10(a) now refers to the Federal Energy Regulatory Commission (FERC). Congress abolished the Federal Power Commission and transfered its hydroelectric licensing functions to FERC in the Department of Energy Reorganization Act of 1977, 42 U.S.C. §§ 7171, 7172(a)(1)(A).

2. ***First Iowa* reaffirmed.** The Court reaffirmed *First Iowa* in California v. FERC, 495 U.S. 490 (1990). FERC issued a license for a hydroelectric project in California that required the licensee to maintain certain minimum streamflows for fish protection. The State Water Resources Control Board wanted to require the licensee to maintain much greater minimum flows for the fish. In rejecting California's argument that *First Iowa* should be overruled so the state could require greater minimum flows, the Court said:

"Were this a case of first impression, petitioner's argument [that FPA § 27 authorizes it to require greater minimum flows] could be said to present a close question. As petitioner argues, California's minimum stream flow requirement might plausibly be thought to 'relat[e] to the control, appropriation, use, or distribution of water used * * * for * * * other uses,' namely the generation of power or the protection of fish. * * * But the meaning of § 27 and the pre-emptive effect of the FPA are not matters of first impression. * * * We decline at this late date to revisit and disturb the understanding of § 27 set forth in *First Iowa.* * * * Adherence to precedent is, in the usual case, a cardinal and guiding principle of adjudication, and '[c]onsiderations of *stare decisis* have special force in the area of statutory interpretation, for here, unlike in the context of constitutional interpretation, the legislative power is implicated, and Congress remains free to alter what we have done.' Patterson v. McLean Credit Union, 491 U.S. 164, 172-73, 109 S.Ct. 2363, 2370, 105 L.Ed.2d 132 (1989). There has been no sufficient intervening change in the law, or indication that *First Iowa* has proved unworkable or has fostered confusion and inconsistency in the law, that warrants our departure from established precedent." Id. at 497-99.

3. **Preemption of state public interest review of water appropriations for hydropower generation.** In Sayles Hydro Associates v. Maughan, 985 F.2d 451 (9th Cir. 1993), Sayles Hydro obtained a FPA license for a hydroelectric project in California but later encountered difficulty getting a state water right for the project. The State Water Resources Control Board refused to process Sayles Hydro's water permit application until it submitted what the Ninth Circuit called "a shifting, expanding range of studies and reports" on how the project would affect recreation, aesthetics, archaeology, sport fishing, and cultural resources. The court interpreted *First Iowa* and *California v. FERC*, supra Note 2, to mean that the FPA occupies the field except for allowing the states under section 27 to "determine proprietary water rights." The court found that requiring the plaintiffs to provide the studies and reports to the State Board "has nothing to do with determining proprietary rights in water." It ruled that the state requirements were preempted: "[M]ost or all of the State Board's concerns were considered by the Federal Energy Regulatory Commission in granting the license, and conditions were imposed in the license to protect these multiple values. * * * There would be no point in Congress requiring the federal agency to consider the state agency recommendations on environmental matters and make its own decisions about which to accept, if the state agencies had the power to impose the requirements themselves." Id. at 456.

The State Board argued the case was not ripe for the Ninth Circuit to hear because the state water permitting process had not been completed, and ultimately the state's substantive permit requirements might not conflict with those in the federal license. The court responded that "the state process itself, regardless of the results, is preempted. * * * The hardship is the process itself. * * * Undue process may impose cost and uncertainty sufficient to thwart the federal determination that a power project should proceed."

In 1991, FERC issued a regulation requiring that every potential FPA license applicant first "consult with the relevant Federal, State, and interstate resource agencies, including * * * the appropriate State water resource management agencies." 18 C.F.R. § 4.38(a)(1). The regulation also requires, unless the federal Office of Energy Projects determines it to be unnecessary, that a "potential applicant must diligently conduct all reasonable studies and obtain all reasonable information requested by resource agencies * * * that are necessary for the Commission to make an informed decision regarding the merits of the application." § 4.38(c)(1).

Suppose Sayles Hydro had sought a FPA license after this regulation became operative. With FPA § 4(e), supra Note 1, requiring FERC to consider "the protection, mitigation, and enhancement of fish and wildlife (including spawning grounds and habitat), the protection of recreational opportunities, and the preservation of other aspects of environmental quality," could the State Board have required Sayles Hydro to do the studies and reports that it desired for submission to FERC?

4. **Relicensing.** FPA licenses cannot be issued for a period exceeding fifty years. 16 U.S.C. § 799. When a license expires, the United States has the right to take over the project upon payment of the licensee's net investment. Id. § 807. If the United States does not take over the project, FERC can issue a new license to the applicant whose proposal is "best adapted to serve the public interest," taking into account the requirements of section 10(a) and other specified considerations. The successful applicant may or may not be the existing licensee, and the new license may be partly or wholly for nonpower use. Insignificant differences in applications, however, must not result in transfer of a project, and transfer requires the new licensee to compensate the old licensee for its net investment. Id. § 808(a), (f)).

FERC has issued the following statement about relicensing:

"[G]enerally, when the license for a project expires, the Commission issues a new license to the existing licensee. However, * * * the Commission concludes that it has the legal authority to deny a new license at the time of relicensing if it determines that, even with ample use of its conditioning authority, no license can be fashioned that will comport with the statutory standard under section 10(a) of the Federal Power Act (the Act) and other applicable law. The commission anticipates that, where existing projects are involved, license denial would rarely occur." Project Decommissioning at Relicensing—Policy Statement, 60 Fed. Reg. 339 (1995).

The determination of what will serve the public interest at relicensing is subject to the section 4(e) requirement, supra Note 1, that in addition to power and development purposes, the Commission must give equal consideration to fish and wildlife, recreational opportunities, and other aspects of environmental quality. Environmental groups have used this requirement to negotiate mitigation of environmental damage associated with a number of nonfederal hydropower projects up for relicensing. Bruce A. Driver, Western Hydropower: Changing Values/New Visions, Report to the Western Water Policy Review Advisory Comm'n 2-3, 9-10 (Aug. 1997).

PUD NO. 1 OF JEFFERSON COUNTY v. WASHINGTON DEPARTMENT OF ECOLOGY

Supreme Court of the United States, 1994.
511 U.S. 700, 114 S. Ct. 1900, 128 L. Ed.2d 716.

JUSTICE O'CONNOR delivered the opinion of the Court.

[Petitioners, a city and a local public utility district, sought a Federal Power Act (FPA) license to build a hydroelectric project on the Dosewallips River in the State of Washington. The river was subject to state water quality standards developed under federal Clean Water Act (CWA) § 303, 33 U.S.C.A. § 1313. Section 303(c) requires that state water quality standards "shall consist of the designated uses of the navigable waters involved and the water quality criteria for such waters based upon such uses." A state water quality standard for certain rivers, including the Dosewallips, listed fish and wildlife habitat among the designated uses and also set out numerical water quality criteria for characteristics such as pH, temperature, and dissolved oxygen. Another state standard for all rivers declared an antidegradation policy calling for protection of existing beneficial water uses and disallowing degradation that would interfere with those uses. Petitioner's proposed project would have greatly reduced the water flow in one stretch of the Dosewallips River. This in turn would have impaired salmon and steelhead habitat and degraded water quality.

CWA § 401, 33 U.S.C.A. § 1341, imposes a state certification requirement for federal licensing:

"(a) * * * Any applicant for a Federal license or permit to conduct any activity including, but not limited to, the construction or operation of facilities, which may result in any discharge into the navigable waters, shall provide the licensing or permitting agency a certification from the State in which the discharge originates or will originate * * * that any such discharge will comply with applicable provisions of sections 301, 302, 303, 306, and 307 of this Act. * * *

"(d) * * * Any certification provided under this section shall set forth any effluent limitations and other limitations, and monitoring requirements necessary to assure that any applicant for a Federal license or permit will comply with any applicable effluent limitations and other limitations, under sections 301 or 302 of this Act, standard of performance under section 306 of this Act, or prohibition, effluent standard, or pretreatment standard under section 307 of this Act, and with any other appropriate requirement of State law set forth in such certification, and shall become a condition on any Federal license or permit subject to the provisions of this section."

The Washington Department of Ecology issued certification for the project under § 401 that imposed a minimum streamflow requirement in order to protect the Dosewallips fishery and to comply with the statewide antidegradation policy. After challenging the minimum streamflow requirement in state court without success, petitioners obtained review by the United States Supreme Court.]

There is no dispute that petitioners were required to obtain a certification from the State pursuant to § 401. Petitioners concede that, at a minimum, the project will result in two possible discharges—the release of dredged and fill material during the construction of the project, and the discharge of water at the end of the tailrace after the water has been used to generate electricity. Petitioners contend, however, that the minimum stream flow requirement imposed by the State was unrelated to these specific discharges, and that as a consequence, the State lacked the authority under § 401 to condition its certification on maintenance of stream flows sufficient to protect the Dosewallips fishery.

If § 401 consisted solely of subsection (a), which refers to a state certification that a "discharge" will comply with certain provisions of the Act, petitioners' assessment of the scope of the State's certification authority would have considerable force. Section 401, however, also contains subsection (d), which expands the State's authority to impose conditions on the certification of a project. Section 401(d) provides that any certification shall set forth "any effluent limitations and other limitations * * * necessary to assure that *any applicant*" will comply with various provisions of the Act and appropriate state law requirements. (Emphasis added.) The language of this subsection contradicts petitioners' claim that the State may only impose water quality limitations specifically tied to a "discharge." The text refers to the compliance of the applicant, not the discharge. Section 401(d) thus allows the State to impose "other limitations" on the project in general to assure compliance with various provisions of the Clean Water Act and with "any other appropriate requirement of State law." * * * [Section] 401(d) is most reasonably read as authorizing additional conditions and limitations on the activity as a whole once the threshold condition, the existence of a discharge, is satisfied. * * *

Although § 401(d) authorizes the State to place restrictions on the activity as a whole, that authority is not unbounded. The State can only ensure that the project complies with "any applicable effluent limitations and other limitations, under section 301 or 302" or certain other provisions of the Act, "and with any other appropriate requirement of State law." The State asserts that the minimum stream flow requirement was imposed to ensure compliance with the state water quality standards adopted pursuant to § 303 of the Clean Water Act.

We agree with the State that ensuring compliance with § 303 is a proper function of the § 401 certification. Although § 303 is not one of the statutory provisions listed in § 401(d), the statute allows states to impose limitations to ensure compliance with § 301 of the Act. Section 301 in turn incorporates § 303 by reference. As a consequence, state water quality standards adopted pursuant to § 303 are among the "other limitations" with which a State may ensure compliance through the § 401 certification process. * * * Moreover, limitations to assure compliance with state water quality standards are also permitted by § 401(d)'s reference to "any other appropriate requirement of State law." We do not speculate on what additional state laws, if any, might be incorporated by this language. But at a minimum, limitations imposed pursuant to state water quality standards adopted pursuant to § 303 are "appropriate" requirements of state law. * * *

Having concluded that, pursuant to § 401, States may condition certification upon any limitations necessary to ensure compliance with state water quality standards or any other "appropriate requirement of State law," we consider whether the minimum flow condition is such a limitation. Under § 303(c)(2)(A), state water quality standards must "consist of the designated uses of the navigable waters involved and the water quality criteria for such waters based upon such uses." In imposing the minimum stream flow requirement, the State determined that construction and operation of the project as planned would be inconsistent with one of the designated uses of Class AA water, namely "[s]almonid [and other fish] migration, rearing, spawning, and harvesting." * * * The designated use of the river as a fish habitat directly reflects the Clean Water Act's goal of maintaining the "chemical, physical, and biological integrity of the Nation's waters." 33 U.S.C. § 1251(a). * * *

Petitioners assert, however, that § 303 requires the State to protect designated uses solely through implementation of specific "criteria." According to petitioners, the State may not require them to operate their dam in a manner consistent with a designated "use"; instead, say petitioners, under § 303 the State may only require that the project comply with specific numerical "criteria."

We disagree with petitioners' interpretation of the language of § 303(c)(2)(A). Under the statute, a water quality standard must "consist of the designated uses of the navigable waters involved *and* the water quality criteria for such waters based upon such uses." (Emphasis added.) The text makes it plain that water quality standards contain two components. We think the language of § 303 is most naturally read to require that a project be consistent with both components, namely the designated use and the water quality criteria. Accordingly, under the literal terms of the statute, a project that does not comply with a designated use of the water does not comply with the applicable water quality standards.

Consequently, pursuant to § 401(d) the State may require that a permit applicant comply with both the designated uses and the water quality criteria of the state standards. * * * A certification requirement that an applicant operate the project consistently with state water quality standards—i.e., consistently with the designated uses of the water body and the water quality criteria—is both a "limitation" to assure "compliance with * * * limitations" imposed under § 303, and an "appropriate" requirement of State law. * * *

The State also justified its minimum stream flow as necessary to implement the "antidegradation policy" of § 303. * * * EPA has promulgated regulations implementing § 303's antidegradation policy, a phrase that is not defined elsewhere in the Act. These regulations require States to "develop and adopt a statewide antidegradation policy and identify the methods for implementing such policy." 40 CFR § 131.12 (1992). * * * The State of Washington's antidegradation policy in turn provides that "[e]xisting beneficial uses shall be maintained and protected and no further degradation which would interfere with or become injurious to existing beneficial uses will be allowed." WAC 173-201-035(8)(a). The State concluded that the reduced streamflows would have just the effect prohibited by this policy. The Solicitor General, representing EPA, asserts, and we agree, that the State's minimum stream flow condition is a proper application of the state and federal antidegradation regulations * * *.

Petitioners also assert more generally that the Clean Water Act is only concerned with water "quality," and does not allow the regulation of water "quantity." This is an artificial distinction. In many cases, water quantity is closely related to water quality; a sufficient lowering of the water quantity in a body of water could destroy all of its designated uses, be it for drinking water, recreation, navigation or, as here, as a fishery. In any event, there is recognition in the Clean Water Act itself that reduced stream flow, i.e., diminishment of water quantity, can constitute water pollution. First, the Act's definition of pollution as "the man-made or man induced alteration of the chemical, physical, biological, and radiological integrity of water" encompasses the effects of reduced water quantity. 33 U.S.C. § 1362(19). This broad conception of pollution—one which expressly evinces Congress' concern with the physical and biological integrity of water—refutes petitioners' assertion that the Act draws a sharp distinction between the regulation of water "quantity" and water "quality." Moreover, § 304 of the Act expressly recognizes that water "pollution" may result from "changes in the movement, flow, or circulation of any navigable waters * * *, including changes caused by the construction of dams. 33 U.S.C. § 1314(f). This concern with the flowage effects of dams and other diversions is also embodied in the EPA regulations, which expressly require existing dams to be operated to attain designated uses.

Petitioners assert that two other provisions of the Clean Water Act, §§ 101(g) and 510(2), 33 U.S.C. §§ 1251(g) and 1370(2), exclude the regulation of water quantity from the coverage of the Act. Section 101(g) provides "that the authority of each State to allocate quantities of water within its jurisdiction shall not be superseded, abrogated or otherwise impaired by this chapter." 33 U.S.C. § 1251(g). Similarly, § 510(2) provides that nothing in the Act shall "be construed as impairing or in any manner affecting any right or jurisdiction of the States with respect to the waters * * * of such States." 33 U.S.C. § 1370. In petitioners' view, these provisions exclude "water quantity issues from direct regulation under the federally controlled water quality standards authorized in § 303."

This language gives the States authority to allocate water rights; we therefore find it peculiar that petitioners argue that it prevents the State from regulating stream flow. In any event, we read these provisions more narrowly than petitioners. Sections 101(g) and 510(2) preserve the authority of each State to allocate water quantity as between users; they do not limit the scope of water pollution controls that may be imposed on users who have obtained, pursuant to state law, a water allocation. * * * Moreover, the certification itself does not purport to determine petitioners' proprietary right to the water of the Dosewallips. In fact, the certification expressly states that a "State Water Right Permit (Chapters 90.03.250 RCW and 508-12 WAC) must be obtained prior to commencing construction of the project." The certification merely determines the nature of the use to which that proprietary right may be put under the Clean Water Act, if and when it is obtained from the State. Our view is reinforced by the legislative history of the 1977 amendment to the Clean Water Act adding § 101(g). See 3 Legislative History of the Clean Water Act of 1977 (Committee Print compiled for the Committee on Environment and Public Works by the Library of Congress), Ser. No. 95-14, p. 532 (1978) ("The requirements [of the Act] may incidentally affect individual water rights. * * * It is not the purpose of this amendment to prohibit those incidental effects. It is the purpose of this amendment to insure that State allocation systems are not subverted, and that effects on individual rights, if any, are prompted by legitimate and necessary water quality considerations").

[Petitioner's last argument is] that we should limit the State's authority to impose minimum flow requirements because FERC has comprehensive authority to license hydroelectric projects pursuant to the FPA. In petitioners' vew, the minimum flow requirement imposed here interferes with FERC's authority under the FPA.

The FPA empowers FERC to issue licenses for projects "necessary or convenient * * * for the development, transmission, and utilization of power across, along, from, or in any of the streams * * * over which Congress has jurisdiction." § 797(e). The FPA also requires FERC to consider a project's effect on fish and wildlife. §§ 797(e), 803(a)(1). In *California v. FERC*, we held that the California Water Resources Control Board, acting pursuant to state law, could not impose a minimum stream flow which conflicted with minimum stream flows contained in a FERC license. We concluded that the FPA did not "save" to the States this authority.

No such conflict with any FERC licensing activity is presented here. FERC has not yet acted on petitioners' license application, and it is possible that FERC will eventually deny petitioners' application altogether. Alternatively, it is quite possible, given that FERC is required to give equal consideration to the protection of fish habitat when deciding whether to issue a license, that any FERC license would contain the same conditions as the State § 401 certification. Indeed, at oral argument the Solicitor General stated that both EPA and FERC were represented in this proceeding, and that the Government has no objection to the stream flow condition contained in the § 401 certification.

Finally, the requirement for a state certification applies not only to applications for licenses from FERC, but to all federal licenses and permits for activities which may result in a discharge into the Nation's navigable waters. For example, a permit from the Army Corps of Engineers is required for the installation of any structure in the navigable waters which may interfere with navigation, including piers, docks, and ramps. Rivers and Harbors Appropriation Act of 1899, § 10, 33 U.S.C. § 403. Similarly, a permit must be obtained from the Army Corps of Engineers for the discharge of dredged or fill material, and from the Secretary of the Interior or Agriculture for the construction of reservoirs, canals and other water storage systems on federal land. See 33 U.S.C. §§ 1344(a), (e); 43 U.S.C. § 1761. We assume that a § 401 certification would also be required for some licenses obtained pursuant to these statutes. Because § 401's certification requirement applies to other statutes and regulatory schemes, and because any conflict with FERC's authority under the FPA is hypothetical, we are unwilling to read implied limitations into § 401. If FERC issues a license containing a stream flow condition with which petitioners disagree, they may pursue judicial remedies at that time.

In summary, we hold that the State may include minimum stream flow requirements in a certification issued pursuant to § 401 of the Clean Water Act insofar as necessary to enforce a designated use contained in a state water quality standard. The judgment of the Supreme Court of Washington, accordingly, is affirmed.

Notes

1. **State certification conditions unrelated to water quality.** Shortly after the Court decided *PUD No. 1*, FERC declared in Tunbridge Mill Corp., 68 F.E.R.C. ¶ 61,078 (1994): "Section 401 authorizes states to impose only conditions that relate to water quality. To the extent that states include conditions that are unrelated to water quality, these condi-

tions are beyond the scope of section 401 and are thus unlawful. We conclude that we have the authority to determine that such conditions do not become terms and conditions of the license we issue." Upon review of *Tunbridge Mill* and several related cases, the Second Circuit agreed that section 401(d) allows states to impose only conditions that relate to water quality. But the court ruled that "the Commission is bound by § 401 to incorporate all state-imposed certification conditions into hydropower licenses and * * * the legality of such conditions can only be challenged by the licensee in a court of appropriate jurisdiction." American Rivers, Inc. v. FERC, 129 F.3d 99, 102 (2d Cir. 1997).

2. **FPA preemption and state certification.** The certifying agency in California for purposes of section 401 is the State Water Resources Control Board. Cal. Water Code § 13160. Sayles Hydro Associates v. Maughan, supra p. 656, Note 3, held that Sayles Hydro's FPA license preempted the State Board when processing its water permit application from requiring studies and reports on how the project would affect recreation, aesthetics, archaeology, sport fishing, and cultural resources. If a project like that were proposed today and would impair water quality in ways harmful to those values, could the State Board successfully impose section 401 certification conditions protecting the values even though FERC wants to license the project without the conditions? In *American Rivers*, supra Note 1, the court said: "The Commission * * * argues that without the authority to reject state-imposed § 401 conditions its Congressionally mandated role under the FPA of ensuring comprehensive planning and development of hydropower would be undermined. * * * The CWA, however, has diminished [the FPA's] preemptive reach by expressly requiring the Commission to incorporate into its licenses state-imposed water-quality conditions." 129 F.3d at 107, 111.

3. **Relicensing and state certification.** *PUD No. 1* concerned the licensing of a new hydroelectric facility. S.D. Warren Co. v. Maine Board of Environmental Protection, 547 U.S. 370 (2006), ruled that the relicensing of an existing facility requires state certification under section 401. S.D. Warren Co. sought to relicense five hydroelectric dams. Each dam impounded water that the company turned into a canal, passed through turbines, and then returned to the river a distance below the dam, so that the water bypassed a section of the river. The company argued that the trigger for section 401 state certification—"any discharge into the navigable waters"—was missing because it was not adding anything to the river that was not already there above the dams. In response, the Court noted that although the CWA defines "discharge of a pollutant," it does not define "discharge" standing alone. Therefore, the Court gave the term its ordinary or natural meaning, which as applied to water is a "flowing or issuing out." Of course, there was a flowing or issuing out of water from the company's turbines into the river.

To support its ruling, the Court explained: "[The CWA] does not stop at controlling the 'addition of pollutants,' but deals with 'pollution' generally, see § 1251(b), which Congress defined to mean 'the man-made or man-induced alteration of the chemical, physical, biological, and radiological integrity of water.' § 1362(19). The alteration of water quality as thus defined is a risk inherent in limiting river flow and releasing water through turbines [e.g., that can cause the river to absorb less oxygen and to be less passable by boaters and fish]. State certifications under § 401 are essential to the scheme to preserve state authority to address the broad range of pollution * * *."

4. **Other federal regulatory programs requiring state certification.** The penultimate paragraph of *PUD No. 1* mentions three federal licensing and permitting programs besides the FPA that might trigger section 401 certification: (1) Rivers and Harbors Appropriation Act of 1899 (RHA) § 10, (2) 33 U.S.C. § 1344, which is CWA § 404, and (3) 43 U.S.C. § 1761, which is the Federal Land Policy and Management Act (FLPMA) § 501.

RHA § 10 reads: "The creation of any obstruction not affirmatively authorized by Congress, to the navigable capacity of any of the waters of the United States is prohibited; and it shall not be lawful to build or commence the building of any wharf, pier, dolphin, boom, weir, breakwater, bulkhead, jetty or other structures in any * * * navigable river, or other water of the United States, outside established harbor lines, or where no harbor lines have been established, except on plans recommended by the Chief of Engineers and authorized by the Secretary of the Army; and it shall not be lawful to excavate or fill, or in any manner to alter or modify the course, location, condition, or capacity * * * of the channel of any navigable water of the United States, unless the work has been recommended by the Chief of Engineers and authorized by the Secretary of the Army prior to beginning the same."

The first clause of section 10, running to the first semicolon, had an essentially identical predecessor in the Rivers and Harbors Act of 1890. The Supreme Court invoked the predecessor provision to enjoin construction of an irrigation dam in the nonnavigable upper reach of the Rio Grande in New Mexico. The dam would have appropriated the entire water flow at its location, thereby diminishing the flow downstream in the navigable reach of the river and impairing navigation. The Court said the statute "is not a prohibition of any obstruction to the navigation, but any obstruction to the navigable capacity, and anything, wherever done or however done, within the limits of the jurisdiction of the United States which tends to destroy the navigable capacity of one of the navigable waters of the United States, is within the terms of the prohibition." United States v. Rio Grande Dam & Irr. Co., 174 U.S. 690, 708 (1899).

The final clause of RHA § 10, beginning after the second semicolon, was involved in *Kaiser Aetna*, supra p. 640. This provision overlaps with CWA § 404. It requires a Corps of Engineers permit to excavate, fill, or otherwise alter the channel of any navigable water of the United States, while section 404 requires a Corps of Engineers permit to discharge dredged or fill material into navigable waters. Permit applicants complete the same Corps of Engineers application form for section 10 and section

404. 33 C.F.R. § 325.1(a), (c). But section 10 applies only to waters that are navigable in the traditional sense, see supra p. 633, Note 3, while section 404 reaches more broadly, see *Rapanos*, supra p. 626. Another difference is that a section 404 permit application but not a section 10 application must meet guidelines developed by the Environmental Protection Agency in conjunction with the Corps of Engineers. 33 U.S.C. § 1344(b).

The RHA § 10 permit process involves full review of the favorable and detrimental impacts on the public interest. 33 C.F.R. § 320.1(a)(1). This is the same public interest review process required for section 404 permits that is described supra pp. 599-601, Note 2.

Although the present materials deal with federal permitting and licensing of nonfederal projects, it might be noted that RHA § 10 and CWA § 404 permits are generally required as well for federal agency projects if they were not specifically authorized by Congress. 33 C.F.R. §§ 322.3(c), 323.3(b).

5. **Federal licenses and permits not requiring state certification.** The section 401 requirement of state certification applies only to discharges from point sources, not discharges from nonpoint sources. Or. Natural Desert Ass'n v. U.S. Forest Serv., 550 F.3d 778 (9th Cir. 2008) (section 401 was not triggered by issuance of a federal livestock grazing permit because livestock runoff is not a point source discharge).

B. Construction and Management of Federal Projects

CALIFORNIA v. UNITED STATES
Supreme Court of the United States, 1978.
438 U.S. 645, 98 S. Ct. 2985, 57 L. Ed.2d 1018.

MR. JUSTICE REHNQUIST delivered the opinion of the Court.

The United States seeks to impound 2.4 million acre-feet of water from California's Stanislaus River as part of its Central Valley Project. The California State Water Resources Control Board ruled that the water could not be allocated to the Government under state law unless it agreed to and complied with various conditions dealing with the water's use. The Government then sought a declaratory judgment in the District Court for the Eastern District of California to the effect that the United States can impound whatever unappropriated water is necessary for a federal reclamation project without complying with state law. * * *

If the term "cooperative federalism" had been in vogue in 1902, the Reclamation Act of that year would surely have qualified as a leading example of it. In that Act, Congress set forth on a massive program to construct and operate dams, reservoirs, and canals for the reclamation of the arid lands in 17 western States. Reflective of the "cooperative federalism" which the Act embodied is § 8, whose exact meaning and scope are the critical inquiries in this case:

> *"[N]othing in this Act shall be construed as affecting or intended to affect or to in any way interfere with the laws of any States or Territory relating to the control, appropriation, use or distribution of water used in irrigation, or any vested rights acquired thereunder, and the Secretary of the Interior, in carrying out the provisions of this Act, shall proceed in conformity with such laws,* and nothing herein shall in any way affect any right of any State or of the Federal Government or of any landowner, appropriator, or user of water in, to or from any interstate stream or the waters thereof: Provided, That the right to use of water acquired under the provisions of this Act shall be appurtenant to the land irrigated, and beneficial use shall be the basis, the measure, and the limit of the right." 43 U.S.C.A. § 383 (emphasis added).

The New Melones Dam, which this litigation concerns, is part of the California Central Valley Project, the largest reclamation project yet authorized under the 1902 Act. The Dam, which will impound 2.4 million acre-feet of water of California's Stanislaus River, has the multiple purposes of flood control, irrigation, municipal use, industrial use, power, recreation, water quality control and the protection of fish and wildlife. * * *

The United States Bureau of Reclamation, as it has with every other federal reclamation project, applied for a permit from the appropriate state agency, here the California State Water Resources Control Board, to appropriate the water that would be impounded by the Dam and later used for reclamation. After lengthy hearings, the State Board found that unappropriated water was available for the New Melones Project during certain times of the year. Although it therefore approved the Bureau's applications, the State Board attached 25 conditions to the permits. The most important conditions prohibit full impoundment until the Bureau is able to show firm commitments, or at least a specific plan, for the use of the water.[8] The State Board concluded that without such a specific plan of beneficial use the Bureau

---

8. Other conditions * * * require that a preference be given to water users in the water basin in which the New Melones Project is located; require storage releases to be made so as to maintain maximum and minimum chemical concentrations in the San Joaquin River and protect fish and wildlife; require the United States to provide means for the release of excess waters and to clear vegetation and structures from the reservoir sites; require the filing of additional reports and studies; and provide for access to the project site by the State Board and the public. Still other conditions reserve jurisdiction to the Board to impose further conditions on the appropriations if necessary to protect the "beneficial use" of the water involved. Respondent did not challenge any of the conditions under state law, but instead filed the federal declaratory action that is now before us.

had failed to meet the California statutory requirements for appropriation. * * *

The history of the relationship between the Federal Government and the States in the reclamation of the arid lands of the western States is both long and involved, but through it runs the consistent thread of purposeful and continued deference to state water law by Congress.* * *

[R]eclamation of the arid lands began almost immediately upon the arrival of pioneers to the western States. Huge sums of private money were invested in systems to transport water vast distances for mining, agriculture, and ordinary consumption. Because a very high percentage of land in the West belonged to the Federal Government, the canals and ditches that carried this water frequently crossed federal land. In 1862, Congress opened the public domain to homesteading. And in 1866, Congress for the first time expressly opened the mineral lands of the public domain to exploration and occupation by miners. Because of the fear that these Acts might in some way interfere with the water rights and systems that had grown up under state and local law, Congress explicitly recognized and acknowledged the local law:

> "[W]henever, by priority of possession, rights to the use of water for mining, agricultural, manufacturing, or other purposes, have vested and accrued, and the same are recognized and acknowledged by the local customs, laws, and the decisions of the courts, the possessors and owners of such vested rights shall be maintained and protected in the same." Mining Act of 1866, § 9, 14 Stat. 251, 253.

The Mining Act of 1866 was not itself a grant of water rights pursuant to federal law. Instead, as this Court observed, the Act was "a voluntary recognition of a preexisting right of possession, constituting a valid claim to its continued use." United States v. Rio Grande Dam & Irrig. Co., 174 U.S. 690, 705 (1899). Congress intended "to recognize as valid the customary law with respect to the use of water which had grown up among the occupants of the public land under the peculiar necessities of their condition." Basey v. Gallagher, 20 Wall. 670, 684 (1874).

In 1877, Congress took its first step towards encouraging the reclamation and settlement of the public desert lands in the West and made it clear that such reclamation would generally follow state water law. In the 1877 Desert Lands Act, 19 Stat. 377, Congress provided for the homesteading of arid public lands in larger tracts

> "by conducting water upon the same, within the period of three years [after filing a declaration to do so], *Provided however* that the right to the use of water by the person so conducting the same * * * shall not exceed the amount of water actually appropriated, and nec-

essarily used for the purpose of irrigation and reclamation: *and all surplus water over and above such actual appropriation and use, together with the water of all lakes, rivers and other sources of water supply upon the public lands and not navigable, shall remain and be held free for the appropriation and use of the public for irrigation, mining and manufacturing purposes subject to existing rights.*" 19 Stat. 377 (emphasis added).

This Court has had an opportunity to construe the 1877 Desert Lands Act before. In California Oregon Power Co. v. Beaver Portland Cement Co., 295 U.S. 142 (1935), Justice Sutherland explained that, through this language, "[Congress] effected a severance of all waters upon the public domain, not theretofore appropriated, from the land itself." Id., at 158. The nonnavigable waters thereby severed were "reserved for the use of the public under the laws of the states and territories." Ibid. Congress' purpose was not to federalize the prior appropriation doctrine already evolving under local law. Quite the opposite:

> "What we hold is that following the act of 1877, if not before, all non-navigable waters then a part of the public domain became *publici juris,* subject to the plenary control of the designated states, including those since created out of the territories named, with the right in each to determine for itself to what extent the rule of appropriation or the common-law rule in respect of riparian rights should obtain. For since 'Congress cannot enforce either rule upon any state,' Kansas v. Colorado, 206 U.S. 46, the full power of choice must remain with the state. The Desert Land Act does not bind or purport to bind the states to any policy. It simply recognizes and gives sanction, in so far as the United States and its future grantees are concerned, to the state and local doctrine of appropriation, and seeks to remove what otherwise might be an impediment to its full and successful operation." Id., at 163-64.

It is against this background that Congress passed the Reclamation Act of 1902. * * *

From the legislative history of the Reclamation Act of 1902, it is clear that state law was expected to control in two important respects. First, and of controlling importance to this case, the Secretary would have to appropriate, purchase, or condemn necessary water rights in strict conformity with state law. According to Representative Mondell, the principal sponsor of the reclamation bill in the House, once the Secretary determined that a reclamation project was feasible and that there was an adequate supply of water for the project, "the Secretary of the Interior would proceed to make the appropriation of the necessary water *by giving the notice and complying with the forms of law of the State or Territory in which the waters were located.*" 35 Cong. Rec. 6678 (1902) (emphasis added). The Secretary of the Interior could not take any action in appropriating the waters of the state streams "which could not be undertaken by an individual or corporation if it were in the position of the Government as regards the ownership of its lands." H.R. Rep. No. 794, 57th Cong., 1st Sess., at 7B8. Thus, in response to the statement of an opponent to the bill that the Secretary would be allowed to condemn water even if in violation of state law, Representative Mondell briskly responded:

> "Whereabouts does the gentleman find any such provision as he is arguing? Whereabouts in the bill is there anything that attempts to give the Federal Government any right to condemn or to take any water right or do anything which an individual could not do? Will the gentleman point out any place or any provision for the Federal Government to do anything that I could not do if I owned the public land?

> "MR. RAY of New York. Do you say there is nothing in this bill that provides for condemnation?

> "MR. MONDELL. *The bill provides explicitly that even an appropriation of water can not be made except under State law.*" 35 Cong. Rec. 6687 (1902) (emphasis added).

Second, once the waters were released from the dam, their distribution to individual landowners would again be controlled by state law. As explained by Senator Clark of Wyoming, one of the principal supporters of the reclamation bill in the Senate, "the control of the water after leaving the reservoirs shall be vested in the State and Territories through which such waters flow." Id., at 2222. * * * As Representative Sutherland, later to be a Justice of this Court, succinctly put it, "if the appropriation and use were not under the provisions of the State law the utmost confusion would prevail." Id., at 6770. Different water rights in the same State would be governed by different laws and would frequently conflict.[21]

---

21. Congress did not intend to relinquish total control of the actual distribution of the reclamation water to the States. Congress provided in § 8 itself that the water right must be appurtenant to the land irrigated and governed by beneficial use, and in § 5 Congress forbade the sale of reclamation water to tracts of land of more than 160 acres. * * *

In previous cases interpreting § 8 of the 1902 Reclamation Act, however, this Court has held that state water law does not control in the distribution of reclamation water *if* inconsistent with other congressional directives to the Secretary. We believe that this reading of the Act is also consistent with the legislative history and indeed is the preferable reading of the Act. Whatever the intent of Congress with respect to state control over the distribution of water, however, Congress in the 1902 Act intended to follow state law as to appropriation of water and condemnation of water rights. * * * Subsequent legislation authorizing a specific project may by its terms signify congressional intent that the Secretary condemn or be permitted to appropriate the necessary water rights for the project in question, but no such legislation was considered by the Court of Appeals in its opinion in this case. That court will be free to consider arguments by the Government to this effect on remand.

For almost half a century, this congressionally mandated division between federal and state authority worked smoothly. No project was constructed without the approval of the Secretary of the Interior, and the United States through this official preserved its authority to determine how federal funds should be expended. But state laws relating to water rights were observed in accordance with the congressional directive contained in § 8 of the Act of 1902. In 1958, however, the first of two cases was decided by this Court in which private land owners or municipal corporations contended that state water law had the effect of overriding specific congressional directives to the Secretary of the Interior as to the operation of federal reclamation projects. In Ivanhoe Irrigation District v. McCracken, 357 U.S. 275, 78 S.Ct. 1174, 2 L.Ed.2d 1313 (1958), the Supreme Court of California decided that California law forbade the 160-acre limitation on irrigation water deliveries expressly written into § 5 of the Reclamation Act of 1902, and that therefore, under § 8 of the Reclamation Act, the Secretary was required to deliver reclamation water without regard to the acreage limitation. Both the State of California and the United States appealed from this judgment, and this Court reversed it, saying:

> "Section 5 is a specific and mandatory prerequisite laid down by the Congress as binding in the operation of reclamation projects, providing that '[no] right to the use of water * * * shall be sold for a tract exceeding one hundred and sixty acres to any one landowner. * * * ' Without passing generally on the coverage of § 8 in the delicate area of federal-state relations in the irrigation field, we do not believe that the Congress intended § 8 to override the repeatedly reaffirmed national policy of § 5." 357 U.S., at 291-292.

Five years later, in City of Fresno v. California, 372 U.S. 627 (1963), this Court affirmed a decision of the United States Court of Appeals for the Ninth Circuit holding that § 8 did not require the Secretary of the Interior to ignore explicit congressional provisions preferring irrigation use over domestic and municipal use.[24]

---

24. "Section 9(c) of the Reclamation Project Act of 1939 * * * provides: 'No contract relating to municipal water supply or miscellaneous purposes * * * shall be made unless, in the judgment of the Secretary [of the Interior], it will not impair the efficiency of the project for irrigation purposes.' * * * It therefore appears clear that Fresno has no preferential rights to contract for project water, but may receive it only if, in the Secretary's judgment, irrigation will not be adversely affected." 372 U.S., at 630-631.

The Court also concluded in a separate portion of its opinion that "§ 8 does not mean that state law may operate to prevent the United States from exercising the power of eminent domain to acquire the water rights of others. * * * Rather, the effect of § 8 in such a case is to leave to state law the definition of the property interests, if any, for which compensation must be made." 372 U.S., at 630. Because no provision of California law was actually inconsistent with the exercise by the United States of its power of eminent domain, this statement was dictum. It also might have been apparent from examination of the congressional authorization of the Central Valley Project

Petitioners [the State of California, the State Board, and its members] do not ask us to overrule these holdings, nor are we presently inclined to do so. Petitioners instead ask us to hold that a State may impose any condition on the "control, appropriation, use or distribution of water" through a federal reclamation project that is not inconsistent with clear congressional directives respecting the project. Petitioners concede, and the Government relies upon, dicta in our cases that may point to a contrary conclusion. Thus, in *Ivanhoe,* the Court went beyond the actual facts of that case and stated:

> "As we read § 8, it merely requires the United States to comply with state law when, in the construction and operation of a reclamation project, it becomes necessary for it to acquire water rights or vested interests therein. * * * We read nothing in § 8 that compels the United States to deliver water on conditions imposed by the State." 357 U.S. 275.

Like dictum was repeated in City of Fresno, 372 U.S., at 630, and in this Court's opinion in Arizona v. California, 373 U.S. 546, (1963), where the Court also said:

> "The argument that § 8 of the Reclamation Act requires the United States in the delivery of water to follow priorities laid down by state law has already been disposed of by this Court in Ivanhoe Irr. Dist. v. McCracken, * * * and reaffirmed in City of Fresno v. California * * *. Since § 8 of the Reclamation Act did not subject the Secretary to state law in disposing of water in [*Ivanhoe*], we cannot, consistently with *Ivanhoe,* hold that the Secretary must be bound by state law in disposing of water under the Project Act." Id., at 586-587.

While we are not convinced that the above language is diametrically inconsistent with the position of petitioners, or that it squarely supports respondent, it undoubtedly goes further than was necessary to decide the cases presented to the Court. *Ivanhoe* and *City of Fresno* involved conflicts between § 8, requiring the Secretary to follow state law as to water rights, and other provisions of Reclamation Acts that placed specific limitations on how the water was to be distributed. Here the United States contends that it may ignore state law even if no explicit congressional directive conflicts with the conditions imposed by the California State Water Control Board.

In *Arizona v. California,* the States had asked the Court to rule that state law would control in the distribution of water from the Boulder Canyon Project, a massive multistate reclamation project on the Colorado river. After reviewing the legislative history of the Boul-

---

that Congress intended the Secretary to have the power to condemn any necessary water rights. We disavow this dictum, however, to the extent that it implies that state law does not control even where not inconsistent with such expressions of congressional intent.

der Canyon Project Act, 43 U.S.C.A. § 617 *et seq.*, the Court concluded that because of the unique size and multistate scope of the Project, Congress did not intend the States to interfere with the Secretary's power to determine with whom and on what terms water contracts would be made. While the Court in rejecting the States' claim repeated the language from *Ivanhoe* and *City of Fresno* as to the scope of § 8, there was no need for it to reaffirm such language except as it related to the singular legislative history of the Boulder Canyon Project Act.

But because there is at least tension between the above quoted dictum and what we conceive to be the correct reading of § 8 of the Reclamation Act of 1902, we disavow the dictum to the extent that it would prevent petitioner from imposing conditions on the permits granted to the United States which are not inconsistent with congressional provisions authorizing the project in question. Section 8 cannot be read to require the Secretary to comply with state law only when it becomes necessary to purchase or condemn vested water rights. That section does, of course provide for the protection of vested water rights, but it also requires the Secretary to comply with state law in the "control, appropriation, use, or distribution of water." * * * The legislative history of the Reclamation Act of 1902 makes it abundantly clear that Congress intended to defer to the substance, as well as the form, of state water law. The Government's interpretation would trivialize the broad language and purpose of § 8. * * *

Because the District Court and the Court of Appeals both held that California could not impose any conditions whatever on the United States' appropriation permits, those courts did not reach the United States' alternative contention that the conditions actually imposed are inconsistent with congressional directives as to the New Melones Project. [R]esolution of their consistency may well require additional fact-finding. We therefore reverse the judgment of the Court of Appeals and remand for further proceedings consistent with this opinion. * * *

Mr. Justice White, with whom Mr. Justice Brennan and Mr. Justice Marshall join, dissenting. * * *

[The majority has] concluded that because of § 8, the United States may not acquire water rights by appropriation or condemnation except in accordance with state law. If, for example, particular water rights are not subject to condemnation under state law by private interests, neither may they be taken by the United States. This issue, going to the acquisition by the United States of water rights by eminent domain, is not among the questions presented in this case, and the views expressed in this respect are no sounder and no less inconsistent with our prior cases than is the majority's view that the distribution of water developed by federal reclamation projects is to be governed by state law. * * *

The short of the matter is that no case in this Court, until this one, has construed § 8 as the present majority insists that it be construed. All of the relevant cases are to the contrary. * * *

Although I do not join the Court in reconstruing the controlling statutes as it does, the Court's work today is a precedent for "setting things right" in the area of statutory water law so as to satisfy the views of a current Court majority. And surely the dicta with which the Court's opinion is laced today deserve no more or no less respect than what it has chosen to label as dicta in past Court decisions. Of course, the matter is purely statutory and Congress could easily put an end to our feuding if it chose to make it clear that local authorities are to control the spending of federal funds for reclamation projects and to control the priorities for the use of water developed by federal projects.

Notes

1. **More on *California v. United States*.** As the Court's references to the Secretary of the Interior imply, the Bureau of Reclamation is located in the Department of the Interior.

The majority opinion regarded Arizona v. California as not being on point because it involved a federal water project of unique size and multi-state scope. This is the same Arizona v. California reprinted in part supra p. 500, where the Court addressed allocation of the lower Colorado River among California, Arizona, and Nevada. In a portion of the opinion not reprinted earlier, the Court ruled state law did not control the distribution of project water to users: "All this vast interlocking machinery—a dozen major works delivering water according to congressionally fixed priorities for home, agricultural, and industrial uses to people spread over thousands of square miles—could function efficiently only under unitary management, able to formulate and supervise a coordinated plan that could take account of the diverse, often conflicting interests of the people and communities of the Lower Basin States. * * * Subjecting the Secretary to the varying, possibly inconsistent, commands of the different state legislatures could frustrate efficient operation of the project and thwart full realization of the benefits Congress intended this national project to bestow." 373 U.S. at 589-90.

California v. United States is critiqued in Amy K. Kelley, Staging a Comeback—Section 8 of the Reclamation Act, 18 U.C. Davis L. Rev. 97 (1984). See also Jerome C. Muys, Section 5 of the Boulder Canyon Project Act and 43 C.F.R. Part 417 Occupy the Field of Determination of Reasonable Beneficial Use of Colorado River Water, 15 Hastings W.-Nw. J. Envt'l L. and Pol'y 197 (2009).

2. **The Reclamation Act and Federal Power Act contrasted regarding preemption.** In *First Iowa*, supra p. 650, the Court gave FPA § 27 extremely limited effect in saving state law from federal preemption. In the principal case, the Court gave Reclamation Act § 8 much greater effect in saving state law from federal preemption. More recently, in Cali-

fornia v. FERC, supra p. 655, Note 2, California pointed out that FPA § 27 and Reclamation Act § 8 are similarly worded state-law savings clauses, and it argued that the principal case's expansive view of Reclamation Act § 8 should require abandoning *First Iowa*'s narrow view of FPA § 27. The Court reaffirmed *First Iowa*, however: "[A]s in *First Iowa*, the Court in *California v. United States* examined the purpose, structure, and legislative history of the entire statute before it and employed those sources to construe the statute's saving clause. Those sources indicate, of course, that the FPA envisioned a considerably broader and more active federal oversight role in hydropower development than did the Reclamation Act." 459 U.S. at 504.

3. **Federal versus state control of water—should "ownership" matter?** In the principal case, the Court noted that California Oregon Power Co. v. Beaver Portland Cement Co. relied on congressional severance of water from public domain land as the basis for state jurisdiction over water rights. Severance explains why states have jurisdiction despite the federal government starting out with "ownership" of all waters in the western states as an incident of its owning the public domain.

Western states have long claimed "ownership" of the waters within their borders and argued the United States should be subject to state control whenever it engages in water resources development activities, under federal reclamation law or otherwise. Merrill v. Bishop, 287 P.2d 620 (Wyo. 1955); National Reclamation Assoc., Preservation of Integrity of State Water Laws (1942). Some logical and historical fallacies of this position were explored in Frank J. Trelease, Government Ownership and Trusteeship of Water, 45 Cal. L. Rev. 638 (1957), and Note, Federal-State Conflicts Over the Control of Western Waters, 60 Colum. L. Rev. 967 (1960), and it seems to have been completely demolished by B. Abbott Goldberg, Interposition—Wild West Water Style, 17 Stan. L. Rev. 1 (1964), and Eva H. Morreale, Federal-State Conflicts over Western Waters—A Decade of Attempted "Clarifying Legislation," 20 Rutgers L. Rev. 423 (1966).

Is "ownership" a useful concept for resolving federal-state jurisdictional conflicts involving water? Consider the following:

"Better results can be reached by sticking to what the Supreme Court has said—that the [United States] had power to dispose of the water. It had that power in 1802, when Ohio became the first state created out of the public domain, but it did not exercise it. Congress might have adopted a federal water law for disposing of water rights as it enacted laws to dispose of the lands, but it did not do so. As the western public lands states were born, they took over the function of establishing water rights by common law and statutes, as had been done in the original thirteen states in which there was no public domain. * * * They did what all states had always done, exercised what the Supreme Court has called their 'traditional jurisdiction' over water. There is no evidence that the legislators or courts of any state from Ohio to California had any thought that they were dealing with water that belonged to the federal government until California's 1886 mistake [in assuming that was so in Lux v. Haggin, 10 P. 674 (Cal. 1886)]. The states filled the vacuum left by federal inaction, and the United States gave its sanction by its 'silent acquiescence,' which means that Congress gave the matter no thought either.

"The holding of [California Oregon Power Co. v. Beaver Portland Cement Co.] gave the western states the rule they had always hoped was law, that each could decide the form of its own water law. Nevertheless, the grounds on which the decision was rested left uneasy doubts as to its universal application. The Court's use of the Desert Land Act in its reasoning creates several difficulties. The act did not cover all the appropriation law states, for it had no force in Kansas, Nebraska and Oklahoma, and it was not applied to Colorado until amended in 1891. The proviso excepts from its operation navigable waters, but surely this could not mean that landowners along the Missouri River in Montana have federal riparian rights. That state recognizes no such rights and inconceivable chaos would result if such rights were held to exist by virtue of federal law. The Act was passed in 1877 and if it in that year severed the water from the federal lands and patents, this could be taken as an indication that patents granted before its enactment did carry riparian rights. Such a ruling would raise havoc with the water law systems of all of the Colorado doctrine states. The Court did leave a way out of this construction by saying that the severance occurred in 1877 'if not before,' and it is commonly supposed that the reference is to the Act of 1866. This is only a less unsatisfactory solution, because much land had been patented in the Colorado doctrine states before that date. Only if 'if not before' refers back to the beginning of state and territorial governments and if each state or territory had from the beginning the right to determine for itself the law of water rights, can the *Beaver* holding be sustained on the reasoning of a severance. And if that is done, we are back to the original proposition here proposed, that the state laws have validity not because of an act of Congress but because of the 'silent acquiescence' of the federal government. Water law was the subject of concurrent federal and state jurisdiction. The states could exercise their traditional jurisdiction unless their laws were superseded by a federal law disposing of the water. Since the federal government never enacted such a law, the state law stood." Frank J. Trelease, Federal-State Relations in Water Law, Nat'l Water Comm'n, Legal Study No. 5, at 147b, 147g-147h (1971).

4. **Origin and evolution of federal reclamation law.** Frank J. Trelease, Reclamation Water Rights, 32 Rocky Mtn. L. Rev. 464, 465 (1960):

"The Reclamation Act [of 1902] marked a departure from [a] pattern of private [water] development. Since the need for large dams and canals was not being fully met by private capital, the act introduced federal financing of projects. A revolving fund was established with moneys received from the sale of public lands, and the Secretary of the Interior was directed to survey the west and locate and construct irrigation projects, opening up the improved public lands to settlement under the homestead laws. * * * Construction costs were to be repaid into the fund by the settlers and landowners in ten annual installments without interest.

"This basic statute has been amended, supplemented, and superseded by a long series of acts, some general in nature, some relating to specific projects. * * * Nowadays the Bureau of Reclamation builds multipurpose projects which include features for production of hydroelectric power, control of floods, navigation improvement, municipal and industrial water supplies, recreation, and fish and wildlife preservation, as well as for irrigation. Projects now encompass the comprehensive development of entire river basins. The revolving fund was long ago exhausted and today's projects are built with general funds. Repayment periods have been stretched out."

One of the acts supplementing the Reclamation Act of 1902 is the Reclamation Project Act of 1939, as amended, 43 U.S.C. §§ 485-485k. It authorizes the construction of multipurpose water projects, provides for allocating project costs to the various purposes undertaken, and makes costs allocated to navigation and flood control nonreimbursable. Costs allocated to the preservation and propagation of fish and wildlife are made nonreimbursable by the Fish and Wildlife Coordination Act, 16 U.S.C. §§ 661-666c. Costs allocated to power and to irrigation and municipal and industrial water supply are reimbursable. They are to be repaid to the United States from net power revenues and by the water users. Costs allocated to irrigation but beyond the irrigators' ability to pay are assigned for repayment from revenues received for power and municipal water supply.

5. **Reclamation law subsidies to irrigators.** The subsidies to irrigators provided by federal reclamation projects were described as follows in National Water Commission, Water Policies for the Future 128 (1973):

"A primary weakness of the Federal water resources development projects is that they have been heavily subsidized by the Federal Government; that is, by all the taxpayers of the Nation, to provide benefits for a few. The water users on some modern Federal Reclamation projects, for example, repay no more than 10 percent of the construction costs attributable to irrigation, the remaining cost being borne by the Federal Government in three ways: by not requiring the water users to reimburse the Treasury for the interest on the capital advanced for project construction, by permitting power revenues and sometimes other nonirrigation revenues to be credited toward irrigation reimbursement, and by allocating an unduly large part of the costs to nonreimbursable purposes."

6. **Acreage limitations.** President Theodore Roosevelt conceived of the Reclamation Act of 1902 as reopening the American frontier—giving a new wave of settlers the opportunity to "go West," settle on family-sized farms, and continue the "agrarian myth" that America's strength lay in its rural population. Consequently, section 5 of the Act provided that no right to the use of water would be sold for land in excess of 160 acres in one ownership.

The Omnibus Adjustment Act of 1926 ended contracts with individual settlers and water user associations and instead required the United States to enter into contracts with irrigation districts—quasi-governmental agencies that would distribute water to eligible landowners, collect charges for water and for operation and maintenance, and reimburse the United States for the allocated costs of construction of the project. The contracts required districts to withhold project water from private land in excess of 160 acres in one ownership unless the owner executed a recordable contract with the Secretary of the Interior obligating the owner to sell the excess land at a price excluding incremental value attributable to the availability of project water. By administrative interpretation, landowners who executed recordable contracts to sell their excess land within ten years were allowed to receive project water for the excess land in the meantime.

The Bureau of Reclamation treated only owned land as subject to the 160-acre limitation, and many large farms circumvented the limitation through leasing, trust, and multiple-ownership arrangements. This led to calls for stricter enforcement of the acreage limitation. After years of debate and trial balloons, Congress passed the Reclamation Reform Act of 1982 (RRA), 43 U.S.C. §§ 390aa to 390zz-1, which made major changes in reclamation law, including the acreage limitation.

The RRA distinguishes between qualified recipients and limited recipients of project water. A qualified recipient is an individual (including a spouse and dependents) or a legal entity benefiting twenty-five persons or less. Id. § 390bb(7). A limited recipient is a legal entity benefiting more than twenty-five persons. Id. § 390bb(9).

A qualified recipient can receive project water for no more than 960 acres of owned land, unless the excess land is made subject to a recordable contract to sell it. A qualified recipient can also receive project water for an unlimited amount of leased land if the lease term, including exercisable options, does not exceed ten years (twenty-five years if the land is used for perennial crops). But a qualified recipient can get water at a subsidized price for no more than 960 acres of land, whether owned or leased, and must pay full cost for any additional leased acres. Id. §§ 390bb(6), 390dd, 390ee, 390yy. A limited recipient can receive project water for up to 640 acres of owned land and for additional leased land. But a limited recipient can get water at a subsidized price for no more than 320 acres, and then only if the entity was receiving water before October 1, 1981. A limited recipient must pay full cost for all other water received. Id. § 390ee.

The acreage limitations are based on the best lands, called Class I lands. Larger acreages are allowed for farmers with less productive lands to give them the equivalent of Class I lands. Id. §§ 390dd, 390gg.

7. The Central Valley Project Improvement Act (CVPIA). Congress continued to reshape reclamation policy in the CVPIA, which is Title XXXIV of the Reclamation Projects Authorization and Adjustment Act of 1992, Pub. L. No. 102-575, 106 Stat. 4600, 4706. Although the CVPIA applies only to the Central Valley Project (CVP) in California, it is important both because of the CVP's massive size and because it may presage greater environmental sensitivity in the operation of reclamation projects throughout the West.

The CVPIA adds fish and wildlife mitigation, protection and restoration as a purpose of the CVP and places it on a par with domestic and agricultural water uses. It also adds fish and wildlife enhancement as a project purpose and places it on a par with power production at a lower priority. Specific fish and wildlife provisions include (1) dedication of 800,000 acre-feet of CVP water annually to general fish and wildlife purposes, dedication of approximately 200,000 acre-feet of water annually for wildlife refuges in the Central Valley, and instream release of 340,000 acre-feet annually to the Trinity River; (2) creation of an annual fish and wildlife restoration fund of $50 million provided primarily by assessments on project contractors; (3) development and implementation of a program to double populations of anadromous fish in ten years; (4) identification of specific measures to be undertaken to mitigate effects of CVP operations on fish and wildlife; and (5) prohibition of new water contracts until fish and wildlife goals are met. The Act also limits long-term renewal contracts to 25 years rather than the 40 years previously used.

The CVPIA contains other innovations. To encourage water conservation, it establishes a tiered pricing structure in which water contractors receive the first 80 percent of their contract amount at the subsidized contract rate, the next 10 percent at a rate halfway between the contract rate and full cost, and the final 10 percent at full cost. It also requires the Secretary of the Interior to develop criteria for assessing water conservation plans developed by water contractors.

To provide flexibility to meet urban water needs, the CVPIA allows the transfer of CVP water by individuals or districts, subject to certain conditions. The conditions include requirements that all transfers must be between willing buyers and willing sellers (condemnation is forbidden), transfers cannot adversely affect groundwater conditions or the fish and wildlife purposes of the Act, transfers must be consistent with state law, and proposed transfers outside the CVP service area are subject to a first right of refusal by entities within the CVP service area. Transfers must be approved by the Secretary of the Interior, and transfers involving more than 20 percent of the CVP water subject to long-term contracts within any contracting district or agency must also be reviewed and approved by the district or agency. Water transferred to an agency or district that is not a CVP contractor must be paid for at the greater of full-cost or cost-of-service rates if used for irrigation and at the greater of cost-of-service or municipal and industrial rates if used for municipal or industrial purposes.

STOCKTON EAST WATER DISTRICT v. UNITED STATES

United States Court of Appeals, Federal Circuit, 2009.

583 F.3d 1344.

PLAGER, Circuit Judge. [The U.S. Bureau of Reclamation contracted in 1983 with the Stockton East Water District and the Central San Joaquin Water Conservation District to supply them with specified minimum quantities of water from the New Melones Unit of the Central Valley Project (CVP) for consumptive uses. The Bureau failed to supply the specified minimum quantities in 1994, 1995, and 1999-2004. The districts sued for breach of contract. After a bench trial, the Court of Federal Claims awarded judgment for the United States.]

[W]hen the CVP was established and for many years after, both federal and state water law and policy gave high priority to making the water resources available for consumptive uses. * * * However, by the late 1980s and early 1990s, as environmental concerns became more pronounced and fish and wildlife interests moved more to the forefront, Government policy began to shift. For example, in 1973 when the [California State Water Resources Control Board] initially approved Reclamation's permit for New Melones, it required 98,000 acre-feet of water to be released annually for fish and wildlife. However, under a 1987 agreement entered into by Reclamation and the California Department of Fish and Game, Reclamation was required to release for the same purpose up to 302,100 acre-feet of water annually. At the same time, while Reclamation anticipated when it signed the 1983 contracts that water quality standards mandated by the state would be attained with annual releases of 70,000 acre-feet from New Melones, significantly greater releases were necessary in later years to meet the standards.

At the federal level, the shift in policy culminated in the Congressional enactment in 1992 of the CVPIA. The CVPIA expressly required the release of substantial quantities of water for fish, wildlife, and habitat restoration needs, directing Reclamation to dedicate annually 800,000 acre-feet of the total CVP yield to those purposes. This legislation significantly affected Reclamation's operation of the CVP. Though no provision of the CVPIA was directed specifically at the operation of the New Melones Unit, * * * Reclamation's decisions regarding implementation of the CVPIA impacted the amount of water made available from New Melones for consumptive uses.

As the trial court found, "the ever-increasing imposition of additional obligations for salinity and fisheries water releases led to a clash of management objectives and priorities, the unpredictability of available water supply, and an inherent conflict between demands for consumptive use by plaintiffs and environmental concerns." *Stockton,* 75 Fed.Cl. at 338. * * *

The Government essentially raises three affirmative defenses to this breach of contract suit. * * *

1. The Inherency Defense: Are the contracts by their inherent nature subject to changes in the law?

The Government's argument is that, because these contracts involve the administration of a government program by a government agency, and the administration of that program is subject to later changes in federal and, in this case state, law and policy, the contracts are effectively adhesion contracts. That is, whatever changes may occur in the Government's law and policies with regard to the contract, for example, the CVPIA and Reclamation's administration of it, the Districts must adhere to them. The Government finds as the source of this doctrine the basic nature of contracts with a sovereign United States, and also cites as authority the basic principles of California water law, including the public trust doctrine, which the Government refers to as "background principles." * * *.

We have no problem rejecting the Government's argument insofar as it pertains to changes in federal law. [T]here is nothing in these contracts to suggest that the Government's reading of the contracts and the claim of inherent law incorporated into them is what either party to the contracts understood was intended. Indeed, the contract provisions suggest quite the contrary. Specific provisions in the contracts afford the Government complete defenses to a failure to perform, but the defenses are circumscribed by the terms in which they are cast, so that the exculpatory provisions apply only in the specified circumstances. If the Government intended or expected to have unilateral control over its legal obligation to perform, control that could be exercised by the simple expedient of a change in its own law or policy, it hardly would need the protections that the provisions in the contracts afford.

Changes in state law, however, present a somewhat different question. [T]he original legislation creating the CVP made the Federal Government's access to the Project's water subject to the State of California's laws and rules governing water rights. [A]s far as the contracting parties were concerned, the Government could only expect to deliver the water that it controlled pursuant to state law, and the two state-created agencies that are the plaintiffs no doubt understood this.

The Government argues accordingly that the Districts' contract rights have always been subordinate to the requirements of state law as provided in the state permits for New Melones, including releases for senior water rights holders, water quality, and fishery. The Districts in fact do not contest that releases of water for these specified uses take priority over the Districts' contracts; the Districts so stipulated.

* * * The Districts respond that the Government did not produce actual evidence that operating New Melones in accordance with state law and pursuant to the state permits necessarily caused a shortage of water for consumptive uses in any given year. They cite as an example the year 1994, the only year at issue designated as a "critical" water year. In that year, releases from New Melones for senior water rights holders and to satisfy state permit requirements totaled some 700,000 acre-feet of water, and CVPIA releases totaled an additional 70,600. The Districts note that, even so, there remained some 425,000 acre-feet in storage at New Melones, and that it was within the discretion of Reclamation to allocate some water to the contracts, rather than, as was the case, provide none.

If the Government chooses to not perform but wishes to avoid having to pay damages, arguing that "the state made me do it," then the Government must prove it was the state mandates that caused the unavailability of water to meet the Government's contract obligations and not simply choices that the Government made.

The Government did not establish nor did the trial court find the critical connection between the state law mandates, whatever they were, and the management practices of Reclamation that caused the shortages. It is a part of the Government's affirmative defense that state law and policy caused the shortages, rather than simply Federal management choices; the burden of persuasion resides with the Government.

[W]e conclude that, since the Government has not carried its burden of proving its affirmative defense that the shortages were entirely or to some specified extent the result of state requirements for fishery and other such uses, the Government's defense on this point fails. Further, the Government's position is not helped by its invocation of "background principles" of California water law. The issue here is not the fundamentals of rights vis-à-vis the United States and the State of California regarding its water, but the obligations, once the water is under the control of the United States, between Reclamation and the Districts pursuant to their contracts.

2. The Contract Provision Defense: Was the failure to perform excused by specific contract provisions?

* * * The Government points to the phrase in Article 9 [of both districts' contracts] that absolves the Government from liability "if a shortage does occur during any year because of drought, or other causes which, in the opinion of the Contracting Officer are beyond the control of the United States." The Government argues that this phrase has the effect of vesting in the contracting officer [the Secretary of the Interior or his representative] discretion over the determination of whether a shortage is beyond the Government's control. * * *

The Districts respond that the provision in Article 9 is simply a typical *force majeure* provision, and that it applies only to drought and other "acts of God." And in any case, the burden of proof of whether the contracting officer correctly invoked the provision is on the Government whose defense it is, and not on the plaintiffs.

The Districts are correct. First, as previously discussed, the burden of proof—the burden of persuasion with regard to this defense—began with and remained with the Government. * * * Second, the plain meaning of the critical part of the phrase at issue, "because of drought, or other causes which * * * are *beyond the control* of the United States," on its face excludes anything that is *within the control* of the United States. [C]hanges in law, or changes in government policy, or changes in management practices brought about by the Government's changes in law or policy, are all causes within the control of the United States. The fact that certain changes in management of the New Melones unit by Reclamation were the result of mandates by Congress regarding the allocation between consumptive and non-consumptive uses of the water in the CVP—mandates that Reclamation may not have had a voice in—is nonetheless a change within the control of the "United States," a term that of course includes Congress as well as the administering agency.

Indeed, it does not matter under this branch of the case if the federal change in management practice was in response to a change in allocation policy by the state, rather than a change mandated by the federal government itself. This is because a federal decision to adjust its management of the CVP to accommodate a change in state allocation policy is a policy decision determined by the Federal Government itself. * * *

Is our reading of the plain meaning of this provision consistent with the intent of the parties at the time the contracts were executed, since contract interpretation is fundamentally a question of the contracting parties' intent? In this case we have the testimony of both parties' representatives on this point, the officials who were responsible for the contracts.

The General Manager of Stockton East and the General Counsel of Central both testified to the effect that Article 9(a) was understood at the time the contract was executed to provide for shortages caused by external circumstances, for example there could be a reduced amount of water in dry years or as a result of other physical problems, such as failure of the reservoir or earthquakes. The official who signed the 1983 contracts on behalf of Reclamation also testified. He responded to a direct question with regard to who bore the risk under Article 9 of future changes in the Reclamation law. He answered in the same vein: though Article 9 did not expressly allocate the risk, "my expectation is that if you have a contract, the United States would live up to its contracts the same way any private party would * * * that everybody will honor their contracts."

The trial court acknowledged the import of that testimony, but considered it trumped by the Ninth Circuit opinion in O'Neill v. United States, 50 F.3d 677 (9th Cir.1995), a case on which the Government placed great weight. *O'Neill* dealt with rights under a similar contract, again involving use of water from the CVP. However, the exculpatory clause in that case—the clause equivalent to Article 9 here—was different in significant respects.

The language there was "in no event shall any liability accrue against the United States * * * for any damage * * * arising from a shortage on account of errors in operation, drought, or any other causes." As plaintiffs note, that language is much broader—the examples offered are not limited to drought or similar causes, but include "operation [and] any other causes." Most significantly, there is no limitation to causes "beyond the control of the United States." * * * And of course the facts of the Ninth Circuit case do not tell us anything about the express intent of the parties regarding the relevant contract provisions in this case.

With this understanding of the contract provisions, we are confronted with the key question that lies at the heart of Article 9(a)—during any of the years at issue in the case, were there circumstances of drought (or other cause within the proper meaning of Article 9(a)) that could excuse the Government's failure to provide the contracted-for quantities of water? * * * With the possible exception of two of the years, 1994 and 1995, there is none.

[F]or the year 1994 the contract required Reclamation to provide at a minimum 23,350 acre-feet of water to Stockton East and 28,000 acre-feet to Central. Reclamation provided no water to either. * * * The trial court held that Reclamation made the determination of shortage on the basis of forecasted hydrology measured against available water storage levels in the New Melones reservoir * * * and concluded that Reclamation validly invoked Article 9's shortage provision, thereby excusing its non-performance. We note, however, that New Melones started the year 1994 with more than 747,000 acre-feet in its reservoir, and ended the year, despite the drought and after providing for other uses, with 425,000. * * * Nevertheless, given the uncertainties of supply in a critically dry year, and in order to accord the trial court the deference it is entitled to, we uphold the court's conclusion and affirm its judgment of no liability for the Government for that year. * * *

The year 1995 is similar. Reclamation cited the general drought and the related water level conditions as the reason for its inability to meet the [districts' rights to water in the range of 25,000-30,000 each], and ultimately delivered only about 4,000 acre-feet to each. The trial court held that "the determination of the contracting officer that the shortage was due to causes outside of the control of the United States is supported adequately by the facts," and again concluded that Reclamation validly invoked the relevant contract provisions so as to excuse its non-performance. Again we note that the year 1995 started with 425,000 acre-feet in the reservoir, and, being a wet year, this time the year concluded with something over 1,800,000 acre-feet, leaving us with a large question about why Reclamation could not meet the relatively minor requests of the Districts for that year. Nevertheless, based on the court's explicit evidentiary findings and conclusions which, under the circumstances, we cannot say are clearly erroneous, we again affirm the trial court's conclusion in favor of the Government for that year.

That, however, is as far as we can go on the record before us. With regard to the remaining years at issue, 1999-2004, the trial court made no such explicit findings and the Government has offered no persuasive explanation for the absence of proof of its defense under Article 9(a) for those years. Furthermore, with the exception of the year 1994 discussed earlier, when New Melones storage was down to 425,504 acre-feet, and the preceding year, 1993, at 747,512 acre-feet, all the years from 1993 to 2004 had storage levels well above 1,000,000 acre-feet. * * * Having failed to make its case, and given the apparent surplus of water in the New Melones Unit for all of the relevant years, which, as the Districts allege, clearly suggests that drought was not the reason for Reclamation's failure to meet the contract requirements, the failure of the Government to prove its affirmative defense with regard to the years 1999-2004 means that judgment for the Districts on this point should have been granted. * * *

3. The Sovereign Acts Defense: Does it absolve the Government of liability?

The Government * * * falls back on the classic government defense invoked whenever a Congressional enactment or other official government action unsettles what were thought to be settled contractual arrangements. The Government argues that the act of Congress in question, the CVPIA, and the implementation of the CVPIA by governmental agencies, are sovereign acts, and any incidental (and presumably unintended) consequences are simply that, for which the Government cannot be held liable. * * *

The basic notion of the sovereign acts doctrine is that the United States as a contracting party acts in a different capacity from its role as a sovereign. As a contractor, it stands in the same shoes as any private party would in dealing with another private party; as a sovereign, it stands apart. The acts of the one are not to be "fused" with the other—if an act of the Government as sovereign would justify non-performance by any other defendant being sued for contract breach, then the Government as contractor is equally free from liability for non-performance. * * *

The Supreme Court's plurality opinion in * * * United States v. Winstar Corp., 518 U.S. 839, 116 S.Ct. 2432, 135 L.Ed.2d 964 (1996), discussed at length the application of the sovereign acts doctrine; that discussion has become the current understanding of the doctrine. * * * The Court posed a two-part test, first asking "whether the sovereign act is properly attributable to the Government as contractor." Id. at 896. That is, is the act simply one designed to relieve the Government of its contract duties, or is it a genuinely public and general act that only incidentally falls upon the contract? If the answer is that the act is a genuine public and general act, the second part of the test asks "whether that act would otherwise release the Government from liability under ordinary principles of contract law." Id. at 896. This second question turns on what is known in contract law as the "impossibility" (sometimes "impracticability") defense.

[T]he Districts argued that performance was not impossible because Reclamation could have fulfilled CVPIA water-release requirements by taking water from other CVP reservoirs rather than from New Melones. [T]he Government contends that the sovereign act at issue includes not only the CVPIA but also the decision by Reclamation and [the U.S. Fish and Wildlife Service] to use water from New Melones to satisfy CVPIA requirements. But even assuming the sovereign act is understood to include the agencies' discretionary implementation of the CVPIA, the Government would have to demonstrate that the agencies' actions made it impossible for Reclamation to deliver to the Districts the full amount of water provided for in the contracts, a showing the Government has not made.

Furthermore, even if the specific implementation of the CVPIA chosen by the agencies rendered performance impossible, the Government cannot rely on the sovereign acts doctrine without returning to the first part of the test and establishing that such implementation is a public and general act. Here it is obvious that Reclamation's operational decisions to comply with the CVPIA by denying water to the Districts in violation of its duties under the contract fail the test of a "public and general" act. The only users affected negatively by Reclamation's actions were the Districts. The conduct of Reclamation in shorting the Districts, presumably in order to make the water available for other users, was directly aimed at the contracts and Reclamation's duties under them, nullifying the rights of the Districts to receive water under the contracts. * * *

Notes

1. **The Government's burden of proof.** The United States has sought rehearing in *Stockton East* based on the following claim: "Precedent of this Court, the Supreme Court, and other federal courts of appeals required the panel to vacate, rather than reverse, the judgment as to 1999-2004 and remand to allow the United States to present the evidence it did not need to present at trial in order to meet its newly allocated burden of proof." United States' Combined Petition for Panel Rehearing and Rehearing En Banc 4, 2009 WL 4863462 (Nov. 20, 2009).

2. **Carryover reservoir storage.** Bureau of Reclamation reservoirs typically smooth out the annual water supply by storing water during wet years and carrying it over for use in dry years. In discussing the *Stockton East* contract exculpatory clause, which excused water delivery because of drought or other causes beyond the control of the United States, the Federal Circuit stated "the apparent surplus of water in the New Melones Unit [during 1999-2004] clearly suggests that drought was not the reason for Reclamation's failure to meet the contract requirements." In managing the New Melones Unit in future years, or if remand is granted as to 1999-2004, how should the Bureau decide upon, or prove in litigation, the proper amount of storage to carry over to prepare for the possibility that the next year or next several years will be dry?

A state administrative hearing officer ruled in a case not involving the Bureau that carryover storage should be limited to one dry year. He reasoned that with the unpredictability of long-term future precipitation, allowing carryover storage for several dry years presented "too great a likelihood for the waste of water to be acceptable." Dep't of Water Resources of the State of Idaho, In the Matter of Distribution of Water Rights, Opinion Constituting Findings of Fact, Conclusions of Law and Recommendation 62 (April 29, 2008).

3. **Contract exculpatory clauses and the ESA.** In rejecting the exculpatory clause defense in *Stockton East*, the Federal Circuit distinguished O'Neill v. United States, where the defense was successful, because the exculpatory clause there was worded more broadly to cover "shortage on account of errors in operation, drought, or any other causes." An exculpatory clause similar to the one in *O'Neill* was at issue in Rio Grande Silvery Minnow v. Keys, 333 F.3d 1109 (10th Cir. 2003). It excused water delivery due to shortage "[o]n account of drought or other causes." The "other causes" were not limited, as they were in *Stockton East*, to those beyond the control of the United States.

Silvery Minnow concerned the Bureau's San Juan-Chama and Middle Rio Grande Projects in New Mexico. Environmental groups obtained a preliminary injunction under ESA § 7 ordering the Bureau to consult with the U.S. Fish and Wildlife Service and curtail contract water deliveries as needed to maintain river flows sufficient to avoid jeopardy to the endangered Rio Grande silvery minnow. The Bureau appealed to the Tenth Circuit, seeking to overturn the injunction on that ground that continued performance of its contractual water delivery obligations came within the exception from ESA § 7 for nondiscretionary agency acts. See supra p. 608-09, Note 2. The appeal turned on whether the exculpatory clause gave the Bureau discretion to reduce water deliveries to contract holders.

The Bureau sought to distinguish *O'Neill* because it concerned a unit of the Central Valley Project in California, and the CVPIA specifically allocated water for fish and wildlife, whereas no similar specific legislation governed the New Mexico projects. But the Tenth Circuit held that general references to fish and wildlife in the legislation authorizing the New Mexico projects and a clause in the water contracts stating that water for fish and wildlife is a beneficial use gave the Bureau discretion to determine the amount of water available for contract holders. Therefore, the Bureau was required to consult under ESA § 7 and reduce water deliveries to contract holders if necessary to protect the silvery minnow.

The decision generated intense opposition. The Bureau denounced it for impeding its collaborative approach to protecting the silvery minnow. The Bureau and other defendants moved for reconsideration en banc and received support though amici briefs filed by a number of western states and large water distribution organizations outside of New Mexico. The New Mexico congressional delegation inserted a provision in the Energy and Water Development Appropriations Act of 2004, Pub. L. No. 108-137, § 208(a), 117 Stat. 1827, prohibiting the expenditure of funds to reallocate water from San Juan-Chama Project contracts to meet the requirements of the ESA unless the water is purchased from a willing seller or lessor. Soon thereafter, the Tenth Circuit panel that issued the *Silvery Minnow* decision avoided en banc reconsideration by vacating its opinion as moot because the preliminary injunction that formed the basis of the appeal covered only the latter part of 2002 plus 2003, and favorable climatic conditions had produced sufficient water flows that the injunction was never invoked. Rio Grande Silvery Minnow v. Keys, 355 F.3d 1215 (10th Cir. 2004).

4. **Types of water contracts.** Section 9(d) of the Reclamation Project Act of 1939 states that no project water may be delivered for irrigation until the irrigation district receiving it has entered into a "repayment contract." 43 U.S.C. § 485h(d). Repayment contracts usually require payment of the irrigators' shares of project costs over a forty year period, after a ten year development period. The necessary charges are assessed to their lands by the district and collected along with annual operation and maintenance charges.

Section 9(e) creates an exception to the section 9(d) requirement of a repayment contract for water delivery. 43 U.S.C. § 485h(e). It authorizes the Secretary to enter into "contracts to furnish water," commonly called water service contracts. These contracts obligate the United States to supply water for up to forty years at rates fixed to cover only an "appropriate share" of construction costs and annual operating and maintenance costs, as the Secretary of the Interior deems proper. They were designed for situations where total repayment of reimbursable construction costs in forty years would be beyond the financial ability of the water users. They have been widely used in the Central Valley Project in California. A statute enacted in 1956 requires long-term section 9(e) contracts, i.e., for more than ten years, to include if requested a provision for renewal under "mutually agreeable" terms. The terms must, however, "provide for an increase or decrease in charges set forth in the contract to reflect, among other things, increases or decreases in construction, operation, and maintenance costs and improvement or deterioration in the party's repayment capacity." 43 U.S.C. § 485h-1(1).

Apart from section 9(d) and 9(e) contracts, the Warren Act, 43 U.S.C. §§ 523, 524, authorizes the Secretary of the Interior to contract to provide water to users outside of a project when the capacity of the project works exceeds project needs. The contracts may provide for temporary water deliveries pending full development of the project or for the "rental" of water on terms making such use secondary and inferior to the right to use the water on the project.

5. **Water right ownership under repayment contracts.** Ickes v. Fox, 300 U.S. 82, 94 (1937), held that irrigators entitled to water under a repayment contract have "a vested right to the perpetual use of the waters as appurtenant to their lands." The Court made this statement after noting that the irrigators had fully repaid their share of project construction costs. Therefore, the opinion did not settle whether irrigators with executory repayment obligations also have vested perpetual rights provided they continue to make their payments.

Nevada v. United States, 463 U.S. 110 (1983), concerned contracts for "a permanent water right" for irrigation. Apparently the contracts were repayment contracts, for the Court described them as "similar" to the *Ickes* contract. The Court declared: "Once these lands were acquired by settlers in the Project, the Government's 'ownership' of the water rights was at most nominal; the beneficial interest in the rights confirmed to the Government resided in the owners of the land within the Project to which these water rights became appurtenant upon the application of Project water to the land." 463 U.S. at 126.

Even if irrigators have vested perpetual rights to project water, they hold those rights subject to the terms of their contracts and explicit directives of federal reclamation law, such as a requirement of approval by the Secretary of the Interior to transfer water use from irrigation to municipal or industrial use. Strawberry Water Users Ass'n v. United States, 576 F.3d 1133 (10th Cir. 2009).

6. **Water service contract renewals and the ESA.** Natural Resources Defense Council v. Houston, 146 F.3d 1118 (9th Cir. 1998), addressed how ESA § 7 affected the renewal of section 9(e) contracts for water from Friant Dam, a part of the Central Valley Project. The Bureau renewed the contracts of various districts on terms substantially similar to their previous contracts. It did no formal ESA consultation before the

renewals. This was because the National Marine Fisheries Service had concluded (erroneously, it was held in *Houston*) that separate consultation was unnecessary because of an ongoing consultation for the entire Central Valley Project.

Environmental groups sued for rescission of the renewal contracts in an effort to get greater releases of water from Friant Dam to improve the degraded downstream habitat of several listed species of fish. The districts defended by arguing no consultation was necessary because the renewals came within the exception from ESA § 7 for nondiscretionary agency acts. They relied on a statute providing that the holder of a long-term section 9(e) contract "shall, during the term of the contract and of any renewal thereof * * *, have a first right (to which right the rights of the holders of any other type of irrigation water contract shall be subordinate) to a stated share or quantity of the project's available water supply * * *." 43 U.S.C. § 485h-1(4). The districts argued this statute deprived the Bureau of discretion to alter contract terms upon renewal regarding the quantity of water to be delivered. The court disagreed. Keying on the word "available" in the statute and citing *O'Neill* for the proposition that an agency can deliver less than a contractually agreed upon amount of water in order to comply with subsequently enacted federal law, it said: "[E]ven if the original contracts guaranteed the [districts] a right to a similar share of available water in the renewal contracts, * * * the Bureau may be able to reduce the amount of water available for sale if necessary to comply with ESA." 146 F.3d at 1126.

7. **Transfer of project water.** Chapter 2, Section 5 considered the transfer of water rights as a method of shifting water to new needs, particularly from agriculture to municipal and industrial use, from the perspective of state law. The transferability of Bureau project water is of great potential importance because the Bureau delivers over twenty-five million acre-feet of water annually for irrigation. Generally reclamation law and repayment contracts and water service contracts have required approval by the Secretary of the Interior for transfer. Historically, absent any firm policy at the national level, regional Bureau offices usually discouraged transfers. Their opposition was based partly on preventing windfall profits to farmers who might in effect sell the irrigation subsidy to the buyer, and partly on the fear of jeopardizing repayment. See Joseph L. Sax, Selling Reclamation Water Rights: A Case Study in Federal Subsidy Policy, 64 Mich. L. Rev. 13 (1965).

More recently, the Department of the Interior has sought to facilitate the transfer of reclamation project water. In 1988, it released a document titled "Principles Governing Voluntary Water Transactions that Involve or Affect Facilities Owned or Operated by the Department of Interior." In general, this document supports the transfer of reclamation water, including the transfer of irrigation water to municipal and industrial use. A supplemental policy addresses the subsidy/windfall profits issue: "When a transfer of project water involves a change in the type of use from irrigation to a different beneficial use, and the capital costs allocable to a project's irrigation purpose have not been repaid, subsidies associated with the provision of project water for irrigation purposes will not follow the transferred project water. Charges payable to Reclamation for transferred project water will be consistent with the new use to which the transferred water is put. On projects where contractual obligations for the repayment of construction costs allocable to irrigation purposes have been fulfilled, charges payable to Reclamation for the transferred project water will be negotiable. In either situation, Reclamation will not attempt to recapture the value of past subsidies in setting charges for transferred project water." Reclamation Manual WTR P02, 6.G.(2).

Also, Congress has shown some inclination in recent years to facilitate transfers of reclamation project water. To alleviate damage from drought conditions, the Reclamation States Emergency Drought Relief Act of 1991, 43 U.S.C. §§ 2201-2247, authorizes the Secretary of the Interior to purchase project water from willing sellers for delivery to willing buyers under temporary contracts (for up to two years) and to participate in state water banks. The CVPIA authorizes and encourages the transfer of project water by districts or individuals in the Central Valley Project, as described supra p. 678, Note 7.

8. **The modern Bureau of Reclamation.** Beginning with the administrations of Presidents Carter and Reagan, federal budget deficits severely curtailed federal investments in water resources projects. Funding for new starts on authorized Bureau of Reclamation projects came virtually to a standstill, and funding for progress on construction of ongoing projects was slowed.

The Bureau has undergone a major mission change during recent decades. In the Reclamation Reform Act of 1982, supra p. 678, Note 6, Congress strengthened the Bureau's role in conservation of project water. It directed the Bureau to encourage nonfederal recipients of irrigation water to implement economically feasible conservation measures, and it required each district with a repayment contract or water service contract to develop a water conservation plan consisting of goals, conservation measures, and a time schedule for meeting the goals. 43 U.S.C. § 390jj.

Five years later, the Bureau issued a report titled "Assessment '87: A New Direction for the Bureau of Reclamation." The report's key conclusion was that "the Bureau's mission must change from one based on federally supported construction to one based on effective and environmentally sensitive resource management." In 1992, the Bureau issued Reclamation's Strategic Plan: A Long-Term Framework for Water Resources Management, Development and Protection (1992), which builds on Assessment '87 and carries forward the theme of shifting emphasis from construction to better management of existing projects.

9. **The Corps of Engineers.** The major federal agency in addition to the Bureau of Reclamation with responsibilities for water project construction and management is the U.S. Army Corps of Engineers. While the Bureau operates only in seventeen western states, the Corps operates

nationwide. Its has responsibilities for improving navigation that go back to 1824, when Congress called upon it to remove snags and sandbars that were interfering with navigation on the Mississippi and Ohio Rivers. In many Rivers and Harbors bills, Congress authorized and appropriated funds for dredging, protective works, locks, and dams to store water for release during low flows. The Corps also has flood control responsibilities through the construction of improvements on main stem rivers. 33 U.S.C. §§ 701a, 701a-1. Projects have been authorized and funded periodically in flood control bills. The Corps' multipurpose dams also generate hydroelectric power and provide water for municipal and industrial use. In 1990, Congress made environmental protection "one of the primary missions of the Corps of Engineers in planning, designing, constructing, operating, and maintaining water resources projects." 33 U.S.C. § 2316.

In the East, the Corps provides large amounts of irrigation water in central and southern Florida. In the West, it supplies water from many of its multipurpose dams to the Bureau of Reclamation for distribution to irrigators under the Flood Control Act of 1944, 43 U.S.C. § 390b. ETSI Pipeline Project v. Missouri, 484 U.S. 495 (1988), held that without approval from the Secretary of the Army, the Bureau lacked authority to remove water stored behind a Corps dam on the Missouri River built under the Flood Control Act of 1944. This was water that the Bureau claimed was available for irrigation and wished to deliver instead for industrial use. The Court stated in dictum that if the Bureau "wishes to remove water from an Army reservoir for *any* purpose, the approval of the Army Secretary must be secured."

10. **Sovereign immunity.** Does the sovereign immunity of the United States bar an aggrieved person or water district from suing a federal agency over its operation of a water project? Any of three general waivers of sovereign immunity might apply. First, the Federal Tort Claims Act, 28 U.S.C. §§ 2671-2680, allows suit for monetary relief in tort actions, such as trespass or negligence, unless the water project operation fits under the "discretionary function" exception to waiver of immunity. Second, the Tucker Act, 28 U.S.C. § 1491(a)(1), allows suit for monetary relief in nontort actions such as inverse condemnation or breach of contract. The suit must be brought in the Court of Federal Claims rather than a federal district court if it is for more than $10,000. Third, the Administrative Procedure Act, 5 U.S.C. § 702, allows suit for nonmonetary relief alleging agency action or inaction in violation of a federal statute.

Reclamation Reform Act of 1982 § 221, 43 U.S.C. § 390uu gives consent "to join the United States as a necessary party defendant in any suit to adjudicate, confirm, validate, or decree the contractual rights of a contracting entity and the United States regarding any contract executed pursuant to Federal reclamation law." The Supreme Court has taken a narrow view of this language: "[It] is best interpreted to grant consent to join the United States in an action between other parties—for example, two water districts, or a water district and its members—when the action requires construction of a reclamation contract and joinder of the United

States is necessary. It does not permit a plaintiff to sue the United States alone." Orff v. United States, 545 U.S. 596 (2005).

Rather than waive sovereign immunity, the Flood Control Act of 1928, 33 U.S.C. § 702c, expressly asserts it: "No liability of any kind shall attach to or rest upon the United States for any damage from or by floods or flood waters at any place * * *." When a dam has multiple purposes, the no-liability rule does not apply to damage from water released for purposes other than flood control, e.g., for hydroelectric power generation. Cent. Green Co. v. United States, 531 U.S. 425 (2001).

SECTION 3. RESERVED WATER RIGHTS

A. Indian Reserved Rights

WINTERS v. UNITED STATES
Supreme Court of the United States, 1908.
207 U.S. 564, 28 S. Ct. 207, 52 L. Ed. 340.

[By the Act of April 15, 1874, ch. 96, 28 Stat. 28 (1875), Congress "set apart" for the use and occupation of the Gros Ventre, Peigan, Blood, Blackfeet, and River Crow Indians a very large area of land in the Territory of Montana. Later, by the Act of May 1, 1888, ch. 213, 25 Stat. 113 (1889), Congress approved an agreement between federal commissioners and the Indians whereby the tribes did "cede and relinquish to the United States" all of this large area of land except for several smaller parcels specifically therein "set apart and reserved" for them. One of these parcels was the Fort Belknap Indian reservation, the northern boundary of which was the middle of the channel of the nonnavigable Milk River. The United States opened the ceded land to settlement, and portions of it upstream from the Fort Belknap reservation came into the hands of the defendants, several individuals and a cattle company. After the reservation was established but before 1898, the defendants appropriated under Montana law 5000 inches of water from the Milk River for the irrigation of hay and grain. Much of the land on the Fort Belknap reservation was usable for grazing, and some of it was suitable for irrigated agriculture. In 1898 an Indian project was constructed on the reservation that required 5000 inches from the Milk for the irrigation of hay, grass, and vegetables. The defendants' water diversions, however, left insufficient water for the Indian project. Upon suit by the United States, the lower court granted an order enjoining the defendants from interfering in any manner with use on the reservation of 5000 inches of water.]

MR. JUSTICE MCKENNA delivered the opinion of the court: * * *

The case, as we view it, turns on the agreement of May, 1888, resulting in the creation of Fort Belknap Reservation. In the construction of this agreement there are certain elements to be considered that are prominent and significant. The reservation was a part of a very much larger tract which the Indians had the right to occupy and use, and which was adequate for the habits and wants of a nomadic and uncivilized people. It was the policy of the government, it was the desire of the Indians, to change those habits and to become a pastoral and civilized people. If they should become such, the original tract was too extensive; but a smaller tract would be inadequate without a change of conditions. The lands were arid, and, without irrigation, were practically valueless. And yet, it is contended, the means of irrigation were deliberately given up by the Indians and deliberately accepted by the government. The lands ceded were, it is true, also arid; and some argument may be urged, and is urged, that with their cession there was the cession of the waters, without which they would be valueless, and "civilized communities could not be established thereon." And this, it is further contended, the Indians knew, and yet made no reservation of the waters. We realize that there is a conflict of implications, but that which makes for the retention of the waters is of greater force than that which makes for their cession. The Indians had command of the lands and the waters—command of all their beneficial use, whether kept for hunting, "and grazing roving herds of stock," or turned to agriculture and the arts of civilization. Did they give up all this? Did they reduce the area of their occupation and give up the waters which made it valuable or adequate? And, even regarding the allegation of the answer as true, that there are springs and streams on the reservation flowing about 2,900 inches of water, the inquiries are pertinent. If it were possible to believe affirmative answers, we might also believe that the Indians were awed by the power of the government or deceived by its negotiators. Neither view is possible. The government is asserting the rights of the Indians. But extremes need not be taken into account. By a rule of interpretation of agreements and treaties with the Indians, ambiguities occurring will be resolved from the standpoint of the Indians. And the rule should certainly be applied to determine between two inferences, one of which would support the purpose of the agreement and the other impair or defeat it. On account of their relations to the government, it cannot be supposed that the Indians were alert to exclude by formal words every inference which might militate against or defeat the declared purpose of themselves and the government, even if it could be supposed that they had the intelligence to foresee the "double sense" which might some time be urged against them.

Another contention of appellants is that if it be conceded that there was a reservation of the waters of Milk river by the agreement of 1888, yet the reservation was repealed by the admission of Montana into the Union, February 22, 1889, "upon an equal footing with the original states." The language of counsel is that "any reservation in the agreement with the Indians, expressed or implied, whereby the waters of Milk river were not to be subject of appropriation by the citizens and inhabitants of said State, was repealed by the act of admission." But to establish the repeal counsel rely substantially upon the same argument that they advance against the intention of the agreement to reserve the waters. The power of the government to reserve the waters and exempt them from appropriation under the state laws is not denied, and could not be. United States v. Rio Grande Ditch & Irrigation Co., 174 U.S. 702, 43 L.Ed. 1141, 19 S.Ct. 770 (1899); United States v. Winans, 198 U.S. 371, 49 L.Ed. 1089, 25 S.Ct. 662 (1905). That the government did reserve them we have decided, and for a use which would be necessarily continued through years. This was done May 1, 1888, and it would be extreme to believe that within a year Congress destroyed the reservation and took from the Indians the consideration of their grant, leaving them a barren waste—took from them the means of continuing their old habits, yet did not leave them the power to change to new ones. * * *

Decree affirmed.

Notes

1. **Who reserved the waters?** Did the Indians cede most of their ancestral lands to the United States but retain some of them, so that for the retained lands the tribes might claim aboriginal water rights dating back to prehistory? Alternatively, did the United States by assuming sovereign authority over the Territory of Montana extinguish prior Indian rights in all the ancestral lands and then grant the reservation lands back to the Indians, so that the tribes could claim only an implied grant of water that would date from the 1874 or 1888 legislation?

Is any light shed on this question by United States v. Winans, cited in *Winters*? That case involved an 1859 treaty between the United States and the Yakima Nation in which the Indians ceded certain lands to the United States. The treaty stated: "The exclusive right of taking fish in all streams where running through or bordering said reservation is further secured to said Confederated Tribes and Bands of Indians, as also the right of taking fish at all usual and accustomed places, in common with citizens of the territory, and of erecting temporary buildings for curing them." Later, non-Indian settlers who obtained title to lands bordering the river sought to exclude the Indians from placing their "fish wheels" (salmon traps) in their accustomed places, now on private lands. The Court said: "The right to resort to the fishing places in controversy was a part of larger rights possessed by the Indians, upon the exercise of which there was not a shadow of impediment, and which were not much less necessary to the existence of the Indians than the atmosphere they breathed * * *. The treaty was not a grant of rights to the Indians, but a grant of rights from them—a reservation of those not granted." 198 U.S. at 381. Why did the Court in *Winters* cite *Winans* for the proposition that "[t]he power of the government to reserve the waters and exempt them from appropriation under the state laws is not denied, and could not be"?

2. *Arizona v. California.* After *Winters*, the Supreme Court did not issue another major Indian water rights opinion until Arizona v. California, 373 U.S. 546, 595–96 (1963): "The Government, on behalf of five Indian Reservations in Arizona, California, and Nevada, asserted rights to water in the mainstream of the Colorado River. The Colorado River Reservation, located partly in Arizona and partly in California, is the largest reservation. It was created by an Act of Congress in 1865, but its area was later increased by Executive Order. Other reservations were created by Executive Orders and amendments to them, ranging in dates from 1870 to 1907. The Special Master found that when the United States created these reservations or added to them, it reserved not only land but also the use of enough water from the Colorado to irrigate the irrigable portions of the reserved lands." The Court agreed and entered a decree fixing the Indian priorities as of the dates the reservations were created or expanded by statute or executive order. 376 U.S. 340 (1964).

The Court, in its 1963 opinion, also addressed several aspects of reserved rights not presented in *Winters*. It established that (1) the implied reservation doctrine applies to navigable waters as well as nonnavigable waters, (2) the doctrine applies to Indian reservations created after statehood as well as those created before statehood, (3) water can be impliedly reserved by executive order as well as by act of Congress, and (4) the amount of water reserved for irrigation and related purposes should be measured not by the reasonably foreseeable needs of the Indians living on the reservation, i.e., not by the number of Indians, but rather by the number of practicably irrigable acres (PIA) on the reservation.

In 1979, the Court entered a supplemental decree upon the joint motion of the parties that quantified the Indian reserved water rights as follows: 131,400 acre-feet for the California reservations, 761,562 acre-feet for the Arizona reservations, and 12,534 acre-feet for the Nevada reservations—for a total of 905,496 acre-feet per year. These quantities represent annual diversions, not consumptive use. 439 U.S. 419 (1979).

Indian tribes in the Lower Colorado River Basin were not parties to the proceedings that resulted in the 1964 and 1979 decrees. Instead, the tribes were represented by the United States. Later, the tribes were allowed to intervene, and they asked the Court to reopen its earlier determination of the amount of PIA on their reservations. They claimed additional water for (1) "boundary lands," which were lands lying outside the reservation boundaries used in the 1964 decree that the tribes alleged should have been included within the reservations, and (2) "omitted lands," which were lands within reservation boundaries that the tribes alleged were practicably irrigable but were not inventoried as such by the United States in the earlier proceeding. The Court held the "boundary lands" question could still be litigated because the earlier proceedings had not determined certain reservation boundaries with finality, and the 1964 decree expressly contemplated future resolution of those boundary issues.

But the Court ruled differently on the "omitted lands" question, despite a general provision in the 1964 decree allowing the parties to file applications to amend it or seek further relief. The Court applied principles akin to res judicata to preclude reopening of that question:

"Certainty of rights is particularly important with respect to water rights in the Western United States. The development of that area of the United States would not have been possible without adequate water supplies in an otherwise water-scarce part of the country. The doctrine of prior appropriation, the prevailing law in the western states, is itself largely a product of the compelling need for certainty in the holding and use of water rights.

"Recalculating the amount of practically irrigable acreage runs directly counter to the strong interest in finality in this case. A major purpose of this litigation, from its inception to the present day, has been to provide the necessary assurance to states of the Southwest and to various private interests, of the amount of water they can anticipate to receive from the Colorado River system. * * * If there is no surplus of water in the Colorado River, an increase in federal reserved water rights will require a 'gallon-for-gallon reduction in the amount of water available for water-needy state and private appropriators.' * * * Not only did the Metropolitan Water District in California and the Central Arizona Project predicate their plans on the basis of the 1964 allocations, but, due to the high priority of Indian water claims, an enlargement of the Tribes' allocation cannot help but exacerbate potential water shortage problems for these projects and their States." 460 U.S. 605, 620-21 (1983).

The Court also stated: "We find no merit in the Tribes' contention that the United States' representation of their interests was inadequate whether because of a claimed conflict of interests arising from the government's interest in securing water rights for other federal property, or otherwise. The United States often represents varied interests in litigation involving water rights, particularly given the large extent and variety of federal land holdings in the West. Indeed, the substantial water allocations awarded the Tribes reflect the competency of the United States' representation. We believe the issue of practically irrigable acreage was fully and fairly litigated in 1963."

3. **The PIA standard in** *Wyoming v. United States.* In Wyoming v. United States, 492 U.S. 406 (1989), the United States Supreme Court was asked to reconsider use of the PIA standard to quantify Indian reserved water rights for irrigation and related uses. The Wyoming Supreme Court had applied the PIA standard in the Wind River Indian Reservation. *In re* Gen. Adjudication of All Rights to Use Water in Big Horn River Sys. (*Big Horn I*), 753 P.2d 76 (Wyo. 1988). The United States Supreme Court issued a one sentence per curiam opinion: "The judgment below is affirmed by an equally divided Court." The Court was divided 4 to 4, with Justice O'Connor not voting because she held a minority interest in a family ranch corporation that was party to a stream adjudication in Arizona involving Indian water rights.

Papers donated by Justice Thurgood Marshall to the Library of Congress after his retirement from the Court included a draft majority opinion in Wyoming v. United States written by Justice O'Connor before she learned of the family ranch matter and recused herself. The draft majority opinion is published as an appendix to Andrew C. Mergen & Sylvia F. Liu, A Misplaced Sensitivity: The Draft Opinions in Wyoming v. United States, 68 U. Colo. L. Rev. 683 (1997), an article strongly critical of the draft majority opinion. The draft opinion declined to discard the PIA standard but would have modified it with a "sensitivity" doctrine and remanded the case for reconsideration in light of that doctrine. Excerpts from the draft opinion follow:

"[Q]uantification of Indian reserved water rights must entail sensitivity to the impact on state and private appropriators of scarce water under state law. * * * The inclusion in the PIA quantification of arable lands not yet irrigated depends on the assumption that necessary future irrigation projects will be built to supply water to those lands. * * * Given that federal reserved water rights will frequently require a gallon-for-gallon reduction in the amount of water available for water-needy state and private appropriators, the existence of future projects cannot be taken for granted. Sensitivity to the impact on prior appropriators necessarily means that there has to be some degree of pragmatism in determining PIA. We think this pragmatism involves a 'practical' assessment—a determination apart from theoretical economic and engineering feasibility—of the reasonable likelihood that future irrigation projects, necessary to enable lands which have never been irrigated to obtain water, will actually be built.

"[M]assive capital outlays are required to fund irrigation projects, and in today's era of budget deficits and excess agricultural production, government officials have to choose carefully what projects to fund in the West. * * *

"By mentioning federal fiscal concerns, we do not mean to suggest that the practicability factor set forth above turns only on funding by the Government. It may be that the Tribes themselves, state agencies, or private investors have the means and intent to construct irrigation projects needed to bring water to future lands. Whether or not such project will be undertaken will also depend in part on the nature of the demand. Thus, the trier of fact must examine the evidence, if any, that additional cultivated acreage is needed to supply food or fibre to resident tribal members, or to meet the realistic needs of tribal members to expand their existing farming operations. The trier must also determine whether there will be a sufficient market for, or economically productive use of, any crops that would be grown on the additional acreage." (Internal citations and quotation marks omitted.)

4. **Lower court cases on reservation purposes, priority date, and the PIA standard.** United States v. Adair, 723 F.2d 1394 (9th Cir. 1983), concerned water rights in the former Klamath Indian Reservation. The reservation was established under an 1864 treaty between the

United States and the Indians. It was terminated under 1954 legislation whereby the United States purchased or condemned the tribal lands. The United States then added some of the former reservation land it acquired to a national forest and made the 15,000 acre Klamath Marsh into a national wildlife refuge. For more than a thousand years, the Indians had lived near the marsh and depended upon it as a source of food in the form of game, wildfowl, and edible plants. The 1864 treaty reserved to the Indians the exclusive right to continue their activities in the marsh, and in other litigation their hunting and fishing rights were held to have survived the termination act.

The court found that the 1864 treaty had the dual essential purposes of encouraging the Indians to take up farming and securing continuation of their traditional hunting and fishing lifestyle. So the court held that water was impliedly reserved for both purposes. The reserved water right for hunting and fishing was a nonconsumptive right entitling the tribe to prevent upstream appropriators from depleting the streamflow below a protected level. Concerning the right's priority date, the court said that "where, as here, a tribe shows its aboriginal use of water to support a hunting and fishing lifestyle, and then enters into a treaty with the United States that reserves this aboriginal water use, the water right thereby established retains a priority date of first or immemorial use." The court limited the aboriginal right, however, to "the amount of water necessary to support * * * hunting and fishing rights as currently exercised to maintain the livelihood of Tribe members, not as those rights once were exercised by the Tribe in 1864." In contrast, the court assigned the reserved right for irrigated agriculture a priority dating only from the 1864 treaty because there was no aboriginal water use for that purpose.

In *Big Horn I,* supra Note 3, the Wyoming court determined that the sole purpose of the 1868 treaty establishing the Wind River Indian Reservation was to encourage agriculture, and therefore water was impliedly reserved only for agriculture and subsumed uses. The court refused to find an implied reservation of water for mineral and industrial uses, for fisheries (because when the treaty was signed the Indians neither depended on fishing for a livelihood nor had a traditional lifestyle involving fishing), or for wildlife and aesthetics (because no tradition of wildlife and aesthetic preservation was shown). The priority date of the reserved right for agriculture and subsumed uses was the date of the treaty.

In State *ex rel.* Martinez v. Lewis, 861 P.2d 235 (N.M. Ct. App. 1993), the court ruled that the priority date of reserved water for irrigation of PIA on the Mescalero Apache Indian Reservation was 1852, when the United States by treaty with the Apaches promised to create a reservation. The tribe claimed an even earlier priority of time immemorial based on aboriginal title. The court noted that the area was not settled by non-Indians until after 1852, so that a priority earlier than 1852 would make no practical difference. It declined to address the tribe's claim of a time-immemorial priority "[b]ecause we will not issue advisory opinions."

In re General Adjudication of All Rights to Use Water in Gila River System & Source, 35 P.3d 68 (Ariz. 2001), eschewed analysis of historic documents to determine the purpose of Indian reservations, largely because the court believed those documents often failed to express the true reasons for creating the reservations. Instead, the court declared that the purpose of Indian reservations is to serve as a homeland for the Native Americans living there. The court also rejected using PIA as the sole standard to quantify the amount of water reserved because that would be inconsistent with the idea of a permanent homeland and would be unfair to tribes inhabiting terrain that is mountainous or otherwise agriculturally marginal. The court provided a nonexclusive list of factors bearing on quantification, including tribal history and culture; the tribal land's geography, topography, and natural resources, including groundwater availability; the tribe's economic base and the optimal manner of creating jobs and income; past water use on the reservation; and present and projected population. Regardless of the relevant factors on a particular reservation, the court said proposed uses must be reasonably feasible both practically and economically.

5. **Lower court cases on reserved rights in groundwater.** The Wyoming Supreme Court declared in *Big Horn I*, supra Note 3, that "the reserved water doctrine does not extend to groundwater." The Montana Supreme Court ruled the reserved rights doctrine extends to groundwater necessary to accomplish the purpose of the reservation. Confederated Salish & Kootenai Tribes v. Stults, 59 P.3d 1093 (Mont. 2002). Similarly, the Arizona Supreme Court said the doctrine extends to groundwater "where other waters are inadequate to accomplish the purpose of a reservation." *In re* Gen. Adjudication of All Rights to Use Water in Gila River Sys. & Source, 989 P.2d 739, 747 (Ariz. 1999).

The Arizona case presented the complication that Arizona has a bifurcated and uncoordinated system of water rights—the appropriation doctrine for surface streams and their subflow and the reasonable use doctrine for other groundwater. A surface appropriator cannot enjoin groundwater pumping even though it depletes the surface appropriator's supply, and the reasonable use doctrine does not allow an overlying owner to enjoin pumping by other overlying owners for reasonable use on their lands even though the pumping interferes with the overlying owner's well. These rules apply to the holders of state water rights as against each other. The court declared that holders of federal reserved rights enjoy greater protection against interference. It said that if state law is inadequate to protect reserved rights in surface water or groundwater, an Indian reservation may invoke federal law to preserve waters necessary to accomplish the reservation purpose. Id. at 749-50. The court added, however, that injunctive protection of reserved rights is limited to the amount needed to meet "minimal need." Id. at 750.

6. **Nature of Indian reserved rights.** A water right is traditionally viewed as a usufruct—a right to use water, not "ownership" of water. A person is usually permitted to use water not being used by someone hav-

ing superior rights. Consequently, it is generally assumed that non-Indians can use water that would ultimately be required to satisfy Indian reserved rights until the Indians actually begin exercising their rights.

Confederated Salish & Kootenai Tribes v. Clinch, 992 P.2d 244 (Mont. 1999), took a different approach. It held that the Montana Department of Natural Resources and Conservation could not issue permits to non-Indians to appropriate water on the Flathead Indian Reservation until the tribes' reserved rights are quantified (see supra pp. 133-35, Note 5). The court rejected the department's position that it should be able to issue permits because some new non-Indian water uses would not diminish instream flow and because by state statute all permits issued before a final determination of existing water rights are only provisional and are subject to being reduced or revoked if necessary to protect senior rights. The court explained:

"The idea that permits can be issued to use water on reservations where that water may have been reserved for the Tribes who occupy those reservations without interfering with tribal rights, ignores the distinction * * * between appropriative water rights provided by Montana's Water Use Act and Indian reserved water rights. Appropriative rights are based on actual use. * * * Reserved rights are established by reference to the purposes of the reservation rather than to actual, present use of water. [B]ecause under federal law, Indian tribes have an ownership interest in the water reserved for them and because that interest does not depend on use of the water it is unpersuasive that the State's permitting process might allow uses of Indian reserved water which in the long-term will not diminish in-stream flows.

"Nor do we agree that the provisional nature of permits issued by the Department is determinative. [U]se of water which may have been reserved by federal law to the Tribes is no less impermissible simply because it is temporary and can be terminated following final quantification of the Tribes' right * * *."

7. **Pueblo Indian water rights.** When the Spaniards came in the sixteenth century to what is now New Mexico, Pueblo Indian communities were practicing irrigated agriculture along the Rio Grande and its tributaries. The Spanish and later the Mexican governments granted the Indians the right to their aboriginal lands. Then in 1848, Mexico ceded territory including New Mexico to the United States in the Treaty of Guadalupe Hidalgo. Pursuant to that treaty, the United States issued patents in 1858 to the various Indian pueblos conveying communal fee simple title to four square leagues of land surrounding the pueblos.

Winters rights do not apply to Indian pueblos because they are not reservations. But Indian pueblo lands have aboriginal rights of *primacia*, first use, measured by the amount customarily used to grow crops for basic life support. The aboriginal rights attached only to lands irrigated between 1846 (when the United States first took control of the territory from Mexico) and 1924 (when the Pueblo Lands Act terminated aboriginal water rights as to lands not previously irrigated).

The Spanish, Mexican, and federal laws relating to the water rights of Pueblo Indian communities are examined in Charles T. DuMars et al., Pueblo Indian Water Rights (1984); Ed Newville, Comment, Pueblo Indian Water Rights: Overview and Update of the Aamodt Litigation, 29 Nat. Resources J. 251 (1989). Water rights for Indian pueblos should be distinguished from the question, explored in Note 5, supra pp. 52-53, of whether modern Southwest cities tracing their origins to Spanish or Mexican grants have paramount rights to water for future municipal growth.

8. **Rancherias.** Rancherias are small plots of land in California purchased by the United States to provide homes for Indians not on reservations or whose reservations lacked sufficient land suitable for cultivation. 35 Stat. 70, 76 (1908); 34 Stat. 325, 333 (1906). Congress authorized the Secretary of the Interior to construct any necessary irrigation ditches, flumes, and reservoirs. Eighty-six such "reservations" were established, ranging in size from 640 acres down to one or two acres, and any Indians, whether or not members of an organized tribe, were entitled to settle on them. Most of the lands remained unoccupied. In 1958, the value of the program was questioned, and Congress directed the Secretary to distribute the lands and water rights on 41 rancherias to the residents or to sell the lands for their benefit, with their approval. 72 Stat. 619 (1958). Before doing so, the Secretary was instructed to install or rehabilitate irrigation or domestic water systems as needed. When the lands were distributed, many of the plots were sold to non-Indians.

The rancheria lands were not reserved or withdrawn from the public lands but, as noted above, were purchased by the United States. Nevertheless, section 4 of the termination statute provided: "Nothing in this act shall abrogate any water right that exists by virtue of the laws of the United States. To the extent that the laws of the State of California are not now applicable to any water right appurtenant to any lands involved herein they shall continue to be inapplicable while the water right is in Indian ownership for a period not to exceed 15 years after the conveyance pursuant to this act of an unrestricted title thereto, and thereafter the applicability of such laws shall be without prejudice to the priority of any such right not theretofore based on state law."

COLVILLE CONFEDERATED TRIBES v. WALTON
United States Court of Appeals, Ninth Circuit, 1981.
647 F.2d 42.

WRIGHT, CIRCUIT JUDGE. * * * In response to a request from the Commissioner of Indian Affairs, President Grant created the Colville Reservation. Executive Order of July 2, 1872. * * * In 1906, Congress ratified an agreement with the Colvilles that provided for distribution of reservation lands to the Indians pursuant to the General Allotment

Act of 1887, 24 Stat. 388, and for disposition of the remainder by entry and settlement. * * *

In 1917, a row of seven allotments was created in the No Name Creek watershed. Walton, a non-Indian, now owns the middle three, numbers 525, 2371 and 894. He bought them in 1948 from an Indian, not a member of the Tribe, who had begun to irrigate the land by diverting water for 32 acres from No Name Creek. Walton immediately procured a permit from the state to irrigate 65 acres by diverting up to 1 cubic foot per second "subject to existing rights." He now irrigates 104 acres and uses additional water for domestic and stock water purposes. The United States holds the remaining allotments in trust for the Colville Indians. * * *

The No Name Creek is a spring-fed creek flowing south into Omak Lake, which has no outlet and is saline. * * * Salmon and trout were traditional foods for the Colville Indians, but the salmon runs have been destroyed by dams on the Columbia River. In 1968, the Tribe, with the help of the Department of the Interior, introduced Lahonton cutthroat trout into Omak Lake. The species thrives in the lake's saline water, but needs fresh water to spawn. The Indians cultivated No Name Creek's lower reach to establish spawning grounds but irrigation use depleted the water flow during spawning season. The federal government has given the Indians fingerlings to maintain the stock of trout.

The trial court found that 1,000 acre feet per year of water were available in No Name Creek Basin in an average year. It calculated the quantity of the Colvilles' reserved water rights on the basis of irrigable acreage. * * * The trial court determined the Indians had a reserved right to 666.4 acre feet per year of water from the No Name Creek Basin. It held that Walton was not entitled to share in the Colvilles' reserved water rights. The trial court found, however, that the Colvilles were irrigating only a portion of the irrigable acres included in its calculation.

Under the district court's findings, in an average year there are 333.6 acre feet per year of water not subject to the Indians' reserved right. There are an additional 237.6 acre feet per year of water to which the Indians have a reserved right, but which they are not currently using. This water is available for appropriation by non-Indians, subject to the Indians' superior right. The court held that Walton had a right to irrigate the 32 acres under irrigation at the time he acquired his land, with a priority date of the actual appropriation of water for that use.

The court also held that the Indians were potentially entitled to use water to propagate trout, but refused to award water for that purpose. It concluded that spawning was unnecessary because fingerlings were provided free by the federal government. * * *

The Tribe's Water Rights

* * * We hold that water was reserved when the Colville Reservation was created. The more difficult question concerns the amount of water reserved. * * * We conclude that, when the Colville reservation was created, sufficient appurtenant water was reserved to permit irrigation of all practicably irrigable acreage on the reservation.

Providing for a land-based agrarian society, however, was not the only purpose for creating the reservation. The Colvilles traditionally fished for both salmon and trout. Like other Pacific Northwest Indians, fishing was of economic and religious importance to them. The Tribe's principal historic fishing grounds on the Columbia River have been destroyed by dams. The Indians have established replacement fishing grounds in Omak Lake by planting a non-indigenous trout. We agree with the district court that preservation of the tribe's access to fishing grounds was one purpose for the creation of the Colville Reservation. Under the circumstances, we find an implied reservation of water from No Name Creek for the development and maintenance of replacement fishing grounds. * * * We affirm the district court's holding that the Colvilles have a reserved right to the quantity of water necessary to maintain the Omak Lake Fishery.

The district court held that water for spawning could not be awarded at this time because the federal government provides the necessary fingerlings. We reverse this holding. The right to water to establish and maintain the Omak Lake Fishery includes the right to sufficient water to permit natural spawning of the trout. When the Tribe has a vested property right in reserved water, it may use it in any lawful manner. As a result, subsequent acts making the historically intended use of the water unnecessary do not divest the Tribe of the right to the water. * * * Finally, we note that permitting the Indians to determine how to use reserved water is consistent with the general purpose for the creation of an Indian reservation—providing a homeland for the survival and growth of the Indians and their way of life.

The General Allotment Act of 1887

We next consider Walton's rights as the fee owner of allotted land, and reverse the district court's judgment that he has no right to reserved water. * * *

The General Allotment Act provided that land on reservations could be allotted for the exclusive use of individual Indians. Remaining land was to be made available for homesteading by non-Indians. After holding allotted lands in trust for individual Indians for a 25-year period, the federal government could convey the land to the allottee in fee, "discharged of said trust and free of all charge or incumbrance whatsoever." 25 U.S.C. § 348.

Because the use of reserved water is not limited to fulfilling the original purposes of the reservation, Congress had the power to allot reserved water rights to individual Indians, and to allow for the transfer of such rights to non-Indians. Whether it did so is a question of congressional intent.

The General Allotment Act represented the shift in federal objectives from segregation of Indians on reservations to assimilation of them in non-Indian culture and society. Its primary sponsor, Senator Dawes, explained that "the quicker [the Indian] is mingled with the whites in every particular the better it will be." The Act was designed to encourage Indians to become self-supporting citizens by making them landowners. Allotted lands were held in trust for a 25 year period because of "the desire to protect the Indian against sharp practices leading to Indian landlessness, the desire to safeguard the certainty of titles, and the urge to continue an important basis of governmental activity [on the Indians' behalf]." F. Cohen, Handbook of Federal Indian Law 221 (1940); U.S. Department of Interior, Federal Indian Law 788–89 (1958).

The only reference to water rights in the Act is found in section 7:

> In cases where the use of water for irrigation is necessary to render the lands within any Indian reservation available for agricultural purposes, the Secretary of the Interior is authorized to prescribe such rules and regulations as he may deem necessary to secure a just and equal distribution thereof among the Indians residing upon any such reservation; and no other appropriation or grant of water by any riparian proprietor shall be authorized or permitted to the damage of any other riparian proprietor.

25 U.S.C. § 381.

The Act was passed over 20 years before the Supreme Court announced the implied-reservation doctrine in *Winters*. There is nothing to suggest Congress gave any consideration to the transferability of reserved water rights. To resolve this issue, we must determine what Congress would have intended had it considered it.

It is settled that Indian allottees have a right to use reserved water. United States v. Powers, 305 U.S. 527 (1939). * * * We must determine whether non-Indian purchasers of allotted lands also obtain a right to some portion of reserved waters.

The general rule is that termination or diminution of Indian rights requires express legislation or a clear inference of Congressional intent gleaned from the surrounding circumstances and legislative history. Upon careful consideration, we conclude this principle supports the proposition that an Indian allottee may sell his right to reserved water.

The district court's holding that an Indian allottee may convey only a right to the water he or she has actually appropriated with a priority date of actual appropriation reduces the value of the allottee's right to reserved water. We think this type of restriction on transferability is a "diminution of Indian rights" that must be supported by a clear inference of Congressional intent.

By placing allotted lands in trust for 25 years, Congress evinced an intent to protect Indians by preventing transfer of those lands. But there is no basis for an inference that some restrictions survived beyond the trust period. Congress provided for extensions of the trust period, but directed that fee title be conveyed to the allottee when the period expired. We think the fee included the appurtenant right to share in reserved waters, and see no basis for limiting the transferability of that right. * * *

In determining the nature of the right acquired by non-Indian purchasers, we consider three aspects of an allottee's right to use reserved waters. First, the extent of an Indian allottee's right is based on the number of irrigable acres he owns. If the allottee owns 10% of the irrigable acreage in the watershed, he is entitled to 10% of the water reserved for irrigation (i.e., a "ratable share"). This follows from the provision for an equal and just distribution of water needed for irrigation. A non-Indian purchaser cannot acquire more extensive rights to reserved water than were held by the Indian seller. Thus, the purchaser's right is similarly limited by the number of irrigable acres he owns.

Second, the Indian allottee's right has a priority as of the date the reservation was created. This is the principal aspect of the right that renders it more valuable than the rights of competing water users, and therefore applies to the right acquired by a non-Indian purchaser. In the event there is insufficient water to satisfy all valid claims to reserved water, the amount available to each claimant should be reduced proportionately.

Third, the Indian allottee does not lose by non-use the right to a share of reserved water. This characteristic is not applicable to the right acquired by a non-Indian purchaser. The non-Indian successor acquires a right to water being appropriated by the Indian allottee at the time title passes. The non-Indian also acquires a right, with a date-of-reservation priority date, to water that he or she appropriates with reasonable diligence after the passage of title. If the full measure of the Indian's reserved water right is not acquired by this means and maintained by continued use, it is lost to the non-Indian successor.

The full quantity of water available to the Indian allottee thus may be conveyed to the non-Indian purchaser. There is no diminution in the right the Indian may convey. We think Congress would have intended, however, that the non-Indian purchaser, under no competitive disability vis-à-vis other water users, may not retain the right to that quantity of water despite non-use.

The district court's holding that Walton has no right to share in water reserved when the Colville reservation was created is reversed. On remand, it will need to determine the number of irrigable acres Walton owns, and the amount of water he appropriated with reasonable diligence in order to determine the extent of his right to share in reserved water. * * *

Notes

1. **The Allotment Act.** The Supreme Court recounted the origin and the demise of the General Allotment (or Dawes) Act in South Dakota v. Yankton Sioux Tribe, 522 U.S. 329 (1998):

"[The mid-nineteenth century was] a period of rapid growth in the United States' population, increasing westward migration, and ensuing demands from non-Indians to open Indian holdings throughout the Western States to settlement. In response * * *, Congress retreated from the reservation concept and began to dismantle the territories that it had previously set aside as permanent and exclusive homes for Indian tribes. The pressure from westward-bound homesteaders, and the belief that the Indians would benefit from private property ownership, promoted passage of the Dawes Act in 1887, 24 Stat. 388. The Dawes Act permitted the Federal Government to allot tracts of tribal land to individual Indians and, with tribal consent, to open the remaining holdings to non-Indian settlement. Within a generation or two, it was thought, the tribes would dissolve, their reservations would disappear, and individual Indians would be absorbed into the larger community of white settlers. * * * [T]he policy favoring assimilation through the allotment of reservation land [was] formally repudiated with the passage of the Indian Reorganization Act in 1934, 48 Stat. 984, 25 U.S.C. § 461 * * *."

2. **"Reasonable diligence after the passage of title."** *Walton* says a non-Indian purchaser of land from an Indian allottee gets a date-of-reservation priority only for (a) water used by the Indian allottee when the title passes and (b) water the purchaser "appropriates with reasonable diligence after the passage of title." The Wyoming Supreme Court addressed the second criterion in *In re* General Adjudication of All Rights to Use Water in Big Horn River System (2002), 48 P.3d 1040 (Wyo. 2002). Various non-Indians bought allotted lands from Indians after the United States commenced constructing the Wind River Irrigation Project but long before it was completed. The lands in question could not be irrigated until the project was finished. The court held that the non-Indian purchasers could have *Walton* rights if they appropriated water "within a

reasonable time and with due diligence, as defined by state law, after the federal project facilities became available to the properties." Id. at 1055.

3. **Use of reserved water on the reservation by Indians for new purposes.** The 1979 supplemental decree in Arizona v. California entered on the joint motion of the parties, supra p. 696, states that while PIA is used to quantify Indian reserved water rights, that method of quantification "shall not constitute a restriction of the usage of [the water rights] to irrigation or other agricultural application. If all or part of the adjudicated water rights of any of the five Indian Reservations is used other than for irrigation or other agricultural application, the total consumptive use * * * for said Reservation shall not exceed the consumptive use that would have resulted if the diversions * * * had been used for irrigation of the number of acres specified for that Reservation * * *."

In *Big Horn I*, supra p. 697, Note 3, the Wyoming court awarded the Wind River Indian Reservation a reserved water right for agricultural and subsumed uses. The award included water for historically irrigated lands and for unirrigated PIA that would require construction of new water project facilities. But the court rejected a tribal claim for instream fishery flows. Later, in *In re* General Adjudication of All Rights to Use Water in Big Horn River System (*Big Horn II*), 835 P.2d 273 (Wyo. 1992), the tribes sought to change their reserved water right for future irrigation projects to the new use of maintaining instream fishery flows. They argued that the PIA standard applied in *Big Horn I* served only as a means to quantify their rights and did not restrict the purposes for which they could use the water. The district court approved the change in use they requested.

The Wyoming Supreme Court reversed by vote of 3 to 2, with the majority split three ways. Justice Macy's lead opinion for the majority said state law governs transfers of reserved rights from a primary reservation purpose (agriculture) to a secondary purpose (instream fish flows), see infra p. 719, Note 1, and the transfer was barred by the Wyoming rule allowing only the state to hold instream appropriations. A second justice agreed state law governed the transfer but said this was only because of the peculiar history of the Wind River Reservation. The third justice said federal law governs transfers of reserved rights, but he thought federal law barred the transfer of a right reserved for irrigation to instream flow maintenance unless the right had first been exercised for its irrigation purpose, and the tribes were seeking transfer of an unexercised irrigation right. The two dissenting justices also thought federal law governed, but they saw no barrier in federal law to the transfer.

United States v. Orr Water Ditch Co., 309 F. Supp. 2d 1245 (D. Nev. 2004), aff'd, United States v. Truckee-Carson Irrigation Dist., 429 F.3d 902 (9th Cir. 2005), involved the temporary transfer to instream fishery use of Indian reserved rights for irrigation that had not been fully exercised. The Nevada State Engineer issued permits to the Pyramid Lake Paiute Tribe to transfer reserved rights decreed by the Orr Ditch Decree, a consent decree that authorized changes in the place or manner of use "in the manner provided by law." The court upheld the transfer. It said "provided by law" means by state law except so far as federal law preempts it, and the court found federal law did preempt a state law limiting transfers to water rights that had been perfected by exercise. The court also accepted the state engineer's finding that both irrigation and fishery use were primary reservation purposes, thus making it unnecessary to decide whether a reserved right can be transferred from a primary to a secondary reservation purpose.

4. **Leasing of reservation land with reserved water to non-Indians.** Congress has authorized the leasing of surplus tribal lands and unallotted irrigable lands on an Indian reservation for farming purposes. 25 U.S.C. §§ 402, 402a. Congress also has authorized the leasing of tribally or individually owned restricted Indian lands (restricted, among other things, in their alienability) for "business purposes, including the development or utilization of natural resources in connection with operations under such leases, * * * and for those farming purposes which require the making of a substantial investment in the improvement of the land for the production of specialized crops." Id. § 415. It is generally thought that these authorizations include the leasing of water rights for the lands. See Skeem v. United States, 273 F. 93 (9th Cir. 1921).

5. **Leasing of reserved water to non-Indians for use off the reservation.** Many tribes with reserved water rights measured by PIA have supplies that might never be fully used to irrigate reservation land and, in any event, often could be used more productively off the reservation by growing municipalities or other entities. Commentators have debated whether and under what conditions a tribe can lease water to non-Indians for use off the reservation. See, e.g., David H. Getches, Management and Marketing of Indian Water: From Conflict to Pragmatism, 58 U. Colo. L. Rev. 515 (1988); Jack D. Palma, II, Considerations and Conclusions Concerning the Transferability of Indian Water Rights, 20 Nat. Resources J. 91 (1980); Lee H. Story, Comment, Leasing Indian Water Off the Reservation: A Use Consistent With the Reservation's Purpose, 76 Cal. L. Rev. 179 (1988).

6. **Indian water right settlements.** Congress has approved a number of negotiated Indian water right settlements during recent decades. Negotiated settlement can be faster and less expensive than litigation of unsettled issues regarding Indian reserved water rights. It can also address broader tribal water concerns such as water quality.

Although the settlements vary in their terms, they typically resolve some of the major legal and factual issues commonly arising from claims of Indian reserved water rights: the purposes for which reserved rights exist on a particular reservation, quantification of the rights, whether reserved rights exist in groundwater, transfer of reserved rights to new uses on the reservation, and transfer for off-reservation uses. Settlements generally protect existing non-Indian uses despite also contemplating an increase in the exercise of Indian reserved rights. Often this is accomplished through water conservation requirements and new federal water storage or other federally financed measures. In an era of generally diminished congressional interest in financing water projects, federal expenditures for Indian water right settlements seem to have been an exception. Various settlements are analyzed in Bonnie G. Colby et al., Negotiating Tribal Water Rights: Fulfilling Promises in the Arid West (2005); Jon C. Hare, Indian Water Rights: An Analysis of Current and Pending Indian Water Rights Settlements (1996); Robert T. Anderson, Indian Water Rights: Litigation and Settlements, 42 Tulsa L. Rev. 43 (2006); Reid P. Chambers & John E. Echohawk, Implementing the *Winters* Doctrine of Indian Reserved Water Rights: Producing Indian Water and Economic Development Without Injuring Non-Indian Water Users?, 27 Gonz. L. Rev. 447 (1991/92).

7. **Abrogation of Indian reserved water rights.** Congress can unilaterally abrogate Indian treaty rights, but abrogation is not lightly inferred. It requires clear evidence the United States actually considered the conflict between its intended action and the treaty rights, and chose to resolve the conflict by abrogating the treaty. State, Dep't of Ecology v. Yakima Reservation Irr. Dist., 850 P.2d 1306 (Wash. 1993). Abrogation requires payment of compensation to the tribe for loss of its rights.

B. Federal Reserved Rights

CAPPAERT v. UNITED STATES
Supreme Court of the United States, 1976.
426 U.S. 128, 96 S. Ct. 2062, 48 L. Ed.2d 523.

MR. CHIEF JUSTICE BURGER delivered the opinion of the Court.

The question presented in this litigation is whether the reservation of Devil's Hole as a national monument reserved federal water rights in unappropriated water.

Devil's Hole is a deep limestone cavern in Nevada. Approximately 50 feet below the opening of the cavern is a pool 65 feet long, 10 feet wide, and at least 200 feet deep, although its actual depth is unknown. The pool is a remnant of the prehistoric Death Valley Lake System and is situated on land owned by the United States since the Treaty of Guadalupe Hidalgo in 1848, 9 Stat. 922. By the Proclamation of January 17, 1952, President Truman withdrew from the public domain a 40-acre tract of land surrounding Devil's Hole, making it a detached component of the Death Valley National Monument. Proclamation No. 2961, 3 CFR 147 (1949-1953 Comp.). The Proclamation was issued under the American Antiquities Preservation Act, 34 Stat. 225, 16 U.S.C.A. § 431, which authorizes the President to declare as national monuments "objects of historic or scientific interest that are situated upon the lands owned or controlled by the Government of the United States * * *."

The 1952 Proclamation notes that Death Valley was set aside as a national monument "for the preservation of the unusual features of scenic, scientific, and educational interest therein contained." The Proclamation also notes that Devil's Hole is near Death Valley and contains a "remarkable underground pool." Additional preambulary statements in the Proclamation explain why Devil's Hole was being added to the Death Valley National Monument:

> "WHEREAS the said pool is a unique subsurface remnant of the prehistoric chain of lakes which in Pleistocene times formed the Death Valley Lake System, and is unusual among caverns in that it is a solution area in distinctly striated limestone, while also owing its formation in part to fault action; and

> "WHEREAS the geologic evidence that this subterranean pool is an integral part of the hydrographic history of the Death Valley region is further confirmed by the presence in this pool of a peculiar race of desert fish, and zoologists have demonstrated that this race of fish, which is found nowhere else in the world, evolved only after the gradual drying up of the Death Valley Lake System isolated this fish population from the original ancestral stock that in Pleistocene times was common to the entire region; and

> "WHEREAS the said pool is of such outstanding scientific importance that it should be given special protection, and such protection can be best afforded by making the said forty-acre tract containing the pool a part of the said monument * * *."

The Cappaert petitioners own a 12,000-acre ranch near Devil's Hole, 4,000 acres of which are used for growing Bermuda grass, alfalfa, wheat, and barley; 1,700 to 1,800 head of cattle are grazed. The ranch represents an investment of more than $7 million; it employs more than 80 people with an annual payroll of more than $340,000.

In 1968 the Cappaerts began pumping groundwater on their ranch on land 2½ miles from Devil's Hole; they were the first to appropriate groundwater. The groundwater comes from an underground basin or aquifer which is also the source of the water in Devil's Hole. After the Cappaerts began pumping from the wells near Devil's Hole, which they do from March to October, the summer water level of the pool in Devil's Hole began to decrease. Since 1962 the level of water in Devil's Hole has been measured with reference to a copper washer installed on one of the walls of the hole by the United States Geological Survey. Until 1968, the water level, with seasonable variations, had been stable at 1.2 feet below the copper marker. In 1969 the water level in Devil's Hole was 2.3 feet below the copper washer; in 1970, 3.17 feet; in 1971, 3.48 feet; and, in 1972, 3.93 feet.

When the water is at the lowest levels, a large portion of a rock shelf in Devil's Hole is above water. However, when the water level is at 3.0 feet below the marker or higher, most of the rock shelf is below water, enabling algae to grow on it. This in turn enables the desert fish (*cyprinodon diabolis,* commonly known as Devil's Hole pupfish), referred to in President Truman's Proclamation, to spawn in the spring. As the rock shelf becomes exposed, the spawning area is decreased, reducing the ability of the fish to spawn in sufficient quantities to prevent extinction.

In August 1971 the United States * * * sought an injunction in the United States District Court for the District of Nevada to limit, except for domestic purposes, the Cappaerts' pumping from six specific wells and from specific locations near Devil's Hole. * * * The District Court found that if the injunction did not issue "there is grave danger that the Devil's Hole pupfish may be destroyed, resulting in irreparable injury to the United States." 375 F. Supp. 456, 460 (1974).

On April 9, 1974, the District Court entered its findings of fact and conclusions of law substantially unchanged in a final decree permanently enjoining pumping that lowers the level of the water below the 3.0-foot level. The Court of Appeals for the Ninth Circuit affirmed, 508 F.2d 313 (1974). We granted certiorari to consider the scope of the implied-reservation-of-water-rights doctrine.

This Court has long held that when the Federal Government withdraws its land from the public domain and reserves it for a federal purpose, the Government, by implication, reserves appurtenant water then unappropriated to the extent needed to accomplish the purpose of the reservation. In so doing the United States acquires a reserved right in unappropriated water which vests on the date of the reservation and is superior to the rights of future appropriators. Reservation of water rights is empowered by the Commerce Clause, Art. I, § 8, which permits federal regulation of navigable streams, and the Property Clause, Art. IV, § 3, which permits federal regulation of federal lands. The doctrine applies to Indian reservations and other federal enclaves, encompassing water rights in navigable and non-navigable streams. * * *

In determining whether there is a federally reserved water right implicit in a federal reservation of public land, the issue is whether the Government intended to reserve unappropriated and thus available water. Intent is inferred if the previously unappropriated waters are necessary to accomplish the purposes for which the reservation was created. Both the District Court and the Court of Appeals held that the 1952 Proclamation expressed an intention to reserve unappropriated water, and we agree. The Proclamation discussed the pool in Devil's Hole in four of the five preambles and recited that the "pool * * * should be given special protection." Since a pool is a body of water, the protection contemplated is meaningful only if the water remains; the water right reserved by the 1952 Proclamation was thus explicit, not implied. * * *

The implied-reservation-of-water-rights doctrine, however, reserves only that amount of water necessary to fulfill the purpose of the reservation, no more. Here the purpose of reserving Devil's Hole Monument is preservation of the pool. Devil's Hole was reserved "for the preservation of the unusual features of scenic, scientific, and educational interest." The Proclamation notes that the pool contains "a peculiar race of desert fish * * * which is found nowhere else in the world" and that the "pool is of * * * outstanding scientific importance * * *." The pool need only be preserved, consistent with the intention expressed in the Proclamation, to the extent necessary to preserve its scientific interest. The fish are one of the features of scientific interest. The preamble noting the scientific interest of the pool follows the preamble describing the fish as unique; the Proclamation must be read in its entirety. Thus, as the District Court has correctly determined, the level of the pool may be permitted to drop to the extent that the drop does not impair the scientific value of the pool as the natural habitat of the species sought to be preserved. The District Court thus tailored its injunction, very appropriately, to minimal need, curtailing pumping only to the extent necessary to preserve an adequate water level at Devil's Hole, thus implementing the stated objectives of the Proclamation. * * *

No cases of this Court have applied the doctrine of implied reservation of water rights to groundwater. Nevada argues that the implied-reservation doctrine is limited to surface water. Here, however, the water in the pool is surface water. The federal water rights were being depleted because, as the evidence showed, the "[g]roundwater and surface water are physically interrelated as integral parts of the hydrologic cycle." C. Corker, Groundwater Law, Management and Administration, National Water Commission Legal Study No. 6, p. xxiv (1971). Here the Cappaerts are causing the water level in Devil's Hole to drop by their heavy pumping. It appears that Nevada itself may recognize the potential interrelationship between surface and groundwater since Nevada applies the law of prior appropriation to both. Nev. Rev. Stat. §§ 533.010 et seq., 534.020, 534.080, 534.090 (1973). Thus, since the implied-reservation-of-water-rights doctrine is based on the necessity of water for the purpose of the federal reservation, we hold that the United States can protect its water from subsequent diversion, whether the diversion is of surface or groundwater. * * *

Accordingly, the judgment of the Court of Appeals is Affirmed.

Note

History of federal reserved water rights. In United States v. Rio Grande Dam & Irrigation Co., 174 U.S. 690, 703 (1899), the Court declared that "a state cannot by its legislation destroy the right of the

United States, as the owner of lands bordering on a stream, to the continued flow of its waters, so far at least as may be necessary for the beneficial uses of the government property."

The Court's first actual allocation of water for non-Indian federal
lands under the reserved rights theory came in its 1963 Arizona v. California opinion: "The Master ruled that the principle underlying the reservation of water rights for Indian Reservations was equally applicable to
other federal establishments such as National Recreation Areas and National Forests. We agree with the conclusions of the Master that the
United States intended to reserve water sufficient for the future requirements of the Lake Mead National Recreation Area, the Havasu Lake National Wildlife Refuge, the Imperial National Wildlife Refuge and the Gila
National Forest." 373 U.S. at 601.

UNITED STATES v. NEW MEXICO
Supreme Court of the United States, 1978.
438 U.S. 696, 98 S. Ct. 3012, 57 L. Ed.2d 1052.

MR. JUSTICE REHNQUIST delivered the opinion of the Court.

The Rio Mimbres rises in the southwestern highlands of New
Mexico and flows generally southward, finally disappearing in a desert sink just north of the Mexican border. The river originates in the
upper reaches of the Gila National Forest, but during its course it
winds more than 50 miles past privately owned lands and provides
substantial water for both irrigation and mining. In 1970, a stream
adjudication was begun by the State of New Mexico to determine the
exact rights of each user to water from the Mimbres. In this adjudication the United States claimed reserved water rights for use in the
Gila National Forest. The State District Court held that the United
States, in setting the Gila National Forest aside from other public
lands, reserved the use of such water "as may be necessary for the
purposes for which [the land was] withdrawn," but that these purposes did not include recreation, aesthetics, wildlife-preservation, or
cattle grazing. The United States appealed unsuccessfully to the Supreme Court of New Mexico. * * * We now affirm.

The question posed in this case—what quantity of water, if any,
the United States reserved out of the Mimbres River when it set aside
the Gila National Forest in 1899—is a question of implied intent and
not power. * * *

Recognition of Congress' power to reserve water for land which is
itself set apart from the public domain, however, does not answer the
question of the amount of water which has been reserved or the purposes for which the water may be used. Substantial portions of the
public domain *have* been withdrawn and reserved by the United
States for use as Indian reservations, forest reserves, national parks,
and national monuments. And water is frequently necessary to

achieve the purposes for which these reservations are made. But Congress has seldom expressly reserved water for use on these withdrawn lands. If water were abundant, Congress' silence would pose no problem. In the arid parts of the West, however, claims to water for use on federal reservations inescapably vie with other public and private claims for the limited quantities to be found in the rivers and streams. This competition is compounded by the sheer quantity of reserved lands in the western States, which lands form brightly colored swaths across the maps of these States.

* * * While many of the contours of what has come to be called the "implied-reservation-of-water doctrine" remain unspecified, the Court has repeatedly emphasized that Congress reserved "only that amount of water necessary to fulfill the purpose of the reservation, no more." Cappaert, 426 U.S., at 141, 96 S.Ct., at 2071. Each time this Court has applied the "implied-reservation-of-water doctrine," it has carefully examined both the asserted water right and the specific purposes for which the land was reserved, and concluded that without the water the purposes of the reservation would be entirely defeated.

This careful examination is required both because the reservation is implied, rather than expressed, and because of the history of congressional intent in the field of federal-state jurisdiction with respect to allocation of water. Where Congress has expressly addressed the question of whether federal entities must abide by state water law, it has almost invariably deferred to the state law. Where water is necessary to fulfill the very purposes for which a federal reservation was created, it is reasonable to conclude, even in the face of Congress' express deference to state water law in other areas, that the United States intended to reserve the necessary water. Where water is only valuable for a secondary use of the reservation, however, there arises the contrary inference that Congress intended, consistent with its other views, that the United States would acquire water in the same manner as any other public or private appropriator. * * *

The quantification of reserved water rights for the national forests is of critical importance to the West, where, as noted earlier, water is scarce and where more than 50% of the available water either originates in or flows through national forests. When, as in the case of the Rio Mimbres, a river is fully appropriated, federal reserved water rights will frequently require a gallon-for-gallon reduction in the amount of water available for water-needy state and private appropriators. This reality has not escaped the attention of Congress and must be weighed in determining what, if any, water Congress reserved for use on the national forests.

The United States contends that Congress intended to reserve minimum instream flows for aesthetic, recreational, and fish-preservation purposes. An examination of the limited purposes for which Congress authorized the creation of national forests, however, provides no support for this claim. In the mid- and late-1800's, many of the forests on the public domain were ravaged and the fear arose that the forest lands might soon disappear, leaving the United States with a shortage both of timber and of watersheds with which to encourage stream flows while preventing floods. It was in answer to these fears that in 1891 Congress authorized the President to "set apart and reserve, in any State or Territory having public lands bearing forests, any part of the public lands wholly or in part covered with timber or undergrowth, whether of commercial value or not, as public reservations." Creative Act of March 3, 1891, 26 Stat. 1095, 1103, 16 U.S.C.A. § 471 (repealed 1976).

The Creative Act of 1891 unfortunately did not solve the forest problems of the expanding Nation. To the dismay of the conservationists, the new national forests were not adequately attended and regulated; fires and indiscriminate timber-cutting continued their toll. To the anguish of Western settlers, reservations were frequently made indiscriminately. President Cleveland, in particular, responded to pleas of conservationists for greater protective measures by reserving some 21 million acres of "generally settled" forest land on February 22, 1897. President Cleveland's action drew immediate and strong protest from Western Congressmen who felt that the "hasty and ill considered" reservation might prove disastrous to the settlers living on or near these lands.

Congress' answer to these continuing problems was three-fold. It suspended the President's Executive order of February 22, 1897; it carefully defined the purposes for which national forests could in the future be reserved; and it provided a charter for forest management and economic uses within the forests. Organic Administration Act of June 4, 1897, 30 Stat. 11, 16 U.S.C.A. § 473 et seq. In particular, Congress provided:

> "No national forest shall be established, except to improve and protect the forest within the boundaries, or for the purpose of securing favorable conditions of water flows, and to furnish a continuous supply of timber for the use and necessities of citizens of the United States; * * *." 30 Stat. 35, as amended, 16 U.S.C.A. § 475 (emphasis added).

The legislative debates surrounding the Organic Administration Act of 1897 and its predecessor bills demonstrate that Congress intended national forests to be reserved for only two purposes—"[t]o conserve the water flows and to furnish a continuous supply of timber for the people." 30 Cong.Rec. 967 (1897) (Cong. McRae). National forests were not to be reserved for aesthetic, environmental, recreational, or wildlife-preservation purposes.

"The objects for which the forest reservation should be made are the protection of the forest growth against destruction by fire and axe and preservation of forest conditions upon which water conditions and water flow are dependent. The purpose, therefore, of this bill is to maintain favorable forest conditions, without excluding the use of these reservations for other purposes. They are not parks set aside for nonuse, but have been established for economic reasons." 30 Cong. Rec. 966 (1897) (Cong. McRae).

Administrative regulations at the turn of the century confirmed that national forests were to be reserved for only these two limited purposes.

Any doubt as to the relatively narrow purposes for which national forests were to be reserved is removed by comparing the broader language Congress used to authorize the establishment of national parks. In 1916, Congress created the National Park Service and provided that the

"fundamental purpose of said parks, monuments, and reservations * * * is to conserve the scenery and the natural and historic objects and the wild life therein and to provide for the enjoyment of the same * * * unimpaired for the enjoyment of future generations." National Park Service Act of 1916, 39 Stat. 535, 16 U.S.C.A. § 1 et seq.

When it was Congress' intent to maintain minimum instream flows within the confines of a national forest, it expressly so directed, as it did in the case of the Lake Superior National Forest:

"In order to preserve the shore lines, rapids, waterfalls, beaches and other natural features of the region in an unmodified state of nature, no further alteration of the natural water level of any lake or stream * * * shall be authorized." 16 U.S.C.A. § 577b. * * *

In 1960, Congress passed the Multiple-Use Sustained-Yield Act of June 12, 1960, 74 Stat. 215, 16 U.S.C.A. § 528 et seq., which provides:

"It is the policy of Congress that the national forests are established and shall be administered for outdoor recreation, range, timber, watershed, and wildlife and fish purposes. The purposes of this Act are declared to be supplemental to, but not in derogation of, the purposes for which the national forests were established as set forth in the [Organic Administration Act of 1897.]"

The Supreme Court of the State of New Mexico concluded that this Act did not give rise to any reserved rights not previously authorized in the Organic Administration Act of 1897. * * * While we conclude that the Multiple-Use Sustained-Yield Act of 1960 was intended to broaden the purposes for which national forests had previously been administered, we agree that Congress did not intend to thereby expand the reserved rights of the United States. * * *

The House Report accompanying the 1960 legislation * * * indicates that recreation, range, and "fish" purposes are "to be supplemental to, but not in derogation of, the purposes for which the national forests were established" in the Organic Administration Act of 1897. * * *

As discussed earlier, the "reserved rights doctrine" is a doctrine built on implication and is an exception to Congress' explicit deference to state water law in other areas. Without legislative history to the contrary, we are led to conclude that Congress did not intend in enacting the Multiple-Use Sustained-Yield Act of 1960 to reserve water for the *secondary* purposes there established. A reservation of additional water could mean a substantial loss in the amount of water available for irrigation and domestic use, thereby defeating Congress' principal purpose of securing favorable conditions of water flow. Congress intended the national forests to be administered for broader purposes after 1960 but there is no indication that it believed the new purposes to be so crucial as to require a reservation of additional water. By reaffirming the primacy of a favorable water flow, it indicated the opposite intent.

What we have said also answers petitioner's contention that Congress intended to reserve water from the Rio Mimbres for stockwatering purposes. Petitioner issues permits to private cattle-owners to graze their stock on the Gila National Forest and provides for stockwatering at various locations along the Rio Mimbres. Petitioner contends that, since Congress clearly foresaw stockwatering on national forests, reserved rights must be recognized for this purpose. The New Mexico courts disagreed and held that any stockwatering rights must be allocated under state law to individual stockwaterers. We agree.

While Congress intended the national forests to be put to a variety of uses, including stockwatering, not inconsistent with the two principal purposes of the forests, stockwatering was not itself a direct purpose of reserving the land. If stockwatering could not take place on the Gila National Forest, Congress' purposes in reserving the land would not be defeated. Congress, of course, did intend to secure favorable water flows, and one of the uses to which the enhanced water supply was intended to be placed was probably stockwatering. But Congress intended the water supply from the Rio Mimbres to be allocated amongst private appropriators under state law. There is no indication in the legislative histories of any of the forest acts that Congress foresaw any need for the Forest Service to allocate water for stockwatering purposes, a task to which state law was well suited. * * *

Mr. Justice Powell, with whom Mr. Justice Brennan, Mr. Justice White, and Mr. Justice Marshall join, dissenting in part.

I agree with the Court that the implied-reservation doctrine should be applied with sensitivity to its impact upon those who have obtained water rights under state law and to Congress' general policy of deference to state water law. I also agree that the Organic Administration Act of 1897 cannot fairly be read as evidencing an intent to reserve water for recreational or stockwatering purposes in the national forests.

I do not agree, however, that the forests which Congress intended to "improve and protect" are the still, silent, lifeless places envisioned by the Court. In my view, the forests consist of the birds, animals, and fish—the wildlife—that inhabit them, as well as the trees, flowers, shrubs, and grasses. I therefore would hold that the United States is entitled to so much water as is necessary to sustain the wildlife of the forests, as well as the plants. * * *

Notes

1. **Indian reserved rights and the primary/secondary purpose distinction.** Justice Macy, who wrote the lead opinion for the three-member majority in *Big Horn II*, supra p. 708, Note 3, concluded that the distinction between primary and secondary reservation purposes in the principal case applies not only to federal land reservations but also to Indian reservations. He said that although water is impliedly reserved for the primary purpose(s) of an Indian reservation, the acquisition of water rights for secondary purposes is governed by state law because of general congressional deference to state water law. He also thought state law should govern transfer from a primary reservation purpose (agriculture) to a secondary purpose (fish habitat). As noted earlier, state law prevented the transfer because it barred anyone except the state from owning an instream flow right.

In Colville Confederated Tribes v. Walton, 647 F.2d 42 (9th Cir. 1981), the Ninth Circuit accepted the primary/secondary purpose distinction of United States v. New Mexico as applicable to an Indian reservation. But it added a telling refinement by recognizing the existence of both general and specific primary purposes. It found that the Colville Reservation had the general purpose of providing a homeland for the Indians, and the more specific purposes of providing for agriculture and preserving access to fishing grounds. The court concluded that the tribe could transfer water reserved for agriculture and fishing to new uses because "permitting the Indians to determine how to use reserved water is consistent with the general purpose for the creation of an Indian reservation—providing a homeland for the survival and growth of the Indians and their way of life." This contrasts with the Wyoming court's rejection in *Big Horn I*, supra p. 697, Note 3, of a general homeland concept.

The Arizona court embraced the homeland concept for Indian reservations and rejected making any distinction between primary and secondary reservation purposes in *In re* General Adjudication of All Rights to Use Water in Gila River Sys. & Source, 35 P.3d 68 (Ariz. 2001).

2. **Reserved rights for instream flows.** United States v. City & County of Denver, 656 P.2d 1 (Colo. 1982) (hereinafter *Denver)* recognized reserved rights to maintain instream flows and lake levels in a national park for scenery, historic and scientific objects, and wildlife. It also recognized reserved rights for insteam flows in three national monuments to support the purposes for which the monuments were formed, but it denied an instream flow right for river rafting in one of them because recreation was not one of the monument's purposes.

Wilderness areas have been a litigation battleground concerning reserved rights to maintain instream flows. Sierra Club v. Block, 622 F. Supp. 842 (D. Colo. 1985), held that the Wilderness Act of 1964 reserved water in wilderness areas for conservation and recreation purposes set forth in the act, including preservation of natural conditions. The Tenth Circuit vacated the judgment and dismissed the case on ripeness grounds without reaching the merits. Sierra Club v. Yeutter, 911 F.2d 1405 (10th Cir. 1990). The Idaho Supreme Court ruled that the Wilderness Act impliedly reserved flows for three wilderness areas and that the quantity reserved was all of the unappropriated water within each area at the time it was established. Potlatch Corp. v. United States, No. 24546, 1999 WL 778325 (Idaho Oct. 1,1999) (3-2 decision). The justice who wrote the opinion for the three-member majority was up for re-election seven months later, and controversy over her opinion was the likely cause of her overwhelming defeat. Gregory J. Hobbs, Jr., State Water Politics Versus an Independent Judiciary: The Colorado and Idaho Experiences, 5 U. Denv. Water L. Rev. 122 (2001). The Idaho Supreme Court reheard the case after the election but before the defeated justice left the bench. Another justice in the former majority changed her vote to create a new 3-2 majority holding that the Wilderness Act does not create implied reserved water rights. Potlatch Corp. v. United States, 12 P.3d 1260 (Idaho 2000). The new majority decided water was not strictly necessary to accomplish the purposes of wilderness areas and relied on remarks by Senator Frank Church of Idaho in support of the Wilderness Act during Senate debate, in which he said the act would not impede water development in the West.

Congress expressly addressed the reserved water issue in several of the more recent acts creating wilderness areas. For example, the Nevada Wilderness Protection Act of 1989, Pub. L. No. 101-195, 103 Stat. 1784 (1989), and the Arizona Wilderness Act of 1990, Pub. L. 101-628, 104 Stat. 4469 (1990), expressly reserve a sufficient quantity of water to fulfill the purposes of the acts. These acts also direct federal officials to take steps necessary to protect the reserved rights, including filing claims in water right adjudications. However, both acts also state that their provisions reserving water shall not be construed as precedent for future wilderness designations nor constitute an interpretation of past acts or designations. The California Desert Protection Act of 1994, Pub. L. No. 103-

433, 108 Stat. 4471 (1994), contains similar provisions expressly reserving water for all but two of the seventy-four wilderness area designations; for the two, it states that "no rights to water of the Colorado River are reserved, either expressly, impliedly, or otherwise." The Clark County Conservation of Public Land and Natural Resources Act of 2002, Pub. L. No. 107-282, 116 Stat. 1994 (2002), creates a number of small wilderness areas in the Mohave Desert within Nevada and declares that nothing in the act shall be construed to constitute an express or implied reservation of water or water rights for the lands.

Wild and Scenic Rivers Act § 13(c), 16 U.S.C. § 1284(c) declares: "Designation of any stream or portion thereof as a national wild, scenic or recreational river area shall not be construed as a reservation of the waters of such streams for purposes other than those specified in this chapter, or in quantities greater than necessary to accomplish these purposes." The Idaho court ruled that although Congress awkwardly expressed its intent in the negative, this language clearly reserves water to fulfill the purposes of the act. Potlatch Corp. v. United States, 12 P.3d 1256 (Idaho 2000).

3. **FLPMA.** The Federal Land Policy and Management Act of 1976 (FLPMA), 43 U.S.C. §§ 1701-1783, directed the Bureau of Land Management (BLM) to undertake a comprehensive program of planning and management of 448 million acres of federal public domain lands—lands not reserved for parks, monuments, forests, and so on—for a multiplicity of purposes. Among the act's directives is a requirement that the BLM manage the public lands in a manner "that will protect the quality of scientific, scenic, historical, ecological, environmental, air and atmospheric, water resource, and archaeological values; that, where appropriate, will preserve and protect certain public lands in their natural condition; that will provide food and habitat for fish and wildlife and domestic animals; and that will provide for outdoor recreation and human occupancy and use." Sierra Club v. Watt, 659 F.2d 203 (D.C. Cir. 1981), held that FLPMA did not create reserved water rights because it did not withdraw land from the public domain and because it expressly disclaimed making any change in federal or state jurisdiction or rights in water resources.

4. **Federal water rights acquired under state law.** In *Denver*, supra Note 2, the court recognized thousands of federal claims for appropriations under state law, mostly for use on public domain lands administered by the BLM. In DeKay v. U.S. Fish & Wildlife Service, 524 N.W.2d 855 (S.D. 1994), the federal Fish & Wildlife Service was allowed to appropriate water under South Dakota law to maintain waterfowl habitat on formerly private land it purchased that is contiguous to a national wildlife refuge.

In California, the United States was held to have riparian rights under state law for the secondary purpose of wildlife enhancement in a national forest. *In re* Water of Hallett Creek Stream Sys., 749 P.2d 324 (Cal. 1988). The rights claimed, however, were for future wildlife enhancement and thus were unexercised riparian rights. As such, said the court, the rights were subject to the rule of *In re* Waters of Long Valley Creek Stream System, supra p. 326, footnote 2, authorizing the State Water Resources Control Board to subordinate unexercised riparian rights to appropriations made before the riparian rights are exercised.

Nevada and Utah have statutes that bar the United States from obtaining instream flow appropriations on public lands for watering livestock owned by persons holding grazing permits under the federal Taylor Grazing Act. Nev. Rev. Stat. § 533.03; Utah Code Ann. § 73-3-31. The Idaho Supreme Court reached the same result absent any such statute, reasoning that it was not the United States but rather the livestock owners that put the water to beneficial use. The court said the livestock owners acquired the appropriations, which were appurtenant to nearby lands that they owned in fee simple. Joyce Livestock Co. v. United States, 156 P.3d 502 (Idaho 2007). In contrast to *Joyce Livestock*, the Utah statute provides that if a grazing permittee ceases to beneficially use water, the water right transfers to the Utah Department of Agriculture and Food, which can sever the right from the federal grazing allotment and sell it to another person for livestock watering.

5. **Federal nonreserved water rights.** If the United States has no reserved water rights for public domain lands or for the secondary purposes of reserved lands, is there any way for it to assure recreational and habitat flows in an appropriation doctrine state that either requires a diversion structure, does not regard such uses as beneficial, or limits instream flow appropriations to state agencies? A possible solution would be a federal nonreserved right to water. The main constitutional basis asserted for the concept is the Supremacy Clause: If a constitutional act of Congress authorizes a federal use of water, the United States must have power under the Supremacy Clause to make that use regardless of state water law. Another asserted constitutional basis is that the United States, by virtue of its "ownership of unappropriated water" (see supra p. 675, Note 3), has power under the Property Clause to use such water as it sees fit without regard to state law. The priority of a nonreserved right would be the date of its first actual use.

The concept of federal nonreserved water rights was created, modified, and repudiated by three successive Solicitors of the Department of the Interior. Solicitor Leo Krulitz made very broad claims to federal nonreserved rights. Federal Water Rights of the National Park Service, Fish and Wildlife Service, Bureau of Reclamation, and Bureau of Land Management, 86 Interior Dec. 553 (1979). The broad claims seemingly ignored the dictum of United States v. New Mexico that where the United States has not reserved water, "there arises the * * * inference that Congress intended * * * that the United States would acquire water in the same manner as any other public or private appropriator." Later Solicitor Clyde Martz opined that federal nonreserved water rights could exist when expressly or impliedly mandated by Congress, but he found no such mandate in the two major federal acts that he addressed, FLPMA and the Taylor Grazing Act. Memorandum of the Solicitor of the Department of the Interior, 88 Interior Dec. 253 (1981). Finally, Solicitor William Coldiron came out flatly against the concept of a nonreserved right: "There is no 'federal non-reserved water right.'" Non-Reserved Water Rights—United States Compliance with State Law, 88 Interior Dec. 1055 (1981).

The third Solicitor's opinion did not end the concept of federal nonreserved water rights. Other agencies of the United States, particularly the Department of Defense and the Forest Service in the Department of Agriculture, could benefit from nonreserved water rights if they exist, so the question of such rights was reviewed by the Department of Justice. Assistant Attorney General Theodore Olson of the Office of Legal Counsel concluded that ownership of unappropriated water was an anomaly "if ownership is understood to mean a proprietary interest in the water," and that "[c]laims of ownership of natural resources by the states or by the federal government are best understood as claims of regulatory jurisdiction over these resources, either under the states' police powers or under the federal government's constitutional powers." He acknowledged that the Supremacy Clause, coupled with the Commerce Clause, the Property Clause and other federal powers, gave ample federal authority to supersede state laws; but in light of California v. United States, supra p. 666, and United States v. New Mexico, supra p. 714, he concluded: "[T]he federal constitutional authority to preempt state water law must be clearly and specifically exercised, * * * otherwise the presumption is that western states retain control over the allocation of unappropriated water within their borders. * * * The exercise of such power must be explicit or clearly implied, however, and federal rights to water will not be found simply by virtue of the ownership, occupation, or use of federal land, without more." Federal "Non-Reserved" Water Rights, 6 U.S. Op. Off. Legal Counsel 328 (1982). See also Frank J. Trelease, Uneasy Federalism — State Water Laws and National Water Uses, 55 Wash. L. Rev. 751 (1980).

Congress explicitly exercised its power to create a federal nonreserved water right for ecosystem protection in the Great Sand Dunes National Park and Preserve Act of 2000, Pub. L. No. 106-530, § 9(b)(2)(B), 114 Stat. 2527, 2533-34. The story of how this occurred is told in John D. Leshy, Water Rights for New Federal Land Conservation Programs: A Turn-of-the Century Evaluation, 4 U. Denv. L. Rev. 271 (2001).

6. **Nonreserved rights for federal uses arising under state law.** Federal agencies, particularly the Forest Service, have made many small diversions on reserved lands over the years without a state permit. Apparently, they relied either on the theory that reserved rights were being exercised or on something like the concept of federal nonreserved rights. In 1983, the California legislature provided a modicum of recognition for such diversions made for secondary forest purposes. It adopted a state version of what it called "nonreserved water rights for federal uses." The legislation gave federal agencies until July 1, 1984, to file for "a priority of right to appropriate water" on reserved land if the water use for secondary purposes was initiated prior to July 3, 1978 (the date United States v. New Mexico held that there are no reserved water rights for secondary

purposes). Each such water right has a priority dating from its initial use, but the priority can be exercised only against other appropriations with a priority on or after July 1, 1984. In other words, a federal secondary water use initiated before July 3, 1978, that was filed by July 1, 1984, would take priority only over appropriations by others made on or after July 1, 1984. Cal. Water Code §§ 1227-1227.4.

7. **A federal regulatory approach to instream flows?** Given the difficulty the United States has had in establishing reserved rights for instream flows in national forests, would a regulatory approach be a viable alternative in some circumstances? Suppose an irrigation company has a right-of-way permit from the Forest Service for a dam and reservoir within a national forest. When the permit comes up for renewal, could the Forest Service condition renewal upon a requirement that the company bypass, i.e., not store, some of the stream flow in order to provide downstream fish habitat? See Note 8, supra p. 604.

C. Adjudication and Administration

COLORADO RIVER WATER CONSERVATION DISTRICT v. UNITED STATES

Supreme Court of the United States, 1976.
424 U.S. 800, 96 S. Ct. 1236, 47 L. Ed.2d 483.

MR. JUSTICE BRENNAN delivered the opinion of the Court.

The McCarran Amendment, 66 Stat. 560, 43 U.S.C.A. § 666, provides that "consent is hereby given to join the United States as a defendant in any suit (1) for the adjudication of rights to the use of water of a river system or other source, or (2) for the administration of such rights, where it appears that the United States is the owner of or is in the process of acquiring water rights by appropriation under State law, by purchase, by exchange, or otherwise, and the United States is a necessary party to such suit." The questions presented by this case concern the effect of the McCarran Amendment upon the jurisdiction of the federal district courts under 28 U.S.C.A. § 1345 over suits for determination of water rights brought by the United States as trustee for certain Indian tribes and as owner of various non-Indian Government claims. * * *

Under the Colorado [Water Rights Determination and Administration] Act, the State is divided into seven Water Divisions, each Division encompassing one or more entire drainage basins for the larger rivers in Colorado. Adjudication of water claims within each Division occurs on a continuous basis. Each month, Water Referees in each Division rule on applications for water rights filed within the preceding five months or refer those applications to the Water Judge of their Division. Every six months, the Water Judge passes on referred applications and contested decisions by Referees. A State Engineer and engineers for each Division are responsible for the administration and distribution of the waters of the State according to the determinations in each Division. * * *

The reserved rights of the United States extend to Indian reservations and other federal lands, such as national parks and forests. The reserved rights claimed by the United States in this case affect waters within Colorado Water Division No. 7. On November 14, 1972, the Government instituted this suit in the United States District Court for the District of Colorado, invoking the court's jurisdiction under 28 U.S.C.A. § 1345. The District Court is located in Denver, some 300 miles from Division 7. The suit, against some 1,000 water users, sought declaration of the Government's rights to waters in certain rivers and their tributaries located in Division 7. In the suit, the Government asserted reserved rights on its own behalf and on behalf of certain Indian tribes, as well as rights based on state law. It sought appointment of a water master to administer any waters decreed to the United States.

Prior to institution of this suit, the Government had pursued adjudication of non-Indian reserved rights and other water claims based on state law in Water Divisions 4, 5, and 6, and the Government continues to participate fully in those Divisions.

Shortly after the federal suit was commenced, one of the defendants in that suit filed an application in the state court for Division 7, seeking an order directing service of process on the United States in order to make it a party to proceedings in Division 7 for the purpose of adjudicating all of the Government's claims, both state and federal. On January 3, 1973, the United States was served pursuant to authority of the McCarran Amendment. Several defendants and intervenors in the federal proceeding then filed a motion in the District Court to dismiss on the ground that under the Amendment, the court was without jurisdiction to determine federal water rights. Without deciding the jurisdictional question, the District Court, on June 21, 1973, granted the motion in an unreported oral opinion stating that the doctrine of abstention required deference to the proceedings in Division 7. On appeal, the Court of Appeals for the Tenth Circuit reversed, United States v. Akin, 504 F.2d 115 (1974), holding that the suit of the United States was within district-court jurisdiction under 28 U.S.C.A. § 1345, and that abstention was inappropriate. We granted certiorari. * * *

We first consider the question of district-court jurisdiction under 28 U.S.C.A. § 1345. That section provides that the district courts shall have original jurisdiction over all civil actions brought by the Federal Government "[e]xcept as otherwise provided by Act of Congress." It is thus necessary to examine whether the McCarran Amendment is such an Act of Congress excepting jurisdiction under § 1345.

The McCarran Amendment does not by its terms, at least, indicate any repeal of jurisdiction under § 1345. * * * Beyond its terms, the legislative history of the Amendment evidences no clear purpose to terminate any portion of § 1345 jurisdiction. * * * Accordingly, we hold that the McCarran Amendment in no way diminished federal-district-court jurisdiction under § 1345 and that the District Court had jurisdiction to hear this case.

We turn next to the question whether this suit nevertheless was properly dismissed in view of the concurrent state proceedings in Division 7.

First, we consider whether the McCarran Amendment provided consent to determine federal reserved rights held on behalf of Indians in state court. This is a question not previously squarely addressed by this Court, and given the claims for Indian water rights in this case, dismissal clearly would have been inappropriate if the state court had no jurisdiction to decide those claims. We conclude that the state court had jurisdiction over Indian water rights under the Amendment.

United States v. District Court for Eagle County, 401 U.S. 520, 91 S.Ct. 998, 28 L.Ed.2d 278 (1971), and United States v. District Court for Water Div. 5, 401 U.S. 527, 91 S.Ct. 1003, 28 L.Ed.2d 284 (1971), held that the provisions of the McCarran Amendment, whereby "consent is * * * given to join the United States as a defendant in any suit (1) for the adjudication * * * or (2) for the administration of [water] rights, where it appears that the United States is the owner * * * by appropriation under State law, by purchase, by exchange, or otherwise," subject federal reserved rights to general adjudication in state proceedings for the determination of water rights. More specifically, the Court held that reserved rights were included in those rights where the United States was "otherwise" the owner. Though *Eagle County* and *Water Div. 5* did not involve reserved rights on Indian reservations, viewing the Government's trusteeship of Indian rights as ownership, the logic of those cases clearly extends to such rights. Indeed, *Eagle County* spoke of non-Indian rights and Indian rights without any suggestion that there was a distinction between them for purposes of the Amendment.

Not only the Amendment's language, but also its underlying policy, dictates a construction including Indian rights in its provisions. *Eagle County* rejected the conclusion that federal reserved rights in general were not reached by the Amendment for the reason that the Amendment "[deals] with an all-inclusive statute concerning 'the adjudication of rights to the use of water of a river system.'" Id., at 524, 91 S.Ct., at 1002, 28 L.Ed.2d, at 282. This consideration applies as well to federal water rights reserved for Indian reservations. * * * Thus, bearing in mind the ubiquitous nature of Indian water rights in the Southwest, it is clear that a construction of the Amendment excluding those rights from its coverage would enervate the Amendment's objective. * * *

The Government argues that because of its fiduciary responsibility to protect Indian rights, any state-court jurisdiction over Indian property should not be recognized unless expressly conferred by Congress. [T]he Government's argument rests on the incorrect assumption that consent to state jurisdiction for the purpose of determining water rights imperils those rights or in some way breaches the special obligation of the Federal Government to protect Indians. Mere subjection of Indian rights to legal challenge in state court, however, would no more imperil those rights than would a suit brought by the Government in district court for their declaration, a suit which, absent the consent of the Amendment, would eventually be necessitated to resolve conflicting claims to a scarce resource. The government has not abdicated any responsibility fully to defend Indian rights in state court, and Indian interests may be satisfactorily protected under regimes of state law. * * * The Amendment in no way abridges any substantive claim on behalf of Indians under the doctrine of reserved rights. Moreover, as *Eagle County* said, "questions [arising from the collision of private rights and reserved rights of the United States], including the volume and scope of particular reserved rights, are federal questions which, if preserved, can be reviewed here after final judgment by the Colorado court." 401 U.S., at 526, 91 S.Ct., at 1003, 28 L.Ed.2d, at 283.

Next, we consider whether the District Court's dismissal was appropriate under the doctrine of abstention. We hold that the dismissal cannot be supported under that doctrine in any of its forms. * * *

Although this case falls within none of the abstention categories, there are principles unrelated to considerations of proper constitutional adjudication and regard for federal-state relations which govern in situations involving the contemporaneous exercise of concurrent jurisdictions, either by federal courts or by state and federal courts. These principles rest on consideration of "wise judicial administration, giving regard to conservation of judicial resources and comprehensive disposition of litigation." Kerotest Mfg. Co. v. C-O-Two Fire Equipment Co., 342 U.S. 180, 183 (1952). * * *

Turning to the present case, a number of factors clearly counsel against concurrent federal proceedings. The most important of these is the McCarran Amendment itself. The clear federal policy evinced by that legislation is the avoidance of piecemeal adjudication of water rights in a river system. * * * The consent to jurisdiction given by the McCarran Amendment bespeaks a policy that recognizes the availability of comprehensive state systems for adjudication of water rights as the means for achieving these goals.

Beyond the congressional policy expressed by the McCarran Amendment and consistent with furtherance of that policy, we also find significant (a) the apparent absence of any proceedings in the District Court, other than the filing of the complaint, prior to the motion to dismiss, (b) the extensive involvement of state water rights occasioned by this suit naming 1,000 defendants, (c) the 300-mile distance between the District Court in Denver and the court in Division 7, and (d) the existing participation by the Government in Division 4, 5, and 6 proceedings. We emphasize, however, that we do not overlook the heavy obligation to exercise jurisdiction. We need not decide, for example, whether, despite the McCarran Amendment, dismissal would be warranted if more extensive proceedings had occurred in the District Court prior to dismissal, if the involvement of state water rights were less extensive than it is here, or if the state proceeding were in some respect inadequate to resolve the federal claims. But the opposing factors here, particularly the policy underlying the McCarran Amendment, justify the District Court's dismissal in this particular case.

The judgment of the Court of Appeals is reversed and the judgment of the District Court dismissing the complaint is affirmed for the reasons here stated.

Notes

1. *Arizona v. San Carlos Apache Tribe.* A sequel to *Colorado River* is Arizona v. San Carlos Apache Tribe, 463 U.S. 545 (1983). This was a consolidated appeal of cases concerning Indian reservations in Arizona and Montana. These two states, like many other western states, have clauses in their statehood enabling acts and state constitutions providing that the state disclaims all right to lands of any Indian or Indian tribe and acknowledges that such lands shall be under the jurisdiction and control of Congress. The tribes argued that the disclaimer clauses barred state court adjudication of their water rights. The Court ruled, however, that the McCarran Amendment removed any barrier to state adjudication possibly arising from disclaimer clauses in the statehood enabling acts. The Court left the meaning of disclaimer clauses in the state constitutions to the state courts. Later the Arizona and Montana courts held that their respective state disclaimer provisions did not bar state court adjudication of Indian water rights. United States v. Superior Court for Maricopa County, 697 P.2d 658 (Ariz. 1985); State *ex rel.* Greely v. Confederated Salish & Kootenai Tribes, 712 P.2d 754 (Mont. 1985).

San Carlos also addressed another post-*Colorado River* issue. The concurrent federal suit in *Colorado River* was brought by the United States and was to adjudicate both Indian and non-Indian reserved rights. In *San Carlos*, the Court held that the *Colorado River* criteria for dismissal of concurrent federal suits apply with full force to those that are brought by tribes, rather than the United States, and that seek only the adjudication of Indian rights.

2. **Consent to a "suit" adjudicating water rights.** The McCarran Amendment consents to joinder of the United States in a "suit" to adjudicate water rights. The Oregon adjudication statutes require water right claims to be submitted to an administrative agency, the Oregon Water Resources Department, rather than to a court. The agency accepts objections to claims and holds hearings on contested claims. It then makes findings and issues an order determining the parties' water rights. The order is filed with a court. If no objections are timely filed, the court must enter judgment affirming the order. If objections are filed, the court holds a hearing and then enters a judgment affirming or modifying the order. In United States v. Oregon, 44 F.3d 758 (9th Cir. 1994), the United States argued this process did not constitute a "suit" within the meaning of the McCarran Amendment. The court disagreed: "Congress had in mind not only traditional suits in equity but also hybrid adjudications taking advantage of the expertise of nonjudicial officials. In fact, the active participation of administrative agencies is at the core of most of the 'comprehensive state systems for adjudication of water rights' contemplated by the McCarran Amendment." Id. at 766.

3. **Consent to adjudication of rights in "a river system or other source."** Another requirement of the McCarran Amendment is that the suit must be to adjudicate rights to use water of "a river system or other source." Dugan v. Rank, 372 U.S. 609 (1963), held that the waiver of immunity does not extend to a private suit to determine the water rights of only some users on a river. Rather, the suit must be a general adjudication of all the rights in "a river system or other source." *Dugan* spawned much litigation about what constitutes a river system or other source.

United States v. District Court for Eagle County, 401 U.S. 520 (1971), concerned a Colorado adjudication of the Eagle River and its tributaries. The Court rejected an argument by the United States that the Eagle River and its tributaries by themselves were not a "river system" because the Eagle River was in turn tributary to the Colorado River. The Court said: "No suit by any State could possibly encompass all of the water rights in the entire Colorado River, which runs through or touches many states. The 'river system' must be read as embracing one within the particular State's jurisdiction." Id. at 523.

In re General Adjudication of Rights to Use of Water from Snake River Basin Water System, 764 P.2d 78 (Idaho 1988), held that the "river system" requirement meant federal sovereign immunity would be waived in the Snake River adjudication only if it included all tributaries of the river within Idaho. The court distinguished *Eagle County*, where the Eagle River adjudication did not include all tributaries of the Colorado River within Colorado. It said *Eagle County* involved a unique system of water adjudication existing in Colorado whereby other tributaries of the Colorado River within that state were the subject of other ongoing adjudication proceedings in the state. (See supra pp. 126-27, Note 2, and pp. 167-68, Note 11, regarding the Colorado adjudication system.) The court also refused to treat the main stem Snake River as a separately adjudicatable "other source" under the McCarran Amendment, saying that this phrase refers to sources like lakes or groundwaters.

In United States v. Oregon, supra Note 2, the United States and the Klamath Tribe asserted that the Klamath River Basin adjudication was not comprehensive enough to comply with the McCarran Amendment for two reasons. First, they objected because rights represented by water certificates issued under the Oregon permit system and rights recognized in earlier statutory adjudications could not be challenged in the adjudication, and holders of those rights did not have to appear unless they wished to contest other claims. The Ninth Circuit saw no merit in this objection: "As was true in *Eagle County*, all existing water rights claims will have been determined when the adjudication is finished. * * * The comprehensiveness standard requires the consolidation of existing controversies, not the reopening of settled determinations." Id. at 768. Additionally, in response to fears of the United States and the tribe that their rights would be insufficiently protected because they would not be allowed in the adjudication to challenge water right certificates issued under the permit system, the court quoted the following passage from *Eagle County*: "The absence of owners of previously decreed rights may present problems going to the merits, in case there develops a collision between them and any reserved rights of the United States. All such questions, including the volume and scope of particular reserved rights, are federal questions which, if preserved, can be reviewed here after final judgment by the [state] court." Id.

Second, the United States and the tribe objected that the adjudication was insufficiently comprehensive because it did not include claims to hydrologically related groundwater. After noting that the McCarran Amendment requires the adjudication of "a river system or other source," the court stated: "Groundwater may be included as an 'other source,' but the use of 'or' strongly suggests that the adjudication may be limited to either a river system or some other source of water, like groundwater, but need not cover both. * * * [W]hile the adjudication must avoid excessively piecemeal litigation of water rights, it need not determine the rights of users of all hydrologically-related water sources." Id. at 769. To explain why the "river system" requirement should not be read to mandate inclusion of hydrologically related groundwater, the court said: "While the trend has been toward a greater legal recognition of the connection between ground and surface waters, that recognition is too recent and too incomplete to infer that Congress intended to require comprehensive stream adjudications under the McCarran Amendment [passed in 1952] to include the adjudication of groundwater rights as well as rights to surface water." Id. at 769-70.

In Arizona, streams and their subflow are subject to the appropriation doctrine, while percolating groundwater is governed by different rules. The exclusion of percolating groundwater from a stream adjudication was approved in *In re* General Adjudication of All Rights to Use Water in Gila River System & Source, 857 P.2d 1236, 1248 (Ariz. 1993): "The McCarran Amendment was not intended to impose on the states a federal definition of 'river system or other source.' * * * We believe that the trial court may adopt a rationally based exclusion for wells having a de minimis effect on the river system. Such a de minimis exclusion effectively allocates to those well owners whatever amount of water is determined to be de minimis. It is, in effect, a summary adjudication of their rights."

4. **Judicial review of federal agency decisions regarding reserved rights claims.** Suppose an environmental group alleges a federal agency entitled to a reserved right is violating federal law by seeking too small a quantity of water in a state court adjudication. Judicial review of the agency's decision about how much water to claim lies exclusively in federal court. The McCarran Amendment's waiver of immunity is not broad enough to allow the state court conducting the adjudication to evaluate the federal agency's decision making processes regarding quantification. *In re* Application for Water Rights of United States, 101 P.3d 1072 (Colo. 2004).

5. **The role of state law under the McCarran Amendment.** The McCarran Amendment does more than consent to the joinder of the United States in general adjudication suits. It also addresses what law governs: "The United States, when a party to any such suit, shall * * * be deemed to have waived any right to plead that the State laws are inapplicable or that the United States is not amenable thereto by reason of its sovereignty, * * * Provided, that no judgment for costs shall be entered against the United States in any such suit."

In United States v. Idaho *ex rel.* Director, Idaho Department of Water Resources, 508 U.S. 1 (1993), an Idaho statute obligated each water right claimant in the Snake River adjudication to pay a filing fee to help finance the cost of the adjudication. The amount of the fee varied with the size of the claim. The United States estimated that the filing fees for its various claims could exceed $10 million. It argued that the McCarran Amendment's waiver of "any right to plead that the State laws are inapplicable" should not be construed to subject it to state adjective law governing procedure, fees, and the like. The Court disagreed because the United States' view "would render the amendment's consent to suit largely nugatory, allowing the Government to argue for some special federal rule defeating established state-law rules governing pleading, discovery, and the admissibility of evidence at trial." Nonetheless, the Court held that Idaho could not require the United States to pay filing fees under state law. The Court relied on the McCarran Amendment proviso prohibiting any "judgment for costs." The Court acknowledged that generally there is a distinction between fees and costs: Fees are amounts paid to a public official for particular charges typically delineated by statute, and costs are expenses incurred in litigation that a prevailing party is allowed by rule to tax against the losing party. But in this case, said the Court, the line was blurred. Before Idaho revised its system for recovering adjudication expenses shortly before commencement of the Snake River adjudication, Idaho courts upon entering final judgment in an adjudication had taxed the costs against all parties, not just the losing parties. Moreover, many of the items that Idaho had formerly taxed as costs were now denominated as fees to be paid upon filing a claim. The court therefore concluded that the McCarran Amendment does not subject "the United States to the payment of the sort of fees that Idaho sought to exact here." 508 U.S. at 8.

In United States v. Bell, 724 P.2d 631 (Colo. 1986), the United States sought to amend a reserved water right claim it filed eleven years earlier in an ongoing Colorado adjudication. The United States wanted to change its claimed point of diversion from small tributaries of the White and Colorado Rivers to the main stem Colorado River. This change would have enabled a substantial increase in the amount that could be diverted. The trial court applied a state rule of civil procedure on the relation back of pleading amendments. The court denied relation back under that rule because the original claim gave no notice to persons who would be adversely affected that the United States claimed a large quantity of main stem water. Without relation back, a state adjudication statute then required that the enlarged portion of the claim be postponed in priority to the date when the pleading was amended rather than the date the reservation was created. The Colorado Supreme Court approved application of the state pleading rule and the postponement statute to the federal claim. It viewed the McCarran Amendment as being intended to "promote certainty in water allocation by subjecting undeclared and unquantified federal water rights to state adjudication." It reasoned that without application of the pleading rule and postponement statute, "the purposes of the McCarran Amendment would be frustrated, and the United States would have avoided the equivalent of a filing deadline."

United States v. Oregon, supra Note 2, dealt not only with the Klamath Basin adjudication but with an Oregon statute requiring the United States to register and describe its reserved right claims to waters *outside* the Klamath Basin by December 31, 1992. Outside the Klamath Basin, no proceedings were under way to adjudicate the water rights of the United States. The Ninth Circuit held that the McCarran Amendment did not consent to make the United States subject to the Oregon registration statute. "While the information obtained by the registration system regarding claims not yet at issue in any proceeding may be useful in future comprehensive adjudications, the process cannot accurately be described as part of the state's adjective law for the adjudication of water rights. * * * It is * * * possible that many years will pass before a registered claim is adjudicated, if it is ever adjudicated at all. The connection between registration and adjudication is too tenuous for the registration provisions to be characterized as part of the adjudications to which the United States has consented to be joined." 44 F.3d at 771.

6. **Water right administration suits.** The McCarran Amendment, as set out at the beginning of the principal case, contains two waivers of sovereign immunity. Clause (1) consents to joinder of the United States in suits to adjudicate water rights in a river system or other source. Clause (2), which has been less in the spotlight, consents to joinder of the United States in suits "for the administration of such rights." The phrase "such rights" in clause (2) refers only to water rights previously adjudicated in a general adjudication. It does not include rights decreed in private suits. S. Delta Water Agency v. Bureau of Reclamation, 767 F.2d 531 (9th Cir. 1985). It does, however, include rights decreed in a general adjudication that predated the McCarran Amendment. State Eng'r v. S. Fork Band of Te-Moak Tribe, 339 F.3d 804 (9th Cir. 2003) (water rights obtained under stated law that were decreed to five ranches the United States purchased after the adjudication in order to create an Indian reservation out of them).

7. **Res judicata effect of previous adjudication of reserved rights.** Nevada v. United States, 463 U.S. 110 (1983), concerned the effect of an earlier adjudication of Indian reserved rights. The Truckee River flows from the Sierra Nevada through Lake Tahoe and then into Pyramid Lake, home of the Lahontan cutthroat trout and the cui-ui sucker. Surrounding the lake is the 1859 reservation of the Paiute Indians, who have always looked to the lake fish as an important source of food. Long ago, the U.S. Bureau of Reclamation diverted a large portion of the Truckee's waters to serve an irrigation project now managed by the Truckee-Carson Irrigation District. A number of private landowners also acquired water rights to the Truckee. In 1913, the United States brought suit in federal district court to assert and protect its water rights for the Indian reservation and the reclamation project. A master's report proposed awarding the Indian reservation an 1859 right for 58.7 c.f.s. to irrigate 3,130 acres and the federal reclamation project a 1902 priority for 1500 c.f.s. In 1926, the district court put this award in force for an experimental period. In 1934 settlement negotiations, the United States demanded an increase in the Indian rights to enable irrigation of an additional 2,745 acres of reservation land. This was accepted and a decree, known as the Orr Ditch decree, was signed in 1935.

In 1973, with the level of Pyramid Lake dropping, the United States instituted a new suit against all users of Truckee water, asserting that the Orr Ditch decree determined only the Indians' reserved rights for irrigation water. The United States claimed on behalf of the Indians an additional reserved right for water to maintain and preserve Pyramid Lake and maintain the lower Truckee as a natural spawning ground. The Court held res judicata barred the United States from asserting this new claim. The Court found that the same cause of action was litigated in both proceedings and that all of the parties in the second suit were bound by the original decree, including the United States and the tribe.

The government had represented both the Indian tribe and the reclamation project landowners in the original suit. Regarding the dual representation, the Court said:

"Today, * * * it may well appear that Congress was requiring the Secretary of the Interior to carry water on at least two shoulders when it delegated to him both the responsibility for the supervision of the Indian tribes and the commencement of reclamation projects in areas adjacent to reservation lands. But Congress chose to do this, and it is simply unrealistic to suggest that the Government may not perform its obligation to represent Indian tribes in litigation when Congress has obliged it to represent other interests as well. In this regard, the Government cannot follow the fastidious standards of a private fiduciary, who would breach his duties to his single beneficiary solely by representing potentially conflicting interests without the beneficiary's consent. The Government does not 'compromise' its obligation to one interest that Congress obliges it to represent by the mere fact that it simultaneously performs another task for another interest that Congress has obligated it by statute to do." 463 U.S. at 128.

UNITED STATES v. ANDERSON
United States Court of Appeals, Ninth Circuit, 1984.
736 F.2d 1358.

J. BLAINE ANDERSON, CIRCUIT JUDGE: * * * The plaintiffs [United States and Spokane Tribe of Indians] sought an adjudication of water rights in the Chamokane Basin, a hydrological system including Chamokane Creek, its tributaries and its ground water basin. The waters of the Chamokane Basin are not wholly within the Spokane Indian Reservation; Chamokane Creek originates north of the reservation and flows south along the eastern boundary. The creek leaves the reservation by discharging into the Spokane River which, in turn, joins with the Columbia River and flows into the Pacific Ocean. * * *

The Spokane Indian Reservation is not exclusively owned and resided upon by Indians. Non-Indian settlement has occurred there, encouraged by various federal programs authorizing allotment of reservation lands to individual Indians and opening excess land to homesteading by non-Indians. * * *

In the case before us, the district court determined that it was permissible for the State of Washington to exercise regulatory jurisdiction over non-Indian use of excess Chamokane Basin waters on lands owned by non-Indians within the Spokane Indian Reservation. The Spokane Tribe takes issue with this determination, arguing that it, not the state, has jurisdiction * * *.

[T]ribal sovereignty is not absolute. In particular, the power to regulate generally the conduct of nonmembers on land no longer owned by or held in trust for the tribe is impliedly withdrawn as a necessary result of tribal dependent status. Montana v. United States, 450 U.S. 544, 564, 101 S.Ct. 1245, 1257, 67 L.Ed.2d 493 (1981). Some exceptions to this implied withdrawal of tribal regulatory authority do exist.

> A tribe may regulate, through taxation, licensing or other means, the activities of nonmembers who enter consensual relationships with the tribe or its members, through commercial dealing, contracts, leases, or other arrangements * * * A tribe may also retain inherent power to exercise civil authority over the conduct of non-Indians on fee lands within the reservation when that conduct threatens or has some direct effect on the political integrity, the economic security, or the health or welfare of the tribe.

Montana v. United States, 450 U.S. at 565-66, 101 S.Ct. at 1258-59.
* * *

Applying these standards, we conclude that the State, not the Tribe, has the authority to regulate the use of excess Chamokane Basin waters by non-Indians on non-tribal, i.e., fee, land. Our review reveals no consensual agreement between the non-Indian water users and the Tribe which would furnish the basis for implication of tribal regulatory authority. We find no conduct which so threatens or has such a "direct effect on the political integrity, the economic security, or the health or welfare of the Tribe," as to confer tribal jurisdiction. Montana v. United States, 450 U.S. at 566, 101 S.Ct. at 1258. The water rights adjudication which furnishes the basis for the instant inquiry quantifies and preserves tribal water rights. The district court appointed a federal water master whose responsibility is to administer the available waters in accord with the priorities of all the water rights as adjudicated. * * * The state may regulate only the use, by non-Indian fee owners, of excess water. Any permits issued by the state would be limited to excess water. If those permits represent rights that may be empty, so be it.

It is evident, however, that the political and economic welfare of the Tribe will not suffer adverse impact from the state-regulated use of surplus waters by nonmembers on non-Indian lands. Instead the factual situation points in favor of state regulation. First, no direct federal preemption of state regulation has occurred. No federal statute or regulatory scheme expressly or impliedly governs water use by non-Indians on the Spokane Reservation. Second, the balance of interest weighs most heavily in favor of the state.

The instant situation is contrary to that addressed by this circuit in Colville Confederated Tribes v. Walton, 647 F.2d 42 (1981). [In a portion of *Walton* not reprinted supra p. 702, the court held that the power of the State of Washington to issue permits to appropriate "water in the No Name system was pre-empted by the creation of the Colville Reservation." 647 F.2d at 52.] The *Walton* decision was compelled by the geography and hydrology of the No Name Basin and its relationship to the Colville Reservation. The reservation lands in question were allotted, not opened for entry and settlement. The No Name hydrological system is non-navigable and is located entirely within the reservation. Validation of the state-issued permits claimed by Walton could have jeopardized the agricultural use of downstream tribal users as well as the existence of the tribal fishery. In essence, the interest of the Tribe in regulation of the waters of the No Name Basin was "critical to the lifestyle of its residents and the development of its resources."

The district court noted, and we agree, that because water per se lies within the exterior boundaries of an Indian reservation does not necessarily negate a state's interest in overseeing its usage along with the other in-state water systems. Washington is obligated to regulate and conserve water consumption for the benefit of all its citizens, including those who own land within a reservation in fee. Therefore, the state's special concern is shared with, not displaced by, similar tribal and federal interests when water is located within the boundaries of both the state and the reservation. The weight of the state's interest depends, in large part, on the extent to which waterways or aquifers transcend the exterior boundaries of Indian country. * * * Chamokane Creek arises outside of the Spokane Indian Reservation and its course, for a good deal of its length, continues outside of that reservation. * * *

The facts in this case are readily distinguishable from the facts in the *Walton* decision. By weighing the competing federal, tribal and state interests involved, it is clear that the state may exercise its regulatory jurisdiction over the use of surplus, non-reserved Chamokane Basin waters by nonmembers on non-Indian fee lands within the Spokane Indian Reservation. Central to our decision is the fact that the interest of the state in exercising its jurisdiction will not infringe on the tribal right to self-government nor impact on the Tribe's economic welfare because those rights have been quantified and will be protected by the federal water master. Additionally, in view of the hydrology and geography of the Chamokane Creek Basin, the State of Washington's interest in developing a comprehensive water program for the allocation of surplus waters weighs heavily in favor of permitting it to extend its regulatory authority to the excess waters, if any, of the Chamokane Basin. State permits issued for any such excess water will be subject to all preexisting rights and those preexisting rights will be protected by the federal court decree and its appointed water master. We do not believe there is any realistic infringement on tribal rights and protected affairs. If there is any intrusion, it is minimal and permissible under all of the circumstances of this case. * * *

Notes

1. **State versus tribal jurisdiction over non-Indian use of surplus water.** Non-Indians own about 8% of the land within the Yakima Indian Reservation. The Yakima Indian Nation adopted a water code purporting to regulate all waters that underlie, arise upon, flow through, or border upon the reservation, including waters used by non-Indians on fee lands both within and outside the reservation. The code required all persons using or claiming the right to divert water to apply for a permit from the tribal water resources council. Any person using water who failed to apply for a permit waived all right to the water. The code established priorities among uses in the following order: (a) tribal or public use dedicated by the Tribal Council, (b) use for tribal enterprises, (c) farming use on Yakima allotments, (d) non-farm use on Yakima allotments, (e) use on allotments held by nonresident Yakimas, (f) use on lands held by non-Yakima Indians, and (g) use on formerly allotted lands now in non-Indian ownership. Within each class, individual users were to receive a just and equitable distribution.

The State of Washington sued to have the tribal water code declared invalid. The parties stipulated that surplus water existed over that needed to satisfy the Yakima Nation's *Winters* rights, though the amount of the excess was not fully quantified. The court granted summary judgment that the code was invalid to the extent it asserted civil regulatory jurisdiction over non-Indian use of the surplus water on fee lands inside or outside the reservation. Holly v. Confederated Tribes & Bands of Yakima Indian Nation, 655 F. Supp. 557 (E.D. Wash. 1985), aff'd sub nom. Holly v. Totus, 812 F.2d 714 (9th Cir. 1987) (no reported opinion). The federal district court applied the Montana v. United States test discussed in the principal case and concluded: "The [Tribes] have not come forward with facts to show [the] existence of a material factual question with respect to whether non-Indian conduct related to non-Indian use of excess waters threatens the political integrity, economic security, or health and welfare of the Tribes. Nor have the non-Indians entered into agreements or dealings with the Tribes with a result of subjecting themselves to tribal civil jurisdiction." 655 F. Supp. at 559.

2. **Integrated administration of Indian reserved rights and appropriative rights.** In *Big Horn II*, supra p. 708, Note 3, the Wyoming Supreme Court by vote of 3 to 2 reversed a trial court order substituting the tribal water agency for the state engineer as the administrator of both the reserved and the state-permitted water rights within the Wind River Indian Reservation. The tribes sought this relief because they believed the state engineer was not adequately recognizing their rights. Justice Macy's lead opinion for the fragmented three-member majority relied on the separation of powers in the state constitution: The state engineer is a constitutionally designated water administration official subject to removal only by the governor, not the judiciary. In apparent recognition of tension between the state engineer and the tribes, Justice Macy admonished the state engineer that if he failed to protect the tribes'

reserved rights, the courts have power to take appropriate enforcement action. He also limited the state engineer's power by saying that if he thinks the tribes are violating the terms of their water rights, he cannot directly shut down their headgates but must seek judicial enforcement. The other two justices making up the majority, in separate concurrences, expressed their conviction that dual management would be unworkable, though their individual reasons for putting management in the state engineer rather than the tribal water agency seem to turn more on quirks of the case than on any broadly applicable principle.

The two dissenting justices each proposed different approaches. One favored dual state and tribal administration of all water rights on the reservation, with judicial resolution of disputes between the joint administrators. He acknowledged, however, that this might result ultimately in judicial administration of the river. The other dissenter urged allowing tribal "monitoring" of non-Indian water use on the reservation. He called this a "lesser regulatory activity" than full tribal administration because non-Indians would not be subject to the jurisdiction of the tribal water agency. Since he thought the state engineer had shown reluctance to enforce the Indian reserved rights, he also urged allowing the tribes to seek judicial enforcement of their rights without first having to request relief from the state engineer.

Compare United States v. City & County of Denver, 656 P.2d 1, 35 (Colo. 1982), which involved the adjudication and integration of non-Indian federal reserved rights into the state water rights systems of several Colorado rivers: "[The United States] agrees that water rights ultimately adjudicated to it are subject to administration by the State Engineer." Should Indian and non-Indian federal reserved rights be treated differently regarding water right administration? If the United States were later to conclude that the state engineer was inadequately protecting its rights, would it have any recourse (would it need any recourse) other than that suggested in *Eagle County*, supra p. 729, Note 3, where the Court said that questions arising from collision of reserved rights and state-created water rights "are federal questions which, if preserved, can be reviewed here after final judgment by the [state] court"? 401 U.S. at 526.

3. **Tribal water quality regulation.** Issues of tribal jurisdiction over activities of nonmembers arise with water quality regulation under the Clean Water Act (CWA). The states have various functions under the CWA, such as development of water quality standards under section 303 and certification in federal licensing or permitting proceedings under section 401. See PUD No. 1 of Jefferson County v. Wash. Dep't of Ecology, supra p. 658. With Environmental Protection Agency (EPA) approval of their programs, states can issue National Pollutant Discharge Elimination (NPDES) permits under section 402 and, in some circumstances, permits for dredged or fill material under section 404. See supra p. 576 and p. 600, Note 2. CWA § 518, 33 U.S.C. § 1377, authorizes EPA to treat an Indian tribe as a state for purposes of performing these functions. EPA

takes a case-by-case approach to approving tribal jurisdiction over activities on lands within reservation boundaries held in fee by nonmembers. Whether the tribe has regulatory jurisdiction depends on how seriously the activity to be regulated affects the tribe's political integrity, economic security, or health and welfare. E.g., Montana v. EPA, 137 F.3d 1135 (9th Cir. 1998); 58 Fed. Reg. 67966, 67970-67971 (various CWA sections); 58 Fed. Reg. 8172, 8173-8176 (CWA § 404); 56 Fed. Reg. 64877-64878 (CWA §§ 303, 401). State ownership of a lakebed does not preclude tribal regulation under CWA § 518. Wisconsin v. EPA, 266 F.3d 741 (7th Cir. 2001).

Tribal water quality standards can impact activities on lands outside the reservation. The Isleta Pueblo in New Mexico issued water quality standards under section 518 for waters of the Rio Grande River flowing through its reservation. The standards protected use of the river for ceremonial purposes involving human immersion and ingestion of water. The standards were more stringent than the state water quality standards for the river. About five miles upstream from the reservation, the City of Albuquerque discharged treated wastes into the river under a NPDES permit. These discharges lowered water quality within the reservation. When EPA undertook to revise the city's permit to ensure compliance with the tribal water quality standards, the city challenged EPA's approval and enforcement of the standards. In City of Albuquerque v. Browner, 97 F.3d 415 (10th Cir. 1996), the court held that (a) a tribe can adopt water quality standards more stringent that those required by federal law and (b) EPA can enforce the tribal standards against point source dischargers located outside the reservation boundaries. Section 518 directs EPA to "provide a mechanism for the resolution of any unreasonable consequences that may arise as a result of differing water quality standards that may be set by States and Indian tribes located on common bodies of water." The court held EPA complied with this directive even though it provided only for resolution by mediation or nonbinding arbitration and authorized only states and tribes, not interested third parties, to initiate the process.

Index

References are to pages.

Private litigation, 474-75

INTERSTATE COMPACTS
See also, Interstate Allocation; Pollution
    Control.
Arkansas River Compact, 498-99
Canadian River Compact, 496
Colorado River Compact, 500
Delaware River Basin Compact, 499-500
Federal-interstate compacts, 499-500
Formation, 495
Pecos River Compact, 496-97
Yellowstone River Compact, 650

IRRIGATION
See Appropriation; Beneficial Use;
    Quantity of Water.

IRRIGATION DISTRICTS
See Water Distribution Organizations.

LAKES
See also, Waters.
Appropriation, 89
Level of water, 246, 270
Ownership of bed, 256, 522-23
Recreation uses, 246, 263, 270
Right to view, 268
Use of surface, 256, 262

LICENSES
See Federal Energy Regulatory
    Commission; Pollution Control.

LOSS OF WATER RIGHTS
See Abandonment; Forfeiture; Prescriptive
    Rights.

MEASUREMENT OF WATER
Methods, 8-9

MEXICAN LAW
Pueblo rights, 52-53, 701-02
Water rights, 19, 320-21

MILL DAM ACTS
Priority in riparian states, 276, 306

MUNICIPAL USE
See also, Preferred Rights.
Condemnation,
  Appropriations, 219
  Riparian rights, 289, 292-96, 331
Eastern permits, 306-15
Future supply, 47, 50-54
Pueblo rights, 52
Quantity of water, 47-53

Relative rights, 299-301
Riparian rights, 245, 292-301

MUTUAL WATER COMPANIES
See Water Distribution Organizations.

NATURAL STREAMS
See Waters.

NAVIGABLE WATERS
  Generally, 515-29
Bed ownership, 520-24
Clean Water Act test, 626
Commerce Clause test, 632-34
Federal test, 632-34
Flood control, 691-92
Navigation servitude, 635-44
  History, 637
  Riparian rights, 639
  State servitude, 639
  Test of navigability, 643
  Waiver of, 638-39
"Pleasure boat" test, 517-18
Pollution control, 573, 576, 583-84
Public access, 257-58, 520-22, 529
Public rights, 515-529
Public trust, 530-39, 542
Riparian rights restricted, 529
"Saw log" test, 303
State license, 650, 656-57
State regulation, 650-66
State tests, 516, 522-23
Superiority of federal law, 650-66

NAVIGATION SERVITUDE
See Navigable Waters.

NON-USE
See Abandonment; Forfeiture.

PERCOLATING WATER
See Groundwater.

PERMITS
See also, Appropriation; Environmental
    Protection; Pollution Control;
    Procedure; Riparian Rights.
Appropriation, 121-151
Dams and reservoirs, 126, 305-06
Eastern states, 306-15
Riparian rights, 306-15

PHREATOPHYTES
  Generally, 78-79, 93-94
Salvaged water, 78-79, 91-94

PLACE OF USE
See also, Transfer of Water Rights.
Appropriation, generally, 97-103
Area of origin, 99-103
County of origin, 99-100
Riparian land, 236-42
State of origin, 644
Watershed limitations,
  Appropriation, 97-101
  Riparian, 236-42

POLICY FACTORS
See Economic Factors; Environmental
  Protection.

POLLUTION CONTROL
  Generally, 571-95
Appropriation law, 141, 571-72, 588-95
Clean Water Act. 573-76
Dredge and fill permits, 626
Effluent limitations, 573-75
Irrigation return flows, 587
Nonpoint sources, 575, 585
NPDES permits, 574-76, 592-94
Planning, 575
Riparian law, 279, 571-73
State control, 658
TMDL, 575-76, 585-86
Tribal regulation, 738-39
Waters protected, 584-85, 626-32

PONDS
See Waters.

PREFERRED RIGHTS
Appropriation, 28-30, 73, 75-76, 158, 215,
  219
Condemnation, 75-76, 219
Domestic and municipal uses, 73, 75-76,
  158, 219, 254-55
Pueblo rights, 52-53
Riparian, 254-55
Transfer without compensation, 73, 75-76,
  278

PRESCRIPTIVE RIGHTS
Appropriations, 192-200
California doctrine, 329-30
Ditch rights, 191, 197
Mutual prescription, 370-75
Riparian rights, 280-85

PRIORITY
See also, Interstate Allocation.
  Generally, 55-82
Cities, 50-54
Date of, 55

Different uses, 73, 75
Diligence, 55, 61-64
Enforcement, 64, 68-71
Groundwater, 356-70
Interstate, 474-75
Means of diversion, 107
Permits, 61
Reasonable diligence, 55, 61-65
Relation back, 55, 61-64
Rights of junior, 79-82
Rights of senior, 79-82
Riparian permits, 309-14
Riparian rights, 274-78
Rotation, 82
Seasonal, 72
Substitution of water, 75, 79
Tributaries, 71-72

PROCEDURE
See also, Adjudication of Water Rights.
Colorado, 126-27, 163, 167-68
Conditional decrees, 126
Conditional permits, 146-49
Denial of permit, 125-159
Permits, 121, 306-15
Plan of augmentation, 76, 79
Posting and filing claims, 124-25
Primary and secondary permits, 126

PROTECTION OF DIVERSION
Appropriation law, 107
Economic consideration, 111-15
Groundwater, 385-94

PUBLIC INTEREST
Appropriation, 135

PUBLIC RIGHTS
See also, Fishing; Navigable Waters.
Non-navigable waters, 515-24
Public trust, 151, 530-51

PUBLIC TRUST
  Generally, 530-51
Appropriation, 151
Planning, 151

PUBLIC UTILITIES
See Water Distribution Organizations.

PUEBLO RIGHTS
See also, Municipal Use.
Indian rights, 701-02

QUALITY OF WATER
See Pollution Control.

STATES' RIGHTS
See Federal-State Relations; Interstate Allocation.

SURFACE WATERS
See Waters.

TRANSFER OF WATER RIGHTS
Generally, 200-20
See also, Condemnation; Prescriptive Rights.
Appropriations,
  Appurtenant to land, 106, 215
  Description of right, 203
  Historic use, 205-06
  No injury to others, 204-05
  Permits, 209
  Procedure for approval, 209
  Quantity transferred, 200-10
  Restrictions, 215
  Temporary, 215
Intradistrict, 450
Interdistrict, 450
Interstate, 644, 648-50
Public interest, 210-14
Reclamation rights, 679, 690-91
Riparian rights, 286-92
By transfer of shares of mutual water
    company, 432
Water banking, 216-17

UNDERGROUND STREAM
See Groundwater.

UNDERGROUND WATER
See Groundwater.

WASTE WATER
See Waters.

WATER COMMISSIONERS
Distribution of water,

WATER COMPANIES
See Water Distribution Organizations.

WATER COURSE
See Waters.

WATER DISTRIBUTION ORGANIZATIONS
Generally, 425-70
Acequias, 431-32, 436
Ad valorem taxation, 453, 458
Carey Act corporations, 429-30
Carrier ditches, 431, 436

Conservancy districts, 453, 458
  Voting, 462, 466-67
Contract water companies, 431
Domestic water supply, 459, 462, 467
Irrigation districts,
  Allocation of water, 448-50
  Assessments, 446
  Charges and tolls, 446
  Constitutionality, 442
  Exclusion of improved land, 450, 453
  Reclamation projects, 446-47
  Water rights of landowners, 447-48
  Water transfers, 450
Joint ditches, 431
Municipalities, 468, 469-70
Mutual water companies, 425-42
  Allocation between stockholders, 430
  Assessments, 430-31
  Stock, 430, 437
  Stock transfers, 437
  Stockholder rights, 432, 435-37
  Water rights of stockholders, 435-37
Public utilities, 438, 440-41
  Rate regulation, 438, 440
  Service requirements, 441, 469-70
State projects, 458-59
Transfers, 437-38
  Interdistrict, 450
Water users' associations, 430

WATER POLICY
See Economic Factors; Environmental
    Protection; Federal Water Policy;
    Pollution Control; Public Rights.

WATER POWER
See also, Federal Energy Regulatory
    Commission.
Beneficial use, 28
Riparian use, 271-74, 302-06
State permits, 650, 656

WATER QUALITY
See Pollution Control.

WATER RIGHTS
Appurtenance, 103-107
Appropriations, 16-235
Federal, 710-34
Groundwater, 334-424
Riparian, 236-333
Territorial extent, 5-8
Types, 5-8
Unadjudicated rights, 133-34

WATERS

See also, Groundwater; Navigable Waters;
  Wild Rivers.
Access to, 115, 244-45, 524-29
Atmospheric, 82-83, 96
Developed water, 92
Diffused surface waters, 84-88, 245-46
Foreign water, see imported water
Hydrologic cycle, 82-83
Imported water, 89, 228-233
Interrelationships, 394-416
Lakes and ponds, 89
Natural streams, 84-88
Return flow,
 Appropriation of, 220-35
 Recapture of, 220-35
Salvaged, 92
Seepage and waste water, 220-35
Sewage, 228-35
Springs, 89
Surface waters, 84-88, 245-46
Unappropriated water, 127-35
Waste water, 220-35
Watercourses, 84-88
Withdrawal from appropriation, 96

WEATHER MODIFICATION

Generally, 96

WETLANDS

See also, Drainage.
 Generally, 595-604
Importance, 598
Regulation, 595-604, 626

WILD RIVERS

Effect on Public and riparian rights, 570-71
Limit on appropriation, 96-97